MANAGERIAL ACCOUNTING

CONCEPTS FOR PLANNING, CONTROL, DECISION MAKING

MANAGERIAL ACCOUNTING

CONCEPTS FOR PLANNING, CONTROL, DECISION MAKING

Sixth Edition

RAY H. GARRISON, D.B.A., CPA

School of Accountancy
Brigham Young University

Homewood, IL 60430
Boston, MA 02116

Associate publisher: Lew Gossage
Developmental editor: Diane M. Van Bakel
Project editor: Margaret Haywood
Production manager: Bette Ittersagen
Designer: Tara L. Bazata
Artist: Precision Graphics
Compositor: Bi-Comp, Incorporated
Typeface: 10/12 Times Roman
Printer: Von Hoffmann Press, Inc.

Library of Congress Cataloging-in-Publication Data

Garrison, Ray H.
Managerial accounting : concepts for planning, control, decision making / Ray H. Garrison.—6th ed.
p. cm.
ISBN 0-256-08120-4 ISBN 0-256-09877-8 (International ed.)
1. Managerial accounting. I. Title.
HF5657.4.G37 1991
658.15′11—dc20 90–4534
CIP

Printed in the United States of America
1 2 3 4 5 6 7 8 9 0 VH 7 6 5 4 3 2 1 0

To my wife,
Mary Jean,

who has contributed greatly to the success of this book through encouragement, assistance in proofing, and the willingness to give up many hours of my time to which she had a clear and rightful claim.

....

The Certified Management Accountant (CMA)

Specific recognition is given to the management accountant as a trained professional in the National Association of Accountants' (NAA) *Certified Management Accountant (CMA)* program. The purpose and operation of the program are described in the following excerpts from a brochure issued by the NAA:

> A Certified Management Accountant is well prepared to be an active participant in management. The CMA program is founded upon the dynamic role the management accountant plays in the management process. The program recognizes all aspects of business, with the focus on the development and analysis of information used in decision making. A CMA has demonstrated the knowledge and professional skills to become an influential member of the management team.
>
> CMAs are found in all levels of management accounting and financial management. Those early in their careers hold staff and supervisory positions. CMAs further along in their careers hold positions of corporate controller, chief financial officer, and CPA firm partners.

To earn the CMA and become a Certified Management Accountant, the following four steps must be completed:

1. Apply for admission to the CMA program and register for the CMA examination.
2. Pass all five parts of the Certified Management Accountant examination within a three-year period.
3. Meet the accounting experience requirement before or within seven years of passing the examination.
4. Comply with the Standards of Ethical Conduct for Management Accountants.

SUMMARY

Understanding organizations and the work of those who manage organizations helps us to understand managerial accounting and its functions. All organizations have basic objectives and a set of strategies for achieving those objectives. Both the setting of strategy, sometimes called strategic planning, and planning of a more short-term nature are basic functions of the manager. In addition to planning, the work of the manager centers on organizing and directing day-to-day operations, controlling, and decision making.

The managers of an organization choose an organizational structure that will permit a decentralization of responsibility by placing managers over specific departments and other units. The responsibility relationships between managers are shown by the organization chart. The organization chart also shows which organizational units are performing line functions and which are performing staff functions. Line functions relate to the specific objectives of the organization, whereas staff functions are supportive in nature, their purpose being to provide specialized services of some type.

A large part of the information needs of management is provided within the structure of the organization itself. Channels of communication exist between various levels of management through which information flows.

Management also calls on various specialists to provide information, including the economist, the engineer, the operations research specialist, and the accountant.

Since managerial accounting is geared to the needs of the manager rather than to the needs of stockholders and others, it differs substantially from financial accounting. Among other things, managerial accounting is oriented more toward the future, it places less emphasis on precision, it emphasizes segments of an organization (rather than the organization as a whole), it draws heavily on other disciplines, it is not governed by generally accepted accounting principles, and it is not mandatory. The role of managerial accounting is expanding rapidly, and managerial accounting has become recognized as a field of professional study through which professional certification can be obtained.

KEY TERMS FOR REVIEW

At the end of each chapter, a list of key terms for review is given, along with the definition of each term. (These terms are set in boldface type where they first appear in the chapter.) Carefully study each term to be sure you understand its meaning, since these terms are used repeatedly in the chapters that follow. The list for Chapter 1 is:

Budget A detailed plan for the future, usually expressed in formal quantitative terms. (p. 11)

Control The process of instituting procedures and then obtaining feedback as needed to ensure that all parts of the organization are functioning effectively and moving toward overall company goals. (p. 4)

Controller The manager in charge of the accounting department in an organization. (p. 8)

Decentralization The delegation of decision-making authority throughout an organization by allowing managers at various operating levels to make key decisions relating to their area of responsibility. (p. 6)

Decision making The process of making rational choices among alternatives. (p. 5)

Directing The overseeing of day-to-day activities in order to keep an organization functioning smoothly. (p. 4)

Feedback Accounting and other reports that help managers monitor performance and focus on problems and/or opportunities that might otherwise go unnoticed. (p. 5)

Financial accounting The phase of accounting that is concerned with providing information to stockholders and others for use in evaluating operations and current financial condition. (p. 2)

Line A position in an organization that is directly related to the achievement of the organization's basic objectives. (p. 7)

Managerial accounting The phase of accounting that is concerned with providing information to managers for use in planning and controlling operations and for use in decision making. (p. 2)

Organization A group of people united for some common purpose. (p. 2)

Organization chart A visual diagram of a firm's organizational structure that depicts formal lines of reporting, communication, and responsibility between managers. (p. 6)

Organizing The process of putting together an organization's human and other resources in such a way as to most effectively carry out established plans. (p. 4)

Performance report A detailed report to management comparing budgeted data against actual data for a specific time period. (p. 11)

Planning The development of objectives in an organization and the preparation of various budgets to achieve these objectives. (p. 4)

Planning and control cycle The flow of management activities through the steps (in sequence) of planning, organizing and directing, controlling, and then back to planning again. (p. 5)

Segment Any part of an organization that can be evaluated independently of other parts and about which the manager seeks cost data. Examples would include a product line, a sales territory, a division, or a department. (p. 14)

Staff A position in an organization that is only indirectly related to the achievement of the organization's basic objectives. Such positions are supportive in nature, in that they provide service or assistance to line positions or to other staff positions. (p. 7)

Strategic planning The planning that leads to the implementation of an organization's objectives. Such planning occurs in two phases: (1) deciding on the products to produce and/or the services to render, and (2) deciding on the marketing and/or manufacturing methods to employ in getting the intended products or services to the proper audience. (p. 3)

QUESTIONS

1–1 Contrast financial and managerial accounting.

1–2 What objectives, other than earning a profit, might be important to the managers of a profit-oriented organization?

1–3 Assume that you are about to go into the retail grocery business. Describe some of the operating strategies that you might follow.

1–4 A labor union is an organization. Describe a labor union in terms of what might be its objectives, its strategies, its organizational structure, the work of its managers, and its need for information.

1–5 Some persons consider strategic planning to be the most important work that a manager does. In what ways might this be true? In what ways might this be false?

1–6 Assume that the central objective of a college basketball team is to win games. What strategies might the team follow to achieve this objective?

1–7 Managerial accounting isn't as important in the government as it is in private industry, since the government doesn't have to worry about earning a profit. Do you agree? Explain.

1–8 What function does *feedback* play in the work of the manager?

1–9 "Essentially, the job of a manager is to make decisions." Do you agree? Explain.

1–10 What is the relationship, if any, between information and decision making?

1–11 Choose an organization with which you are familiar. Prepare an organization chart depicting the structure of the organization you have chosen. (The organization you choose should be sufficiently complex to have at least one staff function.) Be prepared to place your organization chart on the board, if your instructor so directs.

1–12 One of the key responsibilities of an accounting department is to keep records for the entire organization. Why don't line managers keep their own records?

1–13 Managerial accounting information is sometimes described as a means to an end, whereas financial accounting information is described as an end in itself. In what sense is this true?

1–14 A student planning a career in management commented, "Look, I'm going to be a manager, so why don't we just leave the accounting to the accountants?" Do you agree? Explain.

1–15 Accountants are sometimes compared to journalists in that accountants don't just "report" information to the manager; they "editorialize" the information. What implications does this hold for the accountant "managing the news," so to speak?

1–16 Distinguish between line and staff positions in an organization.

1–17 "The term *controller* is a misnomer, because the controller doesn't 'control' anything." Do you agree? Explain.

1–18 A production superintendent once complained, "Accounting is a staff function. Those people have no right to come down here and tell us what to do." Do you agree? Why or why not?

1–19 What are the major differences between financial and managerial accounting? In what ways are the two fields of study similar?

1–20 "If an organization's managerial accounting system functions properly, it will provide management with all the information needed to operate with maximum effectiveness." Do you agree? Explain.

PROBLEMS

P1–1 **Setting Long-Range Objectives** Successful organizations appear to be those that have clearly defined long-range objectives or goals and a well-planned strategy to reach these objectives. Such organizations understand the markets in which they do business and also understand their own internal strengths and weaknesses. They take advantage of this knowledge in order to grow in a consistent and disciplined manner.

Required

1. Discuss the need for long-range objectives or goals in business organizations.
2. Discuss how long-range objectives are set.
3. Define the concepts of strategic planning and management control. Discuss how they relate to each other and contribute to the progress toward attainment of long-range objectives.

(CMA, Adapted)

P1–2 **Preparing an Organization Chart** Bristow University is a large private school located in the Midwest. The university is headed by a president, who has five vice presidents reporting to him. These vice presidents are responsible for, respectively, auxiliary services, admissions and records, academics, financial services (controller), and physical plant.

In addition, the university has managers over several areas who report to these vice presidents. These include managers over central purchasing, the university press, and the university bookstore, all of whom report to the vice president for auxiliary services; managers over computer services and over accounting and finance, who report to the vice president for financial services; and managers over grounds and custodial services and over plant and maintenance, who report to the vice president for physical plant.

The university has four colleges—business, humanities, fine arts, and engineering and quantitative methods—and a law school. Each of these units has a dean who is responsible to the academic vice president. There are several departments in each college.

Required

1. Prepare an organization chart for Bristow University.
2. Which of the positions on your chart would be line positions? Why would they be line positions? Which would be staff positions? Why?

3. Which of the positions on your chart would have need for accounting information? Explain.

P1–3 Line and Staff Positions Special Alloys Corporation is a specialized production firm that manufactures a variety of metal products for industrial use. Most of the revenues are generated by large contracts with companies that have government defense contracts. The company also develops and markets parts to the major automobile companies. The company employs many metallurgists and skilled technicians because most of its products are made from highly sophisticated alloys.

The company recently signed two large contracts; as a result, the work load of Wayne Washburn, the general manager, has become overwhelming. To relieve some of this overload, Mark Johnson was transferred from the research planning department to the general manager's office. Johnson, who has been a senior metallurgist and supervisor in the planning department, was given the title ''assistant to the general manager.''

Washburn assigned several responsibilities to Johnson in their first meeting. Johnson will oversee the testing of new alloys in the product planning department and be given the authority to make decisions as to the use of these alloys in product development; he will also be responsible for maintaining the production schedules for one of the new contracts. In addition to these duties, he will be required to meet with the supervisors of the production departments regularly to consult with them about production problems they may be experiencing. Washburn is expecting that he will be able to manage the company much more efficiently with Johnson's help.

Required

1. Positions within organizations are often described as having *(a)* line authority or *(b)* staff authority. Describe what is meant by these two terms.
2. Of the responsibilities assigned to Mark Johnson as assistant to the general manager, which ones have line authority and which have staff authority?
3. Identify and discuss the conflicts Mark Johnson may experience in the production departments as a result of his new responsibilities.

(CMA, Adapted)

PART I

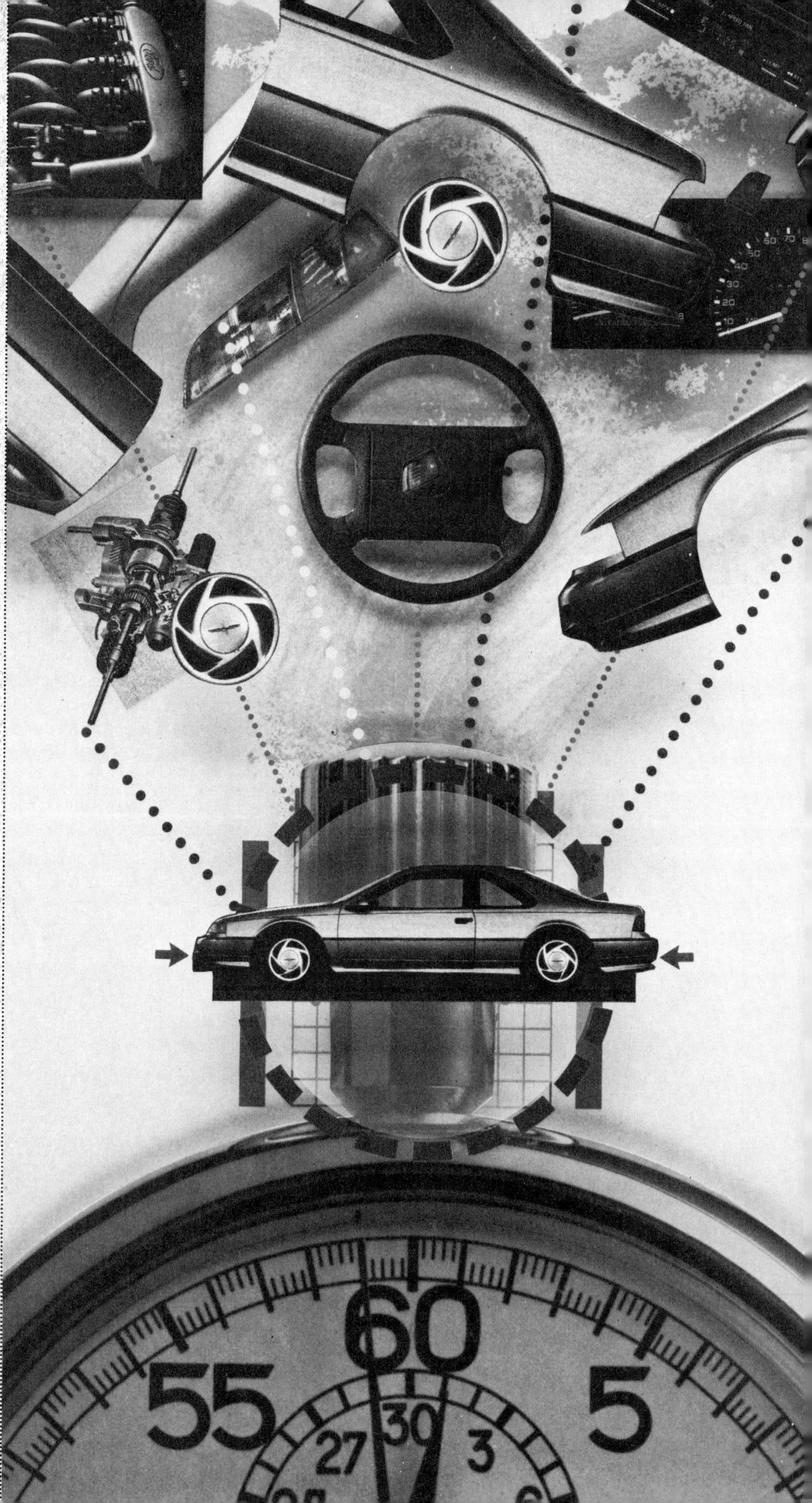

THE FOUNDATION
COST TERMS, COST BEHAVIOR, AND SYSTEMS DESIGN

week, he works 45 hours and has no idle time. His labor cost for the week would be allocated as follows:

Direct labor ($12 × 45 hours)	$540
Manufacturing overhead (overtime premium: $6 × 5 hours). . .	30
Total cost for the week.	$570

Observe from this computation that only the overtime premium of $6 per hour is charged to the overhead account—*not* the entire $18 earned for each hour of overtime work ($12 regular rate × 1.5 = $18).

Labor Fringe Benefits

The proper classification of labor fringe benefits is not so clearly defined in practice as is idle time or overtime premium. Labor fringe benefits are made up of employment-related costs paid by the employer and include the costs of insurance programs, retirement plans, various supplemental unemployment benefits, and hospitalization plans. Many firms treat all such costs as indirect labor by adding them in total to manufacturing overhead. Other firms treat that portion of fringe benefits that relates to direct labor as additional direct labor cost. This approach is conceptually superior since the fringe benefits provided to direct labor workers clearly represent an added cost of their services.

The cost to the employer for fringe benefits is substantial. A recent nationwide survey by the Chamber of Commerce shows that fringe benefits, on the average, cost 37 cents for every dollar of gross wages.

QUESTIONS

2–1 Distinguish between merchandising and manufacturing.

2–2 What are the three major elements in the cost of a manufactured product?

2–3 Distinguish between the following: (*a*) direct materials, (*b*) indirect materials, (*c*) direct labor, (*d*) indirect labor, and (*e*) manufacturing overhead.

2–4 Explain the difference between a product cost and a period cost.

2–5 Describe how the income statement of a manufacturing company differs from the income statement of a merchandising company.

2–6 Of what value is the schedule and cost of goods manufactured? How does it tie into the income statement?

2–7 Distinguish between prime cost and conversion cost. What is meant by conversion cost?

2–8 Describe how the balance sheet of a manufacturing company differs from the balance sheet of a merchandising company so far as current assets are concerned.

2–9 Why are product costs sometimes called inventoriable costs? Describe the flow of such costs in a manufacturing company from the point of incurrence until they finally become expenses on the income statement.

2–10 Is it possible for costs such as salaries or depreciation to end up as assets on the balance sheet? Explain.

2–11 Give at least three terms that may be substituted for the term *manufacturing overhead.*

2–12 In a JIT system, what is meant by a pull approach to the flow of goods, as compared to the push approach used in conventional systems?

2–13 What four key elements are involved in the successful operation of a JIT inventory system?

2–14 What is meant by the "JIT philosophy," and what three ideas underlie its use in an organization?

2–15 What is meant by the term *cost behavior?*

2–16 "A variable cost is a cost that varies per unit of product, whereas a fixed cost is constant per unit of product." Do you agree? Explain.

2–17 How do fixed costs create difficulties in costing units of product?

2–18 Why is manufacturing overhead considered an indirect cost of a unit of product?

2–19 Under what conditions is a cost controllable at a particular level of management?

2–20 Define the following terms: differential cost, opportunity cost, and sunk cost.

2–21 Only variable costs can be differential costs. Do you agree? Explain.

2–22 (Appendix) Mary Adams is employed by Acme Company. Last week she worked 34 hours assembling one of the company's products and was idle 6 hours due to material shortages. Acme's employees are engaged at their workstations for a normal 40-hour week. Ms. Adams is paid $8 per hour. Allocate her earnings between direct labor cost and manufacturing overhead cost.

2–23 (Appendix) John Olsen operates a stamping machine on the assembly line of Drake Manufacturing Company. Last week Mr. Olsen worked 45 hours. His basic wage rate is $5 per hour, with time and a half for overtime (time worked in excess of 40 hours per week). How should last week's wage cost be allocated between direct labor cost and manufacturing overhead cost?

EXERCISES

E2–1 Below are a number of costs that might be incurred in a service, merchandising, or manufacturing company. Copy the list of costs onto your answer sheet, and then place an *X* in the appropriate column for each cost to indicate whether the cost involved would be variable or fixed.

Cost	Cost Behavior	
	Variable	Fixed
1. Small glass plates used for lab tests in a hospital . . .		
2. Straight-line depreciation of a building		
3. Top-management salaries		
4. Electrical costs of running machines		
5. Advertising of products and services		
6. Batteries used in manufacturing trucks		
7. Commissions to salespersons		
8. Insurance on a dentist's office		
9. Leather used in manufacturing footballs		
10. Rent on a medical center		

E2–2 Following are a number of cost terms introduced in the chapter:

Period cost	Fixed cost
Variable cost	Prime cost
Opportunity cost	Conversion cost
Product cost	Sunk cost

Choose the cost term or terms above that most appropriately describe the costs identified in each of the following situations. A cost term can be used more than once.

1. Crown Books, Inc., prints a small book titled *The Pocket Speller* that is popular with college students. The paper going into the manufacture of the book would be called direct materials and classified as a __________ cost. In terms of cost behavior, the paper could also be described as a __________ cost.
2. Instead of compiling the words in the book, the author hired by the company could have spent many hours consulting with business organizations. The consulting fees forgone would be called __________ cost.
3. The paper and other materials used in the manufacture of the book, combined with the direct labor cost involved, would be called __________ cost.
4. The salary of Crown Books' president would be classified as a __________ cost, since the salary will appear on the income statement as an expense in the time period in which it is incurred.
5. Depreciation on the equipment used to print the book would be classified by Crown Books as a __________ cost. However, depreciation on any equipment used by the company in selling and administrative activities would be classified as a __________ cost. In terms of cost behavior, depreciation would probably be classified as a __________ cost.
6. A __________ cost is also known as an inventoriable cost, since such costs go into the Work in Process inventory account and then into the Finished Goods inventory account before appearing on the income statement as part of cost of goods sold.
7. Taken together, the direct labor cost and manufacturing overhead cost involved in the manufacture of the book would be called __________ cost.
8. Crown Books sells the book through agents who are paid a commission on each book sold. The company would classify these commissions as a __________ cost. In terms of cost behavior, commissions would be classified as a __________ cost.
9. Several hundred copies of the book were left over from the prior edition and are stored in a warehouse. The amount invested in these books would be called a __________ cost.
10. Costs can often be classified in several ways. For example, Crown Books pays $4,000 rent each month on the building that houses its printing press. The rent would be part of manufacturing overhead. In terms of cost behavior, it would be classified as a __________ cost. The rent can also be classified as a __________ cost and as part of __________ cost.

E2–3 Ryser Company was organized on May 1, 19x5. On that date the company purchased 35,000 plastic emblems, each with a peel-off adhesive backing. The front of the emblems contained the company's name, accompanied by an attractive logo. Each emblem cost Ryser Company $2.

During May, 31,000 emblems were drawn from the Raw Materials inventory account. Of these, 1,000 were taken by the sales manager to an important sales meeting with prospective customers and handed out as an advertising gimmick. The remaining emblems drawn from inventory were affixed to units of the company's product that were being manufactured during May. Of the units of product having emblems affixed during May, 90 percent were completed and transferred from Work in Process to Finished Goods. Of the units completed during the month, 75 percent were sold and shipped to customers.

Required

1. Determine the cost of emblems that would be in each of the following accounts at May 31, 19x5:

a. Raw Materials.
b. Work in Process.
c. Finished Goods.
d. Cost of Goods Sold.
e. Advertising Expense.

2. Specify whether each of the above accounts would appear on the balance sheet or on the income statement at May 31.

E2–4 The following cost and inventory data are taken from the books of Eccles Company for the year 19x6:

Costs incurred:	
Advertising expense	$100,000
Direct labor cost	90,000
Purchases of raw materials	132,000
Rent, factory building	80,000
Indirect labor	56,300
Sales commissions	35,000
Utilities, factory	9,000
Maintenance, factory equipment	24,000
Supplies, factory	700
Depreciation, office equipment	8,000
Depreciation, factory equipment	40,000

	January 1, 19x6	**December 31, 19x6**
Inventories:		
Raw materials	$ 8,000	$10,000
Work in process	5,000	20,000
Finished goods	70,000	25,000

Required

1. Prepare a schedule of cost of goods manufactured in good form.
2. Prepare the cost of goods sold section of Eccles Company's income statement for the year.

E2–5 A product cost is also known as an inventoriable cost. Classify the following costs as being either product (inventoriable) costs or period (noninventoriable) costs in a manufacturing company:

1. Depreciation on salespersons' cars.
2. Rent on equipment used in the factory.
3. Lubricants used for maintenance of machines.
4. Salaries of finished goods warehouse personnel.
5. Soap and paper towels used by workers at the end of a shift.
6. Factory supervisors' salaries.
7. Heat, water, and power consumed in the factory.
8. Materials used in boxing units of finished product for shipment overseas. (Units are not normally boxed.)
9. Advertising outlays.
10. Workers' compensation insurance on factory employees.
11. Depreciation on chairs and tables in the factory lunchroom.
12. The salary of the switchboard operator for the company.
13. Depreciation on a Lear Jet used by the company's executives.
14. Rent on rooms at a Florida resort for holding of the annual sales conference.
15. Attractively designed box for packaging breakfast cereal.

E2–6 Sherri Masconi operates a retail store. One of the products in the store, product A, costs Sherri $8 per unit and sells for $12 per unit. The store sells 500 units of product

A each year. Sherri is considering dropping product A and selling product B in its place. Product B would cost $10 per unit and sell for $15 per unit. Sherri believes that she could sell 600 units of product B each year, but to do so she would have to rent some special display equipment at a cost of $800 per year. However, she would no longer have to pay $1 per unit to a local repair shop to adjust product A to customers' specifications. Product B would require no adjustments. Each product would require $300 per year in advertising.

Required

1. Compute the differential costs and revenues between product A and product B in terms of total annual revenues, expenses, and net income. Mark each expense as being either variable (V) or fixed (F).
2. Is there an opportunity cost associated with eliminating product A? Explain.

E2–7 (Appendix) Fred Austin is employed by White Company. He works on the company's assembly line and assembles a component part for one of the company's products. Fred is paid $12 per hour for regular time, and he is paid time and a half for all work in excess of 40 hours per week.

Required

1. Assume that during a given week Fred is idle for two hours due to machine breakdowns and that he is idle for four more hours due to material shortages. No overtime is recorded for the week. Allocate Fred's wages for the week as between direct labor cost and manufacturing overhead cost.
2. Assume that during a following week Fred works a total of 50 hours. He has no idle time for the week. Allocate Fred's wages for the week as between direct labor cost and manufacturing overhead cost.
3. Fred's company provides an attractive package of fringe benefits for its employees. This package includes a retirement program and a health insurance program. So far as direct labor workers are concerned, explain two ways that the company could handle the costs of fringe benefits in its cost records.

E2–8 (Appendix) Several weeks ago you called Jiffy Plumbing Company to have some routine repair work done on the plumbing system in your home. The plumber came about two weeks later, at four o'clock in the afternoon, and spent two hours completing your repair work. When you received your bill from the company, it contained a $75 charge for labor—$30 for the first hour and $45 for the second.

When questioned about the difference in hourly rates, the company's service manager explained that the higher rate for the second hour contained a charge for an "overtime premium," since the union required that plumbers be paid time and a half for any work in excess of eight hours per day. The service manager further explained that the company was working overtime to "catch up a little" on its backlog of work orders, but still needed to maintain a "decent" profit margin on the plumbers' time.

Required

1. Do you agree with the company's computation of the labor charge on your job?
2. Assume that the company pays its plumbers $20 per hour. Prepare computations to show how the cost of the plumber's time for the day (nine hours) should be allocated between direct labor cost and general overhead cost on the company's books.
3. Under what circumstances might the company be justified in charging an overtime premium for repair work on your home?

PROBLEMS

P2–9 **Incomplete Data** Supply the missing data in the four cases below. Each case is independent of the others.

	Case			
	1	2	3	4
Direct materials	$ 7,000	$ 9,000	$ 6,000	$ 8,000
Direct labor	2,000	4,000	?	3,000
Manufacturing overhead	10,000	?	7,000	21,000
Total manufacturing costs	?	25,000	18,000	?
Beginning work in process inventory	?	1,000	2,000	?
Ending work in process inventory	4,000	3,500	?	2,000
Cost of goods manufactured	$18,000	$?	$16,000	$?
Sales	$25,000	$40,000	$30,000	$50,000
Beginning finished goods inventory	6,000	?	7,000	9,000
Cost of goods manufactured	?	?	?	31,500
Goods available for sale	?	?	?	?
Ending finished goods inventory	9,000	4,000	?	7,000
Cost of goods sold	?	26,500	18,000	?
Gross margin	?	?	?	?
Operating expenses	6,000	?	?	10,000
Net income	$?	$ 5,500	$ 3,000	$?

P2–10 Cost Classification Various costs associated with manufacturing operations are given below:

1. Plastic washers used in auto production.
2. Production superintendent's salary.
3. Laborers assembling a product.
4. Electricity for operation of machines.
5. Janitorial salaries.
6. Clay used in brick production.
7. Rent on a factory building.
8. Wood used in ski production.
9. Screws used in furniture production.
10. A supervisor's salary.
11. Cloth used in suit production.
12. Depreciation of cafeteria equipment.
13. Glue used in textbook production.
14. Lubricants for machines.
15. Paper used in textbook production.

Required Classify each cost as being either variable or fixed with respect to volume or level of activity. Also classify each cost as being either direct or indirect with respect to units of product. Prepare your answer sheet as shown below:

	Cost Behavior		To Units of Product	
Cost Item	**Variable**	**Fixed**	**Direct**	**Indirect**
Example: Factory insurance		X		X

If you are unsure whether a cost would be variable or fixed, consider how it would behave over fairly wide ranges of activity.

P2–11 Schedule of Cost of Goods Manufactured; Cost Behavior Various cost and sales data for Medco, Inc., are given below for the year 19x5:

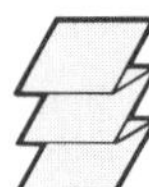

Purchases of raw materials	$ 90,000
Raw materials inventory, January 1	10,000
Raw materials inventory, December 31	17,000
Depreciation, factory	42,000
Insurance, factory	5,000
Direct labor cost	60,000
Maintenance, factory	30,000
Administrative expenses	70,000
Sales	450,000
Utilities, factory	27,000
Supplies, factory	1,000
Selling expenses	80,000
Indirect labor	65,000
Work in process inventory, January 1	7,000
Work in process inventory, December 31	30,000
Finished goods inventory, January 1	10,000
Finished goods inventory, December 31	40,000

Required

1. Prepare a schedule of cost of goods manufactured for 19x5.
2. Prepare an income statement for 19x5.
3. Assume that the company produced the equivalent of 10,000 units of product during 19x5. What was the unit cost for direct materials? What was the unit cost for factory depreciation?
4. Assume that the company expects to produce 15,000 units of product during the coming year. What per unit cost and what total cost would you expect the company to incur for direct materials at this level of activity? For factory depreciation? (In preparing your answer, assume that direct materials is a variable cost and that depreciation is a fixed cost; also assume that depreciation is computed on a straight-line basis.)
5. As the manager responsible for production costs, explain to the president any difference in unit costs between (3) and (4) above.

P2–12 Cost Identification Several years ago Medex Company purchased a small building adjacent to its manufacturing plant in order to have room for expansion when needed. Since the company had no immediate need for the extra space, the building was rented out to another company for a rental revenue of $40,000 per year. The renter's lease will expire next month, and rather than renewing the lease, Medex Company has decided to use the building itself to manufacture a new product.

Direct materials cost for the new product will total $40 per unit. It will be necessary to hire a supervisor to oversee production. His salary will be $1,500 per month. Workers will be hired to manufacture the new product, with direct labor cost amounting to $18 per unit. Manufacturing operations will occupy all of the building space, so it will be necessary to rent space in a warehouse nearby in order to store finished units of product. The rental cost will be $1,000 per month. In addition, the company will need to rent equipment for use in producing the new product; the rental cost will be $3,000 per month. The company will continue to depreciate the building on a straight-line basis, as in past years. Depreciation on the building is $10,000 per year.

Advertising costs for the new product will total $50,000 per year. Costs of shipping the new product to customers will be $10 per unit. Electrical costs of operating machines and other utility costs will be $2 per unit.

In order to have funds to purchase materials, meet payrolls, and so forth, the company will have to liquidate some temporary investments. These investments are presently yielding a return of $6,000 per year.

Required Prepare an answer sheet with the following column headings:

Name of the Cost	Variable Cost	Fixed Cost	Product Cost			Period (selling and administrative) Cost	Opportunity Cost	Sunk Cost
			Direct Materials	Direct Labor	Manufacturing Overhead			

List the different costs associated with the new product decision down the extreme left column (under "Name of the Cost"). Then place an *X* under each heading that helps to describe the type of cost involved. There may be *X*'s under several column headings for a single cost. (For example, a cost may be a fixed cost, a period cost, and a sunk cost; you would place an *X* under each of these column headings opposite the cost.)

P2-13 Cost Identification Heritage Company manufactures a beautiful bookcase that enjoys widespread popularity. The company has a backlog of orders that is large enough to keep production going indefinitely at the plant's full capacity of 4,000 bookcases per year. Annual cost data at full capacity follow:

Materials used (wood and glass)	$430,000
General office salaries	110,000
Factory supervision	70,000
Sales commissions	60,000
Depreciation, factory building	105,000
Depreciation, office equipment	2,000
Indirect materials, factory	18,000
Factory labor (cutting and assembly)	90,000
Advertising	100,000
Insurance, factory	6,000
General office supplies (billing)	4,000
Property taxes, factory	20,000
Utilities, factory	45,000

Required

1. Prepare an answer sheet with the column headings shown below. Enter each cost item on your answer sheet, placing the dollar amount under the appropriate headings. As examples, this has been done already for the first two items in the list above. Note that each cost item is classified in two ways: first, as being either variable or fixed; and second, as being either a selling and administrative cost or a product cost. (If the item is a product cost, it should be classified as being either direct or indirect as shown.)

Cost Item	Cost Behavior		Selling or Administrative Cost	Product Cost	
	Variable	Fixed		Direct	Indirect*
Materials used	$430,000			$430,000	
General office salaries		$110,000	$110,000		

* To units of product.

If you are uncertain whether a cost would be variable or fixed, consider how you would expect it to behave over fairly wide ranges of activity.

2. Total the dollar amounts in each of the columns in (1) above. Compute the cost to produce one bookcase.
3. Due to a recession, assume that production drops to only 2,000 bookcases per year. Would you expect the cost per bookcase to increase, decrease, or remain unchanged? Explain. No computations are necessary.
4. Refer to the original data. The president's next-door neighbor has considered making himself a bookcase and has priced the necessary materials at a building supply store. He has asked the president whether he could purchase a bookcase

from the Heritage Company "at cost," and the president has agreed to let him do so.

a. Would you expect any disagreement between the two men over the price the neighbor should pay? Explain. What price does the president probably have in mind? The neighbor?

b. Since the company is operating at full capacity, what cost term used in the chapter might be justification for the president to charge the full, regular price to the neighbor and still be selling "at cost"? Explain.

P2–14 Classification of Salary Cost You have just been hired by Ogden Company, which was organized on January 2 of the current year. The company manufactures and sells a single product. It is your responsibility to coordinate shipments of the product from the factory to distribution warehouses located in various parts of the United States so that goods will be available as orders are received from customers.

The company is unsure how to classify your $30,000 annual salary in its cost records. The company's cost analyst says that your salary should be classified as a manufacturing (product) cost; the controller says that it should be classified as a selling expense; and the president says that it doesn't matter which way your salary cost is classified.

Required

1. Which viewpoint is correct? Why?
2. From the point of view of the reported net income for the year, is the president correct in his statement that it doesn't matter which way your salary cost is classified? Explain, using the data from Exhibit 2–5 and/or Exhibit 2–6 as needed.

P2–15 Allocating Labor Costs (Appendix) Lynn Bjorland is employed by Southern Laboratories, Inc., and is directly involved in the preparation and packaging of the company's leading antibiotic drug. Lynn's basic wage rate is $12 per hour. The company pays its employees time and a half for any work in excess of 40 hours per week.

Required

1. Suppose that in a given week Lynn works 45 hours. Compute Lynn's total wages for the week. How much of this cost would the company allocate to direct labor cost? To manufacturing overhead cost?
2. Suppose in another week that Lynn works 50 hours but is idle for 4 hours during the week due to equipment breakdowns. Compute Lynn's total wages for the week. How much of this amount would be allocated to direct labor cost? To manufacturing overhead cost?
3. Southern Laboratories has an attractive package of fringe benefits that costs the company $4 for each hour of employee time (either regular time or overtime). During a particular week, Lynn works 48 hours but is idle for 3 hours due to material shortages. Compute Lynn's total wages and fringe benefits for the week. If the company treats all fringe benefits as part of manufacturing overhead cost, how much of Lynn's wages and fringe benefits for the week would be allocated to direct labor cost? To manufacturing overhead cost?
4. Refer to the data in (3) above. If the company treats that part of fringe benefits relating to direct labor as added direct labor cost, how much of Lynn's wages and fringe benefits for the week will be allocated to direct labor cost? To manufacturing overhead cost?

P2–16 Preparing Manufacturing Statements Skyler Company was organized on November 1 of the prior year. After seven months of "start-up" losses, management had expected to earn a profit during June, the most recent month. Management was disappointed, however, when the income statement for June showed that losses were still being realized by the company. June's income statement follows:

SKYLER COMPANY
Income Statement
For the Month Ended June 30, 19x8

Sales		$600,000
Less operating expenses:		
Selling and administrative salaries	$ 35,000	
Rent on facilities	40,000	
Purchases of raw materials	190,000	
Insurance expired	8,000	
Depreciation, sales equipment	10,000	
Utilities costs	50,000	
Indirect labor	108,000	
Direct labor	90,000	
Depreciation, factory equipment	12,000	
Maintenance, factory	7,000	
Advertising	80,000	630,000
Net loss		$(30,000)

After seeing the $30,000 loss for June, Skyler's president stated, "I was sure we'd be profitable within six months, but after eight months we're still spilling out red ink. Maybe it's time for us to throw in the towel and accept one of those offers we've had for the company. To make matters worse, I just heard that Linda won't be back from her surgery for at least six more weeks."

Linda is the company's controller; in her absence, the statement above was prepared by a new assistant who has had little experience in manufacturing operations. Additional information about the company follows:

a. Only 80 percent of the rent on facilities applies to factory operations; the remainder applies to selling and administrative activities.

b. Inventory balances at the beginning and end of the month were as follows:

	June 1	June 30
Raw materials	$17,000	$42,000
Work in process	70,000	85,000
Finished goods	20,000	60,000

c. Some 75 percent of the expired insurance and 90 percent of the utilities cost applies to factory operations; the remaining amounts apply to selling and administrative activities.

The president has asked you to check over the above income statement and make a recommendation as to whether the company should continue operations.

Required

1. As one step in gathering data for a recommendation to the president, prepare a schedule of cost of goods manufactured in good form for June 19x8.
2. As a second step, prepare a new income statement for the month.
3. Based on your statements prepared in (1) and (2) above, would you recommend that the company continue operations?

P2–17 Cost Classification Listed below are a number of costs that might typically be found in a service, merchandising, or manufacturing company.

1. Depreciation, executive jet.
2. Freight-out on merchandise sold.
3. Wood used in furniture manufacturing.
4. Sales manager's salary.

5. Glue used in furniture manufacturing.
6. Secretary, company president.
7. Aerosol attachment placed on a spray can.
8. Billing costs.
9. Packing supplies for shipping products overseas.
10. Sand used in concrete manufacturing.
11. Supervisor's salary, factory.
12. Depreciation of video games in the factory lunchroom.
13. Executive life insurance.
14. Sales commissions.
15. Fringe benefits, assembly-line workers.
16. Advertising costs.
17. Boxes used for packaging breakfast cereal.
18. Property taxes on finished goods warehouses.
19. Security guard, factory.
20. Lubricants for machines.

Required Prepare an answer sheet with column headings as shown below. For each cost item, indicate whether it would be variable or fixed in behavior, and then whether it would be a selling cost, an administrative cost, or a manufacturing cost. If it is a manufacturing cost, indicate whether it would be direct or indirect to units of product. Three sample answers are provided for illustration. If you are unsure about whether a cost would be variable or fixed, consider whether it would fluctuate substantially over a fairly wide range of volume.

Cost Item	Variable or Fixed	Selling Cost	Administrative Cost	Manufacturing (product) Cost	
				Direct	Indirect
Direct labor	V			X	
Executive salaries. . .	F		X		
Factory rent	F				X

P2–18 **Cost Identification** Frieda Bronkowski has invented a new type of flyswatter. After giving the matter much thought, Frieda has decided to quit her $2,000 per month job with a computer firm and produce and sell the flyswatters full time. Frieda will rent a garage that will be used as a production plant. The rent will be $150 per month. She has a number of tools and some equipment purchased several years ago at a cost of $4,000 that will be depreciated and used in production. In addition, Frieda will rent other production equipment at a cost of $500 per month.

The cost of materials for each flyswatter will be $0.30. Frieda will hire workers to produce the flyswatters. They will be paid $0.50 for each completed unit. Frieda will rent a room in the house next door for use as her sales office. The rent will be $75 per month. She has arranged for the telephone company to attach a recording device to her home phone to get off-hours messages from customers. The device will increase her monthly phone bill by $20. In addition, she will be charged $0.50 for each message recorded on the device.

Frieda has some money in savings that is earning interest of $1,000 per year. These savings will be withdrawn and used for about a year to get the business going. In order to sell her flyswatters, Frieda will advertise heavily in the local area. Advertising costs will be $400 per month. In addition, Frieda will pay a sales commission of $0.10 for each flyswatter sold.

For the time being, Frieda does not intend to draw any salary from the new company.

Required 1. Prepare an answer sheet with the following column headings:

Name of the Cost	Variable Cost	Fixed Cost	Product Cost: Direct Materials	Product Cost: Direct Labor	Product Cost: Manufacturing Overhead	Period (selling and administrative) Cost	Opportunity Cost	Sunk Cost

List the different costs associated with the new company down the extreme left column (under "Name of the Cost"). Then place an *X* under each heading that helps to describe the type of cost involved. There may be *X*'s under several column headings for a single cost. (That is, a cost may be a fixed cost, a period cost, and a sunk cost; you would place an *X* under each of these column headings opposite the cost.)

2. All of the costs you have listed above, except one, would be differential costs between the alternatives of Frieda producing flyswatters or staying with the computer firm. Which cost is *not* differential? Explain.

P2–19 Schedule of Cost of Goods Manufactured; Cost Behavior Selected account balances for the year ended December 31, 19x3, are provided below for Valenko Company:

Advertising expense	$215,000
Insurance, factory equipment	8,000
Depreciation, sales equipment	40,000
Rent, factory building	90,000
Utilities, factory	52,000
Sales commissions	35,000
Cleaning supplies, factory	6,000
Depreciation, factory equipment	110,000
Selling and administrative salaries	85,000
Maintenance, factory	74,000
Direct labor	?
Purchases of raw materials	260,000

Inventory balances at the beginning and end of the year were as follows:

	January 1, 19x3	December 31, 19x3
Raw materials	$50,000	$40,000
Work in process	?	33,000
Finished goods	30,000	?

Total manufacturing costs for the year totaled $675,000; the goods available for sale totaled $720,000; and the cost of goods sold totaled $635,000.

Required

1. Prepare a schedule of cost of goods manufactured in the form illustrated in Exhibit 2–3 in the book, and prepare the cost of goods sold section of the company's income statement for the year.
2. Assume that the dollar amounts given above are for the equivalent of 30,000 units produced during the year. Compute the unit cost for direct materials used, and compute the unit cost for rent on the factory building.
3. Assume that in 19x4 (the following year) the company produces 50,000 units. What per unit and total cost would you expect to be incurred for direct materials? For rent on the factory building? (In preparing your answer, you may assume that direct materials is a variable cost and that rent is a fixed cost.)

4. As the manager in charge of production costs, explain to the president the reason for any difference in unit costs between (2) and (3) above.

P2–20 Cost Behavior; Manufacturing Statement; Unit Costs Hickey Company, a manufacturing firm, produces a single product. The following information has been taken from the company's production, sales, and cost records for the year 19x6:

Production in units	30,000
Sales in units	?
Ending finished goods inventory in units	?
Sales in dollars	$650,000
Costs:	
Advertising	$ 90,000
Direct labor	160,000
Indirect labor	60,000
Raw materials purchased	80,000
Building rent (production uses 80% of the space; administrative and sales offices use the rest)	50,000
Utilities, factory	35,000
Royalty paid for use of production patent, $1 per unit produced	?
Maintenance, factory	25,000
Rent for special production equipment, $6,000 per year plus $0.10 per unit produced	?
Selling and administrative salaries	100,000
Other factory overhead costs	11,000
Other selling and administrative expenses	20,000

	January 1, 19x6	**December 31, 19x6**
Inventories:		
Raw materials	$20,000	$10,000
Work in process	30,000	40,000
Finished goods	–0–	?

The finished goods inventory is being carried at the average unit production cost for the year. The selling price of the product is $25 per unit.

Required

1. Prepare a schedule of cost of goods manufactured for the year.
2. Compute the following:
   a. The number of units in the finished goods inventory at December 31.
   b. The cost of the units in the finished goods inventory at December 31.
3. Prepare an income statement for the year.

CASES

C2–21 Missing Data; Statements; Inventory Computation "I know I'm a pretty good scientist, but I guess I still have some things to learn about running a business," said Staci Morales, founder and president of Medical Technology, Inc. "Demand has been so strong for our heart monitor that I was sure we'd be profitable immediately, but just look at the gusher of red ink for the first quarter." The data to which Staci was referring are shown below:

MEDICAL TECHNOLOGY, INC.
Income Statement
For the Quarter Ended June 30, 19x8

Sales (16,000 monitors)		$ 975,000
Less operating expenses:		
Selling and administrative salaries	$ 90,000	
Advertising	200,000	
Cleaning supplies, production	6,000	
Indirect labor cost	135,000	
Depreciation, office equipment	18,000	
Direct labor cost	80,000	
Raw materials purchased	310,000	
Maintenance, production	47,000	
Rental cost, facilities	65,000	
Insurance, production	9,000	
Utilities	40,000	
Depreciation, production equipment	75,000	
Travel, salespersons	60,000	
Total operating expenses		1,135,000
Net loss		$ (160,000)

"At this rate we'll be out of business in a year," said Derek Louganis, the company's accountant. "But I've double-checked these figures, so I know they're right."

Medical Technology was organized on April 1 of the current year to produce and market a revolutionary new heart monitor. The company's accounting system was set up by Herb Stienbeck, an experienced accountant who recently left the company. The statement above was prepared by Louganis, his assistant.

"We may not last a year if the insurance company doesn't pay the $227,000 it owes us for the 4,000 monitors lost in the truck accident last week," said Staci. "The agent says our claim is inflated, but that's a lot of baloney."

Just after the end of the quarter, a truck carrying 4,000 monitors wrecked and burned, destroying the entire load. The monitors were part of the 20,000 units completed during the quarter ended June 30. They were in a warehouse awaiting sale at quarter-end and were sold and shipped on July 3 (this sale is *not* included on the income statement above). The trucking company's insurer is liable for the "cost" of the goods lost. Louganis has determined this cost as follows:

$$\frac{\text{Total costs for the quarter, \$1,135,000}}{\text{Monitors produced during the quarter, 20,000}} = \$56.75 \text{ per unit}$$

$$4{,}000 \text{ monitors} \times \$56.75 = \$227{,}000$$

The following additional information is available on the company's activities over the quarter ended June 30:

a. Inventories at the beginning and end of the quarter were as follows:

	April 1, 19x8	**June 30, 19x8**
Raw materials	–0–	$40,000
Work in process	–0–	.30,000
Finished goods	–0–	?

b. Eighty percent of the rental cost for facilities and 90 percent of the utilities cost relate to manufacturing operations. The remaining amounts relate to selling and administrative activities.

Required

1. What conceptual errors, if any, were made in preparing the income statement above?

2. Prepare a schedule of cost of goods manufactured for the quarter.
3. Prepare a corrected income statement for the quarter. Your statement should show in detail how the cost of goods sold is computed.
4. Do you agree that the insurance company owes Medical Technology, Inc., $227,000? Explain your answer.

C2–22 **Inventory Computations from Incomplete Data** While snoozing at the controls of his Pepper Six airplane, Dunse P. Sluggard leaned heavily against the door; suddenly, the door flew open and a startled Dunse tumbled out. As he parachuted to the ground, Dunse watched helplessly as the empty plane smashed into Operex Products' plant and administrative offices.

"The insurance company will never believe this," cried Mercedes Juliet, the company's controller, as she watched the ensuing fire burn the building to the ground. "The entire company is wiped out!"

"There's no reason to even contact the insurance agent," replied Ford Romero, the company's operations manager. "We can't file a claim without records, and all we have left is this copy of last year's annual report. It shows that raw materials at the beginning of this year (January 1, 19x2) totaled $30,000, work in process totaled $50,000, and finished goods totaled $90,000. But what we need is a record of these inventories as of today, and our records are up in smoke."

"All except this summary page I was working on when the plane hit the building," said Mercedes. "It shows that our sales to date this year have totaled $1,350,000 and that manufacturing overhead cost has totaled $520,000."

"Hey! This annual report is more helpful than I thought," exclaimed Ford. "I can see that our gross margin rate has been 40 percent of sales for years. I can also see that direct labor cost is 20 percent of conversion cost."

"We may have a chance after all," cried Mercedes. "My summary sheet lists prime cost at $510,000 for the year, and it says that our goods available for sale to customers this year has totaled $960,000 at cost. Now if we just knew the amount of raw materials purchased so far this year."

"I know that figure," yelled Ford. "It's $420,000! The purchasing agent gave it to me in our planning meeting yesterday."

"Fantastic," shouted Mercedes. "We'll have our claim ready before the day is over!"

In order to file a claim with the insurance company, Operex Products must determine the amount of cost in its inventories as of October 15, 19x2, the date of the accident. You may assume that all of the materials used in production during the year were direct materials.

Required Determine the amount of cost in the raw materials, work in process, and finished goods inventories as of the date of the accident. (Hint: One way to proceed would be to reconstruct the various schedules and statements that would have been affected by the company's inventories during the year.)

3

Systems Design
Job-Order Costing

LEARNING OBJECTIVES

After studying Chapter 3, you should be able to:

1 Distinguish between process costing and job-order costing and identify companies that would use each costing method.

2 Identify the documents used to control the flow of costs in a job-order costing system.

3 Prepare journal entires to record the flow of direct materials cost, direct labor cost, and manufacturing overhead cost in a job-order costing system.

4 Compute predetermined overhead rates and explain why estimated overhead costs (rather than actual overhead costs) are used in the costing process.

5 Apply overhead cost to Work in Process by use of a predetermined overhead rate.

6 Compute any balance of under- or overapplied overhead cost for a period and prepare the journal entry needed to close the balance into the appropriate accounts.

7 Explain why multiple overhead rates are needed in many organizations.

8 Describe activity-based costing and explain how it improves the accuracy of unit cost data.

9 Prepare journal entries to record the flow of costs in a just-in-time (JIT) inventory system.

10 Define or explain the key terms listed at the end of the chapter.

As discussed in Chapter 2, product costing is the process of assigning manufacturing costs to manufactured goods. An understanding of this process is vital to any manager, since the way in which a product is costed can have a substantial impact on reported net income, as well as on key decisions made by management in day-to-day operations.

In this chapter and in Chapter 4, we look at product costing from the **absorption cost** approach. The approach is so named because it provides for the absorption of all manufacturing costs, fixed and variable, into units of product. It is also known as the **full cost** approach. Later, in Chapter 7, we will look at product costing from another point of view (called *direct costing*) and then discuss the strengths and weaknesses of the two approaches.

As we study product costing, we must keep clearly in mind that *the essential purpose of any costing system is to accumulate costs for managerial use*. A costing system is not an end in itself. Rather, it is a managerial tool in that it exists to provide the manager with the cost data needed to direct the affairs of an organization.

THE NEED FOR UNIT COST DATA

In studying product costing, we will focus initially on *unit cost of production,* an item of cost data that is generally regarded as being highly useful to managers.

Managers need unit cost data for a variety of reasons. First, unit costs are needed to cost inventories on financial statements and to determine a period's net income. If unit costs are incorrectly computed, then both assets and net income will be equally incorrect, as well as the reported profitability of individual product lines.

Second, unit costs are needed to assist management in planning and control of operations. Budgets must be prepared on expected costs at various operating levels, and reports must be generated to provide feedback on where operations can be improved. The usefulness of these budgets and reports will depend in large part on the accuracy of unit cost data.

Finally, unit costs are needed to assist management in a broad range of decision-making situations. Without unit cost data, managers would find it very difficult to set selling prices for products and services.[1] A knowledge of unit costs is also vital in a number of special decision areas, such as whether to add or drop product lines, whether to make or buy production components, whether to expand or contract operations, and whether to accept special orders at special prices. The particular unit costs that are relevant in this variety of decision-making situations will differ, so we need to learn not only how to derive unit costs but also how to differentiate between those costs that are relevant in a particular situation and those that are not. The

[1] We should note here that unit cost represents only one of many factors involved in pricing decisions. Pricing is discussed in depth in Chapter 12.

matter of relevant costs is reserved until later chapters. For the moment, we are concerned with gaining an understanding of the concept of unit cost in its broadest sense.

TYPES OF COSTING SYSTEMS

In computing unit costs, managers are faced with a difficult problem. Many costs (such as rent) are incurred uniformly from month to month whereas production may change frequently, with production going up in one month and then down in another. In addition to variations in the level of production, several different *types* of goods may be produced in a given period. Under these conditions, how is it possible to determine accurate unit costs? The answer is that the computation of unit costs must involve an *averaging* of some type. The way in which this averaging is carried out will depend heavily on the type of manufacturing process involved. Two costing systems have emerged in response to variations in the manufacturing process; these two systems are commonly known as *process costing* and *job-order costing*. Each has its own unique way of averaging costs and thus providing management with unit cost data.

Process Costing

A **process costing system** is employed in those situations where manufacturing involves a single, homogeneous product that is produced for long periods at a time. Examples of industries that use process costing include cement, flour, brick, and various utilities (e.g., natural gas, electricity). All of these industries are characterized by a basically homogeneous product that flows evenly through the production process on a continuous basis.

The basic approach to process costing is to accumulate costs in a particular operation or department for an entire period (month, quarter, year) and then to divide this total by the number of units produced during the period. The basic formula for process costing would be:

$$\frac{\text{Total costs of manufacturing}}{\text{Total units produced (gallons, pounds, bottles)}} = \text{Unit cost (per gallon, pound, bottle)}$$

Since one unit of product (gallon, pound, bottle) is completely indistinguishable from any other unit of product, each unit bears the same average cost as any other unit produced during the period. This costing technique results in a broad, average unit cost figure that applies to many thousands of like units flowing in an almost endless stream off the assembly or processing line.

Job-Order Costing

A **job-order costing system** is used in those manufacturing situations where many *different* products, jobs, or batches of production are being produced each period. Examples of industries that would typically use job-order costing include special-order printing, furniture manufacturing, ship-building, and equipment manufacturing.

Job-order costing is also used extensively in the service industries. Hospitals, law firms, movie studios, accounting firms, advertising agencies, and repair shops, for example, all use job-order costing to accumulate costs for accounting and billing purposes. Although the detailed example of job-order costing provided in the following section deals with a manufacturing firm, the reader should keep in mind that the same basic concepts and procedures are used by many service organizations. More is said on this point later in the chapter.

Because the output of firms involved in the industries mentioned above tends to be heterogeneous, managers need a costing system in which costs can be accumulated *by job (or by client or by customer)* and in which distinct unit costs can be determined for each job completed. Job-order costing provides such a system. However, it is a more complex system than that required by process costing. Under job-order costing, rather than dividing total costs by many thousands of like units, one must somehow divide total costs by a few, basically unlike units. Thus, job-order costing involves certain problems of record keeping and cost assignment that are not found in a process costing system.

Summary of Costing Methods

To summarize this brief introduction to process and job-order costing, regardless of which system one is dealing with, the problem of determining unit costs involves a need for averaging of some type. The essential difference between the process and job-order methods is the way in which this averaging is carried out. In this chapter, we focus on the design of a job-order costing system. In the following chapter, we focus on process costing and also look more closely at the similarities and differences between the two costing methods.

JOB-ORDER COSTING—AN OVERVIEW

In the preceding chapter, the point was made that there are three broad categories of costs involved in the manufacture of any product:

1. Direct materials.
2. Direct labor.
3. Manufacturing overhead.

As we study the design and operation of a job-order costing system, we will look at each of these costs to see how it is involved in the costing of a unit of product. In doing this, we will also look at the various documents involved in job-order costing and give special emphasis to a key document known as a job cost sheet.

Measuring Direct Materials Cost

The production process begins with the transfer of raw materials from the storeroom to the production line. The bulk of these raw materials will be traceable directly to the goods being produced and will therefore be termed

EXHIBIT 3-1
Materials Requisition Form

Materials Requisition Number 14873 Date March 2, 19x2
Job Number to Be Charged 2B47
Department Milling

Description	Quantity	Unit Cost	Total Cost
M46 Housing	2	$123	$246
G7 Connector	8	52	416
			$662

Authorized
Signature Bill White

direct materials. Other materials, generally termed *indirect materials,* will not be charged to a specific job but rather will be included within the general category of manufacturing overhead. As discussed in Chapter 2, indirect materials would include costs of glue, nails, and miscellaneous supplies.

Raw materials are drawn from the storeroom on presentation of a **materials requisition form.** A materials requisition form is shown in Exhibit 3–1.

As shown in the exhibit, the materials requisition form is a detailed source document that specifies the type and quantity of materials that are to be drawn from the storeroom and that identifies the job to which the materials are to be charged. Thus, the form serves as a means both for controlling the flow of materials into production and for making entries in the accounting records.

If the job being worked on involves a product that is frequently manufactured by a company, then any requisition of materials will typically be based on a **bill of materials** that has been prepared for the product. A bill of materials is simply a control sheet that shows the type and quantity of each item of material going into a completed unit.

Job Cost Sheet

The cost of direct materials is entered on a *job cost sheet* similar to the one presented in Exhibit 3–2. A **job cost sheet** is a form prepared for each separate job initiated into production; it serves (1) as a means for accumulating materials, labor, and overhead costs chargeable to a job, and (2) as a means for computing unit costs. Normally, the job cost sheet is not prepared until the accounting department has received notification from the production department that a production order has been issued for a particular job. In turn, a production order is not issued until a definite agreement has been reached with the customer in terms of quantities, prices, and shipment dates.

EXHIBIT 3–2
Job Cost Sheet

JOB COST SHEET

Job Number 2B47

Date Initiated March 2, 19x2

Date Completed

Department Milling

Units Completed

Item Special order coupling

For Stock

Direct Materials		Direct Labor			Manufacturing Overhead		
Req. No.	Amount	Ticket	Hours	Amount	Hours	Rate	Amount
14873	$662						

Cost Summary		Units Shipped		
Direct Materials	$	Date	Number	Balance
Direct Labor	$			
Manufacturing Overhead	$			
Total Cost	$			
Unit Cost	$			

As direct materials are issued, the accounting department makes entries directly on the job cost sheet, thereby charging the specific job noted on the sheet with the cost of materials used in production. When the job is completed, the total cost of materials used can be summarized in the cost summary section as one element involved in determining the total unit cost of the order.

Measuring Direct Labor Cost

Direct labor cost is accumulated and measured in much the same way as direct materials cost. Direct labor includes those labor charges that are directly traceable to the particular job in process. By contrast, those labor charges that cannot be traced directly to a particular job, or that can be traced only with the expenditure of great effort, are treated as part of manufacturing overhead. As discussed in Chapter 2, this latter category of labor costs is termed *indirect labor* and would include such tasks as maintenance, supervision, and cleanup.

Labor costs are generally accumulated by means of some type of work record prepared each day by each employee. These work records, often

EXHIBIT 3–3
Employee Time Ticket

Time Ticket No. 843 Date March 3, 19x2
Employee Mary Holden Station 4

Started	Ended	Time Completed	Rate	Amount	Job Number
7:00	12:00	5.0	$9	$45	2B47
12:30	2:30	2.0	9	18	2B50
2:30	3:30	1.0	9	9	Maintenance
Totals		8.0		$72	

Supervisor R. W. Pace

termed **time tickets,** constitute an hour-by-hour summary of the activities completed during the day by the employee. When working on a specific job, the employee enters the job number on the time ticket and notes the number of hours spent on the particular task involved. When not assigned to a particular job, the employee enters the type of indirect labor tasks to which he or she was assigned (such as cleanup and maintenance) and the number of hours spent on each separate task. An example of an employee time ticket is shown in Exhibit 3–3.

At the end of the day, the time tickets are gathered and the accounting department carefully analyzes each in terms of the number of hours assignable as direct labor to specific jobs and the number of hours assignable to manufacturing overhead as indirect labor. Those hours assignable as direct labor are entered on individual job cost sheets (such as the one shown in Exhibit 3–2), along with the appropriate charges involved. When all direct labor charges associated with a particular job have been accumulated on the job cost sheet, the total can be summarized in the cost summary section. The daily time tickets, in essence, constitute basic source documents used as a basis for labor cost entries into the accounting records.

Application of Manufacturing Overhead

Manufacturing overhead must be considered along with direct materials and direct labor in determining unit costs of production. However, the assignment of manufacturing overhead to units of product is often a difficult task. There are several reasons why this is so.

First, as explained in Chapter 2, manufacturing overhead is an *indirect* cost to units of product and therefore can't be traced directly to a particular product or job. Second, manufacturing overhead consists of many unlike items, involving both variable and fixed costs. It ranges from the grease used in machines to the annual salary of the production superintendent. Finally, firms with large seasonal variations in production often find that even though output is fluctuating, manufacturing overhead costs tend to remain relatively constant. The reason is that fixed costs generally constitute a large part of manufacturing overhead.

Given these problems, about the only acceptable way to assign overhead costs to units of product is to do so through an allocation process. This allocation of overhead costs to products is accomplished by having the manager select an *activity base* that is common to all products that the company manufactures or to all services that the company renders. Then by means of this base, an appropriate amount of overhead cost is assigned to each product or service. The trick, of course, is to choose the right base so that the overhead application will be equitable between jobs.

Historically, the most widely used activity bases have been direct labor-hours (DLH) and direct labor cost, with machine-hours (MH) and even units of product (where a company has only a single product) also used to some extent.

Once an activity base has been chosen, it is divided into the estimated total manufacturing overhead cost of the period in order to obtain a **predetermined overhead rate.** The rate is called predetermined because it is computed *before* the period begins and because it is based entirely on estimated data. After the predetermined overhead rate has been computed, it is then used to apply overhead cost to jobs. In sum, the formula for computing the predetermined overhead rate is:

$$\frac{\text{Estimated total manufacturing overhead costs}}{\text{Estimated total units in the base (MH, DLH, etc.)}} = \text{Predetermined overhead rate}$$

The Need for Estimated Data Actual overhead costs are rarely, if ever, used in overhead costing. The reason is that actual overhead costs are not available until *after* a period is over. This is too late so far as computing unit costs is concerned, since the manager must have unit cost data available at once in order to set prices on products and make other key marketing and operating decisions. The postponing of such decisions until year-end (when actual overhead cost data are available) would destroy an organization's ability to compete effectively. Therefore, in order to have timely data for decision making, most firms *estimate* total overhead costs at the beginning of a year, *estimate* the level of activity for the year, and develop a predetermined overhead rate based on these estimates. Such rates are widely used by both manufacturing and service organizations for costing purposes.

Using the Predetermined Overhead Rate The assigning of overhead cost to jobs (and thereby to units of product) is called **overhead application.** To illustrate the steps involved, assume that a firm has estimated its total manufacturing overhead costs for the year to be $320,000 and has estimated 40,000 total direct labor-hours for the year. Its predetermined overhead rate for the year would be $8 per direct labor-hour, as shown below:

$$\frac{\$320{,}000}{40{,}000 \text{ direct labor-hours}} = \$8 \text{ per direct labor-hour}$$

If a particular job required 27 direct labor-hours to complete, then $216 of overhead cost (27 hours × $8 = $216) would be applied to that job. This overhead application is shown on the job cost sheet in Exhibit 3–4.

Whether the overhead application in Exhibit 3–4 is made slowly as the job is worked on during the period, or in a single application at the time of

EXHIBIT 3–4
A Completed Job Cost Sheet

JOB COST SHEET

Job Number 2B47

Date Initiated March 2, 19x2

Date Completed March 8, 19x2

Department Milling

Item Special order coupling

Units Completed 150

For Stock

Direct Materials		Direct Labor			Manufacturing Overhead		
Req. No.	Amount	Ticket	Hours	Amount	Hours	Rate	Amount
14873	$ 662	843	5	$ 45	27	$8/DLH	$216
14875	504	846	8	60			
14912	238	850	4	21			
	$1,404	851	10	54			
			27	$180			

Cost Summary	
Direct Materials	$1,404
Direct Labor	$ 180
Manufacturing Overhead	$ 216
Total Cost	$1,800
Unit Cost	$ 12*

Units Shipped		
Date	Number	Balance
3/8/x2	—	150

* $1,800 ÷ 150 units = $12 per unit.

completion, is a matter of choice and convenience to the company involved. If a job is not completed at year-end, however, overhead should be applied to the extent needed to properly value the work in process inventory.

Although estimates are involved in the computation of predetermined overhead rates, managers typically become very skilled at making these estimates. As a result, predetermined overhead rates are generally quite accurate, and any difference between the amount of overhead cost that is actually incurred during a period and the amount that is applied to products is usually quite small. This point is discussed further in a following section.

What Drives Overhead Cost?

We stated in Chapter 2 that major shifts are taking place in the structure of costs in some industries. In the past, direct labor has typically accounted for up to 60 percent of the cost of many products with overhead cost making up only a portion of the remainder. With the advent of automation, however, sophisticated new machines are now taking over various functions that used to be performed by direct labor workers. Robots are appearing on the assembly line, and computer-integrated manufacturing (CIM), which requires almost no direct labor input, is being used to control the entire manufacturing process in some companies. As a result of these shifts toward automation, direct labor is becoming less of a factor in the cost of a number of products.

This decrease in the importance of direct labor is accompanied by an increase in the importance of manufacturing overhead, since costly equipment must be depreciated, expensive software must be developed to control manufacturing operations, and so forth. Where processes are largely automated (sometimes referred to as "capital intensive"), direct labor probably has little to do with the incurrence of overhead cost and therefore may not be appropriate as a base for computing overhead rates. Instead, a base should be used that acts as a *cost driver* in the incurrence of overhead cost. A **cost driver** is a measure of activity, such as machine-hours, beds occupied, computer time, flight-hours, or miles driven that is a *causal factor* in the incurrence of cost in an organization. If a base is used to compute overhead rates that does not "drive" overhead costs, then the result will be inaccurate rates and distorted product costs.

We must hasten to add that although direct labor is decreasing in importance in some industries, in other industries it continues to be a significant part of total product cost. In these latter industries, therefore, it remains a viable base for computing overhead rates and for applying overhead cost to products. The key point managers must recognize is that direct labor is not an appropriate allocation base in *every* situation and indeed has become totally irrelevant in some settings. This point is discussed further in a later section.

Computation of Unit Costs

With the application of manufacturing overhead to the job cost sheet, total costs of the job can be summarized in the cost summary section. (See Exhibit 3–4 for an example of a completed job cost sheet.) The cost of the individual units in the job can then be obtained by dividing the total costs by the number of units produced. The completed job cost sheet is then ready to be transferred to the finished goods inventory file, where it will serve as a basis for either costing unsold units in the ending inventory or charging expense for units sold.

Summary of Document Flows

The sequence of events just discussed is summarized in Exhibit 3–5. A careful study of the flow of documents in this exhibit will provide an excellent visual review of the overall operation of a job-order costing system.

JOB-ORDER COSTING—THE FLOW OF COSTS

Having obtained a broad, conceptual perspective of the operation of a job-order costing system, we are now prepared to take a look at the flow of actual costs through the system itself. We shall consider a single month's

EXHIBIT 3–5
The Flow of Documents in a Job-Order Costing System

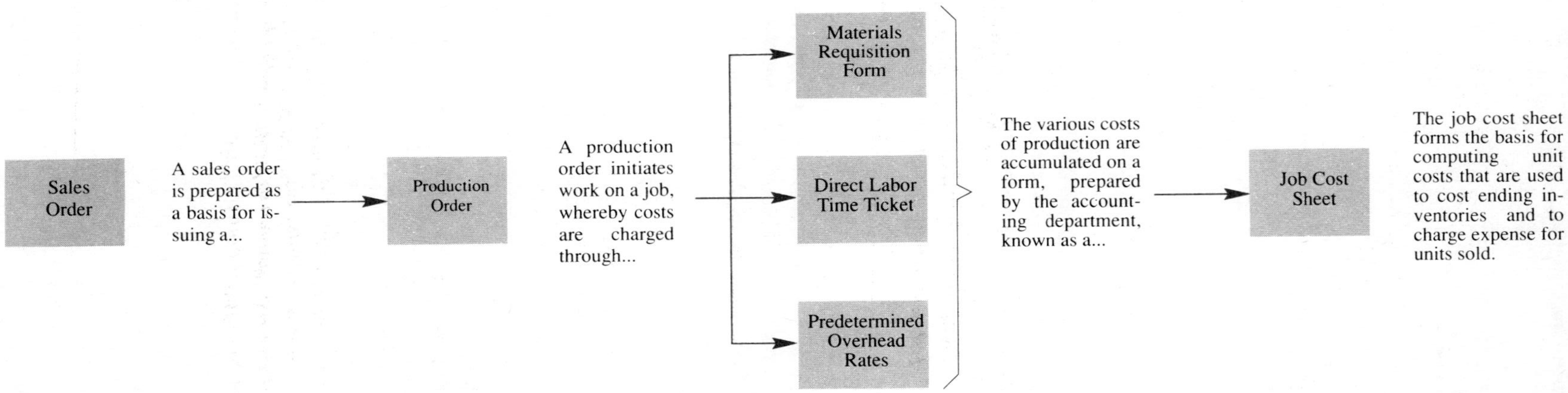

Sales Order

A sales order is prepared as a basis for issuing a...

Production Order

A production order initiates work on a job, whereby costs are charged through...

Materials Requisition Form

Direct Labor Time Ticket

Predetermined Overhead Rates

The various costs of production are accumulated on a form, prepared by the accounting department, known as a...

Job Cost Sheet

The job cost sheet forms the basis for computing unit costs that are used to cost ending inventories and to charge expense for units sold.

activity for a hypothetical company, presenting all data in summary form. As a basis for discussion, let us assume that Rand Company had two jobs in process during April, the first month of its fiscal year. Job A was started during March and had $30,000 in manufacturing costs (materials, labor, and overhead) already accumulated on April 1. Job B was started during April.

The Purchase and Issue of Materials

During April, Rand Company purchased $60,000 in raw materials for use in production. The purchase is recorded in entry (1) below:

(1)

Raw Materials.	60,000	
Accounts Payable		60,000

As explained in Chapter 2, Raw Materials is an inventory account. Thus, any materials remaining in the account at the end of a period will appear on the balance sheet under an inventory classification.

Issue of Direct Materials During the month, Rand Company drew $50,000 in raw materials from the storeroom for use in production. Entry (2) records the issue of the materials to the production departments.

(2)

Work in Process.	50,000	
Raw Materials.		50,000

The materials charged to Work in Process represent direct materials assignable to specific jobs on the production line. As these materials are entered into the Work in Process account, they are also recorded on the separate job cost sheets to which they relate. This point is illustrated in Exhibit 3–6 on the following page.

Notice from the job cost sheets that job A contains the $30,000 in manufacturing cost which we mentioned was carried forward from last month. Also note that the Work in Process account contains the same $30,000 balance. *The reason the $30,000 appears in both places is that the Work in Process account is a control account and the job cost sheets form a subsidiary ledger. Thus, the Work in Process account contains a summarized total of all costs appearing on the individual job cost sheets for all jobs in process at any given point in time.* (Since Rand Company had only job A in process at the beginning of April, job A's $30,000 balance on that date is equal to the balance in the Work in Process account.) Of the $50,000 in materials added to Work in Process during April, $28,000 was chargeable directly to job A and $22,000 was chargeable to job B, as shown in Exhibit 3–6.

Issue of Both Direct and Indirect Materials In entry (2) above, we have assumed that all of the materials drawn from the Raw Materials inventory account were assignable to specific jobs as direct materials. If some of the materials

EXHIBIT 3–6
Raw Materials Cost Flows

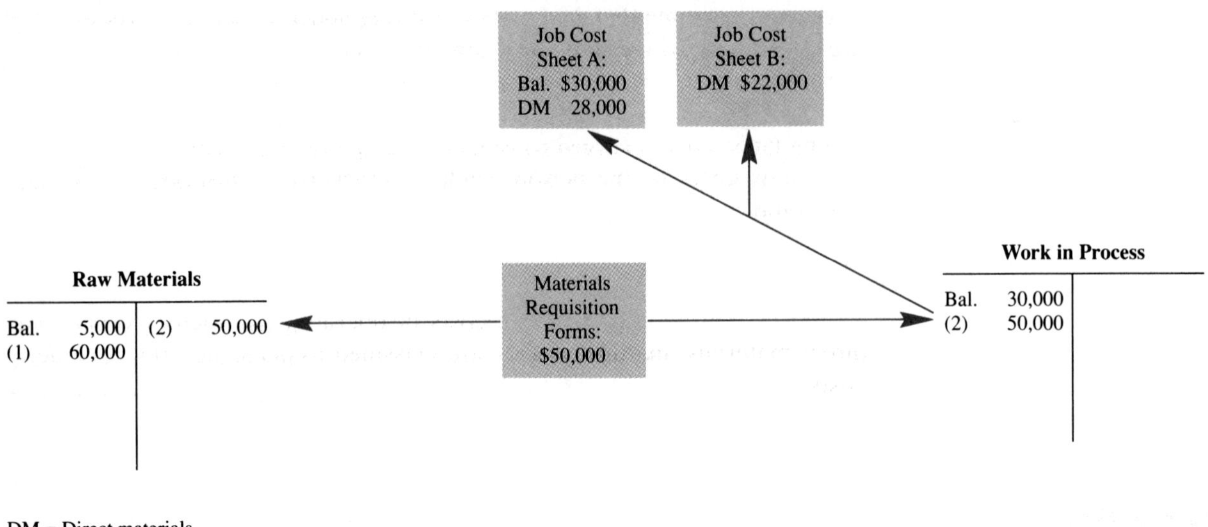

DM = Direct materials

drawn are not assignable to specific jobs, then they must be charged to Manufacturing Overhead as indirect materials. The entry to do this would be:

Work in Process (direct materials)	XXX	
Manufacturing Overhead (indirect materials)	XXX	
Raw Materials		XXX

Observe that the Manufacturing Overhead account is separate from the Work in Process account. The purpose of the Manufacturing Overhead account is to accumulate all manufacturing overhead costs as they are incurred during a period.

Labor Cost

As work is performed in various departments of Rand Company from day to day, employee time tickets are generated, collected, and forwarded to the accounting department. There the tickets are costed according to the various rates paid to the employees, and the resulting costs are classified in terms of being either direct or indirect labor. This costing and classification for the month of April resulted in the following entry:

(3)		
Work in Process	60,000	
Manufacturing Overhead	15,000	
Salaries and Wages Payable		75,000

Only that portion of labor cost that represents direct labor is added to the Work in Process account. For Rand Company, this amounted to $60,000 for April.

At the same time that direct labor costs are added to Work in Process they are also added to the individual job cost sheets, as shown in Exhibit 3–7. During April, $40,000 of direct labor cost was chargeable to job A and the remaining $20,000 was chargeable to job B.

The labor costs charged to Manufacturing Overhead represent the indirect labor costs of the period, such as supervision, janitorial work, and maintenance.

Manufacturing Overhead Costs

As we learned in Chapter 2, all costs of operating the factory other than direct materials and direct labor are classified as manufacturing overhead costs. These costs are entered directly into the Manufacturing Overhead

EXHIBIT 3–7
Labor Cost Flows

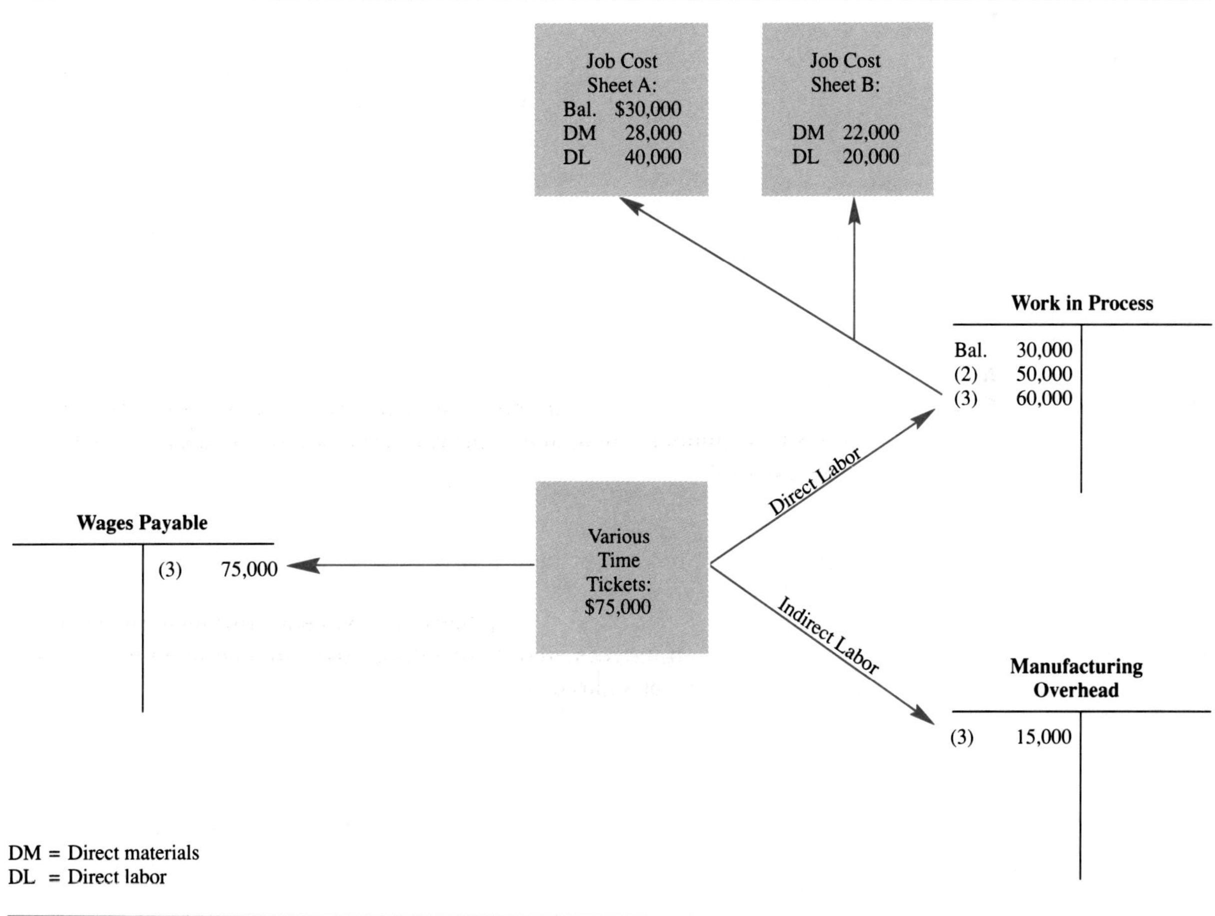

account as they are incurred. To illustrate, assume that Rand Company incurred the following general factory costs during the month of April:

Utilities (heat, water, and power)	$21,000
Rent on equipment	16,000
Miscellaneous factory costs	3,000
Total	$40,000

The entry to record the incurrence of these costs would be:

(4)		
Manufacturing Overhead	40,000	
Accounts Payable		40,000

In addition, let us assume that during April, Rand Company recognized $13,000 in accrued property taxes and $9,000 in insurance expired on factory buildings and equipment. The entry to record these items would be:

(5)		
Manufacturing Overhead	22,000	
Property Taxes Payable		13,000
Prepaid Insurance		9,000

Let us further assume that the company recognized $18,000 in depreciation on factory equipment during April. The entry to record the accrual of depreciation would be:

(6)		
Manufacturing Overhead	18,000	
Accumulated Depreciation		18,000

In short, *all* manufacturing overhead costs are recorded directly into the Manufacturing Overhead account as they are incurred day by day throughout a period. Notice from the entries above that the recording of *actual* manufacturing overhead costs has no effect on the Work in Process account.

The Application of Manufacturing Overhead

How is the Work in Process account charged for manufacturing overhead cost? The answer is, by means of the predetermined overhead rate. Recall from our discussion earlier in the chapter that for costing purposes a predetermined overhead rate is established at the beginning of each year. The rate is calculated by dividing the estimated manufacturing overhead cost for the year by the estimated activity (measured in machine-hours, direct labor-hours, or some other base). As the year progresses, overhead cost is then applied to each job by multiplying the number of hours it requires for completion by the predetermined overhead rate that has been set.

EXHIBIT 3–8
The Flow of Costs in Overhead Application

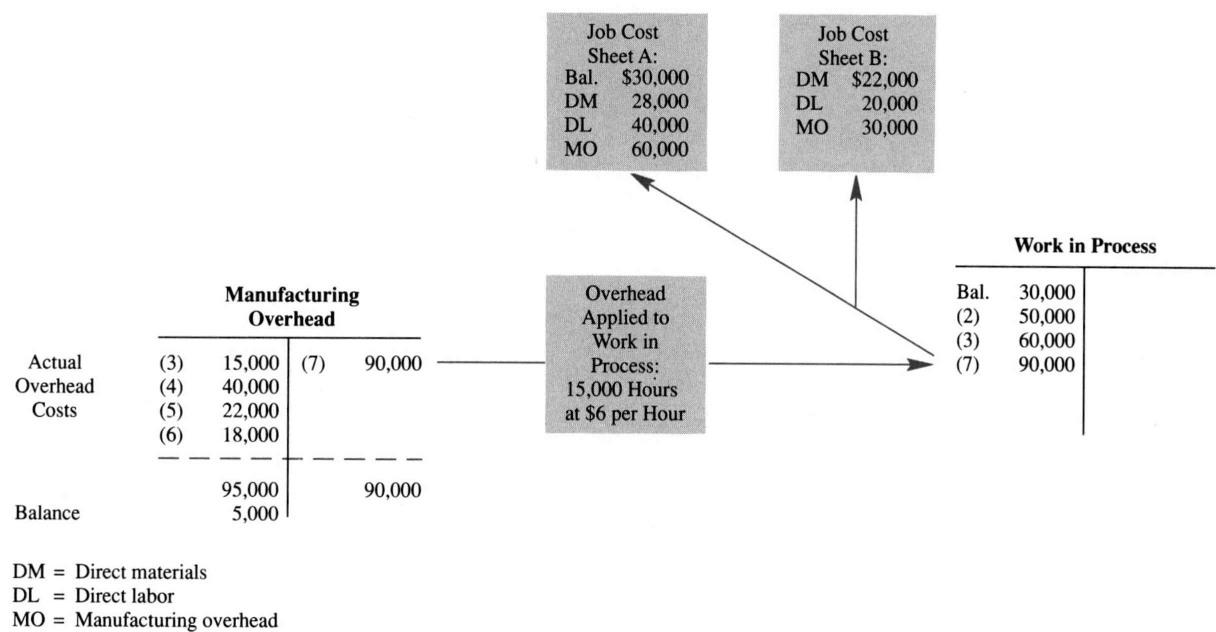

To illustrate the cost flows involved, assume that Rand Company has used machine-hours in computing its predetermined overhead rate and that this rate is $6 per machine-hour. Also assume that during April, 10,000 machine-hours were worked on job A and 5,000 machine-hours were worked on job B (a total of 15,000 machine-hours). Thus, $90,000 in overhead cost (15,000 machine-hours × $6 = $90,000) would be applied to Work in Process. The entry to record the application would be:

(7)		
Work in Process	90,000	
Manufacturing Overhead		90,000

The flow of costs through the Manufacturing Overhead account is shown in T-account format in Exhibit 3–8.

The "actual overhead costs" in the Manufacturing Overhead account in Exhibit 3–8 are the costs that were added to the account in entries (3)–(6). Observe that the incurrence of these actual overhead costs [entries (3)–(6)] and the application of overhead to Work in Process [entry (7)] represent two separate and distinct processes.

The Concept of a Clearing Account The Manufacturing Overhead account operates as a clearing account. As we have noted, actual factory overhead costs are charged to it as they are incurred day by day throughout the year.

At certain intervals during the year, usually when a job is completed, overhead cost is released from the Manufacturing Overhead account and is applied to the Work in Process account by means of the predetermined overhead rate. This sequence of events is illustrated below:

Actual overhead costs are charged to the account as these costs are incurred day by day throughout the period.	→	**Manufacturing Overhead (a clearing account)**	→	Overhead is applied to Work in Process on a periodic basis by means of the predetermined overhead rate.

As we emphasized earlier, the predetermined overhead rate is based entirely on estimates of what overhead costs are *expected* to be, and it is established before the year begins. As a result, the overhead cost applied during a year may turn out to be more or less than the overhead cost that is actually incurred. For example, notice from Exhibit 3–8 that Rand Company's actual overhead costs for the period are $5,000 greater than the overhead cost that has been applied to Work in Process, resulting in a $5,000 debit balance in the Manufacturing Overhead account. We will reserve discussion of what to do with this $5,000 balance until a later section, "Problems of Overhead Application."

For the moment, we can conclude by noting from Exhibit 3–8 that the cost of a completed job consists of the actual materials cost of the job, the actual labor cost of the job, and an *applied* amount of overhead cost to the job. The fact that it is applied overhead cost (not actual overhead cost) that goes into the Work in Process account and onto the job cost sheets is a subtle point that is easy to miss. Thus, this section of the chapter requires special study and consideration.

Nonmanufacturing Costs

In addition to incurring costs such as salaries, utilities, and insurance as part of the operation of the factory, manufacturing companies will also incur these same kinds of costs in relation to other parts of their operations. For example, there will be these types of costs arising from activities in the "front office" where secretaries, top management, and others work. There will be identical kinds of costs arising from the operation of the sales staff. *The costs of these nonfactory operations should not go into the Manufacturing Overhead account because the incurrence of these costs is not related to the manufacture of products.* Rather, these costs should be treated as expenses of the period, as explained in Chapter 2, and charged directly to the income statement. To illustrate, assume that Rand Company incurred selling and administrative costs as follows during the month of April:

Top-management salaries	$21,000
Other office salaries.	9,000
Total salaries.	$30,000

The entry to record these salaries would be:

(8)		
Salaries Expense	30,000	
Salaries and Wages Payable		30,000

Assume that depreciation on office equipment during the month of April was $7,000. The entry would be:

(9)		
Depreciation Expense	7,000	
Accumulated Depreciation		7,000

Pay particular attention to the difference between this entry and entry (6) on page 78 where we recorded depreciation on factory equipment.

Finally, assume that advertising was $42,000 and that other selling and administrative expenses totaled $8,000 for the month. The entry to record these items would be:

(10)		
Advertising Expense	42,000	
Other Selling and Administrative Expense	8,000	
Accounts Payable		50,000

Since the amounts in entries (8) through (10) all go directly into expense accounts, they will have no effect on the costing of Rand Company's production for the month. The same will be true of all other selling and administrative expenses incurred during the month, including sales commissions, depreciation on sales equipment, rent on office facilities, insurance on office facilities, and related costs.

Cost of Goods Manufactured

When a job has been completed, the finished output is transferred from the production departments to the finished goods warehouse. By this time, the accounting department will have charged the job with direct materials and direct labor cost, and the job will have absorbed a portion of manufacturing overhead through the application process discussed earlier. A transfer of these costs must be made within the costing system that *parallels* the physical transfer of the goods to the finished goods warehouse. The transfer within the costing system will be to move the costs of the completed job out of the Work in Process account and into the Finished Goods account. The sum of all amounts transferred between these two accounts represents the cost of goods manufactured for the period. (This point was illustrated earlier in Exhibit 2–5 in Chapter 2. The reader may wish to go back to Exhibit 2–5 and refresh this point before reading on.)

In the case of Rand Company, let us assume that job A was completed during April. The entry to transfer the cost of job A from Work in Process to Finished Goods would be:

(11)		
Finished Goods	158,000	
Work in Process.		158,000

The $158,000 represents the completed cost of job A, as shown on the job cost sheet in Exhibit 3–8. Since job A was the only job completed during April, the $158,000 also represents the cost of goods manufactured for the month.

Job B was not completed by month-end, so its cost will remain in the Work in Process account and carry over to the next month. If a balance sheet is prepared at the end of April, the cost accumulated thus far on job B will appear under the caption "Work in process inventory" in the assets section.

Cost of Goods Sold

As units of product in finished goods are shipped to fill customers orders, the unit cost appearing on the job cost sheets is used as a basis for transferring the cost of the sold items from the Finished Goods account into the Cost of Goods Sold account. If a complete job is shipped, as in the case where a job has been done to a customer's specifications, then it is a simple matter to transfer the entire cost appearing on the job cost sheet into the Cost of Goods Sold account. In most cases, however, only a portion of the units involved in a particular job will be sold. In these situations, the unit cost is particularly important in knowing how much product cost should be removed from Finished Goods and charged into Cost of Goods Sold.

For Rand Company, we will assume that three fourths of the units in job A were shipped to customers by month-end. The total selling price of these units was $225,000. The entries needed to record the sale would be (all sales are on account):

(12)		
Accounts Receivable.	225,000	
Sales.		225,000

(13)		
Cost of Goods Sold	118,500	
Finished Goods		118,500
($158,000 total cost × ¾ = $118,500)		

With entry (13), the flow of costs through our job-order costing system is completed.

Summary of Cost Flows

To pull the entire Rand Company example together, a summary of cost flows is presented in T-account form in Exhibit 3–9. The flows of costs through the

EXHIBIT 3–9

Summary of Cost Flows—Rand Company

Accounts Receivable

	XX		
(12)	225,000		

Accounts Payable

			XX
		(1)	60,000
		(4)	40,000
		(10)	50,000

Capital Stock

			XX

Prepaid Insurance

	XX		
		(5)	9,000

Retained Earnings

			XX

Raw Materials

Bal.	5,000	(2)	50,000
(1)	60,000		
Bal.	15,000		

Salaries and Wages Payable

			XX
		(3)	75,000
		(8)	30,000

Sales

		(12)	225,000

Work in Process

Bal.	30,000	(11)	158,000
(2)	50,000		
(3)	60,000		
(7)	90,000		
Bal.	72,000		

Property Taxes Payable

			XX
		(5)	13,000

Cost of Goods Sold

(13)	118,500		

Salaries Expense

(8)	30,000		

Finished Goods

Bal.	10,000	(13)	118,500
(11)	158,000		
Bal.	49,500		

Depreciation Expense

(9)	7,000		

Advertising Expense

(10)	42,000		

Accumulated Depreciation

			XX
		(6)	18,000
		(9)	7,000

Other Selling and Administrative Expense

(10)	8,000		

Manufacturing Overhead

(3)	15,000	(7)	90,000
(4)	40,000		
(5)	22,000		
(6)	18,000		
Bal.	5,000		

Note: XX = Normal balance in the account (for example, Accounts Receivable normally carries a debit balance).

Explanation of entries:

(1) Raw materials purchased.
(2) Raw materials issued into production.
(3) Factory labor costs incurred.
(4) Utilities and other factory costs incurred.
(5) Property taxes and insurance incurred on the factory.
(6) Depreciation recorded on factory assets.
(7) Overhead cost applied to Work in Process.
(8) Administrative salaries expense incurred.
(9) Depreciation recorded on office equipment.
(10) Advertising and other expense incurred.
(11) Cost of goods manufactured transferred into finished goods.
(12) Sale of job A recorded.
(13) Cost of goods sold recorded for job A.

exhibit are keyed to the numbers (1) through (13). These numbers relate to the numbers of the transactions appearing on the preceding pages.

Exhibit 3–10 presents a schedule of cost of goods manufactured and a schedule of cost of goods sold for Rand Company. Note particularly from Exhibit 3–10 that the cost of goods manufactured for the month ($158,000) agrees with the amount transferred from Work in Process to Finished Goods for the month as recorded earlier in entry (11).

EXHIBIT 3–10

Schedules of Cost of Goods Manufactured and Cost of Goods Sold

Cost of Goods Manufactured		
Direct materials:		
Raw materials inventory, April 1	$ 5,000	
Add: Purchases of raw materials	60,000	
Total raw materials available	65,000	
Deduct: Raw materials inventory, April 30	15,000	
Raw materials used in production		$ 50,000
Direct labor		60,000
Manufacturing overhead:		
Indirect labor	15,000	
Utilities	21,000	
Rent	16,000	
Miscellaneous factory costs	3,000	
Property taxes	13,000	
Insurance	9,000	
Depreciation	18,000	
Actual overhead costs	95,000	
Less underapplied overhead	5,000*	
Overhead applied to work in process		90,000
Total manufacturing costs		200,000
Add: Beginning work in process inventory		30,000
		230,000
Deduct: Ending work in process inventory		72,000
Cost of goods manufactured		$158,000
Cost of Goods Sold		
Opening finished goods inventory		$ 10,000
Add: Cost of goods manufactured		158,000
Goods available for sale		168,000
Ending finished goods inventory		49,500
Cost of goods sold		118,500
Add: Underapplied overhead		5,000
Adjusted cost of goods sold		$123,500

* Note that underapplied overhead must be deducted from actual overhead costs and only the difference ($90,000) is added to direct materials and direct labor. The reason only $90,000 is added to materials and labor is that the schedule of cost of goods manufactured represents a summary of costs flowing through the Work in Process account during a period and therefore must exclude any overhead costs that were incurred but never applied to production. If a reverse situation had existed and overhead had been overapplied during the period, then the amount of overapplied overhead would have been added to actual overhead costs on the schedule. This would have brought the actual overhead costs up to the amount that had been applied to production.

Also note that the underapplied overhead deducted on the schedule of cost of goods manufactured is added to cost of goods sold. The reverse would be true if overhead had been overapplied.

PROBLEMS OF OVERHEAD APPLICATION

Before concluding our discussion of job-order costing, we need to briefly consider two problem areas relating to overhead application. These are: (1) the concept of underapplied and overapplied overhead, and (2) the disposition of any balance remaining in the Manufacturing Overhead account at the end of a period.

The Concept of Underapplied and Overapplied Overhead

Since the predetermined overhead rate is established before a period begins, and since it is based entirely on estimated data, there will generally be a difference between the amount of overhead cost that is applied to the Work in Process account and the amount of overhead cost that is actually incurred during a period. In the case of Rand Company, for example, the predetermined overhead rate of $6 per hour resulted in $90,000 of overhead cost being applied to Work in Process, whereas actual overhead costs proved to be $95,000 for the month (see Exhibit 3–8). The difference between the overhead cost applied to Work in Process and the actual overhead costs of a period is termed either **underapplied** or **overapplied overhead.** For Rand Company, overhead was underapplied because the applied cost ($90,000) was $5,000 less than the actual cost ($95,000). If the tables had been reversed and the company had applied $95,000 in overhead cost to Work in Process while incurring actual overhead costs of only $90,000, then a situation of overapplied overhead would have existed.

Since the amount of overhead applied to Work in Process is dependent on the predetermined overhead rate, any difference between applied overhead cost and actual overhead cost must be traceable to the estimates going into the overhead rate computation. To illustrate, refer again to the formula used in computing the predetermined overhead rate:

$$\frac{\text{Estimated total manufacturing overhead costs}}{\text{Estimated total units in the base (machine-hours, etc.)}} = \text{Predetermined overhead rate}$$

If either the estimated cost or the estimated level of activity used in this formula differs from the actual cost or the actual level of activity for a period, then the predetermined overhead rate will prove to be inaccurate. The result will be either under- or overapplied overhead for the period. Assume, for example, that two companies have prepared the following estimated data for the year 19x1:

	Company	
	A	**B**
Predetermined overhead rate based on	Machine-hours	Direct materials cost
Estimated manufacturing overhead for 19x1	$300,000 (*a*)	$120,000 (*a*)
Estimated machine-hours for 19x1	75,000 (*b*)	—
Estimated direct materials cost for 19x1	—	$ 80,000 (*b*)
Predetermined overhead rate, (*a*) ÷ (*b*)	$4 per machine-hour	150% of direct materials cost

Now assume that the *actual* overhead cost and the *actual* activity recorded during the year in each company are as follows:

	Company	
	A	B
Actual manufacturing overhead costs	$290,000	$130,000
Actual machine-hours	68,000	—
Actual direct materials cost	—	$ 90,000

For each company, notice that the actual cost and activity data differ from the estimates used in computing the predetermined overhead rate. The computation of the resulting under- or overapplied overhead for each company is given below:

	Company	
	A	B
Actual manufacturing overhead costs	$290,000	$130,000
Manufacturing overhead cost applied to Work in Process during 19x1:		
68,000 *actual* machine-hours × $4	272,000	
$90,000 *actual* direct materials cost × 150%		135,000
Underapplied (overapplied) overhead	$ 18,000	$ (5,000)

For Company A, notice that the amount of overhead cost that has been applied to Work in Process ($272,000) is less than the actual overhead cost for the year ($290,000). Therefore, overhead is underapplied. Also notice that the original estimate of overhead in Company A ($300,000) is not directly involved in this computation. Its impact is felt only through the $4 predetermined overhead rate that is used.

For Company B, the amount of overhead cost that has been applied to Work in Process ($135,000) is greater than the actual overhead cost for the year ($130,000), and so a situation of overapplied overhead exists.

A summary of the concepts discussed in this section is presented in Exhibit 3–11.

Disposition of Under- or Overapplied Overhead Balances

What disposition should be made of any under- or overapplied balance remaining in the Manufacturing Overhead account at the end of a period? Generally, any balance in the account is treated in one of two ways:

1. Closed out to Cost of Goods Sold.
2. Allocated between Work in Process, Finished Goods, and Cost of Goods Sold in proportion to the ending balances in these accounts.[2]

The choice between these two approaches depends in large part on the amount of under- or overapplied overhead involved. The greater the amount, the more likely a company is to choose alternative 2.

....

[2] Some firms prefer to make the allocation on a basis of the amount of *overhead cost* in the above accounts at the end of a period. This approach to allocation will yield more accurate results in those situations where the amount of overhead cost differs substantially between jobs. For purposes of consistency, when we allocate in this book it will always be on a basis of the ending balances in the above accounts.

EXHIBIT 3–11
Summary of Overhead Concepts

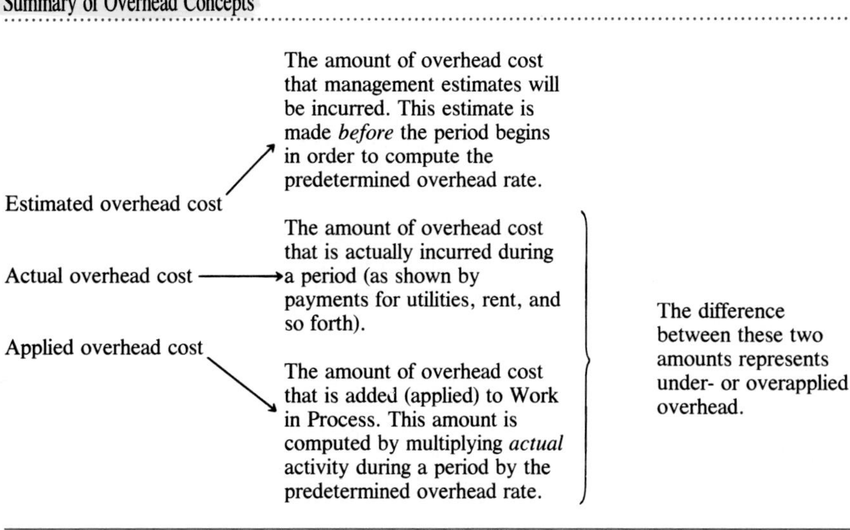

Closed Out to Cost of Goods Sold If the balance in the Manufacturing Overhead account is small, most companies will close it out directly to Cost of Goods Sold, since this approach is simpler than allocation. Returning to the example of Rand Company, the entry to close the underapplied overhead to Cost of Goods sold would be (see Exhibit 3–9 for the $5,000 cost figure):

(14)

Cost of Goods Sold	5,000	
Manufacturing Overhead		5,000

With this entry, the cost of goods sold for the month increases to $123,500, as shown earlier:

Cost of goods sold (from Exhibit 3–9)	$118,500
Add underapplied overhead [entry (14) above]	5,000
Adjusted cost of goods sold	$123,500

After this adjustment has been made, Rand Company's income statement for the month will appear as shown in Exhibit 3–12.

Allocated between Accounts Allocation of under- or overapplied overhead between Work in Process, Finished Goods, and Cost of Goods Sold is more accurate than closing the entire balance into Cost of Goods Sold. The reason is that allocation assigns overhead costs to where they would have gone in the first place had it not been for the errors in the estimates going into the predetermined overhead rate. Although allocation is more accurate than direct write-off, it is used less often in actual practice because of the time and difficulty involved in the allocation process. Most managers believe that the greater accuracy simply isn't worth the extra effort that allocation requires, particularly when the dollar amounts are small.

EXHIBIT 3–12

RAND COMPANY
Income Statement
For the Month of April 19xx

Sales		$225,000
Less cost of goods sold ($118,500 + $5,000)		123,500
Gross margin		101,500
Less selling and administrative expenses:		
Salaries expense	$30,000	
Depreciation expense	7,000	
Advertising expense	42,000	
Other expense	8,000	87,000
Net income		$ 14,500

Had we chosen to allocate the underapplied overhead in the Rand Company example, the computations and entry would have been:

Work in process inventory, April 30	$ 72,000	30.0%
Finished goods inventory, April 30	49,500	20.6
Cost of goods sold	118,500	49.4
Total cost	$240,000	100.0%

Work in Process (30.0% × $5,000)	1,500	
Finished Goods (20.6% × $5,000)	1,030	
Cost of Goods Sold (49.4% × $5,000)	2,470	
Manufacturing Overhead		5,000

If overhead had been overapplied, the entry above would have been just the reverse, since a credit balance would have existed in the Manufacturing Overhead account.

A General Model of Product Cost Flows

The flow of costs in a product costing system can be presented in general model form, as shown in Exhibit 3–13. This model applies as much to a process costing system as it does to a job-order costing system. Visual inspection of the model can be very helpful in gaining a perspective as to how costs enter a system, flow through it, and finally end up as cost of goods sold on the income statement.

JOB-ORDER COSTING IN SERVICE COMPANIES

We stated earlier in the chapter that job-order costing is used extensively in service organizations such as law firms, movie studios, hospitals, and repair shops, as well as in manufacturing companies. In a law firm, for example, each client represents a "job," and the costs of that job are accumulated day by day on a job cost sheet as the client's case is handled by the firm. Paper supplies and similar inputs represent the direct materials for the job; the time expended by attorneys represents the direct labor; and the costs of secretaries, clerks, rent, depreciation, and so forth, represent the overhead.

EXHIBIT 3–13
A General Model of Cost Flows

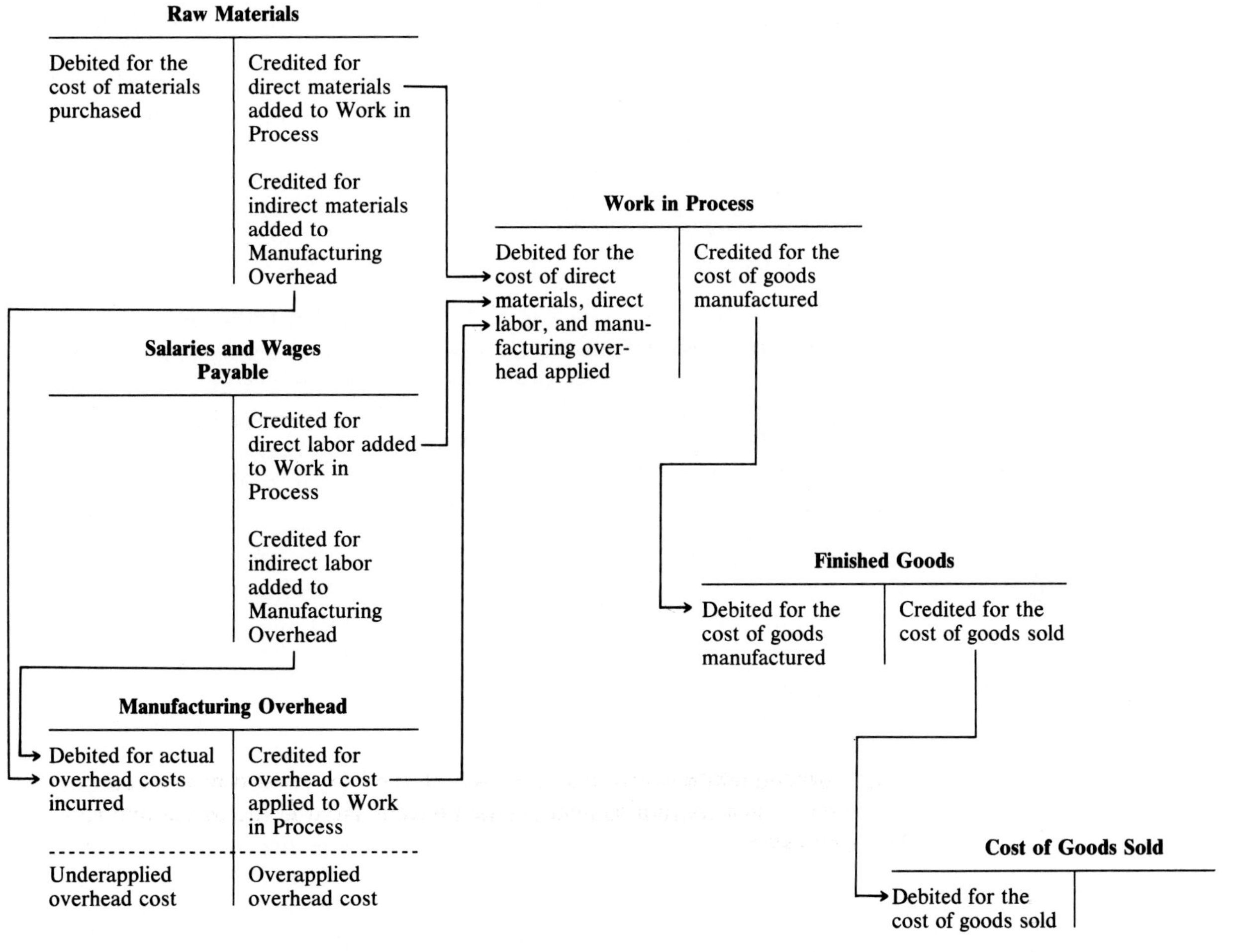

In a movie studio, each picture produced by the studio is a "job," and costs for direct materials (costumes, props, film, etc.) and direct labor (actors, directors, and extras) are carefully accounted for and charged to each picture's job cost sheet. A proportionate share of the studio's overhead costs, such as utilities, depreciation of equipment, salaries of maintenance workers, and so forth, is also charged to each picture. In a movie studio, overhead would typically be applied to jobs on a basis of camera time, or space and time occupied in a studio, rather than applied on a basis of actors' time or cost. On the other hand, in a law firm, an attorney's time may be the most appropriate basis for recognizing overhead cost when determining the cost of a case and billing a client.

In sum, the reader should be aware that job-order costing is a versatile and widely used costing method, and that he or she can expect to encounter it in virtually any organization where the output differs between products, patients, clients, or customers.

ACTIVITY-BASED COSTING

The most difficult task in computing accurate unit costs lies in determining the proper amount of overhead cost to assign to each job or to each unit of product. Three different approaches are available to help the manager in the task of overhead assignment. These approaches differ in terms of level of complexity, ranging from what we term Level One, the least complex, to Level Three, the most complex. Level Three, which deals with *activity-based costing,* is widely viewed as being the most accurate of the three approaches to overhead cost assignment.

Level One: Plantwide Overhead Rate

Our discussion in this chapter has assumed that a single overhead rate was being used throughout an entire factory operation. Such a rate is known formally as a **plantwide overhead rate,** since it encompasses all parts of a company. Historically, such rates have dominated industry practice, but their accuracy is now being called into question because they tend to rely solely on direct labor as an allocation base, which in turn can lead to distorted unit costs.

Direct Labor as a Base In the early part of the 20th century, when cost systems first began to be developed, direct labor constituted a major part of total product cost. Consequently, direct labor was typically chosen as the base for assigning overhead cost to products. Data relating to direct labor were readily available and highly convenient to use, and there was a high correlation in most companies between direct labor and the incurrence of overhead cost. Therefore, direct labor made an excellent allocation base.

Even today, direct labor remains a viable base for applying overhead cost in some companies, both in this country and abroad. In Japan, for example, which has become a world leader in manufacturing technology, direct labor-hours are still widely used as a base in overhead application.[3] Recent studies also reveal high correlations between direct labor and the incurrence of overhead costs in some industries.[4] The circumstances under which direct labor may be appropriate as a base for assigning overhead cost to products include the following:

1. Direct labor is a significant element of total product cost.
2. The amount of direct labor input and the amount of machine input does not differ greatly between products.
3. Products do not differ greatly in terms of volume or individual lot size.
4. A high statistical correlation can be established between direct labor and the incurrence of overhead costs (i.e., direct labor acts as a cost driver for overhead).

[3] Callie Berliner and James A. Brimson (eds.), *Cost Management for Today's Advanced Manufacturing* (Boston: Harvard Business School Press, 1988), p. 232.

[4] George Foster and Mahendra Gupta, "Manufacturing Overhead Cost Driver Analysis," unpublished paper presented at the annual meeting of the American Accounting Association, Orlando, Florida, April 1988.

Changing Manufacturing Environment So long as the above circumstances exist, accurate unit costs can be obtained using direct labor as an allocation base. However, events of the past two decades have made drastic changes in these circumstances in some industries. Automation has greatly decreased the amount of direct labor required; companies have diversified their products both in terms of volume and the amount of machine time required in production; and total overhead cost has increased to the point in some companies that a correlation no longer exists between it and direct labor. Where these changes have prevailed, companies that have continued to use plantwide overhead rates and direct labor as a basis for overhead assignment have experienced major distortions in unit costs. To overcome these distortions and to get better traceability of overhead costs to products, managers have turned to other overhead assignment methods.

Level Two: Departmental Overhead Rates

Rather than use a plantwide overhead rate, some companies use a "two-stage" allocation process. In the first stage, overhead costs are assigned to cost pools, such as individual departments or operations. In the second stage, costs are allocated from the cost pools (departments) to individual jobs. These second stage allocations are made on various bases, according to the nature of the work performed in the department.

One department may be labor intensive, for example, and rely almost solely on the efforts of skilled workers in performing needed functions. Allocation of overhead costs in such a department could, perhaps, be done most equitably on a basis of labor-hours or labor cost. Another department in the same factory may be machine intensive, requiring little in the way of worker effort. Allocation of overhead costs in that department could, perhaps, be done most equitably on a basis of machine-hours. Still another department may find it more equitable to assign overhead costs on a basis of computer time logged or raw materials used.

In short, companies who follow this approach have *many* predetermined overhead rates—perhaps a different one for each department. As a unit of product moves along the production line, overhead is applied in each department according to the various overhead rates that have been set. The accumulation of all of these overhead applications represents the total overhead cost of the job.

Level Three: Activity-Based Costing

Even departmental overhead rates will not be equitable in assigning overhead costs in situations where a company has a number of products that differ in volume and complexity of production. Where differences in volume and complexity exist, *activity-based costing* should be used. **Activity-based costing** involves a two-stage allocation process, as described earlier, with the first stage again assigning overhead costs to cost pools. However, *many* more pools are used under this approach, and they are defined differently. Rather than being defined as departments, the pools represent *activities*, such as setups required, purchase orders issued, and number of inspections completed. In the second stage, costs are assigned to jobs according to the number of these activities required in their completion.

An activity is any event or transaction that is a cost driver—that is, that acts as a causal factor in the incurrence of cost in an organization. Examples of activities that act as cost drivers include the following:

1. Machine setups.
2. Purchase orders.
3. Quality inspections.
4. Production orders (scheduling).
5. Engineering change orders.
6. Shipments.
7. Material receipts.
8. Inventory movements.
9. Maintenance requests.
10. Scrap/rework orders.
11. Machine time.
12. Power consumed.
13. Miles driven.
14. Computer-hours logged.
15. Beds occupied.
16. Flight-hours logged.

The number of these activities in an organization is a function of the complexity of operations. The more complex a company's operations, the more cost-driving activities it is likely to have. As companies have moved from the simple, direct labor-based operations of 30 years ago to the complex, highly automated (and highly competitive) operations of today, the number of cost-driving activities has increased manyfold. Managers have discovered, however, that not all products and services share equally in these activities.

One product in a company, for example, may be a low-volume item that requires frequent machine setups, has many intricate parts requiring numerous purchase orders, and requires constant inspections to maintain quality. Another product in the same company may be a high-volume item that requires few machine setups, few purchase orders, and no quality inspections at all. If this company ignores the impact of these two products on its cost-driving activities, and simply assigns overhead costs on a basis of labor-hours or producing departments, the high-volume product will bear the lion's share of the overhead cost pool. The result will be a serious distortion in unit costs for *both* products.

As stated earlier, activity-based costing overcomes the problem of cost distortion by creating a cost pool for *each* activity or transaction that can be identified as a cost driver, and by assigning overhead cost to products or jobs on a basis of the number of separate activities required in their completion. Thus, in the situation above, the low-volume product would be assigned the bulk of the costs for machine setup, purchase orders, and quality inspections, thereby showing it to have high unit costs as compared to the other product.

Activity-based costing is sometimes referred to as **transactions costing.** Its major advantage over other costing methods is that *it improves the traceability of overhead costs* and thus results in more accurate unit cost data for management.

An Example of Activity-Based Costing

To illustrate how unit costs are computed when activity-based costing is in use, assume the following situation:

> Dillon Company manufactures two products known as product A and product B. Product A is a low-volume item, on which sales are only 5,000 units each year, and product B is a high-volume item, on which sales are 20,000 units each

year. Both products require two direct labor-hours for completion. Therefore, the company works 50,000 direct labor-hours each year, computed as follows:

	Hours
Product A: 5,000 units × 2 hours	10,000
Product B: 20,000 units × 2 hours	40,000
Total hours	50,000

Costs for materials and labor in each product are given below:

	Product	
	A	B
Direct materials	$25	$15
Direct labor (at $5 per hour)	10	10

The company's manufacturing overhead costs total $875,000 each year. Although the same amount of direct labor time is used in each product, product A requires more machine setups and more quality inspections than B because of the complexity of its design. Also, it is necessary to manufacture product A in small lots, so it requires a relatively large number of production orders as compared to product B.

The company has always used direct labor-hours as a basis for assigning overhead cost to its products.

In the two following sections we show allocations of the company's overhead costs to the products, first using direct labor-hours as a base, then using activities as a base.

Direct Labor-Hours as a Base The company's overhead rate will be $17.50 per hour if direct labor-hours are used as a base for assigning overhead costs. This rate is computed as follows:

$$\frac{\text{Manufacturing overhead costs, \$875,000}}{\text{Direct labor-hours, 50,000}} = \$17.50/\text{DLH}$$

Using this rate, the cost to manufacture each of the products is given below:

	Product	
	A	B
Direct materials (above)	$25	$15
Direct labor (above)	10	10
Manufacturing overhead (2 hours × $17.50)	35	35
Total cost to manufacture	$70	$60

As stated earlier, the problem with this costing approach is that it looks only at labor time and does not consider the impact of other factors on the overhead costs of the company. Therefore, since the two products require equal amounts of labor time, they are assigned equal amounts of overhead cost.

Activities as a Base Let us next assume that Dillon Company has analyzed its operations and has determined that five activities act as cost drivers in the incurrence of overhead costs. Data relating to the five activities are presented in Exhibit 3–14.

As shown in the "Basic data" at the top of the exhibit, the company recorded 5,000 machine setups during the year, of which 3,000 setups were traceable to product A and the other 2,000 were traceable to product B. Other activities were as shown in the exhibit. Using an activities approach, Dillon Company has determined an overhead rate for *each activity* and has used the rate as a base for assigning the costs of the activity to the individual products. The rates for the activities and the overhead costs assigned to the products are also given in Exhibit 3–14.

Note from the exhibit that using activities as a base has resulted in $75.44 in overhead cost being assigned to each unit of product A and $24.89 in overhead cost being assigned to each unit of product B. These amounts are

EXHIBIT 3–14

Overhead Allocations by an Activity Approach

Basic Data

Activity	Traceable Costs	Number of Events or Transactions: Total	Product A	Product B
Machine setups	$230,000	5,000	3,000	2,000
Quality inspections	160,000	8,000	5,000	3,000
Production orders	81,000	600	200	400
Machine-hours worked	314,000	40,000	12,000	28,000
Material receipts	90,000	750	150	600
	$875,000			

Overhead Rates by Activity

Activity	(*a*) Traceable Costs	(*b*) Total Events or Transactions	(*a*) ÷ (*b*) Rate per Event or Transaction
Machine setups	$230,000	5,000	$46/setup
Quality inspections	160,000	8,000	$20/inspection
Production orders	81,000	600	$135/order
Machine-hours worked	314,000	40,000	$7.85/hour
Material receipts	90,000	750	$120/receipt

Overhead Cost per Unit of Product

	Product A		Product B	
	Events or Transactions	Amount	Events or Transactions	Amount
Machine setups, at $46/setup	3,000	$138,000	2,000	$ 92,000
Quality inspections, at $20/inspection	5,000	100,000	3,000	60,000
Production orders, at $135/order	200	27,000	400	54,000
Machine-hours worked, at $7.85/hour	12,000	94,200	28,000	219,800
Material receipts, at $120/receipt	150	18,000	600	72,000
Total overhead cost assigned (*a*)		$377,200		$497,800
Number of units produced (*b*)		5,000		20,000
Overhead cost per unit, (*a*) ÷ (*b*)		$75.44		$24.89

used in the table below to determine the cost to manufacture a unit of each product under activity-based costing. For comparison, we also present the unit costs derived earlier when direct labor was used to assign overhead cost to the products.

	Activities Base		Direct Labor Base	
	Product A	Product B	Product A	Product B
Direct materials	$ 25.00	$15.00	$25.00	$15.00
Direct labor	10.00	10.00	10.00	10.00
Manufacturing overhead	75.44	24.89	35.00	35.00
Total cost to manufacture	$110.44	$49.89	$70.00	$60.00

In the past, Dillon Company has been charging $35 in overhead cost to a unit of either product, whereas it should have been charging $75.44 in overhead cost to each unit of product A and only $24.89 to each unit of product B. Thus, as a result of using direct labor as a base for overhead costing, in the past too little overhead cost has been charged to product A and too much has been charged to product B. Consequently, unit costs have been badly distorted. Depending on selling prices, the company may even have been suffering a loss on product A without knowing it (because A's unit cost has been understated). Through activity-based costing, we have been able to identify the overhead costs that are traceable to each product and thus derive more accurate unit cost data.

Summary of Activity-Based Costing

To summarize, activity-based costing improves the costing systems of organizations in three ways:

First, activity-based costing *increases the number of cost pools used to accumulate overhead costs*. Rather than accumulating all overhead costs in a single, companywide pool, or accumulating them in departmental pools, costs are accumulated by activity. As a result, many pools are created according to the number of cost-driving activities that can be identified.

Second, activity-based costing *changes the base used to assign overhead costs to products*. Rather than assigning costs on a basis of direct labor, costs are assigned on a basis of the portion of cost-driving activities that can be traced to the product or job involved.

Third, activity-based costing *changes the nature of many overhead costs* in that costs that were formerly considered to be indirect (such as power, inspection, and machine setup) are identified with specific activities and thereby made directly traceable to individual products.

The Impact of JIT Inventory Methods

We stated in Chapter 2 that companies are implementing JIT inventory methods in order to reduce costs. One reason JIT is effective in reducing costs is that it eliminates (or reduces) *activities* in a company, such as purchase orders issued, quality inspections performed, inventory movements needed, warehousing space required, and so forth. As activities such as these are eliminated (or reduced), the costs that they generate are also reduced accordingly.

Since activity-based costing focuses directly on the activities of a company and views them as being cost drivers that must be controlled, it is not surprising to learn that JIT inventory methods are used hand in hand with the activity costing approach. Indeed, as companies implement JIT and begin to get better control over activities such as those listed above, the need to switch to activity-based costing generally becomes obvious. Thus, JIT has become a significant force in triggering other changes and improvements in the costing systems of organizations.

SUMMARY

Unit cost of production is one of the most useful items of cost data to a manager. There are two methods in widespread use for determining unit costs; these two methods are known as job-order costing and process costing, respectively. Job-order costing is used in those manufacturing situations where products differ from each other, such as in furniture manufacture and shipbuilding. Process costing is used in those situations where units of product are homogeneous, such as in the manufacture of flour or cement. We have also noted that job-order costing is used extensively in the service industries.

Materials requisition forms and labor time tickets control the assignment of direct materials and direct labor cost to production. Indirect manufacturing costs are assigned to production through use of a predetermined overhead rate, which is developed by estimating the level of manufacturing overhead to be incurred during a period and by dividing this estimate by a base common to all the jobs to be worked on during the period. The most frequently used bases are machine-hours and direct labor-hours.

Since the predetermined overhead rate is based on estimates, the actual overhead cost incurred during a period may be somewhat more or somewhat less than the amount of overhead cost applied to production. Such a difference is referred to as under- or overapplied overhead. The under- or overapplied overhead of a period can be either (1) closed out to Cost of Goods Sold or (2) allocated between Work in Process, Finished Goods, and Cost of Goods Sold.

KEY TERMS FOR REVIEW

Absorption cost A costing method that includes all manufacturing costs—direct materials, direct labor, and both variable and fixed overhead—as part of the cost of a finished unit of product. This term is synonymous with *full cost*. (p. 65)

Activity-based costing A costing method that creates a cost pool for each event or transaction (activity) in an organization that acts as a cost driver. Overhead costs are then assigned to products and services on a basis of the number of these events or transactions that the product or service has generated. (p. 91)

Bill of materials A control sheet that shows the type and quantity of each item of material going into a completed unit of product. (p. 68)

Cost driver Machine-hours, direct labor-hours, or a similar base that is a causal factor in the incurrence of overhead cost, or is closely correlated with its incurrence. (p. 73)

Full cost See *Absorption cost.* (p. 65)

Job cost sheet A form prepared for each job initiated into production that serves as a means for accumulating the materials, labor, and overhead costs chargeable to the job and as a means for computing unit costs. (p. 68)

Job-order costing system A costing system used in those manufacturing situations where many different products, jobs, or batches of production are being produced each period. (p. 66)

Materials requisition form A detailed source document that specifies the type and quantity of materials that are to be drawn from the storeroom and identifies the job to which the materials are to be charged. (p. 68)

Overapplied overhead A credit balance in the Manufacturing Overhead account that arises when the amount of overhead cost applied to Work in Process is greater than the amount of overhead cost actually incurred during a period. (p. 85)

Overhead application The charging of manufacturing overhead cost to the job cost sheets and to the Work in Process account. (p. 71)

Plantwide overhead rate A single predetermined overhead rate that is used in all departments of a company, rather than each department having its own separate predetermined overhead rate. (p. 90)

Predetermined overhead rate A rate used to charge overhead cost to jobs in production; the rate is established in advance for each period by use of estimates of manufacturing overhead cost and production activity for the period. (p. 71)

Process costing system A costing system used in those manufacturing situations where a single, homogeneous product (such as cement or flour) is produced for long periods of time. (p. 66)

Time ticket A detailed source document that is used to record an employee's hour-by-hour activities during a day. (p. 70)

Transactions costing See *Activity-based costing.* (p. 92)

Underapplied overhead A debit balance in the Manufacturing Overhead account that arises when the amount of overhead cost actually incurred is greater than the amount of overhead cost applied to Work in Process during a period. (p. 85)

APPENDIX: COST FLOWS IN A JIT SYSTEM

When a company utilizes JIT inventory methods, its cost flows are greatly simplified from those we have discussed on preceding pages. Typically, when JIT is in use only two inventory accounts are utilized. One is a new account titled *Raw and In-Process Inventory,* and the other is the same Finished Goods inventory account with which we are already familiar. Cost flows in a JIT system, as compared to cost flows in a conventional job-order cost system, are illustrated in Exhibit 3A–1.

In the following paragraphs we discuss Exhibit 3A–1 transaction by transaction as we trace the cost flows under JIT. The numbers below relate to the transaction numbers in the exhibit.

Transaction	Comments
1	Under JIT, materials are purchased *only* as needed for production. Thus, only \$350,000 in materials would be purchased under JIT (\$400,000 − \$50,000 = \$350,000) as compared to the entire \$400,000 under a conventional system. (The extra \$50,000 under the conventional system would remain in inventory.) The materials purchased under JIT would go directly into a **Raw and**

EXHIBIT 3A-1
Cost Flows in a JIT System

Transaction	Entries—Conventional System			Entries—JIT System		
1. Purchase of direct materials on account, $400,000 (of which $50,000 is planned for inventory).	Raw Materials	400,000		Raw and In-Process Inventory.	350,000	
	Accounts Payable.		400,000	Accounts Payable		350,000
2. Issue of direct materials to production, $350,000.	Work in Process	350,000		—		
	Raw Materials		350,000			
3. Incurrence of direct labor cost, $40,000.	Work in Process	40,000		—		
	Factory Wages Payable . . .		40,000			
4. Incurrence of manufacturing overhead cost, $160,000.	Manufacturing Overhead.	160,000		Manufacturing Overhead	200,000	
	Accounts Payable.		160,000	Factory Wages Payable.		40,000
				Accounts Payable		160,000
5. Application of manufacturing overhead cost to products, $170,000.	Work in Process	170,000		—		
	Manufacturing Overhead. . .		170,000			
6. Completion of products, $560,000 total cost.	Finished Goods.	560,000		Finished Goods	560,000	
	Work in Process		560,000	Raw and In-Process Inventory. . .		350,000
				Manufacturing Overhead		210,000*

* Under JIT, the overhead applied consists of:

Direct labor cost added to overhead	$ 40,000
Other overhead costs applied, per transaction 5. . .	170,000
Total overhead cost applied.	$210,000

Under both systems, note that overhead cost is overapplied by $10,000 for the period (conventional system: $160,000 incurred − $170,000 applied = $10,000 overapplied; JIT system: $200,000 incurred − $210,000 applied = $10,000 overapplied). This $10,000 would be closed out to Cost of Goods Sold at the end of the period.

Transaction	Comments
	In-Process Inventory account, which is a combination of the Raw Materials and Work In Process inventory accounts found in job-order costing.
2	Purchase of materials and issue of materials into production occur simultaneously in a JIT environment. Therefore, the entry for transaction 1 under JIT encompasses the entries for both transactions 1 and 2 in a conventional system. This greatly simplifies the record-keeping process, since under JIT there are no inventory records to maintain, no requisition forms, no issue slips, and so forth to be concerned with. Also note the absence of a separate Work in Process account under JIT.
3	Direct labor is not treated as a separate cost item in a JIT system. Rather, *it is added to manufacturing overhead* (see the entry for transaction 4 under JIT in the exhibit). There are two

Transaction	Comments
	reasons for this treatment of direct labor. First, it simplifies the costing process. And second, direct labor cost is too small in amount to be dealt with separately in a highly automated, FMS setting where JIT is typically used. Note particularly from the exhibit how few entries are made in a JIT system. When companies adopt JIT, they typically report that *thousands* of journal entries are eliminated each month.
4	Transaction 4, which deals with the incurrence of manufacturing overhead costs, differs in two ways in a JIT system. First, direct labor costs are included, as discussed above. And second, costs are accumulated by *activity* rather than in a single pool for the entire company. The concept of activity-based costing was discussed in the main body of the chapter.
5	Under JIT, overhead cost is applied to products only at the time of completion.
6	Material and conversion costs in a JIT system are not added to products until the products are completed and ready for shipment. This eliminates the need to "track" costs and the need for job cost sheets. When products are completed under JIT, costs are moved from the Raw and In-Process Inventory account and from the Manufacturing Overhead account into Finished Goods. The transfer of costs to Finished Goods under JIT is sometimes referred to as **backflush costing,** since costs are "flushed" out of the system *after* products are completed.

As stated in Chapter 2, the JIT philosophy focuses on simplicity and on the elimination of any activity that does not add value to products. This philosophy is clearly evident in the operation of a JIT system, as described in the preceding paragraphs.

We must emphasize, however, that backflush costing is appropriate *only* in those situations where a *true* JIT system is in operation. If either raw materials or work in process inventories exist at the end of a period, then backflush costing is not appropriate and will be costly to operate. The reason is that when inventories are present, frequent and expensive physical counts of inventory will be necessary to determine the amount of materials and the amount of partially completed goods still on hand. Moreover, with no requisition slips or work orders available, it will be difficult to identify how much cost should be applied to raw materials and work in process inventories and how much should be applied to completed output. Thus, in the absence of a *true* JIT system, backflush costing may result in less timely, less accurate, and more expensive data than a conventional costing system.

KEY TERMS FOR REVIEW (APPENDIX)

Backflush costing A term used under JIT that refers to "flushing" costs out of the system after goods are completed and the charging of these costs directly to the Finished Goods inventory account. (p. 99)

Raw and In-Process Inventory An account used in a JIT system that is a combination of the Raw Materials and Work in Process inventory accounts found in a job-order costing system. (p. 97)

QUESTIONS

3–1 State the purposes for which it is necessary or desirable to compute unit costs.

3–2 Distinguish between job-order costing and process costing.

3–3 What is the essential purpose of any costing system?

3–4 What is the purpose of the job cost sheet in a job-order costing system?

3–5 What is a predetermined overhead rate, and how is it computed?

3–6 Explain how a sales order, a production order, a materials requisition form, and a labor time ticket are involved in the production and costing of products.

3–7 Explain why some production costs must be assigned to products through an allocation process. Name several such costs. Would such costs be classified as *direct* or as *indirect* costs?

3–8 Why do firms use predetermined overhead rates rather than actual manufacturing overhead costs in applying overhead to units of product?

3–9 What factors should be considered in selecting a base to be used in computing the predetermined overhead rate?

3–10 What is meant by the statement that overhead is "absorbed" into units of product? If a company fully absorbs its overhead costs, does this guarantee that a profit will be earned for the period?

3–11 What account is credited when overhead cost is applied to Work in Process? Would you expect the amount applied for a period to equal the actual overhead costs of the period? Why or why not?

3–12 What is underapplied overhead? Overapplied overhead? What disposition is made of these amounts at period end?

3–13 Enumerate several reasons why overhead might be underapplied in a given year.

3–14 What adjustment is made for underapplied overhead on the schedule of cost of goods manufactured, and why is this adjustment necessary? What adjustment is made on the schedule of cost of goods sold?

3–15 What adjustment is made for overapplied overhead on the schedule of cost of goods manufactured, and why is this adjustment necessary? What adjustment is made on the schedule of cost of goods sold?

3–16 Sigma Company applies overhead cost to jobs on a basis of direct labor cost. Job A, which was started and completed during the current period, shows charges of $5,000 for direct materials, $8,000 for direct labor, and $6,000 for overhead on its job cost sheet. Job B, which is still in process at year-end, shows charges of $2,500 for direct materials and $4,000 for direct labor. Should any overhead cost be added to job B at year-end? Explain.

3–17 A company assigns overhead cost to completed jobs on a basis of 125 percent of direct labor cost. The job cost sheet for job 313 shows that $10,000 in direct material has been used on the job and that $12,000 in direct labor cost has been incurred. If 1,000 units were produced in job 313, what is the cost per unit?

3–18 What is a "plantwide" overhead rate? Why are multiple overhead rates, rather than a plantwide rate, used in some companies?

3–19 Why are new approaches to overhead allocation, such as activity-based costing, needed today in many companies and industries?

3–20 In what three ways does activity-based costing improve the costing process when a company is in a highly automated environment?

3–21 (Appendix) How is the purchase of materials and the issue of materials to production handled in a JIT system? In what ways does this approach to the handling of materials save money? What happens to the Work in Process account in a JIT system?

3-22 (Appendix) In what way is direct labor cost handled differently in a JIT system than in a conventional system? What are the reasons for this difference in treatment?

3-23 (Appendix) At what point are materials and overhead costs added to products in a JIT system? Why is this approach to the adding of costs to products sometimes called *backflush costing?*

EXERCISES

E3-1 Which method of accumulating product costs, job-order costing or process costing, would be more appropriate in each of the following situations?

a. A textbook publisher.
b. An oil refinery.
c. A manufacturer of powdered milk.
d. A manufacturer of ready-mix cement.
e. A custom home builder.
f. A shop for customizing vans.
g. A chemical manufacturer.
h. An auto repair shop.
i. A tire manufacturing plant.
j. An advertising agency.

E3-2 Javadi Company manufactures a product that is subject to wide seasonal variations in demand. Unit costs are computed on a quarterly basis by dividing each quarter's manufacturing costs (materials, labor, and overhead) by the quarter's production in units. The company's estimated costs, by quarter, for the coming year are given below:

	Quarter			
	First	Second	Third	Fourth
Direct materials	$240,000	$120,000	$ 60,000	$180,000
Direct labor	96,000	48,000	24,000	72,000
Manufacturing overhead	228,000	204,000	192,000	216,000
Total manufacturing costs	$564,000	$372,000	$276,000	$468,000
Number of units to be produced	80,000	40,000	20,000	60,000
Estimated cost per unit	$7.05	$9.30	$13.80	$7.80

Management finds the variation in unit costs to be confusing and difficult to work with. It has been suggested that the problem lies with manufacturing overhead, since it is the largest element of cost. Accordingly, you have been asked to find a more equitable way of assigning manufacturing overhead cost to units of product. After some analysis, you have determined that the company's overhead costs are mostly fixed and therefore show little sensitivity to changes in the level of production.

Required

1. The company uses a job-order costing system. How would you recommend that manufacturing overhead cost be assigned to production? Be specific, and show computations.
2. Recompute the company's unit costs in accordance with your recommendations in (1) above.

E3-3 Medusa Products is a manufacturing company that operates a job-order costing system. Overhead costs are charged to production on a basis of machine-hours. At the beginning of 19x4, management estimated that the company would incur $170,000 in manufacturing overhead costs for the year and work 85,000 machine-hours.

Required

1. Compute the company's predetermined overhead rate for 19x4.
2. Assume that during the year the company actually works only 80,000 machine-hours and incurs the following costs in the Manufacturing Overhead and Work in Process accounts:

Manufacturing Overhead

	Debit	Credit
(Utilities)	14,000	?
(Insurance)	9,000	
(Maintenance)	33,000	
(Indirect materials)	7,000	
(Indirect labor)	65,000	
(Depreciation)	40,000	

Work in Process

	Debit	Credit
(Direct materials)	530,000	
(Direct labor)	85,000	
(Overhead)	?	

Copy the data in the T-accounts above onto your answer sheet. Compute the amount of overhead cost that should be applied to Work in Process for the year, and make the entry in your T-accounts.

3. Compute the amount of under- or overapplied overhead for the year, and show the balance in your Manufacturing Overhead T-account. Prepare the journal entry that most companies would make to close out the balance in this account.

E3–4 Foley Company uses a job-order costing system. The following data relate to the month of October 19x9, the first month of the company's fiscal year:

a. Raw materials purchased on account, $210,000.
b. Raw materials issued to production, $190,000 (80 percent direct and 20 percent indirect).
c. Direct labor cost incurred, $69,000; and indirect labor cost incurred, $21,000.
d. Depreciation recorded on factory equipment, $105,000.
e. Other manufacturing overhead costs incurred during the month, $130,000 (credit Accounts Payable).
f. The company applies manufacturing overhead cost to production on a basis of $4 per machine-hour. There were 75,000 machine-hours recorded for the month.
g. Production orders costing $510,000 were completed during the month and transferred to Finished Goods.
h. Production orders that had cost $450,000 to complete were shipped to customers during the month. These goods were invoiced at 50 percent above cost to manufacture. The goods were sold on account.

Required

1. Prepare journal entries to record the information given above.
2. Prepare T-accounts for Manufacturing Overhead and Work in Process. Post the relevant information above to each account. Compute the ending balance in each account, assuming that Work in Process has a beginning balance of $35,000.

E3–5 Estimated cost and operating data for three companies for 19x6 are given below:

	Company		
	A	B	C
Direct labor-hours.	60,000	30,000	40,000
Machine-hours	25,000	90,000	18,000
Raw materials cost	$300,000	$160,000	$240,000
Manufacturing overhead cost. . .	432,000	270,000	384,000

Predetermined overhead rates are computed on the following bases in the three companies:

Company	Overhead Rate Based on—
A	Direct labor-hours
B	Machine-hours
C	Raw materials cost

Required

1. Compute the predetermined overhead rate to be used in each company during 19x6.
2. Assume that three jobs are worked on during 19x6 in Company A. Direct labor-hours recorded by job are: job 308, 7,000 hours; job 309, 30,000 hours; and job 310, 21,000 hours. How much overhead cost will the company apply to Work in Process for the year? If actual costs are $420,000 for the year, will overhead be underapplied or overapplied? By how much?

E3–6 Diewold Company has two departments, milling and assembly. The company uses a job-order cost system and computes a predetermined overhead rate in each department. The milling department bases its rate on machine-hours, and the assembly department bases its rate on direct labor cost. At the beginning of 19x1, the company made the following estimates:

	Department	
	Milling	Assembly
Direct labor-hours	8,000	75,000
Machine-hours	60,000	3,000
Manufacturing overhead cost. . .	$510,000	$800,000
Direct labor cost	72,000	640,000

Required

1. Compute the predetermined overhead rate to be used in each department during 19x1.
2. Assume that the overhead rates you computed in (1) above are in effect. The job cost sheet for job 407, which was started and completed during the year, showed the following:

	Department	
	Milling	Assembly
Direct labor-hours	5	20
Machine-hours	90	4
Materials requisitioned . . .	$800	$370
Direct labor cost.	45	160

   Compute the total overhead cost of job 407.
3. Would you expect substantially different amounts of overhead cost to be charged to some jobs if the company used a plantwide overhead rate based on direct labor cost instead of using departmental rates? Explain. No computations are necessary.

E3–7 The following cost data relate to the manufacturing activities of Black Company during 19x5:

Manufacturing overhead costs incurred during the year:	
Property taxes	$ 3,000
Utilities, factory.	5,000
Indirect labor	10,000
Depreciation, factory	24,000
Insurance, factory	6,000
Total actual costs	$48,000

Other costs incurred during the year:	
Purchases of raw materials	$32,000
Direct labor cost	40,000
Inventories:	
Raw materials, January 1.	8,000
Raw materials, December 31	7,000
Work in process, January 1.	6,000
Work in process, December 31	7,500

The company uses a predetermined overhead rate to charge overhead cost to production. The rate for 19x5 was $5 per machine-hour; a total of 10,000 machine-hours was recorded for the year.

Required

1. Compute the amount of under- or overapplied overhead cost for 19x5.
2. Prepare a schedule of cost of goods manufactured for 19x5.

E3–8 Custom Metal Works produces castings and other metal parts to customer specifications, using a job-order costing system. For the year 19x4, the company estimated that it would work 576,000 machine-hours and incur $4,320,000 in manufacturing overhead cost.

The company had no work in process at the beginning of the year. The entire month of January was spent on job 382, which called for 8,000 machine parts. Cost data for January follow:

a. Raw materials purchased on account, $315,000.
b. Raw materials requisitioned for production, $270,000 (80 percent direct and 20 percent indirect).
c. Labor cost incurred in the factory, $190,000, of which $80,000 was direct labor and $110,000 was indirect labor.
d. Depreciation recorded on factory equipment, $63,000.
e. Other manufacturing overhead costs incurred, $85,000 (credit Accounts Payable).
f. Manufacturing overhead cost was applied to production on a basis of 40,000 machine-hours worked during the month.
g. The completed job was moved into the finished goods warehouse on January 31 to await delivery to the customer. (In computing the dollar amount for this entry, remember that the cost of a completed job consists of direct materials, direct labor, and *applied* overhead.)

Required

1. Prepare journal entries to record items *(a)* through *(f)* above. Ignore item *(g)* for the moment.
2. Prepare T-accounts for Manufacturing Overhead and Work in Process. Post the relevant items from your journal entries to these T-accounts.
3. Prepare a journal entry for item *(g)* above, and then compute the unit cost that will appear on the job cost sheet for job 382.

E3–9 The following information is taken from the end-of-year account balances of Latta Company:

Manufacturing Overhead

	Debit	Credit	
(a)	460,000	390,000	*(b)*
Bal.	70,000		

Work in Process

	Debit	Credit	
Bal.	5,000	710,000	*(c)*
	260,000		
	85,000		
(b)	390,000		
Bal.	40,000		

Finished Goods			
Bal.	50,000	640,000	*(d)*
(c)	710,000		
Bal.	120,000		

Cost of Goods Sold		
(d)	640,000	

Required

1. Identify the dollar figures appearing by the letters *(a)*, *(b)*, and so forth.
2. Assume that the company closes any balance in the Manufacturing Overhead account directly to Cost of Goods Sold. Prepare the necessary journal entry.
3. Assume instead that the company allocates any balance in the Manufacturing Overhead account to the other accounts. Prepare the necessary journal entry, with supporting computations.

E3–10 Toronto Company began operations on January 2, 19x2. The following activity was recorded in the company's Work in Process account for the first month of operations:

Work in Process			
Direct materials	200,000	To finished goods	570,000
Direct labor	90,000		
Manufacturing overhead	320,000		

Toronto Company uses a job-order costing system and applies manufacturing overhead cost to Work in Process on a basis of direct materials cost. At the end of January, only one job was still in process. This job (job 15) had been charged with $13,500 in direct materials.

Required

1. Compute the predetermined overhead rate that was in use during January.
2. Complete the following job cost sheet for the partially completed job 15:

Job Cost Sheet—Job 15
As of January 31, 19x2

Direct materials	$?
Direct labor.	?
Manufacturing overhead	?
Total cost to January 31	$?

E3–11 Tyler Company uses a job-order costing system. The table below provides selected data on the three jobs worked on during the company's first month of operations:

	Job Number		
	101	**102**	**103**
Units of product in the job. . . .	2,000	1,800	1,500
Machine-hours worked	1,200	1,000	900
Direct materials cost	$4,500	$3,700	$1,400
Direct labor cost	9,600	8,000	7,200

Actual overhead costs totaling $30,000 were incurred during the month. Manufacturing overhead cost is applied to production on a basis of machine-hours at a predetermined rate of $9 per hour. Jobs 101 and 102 were completed during the month; job 103 was not completed.

Required

1. Compute the amount of manufacturing overhead cost that would have been charged to each job during the month.

2. Compute the unit cost of jobs 101 and 102.
3. Prepare a journal entry showing the transfer of the completed jobs into the finished goods warehouse.
4. What is the balance in the Work in Process account at the end of the month?
5. What is the balance in the Manufacturing Overhead account at the end of the month?

E3–12 (Appendix) Mica Products has an FMS in operation and is considering the use of JIT inventory methods. At present, the company is using conventional job-order costing.

Required

1. For the coming month, the company had planned to purchase $800,000 in raw materials, of which 10 percent is designated for inventory buildup. The remaining amount will be used in production during the month.
   a. Under conventional job-order costing, what entries would be made to record the purchase of the material and the issue of the material to production?
   b. If the company adopts the JIT inventory approach at the beginning of the month, what entry will be made to record the purchase of the material and the issue of the material to production?
2. Assume that direct labor cost for the month totals $110,000 and that actual manufacturing overhead costs total $500,000. What entry would be made under a JIT system to record these costs?
3. Assume that the company does adopt the JIT approach and that $600,000 in overhead cost is applied to the month's production. What entry would be made to record the completed production for the month?

PROBLEMS

P3–13 **Entries Directly into T-Accounts; Income Statement** Durham Company's trial balance as of January 1, 19x7, is given below:

Cash	$ 8,000	
Accounts Receivable	13,000	
Raw Materials	7,000	
Work in Process	18,000	
Finished Goods	20,000	
Prepaid Insurance	4,000	
Plant and Equipment	230,000	
Accumulated Depreciation		$ 42,000
Accounts Payable		30,000
Capital Stock		150,000
Retained Earnings		78,000
Totals	$300,000	$300,000

Durham Company manufactures items to customers' specifications and employs a job-order cost system. During 19x7, the following transactions took place:

a. Raw materials purchased on account, $45,000.
b. Raw materials requisitioned for use in production, $40,000 (80 percent direct and 20 percent indirect).
c. Factory utility costs incurred, $14,600.
d. Depreciation recorded on plant and equipment, $28,000. Three fourths of the depreciation relates to factory equipment, and the remainder relates to selling and administrative equipment.

e. Costs for salaries and wages were incurred as follows:

Direct labor	$40,000
Indirect labor.	18,000
Sales commissions	10,400
Administrative salaries . . .	25,000

f. Insurance expired during the year, $3,000 (80 percent relates to factory operations, and 20 percent relates to selling and administrative activities).

g. Miscellaneous selling and administrative expenses incurred, $18,000.

h. Manufacturing overhead was applied to production. The company applies overhead on a basis of 150 percent of raw materials (direct and indirect) used in production.

i. Goods costing $130,000 to manufacture were transferred to the finished goods warehouse.

j. Goods that had cost $120,000 to manufacture were sold on account for $200,000.

k. Collections from customers during the year totaled $197,000.

l. Payments to suppliers on account during the year, $100,000; and payments to employees for salaries and wages, $90,000.

Required

1. Prepare a T-account for each account in the company's trial balance, and enter the opening balances shown above.
2. Record the transactions above directly into the T-accounts. Prepare new T-accounts as needed. Key your entries to the letters (*a*) through (*l*) above. Find the ending balance in each account.
3. Is manufacturing overhead under- or overapplied for the year? Make an entry in the T-accounts to close any balance in the Manufacturing Overhead account to Cost of Goods Sold.
4. Prepare an income statement for the year. (Do not prepare a schedule of cost of goods manufactured; all of the information needed for the income statement is available in the journal entries and T-accounts you have prepared.)

P3–14 Straightforward Journal Entries; Partial T-Accounts; Income Statement Ravsten Company is a manufacturing firm that uses a job-order cost system. On January 1, 19x9, the company's inventory balances were:

Raw materials.	$16,000
Work in process.	10,000
Finished goods	30,000

The company applies overhead cost to jobs on a basis of direct labor-hours. For 19x9, the company estimated that it would work 36,000 machine-hours and incur $153,000 in manufacturing overhead cost. The following transactions were recorded for the year:

a. Raw materials purchased on account, $200,000.

b. Raw materials requisitioned for use in production, $190,000 (80 percent direct and 20 percent indirect).

c. The following costs were incurred for employee services:

Direct labor.	$160,000
Indirect labor	27,000
Sales commissions.	36,000
Administrative salaries. . . .	80,000

d. Heat, power, and water costs incurred in the factory, $42,000.

e. Insurance expired during the year, $10,000 (90 percent relates to factory operations, and 10 percent relates to selling and administrative activities).

f. Advertising costs incurred, $50,000.
g. Depreciation recorded for the year, $60,000 (85 percent relates to factory operations, and 15 percent relates to selling and administrative activities).
h. Manufacturing overhead cost was applied to production. The company recorded 40,000 machine-hours for the year.
i. Goods costing $480,000 to manufacture were completed during the year.
j. Goods were sold on account to customers during the year at a total selling price of $700,000. These goods cost $475,000 to manufacture.

Required

1. Prepare journal entries to record the transactions given above.
2. Prepare T-accounts for inventories, Manufacturing Overhead, and Cost of Goods Sold. Post relevant data from your journal entries to these T-accounts (don't forget to enter the opening balances in your inventory accounts). Compute an ending balance in each account.
3. Is Manufacturing Overhead underapplied or overapplied for the year? Prepare a journal entry to close any balance in the Manufacturing Overhead account to Cost of Goods Sold.
4. Prepare an income statement for the year. (Do not prepare a schedule of cost of goods manufactured; all of the information needed for the income statement is available in the journal entries and T-accounts you have prepared.)

P3–15 **Video Producer; Entries Directly into T-Accounts; Income Statement** Supreme Videos, Inc., produces short musical videos for sale to retail outlets. The company's balance sheet accounts as of January 1, 19x3, are given below:

SUPREME VIDEOS, INC.
Balance Sheet
January 1, 19x3

Assets

Current assets:		
Cash		$ 63,000
Accounts receivable		102,000
Inventories:		
Raw materials (film, costumes)	$ 30,000	
Videos in process	45,000	
Finished videos awaiting sale	81,000	156,000
Prepaid insurance		9,000
Total current assets		330,000
Studio and equipment	730,000	
Less accumulated depreciation	210,000	520,000
Total assets		$850,000

Liabilities and Stockholders' Equity

Accounts payable		$160,000
Capital stock	$420,000	
Retained earnings	270,000	690,000
Total liabilities and stockholders' equity		$850,000

Since the videos differ in length and in complexity of production, the company uses a job-order costing system to determine the cost of each video produced. Studio (manufacturing) overhead is charged to videos on a basis of camera-hours of activity. For 19x3, the company estimated that it would work 7,000 camera-hours and incur $280,000 in studio overhead cost. The following transactions were recorded for the year:

a. Film, costumes, and similar raw materials purchased on account, $185,000.
b. Film, costumes, and other raw materials issued to production, $200,000 (85

percent of this material was considered direct to the videos in production, and the other 15 percent was considered indirect).

c. Utility costs incurred in the production studio, $72,000.

d. Depreciation recorded on the studio, cameras, and other equipment, $84,000. Three fourths of this depreciation related to actual production of the videos, and the remainder related to equipment used in marketing and administration.

e. Advertising expense incurred, $130,000.

f. Costs for salaries and wages were incurred as follows:

Direct labor (actors and directors)	$ 82,000
Indirect labor (carpenters to build sets, costume designers, and so forth) . . .	110,000
Administrative salaries	95,000

g. Insurance expired during the year, $7,000 (80 percent related to production of videos, and 20 percent related to marketing and administrative activities).

h. Miscellaneous marketing and administrative expenses incurred, $8,600.

i. Studio (manufacturing) overhead was applied to videos in production. The company recorded 7,250 camera-hours of activity during the year.

j. Videos costing $550,000 to produce were transferred to the Finished Videos storeroom to await sale and shipment.

k. Videos that had cost $600,000 to produce were sold on account for $925,000.

l. Collections from customers during the year totaled $850,000.

m. Payments to suppliers on account during the year, $500,000; payments to employees for salaries and wages, $285,000.

Required

1. Prepare a T-account for each account on the company's balance sheet, and enter the opening balances given above.
2. Record the transactions above directly into the T-accounts. Prepare new T-accounts as needed. Key your entries to the letters (*a*) through (*m*) above. Find the ending balance in each account.
3. Is the Studio (manufacturing) Overhead account underapplied or overapplied for the year? Make an entry in the T-accounts to close any balance in the Studio Overhead account to Cost of Goods Sold.
4. Prepare an income statement for the year. (Do not prepare a schedule of cost of goods manufactured; all of the information needed for the income statement is available in the T-accounts.)

P3–16 Multiple Departments; Overhead Rates; Costing Units of Product Clark Technology, Inc., employs a job-order costing system. The company uses predetermined overhead rates in applying manufacturing overhead cost to individual jobs. The predetermined overhead rate in Department A is based on machine-hours, and the rate in Department B is based on direct materials cost. At the beginning of 19x3, the company's management made the following estimates for the year:

	Department	
	A	B
Machine-hours	80,000	21,000
Direct labor-hours	35,000	65,000
Direct materials cost.	$190,000	$400,000
Direct labor cost	280,000	530,000
Manufacturing overhead cost . . .	416,000	720,000

Job 127 was initiated into production on April 1 and completed on May 12. The company's cost records show the following information on the job:

	Department A	Department B
Machine-hours	350	70
Direct labor-hours	80	130
Direct materials cost	$940	$1,200
Direct labor cost	710	980

Required

1. Compute the predetermined overhead rate that should be used during the year in Department A. Compute the rate that should be used in Department B.
2. Compute the total overhead cost applied to job 127.
3. What would be the total cost of job 127? If the job contained 25 units, what would be the cost per unit?
4. At the end of 19x3, the records of Clark Technology, Inc., revealed the following *actual* cost and operating data for all jobs worked on during the year:

	Department A	Department B
Machine-hours	73,000	24,000
Direct labor-hours	30,000	68,000
Direct materials cost	$165,000	$420,000
Manufacturing overhead cost	390,000	740,000

What was the amount of underapplied or overapplied overhead in each department at the end of 19x3?

P3–17 **Law Firm: Multiple Departments; Overhead Rates** Winkle, Kotter, and Zale is a small law firm that contains 10 partners and 10 support persons. The firm employs a job-order costing system to accumulate costs chargeable to each client, and it is organized into two departments—the research and documents department and the litigation department. The firm uses predetermined overhead rates to charge the costs of these departments to its clients. At the beginning of 19x1, the firm's management made the following estimates for the year:

	Department: Research and Documents	Department: Litigation
Research-hours	20,000	—
Direct attorney-hours	9,000	16,000
Materials and supplies	$ 18,000	$ 5,000
Direct attorney cost	430,000	800,000
Departmental overhead cost	700,000	320,000

The predetermined overhead rate in the research and documents department is based on research-hours, and the rate in the litigation department is based on direct attorney cost.

The costs chargeable to each client are made up of three elements: materials and supplies used, direct attorney costs incurred, and an applied amount of overhead from each department in which work is performed on the case.

Case 618-3 was initiated on February 10 and completed on June 30. During this period, the following costs and time were recorded on the case:

	Department: Research and Documents	Department: Litigation
Research-hours	18	—
Direct attorney-hours	9	42
Materials and supplies	$ 50	$ 30
Direct attorney cost	410	2,100

Required

1. Compute the predetermined overhead rate that should be used during the year in the research and documents department. Compute the rate that should be used in the litigation department.
2. Using the rates you computed in (1) above, compute the total overhead cost applied to case 618-3.
3. What would be the total cost charged to case 618-3? Show computations by department and in total for the case.
4. At the end of 19x1, the firm's records revealed the following *actual* cost and operating data for all cases handled during the year:

	Department	
	Research and Documents	Litigation
Research-hours	23,000	—
Direct attorney-hours	8,000	15,000
Materials and supplies	$ 19,000	$ 6,000
Direct attorney cost	400,000	725,000
Departmental overhead cost	770,000	300,000

Determine the amount of underapplied or overapplied overhead cost in each department for 19x1.

P3–18 **Straightforward Journal Entries; Partial T-Accounts; Income Statement** Slater Company manufactures products to customer specifications; a job-order cost system is used to accumulate costs in the company's plant. On July 1, 19x5, the start of Slater Company's fiscal year, inventory balances were as follows:

Raw materials	$25,000
Work in process	10,000
Finished goods	40,000

The company applies overhead cost to jobs on a basis of machine-hours of operating time. For the fiscal year starting July 1, 19x5, it was estimated that the plant would operate 45,000 machine-hours and incur $270,000 in manufacturing overhead cost. During the year, the following transactions were completed:

a. Raw materials purchased on account, $275,000.

b. Raw materials requisitioned for use in production, $280,000 (materials costing $220,000 were chargeable directly to jobs; the remaining materials were indirect).

c. Costs for employee services were incurred as follows:

Direct labor	$180,000
Indirect labor	72,000
Sales commissions	63,000
Administrative salaries	90,000

d. Prepaid insurance expired during the year, $18,000 ($13,000 of this amount related to factory operations, and the remainder related to selling and administrative activities).

e. Utility costs incurred in the factory, $57,000.

f. Advertising costs incurred, $140,000.

g. Depreciation recorded on equipment, $100,000. (Some $88,000 of this amount was on equipment used in factory operations; the remaining $12,000 was on equipment used in selling and administrative activities.)

h. Manufacturing overhead cost was applied to production, $__?__. (The company recorded 50,000 machine-hours of operating time during the year.)

i. Goods costing $675,000 to manufacture were transferred into the finished goods warehouse.

j. Sales (all on account) to customers during the year totaled $1,250,000. These goods had cost $700,000 to manufacture.

Required

1. Prepare journal entries to record the transactions for the year.
2. Prepare T-accounts for inventories, Manufacturing Overhead, and Cost of Goods Sold. Post relevant data from your journal entries to these T-accounts (don't forget to enter the opening balances in your inventory accounts). Compute an ending balance in each account.
3. Is Manufacturing Overhead underapplied or overapplied for the year? Prepare a journal entry to close any balance in the Manufacturing Overhead account to Cost of Goods Sold.
4. Prepare an income statement for the year. (Do not prepare a schedule of cost of goods manufactured; all of the information needed for the income statement is available in the journal entries and T-accounts you have prepared.)

P3–19 **FMS; Activity-Based Costing** Siegel Company manufactures a product that comes in both a deluxe model and a regular model. The company has manufactured the regular model for years; the deluxe model was introduced several years ago to tap a new segment of the market. Since introduction of the deluxe model, the company's profits have steadily declined and management has become increasingly concerned about the accuracy of its costing system. Sales of the deluxe model have been increasing rapidly.

Overhead is assigned to the products on a basis of direct labor-hours. For 19x1, the current year, the company estimated that it would incur $900,000 in overhead cost and produce 5,000 units of the deluxe model and 40,000 units of the regular model. The deluxe model requires two hours of direct labor time, and the regular model requires one hour. Material and labor costs per unit are as follows:

	Model	
	Deluxe	**Regular**
Direct materials . . .	$40	$25
Direct labor	14	7

Required

1. Compute the predetermined overhead rate for 19x1, and determine the cost to manufacture one unit of each model.
2. Assume that the company's overhead costs can be traced to four major activities. These activities, and the amount of overhead cost traceable to each for 19x1, are given below:

		Number of Events or Transactions		
Activity	**Traceable Costs**	**Total**	**Deluxe**	**Regular**
Purchase orders issued.	$204,000	600	200	400
Machine-hours required	182,000	35,000	20,000	15,000
Scrap/rework orders issued. . .	379,000	2,000	1,000	1,000
Shipments made.	135,000	900	250	650
	$900,000			

Determine the amount of overhead cost per event or transaction for each of the four activities above.

3. Using the data presented or computed in (2) above and an activity costing approach, do the following:
   a. Determine the total amount of overhead cost assignable to each model for 19x1. After these totals have been computed, determine the amount of overhead cost per unit of each model.

b. Compute the total cost to manufacture one unit of each model (materials, labor, and overhead).

4. From the data you have developed in (1) through (3) above, identify factors that may account for the company's declining profits.

P3–20 FMS; Activity-Based Costing For many years, Zapro Company manufactured a single product called a mono-relay. Then, three years ago, the company automated its plant and at the same time introduced a second product called a bi-relay. The bi-relay has become increasingly popular, and the company is now producing 10,000 units of it each year as compared to 40,000 units of the mono-relay. The bi-relay is a more complex product, requiring two hours of direct labor time per unit to manufacture; the mono-relay requires only one hour of direct labor time per unit. Overhead costs are assigned to products on a basis of direct labor-hours.

Despite the popularity of the company's new bi-relay, profits have declined steadily since the plant was automated. As a result, management is beginning to think that it was a mistake to automate. Unit costs for materials and labor in the new plant follow:

	Mono-Relay	Bi-Relay
Direct materials . . .	$32	$45
Direct labor	8	16

For 19x2, the current year, the company estimated that it would incur $1,020,000 in manufacturing overhead costs and produce units of the two relays as stated above.

Required

1. Compute the predetermined overhead rate for 19x2, and determine the cost to manufacture one unit of each product.
2. Assume that the company's overhead costs can be traced to four major activities. These activities and the amount of overhead cost traceable to each for 19x2 are given below:

Activity	Traceable Costs	Number of Events or Transactions: Total	Mono-Relay	Bi-Relay
Machine setups required	$ 408,000	2,400	800	1,600
Purchase orders issued	87,000	600	500	100
Machine-hours required	210,000	17,500	7,000	10,500
Maintenance requests issued . . .	315,000	1,500	650	850
	$1,020,000			

Determine the amount of overhead cost per event or transaction for each of the four activities above.

3. Using the data presented or computed in (2) above and an activity costing approach, do the following:
   a. Determine the total amount of overhead cost assignable to each product for 19x2. After these totals have been computed, determine the amount of overhead cost per unit for each product.
   b. Compute the total cost to manufacture one unit of each product.
4. Look at the data you have computed in (3) above. In terms of overhead cost, what factors make the bi-relay so costly to produce as compared to the mono-relay? Is the bi-relay as profitable as the company thinks it is? Explain.

P3–21 Schedule of Cost of Goods Manufactured Alberta Company manufactures a single product. The chief accountant has asked your help in preparing a schedule of cost of goods manufactured for the month ended June 30, 19x3. The following information is available:

a. Ten thousand units were sold at $20 per unit.
b. Twelve thousand units were produced. (One unit of raw materials is required for each finished unit.)
c. The finished goods inventory on June 1 was 3,000 units valued at $16 each.
d. The raw materials inventory on June 1 was 1,000 units valued at $5 each.
e. During June, two purchases of raw materials were made:

June 6.	8,000 units at $6 each
June 22	5,000 units at $5 each

f. The company uses the first-in, first-out method of determining raw materials inventories.
g. The work in process inventories were:

June 1.	2,000 units valued at $18,000
June 30	2,000 units valued at $21,000

h. Depreciation is determined on a straight-line basis, at a rate of 10 percent per annum. Depreciable assets include:

Factory machinery	$240,000 original cost
Office equipment.	6,000 original cost

i. Overhead is applied to production on a basis of 70 percent of direct labor cost.
j. Other information provided:

Direct labor	$100,000
Indirect labor	45,000
Salespersons' salaries.	10,500
Office salaries	16,000
Sales returns and allowances	5,000
Freight-out	2,500
Heat, light, and power	2,000
Factory rent	8,000
Interest expense	2,000
Miscellaneous factory overhead	10,000

Required Prepare a schedule of cost of goods manufactured for the month in good form. Show supporting computations.

(SMA, Adapted)

P3–22 T-Accounts; Periodic Inventory Method; Overhead Balance Allocation Decker Furniture Company employs a job-order costing system. At the beginning of 19x1, the company's records showed inventory balances as follows:

Raw materials	$10,000
Work in process	32,000
Finished goods	60,000

During the year, the following transactions were completed:

a. Raw materials acquired from suppliers on account, $200,000.
b. Raw materials requisitioned for use in production, $185,000 (80 percent direct and 20 percent indirect).
c. Costs for employee services were incurred as follows:

Direct labor.	$160,000
Indirect labor	70,000
Administrative salaries . . .	80,000

d. Depreciation was recorded on equipment, of which $54,000 related to equipment used in the factory and $18,000 related to equipment used in selling and administrative activities.

e. Advertising expense accrued, $150,000.

f. Utility costs accrued, $20,000 (80 percent related to factory operations, and the remainder related to selling and administrative activities).

g. Rent accrued on facilities, $70,000 (90 percent related to factory operations, and the remainder related to selling and administrative activities).

h. Overhead was applied to jobs on a basis of 125 percent of direct labor cost.

i. The ending balance for the year in the Work in Process inventory account was determined to be $30,000.

j. Sales for the year (all on account) were $800,000. The ending balance for the year in the Finished Goods inventory account was determined to be $120,000.

Required

1. Enter the above transactions directly into T-accounts.
2. As stated in (1) above, the ending balance in Work in Process was $30,000. Direct labor constituted $8,000 of this balance. Complete the following schedule:

Direct materials	$?
Direct labor	8,000
Manufacturing overhead . . .	?
Total work in process . . .	$30,000

3. Was manufacturing overhead underapplied or overapplied for the year? By how much?
4. What two options does the company have for disposing of its under- or overapplied overhead? Prepare a journal entry for *each* of these options showing disposition of the under- or overapplied overhead balance for the year.

P3–23 Job Cost Sheets; Overhead Rates; Journal Entries Kenworth Company employs a job-order costing system. Only three jobs—job 105, job 106, and job 107—were worked on during November and December 19x4. Job 105 was completed on December 10; the other two jobs were still in production on December 31, the end of the company's operating year. Job cost sheets on the three jobs are given below:

	Job Cost Sheet		
	Job 105	**Job 106**	**Job 107**
November costs incurred:			
Direct materials	$16,500	$ 9,300	$ —
Direct labor.	13,000	7,000	—
Manufacturing overhead	20,800	11,200	—
December costs incurred:			
Direct materials	—	8,200	21,300
Direct labor.	4,000	6,000	10,000
Manufacturing overhead	?	?	?

The following additional information is available:

a. Manufacturing overhead is assigned to jobs on a basis of direct labor cost.

b. Balances in the inventory accounts at November 30 were:

Raw Materials	$40,000
Work in Process	?
Finished Goods.	85,000

Required

1. Prepare T-accounts for Raw Materials, Work in Process, Finished Goods, and Manufacturing Overhead. Enter the November 30 inventory balances given

above; in the case of Work in Process, compute the November 30 balance and enter it into the Work in Process T-account.

2. Prepare journal entries for the *month of December* as follows:
   a. Prepare an entry to record the issue of materials into production, and post the entry to appropriate T-accounts. (In the case of direct materials, it is not necessary to make a separate entry for each job.) Indirect materials used during December totaled $4,000.
   b. Prepare an entry to record the incurrence of labor cost, and post the entry to appropriate T-accounts. (In the case of direct labor cost, it is not necessary to make a separate entry for each job.) Indirect labor cost totaled $8,000 for December.
   c. Prepare an entry to record the incurrence of $19,000 in various actual manufacturing overhead costs for December (credit Accounts Payable).
3. What apparent predetermined overhead rate does the company use to assign overhead cost to jobs? Using this rate, prepare a journal entry to record the application of overhead cost to jobs for December (it is not necessary to make a separate entry for each job). Post this entry to appropriate T-accounts.
4. As stated earlier, job 105 was completed during December. Prepare a journal entry to show the transfer of this job off of the production line and into the finished goods warehouse. Post the entry to appropriate T-accounts.
5. Determine the balance at December 31 in the Work in Process inventory account. How much of this balance consists of costs traceable to job 106? To job 107?

P3–24 Film Production Studio; Job-Order Cost Journal Entries; Complete T-Accounts; Income Statement

Film Specialties, Inc., operates a small production studio in which advertising films are made for TV and other uses. The company uses a job-order costing system to accumulate costs for each film produced. The company's trial balance as of May 1, 19x5 (the start of its fiscal year), is given below:

Cash	$ 60,000	
Accounts Receivable	210,000	
Materials, Costumes, and Supplies	130,000	
Films in Process	75,000	
Finished Films	860,000	
Prepaid Insurance	90,000	
Studio and Equipment	5,200,000	
Accumulated Depreciation		$1,990,000
Accounts Payable		700,000
Salaries and Wages Payable		35,000
Capital Stock		2,500,000
Retained Earnings		1,400,000
Totals	$6,625,000	$6,625,000

Film Specialties, Inc., uses a Production Overhead account to record all activities relating to overhead costs and applies these costs to jobs on a basis of camera-hours of activity. For the current year, the company estimated that it would incur $1,350,000 in production overhead cost and film 15,000 camera-hours. During the year, the following transactions were completed in the production of films for customers:

a. Materials, costumes, and supplies purchased on account, $690,000.
b. Materials, costumes, and supplies issued from the storeroom for use in production of various films, $700,000 (80 percent direct to the films and 20 percent indirect).
c. Utility costs incurred in the production studio, $90,000.
d. Costs for employee salaries and wages were incurred as follows:

Actors, directors, and extras	$1,300,000
Indirect labor costs of support workers . . .	230,000
Marketing and administrative salaries. . . .	650,000

e. Advertising costs incurred, $800,000.

f. Prepaid insurance expired during the year, $70,000. Of this amount, $60,000 related to the operation of the production studio, and the remaining $10,000 related to the company's marketing and administrative activities.

g. Depreciation recorded for the year, $650,000 (80 percent represented depreciation of the production studio, cameras, and other production equipment; the remaining 20 percent represented depreciation on facilities and equipment used in marketing and administrative activities).

h. Rental costs incurred on various facilities and equipment used in production of films, $360,000; and rental costs incurred on equipment used in marketing and administrative activities, $40,000.

i. Production overhead was applied to jobs filmed during the year. The company recorded 16,500 camera-hours of activity.

j. Films costing $3,400,000 to complete were transferred to the Finished Films storeroom to await delivery to customers.

k. Sales of films for the year (all on account) totaled $6,000,000; these films cost $4,000,000 to produce.

l. Collections on account from customers during the year, $5,400,000.

m. Cash payments made during the year: to creditors on account, $2,500,000; and to employees for salaries and wages, $2,200,000.

Required

1. Prepare journal entries to record the year's transactions.
2. Prepare a T-account for each account in the company's trial balance, and enter the opening balances given above. Post your journal entries to the T-accounts. Prepare new T-accounts as needed. Compute the ending balance in each account.
3. Is production overhead underapplied or overapplied for the year? Prepare the necessary journal entry to close the balance in Production Overhead to Cost of Films Sold.
4. Prepare an income statement for the year. (Do not prepare a schedule of cost of goods manufactured; all of the information needed for the income statement is available in the T-accounts.)

P3–25 Disposition of Under- or Overapplied Overhead Savallas Company is highly automated and uses computers to control manufacturing operations. The company has a job-order costing system in use and applies manufacturing overhead cost to products on a basis of computer-hours of activity. The following estimates were used in preparing a predetermined overhead rate for 19x8:

Computer-hours.	85,000
Manufacturing overhead cost . . .	$1,530,000

During 19x8, a severe economic recession caused a curtailment of production and a buildup of inventory in Savallas Company's warehouses. The company's cost records revealed the following actual cost and operating data for the year:

Computer-hours.	60,000
Manufacturing overhead cost . . .	$1,350,000
Inventories at year-end:	
Raw materials.	400,000
Work in process.	160,000
Finished goods	1,040,000
Cost of goods sold.	2,800,000

Required
1. Compute the company's predetermined overhead rate for 19x8.
2. Compute the under- or overapplied overhead for 19x8.
3. Assume the company closes any under- or overapplied overhead directly to Cost of Goods Sold. Prepare the appropriate entry.
4. Assume that the company allocates any under- or overapplied overhead to the appropriate accounts. Prepare the journal entry to show the allocation for 19x8.
5. How much higher or lower will net income be for 19x8 if the under- or overapplied overhead is allocated rather than closed directly to Cost of Goods Sold?

P3–26 T-Account Analysis of Cost Flows Selected ledger accounts for Rolm Company are given below for the year 19x2:

Raw Materials

Bal. 1/1	30,000	19x2 credits	?
19x2 debits	420,000		
Bal. 12/31	60,000		

Manufacturing Overhead

19x2 debits	385,000	19x2 credits	?

Work in Process

Bal. 1/1	70,000	19x2 credits	810,000
Direct materials	320,000		
Direct labor	110,000		
Overhead	400,000		
Bal. 12/31	?		

Factory Wages Payable

19x2 debits	179,000	Bal. 1/1	10,000
		19x2 credits	175,000
		Bal. 12/31	6,000

Finished Goods

Bal. 1/1	40,000	19x2 credits	?
19x2 debits	?		
Bal. 12/31	130,000		

Cost of Goods Sold

19x2 debits	?		

Required
1. What was the cost of raw materials put into production during the year?
2. How much of the materials in (1) above consisted of indirect materials?
3. How much of the factory labor cost for the year consisted of indirect labor?
4. What was the cost of goods manufactured for the year?
5. What was the cost of goods sold for the year (before considering under- or overapplied overhead)?
6. If overhead is applied to production on a basis of direct materials cost, what rate was in effect for 19x2?
7. Was manufacturing overhead under- or overapplied for 19x2? By how much?
8. Compute the ending balance in the Work in Process inventory account. Assume that this balance consists entirely of goods started during the year. If $32,000 of this balance is direct materials cost, how much of it is direct labor cost? Manufacturing overhead cost?

P3–27 Plantwide versus Departmental Overhead Rates "Don't tell me we've lost another bid!" exclaimed Sandy Kovallas, president of Lenko Products, Inc. "I'm afraid so," replied Doug Martin, the operations vice president. "One of our competitors underbid us by about $10,000 on the Hastings job." "I just can't figure it out," said Kovallas. "It seems we're either too high to get the job or too low to make any money on half the jobs we bid any more. What's happened?"

Lenko Products manufactures specialized goods to customers' specifications and operates a job-order costing system. Manufacturing overhead cost is applied to jobs on a basis of direct labor cost. The following estimates were made at the beginning of 19x6, the current year:

	Department			Total Plant
	Cutting	Machining	Assembly	
Direct labor	$300,000	$200,000	$400,000	$ 900,000
Manufacturing overhead	540,000	800,000	100,000	1,440,000

Jobs require varying amounts of work in the three departments. The Hastings job, for example, would have required manufacturing costs in the three departments as follows:

	Department			Total Plant
	Cutting	Machining	Assembly	
Direct materials	$12,000	$ 900	$ 5,600	$18,500
Direct labor	6,500	1,700	13,000	21,200
Manufacturing overhead	?	?	?	?

The company uses a plantwide overhead rate to apply manufacturing overhead cost to jobs.

Required

1. Assuming use of a plantwide overhead rate:
   a. Compute the rate for the current year.
   b. Determine the amount of manufacturing overhead cost that would have been applied to the Hastings job.
2. Suppose that instead of using a plantwide overhead rate, the company had used a separate predetermined overhead rate in each department. Under these conditions:
   a. Compute the rate for each department for the current year.
   b. Determine the amount of manufacturing overhead cost that would have been applied to the Hastings job.
3. Assume that it is customary in the industry to bid jobs at 150 percent of total manufacturing cost (direct materials, direct labor, and applied overhead). What was the company's bid price on the Hastings job? What would the bid price have been if departmental overhead rates had been used to apply overhead cost?
4. At the end of the current year, the company assembled the following *actual* cost data relating to all jobs worked on during the year:

	Department			Total Plant
	Cutting	Machining	Assembly	
Direct materials	$760,000	$ 90,000	$410,000	$1,260,000
Direct labor	320,000	210,000	340,000	870,000
Manufacturing overhead	560,000	830,000	92,000	1,482,000

Compute the under- or overapplied overhead for the year *(a)* assuming that a plantwide overhead rate is used and *(b)* assuming that departmental overhead rates are used.

P3–28 Comprehensive Problem: Journal Entries; T-Accounts; Statements; Pricing Southworth Company uses a job-order cost system and applies manufacturing overhead cost to jobs on a basis of the cost of direct materials used in production. At the beginning of 19x8, the following estimates were made as a basis for computing a predetermined overhead rate for the year: manufacturing overhead cost, $248,000; direct materials cost, $155,000. The following transactions took place during the year (all purchases and services were acquired on account):

a. Raw materials purchased, $142,000.
b. Raw materials requisitioned for use in production (all direct materials), $150,000.
c. Utility bills incurred in the factory, $21,000.
d. Costs for salaries and wages were incurred as follows:

Direct labor	$216,000
Indirect labor	90,000
Selling and administrative salaries . . .	145,000

e. Maintenance costs incurred in the factory, $15,000.
f. Advertising costs incurred, $130,000.
g. Depreciation recorded for the year, $50,000 (90 percent relates to factory assets, and the remainder relates to selling and administrative assets).
h. Rental cost incurred on buildings, $90,000 (80 percent of the space is occupied by the factory, and 20 percent is occupied by sales and administration).
i. Miscellaneous selling and administrative costs incurred, $17,000.
j. Manufacturing overhead cost was applied to jobs, $____?____.
k. Cost of goods manufactured for the year, $590,000.
l. Sales for the year (all on account) totaled $1,000,000. These goods cost $600,000 to manufacture.

The balances in the inventory accounts at the beginning of 19x8 were:

Raw Materials	$18,000
Work in Process	24,000
Finished Goods.	35,000

Required

1. Prepare journal entries to record the above data.
2. Post your entries to T-accounts. (Don't forget to enter the opening inventory balances above.) Determine the ending balances in the inventory accounts and in the Manufacturing Overhead account.
3. Prepare a schedule of cost of goods manufactured.
4. Prepare a journal entry to close any balance in the Manufacturing Overhead account to Cost of Goods Sold. Prepare a schedule of cost of goods sold.
5. Prepare an income statement for the year. Ignore income taxes.
6. Job 218 was one of the many jobs started and completed during the year. The job required $3,600 in materials and 400 hours of direct labor time at a rate of $11 per hour. If the job contained 500 units and the company billed at 75 percent above the cost to manufacture, what price per unit would have been charged to the customer?

P3–29 Comprehensive Problem: T-Accounts; Job-Order Cost Flows; Statements; Pricing Top-Products, Inc., produces goods to customers' orders and uses a job-order costing system. A trial balance for the company as of January 1, 19x3, is given below:

Cash	$ 18,000	
Accounts Receivable	40,000	
Raw Materials	25,000	
Work in Process	32,000	
Finished Goods	60,000	
Prepaid Insurance	5,000	
Plant and Equipment	400,000	
Accumulated Depreciation.		$148,000
Accounts Payable.		90,000
Salaries and Wages Payable		3,000
Capital Stock		250,000
Retained Earnings		89,000
Totals	$580,000	$580,000

The company applies manufacturing overhead cost to jobs on a basis of direct labor cost. The following estimates were made at the beginning of 19x3 for purposes of computing a predetermined overhead rate for the year: manufacturing overhead cost, $228,000; and direct labor cost, $190,000. Summarized transactions of the company for 19x3 are given below:

a. Raw materials purchased on account, $180,000.
b. Raw materials requisitioned for use in production, $190,000 (all direct materials).
c. Utility costs incurred in the factory, $57,000.
d. Salary and wage costs were incurred as follows:

Direct labor	$200,000
Indirect labor	90,000
Selling and administrative salaries . . .	120,000

e. Insurance expired during the year, $4,000 (75 percent related to factory operations, and 25 percent related to selling and administrative activities).
f. Property taxes incurred on the factory building, $16,000.
g. Advertising costs incurred, $150,000.
h. Depreciation recorded for the year, $50,000 (80 percent related to factory assets, and the remainder related to selling and administrative assets).
i. Other costs were incurred (credit Accounts Payable): for factory overhead, $30,000; for miscellaneous selling and administrative expenses, $18,000.
j. Manufacturing overhead cost applied to jobs, $___?___.
k. Cost of goods manufactured for the year, $635,000.
l. Sales for the year totaled $1,000,000 (all on account); the cost of goods sold was $___?___. (The ending balance in the Finished Goods inventory account was $45,000.)
m. Cash collections from customers during the year, $950,000.
n. Cash payments during the year: to employees, $412,000; on accounts payable, $478,000.

Required

1. Enter the company's transactions for the year directly into T-accounts. (Don't forget to enter the opening balances into the T-accounts.) Key your entries to the letters *(a)* through *(n)* above. Create new T-accounts as needed. Find the ending balance in each account.
2. Prepare a schedule of cost of goods manufactured.
3. Prepare a journal entry to close any balance in the Manufacturing Overhead account to Cost of Goods Sold. Prepare a schedule of cost of goods sold.
4. Prepare an income statement for 19x3. Ignore income taxes.
5. Job 316 was one of the many jobs started and completed during the year. The job required $2,400 in materials and $3,000 in direct labor cost. If the job contained 300 units and the company billed the job at 140 percent of the cost to manufacture, what price per unit would have been charged to the customer?

P3–30 JIT/FMS; Comparison of Costing Systems (Appendix) Tevik Company has just been organized and has constructed a new plant that is equipped with an FMS. Selected transactions for the first month are summarized below.

a. Raw materials costing $420,000 were purchased on account.
b. Direct materials costing $370,000 were issued from the storeroom and placed into production.
c. Direct labor cost totaling $65,000 was incurred during the month.
d. Manufacturing overhead costs totaling $210,000 were incurred during the month (credit Accounts Payable).

e. Manufacturing overhead cost totaling $215,000 was applied to production.
f. Goods were completed during the month at a total cost of $650,000.

Required

1. Assume that the company uses a conventional job-order costing system. Prepare journal entries for items *(a)* through *(f)* above. Allow sufficient space to the right of your entries to make the entries for (3) below.
2. If the company had been using a JIT inventory system, what amount of materials would have been purchased in item *(a)* above?
3. Assume that the company was using a JIT inventory system during the month. Prepare journal entries, as needed, for items *(a)* through *(f)* above. Place these entries to the right of your entries for (1) above.
4. In the case of materials, how does a JIT system provide a cost savings to an organization?
5. Examine your entry to item *(f)* above under the JIT approach. Why is the costing of products under JIT sometimes referred to as *backflush costing?*

P3–31 JIT/FMS; Comparison of Costing Systems (Appendix) "This new, automated plant is marvelous," said Paul Conway, production superintendent of Werke Products, Inc. "It has allowed us to reduce our throughput time by nearly a third."

"I agree," replied Sue Detmer, the executive vice president. "I would never have believed that we would be able to turn out $1.2 million in products during a single month." Data for March 19x1, to which Ms. Detmer was referring, are provided below:

a. Raw materials purchased on account, $550,000.
b. Direct materials drawn from the storeroom and used in production during the month, $490,000.
c. Direct labor cost incurred, $80,000.
d. Manufacturing overhead costs incurred during the month, $620,000 (credit Accounts Payable).
e. Manufacturing overhead cost applied to production, $630,000.
f. Cost of goods manufactured during the month, $1,200,000.

"Now that we have our FMS in operation, I think we should go the rest of the way and switch to JIT inventory and costing methods," said Ms. Detmer. "It would save us a bundle every year in costs."

"JIT makes me nervous," replied Mr. Conway. "Besides, I'll admit that I don't see where the cost savings would come from. We'd have the same total costs flowing through the system either way."

Required

1. Explain to Mr. Conway the ways in which the company could save costs if it changed to a JIT inventory system. Do you agree that the same total costs would flow through the system either way? Explain.
2. Assume that the company is now using a job-order costing system. Prepare journal entries to record items (*a*) through (*f*) above. Leave enough space to the right of your entries to make the entries for (3) below.
3. Assume that the company was using a JIT inventory system during the month. Prepare journal entries, as needed, for items (*a*) through (*f*) above. Place these entries to the right of your entries for (2) above.
4. Examine your entry for item (*f*) above under the JIT approach. Why is the costing of products under JIT sometimes referred to as *backflush costing?*

CASES

C3–32 Incomplete Data; Review of Cost Flows After a dispute concerning wages, Orville Arson tossed an incendiary device into the Sparkle Company's record vault. Within moments, only a few charred fragments were readable from the company's factory ledger, as shown below:

Raw Materials

Bal. 4/1	12,000	

Manufacturing Overhead

Actual costs for April	14,800	

Work in Process

Bal. 4/1	4,500	

Accounts Payable

	Bal. 4/30	8,000

Finished Goods

Bal. 4/30	16,000	

Cost of Goods Sold

Sifting through ashes and interviewing selected employees has turned up the following additional information:

a. The controller remembers clearly that the predetermined overhead rate was based on an estimated 60,000 direct labor-hours to be worked over the year and an estimated $180,000 in manufacturing overhead costs.

b. The production superintendent's cost sheets showed only one job in process on April 30. Materials of $2,600 had been added to the job, and 300 direct labor-hours had been expended at $6 per hour.

c. The accounts payable are for raw material purchases only, according to the accounts payable clerk. He clearly remembers that the balance in the account was $6,000 on April 1. An analysis of cancelled checks (kept in the treasurer's office) shows that payments of $40,000 were made to suppliers during the month. (All materials used during April were direct materials.)

d. A charred piece of the payroll ledger shows that 5,200 direct labor-hours were recorded for the month. The employment department has verified that there were no variations in pay rates among employees. (This infuriated Orville, who felt that his services were underpaid.)

e. Records maintained in the finished goods warehouse indicate that the finished goods inventory totaled $11,000 on April 1.

f. From another charred piece in the vault, you are able to discern that the cost of goods manufactured for April was $89,000.

Required Determine the following amounts:

1. Work in process inventory, April 30.
2. Raw materials purchased during April.
3. Overhead applied to work in process.
4. Cost of goods sold for April.
5. Over- or underapplied overhead for April.
6. Raw materials usage during April.
7. Raw materials inventory, April 30.

(Hint: A good way to proceed is to bring the fragmented T-accounts up-to-date through April 30 by posting whatever entries can be developed from the information provided.)

C3–33 Analysis of Cost Flows and Inventories under Job-Order Costing Kemper Products is a manufacturer of furnishings for infants and children and uses a job-order cost system. The company's work in process inventory at April 30, 19x8, consisted of the following jobs:

Job Number	Items	Number of Units	Accumulated Cost
CBS102	Cribs	20,000	$ 900,000
PLP086	Playpens	15,000	420,000
DRS114	Dressers	25,000	250,000
			$1,570,000

At April 30, the company's finished goods inventory consisted of five items in stock, as follows:

Item	Units on Hand	Unit Cost	Total Cost
Cribs	7,500	$ 64	$ 480,000
Strollers	13,000	23	299,000
Carriages	11,200	102	1,142,400
Dressers	21,000	55	1,155,000
Playpens	19,400	35	679,000
			$3,755,400

Kemper Products applies manufacturing overhead to products on the basis of direct labor-hours. For the fiscal year ending May 31, 19x8, the company estimated that it would incur $4,500,000 in manufacturing overhead cost and that it would work a total of 600,000 direct labor-hours. Through the first 11 months of the year, a total of 555,000 direct labor-hours were worked, and $4,103,000 in actual manufacturing overhead cost was incurred.

At April 30, the balance in Kemper's Raw Materials inventory account totaled $668,000. Purchases of materials and requisitions of materials for use in production during the month of May 19x8 were as follows:

Purchases of raw materials	$638,000
Requisitions of raw materials:	
Job CBS102	155,000
Job PLP086	13,800
Job DRS114	211,000
Job STR077 (10,000 strollers)	143,000
Job CRG098 (5,000 carriages)	252,000
Indirect materials	97,000

During May 19x8, Kemper incurred the following payroll costs:

Job Number	Hours	Total Cost
CBS102	12,000	$122,400
PLP086	4,400	43,200
DRS114	19,500	200,500
STR077	3,500	30,000
CRG098	14,000	138,000
Indirect labor	8,000	72,000
Sales and administration	—	302,000
		$908,100

Listed below are the jobs that were completed and the unit sales for the month of May 19x8:

Job Number		Items	Number of Units: Total Job	Number of Units: Shipped
CBS102	. . . . .	Cribs	20,000	17,500
PLP086	. . . . .	Playpens	15,000	21,000
STR077	. . . . .	Strollers	10,000	14,000
—	. . . . .	Dressers	—	18,000
CRG098	. . . . .	Carriages	5,000	6,000

During May 19x8, the company incurred the following additional costs in its manufacturing facility:

Depreciation	$ 52,000
Utilities	46,000
Insurance	7,000
Property taxes	3,000
Maintenance	18,000
Total	$126,000

The company accounts for all flows of materials and products on a first-in, first-out basis.

Required

1. Describe when it is appropriate for a company to use a job-order cost system.
2. Compute the under- or overapplied overhead cost for the fiscal year ended May 31, 19x8.
3. Determine the dollar balance in Kemper Products' Work in Process inventory account as of May 31, 19x8.
4. Determine the dollar amount related to the playpens in Kemper's Finished Goods as of May 31, 19x8.
5. Explain the proper treatment for under- or overapplied overhead cost when using a job-order cost system.

(CMA, Heavily Adapted)

C3–34 JIT/FMS; Activity-Based Costing "I say it's time we cut back on the X-20 model and shift our resources toward the new Y-30 model," said Cheri Warnick, executive vice president of Cutler Products, Inc. "Just look at this statement I've received from accounting. The Y-30 is generating twice as much in profits as the X-20, and it has only about one fifth as much in sales. I've become convinced that our future depends on the Y-30." The statement to which Cheri was referring follows:

CUTLER PRODUCTS, INC.
Income Statement
For the Year Ended December 31, 19x6

	Total	X-20	Y-30
Sales	$7,250,000	$6,000,000	$1,250,000
Cost of goods sold	4,500,000	3,600,000	900,000
Gross margin	2,750,000	2,400,000	350,000
Less selling and administrative expenses . . .	2,450,000	2,300,000	150,000
Net income	$ 300,000	$ 100,000	$ 200,000
Number of units produced and sold	—	30,000	5,000
Net income per unit sold	—	$3.33	$40.00

"The numbers sure look that way," replied Pete Zayas, the company's sales vice president. "But why aren't our competitors more excited about the Y-30? I know we've only been producing the model for three years, but it seems like more of them would recognize what a money maker it is."

"I think it's our new automated plant," said Cheri. "Now it takes only two direct labor-hours to produce a unit of the X-20 and three hours to produce a unit of the Y-30. That's half of what it used to take us."

"Automation is marvelous," replied Pete. "I suppose that's how we're able to hold down the price on the Y-30. Why, Saki Company in Japan started to bring out a Y-30 but discovered they couldn't touch our price. But Saki is killing us on the X-20; I suppose they'll pick up our X-20 customers as we move out of that market. But who cares? We don't even have to advertise the Y-30; it just seems to sell itself."

"My only concern about automation is how our overhead rate has shot up," said Cheri. "Our total overhead cost was $1,800,000 for 19x6. That comes out to a hefty amount per direct labor-hour, but old Fred down in accounting has been using labor-hours as a base for computing overhead rates for years and doesn't want to change. I don't suppose it matters so long as costs get assigned to products."

"That bookkeeping bores me," replied Pete. "But I think you've got a problem in production. I had lunch with Sally yesterday, and she was complaining about how complex the Y-30 is to produce. Apparently they have to do a lot of machine setups and other work just to keep production moving on the Y-30. And they have to inspect every single unit."

"It'll have to wait," said Cheri. "I'm writing a proposal to the board to phase out the X-20 as rapidly as possible. We've got to bring those profits up or we'll all be looking for jobs."

Required

1. Compute the predetermined overhead rate that the company would have used during 19x6. (You may assume that there was no under- or overapplied overhead for the year.)
2. Materials and labor costs for the two products follow:

	X-20	Y-30
Direct materials . . .	$60	$90
Direct labor	12	18

   Using these data and the rate computed in (1) above, determine the cost to produce one unit of each product.
3. Assume that the company's $1,800,000 in overhead cost is traceable to six activities, as follows:

	Traceable Costs	Number of Events or Transactions		
		Total	X-20	Y-30
Machine setups	$ 560,000	7,000	3,000	4,000
Purchase orders	208,000	1,600	1,000	600
Quality inspections	360,000	9,000	4,000	5,000
Work scheduling orders	90,000	400	280	120
Machine-hours worked	450,000	30,000	9,000	21,000
Shipments	132,000	1,200	800	400
	$1,800,000			

   Given these data, would you support a recommendation to expand sales of the Y-30? Explain your position, and show unit costs, an income statement, and other data to help the board make a decision.
4. From the data you have prepared in (3) above, why do you suppose the Y-30 "just seems to sell itself"?
5. If you were president of Cutler Products, Inc., what strategy would you follow from this point forward to improve the company's overall profits?
6. Examine the costs in (3) above. Which of these costs might be reduced (or even eliminated) if the company adopted the JIT philosophy?

4

Systems Design
Process Costing

LEARNING OBJECTIVES

After studying Chapter 4, you should be able to:

1 Enumerate the major similarities and differences between job-order and process costing.

2 Prepare journal entries to record the flow of materials, labor, and overhead through a process costing system.

3 Compute equivalent units of production by both the weighted-average and FIFO methods.

4 Prepare a quantity schedule and explain its significance.

5 Compute unit costs for a period under both the weighted-average and FIFO methods.

6 Prepare a cost reconciliation for a period under both the weighted-average and FIFO methods.

7 Combine the quantity schedule, the unit costs, and the cost reconciliation into a production report.

8 Explain the impact of a JIT inventory system on process costing.

9 State the conditions under which operation costing is useful to management, and explain the impact of a flexible manufacturing system on job-order and process costing.

10 Define or explain the key terms listed at the end of the chapter.

As explained in the preceding chapter, there are two basic costing systems in use: job-order costing and process costing. We have found that a job-order costing system is used in those situations where many different jobs or batches of production are worked on each period. Examples of industries that would typically use job-order costing include furniture manufacture, special-order printing, shipbuilding, and many types of service organizations.

By contrast, **process costing** is used in those industries that produce basically homogeneous products such as bricks, flour, cement, screws, bolts, and pharmaceutical items. In addition, process costing is employed in assembly-type operations that manufacture typewriters, automobiles, and small appliances, as well as in utilities producing gas, water, and electricity. As suggested by the length of this list, process costing is in widespread use and warrants study by anyone involved in accounting, management, or systems work.

Our purpose in this chapter is to extend the discussion of product costing that was started in the preceding chapter in order to include a process costing system.

COMPARISON OF JOB-ORDER AND PROCESS COSTING

In some ways process costing is very similar to job-order costing, and in some ways it is very different. In the following two sections, we focus on these similarities and differences in order to provide a foundation for the detailed discussion of process costing that follows.

Similarities between Job-Order and Process Costing

It is important to recognize that much of what was learned in the preceding chapter about costing and about cost flows applies equally well to process costing in this chapter. That is, we are not throwing out all that we have learned about costing and starting from ''scratch'' with a whole new system. The similarities that exist between job-order and process costing can be summarized as follows:

1. The same basic purposes exist in both systems, which are: (*a*) to assign material, labor, and overhead costs to products; (*b*) to provide a mechanism for computing unit costs; and (*c*) to provide data essential for planning, control, and decision making.
2. Both systems maintain and use the same basic manufacturing accounts, including Manufacturing Overhead, Raw Materials, Work in Process, and Finished Goods.
3. Costs flow through the manufacturing accounts in basically the same way in both systems.

As can be seen from this comparison, much of the knowledge that we have already acquired about costing is applicable to a process costing system. Our task now is simply to refine and extend this knowledge to meet special process costing needs.

EXHIBIT 4–1
Differences between Job-Order and Process Costing

Job-Order Costing	Process Costing
1. Many different jobs are worked on during each period, with each job having different production requirements.	1. A single product is produced either on a continuous basis or for long periods of time. All units of product are identical.
2. Costs are accumulated by individual job.	2. Costs are accumulated by department.
3. The *job cost sheet* is the key document controlling the accumulation of costs by a job.	3. The *department production report* is the key document showing the accumulation and disposition of costs by a department.
4. Unit costs are computed *by job* on the job cost sheet.	4. Unit costs are computed *by department* on the department production report.

Differences between Job-Order and Process Costing

The differences between job-order and process costing arise from two factors. The first is that the flow of units in a process costing system is more or less continuous, and the second is that these units are indistinguishable from one another. Under process costing, it makes no sense to try to identify materials, labor, and overhead costs with a particular order from a customer (as we did with job-order costing), since each order is just one of many that are filled from a continuous flow of units from the production line. Under process costing, we accumulate costs *by department,* rather than by order, and assign these costs equally to all units that pass through the department during a period.

A further difference between the two costing systems is that the job cost sheet has no use in process costing, since the focal point of that method is on departments. Instead of using job cost sheets, a document known as a **production report** is prepared for each department in which work is done on products. The production report serves several functions. It provides a summary of the number of units moving through a department during a period, and it also provides a computation of unit costs. In addition, it shows what costs were charged to a department during a period and what disposition was made of these costs. As these comments suggest, the department production report is a key document in a process costing system.

The major differences between job-order and process costing are summarized in Exhibit 4–1.

A PERSPECTIVE OF PROCESS COST FLOWS

Before presenting a detailed example of process costing, it will be helpful to gain a visual perspective of how manufacturing costs flow through a process costing system.

Processing Departments

A **processing department** is any location in the factory where work is performed on a product and where materials, labor, or overhead costs are added to the product. For example, a brick factory might have two processing

EXHIBIT 4–2
Sequential Processing Departments

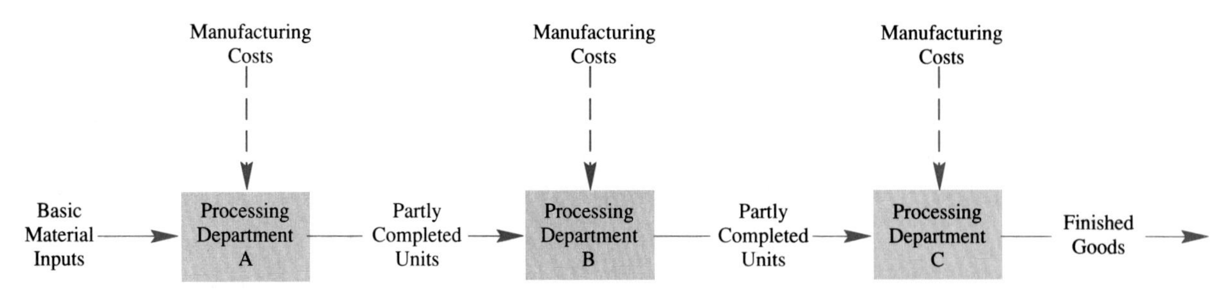

departments—one for mixing and molding clay into brick form and one for firing the molded brick. There can be as many or as few processing departments as are needed to complete the manufacture of a product. Some products may go through several processing departments, while others may go through only one or two. Regardless of the number of departments involved, all processing departments have two essential features. First, the activity performed in the processing department must be performed uniformly on all of the units passing through it. Second, the output of the processing department must be homogeneous.

The processing departments involved in the manufacture of a product such as bricks would probably be organized in a *sequential* pattern. By **sequential processing,** we mean that units flow in sequence from one department to another. An example of processing departments arranged in a sequential pattern is given in Exhibit 4–2.

A different type of processing pattern, known as *parallel processing,* is required in the manufacture of some products. **Parallel processing** is used in those situations where, after a certain point, some units may go through different processing departments than others. For example, the petroleum industry may input crude oil into one processing department and then use the refined output for further processing into several end products. Each end product may undergo several steps of further processing after the initial refining, some of which may be shared with other end products and some of which may not. Exhibit 4–3 illustrates one type of parallel processing. The number of possible variations in parallel processing patterns is virtually limitless. The example given in Exhibit 4–3 is intended as just one sample of the many parallel patterns in use today.

The Flow of Materials, Labor, and Overhead Costs

Cost accumulation is simpler in a process costing system than in a job-order costing system. The reason is that costs need to be identified only by processing department—not by separate job. Thus, in a process costing system, instead of having to trace costs to hundreds of different jobs, costs are traced to only a few processing departments. This means that costs can be accumulated for longer periods of time and that just one allocation is needed at the

EXHIBIT 4–3
Parallel Processing Departments

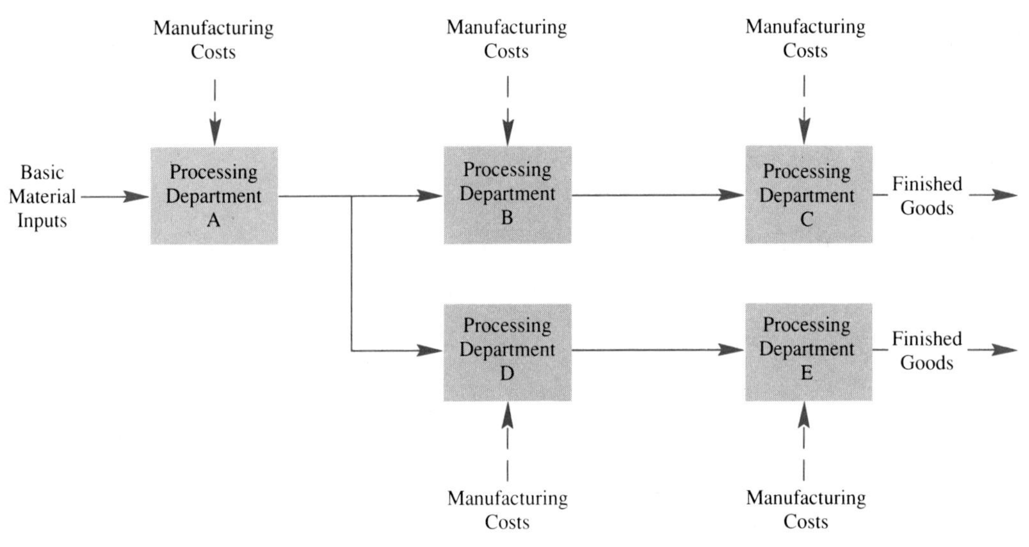

end of a period (week, month, and so forth) in order to assign the accumulated costs to the period's output.

A T-account model of materials, labor, and overhead cost flows in a process costing system is given in Exhibit 4–4 on the following page. Several key points should be noted from this exhibit. First, note that a separate Work in Process account is maintained for *each processing department*, rather than having only a single Work in Process account for the entire company. Second, note that the completed production of the first processing department (Department A in the exhibit) is transferred into the Work in Process account of the second processing department (Department B), where it undergoes further work. After this further work, the completed units are then transferred into Finished Goods. (In Exhibit 4–4, we show only two processing departments; there may be several such departments in some companies.)

Finally, note that materials, labor, and overhead costs can be entered directly into *any* processing department—not just the first. Costs in Department B's Work in Process account would therefore consist of the materials, labor, and overhead costs entered directly into the account plus the costs attached to partially completed units transferred in from Department A (called **transferred-in costs**).

EQUIVALENT UNITS OF PRODUCTION

After materials, labor, and overhead costs have been accumulated in a department, the department's output must be determined so that unit costs can be computed. A department's output is always stated in terms of **equivalent units of production.** Equivalent units can be defined as the number of units

EXHIBIT 4–4
T-Account Model of Process Costing Flows

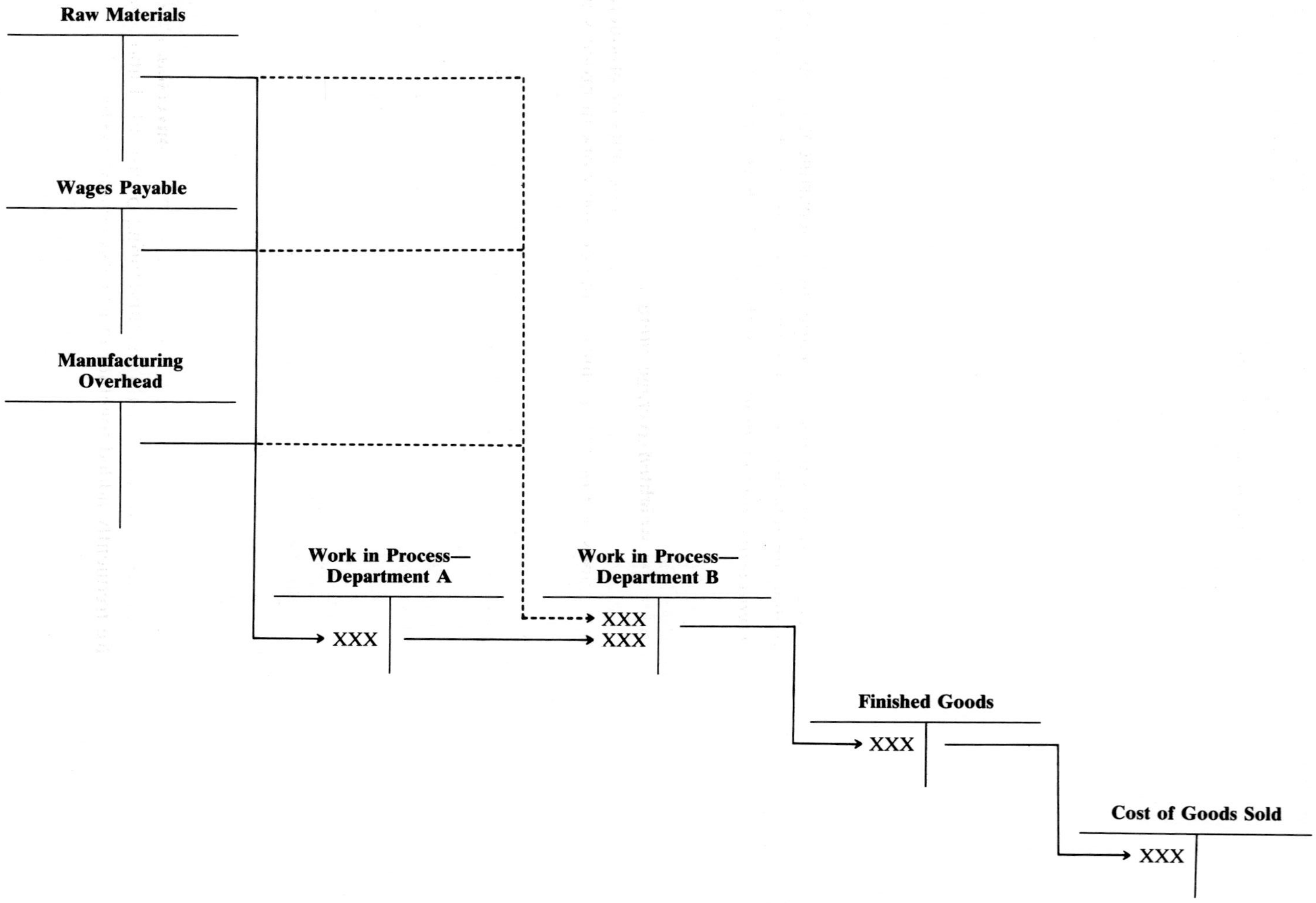

that would have been produced during a period if all of a department's efforts had resulted in completed units of product. Equivalent units are computed by taking completed units and adjusting them for partially completed units in the work in process inventory.

The reasoning behind the computation of equivalent units is as follows: Completed units alone will not accurately measure output in a department, since part of the department's efforts during a period will have been expended on units that are only partially complete. To accurately measure output, these partially completed units must also be considered in the output computation. This is done by mathematically converting the partially completed units into fully completed *equivalent units* and then adjusting the output figure accordingly.

To illustrate, assume that a company has 500 units in its ending work in process inventory that are 60 percent complete. Five hundred units 60 percent complete would be equivalent to 300 fully completed units (500 × 60% = 300). Therefore, the ending inventory would be said to contain 300 *equivalent units*. These equivalent units would be added to the fully completed units in determining the period's output.

There are two ways of computing a department's equivalent units, depending on whether the company is accounting for its cost flows by the *weighted-average method* or by the *first-in, first-out (FIFO) method.*

Weighted-Average Method

Under the **weighted-average method,** a department's equivalent units are computed just as described above: Equivalent units of production = Completed units + Equivalent units in the ending work in process inventory.

To provide an extended example, assume the following data:

Regal Company manufactures a product that goes through two departments—mixing and firing. During 19x1, the following activity took place in the mixing department:

		Percent Completed	
	Units	Materials	Conversion
Work in process, beginning	10,000	100	70
Units started into production during the year	150,000		
Units completed during the year and transferred to the firing department	140,000		
Work in process, ending	20,000	60	25

Recall from our discussion in Chapter 2 that **conversion cost** consists of direct labor combined with manufacturing overhead. Labor and overhead are frequently added together in process costing systems.

Since Regal Company's work in process inventories are at different stages of completion in terms of the amounts of materials cost and conversion cost that have been added, two equivalent unit figures will have to be computed—one for equivalent units in terms of materials and the other for equivalent units in terms of conversion. The equivalent units computations are given in Exhibit 4–5.

EXHIBIT 4–5
Equivalent Units of Production: Weighted-Average Method

	Materials	Conversion
Units transferred to firing	140,000	140,000
Work in process, ending:		
20,000 units × 60%	12,000	
20,000 units × 25%		5,000
Equivalent units of production	152,000	145,000

Note from the computations in Exhibit 4–5 that units in the beginning inventory are ignored and that an adjustment is made only for partially completed units in the ending inventory. This is a key point in the computation of equivalent units under the weighted-average method: *Units in the beginning inventory are always treated as if they were started and completed during the current period.* Thus, no adjustment is made for these units, regardless of how much work was done on them before the period started. Although this procedure may seem illogical and inconsistent, it greatly simplifies the preparation of a department production report, as we shall see shortly.

FIFO Method

The computation of equivalent units under the **FIFO method** differs from the computation under the weighted-average method in two ways.

First, the "units transferred out" figure is divided into two parts. One part consists of the units from the beginning inventory that were completed and transferred out, and the other part consists of the units that were both *started* and *completed* during the current period.

Second, full consideration is given to the amount of work expended during the current period on units in the *beginning* work in process inventory as well as on units in the ending inventory. Thus, under the FIFO method, it is necessary to convert both inventories to an equivalent units basis. For the beginning inventory, the equivalent units represent the work done *to complete* the units; for the ending inventory, the equivalent units represent the work done to bring the units to a stage of partial completion at the end of the period (the same as with the weighted-average method).

In sum, the equivalent units figure under the FIFO method consists of three amounts:

1. The work needed *to complete* the units in the beginning inventory.
2. The work expended on the units *started* and *completed* during the period.
3. The work expended on partially completed units in the ending inventory.

To illustrate, refer again to the Regal Company data. The mixing department completed and transferred 140,000 units to the firing department during the year. Since 10,000 of these units came from the beginning inventory, the mixing department must have started and completed 130,000 units during the

EXHIBIT 4–6
Equivalent Units of Production: FIFO Method

	Materials	Conversion
Work in process, beginning:		
10,000 units × 0%	—	
10,000 units × 30%*		3,000
Units started and completed this year . . .	130,000†	130,000†
Work in process, ending:		
20,000 units × 60%‡	12,000	
20,000 units × 25%‡		5,000
Equivalent units of production	142,000	138,000

* Work needed *to complete* the units in the beginning inventory.
† 140,000 units transferred out − 10,000 units in the beginning inventory = 130,000 units started and completed during the year.
‡ Work *completed* on the units in the ending inventory.

year. The 10,000 units in the beginning inventory had all materials added in the prior year and were 70 percent complete as to conversion costs when the current year started. Thus, during the current year, the mixing department would have added the other 30 percent of conversion cost (100% − 70% = 30%). Given these data, the equivalent units for the mixing department for the year would be computed as shown in Exhibit 4–6.

Comparison of the Weighted-Average and FIFO Methods

The reader should stop at this point and compare the data in Exhibit 4–6 with the data in Exhibit 4–5. Note that the major difference between the two exhibits is that the FIFO method separates the units in the beginning inventory from other units transferred out and converts the units in the beginning inventory to an equivalent units basis. A logical question to ask is, why the difference in the handling of the beginning inventory? The answer lies in what the two methods are trying to accomplish.

The purpose of the weighted-average method is to *simplify the computation of unit costs.* This is accomplished by treating units in the beginning inventory as if they were started and completed during the current period. By treating units in the beginning inventory in this way, the manager is relieved from having to distinguish between which units were on hand at the start of the year and which were not. Thus, he or she is able to treat all units equally when unit costs are computed. This greatly simplifies the costing process.

By contrast, the purpose of the FIFO method is to distinguish between (*a*) units in the beginning inventory and (*b*) units that were started during the period, so that separate unit costs can be computed for each. Under the FIFO method, units in the beginning inventory are assumed to be completed and transferred out first (thus, a ''first-in, first-out'' flow) and to carry their own unit costs. Units started during the year are assumed to be completed next and to carry their own unit costs. This is a more complex costing approach than the weighted-average method, although it can be argued that it is also more accurate.

EXHIBIT 4–7
Visual Perspective of Equivalent Units

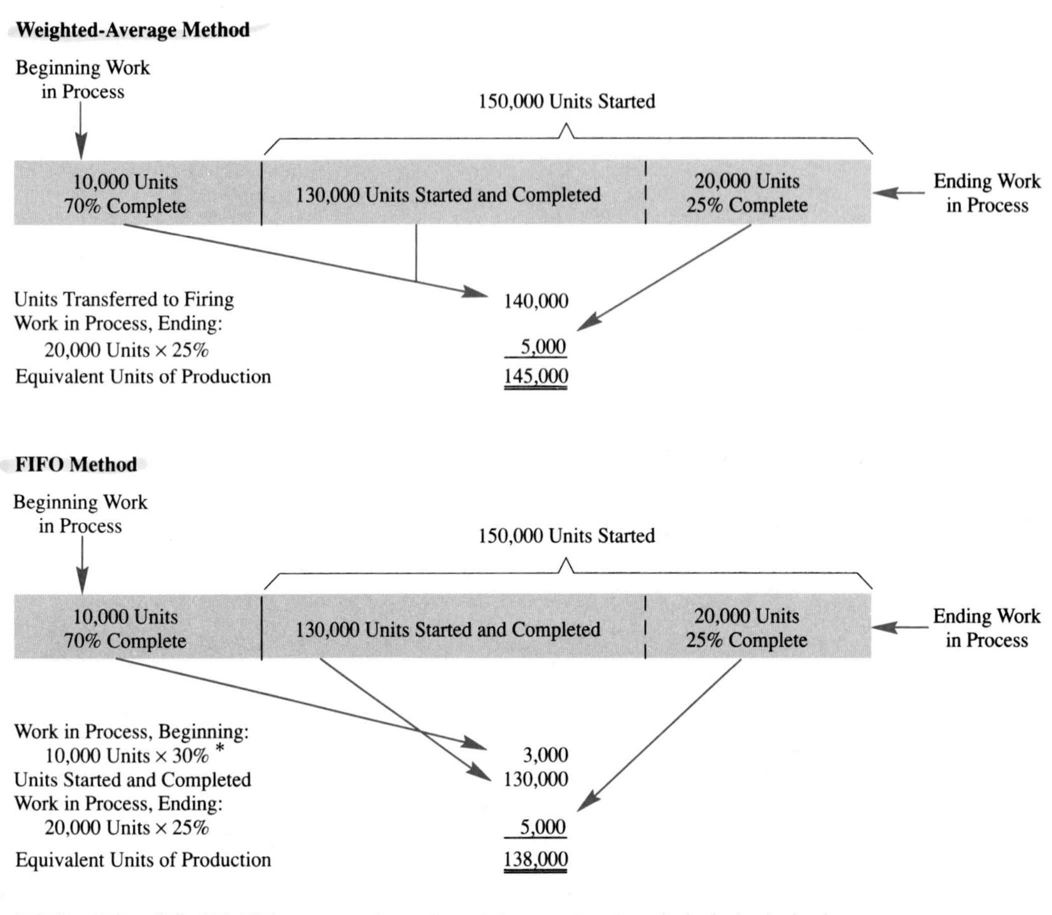

*100% – 70% = 30%. This 30% represents the work needed to complete the units in the beginning inventory.

Visual Perspective of Equivalent Units

To assist in your understanding of equivalent units, Exhibit 4–7 contains a visual perspective of the computation of equivalent units (the data are for Regal Company's conversion costs). The exhibit also shows the relationship between equivalent units as computed by the weighted-average method and equivalent units as computed by the FIFO method. Study Exhibit 4–7 carefully before going on.

PRODUCTION REPORT—WEIGHTED-AVERAGE METHOD

The purpose of the production report is to summarize for the manager all of the activity that takes place in a department's Work in Process account for a period. This activity includes the units that flow through the Work in Process

EXHIBIT 4–8
The Production Report in a Process Costing System

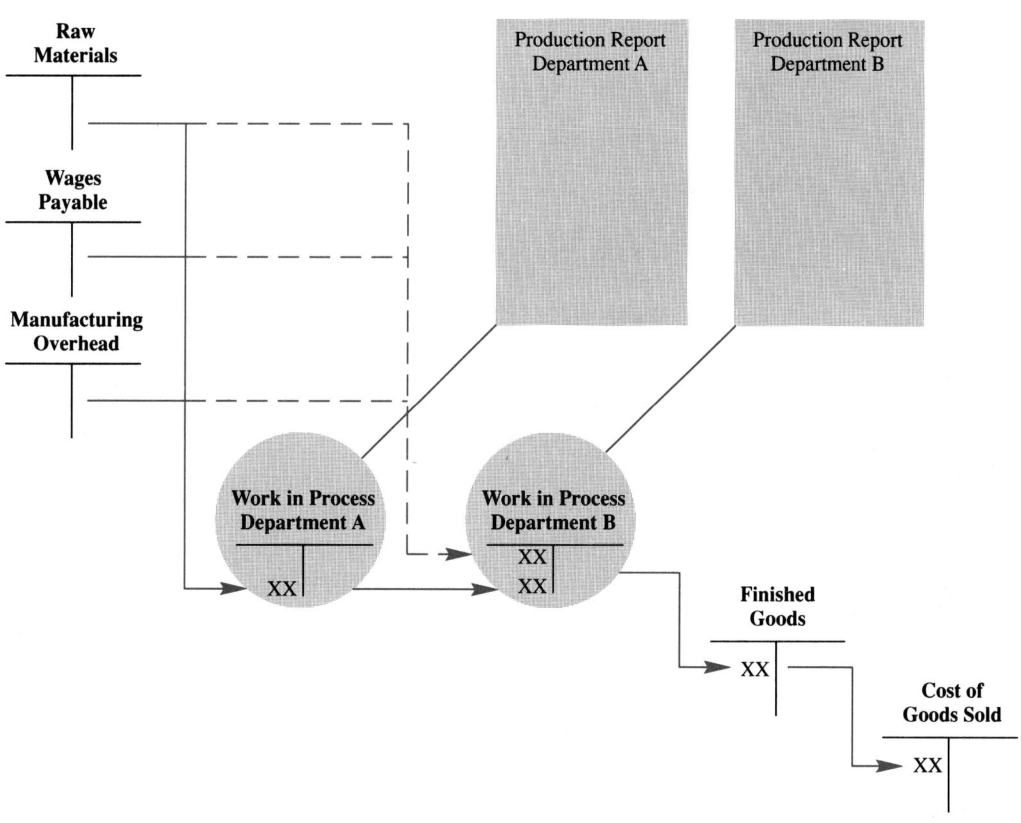

account as well as the costs that flow through it. A separate production report is prepared for each department, as illustrated in Exhibit 4–8.

Earlier, when we outlined the differences between job-order costing and process costing, we stated that the production report takes the place of a job cost sheet in a process costing system. Thus, the production report is a key document for the manager and is vital to the proper operation of the system. There are three separate (though highly interrelated) parts to the production report:

1. A quantity schedule, which shows the flow of units through the department, and a computation of equivalent units.
2. A computation of unit costs.
3. A reconciliation of all cost flows into and out of the department during the period.

We will use the data on the following page to show a numerical example of a production report.

Stabler Chemical Company has two departments—mixing and cooking. Production activity begins in the mixing department; after mixing, the units are transferred to the cooking department. From cooking, the units are transferred to finished goods.

All of the materials involved in mixing are added at the beginning of work in the mixing department. Labor and overhead costs in that department are incurred uniformly as work progresses. Overhead cost is applied at the rate of 150 percent of direct labor cost.

Cost and other data for May 19x1 include the following for the mixing department:

Work in process, beginning:	
Units in process	20,000
Stage of completion	30%
Cost in the beginning inventory:	
Materials cost	$ 8,000
Labor cost	3,600
Overhead cost	5,400
Total cost in process	$ 17,000
Units started into production during the month	180,000
Units completed and transferred to cooking	170,000
Costs added to production during the month:	
Materials cost	$ 63,000
Labor cost	88,000
Overhead cost applied	132,000
Work in process, ending:	
Units in process	30,000
Stage of completion*	40%

* This refers to labor and overhead costs only, since all materials are added at the beginning of work in the mixing department.

In the following sections, we show how a production report is prepared when the weighted-average method is used to compute unit costs. Later in the chapter, we show how a production report is prepared when the FIFO method is used.

Step 1: Prepare a Quantity Schedule and Compute the Equivalent Units

The first section of a production report consists of a **quantity schedule,** which accounts for the physical flow of units through a department, and a computation of the equivalent units for the period. The equivalent units are computed in this section of the production report since the quantity schedule provides the data from which these figures are derived. To illustrate, a quantity schedule combined with a computation of equivalent units is given below for the Stabler Chemical Company. (The quantity schedule is printed in color.)

	Quantity Schedule
Units to be accounted for:	
Work in process, beginning (all materials, 30% labor and overhead added last month)	20,000
Started into production	180,000
Total units to be accounted for	200,000

		Equivalent Units		
		Materials	Labor	Overhead
Units accounted for as follows:				
Transferred to cooking	170,000	170,000	170,000	170,000
Work in process, ending (all materials, 40% labor and overhead added this month)	30,000	30,000	12,000*	12,000*
Total units accounted for	200,000	200,000	182,000	182,000

* 30,000 units × 40% = 12,000 equivalent units.

The quantity schedule permits the manager to see at a glance how many units moved through the department during a period as well as to see the stage of completion of any in-process units. In addition to providing this information, the quantity schedule serves as an essential guide in preparing and tying together the remaining parts of a production report. The equivalent units, for example, are easily computed by simply following the data provided in the quantity schedule, as shown above.

Step 2: Compute the Unit Costs

As stated earlier, the weighted-average method treats units in the beginning work in process inventory as if they were started and completed during the current period. Thus, the cost in the beginning work in process inventory is added in with current period costs in determining unit costs for the period involved. These computations are shown below for the Stabler Chemical Company:

	Total	Materials	Labor	Overhead
Work in process, beginning	$ 17,000	$ 8,000	$ 3,600	$ 5,400
Cost added by the department	283,000	63,000	88,000	132,000
Total cost (*a*)	$300,000	$71,000	$91,600	$137,400
Equivalent units (above) (*b*)	—	200,000	182,000	182,000
Unit cost, (*a*) ÷ (*b*)	$1.613	$0.355	$0.503	$0.755

The units costs that we have computed will be used to apply cost to units that are transferred to the next department and will also be used to compute the cost in the ending work in process inventory. A total of all unit costs from both the mixing and cooking departments will represent the final manufactured cost of a unit of product.

Step 3: Prepare a Cost Reconciliation

The purpose of a **cost reconciliation** is to (*a*) show what costs have been charged to a department during a period and (*b*) show how these costs are accounted for. Typically, the costs charged to a department will consist of:

1. Cost in the beginning work in process inventory.
2. Materials, labor, and overhead cost added during the period.
3. Cost (if any) transferred in from the preceding department.

These costs are accounted for by showing:

1. Cost transferred out to the next department (or into Finished Goods).
2. Cost remaining in the ending work in process inventory.

EXHIBIT 4–9

Graphic Illustration of the Cost Reconciliation Part of a Production Report

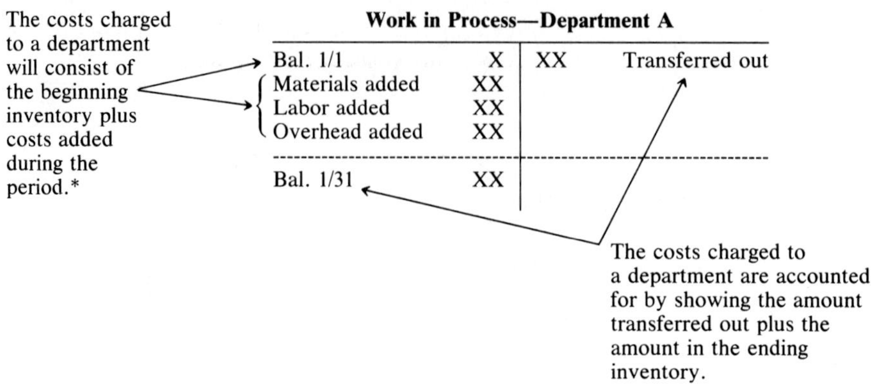

* Departments that follow Department A (Department B and so forth) will also need to show the amount of cost transferred in from the preceding department.

Since this section of the production report is called a cost reconciliation, *the totals of these two groups of cost must always be in agreement.* The content of a cost reconciliation is shown graphically in Exhibit 4–9. Study this exhibit carefully before going on to the next section where we present a cost reconciliation for Stabler Chemical Company.

Example of a Cost Reconciliation The cost reconciliation depends heavily on the quantity schedule that was developed earlier. In fact, *the simplest way to prepare a cost reconciliation is to follow the quantity schedule line for line and show the cost associated with each group of units.* This is done in Exhibit 4–10, where we present a completed production report for Stabler Chemical Company.

Note that the production report has the three sections that we mentioned earlier: (1) a quantity schedule and computation of equivalent units; (2) a computation of unit costs; and (3) a cost reconciliation. As stated, *we follow the quantity schedule line for line in preparing the cost reconciliation.* For example, the quantity schedule shows that 20,000 units were in process at the start of the month and that an additional 180,000 units were started into production. Looking at the cost reconciliation part of the report, notice that the 20,000 units in process at the start of the month had $17,000 in cost attached to them and that the mixing department added another $283,000 in cost to production during the month. Thus, the mixing department has $300,000 in cost to be accounted for.

This cost is accounted for in two ways. As shown on the quantity schedule, 170,000 units were transferred to the cooking department during the month and another 30,000 units were still in process at the end of the month. Thus, part of the $300,000 "cost to be accounted for" goes with the 170,000 units to the cooking department, and part of it remains with the 30,000 units in the ending work in process inventory.

Each of the 170,000 units transferred to the cooking department is assigned $1.613 in cost, for a total of $274,254. The 30,000 units still in process at the end of the month are assigned cost according to their stage of completion. To determine the stage of completion, we refer to the equivalent units computation and bring the equivalent units figures down to the cost reconciliation part of the report. We then assign cost to these units, using the unit cost figures already computed.

EXHIBIT 4–10
Production-Report—Weighted-Average Method

Quantity Schedule and Equivalent Units

	Quantity Schedule			
Units to be accounted for:				
Work in process, beginning (all materials, 30% labor and overhead added last month)	20,000			
Started into production	180,000			
Total units to be accounted for	200,000			
		Equivalent Units		
		Materials	Labor	Overhead
Units accounted for as follows:				
Transferred to cooking	170,000	170,000	170,000	170,000
Work in process, ending (all materials, 40% labor and overhead added this month)	30,000	30,000	12,000*	12,000*
Total units accounted for	200,000	200,000	182,000	182,000

Unit Costs

	Total	Materials	Labor	Overhead
Work in process, beginning	$ 17,000	$ 8,000	$ 3,600	$ 5,400
Cost added by the department	283,000	63,000	88,000	132,000
Total cost *(a)*	$300,000	$ 71,000	$ 91,600	$137,400
Equivalent units *(b)*	—	200,000	182,000	182,000
Unit cost, *(a)* ÷ *(b)*	$1.613	$0.355	$0.503	$0.755

Cost Reconciliation

	Costs	Equivalent Units (EU)		
Cost to be accounted for:				
Work in process, beginning	$ 17,000			
Cost added by the department	283,000			
Total cost to be accounted for	$300,000			
Cost accounted for as follows:				
Transferred to cooking: 170,000 units × $1.613 each	$274,254†	170,000	170,000	170,000
Work in process, ending:				
Materials, at $0.355 per EU	10,650	30,000		
Labor, at $0.503 per EU	6,036		12,000	
Overhead, at $0.755 per EU	9,060			12,000
Total work in process, ending	25,746			
Total cost accounted for	$300,000			

* 40% × 30,000 units = 12,000 equivalent units.
† Rounded upward to avoid a decimal discrepancy in the column totals.

After cost has been assigned to the ending work in process inventory, the total cost that we have accounted for ($300,000) agrees with the amount that we had to account for ($300,000). Thus, the cost reconciliation is complete.

PRODUCTION REPORT—FIFO METHOD

When the FIFO method is used to account for cost flows in a process costing system, the steps followed in preparing a production report are the same as those discussed above for the weighted-average method. However, since the FIFO method makes a distinction between units in the opening inventory and units started during the year, the cost reconciliation portion of the report is more complex under the FIFO method than it is under the weighted-average method. To illustrate the FIFO method, we will again use the data for Stabler Chemical Company found on page 138.

Step 1: Prepare a Quantity Schedule and Compute the Equivalent Units

There is only one difference between a quantity schedule prepared under the FIFO method and one prepared under the weighted-average method. This difference relates to units transferred out. As explained earlier in our discussion of equivalent units, the FIFO method divides units transferred out into two parts. One part consists of the units in the opening inventory, and the other part consists of the units started and completed during the current period. A quantity schedule showing this format for units transferred out is presented below for Stabler Chemical Company, along with a computation of equivalent units for the month. (The quantity schedule is printed in color.)

	Quantity Schedule			
Units to be accounted for:				
Work in process, beginning (all materials, 30% labor and overhead added last month)	20,000			
Started into production	180,000			
Total units to be accounted for	200,000			
		Equivalent Units		
		Materials	**Labor**	**Overhead**
Units accounted for as follows:				
Transferred to cooking:				
From the beginning inventory	20,000	—	14,000*	14,000*
Started and completed this month	150,000†	150,000	150,000	150,000
Work in process, ending (all materials, 40% labor and overhead added this month)	30,000	30,000	12,000‡	12,000‡
Total units accounted for	200,000	180,000	176,000	176,000

* 100% − 30% = 70%; 70% × 20,000 units = 14,000 EU.
† 170,000 units transferred − 20,000 units from the beginning inventory = 150,000 units.
‡ 40% × 30,000 units = 12,000 EU.

We explained earlier that in computing equivalent units under the FIFO method, we must first show the amount of work required *to complete* the units in the beginning inventory. We then show the number of units started and completed during the period, and finally we show the amount of work *completed* on the units still in process at the end of the period. The reader should carefully trace through these computations for Stabler Chemical Company above.

Step 2: Compute the Unit Costs

In computing unit costs under the FIFO method, we use only those costs that were incurred during the current period, and we ignore any costs in the beginning work in process inventory. The reason we ignore costs in the beginning inventory is that under the FIFO method, *unit costs are intended to relate only to work done during the current period.*

	Total	Materials	Labor	Overhead
Cost added by the department *(a)* . . .	$283,000	$ 63,000	$ 88,000	$132,000
Equivalent units (above) *(b)*.	—	180,000	176,000	176,000
Unit cost, *(a)* ÷ *(b)*	$1.60	$0.35	$0.50	$0.75

The unit costs we have computed are used to add cost to units of product as they are transferred to the next department; in addition, they are used to show the amount of cost attached to partially completed units in the ending work in process inventory.

Step 3: Prepare a Cost Reconciliation

We learned earlier that the purpose of a cost reconciliation is *(a)* to show what costs have been charged to a department during a period and *(b)* to show how these costs are accounted for. We also learned that the best way to prepare a cost reconciliation is to follow the quantity schedule line for line and show the cost associated with each group of units.

The first part of the reconciliation (where we show the "cost to be accounted for") is the same under the FIFO method as it was under the weighted-average method. As before, Stabler Chemical Company must account for a total of $300,000 in cost for the month. This $300,000 consists of $17,000 of cost associated with the beginning work in process inventory and an additional $283,000 of cost added during the month. These amounts are shown under the "Cost to be accounted for" part of the cost reconciliation in Exhibit 4–11 on the following page.

The second part of the cost reconciliation (where we show how these costs are accounted for) is more complex under the FIFO method than it is under the weighted-average method. This is because we must again keep units in the beginning inventory separate from units started and completed during the month. For units in the beginning inventory, two cost elements are involved. The first element is the $17,000 of cost carried over from the prior month. The second element is the cost needed to complete these units. As shown in Exhibit 4–11, this second element is computed by multiplying the unit cost figures for the month times the equivalent units completed for materials, labor, and overhead in the beginning inventory. (The equivalent units figures used in this computation are brought down from the "equivalent units" portion of the production report.)

For units started and completed during the month, we simply multiply the number of units started and completed by the total cost per unit to determine

EXHIBIT 4-11
Production-Report—FIFO Method

Quantity Schedule and Equivalent Units

	Quantity Schedule			
Units to be accounted for:				
Work in process, beginning (all materials, 30% labor and overhead added last month)	20,000			
Started into production	180,000			
Total units to be accounted for	200,000			
		Equivalent Units		
		Materials	**Labor**	**Overhead**
Units accounted for as follows:				
Transferred to cooking:				
From the beginning inventory	20,000	—	14,000*	14,000*
Started and completed this month	150,000†	150,000	150,000	150,000
Work in process, ending (all materials, 40% labor and overhead added this month)	30,000	30,000	12,000‡	12,000‡
Total units accounted for	200,000	180,000	176,000	176,000

Unit Costs

	Total	Materials	Labor	Overhead
Cost added by the department *(a)*	$283,000	$·63,000	$ 88,000	$132,000
Equivalent units *(b)*	—	180,000	176,000	176,000
Unit cost, *(a)* ÷ *(b)*	$1.60	$0.35	$0.50	$0.75

Cost Reconciliation

	Costs	**Equivalent Units (EU)**		
Cost to be accounted for:				
Work in process, beginning	$ 17,000			
Cost added by the department	283,000			
Total cost to be accounted for	$300,000			
Cost accounted for as follows:				
Transferred to cooking:				
From the beginning inventory:				
Cost in the beginning inventory	$ 17,000			
Cost to complete these units:				
Materials, at $0.35 per EU	—	—		
Labor, at $0.50 per EU	7,000		14,000	
Overhead, at $0.75 per EU	10,500			14,000
Total cost	34,500			
Units started and completed this month: 150,000 units × $1.60	240,000	150,000	150,000	150,000
Total cost transferred	274,500			
Work in process, ending:				
Materials, at $0.35 per EU	10,500	30,000		
Labor, at $0.50 per EU	6,000		12,000	
Overhead, at $0.75 per EU	9,000			12,000
Total work in process, ending	25,500			
Total cost accounted for	$300,000			

* 100% − 30% = 70%; 70% × 20,000 units = 14,000 equivalent units.
† 170,000 units transferred − 20,000 units in the beginning inventory = 150,000 units.
‡ 40% × 30,000 units = 12,000 equivalent units.

EXHIBIT 4–12
A Comparison of Production Report Content

Weighted-Average Method	FIFO Method
Quantity Schedule and Equivalent Units	
1. The quantity schedule includes all units transferred out in a single figure.	1. The quantity schedule divides the units transferred out into two parts. One part consists of units in the beginning inventory, and the other part consists of units started and completed during the current period.
2. In computing equivalent units, the units in the beginning inventory are treated as if they were started and completed during the current period.	2. Only work needed to *complete* units in the beginning inventory is included in the computation of equivalent units. Units started and completed during the current period is shown as a separate figure.
Unit Costs	
1. Costs in the beginning inventory are added in with current period costs in unit cost computations.	1. Only current period costs are included in unit cost computations.
2. Unit costs will contain some element of cost from the prior period.	2. Unit costs will contain only elements of cost from the current period.
Cost Reconciliation	
1. The "Cost to be accounted for" section of the report is the same for both methods.	1. The "Cost to be accounted for" section of the report is the same for both methods.
2. All units transferred out are treated the same, regardless of whether they were part of the beginning inventory or started and completed during the period.	2. Units transferred out are divided into two groups: *(a)* units in the beginning inventory and *(b)* units started and completed during the period.
3. Units in the ending inventory have cost applied to them in the same way under both methods.	3. Units in the ending inventory have cost applied to them in the same way under both methods.

the amount transferred out. This would be $240,000 (150,000 units × $1.60 = $240,000) for Stabler Chemical Company.

Finally, the amount of cost attached to the ending work in process inventory is computed by multiplying the unit cost figures for the month times the equivalent units for materials, labor, and overhead in the ending inventory. Once again, the equivalent units needed for this computation are brought down from the "equivalent units" portion of the production report.

A Comparison of Production Report Content

The production report is the most difficult part of this chapter, and it will require some effort on the reader's part to master its content and structure. To assist in this study, Exhibit 4–12 summarizes the major similarities and differences between production reports prepared under the weighted-average and FIFO methods.

EVALUATION OF THE WEIGHTED-AVERAGE AND FIFO METHODS

In the two following sections we make a comparison of the weighted-average and FIFO methods and discuss the impact of the JIT inventory approach on process costing.

A Comparison of Costing Methods

Although the weighted-average and FIFO methods seem to be very different, in most process costing situations they will produce unit costs that are nearly the same. Any major difference in unit costs between the two methods is likely to be traceable to erratic movements in raw materials prices. The reason is that conversion costs (labor and overhead) usually will not fluctuate widely from month to month due to the continuous nature of the flow of goods in process costing situations. In addition, inventory levels in most companies tend to remain quite stable, thereby adding to the general stability of unit costs. Raw materials prices can fluctuate considerably from period to period, however, which can result in a difference in unit costs between the two methods. This is because the weighted-average method will always be averaging the costs of one period in with those of the following period.

From the standpoint of cost control, the FIFO method is clearly superior to the weighted-average method. The reason is that current performance should be measured in relation to costs of the current period only, and the weighted-average method inherently mixes these costs in with costs of the prior period. Thus, under the weighted-average method, the manager's performance is influenced to some extent by what happened in a prior period. This problem does not arise under the FIFO method, since it makes a clear distinction between costs in the beginning inventory and costs incurred during the current period.

On the other hand, some managers feel that the weighted-average method is simpler to apply than the FIFO method. Although this may have been true in the past when much accounting work was done by hand, due to the advent of the computer it is doubtful whether it is still true today. The computer can handle either method with ease. The FIFO method would require a more complex programming effort when a process costing system is first set up, but after that there should be little difference between the two methods so far as difficulty in operating the system is concerned.

JIT Inventory Methods and Process Costing

The use of JIT inventory methods in recent years has resulted in a significant narrowing of the difference in unit costs between the FIFO and weighted-average methods, and in some cases this difference has disappeared entirely. The reason is as follows: Recall that under the JIT concept, raw materials are received *just in time* to go into production and parts are completed *just in time* to be assembled into products. As a result, under JIT the raw materials and work in process inventories are either eliminated or reduced to nominal levels. Since the difference between the FIFO and weighted-average methods centers on how costs are handled in work in process inventories, *the elimination of these inventories through JIT automatically eliminates the distinction between the two costing methods*. That is, if a company has no work in process inventories, then all of its costs of production for a period will be traceable to *that* period, and its equivalent units will simply be the units transferred out. Thus, the company's unit costs will be the same regardless of whether the FIFO or the weighted-average method is in use.

EXHIBIT 4–13
JIT Impact on Process Costing

Basic Data
During Year 1 the company operated a traditional process costing system in which there was both a beginning and an ending work in process inventory. During Year 2 the company implemented a JIT inventory approach, so note that there was no ending work in process inventory for that year. By Year 3 the company had the JIT approach fully operational, so in that year the work in process inventories were completely eliminated.

	Year 1			Year 2			Year 3		
		Percent Completed			Percent Completed			Percent Completed	
	Units	Material	Conversion	Units	Material	Conversion	Units	Material	Conversion
Work in process, beginning	50,000	70	60	90,000	80	50	—	—	—
Units started into production	700,000			700,000			700,000		
Units completed and transferred out	660,000			790,000			700,000		
Work in process, ending	90,000	80	50	—	—	—	—	—	—

Equivalent Units Computations

	Year 1 Material	Year 1 Conversion	Year 2 Material	Year 2 Conversion	Year 3 Material	Year 3 Conversion
Weighted-Average Method:						
Units completed and transferred	660,000	660,000	790,000	790,000	700,000	700,000
Work in process, ending*	72,000	45,000	—	—	—	—
Equivalent units of production	732,000	705,000	790,000	790,000	700,000	700,000
FIFO Method:						
Work in process, beginning†	15,000	20,000	18,000	45,000	—	—
Units started and completed	610,000‡	610,000‡	700,000	700,000	700,000	700,000
Work in process, ending*	72,000	45,000	—	—	—	—
Equivalent units of production	697,000	675,000	718,000	745,000	700,000	700,000

* Work completed on the units in the ending inventory.
† Work required to complete the units in the beginning inventory.
‡ 660,000 units − 50,000 units = 610,000 units.

In short, the use of JIT greatly simplifies the production report in that in a pure JIT setting the units started into production, the units completed and transferred out, and the equivalent units will all be the same amount. As shown by Exhibit 4–13, this will be true regardless of whether the company is using the FIFO or weighted-average method. Moreover, with no work in process inventories to account for, the remainder of the production report is also greatly simplified. The "Cost to be accounted for" becomes equal to the "Cost of units transferred out," with no cost in inventory to account for under either FIFO or weighted average. Small wonder that companies find the JIT approach so appealing.

INNOVATIONS IN COSTING SYSTEMS

The costing systems discussed in Chapters 3 and 4 represent the two ends of a continuum. On one end we have job-order costing, which is used by companies that produce many different items—generally to customers' specifications. On the other end we have process costing, which is used by companies that produce basically homogeneous products in large quantities. Between these two extremes there are many "hybrid" systems that include characteristics of both job-order and process costing. One of these hybrids—called *operation costing*—is widely used in actual practice. Also, the ends of the job-order/process continuum are moving closer together as a result of the use of flexible manufacturing systems (FMS) in various industries. Both operation costing and the impact of FMS on job-order and process costing are discussed in following sections.

Operation Costing

Many companies have products that possess some common characteristics and some individual characteristics. Shoes, for example, have certain common characteristics in that all styles involve cutting and sewing that can be done on a repetitive basis, using the same equipment and following the same basic procedures. These same shoes, however, can also have some individual characteristics in that some may be made of expensive leather and others may be made of inexpensive vinyl. When products have some common characteristics and some individual characteristics, such as in the case of shoes, a system known as **operation costing** is often used to determine unit costs for management.

As mentioned above, operation costing is a hybrid system that employs certain aspects of both job-order and process costing. Products are typically handled in batches when operation costing is in use, with each batch charged for the specific materials used in its production. In this sense, operation costing is similar to job-order costing. Labor and overhead costs are accumulated by operation or by department, however, and these costs are assigned to batches on an average per unit basis, as done in process costing. If shoes are being produced, for example, each style is charged the same per unit conversion cost, regardless of the style involved, but charged with its specific materials cost. Thus, the company is able to distinguish between batches in terms of materials, but it is able to employ the simplicity of a process costing system for labor and overhead costs.

Examples of other products for which operation costing is frequently used include electronic equipment (such as semiconductors), textiles, clothing, and jewelry (such as rings, bracelets, and medallions). Products of this type are typically produced in batches, but they can vary considerably from model to model or from style to style in terms of the cost of raw material inputs. Therefore, an operation costing system is well suited for providing necessary cost information for management.

Flexible Manufacturing Systems

In the two preceding chapters, we have discussed the use of the FMS concept, in which plants are heavily automated and the activities are organized around "cells" or "islands" of automated equipment. The FMS concept is having a major impact on costing in several ways. One of these is through the use of activity-based costing, which was discussed in the preceding chapter. Another is through allowing companies to switch their systems from the more costly job-order approach to the less costly process or operation approaches. This switching is made possible through the fact that FMS is proving to be highly efficient in reducing the setup time required between products and jobs. With setup time only a small fraction of previous levels, companies are able to move between products and jobs with about the same speed as if they were working in a continuous, process-type environment. The result is that these companies are able to employ process costing techniques in situations that previously required job-order costing. As the use of FMS grows (and becomes even more efficient), some managers predict that job-order costing will slowly disappear except in a few, selected industries.

A further impact of FMS is through its focus on cells rather than on departments. Although production reports are still prepared in FMS settings, these reports are either much broader to include the entire production process (many cells) or much narrower to include only a single cell or workstation. As stated earlier, if JIT is practiced then the production report becomes greatly simplified, regardless of the level at which it is prepared.

SUMMARY

Process costing is used in those manufacturing situations where homogeneous products are produced on a continuous basis. A process costing system is similar to a job-order costing system in that (1) both systems have the same basic purpose of providing data for the manager, (2) both systems use the same manufacturing accounts, and (3) costs flow through the manufacturing accounts in basically the same way in both systems. A process costing system differs from a job-order system in that (1) a single product is involved, (2) costs are accumulated by department (rather than by job), (3) the department production report replaces the job cost sheet, and (4) unit costs are computed by department (rather than by job).

In order to compute unit costs in a department, the department's equivalent units must be determined. Equivalent units can be computed in two ways—by the weighted-average method and by the FIFO method. The weighted-average method treats partially completed units in the beginning work in process inventory as if they were started and completed during the current period. The FIFO method distinguishes between work completed in the prior period and work completed currently, so that equivalent units represent only work completed during the current period.

The activity in a department is summarized on a production report. There are three separate (though highly interrelated) parts to a production report. The first part is a quantity schedule, which includes a computation of equivalent units and shows the flow of units through a department during a period. The second part consists of a computation of unit costs, with unit costs being provided individually for materials, labor, and overhead as well as in total for the period. The third part consists of a cost reconciliation, which summarizes all cost flows through a department for a period.

Although the weighted-average and FIFO methods are somewhat different, in most process costing situations they will produce unit costs that are nearly the same, except perhaps for raw materials. From the viewpoint of cost control, the FIFO method is superior to the weighted-average method because of its focus on current period costs. Although the FIFO method seems more complex in its operation, this complexity is largely overcome today due to the widespread use of the computer.

KEY TERMS FOR REVIEW

Conversion cost Direct labor cost combined with manufacturing overhead cost. (p. 133)

Cost reconciliation The part of a production report that shows what costs a department has to account for during a period and how those costs are accounted for. (p. 139)

Equivalent units of production The number of units that would have been produced during a period if all of a department's efforts had resulted in completed units of product. (p. 131)

FIFO method A method of accounting for cost flows in a process costing system in which equivalent units and unit costs relate only to work done during the current period. (p. 134)

Operation costing A costing system used when products are manufactured in batches and when the products have some common characteristics and some individual characteristics. This system handles materials the same as in job-order costing and labor and overhead the same as in process costing. (p. 148)

Parallel processing A method of arranging processing departments in which, after a certain point, some units may go through different processing departments than others. (p. 130)

Process costing A costing method used in those industries that produce homogeneous products on a continuous basis. (p. 128)

Processing department Any location in a factory where work is performed on a product and where materials, labor, or overhead costs are added to the product. (p. 129)

Production report A report that summarizes all activity in a department's Work in Process account during a period and that contains three sections: a quantity schedule, a computation of equivalent units and unit costs, and a cost reconciliation. (p. 129)

Quantity schedule The part of a production report that shows the flow of units through a department during a period. (p. 138)

Sequential processing A method of arranging processing departments in which all units flow in sequence from one department to another. (p. 130)

Transferred-in cost The amount of cost attached to units of product that have been received from a prior processing department. (p. 131)

Weighted-average method A method of accounting for cost flows in a process costing system in which units in the beginning work in process inventory are treated as if they were started and completed during the current period. (p. 133)

QUESTIONS

4–1 Under what conditions would it be appropriate to use a process costing system?

4–2 What similarities exist between job-order and process costing?

4–3 Costs are accumulated by job in a job-order costing system; how are costs accumulated in a process costing system?

4–4 What two essential features must characterize any processing department?

4–5 Distinguish between departments arranged in a sequential pattern and departments arranged in a parallel pattern.

4–6 Why is cost accumulation easier under a process costing system than it is under a job-order costing system?

4–7 How many Work in Process accounts are maintained in a company using process costing?

4–8 Assume that a company has two processing departments, mixing and firing. Prepare a journal entry to show a transfer of partially completed units from the mixing department to the firing department.

4–9 Assume again that a company has two processing departments, mixing and firing. Explain what costs might be added to the firing department's Work in Process account during a period.

4–10 What is meant by the term *equivalent units of production?*

4–11 Under the weighted-average method, what assumption is made relative to units in the beginning work in process inventory when equivalent units and unit costs are computed?

4–12 How does the computation of equivalent units under the FIFO method differ from the computation of equivalent units under the weighted-average method?

4–13 What is a quantity schedule, and what purpose does it serve?

4–14 On the cost reconciliation part of the production report, the weighted-average method treats all units transferred out in the same way. How does this differ from the FIFO method of handling units transferred out?

4–15 Under process costing, it is often suggested that a product is like a rolling snowball as it moves from department to department. Why is this an apt comparison?

4–16 From the standpoint of cost control, why is the FIFO method superior to the weighted-average method?

4–17 Watkins Trophies, Inc., produces thousands of medallions made of bronze, silver, and gold. The medallions are identical except for the materials used in their manufacture. What costing system would you advise the company to use?

4–18 Give examples of companies that might use operation costing.

4–19 Job-order costing is likely to increase in importance as a result of the widespread use of flexible manufacturing systems. Do you agree? Explain.

EXERCISES

E4–1 Lindex Company manufactures a product that goes through three departments, A, B, and C. Information relating to activity in Department A during October 19x1 is given below:

	Units	Percent Completed	
		Materials	Conversion
Work in process, October 1	50,000	90	60
Started into production	390,000		
Completed and transferred to Department B	410,000		
Work in process, October 31	30,000	70	50

Required

1. Assume that the company uses the weighted-average method of accounting for units and costs. Compute the equivalent units for the month.
2. Repeat the computations in (1) above, assuming that the company uses the FIFO method of accounting for units and costs.

E4–2 Gulf Fisheries, Inc., processes tuna for various distributors. Two departments are involved—Department 1 and Department 2. Data relating to pounds of tuna processed in Department 1 during May 19x5 are given below:

	Pounds of Tuna	Percent Completed*
Work in process, May 1	30,000	55
Started into processing during May	480,000	—
Work in process, May 31	20,000	90

* Labor and overhead only.

All materials are added at the beginning of processing in Department 1. Labor and overhead costs are incurred uniformly throughout processing.

Required Prepare a quantity schedule and a computation of equivalent units for the month, assuming that the company uses the weighted-average method of accounting for units.

E4–3 Refer to the data for Gulf Fisheries, Inc., in Exercise 4–2.

Required Prepare a quantity schedule and a computation of equivalent units for the month, assuming that the company uses the FIFO method of accounting for units.

E4–4 Kalox, Inc., manufactures an antacid product that passes through two departments. Data for a recent month for Department A follow:

	Gallons	Materials	Labor	Overhead
Work in process, May 1	80,000	$ 69,300	$ 28,000	$ 45,000
Gallons started in process	760,000			
Gallons transferred out	790,000			
Work in process, May 31	50,000			
Cost added during the month	—	907,200	370,000	592,000

The beginning work in process inventory was 80 percent complete as to materials and 75 percent complete as to processing. The ending work in process inventory was 60 percent complete as to materials and 20 percent complete as to processing.

Required

1. Assume that the company uses the weighted-average method of accounting for units and costs. Prepare a quantity schedule and a computation of equivalent units for May's activity.
2. Determine the unit costs for the month.

E4–5 Refer to the data for Kalox, Inc., in Exercise 4–4.

Required
1. Assume that the company uses the FIFO method of accounting for units and costs. Prepare a quantity schedule and a computation of equivalent units for May's activity.
2. Determine the unit costs for the month.

E4–6 Solex Company produces a high-quality insulation material that passes through two production processes. A quantity schedule for a recent month for process A follows:

	Quantity Schedule		
Units to be accounted for:			
Work in process, June 1 (75% materials, 40% conversion cost added last month)	60,000		
Started into production	280,000		
Total units to be accounted for	340,000		
		Equivalent Units	
		Materials	**Conversion**
Units accounted for as follows:			
Transferred to process B	300,000	?	?
Work in process, June 30 (50% materials, 25% conversion cost added this month)	40,000	?	?
Total units accounted for	340,000	?	?

Costs in the beginning work in process inventory were: materials, $57,000; and conversion cost, $16,000. Costs added during the month were: materials, $385,000; and conversion cost, $214,500.

Required
1. Assume that the company uses the weighted-average method of accounting for units and costs. Determine the equivalent units for the month.
2. Compute the unit costs for the month.

E4–7 (This exercise should be assigned only if Exercise 4–6 is also assigned.) Refer to the data in Exercise 4–6 and to the equivalent units and unit costs you have computed there.

Required Complete the following cost reconciliation for process A:

	Costs	Equivalent Units (EU)	
Cost to be accounted for:			
Work in process, June 1	$?		
Cost added during the month	?		
Total cost to be accounted for	$672,500		
Cost accounted for as follows:			
Transferred to process B: ______ units × ______ each	$?	?	?
Work in process, June 30:			
Materials, at ______ per EU	?	?	
Conversion, at ______ per EU	?		?
Total work in process, June 30	?		
Total cost accounted for	$672,500		

E4–8 Refer to the data for Solex Company in Exercise 4–6. Assume that the company uses the FIFO cost method.

Required
1. Prepare a quantity schedule and a computation of equivalent units for the month.
2. Compute the unit costs for the month.

E4–9 (This exercise should be assigned only if Exercise 4–8 is also assigned.) Refer to the data in Exercise 4–6 for Solex Company and to the equivalent units and unit costs that you computed in Exercise 4–8.

Required Complete the following cost reconciliation for process A:

	Costs	Equivalent Units (EU)	
Cost to be accounted for:			
Work in process, June 1	$?		
Cost added during the month.	?		
Total cost to be accounted for	$672,500		
Cost accounted for as follows:			
Transferred to process B:			
From the beginning inventory:			
Cost in the beginning inventory.	$?		
Cost to complete these units:			
Materials, at ______ per EU	?	?	
Conversion, at ______ per EU	?		?
Total cost	?		
Units started and completed this month: ______ units × ______ each . . .	?	?	?
Total cost transferred	?		
Work in process, June 30:			
Materials, at ______ per EU	?	?	
Conversion, at ______ per EU	?		?
Total work in process, June 30	?		
Total cost accounted for	$672,500		

E4–10 Savic Company installed a flexible manufacturing system in one of its plants several months ago. After some effort, the system is now completely operational. As of the beginning of June, the most recent month, the company also switched to JIT for control of inventories. Therefore, no work in process inventories were on hand at the end of June, as shown by the summary of activity below:

		Amount Completed	
	Units	Materials	Conversion
Work in process, June 1	60,000	2/3	1/3
Started into production.	850,000		
Completed and transferred out . . .	910,000		
Work in process, June 30.	—		

Required
1. Assume that the company uses the weighted-average method to account for units. Prepare a quantity schedule and a computation of equivalent units for June.
2. Assume that the company uses the FIFO method to account for units. Prepare a quantity schedule and a computation of equivalent units for June.
3. If the company continues to employ the JIT concept and starts 900,000 units into production during the following month (July), what would be the equivalent units under the weighted-average method? The FIFO method?

PROBLEMS

P4–11 **Quantity Schedule, Equivalent Units, and Unit Costs** Starburst Company manufactures a product that goes through three processes. The following information relates to cost and activity in process A during March 19x4:

	Units	Percent Completed Materials	Percent Completed Conversion
Work in process, March 1	30,000	100	40
Started into production	120,000		
Completed and transferred out	140,000		
Work in process, March 31	10,000	100	80

The beginning work in process inventory contained $24,000 in materials cost and $14,300 in conversion cost. An additional $108,000 in materials cost and $170,000 in conversion cost were added to production during the month.

Required

1. Assume that the company uses the weighted-average method to account for units and costs.
   a. Prepare a quantity schedule and a computation of equivalent units for the month.
   b. Determine the unit costs for the month.
2. Assume that the company uses the FIFO method to account for units and costs.
   a. Prepare a quantity schedule and a computation of equivalent units for the month.
   b. Determine the unit costs for the month.
3. What accounts for most of the difference in unit costs above? Why are unit cost differences between the weighted-average and FIFO methods usually traceable to this cost element?

P4–12 **Partial Production Report** Rolex Company uses a process costing system and manufactures a single product. Activity for July 19x6 has just been completed. A partially completed production report for the month for Department X follows:

Production Report—Department X
For the Month Ended July 31, 19x6

Quantity Schedule and Equivalent Units

	Quantity Schedule	Equivalent Units Materials	Equivalent Units Labor	Equivalent Units Overhead
Units to be accounted for:				
Work in process, July 1 (all materials, 80% labor and overhead added last month) . . .	10,000			
Started into production	100,000			
Total units to account for	110,000			
Units accounted for as follows:				
Transferred to department Y	95,000	?	?	?
Work in process, July 31 (60% materials, 20% labor and overhead added this month) . . .	15,000	?	?	?
Total units accounted for	110,000	?	?	?

Unit Costs

	Total			
Work in process, July 1	$ 8,700	$ 1,500	$ 1,800	$ 5,400
Cost added by the department	245,300	154,500	22,700	68,100
Total cost (*a*)	$254,000	$156,000	$24,500	$73,500
Equivalent units (*b*)	—	104,000	98,000	98,000
Unit cost, (*a*) ÷ (*b*)	$2.50	$1.50	$0.25	$0.75

Cost Reconciliation

Cost to be accounted for:

?

Cost accounted for as follows:

?

Required

1. By scrutinizing the incomplete production report, identify two ways by which you can tell whether the company is using the weighted-average method or the FIFO method.
2. Prepare a schedule showing how the equivalent units were computed.
3. Complete the "Cost reconciliation" part of the production report.

P4–13 Step-by-Step Production Report; Weighted-Average Method The PVC Company manufactures a high-quality plastic pipe in two departments, cooking and molding. Materials are introduced at various points during work in the cooking department. After the cooking is completed, the materials are transferred into the molding department, in which pipe is formed. Materials are accounted for in the cooking department on a pounds basis. Conversion costs are incurred evenly during the cooking process.

Selected data relating to the cooking department during May 19x3 are given below:

Production data:	
Pounds in process, May 1: 100% complete as to materials, 90% complete as to conversion costs	70,000
Pounds started into production during May	350,000
Pounds completed and transferred to molding	?
Pounds in process, May 31: 75% complete as to materials, 25% complete as to conversion costs	40,000
Cost data:	
Work in process inventory, May 1:	
Materials cost	$ 86,000
Conversion cost	36,000
Cost added during May:	
Materials cost	447,000
Conversion cost	198,000

The company uses the weighted-average method to account for units and costs.

Required Prepare a production report for the cooking department. Use the following three steps as a guide in preparing your report:

1. Prepare a quantity schedule and compute the equivalent units.
2. Compute the unit costs for the month.
3. Using the data from (1) and (2) above, prepare a cost reconciliation.

P4–14 Partial Production Report Vitesse Company manufactures a product that is in great demand. The company uses a process costing system and has two processing departments, distilling and blending. Materials are added at stages in the distilling department, whereas labor and overhead costs are incurred evenly as distilling takes place. A partially completed production report for a recent month in the distilling department follows:

Distilling Department—Production Report
For the Month Ended August 31, 19x5

Quantity Schedule and Equivalent Units

	Quantity Schedule			
Gallons to be accounted for:				
Work in process, August 1 (80% materials, 60% labor and overhead added last month)	40,000			
Started into production	310,000			
Total gallons to be accounted for.	350,000			
		Equivalent Units		
		Materials	Labor	Overhead
Gallons accounted for as follows:				
Transferred to blending:				
From the beginning inventory	40,000	?	?	?
Started and completed this month . . .	230,000	?	?	?
Work in process, August 31 (75% materials, 50% labor and overhead added this month)	80,000	?	?	?
Total gallons accounted for	350,000	?	?	?

Unit Costs

Cost added by the department (*a*)	$689,500	$432,100	$ 85,800	$171,600
Equivalent units (*b*).	—	298,000	286,000	286,000
Unit cost, (*a*) ÷ (*b*).	$2.35	$1.45	$0.30	$0.60

Cost Reconciliation

Cost to be accounted for:

?

Cost accounted for as follows:

?

Required

1. By scrutinizing the incomplete production report, identify two ways by which you can tell whether the company is using the weighted-average method or the FIFO method.
2. Prepare a schedule showing how the equivalent units were computed.
3. Assume that the cost in the work in process inventory totaled $62,500 at the beginning of the month (August 1). Complete the "Cost reconciliation" part of the production report above.

P4–15 Step-by-Step Production Report; FIFO Method Reutter Company manufactures a single product and uses a process costing system. The company's product goes through two processes, etching and wiring. The following activity was recorded in the etching department during July 19x6:

Production data:		
Units in process, July 1: 60% complete as to materials, and 30% complete as to conversion costs		60,000
Units started into production		510,000
Units completed and transferred to wiring		?
Units in process, July 31: 80% complete as to materials, and 40% complete as to conversion costs		70,000
Cost data:		
Work in process inventory, July 1:		
Materials cost.	$ 27,000	
Conversion cost	13,000	$ 40,000
Cost added during the month:		
Materials cost.	468,000	
Conversion cost	357,000	825,000
Total cost.		$865,000

Materials are added at several stages during the etching process. Conversion costs are incurred uniformly as the etching takes place. The company uses the FIFO cost method.

Required Prepare a production report for the etching department for the month of July. Use the following three steps as a guide in preparing your report:

1. Prepare a quantity schedule and compute the equivalent units.
2. Compute the unit costs for the month.
3. Using the data from (1) and (2) above, prepare a cost reconciliation.

P4–16 Basic Production Report; Weighted-Average Method (Problem 4–17 uses these same data with the FIFO method.) Honeybutter, Inc., manufactures a product that goes through two departments prior to completion. The following information is available on work in the mixing department during June 19x1:

		Amount Completed	
	Units	Materials	Conversion
Work in process, June 1	70,000	5/7	3/7
Started into production.	460,000		
Completed and transferred out . . .	450,000		
Work in process, June 30.	80,000	3/4	5/8

Cost in the beginning work in process inventory and cost added during the month were as follows:

	Materials	Conversion
Work in process, June 1	$ 35,000	$ 17,000
Cost added during June.	391,000	282,000

The company uses the weighted-average method to compute unit costs. The mixing department is the first department in the production process; after mixing has been completed, the units are transferred to the bottling department.

Required Prepare a production report for the mixing department for the month of June 19x1.

P4–17 Basic Production Report; FIFO Method Refer to the data for Honeybutter, Inc., in Problem 4–16. Assume that the company uses the FIFO method to compute unit costs rather than the weighted-average method.

Required Prepare a production report for the mixing department for the month of June 19x1.

P4–18 Interpreting a Production Report Dolce Company manufactures a product that goes through several departments. A hastily prepared production report for Department A for the month of April is given below:

Quantity Schedule	**Units**
Units to be accounted for:	
Work in process, April 1 (90% materials, 80% conversion cost added last month) . . .	30,000
Started into production.	200,000
Total units to be accounted for	230,000
Units accounted for as follows:	
Transferred to Department B	190,000
Work in process, April 30 (75% materials, 60% conversion cost added this month) . . .	40,000
Total units accounted for	230,000

Cost Reconciliation	Costs
Cost to be accounted for:	
Work in process, April 1	$ 98,000
Cost added during the month	827,000
Total cost to be accounted for.	$925,000
Cost accounted for as follows:	
Transferred to Department B	$805,600
Work in process, April 30	119,400
Total cost accounted for	$925,000

Dolce Company has just been acquired by another organization, and the management of the acquiring company wants some additional information about Dolce's operations.

Required

1. Is Dolce Company using the weighted-average method or the FIFO method to account for units and costs? How can you tell?
2. What were the equivalent units for the month?
3. What were the unit costs for the month? The beginning inventory consisted of the following costs: materials, $67,800; and conversion cost, $30,200. The costs added during the month consisted of: materials, $579,000; and conversion cost, $248,000.
4. How many of the units transferred to Department B were started and completed during the month?
5. The manager of Department A, anxious to make a good impression on Dolce's new owners, stated, "Materials prices jumped from about $2.50 per unit in March to $3 per unit in April, but due to good cost control I was able to hold our materials cost to less than $3 per unit for the month." Should this manager be rewarded for a sterling effort at cost control? Explain.

P4–19 JIT/FMS; Production Report Impact; Weighted-Average Method Over the last year, Lovata Company has installed a flexible manufacturing system in its plant. The company has made extensive changes to the flow of its single product through the various cells, and as of the beginning of last month the company initiated a JIT inventory system. In the past, the company was required to carry a large work in process inventory because of a poor flow of materials between workstations. But JIT, in conjunction with FMS, has allowed the company to control this flow and to avoid any buildup of materials within the cells. Production data for last month follow:

	Units	Materials	Conversion
Work in process, May 1	40,000	$ 53,000	$ 10,000
Started into production.	280,000		
Completed and transferred out . . .	320,000	?	?
Work in process, May 31.	—		
Cost added during the month		491,000	278,000

The May 1 work in process inventory was 75 percent complete as to materials and 25 percent complete as to conversion costs. The company uses the weighted-average method to account for cost flows.

Required

1. Prepare a production report for the month of May.
2. Assume that in June the company begins to experience greater efficiency in its operations so that it is able to introduce 350,000 units into production and operate strictly in accordance with JIT concepts. (That is, work in process is maintained at a zero level.) The company incurs $560,000 in material costs during the month and $280,000 in conversion costs.
   a. Prepare a production report for the month of June.
   b. Examine the report you have just prepared. How (if at all) would the report differ if the company were using the FIFO method to account for cost flows?

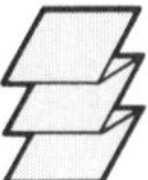

P4–20 JIT/FMS; Production Report Impact; FIFO Method After three months of intensive effort, Century Products has converted its Midvale plant to a FMS layout and has installed necessary automated equipment in the various cells. As of the first of last month the company also initiated a JIT system of inventory control. In the past, work in process inventories have been a problem in that partially completed materials have accumulated in work areas and impeded the efficiency of operations. But during the last month, the company's new JIT system, in conjunction with the FMS layout, has allowed the company to clear out its in-process items and maintain a smooth flow of goods to meet current demand. Production data for last month follow:

	Units	Materials	Conversion
Work in process, March 1	80,000	$ 45,000	$ 21,000
Started into production	530,000		
Completed and transferred out	610,000	?	?
Work in process, March 31	—		
Cost added during the month		385,000	649,000

The March 1 work in process inventory was 75 percent complete as to materials and 25 percent complete as to conversion costs. The company uses the FIFO method to account for cost flows.

Required

1. Prepare a production report for the month of March.
2. During the following month (April), the company is able to increase its efficiency in the Midvale plant so that 630,000 units are started into production. Also, through JIT the company is able to keep work in process inventories from accumulating in the plant. The company incurs $378,000 in cost for materials and $567,000 in conversion cost for the month.
   a. Prepare a production report for the month of April.
   b. Examine the report you have just prepared. How (if at all) would the report differ if the company were using the weighted-average method to account for cost flows?

P4–21 Interpreting a Production Report Flavio Company has a new accountant who has prepared the following production report for the month of May for Department 1:

Quantity Schedule	**Units**
Units to be accounted for:	
Work in process, May 1 (90% materials, 80% conversion cost added last month)	50,000
Started into production	290,000
Total units to be accounted for	340,000
Units accounted for as follows:	
Transferred to Department 2	300,000
Work in process, May 31 (75% materials, 50% conversion cost added this month)	40,000
Total units accounted for	340,000

Cost Reconciliation	**Costs**
Cost to be accounted for:	
Work in process, May 1	$112,000
Cost added during the month	878,000
Total cost to be accounted for	$990,000
Cost accounted for as follows:	
Transferred to Department 2:	
Units from the beginning inventory	$133,000
Units started and completed this month	775,000
Total cost transferred	908,000
Work in process, May 31	82,000
Total cost accounted for	$990,000

The company's management would like some additional information about Department 1's operations for the month.

Required 1. Is the company using the weighted-average method or the FIFO method to account for its activities? What can you see in the report as evidence? (Be sure you look the report over from top to bottom!)
2. How many units were started and completed during the month?
3. What were the equivalent units for the month?
4. What were the unit costs for the month? The following data are available on Department 1's costs:

	Total	Materials	Conversion
Work in process, May 1	$112,000	$ 68,000	$ 44,000
Cost added during the month . . .	878,000	570,000	308,000

5. Prove your answer to (1) above by computing the May 31 work in process inventory figure ($82,000) given in the report. (You may assume that the accountant has properly computed the $82,000 figure.)
6. Flavio Company's executive vice president has secretly obtained a copy of a competitor's production report for May. The competitor's report shows a unit cost of only $1.94 for materials. The vice president is concerned that Flavio's costs aren't being controlled well, even though she is aware that materials costs jumped sharply between April and May. Assuming that neither Flavio nor its competitor had any raw materials on hand at the beginning of the month, what other possible explanation could you give for the difference in unit costs? Provide reasoning to support your answer.

P4–22 Analysis of Work in Process T-Account; Weighted-Average Method Brady Products manufactures a silicone paste wax that goes through three processing departments—cracking, blending, and packing. Raw materials are introduced at the start of work in the cracking department, with conversion costs being incurred uniformly as cracking takes place. The Work in Process T-account for the cracking department for a recent month follows:

Work in Process—Cracking Department

Inventory, May 1 (35,000 lbs., 4/5 processed)	63,700	Completed and transferred to blending (? lbs.)	?
May costs added:			
Raw materials (280,000 lbs.)	397,600		
Labor and overhead	189,700		
Inventory, May 31 (45,000 lbs., 2/3 processed)	?		

The May 1 work in process inventory consists of $43,400 in materials cost and $20,300 in labor and overhead cost. The company uses the weighted-average method to account for units and costs.

Required 1. Prepare a production report for the cracking department for the month.
2. What criticism can be made of the unit costs that you have computed on your production report?

P4–23 Analysis of Work in Process T-Account; FIFO Method Hiko, Inc., manufactures a high-quality pressboard out of wood scraps and sawmill waste. The pressboard goes through two processing departments, shredding and forming. Activity in the shredding department during a recent month is summarized in the department's Work in Process account below:

Work in Process—Shredding Department

Inventory, July 1 (10,000 lbs., 30% processed)	13,400	Completed and transferred to forming (? lbs.)	?
July costs added:			
Wood materials (170,000 lbs.)	139,400		
Labor and overhead	244,200		
Inventory, July 31 (20,000 lbs., 40% processed)	?		

The wood materials are entered into production at the beginning of work in the shredding department. Labor and overhead costs are incurred uniformly throughout the shredding process. The company uses the FIFO cost method.

Required

1. Prepare a production report for the shredding department for the month.
2. In a process costing system, would you expect per unit materials cost or per unit labor and overhead cost to show the greater fluctuation from period to period? Why?

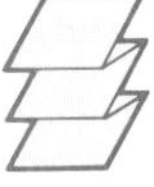

P4–24 Equivalent Units; Costing of Inventories You are employed by Spirit Company, a manufacturer of digital watches. The company's chief financial officer is trying to verify the accuracy of the December 31, 19x6, work in process and finished goods inventories prior to closing the books for the year. You have been asked to assist in this verification. The year-end balances shown on Spirit Company's books are as follows:

	Units	Costs
Work in process (50% complete as to labor and overhead)	300,000	$ 660,960
Finished goods	200,000	1,009,800

Materials are added to production at the beginning of the manufacturing process, and overhead is applied to each product at the rate of 60% of direct labor cost. There was no finished goods inventory on January 1, 19x6. A review of Spirit Company's inventory and cost records has disclosed the following information:

		Costs	
	Units	Materials	Labor
Work in process, January 1, 19x6 (80% complete as to labor and overhead)	200,000	$ 200,000	$ 315,000
Units started into production	1,000,000		
Cost added during 19x6:			
Materials cost		1,300,000	
Labor cost			1,995,000
Units completed during 19x6	900,000		

The company uses the weighted-average cost method.

Required

1. Prepare a computation showing the equivalent units for 19x6 and unit costs for materials, labor, and overhead.
2. Determine the amount of cost that should be assigned to the ending work in process and finished goods inventories.

3. Prepare the necessary correcting journal entry to adjust the work in process and finished goods inventories to the correct balances as of December 31, 19x6.
4. Determine the cost of goods sold for the year.

(CPA, Adapted)

CASES

C4–25 Analysis of Data; Production Report; Weighted-Average Method Durall Company manufactures a plastic gasket that is used in automobile engines. The gaskets go through three processing departments: mixing, forming, and stamping. The company's accountant (who is very inexperienced) has prepared a summary of production and costs for the mixing department as follows for October 19x5:

Mixing department costs:	
Work in process inventory, October 1, 8,000 units, ⅞ complete as to labor and overhead	$ 22,420*
Material A added during the month (added at the start of work in the mixing department)	81,480
Material B added during the month (added when processing is 50 percent complete in the mixing department)	27,600
Conversion costs added during the month	96,900
Total departmental costs	$228,400
Mixing department costs assigned to:	
Units completed and transferred to the forming department, 100,000 units at $2.284 each	$228,400
Work in process inventory, October 31, 5,000 units, ⅖ complete as to labor and overhead	—
Total departmental costs assigned	$228,400

* Consists of material A, $8,820; material B, $3,400; and labor and overhead, $10,200.

Labor and overhead costs are incurred evenly during processing in the mixing department.

After mulling over the data above, Durall's president commented, "I can't understand what's happening here. Despite a concentrated effort at cost reduction, our unit cost actually went up in the mixing department last month. With that kind of performance, year-end bonuses are out of the question for the people in that department."

The company uses the weighted-average method to account for units and costs.

Required

1. Prepare a revised production report for the mixing department for the month.
2. Assume that in order to remain competitive the company undertook a major cost-cutting program during October. Would the effects of this cost-cutting program tend to show up more under the weighted-average method or under the FIFO method? Explain your answer.
3. Explain to the president why the unit cost figure appearing on the report prepared by the accountant is so high.

C4–26 Analysis of Data; Production Report; FIFO Method Refer to the data for Durall Products in the preceding case. Assume that the company uses the FIFO method to account for units and costs.

Required

1. Prepare a production report for the mixing department for the month.
2. Assume as stated in (2) in Case 4–25 that the company has undertaken a major cost-cutting program during the current month. Would you expect unit costs for the current month to be higher under the FIFO method or under the weighted-average method? Why?

5

Cost Behavior
Analysis and Use

LEARNING OBJECTIVES

After studying Chapter 5, you should be able to:

1 Identify examples of variable costs and explain the effect of a change in activity on both total variable costs and per unit variable costs.

2 Identify examples of fixed costs and explain the effect of a change in activity on both total fixed costs and fixed costs expressed on a per unit basis.

3 Define the relevant range and explain its significance in cost behavior analysis.

4 Distinguish between committed and discretionary fixed costs.

5 Analyze a mixed cost by the high-low method, the scattergraph method, and the least-squares method, and enumerate the strengths and weaknesses of each of these analytical approaches.

6 Prepare an income statement using the contribution format.

7 Define or explain the key terms listed at the end of the chapter.

In our discussion of cost terms and concepts in Chapter 2, we stated that one way in which costs can be classified is by behavior. We defined cost behavior as meaning how a cost will react or change as changes take place in the level of business activity. An understanding of cost behavior is the key to many decisions in an organization in that by understanding how costs behave, a manager is better able to predict what costs will be under various operating circumstances. Experience has shown that attempts at decision making without a thorough understanding of the costs involved—and how these costs may change with the activity level—can lead to disaster. A decision to double production of a particular product line, for example, might result in the incurrence of far greater costs than could be generated in additional revenues. To avoid such problems, a manager must be able to accurately predict what costs will be at various activity levels. In this chapter, we shall find that the key to effective cost prediction lies in an understanding of cost behavior patterns.

TYPES OF COST BEHAVIOR PATTERNS

In our brief discussion of cost behavior in Chapter 2, we mentioned only variable and fixed costs. There is a third behavior pattern, generally known as a *mixed* or *semivariable* cost. All three cost behavior patterns—variable, fixed, and mixed—are found in most organizations. The relative proportion of each type of cost present in a firm is known as the firm's **cost structure.** For example, a firm might have many fixed costs but few variable costs or mixed costs. Alternatively, it might have many variable costs but few fixed or mixed costs. A firm's cost structure is very significant in that the decision-making process can be affected by the relative amount of fixed or variable cost that is present in the firm. We must reserve a detailed discussion of cost structure until the next chapter, however, and concentrate for the moment on gaining a full understanding of the behavior of each type of cost that a manager might encounter.

In the following sections, we briefly review the definition of variable costs and fixed costs and then discuss the behavior of these costs in greater depth than we were able to do in Chapter 2. After this review and discussion, we turn our attention to the identification and analysis of mixed costs. We conclude the chapter by introducing a new income statement format—called the contribution format—in which costs are organized by behavior rather than by the traditional functions of production, sales, and administration.

Variable Costs

We found in Chapter 2 that a variable cost is so named because its total dollar amount varies in direct proportion to changes in the activity level. If the activity level doubles, then one would expect the total dollar amount of the variable costs to also double. If the activity level increases by only 10 percent, then one would expect the total dollar amount of the variable costs to increase by 10 percent as well.

EXHIBIT 5–1
Variable Cost Behavior

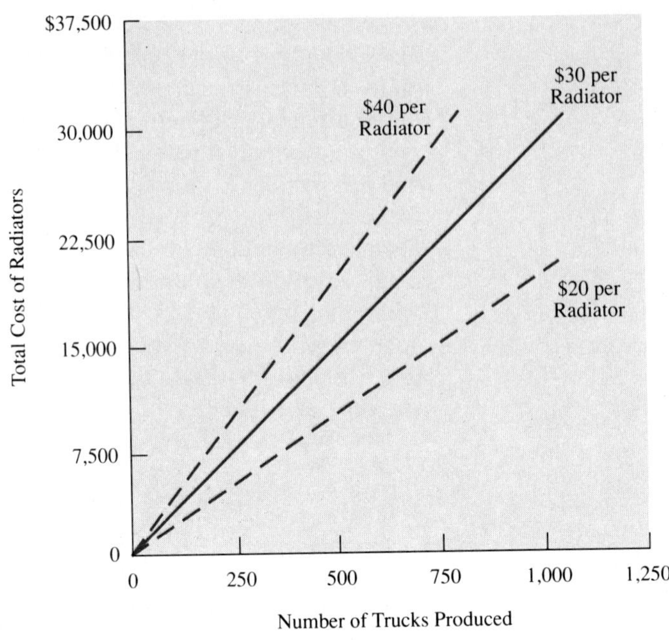

We also found in Chapter 2 that a variable cost remains constant if expressed on a *per unit* basis. To provide an example, assume that Premier Motor Company produces trucks. Each truck has one radiator, and the radiators cost $30 each. Thus, if we look at the cost of radiators on a *per truck* basis, the cost remains constant at $30 per truck. The $30 figure will not change, regardless of how many trucks are produced during a period, unless influenced by some outside factor.[1] The behavior of a variable cost, on both a per unit and a total basis, is illustrated in the following tabulation:

Number of Trucks Produced	Radiator Cost per Truck	Total Radiator Cost
250	$30	$ 7,500
500	30	15,000
750	30	22,500
1,000	30	30,000

The idea that a variable cost is constant per unit but varies in total with the activity level is crucial to an understanding of cost behavior patterns. We shall rely on this concept again and again in this chapter and in chapters ahead.

Exhibit 5–1 provides a graphic illustration of variable cost behavior. The exhibit contains three cost lines—one at $30 per radiator, and then two

[1] Frequently, discounts are allowed on quantity purchases. The handling of such discounts in the cost records of a firm is discussed in Chapter 9.

others showing what would happen to the slope of the line if the cost of radiators increased to $40 each or dropped to $20 each.

The Activity Base For a cost to be variable, it must be variable *with something*. That "something" is its **activity base.** An activity base is a measure of effort that operates as a causal factor in the incurrence of variable cost. In Chapter 3, we mentioned that an activity base is sometimes referred to as a *cost driver*. Some of the most common activity bases are machine-hours, units produced, and units sold. Other activity bases (cost drivers) might include the number of miles driven by salespersons, the number of pounds of laundry processed by a hotel, the number of letters typed by a secretary, the number of hours of labor time logged, and the number of occupied beds in a hospital.

In order to plan and control variable costs, a manager must be well acquainted with the various activity bases within the firm. People sometimes get the notion that if a cost doesn't vary with production or with sales, then it is not really a variable cost. This, of course, is not correct. As suggested by the range of bases listed above, costs can be incurred as a function of many different activities within an organization. Whether a cost is variable depends on whether its incurrence is a function of the activity measure under consideration. For example, if a manager is analyzing the cost of service calls under a product warranty, the relevant activity measure will be the number of service calls made. Those costs that vary in total with the number of service calls made will be variable costs.

Extent of Variable Costs The number and type of variable costs present in an organization will depend in large part on the organization's structure and purpose. A highly capital-intensive organization such as a public utility will tend to have few variable costs. The bulk of its costs will be associated with its plant, and these costs will tend to be quite insensitive to changes in levels of service provided. A manufacturing company, by contrast, will often have many variable costs; these costs will be associated both with the manufacture of its products and with their distribution to customers. A service organization or a merchandising company will tend to fall between these two extremes.

A few of the more frequently encountered variable costs are shown in the tabulation in Exhibit 5–2. The costs listed under "Variable portion of manufacturing overhead" in the exhibit should not be viewed as being inclusive but rather as being representative of the kinds of variable costs found in this classification.

True Variable versus Step-Variable Costs

Not all variable costs have exactly the same behavior pattern. Some variable costs behave in a *true variable* or *proportionately variable* pattern. Other variable costs behave in a *step-variable* pattern.

True Variable Costs Direct materials would be a true or proportionately variable cost because the amount used during a period will vary in direct proportion to the level of production activity. Moreover, any amounts purchased but not used can be stored up and carried forward to the next period as inventory.

EXHIBIT 5–2
Examples of Variable Costs

Type of Organization	Variable Costs
Merchandising company	Cost of goods (merchandise) sold
Manufacturing company	Manufacturing costs: Prime costs: Direct materials Direct labor Variable portion of manufacturing overhead: Indirect materials Lubricants Supplies Utilities Setup time Indirect labor
Both merchandising and manufacturing companies	Selling and administrative costs: Commissions to salespersons Clerical costs, such as invoicing Freight-out
Service organizations	Supplies, travel, clerical

Step-Variable Costs Indirect labor is also considered to be a variable cost, but it doesn't behave in quite the same way as direct materials. As an example, let us consider the labor cost of maintenance workers, which would be part of indirect labor.

Unlike direct materials, the time of maintenance workers is obtainable only in large chunks, rather than in exact quantities. Moreover, any maintenance time not utilized cannot be stored up as inventory and carried forward to the next period. Either the time is used effectively as it expires hour by hour, or it is gone forever. Furthermore, the utilization of indirect labor time can be quite flexible, whereas the utilization of direct materials is usually quite set. A maintenance crew, for example, can work at a fairly leisurely pace if pressures are light, but then the crew can intensify its efforts if pressures build up. For this reason, somewhat small changes in the level of production may have no effect on the number of maintenance people needed to properly carry on maintenance work.

A cost that is obtainable only in large chunks (such as the labor cost of maintenance workers) and that increases or decreases only in response to fairly wide changes in the activity level is known as a **step-variable cost.** The behavior of a step-variable cost, contrasted with the behavior of a true variable cost, is illustrated in Exhibit 5–3.

Notice that the need for maintenance help changes only with fairly wide changes in volume and that when additional maintenance time is obtained, it comes in large, indivisible pieces. The strategy of management in dealing with step-variable costs must be to obtain the fullest use of services possible for each separate step. Great care must be taken in working with these kinds of costs to prevent "fat" from building up in an organization. There is a tendency to employ additional help more quickly than might be needed, and there is generally a reluctance to lay people off when volume declines.

EXHIBIT 5–3
True Variable versus Step-Variable Costs

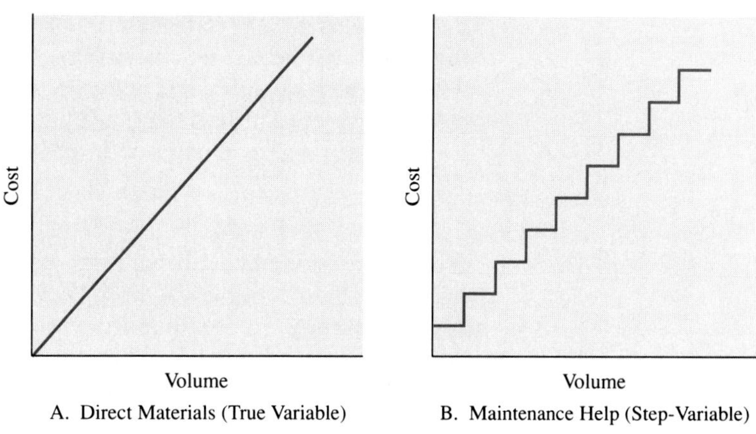

EXHIBIT 5–4
Curvilinear Costs and the Relevant Range

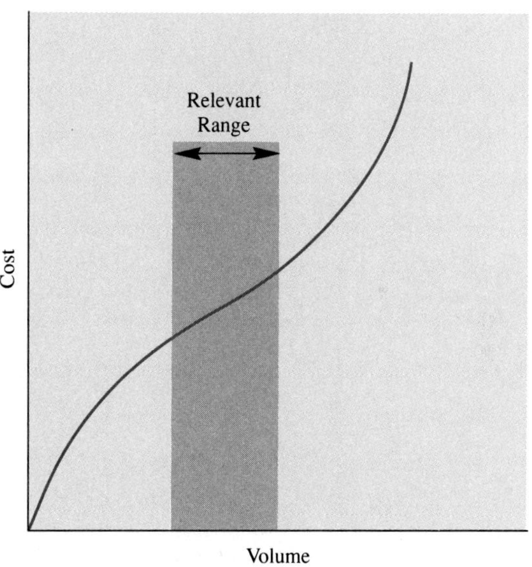

The Linearity Assumption and the Relevant Range

In dealing with variable costs, we have assumed a strictly linear relationship between cost and volume, except in the case of step-variable costs. Economists correctly point out that many costs that the accountant classifies as variable actually behave in a *curvilinear* fashion. The behavior of a **curvilinear cost** is shown in Exhibit 5–4. Notice that a strictly linear relationship between cost and volume does not exist either at very high or at very low levels of activity.

Although the accountant recognizes that many costs are not linear in their relationship to volume at some points, he or she concentrates on their behavior within narrow bands of activity known as the **relevant range.** The relevant range can be defined as that range of activity within which assumptions relative to cost behavior are valid. Generally, the relationship between variable cost and activity is stable enough within this range that an assumption of strict linearity can be used with insignificant loss of accuracy. The concept of the relevant range is illustrated in Exhibit 5–4.

Fixed Costs

In our discussion of cost behavior patterns in Chapter 2, we stated that fixed costs remain constant in total dollar amount regardless of changes in the level of activity. To continue the Premier Motor Company example, if the company rents a factory building for $50,000 per year, the *total* amount of rent paid will not change regardless of the number of trucks produced in a year. This concept is shown graphically in Exhibit 5–5.

Since fixed costs remain constant in total, the amount of cost computed on a *per unit* basis will get progressively smaller as the number of units produced becomes greater. If Premier Motor Company produces only 250 trucks in a year, the $50,000 fixed rental cost would amount to $200 per truck. If 1,000 trucks are produced, the fixed rental cost would amount to only $50 per truck. As we noted in Chapter 2, this aspect of fixed costs can be confusing to the manager, although it is necessary in some contexts to express fixed costs on an average per unit basis. We found in Chapter 3, for

EXHIBIT 5–5
Fixed Cost Behavior

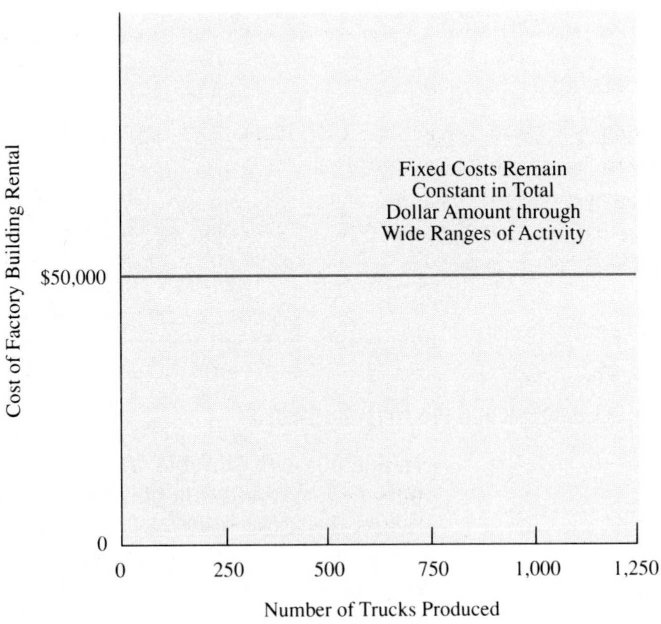

example, that for purposes of preparing financial statements, the manager needs a broad unit cost figure containing both variable and fixed cost elements. For *internal* uses, however, the manager rarely expresses a fixed cost on a per unit basis because of the potential confusion involved. Experience has shown that for internal uses, fixed costs are most easily (and most safely) dealt with on a total basis rather than on a per unit basis.

The Trend toward Fixed Costs

The trend in many companies today is toward greater fixed costs relative to variable costs. At least two factors are responsible for this trend. First, automation is becoming increasingly important in all types of organizations. Although automation has played a significant role in factory operations for well over a century, its role continues to increase. In addition, automation is rapidly becoming a significant factor in some traditionally service-oriented industries as well. Increased automation means increased investment in machinery and equipment, with the attendant fixed depreciation or lease charges.

Second, labor unions have been increasingly successful in stabilizing employment through labor contracts. Labor leaders have set guaranteed annual salaries or guaranteed minimum weeks of work high on their list of goals for the future. Although most people would agree that a stabilization of employment is desirable from a social point of view, guaranteed salaries and workweeks do reduce the response of labor costs to changes in activity.

This shift away from variable costs toward fixed costs has been so significant in some firms that they have become largely "fixed cost" organizations. The textile industry, for example, can be cited as one in which most firms have moved heavily toward automation, with basically inflexible fixed costs replacing flexible, more responsive variable costs to a considerable extent. These shifts are very significant from a managerial accounting point of view in that planning in many ways becomes much more crucial when one is dealing with large amounts of fixed costs. The reason is that when dealing with fixed costs, the manager is much more "locked in" and generally has fewer options available in day-to-day decisions.

Types of Fixed Costs

Fixed costs are sometimes referred to as capacity costs, since they result from outlays made for plant facilities, equipment, and other items needed to provide the basic capacity for sustained operations. For planning purposes, fixed costs can be viewed as being either *committed* or *discretionary*.

Committed Fixed Costs

Committed fixed costs are those that relate to the investment in plant, equipment, and the basic organizational structure of a firm. Examples of such costs include depreciation of plant facilities (buildings and equipment), taxes on real estate, insurance, and salaries of top management and operating personnel.

The two key factors about committed fixed costs are that (1) they are long term in nature, and (2) they can't be reduced to zero even for short periods of time without seriously impairing either the profitability or the long-run goals of a firm. Even if operations are interrupted or cut back, the committed fixed costs will still continue unchanged. During a period of economic recession, for example, a firm can't discharge its key executives or sell off part of the plant. Facilities and the basic organizational structure must be kept intact at all times. In terms of long-run goals, the costs of any other course of action would be far greater than any short-run savings that might be realized.

Since committed fixed costs are basic to the long-run goals of a firm, their planning horizon usually encompasses many years. The commitments involved in these costs are made only after careful analysis of long-run sales forecasts and after relating these forecasts to future capacity needs. Careful control must be exercised by management in the planning stage to ensure that a firm's long-run needs are properly evaluated. Once a decision is made to build a certain size plant, a firm becomes locked into that decision for many years to come.

After a firm becomes committed to a basic plant and organization, how are the associated costs controlled from year to year? Control of committed fixed costs comes through *utilization*. The strategy of management must be to utilize the plant and organization as effectively as possible in bringing about desired goals.

Discretionary Fixed Costs **Discretionary fixed costs** (often referred to as *managed* fixed costs) arise from *annual* decisions by management to spend in certain fixed cost areas. Examples of discretionary fixed costs would include advertising, research, public relations, management development programs, and internships for students.

Basically, two key differences exist between discretionary fixed costs and committed fixed costs. First, the planning horizon for a discretionary fixed cost is fairly short term—usually a single year. By contrast, as we indicated earlier, committed fixed costs have a planning horizon that encompasses many years. Second, under dire circumstances it may be possible to cut certain discretionary fixed costs back for short periods of time with minimal damage to the long-run goals of the organization. For example, a firm that has been spending $50,000 annually on management development programs may be forced because of poor economic conditions to reduce its spending in that area during a given year. Although some unfavorable consequences might result from the cutback, it is doubtful that these consequences would be as great as those that would result if the company decided to economize during the year by disposing of a portion of its plant.

The key factor about discretionary fixed costs is that management is not locked into a decision regarding such costs for any more than a single budget period. Each year a fresh look can be taken at the expenditure level in the various discretionary fixed cost areas. A decision can then be made on whether to continue a particular expenditure, increase it, reduce it, or discontinue it altogether.

Top-Management Philosophy In our discussion of fixed costs, we have drawn a sharp line between committed fixed costs and discretionary fixed costs. As a practical matter, the line between these two classes of costs should be viewed as being somewhat flexible. The reason is that whether a cost is committed or discretionary will depend in large part on the philosophy of top management.

Some management groups prefer to exercise discretion as often as possible on as many costs as possible. They prefer to review costs frequently and to adjust costs frequently, as conditions and needs warrant. Managers who are inclined in this direction tend to view fixed costs as being largely discretionary. Other management groups are slow to make adjustments in costs (especially adjustments downward) as conditions and needs change. They prefer to maintain the status quo and to leave programs and personnel largely undisturbed, even though changing conditions and needs might suggest the desirability of adjustments. Managers who are inclined in this direction tend to view virtually all fixed costs as being committed.

To cite an example, during recessionary periods when the level of home building is down, many construction companies lay off their workers and virtually disband operations for a period of time. Other construction companies continue large numbers of employees on the payroll, even though the workers have little or no work to do. In the first instance, management is viewing its fixed costs as being largely discretionary in nature. In the second instance, management is viewing its fixed costs as being largely committed. The philosophy of most management groups will fall somewhere between these two extremes.

Fixed Costs and the Relevant Range

The concept of the relevant range, which was introduced in our discussion of variable costs, also has application in dealing with fixed costs, particularly those of a discretionary nature. At the beginning of a period, programs are set and budgets established. The level of discretionary fixed costs will depend on the support needs of the programs that have been planned, which in turn will depend at least in part on the level of activity envisioned in the organization overall. At very high levels of activity, programs are usually broadened or expanded to include many things that might not be pursued at lower levels of activity. In addition, the support needs at high levels of activity are usually much greater than the support needs at lower levels of activity. For example, the advertising needs of a company striving to increase sales by 25 percent would probably be much greater than if no sales increase was planned. Thus, fixed costs often move upward in steps as the activity level increases. This concept is illustrated in Exhibit 5–6, which depicts fixed costs and the relevant range.

Although discretionary fixed costs are most susceptible to adjustment according to changing needs, the step pattern depicted in Exhibit 5–6 also has application to committed fixed costs. As a company expands its level of activity, it may outgrow its present plant, or the key management core may need to be expanded. The result, of course, will be increased committed fixed costs as a larger plant is built and as new key management positions are created.

One's first reaction to the step pattern depicted in Exhibit 5–6 is to say that discretionary and committed fixed costs are really just step-variable costs. To some extent this is true, since *all* costs vary in the long-run. There are two major differences, however, between the step-variable costs depicted earlier in Exhibit 5–3 and the fixed costs depicted in Exhibit 5–6.

EXHIBIT 5–6
Fixed Costs and the Relevant Range

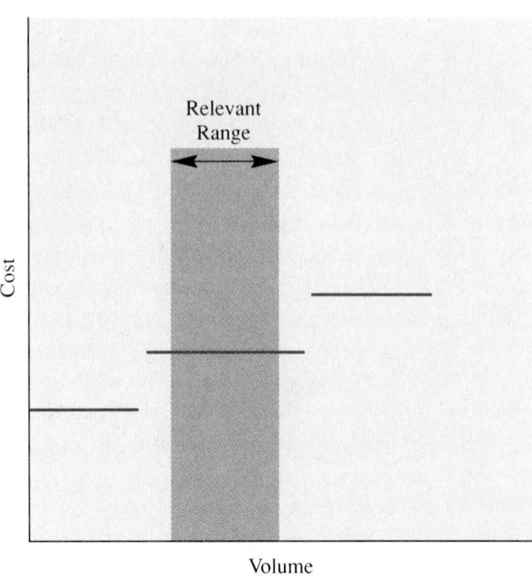

The first difference is that the step-variable costs can be adjusted very quickly as conditions change, whereas once fixed costs have been set, they often can't be changed easily, even if they are discretionary in nature. A step-variable cost such as maintenance labor, for example, can be adjusted upward or downward very quickly by the hiring and firing of maintenance workers. By contrast, once a company has committed itself to a particular program, it becomes locked into the attendant fixed costs, at least for the budget period under consideration. Once an advertising contract has been signed, for example, the company is locked into the attendant costs for the contract period.

The second difference is that the *width of the steps* depicted for step-variable costs is much narrower than the width of the steps depicted for the fixed costs in Exhibit 5–6. The width of the steps relates to volume or level of activity. For step-variable costs, the width of a step may be 40 hours of activity or less if one is dealing, for example, with maintenance labor cost. For fixed costs, however, the width of a step may be *thousands* or even *tens of thousands* of hours of activity. In essence, the width of the steps for step-variable costs is generally so narrow that these costs can be treated essentially as variable costs. The width of the steps for fixed costs, on the other hand, is so wide that these costs must generally be treated as being entirely fixed within the relevant range.

Mixed Costs

A **mixed cost** is one that contains both variable and fixed cost elements. Mixed costs are also known as **semivariable costs.** At certain levels of activity, mixed costs may display essentially the same characteristics as a fixed

EXHIBIT 5–7
Mixed Cost Behavior

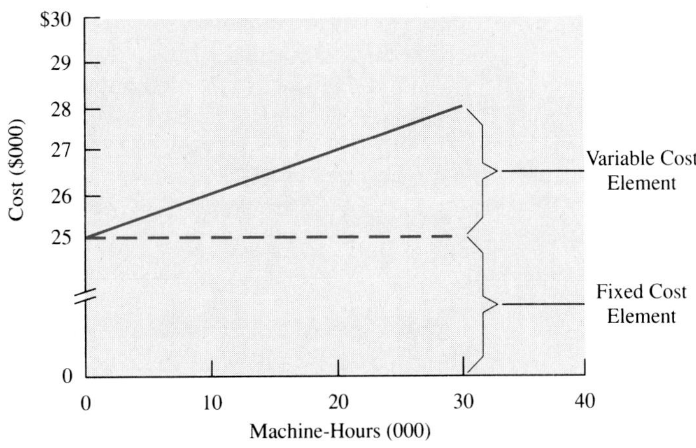

cost; at other levels of activity, they may display essentially the same characteristics as a variable cost.

To continue the Premier Motor Company example, assume that the company leases a large part of the machinery used in its operations. The lease agreement calls for a flat annual lease payment of $25,000, plus 10 cents for each hour that the machines are operated during the year. If during a particular year the machines are operated a cumulative total of 30,000 hours, then the lease cost of the machines will be $28,000, made up of $25,000 in fixed cost plus $3,000 in variable cost. The concept of a mixed cost is shown graphically in Exhibit 5–7.

Even if the machines leased by Premier Motor Company aren't used a single hour during the year, the company will still have to pay the minimum $25,000 charge. This is why the cost line in Exhibit 5–7 intersects the vertical cost axis at the $25,000 point. For each hour that the machines are used, the *total* cost of leasing will increase by 10 cents. Therefore, the total cost line slopes upward as the variable cost element is added onto the fixed cost element.

THE ANALYSIS OF MIXED COSTS

The concept of a mixed cost is important, since mixed costs are common to a wide range of firms. Examples of mixed costs include electricity, heat, repairs, telephone, and maintenance.

The fixed portion of a mixed cost represents the basic, minimum charge for just having a service *ready and available* for use. The variable portion represents the charge made for *actual consumption* of the service. As one would expect, the variable element varies in proportion to the amount of the service that is consumed.

For planning purposes, how does management handle mixed costs? The ideal approach would be to take each invoice as it comes in and break it down into its fixed and variable elements. As a practical matter, even if it were possible to make this type of minute breakdown, the cost of doing so would probably be prohibitive. Analysis of mixed costs is normally done on an aggregate basis, concentrating on the past behavior of a cost at various levels of activity. If this analysis is done carefully, good approximations of the fixed and variable elements of a cost can be obtained with a minimum of effort.

We will examine three methods of breaking mixed costs down into their fixed and variable elements—the *high-low method,* the *scattergraph method,* and the *least-squares method.*

The High-Low Method

The **high-low method** of analyzing mixed costs requires that the cost involved (for example, maintenance) be observed at both the high and low levels of activity within the relevant range. The difference in cost observed at the two extremes is divided by the change in activity in order to determine the amount of variable cost involved.

To illustrate, assume that maintenance costs for Arco Company have been observed as follows within the relevant range of 5,000 to 8,000 direct labor-hours (DLH):

Month	Direct Labor-Hours	Maintenance Cost Incurred
January	5,500	$ 745
February	7,000	850
March	5,000	700
April	6,500	820
May	7,500	960
June	8,000	1,000
July	6,000	825

Since total maintenance cost increases as the activity level increases, it seems obvious that some variable cost element is present. To separate the variable cost element from the fixed cost element, we must relate the change in direct labor-hours between the high and low points to the change that we observe in cost:

	Direct Labor-Hours	Maintenance Cost Incurred
High point observed	8,000	$1,000
Low point observed	5,000	700
Change observed.	3,000	$ 300

$$\text{Variable cost} = \frac{\text{Change in cost}}{\text{Change in activity}} = \frac{\$300}{3{,}000} = \$0.10 \text{ per direct labor-hour}$$

Having determined that the variable rate is 10 cents per direct labor-hour, we can now determine the amount of fixed cost present. This is done by taking total cost at *either* the high or the low point and deducting the variable cost element. In the computation below, total cost at the high point of activity is used in computing the fixed cost element:

$$\begin{aligned}\text{Fixed cost element} &= \text{Total cost} - \text{Variable cost element}\\ &= \$1{,}000 - (\$0.10 \times 8{,}000 \text{ labor-hours})\\ &= \$200\end{aligned}$$

Both the variable and fixed cost elements have now been isolated. The cost of maintenance within the relevant range analyzed can be expressed as being $200 plus 10 cents per direct labor-hour. This is sometimes referred to as a **cost formula.**

$$\left.\begin{array}{c}\text{Cost formula for maintenance—over}\\ \text{the relevant range of 5,000 to}\\ \text{8,000 direct labor-hours}\end{array}\right\} = \begin{array}{c}\text{\$200 fixed cost + \$0.10}\\ \text{per direct labor-hour}\end{array}$$

The data used in this illustration are shown graphically in Exhibit 5–8. Three things should be noted in relation to this exhibit:

1. Notice that cost is always plotted on the vertical axis and that it is represented by the letter *Y*. Cost is known as the **dependent variable,** since the amount of cost incurred during a period will be dependent on the level of activity for the period. (That is, as the level of activity increases, total cost will also increase.)
2. Notice that activity (direct labor-hours in this case) is always plotted on the horizontal axis and that it is represented by the letter *X*. Activity is known as the **independent variable,** since it controls the amount of cost that will be incurred during a period.
3. Notice that the relevant range is highlighted on the exhibit. In using a cost formula, the manager must remember that the formula will not be valid outside the relevant range from which the underlying data have been drawn.

The high-low method is very simple to apply, but it suffers from a major (and sometimes critical) defect in that it utilizes only two points in determining a cost formula. Generally, two points are not enough to produce accurate results in cost analysis work unless the points *happen* to fall in such a way as to represent a true average of all points of cost and activity. As one might suppose, only rarely will the two points in the high-low method happen to fall in just this way. For this reason, other methods of cost analysis that utilize a greater number of points will generally be more accurate than the high-low method in deriving a cost formula. If a manager chooses to use the high-low method, he or she should do so with a full awareness of the method's limitations.

The Scattergraph Method

In mixed cost analysis, the manager is trying to find the *average* rate of variability in a mixed cost. A more accurate way of doing this than the high-low method is to use the **scattergraph method,** which includes all points of observed cost data in the analysis through use of a graph. A graph much like the one that we used in Exhibit 5–8 is constructed, in which cost is shown on the vertical axis and the volume or rate of activity is shown on the horizontal axis. Costs observed at various levels of activity are then plotted on the

EXHIBIT 5–8
High-Low Method of Cost Analysis
Arco Company—Maintenance Cost

Volume	Direct Labor-Hours	Cost Observed
High	8,000	$1,000
Low	5,000	700

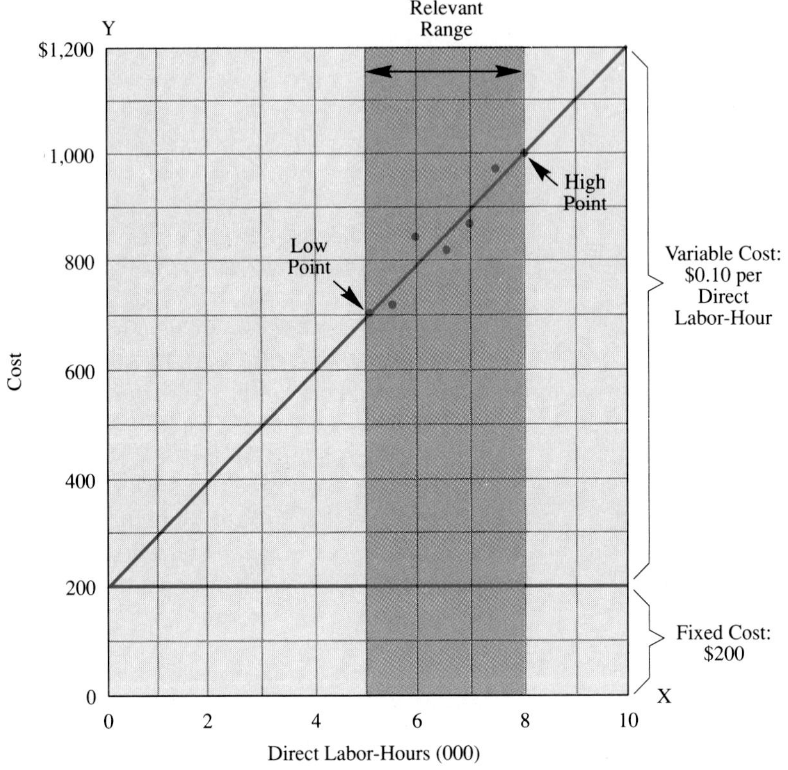

graph, and a line is fitted to the plotted points. However, rather than just fitting the line to the high and low points, *all points* are considered in the placement of the line. This is done through simple visual inspection of the data, with the analyst taking care that the placement of the line is representative of all points, not just the high and low ones. Typically, the line is placed so that approximately equal numbers of points fall above and below it.

A graph of this type is known as a *scattergraph,* and the line fitted to the plotted points is known as a **regression line.** The regression line, in effect, is a line of averages, with the average variable cost per unit of activity represented by the slope of the line and the average fixed cost in total represented by the point where the regression line intersects the cost axis.

To illustrate how a scattergraph is prepared, assume that Western Company has recorded costs for water over the last eight months as follows:

Water Consumed (000 gallons)	Total Cost
12	$260
15	270
10	230
9	215
11	250
13	245
8	220
14	260

The observed costs for water at the various activity levels have been plotted on a graph in Exhibit 5–9, and a regression line has been fitted to the plotted data by visual inspection. Note that the regression line has been placed in such a way that approximately equal numbers of points fall above and below it.

Since the regression line strikes the cost axis at the $150 point, that amount represents the fixed cost element. The variable cost element would be $8 per 1,000 gallons of water consumed, computed as follows:

Total cost observed for 10,000 gallons of water consumed (a point falling on the regression line in Exhibit 5–9)	$230
Less fixed cost element.	150
Variable cost element	$ 80

$80 ÷ 10,000 gallons = $0.008 per gallon, or $8 per thousand gallons.

EXHIBIT 5–9
A Completed Scattergraph
Western Company—Water Cost

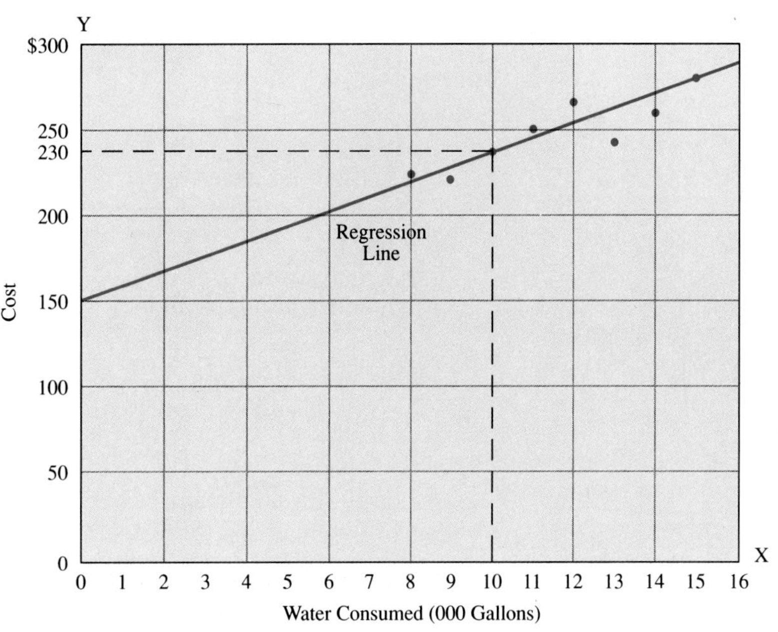

Thus, the cost formula for water would be \$150 per month plus \$8 per thousand gallons of water consumed.

A scattergraph can be an extremely useful tool in the hands of an experienced analyst. Quirks in cost behavior due to strikes, bad weather, breakdowns, and so on, become immediately apparent to the trained observer, who can make appropriate adjustment to the data in fitting the regression line. Many cost analysts would argue that a scattergraph should be the beginning point in all cost analyses, due to the benefits to be gained from having the data visually available in graph form.

The Least-Squares Method

The **least-squares method** is a more sophisticated approach to the scattergraph idea. Rather than fitting a regression line through the scattergraph data by simple visual inspection, the least-squares method fits the line by statistical analysis.

The least-squares method is based on computations that find their foundation in the equation for a straight line. A straight line can be expressed in equation form as:

$$Y = a + bX$$

with Y as the dependent variable; a as the fixed element; b as the degree of variability, or the slope of the line; and X as the independent variable. From this basic equation, and a given set of observations, n, two simultaneous linear equations can be developed that will fit a regression line to a linear array of data. The equations are:[2]

$$\Sigma XY = a\Sigma X + b\Sigma X^2 \qquad (1)$$
$$\Sigma Y = na + b\Sigma X \qquad (2)$$

where

X = activity measure (hours, etc.)
Y = total mixed cost observed
a = fixed cost
b = variable rate
n = number of observations

An Example of Least Squares The application of the least-squares method can best be seen through a detailed example. Let us assume that a company is anxious to break its power (electrical) costs down into basic variable and fixed cost elements. Over the past year, power costs (Y) have been observed as shown in the tabulation below. The number of hours of machine time logged (X) in incurring these costs is also shown in the tabulation.

[2] The appendix at the end of this chapter contains an alternative approach to the least-squares method.

Month	Machine-Hours (000) (X)	Power Costs (Y)	XY	X^2
January.	9	$ 3,000	$ 27,000	81
February	8	2,500	20,000	64
March	9	2,900	26,100	81
April	10	2,900	29,000	100
May	12	3,600	43,200	144
June	13	3,400	44,200	169
July	11	3,200	35,200	121
August	11	3,300	36,300	121
September	10	3,000	30,000	100
October	8	2,600	20,800	64
November	7	2,300	16,100	49
December.	8	2,600	20,800	64
Totals	116	$35,300	$348,700	1,158

Substituting these amounts in the two linear equations given earlier, we have:

$$\Sigma XY = a\Sigma X + b\Sigma X^2 \quad (1)$$
$$\Sigma Y = na + b\Sigma X \quad (2)$$

$$\$348{,}700 = 116a + 1{,}158b \quad (1)$$
$$\$35{,}300 = 12a + 116b \quad (2)$$

In order to solve the equations, it will be necessary to eliminate one of the terms. The a term can be eliminated by multiplying equation (1) by 12, by multiplying equation (2) by 116, and then by subtracting equation (2) from equation (1). These steps are shown below:

Multiply equation (1) by 12:	$\$4{,}184{,}400 = 1{,}392a + 13{,}896b$
Multiply equation (2) by 116:	$\$4{,}094{,}800 = 1{,}392a + 13{,}456b$
Subtract (2) from (1):	$\$89{,}600 = 440b$
	$\$203.64 = b$

Therefore, the variable rate for power cost is $203.64 for each thousand machine-hours of operating time (or $0.20364 per hour). The fixed cost of power can be obtained by substituting the value for term b in either equation (1) or equation (2). We will use equation (2) since the numbers are smaller and easier to deal with:

$$\$35{,}300 = 12a + 116b \quad (2)$$
$$\$35{,}300 = 12a + 116(\$203.64)$$
$$\$35{,}300 = 12a + \$23{,}622.24$$
$$\$11{,}677.76 = 12a$$
$$\$973.15 = a$$

The fixed cost for power is $973.15 per month. The cost formula for the mixed cost is therefore $973.15 per month plus $203.64 per thousand machine-hours worked.

Cost formula for power—over the relevant range of 7,000 to 13,000 machine-hours	=	$973.15 fixed cost + $203.64 per thousand machine-hours ($0.20364 per hour)

In terms of the linear equation $Y = a + bX$, the cost formula can be expressed as:

$$Y = \$973.15 + \$203.64X$$

where activity (X) is expressed in thousands of machine-hours. We can show how the cost formula is used for planning purposes by assuming that 10,500 machine-hours will be worked during the coming month. Under this assumption, the expected power costs will be:

Variable costs:	
10.5 thousand machine-hours × \$203.64 . . .	\$2,138.22
Fixed costs	973.15
Total expected power costs	\$3,111.37

What Does Least Squares Mean? The term *least squares* means that the sum of the squares of the deviations from the plotted points to the regression line *is smaller* than would be obtained from any other line fitted to the data. This idea can be illustrated as shown in Exhibit 5–10.

EXHIBIT 5–10
The Concept of Least Squares

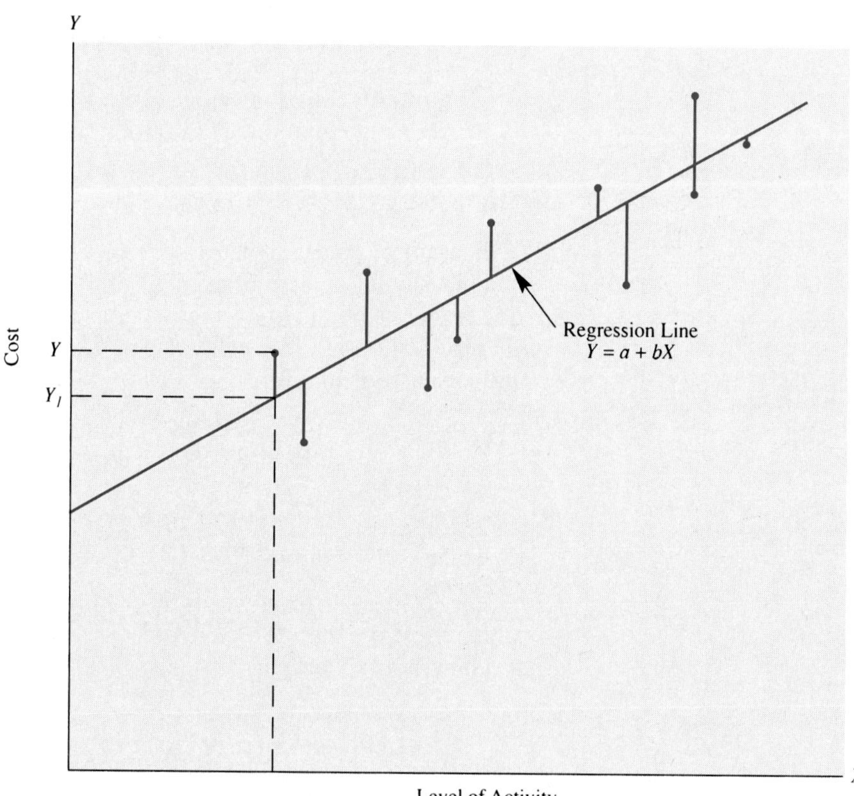

Notice from the exhibit that the deviations from the plotted points to the regression line are measured vertically on the graph. They are not measured perpendicular to the regression line. Least squares will have been attained when $\Sigma(Y - Y_1)^2$ is at the lowest possible figure. At the point of least squares, the best possible fit of a regression line to the plotted points will have been achieved in terms of slope and placement of the line.

The Use of Judgment in Cost Analysis

Although a cost formula has the appearance of exactness, the user should recognize that the breakdown of any mixed cost by any of the three techniques that we have discussed involves a substantial amount of estimating. The breakdowns represent *good approximations* of the fixed and variable cost elements involved; they should not be construed as being precise analyses. Managers must be ready to step in at any point in their analysis of a cost and adjust their computations for judgment factors that in their view are critical to a proper understanding of the mixed cost involved. However, the fact that computations are not exact and involve estimates and judgment factors does not prevent data from being useful and meaningful in decision making. The managers who wait to make a decision until they have perfect data available will rarely have an opportunity to demonstrate their decision-making ability.

Multiple Regression Analysis

In all of our computations involving mixed costs, we have assumed a single causative factor as the basis for the behavior of the variable element. That causative factor has been the volume or rate of some activity, such as direct labor-hours, machine-hours, production, or sales. This assumption is acceptable for many mixed costs, but in some situations there may be more than one causative factor involved in the behavior of the variable element. For example, in a shipping department, the cost of freight-out might depend on both the number of units shipped and the weight of the units as dual causative factors. In a situation such as this, the equation for a simple regression would have to be expanded to include the additional variable:

$$Y = a + bX + cW$$

where c = the factor of variability and W = the weight of a unit. When dealing with an expanded equation such as this one, the simple regression analysis that we have been doing is no longer adequate. A **multiple regression analysis** is necessary. Although the added variable or variables will make the computations more complex, the principles involved are the same as in a simple regression such as we have been doing. Because of the complexity of the computations involved, multiple regression is generally done with the aid of a computer.

Engineering Approach to Cost Study

Some firms use the engineering approach to the study of cost behavior. Essentially, this approach involves a quantitative analysis of what cost behavior should be, based on the industrial engineer's evaluation of the production methods to be used, the materials specifications, labor needs, equipment needs, efficiency of production, power consumption, and so on. The engineering approach must be used in those situations where no past experience is available on activity and costs. In addition, it is often used in tandem with the methods we have discussed above in order to sharpen the accuracy of cost analysis. An NAA (National Association of Accountants) research report of actual business practices describes the use of the engineering approach as follows:

> The industrial engineering approach to determination of how costs should vary with volume proceeds by systematic study of materials, labor, services, and facilities needed at varying volumes. The aim is to find the best way to obtain the desired production. These studies generally make use of past experience, but it is used as a guide or as a check upon the results obtained by direct study of the production methods and facilities. Where no past experience is available, as with a new product, plant, or method, this approach can be applied to estimate the changes in cost that will accompany changes in volume.[3]

THE CONTRIBUTION FORMAT

Once the manager has separated costs into fixed and variable elements, what does he or she do with the data? To answer this question will require most of the remainder of this book, since virtually everything the manager does rests in some way on an understanding of cost behavior. One immediate and very significant application of the ideas we have developed, however, is found in a new format to the income statement known as the **contribution approach.** The unique thing about the contribution approach is that it provides the manager with an income statement geared directly to cost behavior.

Why a New Income Statement Format?

The **traditional approach** to the income statement, such as illustrated in Chapter 2 and such as you studied in financial accounting, is not organized in terms of cost behavior. Rather, it is organized in a "functional" format—emphasizing the functions of production, administration, and sales in the classification and presentation of cost data. No attempt is made to distinguish between the behavior of costs included under each functional heading. Under the heading "Administrative expense," for example, one can expect to find both variable and fixed costs lumped together.

Although an income statement prepared in the functional format may be useful for external reporting purposes, it has serious limitations so far as usefulness internally to the manager is concerned. Internally, the manager needs cost data organized in a format that will facilitate the carrying out of major responsibilities of planning, control, and decision making. As we shall see in chapters ahead, these responsibilities are discharged most effectively when cost data are available in a fixed and variable format. The contribution approach to the income statement has been developed in response to this need.

[3] National Association of Accountants, Research Report No. 16, "The Analysis of Cost-Volume-Profit Relationships" (New York, 1960), p. 17.

EXHIBIT 5–11

Comparison of the Contribution Income Statement with the Traditional Income Statement

Traditional Approach (costs organized by function)

Sales		$12,000
Less cost of goods sold		6,000*
Gross margin		6,000
Less operating expenses:		
Selling	$3,100*	
Administrative	1,900*	5,000
Net income		$ 1,000

Contribution Approach (costs organized by behavior)

Sales		$12,000
Less variable expenses:		
Variable production	$2,000	
Variable selling	600	
Variable administrative	400	3,000
Contribution margin		9,000
Less fixed expenses:		
Fixed production	4,000	
Fixed selling	2,500	
Fixed administrative	1,500	8,000
Net income		$ 1,000

* Contains both variable and fixed expenses. This is the income statement for a *manufacturing* company; thus, when the income statement is placed in the contribution format, the "cost of goods sold" figure is divided between variable production costs and fixed production costs. If this were the income statement for a *merchandising* company (which simply purchases completed goods from a supplier), then the "cost of goods sold" would *all* be variable.

The Contribution Approach

Exhibit 5–11 presents a model of the contribution approach to the income statement, along with the traditional approach with which you are already familiar.

Notice that the contribution approach separates costs into fixed and variable categories, first deducting variable expenses from sales to obtain what is known as the *contribution margin*. The term **contribution margin** can be defined as the amount remaining from sales revenues after variable expenses have been deducted that can be used to *contribute* toward the covering of fixed expenses and then toward profits for the period.

The contribution approach to the income statement is widely used as an internal planning and decision-making tool. Its emphasis on costs by behavior facilitates cost-volume-profit analysis, such as we shall be doing in the following chapter. The approach is also very useful in appraisal of management performance, in segmented reporting of profit data, in budgeting, and in organizing data pertinent to all kinds of special decisions, such as product line analysis, pricing, use of scarce resources, and make or buy analyses. All of these topics are covered in later chapters.

SUMMARY

Managers analyze cost behavior to have a basis for predicting how costs will respond to changes in activity levels throughout the organization. We have looked at three types of cost behavior—variable, fixed, and mixed. In the case of mixed costs, we have studied three methods of breaking a mixed cost into its basic variable and fixed elements. The high-low method is the simplest of the three, having as its underlying assumption that the variable element of a mixed cost can be determined by analyzing the change in cost between two points. In most situations, however, two points are not enough to produce accurate results in cost analysis work, and the manager must therefore use either the scattergraph method or the least-squares method to derive an accurate cost formula. Both of these methods require the construction of a regression line, the slope of which represents the average rate of variability in the mixed cost being analyzed. The least-squares method is the more accurate of the two in that it uses statistical analysis to fit a regression line to an array of data.

Managers use costs organized by behavior as a basis for many decisions. To facilitate this use, costs are often prepared in a contribution format. The unique thing about the contribution format is that it classifies costs on the income statement by cost behavior rather than by the functions of production, administration, and sales.

REVIEW PROBLEM ON COST BEHAVIOR

Neptune Rentals offers a boat rental service. Consider the following costs of the company over a relevant range of 5,000 to 20,000 hours of operating time for its boats:

	Hours of Operating Time			
	5,000	**10,000**	**15,000**	**20,000**
Total costs:				
Variable costs.	$ 20,000	$?	$?	$?
Fixed costs	180,000	?	?	?
Total costs	$200,000	$?	$?	$?
Cost per hour:				
Variable cost	$?	$?	$?	$?
Fixed cost	?	?	?	?
Total cost per hour . . .	$?	$?	$?	$?

Required Compute the missing amounts.

Solution The variable cost per hour of operating time can be computed as follows:

$20,000 ÷ 5,000 hours = $4 per hour

Therefore, in accordance with the behavior of variable and fixed costs, the missing amounts are:

	Hours of Operating Time			
	5,000	**10,000**	**15,000**	**20,000**
Total costs:				
Variable costs.	$ 20,000	$ 40,000	$ 60,000	$ 80,000
Fixed costs	180,000	180,000	180,000	180,000
Total costs	$200,000	$220,000	$240,000	$260,000
Cost per hour:				
Variable cost	$ 4	$ 4	$ 4	$ 4
Fixed cost	36	18	12	9
Total cost per hour . . .	$ 40	$ 22	$ 16	$ 13

Observe that the variable costs increase, in total, proportionately with increases in the number of hours of operating time, but that these costs remain constant at $4 if expressed on a per hour basis.

In contrast, the fixed costs by definition do not change in total with changes in the level of activity. They remain constant at $180,000. With increases in activity, however, the fixed costs decrease on a per hour basis, dropping from $36 per hour when the boats are operated 5,000 hours a period to only $9 per hour when the boats are operated 20,000 hours a period. *Because of this troublesome aspect of fixed costs, they are most easily (and most safely) dealt with on a total basis, rather than on a unit basis, in cost analysis work.*

KEY TERMS FOR REVIEW

Activity base A measure of effort, such as production, sales, or miles driven by salespersons, that operates as a causal factor in the incurrence of variable costs. An activity base is also known as a *cost driver*. (p. 167)

Committed fixed costs Those fixed costs that relate to the investment in plant, equipment, and the basic organizational structure of a firm. (p. 171)

Contribution approach An income statement format that is geared to cost behavior in that costs are separated into variable and fixed categories rather than being separated according to the functions of production, sales, and administration. (p. 184)

Contribution margin The amount remaining from sales revenues after variable expenses have been deducted. (p. 185)

Cost formula A quantitative expression of the fixed and variable elements of a cost. This expression is generally in the form of the linear equation $Y = a + bX$. (p. 177)

Cost structure The relative proportion of fixed, variable, and mixed costs found within an organization. (p. 165)

Curvilinear costs The economist's expression of the relationship between cost and activity in an organization. (p. 169)

Dependent variable A variable that reacts or responds to some controlling factor in a situation; total cost is the dependent variable, as represented by the letter Y, in the equation $Y = a + bX$. (p. 177)

Discretionary fixed costs Those fixed costs that arise from annual decisions by management to spend in certain fixed cost areas, such as advertising and research. (p. 172)

High-low method A method of separating a mixed cost into its fixed and variable elements by analyzing the change in activity and cost between the high and low points of a group of observed data. (p. 176)

Independent variable A variable that acts as the controlling factor in a situation; activity is the independent variable, as represented by the letter X, in the equation $Y = a + bX$. (p. 177)

Least-squares method A method of separating a mixed cost into its fixed and variable elements; under this method, a regression line is fitted to an array of plotted points by statistical analysis. (p. 180)

Mixed cost A cost that contains both variable and fixed cost elements. Also see *Semivariable cost*. (p. 174)

Multiple regression analysis An analytical method required in those situations where more than one causative factor is involved in the behavior of the variable element of a mixed cost. (p. 183)

Regression line A line fitted to an array of plotted points. The slope of the line, denoted by the letter b in the linear equation $Y = a + bX$, represents the average variable cost per unit of activity; the point where the line intersects the cost axis, denoted by the letter a in the equation above, represents the average total fixed cost. (p. 178)

Relevant range That range of activity within which assumptions relative to variable and fixed cost behavior are valid. (p. 170)

Scattergraph method A method of separating a mixed cost into its fixed and variable elements; under this method, a regression line is fitted to an array of plotted points by simple, visual inspection. (p. 177)

Semivariable cost A cost that contains both variable and fixed cost elements. Also see *Mixed cost.* (p. 174)

Step-variable cost A cost (such as the cost of a maintenance worker) that is obtainable only in large pieces and that increases and decreases only in response to fairly wide changes in the activity level. (p. 168)

Traditional approach An income statement format in which costs are organized and presented according to the functions of production, administration, and sales. (p. 184)

APPENDIX: ALTERNATIVE APPROACH TO LEAST SQUARES

Some managers prefer an alternative approach to the least-squares method that does not require use of the equations given in the chapter. Assume that a firm wishes to develop a cost formula for its maintenance expense. The company has determined that the variable portion of maintenance is incurred as a function of the number of machine-hours worked. Data on machine-hours and attendant maintenance expense for the first six months of 19x1 are given in Exhibit 5A–1. The exhibit also contains computations showing how a mixed cost can be broken down into its basic variable and fixed cost elements by the alternative approach.

As shown in the exhibit, the cost formula for maintenance expense is $100 fixed cost plus 20 cents per machine-hour. Or, it can be expressed in equation form as:

$$Y = \$100 + \$0.20X$$

There are six basic steps to computing a cost formula by this method. The reader should trace these six steps back through the computations in Exhibit 5A–1.

EXHIBIT 5A–1

Alternative Approach to Least-Squares Analysis

			Difference from Average			
Month	**Machine-Hours (X)**	**Maintenance Expense (Y)**	**Machine-Hours (X′)**	**Maintenance Expense (Y′)**	**X′Y′**	**X′²**
January	400	$ 180	−100	−$20	+$ 2,000	10,000
February	575	215	+ 75	+ 15	+ 1,125	5,625
March	350	170	−150	− 30	+ 4,500	22,500
April	475	195	− 25	− 5	+ 125	625
May	550	210	+ 50	+ 10	+ 500	2,500
June	650	230	+150	+ 30	+ 4,500	22,500
Totals	3,000	$1,200	-0-	-0-	$12,750	63,750
Average	500 ($\bar{X}$)	$ 200 ($\bar{Y}$)				

Variable rate: $\dfrac{\Sigma X'Y'}{\Sigma X'^2} = \dfrac{\$12{,}750}{63{,}750} = \$0.20$ per machine-hour

Total fixed cost:

$$\bar{Y} = a + b\bar{X}$$
$$\$200 = a + \$0.20(500 \text{ machine-hours})$$
$$a = \$200 - \$100$$
$$a = \$100$$

Step 1: Determine the average level of activity ($\overline{X}$) and the average amount of cost ($\overline{Y}$) for the period of time being analyzed. In Exhibit 5A–1, machine-hours average 500 hours per month (3,000 machine-hours ÷ 6 months = 500 machine-hours) and power costs average $200 per month ($1,200 ÷ 6 months = $200).

Step 2: Compute the difference between the actual activity for each month and the average activity computed in step 1, and enter this difference in a column labeled X'. Then compute the difference between the actual cost for each month and the average cost, and enter this difference in a second column labeled Y'. Use plus (+) and minus (−) notations to signify whether monthly amounts are greater or less than the average.

Step 3: For each month, multiply the amount in the X' column times the amount in the Y' column and enter the result in a column labeled $X'Y'$. (In obtaining the data for the $X'Y'$ column, remember that algebraically a minus times a minus is a plus, but a minus times a plus is a minus.)

Step 4: Square the X' amount for each month, and enter the result in a new column labeled X'^2.

Step 5: Compute the variable rate by the formula:

$$\frac{\Sigma X'Y'}{\Sigma X'^2} = \text{Variable rate}$$

Step 6: Compute the total fixed cost by substituting in the equation:

$$\overline{Y} = a + b\overline{X}$$

where $\overline{Y}$ = the average cost observed, a = the total fixed cost that you are seeking, b = the variable rate computed in step 5, and $\overline{X}$ = the average activity level observed.

QUESTIONS

5–1 Distinguish between *(a)* a variable cost, *(b)* a fixed cost, and *(c)* a mixed cost.

5–2 What effect does an increase in volume have on—

a. Unit fixed costs?

b. Unit variable costs?

c. Total fixed costs?

d. Total variable costs?

5–3 Define the following terms: *(a)* cost behavior and *(b)* relevant range.

5–4 What is meant by an "activity base" when dealing with variable costs? Give several examples of activity bases.

5–5 Distinguish between *(a)* a variable cost, *(b)* a mixed cost, and *(c)* a step-variable cost. Chart the three costs on a graph, with activity plotted horizontally and cost plotted vertically.

5–6 The accountant often assumes a strictly linear relationship between cost and volume. How can this practice be defended in light of the fact that many variable costs are curvilinear in form?

5–7 Distinguish between discretionary fixed costs and committed fixed costs.

5–8 Classify the following fixed costs as normally being either committed (C) or discretionary (D):

a. Depreciation on buildings.

b. Advertising.

c. Research.

d. Insurance.
e. The president's salary.
f. Management development and training.

5–9 What factors are contributing to the trend toward increasing numbers of fixed costs, and why is this trend significant from a managerial accounting point of view?

5–10 Does the concept of the relevant range have application to fixed costs? Explain.

5–11 What is the major disadvantage of the high-low method? Under what conditions would this analytical method provide an accurate cost formula?

5–12 What methods are available for separating a mixed cost into its fixed and variable elements? Which method is most accurate? Why?

5–13 What is meant by a regression line? Give the general formula for a regression line. Which term represents the variable cost? The fixed cost?

5–14 Once a regression line has been drawn, how does one determine the fixed cost element? The variable cost element?

5–15 What is meant by the term *least squares?*

5–16 What is the difference between single regression analysis and multiple regression analysis?

5–17 What is the difference between the contribution approach to the income statement and the traditional approach to the income statement?

5–18 What is meant by contribution margin? How is it computed?

EXERCISES

E5–1 The number of X rays taken and X-ray costs over the last nine months in Beverly Hospital are given below:

Month	X Rays Taken	X Ray Costs
January	6,250	$28,000
February	7,000	29,000
March	5,000	23,000
April.	4,250	20,000
May	4,500	22,000
June	3,000	17,000
July	3,750	18,000
August.	5,500	24,000
September	5,750	26,000

Required
1. Using the high-low method, determine the formula for X-ray costs.
2. What X-ray costs would you expect to be incurred during a month in which 4,600 X rays are taken?

E5–2 Refer to the data in Exercise 5–1.

Required
1. Prepare a scattergraph using the data from Exercise 5–1. Plot cost on the vertical axis and activity on the horizontal axis. Fit a regression line to your plotted points by visual inspection.
2. What is the approximate monthly fixed cost for X rays? The approximate variable cost per X ray taken?
3. Scrutinize the points on your graph, and explain why the high-low method would or would not yield an accurate cost formula in this situation.

E5–3 Zerbel Company has noticed considerable fluctuation in its shipping expense from month to month, as shown on the next page:

Month	Units Shipped	Total Shipping Expense
January	4	$22
February	7	31
March	5	26
April	2	15
May	3	22
June	6	30
July	8	36

Required

1. Using the high-low method, determine the cost formula for shipping expense.
2. The president has no confidence in the high-low method and would like you to "check out" your results using the scattergraph method. Do the following:
   a. Prepare a scattergraph, using the data given above. Plot cost on the vertical axis and activity on the horizontal axis. Fit a regression line to your plotted points by visual inspection.
   b. Using the data from your scattergraph, determine the approximate variable cost per unit shipped and the approximate fixed cost per month.

E5–4 Refer to the data for Zerbel Company in Exercise 5–3.

Required

1. Using the least-squares method, determine the cost formula for shipping expense.
2. If you also completed Exercise 5–3, prepare a simple table comparing the variable and fixed cost elements of shipping expense as computed under the high-low method, the scattergraph method, and the least-squares method.

E5–5 Resort Inns, Inc., has a total of 2,000 rooms in its nationwide chain of motels. On the average, 70 percent of the rooms are occupied each day. The company's operating costs are $21 per occupied room per day at this occupancy level, assuming a 30-day month. This $21 figure contains both variable and fixed cost elements. During October, the occupancy rate dropped to only 45 percent. A total of $792,000 in operating cost was incurred during the month.

Required

1. Determine the variable cost per occupied room per day.
2. Determine the total fixed operating costs per month.
3. Assume that the occupancy rate increases to 60 percent during November. What total operating costs would you expect the company to incur during the month?

E5–6 Parker Company manufactures and sells a single product. The company typically operates within a relevant range of 60,000 to 100,000 units produced and sold each year. A partially completed schedule of the company's total and per unit costs over this range is given below:

	Units Produced and Sold		
	60,000	**80,000**	**100,000**
Total costs:			
Variable costs	$150,000	?	?
Fixed costs	360,000	?	?
Total costs	$510,000	?	?
Cost per unit:			
Variable cost	?	?	?
Fixed cost.	?	?	?
Total cost per unit . . .	?	?	?

Required

1. Complete the schedule of the company's total and unit costs above.
2. Assume that the company produces and sells 90,000 units during a year. The selling price is $7.50 per unit. Prepare an income statement in the contribution format for the year.

E5–7 The data below have been taken from the cost records of the Atlanta Processing Company. The data relate to the cost of operating one of the company's processing facilities at various levels of activity:

Month	Units Processed	Total Cost
January	8,000	$14,000
February	4,500	10,000
March	7,000	12,500
April	9,000	15,500
May	3,750	10,000
June	6,000	12,500
July	3,000	8,500
August	5,000	11,500

Required

1. Prepare a scattergraph by plotting the above data on a graph. Plot cost on the vertical axis and activity on the horizontal axis. Fit a regression line to your plotted points by visual inspection.
2. What is the approximate monthly fixed cost? The approximate variable cost per unit processed? Show computations.

E5–8 One of Varic Company's products goes through a glazing process. The company has observed glazing costs as follows over the last six quarters (the numbers have been simplified for ease of computation):

Quarter	Units Produced	Total Glazing Cost
1	8	$27
2	5	20
3	10	31
4	4	19
5	6	24
6	9	29

For planning purposes, the company's management must know the amount of variable glazing cost per unit and the total fixed glazing cost per quarter.

Required

1. Using the least-squares method, determine the variable and fixed elements of glazing cost as desired by management.
2. Express the cost data in (1) above in the form $Y = a + bX$.
3. If the company processes seven units next quarter, what would be the expected total glazing cost?

E5–9 Speedy Parcel Service operates a fleet of delivery trucks in a large metropolitan area. A careful study by the company's cost analyst has determined that if a truck is driven 120,000 miles during a year, the operating cost is 11.6 cents per mile. If a truck is driven only 80,000 miles during a year, the operating cost increases to 13.6 cents per mile.

Required

1. Using the high-low method, determine the variable and fixed cost elements of the annual cost of truck operation.
2. Express the variable and fixed costs in the form $Y = a + bX$.
3. If a truck were driven 100,000 miles during a year, what total cost would you expect to be incurred?

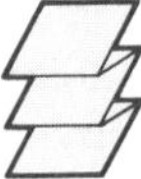

E5–10 Haaki Shop, Inc., is a large retailer of water sports equipment. An income statement for the company's surfboard department for the most recent quarter is presented below.

THE HAAKI SHOP, INC.
Income Statement—Surfboard Department
For the Quarter Ended May 31, 19x6

Sales		$800,000
Less cost of goods sold		300,000
Gross margin		500,000
Less operating expenses:		
Selling expenses	$250,000	
Administrative expenses	160,000	410,000
Net income		$ 90,000

The surfboards sell, on the average, for $400 each. The department's variable selling expenses are $50 per surfboard sold. The remaining selling expenses are fixed. The administrative expenses are 25 percent variable and 75 percent fixed. The company purchases its surfboards from a supplier at a cost of $150 per surfboard.

Required

1. Prepare an income statement for the quarter, using the contribution approach.
2. What was the contribution toward fixed expenses and profits from each surfboard sold during the quarter? (State this figure in a single dollar amount per surfboard.)

PROBLEMS

P5–11 High-Low Method; Contribution Income Statement Frankel Company, a merchandising firm, is the exclusive distributor of a product that is gaining rapid market acceptance. The company's revenues and expenses for the last three months are given below:

FRANKEL COMPANY
Comparative Income Statement
For the Three Months Ended June 30, 19x1

	April	May	June
Sales in units	3,000	3,750	4,500
Sales revenue	$420,000	$525,000	$630,000
Less cost of goods sold	168,000	210,000	252,000
Gross margin	252,000	315,000	378,000
Less operating expenses:			
Shipping expense	44,000	50,000	56,000
Advertising expense	70,000	70,000	70,000
Salaries and commissions	107,000	125,000	143,000
Insurance expense	9,000	9,000	9,000
Depreciation expense	42,000	42,000	42,000
Total operating expenses	272,000	296,000	320,000
Net income (loss)	$(20,000)	$ 19,000	$ 58,000

Required

1. Identify each of the company's expenses (including cost of goods sold) as being either variable, fixed, or mixed.
2. By use of the high-low method, separate each mixed expense into variable and fixed elements. State the cost formula for each mixed expense.
3. Redo the company's income statement at the 4,500-unit level of activity by placing the revenue and expense data in the contribution format.

P5–12 High-Low Method of Cost Analysis Marsden Company's total factory overhead costs fluctuate somewhat from year to year according to the number of machine-hours worked in its production facility. These costs at high and at low levels of activity over recent years are given below:

	Level of Activity	
	Low	High
Machine-hours	60,000	80,000
Total factory overhead costs	$274,000	$312,000

The factory overhead costs above consist of indirect materials, rent, and maintenance. The company has analyzed these costs at the 60,000 machine-hours level of activity and has determined that at this activity level these costs exist in the following amounts:

Indirect materials (V)	$ 90,000
Rent (F)	130,000
Maintenance (M)	54,000
Total factory overhead costs	$274,000

V = variable; F = fixed; M = mixed.

For planning purposes, the company wants to break down the maintenance cost into its variable and fixed cost elements.

Required

1. Determine how much of the $312,000 factory overhead cost at the high level of activity above consists of maintenance cost. (Hint: To do this, it may be helpful to first determine how much of the $312,000 consists of indirect materials and rent. Think about the behavior of variable and fixed costs within the relevant range!)
2. By means of the high-low method of cost analysis, determine the cost formula for maintenance.
3. Express the company's maintenance costs in the linear equation form $Y = a + bX$.
4. What *total* overhead costs would you expect the company to incur at an operating level of 65,000 machine-hours?

P5–13 Least-Squares Method of Cost Analysis; Graphing Amanda King has just been appointed director of recreation programs for Highland city, a rapidly growing community in the East. In the past, the city has sponsored a number of softball leagues in the summer months. From the city's cost records, Amanda has found the following total costs associated with the softball leagues over the last several years:

Year	Number of Leagues	Total Cost
19x1	5	$13,000
19x2	2	7,000
19x3	4	10,500
19x4	6	14,000
19x5	3	10,000

Each league offered requires its own paid supervisor and paid umpires as well as printed schedules and other copy work. Therefore, Amanda knows that there are some variable costs associated with the leagues. She would like to know the amount of variable cost per league and the total fixed cost per year associated with the softball program. This information would help her for planning purposes.

Required

1. Using the least-squares method, compute the variable cost per league and the total fixed cost per year for the softball program.
2. Express the cost data derived in (1) above in the linear equation form $Y = a + bX$.
3. Assume that Amanda would like to expand the softball program during the coming year to involve a total of seven leagues. Compute the expected total cost for the softball program. Can you see any problem with using the cost formula from (2) above to derive this total cost figure?
4. Prepare a scattergraph, and fit a regression line to the plotted points using the cost formula expressed in (2) above.

P5–14 Least-Squares Analysis; Contribution Income Statement "If we expect to stay competitive, we need better information for planning purposes and for control of our costs," said Sal Varney, president of Argyle Company. "The industry literature I've been reading lately says that the way to get better information is to use a contribution-type income statement that separates fixed and variable costs." Accordingly, Mr. Varney has directed the accounting department to prepare the following analysis:

Cost	Cost Formula
Cost of goods sold	$28 per unit
Sales commissions	12% of sales
Advertising expense	$150,000 per month
Administrative salaries	$80,000 per month
Billing expense.	?
Depreciation expense	$31,000 per month

The accounting department feels that billing expense is a mixed cost, containing both fixed and variable cost elements. A tabulation has been made of billing expense and sales over the last several months, as follows:

Month	Units Sold (000)	Billing Expense
January.	8	$15,200
February	10	17,000
March	13	19,400
April	16	21,800
May	14	20,000
June	11	18,200

Mr. Varney would like a cost formula developed for billing expense so that a contribution-type income statement can be prepared for management's use.

Required

1. Using the least-squares method, derive a cost formula for billing expense. (Since the "Units Sold" above are in thousands of units, the variable rate you compute will also be in thousands of units. It can be left in this form, or you can convert your variable rate to a per unit basis by dividing it by 1,000.)
2. Assume that the company plans to sell 15,000 units during July at a selling price of $60 per unit. Prepare a budgeted income statement for the month, using the contribution format.

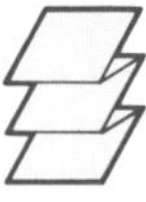

P5–15 High-Low Method of Cost Analysis Golden Company's total overhead costs at various levels of activity are presented below:

Month	Machine-Hours	Total Overhead Costs
March	50,000	$194,000
April	40,000	170,200
May	60,000	217,800
June	70,000	241,600

Assume that the overhead costs above consist of utilities, supervisory salaries, and maintenance. The proportion of these costs at the 40,000 machine-hour level of activity is:

Utilities (V)	$ 52,000
Supervisory salaries (F)	60,000
Maintenance (M)	58,200
Total overhead costs	$170,200

V = variable; F = fixed; M = mixed.

The company wants to break down the maintenance cost into its basic variable and fixed cost elements.

Required

1. As shown above, overhead costs in June amounted to $241,600. Determine how much of this consisted of maintenance cost. (Hint: To do this, it may be helpful to first determine how much of the $241,600 consisted of utilities and supervisory salaries. Think about the behavior of variable and fixed costs within the relevant range!)
2. By means of the high-low method, determine the cost formula for maintenance.
3. Express the company's total overhead costs in the linear equation form $Y = a + bX$.
4. What total overhead costs would you expect to be incurred at an operating activity level of 45,000 machine-hours?

P5–16 Contribution versus Traditional Income Statement House of Organs, Inc., purchases organs from a well-known manufacturer and distributes them at a retail level. The organs sell, on the average, for $2,500 each. The average cost of an organ from the manufacturer is $1,500.

House of Organs, Inc., has always kept careful records of its costs. The costs that the company incurs in a typical month are presented below:

Costs	**Cost Formula**
Selling:	
Advertising	$950 per month
Delivery of organs	$60 per organ sold
Sales salaries and commissions	$4,800 per month, plus 4% of sales
Utilities	$650 per month
Depreciation of sales facilities.	$5,000 per month
Administrative:	
Executive salaries	$13,500 per month
Depreciation of office equipment . . .	$900 per month
Clerical.	$2,500 per month, plus $40 per organ sold
Insurance.	$700 per month

During November 19x3, the company sold and delivered 60 organs.

Required

1. Prepare an income statement for the month of November 19x3, using the traditional format, with costs organized by function.
2. Redo (1) above, this time using the contribution format, with costs organized by behavior. Show costs and revenues on both a total and a per unit basis down through contribution margin.
3. Refer to the income statement you prepared in (2) above. Why might it be misleading to show the fixed costs on a per unit basis?

P5–17 Identifying Cost Patterns Below are a number of cost behavior patterns that might be found in a company's cost structure. The vertical axis on each graph represents cost, and the horizontal axis on each graph represents level of activity (volume).

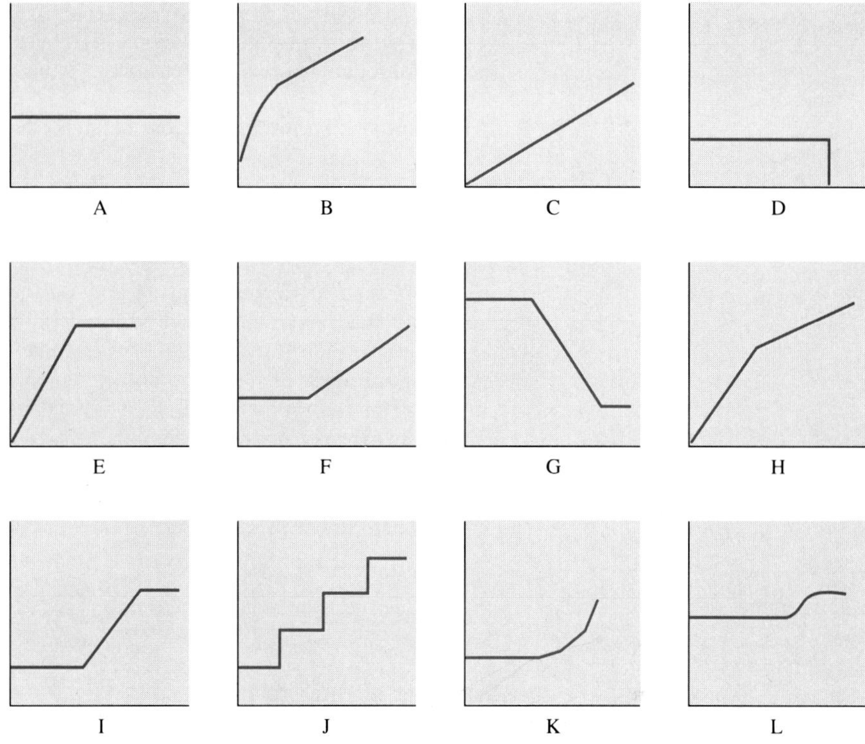

Required 1. For each of the following situations, identify the graph that illustrates the cost pattern involved. Any graph may be used more than once.

a. Cost of raw materials, where the cost decreases by 5 cents per unit for each of the first 100 units purchased, after which it remains constant at $2.50 per unit.

b. Electricity bill—a flat fixed charge, plus a variable cost after a certain number of kilowatt-hours are used.

c. City water bill, which is computed as follows:

First 1,000,000 gallons or less . . .	$1,000 flat fee
Next 10,000 gallons	0.003 per gallon used
Next 10,000 gallons	0.006 per gallon used
Next 10,000 gallons	0.009 per gallon used
Etc..	Etc.

d. Depreciation of equipment, where the amount is computed by the straight-line method. When the depreciation rate was established, it was anticipated that the obsolescence factor would be greater than the wear and tear factor.

e. Rent on a factory building donated by the city, where the agreement calls for a fixed fee payment unless 200,000 labor-hours are worked, in which case no rent need be paid.

f. Salaries of maintenance workers, where one maintenance worker is needed for every 1,000 hours of machine-hours or less (that is, 0 to 1,000 hours requires one maintenance worker, 1,001 to 2,000 hours requires two maintenance workers, etc.)

g. Cost of raw material used.

h. Rent on a factory building donated by the county, where the agreement calls for rent of $100,000 less $1 for each direct labor-hour worked in excess of 200,000 hours, but a minimum rental payment of $20,000 must be paid.

i. Use of a machine under a lease, where a minimum charge of $1,000 is paid for up to 400 hours of machine time. After 400 hours of machine time, an additional charge of $2 per hour is paid up to a maximum charge of $2,000 per period.

2. How would a knowledge of cost behavior patterns such as those above be of help to a manager in analyzing the cost structure of his or her firm?

(CPA, Adapted)

P5–18 Scattergraph and Least Squares In the past, Big Piney Resort has had great difficulty in predicting its costs at various levels of activity through the year. The reason is that the company has never attempted to study its cost structure by analyzing cost behavior patterns. The president has now become convinced that such an analysis is necessary if the company is to maintain its profits and its competitive position. Accordingly, an analysis of cost behavior patterns has been undertaken.

The company has managed to identify variable and fixed costs in all areas of its operation except for food services. Costs in this area do not seem to exhibit either a strictly variable or a strictly fixed pattern. Food costs over the past several months, along with the number of meals served, are given below:

Month	Number of Meals Served (000)	Total Food Cost
January	4	$18,000
February	5	21,000
March	6	24,000
April.	10	33,000
May	12	35,000
June	11	33,000
July	9	30,000
August	8	27,000
September	7	26,000

The president feels that the costs above must contain a mixture of variable and fixed cost elements. He has assigned you the responsibility of determining whether this is correct.

Required

1. Prepare a scattergraph using the data given above. Place cost on the vertical axis and activity (meals served) on the horizontal axis. Fit a regression line to the plotted points by simple visual inspection.
2. Is the president correct in assuming that food costs contain both variable and fixed cost elements? If so, what is the approximate total fixed cost and the approximate variable cost per meal served?
3. By use of the least-squares method, determine the variable and fixed cost elements in total food cost. (Since "Number of meals served" is in thousands of meals, the variable rate you compute will also be in thousands of meals. It can be left in this form, or you can convert your variable rate to a per meal basis by dividing it by 1,000.)
4. From the data determined in (3) above, express the cost formula for food in linear equation form.

P5–19 Manufacturing Statements; High-Low Method of Analysis NuWay, Inc., manufactures a single product. Selected data from the company's cost records for two recent months are given on the next page:

	Level of Activity	
	July—Low	October—High
Equivalent number of units produced	9,000	12,000
Cost of goods manufactured	$285,000	$390,000
Work in process inventory, beginning	14,000	22,000
Work in process inventory, ending	25,000	15,000
Direct materials cost per unit	15	15
Direct labor cost per unit.	6	6
Manufacturing overhead cost, total	?	?

The company's manufacturing overhead cost consists of both variable and fixed cost elements. In order to have data available for planning, management wants to determine how much of the overhead cost is variable with units produced and how much of it is fixed per year.

Required

1. For both July and October, determine the amount of manufacturing overhead cost added to production. The company had no under- or overapplied overhead in either month. (Hint: A useful way to proceed might be to construct a schedule of cost of goods manufactured.)
2. By means of the high-low method of cost analysis, determine the cost formula for manufacturing overhead. Express the variable portion of the formula in terms of a variable rate per unit of product.
3. If 9,500 units are produced during a month, what would be the cost of goods manufactured? (Assume that the company's beginning work in process inventory for the month is $16,000 and that its ending work in process inventory is $19,000. Also assume that there is no under- or overapplied overhead cost for the month.)

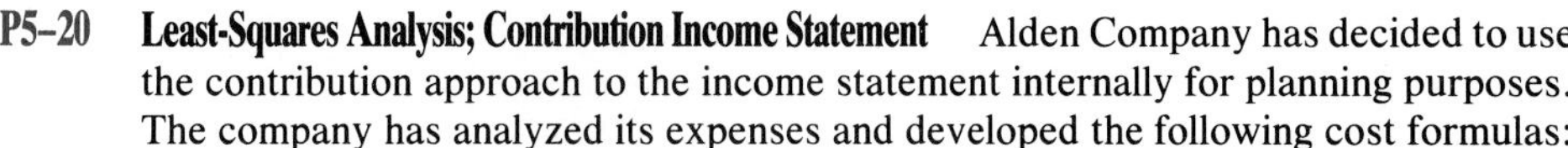

P5–20 Least-Squares Analysis; Contribution Income Statement Alden Company has decided to use the contribution approach to the income statement internally for planning purposes. The company has analyzed its expenses and developed the following cost formulas:

Cost	Cost Formula
Cost of goods sold	$20 per unit sold
Advertising expense	$170,000 per quarter
Sales commissions	5% of sales
Administrative salaries	$80,000 per quarter
Shipping expense.	?
Depreciation expense	$50,000 per quarter

Management has concluded that shipping expense is a mixed cost, containing both variable and fixed cost elements. Units sold and the related shipping expense over the last eight quarters are given below:

Quarter	Units Sold (000)	Shipping Expense
19x1:		
First	16	$160,000
Second	18	175,000
Third	23	210,000
Fourth	19	180,000
19x2:		
First	17	170,000
Second	20	190,000
Third	25	230,000
Fourth	22	205,000

Management would like a cost formula derived for shipping expense so that a budgeted income statement using the contribution approach can be prepared for the next quarter.

Required

1. Using the least-squares method, derive a cost formula for shipping expense. (Since the "Units Sold" above are in thousands of units, the variable rate you compute will also be in thousands of units. It can be left in this form, or you can convert your variable rate to a per unit basis by dividing it by 1,000.)
2. Assume that in the first quarter, 19x3, the company plans to sell 21,000 units at a selling price of $50 per unit. Prepare an income statement for the quarter, using the contribution format.

P5–21 Mixed Cost Analysis by Three Methods Sebolt Wire Company heats copper ingots to very high temperatures by placing the ingots in a large heat coil. The heated ingots are then run through a shaping machine that shapes the soft ingot into wire. Due to the long heat-up time involved, the coil is never turned off. When an ingot is placed in the coil, the temperature is raised to an even higher level, and then the coil is allowed to drop to the "waiting" temperature between ingots. Management needs to know the variable cost of power involved in heating an ingot and to know the fixed cost of power during "waiting" periods. The following data on ingots processed and power costs are available:

Month	Ingots	Power Cost
January	110	$5,500
February	90	4,500
March	80	4,400
April.	100	5,000
May	130	6,000
June	120	5,600
July	70	4,000
August	60	3,200
September	50	3,400
October	40	2,400

Required

1. Using the high-low method, calculate the cost formula for power cost. Express the formula in the form $Y = a + bX$.
2. Prepare a scattergraph by plotting ingots processed and power cost on a graph. Fit a regression line to the plotted points by visual inspection, and determine the cost formula for power cost.
3. Using the least-squares method, calculate the cost formula for power cost. Again express the formula in the form $Y = a + bX$. (Round the variable rate to two decimal places and the fixed rate to the nearest whole dollar.)
4. Prepare a simple table showing the total fixed cost per month and the variable rate per ingot under each of the three methods used above. Then comment on the accuracy and usefulness of the data derived by each method.

CASES

C5–22 Missing Data; Mixed Cost Analysis by Three Methods While you are taking a well-deserved nap, your roommate uses some papers on your desk to soak up some liquid that has spilled on the floor. Upon awakening, you are horrified to discover that part of the papers consisted of a take-home quiz that you had only partially completed before lying down. The quiz itself has been completely destroyed. Only the following bits of information are readable from your answer sheet:

Month	Units Sold (X)	Total Cost (Y)	?	?
March	?	$?	$ 11,200	?
April.	?	?	20,400	36
May	7	?	?	?
June	?	4,100	36,900	81
July	?	3,600	28,800	?
August.	5	?	?	?
September	?	2,000	6,000	9
Totals	?	$?	$142,800	?

(1) $\Sigma XY = a\Sigma X + b\Sigma ?$
(2) $\Sigma Y = ?a + b\Sigma X$

(1) $142,800 = ?a + ?b
(2) $? = ?a + ?b

(1)		$142,800 = ?a + ?b
(2)	Multiply by 6:	$? = ?a + ?b
	Subtract (2) from (1):	$? = ?b
		$? = b

Therefore, the variable rate is ??? per unit sold. To compute the monthly fixed cost, substitute in equation (2):

$? = ?a + ?b
$? = ?a + $12,600
$? = ?a
$1,400 = a

The fixed cost is therefore $1,400 per month.

After chasing your roommate from the apartment with an iron skillet, you suddenly realize that the quiz is due at your instructor's office in just 90 minutes. You also realize that you will have to somehow recreate the data that had been contained on the quiz page and prepare an appropriate solution. Working is especially hard with your roommate pounding on the door trying to get in from the freezing weather, but you are spurred on by the realization that your instructor doesn't accept late work and your grade in the course is already somewhat shaky.

Before starting reconstruction of the data, you remember from your earlier work that the total cost for May can be obtained by applying the cost formula (as derived by the least-squares method) to that month's activity.

Required

1. Copy all of the information above onto a clean, dry piece of paper. Complete the least-squares analysis by finding *all* items of missing data. (Your instructor won't accept incomplete work.)
2. Since you are uncertain whether your answer to (1) is correct, you decide to "check out" your work by doing a high-low analysis of the data. Complete the high-low analysis, and state the cost formula derived by this analytical method.
3. You are shocked to find that the cost formula derived by the high-low method is different from that derived by the least-squares method. Therefore, you decide to prepare a scattergraph as a final check on your work.
   a. Prepare a scattergraph, and fit a regression line to the plotted points by simple visual inspection.
   b. By analyzing the data on your scattergraph, compute the approximate fixed cost per month and the approximate variable rate per unit sold.

4. Looking at the scattergraph prepared in (3) above, you suddenly realize why the cost formula derived by the high-low method is so different from the cost formula derived by the least-squares method. You decide to really impress your instructor by making a clear and concise statement on your answer sheet as to the reason for this difference. Draft an appropriate statement.

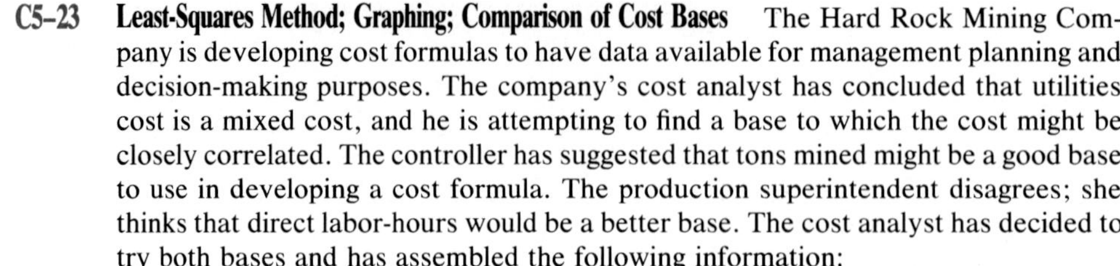

C5–23 Least-Squares Method; Graphing; Comparison of Cost Bases The Hard Rock Mining Company is developing cost formulas to have data available for management planning and decision-making purposes. The company's cost analyst has concluded that utilities cost is a mixed cost, and he is attempting to find a base to which the cost might be closely correlated. The controller has suggested that tons mined might be a good base to use in developing a cost formula. The production superintendent disagrees; she thinks that direct labor-hours would be a better base. The cost analyst has decided to try both bases and has assembled the following information:

Quarter	Tons Mined (000)	Direct Labor-Hours (000)	Utilities Cost
19x4:			
First	15	5	$ 50,000
Second	11	3	45,000
Third	21	4	60,000
Fourth	12	6	75,000
19x5:			
First	18	10	100,000
Second	25	9	105,000
Third	30	8	85,000
Fourth	28	11	120,000

Required

1. Using tons mined as the independent (X) variable:
   a. Determine a cost formula for utilities cost using the least-squares method. (The variable rate you compute will be in thousands of tons. It can be left in this form, or you can convert your variable rate to a per ton basis by dividing it by 1,000.)
   b. Prepare a scattergraph and plot the observed points of tons mined and utilities cost. (Place cost on the vertical axis and tons mined on the horizontal axis.) Fit a regression line to the plotted points using the cost formula determined in (*a*) above.
   c. Scrutinize the data on the scattergraph. Would you expect a high or a low correlation between utilities cost and tons mined?
2. Using direct labor-hours as the independent (X) variable, repeat the computations in (*a*), (*b*), and (*c*) above.
3. Would you recommend that the company use tons mined or direct labor-hours as a base for planning utilities cost?

PART II

THE CENTRAL THEME
PLANNING AND CONTROL

6
Cost-Volume-Profit Relationships

7
Segmented Reporting and the Contribution Approach to Costing

8
Profit Planning

9
Control through Standard Costs

10
Flexible Budgets and Overhead Analysis

11
Control of Decentralized Operations

6

Cost-Volume-Profit Relationships

LEARNING OBJECTIVES

After studying Chapter 6, you should be able to:

1 Explain how changes in activity affect contribution margin and net income.

2 Compute the contribution margin ratio (CM ratio) and use it to compute changes in contribution margin and net income.

3 Compute and explain operating leverage.

4 Show the effects on contribution margin of changes in variable costs, fixed costs, selling price, and volume.

5 Compute the break-even point by both the equation method and the unit contribution method.

6 Prepare a cost-volume-profit (CVP) graph and explain the significance of each of its components.

7 Compute the margin of safety (MS) and explain its significance.

8 Explain the effects of shifts in the sales mix on contribution margin and the break-even point.

9 Define or explain the key terms listed at the end of the chapter.

Cost-volume-profit (CVP) analysis involves a study of the interrelationship between the following factors:

1. Prices of products.
2. Volume or level of activity.
3. Per unit variable costs.
4. Total fixed costs.
5. Mix of products sold.

CVP analysis is a key factor in many decisions, including choice of product lines, pricing of products, marketing strategy, and utilization of productive facilities. The concept is so pervasive in managerial accounting that it touches on virtually everything that a manager does. Because of its wide range of usefulness, CVP analysis is undoubtedly the best tool the manager has for discovering the untapped profit potential that may exist in an organization.

THE BASICS OF COST-VOLUME-PROFIT (CVP) ANALYSIS

Our study of CVP analysis begins where our study of cost behavior in the preceding chapter left off—with the contribution income statement. The contribution income statement has a number of interesting characteristics that can be helpful to the manager in trying to judge the impact on profits of changes in selling price, cost, or volume. To demonstrate these characteristics, we shall use the following income statement of Norton Company, a small manufacturer of microwave ovens:

NORTON COMPANY
Contribution Income Statement
For the Month of June 19x1

	Total	Per Unit
Sales (400 ovens)	$100,000	$250
Less variable expenses	60,000	150
Contribution margin	40,000	$100
Less fixed expenses	35,000	
Net income	$ 5,000	

For purposes of discussion, we shall assume that Norton Company produces only one model of oven.

Notice that the company expresses its sales, variable expenses, and contribution margin on a per unit basis as well as in total. This is commonly done on those income statements prepared for management's use internally, since, as we shall see, it facilitates profitability analysis.

Contribution Margin

As explained in Chapter 5, contribution margin is the amount remaining from sales revenue after variable expenses have been deducted that can be used to contribute toward the covering of fixed expenses and then toward profits for the period. Notice the sequence here—contribution margin is used first to cover the fixed expenses, and then whatever remains after the fixed expenses are covered goes toward profits. If the contribution margin is not sufficient to cover the fixed expenses, then a loss occurs for the period. To illustrate, assume that by the middle of a particular month Norton Company has been able to sell only one oven. At that point, the company's income statement will appear as follows:

	Total	Per Unit
Sales (1 oven)	$ 250	$250
Less variable expenses	150	150
Contribution margin	100	$100
Less fixed expenses	35,000	
Net loss	$(34,900)	

For each additional oven that the company is able to sell during the month, $100 more in contribution margin will become available to help cover the fixed expenses. If a second oven is sold, for example, then the total contribution margin will increase by $100 (to a total of $200) and the company's loss will decrease by $100, to $34,800:

	Total	Per Unit
Sales (2 ovens)	$ 500	$250
Less variable expenses	300	150
Contribution margin	200	$100
Less fixed expenses	35,000	
Net loss	$(34,800)	

If enough ovens can be sold to generate $35,000 in contribution margin, then all of the fixed costs will be covered and the company will have managed to at least *break even* for the month—that is, to show neither profit nor loss but just cover all of its costs. To reach this **break-even point,** the company will have to sell 350 ovens in a month, since each oven sold yields $100 in contribution margin:

	Total	Per Unit
Sales (350 ovens)	$87,500	$250
Less variable expenses	52,500	150
Contribution margin	35,000	$100
Less fixed expenses	35,000	
Net income	$ 0	

Computation of the break-even point is discussed in detail later in the chapter; for the moment, we can note that it can be defined either as the point where total sales revenue equals total expenses, variable and fixed, or as the point where total contribution margin equals total fixed expenses.

Once the break-even point has been reached, net income will increase by the unit contribution margin for each additional unit sold. If 351 ovens are sold in a month, for example, then we can expect that the net income for the month will be $100, since the company will have sold 1 oven more than the number needed to break even:

	Total	Per Unit
Sales (351 ovens)	$87,750	$250
Less variable expenses	52,650	150
Contribution margin	35,100	$100
Less fixed expenses	35,000	
Net income	$ 100	

If 352 ovens are sold (2 ovens above the break-even point), then we can expect that the net income for the month will be $200, and so forth. To know what the profits will be at various levels of activity, therefore, it is not necessary for a manager to prepare a whole series of income statements. The manager can simply take the number of units to be sold over the break-even point and multiply that number by the unit contribution margin. The result will represent the anticipated profits for the period. Or, if an increase in sales is planned and the manager wants to know what the impact of that increase will be on profits, he or she can simply multiply the increase in units sold by the unit contribution margin. The result will be the expected increase in profits. To illustrate, if Norton Company is selling 400 ovens per month and plans to increase sales to 425 ovens per month, the impact on profits will be:

Increased number of ovens to be sold	25
Contribution margin per oven	×$100
Increase in net income	$2,500

As proof:

	Sales Volume			
	400 Ovens	425 Ovens	Difference 25 Ovens	Per Unit
Sales	$100,000	$106,250	$6,250	$250
Less variable expenses	60,000	63,750	3,750	150
Contribution margin	40,000	42,500	2,500	$100
Less fixed expenses	35,000	35,000	–0–	
Net income	$ 5,000	$ 7,500	$2,500	

To summarize the series of examples in this section, we can say that the contribution margin first goes to cover an organization's fixed expenses, and that the potential loss represented by these fixed expenses is reduced successively by the unit contribution margin for each incremental unit sold up to the break-even point. Once the break-even point has been reached, then overall net income is increased by the unit contribution margin for each incremental unit sold from that point forward.

Contribution Margin Ratio (CM Ratio)

In addition to being expressed on a per unit basis, revenues, variable expenses, and contribution margin for Norton Company can also be expressed on a percentage basis:

	Total	Per Unit	Percent
Sales (400 ovens)	$100,000	$250	100
Less variable expenses	60,000	150	60
Contribution margin	40,000	$100	40
Less fixed expenses	35,000		
Net income	$ 5,000		

The percentage of contribution margin to total sales is referred to either as the **contribution margin ratio** (CM ratio) or as the **profit-volume ratio** (P/V ratio). This ratio is extremely useful in that it shows how the contribution margin will be affected by a given dollar change in total sales. To illustrate, notice that Norton Company has a CM ratio of 40 percent. This means that for each dollar increase in sales, total contribution margin will increase by 40 cents ($1 sales × CM ratio of 40 percent). Net income will also increase by 40 cents, assuming that there are no changes in fixed costs.

As this illustration suggests, *the impact on net income of any given dollar change in total sales can be computed in seconds by simply applying the CM ratio to the dollar change*. If Norton Company plans a $30,000 increase in sales during the coming month, for example, management can expect contribution margin to increase by $12,000 ($30,000 increased sales × CM ratio of 40 percent). As we noted above, net income will increase by a like amount if the fixed costs do not change. As proof:

	Sales Volume			
	Present	Expected	Increase	Percent
Sales	$100,000	$130,000	$30,000	100
Less variable expenses	60,000	78,000*	18,000	60
Contribution margin	40,000	52,000	12,000	40
Less fixed expenses	35,000	35,000	–0–	
Net income	$ 5,000	$ 17,000	$12,000	

* $130,000 × 60% = $78,000.

Many managers find the CM ratio easier to work with than the unit contribution margin figure, particularly where a company has multiple product lines. This is because an item in ratio form facilitates comparisons between products. Other things being equal, the manager will search out those product lines that have the highest CM ratios. The reason, of course, is that for a given dollar increase in sales these product lines will yield the greatest amount of contribution margin toward the covering of fixed costs and toward profits.

Cost Structure

We stated in the preceding chapter that *cost structure* refers to the relative proportion of fixed and variable costs in an organization. We also stated that an organization often has some latitude in trading off between fixed and variable costs. Such a trade-off is possible, for example, by automating facilities rather than using direct labor workers.

When the manager does have latitude in trading off between fixed and variable costs, which cost structure is better—high variable costs and low fixed costs, or the opposite? No categorical answer to this question is possible; we can simply note that there may be advantages either way, depending on the specific circumstances involved. To show what we mean by this statement, refer to the income statements given below for Company X and Company Y. Notice that the two companies have very different cost structures—Company X has high variable costs and low fixed costs, with the opposite true for Company Y.

	Company X		Company Y	
	Amount	Percent	Amount	Percent
Sales	$100,000	100	$100,000	100
Less variable expenses	60,000	60	30,000	30
Contribution margin	40,000	40	70,000	70
Less fixed expenses	30,000		60,000	
Net income	$ 10,000		$ 10,000	

The question as to which company has the better cost structure depends on many factors, including the long-run trend in sales, year-to-year fluctuations in the level of sales, and the attitude of the managers toward risk. If sales are expected to trend above $100,000 in the future, then Company Y probably has the better cost structure. The reason is that its CM ratio is higher, and its profits will therefore increase more rapidly as sales increase. To illustrate, assume that each company experiences a 10 percent increase in sales. The new income statements will be:

	Company X		Company Y	
	Amount	Percent	Amount	Percent
Sales	$110,000	100	$110,000	100
Less variable expenses	66,000	60	33,000	30
Contribution margin	44,000	40	77,000	70
Less fixed expenses	30,000		60,000	
Net income	$ 14,000		$ 17,000	

As we would expect, for the same dollar increase in sales, Company Y has experienced a greater increase in net income due to its higher CM ratio.

But what if $100,000 represents maximum sales for the two companies, and what if sales can be expected to drop well below $100,000 from time to time? Under these circumstances, Company X probably has the better cost structure. There are two reasons why this is so. First, due to its lower CM ratio, Company X will not lose contribution margin as rapidly as Company Y when sales fall off. Thus, Company X's income will tend to show more stability. Second, Company X has lower fixed costs, which suggests that it will not incur losses as quickly as Company Y in periods of sharply declining sales.

If sales fluctuate above and below $100,000, it becomes more difficult to tell which company is in a better position.

To summarize, Company Y will experience wider movements in net income as changes take place in sales, with greater profits in good years and greater losses in bad years. Company X will enjoy somewhat greater stability in net income, but it will do so at the risk of losing substantial profits if sales trend upward in the long run.

Operating Leverage

To the scientist, leverage explains how one is able to move a large object with a small force. To the manager, leverage explains how one is able to achieve a large increase in profits (in percentage terms) with only a small increase in sales and/or assets. One type of leverage that the manager uses to do this is known as *operating leverage*.[1]

Operating leverage is a measure of the extent to which fixed costs are being used in an organization. It is greatest in companies that have a high proportion of fixed costs in relation to variable costs. Conversely, operating leverage is lowest in companies that have a low proportion of fixed costs in relation to variable costs. If a company has high operating leverage (that is, a high proportion of fixed costs in relation to variable costs), then profits will be very sensitive to changes in sales. Just a small percentage increase (or decrease) in sales can yield a large percentage increase (or decrease) in profits.

Operating leverage can be illustrated by returning to the data in the preceding section. Company Y has a higher proportion of fixed costs in relation to its variable costs than does Company X, although *total* costs are the same in the two companies at a $100,000 sales level. Observe that with a 10 percent increase in sales (from $100,000 to $110,000 in each company), net income in Company Y increases by 70 percent (from $10,000 to $17,000), whereas net income in Company X increases by only 40 percent (from $10,000 to $14,000). Thus, for a 10 percent increase in sales, Company Y experiences a much greater percentage increase in profits than does Company X. The reason is that Company Y has greater operating leverage as a result of the greater amount of fixed cost used in the production and sale of its product.

The **degree of operating leverage** existing in a company at a given level of sales can be measured by the following formula:

$$\frac{\text{Contribution margin}}{\text{Net income}} = \text{Degree of operating leverage}$$

The degree of operating leverage is a measure, at a given level of sales, of how a percentage change in sales volume will affect profits. To illustrate, the degree of operating leverage existing in Company X and Company Y at a $100,000 sales level would be:

$$\text{Company X: } \frac{\$40{,}000}{\$10{,}000} = 4$$

$$\text{Company Y: } \frac{\$70{,}000}{\$10{,}000} = 7$$

By interpretation, these figures tell us that *for a given percentage change in sales* we can expect a change four times as great in the net income of Company X and a change seven times as great in the net income of Company

[1] There are two types of leverage—operating and financial. Financial leverage is discussed in Chapter 18.

Y. Thus, if sales increase by 10 percent, then we can expect the net income in Company X to increase by four times this amount, or by 40 percent, and the net income in Company Y to increase by seven times this amount, or by 70 percent.

	(1) Percent Increase in Sales	(2) Degree of Operating Leverage	(3) Percent Increase in Net Income (1) × (2)
Company X	10	4	40
Company Y	10	7	70

These computations explain why the 10 percent increase in sales mentioned earlier caused the net income of Company X to increase from $10,000 to $14,000 (an increase of 40 percent) and the net income of Company Y to increase from $10,000 to $17,000 (an increase of 70 percent).

The degree of operating leverage in a company is greatest at sales levels near the break-even point and decreases as sales and profits rise. This can be seen from the tabulation below, which shows the degree of operating leverage for Company X at various sales levels. (Data used earlier for Company X are shown in color.)

Sales	$75,000	$80,000	$100,000	$150,000	$225,000
Less variable expenses	45,000	48,000	60,000	90,000	135,000
Contribution margin (*a*)	30,000	32,000	40,000	60,000	90,000
Less fixed expenses	30,000	30,000	30,000	30,000	30,000
Net income (*b*)	$ -0-	$ 2,000	$ 10,000	$ 30,000	$ 60,000
Degree of operating leverage, (*a*) ÷ (*b*)	∞	16	4	2	1.5

Thus, a 10 percent increase in sales would increase profits by only 15 percent (10% × 1.5) if the company were operating at a $225,000 sales level, as compared to the 40 percent increase we computed earlier at the $100,000 sales level. The degree of operating leverage will continue to decrease the farther the company moves from its break-even point. At the break-even point, the degree of operating leverage will be infinitely large ($30,000 contribution margin ÷ $0 net income = ∞).

The operating leverage concept provides the manager with a tool that can signify quickly what impact various percentage changes in sales will have on profits, without the necessity of preparing detailed income statements. As shown by our examples, the effects of operating leverage can be dramatic. If a company is fairly near its break-even point, then even small increases in sales can yield large increases in profits. *This explains why management will often work very hard for only a nominal increase in sales volume*. If the degree of operating leverage is 5, then a 6 percent increase in sales would translate into a 30 percent increase in profits.

Some Applications of CVP Concepts

The concepts that we have developed on the preceding pages have many applications in planning and decision making. We will now continue with the example of Norton Company (a manufacturer of microwave ovens) to illustrate some of these applications. Norton Company's basic cost and revenue data are:

	Per Unit	Percent
Sales price	$250	100
Less variable expenses	150	60
Contribution margin	$100	40

Recall that fixed expenses are $35,000 per month. We will use these data to show the effects of changes in variable costs, fixed costs, sales price, and sales volume on a company's profitability.

Change in Fixed Costs and Sales Volume Assume that Norton Company is currently selling 400 ovens per month (monthly sales of $100,000). The sales manager feels that a $10,000 increase in the monthly advertising budget would increase monthly sales by $30,000. Should the advertising budget be increased?

Solution

Expected total contribution margin:	
$130,000 × 40% CM ratio	$52,000
Present total contribution margin:	
$100,000 × 40% CM ratio	40,000
Incremental contribution margin	12,000
Change in fixed costs:	
Less incremental advertising expense	10,000
Increased net income	$ 2,000

Yes, the advertising budget should be increased.

Since in this case only the fixed costs and the sales volume are changing, the solution can be presented in an even shorter format, as follows:

Alternative Solution

Incremental contribution margin:	
$30,000 × 40% CM ratio	$12,000
Less incremental advertising expense	10,000
Increased net income	$ 2,000

Notice that this approach does not depend on a knowledge of what sales were previously. Also notice that it is unnecessary under either approach to prepare an income statement. Both of the solutions above involve an **incremental analysis** in that they consider only those items of revenue, cost, and volume that will change if the new program is implemented. Although in each case a new income statement could have been prepared, most managers would prefer the incremental approach. The reason is that it is simpler and more direct, and it permits the decision maker to focus attention on the specific items involved in the decision.

Change in Variable Costs and Sales Volume Refer to the original data. Assume again that Norton Company is currently selling 400 ovens per month. Management is contemplating the use of less costly components in the manufacture of the ovens, which would reduce variable costs by $25 per oven. However, the sales manager predicts that the lower overall quality would reduce sales to only 350 ovens per month. Should the change be made?

Solution The $25 decrease in variable costs will cause the contribution margin per unit to increase from $100 to $125.

Expected total contribution margin:	
350 ovens × $125	$43,750
Present total contribution margin:	
400 ovens × $100	40,000
Increase in total contribution margin	$ 3,750

Yes, the less costly components should be used in the manufacture of the ovens. Since the fixed costs will not change, net income will increase by the $3,750 increase in contribution margin shown above.

Change in Fixed Cost, Sales Price, and Sales Volume Refer to the original data. Assume again that Norton Company is currently selling 400 ovens per month. To increase sales, management would like to cut the selling price by $20 per oven and increase the advertising budget by $15,000 per month. Management feels that if these two steps are taken, unit sales will increase by 50 percent. Should the changes be made?

Solution A decrease of $20 per oven in the selling price will cause the unit contribution margin to decrease from $100 to $80.

Expected total contribution margin:	
400 ovens × 150% × $80	$48,000
Present total contribution margin:	
400 ovens × $100	40,000
Incremental contribution margin	8,000
Change in fixed costs:	
Less incremental advertising expense	15,000
Reduction in net income	$ (7,000)

No, the changes should not be made. The same solution can be obtained by preparing comparative income statements:

	Present 400 Ovens per Month		Expected 600 Ovens per Month		
	Total	**Per Unit**	**Total**	**Per Unit**	**Difference**
Sales	$100,000	$250	$138,000	$230	$38,000
Less variable expenses	60,000	150	90,000	150	30,000
Contribution margin.	40,000	$100	48,000	$ 80	8,000
Less fixed expenses.	35,000		50,000*		15,000
Net income (loss).	$ 5,000		$ (2,000)		$ (7,000)

* $35,000 + $15,000 = $50,000.

Notice that the answer is the same as that obtained by the incremental analysis above.

Change in Variable Cost, Fixed Cost, and Sales Volume Refer to the original data. Assume again that Norton Company is currently selling 400 ovens per month. The sales manager would like to place the sales staff on a commission basis of $15 per oven sold, rather than on flat salaries that now total

$6,000 per month. The sales manager is confident that the change will increase monthly sales by 15 percent. Should the change be made?

Solution Changing the sales staff from a salaried basis to a commission basis will affect both fixed and variable costs. Fixed costs will decrease by $6,000, from $35,000 to $29,000. Variable costs will increase by $15, from $150 to $165, and the unit contribution margin will decrease from $100 to $85.

Expected total contribution margin:	
400 ovens × 115% × $85	$39,100
Present total contribution margin:	
400 ovens × $100	40,000
Decrease in total contribution margin.	(900)
Change in fixed costs:	
Add salaries avoided if a commission is paid . . .	6,000
Increase in net income	$ 5,100

Yes, the changes should be made. Again, the same answer can be obtained by preparing comparative income statements:

	Present 400 Ovens per Month		Expected 460 Ovens per Month		Difference: Increase or (Decrease) in Net Income
	Total	Per Unit	Total	Per Unit	
Sales	$100,000	$250	$115,000*	$250	$ 15,000
Less variable expenses	60,000	150	75,900	165	(15,900)
Contribution margin.	40,000	$100	39,100	$ 85	(900)
Less fixed expenses.	35,000		29,000		6,000
Net income	$ 5,000		$ 10,100		$ 5,100

* 400 ovens × 115% = 460 ovens.
460 ovens × $250 = $115,000.

Change in Regular Sales Price Refer to the original data. Assume again that Norton Company is currently selling 400 ovens per month. The company has an opportunity to make a bulk sale of 150 ovens to a wholesaler if an acceptable price can be worked out. This sale would not disturb regular sales currently being made. What price per oven should be quoted to the wholesaler if Norton Company wants to increase its monthly profits by $3,000?

Solution

Variable cost per oven	$150
Desired profit per oven:	
$3,000 ÷ 150 ovens	20
Quoted price per oven	$170

Notice that no element of fixed cost is included in the computation. This is because Norton Company's regular business puts it beyond the break-even point, and the fixed costs are therefore covered. Thus, the quoted price on the special order only needs to be large enough to cover the variable costs involved with the order and to provide the desired $3,000 contribution margin. As shown above, this is $170 per unit, consisting of $150 in variable costs and $20 per unit in contribution margin.

If Norton Company had been operating at a loss rather than at a profit, how would the price on the new ovens have been computed? A loss would have meant that a portion of the fixed costs was not being covered by regular sales. Therefore, it would have been necessary to quote a price on the 150 new ovens that was high enough to include part or all of these unrecovered fixed costs (as represented by the loss), in addition to the variable costs and the desired profit on the sale.

To illustrate this point, assume that Norton Company is reporting a loss of $6,000 per month and that the company wants to turn this loss into a profit of $3,000 per month. Under these circumstances, the quoted price on the 150 new ovens would be computed as shown below:

Solution

Variable cost per oven	$150
Present net loss:	
$6,000 ÷ 150 ovens	40
Desired profit:	
$3,000 ÷ 150 ovens	20
Quoted price per oven	$210

The $210 price we have computed represents a substantial discount from the $250 regular selling price per oven. Thus, both the wholesaler and the company would benefit from the bulk order.

Importance of the Contribution Margin

As stated in the introduction to the chapter, CVP analysis seeks the most profitable combination of variable costs, fixed costs, selling price, and sales volume. The examples that we have just provided show that the effect on the contribution margin is a major consideration in deciding on the most profitable combination of these factors. We have seen that profits can sometimes be improved by reducing the contribution margin if fixed costs can be reduced by a greater amount. More commonly, however, we have seen that the way to improve profits is to increase the total contribution margin figure. Sometimes this can be done by reducing the selling price and thereby increasing volume; sometimes it can be done by increasing the fixed costs (such as advertising) and thereby increasing volume; and sometimes it can be done by trading off variable and fixed costs with appropriate changes in volume. Many other combinations of factors are possible.

The size of the unit contribution margin figure (and the size of the CM ratio) will have a heavy influence on what steps a company is willing to take to improve profits. For example, the greater the unit contribution margin for a product, the greater is the amount that a company will be willing to spend in order to increase sales of the product by a given percentage. This explains in part why companies with high unit contribution margins (such as auto manufacturers) advertise so heavily, while companies with low unit contribution margins (such as dishware manufacturers) tend to spend much less for advertising.

In short, the effect on the contribution margin holds the key to most cost-revenue decisions in a company.

BREAK-EVEN ANALYSIS

CVP analysis is sometimes referred to simply as break-even analysis. This is unfortunate, because break-even analysis is just one part of the entire CVP concept. However, it is often a key part, and it can give the manager many insights into the data with which he or she is working.

As a basis for discussion, we will continue with the example of Norton Company. Recall that the selling price is $250 per oven, the variable expenses are $150 per oven, and the fixed costs total $35,000 per month.

Break-Even Computations

Earlier in the chapter, we stated that the break-even point can be defined equally well as the point where total sales revenue equals total expenses, variable and fixed, or as the point where total contribution margin equals total fixed expenses. As suggested by these two definitions of the break-even point, break-even analysis can be approached in two ways—first, by the *equation method;* and second, by the *unit contribution method*.

The Equation Method The **equation method** centers on the contribution approach to the income statement illustrated earlier in the chapter. The format of this statement can be expressed in equation form as:

$$\text{Sales} = \text{Variable expenses} + \text{Fixed expenses} + \text{Profits}$$

At the break-even point, profits will be zero. Therefore, the break-even point can be computed by finding that point where sales just equal the total of the variable expenses plus the fixed expenses. For Norton Company, this would be:

$$\text{Sales} = \text{Variable expenses} + \text{Fixed expenses} + \text{Profits}$$

$$\begin{aligned} \$250X &= \$150X + \$35{,}000 + 0 \\ \$100X &= \$35{,}000 \\ X &= 350 \text{ ovens} \end{aligned}$$

where:

$$\begin{aligned} X &= \text{break-even point in ovens} \\ \$250 &= \text{unit sales price} \\ \$150 &= \text{unit variable expenses} \\ \$35{,}000 &= \text{total fixed expenses} \end{aligned}$$

After the break-even point in units sold has been computed, the break-even point in sales dollars can be computed by multiplying the break-even level of units by the sales price per unit:

$$350 \text{ ovens} \times \$250 = \$87{,}500$$

At times, the *dollar* relationship between variable expenses and sales may not be known. In these cases, if one knows the *percentage* relationship between variable expenses and sales, then the break-even point can still be computed, as follows:

$$\text{Sales} = \text{Variable expenses} + \text{Fixed expenses} + \text{Profits}$$

$$\begin{aligned} X &= 0.60X + \$35{,}000 + 0 \\ 0.40X &= \$35{,}000 \\ X &= \$87{,}500 \end{aligned}$$

where:

$$\begin{aligned} X &= \text{break-even point in sales dollars} \\ 0.60 &= \text{variable expenses as a percentage of sales} \\ \$35{,}000 &= \text{total fixed expenses} \end{aligned}$$

Firms often have data available only in percentage form, and the approach we have just illustrated must then be used to find the break-even point. Notice that use of percentages in the equation yields a break-even point in sales dollars rather than in units sold. The break-even point in units sold would be:

$$\$87{,}500 \div \$250 = 350 \text{ ovens}$$

The Unit Contribution Method The **unit contribution method** is actually just a variation of the equation method already described. The approach centers on the idea discussed earlier that each unit sold provides a certain amount of contribution margin that goes toward the covering of fixed costs. To find how many units must be sold to break even, one must divide the total fixed costs by the contribution margin being generated by each unit sold:

$$\frac{\text{Fixed expenses}}{\text{Unit contribution margin}} = \text{Break-even point}$$

Each oven that Norton Company sells generates a contribution margin of \$100 (\$250 selling price, less \$150 variable expenses). Since the total fixed expenses are \$35,000, the break-even point is:

$$\frac{\text{Fixed expenses}}{\text{Unit contribution margin}} = \frac{\$35{,}000}{\$100} = 350 \text{ ovens}$$

If only the percentage relationship between variable expenses, contribution margin, and sales is known, the computation becomes:

$$\frac{\text{Fixed expenses}}{\text{CM ratio}} = \frac{\$35{,}000}{40\%} = \$87{,}500$$

This approach to break-even analysis is particularly useful in those situations where a company has multiple product lines and wishes to compute a single break-even point for the company as a whole. More is said on this point in a later section titled "The Concept of Sales Mix."

CVP Relationships in Graphic Form

The cost data relating to Norton Company's microwave ovens can be expressed in graphic form by preparing a **cost-volume-profit (CVP) graph.** A CVP graph can be very helpful in that it highlights CVP relationships over wide ranges of activity and gives managers a perspective that can be obtained in no other way. Such graphing is sometimes referred to as preparing a **break-even chart.** This is correct to the extent that the break-even point is clearly shown on the graph. The reader should be aware, however, that a graphing of CVP data highlights CVP relationships throughout the *entire* relevant range—not just at the break-even point.

Preparing the CVP Graph Preparing a CVP graph (sometimes called a *break-even chart*) involves three steps. These steps are keyed to the graph in Exhibit 6–1.

1. Draw a line parallel to the volume axis, to represent total fixed expenses. For Norton Company, total fixed expenses are $35,000.
2. Choose some volume of sales, and plot the point representing total expenses (fixed and variable) at the activity level you have selected. In Exhibit 6–1, we have chosen a volume of 600 ovens. Total expenses at that activity level would be:

Fixed expenses	$ 35,000
Variable expenses (600 ovens × $150) . . .	90,000
Total expenses.	$125,000

EXHIBIT 6–1
Preparing the CVP Graph

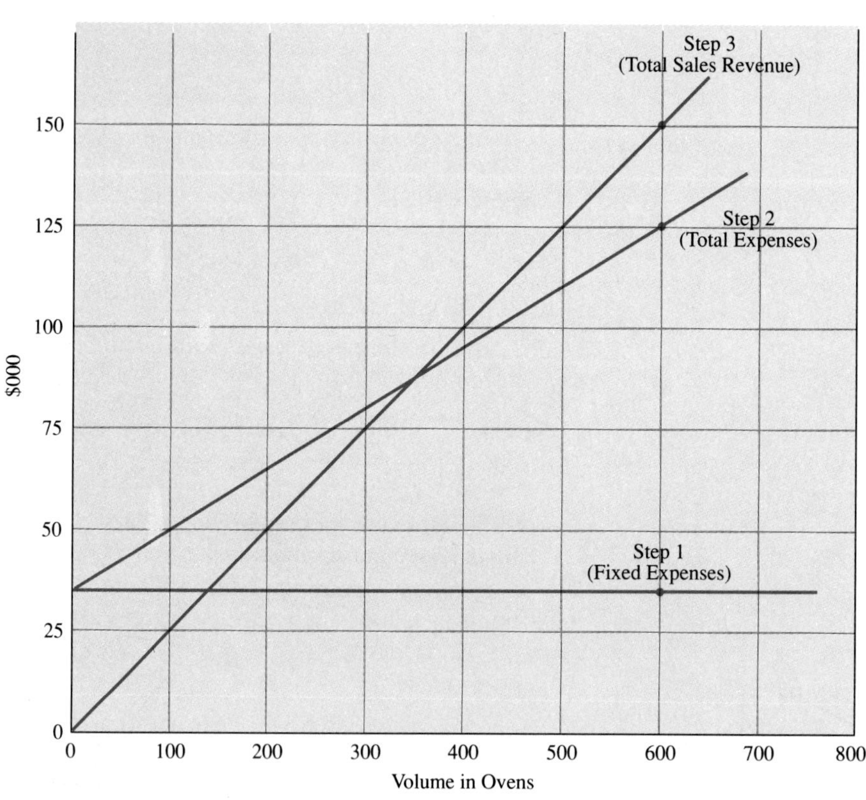

After the point has been plotted, draw a line through it back to the point where the fixed expenses line intersects the dollars axis.

3. Again choose some volume of sales, and plot the point representing total sales dollars at the activity level you have selected. In Exhibit 6–1, we have again chosen a volume of 600 ovens. Sales at that activity level total \$150,000 (600 ovens × \$250). Draw a line through this point back to the origin.

The interpretation of the completed CVP graph is given in Exhibit 6–2. The anticipated profit or loss at any given level of sales is measured by the vertical distance between the total revenue line (sales) and the total expenses line (variable expenses plus fixed expenses).

The break-even point is where the total revenue and total expenses lines cross. The break-even point of 350 ovens in Exhibit 6–2 agrees with the break-even point obtained for Norton Company in earlier computations.

An Alternative Format Some managers prefer an alternative format to the CVP graph, as illustrated in Exhibit 6–3.

Note that the total revenue and total expenses lines are the same as in Exhibit 6–2. However, the new format in Exhibit 6–3 places the fixed expenses above the variable expenses, thereby allowing the contribution

EXHIBIT 6–2
The Completed CVP Graph

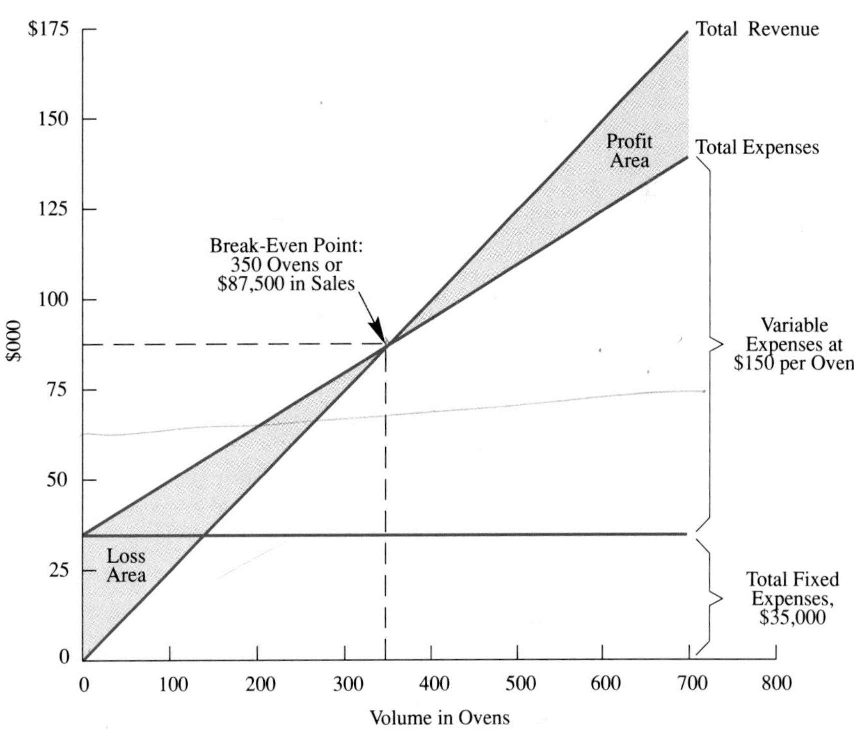

EXHIBIT 6–3
Alternative Format to the CVP Graph

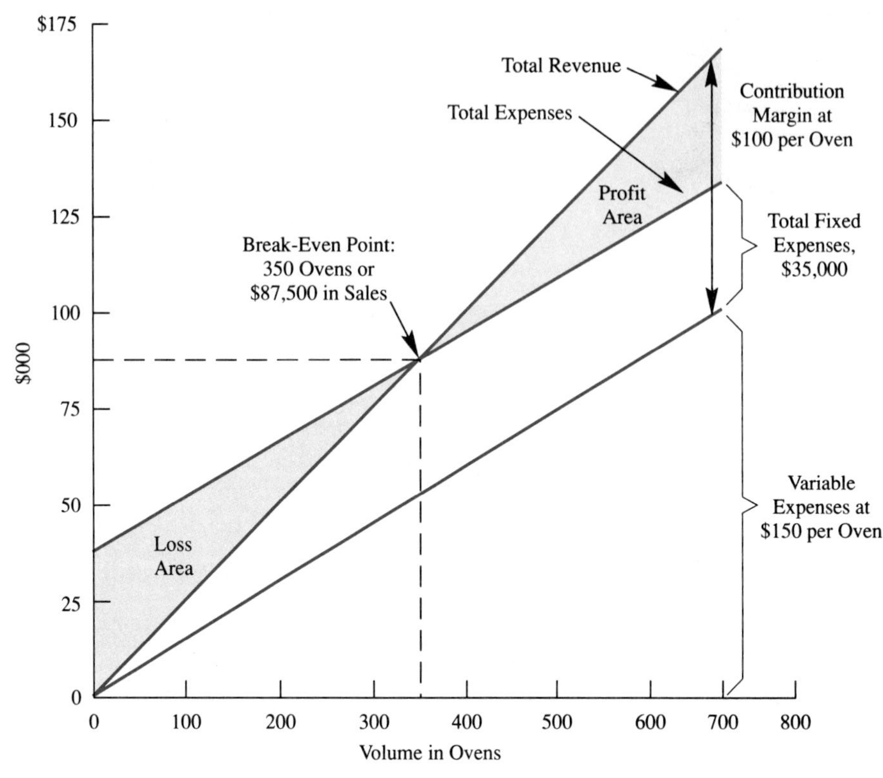

margin to be depicted on the graph. Otherwise, the graphs in the two exhibits are the same.

The Profitgraph Another approach to the CVP graph is presented in Exhibit 6–4. This approach, called a **profitgraph,** is preferred by some managers because it focuses more directly on how profits change with changes in volume. It has the added advantage of being easier to interpret than the more traditional approaches illustrated in Exhibits 6–2 and 6–3. It has the disadvantage, however, of not showing as clearly how costs are affected by changes in the level of sales.

The profitgraph is constructed in two steps. These steps are illustrated in Exhibit 6–4.

1. Locate total fixed expenses on the vertical axis, assuming zero level of activity. This point will be in the "loss area," equal to the total fixed expenses expected for the period.
2. Plot a point representing expected profit or loss at any chosen level of sales. In Exhibit 6–4, we have chosen to plot the point representing expected profits at a sales volume of 600 ovens. At this activity level, expected profits are:

EXHIBIT 6–4
Preparing the Profitgraph

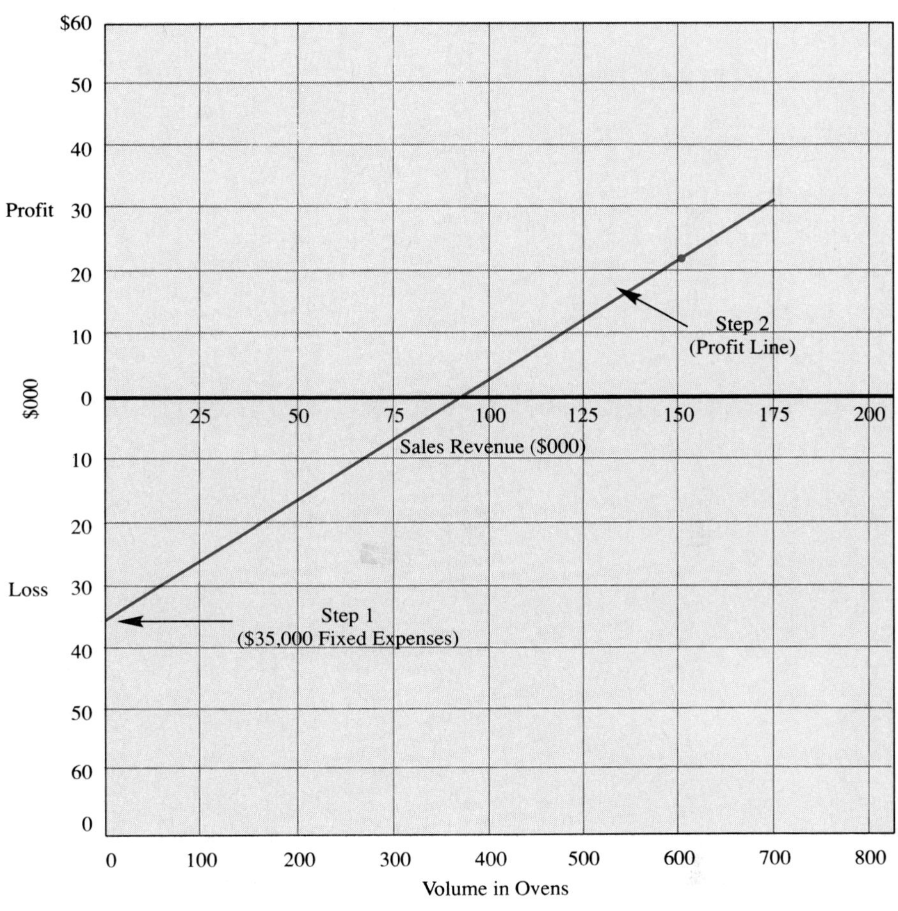

Sales (600 ovens × $250)	$150,000
Less variable expenses (600 ovens × $150)	90,000
Contribution margin.	60,000
Less fixed expenses.	35,000
Net income	$ 25,000

After this point is plotted, draw a line through it back to the point on the vertical axis representing total fixed expenses. The interpretation of the completed profitgraph is given in Exhibit 6–5. The break-even point is where the profit line crosses the break-even line.

The vertical distance between the two lines represents the expected profit or loss at any given level of sales volume. This vertical distance can be translated directly into dollars by referring to the profit and loss figures on the vertical axis.

EXHIBIT 6–5
The Completed Profitgraph

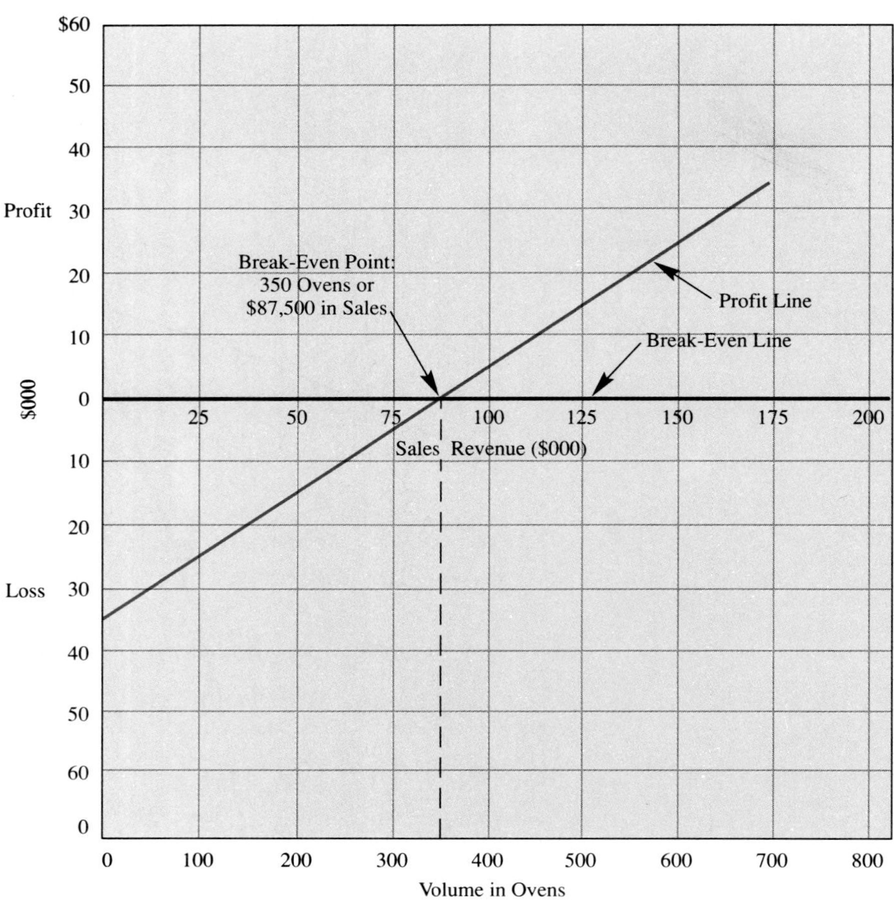

Target Net Profit Analysis

CVP formulas can be used to determine the sales volume required to meet a target net profit figure. Suppose that Norton Company would like to earn a target net profit of $40,000 per month. How many ovens would have to be sold?

The CVP Equation One approach to the solution would be to use the CVP equation. The target net profit requirement can be added into the basic equation data, and the solution will then show what level of sales is necessary to cover all expenses and yield the target net profit.

$$\text{Sales} = \text{Variable expenses} + \text{Fixed expenses} + \text{Profits}$$

$$\$250X = \$150X + \$35{,}000 + \$40{,}000$$
$$\$100X = \$75{,}000$$
$$X = 750 \text{ ovens}$$

where:

X = number of ovens sold
$250 = unit sales price
$150 = unit variable expenses
$35,000 = total fixed expenses
$40,000 = target net profit

Thus, the target net profit can be achieved by selling 750 ovens per month, which represents $187,500 in total sales ($250 × 750 ovens).

The Unit Contribution Approach A second approach would be to expand the unit contribution formula to include the target net profit requirement:

$$\frac{\$35{,}000 \text{ fixed expenses} + \$40{,}000 \text{ target net profit}}{\$100 \text{ contribution margin per oven}} = 750 \text{ ovens}$$

This approach is simpler and more direct than using the CVP equation. In addition, it shows clearly that once the fixed costs are covered, the unit contribution margin is fully available for meeting profit requirements.

The Margin of Safety (MS)

The **margin of safety (MS)** can be defined as the excess of budgeted (or actual) sales over the break-even volume of sales. It states the amount by which sales can drop before losses begin to be incurred in an organization. The formula for its calculation is:

Total sales − Break-even sales = Margin of safety (MS)

Computations involving the MS are presented in Exhibit 6–6. Notice that the two companies in the exhibit have equal sales and net income figures but that Alpha Company has an MS of $40,000, whereas Beta Company has an MS of only $20,000. The difference in the MS can be traced to the fact that the two companies have very different cost structures. Beta Company has higher fixed costs and thus will incur losses more quickly than Alpha Company if sales drop off. As indicated by the MS, if sales drop by only $20,000, Beta Company will be at its break-even point, whereas sales can drop by $40,000 before Alpha Company will be at its break-even point.

The MS can also be expressed in percentage form. This percentage is obtained by dividing the MS in dollar terms by total sales:

$$\frac{\text{MS in dollars}}{\text{Total sales}} = \text{MS percentage}$$

Exhibit 6–6 contains the MS expressed in percentage form for both Alpha Company and Beta Company. The MS can also be expressed in terms of units of product (if a company is a single-product firm) by dividing the MS in dollars by the unit selling price.

If the MS is low, as in Beta Company, what does management do to correct the problem? There is no universal answer to this question, other than to point out that management's efforts must be directed toward either reducing the break-even point or increasing the overall level of sales in the company. In short, the MS is a tool designed to point out a problem (or the lack of one), the solution to which must be found by analyzing the company's cost structure and by applying the general CVP techniques that have been illustrated in this chapter.

EXHIBIT 6–6
Margin of Safety (MS)

	Alpha Company		Beta Company	
	Amount	Percent	Amount	Percent
Sales	$200,000	100	$200,000	100
Less variable expenses	150,000	75	100,000	50
Contribution margin	50,000	25	100,000	50
Less fixed expenses	40,000		90,000	
Net income	$ 10,000		$ 10,000	
Break-even point:				
$40,000 ÷ 25%	$160,000			
$90,000 ÷ 50%			$180,000	
MS in dollars (total sales less break-even sales):				
$200,000 − $160,000	40,000			
$200,000 − $180,000			20,000	
MS in percentage form (MS in dollars divided by total sales):				
$40,000 ÷ $200,000	20%			
$20,000 ÷ $200,000			10%	

AUTOMATION AND CVP ANALYSIS

As stated in the preceding chapter, the move toward flexible manufacturing systems and other uses of automation has resulted in a shift toward greater fixed costs and less variable costs in organizations. In turn, this shift in cost structure has had an impact on product CM ratios, on the break-even point, and on other CVP factors in automated companies. Some of this impact has been favorable and some has been unfavorable, as shown in Exhibit 6–7.

Many benefits can accrue from automation, but as shown in the exhibit, certain risks are introduced when a company moves toward greater amounts of fixed costs. These risks suggest that management must be careful as it automates to ensure that investment decisions are made in accordance with a carefully devised long-run operating strategy. This point is discussed further in Chapter 14 where we deal with investment decisions in an automated environment.

STRUCTURING SALES COMMISSIONS

Some firms base salespersons' commissions on contribution margin generated rather than on sales generated. The reasoning goes like this: Since contribution margin represents the amount of sales revenue available to cover fixed expenses and profits, a firm's well-being will be maximized when contribution margin is maximized. By tying salespersons' commissions to contribution margin, the salespersons are automatically encouraged to concentrate on the element that is of most importance to the firm. There is no

EXHIBIT 6–7

CVP Comparison of Capital-Intensive (automated) and Labor-Intensive Companies

The comparison below is between two companies in the same industry that produce identical products for the same market. One of the companies has chosen to automate its facilities (capital intensive) and the other has chosen to rely heavily on direct labor inputs (labor intensive).

Item	Capital-Intensive (automated) Company	Labor-Intensive Company	Comments
The CM ratio for a given product will tend to be relatively. . .	High	Low	Variable costs in an automated company will tend to be lower than in a labor-intensive company, thereby causing the CM ratio for a given product to be higher.
Operating leverage will tend to be. . .	High	Low	Since operating leverage is a measure of the use of fixed costs in an organization, it will typically be higher in an automated company than in a company that relies on direct labor inputs.
In periods of increasing sales, net income will tend to increase. . .	Rapidly	Slowly	Since both operating leverage and product CM ratios tend to be high in automated companies, net income will increase rapidly after the break-even point has been reached.
In periods of decreasing sales, net income will tend to decrease. . .	Rapidly	Slowly	Just as net income increases rapidly in an automated company after the break-even point has been reached, so will net income decrease rapidly as sales decrease.
The volatility of net income with changes in sales will tend to be. . .	Greater	Less	Due to its higher operating leverage, the net income in an automated company will tend to be much more sensitive to changes in sales than in a labor-intensive company.
The break-even point will tend to be. . .	Higher	Lower	The break-even point in an automated company will tend to be higher because of its greater fixed costs.
The margin of safety at a given level of sales will tend to be. . .	Lower	Higher	The margin of safety in an automated company will tend to be lower because of its higher break-even point.
The latitude available to management in times of economic stress will tend to be. . .	Less	Greater	With high fixed costs in an automated company, management is more "locked in" and has fewer options when dealing with changing economic conditions.
The overall degree of risk associated with operating activities will tend to be. . .	Greater	Less	The risk factor is a summation of all the other factors listed above.

need to worry about what mix of products the salespersons sell, because they will *automatically* sell the mix of products that will maximize the base on which their commissions are to be paid. That is, if salespersons are aware that their commissions will depend on the amount of contribution margin that they are able to generate, then they will use all of the experience, skill, and expertise at their command to sell the mix of products that will maximize the contribution margin base. In effect, by maximizing their own well-being, they automatically maximize the well-being of the firm.

As a further step, some firms deduct from the total contribution margin generated by salespersons the amount of the traveling, entertainment, and other expenses that are incurred. This encourages the salespersons to be sensitive to their own costs in the process of making sales.

THE CONCEPT OF SALES MIX

The preceding sections have given us some insights into the principles involved in CVP analysis, as well as some selected examples of how these principles are used by the manager. Before concluding our discussion, it will be helpful to consider one additional application of the ideas that we have developed—the use of CVP concepts in analyzing sales mix.

The Definition of Sales Mix

The term **sales mix** means the relative combination in which a company's products are sold. Managers try to achieve the combination, or mix, that will yield the greatest amount of profits. Most companies have several products, and often these products are not equally profitable. Where this is true, profits will depend to some extent on the sales mix that the company is able to achieve. Profits will be greater if high-margin items make up a relatively large proportion of total sales than if sales consist mostly of low-margin items.

Changes in the sales mix can cause interesting (and sometimes confusing) variations in a company's profits. A shift in the sales mix from high-margin items to low-margin items can cause total profits to decrease even though total sales may increase. Conversely, a shift in the sales mix from low-margin items to high-margin items can cause the reverse effect—total profits may increase even though total sales decrease. Given the possibility of these types of variations in profits, one measure of the effectiveness of a company's sales force is the sales mix that it is able to generate. It is one thing to achieve a particular sales volume; it is quite a different thing to sell the most profitable mix of products.

Sales Mix and Break-Even Analysis

If a company is selling more than one product, break-even analysis is somewhat more complex than discussed earlier in the chapter. The reason is that different products will have different selling prices, different costs, and different contribution margins. Consequently, the break-even point will depend on the mix in which the various products are sold. To illustrate, assume that a company has two product lines—line A and line B. For 19x1, the company's sales, costs, and break-even point were as shown in Exhibit 6–8.

As shown in the exhibit, the break-even point is $60,000 in sales. This is computed by dividing the fixed costs by the company's *average* CM ratio of 45 percent. But $60,000 in sales represents the break-even point for the company only so long as the sales mix does not change. *If the sales mix changes, then the break-even point will also change*. We can illustrate this by assuming that in 19x2, the following year, the sales mix shifts away from the more profitable line B (which has a 50 percent CM ratio) toward the less profitable line A (which has only a 25 percent CM ratio). Assume that sales in 19x2 are as shown in Exhibit 6–9.

Although sales have remained unchanged at $100,000, the sales mix is exactly the reverse of what it was in Exhibit 6–8, with the bulk of the sales

EXHIBIT 6–8
Multiple-Product Break-Even Analysis

	Line A		Line B		Total	
	Amount	Percent	Amount	Percent	Amount	Percent
Sales	$20,000	100	$80,000	100	$100,000	100
Less variable expenses	15,000	75	40,000	50	55,000	55
Contribution margin.	$ 5,000	25	$40,000	50	45,000	45
Less fixed expenses.					27,000	
Net income					$ 18,000	

Computation of the break-even point:

$$\frac{\text{Fixed expenses, \$27,000}}{\text{Average CM ratio, 45\%}} = \$60{,}000$$

EXHIBIT 6–9
Multiple-Product Break-Even Analysis: A Shift in Sales Mix (see Exhibit 6–8)

	Line A		Line B		Total	
	Amount	Percent	Amount	Percent	Amount	Percent
Sales	$80,000	100	$20,000	100	$100,000	100
Less variable expenses	60,000	75	10,000	50	70,000	70
Contribution margin.	$20,000	25	$10,000	50	30,000	30
Less fixed expenses.					27,000	
Net income					$ 3,000	

Computation of the break-even point:

$$\frac{\text{Fixed expenses, \$27,000}}{\text{Average CM ratio, 30\%}} = \$90{,}000$$

now coming from line A rather than from line B. Notice that this shift in the sales mix has caused both the average CM ratio and total profits to drop sharply from the prior year—the average CM ratio has dropped from 45 percent in 19x1 to only 30 percent in 19x2, and net income has dropped from $18,000 to only $3,000. In addition, with the drop in the average CM ratio, the company's break-even point is no longer $60,000 in sales. Since the company is now realizing less average contribution margin per dollar of sales, it takes more sales to cover the same amount of fixed costs. Thus, the break-even point has increased from $60,000 to $90,000 in sales per year.

In preparing a break-even analysis, some assumption must be made concerning the sales mix. Usually the assumption is that it will not change. However, if the manager knows that shifts in various factors (consumer tastes, market share, and so forth) are causing shifts in the sales mix, then these factors must be explicitly considered in any CVP computations. Otherwise, the manager may be making decisions on the basis of outmoded or faulty data.

EXHIBIT 6–10
Sales Mix and per Unit Contribution Margin Analysis

	Contribution Margin per Unit	Total Units Sold		Total Contribution Margin	
		19x1	19x2	19x1	19x2
Product X	$5	1,000	2,000	$ 5,000	$10,000
Product Y	3	3,000	2,000	9,000	6,000
		4,000	4,000	$14,000	$16,000
Average per unit contribution margin ($14,000 ÷ 4,000 units)				$3.50	
Average per unit contribution margin ($16,000 ÷ 4,000 units)					$4

Sales Mix and per Unit Contribution Margin

Sometimes the sales mix is measured in terms of the average per unit contribution margin. To illustrate, assume that a company has two products—X and Y. During 19x1 and 19x2, sales of products X and Y were as shown in Exhibit 6–10.

Two things should be noted about the data in this exhibit. First, note that the sales mix in 19x1 was 1,000 units of product X and 3,000 units of product Y. This sales mix yielded $3.50 in average per unit contribution margin.

Second, note that the sales mix in 19x2 shifted to 2,000 units for both products, although *total* sales remained unchanged at 4,000 units. This sales mix yielded $4 in average per unit contribution margin, an increase of 50 cents per unit over the prior year.

What caused the increase in average per unit contribution margin between the two years? The answer is the shift in sales mix toward the more profitable product X. Although total volume (in units) did not change, total and per unit contribution margin changed simply because of the change in sales mix.

LIMITING ASSUMPTIONS IN CVP ANALYSIS

Several limiting assumptions must be made when using data for CVP analysis. These assumptions are:

1. The behavior of both revenues and costs is linear throughout the entire relevant range. The economists would differ from this view. They would say that changes in volume will trigger changes in both revenues and costs in such a way that relationships will not remain linear.
2. Costs can be accurately divided into variable and fixed elements.
3. The sales mix is constant.
4. Inventories do not change in break-even computations; that is, the number of units produced equals the number of units sold (this assumption is considered further in Chapter 7).
5. Worker and machine productivity and efficiency do not change throughout the relevant range.

6. The value of a dollar received today is the same as the value of a dollar received in any future year (the time value of money is considered in Chapter 14).

SUMMARY

The analysis of CVP relationships is one of management's most significant responsibilities. Basically, it involves finding the most favorable combination of variable costs, fixed costs, selling price, sales volume, and mix of products sold. We have found that trade-offs are possible between types of costs, as well as between costs and selling price, and between selling price and sales volume. Sometimes these trade-offs are desirable, and sometimes they are not. CVP analysis provides the manager with a powerful tool for identifying those courses of action that will and will not improve profitability.

The concepts developed in this chapter represent a *way of thinking* rather than a mechanical set of procedures. That is, to put together the optimum combination of costs, selling price, and sales volume, the manager must be trained to think in terms of the unit contribution margin, the break-even point, the CM ratio, the sales mix, and the other concepts developed in this chapter. These concepts are dynamic in that a change in one will trigger changes in others—changes that may not be obvious on the surface. Only by learning to *think* in CVP terms can the manager move with assurance toward the firm's profit objectives.

KEY TERMS FOR REVIEW

Break-even chart The relationship between revenues, costs, and level of activity in an organization presented in graphic form. Also see *Cost-volume-profit (CVP) graph*. (p. 220)

Break-even point The level of activity at which an organization neither earns a profit nor incurs a loss. The break-even point can also be defined as the point where total revenue equals total costs and as the point where total contribution margin equals total fixed costs. (p. 208)

Contribution margin ratio The contribution margin per unit expressed as a percentage of the selling price per unit. This term is synonymous with *profit-volume ratio*. (p. 210)

Cost-volume-profit (CVP) graph The relationship between revenues, costs, and level of activity in an organization, presented in graphic form. Also see *Break-even chart*. (p. 219)

Degree of operating leverage A measure, at a given level of sales, of how a percentage change in sales volume will affect profits. The degree of operating leverage is computed by dividing contribution margin by net income. (p. 212)

Equation method A method of computing the break-even point that relies on the equation: Sales = Variable expenses + Fixed expenses + Profits. (p. 218)

Incremental analysis An analytical approach that focuses only on those items of revenue, cost, and volume that will change as a result of a decision in an organization. (p. 214)

Margin of safety (MS) The excess of budgeted (or actual) sales over the break-even volume of sales. (p. 225)

Operating leverage A measure of the extent to which fixed costs are being used in an organization. The greater the fixed costs, the greater is the operating leverage available and the greater is the sensitivity of net income to changes in sales. (p. 212)

Profitgraph An alternative form of the cost-volume-profit graph that focuses more directly on how profits change with changes in volume. (p. 222)

Profit-volume ratio See *Contribution margin ratio*. (p. 210)

Sales mix The relative combination in which a company's products are sold. Sales mix is computed by expressing the sales of each product as a percentage of total sales. (p. 228)

Unit contribution method A method of computing the break-even point in which the fixed costs are divided by the contribution margin per unit. (p. 219)

QUESTIONS

6–1 Cost-volume-profit (CVP) analysis is a study of the interaction of a number of factors. Name the factors involved.

6–2 What is meant by a product's contribution margin ratio (CM ratio)? How is this ratio useful in the planning of business operations?

6–3 Able Company and Baker Company are competing firms. Each company sells a single product, widgets, in the same market at a price of $50 per widget. Variable costs are the same in each company—$35 per widget. Able Company has discovered a way to reduce its variable costs by $4 per unit and has decided to pass half of this cost savings on to its customers in the form of a lower price. Although Baker Company has not been able to reduce its variable costs, it must also lower its selling price to remain competitive with Able Company. If each company sells 10,000 units per year, what will be the effect of the changes on each company's profits?

6–4 Often the most direct route to a business decision is to make an incremental analysis based on the information available. What is meant by an "incremental analysis"?

6–5 Company A's cost structure includes costs that are mostly variable, whereas Company B's cost structure includes costs that are mostly fixed. In a time of increasing sales, which company will tend to realize the most rapid increase in profits? Explain.

6–6 What is meant by the term *operating leverage?*

6–7 A 10 percent decrease in the selling price of a product will have the same impact on net income as a 10 percent increase in the variable expenses. Do you agree? Why or why not?

6–8 "Changes in fixed costs are much more significant to a company than changes in variable costs." Do you agree? Explain.

6–9 What is meant by the term *break-even point?*

6–10 Name three approaches to break-even analysis. Briefly explain how each approach works.

6–11 Why is the term *break-even chart* a misnomer?

6–12 In response to a request from your immediate supervisor, you have prepared a CVP graph portraying the cost and revenue characteristics of your company's product and operations. Explain how the lines on the graph would change if *(a)* the selling price per unit decreased, *(b)* fixed costs increased throughout the entire range of activity portrayed on the graph, and *(c)* variable costs per unit increased.

6–13 Using the following notations, write out the correct formula for computing the break-even level of sales in units: S = sales in units, SP = selling price per unit, FC = total fixed costs, and VC = variable cost per unit. Is the formula you have derived the formula for the equation method or the formula for the unit contribution method?

6–14 Al's Auto Wash charges $4 to wash a car. The variable costs of washing a car are 15 percent of sales. Fixed costs total $1,700 monthly. How many cars must be washed each month for Al to break even?

6–15 What is meant by the margin of safety(MS)?

6–16 Companies X and Y are in the same industry. Company X is highly automated, whereas Company Y relies primarily on labor in the manufacture of its products. If sales in the two companies are about the same, which would you expect to have the lowest MS? Why?

6–17 What is meant by the term *sales mix?* CVP analysis includes some inherent, simplifying assumptions. What assumption is usually made concerning sales mix?

6–18 Explain how a shift in the sales mix could result in both a higher break-even point and a lower net income.

EXERCISES

E6–1 Pringle Company manufactures and sells a single product. The company's sales and expenses for a recent month follow:

	Total	Per Unit
Sales	$600,000	$40
Less variable expenses	420,000	28
Contribution margin	180,000	$12
Less fixed expenses	150,000	
Net income	$ 30,000	

Required

1. What is the monthly break-even point in units sold and in sales dollars?
2. Without resorting to computations, what is the total contribution margin at the break-even point?
3. How many units would have to be sold each month to earn a minimum target net income of $18,000? Use the unit contribution method. Prove your answer by preparing a contribution income statement at the target level of sales.
4. Refer to the original data. Compute the company's MS in both dollar and percentage terms.
5. What is the company's CM ratio? If monthly sales increase by $80,000, by how much would you expect monthly net income to increase?

E6–2 Super Sales Company is the exclusive distributor for a new product. The product sells for $60 per unit and has a CM ratio of 40 percent. The company's fixed expenses are $360,000 per year.

Required

1. What are the variable expenses per unit?
2. Using the equation method:
   a. What is the break-even point in units and in sales dollars?
   b. What sales level in units and in sales dollars is required to earn an annual profit of $90,000?
   c. Assume that through negotiation with the manufacturer the Super Sales Company is able to reduce its variable expenses by $3 per unit. What is the company's new break-even point in units and in sales dollars?
3. Repeat (2) above, using the unit contribution method.

E6–3 Superior Door Company manufactures and sells prehung doors to home builders. The doors are sold for $60 each. Variable costs are $42 per door, and fixed costs total $450,000 per year. The company is currently selling 30,000 doors per year.

Required

1. Compute the degree of operating leverage at the present level of sales.
2. Management is confident that the company can sell 37,500 doors next year (an increase of 7,500 doors, or 25 percent, over current sales). Compute:
   a. The expected percentage increase in net income for next year.
   b. The expected total dollar net income for next year.

E6–4 Chi Omega Sorority is planning its annual Riverboat Extravaganza. The Extravaganza committee has assembled the following expected costs for the event:

Dinner (per person)	$ 7
Favors and program (per person) . . .	3
Orchestra	1,500
Tickets and advertising	700
Riverboat rental	4,800
Floorshow and strolling entertainers	1,000

The committee members would like to charge $30 per person for the evening's activities.

Required

1. Compute the break-even point for the Extravaganza (in terms of the number of persons that must attend).
2. Assume that only 250 persons attended the Extravaganza last year. If the same number attend this year, what price per ticket must be charged in order to break even?
3. Refer to the original data ($30 ticket price per person). Prepare a CVP graph for the Extravaganza from a zero level of activity up to 800 tickets sold. Number of persons should be placed on the horizontal *(X)* axis, and dollars should be placed on the vertical *(Y)* axis. (Note: Exercise 6–5 has further requirements for the data in this exercise.)

E6–5 (This exercise is a continuation of Exercise 6–4.) Refer to the data in Exercise 6–4.

Required

1. Prepare a profitgraph for the Riverboat Extravaganza.
2. The Extravaganza committee has just learned that Brute Springstern, a widely regarded alumnus of the University, will make an appearance during the evening. Accordingly, the committee has decided to raise the ticket price to $35 per person. Will this cause the slope of the profit line to be steeper or flatter on the graph? Explain.

E6–6 Fill in the missing amounts in each of the eight case situations below. Each case is independent of the others. (Hint: One way to find the missing amounts would be to prepare a contribution income statement for each case, enter the known data, and then compute the missing items.)

a. Assume that only one product is being sold in each of the four following case situations:

Case	Units Sold	Sales	Variable Expenses	Contribution Margin per Unit	Fixed Expenses	Net Income (Loss)
1	$ 9,000	$270,000	$162,000	$?	$ 90,000	$?
2	?	350,000	?	15	170,000	40,000
3	20,000	?	280,000	6	?	35,000
4	5,000	160,000	?	?	82,000	(12,000)

b. Assume that more than one product is being sold in each of the four following case situations:

Case	Sales	Variable Expenses	Average Contribution Margin (percent)	Fixed Expenses	Net Income (Loss)
1	$450,000	$?	40	$?	$65,000
2	200,000	130,000	?	60,000	?
3	?	?	80	470,000	90,000
4	300,000	90,000	?	?	(15,000)

E6–7 Porter Company's most recent income statement is shown below:

	Total	Per Unit
Sales (30,000 units).	$150,000	$5
Less variable expenses	90,000	3
Contribution margin	60,000	$2
Less fixed expenses	50,000	
Net income	$ 10,000	

Required Prepare a new income statement under each of the following conditions (consider each case independently):

1. The sales volume increases by 15 percent.
2. The selling price decreases by 50 cents per unit, and the sales volume increases by 20 percent.
3. The selling price increases by 50 cents per unit, fixed expenses increase by $10,000, and the sales volume decreases by 5 percent.
4. Variable expenses increase by 20 cents per unit, the selling price increases by 12 percent, and the sales volume decreases by 10 percent.

E6–8 Reveen Products manufactures and sells camping equipment. One of the company's products, a camp lantern, sells for $90 per unit. Variable expenses are $63 per lantern, and fixed expenses associated with the lantern total $135,000 per month.

Required

1. Compute the company's break-even point in number of lanterns and in total sales dollars.
2. If the variable expenses per lantern increase as a percentage of the selling price, will it result in a higher or a lower break-even point? Why? (Assume that the fixed expenses remain unchanged.)
3. At present, the company is selling 8,000 lanterns per month. The sales manager is convinced that a 10 percent reduction in the selling price will result in a 25 percent increase in the number of lanterns sold each month. Prepare two contribution income statements, one under present operating conditions, and one as operations would appear after the proposed changes. Show both total and per unit data on your statements.
4. Refer to the data in (3) above. How many lanterns would have to be sold at the new selling price to yield a minimum net income of $72,000 per month?

E6–9 Okabee Enterprises sells two products, A and B. Monthly sales and the contribution margin ratios for the two products follow:

	Product A	Product B	Total
Sales	$700,000	$300,000	$1,000,000
Contribution margin ratio . . .	60%	70%	?

The company's fixed expenses total $598,500 per month.

Required

1. Prepare an income statement for the company as a whole. Use the format shown in Exhibit 6–8.
2. Compute the break-even point for the company, based on the current sales mix.

PROBLEMS

P6–10 Basic CVP Analysis, with Graphing Shirts Unlimited operates a chain of shirt stores around the country. The stores carry many styles of shirts that are all sold at the same price. To encourage sales personnel to be aggressive in their sales efforts, the company pays a substantial sales commission on each shirt sold. Sales personnel also receive a small basic salary.

The following cost and revenue data relate to Store 36 and are typical of one of the company's many outlets:

	Per Shirt
Sales price	$40
Variable expenses:	
Invoice cost	$18
Sales commission	7
Total variable expenses . . .	$25
Fixed expenses:	**Per Year**
Rent	$ 80,000
Advertising	150,000
Salaries	70,000
Total fixed expenses	$300,000

Shirts Unlimited is a fairly new organization. The company has asked you, as a member of its planning group, to assist in some basic analysis of its stores and company policies.

Required

1. Calculate the annual break-even point in dollar sales and in unit sales for Store 36.
2. Prepare a CVP graph showing cost and revenue data for Store 36 from a zero level of activity up to 45,000 shirts sold each year. Clearly indicate the break-even point on the graph.
3. If 19,000 shirts are sold in a year, what would be Store 36's net income or loss?
4. The company is considering paying the store manager of Store 36 an incentive commission of $3 per shirt (in addition to the salespersons' commissions). If this change is made, what will be the new break-even point in dollar sales and in unit sales?
5. Refer to the original data. As an alternative to (4) above, the company is considering paying the store manager a $3 commission on each shirt sold in excess of

the break-even point. If this change is made, what will be the store's net income or loss if 23,500 shirts are sold in a year?

6. Refer to the original data. The company is considering eliminating sales commissions entirely in its stores and increasing fixed salaries by $107,000 annually.
   a. If this change is made, what will be the new break-even point in dollar sales and in unit sales in Store 36?
   b. Would you recommend that the change be made? Explain.

P6–11 Basics of CVP Analysis Stratford Company makes a product that sells for $15 per unit. Variable costs are $6 per unit, and fixed costs total $180,000 annually.

Required Answer the following independent questions:

1. What is the product's CM ratio?
2. Use the CM ratio to determine the break-even point in sales dollars.
3. The company estimates that sales will increase by $45,000 during the coming year due to increased demand. By how much should net income increase?
4. Assume that the operating results for last year were:

Sales	$360,000
Less variable expenses . . .	144,000
Contribution margin.	216,000
Less fixed expenses.	180,000
Net income	$ 36,000

   a. Compute the degree of operating leverage at the current level of sales.
   b. The president expects sales to increase by 15 percent next year. By how much should net income increase?

5. Refer to the original data. Assume that the company sold 28,000 units last year. The sales manager is convinced that a 10 percent reduction in the selling price, combined with a $70,000 increase in advertising expenditures, would cause annual sales in units to increase by 50 percent. Prepare two contribution income statements, one showing the results of last year's operations and one showing what the results of operations would be if these changes were made. Would you recommend that the company do as the sales manager suggests?
6. Refer to the original data. Assume again that the company sold 28,000 units last year. The president feels that it would be unwise to change the selling price. Instead, he wants to increase the sales commission by $2 per unit. He thinks that this move, combined with some increase in advertising, would cause annual sales to double. By how much could advertising be increased with profits remaining unchanged? Do not prepare an income statement; use the incremental analysis approach.
7. Refer to the original data. Assume that due to a slack in demand the company is selling only 19,000 units per year. An order has been received from a wholesale distributor who wants to purchase 4,000 units on a special price basis. What unit price would have to be quoted to the distributor if the company wants to earn an overall profit of $15,000 for the year? (Present sales would not be disturbed by this special order.)

P6–12 Sales Mix Assumptions; Break-Even Analysis Marlin Company has been operating for only a few months and is just starting a budgeting and planning program. The company sells three products—A, B, and C. Budgeted sales by product and in total for the coming month are shown below:

	Product						Total	
	A		B		C			
Percentage of total sales .	48%		20%		32%		100%	
Sales	$240,000	100%	$100,000	100%	$160,000	100%	$500,000	100%
Less variable expenses . .	72,000	30	80,000	80	88,000	55	240,000	48
Contribution margin . . .	$168,000	70%	$ 20,000	20%	$ 72,000	45%	260,000	52%
Less fixed expenses . . .							223,600	
Net income							$ 36,400	

$$\text{Break-even sales: } \frac{\text{Fixed expenses, \$223,600}}{\text{CM ratio, 0.52}} = \$430{,}000$$

As shown by these data, net income is budgeted at $36,400 for the month, and break-even sales at $430,000.

Assume that actual sales for the month total $500,000 as planned. Actual sales by product are: A, $160,000; B, $200,000; and C, $140,000.

Required

1. Prepare a contribution income statement for the month based on actual sales data. Present the income statement in the format shown above.
2. Compute the break-even sales for the month, based on your actual data.
3. Considering the fact that the company met its $500,000 sales budget for the month, the president is shocked at the results shown on your income statement in (1) above. Prepare a brief memo for the president explaining why both the operating results and break-even sales are different from what was budgeted.

P6–13 Basics of CVP Analysis; Cost Structure Memofax, Inc., produces a single product. Sales have been very erratic, with some months showing a profit and some months showing a loss. The company's income statement for the most recent month is given below:

Sales (13,500 units at $20) . . .	$270,000
Less variable expenses	189,000
Contribution margin	81,000
Less fixed expenses	90,000
Net loss	$ (9,000)

Required

1. Compute the company's CM ratio and its break-even point in both units and dollars.
2. The sales manager feels that an $8,000 increase in the monthly advertising budget, combined with an intensified effort by the sales staff, will result in a $70,000 increase in monthly sales. If the sales manager is right, what will be the effect on the company's monthly net income or loss? (Use the incremental approach in preparing your answer.)
3. The president is convinced that a 10 percent reduction in the selling price, combined with an increase of $35,000 in the monthly advertising budget, will cause unit sales to double. What will the new income statement look like if these changes are adopted?
4. Refer to the original data. The company's advertising agency thinks that a new package for the company's product would help sales. The new package being proposed would increase packaging costs by $0.60 per unit. Assuming no other changes in cost behavior, how many units would have to be sold each month to earn a profit of $4,500?

5. Refer to the original data. By automating certain operations, the company could slash its variable expenses in half. However, fixed costs would increase by $118,000 per month.
   a. Compute the new CM ratio and the new break-even point in both units and dollars.
   b. Assume that the company expects to sell 20,000 units next month. Prepare two income statements, one assuming that operations are not automated and one assuming that they are.
   c. Would you recommend that the company automate its operations? Explain.
6. Refer to the original data. Assume that sales during the current month are expected to be the same as shown in the income statement above (13,500 units). A large distributor has offered to make a bulk purchase of 5,000 units on a special price basis. Variable selling expenses of $2 per unit could be avoided on this sale. What price per unit should Memofax, Inc., quote to this distributor if Memofax desires to make an overall net income of $11,000 during the month for the company as a whole? (Regular sales would not be disturbed by this order.)

P6–14 Graphing; Incremental Analysis; Operating Leverage Teri Hall has recently opened Sheer Elegance, Inc., a store specializing in fashionable stockings. Ms. Hall has just completed a course in managerial accounting at the state university, and she believes that she can apply certain aspects of the course to her business. She is particularly interested in adopting the cost-volume-profit approach to decision making. Thus, she has prepared the following analysis:

Sales price per pair of stockings	$2.00
Variable expense per pair of stockings	0.80
Contribution margin per pair of stockings	$1.20
Fixed expenses per year:	
Building rental	$12,000
Equipment depreciation	3,000
Selling	30,000
Administrative	15,000
Total fixed expenses	$60,000

Required

1. How many pairs of stockings must be sold to break even? What does this represent in total dollar sales?
2. Prepare a CVP graph for the store from a zero level of activity up to 90,000 pairs of stockings sold each year. Indicate the break-even point on the graph.
3. How many pairs of stockings must be sold to earn a $9,000 target net income for the first year?
4. Ms. Hall now has one full-time and one part-time salesperson working in the store. It will cost her an additional $8,000 per year to convert the part-time position to a full-time position. Ms. Hall believes that the change would bring in an additional $20,000 in sales each year. Should she convert the position? Use the incremental approach (do not prepare an income statement).
5. Refer to the original data. Actual operating results for the first year are as follows:

Sales	$125,000
Less variable expenses	50,000
Contribution margin	75,000
Less fixed expenses	60,000
Net income	$ 15,000

a. What is the store's degree of operating leverage?

b. Ms. Hall is confident that with some effort she can increase sales by 20 percent next year. What would be the expected percentage increase in net income? Use the operating leverage concept to compute your answer.

P6–15 Various CVP Questions: Break-Even Point; Cost Structure; Target Sales Tyrene Products manufactures recreational equipment. One of the company's products, a skateboard, sells for $37.50. The skateboards are manufactured in an antiquated plant that relies heavily on direct labor workers. Thus, variable costs are high, totaling $22.50 per skateboard.

Over the past year the company sold 40,000 skateboards, with the following operating results:

Sales (40,000 skateboards) . . .	$1,500,000
Less variable expenses.	900,000
Contribution margin	600,000
Less fixed expenses	480,000
Net income	$ 120,000

Management is anxious to maintain and perhaps even improve its present level of income from the skateboards.

Required

1. Compute (*a*) the CM ratio and the break-even point in skateboards, and (*b*) the degree of operating leverage at last year's level of sales.
2. Due to an increase in labor rates, the company estimates that variable costs will increase by $3 per skateboard next year. If this change takes place and the selling price per skateboard remains constant at $37.50, what will be the new CM ratio and the new break-even point in skateboards?
3. Refer to the data in (2) above. If the expected change in variable costs takes place, how many skateboards will have to be sold next year to earn the same net income ($120,000) as last year?
4. Refer again to the data in (2) above. The president has decided that the company may have to raise the selling price on the skateboards. If Tyrene Products wants to maintain *the same CM ratio as last year,* what selling price per skateboard must it charge next year to cover the increased labor costs?
5. Refer to the original data. The company is considering the construction of a new, automated plant to manufacture the skateboards. The new plant would slash variable costs by 40 percent, but it would cause fixed costs to increase by 90 percent. If the new plant is built, what would be the company's new CM ratio and new break-even point in skateboards?
6. Refer to the data in (5) above.
   a. If the new plant is built, how many skateboards will have to be sold next year to earn the same net income ($120,000) as last year?
   b. Assume that the new plant is constructed and that next year the company manufactures and sells 40,000 skateboards (the same number as sold last year). Prepare a contribution income statement, and compute the degree of operating leverage.
   c. Explain why the operating leverage figure you have just computed is so much higher than the operating leverage figure computed in (1) above. Given the data in parts (1)–(6), if you were a member of top management, would you have voted in favor of constructing the new plant? Explain.

P6–16 The Case of the Deceptive Fixed Costs The Marbury Stein Shop sells steins from all parts of the world. The owner of the shop, Clint Marbury, is thinking of expanding his operations by hiring local college students, on a commission basis, to sell steins bearing the school emblem at the local college.

These steins must be ordered from the manufacturer three months in advance, and because of the unique emblem of each college, they cannot be returned. The steins would cost Mr. Marbury $15 each with a minimum order of 200 steins. Any additional steins would have to be ordered in increments of 50.

Since Mr. Marbury's plan would not require any additional facilities, the only costs associated with the project would be the cost of the steins and the cost of the sales commissions. The selling price of the steins would be $30 each. Mr. Marbury would pay the students a commission of $6 for each stein sold.

Required

1. To make the project worthwhile in terms of his own time, Mr. Marbury would require a $7,200 profit for the first six months of the venture. What level of sales in units and dollars would be required to meet this target net income figure? Show all computations.
2. Assume that the venture is undertaken and an order is placed for 200 steins. What would be Mr. Marbury's break-even point in units and in sales dollars? Show computations, and explain the reasoning behind your answer.

P6–17 Sales Mix; Break-Even Analysis; Margin of Safety Frutex, Inc., has two products, Hawaiian Fantasy and Tahitian Joy. Present revenue, cost, and sales data on the two products follow:

	Hawaiian Fantasy	Tahitian Joy
Selling price per unit	$15	$100
Variable expenses per unit	9	20
Number of units sold annually . . .	20,000	5,000

Fixed expenses total $475,800 per year.

Required

1. Assuming the sales mix given above, do the following:
   a. Prepare a contribution income statement showing both dollar and percent columns for each product and for the company as a whole.
   b. Compute the break-even point in dollars for the company as a whole and the margin of safety in both dollars and percent.
2. Another product, Samoan Delight, has just come onto the market. Assume that the company could sell 10,000 units at $45 each. The variable expenses would be $36 each. The company's fixed expenses would not change.
   a. Prepare another contribution income statement, including the Samoan Delight (sales of the other two products would not change). Carry percentage computations to one decimal place.
   b. Compute the company's new break-even point in dollars and the new margin of safety in both dollars and percent.
3. The president of the company examines your figures and says, "There's something strange here. Our fixed costs haven't changed and you show greater total contribution margin if we add the new product, but you also show our break-even point going up. With greater contribution margin, the break-even point should go down, not up. You've made a mistake somewhere." Explain to the president what has happened.

P6–18 Interpretive Questions on the CVP Graph A CVP graph, as illustrated below, is a useful technique for showing relationships between costs, volume, and profits in an organization.

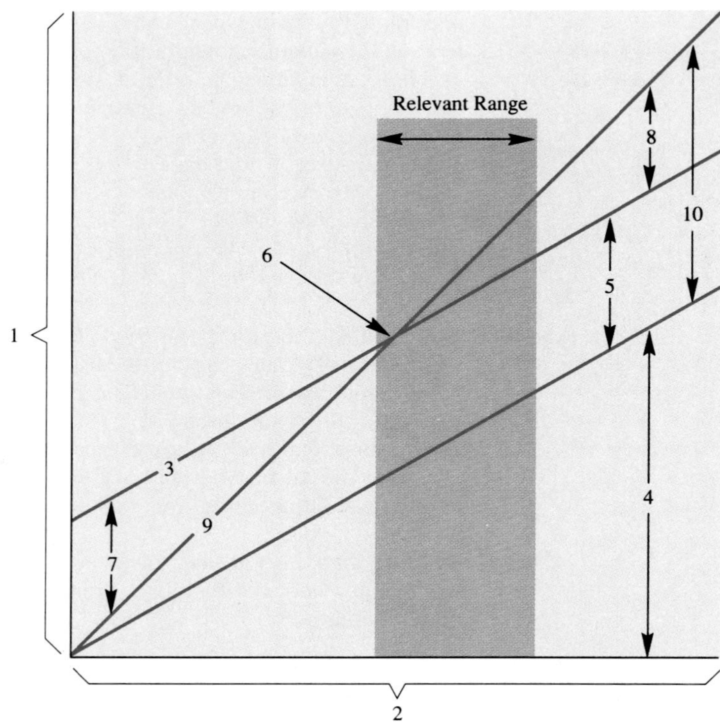

Required

1. Identify the numbered components in the CVP graph.
2. State the effect of each of the following actions on line 3, line 9, and the break-even point. For line 3 and line 9, state whether the action will cause the line to:

   Remain unchanged.
   Shift upward.
   Shift downward.
   Have a steeper slope (i.e., rotate upward).
   Have a flatter slope (i.e., rotate downward).
   Shift upward *and* have a steeper slope.
   Shift upward *and* have a flatter slope.
   Shift downward *and* have a steeper slope.
   Shift downward *and* have a flatter slope.

   In the case of the break-even point, state whether the action will cause the break-even point to:

   Remain unchanged.
   Increase.
   Decrease.
   Probably change, but the direction is uncertain.

   Treat each case independently.

   x. *Example*. Fixed costs are increased by $20,000 each period.
   Answer (see choices above): Line 3: Shift upward.
   Line 9: Remain unchanged.
   Break-even point: Increase.

   a. The unit selling price is decreased from $30 to $27.
   b. The per unit variable costs are increased from $12 to $15.
   c. The total fixed costs are reduced by $40,000.

d. Five thousand less units are sold during the period than were budgeted.
e. Due to purchasing a robot to perform a task that was previously done by workers, fixed costs are increased by $25,000 per period, and variable costs are reduced by $8 per unit.
f. As a result of a decrease in the cost of materials, both unit variable costs and the selling price are decreased by $3.
g. Advertising costs are increased by $50,000 per period, resulting in a 10 percent increase in the number of units sold.
h. Due to paying salespersons a commission rather than a flat salary, fixed costs are reduced by $21,000 per period, and unit variable costs are increased by $6.

P6–19 Sales Mix; Commission Structure; Break-Even Point Carbex, Inc., produces cutlery sets out of high-quality wood and steel. The company makes a standard cutlery set and a deluxe set and sells them to retail department stores throughout the country. The standard set sells for $60, and the deluxe set sells for $75. The variable expenses associated with each set are given below (in cost per set):

	Standard	Deluxe
Production expenses	$15.00	$30.00
Sales commissions (15% of sales price) . . .	9.00	11.25

The company's fixed expenses each month are:

Advertising.	$105,000
Depreciation	21,700
Administrative	63,000

Salespersons are paid on a commission basis to encourage them to be aggressive in their sales efforts. Mary Parsons, the financial vice president, watches sales commissions carefully and has noted that they have risen steadily over the last year. For this reason, she was shocked to find that even though sales have increased, profits for the current month—May 19x2—are down substantially from May of the previous year. Sales, in sets, for May over the last two years are given below:

	Total	Standard	Deluxe
May 19x1	6,000	4,000	2,000
May 19x2	6,000	1,000	5,000

Required

1. Prepare an income statement for May 19x1 and an income statement for May 19x2. Use the contribution format, with the following headings:

	Standard		Deluxe		Total	
	Amount	**Percent**	**Amount**	**Percent**	**Amount**	**Percent**
Sales . . .						
Etc.. . . .						

Place the fixed expenses only in the total column. Carry percentage computations to one decimal place. Do not show percentages for the fixed expenses.

2. Explain why there is a difference in net income between the two months, even though the same *total* number of sets was sold in each month.
3. What can be done to the sales commissions to optimize the sales mix?
4. *a.* Using May 19x1's figures, what was the break-even point for the month in sales dollars?
   b. Has May 19x2's break-even point gone up or down from that of May 19x1?

Explain your answer without calculating the break-even point for May 19x2.

P6–20 Sensitivity Analysis of Net Income; Changes in Volume Detmer Company has just introduced a new product for which the company is trying to find an optimal selling price. Marketing studies suggest that the company can increase sales by 5,000 units for each $2 per unit reduction in the selling price. The company's present selling price is $90 per unit, and variable expenses are $60 per unit. Fixed expenses are $840,000 per year. The present annual sales volume (at the $90 selling price) is 25,000 units.

Required

1. What is the present yearly net income or loss?
2. What is the present break-even point in units and in dollar sales?
3. Assuming that the marketing studies are correct, what is the *maximum* profit that the company can earn yearly? At how many units and at what selling price per unit would the company generate this profit?
4. What would be the break-even point in units and in dollar sales using the selling price you determined in (3) above (e.g., the selling price at the level of maximum profits)? Why is this break-even point different from the break-even point you computed in (1) above?

P6–21 Sales Mix; Break-Even Analysis Topper Sports, Inc., produces high-quality sports equipment. The company's racket division manufactures three tennis rackets—the Standard, the Deluxe, and the Pro—that are widely used in amateur play. Selected information on the rackets is given below:

	Standard	Deluxe	Pro
Selling price per racket	$40.00	$60.00	$90.00
Variable expenses per racket:			
Production.	22.00	27.00	31.50
Selling (5% of selling price) . . .	2.00	3.00	4.50

All sales are made through the company's own retail outlets. The cost records show that the following fixed costs are assignable to the racket division:

	Per Month
Fixed production costs	$120,000
Advertising expense	100,000
Administrative salaries	50,000
Total	$270,000

Sales, in units, over the past two months have been:

	Standard	Deluxe	Pro	Total
April	2,000	1,000	5,000	8,000
May	8,000	1,000	3,000	12,000

Required

1. Using the contribution approach, prepare an income statement for April and an income statement for May, with the following headings:

	Total		Standard		Deluxe		Pro	
	Amount	Percent	Amount	Percent	Amount	Percent	Amount	Percent
Sales . . .								
Etc.. . . .								

Place the fixed expenses only in the total column. Carry percentage computations to one decimal place. Do not show percentages for the fixed expenses.

2. Upon seeing the income statements in (1) above, the president stated, "I can't believe this! We sold 50 percent more rackets in May than in April, yet profits went down. It's obvious that costs are out of control in that division." What other explanation can you give for the drop in net income?
3. Compute the racket division's break-even point in dollars for the month of April.
4. Has May's break-even point in dollars gone up or down from April's break-even point? Explain without computing a break-even point for May.
5. Assume that sales of the Standard racket increase by $20,000. What would be the effect on net income? What would be the effect if Pro racket sales increased by $20,000? Do not prepare income statements; use the incremental analysis approach in determining your answer.

P6–22 Changing Levels of Fixed and Variable Costs Novelties, Inc., produces and sells highly faddish products directed toward the teenage market. A new product has come onto the market that the company is anxious to produce and sell. Enough capacity exists in the company's plant to produce 30,000 units each month. Variable costs to manufacture and sell one unit would be $1.60, and fixed costs would total $40,000 per month.

The marketing department predicts that demand for the product will exceed the 30,000 units that the company is able to produce. Additional production capacity can be rented from another company at a fixed cost of $2,000 per month. Variable costs in the rented facility would total $1.75 per unit, due to somewhat less efficient operations than in the main plant. The product would sell for $2.50 per unit.

Required

1. Compute the monthly break-even point for the new product in units and in total dollar sales. Show all computations in good form.
2. How many units must be sold each month in order to make a monthly profit of $9,000?
3. If the sales manager receives a bonus of 15 cents for each unit sold in excess of the break-even point, how many units must be sold each month in order to earn a return of 25 percent on the monthly investment in fixed costs? Show all computations in good form.

P6–23 Changes in Cost Structure Frieden Company's income statement for the most recent month is given below:

Sales (40,000 units)	$800,000
Less variable expenses	560,000
Contribution margin.	240,000
Less fixed expenses.	192,000
Net income	$ 48,000

The industry in which Frieden Company operates is quite sensitive to cyclical movements in the economy. Thus, profits vary considerably from year to year according to general economic conditions. The company has a large amount of unused capacity and is studying ways of improving profits.

Required

1. New equipment has come onto the market that would allow Frieden company to automate a portion of its operations. Variable costs would be reduced by $6 per unit. However, fixed costs would increase to a total of $432,000 each month. Prepare two contribution type income statements, one showing present operations and one showing how operations would appear if the new equipment is purchased. Show an amount column, a per unit column, and a percent column on each statement. Do not show percentages for the fixed costs.
2. Refer to the income statements in (1) above. For both present operations and the proposed new operations, compute *(a)* the degree of operating leverage, *(b)* the

break-even point in dollars, and *(c)* the margin of safety in both dollar and percentage terms.

3. Refer again to the data in (1) above. As a manager, what factor would be paramount in your mind in deciding whether to purchase the new equipment? (You may assume that ample funds are available to make the purchase.)
4. Refer to the original data. Rather than purchase new equipment, the president is thinking about changing the company's marketing method. Under the new method, the president estimates that sales would increase by 50 percent each month and that net income would increase by two thirds. Fixed costs would be slashed to only $160,000 per month. Using the president's estimates, compute the break-even point in dollars for the company after the change in marketing method. What risks can you see in the president's proposal?

P6–24 Break-Even Analysis with Step Fixed Costs Wymont Hospital operates a general hospital that rents space and beds to separate departments such as pediatrics, maternity, and surgery. Wymont Hospital charges each separate department for common services to its patients such as meals and laundry and for administrative services such as billing and collections. Space and bed rentals are fixed for the year.

For the year ended June 30, 19x7, the pediatrics department at Wymont Hospital charged its patients an average of $65 per day, had a capacity of 80 beds, operated 24 hours per day for 365 days, and had total revenue of $1,138,800.

Expenses charged by the hospital to the pediatrics department for the year were as follows:

	Basis for Allocation	
	Patient-Days (variable)	**Bed Capacity (fixed)**
Dietary	$ 42,952	
Janitorial		$ 12,800
Laundry	28,000	
Laboratory	47,800	
Pharmacy	33,800	
Repairs and maintenance	5,200	7,140
General administrative services		131,760
Rent		275,320
Billings and collections	87,000	
Other	18,048	25,980
	$262,800	$453,000

The only personnel directly employed by the pediatrics department are supervising nurses, nurses, and aides. The hospital has minimum personnel requirements based on total annual patient-days. Hospital requirements, beginning at the minimum expected level of operation, follow:

Annual Patient-Days	Aides	Nurses	Supervising Nurses
10,000–14,000	21	11	4
14,001–17,000	22	12	4
17,001–23,725	22	13	4
23,726–25,550	25	14	5
25,551–27,375	26	14	5
27,376–29,200	29	16	6

These staffing levels represent full-time equivalents, and it should be assumed that the pediatrics department always employs only the minimum number of required full-time equivalent personnel.

Annual salaries for each class of employee are: supervising nurses, $18,000; nurses, $13,000; and aides, $5,000. Salary expense for the year ended June 30, 19x7, was $72,000, $169,000, and $110,000 for supervising nurses, nurses, and aides, respectively.

Required

1. Compute the following:
   a. The number of patient-days in the pediatrics department for the year ended June 30, 19x7. (Each day a patient is in the hospital is known as a "patient-day.")
   b. The variable cost per patient-day for the year ended June 30, 19x7.
   c. The total fixed costs, including both allocated fixed costs and personnel costs, in the pediatrics department for each level of operation shown above (i.e., total fixed costs at the 10,000–14,000 patient-day level of operation, total fixed costs at the 14,001–17,000 patient-day level of operation, etc.).
2. Using the data computed in (1) above and any other data as needed, compute the *minimum* number of patient-days required for the pediatrics department to break even. You may assume that variable and fixed cost behavior and that revenue per patient-day will remain unchanged in the future.
3. Determine the minimum number of patient-days required for the pediatrics department to earn an annual profit of $200,000.

(CPA, Heavily Adapted)

P6–25 Missing Data; Integration of CVP Factors After being fired for padding his travel expense reports, a distraught employee of Putrex Company grabbed a large fire extinguisher and proceeded to spray foam into numerous offices before he was forcibly ejected from the company's premises. The foam damaged many important papers, among which was a report containing an analysis of one of the company's products that you had just completed and placed on your supervisor's desk. This report is needed for a meeting of the company's planning committee later in the day. The report contained the following *projected* income statement for next month on the product (the question marks indicate obliterated data):

PUTREX COMPANY
Projected Income Statement
For the Month Ended August 31, 19x1

	Total	Per Unit	Percent
Sales (90,000 units)	$?	$?	?
Less variable expenses	?	?	?
Contribution margin	?	$?	?
Less fixed expenses	?		
Net income	$243,000		

The report also contained the results of sales and expenses for the product for the month just completed, as well as certain analytical data that you had prepared. These data are given on the next page:

PUTREX COMPANY
Actual Income Statement
For the Month Ended July 31, 19x1

	Total	Per Unit	Percent
Sales (? units)	$?	$?	100
Less variable expenses	?	?	?
Contribution margin	?	$?	?
Less fixed expenses	?		
Net income	$?		
Degree of operating leverage		?	
Break-even point:			
In units		? units	
In dollars		$1,012,500	
Margin of safety:			
In dollars		$?	
In percentage		25%	

The supervisor has just given the report back to you with instructions to "work up" the missing information and have the completed report back within the hour. You are spurred on by the realization that the fired employee's position will need to be filled quickly, and a sterling effort on your part could make you a leading candidate for the job.

You recall from your prior work on the report that the net income for July on the product was $135,000 (the same as the cost of your new home). You also remember that sales for August are projected to increase by 20 percent over sales for July. Finally, you remember that your supervisor likes to use the degree of operating leverage as a predictive tool.

Total fixed expenses, the unit selling price, and the unit variable expenses are planned to be the same in August as they were in July.

Required

1. For the July 19x1 actual data, do the following:
   a. Complete the July 19x1 income statement (all three columns).
   b. Compute the break-even point in units, and prove the break-even point in dollars. Use the unit contribution method.
   c. Compute the margin of safety in dollars, and prove the margin of safety percentage.
   d. Compute the degree of operating leverage as of July 31, 19x1.
2. For the August 19x1 data, do the following:
   a. Complete the August 19x1 projected income statement (all three columns).
   b. Compute the margin of safety in dollars and percent, and compute the degree of operating leverage. Why has the margin of safety gone up and the degree of operating leverage gone down?
3. Excited over the fact that you were able to complete (1) and (2) above so quickly, you decide to "lock up" the new job by providing your supervisor with some valuable, additional information. You have just learned from the purchasing agent that the cost of direct materials may increase by $0.90 per unit next year. Assuming that this cost increase takes place and that selling price and other cost factors remain unchanged, how many units will the company have to sell in a month to earn a net income equal to 15 percent of sales?

CASES

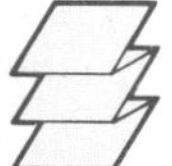

C6–26 Detailed Income Statement; CVP Analysis Alpine, Inc., has been experiencing losses for some time, as shown by its most recent income statement:

ALPINE, INC.
Income Statement
For the Year Ended June 30, 19x1

Sales (40,000 units at $12)			$480,000
Less cost of goods sold:			
Direct materials		$120,000	
Direct labor		65,600	
Manufacturing overhead		90,000	275,600
Gross margin			204,400
Less operating expenses:			
Selling expenses:			
Variable:			
Sales commissions	$38,400		
Shipping	14,000	52,400	
Fixed (advertising, salaries)		110,000	
Administrative expenses:			
Variable (billing, other)		3,200	
Fixed (salaries, other)		85,000	250,600
Net loss			$ (46,200)

All variable expenses in the company vary in terms of units sold, except for sales commissions, which are based on sales dollars. Variable manufacturing overhead is 50 cents per unit. The company's plant has a capacity of 70,000 units.

Management is particularly disappointed with 19x1's operating results. Several possible courses of action are being studied to determine what should be done to make 19x2 profitable.

Required

1. Redo Alpine, Inc.'s 19x1 income statement in the contribution format. Show both a total column and a per unit column on your statement. Leave enough space to the right of your numbers to enter the solution to both parts of (2) below.
2. In an effort to make 19x2 profitable, the president is considering two proposals prepared by members of her staff:
   a. The sales manager would like to reduce the unit selling price by 25 percent. He is certain that this would fill the plant to capacity.
   b. The executive vice president would like to *increase* the unit selling price by 25 percent, increase the sales commissions to 12 percent of sales, and increase advertising by $90,000. Based on experience in another company, he is confident this would trigger a 50 percent increase in unit sales.

   Prepare two contribution income statements, one showing what profits would be under the sales manager's proposal and one showing what profits would be under the vice president's proposal. On each statement, include both total and per unit columns (do not show per unit data for the fixed costs).
3. Refer to the original data. The president thinks it would be unwise to change the selling price. Instead, she wants to use less costly materials in manufacturing units of product, thereby reducing costs by $1.73 per unit. How many units would have to be sold during 19x2 to earn a target profit of $59,000 for the year?
4. Refer to the original data. Alpine, Inc.'s advertising agency thinks that the problem lies in inadequate promotion. By how much can advertising be increased and still allow the company to earn a target return of 4.5 percent on sales of 60,000 units?
5. Refer to the original data. The company has been approached by an overseas distributor who wants to purchase 15,000 units on a special price basis. There would be no sales commission on these units. However, shipping costs would be increased by 80 percent, and variable administrative costs would be reduced by 50 percent. Alpine, Inc., would have to pay a foreign import duty of $3,150 on

behalf of the overseas distributor in order to get the goods into the country. Given these data, what unit price would have to be quoted on the 15,000 units by Alpine, Inc., to allow the company to earn a profit of $18,000 on total operations? Regular business would not be disturbed by this special order.

C6–27 **Cost Structure; Break-Even Point; Target Profits** "In my opinion, it will be a mistake if that new plant is built," said Carl Roberts, controller of Tanka Toys. "Why, if that plant was in existence right now, we would be reporting a loss of $100,000 for the year (1990) rather than a profit, and 1990 sales have been the best in the history of the company."

Mr. Roberts was speaking of a new, automated production facility that Tanka Toys is considering building. The company was organized only seven years ago, but it is growing rapidly due to its innovative new toys. Annual sales since inception of the company, along with net income as a percentage of sales, are presented below:

Year	Sales	Income as a Percent of Sales
1984	$ 800,000	7.4
1985	1,900,000	7.0
1986	2,600,000	6.1
1987	3,000,000	5.3
1988	2,400,000	1.2
1989	3,700,000	3.8
1990	4,000,000	3.0

Although the company has always been profitable, in recent years rising costs have cut into its profit margins. The main production plant was constructed in 1984, but growth has been greater than anyone anticipated, making it necessary to rent additional production and storage space in various locations around the country. This spreading out of production facilities has caused costs to rise, particularly since the company is somewhat limited in the amount of automated equipment that it can use and therefore must rely on training a large number of new workers each year during peak production seasons.

Tanka Toys produces about 75 percent of its toys between April and September and only about 25 percent during the remainder of the year. This seasonal production pattern is followed by many toy manufacturers, since it saves on storage costs and reduces the chances of toy obsolescence due to style changes. Other toy manufacturers produce evenly throughout the year, thereby maintaining a stable work force. Alice Clark, manufacturing vice president of Tanka Toys, is pushing the new plant very hard, since it would permit Tanka Toys to produce on a more even basis, as well as to automate many hand operations and thereby dramatically reduce variable costs.

Tanka's management recognizes that much of the company's success is due to the creative efforts of Golda Frieburg, head of the company's new products department. Golda has developed new toys that have revolutionized some areas of the toy market. Her talents are now becoming recognized by competitors, and Tanka's management is concerned that one of these competitors may be successful in "buying" her away from the company.

Although total toy sales are quite stable, individual toy manufacturers can experience wide fluctuations from year to year according to how well their toys are received by the market. For example, Tanka Toys "missed the market" on one of its toy lines in 1988, causing a 20 percent drop in sales and a sharp drop in profits, as shown above. Other manufacturers have experienced even sharper drops in sales, some on a prolonged basis, and Tanka Toys feels fortunate in the sales stability that it has enjoyed.

Mr. Roberts points out that although variable costs will be reduced by the new plant, fixed costs will rise steeply, to $1,700,000 per year. On the other hand, fixed costs are now only $450,000 per year. Mr. Roberts is confident (and Ms. Clark agrees) that with stringent cost controls variable expenses can be held at 82 percent of sales if the company continues with its present production setup. Variable expenses will be 60 percent of sales if the new plant is built.

Ms. Clark points out that marketing projections predict only a 10 percent annual growth rate in sales if the company continues with its present production setup, whereas sales growth is expected to be as much as 15 percent annually if the new plant is built. The new plant would provide ample capacity to meet projected sales needs for many years into the future. Economies of expansion dictate, however, that any expansion undertaken be made in one step, since expansion by stages is too costly to be a feasible alternative.

Required

1. Assuming that the company continues with its present production setup:
   a. Compute the break-even point in sales dollars.
   b. Prepare a contribution income statement for each of the next three years (1991–93) using projected sales as follows (these figures assume a 10 percent growth rate in sales each year):

Year	Sales
1991	$4,400,000
1992	4,840,000
1993	5,324,000

   Assume that cost behavior patterns remain stable over the three-year period.
   c. Refer to the computations in *(b)* above. Compute the operating leverage and the margin of safety for each year. The MS should be expressed in percentage terms. Carry computations to one decimal place.
2. Assuming that the company builds the new plant, redo the computations in (1)*(a)*, (1)*(b)*, and (1)*(c)* above. Use projected sales as follows (these figures assume a 15 percent growth rate in sales each year):

Year	Sales
1991	$4,600,000
1992	5,290,000
1993	6,083,500

3. Compute the level of sales at which profits would be equal with either the old or the new plant.
4. Refer to the original data. Assume that Tanka Toys "misses the market" with its toy lines in 1991 and that sales fall by 20 percent to only $3,200,000 for the year. Compute the net profit or loss for the year with and without the new plant.
5. Refer to the original data. Suppose that the company is anxious to earn a target profit of at least 12 percent on sales.
   a. At what sales level will the 12 percent target profit on sales be achieved if the new plant is built? According to the company's projected sales growth, in what year will this sales level be reached?
   b. At what sales level will the 12 percent target profit on sales be achieved if the company keeps its old plant? How long does it appear that it will take the company to reach this sales level?
6. Based on the data in (1)–(5) above, evaluate the risks and merits of building the new plant and recommend to management the course of action that you think should be taken. *Be prepared to defend your recommendation in class.*

7

Segmented Reporting and the Contribution Approach to Costing

LEARNING OBJECTIVES

After studying Chapter 7, you should be able to:

1 Explain how costs are allocated to segments of an organization when the contribution approach is used.

2 Differentiate between traceable fixed costs and common fixed costs.

3 Compute the segment margin and explain how it differs from the contribution margin.

4 Prepare a segmented income statement using the contribution approach.

5 Explain how direct costing differs from absorption costing and compute the cost of a unit of product under each method.

6 Describe how fixed overhead costs are deferred in inventory and released from inventory under absorption costing.

7 Prepare income statements using both absorption costing and direct costing and reconcile the two net income figures.

8 Define or explain the key terms listed at the end of the chapter.

One aspect of the accountant's work centers on the problem of assigning costs to various parts of an organization. Cost assignment is necessary to provide useful and relevant data for three purposes:

1. For product costing and for pricing.
2. For appraisal of managerial performance.
3. For making special decisions.

In assigning costs for these purposes, the accountant can use either of two approaches. One approach, known as absorption costing, was discussed at length in Chapter 3. The other, generally called the contribution approach to costing, was introduced in the preceding chapter in conjunction with our discussion of cost-volume-profit (CVP) analysis. The purpose of this chapter is to study the contribution approach in greater depth. We have already seen how it can be used in making a variety of special decisions. We shall now see how it can be used in preparing segmented statements for management's use, and how the cost of a unit of product or the cost of a service is computed under this costing method.

SEGMENTED REPORTING

To operate effectively, managers must have a great deal more information available to them than the information provided by a single, companywide income statement. The reason is that such a statement usually provides only a summary of overall operations; as such, it typically does not contain enough detail to allow the manager to detect problems that may exist in the organization. For example, some product lines may be profitable while others may be unprofitable; some salespersons may be more effective than others; some sales territories may have a poor sales mix or may be overlooking sales opportunities; or some producing divisions may be ineffectively using their capacity and/or resources. To uncover problems such as these, the manager needs not just one but several income statements, and these statements must be designed to focus on the *segments* of the company. The preparation of income statements of this type is known as **segmented reporting.**

A **segment** can be defined as any part or activity of an organization about which a manager seeks cost or revenue data. Examples of segments would include sales territories, individual stores or other retail outlets, service centers, manufacturing divisions or plants, sales departments, and individual product lines. How does the manager prepare income statements that show the results of segment activities? As illustrated in the pages that follow, such statements are generally prepared using the contribution approach with which we are already familiar. Statements prepared in this format are indispensable to the manager in analyzing the parts of an organization as well as operations for the company as a whole.

Differing Levels of Segmented Statements

Segmented statements can be prepared for activity at many different levels in an organization and in differing formats. Exhibit 7–1 illustrates three levels of segmented statements presented in a format that is widely used. Observe from this exhibit that the total company is first segmented in terms of divisions. Then one of these divisions, Division 2, is further segmented in terms of the product lines sold within the division. In turn, one of these product lines, the regular model, is further segmented in terms of the territories in which it is sold.

Notice that as we go from one segmented statement to another, we are looking at smaller and smaller pieces of the company. This is a widely used approach to segmented reporting. If management desired, Division 1 could also be segmented into smaller pieces in the same way as we have segmented Division 2, thereby providing a detailed look at all aspects and levels of the company's operations.

The benefits accruing to the manager from a series of statements such as those contained in Exhibit 7–1 are very great. By carefully examining trends and results in each segment, the manager will be able to gain considerable insight into the company as a whole, and perhaps will discover opportunities and courses of action that would otherwise have remained hidden from view.

Assigning Costs to Segments

Segmented statements for internal use are typically prepared in the contribution format, as stated earlier. The same costing guidelines are used in preparing these statements as are used in preparing contribution-type statements generally, with one exception. This lies in the handling of the fixed costs. Notice from Exhibit 7–1 that the fixed costs are divided into two parts on a segmented statement—one part labeled *traceable* and the other part labeled *common*. Only those fixed costs labeled traceable are charged to the various segments. If a fixed cost is not traceable directly to some segment, then it is treated as a common cost and kept separate from the segments themselves. Thus, under the contribution approach, a cost is never arbitrarily assigned to a segment of an organization.

In sum, two guidelines are followed in assigning costs to the various segments of a company under the contribution approach:

1. First, according to cost behavior patterns (that is, variable and fixed).
2. Second, according to whether the costs are *directly traceable* to the segments involved.

We will now consider various parts of Exhibit 7–1 in greater depth.

Sales and Contribution Margin

In order to prepare segmented statements, it is necessary to keep records of sales by individual segment, as well as in total for the organization. After deducting related variable expenses, a contribution margin figure can then be computed for each segment, as illustrated in Exhibit 7–1.

Recall from the prior chapter that the contribution margin is an extremely useful piece of data to the manager—particularly for determining the effect

EXHIBIT 7-1
Segmented Income Statements

Segments Defined as Divisions

	Total Company	Segment: Division 1	Segment: Division 2
Sales	$500,000	$300,000	$200,000
Less variable expenses:			
Variable cost of goods sold	180,000	120,000	60,000
Other variable expenses	50,000	30,000	20,000
Total variable expenses	230,000	150,000	80,000
Contribution margin	270,000	150,000	120,000
Less traceable fixed expenses	170,000	90,000	80,000*
Divisional segment margin	100,000	$ 60,000	$ 40,000
Less common fixed expenses	25,000		
Net income	$ 75,000		

Segments Defined as Product Lines of Division 2

	Division 2	Segment: Deluxe Model	Segment: Regular Model
Sales	$200,000	$75,000	$125,000
Less variable expenses:			
Variable cost of goods sold	60,000	20,000	40,000
Other variable expenses	20,000	5,000	15,000
Total variable expenses	80,000	25,000	55,000
Contribution margin	120,000	50,000	70,000
Less traceable fixed expenses	70,000	30,000	40,000
Product line segment margin	50,000	$20,000	$ 30,000
Less common fixed expenses	10,000		
Divisional segment margin	$ 40,000		

Segments Defined as Sales Territories for One Product Line of Division 2

	Regular Model	Segment: Home Sales	Segment: Foreign Sales
Sales	$125,000	$100,000	$25,000
Less variable expenses:			
Variable cost of goods sold	40,000	32,000	8,000
Other variable expenses	15,000	5,000	10,000
Total variable expenses	55,000	37,000	18,000
Contribution margin	70,000	63,000	7,000
Less traceable fixed expenses	25,000	15,000	10,000
Territorial segment margin	45,000	$ 48,000	$(3,000)
Less common fixed expenses	15,000		
Product line segment margin	$ 30,000		

* Notice that this $80,000 in traceable fixed expense is divided into two parts—$70,000 traceable and $10,000 common—when Division 2 is broken down into product lines. The reasons for this are discussed in a later section, "Traceable Costs Can Become Common Costs."

on net income of increases and decreases in sales volume. If sales volume goes up or down, the impact on net income can easily be computed by simply multiplying the unit contribution margin figure by the change in units sold or by multiplying the change in sales dollars by the CM ratio. Segmented statements give the manager the ability to make such computations on a product-by-product, division-by-division, or territory-by-territory basis, thereby providing the information needed to shore up areas of weakness or to capitalize on areas of strength.

It is important to keep in mind that *the contribution margin is basically a short-run planning tool.* As such, it is especially valuable in decisions relating to temporary uses of capacity, to special orders, and to short-run product line promotion. Decisions relating to the short run usually involve only variable costs and revenues, which of course are the very elements involved in contribution margin. By carefully monitoring segment contribution margins and segment contribution margin ratios, the manager will be in a position to make those short-run decisions that will maximize the contribution of each segment to the overall profitability of the organization.

The Importance of Fixed Costs

The emphasis that we place on the usefulness of the contribution margin should not be taken as a suggestion that fixed costs are not important. *Fixed costs are very important in any organization.* What the contribution approach does imply is that *different costs are needed for different purposes.* For one purpose, variable costs and revenues alone may be adequate for a manager's needs; for another purpose, his or her needs may encompass the fixed costs as well.

The breaking apart of fixed and variable costs also emphasizes to management that the costs are controlled differently and that these differences must be kept clearly in mind for both short-run and long-run planning. Moreover, the grouping of fixed costs under the contribution approach highlights the fact that net income emerges only after the fixed costs have been covered. It also highlights the fact that after the fixed costs have been covered, net income will increase to the extent of the contribution margin generated on each additional unit sold. All of these concepts are useful to the manager *internally* for planning purposes.

Traceable and Common Fixed Costs

Traceable fixed costs can be defined as those fixed costs that can be identified with a particular segment and that arise because of the existence of the segment. **Common fixed costs** can be defined as those fixed costs that cannot be identified with any particular segment but rather arise because of overall operating activities. In order to be assigned to segments, a common fixed cost would have to be allocated on some highly arbitrary[1] basis, such as sales dollars. Common costs are also known as *indirect costs.*

[1] It can be argued that *all* cost allocations are arbitrary. The use of the term *arbitrary* in this chapter is intended to convey the thought that a particular cost is not traceable to a segment, but yet it is being charged to that segment on some basis chosen solely by management.

Examples of traceable fixed costs would include advertising outlays made on behalf of a particular segment, the salary of a segment manager (such as a product line supervisor), and depreciation of buildings and equipment acquired for use in a particular segment. Examples of common fixed costs would include corporate image advertising (from which many segments may benefit), salaries of top administrative officers, and depreciation of facilities shared by more than one segment.

Identifying Traceable Fixed Costs

The distinction that we have drawn between traceable and common fixed costs is crucial in segmented reporting, since traceable fixed costs are charged to the segments, whereas common fixed costs are not, as mentioned earlier. As the reader may suppose, in an actual situation it is sometimes hard to determine whether a cost should be classified as traceable or common. One widely used rule of thumb is to treat as traceable costs *only those costs that would disappear over time if the segment itself disappeared.* For example, if Division 1 in Exhibit 7–1 were discontinued, then it is unlikely that the division manager would be retained. Since she would disappear with her division, then her salary should be classified as a traceable fixed cost of the division. On the other hand, the president of the company undoubtedly would continue even if Division 1 were dropped. Therefore, his salary is common to both divisions. The same idea can be expressed in another way: *treat as traceable costs only those costs that are added as a result of the creation of a segment.*

There will always be some costs that fall between the traceable and common categories, and considerable care and good judgment will be required for their proper classification. The important point is to resist the temptation to allocate the common costs. From a managerial point of view, *any allocation of common costs to segments would simply destroy the value of the segment margin as a guide to long-run segment profitability.*

Traceable Costs Can Become Common Costs

Fixed costs that are traceable on one segmented statement may become common if the company is divided into smaller segments. This is because there are limits to how finely a cost can be separated without resorting to arbitrary allocation. The more finely segments are defined, the more costs there are that become common.

This concept can be seen from the diagram below. Notice from the diagram that when segments are defined as divisions, Division 2 has $80,000 in traceable fixed expenses. Only $70,000 of this amount remains traceable, however, when we narrow our definition of a segment from divisions to that of the product lines within Division 2. Notice that the other $10,000 then becomes a common cost of these product lines.

Why would $10,000 of traceable fixed costs become common costs when the division is divided into product lines? The $10,000 could be depreciation on Division 2's plant building. This depreciation would be a *traceable* cost when we are speaking of the division as a whole, but it would be *common* to

	Total Company	Segment: Division 1	Segment: Division 2
Contribution margin.	$270,000	$150,000	$120,000
Less traceable fixed expenses	170,000	90,000	80,000

	Division 2	Segment: Deluxe Model	Segment: Regular Model
Contribution margin.	$120,000	$50,000	$70,000
Less traceable fixed expenses	70,000	30,000	40,000
Product line segment margin	50,000	$20,000	$30,000
Less common fixed expenses	10,000		
Divisional segment margin	$ 40,000		

the product lines produced within the building because both lines would share in the building's use. Any allocation of the depreciation between the two product lines would have to be on some arbitrary basis. To avoid this, we would treat the depreciation on the building as a common cost when Division 2 is segmented into product lines.

The $70,000 that remains a traceable fixed cost even after the division is segmented into product lines would consist of amounts that can be identified directly with the product lines on a nonarbitrary basis. This $70,000 might consist of advertising, for example, expended for product line promotion, of which $30,000 was expended for promotion of the deluxe model and $40,000 was expended for promotion of the regular model. Product line advertising would be a traceable fixed cost of the division as a whole, and it would still be a traceable cost when looking only at the product lines within the division, since it could be assigned to the lines without the necessity of making an arbitrary allocation.

Segment Margin

Observe from Exhibit 7–1 that the **segment margin** is obtained by deducting the traceable fixed costs of a segment from the segment's contribution margin. It represents the margin available after a segment has covered all of its own costs that can be applied toward the organization's common costs and then toward profits. *The segment margin is viewed as being the best gauge of the long-run profitability of a segment,* since only those costs that are assignable to the segment are used in its computation. If in the long run a segment can't cover its own costs, then that segment probably should not be retained (unless it is essential to sales in other segments). Notice from Ex-

EXHIBIT 7–2

Income Statement Segmented by Products

	Total Company		Product					
			A		B		C	
Sales	$100,000	100%	$30,000	100%	$50,000	100%	$20,000	100%
Less variable expenses	46,000	46	9,000	30	25,000	50	12,000	60
Contribution margin	54,000	54	21,000	70	25,000	50	8,000	40
Less traceable fixed expenses	30,000	30	15,000	50	10,000	20	5,000	25
Product segment margin	24,000	24	$ 6,000	20%	$15,000	30%	$ 3,000	15%
Less common fixed expenses	15,000	15						
Net income	$ 9,000	9%						

hibit 7–1, for example, that one sales territory (foreign) has a negative segment margin. This means that the segment is not covering its own costs and thus is not contributing to the overall profits of the company. In fact, it is detracting from profits in that its loss must be covered by other segments.[2]

From a decision-making point of view, the segment margin is most useful in those decisions relating to long-run needs and performance, such as capacity changes, long-run pricing policy, and segment return on investment. By contrast, as we noted earlier, the contribution margin is most useful in decisions relating to the short run, such as pricing of special orders and utilization of existing capacity through short-term promotional campaigns.

To emphasize these ideas, refer to the data in Exhibit 7–2. Here we have an income statement segmented by products. Notice that all three products are covering their own costs and thus have positive segment margins.

Which is the company's best product? The answer depends on your point of reference. In terms of *long-run performance,* product B is the company's best product. Note that it is generating a $15,000 segment margin each period, which by itself is adequate to cover all of the company's common fixed costs. Product B's segment margin ratio is also very high (30 percent), which indicates that its overall costs are low in relation to sales. Thus, as shown by its segment margin data, product B represents the company's best product in terms of long-run performance.

In terms of *short-run* promotional campaigns or *short-run* capacity utilization, however, management might prefer product A over product B. The reason is that product A has a higher contribution margin (CM) ratio. Note that product A's CM ratio is 70 percent as compared to only 50 percent for product B. Thus, product A will generate a greater amount of contribution margin for a given increase in sales. As we learned in Chapter 6, the greater the amount of contribution margin that a company is able to generate, the more quickly it will cover its fixed costs or increase its profits.

Of course, in making short-run decisions of this type, management must consider other factors as well, such as available capacity, the degree of

[2] Retention or elimination of product lines and other segments is covered in depth in Chapter 13.

market saturation, and the amount of sales that can be generated per dollar of advertising. But other factors being equal, in short-run promotional decisions or in capacity utilization decisions, management will focus on those products that will generate the greatest amount of contribution margin toward the covering of fixed costs.

To summarize, in evaluating the long-run performance of a segment, the manager will look at the segment margin and at the segment margin ratio. In short-run decision making, however (such as a two-week promotional campaign), the manager will look for the segments that will generate the greatest amount of contribution margin for the effort expended. Typically, this will be the segments that have the highest CM ratios.

Breakdown of Traceable Fixed Costs

In preparing segmented income statements, some managers like to separate the traceable fixed costs into two classes—discretionary and committed. As discussed in Chapter 5, discretionary fixed costs are under the immediate control of the manager, whereas committed fixed costs are not. Therefore, a breakdown of the traceable fixed costs into these two classes *allows a company to make a distinction between the performance of the segment manager and the performance of the segment as a long-term investment.*

In some situations, this distinction in performance can be very important. A top-flight manager, for example, may be assigned to a division that has an antiquated plant or that is saddled with other committed fixed costs that are beyond the segment manager's control. Under these conditions, it would be unfair to judge the segment manager's performance simply on a basis of the overall margin generated by the segment. Rather, in these circumstances, the discretionary fixed costs should be separated from the committed fixed costs and deducted as a separate group from the segment's contribution margin. The amount remaining after deducting the discretionary fixed costs, sometimes called a *segment performance margin,* should then be used as a basis for evaluating the segment manager's performance. This would be a valid measure of performance, since the amount involved would represent the margin generated by the segment after deducting all costs controllable by the segment manager. The committed fixed costs would then be deducted from the segment performance margin to determine the overall segment margin for the period.

The traceable costs of a segment can be broken down in still other ways. However, the discussion above is adequate for our purposes. Any further discussion, as well as numerical examples, is reserved for more advanced books.

Common Fixed Costs

Common fixed costs are not allocated to segments but simply deducted in total amount to arrive at the net income for the company as a whole.[3] (See Exhibits 7–1 and 7–2.) The managerial accountant contends that nothing is

[3] For external reporting purposes, the Financial Accounting Standards Board requires that all common costs be allocated among segments on a "reasonable" basis. FASB, *Statement of Financial Accounting Standards No. 14,* "Financial Reporting for Segments of a Business Enterprise" (Stamford, Conn., 1976), par. 10(d).

added to the overall usefulness of a segmented statement by allocating the common costs among segments. Rather, the accountant would argue that such allocations tend to *reduce* the usefulness of segmented statements. The reason is that arbitrary allocations draw attention away from those costs that are traceable to a segment and that should form a basis for appraising performance.

Moreover, it is argued that any attempt to allocate common costs among segments may result in misleading data or may obscure important relationships between segment revenues and segment earnings. Backer and McFarland state the problem as follows:

> A characteristic of all arbitrary allocations is that they lack universality. Sooner or later circumstances arise in which allocation procedures break down and yield misleading or even absurd results.[4]

Backer and McFarland point out that any allocation of a common cost to a segment may result in the segment's *appearing* to be unprofitable, whereas it may be contributing substantially above its own traceable costs toward the overall profitability of the firm. In such cases, the allocated costs may lead to the unwise elimination of a segment and to a *decrease* in profits for the company as a whole.

Varying Breakdowns of Total Sales

In order to obtain more detailed information, a company may show total sales broken down into several different segment arrangements. For example, a company may show total sales segmented in three different ways: (1) segmented according to divisions; (2) segmented according to product lines, without regard to the divisions in which the products are sold; and (3) segmented according to the sales territories in which the sales were made. In each case, the sum of the sales by segments would add up to total company sales; the variation in segment arrangements would simply give management the power to look at the total company from several different directions. This type of segmented reporting provides much the same perspective as looking at a beautiful landscape from several different views—from each view you see something you didn't see before.

After this type of segmentation of total sales has been made, many companies then go ahead and break each segment down more finely, such as we illustrated earlier in Exhibit 7–1 and such as is illustrated graphically in Exhibit 7–3. With the availability of the computer, the type of segmentation that we describe here is well within the reach of most companies today.

Sales Segmented by Products and Territories

To provide an example of how total sales can be divided into more than one segment arrangement, assume that Fairfield Company sells two products, X and Y, in two sales territories, the East and the West. Cost and revenue data on the products and the sales territories follow:

[4] Morton Backer and Walter B. McFarland, *External Reporting for Segments of a Business* (New York: National Association of Accountants, 1968), p. 23.

EXHIBIT 7–3
Graphic Presentation of Segmented Reporting—Detroit Motor Company

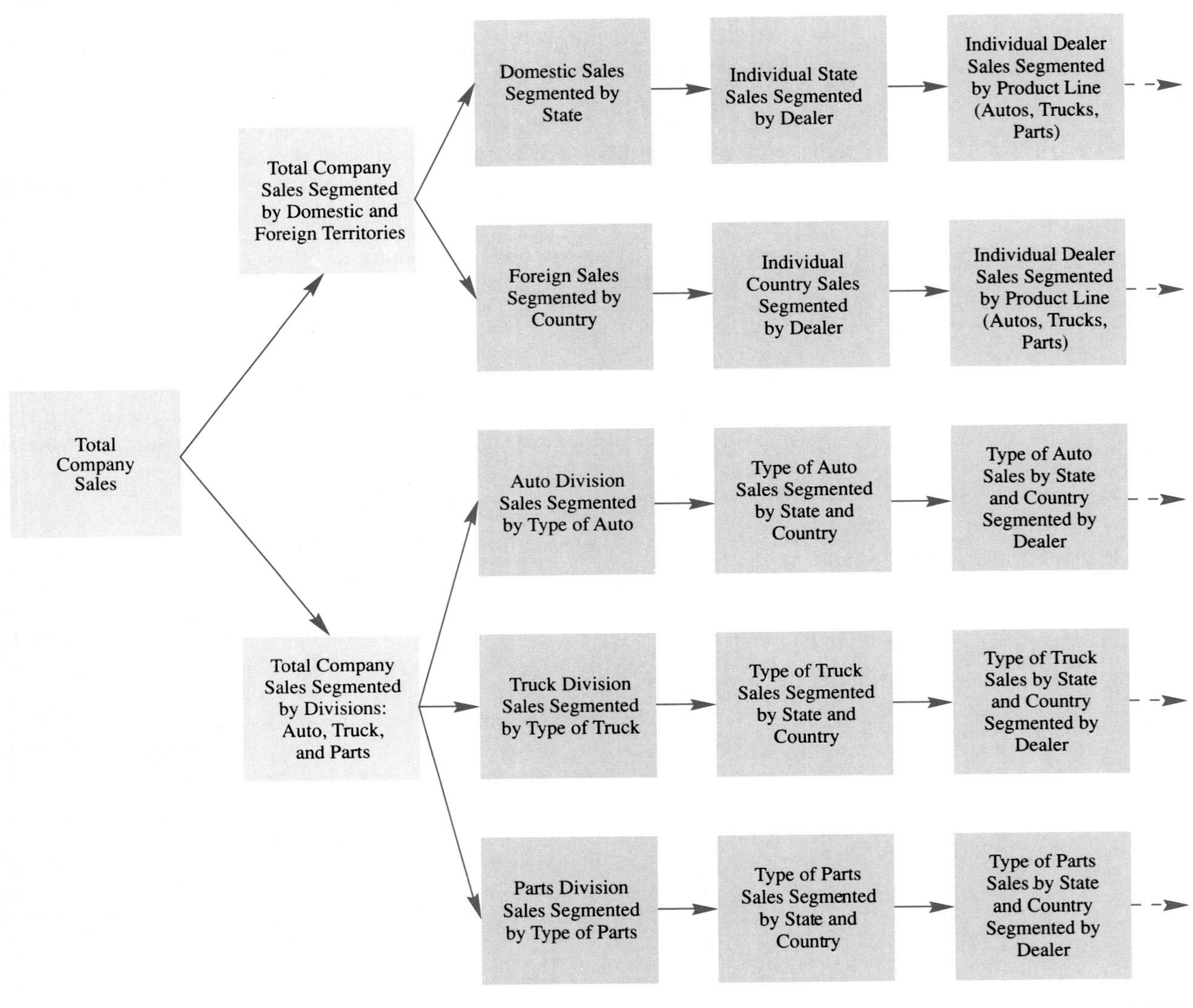

1. Selling price, variable expenses, and contribution margin per unit:

	Product	
	X	Y
Selling price per unit	$10	$6
Variable expense per unit.	6	4
Contribution margin per unit . . .	$ 4	$2

EXHIBIT 7–4

Total Sales Segmented by Products and by Sales Territories

Total Sales Presented by Products

	Total Company	Product X	Product Y
Sales	$190,000	$100,000	$90,000
Less variable expenses	120,000	60,000	60,000
Contribution margin	70,000	40,000	30,000
Less traceable fixed expenses:			
Production	14,000	8,000	6,000
Administration—products	3,500	2,000	1,500
Total traceable fixed expenses	17,500	10,000	7,500
Product segment margin	52,500	$ 30,000	$22,500
Less common fixed expenses:			
Selling—sales territories	22,000		
Administration—sales territories	4,500		
General administration	9,000		
Total common fixed expenses	35,500		
Net income	$ 17,000		

Total Sales Presented by Sales Territories

	Total Company	Sales Territory East	Sales Territory West
Sales	$190,000	$66,000*	$124,000*
Less variable expenses	120,000	42,000†	78,000†
Contribution margin	70,000	24,000	46,000
Less traceable fixed expenses:			
Selling—sales territories	22,000	12,000	10,000
Administration—sales territories	4,500	2,200	2,300
Total traceable fixed expenses	26,500	14,200	12,300
Territorial segment margin	43,500	$ 9,800	$ 33,700
Less common fixed expenses:			
Production	14,000		
Administration—products	3,500		
General administration	9,000		
Total common fixed expenses	26,500		
Net income	$ 17,000		

	Total Company	Sales Territory East	Sales Territory West
* Sales by sales territories:			
Product X sales at $10 per unit	$100,000	$30,000	$ 70,000
Product Y sales at $6 per unit	90,000	36,000	54,000
Total sales, as above	$190,000	$66,000	$124,000
† Variable expenses by sales territories:			
Product X variable expenses, at $6 per unit	$ 60,000	$18,000	$ 42,000
Product Y variable expenses, at $4 per unit	60,000	24,000	36,000
Total variable expenses, as above	$120,000	$42,000	$ 78,000

2. Sales in units during 19x1 were:

	Sales Territory		
	East	West	Total Sales
Product X sales	3,000	7,000	10,000
Product Y sales	6,000	9,000	15,000

3. Fixed costs incurred during 19x1 were:

	Product		Sales Territory	
	X	Y	East	West
Fixed production costs	$8,000	$6,000	—	—
Fixed selling costs	—	—	$12,000	$10,000
Fixed administrative costs	2,000	1,500	2,200	2,300

In addition, the company had $9,000 in fixed general administrative costs during 19x1 that cannot be charged directly to any segment.

Exhibit 7–4 presents total sales for the company for 19x1, broken down first between products and then between sales territories. Notice from the exhibit that although the products are about equally profitable, this equality does not carry over to the sales territories. The West is much more profitable than the East. Thus, the segmented statements point out to management those areas that may be in need of attention.

In summary, segmented reporting gives a company the ability to look at itself from many different directions. Some of the ways in which cost and profitability data can be generated include:

1. By division.
2. By company.
3. By store or other retail outlet.
4. By service center.
5. By product or product line.
6. By salesperson.
7. By sales territory.
8. By region of the country.
9. By domestic and foreign operations.

As we have noted, each of these segments can in turn be broken down into many parts. Indeed, the number of possible directions in which segments can be defined is limited only by one's imagination or by the needs of the firm.

INVENTORY VALUATION UNDER THE CONTRIBUTION APPROACH—DIRECT COSTING

As discussed in Chapter 3, absorption costing allocates a portion of fixed manufacturing overhead to each unit produced during a period, along with variable manufacturing costs. Since absorption costing mingles variable and fixed costs together, units of product costed by that method are not well suited for inclusion in a contribution-type income statement. This has led to an alternative costing method that focuses on cost behavior in computing unit costs. This alternative method is called *direct costing*. It harmonizes fully with the contribution approach and is widely used by manufacturing companies and other organizations in their preparation of contribution-type income statements.

Direct Costing

Under **direct costing,** only those costs of production that vary directly with activity are treated as product costs. This would include direct materials, direct labor, and the variable portion of manufacturing overhead. Fixed manufacturing overhead is not treated as a product cost under this method. Rather, fixed manufacturing overhead is treated as a period cost and, like selling and administrative expenses, it is charged off in its entirety against revenue each period. Consequently, the inventory cost of a unit of product under the direct costing method contains no element of fixed overhead cost.

Although it is widely used, the term *direct costing* is really a misnomer. More accurate terms for this costing method would be **variable** or **marginal costing,** since the method centers on the notion that only variable production costs should be added to the cost of goods produced. The term *direct costing* is so firmly embedded in the literature and in everyday usage, however, that it seems unlikely that any change in terminology will be made.

Absorption Costing

As we learned in Chapter 3, **absorption costing** treats *all* costs of production as product costs, regardless of whether they are variable or fixed in nature. Thus, unlike direct costing, absorption costing allocates a portion of the fixed manufacturing overhead to each unit of product, along with the variable manufacturing costs. The cost of a unit of product under the absorption costing method therefore consists of direct materials, direct labor, and *both* variable and fixed overhead. Because absorption costing includes all costs of production as product costs, it is frequently referred to as the **full cost method.**

To complete this summary comparison of direct and absorption costing, we need to consider briefly the handling of selling and administrative expenses. These expenses are never treated as product costs, regardless of the costing method in use. Thus, under either direct or absorption costing, selling and administrative expenses are always treated as period costs and deducted from revenues as incurred.

The concepts discussed in this and in the preceding section are illustrated in Exhibit 7–5, which shows the classification of costs under both absorption and direct costing.

Unit Cost Computations

To illustrate the computation of unit costs under both direct and absorption costing, assume the following data:

Boley Company produces a single product. The cost characteristics of the product and of the manufacturing plant are given on the next page:

EXHIBIT 7–5

Cost Classifications—Absorption versus Direct Costing

Absorption Costing		Direct Costing
Product costs	Direct materials	Product costs
	Direct labor	
	Variable manufacturing overhead	
	Fixed manufacturing overhead	Period costs
Period costs	Selling and administrative expenses	

Number of units produced each year	6,000
Variable costs per unit:	
Direct materials	$ 2
Direct labor	4
Variable manufacturing overhead	1
Variable selling and administrative expenses	3
Fixed costs per year:	
Manufacturing overhead	30,000
Selling and administrative expenses	10,000

Required

1. Compute the cost of a unit of product under absorption costing.
2. Compute the cost of a unit of product under direct costing.

Solution

Absorption Costing

Direct materials	$ 2
Direct labor	4
Variable overhead	1
Total variable production cost	7
Fixed overhead ($30,000 ÷ 6,000 units of product)	5
Total cost per unit	$12

Direct Costing

Direct materials	$ 2
Direct labor	4
Variable overhead	1
Total cost per unit	$ 7

(The $30,000 fixed overhead will be charged off in total against income as a period expense along with the fixed selling and administrative expenses.)

Under the absorption costing method, notice that *all* production costs, variable and fixed, have been added to the cost of units produced during the period. Thus, if the company sells a unit of product and absorption costing is being used, then $12 (consisting of $7 variable cost and $5 fixed cost) will be deducted on the income statement as cost of goods sold. Similarly, any unsold units will be carried as inventory on the balance sheet at $12 each.

Under the direct costing method, notice that only the variable production costs have been added to the cost of units produced during the period. Thus, if the company sells a unit of product, only $7 will be deducted as cost of goods sold, and unsold units will be carried in the balance sheet inventory account at only $7 each.

The Controversy over Fixed Overhead Cost

Probably no subject in all of managerial accounting has created as much controversy among accountants as has direct costing. The controversy isn't over whether costs should be separated as between variable and fixed in matters relating to planning and control. Rather, the controversy is over the theoretical justification for excluding fixed overhead costs from the cost of units produced and therefore from inventory.

Advocates of direct costing argue that fixed overhead costs relate to the *capacity* to produce rather than to the actual production of units of product in a given year. That is, they argue that costs for facilities and equipment, insurance, supervisory salaries, and the like, represent costs of being *ready* to produce and therefore will be incurred regardless of whether any actual production takes place during the year. For this reason, advocates of direct costing feel that such costs should be charged against the period rather than against the product.

Advocates of absorption costing argue, on the other hand, that so far as product costing is concerned, it makes no difference whether a manufacturing cost is variable or fixed. They argue that fixed overhead costs such as depreciation and insurance are just as essential to the production process as are the variable costs, and therefore cannot be ignored in costing units of product. They argue that to be fully costed, each unit of product must bear an equitable portion of *all* manufacturing costs.

Although this difference in the handling of fixed overhead might seem slight, it can have a substantial impact on both the clarity and the usefulness of statement data, as we shall see in the following sections.

Comparison of Absorption and Direct Costing

Income statements prepared under the absorption and direct costing approaches are shown in Exhibit 7–6. In preparing these statements, we use the data for Boley Company presented earlier, along with other information about the company as given below:

Beginning inventory in units	-0-
Units produced	6,000
Units sold	5,000
Ending inventory in units	1,000
Selling price per unit	$ 20
Selling and administrative expenses:	
Variable per unit	3
Fixed per year	10,000

	Absorption Costing	Direct Costing
Cost of a unit of product:		
Direct materials	$ 2	$2
Direct labor	4	4
Variable overhead	1	1
Fixed overhead ($30,000 ÷ 6,000 units)	5	–
Total cost per unit	$12	$7

Several points can be made from the statements in Exhibit 7–6:

1. Under the absorption costing method, it is possible to defer a portion of the fixed overhead costs of the current period to future periods through the inventory account. Such a deferral is known as **fixed overhead cost deferred in inventory.** The process involved can be explained by referring to the data for Boley Company. During the current period, Boley Company produced 6,000 units but sold only 5,000 units, thus leaving 1,000 units in the ending inventory. Under the absorption costing method, each unit produced was assigned $5 in fixed overhead cost (see the unit cost computations above). Therefore, each of the 1,000 units going into inventory at the end of the period has $5 in fixed overhead cost attached to it, or a total of $5,000 for the 1,000 units involved. *This amount of fixed overhead cost of the current period has thereby been deferred in inventory to the next period, when, hopefully, these units will be taken out of inventory and sold.* The deferral of fixed overhead cost we are talking about can be seen clearly by analyzing the $12,000 ending inventory figure under the absorption costing method:

Variable manufacturing costs: 1,000 units × $7 . . .	$ 7,000
Fixed overhead costs: 1,000 units × $5.	5,000
Total inventory value.	$12,000

In summary, of the $30,000 in fixed overhead cost incurred during the period, only $25,000 (5,000 units sold × $5) has been included in cost of goods sold. The remaining $5,000 (1,000 units *not* sold × $5) has been deferred in inventory to the next period.

2. Under the direct costing method, the entire $30,000 in fixed overhead cost has been treated as an expense of the current period (see the bottom portion of the direct costing income statement).

3. The ending inventory figure under the direct costing method is $5,000 lower than it is under the absorption costing method. The reason is that under direct costing, only the variable manufacturing costs have been added to units of product and therefore included in inventory:

Variable manufacturing costs: 1,000 units × $7	$7,000

The $5,000 difference in ending inventories explains the difference in net income reported between the two costing methods. Net income is $5,000 *higher* under absorption costing since, as explained above, $5,000 of fixed overhead cost has been deferred in inventory to the next period under that costing method.

4. The absorption costing income statement makes no distinction between fixed and variable costs; therefore, it is not well suited for CVP computations, which we have emphasized as being important to good planning and control. In order to generate data for CVP analysis, it would be necessary to spend considerable time reworking and reclassifying the absorption statement.

5. The direct costing approach to costing units of product blends very well with the contribution approach to the income statement, since both concepts are based on the idea of classifying costs by behavior. The direct costing data in Exhibit 7–6 could be used immediately in CVP computations.

EXHIBIT 7–6
Comparison of Absorption and Direct Costing

Absorption Costing		
Sales (5,000 units × $20)		$100,000
Cost of goods sold:		
Beginning inventory	$ -0-	
Cost of goods manufactured (6,000 units × $12)	72,000	
Goods available for sale	72,000	
Less ending inventory (1,000 units × $12)	12,000	60,000
Gross margin		40,000
Less selling and administrative expenses ($15,000 total variable plus $10,000 fixed)		25,000
Net income		$ 15,000
Direct Costing		
Sales (5,000 units × $20)		$100,000
Less variable expenses:		
Variable cost of goods sold:		
Beginning inventory	$ -0-	
Variable manufacturing costs (6,000 units × $7)	42,000	
Goods available for sale	42,000	
Less ending inventory (1,000 units × $7)	7,000	
Variable cost of goods sold	35,000	
Variable selling and administrative expenses (5,000 units × $3)	15,000	50,000
Contribution margin		50,000
Less fixed expenses:		
Fixed overhead costs	30,000	
Fixed selling and administrative expenses	10,000	40,000
Net income		$ 10,000

Note the difference in ending inventories. Fixed overhead cost at $5 per unit is included under the absorption approach. This explains the difference in ending inventory and in net income (1,000 units × $5 = $5,000).

The Definition of an Asset

Essentially, the difference between the absorption costing method and the direct costing method centers on the matter of timing. Advocates of direct costing say that fixed manufacturing costs should be released against revenues immediately in total, whereas advocates of absorption costing say that fixed manufacturing costs should be released against revenues bit by bit as units of product are sold. Any units of product not sold under absorption costing result in fixed costs being inventoried and carried forward *as assets* to the next period. The solution to the controversy as to which costing method is "right" should therefore rest in large part on whether fixed costs added to inventory fall within the definition of an asset as this concept is generally viewed in accounting theory.

What Is an Asset? A cost is normally viewed as being an asset if it can be shown that it has revenue-producing powers, or if it can be shown that it will be beneficial in some way to operations in future periods. In short, a cost is an asset if it can be shown that it has *future service potential* that can be identified. For example, insurance prepayments are viewed as being assets, since they have future service potential. The prepayments acquire protection that can be used in future periods to guard against losses that might otherwise hinder operations. If fixed production costs added to inventory under absorption costing are indeed properly called assets, then they too must meet this test of service potential.

The Absorption Costing View Advocates of absorption costing argue that fixed production costs added to inventory do, indeed, have future service potential. They take the position that if production exceeds sales, then a benefit to future periods is created in the form of an inventory that can be carried forward and sold, resulting in a future inflow of revenue. They argue that *all costs* involved in the creation of inventory should be carried forward as assets—not just the variable costs. The fixed costs of depreciation, taxes, insurance, supervisory salaries, and so on, are just as essential to the creation of units of product as are the variable costs. It would be just as impossible to create units of product in the absence of equipment as it would be to create them in the absence of raw materials or in the absence of workers to operate the machines.

In sum, proponents of absorption costing argue that until the fixed production costs have been recognized and attached, units of product have not been fully costed. Both variable and fixed costs become inseparably attached as units are produced and *remain* inseparably attached regardless of whether the units are sold immediately or carried forward as inventory to generate revenue in future periods.

The Direct Costing View Advocates of direct costing argue that a cost has service potential and is therefore an asset *only if its incurrence now will make it unnecessary to incur the same cost again in the future.* Service potential is therefore said to hinge on the matter of *future cost avoidance*. If the incurrence of a cost now will have no effect on whether or not the same cost will be incurred again in the future, then that cost is viewed as having no relevance to future events. It is argued that such a cost can in no way represent a future benefit or service.

For example, the prepayment of insurance is viewed as being an asset because the cash outlays made when the insurance is acquired make it unnecessary to sustain the same outlays again in the future periods for which insurance protection has been purchased. In short, by making insurance payments now, a company *avoids* having to make payments in the future. Since prepayments of insurance result in *future cost avoidance,* the prepayments qualify as assets.

This type of cost avoidance does not exist in the case of fixed production costs. The incurrence of fixed production costs in one year in no way reduces the necessity to incur the same costs again in the following year. Since the incurrence of fixed production costs does not result in *future cost avoidance,* the costs of one year can have no relevance to future events and therefore cannot possibly represent a future benefit or service. Direct costing advocates argue, therefore, that no part of the fixed production costs of one year should ever be carried forward as an asset to the following year. Such costs do not result in future cost avoidance—the key test for any asset.

Extended Comparison of Income Data

Having gained some insights into the conceptual differences between absorption and direct costing, we are now prepared to take a more detailed look at the differences in the income data generated by these two approaches to cost allocation. Exhibit 7–7 presents data covering a span of three years. In the first year, production and sales are equal. In the second year, production exceeds sales. In the third year, the tables are reversed, with sales exceeding production.

Certain generalizations can be drawn from the data in Exhibit 7–7.

1. When production and sales are equal, the same net income will be realized regardless of whether absorption or direct costing is being used (see year 1 in Exhibit 7–7). The reason is that when production and sales are equal, there is no chance for fixed overhead costs to be deferred in inventory or released from inventory under absorption costing.

2. When production exceeds sales, the net income reported under absorption costing will generally be greater than the net income reported under direct costing (see year 2 in Exhibit 7–7). The reason is that when more is produced than is sold, part of the fixed overhead costs of the current period are deferred in inventory to the next period under absorption costing, as discussed earlier. In year 2, for example, \$30,000 of fixed overhead cost (5,000 units × \$6 per unit) has been deferred in inventory to year 3 under the absorption approach. Only that portion of the fixed overhead costs of year 2 under absorption costing that is associated with *units sold* is charged against income for that year.

Under direct costing, however, *all* of the fixed overhead costs of year 2 have been charged immediately against income as a period cost. As a result, the net income for year 2 under direct costing is \$30,000 *lower* than it is under absorption costing. Exhibit 7–8 contains a reconciliation of the direct costing and absorption costing net income figures.

3. When sales exceed production, the net income reported under the absorption costing approach will generally be less than the net income reported under the direct costing approach (see year 3 in Exhibit 7–7). The reason is that when more is sold than is produced, inventories are drawn down and fixed overhead costs that were previously deferred in inventory under absorption costing are released and charged against income (known as **fixed overhead cost released from inventory**). In year 3, for example, the \$30,000 in fixed overhead cost deferred in inventory under the absorption approach from year 2 to year 3 is released from inventory through the sales process and charged against income. As a result, the cost of goods sold for year 3 contains not only all of the fixed overhead costs for year 3 (since all that was produced in year 3 was sold in year 3) but \$30,000 of fixed overhead cost from year 2 as well.

By contrast, under direct costing only the fixed overhead costs of year 3 have been charged against year 3. The result is that net income under direct costing is \$30,000 *higher* than it is under absorption costing. Exhibit 7–8 contains a reconciliation of the direct costing and absorption costing net income figures.

EXHIBIT 7–7

Absorption Costing versus Direct Costing—Extended Income Data

Basic Data

Sales price per unit	$ 20
Variable manufacturing costs per unit (direct materials, direct labor, and variable overhead)	11
Fixed manufacturing overhead costs (total)	150,000
Cost of producing one unit of product:	
Under direct costing:	
Variable manufacturing costs	$ 11
Under absorption costing:	
Variable manufacturing costs	$ 11
Fixed overhead costs (based on a normal production volume of 25,000 units per year—$150,000 ÷ 25,000)	6
Total absorption costs	$ 17

Selling and administrative expenses are assumed, for simplicity, to be all fixed at $30,000 per year.

	Year 1	Year 2	Year 3	Three Years Together
Beginning inventory in units	–0–	–0–	5,000	–0–
Number of units produced	25,000	25,000	25,000	75,000
Number of units sold	25,000	20,000	30,000	75,000
Ending inventory in units	–0–	5,000	–0–	–0–
Direct Costing				
Sales	$500,000	$400,000	$600,000	$1,500,000
Less variable expenses	275,000*	220,000*	330,000*	825,000
Contribution margin	225,000	180,000	270,000	675,000
Less fixed expenses:				
Manufacturing overhead	150,000	150,000	150,000	450,000
Selling and administrative expenses	30,000	30,000	30,000	90,000
Total fixed expenses	180,000	180,000	180,000	540,000
Net income	$ 45,000	$ –0–	$ 90,000	$ 135,000
Absorption Costing				
Sales	$500,000	$400,000	$600,000	$1,500,000
Beginning inventory	–0–	–0–	85,000	–0–
Add cost of goods manufactured	425,000†	425,000	425,000	1,275,000
Goods available for sale	425,000	425,000	510,000	1,275,000
Less ending inventory	–0–	85,000‡	–0–	–0–
Cost of goods sold	425,000	340,000	510,000	1,275,000
Gross margin	75,000	60,000	90,000	225,000
Less selling and administrative expenses	30,000	30,000	30,000	90,000
Net income	$ 45,000	$ 30,000	$ 60,000	$ 135,000

* Year 1: 25,000 units sold × $11 = $275,000.
Year 2: 20,000 units sold × $11 = $220,000.
Year 3: 30,000 units sold × $11 = $330,000.

† 25,000 units produced × $17 = $425,000.

‡ 5,000 units in inventory × $17 = $85,000.

EXHIBIT 7–8

Reconciliation of Direct Costing and Absorption Costing—Net Income Data from Exhibit 7–7

	Year 1	Year 2	Year 3
Direct costing net income	$45,000	$ –0–	$ 90,000
Add fixed overhead costs deferred in inventory under absorption costing (5,000 units × $6 per unit)	—	30,000	—
Deduct fixed overhead costs released from inventory under absorption costing (5,000 units × $6 per unit)	—	—	(30,000)
Absorption costing net income	$45,000	$30,000	$ 60,000

4. Over an *extended* period of time, the net income figures reported under absorption costing and direct costing will tend to be the same. The reason is that over the long run sales can't exceed production, nor can production much exceed sales. The shorter the time period, the more the net income figures will tend to vary.

Sales Constant, Production Fluctuates

Exhibit 7–9 presents a reverse situation from that depicted in Exhibit 7–7. In Exhibit 7–7, we made production constant and allowed sales to fluctuate from period to period. In Exhibit 7–9, sales are constant and production fluctuates. Our purpose in Exhibit 7–9 is to observe the effect of changes in production on net income under both absorption and direct costing.

Direct Costing Net income is *not* affected by changes in production under direct costing. Notice from Exhibit 7–9 that net income is the same for all three years under the direct costing approach, although production exceeds sales in one year and is less than sales in another year. In short, the only thing that can affect net income under direct costing is a change in sales—a change in production has no impact when direct costing is in use.

Absorption Costing Net income *is* affected by changes in production when absorption costing is in use, however. As shown in Exhibit 7–9, net income under the absorption approach goes up in year 2, in response to the increase in production for that year, and then goes down in year 3, in response to the drop in production for that year. Note particularly that net income goes up and down between these two years *even though the same number of units is sold in each year*. The reason for this effect can be traced to the shifting of fixed overhead cost between periods under the absorption costing method.

Since this shifting of fixed overhead cost has already been discussed in preceding sections, at this point all we need to consider is how it affects the data in Exhibit 7–9. As shown in the exhibit, production exceeds sales in year 2, thereby causing 10,000 units to be carried forward as inventory to year 3. Each unit produced during year 2 has $6 in fixed overhead cost attached to it (see the unit cost computations at the top of Exhibit 7–9). Therefore, $60,000 (10,000 units × $6) of the fixed overhead costs of year 2 are not charged against that year but rather are added to the inventory account (along with the variable manufacturing costs). As a result, the net

EXHIBIT 7–9
Sensitivity to Changes in Production and Sales

Basic Data

Sales price per unit	$ 25
Variable manufacturing costs per unit	10
Fixed manufacturing overhead costs (total)	300,000
Selling and administrative expenses (all assumed, for simplicity, to be fixed)	210,000

	Year 1	Year 2	Year 3
Number of units produced	40,000	50,000	30,000
Number of units sold	40,000	40,000	40,000
Cost of producing one unit:			
Under direct costing (variable manufacturing costs only)	$10.00	$10.00	$10.00
Under absorption costing:			
Variable manufacturing costs	$10.00	$10.00	$10.00
Fixed overhead costs ($300,000 total spread in each year over the number of units produced)	7.50	6.00	10.00
Total cost per unit	$17.50	$16.00	$20.00
Direct Costing			
Sales (40,000 units)	$1,000,000	$1,000,000	$1,000,000
Less variable expenses (40,000 units)	400,000	400,000	400,000
Contribution margin	600,000	600,000	600,000
Less fixed expenses:			
Manufacturing overhead	300,000	300,000	300,000
Selling and administrative expenses	210,000	210,000	210,000
Total fixed expenses	510,000	510,000	510,000
Net income	$ 90,000	$ 90,000	$ 90,000
Absorption Costing			
Sales (40,000 units)	$1,000,000	$1,000,000	$1,000,000
Beginning inventory	–0–	–0–	160,000
Add cost of goods manufactured	700,000*	800,000*	600,000*
Goods available for sale	700,000	800,000	760,000
Less ending inventory	–0–	160,000†	–0–
Cost of goods sold (40,000 units)	700,000	640,000	760,000
Gross margin	300,000	360,000	240,000
Less selling and administrative expenses	210,000	210,000	210,000
Net income	$ 90,000	$ 150,000	$ 30,000

* Cost of goods manufactured:
Year 1: 40,000 units × $17.50 = $700,000.
Year 2: 50,000 units × $16.00 = $800,000.
Year 3: 30,000 units × $20.00 = $600,000.

† Observe that 50,000 units are produced in year 2, but only 40,000 units are sold. The 10,000 units going into the ending inventory have the following costs attached to them:

Variable manufacturing costs: 10,000 units × $10	$100,000
Fixed manufacturing overhead costs: 10,000 units × $6	60,000
Total inventory cost	$160,000

income of year 2 rises sharply, even though the same number of units is sold in year 2 as in the other years.

The reverse effect occurs in year 3. Since sales exceed production in year 3, that year is forced to cover all of its own fixed overhead costs as well as the fixed overhead costs carried forward in inventory from year 2. The result is a substantial drop in net income during year 3, although, as we have noted, the same number of units is sold in that year as in the other years.

Opponents of absorption costing argue that this shifting of fixed overhead cost between periods can be confusing to a manager and can cause him or her either to misinterpret data or to make faulty decisions. To avoid mistakes, the manager must be alert to any changes that may take place during a period in the level of inventory or in unit costs. By this means, he or she should be able to properly interpret any erratic movement in net income that may occur under the absorption costing method.

One way to overcome problems such as those discussed above is to use normalized overhead rates. A **normalized overhead rate** is a rate based on the *average* activity of many periods—past and present—rather than based only on the expected activity of the current period. Thus, unit costs are stable from year to year. Even if normalized overhead rates are used, however, net income can still be erratic if the under- or overapplied overhead that results from an imbalance between production and sales is taken to cost of goods sold. The only way to avoid the problems entirely is to use normalized overhead rates and to place any under- or overapplied overhead in a balance sheet clearing account of some type. However, this is rarely done in practice.

CVP Analysis and Absorption Costing

Absorption costing is widely regarded as a product costing method. Many firms use the absorption approach exclusively because of its focus on "full" costing of units of product. If the approach has a weakness, it is to be found in its inability to dovetail well with CVP analysis under certain conditions.

To illustrate, refer again to Exhibit 7–7. Let us compute the break-even point for the firm represented by the data in this exhibit. To obtain the break-even point, we divide total fixed costs by the contribution margin per unit:

Sales price per unit	$20
Variable costs per unit	11
Contribution margin per unit	$ 9
Fixed overhead costs	$150,000
Fixed selling and administrative costs	30,000
Total fixed costs	$180,000

$$\frac{\text{Total fixed costs}}{\text{Contribution margin per unit}} = \frac{\$180{,}000}{\$9} = 20{,}000 \text{ units}$$

We have computed the break-even point to be 20,000 units sold. Notice from Exhibit 7–7 that in year 2 the firm sold exactly 20,000 units, the break-even volume. Under the contribution approach, using direct costing, the firm does break even in year 2, showing zero net income or loss. *Under absorption costing, however, the firm shows a positive net income of $30,000 for* *year 2*. How can this be so? How can absorption costing produce a positive net income when the firm sold exactly the break-even volume of units?

The answer lies in the fact that in year 2 under absorption costing, $30,000 in fixed overhead costs were deferred in inventory and did not appear as charges against income. By deferring these fixed overhead costs in inventory, the firm was able to show a profit even though it sold exactly the break-even volume of units. This leads us to a general observation about absorption costing. The only way that absorption costing data can be used in a break-even analysis is to assume that inventories will not change. Unfortunately, such an assumption often falls far short of reality.

Absorption costing runs into similar kinds of difficulty in other aeas of CVP analysis and often requires considerable manipulation of data before figures are available that are usable for decision-making purposes.

External Reporting and Income Taxes

For external reporting on financial statements, a company is required to cost units of product by the absorption costing method. In like manner, the absorption costing method must be used in preparing tax returns. In short, the contribution approach is limited to *internal* use by the managers of a company.

The majority of accountants would agree that absorption costing *should* be used in external reporting. That is, most accountants feel that for *external reporting purposes,* units of product *should* contain a portion of fixed manufacturing overhead, along with variable manufacturing costs. The absorption costing argument that a unit of product is not fully costed until it reflects a portion of the fixed costs of production is difficult to refute, particularly as it applies to the preparing of information to be reported to stockholders and others.

The contribution approach finds its greatest application internally as an assist to the manager in those situtions where the absorption costing data are not well suited for CVP analysis or are not well suited for a segment-type analysis, such as was covered earlier in the chapter. No particular problems are created by using *both* costing methods—the contribution method internally and the absorption method externally. As we demonstrated earlier in Exhibit 7–8, the adjustment from direct costing net income to absorption costing net income is a simple one and can be made in a few hours' time at year-end in order to produce an absorption costing net income figure for use on financial statements.

ADVANTAGES OF THE CONTRIBUTION APPROACH

As stated in the preceding section, many accountants feel that under the appropriate circumstances there are certain advantages to be gained from using the contribution approach (with direct costing) internally, even if the absorption approach is used externally for reporting purposes. These advantages have been summarized by the National Association of Accountants as follows:[5]

[5] National Association of Accountants, *Research Series No. 23,* "Direct Costing" (New York, 1953), p. 55.

1. CVP relationship data wanted for profit planning purposes are readily obtained from the regular accounting statements. Hence management does not have to work with two separate sets of data to relate one to the other.
2. The profit for a period is not affected by changes in absorption of fixed expenses resulting from building or reducing inventory. Other things remaining equal (for example, selling prices, costs, sales mix), profits move in the same direction as sales when direct costing is in use.
3. Manufacturing cost and income statements in the direct cost form follow management's thinking more closely than does the absorption cost form for these statements. For this reason, management finds it easier to understand and to use direct cost reports.
4. The impact of fixed costs on profits is emphasized because the total amount of such cost for the period appears in the income statement.
5. Marginal income figures facilitate relative appraisal of products, territories, classes of customers, and other segments of the business without having the results obscured by allocation of joint (common) fixed costs.
6. Direct costing ties in with such effective plans for cost control as standard costs and flexible budgets.[6] In fact, the flexible budget is an aspect of direct costing, and many companies thus use direct costing methods for this purpose without recognizing them as such.
7. Direct cost constitutes a concept of inventory cost that corresponds closely with the current out-of-pocket expenditure necessary to manufacture the goods.

IMPACT OF JIT INVENTORY METHODS

We have learned in this chapter that direct and absorption costing will provide different net income figures whenever the number of units produced is different from the number of units sold. We have also learned that the absorption costing net income figure can be erratic, sometimes moving in a direction that is different from the movement in sales.

When companies employ JIT inventory methods, these problems with net income under absorption costing are either eliminated or reduced to insignificant proportions. The reason is as follows: The erratic movement of net income under absorption costing and the differences in net income between absorption and direct costing arise *because of changing levels of inventory*. Under JIT, goods are produced strictly to customers' orders. As a result, there are no goods in process at year-end, or no goods produced and confined to warehouses, awaiting orders from customers. Thus, with production geared strictly to sales, inventories are largely (or entirely) eliminated, thereby eliminating also any opportunity for fixed overhead costs to be shifted between periods under absorption costing. When JIT is in operation, therefore, both direct and absorption costing will show the same net income figure, and the net income under absorption costing will move in the same direction as movements in sales.

Of course, the cost of a unit of product will still be different between direct and absorption costing, as explained earlier in the chapter. But the

[6] Standard costs and flexible budgets are covered in Chapters 9 and 10.

differences in net income will disappear when JIT is used, thereby making it easier for management to interpret the data produced on an absorption costing income statement. This is an important point, since we have already stated that absorption costing must be used for external reporting purposes. Thus, by employing the JIT concept, companies gain a major advantage in the form of an income statement that is clearer and easier to understand.

SUMMARY

Cost allocation problems exist in every company. The contribution approach attempts to handle these problems by defining segments of an organization and by classifying costs as being either traceable or common to the segments. Only those costs that are traceable to the segments are allocated. Costs that are not traceable to the segments are treated as common costs and are not allocated.

The contribution approach also classifies costs by behavior. For this reason, those costs traceable to a segment are classified as between variable and fixed. Deducting total variable costs from sales yields a contribution margin, which is highly useful in short-run planning and decision making. The traceable fixed costs of a segment are then deducted from the contribution margin, yielding a segment margin. The segment margin is highly useful in long-run planning and decision making. Segments can be arranged in many ways—by sales territory, by division, by product line, by salesperson, and so on.

In costing units of product in a manufacturing company, the contribution method with direct costing adds only the variable manufacturing costs to units of product. The fixed manufacturing costs are taken immediately to the income statement as expenses of the period.

Although the contribution approach cannot be used externally either for financial reporting or for tax purposes, it is often used internally by management. Its popularity internally can be traced in large part to the fact that it dovetails well with CVP concepts that are often indispensable in profit planning and decision making.

REVIEW PROBLEM ON ABSORPTION AND DIRECT COSTING

Dexter Company produces and sells a single product. Selected cost and operating data relating to the product for a recent year are given below:

Beginning inventory in units	–0–
Units produced during the year. . .	10,000
Units sold during the year	8,000
Ending inventory in units	2,000
Selling price per unit	$ 50
Selling and administrative costs:	
Variable per unit	5
Fixed per year	70,000
Manufacturing costs:	
Variable per unit:	
Direct materials.	11
Direct labor	6
Variable overhead.	3
Fixed per year	100,000

Required

1. Assume that the company uses absorption costing.
   a. Compute the manufactured cost of one unit of product.
   b. Prepare an income statement for the year.
2. Assume that the company uses direct costing.
   a. Compute the manufactured cost of one unit of product.
   b. Prepare an income statement for the year.
3. Reconcile the direct costing and absorption costing net income figures.

Solution

1. a. Under absorption costing, all manufacturing costs, variable and fixed, are added to the cost of a unit of product:

Direct materials	$11
Direct labor	6
Variable overhead	3
Fixed overhead ($100,000 ÷ 10,000 units)	10
Total cost per unit	$30

b. The absorption costing income statement follows:

Sales (8,000 units × $50)		$400,000
Cost of goods sold:		
Beginning inventory	$ -0-	
Add cost of goods manufactured (10,000 units × $30)	300,000	
Goods available for sale	300,000	
Less ending inventory (2,000 units × $30)	60,000	240,000
Gross margin		160,000
Less selling and administrative expenses		110,000*
Net income		$ 50,000

* Variable (8,000 units × $5)	$ 40,000
Fixed per year	70,000
Total	$110,000

2. a. Under direct costing, only the variable manufacturing costs are added to the cost of a unit of product:

Direct materials	$11
Direct labor	6
Variable overhead	3
Total cost per unit	$20

b. The direct costing income statement follows. Notice that the variable cost of goods sold is computed in a simpler, more direct manner than in the example provided earlier in Exhibit 7–6. On a direct costing income statement, either approach is acceptable.

Sales (8,000 units × $50)		$400,000
Less variable expenses:		
Variable cost of goods sold (8,000 units × $20)	$160,000	
Variable selling and administrative expenses (8,000 units × $5)	40,000	200,000
Contribution margin		200,000
Less fixed expenses:		
Fixed overhead cost for the year	100,000	
Fixed selling and administrative expenses	70,000	170,000
Net income		$ 30,000

3. The reconciliation of the direct and absorption costing net income figures follows:

Direct costing net income	$30,000
Add fixed overhead costs deferred in inventory under absorption costing (2,000 units × $10)	20,000
Absorption costing net income	$50,000

KEY TERMS FOR REVIEW

Absorption costing A costing method that includes all manufacturing costs—direct materials, direct labor, and both variable and fixed manufacturing overhead—in the cost of a unit of product. Absorption costing is also referred to as the *full cost* method. (p. 265)

Common fixed cost A cost that cannot be identified with any particular segment of an organization. Such costs, which are also known as *indirect costs,* exist to serve the combined needs of two or more segments. (p. 256)

Direct costing A costing method that includes only variable manufacturing costs—direct materials, direct labor, and variable overhead—in the cost of a unit of product. Also see *Marginal costing* or *Variable costing*. (p. 265)

Fixed overhead cost deferred in inventory The portion of the fixed overhead cost of a period that goes into inventory under the absorption costing method as a result of production exceeding sales. (p. 268)

Fixed overhead cost released from inventory The portion of the fixed overhead cost of a *prior* period that becomes an expense of the current period under the absorption costing method as a result of sales exceeding production. (p. 271)

Full cost See *Absorption costing*. (p. 265)

Marginal costing Another term for direct costing. See *Direct costing*. (p. 265)

Normalized overhead rate A rate based on the average activity of many periods—past and present—rather than based only on the expected activity of the current period. (p. 275)

Segment Any part or activity of an organization about which the manager seeks cost or revenue data. (p. 253)

Segment margin The amount remaining from the sales of a segment after the segment has covered all of its own costs, variable and fixed. (p. 258)

Segmented reporting An income statement or other report in an organization in which data are divided according to product lines, divisions, territories, or similar organizational segments. (p. 253)

Traceable fixed cost A cost that can be identified with a particular segment and that arises because of the existence of that segment. (p. 256)

Variable costing Another term for direct costing. See *Direct costing*. (p. 265)

QUESTIONS

7–1 Define a segment of an organization. Give several examples of segments.

7–2 How does the contribution approach attempt to assign costs to segments of an organization?

7–3 Distinguish between a traceable cost and a common cost. Give several examples of each.

7–4 How does the manager benefit from having the income statement in a segmented format?

7–5 Explain how the segment margin differs from the contribution margin. Which concept is most useful to the manager? Why?

7–6 Why aren't common costs allocated to segments under the contribution approach?

7–7 How is it possible for a cost that is traceable under one segment arrangement to become a common cost under another segment arrangement?

7–8 What is the basic difference between absorption costing and direct costing?

7–9 Are selling and administrative expenses treated as product costs or as period costs under direct costing?

7–10 Explain how fixed overhead costs are shifted from one period to another under absorption costing.

7–11 What arguments can be advanced in favor of treating fixed overhead costs as product costs?

7–12 What arguments can be advanced in favor of treating fixed overhead costs as period costs?

7–13 If production and sales are equal, which method would you expect to show the highest net income, direct costing or absorption costing? Why?

7–14 If production exceeds sales, which method would you expect to show the highest net income, direct costing or absorption costing? Why?

7–15 If fixed overhead costs are released from inventory under absorption costing, what does this tell you about the level of production in relation to the level of sales?

7–16 What special assumption must be made in order to compute a break-even point under absorption costing?

7–17 Under absorption costing, how is it possible to increase net income without increasing sales?

7–18 What limitations are there to the use of direct costing?

EXERCISES

E7–1 Caltec, Inc., produces and sells two products. Revenue and cost information relating to the products follow:

	Product	
	A	B
Selling price per unit	$ 8.00	$ 25.00
Variable expenses per unit.	3.20	17.50
Traceable fixed expenses per year . . .	138,000	45,000

Common fixed expenses in the company total $105,000 annually. During 19x3, the company produced and sold 37,500 units of product A and 18,000 units of product B.

Required Prepare an income statement for 19x3 segmented by product lines. Show both "Amount" and "Percent" columns for the company as a whole and for each of the product lines. Carry percentage computations to one decimal place.

E7–2 Marple Company operates two divisions, X and Y. A segmented income statement for the company's most recent year is given below:

	Total Company		Segment: Division X		Division Y	
Sales	$750,000	100.0%	$150,000	100%	$600,000	100%
Less variable expenses	405,000	54.0	45,000	30	360,000	60
Contribution margin	345,000	46.0	105,000	70	240,000	40
Less traceable fixed expenses	168,000	22.4	78,000	52	90,000	15
Divisional segment margin	177,000	23.6	$ 27,000	18%	$150,000	25%
Less common fixed expenses	120,000	16.0				
Net income	$ 57,000	7.6%				

Required

1. By how much would the company's net income increase if Division Y increased its sales by $75,000 per year? Assume no change in cost behavior patterns in the company.
2. Refer to the original data. Assume that sales in Division X increase by $50,000 next year and that sales in Division Y remain unchanged. Assume no change in fixed costs in the divisions or in the company.
   a. Prepare a new segmented income statement for the company, using the format above. Show both amounts and percentages.
   b. Observe from the income statement you have prepared that the CM ratio for Division X has remained unchanged at 70 percent (the same as in the data above) but that the segment margin ratio has changed. How do you explain the change in the segment margin ratio?

E7–3 Refer to the data in Exercise 7–2. Assume that Division Y's sales by product line are:

	Division Y		Segment: Product A		Product B	
Sales	$600,000	100%	$400,000	100%	$200,000	100%
Less variable expenses	360,000	60	260,000	65	100,000	50
Contribution margin	240,000	40	140,000	35	100,000	50
Less traceable fixed expenses	72,000	12	20,000	5	52,000	26
Product line segment margin	168,000	28	$120,000	30%	$ 48,000	24%
Less common fixed expenses	18,000	3				
Divisional segment margin	$150,000	25%				

The company would like to initiate an intensive advertising campaign on one of the two products during the next month. The campaign would cost $8,000. Marketing studies indicate that such a campaign would increase sales of product A by $70,000 or increase sales of product B by $60,000.

Required

1. On which of the products would you recommend that the company focus its advertising campaign? Show computations to support your answer.
2. In Exercise 7–2, Division Y shows $90,000 in traceable fixed expenses. What happened to the $90,000 in this exercise?

E7–4 You have a client who operates a large retail self-service grocery store that has a full range of departments. The mangement has encountered difficulty in using accounting data as a basis for decisions as to possible changes in departments operated, products, marketing methods, and so forth. List several overhead costs, or costs not applicable to a particular department, and explain how the existence of such costs (sometimes called *common costs* or *joint costs*) complicates and limits the use of accounting data in making decisions in such a store.

(CPA Adapted)

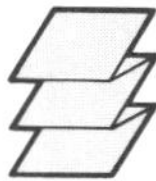

E7–5 Bovine Company has been experiencing losses for some time, as shown by its most recent monthly income statement below:

Sales	$1,500,000
Less variable expenses	588,000
Contribution margin	912,000
Less fixed expenses	945,000
Net loss	$ (33,000)

In an effort to isolate the problem, the president has asked for an income statement segmented by product lines. Accordingly, the accounting department has developed the following cost and revenue data:

	Product		
	A	B	C
Sales	$400,000	$600,000	$500,000
Variable expenses as a percentage of sales	52%	30%	40%
Traceable fixed expenses	$240,000	$330,000	$200,000

Required

1. Prepare an income statement segmented by product lines, as desired by the president. Show both "Amount" and "Percent" columns for the company as a whole and for each product line. Carry percentage computations to one decimal place.
2. The company's sales manager believes that sales of product B could be increased by 15 percent if advertising were increased by $25,000 each month. Would you recommend the increased advertising? Show computations to support your answer.

E7–6 Hartley Company manufactures two products, Meps and Zins. The Zins product is a relatively new line and is manufactured in a highly automated plant. Sal Monson, a very capable manager hired just a few months ago by Hartley Company, is serving as the manager of the Zins line. Cost and revenue data on the two products for last month follow:

	Product	
	Meps	Zins
Sales	$300,000	$200,000
Contribution margin ratio	60%	75%
Traceable fixed expenses:		
Committed	$ 30,000	$ 90,000
Discretionary	105,000	40,000

In addition to the costs given above, the company incurs $60,000 in common fixed expenses each month.

Required

1. Prepare a segmented income statement for last month. Show both "Amount" and "Percent" columns for the company as a whole and for each product. Present the statement in enough detail to allow the company to evaluate the performance of the manager over each product.
2. From a standpoint of cost control, which segment manager seems to be doing the best job?

E7–7 Selected information on the operations of Diston Company for 19x8 follows:

Beginning inventory in units	–0–
Units produced during the year	25,000
Units sold during the year	20,000
Ending inventory in units	5,000
Variable costs per unit:	
Direct materials	$4
Direct labor	7
Variable overhead	1
Variable selling expenses	2
Fixed costs per year:	
Manufacturing overhead	$200,000
Selling and administrative expenses	90,000

The company produces and sells a single product. Work in process inventories are nominal and can be ignored.

Required

1. Assume that the company uses absorption costing. Compute the cost of one unit of product.
2. Assume that the company uses direct costing. Compute the cost of one unit of product.

E7–8 Refer to the data in Exercise 7–7. An income statement prepared under the absorption costing method for 19x8 follows:

Sales (20,000 units × $30)		$600,000
Cost of goods sold:		
Beginning inventory	$ –0–	
Cost of goods manufactured (25,000 units × $?)	500,000	
Goods available for sale	500,000	
Less ending inventory (5,000 units × $?)	100,000	400,000
Gross margin		200,000
Less selling and administrative expenses:		
Variable selling	40,000	
Fixed selling and administrative expenses	90,000	130,000
Net income		$ 70,000

Required

1. Determine how much of the $100,000 ending inventory above consists of fixed overhead cost deferred in inventory to the next period.
2. Prepare an income statement for 19x8, using the direct costing method. How do you explain the difference in net income between the two costing methods?

E7–9 Amcor, Inc., produces and sells a single product. The following costs relate to its production and sale:

Variable costs per unit:	
Direct materials	$10
Direct labor	5
Variable manufacturing overhead	2
Variable selling and administrative expenses	4
Fixed costs per year:	
Manufacturing overhead	$ 90,000
Selling and administrative expenses	300,000

During the last year, 30,000 units were produced and 25,000 units were sold. The Finished Goods inventory account at the end of the year shows a balance of $85,000 for the 5,000 unsold units.

Required

1. Is the company using absorption costing or direct costing to cost units in the Finished Goods inventory account? Show computations to support your answer.
2. Assume that the company wishes to prepare financial statements for the year to issue to its stockholders.
   a. Is the $85,000 figure for Finished Goods inventory the correct figure to use on these statements for external reporting purposes? Explain.
   b. At what dollar amount *should* the 5,000 units be carried in inventory for external reporting purposes?

E7–10 Morey Company was organized just one year ago. The results of the company's first year of operations are shown below (absorption costing basis):

MOREY COMPANY
Income Statement
For the Year 19x1

Sales (40,000 units at $33.75)		$1,350,000
Less cost of goods sold:		
Beginning inventory	$ –0–	
Cost of goods manufactured (50,000 units at $21)	1,050,000	
Goods available for sale	1,050,000	
Ending inventory (10,000 units at $21)	210,000	840,000
Gross margin		510,000
Less selling and administrative expenses		420,000
Net income		$ 90,000

The company's selling and administrative expenses consist of $300,000 per year in fixed expenses and $3 per unit sold in variable expenses. The company's $21 manufacturing cost per unit given above is computed as follows:

Direct materials	$10
Direct labor	4
Variable manufacturing overhead	2
Fixed manufacturing overhead ($250,000 ÷ 50,000 units)	5
Total cost per unit	$21

Required

1. Redo the company's income statement in the contribution format, using direct costing.
2. Reconcile any difference between the net income figure on your direct costing income statement and the net income figure on the absorption costing income statement above.

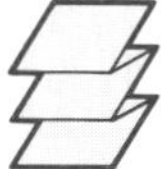

E7–11 Maxwell Company manufactures and sells a single product. The following costs were incurred during 19x5, the company's first year of operations:

Variable costs per unit:	
Production:	
Direct materials	$18
Direct labor	7
Variable manufacturing overhead	2
Selling and administrative	5
Fixed costs per year:	
Manufacturing overhead	$160,000
Selling and administrative	110,000

During 19x5, the company produced 20,000 units and sold 16,000 units. The selling price of the company's product is $50 per unit.

Required
1. Assume that the company uses the absorption costing method:
   a. Compute the cost to produce one unit of product.
   b. Prepare an income statement for 19x5.
2. Assume that the company uses the direct costing method:
   a. Compute the cost to produce one unit of product.
   b. Prepare an income statement for 19x5.

PROBLEMS

Problems 7–12 through 7–19 deal primarily with segmented reporting issues; Problems 7–20 through 7–28 deal primarily with absorption versus direct costing issues.

P7–12 Segment Reporting The most recent monthly income statement for Reston Company is given below:

RESTON COMPANY
Income Statement
For the Month Ended May 31, 19x1

Sales	$900,000	100.0%
Less variable expenses	408,000	45.3
Contribution margin	492,000	54.7
Less fixed expenses	465,000	51.7
Net income	$ 27,000	3.0%

Management is disappointed with the company's performance and is wondering what can be done to improve profits. By examining sales and cost records, you have determined the following:

a. The company is divided into two sales territories—Central and Eastern. The Central Territory recorded $400,000 in sales and $208,000 in variable expenses during May. The remaining sales and variable expenses were recorded in the Eastern Territory. Fixed expenses of $160,000 and $130,000 are traceable to the Central and Eastern Territories, respectively. The rest of the fixed expenses are common to the two territories.

b. The company sells two products—Awls and Pows. Sales of Awls and Pows totaled $100,000 and $300,000, respectively, in the Central Territory during May. Variable expenses are 25 percent of the selling price for Awls and 61 percent for Pows. Cost records show that $60,000 of the Central Territory's fixed expenses are traceable to Awls and $54,000 to Pows, with the remainder common to the two products.

Required
1. Prepare segmented income statements such as illustrated in Exhibit 7–1, first showing the total company broken down between sales territories and then showing the Central Territory broken down by product line. Show both "Amount" and "Percent" columns for the company in total and for each segment. Round percentage computations to one decimal place.
2. Look at the statement you have prepared showing the total company segmented by sales territory. What points revealed by this statement should be brought to the attention of management?
3. Look at the statement you have prepared showing the Central Territory segmented by product lines. What points revealed by this statement should be brought to the attention of management?

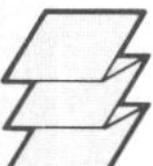

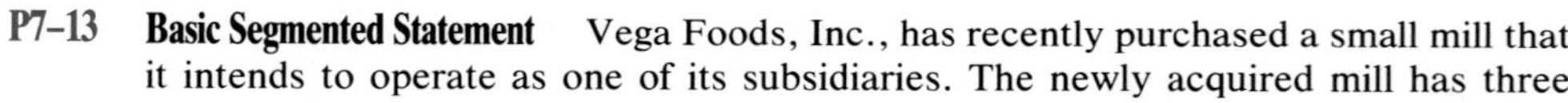

P7–13 Basic Segmented Statement Vega Foods, Inc., has recently purchased a small mill that it intends to operate as one of its subsidiaries. The newly acquired mill has three products that it offers for sale—wheat cereal, pancake mix, and flour. Each product sells for $10 per package. Materials, labor, and other variable production costs are $3 per bag of wheat cereal, $4.20 per bag of pancake mix, and $1.80 per bag of flour. Sales commissions are 10 percent of sales for any product. All other costs are fixed.

The mill's income statement for the most recent month is given below:

	Total Company		Product Line		
			Wheat Cereal	Pancake Mix	Flour
Sales	$600,000	100.0%	$200,000	$300,000	$100,000
Less expenses:					
Materials, labor, and other	204,000	34.0	60,000	126,000	18,000
Sales commissions	60,000	10.0	20,000	30,000	10,000
Advertising	123,000	20.5	48,000	60,000	15,000
Salaries	66,000	11.0	34,000	21,000	11,000
Equipment depreciation	30,000	5.0	10,000	15,000	5,000
Warehouse rent	12,000	2.0	4,000	6,000	2,000
General administration	90,000	15.0	30,000	30,000	30,000
Total expenses	585,000	97.5	206,000	288,000	91,000
Net income (loss)	$ 15,000	2.5%	$ (6,000)	$ 12,000	$ 9,000

The following additional information is available about the company:

a. The same equipment is used to mill and package all three products, and the same warehouse facilities are used to store the products while they await sale. Therefore, the equipment depreciation and the warehouse rent have been allocated to the products on a basis of sales dollars.

b. The general administration costs relate to administration of the company as a whole; therefore, these costs have been allocated equally between the three product lines.

c. All other costs are traceable to the product lines.

Vega Foods' management is anxious to improve on the mill's 2.5 percent margin on sales.

Required

1. Prepare a new segmented income statement for the month, using the contribution approach. Show both "Amount" and "Percent" columns for the company as a whole and for each product line. Carry percentage computations to one decimal place.
2. After seeing the statement in the main body of the problem, management has decided to eliminate the wheat cereal, since it is not returning a profit, and to focus all available resources on promoting the pancake mix.
   a. Based on the statement you have prepared, do you agree with the decision to eliminate the wheat cereal? Explain.
   b. Based on the statement you have prepared, do you agree with the decision to focus all available resources on promoting the pancake mix? Explain. (You may assume that ample market is available for all three products.)
3. What additional points would you bring to the attention of management that might help to improve profits?

P7–14 Restructuring a Segmented Income Statement Profits in Wiley Company have either been poor or nonexistent for some time. In an effort to improve the company's operating performance, the executive committee has requested that the monthly income statement be segmented by sales territory. Accordingly, the company's accounting department has prepared the following statement for March 19x1, the most recent month of activity:

	Territory		
	A	B	C
Sales	$300,000	$800,000	$ 700,000
Less territorial expenses:			
Cost of goods sold	93,000	240,000	315,000
Salaries	54,000	56,000	112,000
Insurance	9,000	16,000	14,000
Advertising	105,000	240,000	245,000
Depreciation	21,000	32,000	28,000
Shipping	15,000	32,000	42,000
Total territorial expenses	297,000	616,000	756,000
Territorial income (loss) before corporate expenses	3,000	184,000	(56,000)
Less corporate expenses:			
Advertising (general)	15,000	40,000	35,000
General administrative	20,000	20,000	20,000
Total corporate expenses	35,000	60,000	55,000
Net income (loss)	$ (32,000)	$124,000	$(111,000)

Cost of goods sold and shipping expense are both variable; other costs are all fixed.

Wiley Company is a wholesale distributor of hardware products. It purchases various hardware products from the manufacturer and distributes them in the three territories given above. The three territories are about the same size, and each has its own manager and sales staff. The products that the company distributes vary widely in profitability, some having a high margin and some having a low margin.

Required

1. List any disadvantages or weaknesses that you see to the statement format illustrated above.
2. Explain the basis being used to allocate the corporate expenses to the sales territories. Do you agree with these allocations? Explain.
3. Prepare a new segmented income statement for March 19x1, using the contribution approach. Show a "Total" column as well as data for each territory. Include percentages on your statement for all columns. Carry percentages to one decimal place.
4. Analyze the statement that you prepared in (3) above. What points that might help to improve the company's performance would you be particularly anxious to bring to the attention of management?

P7–15 Multiple Segmented Income Statements Rolnick Products, Inc., is organized into two divisions. The company's income statement for last month is given below:

	Total Company	Division: Cloth	Division: Leather
Sales	$3,500,000	$2,000,000	$1,500,000
Less variable expenses	1,721,000	960,000	761,000
Contribution margin	1,779,000	1,040,000	739,000
Less traceable fixed expenses:			
Advertising	612,000	300,000	312,000
Administration	427,000	210,000	217,000
Depreciation	229,000	115,000	114,000
Total traceable fixed expenses	1,268,000	625,000	643,000
Divisional segment margin	511,000	$ 415,000	$ 96,000
Less common fixed expenses	390,000		
Net income	$ 121,000		

Top management can't understand why the Leather Division has such a low segment margin when its sales are only 25 percent less than sales in the Cloth Division. As one step in isolating the problem, management has directed that the Leather Division be further segmented into product lines. The following information is available on the product lines in the Leather Division:

	Product Line		
	A	**B**	**C**
Sales	$500,000	$700,000	$300,000
Traceable fixed expenses:			
Advertising	80,000	112,000	120,000
Administration	30,000	35,000	42,000
Depreciation	25,000	56,000	33,000
Variable expenses as a percentage of sales	65%	40%	52%

Analysis shows that $110,000 of the Leather Division's administrative expenses are common to the product lines.

Required

1. Prepare a segmented income statement for the Leather Division, with segments defined as product lines. Use the contribution approach and the format shown in Exhibit 7–1. Show both "Amount" and "Percent" columns for the division in total and for each product line. Carry percentage figures to one decimal place.
2. Management is surprised by product line C's poor showing and would like to have the product line segmented by market. The following information is available about the two markets in which product line C is sold:

	Market	
	Domestic	**Foreign**
Sales	$200,000	$100,000
Traceable fixed expenses:		
Advertising	40,000	80,000
Variable expenses as a percentage of sales	43%	70%

All of product line C's administrative expenses and depreciation are common to the markets in which the product is sold. Prepare a segmented income statement for product line C, with segments defined as markets. Again use the format in Exhibit 7–1 and show both "Amount" and "Percent" columns.

3. Refer to the statement prepared in (1) above. The sales manager wants to run a special promotional campaign on one of the products over the next month. A marketing study indicates that such a campaign would increase sales of product line A by $200,000 or sales of product line B by $145,000. The campaign would cost $30,000. Show computations to determine which product line should be chosen.

P7–16 **Multiple Segmented Income Statements** Heritage Company started segmenting its income statements several months ago as a way to provide more useful data to management. The company's income statement segmented by divisions for May 19x6 follows:

	Total Company	Division: Office Products	Division: Home Products
Sales	$4,000,000	$2,200,000	$1,800,000
Less variable expenses:			
Production	1,608,000	790,000	828,000
Other	340,000	160,000	180,000
Total variable expenses	1,958,000	950,000	1,008,000
Contribution margin	2,042,000	1,250,000	792,000
Less traceable fixed expenses	1,390,000	690,000	700,000
Divisional segment margin	652,000	$ 560,000	$ 92,000
Less common fixed expenses	410,000		
Net income	$ 242,000		

Management is concerned about the poor performance of the Home Products Division. To help pinpoint the problem, the president has asked for additional information about the Home Products Division in terms of the products and markets involved. The following data have been assembled on the three products that the division manufactures and sells:

	Total	Product Line: A	B	C
Sales	$1,800,000	$900,000	$300,000	$600,000
Variable production costs as a percentage of sales	—	42%	38%	56%
Other variable expenses as a percentage of sales	—	10%	12%	9%
Traceable fixed expenses	$ 570,000	$189,000	$135,000	$246,000

Required

1. Prepare a segmented income statement for the Home Products Division, with segments defined by products. Use the contribution approach and the format shown in Exhibit 7–1. Show both "Amount" and "Percent" columns for the division in total and for each product line.
2. The president now wants more information about product line C. This product is sold in two sales markets—the East and the West. Sales and other data about the two markets follow:

	Total	Market: East	West
Sales	$600,000	$400,000	$200,000
Variable production costs as a percentage of sales	—	56%	56%
Other variable expenses as a percentage of sales	—	4%	19%
Traceable fixed expenses	$198,000	$ 68,000	$130,000

   Prepare a segmented income statement for product line C, with segments defined as markets. Again use the format in Exhibit 7–1 and show both "Amount" and "Percent" columns.
3. Scrutinize the statements you have prepared in (1) and (2) above. What points should be brought to the attention of management?
4. Assume that the president wants more information about the West sales market. Suggest ways in which this market might be further segmented.

P7–17 Segmented Reporting; Expansion Analysis Meredith Company produces and sells three products (A, B, and C) that are sold in a local market and a regional market. At the end of the first quarter of the current year, the following absorption basis income statement has been prepared:

MEREDITH COMPANY
Income Statement
For the First Quarter

	Total Company	Market: Local	Market: Regional
Sales	$1,300,000	$1,000,000	$300,000
Cost of goods sold	1,010,000	777,000	233,000
Gross margin	290,000	223,000	67,000
Less operating expenses:			
Selling	105,000	60,000	45,000
Administrative	52,000	40,000	12,000
Total operating expenses	157,000	100,000	57,000
Net income	$ 133,000	$ 123,000	$ 10,000

Management has expressed special concern with the regional market because of the extremely poor return on sales. This market was entered a year ago because of excess capacity. It was originally believed that the return on sales would improve with time, but after a year no noticeable improvement can be seen from the results in the above quarterly statement.

In attempting to decide whether to eliminate the regional market, the following information has been gathered:

	Product Line: A	B	C
Sales	$500,000	$400,000	$400,000
Variable manufacturing expenses as a percentage of sales	40%	35%	30%
Variable selling expenses as a percentage of sales	3%	2%	2%
Fixed manufacturing expenses traceable directly to the product lines	$190,000	$150,000	$210,000

Product Line	Sales by Markets: Local	Regional
A	$ 400,000	$100,000
B	300,000	100,000
C	300,000	100,000
Total sales	$1,000,000	$300,000

The administrative expenses shown on the income statement above are common to both the markets and the product lines. They have been allocated to the markets above on a basis of sales dollars. The selling expenses shown on the income statement above are all traceable to the markets, as shown. Inventory levels are nominal and can be ignored.

Required

1. Prepare a segmented income statement for the quarter using the contribution approach, segmented into local and regional markets. Show both ''Amount''

and "Percent" columns for the company in total and for each market. (Carry percentages to one decimal place.)

2. Assuming that there are no alternative uses for the company's present capacity, would you recommend that the regional market be dropped? Why or why not?
3. Prepare another segmented income statement for the quarter, again using the contribution approach, but this time segmented by product line. (Do not allocate the fixed selling expenses to the product lines; treat these as common costs.) Show both "Amount" and "Percent" columns for the company in total and for each product line.
4. Assume that product lines B and C are both at full capacity. The company would like to add sufficient additional capacity to double the output of one of these product lines. Overall cost relationships for the added capacity would follow the same cost behavior patterns as with present capacity for each product line. The company's executive committee has decided to double the capacity of product C because of its higher CM ratio. Explain why you do or do not agree with this decision.

(CMA, Adapted)

P7–18 Segmented Statements; Product Line Analysis "The situation is slowly turning around," declared Bill Aiken, president of Datex, Inc. "This $42,500 loss for June is our smallest yet. If we can just strengthen product lines A and C somehow, we'll soon be making a profit." Mr. Aiken was referring to the company's latest monthly income statement presented below (absorption costing basis):

DATEX, INC.
Income Statement

	Total	Line A	Line B	Line C
Sales	$1,000,000	$400,000	$250,000	$350,000
Cost of goods sold	742,500	300,000	180,000	262,500
Gross margin	257,500	100,000	70,000	87,500
Less operating expenses:				
Selling	150,000	60,000	22,500	67,500
Administrative	150,000	60,000	37,500	52,500
Total operating expenses	300,000	120,000	60,000	120,000
Net income (loss)	$ (42,500)	$ (20,000)	$ 10,000	$ (32,500)

"How's that new business graduate doing that we just hired?" asked Mr. Aiken. "He's supposed to be well trained in internal reporting; can he help us pinpoint what's wrong with lines A and C?" "He claims it's partly the way we make up our segmented statements," declared Margie Nelson, the controller. "Here are a lot of data he's prepared on what he calls traceable and common costs that he thinks we ought to be isolating in our reports." The data to which Ms. Nelson was referring are shown below:

	Line A	Line B	Line C
Variable costs:*			
Production (materials, labor, and variable overhead)	20%	30%	25%
Selling	5%	5%	5%
Traceable fixed costs:			
Production	$107,000	$30,000	$63,000
Selling†	40,000	10,000	50,000

* As a percentage of line sales.
† Salaries and advertising. Advertising contracts are signed annually.

a. Fixed production costs total $500,000 per month. Part of this amount is traceable directly to the product lines, as shown in the tabulation above. The remainder is common to the product lines.
b. All administrative costs are common to the three product lines.
c. Work in process and finished goods inventories are nominal and can be ignored.
d. Lines A and B each sell for $100 per unit, and line C sells for $80 per unit. Strong market demand exists for all three products.

"I don't get it," said Mr. Aiken. "Our CPAs assure us that we're following good absorption costing methods in our cost allocations, and we're segmenting our statements like they want us to do. So what could be wrong?"

At that moment, John Young, the production superintendent, came bursting into the room. "Word has just come that Fairchild Company, the supplier of our type B4 chips, has just gone out on strike. The trade says that they'll be out for at least a month, and our inventory of B4 chips is low. We'll have to cut back production of either line A or B, since that chip is used in both products." (A single B4 chip is used per unit of each product.) Mr. Aiken looked at the latest monthly statement and declared, "Thank goodness for these segmented statements. It's pretty obvious that we should cut back production of line A. Pass the word, and concentrate all of our B4 chip inventory on production of line B."

Required

1. Prepare a new income statement segmented by product lines, using the contribution approach. Show both "Amount" and "Percent" columns for the company in total and for each of the product lines. (Carry percentages to one decimal place.)
2. Do you agree with Mr. Aiken's decision to cut back production of line A? Why or why not?
3. Assume that the company's executive committee is considering the elimination of line C, due to its poor showing. If you were serving on this committee, what points would you make for or against elimination of the line?
4. Line C is sold in both a home and a foreign market, with sales and cost data as follows:

	Home Market	Foreign Market
Sales	$300,000	$50,000
Traceable fixed costs:		
Selling	10,000	40,000

The fixed production costs of line C are considered to be common to the markets in which the product is sold. Variable expense relationships in the markets are the same as those shown in the main body of the problem for line C.

a. Prepare a segmented income statement showing line C segmented by markets. Show both "Amount" and "Percent" columns for line C in total and for both of the markets.
b. What points revealed by this statement would you be particularly anxious to bring to the attention of management?

P7–19 Preparing Various Segment Reports; Segment Profit Analysis "Wow! Just look at this statement," exclaimed Karma Lechner, president of Ipson Company. "Our 5.5 percent return on sales is a full percentage point above the industry average." The statement to which Ms. Lechner was referring is shown below, which gives the company's operating performance for the most recent month.

Sales		$3,000,000	100.0%
Less production and packaging expenses		2,019,000	67.3
Gross margin		981,000	32.7
Less operating expenses:			
Marketing	$528,000		
Administration	288,000	816,000	27.2
Net income		$ 165,000	5.5%

Ipson Company produces and distributes three product lines throughout the continental United States. To facilitate distribution, the country is divided into three sales regions—the East, the Midwest, and the West.

"Has that consulting company completed its appraisal of our operations yet?" asked Ms. Lechner. "We need to have a firm grasp of what's going on with our products and with our sales regions if we expect to maintain our leadership position in the industry."

"Frankly, I'm not too impressed with what the consulting company is recommending," replied Brent Atwater, the controller. "They want us to break our income statement down two or three different ways. I've been doing these statements for nearly 20 years, and by this time it's pretty obvious that line A is our best line and that the East is our best sales region. The consultants have worked up a lot of figures showing what they call 'traceable' and 'common' costs that they say we ought to be isolating in our reports. It just looks like a lot of busy work to me and maybe a way to justify their $200 per hour fee." The data to which the controller was referring are shown below:

	Total Sales	Production and Packaging	Marketing	Administration
Sales and variable expenses:				
Line A	$1,500,000	55%	5%	—
Line B	600,000	47%	5%	—
Line C	900,000	35%	5%	—
Traceable fixed expenses:				
Line A		$ 60,000	$90,000	—
Line B		270,000	54,000	—
Line C		267,000	30,000	—
West Region			60,000	$57,000
Midwest Region			81,000	42,000
East Region			63,000	99,000
Common fixed expenses:				
General administration				90,000

The percentage figures above are in terms of total sales. Corporate headquarters does some advertising directly for each product line on a national basis, which is supplemented by each sales region doing whatever additional advertising it deems necessary. The sales by region (which have been constant in terms of mix for some time) are shown below:

	Percentage of Product Line Sales		
	Line A	Line B	Line C
West Region	15	50	60
Midwest Region	25	20	30
East Region	60	30	10
	100	100	100

Required

1. Prepare segmented income statements, as follows:
   a. For the company as a whole, broken down into product line segments. Use the contribution format. Show both amount and percent columns, with the percentages rounded to one decimal place.
   b. For the company as a whole, broken down into regional markets. Use the contribution format. Show both "Amount" and "Percent" columns, with the percentages rounded to one decimal place. (Do not allocate the traceable fixed expenses of the product lines to the regions; treat these as common costs.)
2. Refer to the statement you prepared in (1*a*) above.
   a. Analyze the statement and indicate the points you would be particularly anxious to bring to the attention of management.
   b. The company is about to launch a national promotional campaign for one of the product lines. Assuming that ample capacity exists and that none of the product lines has reached market saturation, which product line would you recommend to management? Explain the reason for your choice.
3. Refer to the statement you prepared in (1*b*) above. Analyze the statement and indicate the points you would be particularly anxious to bring to the attention of management.

P7–20 Straightforward Direct Costing Statements Denton Company was organized on January 2, 19x4. During its first two years of operations, the company reported net income as follows (absorption costing basis):

	19x4	19x5
Sales (at $50).	$1,000,000	$1,500,000
Less cost of goods sold:		
Opening inventory	-0-	170,000
Add cost of goods manufactured (at $34)	850,000	850,000
Goods available for sale	850,000	1,020,000
Less ending inventory (at $34)	170,000	-0-
Cost of goods sold	680,000	1,020,000
Gross margin	320,000	480,000
Less selling and administrative expenses*	310,000	340,000
Net income	$ 10,000	$ 140,000

* $3 per unit variable; $250,000 fixed each year.

The company's $34 unit cost is computed as follows:

Direct materials	$ 8
Direct labor	10
Variable manufacturing overhead	2
Fixed manufacturing overhead ($350,000 ÷ 25,000 units)	14
Total cost per unit	$34

Production and cost data for the two years are given below:

	19x4	19x5
Units produced	25,000	25,000
Units sold	20,000	30,000

Required

1. Prepare an income statement for each year in the contribution format, using direct costing.
2. Reconcile the absorption costing and direct costing net income figures for each year.

P7–21 **Straightforward Comparison of Costing Methods** Wiengot Antennas, Inc., produces and sells a unique type of TV antenna. The company has just opened a new plant to manufacture the antenna, and the following cost and revenue data have been reported for May 19x1, the first month of the plant's operation:

Opening inventory	-0-
Units produced	40,000
Units sold	35,000
Selling price per unit	$ 60
Selling and administrative expenses:	
Variable per unit	2
Fixed (total)	560,000
Manufacturing costs:	
Direct materials cost per unit	15
Direct labor cost per unit	7
Variable overhead cost per unit	2
Fixed overhead cost (total)	640,000

Since the new antenna is unique in design, management is anxious to see how profitable it will be and has asked that an income statement be prepared for the month.

Required

1. Assume that the company uses absorption costing.
   a. Determine the cost to produce one unit of product.
   b. Prepare an income statement for the month.
2. Assume that the company uses the contribution approach with direct costing.
   a. Determine the cost to produce one unit of product.
   b. Prepare an income statement for the month.
3. Explain the reason for any difference in the ending inventory under the two costing methods and the impact of this difference on reported net income.

P7–22 **A Comparison of Costing Methods** Advance Products, Inc., has just organized a new division to manufacture and sell specially designed tables for mounting and using personal computers. The company's new plant is highly automated and thus requires high monthly fixed costs, as shown in the schedule below:

Manufacturing costs:	
Variable costs per unit:	
Direct materials	$ 50
Direct labor	36
Variable overhead	4
Fixed overhead costs (total)	240,000
Selling and administrative costs:	
Variable	15% of sales
Fixed (total)	$160,000

During June 19x9, the first month of operations, the following activity was recorded:

Units produced	4,000
Units sold	3,200
Selling price per unit	$250

Required

1. Compute the cost of a single unit of product under:
   a. Absorption costing.
   b. Direct costing.
2. Prepare an income statement for the month, using absorption costing.
3. Prepare an income statement for the month, using direct costing.
4. Assume that in order to continue operations, the company must obtain additional financing. As a member of top management, which of the statements that

you have prepared in (2) and (3) above would you prefer to take with you as you negotiate with the bank?

5. Reconcile the absorption costing and direct costing net income figures in (2) and (3) above for the month.

P7–23 **Preparation and Reconciliation of Direct Costing Statements** Linden Company was organized on May 1, 19x1. The company manufactures and sells a single product. Cost data for the product follow:

Variable costs per unit:	
Direct materials	$ 6
Direct labor	12
Variable factory overhead	4
Variable selling and administrative	3
Total variable costs per unit	$25
Fixed costs per month:	
Factory overhead	$240,000
Selling and administrative	180,000
Total fixed costs per month	$420,000

The product sells for $40 per unit. Production and sales data for May and June are:

	Units Produced	Units Sold
May	30,000	26,000
June	30,000	34,000

Income statements prepared by the accounting department, using absorption costing, are presented below:

	May 19x1	June 19x1
Sales	$1,040,000	$1,360,000
Less cost of goods sold:		
Beginning inventory	-0-	120,000
Cost of goods manufactured	900,000	900,000
Goods available for sale	900,000	1,020,000
Less ending inventory	120,000	-0-
Cost of goods sold	780,000	1,020,000
Gross margin	260,000	340,000
Less selling and administrative expenses	258,000	282,000
Net income	$ 2,000	$ 58,000

Required

1. Determine the cost of a single unit of product under:
   a. Absorption costing.
   b. Direct costing.
2. Prepare income statements for May and June using the contribution approach with direct costing.
3. Reconcile the direct costing and absorption costing net income figures.
4. The company's accounting department has determined the break-even point to be 28,000 units per month, computed as follows:

$$\frac{\text{Fixed cost per month}}{\text{Unit contribution margin}} = \frac{\$420{,}000}{\$15} = 28{,}000 \text{ units}$$

Upon receiving this figure, the president commented, "There's something peculiar here. The controller says that the break-even point is 28,000 units per month.

Yet we sold only 26,000 units in May, and the income statement we received showed a $2,000 profit. Which figure do we believe?'' Prepare a brief explanation of what happened on the May income statement.

P7–24 Absorption and Direct Costing; Production Constant, Sales Fluctuate Sandi Scott obtained a patent on a small electronic device and organized Scott Products, Inc., in order to produce and sell the device. During the first month of operations, the device was very well received on the market, so Ms. Scott looked forward to a healthy profit from sales. For this reason, she was surprised to see a loss for the month on her income statement. This statement was prepared by her accounting service, which takes great pride in providing its clients with timely financial data. The statement follows:

SCOTT PRODUCTS, INC.
Income Statement

Sales (40,000 units)		$200,000
Less variable expenses:		
Variable cost of goods sold*	$80,000	
Selling and administrative expenses	30,000	110,000
Contribution margin		90,000
Less fixed expenses:		
Fixed manufacturing overhead	75,000	
Selling and administrative expenses	20,000	95,000
Net loss		$ (5,000)

* Consists of direct materials, direct labor, and variable overhead.

Ms. Scott is discouraged over the loss shown for the month, particularly since she had planned to use the statement to encourage investors to purchase stock in the new company. A friend, who is a CPA, insists that the company should be using absorption costing rather than direct costing. He argues that if absorption costing had been used, the company would probably have reported a nice profit for the month.

Selected cost data relating to the product and to the first month of operations follow:

Units produced	50,000
Units sold	40,000
Variable costs per unit:	
Direct materials	$1.00
Direct labor	0.80
Variable overhead	0.20
Variable selling and administrative expenses	0.75

Required

1. Complete the following:
   a. Compute the cost of a unit of product under absorption costing.
   b. Redo the company's income statement for the month, using absorption costing.
   c. Reconcile the direct and absorption costing net income figures.
2. Was the CPA correct in suggesting that the company really earned a ''profit'' for the month? Explain.
3. During the second month of operations, the company again produced 50,000 units but sold 60,000 units. (Assume no change in total fixed costs.)
   a. Prepare an income statement for the month, using direct costing.
   b. Prepare an income statement for the month, using absorption costing.
   c. Reconcile the direct costing and absorption costing net income figures.

P7–25 Prepare Direct Costing Statements; Sales Constant, Production Varies; Automation; JIT Impact "Can someone explain to me what's wrong with these statements?" asked Cheri Reynolds, president of Milex Company. "They just don't make any sense. We sold the same number of units this year as we did last year, yet our profits have tripled! I know this new, automated plant is supposed to do marvels, but how can it increase our profits if our sales stay flat?"

The statements to which Ms. Reynolds was referring are shown below (absorption costing basis):

	19x1	19x2
Sales (40,000 units each year)	$1,250,000	$1,250,000
Less cost of goods sold	840,000	720,000
Gross margin	410,000	530,000
Less selling and administrative expenses	350,000	350,000
Net income	$ 60,000	$ 180,000

The company moved into a new, automated plant on January 2, 19x1, so the statements above show the results of operations after two years of the plant's use. In the first year, the company produced and sold 40,000 units; in the second year, the company again sold 40,000 units, but it increased production in order to have a stock of units on hand, as shown below:

	19x1	19x2
Production in units	40,000	50,000
Sales in units	40,000	40,000
Variable production cost per unit	$6	$6
Fixed overhead costs (total)	$600,000	$600,000

Milex Company produces a single product in the plant, and fixed overhead costs are applied to the product on the basis of *each year's production*. (Thus, a new fixed overhead rate is computed each year, as in Exhibit 7–9.) Variable selling and administrative expenses are $2 per unit sold.

Required

1. Compute the cost of a single unit of product for each year under:
   a. Absorption costing.
   b. Direct costing.
2. Prepare an income statement for each year, using the contribution approach with direct costing.
3. Reconcile the direct costing and absorption costing net income figures for each year.
4. Explain to the president why the net income for 19x2 under absorption costing was higher than the net income for 19x1, although the same number of units was sold in each year.
5. *a.* Explain how operations would have differed in 19x2 if the company had been using JIT inventory methods.
   b. If JIT had been in use during 19x2, what would the company's net income have been under the absorption costing method? Explain the reason for any difference between this income figure and the figure reported by the company in the statements above.

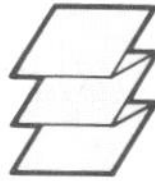

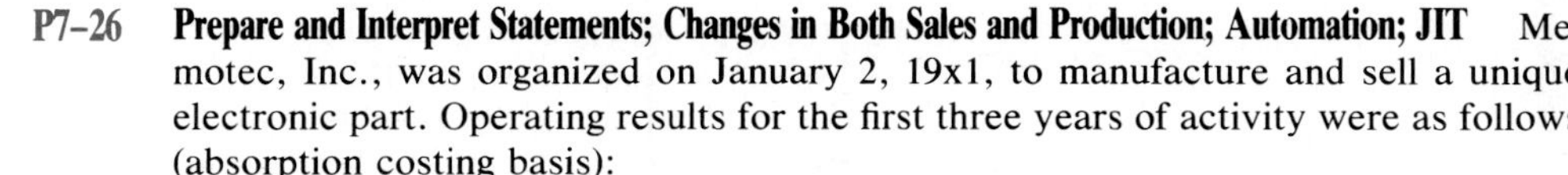

P7–26 Prepare and Interpret Statements; Changes in Both Sales and Production; Automation; JIT Memotec, Inc., was organized on January 2, 19x1, to manufacture and sell a unique electronic part. Operating results for the first three years of activity were as follows (absorption costing basis):

	19x1	19x2	19x3
Sales	$1,000,000	$800,000	$1,000,000
Cost of goods sold:			
Beginning inventory	-0-	-0-	280,000
Cost of goods manufactured. . . .	800,000	840,000	760,000
Goods available for sale	800,000	840,000	1,040,000
Less ending inventory	-0-	280,000	190,000
Cost of goods sold	800,000	560,000	850,000
Gross margin	200,000	240,000	150,000
Less selling and administrative expenses	170,000	150,000	170,000
Net income (loss)	$ 30,000	$ 90,000	$ (20,000)

Sales dropped by 20 percent during 19x2 due to the entry of several foreign competitors into the market. Memotec had not expected this competition, so production increased during the year even though sales were down. In order to work off the excessive inventories, Memotec cut back production during 19x3, as shown below:

	19x1	19x2	19x3
Production in units . . .	50,000	60,000	40,000
Sales in units	50,000	40,000	50,000

Additional information about the company follows:

a. The company's plant is highly automated. Variable manufacturing costs (direct materials, direct labor, and variable overhead) total only $4 per unit, and fixed manufacturing costs total $600,000 per year.
b. Fixed manufacturing costs are applied to units of product on the basis of each year's production. (That is, a new fixed overhead rate is computed each year, as in Exhibit 7–9.)
c. Variable selling and administrative expenses are $2 per unit sold. Fixed selling and administrative expenses total $70,000 per year.
d. The company uses a FIFO inventory flow.

Memotec's management can't understand why profits tripled during 19x2 when sales dropped by 20 percent, and why a loss was incurred during 19x3 when sales recovered to previous levels.

Required

1. Prepare a new income statement for each year using the contribution approach with direct costing.
2. Refer to the absorption costing income statements above.
   a. Compute the cost to produce one unit of product in each year under absorption costing. (Show how much of this cost is variable and how much is fixed.)
   b. Reconcile the direct costing and absorption costing net income figures for each year.
3. Refer again to the absorption costing income statements. Explain why net income was higher in 19x2 than it was in 19x1 under the absorption approach, in light of the fact that fewer units were sold in 19x2 than in 19x1.
4. Refer again to the absorption costing income statements. Explain why the company suffered a loss in 19x3 but reported a profit in 19x1, although the same number of units was sold in each year.
5. *a.* Explain how operations would have differed in 19x2 and 19x3 if the company had been using JIT inventory methods.
   b. If JIT had been in use during 19x2 and 19x3, what would the company's net income (or loss) have been in each year under absorption costing? Explain

the reason for any differences between these income figures and the figures reported by the company in the statements above.

CASES

C7–27 The Case of the Perplexed President; Automation; JIT Impact John Ovard, president of Mylar, Inc., was looking forward to receiving the company's second quarter income statement. He knew that the sales budget of 20,000 units sold had been met during the second quarter and that this represented a 25 percent increase in sales over the first quarter. He was especially happy about the increase in sales, since Mylar was about to approach its bank for additional loan money for expansion purposes. He anticipated that the strong second-quarter results would be a real plus in persuading the bank to extend the additional credit.

For this reason Mr. Ovard was shocked when he received the second-quarter income statement below, which showed a substantial drop in net income from the first quarter.

MYLAR, INC.
Income Statements
For the First Two Quarters

	First Quarter		Second Quarter	
Sales		$1,600,000		$2,000,000
Less cost of goods sold:				
Beginning inventory	$ 210,000		$ 490,000	
Cost of goods manufactured	1,400,000		980,000	
Goods available for sale	1,610,000		1,470,000	
Less ending inventory	490,000		70,000	
Cost of goods sold	1,120,000		1,400,000	
Add underapplied overhead	—	1,120,000	240,000	1,640,000
Gross margin		480,000		360,000
Less selling and administrative expenses		310,000		330,000
Net income		$ 170,000		$ 30,000

Mr. Ovard was certain there had to be an error somewhere and immediately called the controller into his office to find the problem. The controller stated, "That net income figure is correct, John. I agree that sales went up during the second quarter, but the problem is in production. You see, we budgeted to produce 20,000 units each quarter, but a strike in one of our supplier's plants forced us to cut production back to only 14,000 units in the second quarter. That's what caused the drop in net income."

Mr. Ovard was angered by the controller's explanation. "I call you in here to find out why income dropped when sales went up, and you talk about production! So what if production was off? What does that have to do with the sales that we made? If sales go up, then income ought to go up. If your statements can't show a simple thing like that, then we're due for some changes in your area!"

Budgeted production and sales for the year, along with actual production and sales for the first two quarters, are given below:

	Quarter			
	First	Second	Third	Fourth
Budgeted sales (units)	16,000	20,000	20,000	24,000
Actual sales (units)	16,000	20,000	—	—
Budgeted production (units)	20,000	20,000	20,000	20,000
Actual production (units)	20,000	14,000	—	—

The company's plant is heavily automated, so fixed overhead costs total $800,000 per quarter. Variable manufacturing costs are $30 per unit. The fixed overhead cost is applied to units of product at the rate of $40 per unit (based on the budgeted production shown above). Any under- or overapplied overhead is taken directly to cost of goods sold for the quarter.

The company had 3,000 units in inventory to start the first quarter and uses the FIFO inventory method. Variable selling and administrative expenses are $5 per unit sold.

Required

1. What characteristic of absorption costing caused the drop in net income for the second quarter and what could the controller have said to explain the problem more fully?
2. Prepare income statements for each quarter using the contribution approach, with direct costing.
3. Reconcile the absorption costing and the direct costing net income figures for each quarter.
4. Identify and discuss the advantages and disadvantages of using the direct costing method for internal reporting purposes.
5. Assume that the company had introduced JIT inventory methods at the beginning of the second quarter. (Sales and production during the first quarter were as shown above.)
   a. How many units would have been produced during the second quarter under JIT?
   b. Starting with the third quarter, would you expect any difference between the net income reported under absorption costing and under direct costing? Explain why there would or would not be any difference.

C7–28 Absorption and Direct Costing; Uneven Production; Break-Even Analysis; Automation; JIT Impact "I thought that new, automated plant was supposed to make us more efficient and therefore more profitable," exclaimed Marla Warner, president of Visic Company. "Just look at these monthly income statements for the second quarter. Sales have risen steadily month by month, but income is going in the opposite direction, and we even show a loss for June! Can someone explain what's happening?"

The statements to which Ms. Warner was referring are given below:

VISIC COMPANY
Monthly Income Statements
For the Second Quarter

	April	May	June
Sales (at $25)	$1,500,000	$1,625,000	$1,750,000
Less cost of goods sold:			
Opening inventory	70,000	280,000	350,000
Cost applied to production:			
Variable manufacturing costs (at $6)	450,000	420,000	300,000
Fixed manufacturing overhead	600,000	560,000	400,000
Cost of goods manufactured	1,050,000	980,000	700,000
Goods available for sale	1,120,000	1,260,000	1,050,000
Less ending inventory	280,000	350,000	70,000
Cost of goods sold	840,000	910,000	980,000
Underapplied or (overapplied) overhead cost	(40,000)	—	160,000
Adjusted cost of goods sold	800,000	910,000	1,140,000
Gross margin	700,000	715,000	610,000
Less selling and administrative expenses	620,000	665,000	710,000
Net income (loss)	$ 80,000	$ 50,000	$ (100,000)

"Fixed costs associated with the new plant are very high," replied Brian Hauber, the controller. "We're just following good absorption costing, as we have for years."

"Maybe the costing method *is* the problem," responded Teri Carlyle, the financial vice president. "A management development seminar I just attended suggested that the contribution approach, with direct costing, is the best way to report profit data to management. The contribution approach is particularly good when production is erratic, as ours has been lately."

Production and sales data for the second quarter follow:

	April	May	June
Production in units . . .	75,000	70,000	50,000
Sales in units	60,000	65,000	70,000

Additional information about the company's operations is given below:

a. Five thousand units were in inventory on April 1.
b. Fixed manufacturing overhead costs total $1,680,000 per quarter and are incurred evenly throughout the quarter. This fixed overhead cost is applied to units of product on the basis of a budgeted production volume of 70,000 units per month.
c. Variable selling and administrative expenses are $9 per unit sold. The remainder of the selling and administrative expenses on the statements above are fixed.
d. The company uses a FIFO inventory flow. Work in process inventories are nominal and can be ignored.

"We had to build inventory early in the year in anticipation of a strike in June," said Mr. Hauber. "Since the union settled without a strike, we then had to cut back production in June in order to work off the excess inventories. The income statements you have are completely accurate."

Required

1. Prepare an income statement for each month, using the contribution approach with direct costing.
2. Compute the monthly break-even point in units under:
   a. Direct costing.
   b. Absorption costing.
3. Explain to Ms. Warner why profits have moved erratically over the three-month period shown in the absorption costing income statements above and why profits have not been more closely correlated with changes in sales volume.
4. Reconcile the direct costing and absorption costing net income (loss) figures for each month. Show all computations, and show how you derive each figure used in your reconciliation.
5. Assume that the company had decided to introduce JIT inventory methods at the beginning of June. (Sales and production during April and May were as shown above.)
   a. How many units would have been produced during June under JIT?
   b. Starting with the next quarter (July, August, and September), would you expect any difference between the income reported under absorption costing and under direct costing? Explain why there would or would not be any difference.
   c. Refer to your computations in (2) above. How would JIT help break-even analysis "make sense" under absorption costing?

8

Profit Planning

LEARNING OBJECTIVES

After studying Chapter 8, you should be able to:

1. Define budgeting and explain the difference between planning and control.
2. Enumerate the principal advantages of budgeting.
3. Diagram and explain the master budget interrelationships.
4. Prepare a sales budget, including a computation of expected cash receipts.
5. Prepare a production budget.
6. Prepare a direct materials purchases budget, including a computation of expected cash disbursements.
7. Prepare a manufacturing overhead budget and a selling and administrative expense budget.
8. Prepare a cash budget, along with a budgeted income statement and a budgeted balance sheet.
9. Describe JIT purchasing and explain how it differs from JIT production.
10. Compute the economic order quantity (EOQ) and the reorder point.
11. Define or explain the key terms listed at the end of the chapter.

In this chapter, we focus our attention on those steps taken by business organizations to achieve certain desired levels of profits—a process that is generally called *profit planning*. In our study, we shall see that profit planning is accomplished through the preparation of a number of budgets, which, when brought together, form an integrated business plan known as the *master budget*. We shall find that the data going into the preparation of the master budget focus heavily on the future, rather than on the past.

THE BASIC FRAMEWORK OF BUDGETING

Definition of Budgeting

A **budget** is a detailed plan outlining the acquisition and use of financial and other resources over some given time period. It represents a plan for the future expressed in formal quantitative terms. The act of preparing a budget is called *budgeting*. The use of budgets to control a firm's activities is known as *budgetary control*.

The **master budget** is a summary of all phases of a company's plans and goals for the future. It sets specific targets for sales, production, distribution, and financing activities, and it generally culminates in a projected statement of net income and a projected statement of cash position. In short, it represents a comprehensive expression of management's plans for the future and how these plans are to be accomplished.

Personal Budgets

Nearly everyone budgets to some extent, even though many of the people who prepare and use budgets do not recognize what they are doing as budgeting. For example, most people make estimates of the income to be realized over some future time period and plan expenditures for food, clothing, housing, and so on, accordingly. As a result of this planning, spending will usually be restricted by limiting it to some predetermined, allowable amount. In taking these steps, the individual clearly goes through a budget process in that he or she (1) makes an estimate of income, (2) plans expenditures, and (3) restricts spending in accordance with the plan. In other situations, individuals use estimates of income and expenditures to predict what their financial condition will be in the future. The budgets involved here may exist only in the mind of the individual, but they are budgets nonetheless in that they involve plans of how resources will be acquired and used over some specific time period.

The budgets of a business firm serve much the same functions as the budgets prepared informally by individuals. Business budgets tend to be more detailed and to involve more work in preparation (mostly because they are formal rather than informal), but they are similar to the budgets prepared by individuals in most other respects. Like personal budgets, they assist in planning and controlling expenditures; they also assist in predicting operating results and financial condition in future periods.

Difference between Planning and Control

The terms *planning* and *control* are often confused, and occasionally these terms are used in such a way as to suggest that they mean the same thing. Actually, planning and control are two quite distinct concepts. **Planning** involves the development of future objectives and the preparation of various budgets to achieve these objectives. **Control** involves the steps taken by management to ensure that the objectives set down at the planning stage are attained, and to ensure that all parts of the organization function in a manner consistent with organizational policies. To be completely effective, a good budgeting system must provide for *both* planning and control. Good planning without effective control is time wasted. On the other hand, unless plans are laid down in advance, there are no objectives toward which control can be directed.

Advantages of Budgeting

There is an old saying to the effect that "a man is usually down on what he isn't up on." Managers who have never tried budgeting or attempted to find out what benefits might be available through the budget process are usually quick to state that budgeting is a waste of time. These managers may argue that even though budgeting may work well in *some* situations, it would never work well in their companies because operations are too complex or because there are too many uncertainties involved. In reality, however, managers who argue this way usually will be deeply involved in planning (albeit on an informal basis). These managers will have clearly defined thoughts about what they want to accomplish and when they want it accomplished. The difficulty is that unless they have some way of communicating their thoughts and plans to others, the only way their companies will ever attain the desired objectives will be through accident. In short, even though companies may attain a certain degree of success without budgets, they never attain the heights that could have been reached had a coordinated system of budgets been in operation.

One of the great values of budgeting is that it requires managers to give planning top priority among their duties. Moreover, budgeting provides managers with a vehicle for communicating their plans in an orderly way throughout an entire organization. When budgets are in use, no one has any doubt about what the managers want to accomplish or how they want it done. Other benefits of budgeting are:

1. It provides managers with a way to *formalize* their planning efforts.
2. It provides definite goals and objectives that serve as *benchmarks* for evaluating subsequent performance.
3. It uncovers potential *bottlenecks* before they occur.
4. It *coordinates* the activities of the entire organization by *integrating* the plans and objectives of the various parts. By so doing, budgeting ensures that the plans and objectives of the parts are consistent with the broad goals of the entire organization.

Consider the following situation encountered by the author:

Company X is a mortgage banking firm. For years, the company operated with virtually no system of budgets whatever. Management contended that budgeting wasn't well suited to the firm's type of operation. Moreover, management pointed out that the firm was already profitable. Indeed, outwardly the company gave every appearance of being a well-managed, smoothly operating organization. A careful look within, however, disclosed that day-to-day operations were far from smooth, and often approached chaos. The average day was nothing more than an exercise in putting out one brush fire after another. The Cash account was always at crisis levels. At the end of a day, no one ever knew whether enough cash would be available the next day to cover required loan closings. Departments were uncoordinated, and it was not uncommon to find that one department was pursuing a course that conflicted with the course pursued by another department. Employee morale was low, and turnover was high. Employees complained bitterly that when a job was well done, nobody ever knew about it.

Company X was bought out by a new group of stockholders who required that the company establish an integrated budgeting system to control operations. Within one year's time, significant changes were evident. Brush fires were rare. Careful planning virtually eliminated the problems that had been experienced with cash, and departmental efforts were coordinated and directed toward predetermined overall company goals. Although the employees were wary of the new budgeting program initially, they became "converted" when they saw the positive effects that it brought about. The more efficient operations caused profits to jump dramatically. Communication increased throughout the organization. When a job was well done, everybody knew about it. As one employee stated, "For the first time, we know what the company expects of us."

Responsibility Accounting

Most of what we say in the remainder of this chapter and in Chapters 9, 10, and 11 centers on the concept of *responsibility accounting*. The basic idea behind **responsibility accounting** is that each manager's performance should be judged by how well he or she manages those items directly under his or her control. To judge a manager's performance in this way, the costs (and revenues) of an organization must be carefully scrutinized and classified according to the various levels of management under whose control the costs rest. Each level of management is then charged with those costs under its care, and the managers at each level are held responsible for variations between budgeted goals and actual results. In effect, responsibility accounting *personalizes* the accounting system by looking at costs from a *personal control* standpoint, rather than from an *institutional* standpoint. This concept is central to any effective profit planning and control system.

We will look at responsibility accounting in more detail in Chapters 9, 10, and 11. For the moment, we can summarize the overall idea by noting that it rests on three basic premises. The first premise is that costs can be organized in terms of levels of management responsibility. The second premise is that the costs charged to a particular level are controllable at that level by its managers. And the third premise is that effective budget data can be generated as a basis for evaluating actual performance. This chapter on profit planning is concerned with the third of these premises, in that the purpose of the chapter is to show the steps involved in budget preparation.

Choosing a Budget Period

Budgets covering acquisition of land, buildings, and other items of capital equipment (often called **capital budgets**) generally have quite long time horizons and may extend 30 years or more into the future. The later years covered by such budgets may be quite indefinite, but at least management is kept planning ahead sufficiently to ensure that funds will be available when purchases of equipment become necessary. As time passes, capital equipment plans that were once somewhat indefinite come more sharply into focus, and the capital budget is updated accordingly. Without such long-term planning, an organization can suddenly come to the realization that substantial purchases of capital equipment are needed, but find that no funds are available to make the purchases.

Operating budgets are ordinarily set to cover a one-year period. The one-year period should correspond to the company's fiscal year so that the budget figures can be compared with the actual results. Many companies divide their budget year into four quarters. The first quarter is then subdivided into months, and monthly budget figures are established. These near-term figures can usually be established with considerable accuracy. The last three quarters are carried in the budget at quarterly totals only. As the year progresses, the figures for the second quarter are broken down into monthly amounts, then the third quarter figures are broken down, and so forth. This approach has the advantage of requiring a constant review and reappraisal of budget data.

Continuous or perpetual budgets are becoming very popular. A continuous or perpetual budget is one that covers a 12-month period but which is constantly adding a new month on the end as the current month is completed. Advocates of continuous budgets state that this approach to budgeting is superior to other approaches in that it keeps management thinking and planning a full 12 months ahead. Thus, it stabilizes the planning horizon. Under other budget approaches, the planning horizon becomes shorter as the year progresses.

The Self-Imposed Budget

The success of any budget program will be determined in large part by the way in which the budget itself is developed. Generally, the most successful budget programs are those that permit managers with responsibility over cost control to prepare their own budget estimates, as illustrated in Exhibit 8–1. This approach to preparing budget data is particularly important if the budget is to be used in controlling a manager's activities after it has been developed. If a budget is forced on a manager from above, it will probably generate resentment and ill will rather than cooperation and increased productivity.

When managers prepare their own budget figures, the budgets that they prepare become *self-imposed* in nature. Certain distinct advantages arise from the **self-imposed budget** (also called a **participative budget**):

1. Individuals at all levels of the organization are recognized as members of the team, whose views and judgments are valued by top management.

EXHIBIT 8–1
The Initial Flow of Budget Data

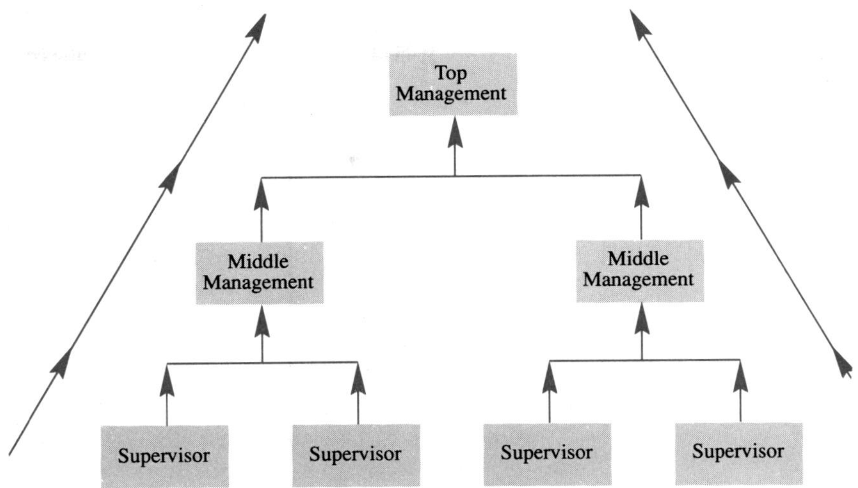

The initial flow of budget data is from lower levels of responsibility to higher levels of responsibility. Each person with responsibility for cost control will prepare his or her own budget estimates and submit them to the superior. These estimates are consolidated as they move upward in the organization.

2. The person in direct contact with an activity is in the best position to make budget estimates. Therefore, budget estimates prepared by such persons tend to be more accurate and reliable.
3. A person is more apt to work at fulfilling a budget that he has set himself than he is to work at fulfilling a budget imposed on him from above.
4. A self-imposed budget contains its own unique system of control in that if people are not able to meet budget specifications, they have only themselves to blame. On the other hand, if a budget is imposed on them from above, they can always say that the budget was unreasonable or unrealistic to start with, and therefore was impossible to meet.

Once self-imposed budgets are prepared, are they subject to any kind of review? The answer is yes. Even though individual preparation of budget estimates is critical to a successful budgeting program, such budget estimates cannot necessarily be accepted without question by higher levels of management. If no system of checks and balances is present, the danger exists that self-imposed budgets will be too loose and allow too much freedom in activities. The result will be inefficiency and waste. Therefore, before budgets are accepted, they must be carefully reviewed by immediate superiors. If changes from the original budget seem desirable, the items in question are discussed, and compromises are reached that are acceptable to all concerned.

In essence, all levels of an organization work together to produce the budget. Since top management is generally unfamiliar with detailed, day-to-day cost matters, it will rely on subordinates to provide detailed budget information. On the other hand, top management has a perspective on the company as a whole that is vital in making broad policy decisions in budget preparation. Each level of responsibility in an organization contributes in the way that it best can in a *cooperative* effort to develop an integrated budget document.

The Matter of Human Relations

Whether or not a budget program is accepted by lower management personnel will be reflective of (1) the degree to which top management accepts the budget program as a vital part of the company's activities, and (2) the way in which top management uses budgeted data.

If a budget program is to be successful, it must have the complete acceptance and support of the persons who occupy key management positions. If lower or middle management personnel sense that top management is lukewarm about budgeting, or if they sense that top management simply tolerates budgeting as a necessary evil, then their own attitudes will reflect a similar lack of enthusiasm. Budgeting is hard work, and if top management is not enthusiastic about and committed to the budget program, then it is unlikely that anyone else in the organization will be either.

In administering the budget program, it is particularly important that top management not use the budget as a "club" to pressure employees or as a way to find someone to "blame" for a particular problem. This type of negative emphasis will simply breed hostility, tension, and mistrust rather than greater cooperation and productivity. Unfortunately, research suggests that the budget is often used as a pressure device and that great emphasis is placed on "meeting the budget" under all circumstances.[1]

Rather than being used as a pressure device, the budget should be used as a positive instrument to assist in establishing goals, in measuring operating results, and in isolating areas that are in need of extra effort or attention. Any misgivings that employees have about a budget program can be overcome by meaningful involvement at all levels and by proper use of the program over a period of time. Administration of a budget program requires a great deal of insight and sensitivity on the part of management. The ultimate objective must be to develop the realization that the budget is designed to be a positive aid in achieving both individual and company goals.

Management must keep clearly in mind that the human dimension in budgeting is of key importance. It is easy for the manager to become preoccupied with the technical aspects of the budget program to the exclusion of the human aspects. Accountants are particularly open to criticism in this regard. Indeed, the study cited earlier found that use of budget data in a rigid and inflexible manner was the greatest single complaint of persons whose performance was being evaluated through the budget process.[2] In light of these facts, management should remember that the purposes of the budget are to motivate employees and to coordinate efforts. Preoccupation with the

[1] Paul J. Carruth, Thurrell O. McClendon, and Milton R. Ballard, "What Supervisors Don't Like about Budget Evaluations," *Management Accounting* 64, no. 8 (February 1983), p. 42.

[2] Ibid.

dollars and cents in the budget, or being rigid and inflexible in budget administration, can only lead to frustration of these purposes.

The Budget Committee

A standing **budget committee** will usually be responsible for overall policy matters relating to the budget program and for coordinating the preparation of the budget itself. This committee generally consists of the president; vice presidents in charge of various functions such as sales, production, and purchasing; and the controller. Difficulties and disputes between segments of the organization in matters relating to the budget are resolved by the budget committee. In addition, the budget committee approves the final budget and receives periodic reports on the progress of the company in attaining budgeted goals.

The Master Budget—A Network of Interrelationships

The master budget is a network consisting of many separate budgets that are interdependent. This network is illustrated in Exhibit 8–2.

The Sales Budget A **sales budget** is a detailed schedule showing the expected sales for coming periods; typically, it is expressed in both dollars and units of product. Much time and effort is put into preparing an accurate sales budget, since it is the key to the entire budgeting process. The reason it is the key is that all other parts of the master budget are dependent on the sales budget in some way, as illustrated in Exhibit 8–2. Thus, if the sales budget is sloppily done, then the rest of the budgeting process is largely a waste of time.

After the sales budget has been set, a decision can be made on the level of production that will be needed for the period to support sales, and the production budget can be set as well. The production budget then becomes a key factor in the determination of other budgets, including the direct materials budget, the direct labor budget, and the manufacturing overhead budget. These budgets, in turn, are needed to assist in formulating a cash budget for the budget period. In essence, the sales budget triggers a chain reaction that leads to the development of many other budget figures in an organization.

As shown in Exhibit 8–2, the selling and administrative expense budget is both dependent on and a determinant of the sales budget. This reciprocal relationship arises from the fact that sales will in part be determined by the funds available for advertising and sales promotion.

The Cash Budget Once the operating budgets (sales, production, and so on) have been established, the cash budget and other financial budgets can be prepared. A **cash budget** is a detailed plan showing how cash resources will be acquired and used over some specified time period. Observe from Exhibit 8–2 that all of the operating budgets, including the sales budget, have an impact of some type on the cash budget. In the case of the sales budget, the impact comes from the planned cash receipts to be received on sales. In the case of the other budgets, the impact comes from the planned cash expenditures within the budgets themselves.

EXHIBIT 8–2
The Master Budget Interrelationships

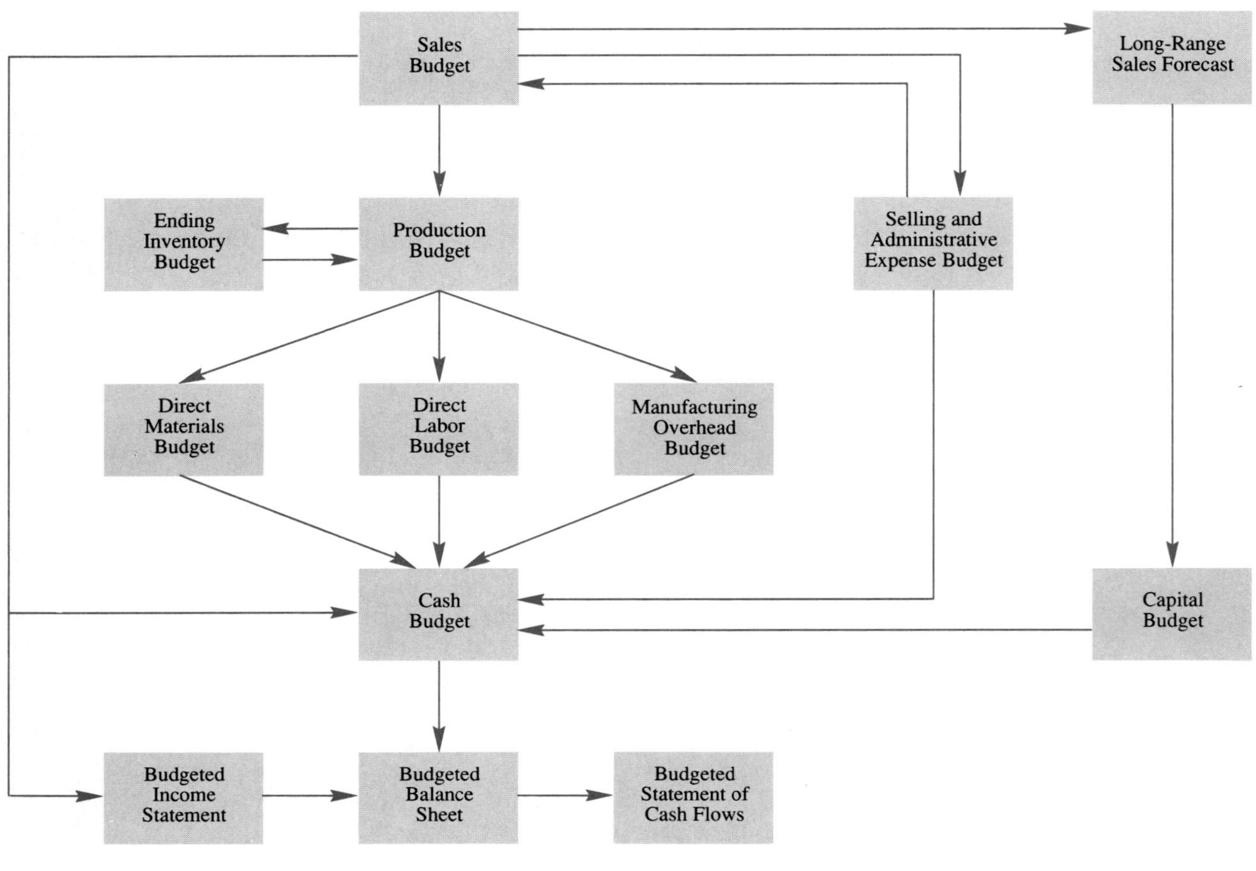

Sales Forecasting—A Critical Step

The sales budget is prepared from the *sales forecast*. A **sales forecast** is broader than a sales budget, generally encompassing potential sales for the entire industry, as well as potential sales for the firm preparing the forecast. Factors that are considered in making a sales forecast include the following:

1. Past experience in terms of sales volume.
2. Prospective pricing policy.
3. Unfilled order backlogs.
4. Market research studies.
5. General economic conditions.
6. Industry economic conditions.
7. Movements of economic indicators such as gross national product, employment, prices, and personal income.
8. Advertising and product promotion.
9. Industry competition.
10. Market share.

Sales results from prior years are used as a starting point in preparing a sales forecast. Forecasters examine sales data in relation to various factors, including prices, competitive conditions, availability of supplies, and general economic conditions. Projections are then made into the future, based on those factors that the forecasters feel will be significant over the budget period. In-depth discussions generally characterize the gathering and interpretation of all data going into the sales forecast. These discussions, held at all levels of the organization, develop perspective and assist in assessing the significance and usefulness of data.

Statistical tools such as regression analysis, trend and cycle projection, and correlation analysis are widely used in sales forecasting. In addition, some firms have found it useful to build econometric models of their industry or of the nation to assist in forecasting problems. Such models hold great promise for improving the overall quality of budget data.

PREPARING THE MASTER BUDGET

To show how the separate budgets making up the master budget are developed and integrated, we focus now on Meredith Company. Meredith Company produces and sells a single product that we will call product A. Each year the company prepares the following budget documents:

1. A sales budget, including a computation of expected cash receipts.
2. A production budget (or merchandise purchases budget for a merchandising company).
3. A direct materials budget, including a computation of expected cash payments for raw materials.
4. A direct labor budget.
5. A manufacturing overhead budget.
6. An ending finished goods inventory budget.
7. A selling and administrative expense budget.
8. A cash budget.
9. A budgeted income statement.
10. A budgeted balance sheet.

These budgets for the year 19x1 are illustrated in Schedules 1 through 10 following.

The Sales Budget

The sales budget is the starting point in preparing the master budget. As shown earlier in Exhibit 8–2, nearly all other items in the master budget, including production, purchases, inventories, and expenses, depend on it in some way.

The sales budget is constructed by multiplying the expected sales in units by the sales price. Schedule 1 on the following page contains the sales budget for Meredith Company for 19x1, by quarters. Notice from the schedule that the company plans to sell 100,000 units during the year, with sales peaking out in the third quarter.

SCHEDULE 1

MEREDITH COMPANY
Sales Budget
For the Year Ended December 31, 19x1

	Quarter				
	1	2	3	4	Year
Expected sales in units	10,000	30,000	40,000	20,000	100,000
Selling price per unit	× $20	× $20	× $20	× $20	× $20
Total sales	$200,000	$600,000	$800,000	$400,000	$2,000,000

Schedule of Expected Cash Collections

	1	2	3	4	Year
Accounts receivable, 12/31/x0	$ 90,000				$ 90,000
First-quarter sales ($200,000)	140,000	$ 60,000			200,000
Second-quarter sales ($600,000)		420,000	$180,000		600,000
Third-quarter sales ($800,000)			560,000	$240,000	800,000
Fourth-quarter sales ($400,000)				280,000	280,000
Total cash collections	$230,000	$480,000	$740,000	$520,000	$1,970,000

Note: Seventy percent of a quarter's sales is collected in the quarter of sale; the remaining 30 percent is collected in the quarter following.

Generally, the sales budget is accompanied by a computation of expected cash receipts for the forthcoming budget period. This computation is needed to assist in preparing the cash budget for the year. Expected cash receipts are composed of collections on sales made to customers in prior periods, plus collections on sales made in the current budget period. Schedule 1 above contains a computation of expected cash collections for Meredith Company.

The Production Budget

After the sales budget has been prepared, the production requirements for the forthcoming budget period can be determined and organized in the form of a **production budget.** Sufficient goods will have to be available to meet sales needs and provide for the desired ending inventory. A portion of these goods will already exist in the form of a beginning inventory. The remainder will have to be produced. Therefore, production needs can be determined by adding budgeted sales (in units or in dollars) to the desired ending inventory (in units or in dollars) and deducting the beginning inventory (in units or in dollars) from this total. Schedule 2 contains a production budget for Meredith Company.

Students are often surprised to learn that firms budget the level of their ending inventories. Budgeting of inventories is a common practice, however. If inventories are not carefully planned, the levels remaining at the end of a period may be excessive, causing an unnecessary tie-up of funds and an unneeded expense of carrying the unwanted goods. On the other hand, without proper planning, inventory levels may be too small, thereby requiring crash production efforts in following periods, and perhaps loss of sales due to inability to meet shipping schedules.

SCHEDULE 2

MEREDITH COMPANY
Production Budget
For the Year Ended December 31, 19x1
(in units)

	Quarter				
	1	**2**	**3**	**4**	**Year**
Expected sales (Schedule 1)	10,000	30,000	40,000	20,000	100,000
Add desired ending inventory of finished goods*	6,000	8,000	4,000	3,000	3,000†
Total needs	16,000	38,000	44,000	23,000	103,000
Less beginning inventory of finished goods‡	2,000	6,000	8,000	4,000	2,000
Units to be produced	14,000	32,000	36,000	19,000	101,000

* Twenty percent of the next quarter's sales.
† Estimated.
‡ The same as the prior quarter's *ending* inventory.

Inventory Purchases—Merchandising Firm

Meredith Company prepares a production budget since it is a *manufacturing* firm. If it were a *merchandising* firm, then instead of a production budget it would prepare a **merchandise purchases budget** showing the amount of goods to be purchased from its suppliers during the period. The merchandise purchases budget is in the same basic format as the production budget, except that it shows goods to be purchased rather than goods to be produced, as shown below:

Budgeted cost of goods sold (in units or in dollars)	XXXXX
Add desired ending merchandise inventory	XXXXX
Total needs	XXXXX
Less beginning merchandise inventory	XXXXX
Required purchases (in units or in dollars)	XXXXX

The merchandising firm would prepare an inventory purchases budget such as this one for each item carried in stock. Some large retail organizations make such computations on a frequent basis (particularly at peak seasons) to ensure that adequate stocks are on hand to meet customer needs.

The Direct Materials Budget

Returning to the Meredith Company example, after production needs have been computed, a **direct materials budget** should be prepared to show the materials that will be required in the production process. Sufficient raw materials will have to be available to meet production needs, and to provide for the desired ending raw materials inventory for the budget period. Part of this raw materials requirement will already exist in the form of a beginning raw materials inventory. The remainder will have to be purchased from suppliers. In sum, the format for computing raw materials needs is:

Raw materials needed to meet the production schedule	XXXXX
Add desired ending inventory of raw materials	XXXXX
Total raw materials needs	XXXXX
Less beginning inventory of raw materials	XXXXX
Raw materials to be purchased	XXXXX

Preparing a budget of this kind is one step in a company's overall **material requirements planning (MRP).** MRP is an operations research tool that employs the computer to assist the manager in overall materials and inventory planning. The objective of MRP is to ensure that the right materials are on hand, in the right quantities, and at the right time to support the production process. The detailed operation of MRP is covered in most operations research textbooks; for this reason, it will not be considered further here, other than to point out that the concepts we are discussing are an important part of the overall MRP technique.

Schedule 3 contains a direct materials purchases budget for Meredith Company. Notice that materials requirements are first determined in units (pounds, gallons, and so on) and then translated into dollars by multiplying by the appropriate unit cost.

SCHEDULE 3

MEREDITH COMPANY
Direct Materials Budget
For the Year Ended December 31, 19x1

	Quarter 1	Quarter 2	Quarter 3	Quarter 4	Year
Units to be produced (Schedule 2)	14,000	32,000	36,000	19,000	101,000
Raw materials needed per unit (pounds)	× 5	× 5	× 5	× 5	× 5
Production needs (pounds)	70,000	160,000	180,000	95,000	505,000
Add desired ending inventory of raw materials* (pounds)	16,000	18,000	9,500	7,500	7,500
Total needs (pounds)	86,000	178,000	189,500	102,500	512,500
Less beginning inventory of raw materials (pounds)	7,000	16,000	18,000	9,500	7,000
Raw materials to be purchased (pounds)	79,000	162,000	171,500	93,000	505,500
Cost of raw materials to be purchased at $0.60 per pound	$47,400	$ 97,200	$102,900	$ 55,800	$303,300

* Ten percent of the next quarter's production needs. For example, the second-quarter production needs are 160,000 pounds. Therefore, the desired ending inventory for the first quarter would be 10 percent × 160,000 pounds = 16,000 pounds. The ending inventory of 7,500 pounds for the fourth quarter is estimated.

Schedule of Expected Cash Disbursements

	1	2	3	4	Year
Accounts payable, 12/31/x0	$25,800				$ 25,800
First-quarter purchases ($47,400)	23,700	$ 23,700			47,400
Second-quarter purchases ($97,200)		48,600	$ 48,600		97,200
Third-quarter purchases ($102,900)			51,450	$ 51,450	102,900
Fourth-quarter purchases ($55,800)				27,900	27,900
Total cash disbursements	$49,500	$ 72,300	$100,050	$ 79,350	$301,200

Note: Fifty percent of a quarter's purchases is paid for in the quarter of purchase; the remaining 50 percent is paid for in the quarter following.

The direct materials budget is usually accompanied by a computation of expected cash disbursements for raw materials. This computation is needed to assist in developing a cash budget. Disbursements for raw materials will consist of payments for prior periods, plus payments for purchases for the current budget period. Schedule 3 contains a computation of expected cash disbursements for Meredith Company.

The Direct Labor Budget

The **direct labor budget** is also developed from the production budget. Direct labor requirements must be computed so that the company will know whether sufficient labor time is available to meet production needs. By knowing in advance just what will be needed in the way of labor time throughout the budget year, the company can develop plans to adjust the labor force as the situation may require. Firms that neglect to budget run the risk of facing labor shortages or having to hire and fire at awkward times. Erratic labor policies lead to insecurity and inefficiency on the part of employees.

To compute direct labor requirements, the number of units of finished product to be produced each period (month, quarter, and so on) is multiplied by the number of direct labor-hours required to produce a single unit. Many different types of labor may be involved. If so, then computations should be by type of labor needed. The hours of direct labor time resulting from these computations can then be multiplied by the direct labor cost per hour to obtain budgeted total direct labor costs. Schedule 4 contains such computations for Meredith Company.

The Manufacturing Overhead Budget

The **manufacturing overhead budget** should provide a schedule of all costs of production other than direct materials and direct labor. These costs should be broken down by cost behavior for budgeting purposes, and a predetermined overhead rate developed. This rate will be used to apply manufacturing overhead to units of product throughout the budget period.

A computation showing budgeted cash disbursements for manufacturing overhead should be made for use in developing the cash budget. The critical

SCHEDULE 4

MEREDITH COMPANY
Direct Labor Budget
For the Year Ended December 31, 19x1

	Quarter				
	1	**2**	**3**	**4**	**Year**
Units to be produced (Schedule 2)	14,000	32,000	36,000	19,000	101,000
Direct labor time per unit (hours)	× 0.8	× 0.8	× 0.8	× 0.8	× 0.8
Total hours of direct labor time needed	11,200	25,600	28,800	15,200	80,800
Direct labor cost per hour	× $7.50	× $7.50	× $7.50	× $7.50	× $7.50
Total direct labor cost	$84,000	$192,000	$216,000	$114,000	$606,000

SCHEDULE 5

MEREDITH COMPANY
Manufacturing Overhead Budget
For the Year Ended December 31, 19x1

	Quarter				
	1	2	3	4	Year
Budgeted direct labor-hours	11,200	25,600	28,800	15,200	80,800
Variable overhead rate	× $2	× $2	× $2	× $2	× $2
Budgeted variable overhead	$22,400	$ 51,200	$ 57,600	$30,400	$161,600
Budgeted fixed overhead	60,600	60,600	60,600	60,600	242,400
Total budgeted overhead	83,000	111,800	118,200	91,000	404,000
Less depreciation	15,000	15,000	15,000	15,000	60,000
Cash disbursements for overhead	$68,000	$ 96,800	$103,200	$76,000	$344,000

thing to remember in making this computation is that depreciation is a non-cash charge. Therefore, any depreciation charges included in manufacturing overhead must be deducted from the total in computing expected cash payments.

We will assume that the variable overhead rate is $2 per direct labor-hour, and that fixed overhead costs are budgeted at $60,600 per quarter, of which $15,000 represents depreciation. All overhead costs involving cash disbursements are paid for in the quarter incurred. The manufacturing overhead budget, by quarters, and the expected cash disbursements, by quarters, are both shown in Schedule 5.

Ending Finished Goods Inventory Budget

After completing Schedules 1–5, sufficient data will have been generated to compute the cost of a unit of finished product. This computation is needed for two reasons: first, to know how much to charge as cost of goods sold on the budgeted income statement; and second, to know what amount to place on the balance sheet for unsold units. The dollar amount of the unsold units planned to be on hand is known as the **ending finished goods inventory budget.**

For Meredith Company, the cost of a unit of finished product is $13—consisting of $3 of direct materials, $6 of direct labor, and $4 of manufacturing overhead—and the ending finished goods inventory is budgeted to be $39,000. The computations behind these figures are shown in Schedule 6.

The Selling and Administrative Expense Budget

The **selling and administrative expense budget** contains a list of anticipated expenses for the budget period that will be incurred in areas other than manufacturing. The budget will be made up of many smaller, individual budgets submitted by various persons having responsibility for cost control in selling and administrative matters. If the number of expense items is very

SCHEDULE 6

MEREDITH COMPANY
Ending Finished Goods Inventory Budget
For the Year Ended December 31, 19x1

Item	Quantity	Cost	Total
Production cost per unit:			
Direct materials	5.0 pounds	$0.60 per pound	$ 3
Direct labor	0.8 hours	7.50 per hour	6
Manufacturing overhead	0.8 hours	5.00 per hour*	4
			$13
Budgeted finished goods inventory:			
Ending finished goods inventory in units (Schedule 2)			3,000
Total production cost per unit (see above)			× $13
Ending finished goods inventory in dollars			$39,000

* $404,000 ÷ 80,800 hours = $5.

SCHEDULE 7

MEREDITH COMPANY
Selling and Administrative Expense Budget
For the Year Ended December 31, 19x1

	Quarter				
	1	2	3	4	Year
Budgeted sales in units	10,000	30,000	40,000	20,000	100,000
Variable selling and administrative expense per unit*	× $1.80	× $1.80	× $1.80	× $1.80	× $1.80
Budgeted variable expense	$18,000	$ 54,000	$ 72,000	$ 36,000	$180,000
Budgeted fixed selling and administrative expenses:					
Advertising	40,000	40,000	40,000	40,000	160,000
Executive salaries	35,000	35,000	35,000	35,000	140,000
Insurance	—	1,900	37,750	—	39,650
Property taxes	—	—	—	18,150	18,150
Total budgeted selling and administrative expenses	$93,000	$130,900	$184,750	$129,150	$537,800

* Commissions, clerical, and freight-out.

large, separate budgets may be needed for the selling and administrative functions.

Schedule 7 contains the selling and administrative expense budget for Meredith Company for 19x1.

The Cash Budget

The cash budget pulls together much of the data developed in the preceding steps, as illustrated earlier in Exhibit 8–2. The reader should restudy this exhibit before reading on.

The cash budget is composed of four major sections:

1. The receipts section.
2. The disbursements section.
3. The cash excess or deficiency section.
4. The financing section.

The receipts section consists of the opening cash balance added to whatever is expected in the way of cash receipts during the budget period. Generally, the major source of receipts will be from sales, as discussed earlier.

The disbursements section consists of all cash payments that are planned for the budget period. These payments will include raw materials purchases, direct labor payments, manufacturing overhead costs, and so on, as contained in their respective budgets. In addition, other cash disbursements such as income taxes, capital equipment purchases, and dividend payments will also be included.

The cash excess or deficiency section consists of the difference between the cash receipts section totals and the cash disbursements section totals. If a deficiency exists, the company will need to arrange for borrowed funds from its bank. If an excess exists, funds borrowed in previous periods can be repaid or the idle funds can be placed in short-term investments.

The financing section provides a detailed account of the borrowings and repayments projected to take place during the budget period. It also includes a detail of interest payments that will be due on money borrowed. Banks are becoming increasingly insistent that firms in need of borrowed money give long advance notice of the amounts and times that funds will be needed. This permits the banks to plan and helps to assure that funds will be ready when needed. Moreover, careful planning of cash needs via the budgeting process avoids unpleasant surprises for companies as well. Few things are more disquieting to an organization than to run into unexpected difficulties in the Cash account. A well-coordinated budgeting program eliminates uncertainty as to what the cash situation will be two months, six months, or a year from now.

The cash budget should be broken down into time periods that are as short as feasible. Many firms budget cash on a weekly basis, and some larger firms go so far as to plan daily cash needs. The more common planning horizons are geared to monthly or quarterly figures. The cash budget for Meredith Company for 19x1 is shown on a quarterly basis in Schedule 8.[3]

The Budgeted Income Statement

A budgeted income statement can be prepared from the data developed in Schedules 1–8. *The budgeted income statement is one of the key schedules in the budget process.* It is the document that tells how profitable operations are anticipated to be in the forthcoming period. After it has been developed, it stands as a benchmark against which subsequent company performance can be measured.

Schedule 9 on page 322 contains a budgeted income statement for Meredith Company for 19x1.

[3] Meredith Company has an open line of credit with its bank, which can be used as needed to bolster the cash position. Borrowings and repayments must be in round $1,000 amounts, and interest is 10 percent per annum. Interest is computed and paid on the principal as the principal is repaid. All borrowings take place at the beginning of a quarter, and all repayments are made at the end of a quarter.

SCHEDULE 8

MEREDITH COMPANY
Cash Budget
For the Year Ended December 31, 19x1

	Schedule	Quarter 1	Quarter 2	Quarter 3	Quarter 4	Year
Cash balance, beginning		$ 42,500	$ 40,000	$ 40,000	$ 40,500	$ 42,500
Add receipts:						
Collections from customers	1	230,000	480,000	740,000	520,000	1,970,000
Total cash available before current financing		272,500	520,000	780,000	560,500	2,012,500
Less disbursements:						
Direct materials	3	49,500	72,300	100,050	79,350	301,200
Direct labor	4	84,000	192,000	216,000	114,000	606,000
Manufacturing overhead	5	68,000	96,800	103,200	76,000	344,000
Selling and administrative	7	93,000	130,900	184,750	129,150	537,800
Income taxes	9	18,000	18,000	18,000	18,000	72,000
Equipment purchases		30,000	20,000	—	—	50,000
Dividends		10,000	10,000	10,000	10,000	40,000
Total disbursements		352,500	540,000	632,000	426,500	1,951,000
Excess (deficiency) of cash available over disbursements		(80,000)	(20,000)	148,000	134,000	61,500
Financing:						
Borrowings (at beginning)		120,000*	60,000	—	—	180,000
Repayments (at ending)		—	—	(100,000)	(80,000)	(180,000)
Interest (at 10% per annum)		—	—	(7,500)†	(6,500)†	(14,000)
Total financing		120,000	60,000	(107,500)	(86,500)	(14,000)
Cash balance, ending		$ 40,000	$ 40,000	$ 40,500	$ 47,500	$ 47,500

* The company requires a minimum cash balance of $40,000. Therefore, borrowing must be sufficient to cover the cash deficiency of $80,000 and to provide for the minimum cash balance of $40,000. All borrowings and all repayments of principal are in round $1,000 amounts.

† The interest payments relate only to the principal being repaid at the time it is repaid. For example, the interest in quarter 3 relates only to the interest due on the $100,000 principal being repaid from quarter 1 borrowing, as follows: $100,000 × 10% × ¾ = $7,500. The interest paid in quarter 4 is computed as follows:

$20,000 × 10% × 1 year	$2,000
$60,000 × 10% × ¾	4,500
Total interest paid	$6,500

SCHEDULE 9

MEREDITH COMPANY
Budgeted Income Statement
For the Year Ended December 31, 19x1

	Schedule	
Sales (100,000 units at $20)	1	$2,000,000
Less cost of goods sold (100,000 units at $13)	6	1,300,000
Gross margin		700,000
Less selling and administrative expenses	7	537,800
Net operating income		162,200
Less interest expense	8	14,000
Income before taxes		148,200
Less income taxes	*	72,000
Net income		$ 76,200

* Estimated.

The Budgeted Balance Sheet

The budgeted balance sheet is developed by beginning with the current balance sheet and adjusting it for the data contained in the other budgets. A budgeted balance sheet for Meredith Company for 19x1 is presented in Schedule 10. The company's beginning-of-year balance sheet, from which the budgeted balance sheet in Schedule 10 has been derived in part, is presented below:

MEREDITH COMPANY
Balance Sheet
December 31, 19x0

Assets

Current assets:		
Cash	$ 42,500	
Accounts receivable	90,000	
Raw materials inventory (7,000 pounds)	4,200	
Finished goods inventory (2,000 units)	26,000	
Total current assets		$162,700
Plant and equipment:		
Land	80,000	
Buildings and equipment	700,000	
Accumulated depreciation	(292,000)	
Plant and equipment, net		488,000
Total assets		$650,700

Liabilities and Stockholders' Equity

Current liabilities:		
Accounts payable (raw materials)		$ 25,800
Stockholders' equity:		
Common stock, no par	$175,000	
Retained earnings	449,900	
Total stockholders' equity		624,900
Total liabilities and stockholders' equity		$650,700

SCHEDULE 10

MEREDITH COMPANY
Budgeted Balance Sheet
December 31, 19x1

Assets

Current assets:		
Cash	$ 47,500 *(a)*	
Accounts receivable	120,000 *(b)*	
Raw materials inventory	4,500 *(c)*	
Finished goods inventory	39,000 *(d)*	
Total current assets		$211,000
Plant and equipment:		
Land	80,000 *(e)*	
Buildings and equipment	750,000 *(f)*	
Accumulated depreciation	(352,000) *(g)*	
Plant and equipment, net		478,000
Total assets		$689,000

Liabilities and Stockholders' Equity

Current liabilities:		
Accounts payable (raw materials)		$ 27,900 *(h)*
Stockholders' equity:		
Common stock, no par	$175,000 *(i)*	
Retained earnings	486,100 *(j)*	
Total stockholders' equity		661,100
Total liabilities and stockholders' equity		$689,000

Explanation of December 31, 19x1, balance sheet figures:

a. The ending cash balance, as projected by the cash budget in Schedule 8.
b. Thirty percent of fourth-quarter sales, from Schedule 1 ($400,000 × 30% = $120,000).
c. From Schedule 3, the ending raw materials inventory will be 7,500 pounds. This material costs $0.60 per pound. Therefore, the ending inventory in dollars will be 7,500 pounds × $0.60 = $4,500.
d. From Schedule 6.
e. From the December 31, 19x0, balance sheet (no change).
f. The December 31, 19x0, balance sheet indicated a balance of $700,000. During 19x1, $50,000 additional equipment will be purchased (see Schedule 8), bringing the December 31, 19x1, balance to $750,000.
g. The December 31, 19x0, balance sheet indicated a balance of $292,000. During 19x1, $60,000 of depreciation will be taken (see Schedule 5), bringing the December 31, 19x1, balance to $352,000.
h. One half of the fourth-quarter raw materials purchases, from Schedule 3.
i. From the December 31, 19x0, balance sheet (no change).
j.

December 31, 19x0, balance	$449,900
Add net income, from Schedule 9	76,200
	526,100
Deduct dividends paid, from Schedule 8	40,000
December 31, 19x1, balance	$486,100

Expanding the Budgeted Income Statement

The master budget income statement in Schedule 9 focuses on a single level of activity and has been prepared using absorption costing. Some managers prefer an alternate format that focuses on a *range* of activity and that is prepared using the contribution approach. A master budget income statement using this alternative format is presented in Exhibit 8–3.

EXHIBIT 8–3

EXAMPLE COMPANY
Master Budget Income Statement

	Budget Formula (per unit)	Sales in Units			
		800	1,400	2,000	2,800
Sales	$75.00	$ 60,000	$105,000	$150,000	$210,000
Less variable expenses:					
Direct materials	12.00	9,600	16,800	24,000	33,600
Direct labor	31.00	24,800	43,400	62,000	86,800
Variable overhead	7.50	6,000	10,500	15,000	21,000
Variable selling and other	4.00	3,200	5,600	8,000	11,200
Total variable expenses	54.50	43,600	76,300	109,000	152,600
Contribution margin	$20.50	16,400	28,700	41,000	57,400
Less fixed expenses:					
Manufacturing overhead		18,000	18,000	18,000	18,000
Selling and administrative		9,000	9,000	9,000	9,000
Total fixed expenses		27,000	27,000	27,000	27,000
Net income (loss)		$(10,600)	$ 1,700	$ 14,000	$ 30,400

A statement such as that in Exhibit 8–3 is *flexible* in its use since it is geared to more than one level of activity. If, for example, the company planned to sell 2,000 units during a period but actually sold only 1,400 units, then the budget figures at the 1,400-unit level would be used to compare against actual costs and revenues. Other columns could be added to the budget as needed by simply applying the budget formulas provided.

In short, a master budget income statement in this expanded format can be very useful to the manager in the planning and control of operations. The concepts underlying a flexible approach to budgeting are covered in the following two chapters.

JIT PURCHASING

It is important that we distinguish between JIT production and JIT purchasing. JIT *production* can only be used by manufacturing companies, since it focuses on the manufacture of goods. We have learned that it is based on a demand-pull concept, where inventories are largely (or entirely) eliminated and where all production activities respond to the "pull" exerted by the final assembly stage. JIT *purchasing,* on the other hand, can be used by *any* organization—retail, wholesale, distribution, or manufacturing. It focuses on the *acquisition* of goods. These goods might either be resold to customers (such as in a retail store) or be used as raw materials in the production process.

In Chapter 2, we stated that the central thrust of the JIT philosophy was toward simplification and elimination of waste. This philosophy is just as applicable to JIT purchasing as it is to JIT production. Below we outline the key features relating to JIT purchasing in an organization. (Some of these features were touched on briefly in Chapter 2.)

Under JIT purchasing:

1. *Goods are delivered immediately before demand or use.* Companies that have adopted JIT purchasing require an increase in the number of deliveries, accompanied by a decrease in the number of items per delivery. We have already stated that a manufacturing company might receive several deliveries of a particular raw material each day. This concept of daily (or at least frequent) delivery also has application at the retail level. For many years, retail food stores have received daily deliveries of milk and bread. Various other retail organizations are now moving toward this concept for their goods as well. Food outlets are guaranteeing that baked goods are no more than a few *hours* old, which means that output must be geared to anticipated demand at various times of the day. Even in those manufacturing or retailing situations where some inventories must be maintained, the level of these inventories under JIT purchasing can be reduced to only a fraction of previous amounts.

2. *The number of suppliers is greatly decreased.* All purchases are concentrated on a few, highly dependable suppliers who can meet stringent delivery requirements. IBM, for example, eliminated *95 percent* of the suppliers from one of its plants, reducing the number from 640 to only 32.[4] With this decrease in suppliers comes a corresponding decrease in the amount of resources needed for purchase negotiations and for processing of purchasing data.

3. *Long-term agreements are signed with suppliers; these agreements stipulate the delivery schedule, the quality of the goods, and the price to be paid.* Long-term agreements make it unnecessary to have separate negotiations for each purchase. Thus, minimal paperwork is involved with individual purchase transactions. Delivery schedules are set far in advance, and these schedules must be strictly adhered to by suppliers. Although adhering to a preset delivery schedule is important, the real key to the successful operation of JIT is *quality*. In the absence of an absolute standard for high quality, JIT would be impossible to use.

4. *Little or no inspection is made as to the quantity of goods received in a shipment, nor is the shipment inspected for defects.* Through the long-term agreements that have been signed, suppliers are fully aware of the importance of exact quantities and "zero defect" quality. This eliminates the need for inspection, which JIT views as being a non-value-added activity. Many companies require that suppliers deliver goods in "shop-ready" containers. A shop-ready container is one that contains exactly the number and type of items needed for a particular cell. Such containers eliminate the need for packing and unpacking of materials, which JIT views as being another non-value-added activity.

5. *Payments are not made for each individual shipment; rather, payments are "batched" for each supplier.* Since a supplier may be making several shipments each day to a manufacturer or several shipments each week to a

[4] George Foster and Charles T. Horngren, "JIT: Cost Accounting and Cost Management Issues," *Management Accounting* 68 (June 1987), p. 20.

retailer, it would be costly to make payments for these shipments individually. Typically, invoices are "batched" into a single monthly payment for each supplier. The computer is used to track the shipments, to match the ensuing invoices to the goods received, and to determine the amount due.

Companies that have adopted JIT purchasing have realized substantial savings in the cost of placing purchase orders and administering the purchasing function. Note particularly that the adoption of purchasing practices such as those outlined above does not require that a company eliminate *all* inventories. Indeed, retail organizations must maintain *some* inventories or they couldn't operate. But the amount of time a good spends on the shelf or in the warehouse can be greatly reduced even in a retail organization through the JIT approach.

ZERO-BASE BUDGETING

Zero-base budgeting has received considerable attention recently as a new approach to preparing budget data, particularly for use in not-for-profit, governmental, and service-type organizations. The type of budget prepared under this approach—called a **zero-base budget**—is so named because managers are required to start at zero budget levels every year and justify all costs as if the programs involved were being initiated for the first time. By "justify," we mean that no costs are viewed as being ongoing in nature; the manager must start at the ground level each year and present justification for all costs in the proposed budget, regardless of the type of cost involved. This is done in a series of "decision packages" in which the manager ranks all of the activities in the department according to relative importance, going from those that he or she considers essential to those that he or she considers of least importance. Presumably, this allows top management to evaluate each decision package independently and to pare back in those areas that appear less critical or that do not appear to be justified in terms of the cost involved.

This process differs from traditional budgeting, in which budgets are generally initiated on an incremental basis; that is, the manager starts with last year's budget and simply adds to it (or subtracts from it) according to anticipated needs. The manager doesn't have to start at the ground each year and justify ongoing costs (such as salaries) for existing programs.

In a broader sense, zero-base budgeting isn't really a new concept at all. Managers have always advocated in-depth reviews of departmental costs. The only difference is the frequency with which this review is carried out. Zero-base budgeting says that it should be done annually; critics of the zero-base idea say that this is too often and that such reviews should be made only every five years or so. These critics say that annual in-depth reviews are too time-consuming and too costly to be really feasible, and that in the long run such reviews probably cannot be justified in terms of the cost savings involved. In addition, it is argued that annual reviews soon become mechanical and that the whole purpose of the zero-base idea is then lost.

The question of frequency of zero-base reviews must be left to the judgment of the individual manager. In some situations, annual zero-base reviews may be justified; in other situations, they may not because of the time and cost involved. Whatever the time period chosen, however, most managers would agree that zero-base reviews can be helpful and should be an integral part of the overall budgeting process.

THE NEED FOR FURTHER BUDGETING MATERIAL

The material covered in this chapter represents no more than an introduction into the vast area of budgeting and profit planning. Our purpose has been to present an overview of the budgeting process and to show how the various operating budgets build on each other in guiding a firm toward its profit objectives. However, the matter of budgeting and profit planning is so critical to the intelligent management of a firm in today's business environment that we can't stop with simply an overview of the budgeting process. We need to look more closely at budgeting to see how it helps managers in the day-to-day conduct of business affairs. We will do this by studying standard costs and flexible budgets in the following two chapters and by introducing the concept of performance reporting. In Chapter 11, we will expand on these ideas by looking at budgeting and profit planning as tools for control of decentralized operations and as facilitating factors in judging managerial performance.

In sum, the materials in the following two chapters build on the budgeting and profit planning foundation that has been laid in this chapter by expanding on certain concepts that have been introduced and by refining others. The essential thing to keep in mind at this point is that the material covered in this chapter does not conclude our study of budgeting and profit planning, but rather just introduces the ideas.

KEY TERMS FOR REVIEW

Budget A detailed plan outlining the acquisition and use of financial and other resources over some given time period. (p. 305)

Budget committee A group of key management persons who are responsible for overall policy matters relating to the budget program and for coordinating the preparation of the budget itself. (p. 311)

Capital budget A budget covering the acquisition of land, buildings, and items of equipment; such a budget may have a time horizon extending 30 years or more into the future. (p. 308)

Cash budget A detailed plan showing how cash resources will be acquired and used over some specific time period. (p. 311)

Continuous or perpetual budget A budget that covers a 12-month period but is constantly adding a new month on the end as the current month is completed. (p. 308)

Control Those steps taken by management to ensure that the objectives set down at the planning stage are attained and to ensure that all parts of the organization function in a manner consistent with organizational policies. (p. 306)

Direct labor budget A detailed plan showing labor requirements over some specific time period. (p. 317)

Direct materials budget A detailed plan showing the amount of raw materials that must be purchased during a period to meet both production and inventory needs. (p. 315)

Ending finished goods inventory budget A budget showing the dollar amount of cost expected to appear on the balance sheet for unsold units at the end of a period. (p. 318)

Manufacturing overhead budget A detailed plan showing the production costs, other than direct materials and direct labor, that will be incurred in attaining the output budgeted for a period. (p. 317)

Master budget A summary of all phases of a company's plans and goals for the future in which specific targets are set for sales, production, and financing activities and that generally culminates in a projected statement of net income and a projected statement of cash position. (p. 305)

Material requirements planning (MRP) An operations research tool that employs the computer to assist the manager in overall materials and inventory planning. (p. 316)

Merchandise purchases budget A budget used by a merchandising company that shows the amount of goods that must be purchased from suppliers during the period. (p. 315)

Participative budget See *Self-imposed budget*. (p. 308)

Planning The development of objectives in an organization and the preparation of various budgets to achieve these objectives. (p. 306)

Production budget A detailed plan showing the number of units that must be produced during a period in order to meet both sales and inventory needs. (p. 314)

Responsibility accounting A system of accounting in which costs are assigned to various managerial levels according to where control of the costs is deemed to rest, with the managers then held responsible for differences between budgeted and actual results. (p. 307)

Sales budget A detailed schedule showing the expected sales for coming periods; these sales are typically expressed in both dollars and units. (p. 311)

Sales forecast A schedule of expected sales for an entire industry. (p. 312)

Self-imposed budget A method of budget preparation in which managers with responsibility over cost control prepare their own budget figures; these budget figures are reviewed by the managers' supervisors, and any questions are then resolved in face-to-face meetings. (p. 308)

Selling and administrative expense budget A detailed schedule of planned expenses that will be incurred in areas other than manufacturing during a budget period. (p. 318)

Zero-base budget A method of budgeting in which managers are required to start at zero budget levels every year and to justify all costs as if the programs involved were being initiated for the first time. (p. 326)

APPENDIX: ECONOMIC ORDER QUANTITY AND THE REORDER POINT

As stated in the main body of the chapter, inventory planning and control are an essential part of a budgeting system. We have seen that inventory levels are not left to chance but rather are carefully planned for, in terms of both opening and closing balances. Major questions that we have left unanswered are, "How does the manager know what inventory level is 'right' for the firm?'' and ''Won't the level that is 'right' vary from organization to organization?'' The purpose of this section is to examine the inventory control methods available to the manager for answering these questions.

Costs Associated with Inventory

Three groups of costs are associated with inventory. The first group, known as **inventory ordering costs,** consists of costs associated with the acquisition of inventory. Examples include:

1. Clerical costs.
2. Transportation costs.

The second group, known as **inventory carrying costs,** consists of costs that arise from having inventory in stock. Examples include:

1. Storage space costs.
2. Handling costs.
3. Property taxes.
4. Insurance.
5. Obsolescence losses.
6. Interest on capital invested in inventory.

The third group, known as **costs of not carrying sufficient inventory,** consists of costs that result from not having enough inventory in stock to meet customers' needs. Costs in this group are more difficult to identify than costs in the other two groups, but nevertheless they can include items that are very significant to a firm. Examples of costs in this group are:

1. Customer ill will.
2. Quantity discounts foregone.
3. Erratic production (expediting of goods, extra setup, etc.).
4. Inefficiency of production runs.
5. Added transportation charges.
6. Lost sales.

In a broad conceptual sense, the ''right'' level of inventory to carry is the level that will minimize the total of these three groups of costs. Such a minimization is difficult to achieve, however, since certain of the costs involved are in direct conflict with one another. Notice, for example, that as inventory levels increase, the costs of carrying inventory will also increase, but the costs of not carrying sufficient inventory will decrease. In working toward total cost minimization, therefore, the manager must balance off the three groups of costs against one another. The problem really has two dimensions—how much to order (or how much to produce in a production run) and how often to do it.

Computing the Economic Order Quantity (EOQ)

The ''how much to order'' is commonly referred to as the **economic order quantity (EOQ).** It is the order size that will result in a minimization of the first two groups of costs above. We will consider two approaches to computing the EOQ—the tabular approach and the formula approach.

EXHIBIT 8A–1

Tabulation of Costs Associated with Various Order Sizes

		Order Size in Units								
Symbol*		**25**	**50**	**100**	**200**	**250**	**300**	**400**	**1,000**	**3,000**
$O/2$	Average inventory in units	12.5	25	50	100	125	150	200	500	1,500
Q/O	Number of purchase orders	120	60	30	15	12	10	7.5	3	1
$C(O/2)$	Annual carrying cost at $0.80 per unit	$ 10	$ 20	$ 40	$ 80	$100	$120	$160	$400	$1,200
$P(Q/O)$	Annual purchase order cost at $10 per order	1,200	600	300	150	120	100	75	30	10
T	Total annual cost.	$1,210	$620	$340	$230	$220	$220	$235	$430	$1,210

* Symbols:

O = Order size in units (see headings above).

Q = Annual quantity used in units (3,000 in this example).

C = Annual cost of carrying one unit in stock.

P = Cost of placing one order.

T = Total annual cost.

The Tabular Approach Given a certain annual consumption of an item, a firm might place a few orders each year of a large quantity each, or it might place many orders of a small quantity each. Placing only a few orders would result in low inventory ordering costs but in high inventory carrying costs, since the average inventory level would be very large. On the other hand, placing many orders would result in high inventory ordering costs but in low inventory carrying costs, since in this case the average inventory level would be quite small. As stated above, the EOQ seeks the order size that will balance off these two groups of costs. To show how it is computed, assume that a manufacturer uses 3,000 subassemblies in the manufacturing process each year. The subassemblies are purchased from a supplier at a cost of $20 each. Other cost data are given below:

Inventory carrying costs, per unit, per year . . .	$ 0.80
Cost of placing a purchase order	10.00

Exhibit 8A–1 contains a tabulation of the total costs associated with various order sizes for the subassemblies. Notice that total annual cost is lowest (and is equal) at the 250- and 300-unit order sizes. The EOQ will lie somewhere between these two points. We could locate it precisely by adding more columns to the tabulation, and we would in time zero in on 274 units as being the exact EOQ.

The cost relationships from this tabulation are shown graphically in Exhibit 8A–2. Notice from the graph that total annual cost is minimized at that point where annual carrying costs and annual purchase order costs are equal. The same point identifies the EOQ, since the purpose of the computation is to find the point of exact trade-off between these two classes of costs.

Observe from the graph that total cost shows a tendency to flatten out between 200 and 400 units. Most firms look for this minimum cost range and choose an order size that falls within it, rather than choosing the exact EOQ. The primary reason is that suppliers will often ship goods only in round-lot sizes.

EXHIBIT 8A–2
Graphic Solution to Economic Order Quantity

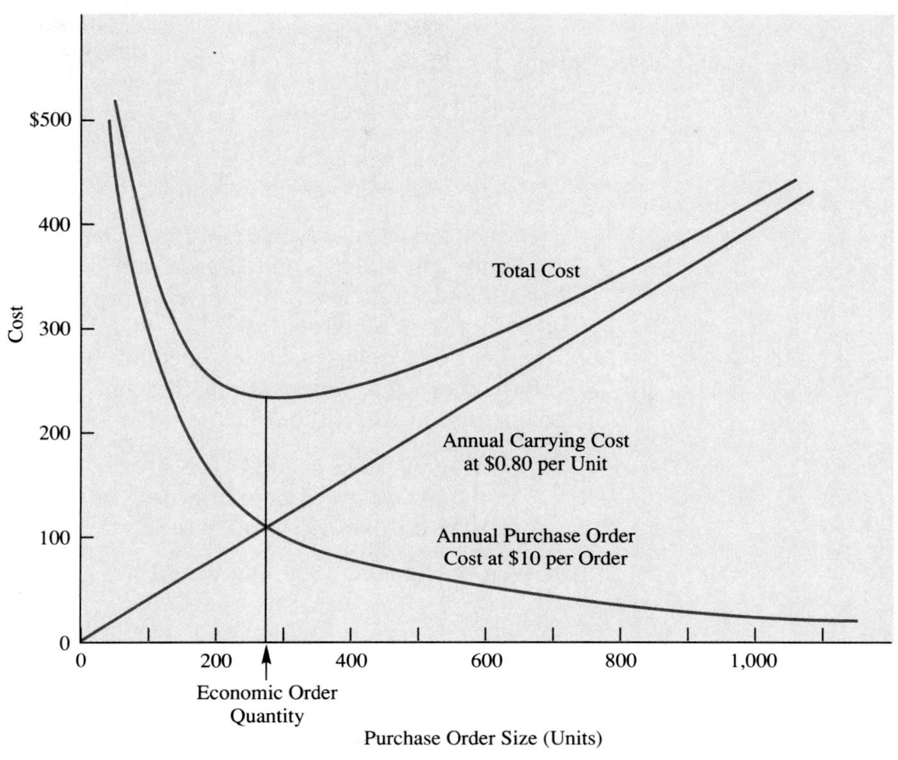

The Formula Approach The EOQ can also be found by means of a formula. The formula is (derived by calculus):

$$E = \sqrt{\frac{2\ QP}{C}}$$

where:

E = economic order quantity (EOQ)
Q = annual quantity used in units
P = cost of placing one order
C = annual cost of carrying one unit in stock

Substituting with the data used in our preceding example, we have:

Q = 3,000 subassemblies used per year
P = \$10 cost to place one order
C = \$0.80 cost to carry one subassembly in stock for one year

$$E = \sqrt{\frac{2\ QP}{C}} = \sqrt{\frac{2(3{,}000)(\$10)}{\$0.80}} = \sqrt{\frac{\$60{,}000}{\$0.80}} = \sqrt{75{,}000}$$

E = 274 (the EOQ)

Although data can be obtained very quickly using the formula approach, it has the drawback of not providing as great a range of information as the methods discussed above.

JIT and the Economic Order Quantity

The EOQ will decrease if:

1. The cost of placing an order decreases, or
2. The cost of carrying inventory in stock increases.

Managers who advocate JIT purchasing argue that the cost of carrying inventory in stock is much greater than generally realized because of the waste and inefficiency that inventories create. These managers argue that this fact, combined with the fact that JIT purchasing dramatically reduces the cost of placing an order, is solid evidence that companies should purchase more frequently in smaller amounts. Assume, for example, that a company has used the following data to compute its EOQ:

Q = 1,000 units needed each year
P = $60 cost to place one order
C = $3 cost to carry one unit in stock for one year

Given these data, the EOQ would be:

$$E = \sqrt{\frac{2\,QP}{C}} = \sqrt{\frac{2(1{,}000)(\$60)}{\$3}} = \sqrt{40{,}000}$$

$$E = 200 \text{ units}$$

Now assume that as a result of JIT purchasing the company is able to decrease the cost of placing an order to only $10. Also assume that due to the waste and inefficiency caused by inventories, the true cost of carrying a unit in stock is $8 per year. The revised EOQ would be:

$$E = \sqrt{\frac{2\,QP}{C}} = \sqrt{\frac{2(1{,}000)(\$10)}{\$8}} = \sqrt{2{,}500}$$

$$E = 50 \text{ units}$$

Under JIT purchasing, the company would *not* necessarily order in 50-unit lots since purchases would be geared to current demand. This example shows quite dramatically, however, the economics behind the JIT concept so far as the purchasing of goods is concerned.

Production Runs

The EOQ concept can also be applied to the problem of determining the **economic production-run size.** Deciding when to start and when to stop production runs is a problem that has plagued manufacturers for years. The problem can be solved quite easily by inserting the **setup cost** for a new production run into the EOQ formula in place of the purchase order cost. The setup cost includes the labor and other costs involved in getting facilities ready for a run of a different production item.

To illustrate, assume that Chittenden Company has determined that the following costs are associated with one of its product lines:

Q = 15,000 units produced each year
P = \$150 setup costs to change a production run
C = \$2 to carry one unit in stock for one year

What is the optimal production-run size for this product line? It can be determined by using the same formula as is used to compute the EOQ:

$$E = \sqrt{\frac{2\,QP}{C}} = \sqrt{\frac{2(15{,}000)(\$150)}{\$2}} = \sqrt{\frac{\$4{,}500{,}000}{\$2}} = \sqrt{2{,}250{,}000}$$

E = 1,500 (economic production-run size in units)

Chittenden Company will minimize its overall costs by producing in runs of 1,500 units each.

Reorder Point and Safety Stock

We stated earlier that the inventory problem has two dimensions—how much to order and how often to do it. The "how often to do it" involves what are commonly termed the *reorder point* and the *safety stock,* and seeks to find the optimal trade-off between the second two groups of inventory costs outlined earlier (the costs of carrying inventory and the costs of not carrying sufficient inventory). First, we will discuss the reorder point and the factors involved in its computation. Then, we will discuss the circumstances under which a safety stock must be maintained.

The **reorder point** tells the manager when to place an order or when to initiate production to replenish depleted stocks. It is dependent on three factors—the EOQ (or economic production-run size), the *lead time,* and the rate of usage during the lead time. The **lead time** can be defined as the interval between the time that an order is placed and the time that the order is finally received from the supplier or from the production line.

Constant Usage during the Lead Time If the rate of usage during the lead time is known with certainty, the reorder point can be determined by the following formula:

$$\text{Reorder point} = \text{Lead time} \times \text{Average daily or weekly usage}$$

To illustrate the formula's use, assume that a company's EOQ is 500 units, that the lead time is 3 weeks, and that the average weekly usage is 50 units.

$$\text{Reorder point} = 3\text{ weeks} \times 50\text{ units per week} = 150\text{ units}$$

The reorder point would be 150 units. That is, the company will automatically place a new order for 500 units when inventory stocks drop to a level of 150 units, or three weeks' supply, left on hand.

Variable Usage during the Lead Time The previous example assumed that the 50 units per week usage rate was constant and was known with certainty. Although some firms enjoy the luxury of certainty, the more common situation is to find considerable variation in the rate of usage of inventory items from period to period. If usage varies from period to period, the firm that reorders in the way computed above may soon find itself out of stock. A sudden spurt in demand, a delay in delivery, or a snag in processing an order may cause inventory levels to be depleted before a new shipment arrives.

Companies that experience problems in demand, delivery, or processing of orders have found that they need some type of buffer to guard against stockouts. Such a buffer is usually called a **safety stock**. A safety stock serves as a kind of insurance against greater than usual demand and against problems in the ordering and delivery of goods. Its size is determined by deducting *average usage* from the *maximum usage* that can reasonably be expected during a period. For example, if the firm in the preceding example was faced with a situation of variable demand for its product, it would compute a safety stock as follows:

Maximum expected usage per week . . .	65 units
Average usage per week	50 units
Excess	15 units
Lead time	× 3 weeks
Safety stock	45 units

The reorder point is then determined by *adding the safety stock to the average usage during the lead time*. In formula form, the reorder point would be:

Reorder point
= (Lead time × Average daily or weekly usage) + Safety stock

Computation of the reorder point by this approach is shown both numerically and graphically in Exhibit 8A–3. As shown in the exhibit, the company will place a new order for 500 units when inventory stocks drop to a level of 195 units left on hand.

EXHIBIT 8A–3
Determining the Reorder point—Variable Usage

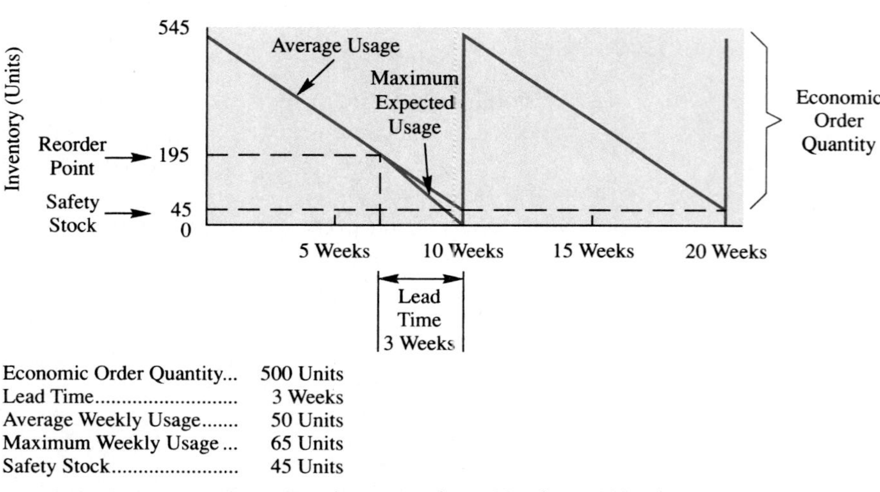

Economic Order Quantity...	500 Units
Lead Time..........................	3 Weeks
Average Weekly Usage.......	50 Units
Maximum Weekly Usage ...	65 Units
Safety Stock........................	45 Units

Reorder point = (3 weeks × 50 units per week) + 45 units = 195 units

KEY TERMS FOR REVIEW (APPENDIX)

Costs of not carrying sufficient inventory Those costs that result from not having enough inventory in stock to meet customers' needs; such costs would include customer ill will, quantity discounts forgone, erratic production, added transportation charges, and lost sales. (p. 329)

Economic order quantity (EOQ) The order size for materials that will result in a minimization of the costs of ordering inventory and carrying inventory. (p. 329)

Economic production-run size The number of units produced in a production run that will result in a minimization of setup costs and the costs of carrying inventory. (p. 332)

Inventory carrying costs Those costs that result from having inventory in stock, such as rental of storage space, handling costs, property taxes, insurance, and interest on funds. (p. 329)

Inventory ordering costs Those costs associated with the acquisition of inventory, such as clerical costs and transportation costs. (p. 329)

Lead time The interval between the time that an order is placed and the time that the order is finally received from the supplier. (p. 333)

Reorder point The point in time when an order must be placed to replenish depleted stocks; it is determined by multiplying the lead time by the average daily or weekly usage. (p. 333)

Safety stock The difference between average usage of materials and maximum usage of materials that can reasonably be expected during the lead time. (p. 334)

Setup costs Labor and other costs involved in getting facilities ready for a run of a different production item. (p. 332)

QUESTIONS

8–1 What is a budget? What is budgetary control?

8–2 Discuss some of the major benefits to be gained from budgeting.

8–3 What is meant by the term *responsibility accounting?*

8–4 "Budgeting is designed primarily for organizations that have few complexities and uncertainties in their day-to-day operations." Do you agree? Why or why not?

8–5 What is a master budget? Briefly describe its contents.

8–6 Which is a better basis for judging actual results, budgeted performance or past performance? Why?

8–7 Why is the sales forecast always the starting point in budgeting?

8–8 Is there any difference between a sales forecast and a sales budget? Explain.

8–9 "As a practical matter, planning and control mean exactly the same thing." Do you agree? Explain.

8–10 Describe the flow of budget data in an organization. Who are the participants in the budgeting process, and how do they participate?

8–11 "To a large extent, the success of a budget program hinges on education and good salesmanship." Do you agree? Explain.

8–12 What is a self-imposed budget? What are the major advantages of self-imposed budgets? What caution must be exercised in their use?

8–13 How can budgeting assist a firm in its employment policies?

8–14 "The principal purpose of the cash budget is to see how much cash the company will have in the bank at the end of the year." Do you agree? Explain.

8–15 How does JIT purchasing differ from JIT production?

8–16 What are the five key ideas associated with JIT purchasing?

8–17 Does a company have to eliminate all inventories in order to adopt JIT purchasing?

8–18 How does zero-base budgeting differ from traditional budgeting?

8–19 (Appendix) What three classes of costs are associated with a company's inventory policy? Which of these classes of costs is the most difficult to quantify?

8–20 (Appendix) List at least three costs associated with a company's inventory policy that do not appear as an expense on the income statement.

8–21 (Appendix) What trade-offs in costs are involved in computing the economic order quantity (EOQ)?

8–22 (Appendix) "Managers are more interested in a minimum cost *range* than they are in a minimum cost point." Explain.

8–23 (Appendix) Define *lead time* and *safety stock.*

EXERCISES

E8–1 Peak sales for Midwest Products, Inc., occur in August. The company's sales budget for the third quarter of 19x8, showing these peak sales, is given below:

	July	August	September	Total
Budgeted sales	$600,000	$900,000	$500,000	$2,000,000

From past experience, the company has learned that 20 percent of a month's sales are collected in the month of sale, that another 70 percent is collected in the month following sale, and that the remaining 10 percent is collected in the second month following sale. Bad debts are negligible and can be ignored. May sales totaled $430,000, and June sales totaled $540,000.

Required
1. Prepare a schedule of budgeted cash collections from sales, by month and in total, for the third quarter.
2. Assume that the company will prepare a budgeted balance sheet as of September 30. Compute the accounts receivable as of that date.

E8–2 Warner Company has budgeted the sales of its product over the next four months as follows:

	Sales in Units
July	30,000
August	45,000
September	60,000
October	50,000

The company is now in the process of preparing a production budget for the third quarter. Past experience has shown that end-of-month inventories of finished goods must equal 10 percent of the next month's sales. The inventory at the end of June was 3,000 units.

Required Prepare a production budget for the third quarter showing the number of units to be produced each month and for the quarter in total.

E8–3 Micro Products, Inc., has developed a very powerful electronic calculator. Each calculator requires three small "chips" in its manufacture. The chips cost $2 each and are purchased from an overseas supplier. Micro Products has prepared a production budget for the calculator by quarters for 19x5 and for the first quarter of 19x6, as shown below:

	19x5				19x6
	First	Second	Third	Fourth	First
Budgeted production, in calculators	60,000	90,000	150,000	100,000	70,000

The chip used in production of the calculator is sometimes hard to get, so it is necessary to carry large inventories as a precaution against stockouts. For this reason, the inventory of chips at the end of a quarter must be equal to 20 percent of the following quarter's production needs. Some 36,000 chips will be on hand to start the first quarter of 19x5.

Required Prepare a materials purchases budget for chips, by quarter and in total, for 19x5. At the bottom of your budget, show the dollar amount of purchases for each quarter and for the year in total.

E8–4 A cash budget, by quarters, is given below (000 omitted). The company requires a minimum cash balance of $5,000 to start each quarter.

	Quarter				
	1	2	3	4	Year
Cash balance, beginning	$ 9	$?	$?	$?	$?
Add collections from customers.	?	?	125	?	391
Total cash available	85	?	?	?	?
Less disbursements:					
Purchase of inventory	40	58	?	32	?
Operating expenses	?	42	54	?	180
Equipment purchases	10	8	8	?	36
Dividends	2	2	2	2	?
Total disbursements	?	110	?	?	?
Excess (deficiency) of cash available over disbursements	(3)	?	30	?	?
Financing:					
Borrowings	?	20	—	—	?
Repayments (including interest)* . . .	—	—	(?)	(7)	(?)
Total financing	?	?	?	?	?
Cash balance, ending	$?	$?	$?	$?	$?

* Interest will total $4,000 for the year.

Required Fill in the missing amounts in the table above.

E8–5 Calgon Products needs a cash budget for the month of September 19x4. The following information is available:

a. The cash balance at the beginning of September is $9,000.
b. Actual sales for July and August and expected sales for September are:

	July	August	September
Cash sales	$ 6,500	$ 5,250	$ 7,400
Sales on account . . .	20,000	30,000	40,000
Total sales	$26,500	$35,250	$47,400

Sales on account are collected over a three-month period in the following ratio: 10 percent collected in the month of sale, 70 percent collected in the month following sale, and 18 percent collected in the second month following sale. The remaining 2 percent is uncollectible.

c. Purchases of inventory will total $25,000 for September. Twenty percent of a month's inventory purchases are paid for during the month of purchase. The accounts payable remaining from August's inventory purchases total $16,000, all of which will be paid in September.

d. Selling and administrative expenses are budgeted at $13,000 for September. Of this amount, $4,000 is for depreciation.

e. Equipment costing $18,000 will be purchased for cash during September, and dividends totaling $3,000 will be paid during the month.

f. The company must maintain a minimum cash balance of $5,000. An open line of credit is available from the company's bank to bolster the cash position as needed.

Required

1. Prepare a schedule of expected cash collections for the month of September.
2. Prepare a schedule of expected cash payments to suppliers during September for inventory purchases.
3. Prepare a cash budget for the month of September. Indicate in the financing section any borrowing that will be needed during the month.

E8–6 Greenup, Inc., manufactures a product that has peak sales in March of each year. The company's budgeted sales for the first quarter of 19x6 are given below:

	January	February	March	Total
Budgeted sales . . .	$500,000	$700,000	$1,800,000	$3,000,000

The company is in the process of preparing a cash budget for the first quarter and must determine the expected cash collections by month. To this end, the following information has been assembled:

Collections on sales:
60% in month of sale
30% in month following sale
8% in second month following sale
2% uncollectible

The company gives a 2 percent cash discount for payments made by customers during the month of sale. The accounts receivable balance to start the year is $220,000, of which $40,000 represents uncollected November 19x5 sales and $180,000 represents uncollected December 19x5 sales.

Required

1. What were the total sales for November 19x5? For December 19x5?
2. Prepare a schedule showing the budgeted cash collections from sales, by month and in total, for the first quarter of 19x6.

E8–7 (Appendix) Classify the following as either *(a)* costs of carrying inventory or *(b)* costs of not carrying sufficient inventory:

1. Airfreight on a rush order of a critical part needed in production.
2. Interest paid on investment funds.
3. State and local taxes on personal property.
4. Spoilage of perishable goods.
5. Excessive setup costs.
6. Customers lost through inability of the company to make prompt delivery.
7. Quantity discounts lost as a result of purchasing in small lots.
8. Fire insurance on inventory.

9. Loss sustained when a competitor comes out with a less expensive, more efficient product.
10. A general feeling of ill will among customers, due to broken delivery promises.

E8–8 (Appendix) Castleberry Manufacturing Company uses 5,400 units of part MV–4 each year. The cost of placing one order for part MV–4 is $10. Other costs associated with part MV–4 are:

	Annual Cost per Part
Insurance	$0.12
Property taxes	0.05
Interest on funds invested	0.10
Other	0.03
Total cost	$0.30

Required

1. Compute the EOQ for part MV–4.
2. Assume that the company has adopted JIT purchasing policies and has been able to reduce the cost of placing an order to only $1. Also assume that when the waste and inefficiency caused by inventories is considered, the cost to carry a part in inventory jumps to $1.20 per unit. Under these conditions, what would be the EOQ?

E8–9 (Appendix) Selected information relating to an inventory item carried by the Santos Company is given below:

Economic order quantity	700 units
Maximum weekly usage	60 units
Lead time	4 weeks
Average weekly usage	50 units

Santos Company is trying to determine the proper safety stock to carry on this inventory item, and to determine the proper reorder point.

Required

1. Assume that no safety stock is to be carried. What is the reorder point?
2. Assume that a full safety stock is to be carried.
   a. What would be the size of the safety stock in units?
   b. What would be the reorder point?

E8–10 (Appendix) Baldwin Company uses 8,000 units of a certain part each year.

Required

1. The company has determined that it costs $40 to place an order for the part from the supplier and $4 to carry one part in inventory each year. Compute the EOQ for the part.
2. Assume that Baldwin Company's ordering costs increase to $50 per order. What will be the effect on the EOQ? Show computations.
3. Assume that Baldwin Company's carrying costs increase to $5 per part. (Ordering costs remain unchanged at $40.) What will be the effect on the EOQ? Show computations.
4. In (2) and (3) above, why does an increase in cost cause the EOQ to go up in one case and to go down in the other?

PROBLEMS

P8–11 **Production and Purchases Budgets** Tonga Toys manufactures and distributes a number of products to retailers. One of these products, Playclay, requires three pounds of material A in the manufacture of each unit. The company is now planning raw materials needs for the third quarter of 19x7. Peak sales of Playclay occur in the third quarter of each year. In order to keep production and shipments moving smoothly, the company has the following inventory requirements:

a. The finished goods inventory on hand at the end of each month must be equal to 5,000 units plus 30 percent of the next month's sales. The finished goods inventory on June 30 is budgeted to be 17,000 units.

b. The raw materials inventory on hand at the end of each month must be equal to one half of the following month's production needs for raw materials. The raw materials inventory on June 30 for material A is budgeted to be 64,500 pounds.

c. The company maintains no work in process inventories.

A sales budget for Playclay for the last six months of 19x7 is given below:

	Budgeted Sales in Units
July	40,000
August	50,000
September	70,000
October	35,000
November	20,000
December.	10,000

Required

1. Prepare a production budget for Playclay for the months July–October.
2. Examine the production budget that you have prepared. Why will the company produce more units than it sells in July and August and less units than it sells in September and October?
3. Prepare a budget showing the quantity of material A to be purchased for July, August, and September 19x7 and for the quarter in total.

P8–12 **Cash Budget** Jodi Horton, president of Crestline Products, has just approached the company's bank with a request for a $30,000, 90-day loan. The purpose of the loan is to assist the company in building inventories in support of peak April sales. Since the company has had some difficulty in paying off its loans in the past, the loan officer has asked for a cash budget to help determine whether the loan should be made. The following data are available for the months April–June, during which the loan will be used:

a. On April 1, the start of the loan period, the cash balance will be $26,000. Accounts receivable on April 1 will total $151,500, of which $141,000 will be collected during April and $7,200 will be collected during May. The remainder will be uncollectible.

b. Past experience shows that 20 percent of a month's sales are collected in the month of sale, 75 percent in the month following sale, and 4 percent in the second month following sale. Budgeted sales and expenses for the period follow:

	April	May	June
Sales	$200,000	$300,000	$250,000
Merchandise purchases . . .	120,000	180,000	150,000
Payroll.	9,000	9,000	8,000
Lease payments	15,000	15,000	15,000
Advertising.	70,000	80,000	60,000
Equipment purchases	8,000	—	—
Depreciation	10,000	10,000	10,000

c. Merchandise purchases are paid in full during the month following purchase. Accounts payable for merchandise purchases on March 31, which will be paid during April, total $108,000.

d. In preparing the cash budget, assume that the $30,000 loan will be made in April and repaid in June. Interest on the loan will total $1,200.

Required
1. Prepare a schedule of budgeted cash collections for April, May, and June and for the three months in total.
2. Prepare a cash budget, by month and in total, for the three-month period.
3. If the company needs a minimum cash balance of $20,000 to start each month, can the loan be repaid as planned? Explain.

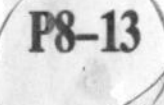

P8–13 Production and Direct Materials Budgets A sales budget is given below for one of the products manufactured by Vincent, Ltd.:

Month	Sales Budget in Units
July	20,000
August	35,000
September	60,000
October	40,000
November	30,000
December.	25,000

The inventory of finished goods at the end of each month must equal 20 percent of the next month's sales. On June 30, the finished goods inventory totaled 4,000 units.

Each unit of product requires three ounces of a special liquid extract known as SV-6. Sometimes this extract is in short supply; for this reason, the company has a policy of maintaining an inventory at the end of each month equal to 30 percent of the next month's production needs. This requirement was met on July 1 of the current year.

Required Prepare a budget showing the quantity of SV-6 to be purchased each month for July, August, and September and in total for the three-month period. (Hint: Remember that a production budget must be prepared before a materials purchases budget can be prepared.)

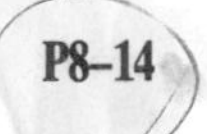

P8–14 Master Budget Preparation The balance sheet of Phototec, Inc., as of May 31, 19x4, is given below:

PHOTOTEC, INC.
Balance Sheet
May 31, 19x4

Assets	
Cash	$ 8,000
Accounts receivable	72,000
Inventory	30,000
Plant and equipment, net of depreciation . . .	500,000
Total assets	$610,000
Liabilities and Stockholders' Equity	
Accounts payable, suppliers	$ 90,000
Note payable.	15,000
Capital stock, no par	420,000
Retained earnings.	85,000
Total liabilities and stockholders' equity . . .	$610,000

Phototec, Inc., has not budgeted previously, and for this reason it is limiting its master budget planning horizon to just one month—June 19x4. The company has assembled the following budgeted data relating to the month of June:

a. Sales are budgeted at $250,000. Of these sales, $60,000 will be for cash; the remainder will be credit sales. One half of a month's credit sales are collected in the month the sales are made, and the remainder is collected in the month following. All of the May 31 accounts receivable will be collected in June.
b. Purchases of inventory are expected to total $200,000 during June. These purchases will all be on account. Forty percent of all inventory purchases are paid for in the month of purchase; the remainder is paid in the following month. All of the May 31 accounts payable to suppliers will be paid during June.
c. The June 30 inventory balance is budgeted at $40,000.
d. Operating expenses for June are budgeted at $51,000, exclusive of depreciation. These expenses will all be paid in cash. Depreciation is budgeted at $2,000 for the month.
e. The note payable on the May 31 balance sheet will be paid during June. The company's interest expense for June (on all borrowing) will be $500, which will be paid in cash.
f. New equipment costing $9,000 will be purchased for cash during June.
g. During June, the company will borrow $18,000 from its bank by giving a new note payable to the bank for that amount. The new note will be due in one year.

Required

1. Prepare a cash budget for June 19x4. Support your budget with schedules showing budgeted cash receipts from sales and budgeted cash payments for inventory purchases.
2. Prepare a budgeted income statement for June 19x4. Use the traditional income statement format, as shown in Schedule 9. Ignore income taxes.
3. Prepare a budgeted balance sheet as of June 30, 19x4.

P8–15 Behavioral Impact of Budgeting Methods An effective budget converts the objectives and goals of management into data. Once completed, the budget serves as a blueprint that represents management's plan for operating the organization. Moreover, the budget frequently is a basis for control in that management performance can be evaluated by comparing actual results with the budget.

Given the importance of budgeting, the creation of an effective budget is essential for the successful operation of an organization. There are several ways in which budget data can be generated, and all of these ways involve extensive contacts with people at various operating levels. The manner in which the people involved perceive their roles in the budget process is important to the successful use of the budget as a management tool.

Required

1. Discuss the behavioral implications associated with preparing the budget and with using the budget as a method to control activities when a company employs:
   a. A budgetary approach in which budget data are imposed from above.
   b. A budgetary approach in which budget data are prepared at various levels in a self-imposed (participative) manner.
2. Communication plays an important part in the budget process regardless of whether the budget is imposed from above or a participative budget approach is used. Describe the differences in communication flows between these two approaches to budget preparation.

(CMA, Heavily Adapted)

P8–16 Integration of the Sales, Production, and Purchases Budgets Milo Company manufactures a single product for which peak sales occur in August of each year. The company is now preparing detailed budgets for the third quarter and has assembled the following information to assist in the budget preparation:

a. The marketing department has estimated sales as follows for the remainder of the year (in units):

July	30,000	October	20,000
August.	70,000	November	10,000
September	50,000	December	10,000

The selling price of the company's product is $12 per unit.

b. All sales are on account. Based on past experience, sales are collected in the following pattern:

30 percent in the month of sale
65 percent in the month following sale
5 percent uncollectible

Sales for June 19x6 totaled $300,000.

c. The company maintains finished goods inventories equal to 15 percent of the following month's sales. This requirement will be met at the end of June.

d. Each finished unit of product requires 4 feet of Gilden, a material that is sometimes hard to get. Therefore, the company requires that the inventory of Gilden on hand at the end of each month be equal to 50 percent of the following month's production needs. The inventory of Gilden on hand at the beginning and end of the quarter will be:

June 30	72,000 feet
September 30 . . .	? feet

e. The Gilden costs $0.80 per foot. One half of a month's purchases of Gilden is paid for in the month of purchase; the remainder is paid for in the following month. The accounts payable on July 1 for purchases of Gilden during June will be $76,000.

Required

1. Prepare a sales budget, by month and in total, for the third quarter. (Show your budget in both units and dollars.) Also prepare a schedule of expected cash collections, by month and in total, for the third quarter.
2. Prepare a production budget for each of the months July–October.
3. Prepare a materials purchases budget for Gilden, by month and in total, for the third quarter. Also prepare a schedule of expected cash payments for Gilden, by month and in total, for the third quarter.

P8–17 Planning Bank Financing by Means of a Cash Budget The president of Univax, Inc., has just approached the company's bank seeking short-term financing for the coming year, 19x2. The bank has stated that the loan request must be accompanied by a detailed cash budget that shows the quarters in which financing will be needed, as well as the amounts that will be needed and the quarters in which repayments can be made.

In order to provide this information for the bank, the president has directed that the following data be gathered from which a cash budget can be prepared:

a. Budgeted sales and merchandise purchases for 19x2, as well as actual sales and purchases for the last quarter of 19x1, are:

	Sales	Merchandise Purchases
19x1:		
Fourth quarter actual	$300,000	$180,000
19x2:		
First quarter budgeted	400,000	260,000
Second quarter budgeted	500,000	310,000
Third quarter budgeted	600,000	370,000
Fourth quarter budgeted	480,000	240,000

b. The company typically collects 33 percent of a quarter's sales before the quarter ends and another 65 percent in the following quarter. The remainder is uncollectible. This pattern of collections is now being experienced in the actual data for the 19x1 fourth quarter.

c. Some 20 percent of a quarter's merchandise purchases are paid for within the quarter. The remainder is paid in the quarter following.

d. Operating expenses for 19x2 are budgeted quarterly at $90,000 plus 12 percent of sales. Of the fixed amount, $20,000 each quarter is depreciation.

e. The company will pay $10,000 in cash dividends each quarter.

f. Equipment purchases will be made as follows during the year: $80,000 in the second quarter and $48,500 in the third quarter.

g. The Cash account contained $20,000 at the end of 19x1. The company must maintain a minimum cash balance of at least $18,000.

h. Any borrowing will take place at the beginning of a quarter, and any repayments will be made at the end of a quarter at an annual interest rate of 10 percent. Interest is paid only when principal is repaid. All borrowings and all repayments of principal must be in round $1,000 amounts. Interest payments can be in any amount.

i. At present, the company has no loans outstanding.

Required

1. Prepare the following, by quarter and in total, for the year 19x2:
   a. A schedule of budgeted cash collections on sales.
   b. A schedule of budgeted cash payments for merchandise purchases.
2. Compute the expected cash payments for operating expenses, by quarter and in total, for the year 19x2.
3. Using the data from (1) and (2) above and other data as needed, prepare a cash budget for 19x2, by quarter and in total for the year. Show clearly on your budget the quarter(s) in which borrowing will be needed and the quarter(s) in which repayments can be made, as requested by the company's bank.

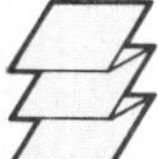

P8–18 Master Budget Preparation Nordic Company prepares its master budget on a quarterly basis. The following data have been assembled to assist in preparation of the master budget for the second quarter of 19x6:

a. As of March 31, 19x6 (the end of the prior quarter), the company's balance sheet showed the following account balances:

Cash	$ 9,000	
Accounts Receivable	48,000	
Inventory	12,600	
Plant and Equipment (net)	214,100	
Accounts Payable		$ 18,300
Capital Stock		190,000
Retained Earnings		75,400
	$283,700	$283,700

b. Actual sales for March and budgeted sales for April-July are as follows:

March (actual)	$60,000
April	70,000
May	85,000
June	90,000
July	50,000

c. Sales are 20 percent for cash and 80 percent on credit. All credit sale terms are n/30; therefore, accounts are collected in the month following sale. The accounts receivable at March 31 are a result of March credit sales.

d. The company's gross profit rate is 40 percent of sales.

e. Monthly expenses are budgeted as follows: salaries and wages, $7,500 per month; freight-out, 6 percent of sales; advertising, $6,000 per month; depreciation, $2,000 per month; other expense, 4 percent of sales.

f. At the end of each month, inventory is to be on hand equal to 30 percent of the following month's sales needs, stated at cost.

g. Half of a month's inventory purchases are paid for in the month of purchase and half in the following month.

h. Equipment purchases during the quarter will be as follows: April, $11,500; and May, $3,000.

i. Dividends totaling $3,500 will be declared and paid in June.

j. The company must maintain a minimum cash balance of $8,000. An open line of credit is available at a local bank. All borrowing is done at the beginning of a month, and all repayments are made at the end of a month. Borrowings and repayments of principal must be in multiples of $1,000. Loan repayments are on a FIFO basis. Interest is paid only at the time of repayment of principal. The interest rate is 12 percent per annum. (Figure interest on whole months, e.g., 1/12, 2/12.)

Required Using the data above, complete the following statements and schedules for the second quarter:

1. Schedule of expected cash collections:

	April	May	June	Total
Cash sales	$14,000			
Credit sales	48,000			
Total collections	$62,000			

2. *a.* Inventory purchases budget:

	April	May	June	Total
Budgeted cost of goods sold	$42,000*	$51,000		
Add: Desired ending inventory	15,300†			
Total needs	57,300			
Deduct: Opening inventory	12,600			
Required purchases	$44,700			

* For April sales: $70,000 sales × 60% cost ratio = $42,000.
† $51,000 × 30% = $15,300.

b. Schedule of cash disbursements for purchases:

	April	May	June	Total
For March purchases	$18,300			$18,300
For April purchases	22,350	$22,350		44,700
For May purchases				
For June purchases				
Total cash disbursements	$40,650			

3. Schedule of cash disbursements for expenses:

	April	May	June	Total
Salaries and wages	$ 7,500			
Freight-out	4,200			
Advertising	6,000			
Other expenses	2,800			
Total cash disbursements	$20,500			

4. Cash budget:

	April	May	June	Total
Cash balance, beginning	$ 9,000			
Add cash collections	62,000			
Total cash available	71,000			
Less disbursements:				
For inventory purchases	40,650			
For operating expenses	20,500			
For equipment purchases	11,500			
For dividends	—			
Total disbursements	72,650			
Excess (deficiency) of cash	(1,650)			
Financing:				
Etc.				

5. Prepare an income statement for the quarter ending June 30. (Use the functional format in preparing your income statement, as shown in Schedule 9. Ignore income taxes.)
6. Prepare a balance sheet as of June 30.

P8–19 Cash Budget with Supporting Schedules Janus Products, Inc., is a merchandising company that sells binders, paper, and other school supplies. The company is planning its cash needs for the third quarter of 19x6. In the past, Janus Products has had to borrow money during the third quarter in order to support peak sales of back-to-school materials, which occur during August. The following information has been assembled to assist in preparing a cash budget for the quarter:

a. Budgeted monthly income statements for July–October 19x6 are:

	July	August	September	October
Sales	$40,000	$70,000	$50,000	$45,000
Cost of goods sold	24,000	42,000	30,000	27,000
Gross margin	16,000	28,000	20,000	18,000
Less operating expenses:				
Selling expense	7,200	11,700	8,500	7,300
Administrative expense*	5,600	7,200	6,100	5,900
Total operating expenses	12,800	18,900	14,600	13,200
Net income	$ 3,200	$ 9,100	$ 5,400	$ 4,800

* Includes $2,000 depreciation each month.

b. Sales are 20 percent for cash and 80 percent on credit.

c. Credit sales are collected over a three-month period in the ratio of 10 percent in the month of sale, 70 percent in the month following sale, and 20 percent in the second month following sale. May sales totaled $30,000, and June sales totaled $36,000.

d. Inventory purchases are paid for within 15 days. Therefore, 50 percent of a month's inventory purchases are paid for in the month of purchase. The remaining 50 percent is paid in the following month. Accounts payable for inventory purchases at June 30 total $11,700.

e. The company maintains its ending inventory levels at 75 percent of the cost of the merchandise to be sold in the following month. The merchandise inventory at June 30 is $18,000.

f. Equipment costing $4,500 will be purchased in July.
g. Dividends of $1,000 will be declared and paid in September.
h. The cash balance on June 30 is $8,000; the company must maintain a cash balance of at least this amount at all times.
i. The company can borrow from its bank as needed to bolster the Cash account. Borrowings must be in multiples of $1,000. All borrowings take place at the beginning of a month, and all repayments are made at the end of a month. The interest rate is 12 percent per annum. Compute interest on whole months (1/12, 2/12, and so on).

Required

1. Prepare a schedule of budgeted cash collections from sales for each of the months July, August, and September and for the quarter in total.
2. Prepare the following for merchandise inventory:
   a. An inventory purchases budget for each of the months July, August, and September.
   b. A schedule of expected cash disbursements for inventory for each of the months July, August, and September and for the quarter in total.
3. Prepare a cash budget for the third quarter of 19x6. Show figures by month as well as for the quarter in total. Show borrowings from the company's bank and repayments to the bank as needed to maintain the minimum cash balance.

P8–20 Production Budget; Purchases Budget; Income Statement Amcor Products, Inc., produces and sells a very popular fertilizer called Greenex. The company is in the process of preparing budgeted data on Greenex for the second quarter of 19x4. The following data are available:

a. The company expects to sell 45,000 bags of Greenex during the second quarter of 19x4. The selling price is $10 per bag.
b. Each bag of Greenex requires 5 pounds of a material called Nitro and 15 pounds of a material called Mixo.
c. The finished goods inventory of Greenex is planned to be reduced by 25 percent by the end of the second quarter. The inventory at the beginning of the quarter will be 12,000 bags. Other inventory levels are planned as follows:

	Beginning of Quarter	End of Quarter
Material Nitro—pounds . . .	65,000	52,500
Material Mixo—pounds . . .	115,000	95,000
Empty bags.	30,000	20,000

d. Nitro costs 60 cents per pound; Mixo costs 10 cents per pound; and empty bags cost 80 cents each.
e. It requires six minutes of direct labor time to process and fill one bag of Greenex. Labor cost is $7.50 per hour.
f. Variable manufacturing overhead costs are 45 cents per bag. Fixed manufacturing overhead costs total $60,000 per quarter.
g. Variable selling and administrative expenses are 5 percent of sales. Fixed selling and administrative expenses total $35,000 per quarter.

Required

1. Prepare a production budget for Greenex for the second quarter.
2. Prepare a raw materials purchases budget for Nitro, Mixo, and empty bags for the second quarter. Show the budgeted purchases in dollars as well as in pounds or bags.

3. Compute the budgeted cost to manufacture one bag of finished Greenex. (Include only variable manufacturing costs in your computation.)
4. Prepare a budgeted income statement for Greenex for the second quarter. Use the contribution approach, and show both per unit and total cost data.

P8–21 Master Budget Preparation Actual sales for June and budgeted sales for July–October 19x2 are presented below for the Newark Company:

June (actual)	$40,000
July	50,000
August	64,000
September	80,000
October	36,000

The company is preparing its master budget for the third quarter. The following information is available:

a. Sales are 40 percent for cash and 60 percent on credit. All credit sale terms are n/30; therefore, accounts are collected in the month following sale. The accounts receivable at June 30 are a result of June credit sales.
b. The gross profit rate is 30 percent of sales.
c. Monthly expenses are as follows: salaries and wages, 15 percent of sales; rent, $2,200 per month; and other expenses (excluding depreciation), 5 percent of sales. Depreciation is $1,000 per month.
d. At the end of each month, inventory is to be on hand equal to 75 percent of the following month's sales needs, stated at cost.
e. One half of a month's inventory purchases are paid for in the month of purchase; the other half is paid for in the following month. The accounts payable at June 30 are a result of June purchases of inventory.
f. Equipment costing $2,625 will be purchased in August.
g. The company must maintain a minimum cash balance of $5,000. An open line of credit is available at a local bank. All borrowing is done at the beginning of a month, and all repayments are made at the end of a month. Borrowings and repayments of principal must be in multiples of $1,000. Loan repayments are on a FIFO basis. Interest is paid at the end of each quarter on all amounts outstanding during the quarter. The interest rate is 18 percent per annum. (Figure interest on whole months—1⁄12, 2⁄12, and so forth.)
h. Dividends of $1,500 will be declared and paid in September.
i. The amounts in various balance sheet accounts at June 30 follow:

Cash	$ 7,000
Accounts Receivable	24,000
Inventory	26,250
Plant and Equipment (net)	150,000
Accounts Payable	16,625
Capital Stock	175,000
Retained Earnings	15,625

Required Using the data above, complete the following statements and schedules:

1. Schedule of expected cash collections:

	July	August	September	Total
Cash sales	$20,000			
Credit sales	24,000			
Total collections	$44,000			

2. *a.* Purchases budget:

	July	August	September	Total
Budgeted cost of goods sold	$35,000*	$44,800		
Add: Desired ending inventory . . .	33,600†			
Total needs	68,600			
Deduct: Opening inventory	26,250			
Required purchases	$42,350			

* For July sales: $50,000 sales × 70% cost ratio = $35,000.
† $44,800 × 75% = $33,600.

b. Schedule of cash disbursements for purchases:

	July	August	September	Total
For June purchases	$16,625			$16,625
For July purchases.	21,175	$21,175		42,350
For August purchases				
For September purchases.				
Total.	$37,800			

3. Schedule of cash disbursements for expenses:

	July	August	September	Total
Salaries and wages.	$ 7,500			
Rent	2,200			
Other expenses	2,500			
Total cash disbursements.	$12,200			

4. Cash budget:

	July	August	September	Total
Cash balance, beginning	$ 7,000			
Add cash collections.	44,000			
Total cash available	51,000			
Less disbursements:				
For inventory purchases	37,800			
For expenses	12,200			
For equipment purchases.	—			
For dividends	—			
Total disbursements	50,000			
Excess (deficiency) of cash	1,000			
Financing:				
Etc.				

5. Prepare an income statement for the quarter ending September 30. (Use the functional format in preparing your income statement, as shown in Schedule 9. Ignore income taxes.)
6. Prepare a balance sheet as of September 30.

P8–22 **Cash Budget for Month** The treasurer of Househall Company, Ltd., states, "Our monthly financial budget shows me our cash surplus or deficiency and assures me that an unexpected cash shortage will not occur."

A cash budget is now being prepared for the month of May 19x5. The following information has been gathered to assist in preparing the budget:

a. Budgeted sales and production requirements are:

Budgeted sales.	$650,000
Production requirements:	
Raw materials to be used	301,000
Direct labor cost	85,000

The raw materials inventory is budgeted to increase by $6,000 during the month; other inventories will not change.

b. Customers are allowed a 2 percent cash discount on accounts paid within 10 days after the end of the month of sale. Only 50 percent of the payments made in the month following sale fall within the discount period.

c. Accounts receivable outstanding at April 30 were:

Month	Sales	Accounts Receivable at April 30	Percentage of Sales Uncollected at April 30	Percentage to Be Collected in May
January.	$340,000	$ 8,500	2½	?
February	530,000	31,800	6	?
March	470,000	47,000	10	?
April	550,000	550,000	100	?

Bad debts are negligible. All January receivables outstanding will have been collected by the end of May, and the collection pattern since the time of sale will be the same in May as in previous months.

d. Raw materials purchases are paid in the month following purchase, and $320,000 in accounts payable for purchases was outstanding at the end of April.

e. Accrued wages on April 30, 19x5, were $11,000. All May payroll amounts will be paid within the month of May.

f. Budgeted operating expenses and overhead costs for May are:

Overhead and other charges:		
Indirect labor	$34,000	
Real estate taxes	1,500	
Depreciation	25,000	
Utilities	1,500	
Wage benefits	9,000	
Fire insurance	1,500	
Amortization of patents	5,000	
Spoilage of materials in the warehouse . . .	1,500	$79,000
Sales salaries.		45,000
Administrative salaries		15,000

g. Real estate taxes are paid in August each year.

h. Utilities are billed and paid within the month.

i. The $9,000 monthly charge above for "Wage benefits" includes:

Unemployment insurance (payable monthly)	$1,350
Canada pension plan (payable monthly)	820
Holiday pay, which represents 1/12 of the annual cost (May holidays will require $2,040).	1,100
Company pension fund, including 1/12 of a $10,800 adjustment paid in January 19x5	5,000
Group insurance (payable quarterly, with the last payment having been made in February)	730

j. Fire insurance premiums are payable in January, in advance.

k. Freight-out costs for May will be $1,000, all payable during the month.

l. The cash balance on April 30, 19x5, was $5,750.

Required 1. Prepare a schedule showing expected cash collections for May 19x5.
2. Prepare a cash budget for May 19x5 in good form. Ignore income taxes.
3. Comment briefly on the treasurer's statement quoted at the beginning of the problem.

(SMA, Adapted)

P8–23 **Integrated Operating Budgets** The East Division of Kensic Company manufactures a vital component that is used in one of Kensic's major product lines. The East Division has been experiencing some difficulty in coordinating activities between its various departments, which has resulted in some shortages of the component at critical times. To overcome the shortages, the manager of East Division has decided to initiate a monthly budgeting system that is integrated between departments.

The first budget is to be for the second quarter of the current year. To assist in developing the budget figures, the divisional controller has accumulated the following information:

Sales

Sales through March 31, 19x5, the first three months of the current year, were 30,000 units. Actual sales in units for February and March, and planned sales in units over the next five months, are given below:

February (actual)	10,000
March (actual)	14,000
April (planned)	20,000
May (planned)	35,000
June (planned)	50,000
July (planned).	45,000
August (planned)	30,000

In total, the East Division expects to product and sell 250,000 units during 19x5.

Direct Material

Two different materials are used in the production of the component. Data regarding these materials are given below:

Direct Material	Units of Direct Materials per Finished Component	Cost per Unit	Inventory at March 31, 19x5
No. 208	4 pounds	$5.00	46,000 pounds
No. 311	9 feet	2.00	69,000 feet

Material No. 208 is sometimes in short supply. Therefore, the East Division requires that enough of the material be on hand at the end of each month to provide for 50 percent of the following month's production needs. Material No. 311 is easier to get, so only one third of the following month's production must be on hand at the end of each month.

Direct Labor

The East Division has three departments through which the components must pass before they are completed. Information relating to direct labor in these departments is given below:

Department	Direct Labor-Hours per Finished Component	Cost per Direct Labor-Hour
Shaping	0.75	$6.00
Assembly	2.80	4.00
Finishing	0.25	8.00

Manufacturing Overhead

East Division manufactured 32,000 components during the first three months of 19x5. The actual variable overhead costs incurred during this three-month period are shown below. East Division's controller believes that the variable overhead costs incurred during the last nine months of the year will be at the same rate per component as experienced during the first three months.

Utilities	$ 57,000
Indirect labor	31,000
Supplies	16,000
Other	8,000
Total variable overhead	$112,000

The actual fixed overhead costs incurred during the first three months of 19x5 amounted to $1,170,000. The East Division has planned fixed overhead costs for the entire year as follows:

Supervision	$ 872,000
Property taxes	143,000
Depreciation	2,910,000
Insurance	631,000
Other	72,000
Total fixed overhead	$4,628,000

Finished Goods Inventory

The desired monthly ending inventory of completed components is 20 percent of the next month's estimated sales. The East Division has 4,000 units in the finished goods inventory on March 31, 19x5.

Required

1. Prepare a production budget for the East Division for the second quarter ending June 30, 19x5. Show computations by month and in total for the quarter.
2. Prepare a direct materials purchases budget in units and in dollars for each type of material for the second quarter ending June 30, 19x5. Again show computations by month and in total for the quarter.
3. Prepare a direct labor budget in hours and in dollars for the second quarter ending June 30, 19x5. This time it is *not* necessary to show monthly figures; show quarterly totals only.
4. Assume that the company plans to manufacture a total of 250,000 units for the year. Prepare a manufacturing overhead budget for the nine-month period ending December 31, 19x5. Again, it is *not* necessary to show monthly figures.

P8–24 Tabulation Approach to Economic Order Quantity (Appendix) Yales Jewelers, Inc., purchases 30,000 one-quarter-carat diamonds each year for various mountings. Pertinent information relating to the diamonds is given below:

Purchase cost per diamond	$200
Cost to carry one diamond in inventory for one year	5
Cost of placing one order to the company's supplier	40

The maximum order that the insurance company will permit is 1,500 diamonds. The minimum order that the supplier will permit is 300 diamonds, with all orders required to be in multiples of 300 diamonds. The company has been purchasing in the maximum allowable volume of 1,500 diamonds per order.

Required

1. By use of the tabulation approach to EOQ, determine the volume in which the company should be placing its diamond orders.

2. Compute the annual cost savings that will be realized if the company purchases in the volume you have determined in (1) above, as compared to its present purchase policy.

P8–25 **Economic Order Quantity; Safety Stock; JIT Purchasing Impact** (Appendix) Hillclimber, Inc., manufactures a four-wheeler, off-road vehicle. The company purchases one of the parts used in the manufacture of the vehicle from a supplier located in another state. In total, Hillclimber purchases 18,000 parts per year at a cost of $30 per part.

The parts are used evenly throughout the year in the production process on a 360-day-per-year basis. The company estimates that it costs $75 to place a single purchase order and about $1.20 to carry one part in inventory for a year.

Delivery from the supplier generally takes 9 days, but it can take as much as 13 days. The days of delivery time and the percentage of their occurrence are shown in the following tabulation:

Delivery Time (days)	Percentage of Occurrence
9	70
10	12
11	6
12	6
13	6

Required

1. Compute the EOQ.
2. Assume that the company is willing to assume an 18 percent risk of being out of stock. What would be the safety stock? The reorder point?
3. Assume that the company is willing to assume only a 6 percent risk of being out of stock. What would be the safety stock? The reorder point?
4. Assume a 6 percent stockout risk as stated in (3) above. What would be the total cost of ordering and carrying inventory for one year?
5. Refer to the original data. Assume that the company decides to adopt JIT purchasing policies, as stated in the chapter. This change allows the company to reduce its cost of placing a purchase order to only $6. Also, the company estimates that when the waste and inefficiency caused by inventories is considered, the true cost of carrying a unit in stock is $5.40 per year.
   a. Compute the new EOQ.
   b. How frequently would the company be placing an order, as compared to the old purchasing policy?

P8–26 **Economic Order Quantity; Safety Stock; JIT Purchasing Impact** (Appendix) Stoffer Manufacturing Company uses 7,200 units of material X each year. The material is used evenly throughout the year in the company's production process. A recent cost study indicates that it costs $3.20 to carry one unit in stock for a year. The company estimates that the cost of placing an order for material X is $180.

On the average, it takes 7 days to receive an order from the supplier. Sometimes, orders do not arrive for 10 days, and at rare intervals (about 2 percent of the time) they do not arrive for 12 days. Each unit of material X costs the company $15. Stoffer works an average of 360 days per year.

Required

1. Compute the EOQ.
2. What size safety stock would you recommend for material X? Why?
3. What is the reorder point for material X in units?
4. Compute the total cost associated with ordering and carrying material X in stock for a year. (Do *not* include the $15 purchase cost in this computation.)
5. Refer to the original data. Assume that as a result of adopting JIT purchasing policies, the company is able to reduce the cost of placing a purchase order to

only $5. Also assume that after considering the waste and inefficiency caused by inventories, the actual cost of carrying one unit of material X in stock for a year is $18.

a. Compute the new EOQ.

b. How frequently would the company be placing a purchase order, as compared to the old purchasing policy?

P8–27 Tabulation Approach; Economic Order Quantity; Reorder Point (Appendix) You have been engaged to install an inventory control system for Dexter Company. Among the inventory control features that Dexter desires in the system are indicators of "how much" to order "when." The following information is furnished for one item, called a duosonic, that is carried in inventory:

a. Duosonics are sold by the gross (12 dozen) at a list price of $800 per gross, FOB shipper. Dexter receives a 40 percent trade discount off list price on purchases in gross lots.

b. Freight cost is $20 per gross from the shipping point to Dexter's plant.

c. Dexter uses about 5,000 duosonics during a 259-day production year but must purchase a total of 36 gross per year to allow for normal breakage. Minimum and maximum usages are 12 and 28 duosonics per day, respectively.

d. Normal delivery time to receive an order is 20 working days from the date that a purchase request is initiated. A stockout (complete exhaustion of the inventory) of duosonics would stop production, and Dexter would purchase duosonics locally at list price rather than shut down.

e. The cost of placing an order is $30.

f. Space storage cost is $24 per year per average gross in storage.

g. Insurance and taxes are approximately 12 percent of the net delivered cost of average inventory, and Dexter expects a return of at least 8 percent on its average investment. (Ignore ordering costs and carrying costs in making these computations.)

Required

1. Prepare a schedule computing the total annual cost of duosonics based on uniform order lot sizes of one, two, three, four, five, and six gross of duosonics. (The schedule should show the total annual cost according to each lot size.) Indicate the EOQ.
2. Prepare a schedule computing the minimum stock reorder point for duosonics. This is the point below which reordering is necessary to guard against a stockout. Factors to be considered include average lead period usage and safety stock requirements.

(CPA, Adapted)

CASES

C8–28 Evaluating a Company's Budget Procedures Rouge Corporation is a medium-sized company in the steel fabrication industry with six divisions located in different geographic sectors of the United States. Considerable autonomy in operational management is permitted in the divisions, due in part to the distance between corporate headquarters in St. Louis and five of the six divisions. Corporate management establishes divisional budgets using data for the prior year adjusted for industry and economic changes expected for the coming year. Budgets are prepared by year and by quarter, with top management attempting to recognize problems unique to each division in the divisional budget-setting process. Once the year's divisional budgets have been set by corporate management, they cannot be modified by division management.

The budget for calendar year 1991 projects total corporate net income before taxes of $3,750,000 for the year, including $937,500 for the first quarter. Results of first-quarter operations presented to corporate management in early April showed corporate net income of $865,000, which was $72,500 below the projected net income for the quarter. The St. Louis division operated at 4.5 percent above its projected divisional net income, while the other five divisions showed net incomes with variances ranging from 1.5 to 22 percent below budgeted net income.

Corporate management is concerned with the first-quarter results because it believes strongly that differences between divisions had been recognized. An entire day in late November of last year had been spent presenting and explaining the corporate and divisional budgets to the division managers and their division controllers. A mid-April meeting of corporate and division management generated unusual candor. All five out-of-state division managers cited reasons why the first-quarter results in their respective divisions represented effective management and was the best that could be expected. Corporate management has remained unconvinced and informs division managers that "results will be brought into line with the budget by the end of the second quarter."

Required

1. Identify the major defects in the procedures employed by Rouge Corporation's corporate management in preparing and implementing the divisional budgets.
2. Discuss the behavioral problems that may arise by requiring Rouge Corporation's division managers to meet the quarterly budgeted net income figures as well as the annual budgeted net income.

(CMA, Adapted)

C8–29 **Master Budget with Supporting Budgets** You have just been hired as a new management trainee by Quik-Flik Sales Company, a nationwide distributor of a revolutionary new cigarette lighter. The company has an exclusive franchise on distribution of the lighter, and sales have grown so rapidly over the last few years that it has become necessary to add new members to the management team. You have been given direct responsibility for all planning and budgeting. Your first assignment is to prepare a master budget for the next three months, starting April 1. You are anxious to make a favorable impression on the president and have assembled the information below.

The company desires a minimum ending cash balance each month of $10,000. The lighters are forecast to sell for $8 each. Recent and forecast sales in units are:

January (actual)	20,000	June	60,000
February (actual)	24,000	July	40,000
March (actual)	28,000	August	36,000
April	35,000	September	32,000
May	45,000		

The large buildup in sales before and during the month of June is due to Father's Day. Ending inventories are supposed to equal 90 percent of the next month's sales in units. The lighters cost the company $5 each.

Purchases are paid for as follows: 50 percent in the month of purchase and the remaining 50 percent in the following month. All sales are on credit, with no discount, and payable within 15 days. The company has found, however, that only 25 percent of a month's sales are collected by month-end. An additional 50 percent is collected in the month following, and the remaining 25 percent is collected in the second month following. Bad debts have been negligible.

The company's monthly operating expenses are given below:

Variable:	
Sales commissions	$1 per lighter
Fixed:	
Wages and salaries	$22,000
Utilities	14,000
Insurance expired	1,200
Depreciation	1,500
Miscellaneous	3,000

All operating expenses are paid during the month, in cash, with the exception of depreciation and insurance expired. New fixed assets will be purchased during May for $25,000 cash. The company declares dividends of $12,000 each quarter, payable in the first month of the following quarter. The company's balance sheet at March 31 is given below:

Assets	
Cash	$ 14,000
Accounts receivable ($48,000 February sales; $168,000 March sales)	216,000
Inventory (31,500 units)	157,500
Unexpired insurance	14,400
Fixed assets, net of depreciation	172,700
Total assets	$574,600
Liabilities and Stockholders' Equity	
Accounts payable, purchases	$ 85,750
Dividends payable	12,000
Capital stock, no par	300,000
Retained earnings	176,850
Total liabilities and stockholders' equity	$574,600

The company can borrow money from its bank at 12 percent annual interest. All borrowing must be done at the beginning of a month, and repayments must be made at the end of a month. Repayments of principal must be in round $1,000 amounts. Borrowing (and payments of interest) can be in any amount.

Interest is computed and paid at the end of each quarter on all loans outstanding during the quarter. Round all interest payments to the nearest whole dollar. Compute interest on whole months (1/12, 2/12, and so forth). The company wishes to use any excess cash to pay loans off as rapidly as possible.

Required Prepare a master budget for the three-month period ending June 30. Include the following detailed budgets:

1. *a.* A sales budget by month and in total.
   b. A schedule of budgeted cash collections from sales and accounts receivable, by month and in total.
   c. A purchases budget in units and in dollars. Show the budget by month and in total.
   d. A schedule of budgeted cash payments for purchases, by month and in total.
2. A cash budget. Show the budget by month and in total.
3. A budgeted income statement for the three-month period ending June 30. Use the contribution approach.
4. A budgeted balance sheet as of June 30.

C8–30 Evaluating a Company's Budget Procedures Tom Emory and Jim Morris strolled back to their plant from the administrative offices of Ferguson & Son Mfg. Company. Tom was manager of the machine shop in the company's factory; Jim was manager of the equipment maintenance department.

The men had just attended the monthly performance evaluation meeting for plant department heads. These meetings had been held on the third Tuesday of each month since Robert Ferguson, Jr., the president's son, had become plant manager a year earlier.

As they were walking, Tom Emory spoke. "Boy, I hate those meetings! I never know whether my department's accounting reports will show good or bad performance. I'm beginning to expect the worst. If the accountants say I saved the company a dollar, I'm called 'Sir,' but if I spend even a little too much—boy, do I get in trouble. I don't know if I can hold on until I retire."

Tom had just been given the worst evaluation he had ever received in his long career with Ferguson & Son. He was the most respected of the experienced machinists in the company. He had been with Ferguson & Son for many years and was promoted to supervisor of the machine shop when the company expanded and moved to its present location. The president (Robert Ferguson, Sr.) had often stated that the company's success was due to the high quality of the work of machinists like Tom. As supervisor, Tom stressed the importance of craftsmanship and told his workers that he wanted no sloppy work coming from his department.

When Robert Ferguson, Jr., became the plant manager, he directed that monthly performance comparisons be made between actual and budgeted costs for each department. The departmental budgets were intended to encourage the supervisors to reduce inefficiencies and to seek cost reduction opportunities. The company controller was instructed to have his staff "tighten" the budget slightly whenever a department attained its budget in a given month; this was done to reinforce the plant supervisor's desire to reduce costs. The young plant manager often stressed the importance of continued progress toward attaining the budget; he also made it known that he kept a file of these performance reports for future reference when he succeeded his father.

Tom Emory's conversation with Jim Morris continued as follows:

Emory: I really don't understand. We've worked so hard to get up to budget, and the minute we make it they tighten the budget on us. We can't work any faster and still maintain quality. I think my men are ready to quit trying. Besides, those reports don't tell the whole story. We always seem to be interrupting the big jobs for all those small rush orders. All that setup and machine adjustment time is killing us. And quite frankly, Jim, you were no help. When our hydraulic press broke down last month, your people were nowhere to be found. We had to take it apart ourselves and got stuck with all that idle time.

Morris: I'm sorry about that, Tom, but you know my department has had trouble making budget, too. We were running well behind at the time of that problem, and if we'd spent a day on that old machine, we would never have made it up. Instead we made the scheduled inspections of the forklift trucks because we knew we could do those in less than the budgeted time.

Emory: Well, Jim, at least you have some options. I'm locked into what the scheduling department assigns to me and you know they're being harrassed by sales for those special orders. Incidentally, why didn't your report show all the supplies you guys wasted last month when you were working in Bill's department?

Morris: We're not out of the woods on that deal yet. We charged the maximum we could to our other work and haven't even reported some of it yet.

Emory: Well, I'm glad you have a way of getting out of the pressure. The accountants seem to know everything that's happening in my department, sometimes even before I do. I thought all that budget and accounting stuff was supposed to help, but it just gets me into trouble. Its all a big pain. I'm trying to put out quality work; they're trying to save pennies.

Required

1. Identify the problems which appear to exist in Ferguson & Son Mfg. Company's budgetary control system and explain how the problems are likely to reduce the effectiveness of the system.
2. Explain how Ferguson & Son Mfg. Company's budgetary control system could be revised to improve its effectiveness.

(CMA, Adapted)

C8–31 Economic Order Quantity Computations (Appendix) SaPane Company is a regional distributor of automobile window glass. With the introduction of the new subcompact car models and the expected high level of consumer demand, management recognizes a need to determine the total inventory cost associated with maintaining an optimal supply of replacement windshields for the new subcompact cars introduced by each of the three major manufacturers. SaPane is expecting a daily demand for 36 windshields. The purchase price of each windshield is $50.

Other costs associated with ordering and maintaining an inventory of these windshields are as follows:

a. The historical ordering costs incurred in the purchase order department for placing and processing orders are shown below:

Year	Orders Placed and Processed	Total Ordering Costs
1989	20	$12,300
1990	55	12,475
1991	100	12,700

Management expects the ordering costs to increase 16 percent over the amounts and rates experienced during the last three years.

b. The windshield manufacturer charges SaPane a $75 shipping fee per order.

c. A clerk in the receiving department receives, inspects, and secures the windshields as they arrive from the manufacturer. This activity requires eight hours per order received. This clerk has no other responsibilities and is paid at the rate of $9 per hour. Related variable overhead costs in this department are applied at the rate of $2.50 per hour.

d. Additional warehouse space will have to be rented to store the new windshields. Space can be rented as needed in a public warehouse at an estimated cost of $2,500 per year plus $5.35 per windshield.

e. Breakage cost is estimated to be 6 percent of the cost per windshield.

f. Taxes and fire insurance on the inventory are $1.15 per windshield.

g. The desired rate of return on the investment in inventory is 21 percent of the purchase price.

Six working days are required from the time an order is placed with the manufacturer until it is received. SaPane uses a 300-day workyear when making economic order quantity computations.

Required

Calculate the following values for SaPane Company.

1. Value for ordering cost that should be used in the EOQ formula.
2. Value for storage cost that should be used in the EOQ formula.
3. Economic order quantity.
4. Minimum annual cost at the economic order quantity point.
5. Reorder point in units.

(CMA, Adapted)

9

Standard Costs and JIT/FMS Performance Measures

LEARNING OBJECTIVES

After studying Chapter 9, you should be able to:

1 Distinguish between ideal standards and practical standards.

2 Explain how direct materials standards and direct labor standards are set.

3 Enumerate the advantages and disadvantages of using standard costs.

4 Compute the direct materials price and quantity variances and explain their significance.

5 Compute the direct labor rate and efficiency variances and explain their significance.

6 Compute the variable overhead spending and efficiency variances.

7 Explain how the manager would determine whether a variance constituted an ''exception'' that would require his or her attention.

8 Explain how the performance measures used in an automated setting differ from standard costs.

9 Enumerate the JIT/FMS performance measures and explain how they are used.

10 Compute the throughput time, the delivery cycle time, and the velocity of production as these measures relate to JIT/FMS.

11 Prepare journal entries to record standard costs and variances.

12 Define or explain the key terms listed at the end of the chapter.

In attempting to control costs, managers have two types of decisions to make—decisions relating to prices paid and decisions relating to quantities used. To attain the objectives of their firms, managers are expected to pay the lowest possible prices that are consistent with the quality of output desired. In attaining these objectives, managers are also expected to consume the minimum quantity of whatever resources they have at their command, again consistent with the quality of output desired. Breakdowns in control over either price or quantity will lead to excessive costs and to deteriorating profit margins.

How do managers attempt to control price paid and quantity used? Managers could personally examine every transaction that takes place, but this obviously would be an inefficient use of management time. The answer to the control problem lies in *standard costs*.

STANDARD COSTS—MANAGEMENT BY EXCEPTION

A *standard* can be defined as a benchmark or "norm" for measuring performance. Standards are found in many facets of day-to-day life. Students who wish to enter a college or university are often required to perform at a certain level on a standard achievement exam as a condition for admittance; the autos we drive are built under exacting engineering standards; and the food we eat is prepared under standards of both cleanliness and nutritional content. Standards are also widely used in managerial accounting. Here the standards relate to the *quantity* and *cost* of inputs used in manufacturing goods or providing services.

Quantity and cost standards are set by managers for the three elements of cost input—materials, labor, and overhead—that we have discussed in preceding chapters. *Quantity standards* say how much of a cost element, such as labor time or raw materials, should be used in manufacturing a unit of product or in providing a unit of service. *Cost standards* say what the cost of the time or the materials should be. Actual quantities and actual costs of inputs are measured against these standards to see whether operations are proceeding within the limits that management has set. If either the quantity or the cost of inputs exceeds the bounds that management has set, attention is directed to the difference, thereby permitting the manager to focus his or her efforts where they will do the most good. This process is called **management by exception.**

Who Uses Standard Costs?

Manufacturing, service, food, and not-for-profit organizations all make use of standards (in terms of either costs or quantities) to some extent. Auto service centers, for example, often set specific labor time standards for the completion of certain work tasks, such as installing a carburetor or doing a valve job, and then measure actual performance against these standards. Fast-food outlets such as McDonald's have exacting standards as to the quantity of meat going into a sandwich, as well as standards for the cost of the meat. Hospitals have standard costs (for food, laundry, and other items) for each occupied bed per day, as well as standard time allowances for the performing of certain routine activities, such as laboratory tests. In short, the business student is likely to run into standard cost concepts in virtually any line of business that she or he may enter.

The broadest application of the standard cost idea is probably found in manufacturing companies, where standards relating to materials, labor, and overhead are developed in detail for each separate product line. These standards are then organized into a **standard cost card** that tells the manager what the final, manufactured cost should be for a single unit of product. In the following section, we provide a detailed example of the setting of standard costs and the preparation of a standard cost card.

SETTING STANDARD COSTS

The setting of standard costs is more an art than a science. It requires the combined thinking and expertise of all persons who have responsibility over prices and quantities of inputs. In a manufacturing setting, this would include the managerial accountant, the purchasing agent, the industrial engineer, production supervisors, and line managers.

The beginning point in setting standard costs is a rigorous look at past experience. The managerial accountant can be of great help in this task by preparing data on the cost characteristics of prior years' activities at various levels of operations. A standard for the future must be more than simply a projection of the past, however. Data must be adjusted and modified in terms of changing economic patterns, changing demand and supply characteristics, and changing technology. Past experience in certain costs may be distorted due to inefficiencies. To the extent that such inefficiencies can be identified, the data must be appropriately adjusted. The manager must realize that the past is of value only insofar as it helps to predict the future. In short, standards must be reflective of efficient *future* operations, not inefficient *past* operations.

Ideal versus Practical Standards

Should standards be attainable all of the time, should they be attainable only part of the time, or should they be so tight that they become, in effect, "the impossible dream"? Opinions among managers vary, but standards tend to fall into one of two categories—either ideal or practical.

Ideal standards are those that can be attained only under the best circumstances. They allow for no machine breakdowns or other work interruptions, and they call for a level of effort that can be attained only by the most skilled and efficient employee working at peak effort 100 percent of the time. Some managers feel that such standards have a motivational value. These managers argue that even though an employee knows he will never stay within the standard set, it is a constant reminder to him of the need for ever-increasing efficiency and effort. Few firms use ideal standards. Most managers are of the opinion that ideal standards tend to discourage even the most diligent workers. Moreover, when ideal standards are used, variances from standards have little meaning. The reason is that the variances contain elements of "normal" inefficiencies, not just the abnormal inefficiencies that managers would like to have isolated and brought to their attention.

Practical standards can be defined as standards that are "tight but attainable." They allow for normal machine downtime and employee rest periods, and are such that they can be attained through reasonable, though highly efficient, efforts by the average worker at a task. Variances from such a standard are very useful to management in that they represent deviations that fall outside of normal, recurring inefficiencies and signal a need for management attention. Furthermore, practical standards can serve multiple purposes. In addition to signaling abnormal deviations in costs, they can also be used in forecasting cash flows and in planning inventory. By contrast, ideal standards cannot be used in forecasting and planning; they do not allow for normal inefficiencies, and therefore they result in unrealistic planning and forecasting figures.

Throughout the remainder of this chapter, we will assume the use of practical rather than ideal standards.

Setting Direct Materials Standards

As stated earlier, managers prepare separate standards for the price and quantity of inputs. The **standard price per unit** for direct materials should reflect the final, delivered cost of the materials, net of any discounts taken. For example, the standard price of a pound of material A might be determined as follows:

Purchase price, top grade, in 500-pound quantities . . .	$3.60
Freight, by truck, from the supplier's plant	0.44
Receiving and handling	0.05
Less purchase discount	(0.09)
Standard price per pound	$4.00

Notice that the standard price reflects a particular grade of material (top grade), purchased in particular lot sizes (500 pounds), and delivered by a particular type of carrier (truck). Allowances have also been made for handling and discounts. If all proceeds according to plans, the net standard price of a pound of material A should therefore be $4.

The **standard quantity per unit** for direct materials should reflect the amount of material going into each unit of finished product, as well as an allowance for unavoidable waste, spoilage, and other normal inefficiencies. To illustrate, the standard quantity of material A going into a unit of product might be determined as follows:

Per bill of materials, in pounds	2.7
Allowance for waste and spoilage, in pounds	0.2
Allowance for rejects, in pounds	0.1
Standard quantity per unit of product, in pounds . . .	3.0

A **bill of materials** is simply a list that shows the type and quantity of each item of material going into a unit of finished product. It is a handy source for determining the basic material input per unit, but it must be adjusted for waste and other factors, as shown above, in determining the full standard quantity per unit of product. "Rejects" represent the direct material contained in units of product that are rejected at final inspection. The cost of this material must be added back to good units.

Once the price and quantity standards have been set, the standard cost of material A per unit of finished product can be computed as follows:

$$3.0 \text{ pounds} \times \$4 = \$12 \text{ per unit}$$

This $12 cost figure will appear as one item on the standard cost card of the product under consideration.

Setting Direct Labor Standards

Direct labor price and quantity standards are usually expressed in terms of labor rate and labor-hours. The **standard rate per hour** for direct labor would include not only wages earned but also an allowance for fringe benefits and other labor-related costs. The computation might be as follows:

Basic wage rate per hour	$10
Employment taxes at 10% of the basic rate . . .	1
Fringe benefits at 30% of the basic rate	3
Standard rate per direct labor-hour	$14

Many companies prepare a single standard rate for all employees in a department, even though the actual wage rates may vary somewhat between employees due to seniority or other reasons. This simplifies the use of standard costs and also permits the manager to monitor the use of employees within departments. More is said on this point a little later. If all proceeds according to plans, the direct labor rate for our mythical company should average $14 per hour.

The standard direct labor time required to complete a unit of product (generally called the **standard hours per unit**) is perhaps the single most difficult standard to determine. One approach is to divide each operation performed on the product into elemental body movements (such as reaching, pushing, and turning over). Published tables of standard times for such movements are available. These times can be applied to the movements and then added together to determine the total standard time allowed per operation. Another approach is for an industrial engineer to do a time and motion study, actually clocking the time required for certain tasks. As stated earlier, the standard time developed must include allowances for coffee breaks, personal needs of employees, cleanup, and machine downtime. The resulting standard time might appear as follows:

Basic labor time per unit, in hours.	1.9
Allowance for breaks and personal needs	0.1
Allowance for cleanup and machine downtime . . .	0.3
Allowance for rejects	0.2
Standard hours per unit of product	2.5

Once the rate and time standards have been set, the standard labor cost per unit of product can be computed as follows:

$$2.5 \text{ hours} \times \$14 = \$35 \text{ per unit}$$

This $35 cost figure will appear along with direct materials as one item on the standard cost card of the product under consideration.

EXHIBIT 9–1
Standard Cost Card—Variable Production Cost

Inputs	(1) Standard Quantity or Hours	(2) Standard Price or Rate	(3) Standard Cost (1) × (2)
Direct materials.	3.0 pounds	$ 4.00	$12.00
Direct labor	2.5 hours	14.00	35.00
Variable overhead	2.5 hours	3.00	7.50
Total standard cost per unit . . .			$54.50

Setting Variable Overhead Standards

As with direct labor, the price and quantity standards for variable overhead are generally expressed in terms of rate and hours. The rate represents *the variable portion of the predetermined overhead rate* discussed in Chapter 3; the hours represent whatever hours base is used to apply overhead to units of product (often machine-hours, computer time, or direct labor-hours, as we learned in Chapter 3). To illustrate, if the variable portion of the predetermined overhead rate was $3 and if overhead was applied to units of product on a basis of direct labor-hours, the standard variable overhead cost per unit of product in our example would be:

$$2.5 \text{ hours} \times \$3.00 = \$7.50 \text{ per unit}$$

A more detailed look at the setting of overhead standards is reserved until Chapter 10.

To summarize our example on the setting of standard costs, the completed standard cost card for one unit of product in our mythical company is presented in Exhibit 9–1. Observe that the **standard cost per unit** is computed by multiplying the standard quantity or hours by the standard price or rate.

Are Standards the Same as Budgets?

Essentially, standards and budgets are the same thing. The only distinction between the two terms is that a standard is a *unit* amount, whereas a budget is a *total* amount. That is, the standard cost for materials in a unit of product may be $5. If 1,000 units of the product are to be produced during a period, then the budgeted cost of materials is $5,000. In effect, a standard may be viewed as being the *budgeted cost for one unit of product*.

A GENERAL MODEL FOR VARIANCE ANALYSIS

One reason for separating standards into two categories—price and quantity—is that control decisions relating to price paid and quantity used will generally fall at different points in time. In the case of raw materials, for example, control over price paid comes at the time of purchase. By contrast, control over quantity used does not come until the raw materials are used in

EXHIBIT 9–2

A General Model for Variance Analysis—Variable Production Costs

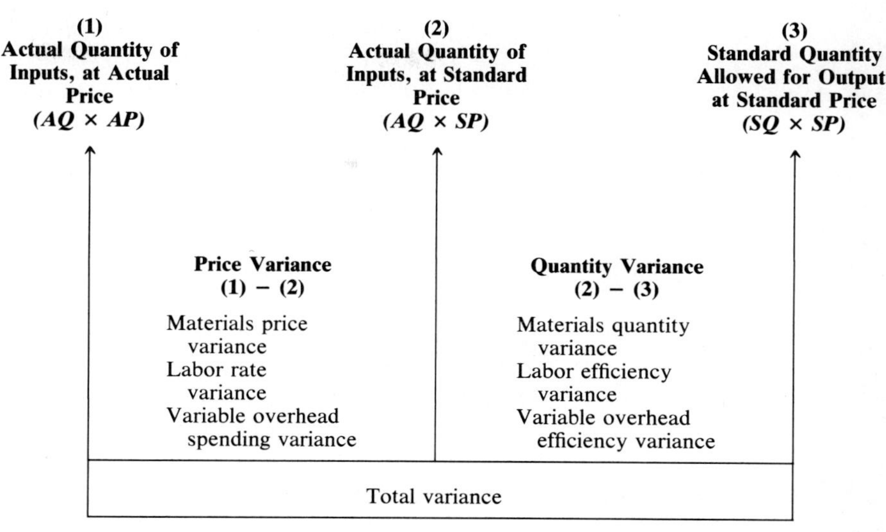

production, which may be many weeks or months after the purchase date. In addition, control over price paid and quantity used will generally be the responsibility of two different managers and will therefore need to be assessed independently. As we have stressed earlier, no manager should be held responsible for a cost over which he or she has no control. It is important, therefore, that we separate price considerations from quantity considerations in our approach to the control of costs.

Price and Quantity Variances

The manager separates price considerations from quantity considerations in the control of costs through the use of a general model that distinguishes between these two cost elements and that provides a base for *variance* analysis. A **variance** is the difference between *standard* prices and quantities and *actual* prices and quantities. This model, which deals with variable costs, isolates price variances from quantity variances and shows how each of these variances is computed.[1] The model is presented in Exhibit 9–2.

Three things should be noted from Exhibit 9–2. First, note that a price variance and a quantity variance can be computed for all three variable cost elements—direct materials, direct labor, and variable manufacturing overhead—even though the variance is not called by the same name in all cases. For example, a price variance is called a *materials price variance* in the case of direct materials but a *labor rate variance* in the case of direct labor and an *overhead spending variance* in the case of variable manufacturing overhead.

[1] Variance analysis of fixed costs is reserved until Chapter 10.

Second, note that even though a price variance may be called by different names, it is computed in exactly the same way regardless of whether one is dealing with direct materials, direct labor, or variable manufacturing overhead. The same is true with the quantity variance.

Third, note that variance analysis is actually a matter of input-output analysis. The inputs represent the actual quantity of direct materials, direct labor, and variable manufacturing overhead used; the output represents the good production of the period, expressed in terms of the *standard quantity (or the standard hours) allowed* in its manufacture (see column 3 in Exhibit 9–2). By **standard quantity allowed** or **standard hours allowed,** we mean the amount of direct materials, direct labor, or variable manufacturing overhead *that should have been used* to produce what was produced during the period. This might be more or less than what was *actually* used, depending on the efficiency or inefficiency of operations.

With this general model as a foundation, we will now examine the price and quantity variances in more detail.

USING STANDARD COSTS—DIRECT MATERIAL VARIANCES

To illustrate the computation and use of direct material variances, we will return to the standard cost data for direct materials contained in Exhibit 9–1. This exhibit shows the standard cost of direct materials per unit of product in our mythical company to be:

$$3.0 \text{ pounds} \times \$4 = \$12$$

We will assume that during June the company purchased 6,500 pounds of material at a cost of $3.80 per pound, including freight and handling costs, and net of the quantity discount. All of the material was used in the manufacture of 2,000 units of product. The computation of the price and quantity variances for the month is shown in Exhibit 9–3.[2]

A variance is unfavorable if the actual price or quantity exceeds the standard price or quantity; a variance is favorable if the actual price or quantity is less than the standard.

Materials Price Variance—A Closer Look

A **materials price variance** measures the difference between what is paid for a given quantity of materials and what should have been paid according to the standard that has been set. From Exhibit 9–3, this difference can be expressed by the following formula:

$$(AQ \times AP) - (AQ \times SP) = \text{Materials price variance}$$

The formula can be factored into simpler form as:

$$AQ(AP - SP) = \text{Materials price variance}$$

[2] Exhibit 9–3 shows the computation of the price and quantity variances when all materials purchased during a period are used in production and none remains in inventory at period-end. See the review problem at the end of the chapter for a computation of the price and quantity variances when only part of the materials purchased during a period is used in production during that period.

EXHIBIT 9–3
Variance Analysis—Direct Materials

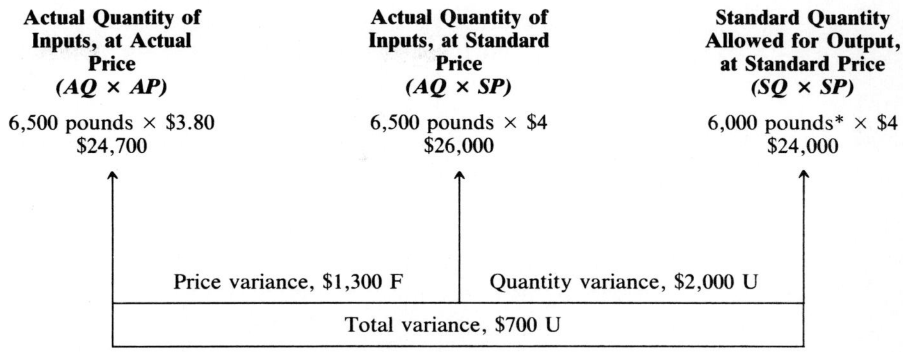

* 2,000 units × 3.0 pounds per unit = 6,000 pounds.
F = Favorable.
U = Unfavorable.

Some managers prefer this simpler formula, since it permits variance computations to be made very quickly. Using the data from Exhibit 9–3 in this formula, we have:

$$6{,}500 \text{ pounds } (\$3.80 - \$4.00) = \$1{,}300 \text{ F}$$

Notice that the answer is the same as that yielded in Exhibit 9–3. If the company wanted to put these data into a performance report, the data would appear as follows:

MYTHICAL COMPANY
Performance Report—Purchasing Department

Item Purchased	(1) Quantity Purchased	(2) Actual Price	(3) Standard Price	(4) Difference in Price (2) − (3)	(5) Total Price Variance (1) × (4)	Explanation
Material A	6,500 pounds	$3.80	$4.00	$0.20	$1,300 F	Second-grade materials purchased, rather than top grade

F = Favorable.
U = Unfavorable.

Isolation of Variances At what point should variances be isolated and brought to the attention of management? The answer is, the earlier the better. One of the basic reasons for utilizing standard costs is to facilitate cost control. Therefore, the sooner deviations from standard are brought to the attention of management, the sooner problems can be evaluated and corrected. If long periods are allowed to elapse before variances are computed, costs that could otherwise have been controlled may accumulate to the point of doing significant damage to profits. Most firms compute the materials price variance, for example, when materials *are purchased* rather than when the materials are placed into production. This permits earlier isolation of the variance, since materials may lay in the warehouse for many months before being used in production. Isolating the price variance when materials are purchased also permits the company to carry its raw materials in the inventory accounts at standard cost. This greatly simplifies the process of costing materials as they are later placed into production.[3]

Once a performance report has been prepared, what does management do with the price variance data? The variances should be viewed as "red flags," calling attention to the fact that an exception has occurred that will require some follow-up effort. Normally, the performance report itself will contain some explanation of the reason for the variance, as shown above.

Responsibility for the Variance Who is responsible for the materials price variance? Generally speaking, the purchasing agent has control over the price to be paid for goods and is therefore responsible for any price variances. Many factors control the price paid for goods, including size of lots purchased, delivery method used, quantity discounts available, rush orders, and the quality of materials purchased. To the extent that the purchasing agent can control these factors, he or she is responsible for seeing that they are kept in agreement with the factors anticipated when the standard costs were initially set. A deviation in any factor from what was intended in the initial setting of a standard cost can result in a price variance. For example, purchase of second-grade materials rather than top-grade materials would result in a favorable price variance, since the lower-grade materials would generally be less costly (but perhaps less suitable for production).

There may be times, however, when someone other than the purchasing agent is responsible for a materials price variance. Production may be scheduled in such a way, for example, that the purchasing agent is required to obtain delivery by airfreight, rather than by truck, or he or she may be forced to buy in uneconomical quantities. In these cases, the production manager would bear responsibility for the variances that develop.

A word of caution is in order. Variance analysis should not be used as an excuse to conduct witch hunts or as a means of beating line managers over the head. The emphasis must be on the control function in the sense of *supporting* the line managers and *assisting* them in meeting the goals that they have participated in setting for the company. In short, the emphasis must be positive rather than negative. Excessive dwelling on what has already happened, particularly in terms of trying to find someone to "blame," can often be destructive to the goals of an organization.

Materials Quantity Variance—A Closer Look

The **materials quantity variance** measures the difference between the quantity of materials used in production and the quantity that should have been used according to the standard that has been set. Although the variance is concerned with the physical usage of materials, it is generally stated in dollar terms, as shown in Exhibit 9–3. The formula for the materials quantity variance is:

$$(AQ \times SP) - (SQ \times SP) = \text{Materials quantity variance}$$

[3] See the appendix at the end of the chapter for an illustration of journal entries in a standard cost system.

Again, the formula can be factored into simpler terms:

$$SP(AQ - SQ) = \text{Materials quantity variance}$$

Using the data from Exhibit 9–3 in the formula, we have:

$$\$4(6{,}500 \text{ pounds} - 6{,}000 \text{ pounds*}) = \$2{,}000 \text{ U}$$

* 2,000 units × 3.0 pounds per unit = 6,000 pounds.

The answer, of course, is the same as that yielded in Exhibit 9–3. The data would appear as follows if a formal performance report were prepared:

MYTHICAL COMPANY
Performance Report—Production Department

Type of Materials	(1) Standard Price	(2) Actual Quantity	(3) Standard Quantity Allowed	(4) Difference in Quantity (2) − (3)	(5) Total Quantity Variance (1) × (4)	Explanation
Material A . . .	$4	6,500 pounds	6,000 pounds	500 pounds	$2,000 U	Second-grade materials, unsuitable for production

F = Favorable.
U = Unfavorable.

The materials quantity variance is best isolated at the time that materials are placed into production.[4] Materials are drawn for the number of units to be produced, according to the standard bill of materials for each unit. Any additional materials are usually drawn on an excess materials requisition slip, which is different in color from the normal requisition slips. This procedure calls attention to the excessive usage of materials *while production is still in process* and permits opportunity for early control of any developing problem.

Excessive usage of materials can result from many factors, including faulty machines, inferior quality of materials, untrained workers, and poor supervision. Generally speaking, it is the responsibility of the production department to see that material usage is kept in line with standards. There may be times, however, when the *purchasing* department may be responsible for an unfavorable material quantity variance. If the purchasing department obtains materials of inferior quality in an effort to economize on price, the materials may prove to be unsuitable for use on the production line and may result in excessive waste. Thus, purchasing rather than production would be responsible for the quantity variance.

USING STANDARD COSTS—DIRECT LABOR VARIANCES

To illustrate the computation and use of direct labor variances, we will use the standard cost data for direct labor contained in Exhibit 9–1. This exhibit

[4] If a company uses process costing, then it may be necessary in some situations to compute the materials quantity variance on a periodic basis as production is *completed*. This is because under process costing it is sometimes difficult to know in advance what the output will be for a period. We assume the use of a job-order costing system throughout this chapter (including all assignment materials).

EXHIBIT 9–4
Variance Analysis—Direct Labor

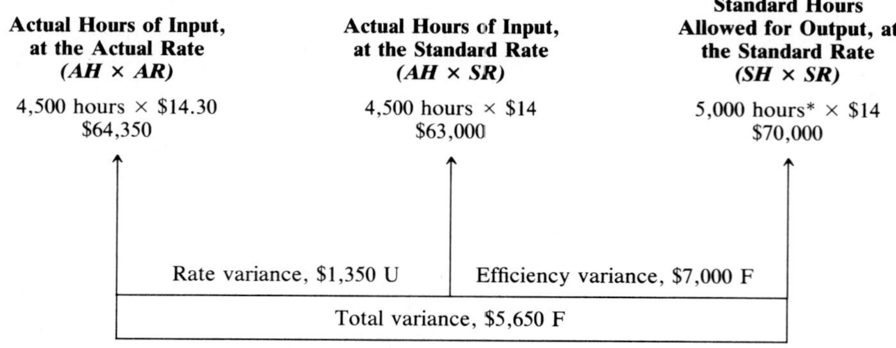

* 2,000 units × 2.5 hours per unit = 5,000 hours.
F = Favorable.
U = Unfavorable.

shows the standard cost of direct labor per unit of product in our mythical company to be:

$$2.5 \text{ hours} \times \$14 = \$35$$

We will assume that during June the company recorded 4,500 hours of direct labor time. The actual cost of this labor time was $64,350 (including employment taxes and fringe benefits), or an average of $14.30 per hour. Recall that the company produced 2,000 units of product during June. The computation of the labor rate and efficiency variances for the month is shown in Exhibit 9–4.

Notice that the column headings in Exhibit 9–4 are the same as those used in the prior two exhibits, except that in Exhibit 9–4 the terms *hours* and *rate* are used in place of the terms *quantity* and *price*.

Labor Rate Variance—A Closer Look

As explained earlier, the price variance for direct labor is commonly termed a **labor rate variance**. This variance measures any deviation from standard in the average hourly rate paid to direct labor workers. From Exhibit 9–4, the formula for the labor rate variance would be expressed as follows:

$$(AH \times AR) - (AH \times SR) = \text{Labor rate variance}$$

The formula can be factored into simpler form as:

$$AH(AR - SR) = \text{Labor rate variance}$$

Using the data from Exhibit 9–4 in the formula, we have:

$$4{,}500 \text{ hours } (\$14.30 - \$14.00) = \$1{,}350 \text{ U}$$

In many firms, the rates paid workers are set by union contract; therefore, rate variances, in terms of amounts paid to workers, tend to be almost nonexistent. Rate variances can arise, though, through the way labor is used. Skilled workers with high hourly rates of pay can be given duties that require little skill and call for low hourly rates of pay. This type of misallocation of the work force will result in unfavorable labor rate variances, since the actual hourly rate of pay will exceed the standard rate authorized for the particular task being performed. A reverse situation exists when unskilled or untrained workers are assigned to jobs. The lower pay scale for these workers will result in favorable rate variances, although the workers may be highly inefficient in terms of output. Finally, unfavorable rate variances can arise from overtime work at premium rates if any portion of the overtime premium is added to the direct labor account.

Who is responsible for controlling the labor rate variance? Since rate variances generally arise as a result of how labor is used, those supervisors in charge of effective utilization of labor time bear responsibility for seeing that labor rate variances are kept under control.

Labor Efficiency Variance—A Closer Look

The quantity variance for direct labor, more commonly called the **labor efficiency variance,** measures the productivity of labor time. No variance is more closely watched by management, since increasing productivity of labor time is a vital key to reducing unit costs of production. From Exhibit 9–4, the formula for the labor efficiency variance would be expressed as follows:

$$(AH \times SR) - (SH \times SR) = \text{Labor efficiency variance}$$

Factored into simpler terms, the formula is:

$$SR(AH - SH) = \text{Labor efficiency variance}$$

Using the data from Exhibit 9–4 in the formula, we have:

$$\$14(4{,}500 \text{ hours} - 5{,}000 \text{ hours*}) = \$7{,}000 \text{ F}$$

* 2.000 units × 2.5 hours per unit = 5,000 hours.

Causes of the labor efficiency variance include poorly trained workers; poor quality materials, requiring more labor time in processing; faulty equipment, causing breakdowns and work interruptions; and poor supervision of workers. The managers in charge of production would generally be responsible for control of the labor efficiency variance. However, the variance might be chargeable to purchasing if the acquisition of poor materials resulted in excessive labor processing time.

USING STANDARD COSTS—VARIABLE OVERHEAD VARIANCES

The variable portion of manufacturing overhead can be analyzed and controlled using the same basic variance formulas that are used in analyzing direct materials and direct labor. To lay a foundation for the following chapter, where we discuss overhead control at length, it will be helpful at this time to illustrate the analysis of variable overhead using these basic formulas. As a basis for discussion, we will again use the cost data found in Exhibit

EXHIBIT 9–5
Variance Analysis—Variable Overhead

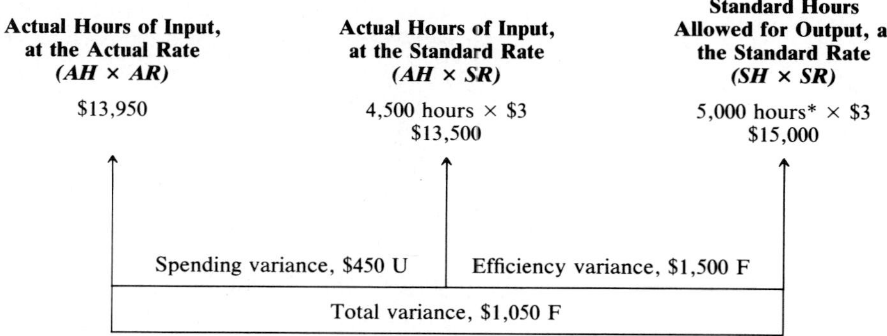

* 2,000 units × 2.5 hours per unit = 5,000 hours.
F = Favorable.
U = Unfavorable.

9–1. The exhibit shows the standard variable overhead cost per unit of product in our mythical company to be:

$$2.5 \text{ hours} \times \$3.00 = \$7.50$$

We will assume that the total actual variable overhead cost for the month of June was $13,950. Recall from our earlier discussion that 4,500 hours of direct labor time were recorded during the month and that the company produced 2,000 units of product. Exhibit 9–5 contains an analysis of the variable overhead variances.

Notice the similarities between Exhibits 9–4 and 9–5. These similarities arise from the fact that direct labor-hours are being used as a base for allocating overhead to units of product; thus, the same hours figures appear in Exhibit 9–5 for variable overhead as in Exhibit 9–4 for direct labor. The main difference between the two exhibits is in the standard hourly rate being used, which is much lower for variable overhead.

Overhead Variances—A Closer Look

As its name implies, the **variable overhead spending variance** measures deviations in amounts spent for overhead inputs such as lubricants and utilities. The formula for the variance can be expressed as:

$$(AH \times AR) - (AH \times SR) = \text{Variable overhead spending variance}$$

Or, factored into simpler terms:

$$AH(AR - SR) = \text{Variable overhead spending variance}$$

Using the data from Exhibit 9–5 in the formula, we have:

$$4{,}500 \text{ hours}(\$3.10^* - \$3.00) = \$450 \text{ U}$$

* $13,950 ÷ 4,500 hours = $3.10.

The **variable overhead efficiency variance** is a measure of the difference between the actual activity of a period and the standard activity allowed, multiplied by the variable part of the predetermined overhead rate. The formula for the variance can be expressed as:

$$(AH \times SR) - (SH \times SR) = \text{Variable overhead efficiency variance}$$

Or, factored into simpler terms:

$$SR(AH - SH) = \text{Variable overhead efficiency variance}$$

Again using the data from Exhibit 9–5, the computation of the variance would be:

$$\$3(4{,}500 \text{ hours} - 5{,}000 \text{ hours*}) = \$1{,}500 \text{ F}$$

* 2,000 units × 2.5 hours per unit = 5,000 hours.

We will reserve further discussion of the variable overhead spending and efficiency variances until Chapter 10, where overhead analysis is discussed in depth.

Before proceeding further, it will be helpful for the reader to pause at this point and go back and review the data contained in Exhibits 9–1 through 9–5. These exhibits and the accompanying text discussion represent a comprehensive, integrated illustration of standard setting and variance analysis.

VARIANCE ANALYSIS AND MANAGEMENT BY EXCEPTION

Variance analysis and performance reports provide a vehicle for implementation of the concept of *management by exception*. Simply put, management by exception means that the manager's attention must be directed toward those parts of the organization where things are not proceeding according to plans. Since a manager's time is limited, every hour must be used as effectively as possible, and time and effort must not be wasted looking after those parts of the organization where things are going smoothly.

The budgets and standards discussed in this chapter and in the preceding chapter represent the "plans" of management. If all goes smoothly, then costs would be expected to fall within the budgets and standards that have been set. To the extent that this happens, the manager is free to spend time elsewhere, with the assurance that at least in the budgeted areas all is proceeding according to expectations. To the extent that actual costs and revenues do not conform to the budget, however, a signal comes to the manager that an "exception" has occurred. This exception comes in the form of a variance from the budget or standard that was originally set.

The major question at this point is, "Are *all* variances to be considered exceptions that will require the attention of management?" The answer is no. If every variance were considered an exception, then management would get little else done other than chasing down nickel-and-dime differences. It is probably safe to say that only by the rarest of coincidences will actual costs and revenues ever conform exactly to the budgeted pattern. The reason is that even though budgets may be prepared with the greatest of care, it will never be possible to develop budgeted data that contain the precise allowances necessary for each of the multitude of variables that can

EXHIBIT 9–6
A Statistical Control Chart

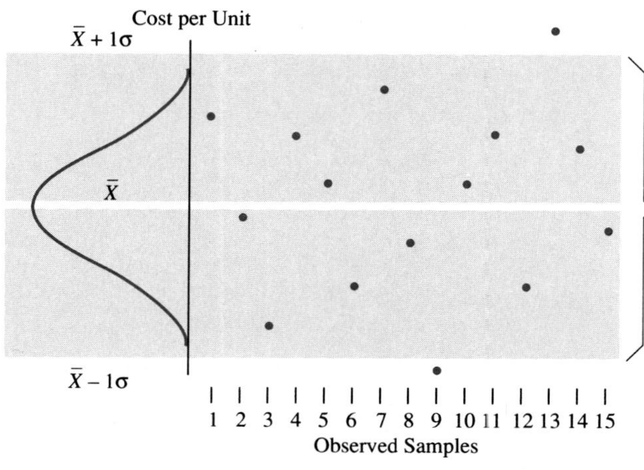

affect actual costs and revenues. For this reason, one can expect that in every period virtually every budgeted figure will produce a variance of some type when compared to actual cost data. How do managers decide which variances are really "exceptions" and which are due simply to chance or random causes? The most dependable approach to separating "exceptions" from random variances can be found in statistical analysis.

The statistical approach to separating variances has its basis in the idea that a budget or standard represents a *range* of activity, rather than a single point. Any variance falling within this range is considered to be due solely to random causes that either are not within the ability of management to control or that would be impractical to control. One author puts the idea this way:

> Measured quality of manufactured product is always subject to a certain amount of variation as a result of chance. Some stable "system of chance causes" is inherent in any particular scheme of production and inspection. Variation within this stable pattern is inevitable. The reasons for variation outside this stable pattern [should] be discovered and corrected.[5]

How does a firm isolate the range within which variances from budget will be due to chance or random causes? This is done by means of statistical sampling of the population represented by the budgeted data. Random samples of the population are drawn, and the variances found in these samples are plotted on a *control chart* such as that illustrated in Exhibit 9–6. In effect, the upper and lower limits on the chart represent the normal distribution (bell-shaped curve), with the upper and lower limits generally being at least one standard deviation from the grand mean. Any variances falling within the upper and lower control limits will be due simply to chance

[5] Eugene L. Grant and Richard L. Leavenworth, *Statistical Quality Control,* 4th ed. (New York: McGraw-Hill, 1972), p. 3. Used with permission of McGraw-Hill Book Company.

occurrences and, therefore, either will not be within the ability of management to control or will not be large enough to warrant management time. Any variances falling outside these limits will not be due to random or chance causes and will be considered "exceptions" toward which management attention will need to be directed.[6]

PERFORMANCE MEASURES IN AN AUTOMATED ENVIRONMENT

As stated earlier, standard costs are widely used in manufacturing, service, food, and not-for-profit organizations. Indeed, the list of companies that employ standards as a method for controlling costs and for measuring performance continues to grow. In an automated environment, however, the traditional standards discussed on preceding pages are being used less frequently and in many cases are deemed inappropriate for management's needs. In place of these standards, a wide range of new performance measures is emerging.

Standard Costs and Automation

There are several reasons why traditional standards are deemed to be inappropriate in an automated environment. First, in this new environment, labor is less significant and tends to be more fixed. Thus, the traditional labor variances are of little value to management, and a focus on items such as the labor efficiency variance may even prompt companies to overproduce and create needless inventories. Second, a key objective in the new manufacturing environment is to increase quality rather than to just minimize cost. Managers argue that a preoccupation with items such as the materials price variance often results in the purchase of low-quality materials or in the stockpiling of materials in order to take advantage of quantity discounts. Finally, the manufacturing process is more reliable and consistent in an automated environment, and as a result the traditional variances are either minimal or cease to exist.

New Performance Measures

Many new performance measures are emerging as managers seek to streamline their operations, to improve quality and service, and to employ sophisticated new concepts such as JIT and FMS. These new measures can be classified into five general groupings consisting of quality control, material control, inventory control, machine performance, and delivery performance. These groupings, along with the specific measures that they encompass, are provided in Exhibit 9–7.

The new performance measures listed in the exhibit are more subjective than traditional standard costs, and they tend to be nonfinancial in nature. Also, their computation and use differs in several ways from standard costs. First, these new measures are often computed on an *on-line* basis so that management is able to monitor activities continually. On-line access to data

[6] For further discussion of this and other statistical uses in cost analysis, see Joel S. Demski, *Information Analysis,* 2nd ed. (Reading, Mass: Addison-Wesley Publishing, 1980), chap. 6.

allows problems to be identified and corrected "on the factory floor" as the problems occur, rather than waiting several days for a report to be generated. This approach to the control process is easy when managers routinely use PCs in their work, as is true in many companies today. Second, many of the measures are computed at the *plant* level in order to emphasize the concept of an integrated, interdependent operation. Although performance is also measured at the cell level, plantwide performance is especially important in an automated setting. And third, in using the measures, managers focus more directly on *trends* over time than on any particular change during the current period. The key objectives are *progress* and *improvement*, rather than meeting any specific standards.

In the following sections, we look at each of these groupings in more detail. The reader should be aware that the measures included in these groupings are representative and not exhaustive of the possibilities. Many other measures are possible, depending on individual company needs.

EXHIBIT 9–7
Operating Measures in a JIT/FMS Setting

Measures	**Desired Change**
Quality Control Measures	
Number of Warranty Claims	Decrease
Number of Customer Complaints	Decrease
Number of Defects	Decrease
Cost of Rework	Decrease
Material Control Measures	
Material as a Percentage of Total Cost	Decrease
Lead Time	Decrease
Scrap as a Percentage of Good Pieces	Decrease
Scrap as a Percentage of Total Cost	Decrease
Actual Scrap Loss	Decrease
Inventory Control Measures	
Inventory Turnover:	
Raw Materials (By Type)	Increase
Finished Goods (By Product)	Increase
Number of Inventoried Items	Decrease
Machine Performance Measures	
Percentage of Machine Availability	Increase
Percentage of Machine Downtime	Decrease
Setup Time	
Machine Stops (Breakdowns)	
Preventative Maintenance	
Use as a Percentage of Availability	Increase
Setup Time	Decrease
Delivery Performance Measures	
Percentage of On-Time Deliveries	Increase
Delivery Cycle Time	Decrease
Throughput Time, or Velocity	Decrease
Manufacturing Cycle Efficiency (MCE)	Increase
Order Backlog	Decrease
Total Throughput	Increase

Quality Control Measures

We have stated several times in preceding chapters that high quality is a major objective in the new manufacturing environment. To monitor quality, managers look at measures such as warranty claims, customer complaints, and defects in units. Although such items have always been watched by management, the difference today is *speed*. Immediate steps are taken to correct defects in design that may result in claims, and immediate steps are taken to resolve complaints. Managers have learned that insensitivity to such matters can be disastrous in markets that have become worldwide in scope.

In addition to the measures listed in Exhibit 9–7, some companies compute another measure called the **cost of quality.** This measure, which is stated in dollar amount, is a summation of all four quality measures given in the exhibit. It represents a total of all the specific costs that can be traced to producing a *non*quality product.

Material Control Measures

We stated above that traditional standard costing seeks to control material cost through the materials price variance. In an automated setting, the focus is in a different direction—it is toward higher quality, shorter lead time, and greater control over scrap. We have already discussed the quality issue at length so we will direct our comments toward the other two factors.

In Chapter 8, we defined the lead time as the interval between when an order is placed and when the order is finally received from the supplier. Where JIT is in use, the goal is to reduce the lead time to only a few hours so that materials are available immediately as needed all along the production line. Lead time is computed by supplier and by type of material so that undependable suppliers can be identified and eliminated.

A major difference between traditional standard costing and the new performance measures is the focus of the latter on the cost of scrap. Under standard costing, the cost of scrap is included as part of the materials quantity variance. But this variance doesn't include *all* the cost of scrap, since some "acceptable" level is built right into the standard itself. Under the new performance measures, scrap is treated as a separate item and there is no "acceptable" level. *Any* amount of scrap is viewed as a loss that must be eliminated. As shown in Exhibit 9–7, managers monitor progress toward achieving zero scrap by computing the dollar amount and the number of scrap parts to good parts.

Inventory Control Measures

Historically, companies have operated under the assumption that some level of inventory was needed to act as a buffer against stockouts. Now managers are recognizing that the cost of carrying inventory is much greater than was previously supposed. As a result, we have learned that orders are placed more frequently and in smaller amounts. We have also learned that the goal of JIT is to have zero inventories on hand. To monitor progress toward this goal, companies compute inventory turnover by type of material and also by individual product. Broadly defined, **inventory turnover** means how many times the average inventory balance has been used (and thereby replaced) during the period. The smaller the inventory balance, the greater the number of times that turnover will occur. Therefore, an increase in the turnover rate is a positive indicator of progress toward reducing the amount of inventory on hand.

Machine Performance Measures

The most significant trend in the new manufacturing environment is toward greater use of automation. With greater automation comes a massive, fixed investment in equipment that requires considerably more attention from management than is needed in a nonautomated setting. Several measures have been developed to determine the availability and use of equipment, as shown in Exhibit 9–7.

The first two of these measures, which focus on machine availability and machine downtime, are the inverse of each other. That is, if a machine isn't available, then it's down for some reason; the reasons for being down are given in the exhibit. The goal, of course, is to minimize the amount of downtime so that machines are available as much as possible.

The third measure, "Use as a percentage of available capacity," is designed primarily for control of bottleneck operations, which hinder throughput. The goal in a bottleneck operation is to keep machine use at 100 percent of available capacity so that maximum output can be achieved. This measure has less significance in a *non*bottleneck operation since the goal there should be to use the equipment *only* as needed to support JIT production. Trying to achieve 100 percent use in a nonbottleneck operation might result in producing more than is required to maintain a smooth JIT flow, and thereby precipitate a needless buildup of inventory.

Setup time is a key element relating to all equipment. We learned in Chapter 2 that one of the central benefits of a flexible manufacturing system is the reduction in time required to change from one production run to another or to change from one job to another. Through FMS, companies have been able to reduce setup time in many cases from several hours to only a few minutes. Since setup time constitutes part of non-value-added time, throughput is increased in a cell or plant as it is reduced. Thus, setup time is carefully monitored to allow maximum machine availability.

Delivery Performance Measures

The purpose of production is to get a high-quality product into the hands of a customer as quickly as possible. If a customer has to wait months for a delivery and a competitor can provide the needed item in a few weeks, then the competitor probably will get the business. Thus, in the new manufacturing environment with its worldwide competition, speed has become equally as important as quality in gaining (or retaining) customers. Moreover, an automated plant has high operating leverage (due to its high fixed costs), and therefore it must obtain a large number of orders and fill them quickly if it expects to generate a satisfactory profit margin.

There are several key measures of delivery performance. As shown in Exhibit 9–7, the first of these is the percentage of on-time deliveries. Companies strive for 100 percent on-time deliveries, but whether or not this goal is

EXHIBIT 9–8
Delivery Cycle Time and Throughput (Manufacturing Cycle) Time

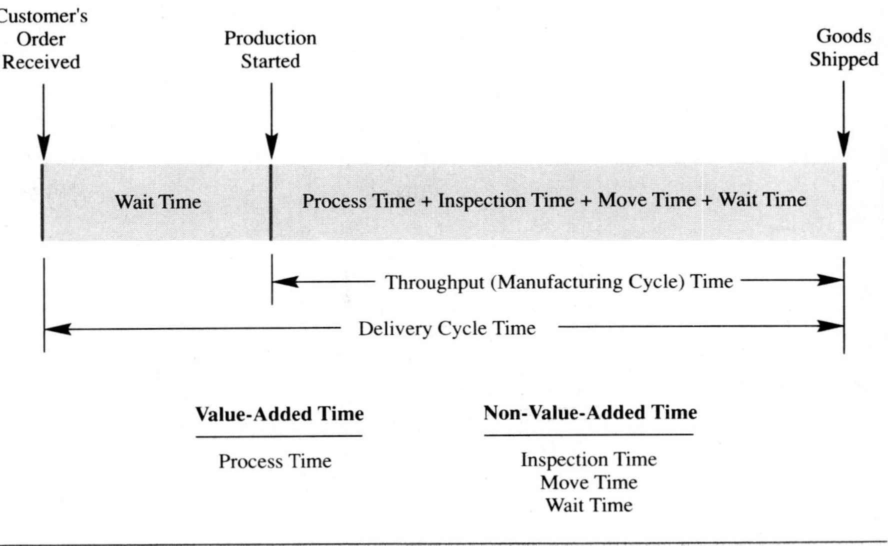

achieved depends on several other factors. One of these is the **delivery cycle time,** which represents the amount of time required from receipt of an order from a customer to shipment of the completed goods.[7] Another factor is the **throughput time,** which measures the amount of time required to turn raw materials into completed products. The throughput time is also known as the **manufacturing cycle time** or **velocity** of production. The relationship between the delivery cycle time and the throughput (manufacturing cycle) time is illustrated in Exhibit 9–8.

Through concerted efforts to eliminate waste and improve efficiency, some companies have reduced the delivery cycle time from five or six months to only a few weeks, and they have cut the throughput time to only a fraction of previous levels. The throughput time, which is considered to be a key measure in delivery performance, can be put into better perspective by computing the **manufacturing cycle efficiency (MCE).** The MCE is computed by relating the value-added time to the throughput time. The formula is:

$$\text{MCE} = \frac{\text{Value-added time}}{\text{Throughput (manufacturing cycle) time}}$$

If the MCE is less than 1, then it means that non-value-added time is present in the production process. An MCE of 0.5, for example, would mean that half of the total production time consisted of waiting, inspection, and similar non-value-added activities. In many manufacturing companies today, the MCE is less than 0.1 (10 percent), which means that 90 percent of the time a unit is in process is spent on activities that do not add value to the

[7] Sometimes the delivery cycle time is improperly referred to as the lead time. The term *lead time* should be used only in conjunction with the purchase of raw materials.

product.[8] By monitoring the MCE, companies are able to pare away non-value-added activities and thus get products into the hands of customers more quickly.

To provide a numeric example of these measures, assume the following data for Novex Company:

Novex Company keeps careful track of the time relating to orders and to the production of goods. During the most recent quarter, the following average times were recorded for each unit or order:

Inspection time	0.4 days
Process time	2.0 days
Move time	0.6 days
Wait time:	
From order to start of production	17.0 days
From start to completion of production	5.0 days

Goods are shipped as soon as production is completed.

Required

1. Compute the throughput time, or velocity of production.
2. Compute the manufacturing cycle efficiency (MCE).
3. What percentage of the production time is spent in non-value-added activities?
4. Compute the delivery cycle time.

Solution

1. Throughput time = Process time + Inspection time + Move time + Wait time
   = 2.0 days + 0.4 days + 0.6 days + 5.0 days
   = 8.0 days
2. Only process time represents value-added time; therefore, the computation of the MCE would be:

$$\text{MCE} = \frac{\text{Value-added time, 2.0 days}}{\text{Throughput time, 8.0 days}}$$
$$= 0.25$$

   As stated earlier in the chapter, the MCE puts the throughput time into perspective by showing how efficiently units are being produced. Thus, the MCE is 0.25, or 25%.
3. Since the MCE is 25%, the reciprocal of this figure, or 75% of the total production time, is spent in non-value-added activities.
4. Delivery cycle time = Wait time + Throughput time
   = 17.0 days + 8.0 days
   = 25.0 days

Use in a Nonautomated Environment

Although the new performance measures discussed on the preceding pages were developed specifically for use in the new manufacturing environment, many nonautomated companies are also beginning to use them. The reader should refer again to the list of performance measures given in Exhibit 9–7

[8] Callie Berlinger and James A. Brimson (eds.), *Cost Management for Today's Advanced Manufacturing* (Boston: Harvard Business School Press, 1988), p. 4.

and note that most of these measures would benefit nearly any organization. Moreover, these measures can be (and are) used side by side in some companies along with the standard costs developed earlier in the chapter.[9] In a nonautomated environment, such measures actually complement the use of standard costs since they focus on many key areas (such as warranty claims, on-time deliveries, and delivery cycle time) that traditional standards do not cover. In sum, there is nothing exclusive about the new performance measures; they simply represent added tools available to managers in the planning and control of operations.

SUMMARY

A standard is a benchmark or "norm" for measuring performance. Standards are found in many facets of life, including in the business community. In business organizations, standards are set for both the cost and the quantity of inputs needed to manufacture goods or to provide services. Quantity standards say how much of a cost element, such as labor time or raw materials, should be used in manufacturing a unit of product or in providing a unit of service. Cost standards say what the cost of the time or the materials should be.

Generally, standards are set by the cooperative effort of many people in an organization, including the accountant, the industrial engineer, and various levels of management. Standards are normally "practical" in nature, meaning that they can be attained by reasonable, though highly efficient, efforts. Such standards are generally felt to have a favorable motivational impact on employees.

When standards are compared against actual performance, the difference is referred to as a variance. Variances are computed and reported to management on a regular basis for both the price and the quantity elements of materials, labor, and overhead. Specific formulas are available to assist in these computations.

Not all variances are considered to be "exceptions" that require management time or attention. Rather, parameters or limits are set within which variances are considered to be due to chance causes. If a variance falls outside the limits set by management, it is then considered to be an exception toward which management time and attention must be directed.

In automated environments, the traditional standard costs are being used less frequently, and in many cases they are thought to be inappropriate for management's needs. In place of standard costs, managers have developed new performance measures that can be classified into five general groupings. These groupings consist of quality control measures, material control measures, inventory control measures, machine performance measures, and delivery performance measures. These new measures are generally computed on an on-line basis, with managers looking at the trend over time rather than toward the attainment of a specific standard.

[9] James A. Hendricks, "Applying Cost Accounting to Factory Automation," *Management Accounting* 70, no. 6 (December 1988), p. 28. This is an excellent study that provides many insights into current practice.

REVIEW PROBLEM ON STANDARD COSTS

Xavier Company produces a single product. The standard costs for one unit of product are:

Direct material: 6 ounces at $0.50 per ounce . . .	$ 3
Direct labor: 1.8 hours at $10 per hour	18
Variable overhead: 1.8 hours at $5 per hour . . .	9
Total standard variable cost per unit	$30

During June, 2,000 units were produced. The costs associated with the month were:

Material purchased: 18,000 ounces at $0.60 . . .	$10,800
Material used in production: 14,000 ounces . . .	—
Direct labor: 4,000 hours at $9.75.	39,000
Variable overhead costs incurred	20,800

Materials Variances

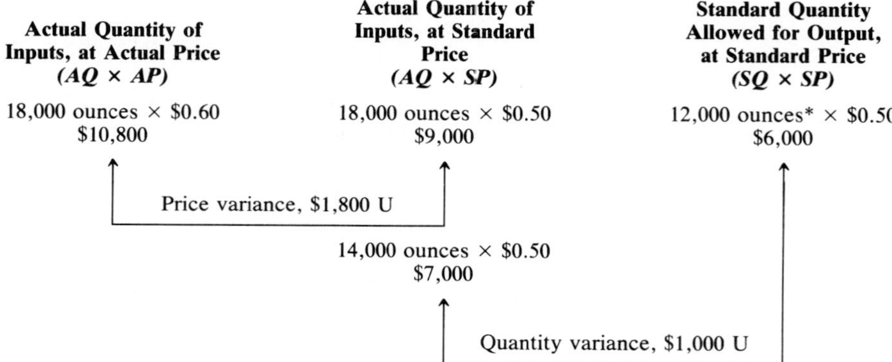

A total variance can't be computed in this situation, since the amount of materials purchased (18,000 ounces) differs from the amount of materials used in production (14,000 ounces).

* 2,000 units × 6 ounces = 12,000 ounces.

The same variances in shortcut format would be:

$$AQ(AP - SP) = \text{Materials price variance}$$
$$18{,}000 \text{ ounces}(\$0.60 - \$0.50) = \$1{,}800 \text{ U}$$
$$SP(AQ - SQ) = \text{Materials quantity variance}$$
$$\$0.50(14{,}000 \text{ ounces} - 12{,}000 \text{ ounces}) = \$1{,}000 \text{ U}$$

Notice that the price variance is computed on the entire amount of material purchased (18,000 ounces), whereas the quantity variance is computed only on the portion of this material used in production during the period (14,000 ounces). This is a common situation. The price variance is usually computed on whatever materials have been purchased. The quantity variance, however, is computed only on that portion of the purchased materials *actually used* during the period. In the example above, a quantity variance on the 4,000 ounces of materials that were purchased during the period but *not* used in production (18,000 ounces purchased − 14,000 ounces used = 4,000 ounces unused) will be computed in a future period when these materials are drawn out of inventory and used in the production process.

Labor Variances

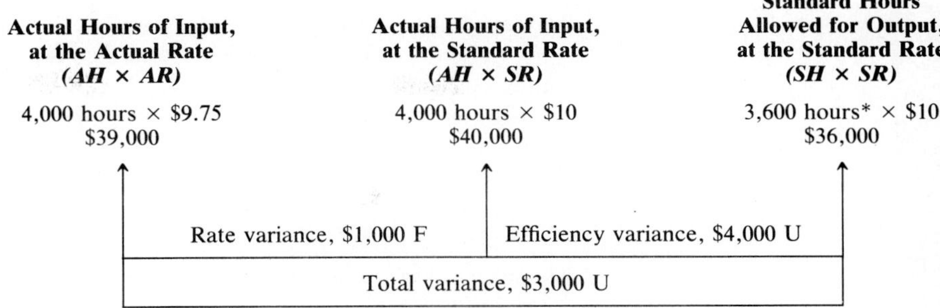

* 2,000 units × 1.8 hours = 3,600 hours.

The same variances in shortcut format would be:

$AH(AR - SR)$ = Labor rate variance
4,000 hours($9.75 − $10) = $1,000 F

$SR(AH - SH)$ = Labor efficiency variance
$10(4,000 hours − 3,600 hours) = $4,000 U

Variable Overhead Variances

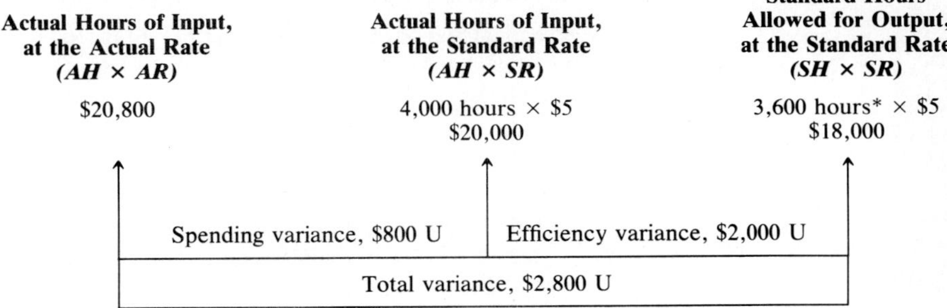

* 2,000 units × 1.8 hours = 3,600 hours.

The same variances in shortcut format would be:

$AH(AR - SR)$ = Variable overhead spending variance
4,000 hours($5.20* − $5.00) = $800 U

*$20,800 ÷ 4,000 hours = $5.20.

$SR(AH - SH)$ = Variable overhead efficiency variance
$5(4,000 hours − 3,600 hours) = $2,000 U

KEY TERMS FOR REVIEW

Bill of materials A listing of the type and quantity of each item of material required in the manufacture of a unit of product. (p. 362)

Cost of quality A summation of all quality measures. It represents a total of all the specific costs that can be traced to producing a nonquality product. (p. 377)

Delivery cycle time The amount of time required from receipt of an order from a customer to shipment of the completed goods. (p. 379)

Ideal standards Standards that allow for no machine breakdowns or other work interruptions and that require peak efficiency at all times. (p. 361)

Inventory turnover The number of times the average inventory balance has been used (and thereby replaced) during the period. (p. 377)

Labor efficiency variance A measure of the difference between the actual hours required to complete a task and the standard hours allowed, multiplied by the standard hourly rate. (p. 370)

Labor rate variance A measure of the difference between the actual hourly labor rate and the standard rate allowed, multiplied by the number of hours worked during the period. (p. 370)

Management by exception A system of management in which standards are set for various operating activities, with actual results then compared against these standards and any differences that are deemed significant brought to the attention of management as "exceptions." (p. 360)

Manufacturing cycle efficiency (MCE) Process (value-added) time as a percentage of throughput time. (p. 379)

Manufacturing cycle time See *Throughput time*. (p. 379)

Materials price variance A measure of the difference between the actual unit price paid for an item and the standard price that should have been paid, multiplied by the quantity purchased. (p. 366)

Materials quantity variance A measure of the difference between the actual quantity of materials used in production and the standard quantity allowed, multiplied by the standard price per unit of materials. (p. 368)

Practical standards Standards that allow for normal machine downtime and other work interruptions and that can be attained through reasonable, though highly efficient, efforts by the average worker at a task. (p. 362)

Standard cost card A detailed listing of the standard amounts of materials, labor, and overhead that should go into a unit of product, multiplied by the standard price or rate that has been set. (p. 361)

Standard cost per unit The expected cost of a unit of product as shown on the standard cost card; it is computed by multiplying the standard quantity or hours by the standard price or rate. (p. 364)

Standard hours allowed The time that should have been taken to complete the period's output as computed by multiplying the number of units produced by the standard hours per unit. (p. 366)

Standard hours per unit The amount of labor time that should be required to complete a single unit of product, including allowances for breaks, machine downtime, cleanup, rejects, and other normal inefficiencies. (p. 363)

Standard price per unit The price that should be paid for a single unit of materials, including allowances for quality, quantity purchased, freight-in, receiving, and other such costs, net of any discounts allowed. (p. 362)

Standard quantity allowed The amount of materials that should have been used to complete the period's output as computed by multiplying the number of units produced by the standard quantity per unit. (p. 366)

Standard quantity per unit The amount of materials that should be required to complete a single unit of product, including allowances for normal waste, spoilage, rejects, and similar inefficiencies. (p. 362)

Standard rate per hour The labor rate that should be incurred per hour of labor time, including allowances for employment taxes, fringe benefits, and other such labor costs. (p. 363)

Throughput time The amount of time required to turn raw materials into completed products. (p. 379)

Variable overhead efficiency variance A measure of the difference between the actual activity (direct labor-hours, machine-hours, or some other base) of a period and the standard activity allowed, multiplied by the variable part of the predetermined overhead rate. (p. 373)

Variable overhead spending variance A measure of the difference between the actual variable overhead cost incurred during a period and the standard cost that should have been incurred, based on the actual activity of the period. (p. 372)

Variance The difference between standard prices and quantities and actual prices and quantities. (p. 365)

Velocity A measure of the speed that goods move through the production process. See *Throughput time*. (p. 379)

APPENDIX: GENERAL LEDGER ENTRIES TO RECORD VARIANCES

Although standard costs and variances can be computed and used by management without being formally entered into the accounting records, most organizations prefer to make formal entries for three reasons. First, entry into the accounting records encourages early recognition of variances. As mentioned in the main body of the chapter, the earlier that variances can be recognized, the greater is their value to management in the control of costs. Second, formal entry tends to give variances a greater emphasis than is generally possible through informal, out-of-record computations. This emphasis gives a clear signal of management's desire to keep costs within the limits that have been set. Third, formal use of standard costs simplifies the bookkeeping process. By using standard costs within the accounting system itself, management eliminates the need to keep track of troublesome variations in actual costs and quantities, thereby providing for a flow of costs that is smoother, simpler, and more easily accounted for.

Direct Materials Variances

To illustrate the general ledger entries needed to record standard cost variances, we will return to the data contained in the review problem at the end of the chapter. The entry to record the purchase of direct materials would be:

Raw Materials (18,000 ounces at $0.50)	9,000	
Materials Price Variance (18,000 ounces at $0.10 U)	1,800	
Accounts Payable (18,000 ounces at $0.60)		10,800

Notice that the price variance is recognized when purchases are made, rather than when materials are actually used in production. This permits the price variance to be isolated early, and it also permits the materials to be carried in the inventory account at standard cost. As direct materials are later drawn from inventory and used in production, the quantity variance is isolated as follows:

Work in Process (12,000 ounces at $0.50)	6,000	
Materials Quantity Variance (2,000 ounces U at $0.50)	1,000	
Raw Materials (14,000 ounces at $0.50)		7,000

Thus, direct materials enter into the Work in Process account at standard cost, in terms of both price and quantity.

Notice that both the price variance and the quantity variance above are unfavorable, thereby showing up as debit (or additional cost) balances. If these variances had been favorable, they would have appeared as credit (or reduction in cost) balances, as in the case of the direct labor rate variance below.

Direct Labor Variances

Referring again to the cost data in the review problem at the end of the chapter, the general ledger entry to record the incurrence of direct labor cost would be:

Work in Process (3,600 hours at $10)	36,000	
Labor Efficiency Variance (400 hours U at $10).	4,000	
Labor Rate Variance (4,000 hours at $0.25 F).		1,000
Wages Payable (4,000 hours at $9.75)		39,000

Thus, as with direct materials, direct labor costs enter into the Work in Process account at standard, both in terms of the rate and in terms of the hours allowed for the production of the period.

Variable Overhead Variances

Variable overhead variances generally are not recorded in the accounts separately but rather are determined as part of the general analysis of overhead, which is discussed in Chapter 10.

QUESTIONS

9–1 What types of organizations make use of standard costs?

9–2 What is a quantity standard? What is a price standard?

9–3 What is the beginning point in setting a standard? Where should final responsibility for standard setting fall?

9–4 Why must a standard for the future be more than simply a projection of the past?

9–5 Distinguish between ideal and practical standards.

9–6 If employees are unable to meet a standard, what effect would you expect this to have on their productivity?

9–7 What is the difference between a standard and a budget?

9–8 What is meant by the term *variance?*

9–9 What is meant by the term *management by exception?*

9–10 Why are variances generally segregated in terms of a price variance and a quantity variance?

9–11 Who is generally responsible for the materials price variance? The materials quantity variance? The labor efficiency variance?

9–12 The materials price variance can be computed at what two different points in time? Which point is better? Why?

9–13 An examination of the cost records of the Chittenden Furniture Company indicates that the materials price variance is favorable but that the materials quantity variance is unfavorable by a substantial amount. What might this indicate?

9–14 What dangers lie in using standards as punitive tools?

9–15 "Our workers are all under labor contracts; therefore, our labor rate variance is bound to be zero." Discuss.

9–16 What effect, if any, would you expect poor quality materials to have on direct labor variances?

9–17 If variable manufacturing overhead is applied to production on a basis of direct labor-hours and the direct labor efficiency variance is unfavorable, will the variable overhead efficiency variance be favorable or unfavorable, or could it be either? Explain.

9–18 What factors are considered by management in determining whether a variance is properly called an exception?

9–19 What is a statistical control chart, and how is it used?

9–20 How does the nature, computation, and use of performance measures in an automated environment differ from the nature, computation, and use of standard costs?

9–21 Into what five general groupings can the JIT/FMS performance measures be placed?

9–22 What danger is there in trying to keep the use of equipment at 100 percent of available capacity in all operations?

9–23 What is the difference between the delivery cycle time and the throughput time? What four elements make up the throughput time? Into what two classes can these four elements be placed?

9–24 If a company has an MCE of less than 1, what does it mean? How would you interpret an MCE of 0.40?

9–25 (Appendix) What advantages can be cited in favor of making formal journal entries in the accounting records for variances?

EXERCISES

E9–1 Sonne Company produces a perfume called Whim. The direct materials and direct labor standards for one bottle of Whim are given below:

	Standard Quantity or Hours	Standard Price or Rate	Standard Cost
Direct materials . . .	7.2 ounces	$2.50 per ounce	$18
Direct labor	0.4 hours	$10 per hour	4

During the most recent month, the following activity was recorded:

a. Twenty thousand ounces of material were purchased at a cost of $2.40 per ounce.

b. All of the material was used to produce 2,500 bottles of Whim.

c. Nine hundred hours of direct labor time were recorded at a total labor cost of $10,800.

Required

1. Compute the direct materials price and quantity variances for the month.
2. Compute the direct labor rate and efficiency variances for the month.

E9–2 Refer to the data in Exercise 9–1. Assume that instead of producing 2,500 bottles of Whim during the month, the company produced only 2,000 bottles, using 16,000 ounces of material in the production process. (The rest of the material purchased remained in inventory.)

Required Compute the direct materials price and quantity variances for the month.

E9–3 Topper Toys has developed a new toy called the Brainbuster. The company has a standard cost system to help control costs and has established the following standards for the Brainbuster toy:

Direct materials: 8 pieces per toy at $0.30 per piece
Direct labor: 1.2 hours per toy at $7 per hour

During the month of August 19x4, the company produced 5,000 Brainbuster toys. Production data for the month on the toy follow:

Direct materials: 70,000 pieces were purchased for use in production at a cost of $0.28 per piece. Some 20,000 of these pieces were still in inventory at the end of the month.

Direct labor: 6,400 direct labor-hours were worked at a cost of $48,000.

Required

1. Compute the following variances for the month:
   a. Direct materials price and quantity variances.
   b. Direct labor rate and efficiency variances.
2. Prepare a brief explanation of the significance and possible causes of each variance.

E9–4 As business organizations grow in size and complexity, cost control becomes more difficult. A system to provide information and assist in cost control is imperative for effective management. Management by exception is one technique that is often used to foster cost control.

Required

1. Describe how a standard cost system helps to make management by exception possible.
2. Discuss the potential benefits of management by exception to an organization.
3. Identify and discuss the behavioral problems that might occur in an organization using standard costs and management by exception.

(CMA, Adapted)

E9–5 Harmon Household Products, Inc., manufactures a number of consumer items for general household use. One of these products, a chopping board, requires an expensive hardwood in its manufacture. During a recent month, the company manufactured 4,000 chopping boards, using 11,000 board feet of hardwood in the process. The hardwood cost the company $18,700.

The company's standards for one chopping board are 2.5 board feet of hardwood, at a cost of $1.80 per board foot.

Required

1. What cost for wood should have been incurred in the manufacture of the 4,000 chopping blocks? How much greater or less is this than the cost that was incurred?
2. Break down the difference computed in (1) above in terms of a materials price variance and a materials quantity variance.

E9–6 Hollowell Audio, Inc., manufactures compact discs. The company uses standards to control its costs. The labor standards that have been set for one disc are as follows:

Standard Hours	Standard Rate per Hour	Standard Cost
24 minutes	$6.00	$2.40

During July, 8,500 hours of direct labor time were recorded in the manufacture of 20,000 discs. The direct labor cost totaled $49,300 for the month.

Required

1. What direct labor cost should have been incurred in the manufacture of the 20,000 discs? By how much does this differ from the cost that was incurred?
2. Break down the difference in cost from (1) above into a labor rate variance and a labor efficiency variance.
3. The budgeted variable overhead rate is $4 per direct labor-hour. During July, the company incurred $39,100 in variable overhead cost. Compute the variable overhead spending and efficiency variances for the month.

E9–7 Kelson Products manufactures a gasoline additive. Each bottle of additive requires two items of material, Benol and Protex, as described below:

a. Benol is purchased in 10-gallon containers at a cost of $60 per container. Freight is paid by the supplier. Discount terms of 2/10, n/30 are offered by the supplier, and Kelson Products takes all discounts.

b. Protex is purchased in 80-pound boxes at a cost of $30 per box. Kelson Products must pay all freight charges, which amount to $420 for an average shipment of 100 boxes. About 5 percent of the Protex is lost in shipment to Kelson's warehouse.

Required

1. Compute the following:
   a. The standard price of a quart of Benol.
   b. The standard price of a pound of Protex.
2. Assume that each bottle of additive requires 1.2 quarts of Benol and 0.6 pounds of Protex. Prepare a standard cost card showing the standard cost of material in a bottle of additive. (Carry computations to three decimal places.)

E9–8 The Worldwide Credit Card, Inc., uses standards to control the labor time involved in opening mail from card holders and recording the enclosed remittances. Incoming mail is gathered into batches, and a standard time is set for opening and recording each batch. The labor standards relating to one batch are given below:

	Standard Hours	Standard Rate	Standard Cost
Per batch	2.5	$6	$15

The record showing the time spent last week in opening batches of mail has been misplaced. However, the batch supervisor recalls that 168 batches were received and opened during the week, and the controller recalls the following variance data relating to these batches:

Total labor variance	$330 U
Labor rate variance	150 F

Required

1. Determine the number of actual labor-hours spent opening batches during the week.
2. Determine the actual hourly rate paid to employees for opening batches last week.

(Hint: A useful way to proceed would be to work from known to unknown data either by using the variance formulas or by using the columnar format shown in Exhibit 9–4.)

E9–9 Lipex, Inc., has automated one of its plants and employs both JIT and FMS concepts. For the first quarter of operations, the following data were reported for each unit or each order processed:

Inspection time	0.5 days
Process time	2.8 days
Wait time:	
From order to start of production	16.0 days
From start to completion of production . . .	4.0 days
Move time	0.7 days

Management is unsure how to use these data to measure performance and control operations.

Required

1. Compute the throughput time, or velocity of production.
2. Compute the manufacturing cycle efficiency (MCE) for the quarter. How do you interpret the MCE?
3. What percentage of the throughput time was spend in non-value-added activities?
4. Compute the delivery cycle time.
5. If by use of JIT all wait time can be eliminated in production, what would be the new MCE?

E9–10 (Appendix) Aspen Products, Inc., began production of product A on April 1, 19x8. The company uses a standard cost system and has established the following standards for one unit of product A:

	Standard Quantity	Standard Price or Rate	Standard Cost
Direct materials . . .	3.5 feet	$6 per foot	$21
Direct labor	0.4 hours	$10 per hour	4

During the month of April, the following activity was recorded relative to product A:

a. Purchased 7,000 feet of material at a cost of $5.75 per foot.
b. Used 6,000 feet of material to produce 1,500 units of product A.
c. Worked 725 direct labor-hours on product A at a cost of $8,120.

Required

1. For materials:
   a. Compute the direct materials price and quantity variances.
   b. Prepare journal entries to record the purchase of materials and the use of materials in production.
2. For direct labor:
   a. Compute the direct labor rate and efficiency variances.
   b. Prepare journal entries to record the incurrence of direct labor cost for the month.
3. Post the entries you have prepared to the T-accounts below:

Raw Materials

	Debit	Credit
	?	?
Bal.	?	

Accounts Payable

Debit	Credit
	40,250

Materials Price Variance

Debit	Credit

Wages Payable

Debit	Credit
	8,120

Materials Quantity Variance

Debit	Credit

Labor Rate Variance

Debit	Credit

Work in Process—Product A	
Materials used ?	
Labor cost ?	

Labor Efficiency Variance	

PROBLEMS

P9–11 **Straightforward Variance Analysis** Barberry, Inc., manufactures a product called Fruta. The company uses a standard cost system and has established the following standards for one unit of Fruta:

	Standard Quantity	Standard Price or Rate	Standard Cost
Direct materials	1.5 pounds	\$6 per pound	\$ 9.00
Direct labor	0.6 hours	\$12 per hour	7.20
Variable overhead . . .	0.6 hours	\$2.50 per hour	1.50
			\$17.70

During June 19x8, the following activity was recorded by the company relative to production of Fruta:

a. The company produced 3,000 units during the month.
b. A total of 8,000 pounds of material were purchased at a cost of \$46,000.
c. There was no beginning inventory of materials on hand to start the month; at the end of the month, 2,000 pounds of material remained in the warehouse unused.
d. The company employs 10 persons to work on the production of Fruta. During June, each worked an average of 160 hours at an average rate of \$12.50 per hour.
e. Variable overhead is assigned to Fruta on a basis of direct labor-hours. Variable overhead costs during June totaled \$3,600.

The company's management is anxious to determine the efficiency of the activities surrounding the production of Fruta.

Required

1. For materials used in the production of Fruta:
   a. Compute the price and quantity variances.
   b. The materials were purchased from a new supplier who is anxious to enter into a long-term purchase contract. Would you recommend that the company sign the contract? Explain.
2. For labor employed in the production of Fruta:
   a. Compute the rate and efficiency variances.
   b. In the past, the 10 persons employed in the production of Fruta consisted of four senior workers and six assistants. During June, the company experimented with five senior workers and five assistants. Would you recommend that the new labor mix be continued? Explain.
3. Compute the variable overhead spending and efficiency variances. What relationship can you see between this efficiency variance and the labor efficiency variance?

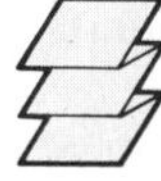

P9–12 **Computations from Incomplete Data** Topaz Company produces a single product. The company has set standards as follows for materials and labor:

	Direct Materials	Direct Labor
Standard quantity or hours per unit . . .	? pounds	2.5 hours
Standard price or rate	? per pound	\$9 per hour
Standard cost per unit	?	\$22.50

During the past month, the company purchased 6,000 pounds of direct materials at a cost of $16,500. All of this material was used in the production of 1,400 units of product. Direct labor cost totaled $28,500 for the month. The following variances have been computed:

Materials quantity variance	$1,200 U
Total materials variance	300 F
Labor efficiency variance	4,500 F

Required

1. For direct materials:
   a. Compute the standard price per pound for materials.
   b. Compute the standard quantity allowed for materials for the month's production.
   c. Compute the standard quantity of materials allowed per unit of product.
2. For direct labor:
   a. Compute the actual direct labor cost per hour for the month.
   b. Compute the labor rate variance.

(Hint: In completing the problem, it may be helpful to move from known to unknown data either by using the variance formulas or by using the columnar format shown in Exhibits 9–3 and 9–4.)

P9–13 **Setting Labor Standards** Mason Company is going to expand its punch press department. The company is about to purchase several new punch presses from Equipment Manufacturers, Inc. Equipment Manufacturers' engineers report that their mechanical studies indicate that for Mason's intended use, the output rate for one press should be 1,000 pieces per hour. Mason Company has similar presses now in operation. At present, production from these presses averages 600 pieces per hour.

A detailed study of Mason Company's experience shows that the average is derived from the following individual outputs:

Worker	**Output per Hour (pieces)**
J. Smith	750
H. Brown	750
R. Jones	600
J. Hardy	550
P. Clark	500
B. Randall	450
Total	3,600
Average	600

Mason's management also plans to institute a standard cost accounting system in the near future. The company's engineers are supporting a standard based on 1,000 pieces per hour; the accounting department is arguing for a standard of 750 pieces per hour; and the department supervisor is arguing for a standard of 600 pieces per hour.

Required

1. What arguments would each proponent be likely to use to support his or her case?
2. Which alternative best reconciles the needs of cost control and motivation for improved performance? Explain the reasons for your choice.

(CMA, Adapted)

P9–14 **Hospital; Basic Variance Analysis** "What's going on in that lab?" asked Derek Warren, chief administrator for Cottonwood Hospital, as he studied the prior month's reports. "Every month the lab teeters between a profit and a loss. Are we going to have to increase our lab fees again?"

"We can't," replied Lois Ankers, the controller. "We're getting *lots* of complaints about the last increase, particularly from the insurance companies and governmental health units. They're now paying only about 80 percent of what we bill. I'm beginning to think the problem is on the cost side."

To determine if lab costs are in line with other hospitals, Mr. Warren has asked you to evaluate the costs for the past month. Ms. Ankers has provided you with the following information:

a. Two basic types of tests are performed in the lab—smears and blood tests. During the past month, 2,700 smears and 900 blood tests were performed in the lab.

b. Small glass plates are used in both types of tests. During the past month, the hospital purchased 16,000 plates at a cost of $38,400 (net of a 4 percent quantity discount). A total of 2,000 of these plates were still on hand unused at the end of the month; there were no plates on hand at the beginning of the month.

c. During the past month, 1,800 hours of labor time were used in performing smears and blood tests. The cost of this labor time was $18,450.

d. Variable overhead cost last month in the lab for utilities and supplies totaled $11,700.

Cottonwood Hospital has never used standard costs. By searching industry literature, however, you have determined the following nationwide averages for hospital labs:

Plates: Three plates are required per lab test. These plates cost $2.50 each and are disposed of after the test is completed.

Labor: Each smear should require 0.3 hours to complete, and each blood test should require 0.6 hours to complete. The average cost of this lab time is $12 per hour.

Overhead: Overhead cost is based on direct labor-hours. The average rate for variable overhead is $6 per hour.

Mr. Warren would like a complete analysis of the cost of plates, labor, and variable overhead in the lab for last month so that he can determine if costs in the lab are indeed out of line.

Required

1. Compute the materials price variance for the plates purchased last month, and compute a materials quantity variance for the plates used last month.
2. For labor cost in the lab:
   a. Compute a labor rate variance and a labor efficiency variance.
   b. In most hospitals, three fourths of the workers in the lab are certified technicians and one fourth are assistants. In an effort to reduce costs, Cottonwood Hospital employs only one half certified technicians and one half assistants. Would you recommend that this policy be continued? Explain.
3. Compute the variable overhead spending and efficiency variances. Is there any relationship between the variable overhead efficiency variance and the labor efficiency variance? Explain.

P9–15 The Impact of Variances on Unit Costs; Basic Variance Analysis Sparks Company produces a number of products. The standards relating to one of these products are shown below, along with actual cost data for July 19x8 (per unit):

	Standard Cost		Actual Cost
Direct materials:			
Standard: 2.8 yards at $3.50 per yard	$ 9.80		
Actual: 2.75 yards at $3.60 per yard			$ 9.90
Direct labor:			
Standard: 0.8 hours at $9 per hour	7.20		
Actual: 0.9 hours at $8.50 per hour			7.65
Variable overhead:			
Budget: 0.8 hours at $2.50 per hour	2.00		
Actual: 0.9 hours at $2.40 per hour			2.16
Total cost per unit.	$19.00		$19.71
Excess of actual unit cost over standard		$0.71	

The production superintendent was disturbed when he saw these cost figures. He explained to one of his assistants, "This 71-cent variance doesn't look like much when you're talking about only one unit of product, but when you consider that we produce thousands of these a year, it can really add up fast. We need to isolate and correct the cost problem before any real damage is done to profits."

Actual production for the month was 4,000 units. Overhead is assigned to products on a basis of direct labor-hours.

Required

1. Compute the following variances for the month of July:
   a. Materials price and quantity.
   b. Labor rate and efficiency.
   c. Overhead spending and efficiency.
2. Show how much of the 71 cents excessive unit cost is traceable to each of the variances computed in (1) above.
3. Show how much of the 71 cents excessive unit cost is traceable to the inefficient use of labor time.

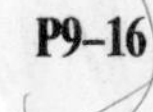

P9–16 **JIT/FMS Performance Measures** Devani Products, Inc., has automated its plant and set up a flexible manufacturing system. The company is also trying to move toward a JIT inventory system. This has been a dramatic move for the company after operating a traditional, labor-based facility for many years. Progress has been slow, particularly in trying to measure performance in the factory.

The company has gathered the following data relating to operating activities over the last four months:

	Month			
	1	2	3	4
Quality control measures:				
Number of warranty claims	27	24	19	16
Number of customer complaints	31	32	24	18
Material control measures:				
Purchase order lead time	6 days	6 days	5 days	4 days
Scrap as a percent of good pieces . . .	3%	3%	4%	5%
Inventory control measures:				
Raw material turnover (times)	20	19	17	15
Finished goods turnover (times)	11	10	8	6
Machine performance measures:				
Percentage of machine availability . . .	98%	96%	92%	90%
Use as a percentage of availability . . .	95%	89%	88%	85%
Setup time (hours)	1.9	2.3	2.5	2.7
Delivery performance measures:				
Percentage of on-time deliveries	93%	91%	89%	84%
Delivery cycle time	?	?	?	?
Throughput time, or velocity.	?	?	?	?
Manufacturing cycle efficiency (MCE) .	?	?	?	?

Management is uncertain how to compute the delivery cycle time, the throughput time, and the MCE, and has asked for your assistance. You have gathered the following data from the computer relating to these measures:

	Average per Month (in days)			
	1	2	3	4
Inspection time per unit	0.9	0.8	0.9	0.9
Process time per unit	1.7	1.6	1.7	1.8
Wait time per unit during production	5.6	6.2	7.0	8.0
Wait time per order before start of production	16.5	18.0	19.0	21.0
Move time per unit	0.3	0.4	0.4	0.3

Required

1. For each month, compute the following performance measures:
   a. The throughput time, or velocity of prodution.
   b. The manufacturing cycle efficiency (MCE).
   c. The delivery cycle time.
2. Using the performance measures given in the main body of the problem and the performance measures computed in (1) above, do the following:
   a. Identify the areas where the company seems to be improving.
   b. Identify the areas where performance seems to be deteriorating and, from scrutiny of the various measures, explain why this deterioration is taking place.
3. Refer to the inspection time, process time, and so forth given above for month 4.
   a. Assume in month 5 the inspection time, process time, and so forth are the same as in month 4, except that through the use of JIT the company is able to completely eliminate the wait time during production. Compute the new throughput time and MCE.
   b. Assume in month 6 the inspection time, process time, and so forth are again the same as in month 4, except that the company is able to eliminate both the wait time during production and the inspection time. Compute the new throughput time and MCE.

P9–17 Basic Variance Analysis Portland Company's Ironton Plant produces precast ingots for industrial use. Carlos Santiago, who was recently appointed general manager of the Ironton Plant, has just been handed the plant's income statement for October 19x4. The statement is shown below:

	Budgeted	Actual
Sales (5,000 ingots)	$250,000	$250,000
Less variable expenses:		
Variable cost of goods sold*	80,000	96,390
Variable selling expenses	20,000	20,000
Total variable expenses	100,000	116,390
Contribution margin	150,000	133,610
Less fixed expenses:		
Manufacturing overhead	60,000	60,000
Selling and administrative	75,000	75,000
Total fixed expenses	135,000	135,000
Net income (loss)	$ 15,000	$ (1,390)

* Contains direct materials, direct labor, and variable overhead.

Mr. Santiago was shocked to see the loss for the month, particularly since sales were exactly as budgeted. He stated, "I sure hope the plant has a standard cost system in operation. If it doesn't, I won't have the slightest idea of where to start looking for the problem.''

The plant does use a standard cost system, with the following standard variable cost per ingot:

	Standard Quantity or Hours	Standard Price or Rate	Standard Cost
Direct materials	4.0 pounds	$2.50 per pound	$10.00
Direct labor	0.6 hours	$9.00 per hour	5.40
Variable overhead	0.3 hours*	$2.00 per hour	0.60
Total standard variable cost			$16.00

* Based on machine-hours.

Mr. Santiago has determined that during the month of October the plant produced 5,000 units and incurred the following costs:

a. Purchased 25,000 pounds of materials at a cost of $2.95 per pound. There were no raw materials in inventory at the beginning of the month.
b. Used 19,800 pounds of materials in production. (Finished goods and work in process inventories are nominal and can be ignored.)
c. Worked 3,600 direct labor-hours at a cost of $8.70 per hour.
d. Incurred a total variable overhead cost of $4,320 for the month. A total of 1,800 machine-hours was recorded.

It is the company's policy to close all variances to cost of goods sold on a monthly basis.

Required

1. Compute the following variances for the month:
   a. Direct materials price and quantity variances.
   b. Direct labor rate and efficiency variances.
   c. Variable overhead spending and efficiency variances.
2. Summarize the variances that you computed in (1) above by showing the net overall favorable or unfavorable variance for the month. What impact did this figure have on the company's income statement?
3. Pick out the two most significant variances that you computed in (1) above. Explain to Mr. Santiago the possible causes of these variances, so that he will know where to concentrate his and his subordinates' time.

P9–18 Standards and Variances from Incomplete Data Vitalite, Inc., produces a number of products, including a body-wrap kit. Standard variable costs relating to a single kit are given below:

	Standard Quantity or Hours	Standard Price or Rate	Standard Cost
Direct materials	?	$6 per yard	$?
Direct labor	?	?	?
Variable overhead	?	$2 per hour	?
Total standard cost per kit			$42

During August 19x9, 500 kits were manufactured and sold. Selected information relating to the month's production is given below:

	Materials Used	Direct Labor	Variable Overhead
Total standard cost*	$?	$8,000	$1,600
Actual costs incurred	10,000	?	1,620
Materials price variance	?		
Materials quantity variance	600 U		
Labor rate variance		?	
Labor efficiency variance		?	
Overhead spending variance			?
Overhead efficiency variance			?

* For the month's production.

The following additional information is available for August production of kits:

Actual direct labor-hours	900
Overhead is based on	Direct labor-hours
Difference between standard and actual cost per kit produced during August	$0.14 U

Required

1. What was the total standard cost of the materials used during August?
2. How many yards of material are required at standard per kit?
3. What was the materials price variance for August?
4. What is the standard direct labor rate per hour?
5. What was the labor rate variance for the month? The labor efficiency variance?
6. What was the overhead spending variance for the month? The overhead efficiency variance?
7. Complete the standard cost card for one kit shown at the beginning of the problem.

P9–19 **JIT/FMS Performance Measures** After operating for many years as a labor-based facility, DataSpan, Inc., automated its plant at the start of the current year and installed a flexible manufacturing system. The company is also evaluating its suppliers and moving toward a JIT inventory system. Many adjustment problems have been encountered, among which are problems relating to performance measurement. After much study, the company has decided to use the performance measures below, and it has gathered data relating to these measures for the first four months of operations.

	Month			
	1	2	3	4
Quality control measures:				
Number of customer complaints	75	68	59	45
Number of warranty claims	42	39	30	27
Cost of rework	$6,402	$6,910	$7,215	$8,130
Material control measures:				
Purchase order lead time (days)	8	6	5	3
Scrap as a percentage of total cost	1.3%	1.7%	2.4%	2.8%
Inventory control measures:				
Raw material turnover (times)	27	20	18	14
Finished goods turnover (times)	16	13	11	10
Machine performance measures:				
Percentage of machine downtime	4.3%	5.1%	6.2%	7.0%
Use as a percentage of availability	97%	92%	89%	86%
Setup time (hours)	1.3	1.8	2.5	3.0
Delivery performance measures:				
Throughput time (days)	?	?	?	?
Delivery cycle time (days)	?	?	?	?
Manufacturing cycle efficiency	?	?	?	?
Percentage of on-time deliveries	91%	86%	83%	79%
Total throughput (units)	3,210	3,072	2,915	2,806

Management has heard that throughput time, delivery cycle time, and manufacturing cycle efficiency (MCE) are important measures in an automated environment, but no one knows how to compute the figures. Fortunately, the company's computer logs time by element as a unit goes through the production process. The following average times have been logged over the last four months:

	Average per Month (in days)			
	1	2	3	4
Move time per unit	0.4	0.3	0.4	0.4
Process time per unit	2.1	2.0	1.9	1.8
Wait time per order before start of production	16.0	17.5	19.0	20.5
Wait time per unit during production	4.3	5.0	5.8	6.7
Inspection time per unit	0.6	0.7	0.7	0.6

Required

1. For each month, compute the following performance measures:
   a. The throughput time, or velocity of production.
   b. The manufacturing cycle efficiency (MCE).
   c. The delivery cycle time.
2. Copy the performance measures above onto your answer sheet, and evaluate the company's performance over the last four months as follows:

Measure	Trend	Probable Cause
Quality control measures:		
Number of customer complaints	Favorable	Use of automated equipment; more care in production; better quality materials.
Cost of rework	Unfavorable	Poorly adjusted machines; poorly trained employees.
Number of warranty claims	?	?
Material control measures:		
Etc.		

3. Refer to the move time, process time, and so forth given above for month 4.
   a. Assume in month 5 that the move time, process time, and so forth are the same as in month 4, except that through the use of JIT inventory methods the company is able to completely eliminate the wait time during production. Compute the new throughput time and MCE.
   b. Assume in month 6 that the move time, process time, and so forth are again the same as in month 4, except that the company is able to eliminate both the wait time during production and the inspection time. Compute the new throughput time and MCE.

P9–20 Variance Analysis; Multiple Lots Ricardo Shirts, Inc., manufactures short- and long-sleeved men's shirts for large stores. Ricardo produces a single-quality shirt in lots to each customer's order and attaches the store's label to each shirt. The standard direct costs for a dozen long-sleeved shirts include:

Direct materials:	24 yards at \$0.65	\$15.60
Direct labor:	3 hours at \$7.25	21.75

During April, Ricardo worked on three orders for long-sleeved shirts. Job cost records for the month disclose the following:

Lot	Units in Lot (dozens)	Materials Used (yards)	Hours Worked
30	1,000	24,100	2,980
31	1,700	40,440	5,130
32	1,200	28,825	2,890

The following additional information is available:

a. Ricardo purchased 95,000 yards of material during the month at a cost of $66,500.
b. Direct labor cost incurred amounted to $80,740 during April.
c. There was no work in process at April 1. During April, lots 30 and 31 were completed. At April 30, lot 32 was 100 percent complete as to materials but only 80 percent complete as to labor.

Required

1. Compute the materials price variance for April, and show whether the variance was favorable or unfavorable.
2. Determine the materials quantity variance for the month in both yards and dollars:
   a. For the company in total.
   b. For each lot worked on during the month.
3. Compute the labor rate variance for April, and show whether the variance was favorable or unfavorable.
4. Determine the labor efficiency variance for the month in both hours and dollars:
   a. For the company in total.
   b. For each lot worked on during the month.
5. In what situations might it be better to express variances in units (hours, yards, and so on) rather than in dollars? In dollars rather than in units?

(CPA, Adapted)

P9–21 Missing Data; Variance Analysis; Standard Cost Card Astro Company's Southland Plant manufactures a small computer table. A partial standard cost card on the table is given below:

	Standard Quantity or Hours	Standard Price or Rate	Standard Cost
Direct materials.	? board feet	$4 per board foot	$?
Direct labor	? hours	? per hour	?
Variable overhead.	? hours*	3 per hour	?
Total standard cost . . .			$45

* Based on direct labor-hours.

The plant has just completed operations for the first quarter of 19x2. Retch P. Clod, the plant's production supervisor (who prides himself for "telling it like it is"), has summarized operations for the first quarter as follows in a memo to the plant manager:

"As usual, those incompetents at headquarters are trying to blame production for the excess cost on last quarter's output. Total cost for the 8,000 tables produced during the quarter came to $403,500. That's $50.4375 per table, or 12.1 percent over the standard cost of $45. A lot of the problem was those big spenders in purchasing. They paid $0.20 per board foot over standard for the 50,000 board feet of material that was purchased and used during the quarter. Twenty cents may not sound like much, but it was the cause of most of the $18,000 total variance (unfavorable) that the pencil pushers say we had with materials. To top that off, those wimps in personnel caved in to the union (again!) and agreed to a $0.50 per hour wage increase over standard. That really blew the budget!!

"But, like always, production saved the day. We managed to pare variable overhead back to only $2.75 per hour or a total of $49,500 for the quarter. That gave variable overhead a great, big $4,500 favorable spending variance! Can you believe, though, that the bean counters in the front office griped because the total variable overhead variance was a measly $1,500 unfavorable? It seems to me that instead of complaining, they should have given big, fat bonuses to me and the production crew for a job well done."

The plant had no inventory of materials on hand at either the beginning or end of the quarter.

Required

1. Compute the following variances (show all computations):
   a. Materials price and quantity variances.
   b. Direct labor rate and efficiency variances.
   c. Variable overhead spending and efficiency variances.
2. Scrutinize the variances you prepared in (1) above. Do you agree that Retch and the production crew deserve "big, fat bonuses for a job well done"? Explain.
3. Complete the standard cost card shown at the beginning of the problem. Again, show all computations.

P9–22 Setting Materials and Labor Standards Scera Company manufactures trivets. The company is just starting to use standard costs. From accounting records, industrial engineering studies, and other sources, the following information has been developed:

a. The clocked labor time to produce one trivet (good or defective) is 1.5 hours.
b. Ten percent of all completed trivets are scrapped as defective. The scrapped trivets have no monetary value.
c. The materials required in the production of one trivet (good or defective) are:

Material	Quantity Required per Trivet	Invoice Cost	Freight
H–4	3.6 qts.*	$3 per qt.	$0.10 per qt.
H–11	2.7 lbs.	4 per lb.	0.20 per lb.

* After spillage or evaporation loss.

d. All materials are purchased subject to a 2 percent cash discount if paid within 10 days. All discounts are taken.
e. Only 80 percent of material H–4 finds its way into a trivet. The remainder is lost through spillage or evaporation.
f. The labor rate is $6 per hour.
g. Coffee breaks, cleanup, and so on, consume about 0.8 hours of labor time each eight-hour day. The company works a 40-hour week.

Required

1. Compute the following for material:
   a. The standard quantity of material H–4 and the standard quantity of material H–11 for each acceptable trivet, allowing for the normal loss factors mentioned above.
   b. The standard cost per quart or pound for each type of material.
   c. Using the data from *(a)* and *(b)* above, compute the standard cost of each type of material per acceptable trivet.
2. Compute the following for labor:
   a. The standard labor time per acceptable trivet, again allowing for normal loss factors.
   b. The standard labor cost per acceptable trivet.

P9–23 Preparation of a Variance Report Dolby, Inc., produces and sells high-quality cabinets for stereo speakers. The company's most recent income statement is given below:

DOLBY, INC.
Income Statement
For the Month Ended July 31, 19x7

	Budget	Actual	Variance
Sales (2,500 units)	$200,000	$200,000	—
Less variable expenses:			
Variable production costs	90,000	96,000	$6,000 U
Other variable expenses	30,000	30,000	—
Total variable expenses	120,000	126,000	
Contribution margin	80,000	74,000	
Less fixed expenses:			
Production	28,000	28,000	—
Selling and administrative	32,000	32,000	—
Total fixed expenses	60,000	60,000	
Net income	$ 20,000	$ 14,000	$6,000 U

The company uses a standard cost system for planning and control purposes. The standard cost for one unit of product is given below:

Wood: 3.2 feet at $6 per foot	$19.20
Direct labor: 1.4 hours at $10 per hour	14.00
Variable overhead: 0.7 machine-hours at $4 per hour	2.80
Total standard variable cost	$36.00

As indicated above, variable overhead cost is applied to products on a basis of machine-hours of activity.

Management is somewhat unhappy with the standard cost system because difficulty is being experienced in interpreting the cost variance reports coming from accounting. A typical cost variance report is given below. The report relates to the $6,000 variance above for July:

DOLBY, INC.
Cost Variance Report—Variable Production Costs
For the Month of July 19x7

	Total	Per Unit
Excess wood used in production	$1,400	$0.56
Excess direct labor cost incurred	4,400	1.76
Excess variable overhead cost incurred	200	0.08
Total excess cost incurred	$6,000	$2.40

The company has hired you, as an expert in cost analysis, to help management clarify the reports coming from accounting. You have found that 2,500 units of product were produced and sold during the month and that the following actual unit costs were incurred:

Wood: 3.04 feet at $6.50 per foot.
Direct labor: 1.6 hours at $9.85 per hour.
Variable overhead: 0.8 machine-hours at $3.60 per hour.

Required

1. What criticisms can be made of the cost variance reports currently being prepared by accounting?

2. Compute the following variances for July 19x7:
   a. Materials price and quantity.
   b. Labor rate and efficiency.
   c. Variable overhead spending and efficiency.
3. Prepare a new cost variance report for management; show your variances on both a total and a per unit basis.

P9–24 Determining Standard Costs; Variance Analysis Helix Company produces several products in its factory, including a karate robe. The company uses a standard cost system to assist in the control of costs. According to the standards that have been set for the robes, the factory should work 780 direct labor-hours each month and produce 1,950 robes. The standard costs associated with this level of production activity are:

	Total	Per Unit of Product
Direct materials	$35,490	$18.20
Direct labor.	7,020	3.60
Variable overhead (based on direct labor-hours) . . .	2,340	1.20
		$23.00

During April 19x8, the factory worked only 760 direct labor-hours and produced 2,000 robes. The following actual costs were recorded during the month:

	Total	Per Unit of Product
Direct materials (6,000 yards) . . .	$36,000	$18.00
Direct labor	7,600	3.80
Variable overhead	3,800	1.90
		$23.70

At standard, each robe should require 2.8 yards of material. All of the materials purchased during the month were used in production.

Required Compute the following variances for April 19x8:

1. The materials price and quantity variances.
2. The labor rate and efficiency variances.
3. The variable overhead spending and efficiency variances.

P9–25 Development of Standard Costs ColdKing Company is a small producer of fruit-flavored frozen desserts. For many years, ColdKing's products have had strong regional sales on the basis of brand recognition; however, other companies have begun marketing similar products in the area, and price competition has become increasingly important. John Wakefield, the company's controller, is planning to implement a standard cost system for ColdKing and has gathered considerable information from his co-workers on production and material requirements for ColdKing's products. Wakefield believes that the use of standard costing will allow ColdKing to improve cost control and make better pricing decisions.

ColdKing's most popular product is raspberry sherbert. The sherbert is produced in 10-gallon batches, and each batch requires 6 quarts of good raspberries. The fresh raspberries are sorted by hand before they enter the production process. Because of imperfections in the raspberries and normal spoilage, 1 quart of berries is discarded for every 4 quarts of acceptable berries. Three minutes is the standard direct labor time for the sorting that is required to obtain 1 quart of acceptable raspberries. The acceptable raspberries are then blended with the other ingredients; blending requires

12 minutes of direct labor time per batch. After blending, the sherbert is packaged in quart containers. Wakefield has gathered the following pricing information.

a. ColdKing purchases raspberries at a cost of $0.80 per quart. All other ingredients cost a total of $0.45 per gallon.
b. Direct labor is paid at the rate of $9 per hour.
c. The total cost of material and labor required to package the sherbert is $0.38 per quart.

Required

1. Develop the standard cost for the direct cost components (materials, labor, and packaging) of a 10-gallon batch of raspberry sherbert. The standard cost should identify the standard quantity, standard rate, and standard cost per batch for each direct cost component of a batch of raspberry sherbert.
2. As part of the implementation of a standard cost system at ColdKing, John Wakefield plans to train those responsible for maintaining the standards on how to use variance analysis. Wakefield is particularly concerned with the causes of unfavorable variances.
   a. Discuss the possible causes of unfavorable material price variances, and identify the individual(s) who should be held responsible for these variances.
   b. Discuss the possible causes of unfavorable labor efficiency variances, and identify the individual(s) who should be held responsible for these variances.

(CMA, Adapted)

P9–26 **Variances; Unit Costs; Journal Entries** (Appendix) Vermont Mills, Inc., is a large producer of men's and women's clothing. The company uses standard costs for all of its products. The standard costs and actual costs for a recent period are given below for one of the company's product lines (per unit of product):

	Standard Cost	Actual Cost
Direct materials:		
Standard: 4.0 yards at $3.60 per yard	$14.40	
Actual: 4.4 yards at $3.35 per yard		$14.74
Direct labor:		
Standard: 1.6 hours at $4.50 per hour	7.20	
Actual: 1.4 hours at $4.85 per hour		6.79
Variable overhead:		
Standard: 1.6 hours at $1.80 per hour	2.88	
Actual: 1.4 hours at $2.15 per hour		3.01
Total cost per unit.	$24.48	$24.54

During this period, the company produced 4,800 units of product. A comparison of standard and actual costs for the period on a total cost basis is given below:

Actual costs: 4,800 units at $24.54	$117,792
Standard costs: 4,800 units at $24.48	117,504
Difference in cost—unfavorable	$ 288

There was no inventory of materials on hand to start the period. During the period, 21,120 yards of materials were purchased, all of which were used in production.

Required

1. For direct materials:
   a. Compute the price and quantity variances for the period.
   b. Prepare journal entries to record all activity relating to direct materials for the period.

2. For direct labor:
   a. Compute the rate and efficiency variances.
   b. Prepare a journal entry to record the incurrence of direct labor cost for the period.
3. Compute the variable overhead spending and efficiency variances.
4. On seeing the $288 total cost variance, the company's president stated, "This variance of $288 is only 0.2 percent of the $117,504 standard cost for the period. It's obvious that our costs are well under control." Do you agree? Explain.
5. State the possible causes of each variance that you have computed.

P9–27 Variance Analysis; Incomplete Data; Journal Entries (Appendix) Topline Surf Boards manufactures a single product. The standard cost of one unit of this product is:

Direct materials: 6 feet at $1	$ 6.00
Direct labor: 1 hour at $4.50	4.50
Variable overhead: 1 hour at $3	3.00
Total standard variable cost per unit . . .	$13.50

During the month of October, 6,000 units were produced. Selected cost data relating to the month's production follow:

Material purchased: 60,000 feet at $0.95	$57,000
Material used in production: 38,000 feet	—
Direct labor: __?__ hours at $__?__ per hour . . .	27,950
Variable overhead cost incurred	20,475
Variable overhead efficiency variance	1,500 U

There was no beginning inventory of raw materials. The variable overhead rate is based on direct labor-hours.

Required

1. For direct materials:
   a. Compute the price and quantity variances for the month.
   b. Prepare journal entries to record activity for the month.
2. For direct labor:
   a. Compute the rate and efficiency variances for the month.
   b. Prepare a journal entry to record labor activity for the month.
3. For variable overhead:
   a. Compute the spending variance for the month, and prove the efficiency variance given above.
   b. If overhead is applied to production on a basis of direct labor-hours, is it possible to have a favorable direct labor efficiency variance and an unfavorable overhead efficiency variance? Explain.
4. State the possible causes of each variance that you have computed.

CASES

C9–28 JIT/FMS Performance Measures; Missing Data "I'm having a really hard time with these new production measures," said Ruth Dancie, president of Kendrix Products. "I understood standard costs and variances, because we were always aiming for a specific figure. But with no standards to shoot for, what's good and what's bad? To make matters worse, the computer garbled some of the numbers in this report on the first four months of our fiscal year."

The report to which Ms. Dancie was referring is shown below:

Production and Cycle Times
April–July 19x1

	April	May	June	July
Average time required per unit, in days:				
Inspection time	0.6	0.5	0.5	0.4
Process time	1.3	?	?	?
Wait time:				
From order to start of production	27.0	24.5	19.0	14.0
During production	6.4	5.9	4.2	2.7
Move time	0.9	0.8	0.8	?

General Performance Measures
April–July 19x1

	April	May	June	July
Quality control measures:				
Number of warranty claims	105	96	81	72
Number of customer complaints	76	61	53	39
Number of defects in parts	27	30	34	40
Material control measures:				
Purchase order lead time (days)	10	7	6	4
Scrap as a percentage of total cost	2.1%	2.8%	3.4%	3.9%
Inventory control measures:				
Raw material turnover (times)	35	29	21	18
Finished goods turnover (times)	9	10	13	16
Number of items of raw material carried in inventory	4,806	5,210	6,724	7,805
Machine performance measures:				
Percentage of machine availability	95%	91%	87%	84%
Use as a percentage of availability	86%	90%	94%	100%
Setup time (hours)	4.3	3.9	3.1	2.5
Delivery performance measures:				
Throughput time, or velocity (days)	?	8.5	?	?
Manufacturing cycle efficiency (MCE)	?	?	?	22.0%
Delivery cycle time (days)	?	?	25.7	19.0
Percentage of on-time deliveries	?	?	?	?

Kendrix Products moved into a new, automated facility four months ago, at the start of its fiscal year. The company is now in the process of moving toward JIT purchasing and production. Management has been so busy with the new system that little time has been available to develop or interpret any new performance measures. Accordingly, you have been asked to supply the missing data in the report above, and to give a line-by-line critique to management as to how the company is doing.

Required

1. For each month, determine the following items:
   a. The throughput time (velocity) per unit, including all elements that make up the throughput time.
   b. The manufacturing cycle efficiency (MCE), including all elements from which the MCE is computed.
   c. The delivery cycle time, including all elements that make up the delivery cycle time.
2. Refer to the "General Performance Measures" given above. Copy these measures down on your answer sheet, and for each measure indicate the trend (either favorable or unfavorable) and the probable cause of the trend that you observe. Use the following format:

Measure	Trend	Probable Cause
Quality control measures:		
Number of warranty claims	Favorable	Better quality equipment, materials, and construction.
Number of customer complaints . . .	?	?

3. Refer again to the "General Performance Measures" given above, and to the "Percentage of on-time deliveries." In view of your analysis in (2) above, would you expect the percentage of on-time deliveries to be increasing or decreasing? Explain.
4. Refer to the "Production and Cycle Times" given above for July.
   a. Assume in August that these times are the same as for July, except that through the use of JIT production the company is able to completely eliminate the wait time during production. Compute the new throughput time and MCE.
   b. Assume in September that the "Production and Cycle Times" again are the same as in July, except that the company is able to eliminate both the wait time during production and the move time. Compute the new throughput time and MCE.
   c. What do you think is the purpose of the computations in *(a)* and *(b)* above?

C9–29 **Fragmentary Data; Journal Entries; Unit Costs** (Appendix) You have just been hired by Barfex Company, which manufactures cough syrup. The syrup requires two materials, A and B, in its manufacture, and it is produced in batches. The company uses a standard cost system, with the controller preparing variances on a weekly basis. These variances are discussed at a meeting attended by all relevant managers. The meeting to discuss last week's variances is tomorrow. Since you will be working initially in the planning and control area, the president thinks that this would be a good chance for you to get acquainted with the company's control system and has asked that you attend and be prepared to participate fully in the discussion. Accordingly, you have taken home the controller's figure sheet containing last week's variances, as well as the ledger pages from which these variances were derived. You are sure that with a little study you will be able to make a sterling impression and be launched into a bright and successful career.

After completing your study that night, the weather being warm and humid, you leave your windows open upon retiring, only to arise the next morning horrified to discover that a sudden shower has obliterated most of the controller's figures (left lying on a table by an open window). Only the following fragments are readable:

Raw Materials—A

	Debit	Credit
Bal. 6/1	720	
Bal. 6/7	1,500	

Wages Payable

Debit	Credit
	1,725

Raw Materials—B

	Debit	Credit
Bal. 6/1	0	600
Bal. 6/7	200	

Material A—Price Variance

Debit	Credit
220	

Work in Process

Debit		Credit
Bal. 6/1	0	
Material A	2,400	
Bal. 6/7	0	

Material B—Quantity Variance

Debit	Credit
	40

Accounts Payable

Debit	Credit
	4,240

Labor Efficiency Variance

Debit	Credit
240	

Not wanting to admit your carelessness to either the president or the controller, you have decided that your only alternative is to reproduce the obliterated data. From your study last night, you recall the following:

a. The wages payable are only for direct labor.
b. The accounts payable are for purchases of both material A and material B.
c. The standard cost of material A is $6 per gallon, and the standard quantity is 5 gallons per batch of syrup.
d. Purchases last week were: material A, 550 gallons; and material B, 200 pounds.
e. The standard rate for direct labor is $8 per hour; a total of 230 actual hours were worked last week.

Required

1. How many batches of syrup were produced last week? (Double-check this figure before going on!)
2. For material A:
   a. How many gallons were used in production last week?
   b. What was the quantity variance?
   c. What was the cost of material A purchased during the week?
   d. Prepare journal entries to record all activity relating to material A during the week.
3. For material B:
   a. What is the standard cost per pound of material B?
   b. How many pounds of material B were used in production last week? How many pounds should have been used at standard?
   c. What is the standard quantity of material B per batch?
   d. What was the price variance for material B?
   e. Prepare journal entries to record all activity relating to material B during the week.
4. For direct labor:
   a. What were the standard hours allowed for last week's production?
   b. What are the standard hours per batch?
   c. What was the direct labor rate variance?
   d. Prepare a journal entry to record all activity relating to direct labor during the week.
5. In terms of materials and labor, compute the standard cost of one batch of syrup.

10

Flexible Budgets and Overhead Analysis

LEARNING OBJECTIVES

After studying Chapter 10, you should be able to:

1. Prepare a flexible budget, and explain the advantages of the flexible budget approach over the static budget approach.
2. Use the flexible budget to prepare a variable overhead performance report containing *(a)* only a spending variance and *(b)* both a spending and an efficiency variance.
3. Explain the cause of the spending and efficiency variances and how they are controlled.
4. Explain the significance of the denominator activity figure in determining the standard cost of a unit of product.
5. Properly apply overhead cost to units of product in a standard cost system.
6. Compute and properly interpret the fixed overhead budget and volume variances.
7. Define or explain the key terms listed at the end of the chapter.

There are four problems involved in overhead cost control. First, manufacturing overhead is usually made up of many separate costs. Second, these separate costs are often very small in dollar amount, making it highly impractical to control them in the same way that direct materials and direct labor costs are controlled. Third, these small, separate costs are often the responsibility of different managers. And fourth, manufacturing overhead costs vary in behavior, some being variable, some fixed, and some mixed in nature.

Most of these problems can be overcome by use of a *flexible budget*. Flexible budgets were touched on briefly in Chapter 8. In this chapter, we study flexible budgets in greater detail and learn how they are used to control costs. We also expand the study of overhead variances that we started in Chapter 9.

FLEXIBLE BUDGETS

Characteristics of a Flexible Budget

The budgets that we studied in Chapter 8 were essentially static budgets in nature. A **static budget** has two characteristics:

1. It is geared toward only one level of activity.
2. Actual results are always compared against budgeted costs at the *original* budget activity level.

A **flexible budget** differs from a static budget on both of these points. First, it does not confine itself to only one level of activity, but rather is geared toward a *range* of activity. Second, actual results do not have to be compared against budgeted costs at the original budget activity level. Since the flexible budget covers a *range* of activity, if actual costs are incurred at a different activity level from what was originally planned, then the manager is able to construct a new budget, as needed, to compare against actual results. Hence, the term *flexible budget*. In sum, the characteristics of a flexible budget are:

1. It is geared toward *all* levels of activity within the relevant range, rather than toward only one level of activity.
2. It is *dynamic* in nature rather than static. A budget can be tailored for any level of activity within the relevant range, even after the period is over. That is, a manager can look at what activity level *was attained* during a period and then turn to the flexible budget to determine what costs *should have been* at that activity level.

Deficiencies of the Static Budget

To illustrate the difference between a static budget and a flexible budget, let us assume that the assembly operation of Rocco Company has budgeted to produce 10,000 units during March. The variable overhead budget that has been set is shown in Exhibit 10–1.

EXHIBIT 10–1

ROCCO COMPANY
Static Budget
Assembly Operation
For the Month Ended March 31, 19x1

Budgeted production in units	10,000
Budgeted variable overhead costs:	
Indirect materials	$4,000
Lubricants	1,000
Power	3,000
Total	$8,000

EXHIBIT 10–2

ROCCO COMPANY
Static Budget Performance Report
Assembly Operation
For the Month Ended March 31, 19x1

	Actual	Budget	Variance
Production in units	9,400	10,000	600 U
Variable overhead costs:			
Indirect materials	$3,800	$4,000	$200 F*
Lubricants	950	1,000	50 F*
Power	2,900	3,000	100 F*
Total	$7,650	$8,000	$350 F*

* These cost variances are useless, since they have been derived by comparing actual costs at one level of activity against budgeted costs at a *different* level of activity.

Let us assume that the production goal of 10,000 units is not met. The company is able to produce only 9,400 units during the month. *If a static budget approach is used,* the performance report for the month will appear as shown in Exhibit 10–2.

What's wrong with this report? The deficiencies of the static budget can be explained as follows. A production manager has two prime responsibilities to discharge in the performance of his or her duties—*production control* and *cost control*. Production control is involved with seeing that production goals in terms of output are met. Cost control is involved with seeing that output is produced at the least possible cost, consistent with quality standards. These are different responsibilities, and they must be kept separate in attempting to assess how well the production manager is doing his or her job. The main difficulty with the static budget is that it fails completely to distinguish between the production control and the cost control dimensions of a manager's performance.

Of the two, the static budget does a good job of measuring only whether production control is being maintained. Look again at the data in Exhibit 10–2. The data on the top line relate to the production superintendent's responsibility for production control. These data for Rocco Company properly reflect the fact that production control was not maintained during the month. The company failed to meet its production goal by 600 units.

The remainder of the data in the report deal with cost control. These data are useless in that they are comparing apples with oranges. Although the production manager may be very proud of the favorable cost variances, they tell nothing about how well costs were controlled during the month. The problem is that the budget costs are based on an activity level of 10,000 units, whereas the actual costs were incurred at an activity level substantially below this (only 9,400 units). From a cost control point of view, it is total nonsense to try to compare costs at one activity level with costs at a different activity level. Such comparisons will always make a production manager look good so long as the actual production is less than the budgeted production.

How the Flexible Budget Works

The basic idea of the flexible budget approach is that through a study of cost behavior patterns, a budget can be prepared that is geared to a *range* of activity, rather than to a single level. The basic steps in preparing a flexible budget are:

1. Determine the relevant range over which activity is expected to fluctuate during the coming period.
2. Analyze costs that will be incurred over the relevant range in terms of determining cost behavior patterns (variable, fixed, or mixed).
3. Separate costs by behavior, determining the formula for variable and mixed costs, as discussed in Chapter 5.
4. Using the formula for the variable portion of the costs, prepare a budget showing what costs will be incurred at various points throughout the relevant range.

To illustrate, let us assume that Rocco Company's production normally fluctuates between 8,000 and 11,000 units each month. A study of cost behavior patterns over this relevant range has revealed the following formulas for the variable portion of overhead:

Overhead Costs	Variable Cost Formula (per unit)
Indirect materials	$0.40
Lubricants	0.10
Power	0.30

Based on these cost formulas, a flexible budget for Rocco Company would appear as shown in Exhibit 10–3.

Using the Flexible Budget Once the flexible budget has been prepared, the manager is ready to compare actual results for a period against the comparable budget level anywhere within the relevant range. The manager isn't limited to a single budget level as with the static budget. To illustrate, let us again assume that Rocco Company is unable to meet its production goal of 10,000 units during the month of March. As before, we will assume that only

EXHIBIT 10–3

ROCCO COMPANY
Flexible Budget
Assembly Operation
For the Month Ended March 31, 19x1

Budgeted production in units. 10,000

Overhead Costs	Cost Formula (per unit)	Range of Production in Units 8,000	9,000	10,000	11,000
Variable costs:					
Indirect materials	$0.40	$3,200	$3,600	$4,000	$4,400
Lubricants	0.10	800	900	1,000	1,100
Power	0.30	2,400	2,700	3,000	3,300
Total variable costs	$0.80	$6,400	$7,200	$8,000	$8,800

EXHIBIT 10–4

ROCCO COMPANY
Performance Report
Assembly Operation
For the Month Ended March 31, 19x1

Budgeted production in units 10,000
Actual production in units 9,400

Overhead Costs	Cost Formula	Actual Costs Incurred 9,400 Units	Budget Based on 9,400 Units	Variance
Variable costs:				
Indirect materials	$0.40	$3,800	$3,760*	$ 40 U†
Lubricants	0.10	950	940	10 U†
Power	0.30	2,900	2,820	80 U†
Total variable costs	$0.80	$7,650	$7,520	$130 U†

* 9,400 units × $0.40 = $3,760. Other budget allowances are computed in the same way.
† These cost variances are usable in evaluating cost control, since they have been derived by comparing actual costs and budgeted costs at the *same* level of activity.

9,400 units are produced. Under the flexible budget approach, the performance report would appear as shown in Exhibit 10–4.

In contrast to the performance report prepared earlier under the static budget approach (Exhibit 10–2), this performance report distinguishes clearly between production control and cost control. The production data at the top of the report indicate whether the production goal was met. The cost data at the bottom of the report tell how well costs were controlled for the 9,400 units that were actually produced.

Notice that all cost variances are *unfavorable*, as contrasted to the *favorable* cost variances on the performance report prepared earlier under the static budget approach. The reason for the change in variances is that by means of the flexible budget approach we are able to compare budgeted and actual costs at *the same activity level* (9,400 units produced), rather than being forced to compare budgeted costs at one activity level against actual costs at a different activity level. Herein lies the strength and dynamic nature of the flexible budget approach. By simply applying the cost formulas, it is possible to develop a budget *at any time* for *any* activity level within the relevant range. Thus, even if actual activity results in some odd figure that does not appear in the flexible budget, such as the 9,400 units above, budgeted costs can still be prepared to compare against actual costs. One simply develops a budget at the 9,400-unit level, as we have done, by using the cost formulas contained in the flexible budget. The result shows up in more usable variances.

The Measure of Activity—A Critical Choice

In the Rocco Company example, we chose to use units of production as the activity base for developing a flexible budget. Rather than use units, which are a measure of output, most companies find it more practical to use some *input* measure, such as machine-hours (MH) or direct labor-hours (DLH), to plan and control overhead costs. This is especially true when more than one product is manufactured. At least three factors should be considered in selecting an activity base for an overhead flexible budget:

1. The existence of a causal relationship between the activity base and overhead costs.
2. The avoidance of dollars in the activity base itself.
3. The selection of an activity base that is simple and easily understood.

Causal Relationship There should be a direct causal relationship between the activity base and a company's variable overhead costs. That is, the variable overhead costs should vary as a result of changes in the activity base. In a machine shop, for example, one would expect power usage and other variable overhead costs to vary in relationship to the number of machine-hours worked. Machine-hours would therefore be the proper base to use in the flexible budget. As explained in Chapter 3, an activity base is frequently referred to as a "cost driver," since it is the controlling factor in the incurrence of cost.

Other common activity bases (cost drivers) include direct labor-hours, miles driven by salespersons, contacts made by salespersons, number of invoices processed, number of occupied beds in a hospital, and number of X rays given. Any one of these could be used as the base for preparing a flexible budget in the proper situation.

Do Not Use Dollars Whenever possible, the activity base should be expressed in units rather than in dollars. If dollars are used, they should be standard dollars rather than actual dollars.

The problem with dollars is that they are subject to price-level changes, which can cause a distortion in the activity base if it is expressed in dollar terms. A similar problem arises when wage-rate changes take place if direct labor cost is being used as the activity base in a flexible budget. The change in wage rates will cause the activity base to change, even though a proportionate change may not take place in the overhead costs themselves. These types of fluctuations generally make dollars difficult to work with, and argue strongly for units rather than dollars in the activity base. The use of *standard* dollar costs rather than *actual* dollar costs overcomes the problem to some degree, but standard costs still have to be adjusted from time to time as changes in actual costs take place. On the other hand, *units* as a measure of activity (beds, hours, miles, and so on) are subject to few distorting influences and are less likely to cause problems in preparing and using a flexible budget.

Keep the Base Simple The activity base should be simple and easily understood. A base that is not easily understood by the manager who works with it day by day will probably result in confusion and misunderstanding rather than serve as a positive means of cost control.

THE OVERHEAD PERFORMANCE REPORT—A CLOSER LOOK

A special problem arises in preparing overhead performance reports when the flexible budget is based on *hours* of activity (such as direct labor-hours) rather than on units of product. The problem relates to what hour base to use in constructing budget allowances on the performance report.

The Problem of Budget Allowances

The nature of the problem can best be seen through a specific example. Assume that Donner Company is budgeting its activities for the year 19x1. The flexible budget that has been prepared is shown in Exhibit 10–5.

As shown in Exhibit 10–5, the company uses machine-hours as an activity base in its flexible budget and has budgeted to operate at an activity level of 50,000 machine-hours for the year. Let us assume that two machine-hours are required to produce one unit of output. Under this assumption, budgeted production for the year is 25,000 units (50,000 budgeted machine-hours ÷ 2 hours per unit = 25,000 units). After the year is over, suppose the company finds that actual production for the year was only 20,000 units and that it required 42,000 hours of machine time to produce these units. A summary of the year's activities follows:

Budgeted machine-hours	50,000
Actual machine-hours	42,000
Standard machine-hours allowed	40,000*
Actual variable overhead costs:	
Indirect labor	$36,000
Lubricants	11,000
Power	24,000
Total actual costs	$71,000

* 20,000 units produced × 2 hours per unit = 40,000 standard hours allowed for the year's output.

In preparing a performance report for the year, what hour base should Donner Company use in computing budget allowances to compare against actual results? There are two alternatives. The company could use:

1. The 42,000 hours *actually worked* during the year.
2. The 40,000 hours that *should have been worked* during the year to produce 20,000 units of output.

EXHIBIT 10–5

DONNER COMPANY
Flexible Budget

Budgeted machine-hours	50,000				
	Cost Formula	**Machine-Hours**			
Overhead Costs	**(per hour)**	**30,000**	**40,000**	**50,000**	**60,000**
Variable costs:					
Indirect labor	$0.80	$24,000	$32,000	$40,000	$48,000
Lubricants	0.30	9,000	12,000	15,000	18,000
Power	0.40	12,000	16,000	20,000	24,000
Total variable costs	$1.50	$45,000	$60,000	$75,000	$90,000

Which base the company chooses will depend on how much detailed variance information it wants. As we learned in the preceding chapter, variable overhead can be analyzed in terms of a *spending* variance and an *efficiency* variance. The two bases provide different variance output.

Spending Variance Alone

If Donner Company chooses alternative 1 and bases its performance report on the 42,000 machine-hours actually worked during the year, then the performance report will show only a spending variance for variable overhead. A performance report prepared in this way is shown in Exhibit 10–6.

EXHIBIT 10–6

DONNER COMPANY
Variable Overhead Performance Report
For the Year Ended March 31, 19x1

Budget allowances are based on 42,000 machine-hours actually worked.

Comparing the budget against actual overhead cost yields only a spending variance.

Budgeted machine-hours	50,000			
Actual machine-hours	42,000			
Standard machine-hours allowed . . .	40,000			
Overhead Costs	**Cost Formula (per hour)**	**Actual Costs Incurred 42,000 Hours**	**Budget Based on 42,000 Hours**	**Spending Variance**
Variable costs:				
Indirect labor	$0.80	$36,000	$33,600*	$2,400 U
Lubricants	0.30	11,000	12,600	1,600 F
Power	0.40	24,000	16,800	7,200 U
Total variable costs	$1.50	$71,000	$63,000	$8,000 U

* 42,000 hours × $0.80 = $33,600. Other budget allowances are computed in the same way.

The formula behind the spending variance was introduced in the preceding chapter. For review, that formula is:

$$(AH \times AR) - (AH \times SR) = \text{Variable overhead spending variance}$$

Or, in factored form:

$$AH(AR - SR) = \text{Variable overhead spending variance}$$

The report in Exhibit 10–6 is prepared around the first, or unfactored, format.

Interpreting the Spending Variance The overhead spending variance is affected by two things. First, a spending variance may occur simply because of price increases over what is shown in the flexible budget. For Donner Company, this means that prices paid for overhead items may have gone up during the year, resulting in unfavorable spending variances. This portion of the overhead spending variance is just like the price variance for raw materials.

Second, the overhead spending variance is affected by waste or excessive usage of overhead materials. A first reaction is to say that waste or excessive usage of materials ought to show up as part of the efficiency variance. But this isn't true so far as overhead is concerned. Waste or excessive usage will show up as part of the spending variance. The reason is that the Manufacturing Overhead account is charged with *all* overhead costs incurred during a period, including those costs that arise as a result of waste. Since the spending variance represents any difference between the standard rate per hour and the actual costs incurred, waste will automatically show up as part of this variance, along with any excessive prices paid for variable overhead items.

In sum, the overhead spending variance contains both price and quantity (waste) elements. These two elements could be broken out and shown separately on the performance report, but this is rarely done in actual practice.

Usefulness of the Spending Variance Most firms consider the overhead spending variance to be highly useful. Generally, the price element in this variance will be small, so the variance permits a focusing of attention on that thing over which the supervisor probably has the greatest control—usage of overhead in production. In many cases, firms will limit their overhead analysis to the spending variance alone, feeling that the information it yields is sufficient for overhead cost control.

Both Spending and Efficiency Variances

If Donner Company wants both a spending and an efficiency variance for overhead, then it should compute budget allowances for *both* the 40,000 machine-hour and the 42,000 machine-hour levels of activity. A performance report prepared in this way is shown in Exhibit 10–7.

Note from Exhibit 10–7 that the spending variance is the same as the spending variance shown in Exhibit 10–6. The performance report in Exhibit 10–7 has simply been expanded to include an efficiency variance as well. Together, the spending and efficiency variances make up the total variance, as explained in the preceding chapter.

Interpreting the Efficiency Variance The term *overhead efficiency variance* is a misnomer, since this variance has nothing to do with efficiency in the use of overhead. What the variance really measures is how efficiently the *base* underlying the flexible budget is being utilized in production. Recall from the preceding chapter that the variable overhead efficiency variance is a function of the difference between the actual hours utilized in production and the hours that should have been taken to produce the period's output:

$$(AH \times SR) - (SH \times SR) = \text{Variable overhead efficiency variance}$$

Or, in factored form:

$$SR(AH - SH) = \text{Variable overhead efficiency variance}$$

If more hours are worked than are allowed at standard, then the overhead efficiency variance will be unfavorable to reflect this inefficiency. As a practical matter, however, the inefficiency is not in the use of overhead *but rather in the use of the base itself.*

This point can be illustrated by looking again at Exhibit 10–7. Two thousand more machine-hours were used during the period than should have been used to produce the period's output. Each of these hours required the incurrence of $1.50 of variable overhead cost, resulting in an unfavorable variance of $3,000 (2,000 hours × $1.50 = $3,000). Although this $3,000 variance is called an overhead efficiency variance, it could better be called a

EXHIBIT 10–7

DONNER COMPANY
Variable Overhead Performance Report
For the Year Ended March 31, 19x1

Budget allowances are based on 40,000 machine-hours—the time it *should have taken* to produce 20,000 units of output—as well as on the 42,000 *actual* machine-hours worked.

This approach yields both a spending and an efficiency variance.

Budgeted machine-hours	50,000
Actual machine-hours	42,000
Standard machine-hours allowed	40,000

Overhead Costs	Cost Formula (per hour)	(1) Actual Costs Incurred 42,000 Hours	(2) Budget Based on 42,000 Hours	(3) Budget Based on 40,000 Hours	(4) Total Variance (1) − (3)	Breakdown of the Total Variance: Spending Variance (1) − (2)	Efficiency Variance (2) − (3)
Variable costs:							
Indirect labor	$0.80	$36,000	$33,600*	$32,000	$ 4,000 U	$2,400 U	$1,600 U
Lubricants	0.30	11,000	12,600	12,000	1,000 F	1,600 F	600 U
Power	0.40	24,000	16,800	16,000	8,000 U	7,200 U	800 U
Total variable costs	$1.50	$71,000	$63,000	$60,000	$11,000 U	$8,000 U	$3,000 U

* 42,000 hours × $0.80 = $33,600. Other budget allowances are computed in the same way.

machine-hours efficiency variance, since it measures the efficiency of utilization of machine time. However, the term *overhead efficiency variance* is so firmly ingrained in day-to-day use that a change is unlikely. Even so, the user must be careful to interpret the variance with a clear understanding of what it really measures.

Control of the Efficiency Variance Who is responsible for control of the overhead efficiency variance? Since the variance really measures efficiency in the utilization of the base underlying the flexible budget, whoever is responsible for control of this base is responsible for control of the variance. If the base is direct labor-hours, then the supervisor responsible for the use of labor time will be chargeable for any overhead efficiency variance.

FIXED COSTS AND THE FLEXIBLE BUDGET

Should the flexible budget contain fixed costs as well as variable costs? The term *flexible budget* implies variable costs only. As a practical matter, however, most firms include fixed overhead costs in the budget as well.

Exhibit 10–8 illustrates the flexible budget of Donner Company, which has been expanded to include the company's fixed overhead costs as well as its variable overhead costs. Actually, the fixed portion of the budget is a *static budget* in that the amounts remain unchanged throughout the relevant range.

Fixed costs are often included in the flexible budget for at least two reasons. First, to the extent that a fixed cost is controllable by a manager, it should be included in the evaluation of his or her performance. Such costs should be placed on the manager's performance report, along with the variable costs for which he or she is responsible. And second, fixed costs are needed in the flexible budget for product costing purposes. Recall from

EXHIBIT 10–8

DONNER COMPANY
Flexible Budget

Budgeted machine-hours	50,000				
	Cost Formula	**Machine-Hours**			
Overhead Costs	**(per hour)**	**30,000**	**40,000**	**50,000**	**60,000**
Variable costs:					
Indirect labor	$0.80	$ 24,000	$ 32,000	$ 40,000	$ 48,000
Lubricants	0.30	9,000	12,000	15,000	18,000
Power	0.40	12,000	16,000	20,000	24,000
Total variable costs	$1.50	45,000	60,000	75,000	90,000
Fixed costs:					
Depreciation		100,000	100,000	100,000	100,000
Supervisory salaries		160,000	160,000	160,000	160,000
Insurance.		40,000	40,000	40,000	40,000
Total fixed costs.		300,000	300,000	300,000	300,000
Total overhead costs.		$345,000	$360,000	$375,000	$390,000

Chapter 3 that overhead costs are added to units of product by means of the predetermined overhead rate. *The flexible budget provides the manager with the information needed to compute this rate.* In the remainder of this chapter, we discuss the use of the flexible budget for this purpose; in the process, we also demonstrate the preparation and use of fixed overhead variances.

FIXED OVERHEAD ANALYSIS

The analysis of fixed overhead differs considerably from the analysis of variable overhead, simply because of the difference in the nature of the costs involved. To provide a background for our discussion, we will first review briefly the need for, and computation of, predetermined overhead rates. This review will be helpful since the predetermined overhead rate plays a role in fixed overhead analysis. We will then show how fixed overhead variances are computed and make certain observations as to their usefulness to the manager.

Flexible Budgets and Overhead Rates

Fixed costs come in large, indivisible pieces that by definition do not change with changes in the level of activity. As we learned in Chapter 3, this creates a problem in product costing, since a given level of fixed overhead cost spread over a small number of units will result in a higher cost per unit than if the same amount of cost is spread over a large number of units. Consider the data in the table below:

Month	(1) Fixed Overhead Cost	(2) Number of Units Produced	(3) Unit Cost (1) ÷ (2)
January	$6,000	1,000	$6.00
February	6,000	1,500	4.00
March	6,000	800	7.50

Notice that the large number of units produced in February results in a low unit cost ($4), whereas the small number of units produced in March results in a high unit cost ($7.50). This problem arises only in connection with the fixed portion of overhead, since by definition the variable portion of overhead remains constant on a per unit basis, rising and falling in total proportionately with changes in the activity level. For product costing purposes, managers need to stabilize the fixed portion of unit cost so that a single unit cost figure can be used throughout the year without regard to month-by-month changes in activity levels. As we learned in Chapter 3, this stability can be accomplished through use of the predetermined overhead rate.

Denominator Activity The formula that we used in Chapter 3 to compute the predetermined overhead rate is given below, with one added feature. We have titled the estimated activity portion of the formula as being the **denominator activity:**

$$\frac{\text{Estimated total manufacturing overhead costs}}{\text{Estimated total units in the base (MH, DLH, etc.)}} = \begin{array}{c}\text{Predetermined}\\ \text{overhead rate}\end{array}$$

(denominator activity)

Recall from our discussion in Chapter 3 that once an estimated activity level (denominator activity) has been chosen, it remains unchanged throughout the year, even if actual activity later proves the estimate (denominator) to be somewhat in error. The reason for not changing the denominator, of course, is to maintain stability in the amount of overhead applied to each unit of product regardless of when it is produced during the year.

Computing the Overhead Rate When we discussed predetermined overhead rates in Chapter 3, we did so without elaboration as to the source of the estimated data going into the formula. These data are normally derived from the flexible budget. To illustrate, refer to Donner Company's flexible budget in Exhibit 10–8. Notice that the budgeted activity level for 19x1 is 50,000 machine-hours. These 50,000 hours *become the denominator activity in the formula,* with the overhead cost (variable and fixed) at this activity level becoming the estimated overhead cost in the formula ($375,000 from Exhibit 10–8). In sum, the 19x1 predetermined overhead rate for Donner Company will be:

$$\frac{\$375{,}000}{50{,}000\text{ MH}} = \$7.50\text{ per machine-hour}$$

Or, the company can break its predetermined overhead rate down into variable and fixed elements rather than using a single combined figure:

$$\text{Variable element } \frac{\$75{,}000}{50{,}000\text{ MH}} = \$1.50\text{ per machine-hour}$$

$$\text{Fixed element } \frac{\$300{,}000}{50{,}000\text{ MH}} = \$6\text{ per machine-hour}$$

For every standard machine-hour of operation, work in process will be charged with $7.50 of overhead, of which $1.50 will be variable overhead and $6 will be fixed overhead. If a unit of product takes two machine-hours to complete, then its cost will include $3 variable overhead and $12 fixed overhead, as shown on the standard cost card below:

Standard Cost Card—Per Unit

Direct materials (assumed)	$14
Direct labor (assumed)	6
Variable overhead (2 machine-hours at $1.50)	3
Fixed overhead (2 machine-hours at $6)	12
Total standard cost per unit	$35

In sum, the flexible budget provides the manager with both the overhead cost figure and the denominator activity figure needed in computing the predetermined overhead rate. Thus, the flexible budget plays a key role in determining the amount of fixed and variable overhead cost that will be charged to units of product.

EXHIBIT 10–9

Applied Overhead Costs: Actual Cost System versus Standard Cost System

Actual Cost System

Manufacturing Overhead

Actual overhead costs incurred.	Applied overhead costs: Actual hours × Predetermined overhead rate.
Under- or overapplied overhead	

Standard Cost System

Manufacturing Overhead

Actual overhead costs incurred.	Applied overhead costs: Standard hours allowed for output × Predetermined overhead rate.
Under- or overapplied overhead	

Overhead Application in a Standard Cost System

To understand the fixed overhead variances, it is necessary first to understand how overhead is applied to work in process in a standard cost system. In Chapter 3, recall that we applied overhead to work in process on a basis of actual hours of activity (multiplied by the predetermined overhead rate). This procedure was correct, since at the time we were dealing with an actual cost system. However, we are now dealing with a standard cost system; and when standards are in operation, overhead is applied to work in process on a basis of the *standard hours allowed for the output of the period* rather than on a basis of the actual number of hours worked. This point is illustrated in Exhibit 10–9.

The reason for using standard hours to apply overhead to production in a standard cost system is to assure that every unit of product moving along the production line bears the same amount of overhead cost, regardless of any time variations that may be involved in its manufacture.

The Fixed Overhead Variances

To illustrate the computation of fixed overhead variances, we will refer again to the flexible budget data for Donner Company contained in Exhibit 10–8.

Denominator activity in machine-hours	50,000
Budgeted fixed overhead costs	$300,000
Fixed portion of the predetermined overhead rate (computed earlier)	$6

Let us assume that the following actual operating results were recorded for the year:

Actual machine-hours	42,000
Standard machine-hours allowed*	40,000
Actual fixed overhead costs:	
Depreciation	$100,000
Supervisory salaries	172,000
Insurance	36,000
Total actual costs	$308,000

* For the actual production of the year.

EXHIBIT 10–10
Computation of the Fixed Overhead Variances

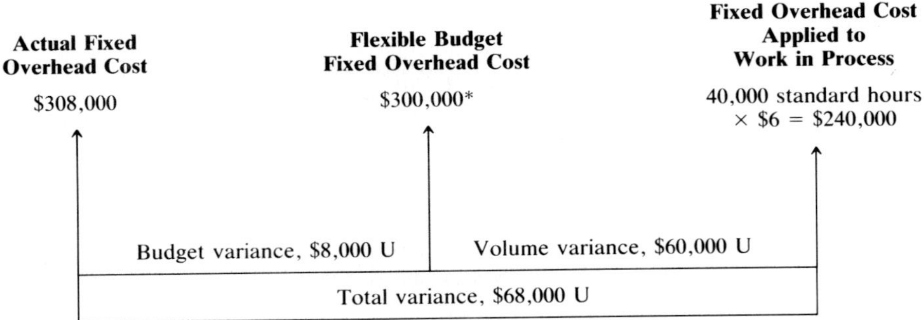

* As originally budgeted (see Exhibit 10–8). This figure can also be expressed as 50,000 denominator hours × $6 = $300,000.

From these data, two variances can be computed for fixed overhead—a *budget variance* and a *volume variance*. The variances are shown in Exhibit 10–10.

Notice from the exhibit that overhead has been applied to work in process on a basis of 40,000 standard hours allowed for the output of the year rather than on a basis of 42,000 actual hours worked. As stated earlier, this keeps unit costs from being affected by any efficiency variations.

The Budget Variance—A Closer Look

The **budget variance** represents the difference between actual fixed overhead costs incurred during the period and budgeted fixed overhead costs as contained in the flexible budget. The variance can also be presented in the following format:

Actual fixed overhead costs	$308,000
Budgeted fixed overhead costs (from the flexible budget in Exhibit 10–8)	300,000
Budget variance	$ 8,000 U

Although the budget variance is somewhat similar to the variable overhead spending variance, care must be exercised in how it is used. One must keep in mind that fixed costs are often beyond immediate managerial control. Therefore, rather than serving as a measure of managerial performance, in many cases the budget variance will be computed simply for information purposes in order to call management's attention to changes in price factors.

Fixed overhead costs and variances are often presented on the overhead performance report, along with the variable overhead costs. To show how this is done, an overhead performance report for Donner Company containing the fixed overhead budget variance is found in Exhibit 10–11. (The variable overhead cost data in the exhibit are taken from Exhibit 10–6.)

EXHIBIT 10–11

Fixed Overhead Costs on the Overhead Performance Report

DONNER COMPANY
Overhead Performance Report
For the Year Ended March 31, 19x1

Budgeted machine-hours	50,000
Actual machine-hours	42,000
Standard machine-hours allowed	40,000

Overhead Costs	Cost Formula (per hour)	Actual Costs 42,000 Hours	Budget Based on 42,000 Hours	Spending or Budget Variance
Variable costs:				
Indirect labor	$0.80	$ 36,000	$ 33,600	$ 2,400 U
Lubricants	0.30	11,000	12,600	1,600 F
Power	0.40	24,000	16,800	7,200 U
Total variable costs	$1.50	71,000	63,000	8,000 U
Fixed costs:				
Depreciation		100,000	100,000	—
Supervisory salaries		172,000	160,000	12,000 U
Insurance		36,000	40,000	4,000 F
Total fixed costs		308,000	300,000	8,000 U
Total overhead costs		$379,000	$363,000	$16,000 U

The Volume Variance—A Closer Look

The **volume variance** is a measure of utilization of plant facilities. The variance arises whenever the standard hours allowed for the output of a period are different from the denominator activity level that was planned when the period began. It can be computed as shown in Exhibit 10–10 or by means of the formula below:

$$\begin{array}{c}\text{Fixed portion of}\\ \text{the predetermined}\\ \text{overhead rate}\end{array} \times \left(\begin{array}{c}\text{Denominator}\\ \text{hours}\end{array} - \begin{array}{c}\text{Standard hours}\\ \text{allowed}\end{array}\right) = \begin{array}{c}\text{Volume}\\ \text{variance}\end{array}$$

Applying this formula to Donner Company, the volume variance would be:

$$\$6\ (50{,}000\text{ MH} - 40{,}000\text{ MH}) = \$60{,}000\text{ unfavorable}$$

Note that this computation agrees with the volume variance as shown in Exhibit 10–10. As stated earlier, the volume variance is a measure of utilization of available plant facilities. An unfavorable variance, as above, means that the company operated at an activity level *below* that planned for the period. A favorable variance would mean that the company operated at an activity level *greater* than that planned for the period.

It is important to note that the volume variance does not measure over- or underspending. A company normally would incur the same dollar amount of fixed overhead cost regardless of whether the period's activity was above or below the planned (denominator) level. In short, the volume variance is an activity-related variance in that it is explainable only by activity and is controllable only through activity.

To summarize:

1. If the denominator activity and the standard hours allowed for the output of the period are the same, then there is no volume variance.
2. If the denominator activity is greater than the standard hours allowed for the output of the period, then the volume variance is unfavorable, signifying an underutilization of available facilities.
3. If the denominator activity is less than the standard hours allowed for the output of the period, then the volume variance is favorable, signifying an overutilization of available facilities.

Graphic Analysis of Fixed Overhead Variances

Some insights into the budget and volume variances can be gained through graphic analysis. The needed graph is presented in Exhibit 10–12.

EXHIBIT 10–12
Graphic Analysis of Fixed Overhead Variances

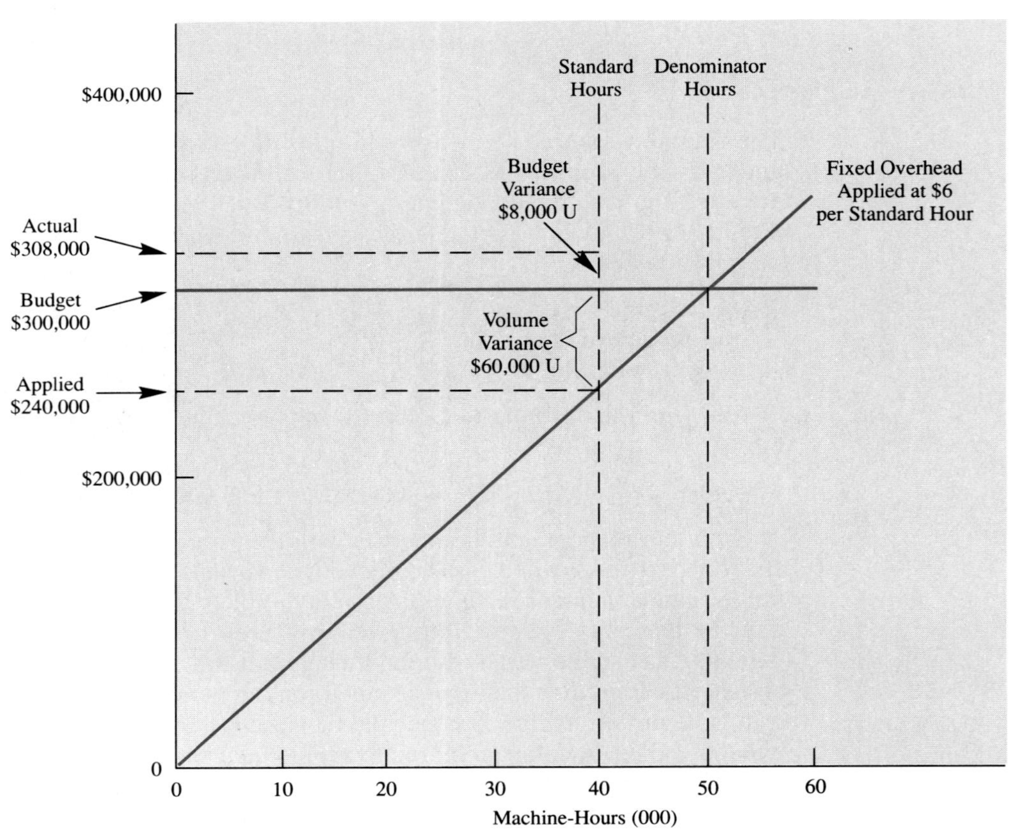

As shown in the graph, fixed overhead cost is applied to work in process at the predetermined rate of $6 for each standard hour of activity. (The applied-cost line is the upward-sloping line on the graph.) Since a denominator level of 50,000 machine-hours was used in computing the $6 rate, the applied-cost line crosses the budget-cost line at exactly the 50,000 machine-hour point. Thus, if the denominator hours and the standard hours allowed for output are the same, there can be no volume variance, since the applied-cost line and the budget-cost line will exactly meet on the graph. It is only when the standard hours differ from the denominator hours that a volume variance can arise.

In the case at hand, the standard hours allowed for output (40,000 hours) are less than the denominator hours (50,000 hours); the result is an unfavorable volume variance, since less cost was applied to production than was originally budgeted. If the tables had been reversed and the standard hours allowed for output had exceeded the denominator hours, then the volume variance on the graph would have been favorable.

Cautions in Fixed Overhead Analysis

There can be no volume variance for variable overhead, since applied costs and budgeted costs are both dependent on activity and thus will always be moving together. The reason we get a volume variance for fixed overhead is that the incurrence of the fixed costs does not depend on activity; yet when applying the costs to work in process, we do so *as if* the costs were variable and depended on activity. This point can be seen from the graph in Exhibit 10–12. Notice from the graph that the fixed overhead costs are applied to work in process at a rate of $6 per hour *as if* they were indeed variable. Treating these costs as if they were variable is necessary for product costing purposes, but there are some real dangers here. The manager can easily become misled and start thinking of the fixed costs as if they were *in fact* variable.

The manager must keep clearly in mind that fixed overhead costs come in large, indivisible pieces. Any breakdown of such costs, though necessary for product costing purposes, is artificial in nature and has no significance in matters relating either to actual cost behavior or to cost control. This is why the volume variance, which arises as a result of treating fixed costs as if they were variable, is not a controllable variance from a spending point of view. The fixed overhead rate used to compute the variance is simply a derived figure needed for product costing purposes, but it has no significance in terms of cost control.

Because of these factors, some companies present the volume variance in physical units (hours) rather than in dollars. These companies feel that stating the variance in physical units gives management a clearer signal as to the cause of the variance and how it can be controlled.

PRESENTATION OF VARIANCES ON THE INCOME STATEMENT

To complete our discussion of standard costs and variance analysis, we will show how variances can be presented on the income statement. Even though the variances may have already been presented on individual managers' performance reports and fully analyzed as to causes, many companies find it helpful to present them on the income statement as well, so that top management can see the cumulative effect on profits.

To illustrate, assume that Donner Company had the following variances for the most recent month. (The variances for materials and labor are assumed; the variances for variable and fixed overhead are the ones computed for Donner Company on preceding pages.)

Direct materials price variance	$ 5,000 F
Direct materials quantity variance	19,000 U
Direct labor rate variance	7,000 U
Direct labor efficiency variance	10,000 F
Variable overhead spending variance (p. 415)	8,000 U
Variable overhead efficiency variance (p. 417)	3,000 U
Fixed overhead budget variance (p. 422)	8,000 U
Fixed overhead volume variance (p. 422)	60,000 U
Total variances	$90,000 U

An income statement for Donner Company containing the total of these variances is presented in Exhibit 10–13. Note that the actual cost of goods sold on the statement exceeds the budgeted amount by $90,000, which agrees with the total of the variances summarized above. This type of presentation provides management with a clear picture of the impact of the variances on profits—a picture that could not be obtained by looking at performance reports alone. In the case at hand, Donner Company's profits have been dramatically reduced by the variances that developed during the period.

We should note that separate presentation of variances on the income statement is generally done only on those income statements that are prepared for management's own internal use. Income statements prepared for external use (for stockholders and others) typically show only actual cost figures.

EXHIBIT 10–13

Variances on the Income Statement

DONNER COMPANY
Income Statement
For the Year Ended March 31, 19x1

	20,000 Units		
	Actual	**Budgeted**	**Variance**
Sales ($50 per unit)	$1,000,000	$1,000,000	—
Less cost of goods sold (standard cost, $35 per unit*)	790,000	700,000	$90,000 U
Gross margin	210,000	300,000	90,000 U
Less operating expenses:			
Selling expense	105,000	105,000	—
Administrative expense	65,000	65,000	—
Total operating expenses	170,000	170,000	—
Net income	$ 40,000	$ 130,000	$90,000 U

* The $35 standard cost is taken from Donner Company's standard cost card found on page 420.

REVIEW PROBLEM ON OVERHEAD ANALYSIS

(This problem provides a comprehensive review of all parts of Chapter 10, including the computation of under- or overapplied overhead and its breakdown into the four overhead variances.)

A flexible budget for Aspen Company is given below:

Overhead Costs	Cost Formula (per hour)	Machine-Hours 4,000	6,000	8,000
Variable costs:				
Supplies	$0.20	$ 800	$ 1,200	$ 1,600
Indirect labor	0.30	1,200	1,800	2,400
Total variable costs	$0.50	2,000	3,000	4,000
Fixed costs:				
Depreciation		4,000	4,000	4,000
Supervision		5,000	5,000	5,000
Total fixed costs		9,000	9,000	9,000
Total overhead costs		$11,000	$12,000	$13,000

Five hours of machine time are required per unit of product. The company has set denominator activity for the coming period at 6,000 hours (or 1,200 units). The computation of the predetermined overhead rate would be:

$$\text{Total } \frac{\$12,000}{6,000 \text{ MH}} = \$2 \text{ per MH}$$

$$\text{Variable element } \frac{\$3,000}{6,000 \text{ MH}} = \$0.50 \text{ per MH}$$

$$\text{Fixed element } \frac{\$9,000}{6,000 \text{ MH}} = \$1.50 \text{ per MH}$$

Assume the following actual results for the period:

Number of units produced	1,300
Actual machine-hours	6,800
Standard machine-hours allowed*	6,500
Actual variable overhead cost	$4,200
Actual fixed overhead cost	9,400

* For 1,300 units of product.

Therefore, the company's Manufacturing Overhead account would appear as follows at the end of the period:

Manufacturing Overhead

	Debit	Credit	
Actual overhead costs	13,600*	13,000†	Applied overhead costs
Underapplied overhead	600		

* $4,200 variable + $9,400 fixed = $13,600.
† 6,500 standard hours × $2 = $13,000.

Required Analyze the $600 underapplied overhead in terms of:

1. A variable overhead spending variance.
2. A variable overhead efficiency variance.
3. A fixed overhead budget variance.
4. A fixed overhead volume variance.

Variable Overhead Variances

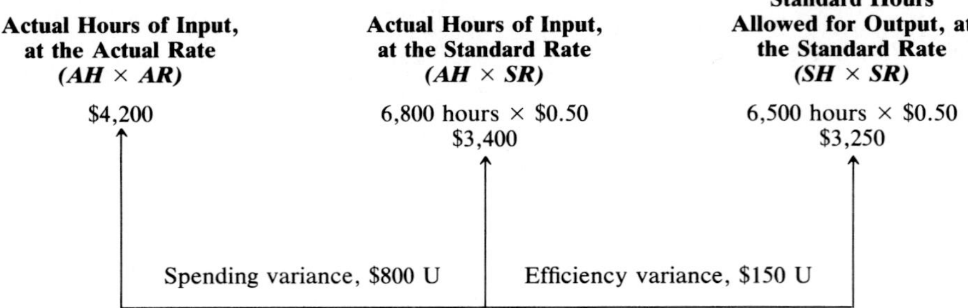

These same variances in the alternative format would be:

Variable overhead spending variance:

Actual variable overhead cost	$4,200
Actual inputs at the standard rate:	
6,800 hours × $0.50.	3,400
Spending variance	$ 800 U

Variable overhead efficiency variance:

$$SR(AH - SH) = \text{Efficiency variance}$$

$$\$0.50(6{,}800 \text{ hours} - 6{,}500 \text{ hours}) = \$150 \text{ U}$$

Fixed Overhead Variances

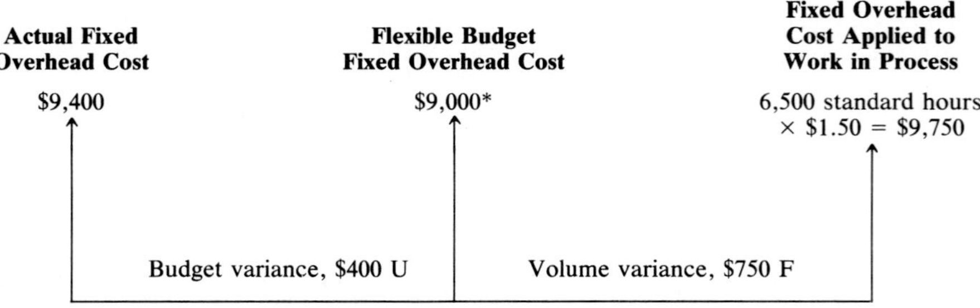

* Can be expressed as: 6,000 denominator hours × $1.50 = $9,000.

These same variances in the alternative format would be:

Fixed overhead budget variance:

Actual fixed overhead	$9,400
Budgeted fixed overhead	9,000
Budget variance	$ 400 U

Fixed overhead volume variance:

$$\begin{matrix}\text{Fixed portion of} \\ \text{the predetermined} \\ \text{overhead rate}\end{matrix} \times \left(\begin{matrix}\text{Denominator} \\ \text{hours}\end{matrix} - \begin{matrix}\text{Standard} \\ \text{hours}\end{matrix}\right) = \begin{matrix}\text{Volume} \\ \text{variance}\end{matrix}$$

$$\$1.50\ (6{,}000 \text{ hours} - 6{,}500 \text{ hours}) = \$750 \text{ F}$$

Summary of Variances

A summary of the four overhead variances is given below:

Variable overhead:	
Spending variance	$800 U
Efficiency variance	150 U
Fixed overhead:	
Budget variance	400 U
Volume variance	750 F
Underapplied overhead	$600

Notice that the $600 summary variance figure agrees with the underapplied balance in the company's Manufacturing Overhead account. This agreement stands as proof of the accuracy of our variance analysis. *Each period* the under- or overapplied overhead balance should be analyzed as we have done above. These variances will help the manager to see where his or her time and the time of the subordinates should be directed for better control of costs and operations.

KEY TERMS FOR REVIEW

Budget variance A measure of the difference between the actual fixed overhead costs incurred during the period and budgeted fixed overhead costs as contained in the flexible budget. (p. 422)

Denominator activity The estimated activity figure used to compute the predetermined overhead rate. (p. 419)

Flexible budget A budget that is designed to cover a range of activity and that can be used to develop budgeted costs at any point within that range to compare against actual costs incurred. (p. 409)

Static budget A budget designed to cover only one level of activity and in which actual costs are always compared against budgeted costs at this one activity level. (p. 409)

Volume variance A measure of utilization of plant facilities. The variance arises whenever the standard hours allowed for the output of a period are different from the denominator activity level that was planned when the period began. (p. 423)

QUESTIONS

10–1 What is a static budget?

10–2 What is a flexible budget, and how does it differ from a static budget? What is the main deficiency of the static budget?

10–3 What are the two prime responsibilities of the production manager? How do these two responsibilities differ?

10–4 Name three criteria that should be considered in choosing an activity base on which to construct a flexible budget.

10–5 In comparing budgeted data with actual data in a performance report for variable manufacturing overhead, what variance(s) will be produced if the budgeted data are based on actual hours worked? On both actual hours worked and standard hours allowed?

10–6 What is meant by the term *standard hours allowed?*

10–7 How does the variable manufacturing overhead spending variance differ from the materials price variance?

10–8 Why is the term *overhead efficiency variance* a misnomer?

10–9 "Fixed costs have no place in a flexible budget." Discuss.

10–10 In what way is the flexible budget involved in product costing?

10–11 What costing problem is created by the fact that fixed overhead costs come in large, indivisible chunks?

10–12 What is meant by the term *denominator level of activity?*

10–13 Why do we apply overhead to work in process on a basis of standard hours allowed in Chapter 10, when we applied it on a basis of actual hours in Chapter 3? What is the difference in costing systems between the two chapters?

10–14 In a standard cost system, what two variances can be computed for fixed overhead?

10–15 What does the fixed overhead budget variance measure? Is the variance controllable by management? Explain.

10–16 Under what circumstances would you expect the volume variance to be favorable? Unfavorable? Does the variance measure deviations in spending for fixed overhead items? Explain.

10–17 How might the volume variance be measured, other than in dollars?

10–18 What dangers are there in expressing fixed costs on a per unit basis?

10–19 In Chapter 3, you became acquainted with the concept of under- or overapplied overhead. What four variances can be computed from the under- or overapplied overhead total?

10–20 If factory overhead is overapplied for the month of August, would you expect the total of the overhead variances to be favorable or unfavorable? Why?

EXERCISES

E10–1 An incomplete flexible budget is given below:

Overhead Costs	Cost Formula (per hour)	Machine-Hours			
		6,000	8,000	10,000	12,000
Variable costs:					
Indirect materials			$ 6,000		
Maintenance			4,800		
Utilities			1,200		
Total variable costs					
Fixed costs:					
Rent			10,000		
Supervisory salaries			20,000		
Insurance.			8,000		
Total fixed costs.					
Total overhead costs.					

Required Provide the missing information in the budget.

E10–2 The cost formulas for Swan Company's overhead costs are given below. The costs cover a range of 8,000 to 10,000 machine-hours.

Overhead Costs	Cost Formula
Supplies	$0.20 per machine-hour
Indirect labor	10,000 plus $0.25 per machine-hour
Utilities	0.15 per machine-hour
Maintenance.	7,000 plus $0.10 per machine-hour
Depreciation.	8,000

Required Prepare a flexible budget in increments of 1,000 machine-hours. Include the fixed costs in your flexible budget.

E10–3 The variable portion of Whaley Company's flexible budget is given below:

Overhead Costs	Cost Formula (per hour)	Machine-Hours 10,000	18,000	24,000
Utilities	$1.20	$12,000	$21,600	$ 28,800
Supplies	0.30	3,000	5,400	7,200
Maintenance	2.40	24,000	43,200	57,600
Rework time	0.60	6,000	10,800	14,400
Total variable costs	$4.50	$45,000	$81,000	$108,000

During a recent period, the company recorded 16,000 machine-hours of activity. The variable overhead costs incurred were as follows:

Utilities	$20,000
Supplies	4,700
Maintenance	35,100
Rework time	12,300

The budgeted activity for the period had been 18,000 machine-hours.

Required

1. Prepare a variable overhead performance report for the period. Indicate whether variances are favorable (F) or unfavorable (U). Show only a spending variance on your report.
2. Discuss the significance of the variances. Might some variances be the result of others? Explain.

E10–4 Operating at a normal level of 24,000 direct labor-hours, Trone Company produces 8,000 units of product. The direct labor wage rate is $6.30 per hour. Two pounds of raw materials go into each unit of product at a cost of $4.20 per pound. A flexible budget is used to plan and control overhead costs:

Flexible Budget Data

Overhead Costs	Cost Formula (per hour)	Direct Labor-Hours 20,000	22,000	24,000
Variable costs	$1.60	$ 32,000	$ 35,200	$ 38,400
Fixed costs		84,000	84,000	84,000
Total overhead costs		$116,000	$119,200	$122,400

Required

1. Using 24,000 direct labor-hours as the denominator activity, compute the predetermined overhead rate and break it down into fixed and variable elements.

2. Complete the standard cost card below for one unit of product:

Direct materials, 2 pounds at $4.20 . . .	$8.40
Direct labor, ?.	?
Variable overhead, ?.	?
Fixed overhead, ?.	?
Total standard cost per unit	$?

E10–5 Kohler Company's flexible budget (in condensed form) is given below:

Overhead Costs	Cost Formula (per hour)	Machine-Hours 12,000	15,000	18,000
Variable costs	$1.80	$21,600	$27,000	$32,400
Fixed costs		60,000	60,000	60,000
Total overhead costs		$81,600	$87,000	$92,400

The following information is available for 19x8:

a. For 19x8, the company chose 15,000 machine-hours as the denominator level of activity for computing the predetermined overhead rate.
b. During 19x8, the company produced 9,500 units of product and worked 14,000 actual hours. The standard machine time per unit is 1.5 hours.
c. Actual overhead costs incurred during 19x8 were: variable overhead, $26,000; and fixed overhead, $60,450.

Required

1. Compute the predetermined overhead rate used during 19x8. Divide it into fixed and variable elements.
2. Compute the standard hours allowed for the output of 19x8.
3. Compute the fixed overhead budget and volume variances for 19x8.

E10–6 Selected operating information on four different companies for the year 19x6 is given below:

	Company A	B	C	D
Full-capacity machine-hours	10,000	18,000	20,000	15,000
Budgeted machine-hours*	9,000	17,000	20,000	14,000
Actual machine-hours	9,000	17,800	19,000	14,500
Standard machine-hours allowed for actual production	9,500	16,000	20,000	13,000

* Denominator activity.

Required

In each case, state whether the company would have:

1. No volume variance.
2. A favorable volume variance.
3. An unfavorable volume variance.

Also state in each case why you chose (1), (2), or (3).

E10–7 Weller Company's flexible budget (in condensed form) follows:

Overhead Costs	Cost Formula (per hour)	Machine-Hours 8,000	9,000	10,000
Variable costs	$1.05	$ 8,400	$ 9,450	$10,500
Fixed costs		24,800	24,800	24,800
Total overhead costs		$33,200	$34,250	$35,300

The following information is available:

a. For 19x1, a denominator activity of 8,000 machine-hours was chosen to compute the predetermined overhead rate.
b. At the 8,000 standard machine-hours level of activity, the company should produce 3,200 units of product.
c. During 19x1, the company's actual operating results were:

Number of units produced	3,500
Actual machine-hours	8,500
Actual variable overhead costs	$ 9,860
Actual fixed overhead costs.	25,100

Required
1. Compute the predetermined overhead rate for 19x1, and break it down into variable and fixed cost elements.
2. What were the standard hours allowed for the output of 19x1?
3. Compute the variable overhead spending and efficiency variances and the fixed overhead budget and volume variances for 19x1.

E10–8 Selected information relating to the fixed overhead costs of Westwood Company for 19x7 is given below:

Activity:	
Number of units produced	9,500
Standard hours allowed per unit	2
Denominator activity (machine-hours) . . .	20,000
Costs:	
Actual fixed overhead costs incurred . . .	$79,000
Budget variance	1,000 F

Overhead cost is applied to products on a basis of machine-hours.

Required
1. What was the fixed portion of the predetermined overhead rate for 19x7?
2. What were the standard hours allowed for 19x7 production?
3. What was the volume variance for 19x7?

E10–9 The standard cost card for the single product manufactured by Prince Company is given below:

Standard Cost Card—Per Unit

Direct materials, 3.5 feet at $4	$14.00
Direct labor, 0.8 hours at $9	7.20
Variable overhead, 0.8 hours at $2.50	2.00
Fixed overhead, 0.8 hours at $6	4.80
Total standard cost per unit.	$28.00

During 19x8, the company produced 10,000 units of product and worked 8,200 actual direct labor-hours. Overhead cost is applied to production on a basis of direct labor-hours. Selected data relating to the company's operations for the year are shown below:

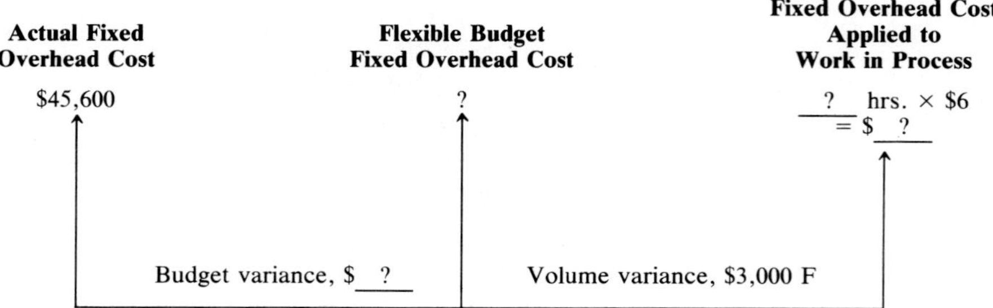

Required

1. What were the standard hours allowed for 19x8 production?
2. What was the amount of fixed overhead cost contained in the flexible budget for the year?
3. What was the budget variance for the year?
4. What denominator activity level did the company use in setting the predetermined overhead rate for the year?

PROBLEMS

P10–10 Standard Cost Card; Materials, Labor, and Overhead Variances Dresser Company uses a standard cost system and sets predetermined overhead rates on a basis of direct labor-hours. The following data are taken from the company's flexible budget for 19x5:

Denominator activity (direct labor-hours) . . .	9,000
Variable overhead cost	$34,200
Fixed overhead cost	63,000

A standard cost card showing the standard cost to produce one unit of the company's product is given below:

Direct materials, 4 pounds at $2.60	$10.40
Direct labor, 2 hours at $9	18.00
Overhead, 120% of direct labor cost	21.60
Standard cost per unit	$50.00

During 19x5, the company produced 4,800 units of product and incurred the following costs:

Materials purchased, 30,000 pounds at $2.50	$75,000
Materials used in production (in pounds)	20,000
Direct labor cost incurred, 10,000 hours at $8.60	$86,000
Variable overhead cost incurred	35,900
Fixed overhead cost incurred	64,800

Required

1. Redo the standard cost card in a clearer, more usable format by detailing the variable and fixed overhead cost elements.

2. Prepare an analysis of the variances for materials and labor for the year.
3. Prepare an analysis of the variances for variable and fixed overhead for the year.
4. What effect, if any, does the choice of a denominator activity level have on unit costs? Is the volume variance a controllable variance from a spending point of view? Explain.

P10–11 Basic Overhead Analysis High-Tech, Inc., produces a single product and uses a standard cost system to help in the control of costs. Overhead is applied to production on a basis of machine-hours. According to the company's flexible budget, the following overhead costs should be incurred at an activity level of 18,000 machine-hours (the denominator activity level chosen for 19x8):

Variable overhead costs	$ 31,500
Fixed overhead costs	72,000
Total overhead costs	$103,500

During 19x8, the following operating results were recorded:

Actual machine-hours worked	15,000
Standard machine-hours allowed	16,000
Actual variable overhead cost incurred	$26,500
Actual fixed overhead cost incurred	70,000

At the end of the year, the company's Manufacturing Overhead account contained the following data:

Manufacturing Overhead

Actual costs	96,500	92,000	Applied costs
	4,500		

Management would like to determine the cause of the $4,500 underapplied overhead before closing the amount to cost of goods sold.

Required

1. Compute the predetermined overhead rate that would have been used during 19x8. Break it down into variable and fixed cost elements.
2. Show how the $92,000 "Applied Costs" figure in the Manufacturing Overhead account was computed.
3. Analyze the $4,500 underapplied overhead figure in terms of the variable overhead spending and efficiency variances and the fixed overhead budget and volume variances.
4. Explain the meaning of each variance that you computed in (3) above, and indicate how each variance is controlled.

P10–12 Absorption Costing Statement; Integration of Materials, Labor, and Overhead Variances "It certainly is nice to see that small variance on the income statement after all the trouble we've had lately in controlling manufacturing costs," said Linda White, vice president of Molina Company. "The $2,250 variance reported last period is well below the 3 percent parameter we have set for variances. We need to congratulate everybody on a job well done." The income statement to which Ms. White was referring is shown on the following page:

	20,000 Units		
	Actual	Budgeted	Variance
Sales	$1,200,000	$1,200,000	$ —
Less cost of goods sold (standard cost, $38 per unit)	762,250	760,000	2,250
Gross margin	437,750	440,000	(2,250)
Less operating expenses:			
Selling expenses	200,000	200,000	—
Administrative expenses	150,000	150,000	—
Total operating expenses	350,000	350,000	—
Net income	$ 87,750	$ 90,000	$(2,250)

The company produces and sells a single product. A standard cost card for the product follows:

Standard Cost Card—Per Unit of Product

Direct materials, 4 yards at $3.50	$14
Direct labor, 1.5 hours at $8	12
Variable overhead, 1.5 hours at $2	3
Fixed overhead, 1.5 hours at $6	9
Standard cost per unit	$38

The following additional information is available for the year just completed:

a. The company manufactured and sold 20,000 units of product during the year.
b. A total of 78,000 yards of material were purchased during the year at a cost of $3.75 per yard. All of this material was used to manufacture the 20,000 units. There were no beginning or ending inventories for the year.
c. The company worked 32,500 direct labor-hours during the year at a cost of $7.80 per hour.
d. Overhead cost is applied to products on a basis of direct labor-hours. Data relating to overhead costs follow:

Denominator activity level (direct labor-hours) . . .	25,000
Budgeted fixed overhead costs (from the flexible budget)	$150,000
Actual fixed overhead costs	148,000
Actual variable overhead costs	68,250

e. All variances are closed to cost of goods sold at the end of each year.

Required

1. Compute the direct materials price and quantity variances for the year.
2. Compute the direct labor rate and efficiency variances for the year.
3. For overhead compute:
   a. The variable overhead spending and efficiency variances for the year.
   b. The fixed overhead budget and volume variances for the year.
4. Total the variances you have computed, and compare the net amount with the $2,250 variance on the income statement. Do you agree that everyone should be congratulated for a job well done? Explain.

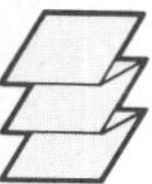

P10–13 Flexible Budgets and Overhead Analysis Rowe Company manufactures a variety of products in several departments. Budgeted costs for the company's finishing department have been set as follows for 19x2:

Variable costs:	
Direct materials	$ 600,000
Direct labor	450,000
Indirect labor	30,000
Utilities	50,000
Maintenance	20,000
Total variable costs	1,150,000
Fixed costs:	
Supervisory salaries	60,000
Insurance	5,000
Depreciation	190,000
Equipment rental	45,000
Total fixed costs	300,000
Total budgeted costs	$1,450,000
Budgeted direct labor-hours	?

After careful study, the company has determined that operating activity in the finishing department is best measured in direct labor-hours. Direct labor cost is budgeted at $9 per hour. The cost formulas used to develop the budgeted costs above are valid over a relevant range of 40,000 to 60,000 direct labor-hours per year.

Required

1. Prepare an overhead flexible budget in good form for the finishing department. Make your budget in increments of 10,000 hours. (The company does not include direct materials and direct labor costs in the flexible budget.)
2. Assume that the company computes predetermined overhead rates by department. Compute the rates, variable and fixed, that will be used by the finishing department during 19x2 to apply overhead costs to production.
3. Suppose that during 19x2 the following actual activity and costs are recorded in the finishing department:

Actual direct labor-hours worked	46,000
Standard direct labor-hours allowed for the output of the year	45,000
Actual variable overhead cost incurred	$ 89,700
Actual fixed overhead cost incurred	296,000

a. A T-account for manufacturing overhead costs for 19x2 in the finishing department is given below. Determine the amount of applied overhead cost for the year, and compute the under- or overapplied overhead.

Manufacturing Overhead

Actual costs 385,700	

b. Analyze the under- or overapplied overhead figure in terms of the variable overhead spending and efficiency variances and the fixed overhead budget and volume variances.

P10–14 Standard Cost Card and Overhead Analysis Wymont Company produces a single product that requires a large amount of labor time. Therefore, overhead cost is applied on a basis of direct labor-hours. The company's condensed flexible budget is given below:

Overhead Costs	Cost Formula (per hour)	Direct Labor-Hours 24,000	30,000	36,000
Variable costs	$2	$ 48,000	$ 60,000	$ 72,000
Fixed costs		180,000	180,000	180,000
Total overhead costs		$228,000	$240,000	$252,000

The company's product requires 4 feet of direct material that has a standard cost of $3 per foot. The product requires 1.5 hours of direct labor time. The standard labor rate is $7 per hour.

During 19x7, the company had planned to operate at a denominator activity level of 30,000 direct labor-hours and to produce 20,000 units of product. Actual activity and costs for the year were as follows:

Number of units produced	22,000
Actual direct labor-hours worked	35,000
Actual variable overhead cost incurred	$ 63,000
Actual fixed overhead cost incurred	181,000

Required

1. Compute the predetermined overhead rate that would have been used during 19x7. Break the rate down into variable and fixed elements.
2. Prepare a standard cost card for the company's product; show the details for all manufacturing costs on your standard cost card.
3. *a.* Compute the standard hours allowed for 19x7 production.
   b. Complete the following Manufacturing Overhead T-account for the year:

Manufacturing Overhead

?	?
?	?

4. Determine the reason for the under- or overapplied overhead from (3) above by computing the variable overhead spending and efficiency variances and the fixed overhead budget and volume variances.
5. Suppose the company had chosen 36,000 direct labor-hours as the denominator activity rather than 30,000 hours. State which, if any, of the variances computed in (4) above would have changed, and explain how the variance(s) would have changed. No computations are necessary.

P10–15 Absorption Costing Statement; Integration of Materials, Labor, and Overhead Variances "What a disaster!" exclaimed Kori Ortega, president of Oyler Company. "Our variances have almost wiped out our income for the last year. Just look at this statement. It's bad enough that our sales were off for the year, and now our costs are completely out of control." The statement to which Ms. Ortega was referring is given below:

	Actual	Budgeted	Variance
Sales	$1,300,000	$1,300,000	$ —
Less cost of goods sold (standard cost, $60 per unit)	863,500	780,000	83,500*
Gross margin	436,500	520,000	(83,500)
Less operating expenses:			
Selling expenses	270,000	270,000	—
Administrative expenses	160,000	160,000	—
Total operating expenses	430,000	430,000	—
Net income	$ 6,500	$ 90,000	$(83,500)

* Consists of the following variances:

Direct materials	$ 4,000 U
Direct labor	5,400 F
Manufacturing overhead	84,900 U
Total variance	$83,500 U

The company produces and sells a single product. A standard cost card for the product follows:

Standard Cost Card—Per Unit of Product

Direct materials: 3 feet at $10 per foot	$30
Direct labor: 1.5 hours at $6 per hour	9
Variable manufacturing overhead: 1.5 hours at $2 per hour . . .	3
Fixed manufacturing overhead: 1.5 hours at $12 per hour* . . .	18
Total standard cost per unit	$60

* Based on a denominator activity of 26,250 hours.

The following additional information is available for the period:

a. The company purchased 40,000 feet of materials during the year, at a cost of $9.85 per foot. All of the material was used to produce 13,000 units. There were no beginning or ending inventories.
b. The company worked 18,000 direct labor-hours during the year, at an average cost of $6.20 per hour.
c. The company incurred $31,500 in variable overhead cost during the year. Overhead is applied to products on a basis of direct labor-hours.
d. The company incurred $326,400 in fixed overhead costs during the year; according to the flexible budget, the company had planned to incur $315,000 in fixed overhead cost. A denominator activity of 26,250 hours is used to set overhead rates.
e. The company closes all variances to cost of goods sold each year, as shown in the income statement above.

Required

1. Compute the direct materials price and quantity variances for the year.
2. Compute the direct labor rate and efficiency variances for the year.
3. Compute the variable overhead spending and efficiency variances and the fixed overhead budget and volume variances for the year.
4. Is the company's problem primarily one of poor control over costs? Explain.

P10–16 Standard Cost Card; Fixed Overhead Analysis; Graphing For the year 19x3, Eastwood Company chose a denominator activity level of 15,000 direct labor-hours. According to the company's flexible budget, the following overhead costs should be incurred at this activity level:

Variable overhead costs . . .	$ 18,000
Fixed overhead costs	135,000

The company manufactures a single product that requires 2.5 hours to complete. The direct labor rate is $7 per hour. The product requires 4 pounds of raw materials; this material has a standard cost of $8 per pound. Overhead is applied to production on a basis of direct labor-hours.

Required

1. Compute the predetermined overhead rate that the company will use during 19x3. Break the rate down into variable and fixed cost elements.
2. Prepare a standard cost card for one unit of product, using the following format:

Direct materials, 4 pounds at $8.00 . . .	$32.00
Direct labor, ?	?
Variable overhead, ?.	?
Fixed overhead, ?	?
Total standard cost per unit	$?

3. Prepare a graph with cost on the vertical *(Y)* axis and direct labor-hours on the horizontal *(X)* axis. Plot a line on your graph from a zero level of activity to 20,000 direct labor-hours for each of the following costs:
   a. Budgeted fixed overhead cost (in total).
   b. Applied fixed overhead cost applied at the hourly rate computed in (1) above.
4. Assume that during 19x3 the company's actual activity is as follows:

Number of units produced	5,600
Actual direct labor-hours worked	14,500
Actual fixed overhead cost incurred . . .	$137,400

   a. Compute the fixed overhead budget and volume variances for the year.
   b. Show the volume variance on the graph you prepared in (3) above.
5. Disregard the data in (4) above. Assume instead that the company's actual activity for the year 19x3 is as follows:

Number of units produced	6,200
Actual direct labor-hours worked	15,800
Actual fixed overhead costs incurred . . .	$137,400

   a. Compute the fixed overhead budget and volume variances for the year.
   b. Show the volume variance on the graph you prepared in (3) above.

P10–17 Selection of a Denominator; Overhead Analysis The condensed flexible budget of the Scott Company for 19x2 is given below:

Overhead Costs	Cost Formula (per hour)	Direct Labor-Hours		
		30,000	40,000	50,000
Variable costs	$2.50	$ 75,000	$100,000	$125,000
Fixed costs		320,000	320,000	320,000
Total overhead costs		$395,000	$420,000	$445,000

The company produces a single product that requires 2.5 direct labor-hours to complete. The direct labor wage rate is $7.50 per hour. Three yards of raw material are required for each unit of product, at a cost of $5 per yard.

Demand for the company's product differs widely from year to year. Expected actual activity for 19x2 is 50,000 direct labor-hours; long-run normal activity is 40,000 direct labor-hours per year.

Required

1. Assume that the company chooses 40,000 direct labor-hours as the denominator level of activity. Compute the predetermined overhead rate, breaking it down into fixed and variable cost elements.
2. Assume that the company chooses 50,000 direct labor-hours as the denominator level of activity. Repeat the computations in (1) above.
3. Complete two standard cost cards as outlined below. Each card should relate to a single unit of product.

Denominator Activity: 40,000 DLH

Direct materials, 3 yards at $5	$15.00
Direct labor, ?	?
Variable overhead, ?	?
Fixed overhead, ?	?
Total standard cost per unit	$?

Denominator Activity: 50,000 DLH	
Direct materials, 3 yards at $5	$15.00
Direct labor, ?	?
Variable overhead, ?	?
Fixed overhead, ?	?
Total standard cost per unit	$?

4. Assume that 48,000 actual hours are worked during 19x2, and that 18,500 units are produced. Actual overhead costs for the year are:

Variable costs	$124,800
Fixed costs	321,700
Total overhead costs . . .	$446,500

   a. Compute the standard hours allowed for 19x2 production.
   b. Compute the missing items from the manufacturing overhead account below. Assume that the company uses 40,000 direct labor-hours (long-run normal activity) as the denominator activity figure in computing overhead rates, as you have used in (1) above.

Manufacturing Overhead

Actual costs	446,500	?
?		?

   c. Analyze your under- or overapplied overhead balance in terms of variable overhead spending and efficiency variances and fixed overhead budget and volume variances.

5. Looking at the variances that you have computed, what appears to be the major disadvantage of using long-run normal activity rather than expected actual activity as a denominator in computing the predetermined overhead rate? What advantages can you see to offset this disadvantage?

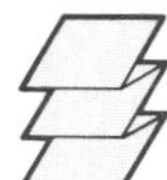

P10–18 Standard Cost Card; Overhead Analysis; Graphing A condensed flexible budget for Eaton Company is given below:

Overhead Costs	Cost Formula (per hour)	Direct Labor-Hours 8,000	10,000	12,000
Variable costs	$1.50	$ 12,000	$ 15,000	$ 18,000
Fixed costs		90,000	90,000	90,000
Total overhead costs		$102,000	$105,000	$108,000

The company produces a single product, which requires 2 hours of direct labor time to complete, at a rate of $5 per hour. Each unit of product requires 3 yards of material at $5.60 per yard. Overhead is applied to units of product on a basis of direct labor-hours. During the most recent period, the following actual costs and output were recorded:

Number of units produced	4,250
Actual direct labor-hours	9,000
Actual fixed overhead cost	$88,500

Required

1. Assume that the company computes predetermined overhead rates by using a denominator activity of 8,000 direct labor-hours.
   a. Compute the predetermined overhead rate, and break it down into variable and fixed cost elements.
   b. Prepare a standard cost card, showing the cost to produce one unit of product.
2. Refer to the original data. Assume that the company computes predetermined overhead rates by using a denominator activity of 12,000 direct labor-hours.
   a. Compute the predetermined overhead rate under this assumption, and break it down into variable and fixed cost elements.
   b. Prepare a standard cost card, showing the cost to produce one unit of product.
3. Refer to your computations in (1) above.
   a. Using these data, compute the budget and volume variances for the most recent period.
   b. Prepare a graph showing budgeted fixed costs throughout the relevant range and showing an applied overhead line for fixed costs from a zero level of activity through the denominator level of activity. Indicate on your graph the volume variance that you have just computed. In your own words, explain why a volume variance arises.
4. Refer to your computations in (2) above.
   a. Using these data, compute the budget and volume variances for the most recent period.
   b. Prepare another graph showing budgeted fixed overhead and applied fixed overhead, as well as the volume variance that you have just computed.
5. What are the implications of this problem regarding the setting of fixed overhead rates for product costing purposes? Are such rates useful control tools? Explain.

P10–19 **Comprehensive Overhead Analysis** Pallas Company manufactures and sells a single product. Each unit requires 6 pounds of raw material, which has a standard cost of \$3.75 per pound, and 2.5 hours of direct labor time, which has a standard rate of \$4 per hour. Overhead costs are planned and controlled through a flexible budget, which is shown in condensed form below:

Overhead Costs	Cost Formula (per hour)	Direct Labor-Hours 15,000	30,000	45,000
Variable costs	\$3	\$ 45,000	\$ 90,000	\$135,000
Fixed costs		360,000	360,000	360,000
Total overhead costs		\$405,000	\$450,000	\$495,000

Actual operating results for the most recent period are shown below:

Activity:	
Number of units produced	14,000
Standard hours allowed for output	?
Actual direct labor-hours worked	36,000
Cost:	
Actual variable overhead cost	\$107,100
Actual fixed overhead cost	362,500

Required

1. Assume that the company normally operates at an activity level of 30,000 standard direct labor-hours each period and that this figure is used as the denominator activity in computing predetermined overhead rates.
   a. Compute the predetermined overhead rate, and break it down into fixed and variable cost elements.

   b. Prepare a standard cost card, showing the standard cost to produce one unit of product.

2. Refer to the original data. Assume that the company decides to use 45,000 standard direct labor-hours as the denominator activity in computing predetermined overhead rates.
   a. Under this assumption, compute the predetermined overhead rate and break it down into fixed and variable cost elements.
   b. Prepare another standard cost card, showing the standard cost to produce one unit of product.
3. Refer to the computations you made in (1) above.
   a. Prepare a T-account for manufacturing overhead, and enter the actual overhead costs for the most recent period as shown in the original data to the problem. Determine the amount of overhead that would have been applied to production during the period, and enter this amount into the T-account.
   b. Compute the amount of under- or overapplied overhead for the period, and then analyze it in terms of the variable overhead spending and efficiency variances and the fixed overhead budget and volume variances.
4. Refer to the computations you made in (2) above.
   a. Prepare another T-account for manufacturing overhead, and again enter the actual overhead costs for the most recent period. Determine the amount of overhead that would have been applied to production during the period, and enter this amount into the T-account.
   b. Compute the amount of under- or overapplied overhead for the period, and then analyze it in terms of the variable overhead spending and efficiency variances and the fixed overhead budget and volume variances.
5. Firms are sometimes accused by competitors and others of selling products "below cost." What implications does this problem have for the "cost" of a unit of product so far as the setting of fixed overhead rates is concerned?

P10–20 Preparing a Revised Overhead Performance Report Shipley Company has had a comprehensive budgeting system in operation for several years. Feelings vary among the managers as to the value and benefit of the system. The line supervisors are very happy with the reports being prepared on their performance, but upper management often expresses dissatisfaction over the reports being prepared on various phases of the company's operations. A typical overhead performance report for a recent period is shown below:

SHIPLEY COMPANY
Overhead Performance Report—Milling Department
For the Quarter Ended June 30, 19x6

	Actual	Budget	Variance
Machine-hours	25,000	30,000	
Variable overhead:			
Indirect labor	$ 20,000	$ 22,500	$2,500 F
Supplies	5,400	6,000	600 F
Utilities	27,000	30,000	3,000 F
Rework time	14,000	15,000	1,000 F
Total variable costs	66,400	73,500	7,100 F
Fixed overhead:			
Maintenance	61,900	60,000	1,900 U
Inspection	90,000	90,000	—
Total fixed costs	151,900	150,000	1,900 U
Total overhead costs	$218,300	$223,500	$5,200 F

After receiving a copy of this performance report, the supervisor of the milling department stated, "No one can complain about my department; our variances have been favorable for over a year now. We've saved the company thousands of dollars by our excellent cost control."

The "budget" data above are taken from the department's flexible budget and represent the original planned level of activity for the quarter.

Required

1. The production superintendent is uneasy about the performance reports being prepared and would like you to evaluate their usefulness to the company.
2. What changes, if any, would you recommend be made in the overhead performance report above in order to give the production superintendent better insight into how well the supervisor is doing his job?
3. Prepare a new overhead performance report for the quarter, incorporating any changes you suggested in (2) above.

P10–21 Flexible Budget and Overhead Performance Report Durrant Company has had great difficulty in controlling overhead costs. At a recent convention, the president heard about a control device for overhead costs known as a flexible budget, and he has hired you to implement this budgeting program in Durrant Company. After some effort, you develop the following cost formulas for the company's machining department. These costs are based on a normal operating range of 10,000 to 20,000 machine-hours per month:

Cost	Cost Formula
Utilities	$0.70 per machine-hour
Lubricants	1.00 per machine-hour plus $8,000 per month
Machine setup	0.20 per machine-hour
Indirect labor	0.60 per machine-hour plus $120,000 per month
Depreciation	32,000 per month

During March 19x3, the first month after your preparation of the above data, the machining department worked 18,000 machine-hours and produced 9,000 units of product. The actual costs of this production were:

Utilities	$ 12,000
Lubricants	24,500
Machine setup	4,800
Indirect labor	132,500
Depreciation	32,000
Total costs	$205,800

There were no variances in the fixed costs. The department had originally been budgeted to work 20,000 machine-hours during March 19x3.

Required

1. Prepare a flexible budget for the machining department in increments of 5,000 hours. Include both variable and fixed costs in your budget.
2. Prepare an overhead performance report for the machining department for the month of March. Include both variable and fixed costs in the report (in separate sections). Show only a spending variance on the report.
3. What additional information would you need to have in order to compute an overhead efficiency variance for the department?
4. Explain to the president how the flexible budget might be used for product costing purposes as well as for cost control purposes.

P10–22 Spending and Efficiency Variances; Evaluating an Overhead Performance Report Ronald Davis, superintendent of Mason Company's milling department, is very happy with his performance report for the past month. The report follows:

MASON COMPANY
Overhead Performance Report—Milling Department

	Actual	Budget	Variance
Machine-hours	30,000	35,000	
Variable overhead:			
Indirect labor	$ 19,700	$ 21,000	$ 1,300 F
Utilities	50,800	59,500	8,700 F
Supplies	12,600	14,000	1,400 F
Maintenance	24,900	28,000	3,100 F
Total variable costs	108,000	122,500	14,500 F
Fixed overhead:			
Maintenance	52,000	52,000	—
Supervision	110,000	110,000	—
Depreciation	80,000	80,000	—
Total fixed costs	242,000	242,000	—
Total overhead costs	$350,000	$364,500	$14,500 F

Upon receiving a copy of this report, John Arnold, the production manager, commented, "I've been getting these reports for months now, and I still can't see how they help me assess efficiency and cost control in that department. I agree that the budget for the month was 35,000 machine-hours, but that represents 17,500 units of product (since it should take two hours to produce one unit). The department produced only 14,000 units during the month, and took 30,000 machine-hours of time to do it. Why do all the variances turn up favorable?"

Required

1. In answer to Mr. Arnold's question, why do all the variances turn up favorable? Evaluate the performance report.
2. Prepare a new overhead performance report that will help Mr. Arnold assess efficiency and cost control in the milling department. (Hint: Exhibit 10–7 may be helpful in structuring your report; include both variable and fixed costs in the report.)

P10–23 Preparing and Analyzing a Detailed Overhead Performance Report Weil Products, Inc., operates a number of production plants throughout the country. The company's Lindon Plant has been in operation for 15 months. Performance in the plant during the first six months was affected by the usual problems associated with a new operation. Although operations are now running smoothly, the Lindon Plant has not been able to produce profits on a consistent basis. As the production requirements to meet sales demand have increased, the profit performance has deteriorated.

At a staff meeting attended by the plant general manager, the corporate controller, and the corporate budget director, the plant production manager commented that production in the plant changes somewhat from month to month according to sales demand. He noted that this makes it more difficult to control manufacturing expenses. He further noted that the overhead budget for the plant, included in the company's annual profit plan, was static in nature and thus was not useful for judging the plant's performance because of the month-to-month changes in operating levels. The meeting resulted in a decision to redo the budget on a flexible basis and to prepare a report each month that would compare actual manufacturing expenses with budgeted expenses based on actual machine-hours in the plant.

The plant production manager and the plant accountant studied the cost patterns for recent months, as well as volume and cost data from other Weil plants. Then they prepared the following flexible budget schedule:

Overhead Costs	Per Machine-Hour	Machine-Hours 150,000	200,000	250,000
Variable costs:				
Indirect labor	$0.80	$120,000	$160,000	$200,000
Supplies	0.13	19,500	26,000	32,500
Power	0.07	10,500	14,000	17,500
Total variable costs	$1.00	150,000	200,000	250,000
Fixed costs:				
Supervisory labor		64,000	64,000	64,000
Heat and light		15,000	15,000	15,000
Property taxes		5,000	5,000	5,000
Total fixed costs		84,000	84,000	84,000
Total overhead costs		$234,000	$284,000	$334,000

The plant expected to work 200,000 planned production hours in a typical month, which at standard would result in 50,000 units of output.

The manufacturing expense reports prepared for the first three months after the flexible budget program was approved were pleasing to the plant production manager. They showed that except for small variations, the manufacturing expenses were in line with the flexible budget allowances. This is also reflected in the report prepared for November, which is presented below, when 50,500 units were manufactured. However, the plant is still not producing an adequate profit (due in part to excessive overhead costs), and management is beginning to wonder whether the flexible budget was a good idea after all.

LINDON PLANT
Manufacturing Expense Report
November 19x5

220,000 actual machine production hours

Overhead Costs	Actual Costs	Budgeted Costs	(Over) Under Budget
Variable costs:			
Indirect labor	$177,000	$176,000	$(1,000)
Supplies	27,400	28,600	1,200
Power	16,000	15,400	(600)
Total variable costs	220,400	220,000	(400)
Fixed costs:			
Supervisory labor	65,000	64,000	(1,000)
Heat and light	15,500	15,000	(500)
Property taxes	5,000	5,000	—
Total fixed costs	85,500	84,000	(1,500)
Total overhead costs	$305,900	$304,000	$(1,900)

Required

1. From the standpoint of cost control, explain the advantages of the flexible budget approach over the static budget approach.
2. Criticize the overhead expense report above. How could the report be improved to provide management with more information about overhead costs?
3. Prepare a new overhead expense report for November. On your report, show the total excess over standard incurred for manufacturing expense items during the month. Analyze this total excess amount into those variances due to:

   a. Spending (or budget).
   b. Efficiency.
4. Explain what the management of the Lindon Plant should do to reduce:
   a. The spending (or budget) variance.
   b. The efficiency variance.

(CMA, Adapted)

P10–24 Comprehensive Problem: Flexible Budget; Overhead Performance Report Elgin Company has recently introduced budgeting as an integral part of its corporate planning process. An inexperienced member of the accounting staff was given the assignment of constructing a flexible budget for overhead costs and prepared it in the format shown below:

Percentage of Capacity	**80%**	**100%**
Machine-hours	40,000	50,000
Utilities	$ 41,000	$ 49,000
Supplies	4,000	5,000
Indirect labor	8,000	10,000
Maintenance	37,000	41,000
Supervision	10,000	10,000
Total overhead costs	$100,000	$115,000

The company assigns overhead costs to production on a basis of machine-hours. The cost formulas used to prepare the budgeted figures above are relevant over a range of 80 to 100 percent of capacity and relate to monthly usage of overhead cost items. The managers who will be working under these budgets have control over both fixed and variable overhead costs.

Required

1. Redo the company's flexible budget, presenting it in better format as illustrated in Exhibit 10–8. Show the budgeted costs at 80, 90, and 100 percent levels of capacity. (Use the high-low method to separate fixed and variable costs.)
2. Express the flexible budget prepared in (1) above in cost formula form, using a single cost formula to express all overhead costs.
3. During May 19x7, the company operated at 86 percent of capacity in terms of actual machine-hours recorded in the factory. Actual overhead costs incurred during the month were:

Utilities	$ 42,540
Supplies	6,450
Indirect labor	9,890
Maintenance	35,190
Supervision	10,000
Total actual costs	$104,070

   There were no variances in the fixed costs. Prepare a performance report for May 19x7. Include both fixed and variable costs in your report (in separate sections). Structure your report so that it shows only a spending variance for overhead. The company originally budgeted to work 40,000 machine-hours during the month; standard hours allowed for the month's production totaled 41,000 machine-hours.
4. Explain the possible causes of the spending variance for supplies.
5. Compute an efficiency variance for *total* variable overhead cost, and explain the nature of the variance.

CASES

C10–25 Integrative Case; Working Backwards from Variance Data You have recently accepted a position with Dork Company, the manufacturer of an unusual product that is popular with some people. As part of your duties, you review the variances that are reported for each period and make a presentation on the variances to the company's executive committee.

Earlier this morning you received the variances for the most recent period. After reviewing the variances and organizing the data for your presentation, you accidently placed the material on top of some papers that were going to the shredder. In the middle of lunch you suddenly realized your mistake and dashed from the executive lunchroom to the shredding room. There you found the operator busily feeding your pages through the machine. You managed to pull only part of one page from the feeding chute, which contains the following information:

Standard Cost Card

Direct materials, 2 yards at $16	$32.00
Direct labor, 3 hours at $5	15.00
Variable overhead, 3 hours at $3 . . .	9.00
Fixed overhead, 3 hours at $8	24.00
Standard cost per unit	$80.00

	Total Standard Cost*	Variances Reported			
		Price or Rate	Spending or Budget	Quantity or Efficiency	Volume
Direct materials	$608,000	$11,600 F		$32,000 U	
Direct labor	285,000	8,540 U		20,000 U	
Variable overhead . . .	171,000		$3,700 F	?†	
Fixed overhead	456,000		1,500 F		$24,000 U

* Applied to Work in Process during the period.
† Figure obliterated by the shredder.

You recall that overhead cost is applied to production on a basis of direct labor-hours and that all of the materials purchased during the period were used in production. Since the company uses JIT to control work flows, work in process inventories are nominal and can be ignored.

At lunch your supervisor told you how pleased she was with your work and that she was looking forward to your presentation that afternoon. You realize that to avoid looking like a bungling fool you must somehow generate necessary "backup" data for the variances before the executive committee meeting starts in one hour.

Required

1. How many units were produced last period? (You'll have to think a bit to derive this figure from the data.)
2. How many yards of direct materials were purchased and used in production?
3. What was the actual cost per yard of material?
4. How many actual direct labor-hours were worked during the period?
5. What was the actual rate per direct labor-hour?
6. How much actual variable overhead cost was incurred during the period?
7. What is the total fixed cost in the company's flexible budget?
8. What were the denominator hours for last period?

C10–26 Incomplete Data Each of the cases below is independent. You may assume that each company uses a standard cost system and that each company's flexible budget is based on standard machine-hours.

Item	Company X	Company Y
1. Denominator activity in hours	18,000	?
2. Standard hours allowed for units produced	?	28,000
3. Actual hours worked	?	27,500
4. Flexible budget variable overhead per machine-hour	$ 1.60	$?
5. Flexible budget fixed overhead (total)	?	?
6. Actual variable overhead cost	30,000	55,275
7. Actual fixed overhead cost	72,500	134,600
8. Variable overhead cost applied to production*	31,200	?
9. Fixed overhead cost applied to production*	?	126,000
10. Variable overhead spending variance	?	?
11. Variable overhead efficiency variance	800 U	1,000 F
12. Fixed overhead budget variance	500 U	?
13. Fixed overhead volume variance	?	9,000 U
14. Variable portion of the predetermined overhead rate	?	?
15. Fixed portion of the predetermined overhead rate	?	?
16. Underapplied or (overapplied) overhead	?	?

* Based on standard hours allowed for units produced.

Required Compute the unknown amounts. (Hint: One way to proceed would be to use the columnar format for variance analysis found in Exhibit 9–5 for variable overhead and in Exhibit 10–10 for fixed overhead.)

C10–27 Selling Expense Flexible Budget Mark Fletcher, president of SoftGro Inc., was looking forward to seeing the performance reports for the month of November because he knew the company's sales for the month had exceeded budget by a considerable margin. SoftGro, a distributor of educational software packages, had been growing steadily for approximately two years. Fletcher's biggest challenge at this point was to ensure that the company did not lose control of expenses during this growth period. When Fletcher received the November reports, he was dismayed to see the large unfavorable variance in the company's monthly selling expense report that is presented below:

SOFTGRO INC.
Monthly Selling Expense Report
November 19x7

	Annual Budget	November Budget	November Actual	November Variance
Unit sales	2,000,000	280,000	310,000	30,000 F
Dollar sales	$80,000,000	$11,200,000	$12,400,000	$1,200,000 F
Orders processed	54,000	6,500	5,800	700 U
Salespersons per month	90	90	96	6 U
Expenses:				
Advertising	$19,800,000	$ 1,650,000	$ 1,660,000	$ 10,000 U
Staff salaries	1,500,000	125,000	125,000	—
Sales salaries	1,296,000	108,000	115,400	7,400 U
Commissions	3,200,000	448,000	496,000	48,000 U
Per diem expense	1,782,000	148,500	162,600	14,100 U
Office expense	4,080,000	340,000	358,400	18,400 U
Shipping expense	6,750,000	902,500	976,500	74,000 U
Total expenses	$38,408,000	$ 3,722,000	$ 3,893,900	$ 171,900 U

Fletcher called in the company's new controller, Susan Porter, to discuss the implications of the variances reported for November and to plan a strategy for improving performance. Porter suggested that the reporting format that the company had been using might not be giving Fletcher a true picture of the company's operations and proposed that SoftGro implement flexible budgeting for reporting purposes. Porter offered to redo the monthly selling expense report for November using flexible budgeting so that Fletcher could compare the two reports and see the advantages of flexible budgeting.

After some analysis, Porter has determined the following data about the company's selling expenses:

a. The total compensation paid to the sales force consists of both a monthly base salary and a commission. The commission varies with sales dollars.

b. Sales office expense is a mixed cost with the variable portion related to the number of orders processed. The fixed portion of office expense is $3,000,000 annually and is incurred uniformly throughout the year.

c. Subsequent to the adoption of the annual budget for the current year, SoftGro decided to open a new sales territory. As a consequence, approval was given to hire six additional salespersons effective November 1, 19x7. Porter decided that these additional six people should be recognized in her revised report.

d. Per diem reimbursement to the sales force, while a fixed stipend per day, is variable with the number of salespersons and the number of days spent traveling. SoftGro's original budget was based on an average sales force of 90 persons throughout the year with each salesperson traveling 15 days per month.

e. The company's shipping expense is a mixed cost with the variable portion, $3 per unit, dependent on the number of units sold. The fixed portion is incurred uniformly throughout the year.

Using the data above, Porter believed she would be able to redo the November report and present it to Fletcher for his review.

Required

1. Cite the benefits of flexible budgeting, and explain why Susan Porter would propose that SoftGro use flexible budgeting in this situation.
2. Prepare a revised monthly selling expense report for November that would permit Mark Fletcher to more clearly evaluate SoftGro's control over selling expenses. The report should have a line for *each* selling expense item showing the appropriate budgeted amount, the actual selling expense, and the variance for the month.

(CMA, Adapted)

11

Control of Decentralized Operations

LEARNING OBJECTIVES

After studying Chapter 11, you should be able to:

1. Explain how a pyramiding system of reports is used to communicate information between various levels of responsibility in an organization.
2. Enumerate the benefits to be gained by decentralization in an organization.
3. Differentiate between cost centers, profit centers, and investment centers, and explain how performance is measured in each.
4. Compute return on investment (ROI) by means of the ROI formula and show how changes in sales, expenses, and assets affect an organization's ROI.
5. Compute the residual income and enumerate the strengths and weaknesses of this method of measuring managerial performance.
6. Use the transfer pricing formula to compute an appropriate transfer price between segments of an organization under conditions of *(a)* full capacity and *(b)* idle capacity.
7. Define or explain the key terms listed at the end of the chapter.

In this chapter, we expand our knowledge of performance reports by looking more closely at responsibility accounting. This concept was first introduced in Chapter 8 and has been the "why" behind most of our work with budgets and performance reports in preceding chapters. We shall now use the responsibility accounting concept to show how the reports developed in these chapters fit together into an integrated reporting system. In the process, we will extend the technique of performance reporting to the company as a whole and demonstrate methods of evaluating the performance of top management.

RESPONSIBILITY ACCOUNTING

Responsibility accounting centers on the idea that an organization is simply a group of individuals working toward common goals. The more each individual can be assisted in the performance of his or her tasks, the better chance the organization has of reaching the goals it has set. As we have seen in preceding chapters, responsibility accounting recognizes each person in an organization who has any control over cost or revenue to be a *separate responsibility center* whose stewardship must be defined, measured, and reported upward in the organization. One author expresses the idea this way:

> In effect, the system personalizes the accounting statements by saying, "Joe, this is what you originally budgeted and this is how you performed for the period with actual operations as compared against your budget." By definition it [responsibility accounting] is a system of accounting which is tailored to an organization so that costs are accumulated and reported by levels of responsibility within the organization. Each supervisory area in the organization is charged *only* with the cost for which it is responsible and over which it has control.[1]

Although the idea behind responsibility accounting is not new, the implementation of the idea on a widespread basis is quite recent and has come about in response to the manager's need for better and more efficient ways to control operations.

The Functioning of the System

In order to broaden our perspective of how a responsibility accounting system functions, we will consider selected data relating to Potter Company. Potter Company is part of the Western Division of General Products, Inc., a broadly diversified firm with interests in many product areas. A partial organization chart for Potter Company is shown in Exhibit 11–1. The data on this chart form the basis for exhibits found on the following pages.

Although the concepts underlying responsibility accounting apply equally well to all parts of an organization, we will concentrate our discussion on the shaded area of Potter Company's organization chart. It depicts the line of

[1] John A. Higgins, "Responsibility Accounting," *Arthur Andersen Chronicle*, April 1952, p. 94.

EXHIBIT 11–1
Organization Chart—Potter Company

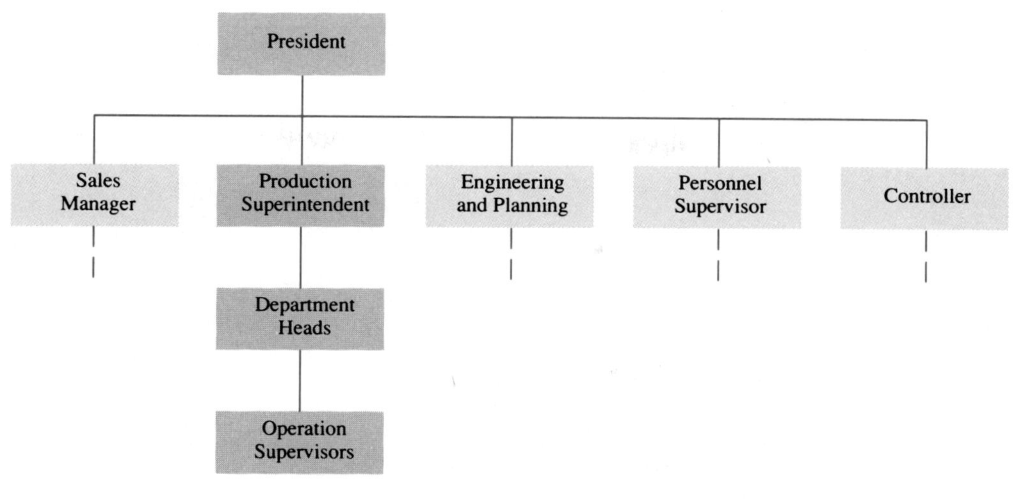

responsibility for the production activities of the firm. This line of responsibility begins with the operation supervisors and moves upward in the organization, with each successive level having greater overall responsibility than the level that preceded it. To see how this concept of an upward-flowing, broadening line of responsibility can be integrated into the accounting statements, refer to Exhibit 11–2.

Exhibit 11–2 provides us with a bird's-eye view of the structuring of reports in a responsibility accounting system. Notice that the performance reports *start at the bottom and build upward,* with each manager receiving information on his own performance as well as on the performance of each manager under him in the chain of responsibility. We will now start at the bottom of this chain and follow it upward to show how the reports are used by the various levels of management.

The Flow of Information

The responsibility accounting system depicted in Exhibit 11–2 is structured around four levels of responsibility. The number of levels of responsibility will vary from company to company, according to organizational structure and needs.

Fourth Level of Responsibility The fourth, or lowest, level of responsibility is that of the wiring operation supervisor. The performance report prepared for the supervisor will be similar to the performance reports discussed in the two preceding chapters. This report will show budgeted data, actual data, and variances in terms of materials, labor, and overhead. This information will be communicated upward to the department head, along with detailed variance analyses.

EXHIBIT 11–2

POTTER COMPANY
An Overview of Responsibility Accounting

President's Report

The president's performance report summarizes all company data. Since variances are given, the president can trace the variances downward through the company as needed to determine where his and his subordinates' time can best be spent.

	Budget	Actual	Variance
Responsibility center:			
Sales manager	X	X	X
Production superintendent	$26,000	$29,000	$3,000 U
Engineering and planning	X	X	X
Personnel supervisor	X	X	X
Controller	X	X	X
	$54,000	$61,000	$7,000 U

Production Superintendent

The performance of each department head is summarized for the production superintendent. The totals on the superintendent's performance report are then passed upward to the next level of responsibility.

	Budget	Actual	Variance
Responsibility center:			
Cutting department	X	X	X
Machining department	X	X	X
Finishing department	$11,000	$12,500	$1,500 U
Packaging department	X	X	X
	$26,000	$29,000	$3,000 U

Finishing Department Head

The performance report of each supervisor is summarized on the performance report of the department head. The department totals are then summarized upward to the production superintendent.

	Budget	Actual	Variance
Responsibility center:			
Sanding operation	X	X	X
Wiring operation	$ 5,000	$ 5,800	$ 800 U
Assembly operation	X	X	X
	$11,000	$12,500	$1,500 U

Wiring Operation Supervisor

The supervisor of each operation receives a performance report on his or her center of responsibility. The totals on these reports are then communicated upward to the next higher level of responsibility.

	Budget	Actual	Variance
Variable costs:			
Direct materials	X	X	X
Direct labor	X	X	X
Manufacturing overhead	X	X	X
	$ 5,000	$ 5,800	$ 800 U

Third Level of Responsibility The third level of responsibility is that of the finishing department head who oversees the work of the wiring operation supervisor as well as the work of the other supervisors in this department. Notice from Exhibit 11–2 that the department head will receive summarized data from each of the operations within the department. If the department head desires to know the reasons behind the variances reported in these summaries (such as the $800 variance in the wiring operation), he or she can look at the detailed, individual performance reports prepared on the separate operations.

Second Level of Responsibility The second level of responsibility is that of the production superintendent who has responsibility for all producing department activities. Notice from Exhibit 11–2 that the summarized totals from the performance report of the finishing department head are reported upward to the production superintendent, along with summarized totals from the performance reports of other departments. In addition to the summarized totals, the production superintendent will undoubtedly also require that detailed copies of the performance reports themselves be furnished to him, as well as detailed copies of the performance reports from all separate operations within the departments. The availability of these reports will permit the production superintendent to go right to the heart of any problem in cost control. This, of course, is the implementation of the management by exception principle discussed in earlier chapters. By having variances from budget highlighted on each performance report, the production superintendent is able to see where his or her time and the time of the department heads and supervisors can best be spent.

First Level of Responsibility The president of a company has ultimate responsibility for all costs and revenues. On his or her performance report, therefore, the activities of all phases of the business must be summarized for review.

The president may require that copies of the detailed performance reports from *all* levels of responsibility be supplied to him. On the other hand, he may concern himself only with broad results, leaving the more detailed data for the scrutiny of the managers of the lower responsibility centers, such as the production superintendent. Thus, the system provides a great deal of flexibility and can be expanded or contracted in terms of data provided to suit the needs and interests of the particular manager involved.

In the absence of a responsibility accounting system, managers are left with little more than a "seat-of-the-pants" feel for what is going on in their own areas of responsibility, as well as those of their subordinates. In today's highly competitive business environment, a seat-of-the-pants feel for how well costs are being controlled is rarely sufficient to sustain profitable operations.

Expanding the Responsibility Accounting Idea

We have indicated earlier that Potter Company is a part of the Western Division of General Products, Inc. Exhibit 11–3 on the following page shows more clearly just how Potter Company fits into the structure of the General Products, Inc., organization.

This exhibit illustrates a further expansion of the responsibility accounting idea. Notice from the exhibit that contribution income statements are used to report company-level performance to the divisional manager and to report divisional performance to corporate headquarters.

On a corporate headquarters level, all data are summarized into various segment arrangements for an overall performance evaluation of the entire corporate structure (see Exhibit 11–3). Since variances from budgeted sales and costs are shown on the contribution income statements, managers at the various levels of responsibility can see clearly where profit objectives are not being met. An illustration of a contribution income statement with variances is presented in Exhibit 11–4. Income statements of this type are prepared at both the company and division levels and then consolidated on a corporate level.

EXHIBIT 11–3

General Products, Inc., Organization—An Expansion of the Responsibility Accounting Concept

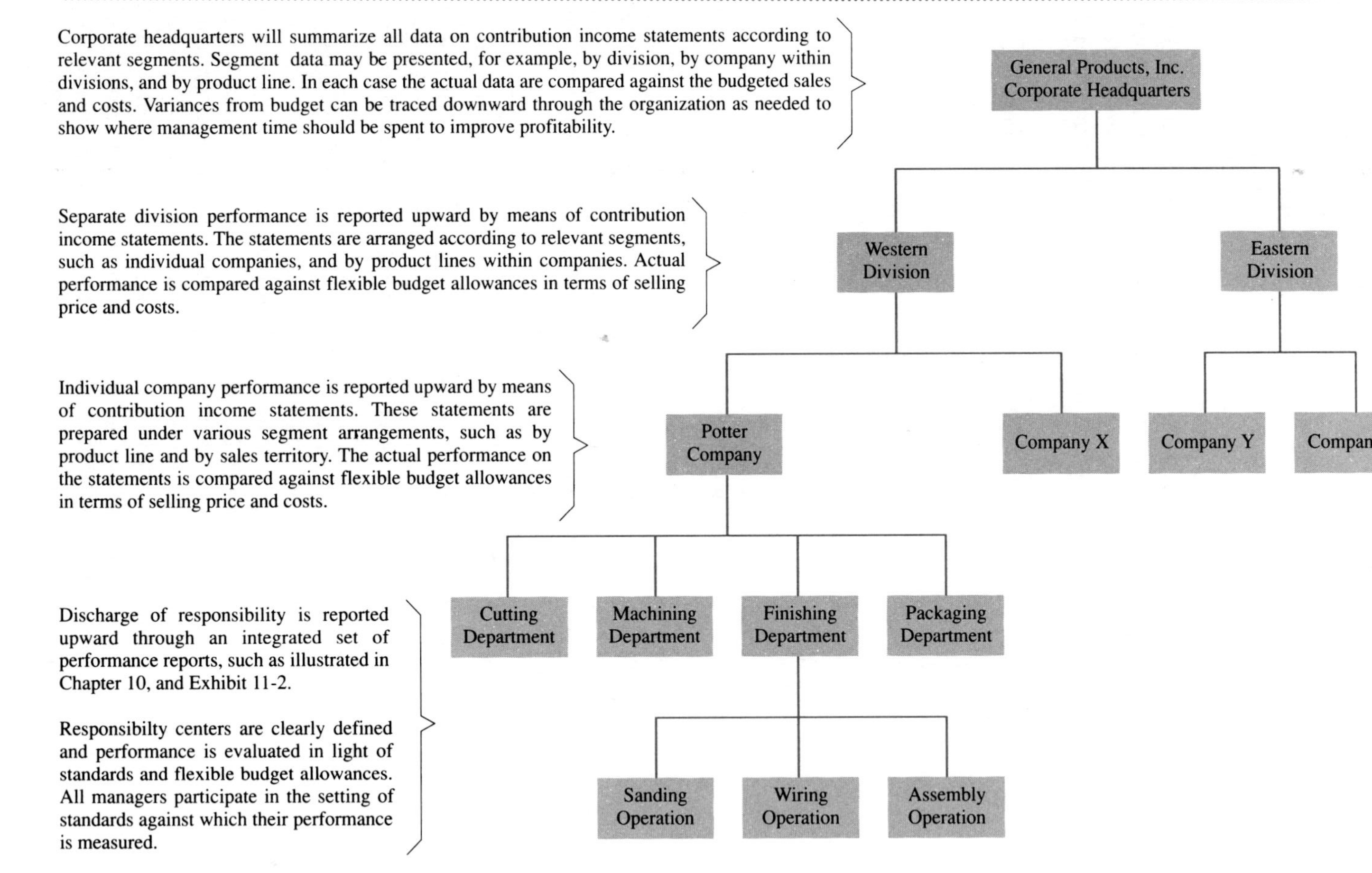

EXHIBIT 11-4

GENERAL PRODUCTS, INC.
Contribution Income Statement Comparing
Budgeted Data with Actual Data
(in thousands)

	Budget	Actual	Variance
Sales	$100,000	$97,000	$3,000 U
Variable expenses:			
Variable cost of sales	45,000	46,000	1,000 U
Other variable expenses	15,000	14,500	500 F
Total variable expenses	60,000	60,500	500 U
Contribution margin	40,000	36,500	3,500 U
Less fixed expenses:			
Selling	13,000	13,000	—
Administrative	4,000	4,300	300 U
Manufacturing	13,000	13,700	700 U
Total fixed expenses	30,000	31,000	1,000 U
Net income	$ 10,000	$ 5,500	$4,500 U

The Benefits of Decentralization

Managers have found that a responsibility accounting system functions most effectively in an organization that is *decentralized*. A **decentralized organization** is one in which decision making is not confined to a few top executives but rather is spread throughout the organization, with managers at various levels making key operating decisions relating to their sphere of responsibility. Decentralization must be viewed in terms of degree, since all organizations are decentralized to some extent out of economic necessity. At one extreme, a strongly decentralized organization is one in which there are few, if any, constraints on the freedom of a manager to make a decision, even at the lowest levels. At the other extreme, a strongly centralized organization is one in which little freedom exists to make a decision other than at top levels of management. Although most firms today fall somewhere between these two extremes, there is a pronounced tendency toward the decentralized end of the spectrum.

Many benefits are felt to accrue from decentralization. These benefits include the following:

1. By spreading the burden of decision making among many levels of management, top management is relieved of much day-to-day problem solving and is left free to concentrate on long-range planning and on coordination of efforts.
2. Allowing managers greater decision-making control over their segments provides excellent training as these managers rise in the organization. In the absence of such training, managers may be ill-prepared to function in a decision-making capacity as they are given greater responsibility.
3. Added responsibility and decision-making authority often result in increased job satisfaction and provide greater incentive for the manager to put forth his or her best efforts.

4. Decisions are best made at that level in an organization where a problem arises. Members of top management are often in a poor position to make decisions in matters relating to the everyday operation of a given segment, since they are not intimately acquainted with the problems or local conditions that may exist.
5. Decentralization provides a more effective basis for measuring a manager's performance, since it typically leads to the creation of profit and investment centers. Profit and investment centers and the measurement of management performance are discussed in the following section.

Investment, Profit, and Cost Centers

In a decentralized organization, the responsibility accounting system is structured around a number of centers, such as are depicted in Exhibit 11–5 for General Products, Inc. These consist of investment centers, profit centers, and cost centers, each of which defines a particular area of responsibility in an organization.[2]

Responsibility Center A **responsibility center** is any point within an organization where control over the incurrence of cost, the generating of revenue, or the use of investment funds is found. Such a point could be an individual, an operation, a department, a company, a division, or the entire organization itself.

Cost Center A **cost center** is any responsibility center that has control over the incurrence of cost. A cost center has no control over either the generating of revenue or the use of investment funds.

Profit Center By contrast to a cost center, a **profit center** has control over both cost and revenue. Potter Company, for example, would be a profit center in the General Products, Inc., organization, since it would be concerned with marketing its goods as well as producing them. Like a cost center, however, a profit center generally does not have control over how investment funds are used.

Investment Center An **investment center** is any responsibility center within an organization that has control over cost and revenue and also over the use of investment funds. The corporate headquarters of General Products, Inc., would clearly be an example of an investment center. Corporate officers have ultimate responsibility for seeing that production and marketing goals are met. In addition, they have responsibility for seeing that adequate facilities are available to carry out the production and marketing functions, and for seeing that adequate working capital is available for operating needs. Whenever a segment of an organization has control over investment in such areas as physical plant and equipment, receivables, inventory, and entry into new markets, then it is termed an *investment center*. Potter Company itself

[2] Some organizations also identify "revenue centers," which are responsible for sales activities only (products are shipped directly from the plant or from a warehouse as orders are submitted). An example of such a revenue center would be a Sears catalog outlet. Other companies would consider this to be just another type of profit center, since costs of some kind (salaries, rent, utilities) are usually present.

EXHIBIT 11–5

Investment, Profit, and Cost Centers—General Products, Inc.

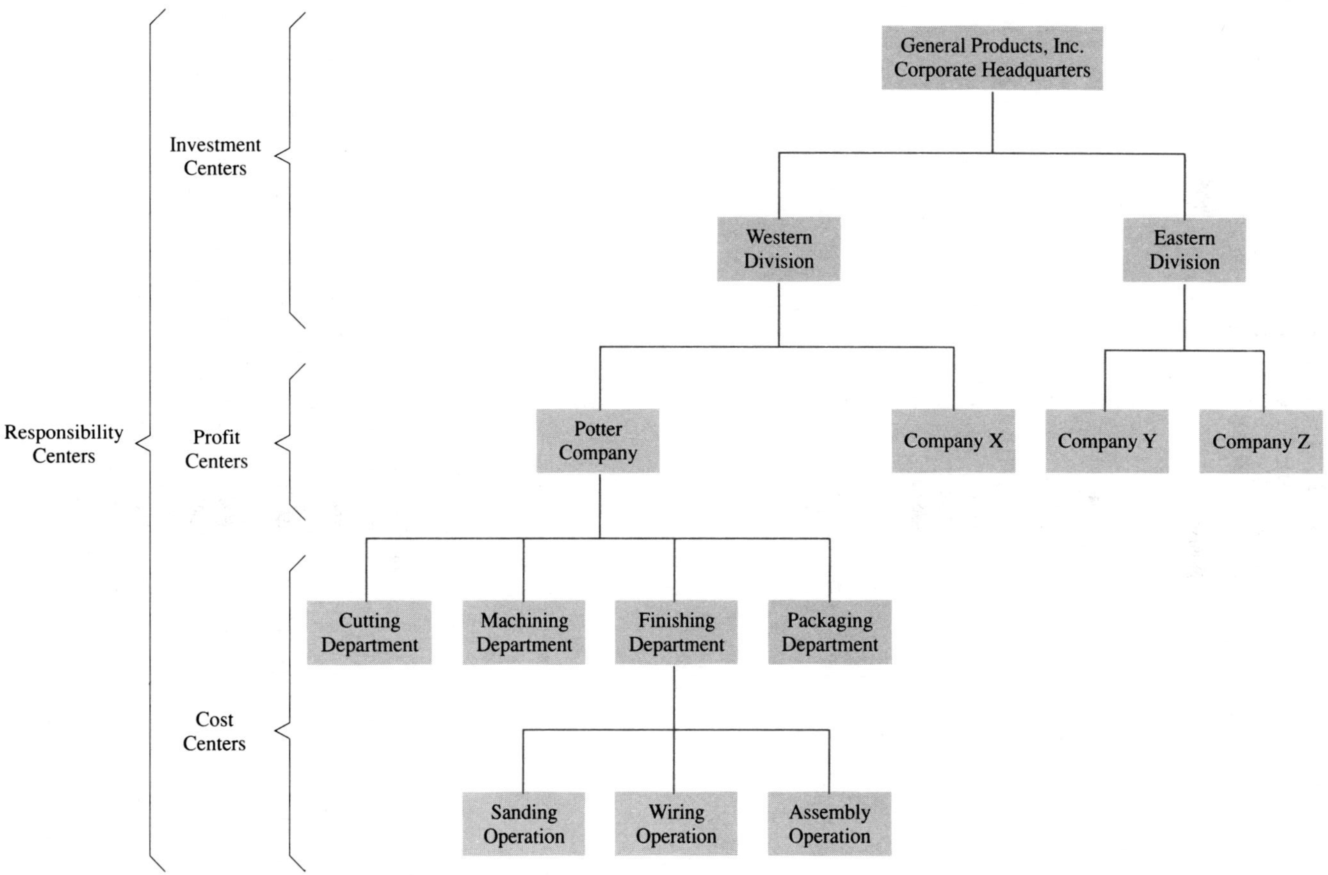

could be an investment center if it were given control over investment funds for some of these purposes. In the more usual situation, however, Potter Company would be a profit center within the larger organization, with most (or all) investment decisions being made at the divisional or central headquarters levels.

The reader should be cautioned that in everyday business practice the distinction between a profit center and an investment center is sometimes blurred, and the term *profit center* is often used to refer to either one. Thus, a company may refer to one of its segments as being a profit center when in fact the manager has full control over investment decisions in the segment. For purposes of our discussion, we will continue to maintain a distinction between the two, as made above.

Measuring Management Performance

These concepts of responsibility accounting are very important, since they assist in defining a manager's sphere of responsibility and also in determining how performance will be evaluated.

Cost centers are evaluated by means of performance reports, in terms of meeting cost standards that have been set. Profit centers are evaluated by means of contribution income statements, in terms of meeting sales and cost objectives. Investment centers are also evaluated by means of contribution income statements, but normally in terms of the *rate of return* that they are able to generate on *invested funds*. In the following section, we discuss rate of return as a tool for measuring managerial performance in an investment center.

RATE OF RETURN FOR MEASURING MANAGERIAL PERFORMANCE

The development of concepts such as investment centers, profit centers, and cost centers is largely a result of the rapid growth of decentralization in corporate structures. As mentioned earlier, in a decentralized organization, managers are given a great deal of autonomy in directing the affairs in their particular areas of responsibility. So great is this autonomy that the various profit and investment centers are often viewed as being virtually independent businesses, with their managers having about the same control over decisions as if they were in fact running their own independent firms. With this autonomy, fierce competition often develops among managers, with each striving to make his or her operation the "best" in the company.

Competition is particularly keen when it comes to passing out funds for expansion of product lines, or for introduction of new product lines. How do top managers in corporate headquarters go about deciding who gets new investment funds as they become available, and how do these managers decide which investment centers are most profitably using the funds that have already been entrusted to their care? One of the most popular ways of making these judgments is to measure the rate of return that investment center managers are able to generate on their assets. This can be done through the *return on investment (ROI)* formula.

The Return on Investment (ROI) Formula

To understand the elements behind the ROI formula, refer to the data in Exhibit 11–6. As shown in the exhibit, **return on investment (ROI)** is a product of an investment center's *margin* multiplied by its *turnover*. The

EXHIBIT 11–6
Elements of Return on Investment

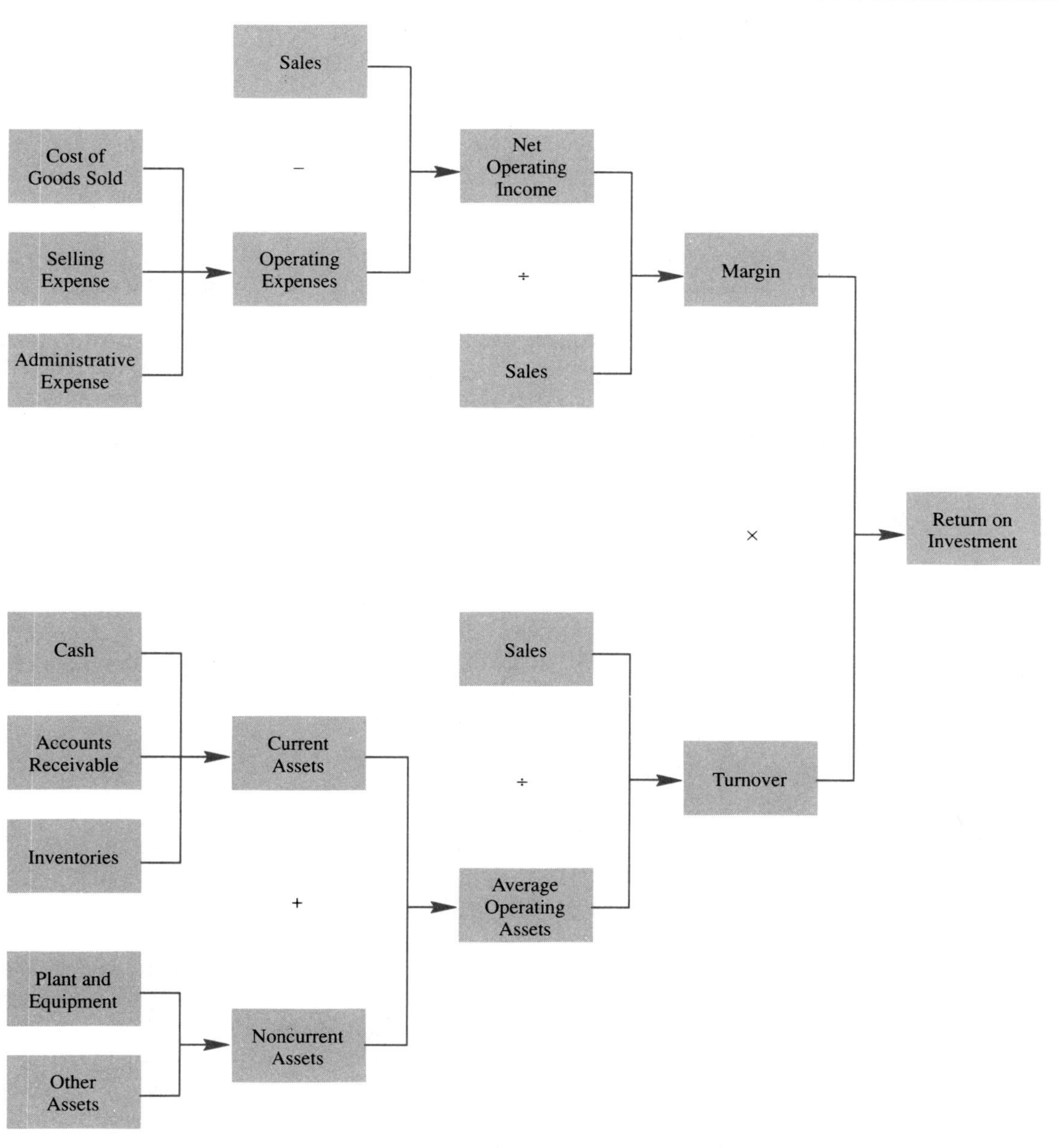

margin portion of the ROI formula is a measure of management's ability to control operating expenses in relation to sales. The lower the operating expenses per dollar of sales, the higher the margin earned. The **turnover** portion of the ROI formula is a measure of the amount of sales that can be generated in an investment center for each dollar invested in operating assets. In sum, the ROI formula can be expressed as follows:

$$\text{Margin} \times \text{Turnover} = \text{ROI}$$

$$\text{Margin} = \frac{\text{Net operating income}}{\text{Sales}} \qquad \text{Turnover} = \frac{\text{Sales}}{\text{Average operating assets}}$$

Therefore,

$$\frac{\text{Net operating income}}{\text{Sales}} \times \frac{\text{Sales}}{\text{Average operating assets}} = \text{ROI}$$

In the past, managers have tended to focus only on the margin earned and have ignored the turnover of assets. To some degree at least, the margin earned can be a valuable measure of a manager's performance. Standing alone, however, it overlooks one very crucial area of a manager's responsibility—the control of investment in operating assets. Excessive funds tied up in operating assets can be just as much of a drag on profitability as excessive operating expenses. One of the real advantages of the ROI formula is that it forces the manager to control his or her investment in operating assets as well as to control expenses and the margin earned.

Du Pont was the first major corporation to recognize the importance of looking at both margin *and* turnover in assessing the performance of a manager. To it must go the credit for pioneering the ROI concept. Monsanto Company and other major corporations have followed Du Pont's lead, and the ROI formula is now recognized as one of the best single measures of a manager's performance when that manager has control of an investment center. The ROI formula blends together many aspects of the manager's responsibilities into a single figure that can be compared against the return of competing investment centers, as well as against that of other firms in the industry.

Net Operating Income and Operating Assets Defined

The reader may have noted that *net operating income,* rather than net income, was used in the ROI formula in computing the margin percentage. **Net operating income** is income before interest and taxes. In business jargon, it is sometimes referred to as EBIT (earnings before interest and taxes). The reader should become familiar with these terms. The reason for using net operating income in the formula is that the income figure used should be consistent with the base to which it is applied. Notice that the base in the turnover part of the formula consists of *operating assets*. Thus, to be consistent we use net operating income in computing the margin figure.

Operating assets would include cash, accounts receivable, inventory, plant and equipment, and all other assets held for productive use in the organization. Examples of assets that would not be included in the operating assets category (that is, examples of nonoperating assets) would include land being held for future use, or a factory building being rented to someone else. The operating assets base used in the formula is typically computed as the average between the beginning and the end of the year.

Plant and Equipment: Net Book Value or Gross Cost?

A major consideration in ROI computations is the dollar amount of plant and equipment that should be included in the operating assets base. To illustrate the problem involved, assume that a company reports the following amounts for plant and equipment on its balance sheet:

Plant and equipment	$3,000,000
Less accumulated depreciation . . .	900,000
Net book value	$2,100,000

What dollar amount of plant and equipment should the company include with its operating assets in computing ROI? One widely used approach is to include only the plant and equipment's *net book value*—that is, the plant's original cost less accumulated depreciation ($2,100,000 in the example above). A second approach is to ignore depreciation and include the plant's entire *gross cost* in the operating assets base ($3,000,000 in the example above). Both of these approaches are used in actual practice, even though they will obviously yield very different operating asset and ROI figures.

The following arguments can be raised for and against including only a plant's net book value as part of operating assets:

Arguments for Net Book Value

1. It is consistent with how plant and equipment items are reported on the balance sheet (that is, cost less accumulated depreciation to date).
2. It is consistent with the computation of net operating income, which includes depreciation as an operating expense.

Arguments against Net Book Value

1. It allows ROI to increase over time as assets get older and therefore have increasingly smaller net book values.
2. It discourages the replacement of old, worn-out equipment in that the purchase of new equipment can have a dramatic, adverse effect on ROI.

The following arguments can be raised for and against including a plant's entire gross cost as part of operating assets:

Arguments for Gross Cost

1. It eliminates both age of equipment and method of depreciation as factors in ROI computations.
2. It allows the manager to replace old, worn-out equipment with a minimum adverse impact on ROI.

Arguments against Gross Cost

1. It is not consistent with either the income statement or the balance sheet in that it ignores depreciation.

2. It involves double counting in that the original cost of an asset plus any recovery of that original cost (through the depreciation process) are both included in the operating assets base.

Managers generally view consistency as the most important of the considerations above. As a result, a majority of companies use the net book value approach in ROI computations.[3] In this book, we will also use the net book value approach unless a specific exercise or problem directs otherwise.

CONTROLLING THE RATE OF RETURN

When being measured by the ROI formula, a manager can improve profitability in three ways:

1. By increasing sales.
2. By reducing expenses.
3. By reducing assets.

To illustrate how the rate of return can be controlled by each of these three actions, let us assume the following data for an investment center:

Net operating income	$ 10,000
Sales	100,000
Average operating assets . . .	50,000

The rate of return generated by the investment center would be:

$$\frac{\text{Net operating income}}{\text{Sales}} \times \frac{\text{Sales}}{\text{Average operating assets}} = \text{ROI}$$

$$\frac{\$10{,}000}{\$100{,}000} \times \frac{\$100{,}000}{\$50{,}000} = \text{ROI}$$

$$10\% \times 2 = 20\%$$

As we stated above, to improve the ROI figure the manager must either (1) increase sales, (2) reduce expenses, or (3) reduce the operating assets.

Approach 1: Increase Sales Assume that the manager in our example is able to increase sales from $100,000 to $110,000. Assume further that either because of good cost control or because most costs in the company are fixed, the net operating income increases even more rapidly, going from $10,000 to $12,000 per period. The operating assets remain constant.

$$\frac{\$12{,}000}{\$110{,}000} \times \frac{\$110{,}000}{\$50{,}000} = \text{ROI}$$

$$10.91\% \times 2.2 = 24\% \text{ (as compared to 20\% above)}$$

Approach 2: Reduce Expenses Assume that the manager is able to reduce expenses by $1,000, so that net operating income increases from $10,000 to $11,000. Both sales and operating assets remain constant.

[3] For an excellent study of net book value and gross cost, and for additional discussion, see James S. Reese and William R. Cool, "Measuring Investment Center Performance," *Harvard Business Review,* May–June 1978, p. 28.

$$\frac{\$11{,}000}{\$100{,}000} \times \frac{\$100{,}000}{\$50{,}000} = \text{ROI}$$

$$11\% \times 2 = 22\% \text{ (as compared to 20\% above)}$$

Approach 3: Reduce Assets Assume that the manager is able to reduce operating assets from $50,000 to $40,000. Sales and net operating income remain unchanged.

$$\frac{\$10{,}000}{\$100{,}000} \times \frac{\$100{,}000}{\$40{,}000} = \text{ROI}$$

$$10\% \times 2.5 = 25\% \text{ (as compared to 20\% above)}$$

A clear understanding of these three approaches to improving the ROI figure is critical to the effective management of an investment center. We will now look at each approach in more detail.

Increase Sales

In first looking at the ROI formula, one is inclined to think that the sales figure is neutral, since it appears as the denominator in the margin computation and as the numerator in the turnover computation. We *could* cancel out the sales figure, but we don't do so for two reasons. First, this would tend to draw attention away from the fact that the rate of return is a function of *two* variables, margin and turnover. And second, it would tend to conceal the fact that a change in sales can affect *either* the margin or the turnover in an organization. To explain, a change in sales can affect the *margin* if expenses increase or decrease at a different rate than sales. For example, a company may be able to keep a tight control on its costs as its sales go up, thereby allowing the net operating income to increase more rapidly than sales and thus allowing the margin percentage to rise. Or, a company may have many fixed expenses that will remain constant as sales go up, thereby again allowing a rapid increase in the net operating income and causing the margin percentage to rise. Either (or both) of these factors could have been responsible for the increase in the margin percentage from 10 percent to 10.91 percent illustrated in approach 1 above.

Further, a change in sales can affect the *turnover* if sales either increase or decrease without a proportionate increase or decrease in the operating assets. In the first approach above, for example, sales increased from $100,000 to $110,000, but the operating assets remained unchanged. As a result, the turnover increased from 2 to 2.2 for the period.

In sum, because a change in sales can affect either the margin or the turnover in a company, such changes are particularly significant to the manager in his or her attempts to control the ROI figure.

Reduce Expenses

Often the easiest route to increased profitability and to a stronger ROI figure is to simply cut the "fat" out of an organization through a concerted effort to control expenses. When profit margins begin to be squeezed, this is generally the first line of attack by a manager. The discretionary fixed costs usually come under scrutiny first, and various programs are either curtailed or eliminated in an effort to cut costs. Firms under extreme pressures to reduce expenses have gone so far as to eliminate coffee breaks, under the reasoning that nothing could more emphatically impress the staff with the need to be cost conscious.

One of the most common ways to reduce variable expenses is to use less costly inputs of materials. Another way is to automate processes as much as possible, particularly where large volumes of units are involved.

Reduce Operating Assets

Managers have always been sensitive to the need to control sales, operating expenses, and operating margins. They have not always been equally sensitive, however, to the need to control investment in operating assets. Firms that have adopted the ROI approach to measuring managerial performance report that one of the first reactions on the part of investment center managers is to trim down their investment in operating assets. The reason, of course, is that these managers soon realize that an excessive investment in operating assets will reduce the asset turnover and hurt the rate of return. As these managers pare down their investment in operating assets, funds are released that can be used elsewhere in the organization. Consider the following actual situation:

> X Company, a firm located in a western state, is a manufacturer of high-quality cast-iron pipe. A few years ago a large conglomerate acquired a controlling interest in the stock of X Company, and X Company became an investment center of the larger organization. The parent company measured the performance of the investment center managers by the ROI formula. X Company managers quickly found that their performance was below that of other investment centers within the organization. Because of their mediocre performance, X Company managers realized that they were in a poor position to compete for new investment funds. As one step in an effort to improve the rate of return, the company took a hard look at its investment in operating assets. As a result, it was able to reduce inventory alone by nearly 40 percent. This resulted in several million dollars becoming available for productive use elsewhere in the company. Within two years' time, the rate of return being generated by X Company improved dramatically. The controller of X Company, speaking at a management development conference, stated that the company had always been profitable in terms of net income to sales, so there really had been no incentive to watch the investment in operating assets prior to being put under the ROI microscope.

What approaches are open to an investment center manager in attempts to control the investment in operating assets? One approach is to pare out unneeded inventory. JIT purchasing and JIT manufacturing have been extremely helpful in reducing inventories of all types, with the result that ROI figures have improved dramatically in some companies. Another approach is to devise various methods of speeding up the collection of receivables. For example, many firms now employ the lockbox technique by which customers in distant states remit directly to local post office boxes. The funds are received and deposited by a local banking institution in behalf of the payee firm. This can greatly speed up the collection process, thereby reducing the total investment required to carry accounts receivable. (The released funds are typically used to pay amounts due to short-term creditors.) As the level of investment in receivables is reduced, the asset turnover is increased.

The Problem of Allocated Expenses and Assets

In decentralized organizations such as General Products, Inc., it is common practice to allocate to the separate divisions the expenses incurred in operating corporate headquarters. When such allocations are made, a very thorny question arises as to whether these allocated expenses should be considered in the divisions' rate of return computations.

It can be argued on the one hand that allocated expenses should be included in rate of return computations, since they represent the value of services rendered to the divisions by central headquarters. On the other hand, it can be argued that they should not be included, since the divisional managers have no control over the incurrence of the expenses and since the "services" involved are often of questionable value, or are hard to pin down.

At the very least, *arbitrary* allocations should be avoided in rate of return computations. If arbitrary allocations are made, great danger exists of creating a bias for or against a particular division. Expense allocations should be limited to the cost of those *actual* services provided by central headquarters that the divisions would *otherwise* have had to provide for themselves. The amount of expense allocated to a division should not exceed the cost that the division would have incurred if it had provided the service for itself.

These same guidelines apply to asset allocations from central corporate headquarters to the separate divisions. Assets relating to overall corporate operations should not be included as part of the divisional operating assets in divisional ROI computations, unless there are clear and traceable benefits to the divisions from the assets involved. As before, any type of arbitrary allocations (such as allocations on the basis of sales dollars) should be avoided.

Criticisms of ROI

Although ROI is widely used in evaluating performance, it is far from being a perfect tool. The method is subject to the following criticisms:

1. ROI tends to emphasize short-run performance rather than long-run profitability. In an attempt to protect the current ROI, a manager may be motivated to reject otherwise profitable investment opportunities. (This point is discussed further in the following section.)
2. ROI is not consistent with the cash flow models used for capital expenditure analysis. (Cash flow models are discussed in Chapters 14 and 15.)
3. ROI may not be fully controllable by the division manager due to the presence of committed costs. This inability to control the ROI can make it difficult to distinguish between the performance of the manager and the performance of the division as an investment.

In an effort to overcome these problems, some companies use multiple criteria in evaluating performance rather than relying on ROI as a single measure. Other criteria used include the following:

Growth in market share.
Increases in productivity.
Dollar profits.
Receivables turnover.

Inventory turnover.
Product innovation.
Ability to expand into new and profitable areas.

It is felt that the use of multiple performance measures such as those above provide a more comprehensive picture of a manager's performance than can be obtained by relying on ROI alone.

The Concept of Residual Income

In our discussion, we have assumed that the purpose of an investment center should be to maximize the rate of return that it is able to generate on operating assets. There is another approach to measuring performance in an investment center that focuses on a concept known as *residual income*. **Residual income** is the net operating income that an investment center is able to earn *above* some minimum rate of return on its operating assets. When residual income is used to measure performance, the purpose is to maximize the total amount of residual income, *not* to maximize the overall ROI figure.

Consider the following data for two comparable divisions:

	Performance Measured by—	
	Rate of Return (Division A)	**Residual Income (Division B)**
Average operating assets	$100,000 *(a)*	$100,000
Net operating income	$ 20,000 *(b)*	$ 20,000
ROI, *(b)* ÷ *(a)*	20%	
Minimum required rate of return is assumed to be 15% (15% × $100,000)		15,000
Residual income		$ 5,000

Notice that Division B has a positive residual income of $5,000. The performance of the manager of Division B is assessed according to how large or how small this residual income figure is from year to year. The larger the residual income figure, the better is the performance rating received by the division's manager.

Motivation and Residual Income

Many companies view residual income as being a better measure of performance than rate of return. They argue that the residual income approach encourages managers to make profitable investments that would be rejected by managers being measured by the ROI formula. To illustrate, assume that each of the divisions above is presented with an opportunity to make an investment of $25,000 in a new project that would generate a return of 18 percent on invested assets. The manager of Division A would probably reject this opportunity. Note from the tabulation above that his division is already earning a return of 20 percent on its assets. If he takes on a new project that provides a return of only 18 percent, then his overall ROI will be reduced, as shown on the next page:

	Present	New Project	Overall
Average operating assets *(a)* . . .	$100,000	$25,000	$125,000
Net operating income *(b)*	$ 20,000	$ 4,500*	$ 24,500
ROI, *(b)* ÷ *(a)*	20%	18%	19.6%

* $25,000 × 18% = $4,500.

Since the performance of the manager of this division is being measured according to the *maximum* rate of return that he is able to generate on invested assets, he will be unenthused about any investment opportunity that reduces his current ROI figure. He will tend to think and act along these lines, even though the opportunity he rejects might have benefited the company *as a whole*.

On the other hand, the manager of Division B will be very anxious to accept the new investment opportunity. The reason is that she isn't concerned about maximizing her rate of return. She is concerned about maximizing her residual income. Any project that provides a return greater than the minimum required 15 percent will be attractive, since it will add to the *total amount* of the residual income figure. Under these circumstances, the new investment opportunity with its 18 percent return will clearly be attractive, as shown below:

	Present	New Project	Overall
Average operating assets.	$100,000	$25,000	$125,000
Net operating income	$ 20,000	$ 4,500*	$ 24,500
Minimum required rate of return is again assumed to be 15%	15,000	3,750†	18,750
Residual income	$ 5,000	$ 750	$ 5,750

* $25,000 × 18% = $4,500.
† $25,000 × 15% = $3,750.

Thus, by accepting the new investment project, the manager of Division B will increase her division's overall residual income figure and thereby show an improved performance as a manager. The fact that her division's overall ROI might be lower as a result of accepting the project is immaterial, since performance is being evaluated by residual income, not ROI. The well-being of both the manager and the company as a whole will be maximized by accepting all investment opportunities down to the 15 percent cutoff rate.

Divisional Comparison and Residual Income

The residual income approach has one major disadvantage. It can't be used to compare the performance of divisions of different sizes, since by its very nature it creates a bias in favor of larger divisions. That is, one would expect larger divisions to have more residual income than smaller divisions, not necessarily because they are better managed but simply because of the bigger numbers involved.

As an example, consider the following residual income computations for Division X and Division Y:

	Division	
	X	Y
Average operating assets *(a)*	$1,000,000	$250,000
Net operating income	$ 120,000	$ 40,000
Minimum required return: 10% × *(a)*	100,000	25,000
Residual income	$ 20,000	$ 15,000

Observe that Division X has slightly more residual income than Division Y, but that Division X has $1,000,000 in operating assets as compared to only $250,000 in operating assets for Division Y. Thus, Division X's greater residual income is probably more a result of its size than the quality of its management. In fact, it appears that the smaller division is better managed, since it has been able to generate nearly as much residual income with only one fourth as much in operating assets to work with.

TRANSFER PRICING

Special problems arise in applying the rate of return or residual income approaches to performance evaluation whenever segments of a company do business with each other. The problems revolve around the question of what transfer price to charge between the segments. A **transfer price** can be defined as the price charged when one segment of a company provides goods or services to another segment of the company.

The Need for Transfer Prices

Assume that a vertically integrated firm has three divisions. The three divisions are:

Mining Division.
Processing Division.
Manufacturing Division.

The Mining Division mines raw materials that are transferred to the Processing Division. After processing, the Processing Division transfers the processed materials to the Manufacturing Division. The Manufacturing Division then includes the processed materials as part of its finished product.

In this example, we have two transfers of goods between divisions within the same company. What price should control these transfers? Should the price be set so as to include some "profit" element to the selling division? Should it be set so as to include only the accumulated costs to that point? Or should it be set at yet another figure? The choice of a transfer price can be complicated by the fact that each division may be supplying portions of its output to outside customers, as well as to sister divisions. Another complication is that the price charged by one division becomes a cost to the other division, and the higher this cost, the lower will be the purchasing division's rate of return. Thus, the purchasing division would like the transfer price to be low, whereas the selling division would like it to be high. The selling division may even want to charge the same "market" price internally as it charges to outside customers.

As the reader may guess, the problem of what transfer price to set between segments of a company has no easy solution and often leads to protracted and heated disputes between investment center managers. Yet some transfer price *must* be set if data are to be available for performance evaluation of the various parts or divisions of a company. In practice, three general approaches are used in setting transfer prices:

1. Set transfer prices at cost using:
   a. Variable cost.
   b. Full (absorption) cost.
2. Set transfer prices at the market price.
3. Set transfer prices at a negotiated market price.

In the following sections, we consider each of these approaches to the transfer pricing problem.

Transfer Prices at Cost

Many firms make transfers between divisions on a basis of the accumulated cost of the goods being transferred, thus ignoring any profit element to the selling division. A transfer price computed in this way might be based only on the variable costs involved, or fixed costs might also be considered and the transfer price thus based on full (absorption) costs accumulated to the point of transfer. Although the cost approach to setting transfer prices is relatively simple to apply, it has some major defects. These defects can be brought out by the following illustration:

> Assume that a multidivisional company has a Relay Division that manufactures an electrical relay widely used as a component part by various governmental contractors. The relay requires $12 in variable costs to manufacture and sells for $20. Each relay requires one direct labor-hour to complete, and the division has a capacity of 50,000 relays per year.
>
> The company also has a Motor Division. This division has developed a new motor requiring an electrical relay, but this relay is different from the one presently being manufactured by the Relay Division. In order to acquire the needed relay, the Motor Division has two alternatives:
>
> 1. The new relay can be purchased from an outside supplier at a price of $15 per relay, based on an order of 50,000 relays per year.
> 2. The new relay can be manufactured by the company's Relay Division. This would require that the Relay Division give up its present business, since manufacture of the new relay would require all of its capacity. One direct labor-hour would be required to produce each relay (the same time as that required by the old relay). Variable manufacturing costs would total $10 per relay.
>
> In addition to the relay, each motor would require $25 in other variable cost inputs. The motors would sell for $60 each.

Should the Relay Division give up its present relay business and start producing the new relays for the Motor Division, or should it continue its present business and let the Motor Division purchase the new relays from the outside supplier? Let us assume first that the Motor Division decides to purchase the new relays from the outside supplier at $15 each, thereby permitting the Relay Division to continue to produce and sell the old relay.

EXHIBIT 11–7
Effects of Pricing Transfers between Divisions at Cost

Alternative 1: The Motor Division purchases the new relays from the outside supplier at $15 each; the Relay Division continues to produce and sell the old relays.

	50,000 Units per Year		
	Relay Division	Motor Division	Total Company
Sales (at $20 per old relay and $60 per motor, respectively)	$1,000,000	$3,000,000	$4,000,000
Less variable expenses (at $12 per old relay and $40* per motor, respectively)	600,000	2,000,000	2,600,000
Contribution margin	$ 400,000	$1,000,000	$1,400,000

Alternative 2: The Motor Division purchases the new relays from the Relay Division at an internal transfer price of $10 per relay (the Relay Division's variable cost of producing the new relay). This requires that the Relay Division give up its present outside business.

	Relay Division	Motor Division	Total Company
Sales (at $10 per new relay and $60 per motor, respectively)	$ 500,000	$3,000,000	$3,000,000‡
Less variable expenses (at $10 per new relay and $35† per motor, respectively)	500,000	1,750,000	1,750,000‡
Contribution margin	$ -0-	$1,250,000	$1,250,000
Decrease in contribution margin for the company as a whole if alternative 2 is accepted			$ 150,000

* $15 outside supplier's cost per new relay + Other variable costs of $25 per motor = $40 per motor.
† $10 internal transfer price per new relay + Other variable costs of $25 per motor = $35 per motor.
‡ The $500,000 in intracompany sales has been eliminated.

Partial income statements are given at the top of Exhibit 11–7 to show the effects of this decision on each division and on the company as a whole. Notice from the exhibit (alternative 1) that each division will have a positive contribution margin, and that the company as a whole will have a contribution margin of $1,400,000 for the year if this alternative is accepted.

Let us assume second that the Motor Division purchases the new relays internally from the Relay Division at a transfer price of $10 per relay (the Relay Division's variable costs per unit). This would require that the Relay Division give up its present outside business. On the surface this would seem to be a good decision, since the variable costs to the Relay Division would be only $10 for the new relay as compared to $12 for the old relay, and since the Motor Division would otherwise have to purchase the new relays from the outside supplier at $15 each. But this illusion quickly vanishes when we look at the data at the bottom of Exhibit 11–7 (alternative 2). Notice that this alternative would reduce the contribution margin for the company as a whole by $150,000 per year.

Herein lies one of the defects of the cost approach to setting transfer prices: Cost-based transfer prices can lead to dysfunctional decisions in a company because this approach has no built-in mechanism for telling the manager when transfers should or should not be made between divisions. In the case at hand, transfers should *not* be made; the Relay Division should go on selling the old relay to the governmental contractors, and the Motor Division should buy the new relay from the outside supplier. Although this is obvious after seeing the income statement data in Exhibit 11–7, such matters can be obscured when dealing with multiproduct divisions. Thus, as a result of using cost as a transfer price, profits for the company as a whole may be adversely affected and the manager may never know about it.

Exhibit 11–7 also illustrates another defect associated with cost-based transfer prices: The only division that will show any profits is the one that makes the final sale to an outside party. Other divisions, such as the Relay Division in the bottom portion of Exhibit 11–7, will show no profits for their efforts; thus, evaluation by the ROI formula or by the residual income approach will not be possible.

Another serious criticism of cost-based transfer prices lies in their general inability to provide incentive for control of costs. If the costs of one division are simply passed on to the next, then there is little incentive for anyone to control costs. The final selling division is simply burdened with the accumulated waste and inefficiency of intermediate processors and will be penalized with a rate of return that is deficient in comparison to that of competitors. Experience has shown that unless costs are subject to some type of competitive pressures at transfer points, waste and inefficiency almost invariably develop.

Despite these shortcomings, cost-based transfer prices are in fairly common use. Advocates argue that they are easily understood and highly convenient to use. If transfer prices are to be based on cost, then the costs should be standard costs rather than actual costs. This will at least avoid the passing on of inefficiency from one division to another.

A General Formula for Computing Transfer Prices

A general formula exists that can be used by the manager as a starting point in computing the appropriate transfer price between divisions or segments in a multidivisional company.[4] The formula is that *the transfer price should be equal to the unit variable costs of the good being transferred, plus the contribution margin per unit that is lost to the selling division as a result of giving up outside sales*. The formula can be expressed as:

$$\text{Transfer price} = \text{Variable costs per unit} + \begin{array}{c}\text{Lost contribution margin per}\\ \text{unit on outside sales}\end{array}$$

Applying this formula to the data in the preceding section, the proper transfer price for the Relay Division to charge for the new relay would be:

Transfer price = \$10 (the variable costs of the new relay) + \$8 (the contribution margin per unit lost to the Relay Division as a result of giving up outside relay sales: \$20 selling price − \$12 variable costs = \$8 lost contribution margin on the old relays)

Transfer price = \$18 per unit

[4] For background discussion, see Ralph L. Benke, Jr., and James Don Edwards, "Transfer Pricing: Techniques and Uses," *Management Accounting* 61, no. 12 (June 1980), pp. 44–46.

Upon seeing this transfer price, it becomes immediately obvious to management that no transfers should be made between the two divisions, since the Motor Division can buy its relays from an outside supplier at only $15 each. Thus, the transfer price enables management to reach the correct decision and to avoid any adverse effect on profits.

Two additional points should be noted before going on. First, *the price set by the transfer pricing formula always represents a lower limit for a transfer price, since the selling division must receive at least the amount shown by the formula in order to be as well off as if it only sold to outside customers.* Under certain conditions (discussed later), the price can be more than the amount shown by the formula, but it can't be less or the selling division and the company as a whole will suffer. Second, the transfer price computed by using the formula is a price based on competitive market conditions. The remainder of our discussion will focus on the setting of market-based transfer prices.

Transfers at Market Price: General Considerations

Some form of competitive **market price** (that is, the price charged for an item on the open market) is generally regarded as the best approach to the transfer pricing problem. The reason is that the use of market prices dovetails well with the profit center concept and makes profit-based performance evaluation feasible at many levels of an organization. By using market prices to control transfers, *all* divisions or segments are able to show profits for their efforts—not just the final division in the chain of transfers. The market price approach also helps the manager to decide when transfers should be made, as we saw earlier, and tends to lead to the best decisions involving transfer questions that may arise on a day-to-day basis.

The market price approach is designed for use in highly decentralized organizations. By this we mean that it is used in those organizations where divisional managers have enough autonomy in decision making so that the various divisions can be viewed as being virtually independent businesses with independent profit responsibility. The idea in using market prices to control transfers is to create the competitive market conditions that would exist if the various divisions were *indeed* separate firms and engaged in arm's-length, open-market bargaining. To the extent that the resulting transfer prices reflect actual market conditions, divisional operating results provide an excellent basis for evaluating managerial performance.

The National Association of Accountants describes other advantages and the overall operation of the market price approach as follows:

> Internal procurement is expected where the company's products and services are superior or equal in design, quality, performance, and price, and when acceptable delivery schedules can be met. So long as these conditions are met, the receiving unit suffers no loss and the supplier unit's profit accrues to the company. Often the receiving division gains advantages such as better control over quality, assurance of continued supply, and prompt delivery.[5]

[5] National Association of Accountants, *Research Series No. 30,* "Accounting for Intra-Company Transfers" (New York: National Association of Accountants, June 1956), pp. 13–14.

In addition to the formula given earlier, there are certain guidelines that should be followed when using market prices to control transfers between divisions. These guidelines are:

1. The buying division must purchase internally so long as the selling division meets all bona fide outside prices and wants to sell internally.
2. If the selling division does not meet all bona fide outside prices, then the buying division is free to purchase outside.
3. The selling division must be free to reject internal business if it prefers to sell outside.[6]
4. An impartial board must be established to help settle disagreements between divisions over transfer prices.

Transfers at Market Price: Well-Defined Intermediate Market

Not all companies or divisions face the same market conditions. Sometimes the only customer a division has for its output is a sister division. In other situations, an **intermediate market** may exist for part or all of a division's output. By intermediate market, we mean that a market exists in which an item can be sold *immediately* and *in its present form* to outside customers, if desired, rather than being transferred to another division for use in its manufacturing process. Thus, if an intermediate market exists, a division will have a choice between selling its products to outside customers on the intermediate market or selling them to other divisions within the company. In this section, we consider transfer pricing in those situations where intermediate markets are strong and well defined.

Let us assume that Division A of International Company has a product that can be sold either to Division B or to outside customers in an intermediate market. The cost and revenue structures of the two divisions are given below:

Division A		**Division B**	
Intermediate selling price if sold outside	$25	Final market price outside	$100
Variable costs	15	Transfer price from Division A (or outside purchase price)	25
		Variable costs added in Division B . .	40

What transfer price should control transfers between the two divisions? In this case, the answer is easy; the transfer price should be $25—the price that Division A can get by selling in the intermediate market and the price that Division B would otherwise have to pay to purchase the desired goods from an outside supplier in the intermediate market. This price can also be obtained by applying the formula developed earlier:

$$\text{Transfer price} = \text{Variable costs per unit} + \begin{array}{c}\text{Lost contribution margin per}\\ \text{unit on outside sales}\end{array}$$

$$\text{Transfer price} = \$15 + (\$25 - \$15 = \$10)$$
$$\text{Transfer price} = \$25$$

The choices facing the two divisions are shown graphically in Exhibit 11–8.

....

[6] Ibid., p. 14. Outside sales may provide the selling division with a greater return (as in the case of the Relay Division in our earlier example).

EXHIBIT 11–8
Transfers at Market Price: Well-Defined Intermediate Market

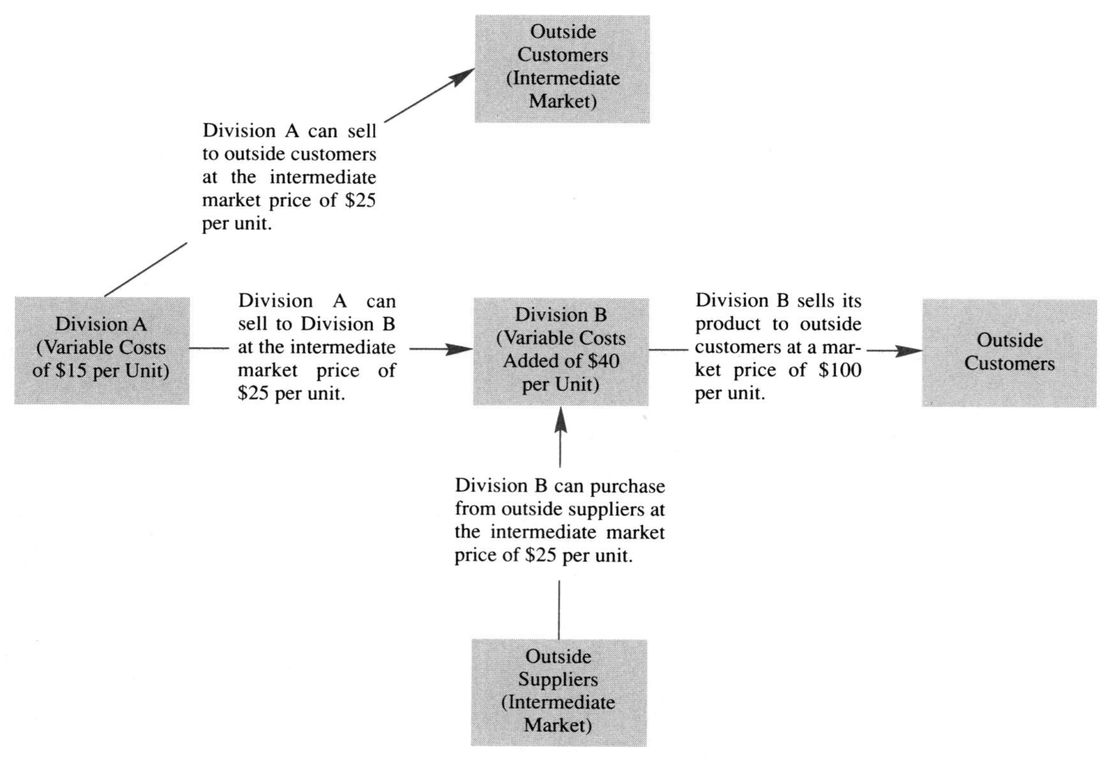

So long as Division A receives a transfer price of $25 per unit from Division B, it will be willing to sell all of its output internally. In selling to Division B, Division A will be just as well off as if it had sold its product outside at the $25 price. In like manner, so long as the price charged by outside suppliers is not less than $25 per unit, Division B will be willing to pay that price to Division A. The $25 per unit intermediate market price therefore serves as an acceptable transfer price between the two divisions. The results of transfers at this price can be summarized as follows:

	Division		
	A	**B**	**Total Company**
Sales price per unit	$25	$100	$100
Variable costs added per unit . . .	15	40	55
Transfer cost per unit.	—	25	—
Contribution margin per unit. . . .	$10	$ 35	$ 45

The contribution margin realized for the entire company is $45 per unit. By using the $25 intermediate market price to control intracompany transfers, the firm is able to show that a portion of this margin accrues from the efforts of Division A and that a portion accrues from the efforts of Division B. These data will then serve as an excellent basis for evaluating managerial performance in the divisions, using the rate of return or residual income approaches.

Transfers at Market Price: Price Changes in the Intermediate Market

In the preceding section, we assumed that there was complete price agreement in the intermediate market, and therefore that Division B could purchase the needed goods from an outside supplier at the same $25 price as being charged by Division A. In reality, complete price agreement often doesn't exist, or it may be upset by some suppliers deciding to cut their prices for various reasons. Returning to the example in the preceding section, let us assume that an outside supplier has offered to supply the goods to Division B for only $20 per unit, rather than at the normal $25 intermediate market price being charged by Division A. Should Division B accept this offer, or should Division A cut its price to $20 in order to get Division B's business? The answer will depend on whether Division A (the selling division) is operating at full or at partial capacity.

Selling Division at Full Capacity If Division A (the selling division) is operating at capacity, then it will have to give up outside sales in order to sell to Division B. Under these circumstances, the transfer price will be computed in the same way as we computed it earlier:

Transfer price = Variable costs per unit + Lost contribution margin per unit on outside sales

Transfer price = $15 + ($25 outside selling price − $15 variable costs = $10 lost contribution margin per unit)

Transfer price = $25

Recall that the price set by the formula always represents a *lower limit* for a transfer price, since the selling division must receive at least the amount shown by the formula in order to be as well off as if it sold only to outside customers. Therefore, Division A should not cut its price to $20 in order to sell to Division B. If Division A cuts its price, it will lose $5 per unit in contribution margin, and both it and the company as a whole will be worse off.

In short, whenever the selling division must give up outside sales in order to sell internally, it has an opportunity cost that must be considered in setting the transfer price. As shown by the formula, this opportunity cost is the contribution margin that will be lost as a result of giving up outside sales. Unless the transfer price can be set high enough to cover this opportunity cost, along with the variable costs associated with the sale, then no transfers should be made.

Selling Division with Idle Capacity If the selling division has idle capacity, then a different situation exists. Under these conditions, the selling division's opportunity cost *may* be zero (depending on what alternative uses it has for its idle capacity). Even if the opportunity cost is zero, many managers would argue that the transfer price should still be based on prevailing market prices, to the extent that these prices can be determined accurately and fairly. Other managers would argue that idle capacity combined with an opportunity cost of zero, or near zero, calls for a negotiation of the transfer price downward from prevailing market rates, so that both the buyer and the seller can profit from the intracompany business.

Under idle capacity conditions, so long as the selling division can receive a price greater than its variable costs (at least in the short run), all parties will benefit by keeping business inside the company rather than having the buying division go outside. The accuracy of this statement can be shown by returning to the example in the preceding section. Assume again that an outside supplier offers to sell the needed goods to Division B at $20 per unit. In this case, however, we will assume that Division A has enough idle capacity to supply all of Division B's needs, with no prospects for additional outside sales at the current $25 intermediate market price. Using our formula, the transfer price between Divisions A and B would be:

Transfer price = Variable costs per unit + Lost contribution margin per unit on outside sales
Transfer price = $15 + –0–
Transfer price = $15

As stated before, the $15 figure represents a lower limit for a transfer price. Actually, the transfer price can be anywhere between this figure and the $20 price being quoted to Division B from the outside. In this situation, therefore, we have a transfer price *range* in which to operate, as shown below:

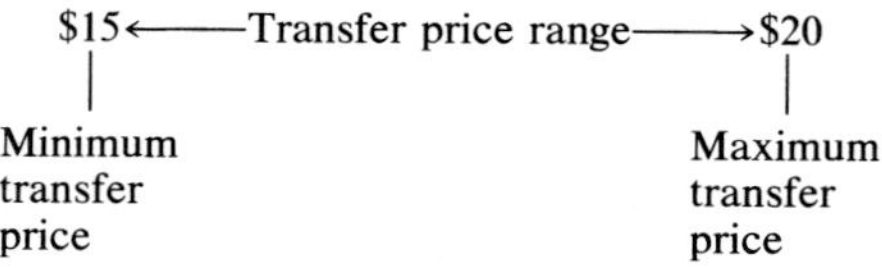

If Division A (the selling division) is hesitant to reduce its price, should it be required to at least meet the $20 figure to supply Division B's needs? The answer is no. The guidelines given earlier indicate that the selling division is not required to sell internally. Rather than accept a $20 price for its goods, Division A may prefer to let its capacity remain idle and search for other, more profitable products.

If Division A decides not to reduce its price to $20 to meet outside competition, should Division B be forced to continue to pay $25 and to buy internally? The answer again is no. The guidelines given earlier state that if the selling division is not willing to meet all bona fide outside prices, then the buying division is free to go outside to get the best price it can. However, if the selling division has idle capacity and the buying division purchases from an outside supplier, then **suboptimization**[7] will result for the selling division, possibly for the buying division, and certainly for the company as a whole. In our example, if Division A refuses to meet the $20 price, then *both it and the company as a whole will lose $5 per unit in potential contribution margin ($20 − $15 = $5)*. In short, where idle capacity exists, every effort should be made to negotiate a price acceptable to both the buyer and the seller that will keep business within the company as a whole.

[7] By *suboptimization*, we mean that overall profitability will be less than an organization is capable of earning.

Transfers at Negotiated Market Price

There are some situations where a transfer price below the intermediate market price can be justified. For example, selling and administrative expenses may be less when intracompany sales are involved, or the volume of units may be large enough to justify quantity discounts. In addition, we have already seen that a price below the prevailing market price may be justified when the selling division has idle capacity. Situations such as these can probably be served best by some type of **negotiated market price.** A negotiated market price is one agreed on between the buying and selling divisions that reflects unusual or mitigating circumstances.

Possibly the widest use of negotiated market prices is in those situations where no intermediate market prices are available. For example, one division may require an item that is not available from any outside source and therefore must be produced internally. Under these circumstances, the buying division must negotiate with another division in the company and agree to a transfer price that is attractive enough to the other division to cause it to take on the new business. To provide an example of how a transfer price would be set in such a situation, consider the following data:

> Division X has developed a new product that requires a custom-made fitting. Another division in the company, Division Y, has both the experience and the equipment necessary to produce the fitting. Division X has approached Division Y for a quoted unit price based on the production of 5,000 fittings per year.
>
> Division Y has determined that the fitting would require variable costs of $8 per unit. However, in order to have time to produce the fitting, Division Y would have to reduce production of a different product, product A, by 3,500 units per year. Product A sells for $45 per unit and has variable costs of $25 per unit. What transfer price should Division Y quote to Division X for the new fittings? Employing our formula, we get:

$$\text{Transfer price} = \text{Variable costs per unit} + \frac{\text{Lost contribution margin per unit on}}{\text{outside sales}}$$

The lost contribution margin per unit would be:

Selling price of product A	$ 45
Variable costs of product A	25
Contribution margin of product A . . .	20
Unit sales of product A given up. . . .	× 3,500
Total lost contribution margin	$70,000

$$\frac{\$70{,}000 \text{ lost contribution margin on product A}}{5{,}000 \text{ fittings to be manufactured for Division X}} = \begin{array}{c}\$14 \text{ lost contribution}\\ \text{margin per fitting}\end{array}$$

Transfer price = $8 variable costs + $14 lost contribution margin
Transfer price = $22 per fitting

Thus, the transfer price quoted by Division Y should not be less than $22 per fitting. Division Y might quote a higher price if it wants to increase its overall profits (at the expense of Division X), but it should not quote less than $22, or the profits of the company as a whole will suffer. If Division X is not happy with the $22 price, it can get a quote from an outside manufacturer for the fitting.

If Division Y in our example has idle capacity, then the appropriate transfer price is less clear. The lower limit for a transfer price would be the $8 variable costs, as discussed earlier. However, no division wants to simply recover its costs, so the actual transfer price would undoubtedly be greater than $8, according to what could be negotiated between the two divisional managers. In situations such as this, the selling division will often add some "target" markup figure to its costs in quoting a transfer price to the buying division.

Divisional Autonomy and Suboptimization

A question often arises as to how much autonomy should be granted to divisions in setting their own transfer prices and in making decisions concerning whether to sell internally or to sell outside. Should the divisional heads have complete authority to make these decisions, or should top corporate management step in if it appears that a decision is about to be made that would result in suboptimization? For example, if idle capacity exists in the selling division and divisional managers are unable to agree on a transfer price, should top corporate management step in and *force* settlement of the dispute?

Efforts should always be made, of course, to bring disputing managers together. But the almost unanimous feeling among top corporate executives is that divisional heads should not be forced into an agreement over a transfer price. That is, if a particular divisional head flatly refuses to change his or her position in a dispute, *then this decision should be respected* even if it results in suboptimization. This is simply the price that is paid for the concept of divisional autonomy. If top corporate management steps in and forces the decisions in difficult situations, then the concepts that we have been developing in this chapter largely evaporate and the company simply becomes a centralized operation with decentralization of only minor decisions and responsibilities. In short, if a division is to be viewed as an autonomous unit with independent profit responsibility, then it must have control over its own destiny—even to the extent of having the right to make bad decisions.

We should note, however, that if a division consistently makes bad decisions, the results will soon have an impact on its rate of return, and the divisional manager may find himself having to defend the division's performance. Even so, his right to get himself into an embarrassing situation must be respected if the divisional concept is to operate successfully. The overwhelming experience of multidivisional companies is that divisional autonomy and independent profit responsibility lead to much greater success and profitability than do closely controlled, centrally administered operations. Part of the price of this success and profitability is an occasional situation of suboptimization due to pettiness, bickering, or just plain managerial stubbornness.

SUMMARY

Responsibility accounting centers on the notion that any point within an organization having control over cost or revenue is a responsibility center. The way in which the various responsibility centers discharge their control over cost or revenue is communicated upward in an organization, from lower levels of responsibility to higher levels of responsibility, through a system of integrated performance reports.

Those responsibility centers having control over cost are known as cost centers; those having control over both cost and revenue are known as profit centers; and those having control over cost, revenue, and investment funds are known as investment centers. The ROI formula is widely regarded as a method of evaluating performance in an investment center because it summarizes into one figure many aspects of an investment center manager's responsibilities. As an alternative to the ROI formula, some companies use residual income as a measure of investment center performance. These companies argue that the residual income approach encourages profitable investment in many situations where the ROI approach might discourage investment.

Transfer pricing relates to the price to be charged in a transfer of goods or an exchange of services between two units (such as divisions) within an organization. A transfer price can be based on the cost of the goods being transferred, on the intermediate market price of the goods being transferred, or on a price negotiated between the buying and selling divisions. The predominant feeling is that the best transfer price is some version of market price—either intermediate or negotiated—to the extent that such a price exists or can be determined for the good or service involved. The use of market price or negotiated market price in transfers between units facilitates performance evaluation by permitting both the buyer and the seller to be treated as independent, autonomous units.

REVIEW PROBLEM ON TRANSFER PRICING

Situation A

Collyer Products, Inc., has a Valve Division that manufactures and sells a standard valve as follows:

Capacity in units.	100,000
Selling price to outside customers on the intermediate market	$30
Variable costs per unit	16
Fixed costs per unit (based on capacity) . . .	9

The company has a Pump Division that could use this valve in the manufacture of one of its pumps. The Pump Division is currently purchasing 10,000 valves per year from an overseas supplier at a cost of $29 per valve.

Required

1. Assume that the Valve Division has ample idle capacity to handle all of the Pump Division's needs. What should be the transfer price between the two divisions?
2. Assume that the Valve Division is selling all that it can produce to outside customers on the intermediate market. What should be the transfer price between the two divisions? At this price, will any transfers be made?
3. Assume again that the Valve Division is selling all that it can produce to outside customers on the intermediate market. Also assume that $3 in variable expenses can be avoided on intracompany sales, due to reduced selling costs. What should be the transfer price between the two divisions?

Solution—Situation A

1. Since the Valve Division has idle capacity, it does not have to give up any outside sales in order to take on the Pump Division's business. Therefore, applying the transfer pricing formula, we get:

   Transfer price = Variable costs per unit + Lost contribution margin per unit on outside sales
   Transfer price = $16 + $–0–
   Transfer price = $16

   However, a transfer price of $16 represents a minimum price to cover the Valve Division's variable costs. The actual transfer price would undoubtedly fall somewhere between this amount and the $29 that the Pump Division is currently paying for its valves. Thus, we have a transfer price range in this case of from $16 to $29 per unit, depending on negotiations between the two divisions.
2. Since the Valve Division is selling all that it can produce on the intermediate market, it would have to give up some of these outside sales in order to take on the Pump Division's business. Applying the transfer pricing formula, we get:

   Transfer price = Variable costs per unit + Lost contribution margin per unit on outside sales
   Transfer price = $16 + $14*
   Transfer price = $30

   * $30 selling price − $16 variable costs = $14 contribution margin per unit.

   Since the Pump Division can purchase valves from an outside supplier at only $29 per unit, no transfers will be made between the two divisions.
3. Applying the transfer pricing formula, we get:

   Transfer price = Variable costs per unit + Lost contribution margin per unit on outside sales
   Transfer price = $13* + $14
   Transfer price = $27

   * $16 variable expenses − $3 variable expenses avoided = $13.

   In this case, we again have a transfer price range; it is between $27 (the lower limit) and $29 (the Pump Division's outside price) per unit.

Situation B

Refer to the original data in situation A above. Assume that the Pump Division needs 20,000 special valves per year that are to be supplied by the Valve Division. The Valve Division's variable costs to manufacture and ship the special valve would be $20 per unit. To produce these special valves, the Valve Division would have to give up one half of its production of the regular valves (that is, cut its production of the regular valves from 100,000 units per year to 50,000 units per year). You can assume that the Valve Division is selling all of the regular valves that it can produce to outside customers on the intermediate market.

Required

If the Valve Division decides to produce the special valves for the Pump Division, what transfer price should it charge per valve?

Solution—Situation B

In order to produce the 20,000 special valves, the Valve Division will have to give up sales of 50,000 regular valves to outside customers. The lost contribution margin on the 50,000 regular valves will be:

50,000 valves × $14 per unit = $700,000

Spreading this lost contribution margin over the 20,000 special valves, we get:

$$\frac{\$700{,}000 \text{ lost contribution margin}}{20{,}000 \text{ special valves}} = \$35 \text{ per unit}$$

Using this amount in the transfer pricing formula, we get the following transfer price per unit on the special valves:

$$\text{Transfer price} = \text{Variable costs per unit} + \begin{array}{c}\text{Lost contribution margin per}\\ \text{unit on outside sales}\end{array}$$

$$\text{Transfer price} = \$20 + \$35$$

$$\text{Transfer price} = \$55$$

Thus, the Valve Division must charge a transfer price of $55 per unit on the special valves in order to be as well off as if it just continued to manufacture and sell the regular valves on the intermediate market. If the Valve Division wishes to increase its profits, it could charge more than $55 per valve, but it must charge at least $55 in order to maintain its present level of profits.

KEY TERMS FOR REVIEW

Cost center A responsibility center that has control over the incurrence of cost but has no control over the generation of revenue or the use of investment funds. (p. 458)

Decentralized organization An organization in which decision making is not confined to a few top executives but rather is spread throughout the organization. (p. 457)

Intermediate market A market in which an item can be sold immediately and in its present form to outside customers rather than just being transferred to another division for use in its manufacturing process. (p. 475)

Investment center A responsibility center that has control over the incurrence of cost and over the generating of revenue and that also has control over the use of investment funds. (p. 458)

Margin A measure of management's ability to control operating expenses in relation to sales. It is computed by dividing net operating income by the sales figure. (p. 462)

Market price The price being charged for an item on the open (intermediate) market. (p. 474)

Negotiated market price A transfer price agreed on between buying and selling divisions that reflects unusual or mitigating circumstances. (p. 479)

Net operating income The income of an organization before interest and income taxes have been deducted. (p. 462)

Operating assets Cash, accounts receivable, inventory, plant and equipment, and all other assets held for productive use in an organization. (p. 462)

Profit center A responsibility center that has control over the incurrence of cost and the generating of revenue but has no control over the use of investment funds. (p. 458)

Residual income The net operating income that an investment center is able to earn above some minimum rate of return on its operating assets. (p. 468)

Responsibility center Any point in an organization that has control over the incurrence of cost, the generating of revenue, or the use of investment funds. (p. 458)

Return on investment (ROI) A measure of profitability in an organization that is computed by multiplying the margin by the turnover. (p. 461)

Suboptimization An overall level of profitability that is less than an organization is capable of earning. (p. 478)

Transfer price The price charged when one division or segment provides goods or services to another division or segment of an organization. (p. 470)

Turnover A measure of the amount of sales that can be generated in an investment center for each dollar invested in operating assets. It is computed by dividing sales by the average operating assets figure. (p. 462)

QUESTIONS

11–1 Describe the general flow of information in a responsibility accounting system.

11–2 What is meant by the term *responsibilty center?* Could a responsibility center be a person as well as a department, and so on? Does the concept of a responsibility center apply to nonmanufacturing as well as to manufacturing activities?

11–3 What is meant by the term *decentralization?*

11–4 What benefits are felt to result from decentralization in an organization?

11–5 Distinguish between a cost center, a profit center, and an investment center.

11–6 How is performance in a cost center generally measured? Performance in a profit center? Performance in an investment center?

11–7 What is meant by the terms *margin* and *turnover?*

11–8 In what way is the ROI formula a more exacting measure of performance than the ratio of net income to sales?

11–9 When the ROI formula is being used to measure performance, what three approaches to improving the overall profitability are open to the manager?

11–10 The sales figure could be canceled out in the ROI formula, leaving simply net operating income over operating assets. Since this abbreviated formula would yield the same ROI figure, why leave sales in?

11–11 A student once commented to the author, ''It simply is not possible for a decrease in operating assets to result in an increase in profitability. The way to increase profits is to *increase* the operating assets.'' Discuss.

11–12 X Company has high fixed expenses and is currently operating somewhat above the break-even point. From this point on, will percentage increases in net income tend to be greater than, about equal to, or less than percentage increases in total sales? Why? (Ignore income taxes.)

11–13 What is meant by residual income?

11–14 In what way can ROI lead to dysfunctional decisions on the part of the investment center manager? How does the residual income approach overcome this problem?

11–15 Division A has operating assets of $100,000, and Division B has operating assets of $1,000,000. Can residual income be used to compare performance in the two divisions? Explain.

11–16 What is meant by the term *transfer price,* and why are transfer pricing systems needed?

11–17 Why are cost-based transfer prices in widespread use? What are the disadvantages of cost-based transfer prices?

11–18 If a market price for a product can be determined, why is it generally considered to be the best transfer price?

11–19 Under what circumstances might a negotiated market price be a better approach to pricing transfers between divisions than the actual market price?

11–20 In what ways can suboptimization result if divisional managers are given full autonomy in setting, accepting, and rejecting transfer prices?

EXERCISES

E11–1 Selected operating data for two divisions of York Company are given below:

	Division	
	Eastern	Western
Sales	$1,000,000	$1,750,000
Average operating assets	500,000	500,000
Net operating income	90,000	105,000
Property, plant, and equipment	250,000	200,000

Required

1. Compute the rate of return for each division, using the ROI formula.
2. So far as you can tell from the data available, which divisional manager seems to be doing the better job? Why?

E11–2 Provide the missing data in the following tabulation:

	Division		
	A	B	C
Sales	$800,000	$?	$?
Net operating income	72,000	?	40,000
Average operating assets	?	130,000	?
Margin	?	4%	8%
Turnover	?	5	?
ROI	18%	?	20%

E11–3 Melbourne Company has two divisions, A and B. Selected data on the two divisions follow:

	Division	
	A	B
Sales	$9,000,000	$20,000,000
Net operating income	630,000	1,800,000
Average operating assets	3,000,000	10,000,000

Required

1. Compute the ROI for each division.
2. Assume that the company evaluates performance by use of residual income and that the minimum required return for any division is 16 percent. Compute the residual income for each division.
3. Is Division B's greater residual income an indication that it is better managed? Explain.

E11–4 Nelcro Company's Electrical Division produces a high-quality transformer. Sales and cost data on the transformer follow:

Selling price per unit on the intermediate market	$40
Variable costs per unit	21
Fixed costs per unit (based on capacity)	9
Capacity in units	60,000

Nelcro Company has an Audio Division that would like to begin purchasing this transformer from the Electrical Division. The Audio Division is currently purchasing 10,000 transformers each year from another manufacturer at a cost of $40 per transformer, less a 5 percent quantity discount.

Required

1. Assume that the Electrical Division is now selling only 50,000 transformers each year to outside customers on the intermediate market. If it begins to sell to the Audio Division, and if each division is to be treated as an independent investment center, what transfer price would you recommend? Why?
2. Assume that the Electrical Division is selling all of the transformers it can produce to outside customers on the intermediate market. Would this change your recommended transfer price? Explain.

E11–5 Listed below are three charges found on the monthly report of a division that manufactures and sells products primarily to outside customers. Divisional performance is evaluated by the use of ROI. You are to state which, if any, of the following charges are consistent with the responsibility accounting concept. Support each answer with a brief explanation.

1. A charge (at 10 percent of division sales) for the cost of operating general corporate headquarters.
2. A charge for goods purchased from another division. The charge is based on the competitive market price for the goods.
3. A charge for the use of the corporate computer facility. The charge is determined by taking actual annual computer department costs and allocating an amount to each division based on the ratio of its use to total corporate use.

(CMA, Adapted)

E11–6 Supply the missing data in the tabulation below:

	Division		
	A	**B**	**C**
Sales	$400,000	$750,000	$600,000
Net operating income	?	45,000	?
Average operating assets	160,000	?	150,000
ROI	20%	18%	?
Minimum required rate of return:			
Percentage	15%	?	12%
Dollar amount	$?	$ 50,000	$?
Residual income	?	?	6,000

E11–7 Division A manufactures picture tubes for TVs. The tubes can be sold either to Division B or to outside customers. During 19x3, the following activity was recorded in Division A:

Selling price per tube	$175
Production cost per tube	130
Number of tubes:	
Produced during the year	20,000
Sold to outside customers	16,000
Sold to Division B	4,000

Sales to Division B were at the same price as sales to outside customers. The tubes purchased by Division B were used in a TV set manufactured by that division. Division B incurred $300 in additional cost per TV and then sold the TVs for $600 each.

Required

1. Prepare income statements for 19x3 for Division A, Division B, and the company as a whole.
2. Assume that Division A's manufacturing capacity is 20,000 tubes per year. In 19x4, Division B wants to purchase 5,000 tubes from Division A, rather than only 4,000 tubes as in 19x3. (Tubes of this type are not available from outside

sources.) Should Division A sell the 1,000 additional tubes to Division B, or should it continue to sell them to outside customers? Explain why this would or would not make any difference from the point of view of the company as a whole.

E11–8 In each of the cases below, assume that Division X has a product that can be sold either to outside customers on an intermediate market or to Division Y for use in its production process.

	Case	
	A	**B**
Division X:		
Capacity in units	100,000	100,000
Number of units being sold on the intermediate market	100,000	80,000
Selling price per unit on the intermediate market	$50	$35
Variable costs per unit	30	20
Fixed costs per unit (based on capacity)	8	6
Division Y:		
Number of units needed for production	20,000	20,000
Purchase price per unit now being paid to an outside supplier	$47	$34

Required

1. Refer to the data in case A above. Assume that $2 per unit in variable selling costs can be avoided on intracompany sales.
   a. Using the transfer pricing formula, determine the transfer price that Division X should charge on any sales to Division Y.
   b. Will any transfers be made between the two divisions? Explain.
2. Refer to the data in case B above. Within what range should the transfer price be set for any sales between the two divisions? (Use the transfer pricing formula as needed.)

E11–9 Selected sales and operating data for three companies are given below:

	Company		
	A	**B**	**C**
Sales	$6,000,000	$10,000,000	$8,000,000
Average operating assets	1,500,000	5,000,000	2,000,000
Net operating income	300,000	900,000	180,000
Stockholders' equity	1,000,000	3,500,000	1,500,000
Minimum required rate of return	15%	18%	12%

Required

1. Compute the ROI for each company.
2. Compute the residual income for each company.
3. Assume that each company is presented with an investment opportunity that would yield a rate of return of 17 percent.
   a. If performance is being measured by ROI, which company or companies will probably accept the opportunity? Reject? Why?
   b. If performance is being measured by residual income, which company or companies will probably accept the opportunity? Reject? Why?

PROBLEMS

P11–10 ROI; Comparison of Company Performance Comparative data on three companies in the same industry are given on the next page:

	Company		
	A	B	C
Sales	$4,000,000	$1,500,000	$?
Net operating income	560,000	210,000	?
Average operating assets	2,000,000	?	3,000,000
Margin	?	?	3.5%
Turnover	?	?	2
ROI	?	7%	?

Required

1. What advantages can you see in breaking down the ROI computation into two separate elements, margin and turnover?
2. Fill in the missing information above, and comment on the relative performance of the three companies in as much detail as the data permit. Make *specific recommendations* on steps to be taken to improve the return on investment, where needed.

(Adapted from National Association of Accountants, *Research Report No. 35,* p. 34)

P11-11 The Appropriate Transfer Price; Well-Defined Intermediate Market Galati Products, Inc., has just purchased a small company that specializes in the manufacture of electronic tuners that are used as a component part in TV sets. Galati Products, Inc., is a decentralized company, and it will treat the newly acquired company as an autonomous division with full profit responsibility. The new division, called the Tuner Division, has the following revenue and costs associated with each tuner that it manufactures and sells:

Selling price		$20
Less expenses:		
Variable	$11	
Fixed (based on a capacity of 100,000 tuners per year)	6	17
Net income		$ 3

Galati Products also has an Assembly Division that assembles TV sets. The division is currently purchasing 30,000 tuners per year from an overseas supplier at a cost of $20 per tuner, less a 10 percent quantity discount. The president of Galati Products is anxious to have the Assembly Division begin purchasing its tuners from the newly acquired Tuner Division in order to "keep the profits within the corporate family."

Required For (1) through (4) below, assume that the Tuner Division can sell all of its output to outside TV manufacturers at the normal $20 price.

1. If the Assembly Division purchases 30,000 tuners each year from the Tuner Division, what price should control the transfers? Why?
2. Refer to the computations in (1) above. What is the lower limit and the upper limit for a transfer price? Is an upper limit relevant in this situation?
3. If the Tuner Division meets the price that the Assembly Division is currently paying to its overseas supplier and sells 30,000 tuners to the Assembly Division each year, what will be the effect on the profits of the Tuner Division, the Assembly Division, and the company as a whole?
4. If the intermediate market price for tuners is $20, is there any reason why the Tuner Division should sell to the Assembly Division for less than $20? Explain.

For (5) through (8) below, assume that the Tuner Division is currently selling only 60,000 tuners each year to outside TV manufacturers at the stated $20 price.

5. If the Assembly Division purchases 30,000 tuners each year from the Tuner Division, what price should control the transfers? Why?
6. Suppose that the Assembly Division's overseas supplier drops its price (net of the quantity discount) to only $16 per tuner. Should the Tuner Division meet this price? Explain. If the Tuner Division does *not* meet this price, what will be the effect on the profits of the company as a whole?
7. Refer to (6) above. If the Tuner Division refuses to meet the $16 price, should the Assembly Division be required to purchase from the Tuner Division at a higher price, for the good of the company as a whole? Explain.
8. Refer to (6) above. Assume that due to inflexible management policies, the Assembly Division is required to purchase 30,000 tuners each year from the Tuner Division at $20 per tuner. What will be the effect on the profits of the company as a whole?

P11–12 **Basic Transfer Pricing Computations** In cases 1–3 below, assume that Division A has a product that can be sold either to Division B or to outside customers on an intermediate market. (Further information on case 4 is given in the "Required" material.) Treat each case independently.

	Case			
	1	**2**	**3**	**4**
Division A:				
Capacity in units	50,000	300,000	100,000	200,000
Number of units now being sold to outside customers on the intermediate market	50,000	300,000	75,000	200,000
Selling price per unit on the intermediate market	$100	$40	$60	$45
Variable costs per unit	63	19	35	30
Fixed costs per unit (based on capacity)	25	8	17	6
Division B:				
Number of units needed annually	10,000	70,000	20,000	60,000
Purchase price now being paid to an outside supplier	$92	$39	$60*	—

* Before any quantity discount.

Required

1. Refer to case 1 above. A study has indicated that Division A can avoid $5 per unit in variable costs on any sales to Division B. Use the transfer pricing formula to determine what transfer price should be charged on any sales between the two divisions. Will any transfers be made? Explain.
2. Refer to case 2 above. Assume that Division A can avoid $4 per unit in variable costs on any sales to Division B.
   a. Again use the transfer pricing formula to compute an appropriate transfer price. Would you expect any disagreement between the two divisional managers over what transfer price should be paid? Explain.
   b. Assume that Division A offers to sell 70,000 units to Division B for $38 per unit and that Division B refuses this price. What will be the loss in potential profits for the company as a whole?
3. Refer to case 3 above. Assume that Division B is now receiving a 5 percent quantity discount from the outside supplier.
   a. Within what range should the transfer price be set for any sales between the two divisions?
   b. Assume that Division B offers to purchase 20,000 units from Division A at $52 per unit. If Division A accepts this price, would you expect its ROI to increase, decrease, or remain unchanged? Why?

4. Refer to case 4 above. Assume that Division B wants Division A to provide it with 60,000 units of a *different* product from the one that Division A is now producing. The new product would require $25 per unit in variable costs and would require that Division A cut back production of its present product by 30,000 units annually. Use the transfer pricing formula to determine what transfer price per unit Division A should charge Division B for the new product.

P11–13 ROI and Residual Income "I know headquarters wants us to add on that new product line," said Fred Halloway, manager of Kirsi Products' East Division. "But I want to see the numbers before I make a move. Our division has led the company for three years, and I don't want any letdown."

Kirsi Products is a decentralized company with four autonomous divisions. The divisions are evaluated on a basis of the return that they are able to generate on invested assets, with year-end bonuses given to the divisional managers who have the highest ROI figures. Operating results for the company's East Division for last year are given below:

Sales	$21,000,000
Less variable expenses	13,400,000
Contribution margin	7,600,000
Less fixed expenses	5,920,000
Net operating income	$ 1,680,000
Divisional operating assets	$ 5,250,000

The company had an overall ROI of 18 percent last year (considering all divisions). The company's East Division has an opportunity to add a new product line that would require an investment of $3,000,000. The cost and revenue characteristics of the new product line per year would be as follows:

Sales	$9,000,000
Variable expenses	65% of sales
Fixed expenses	$2,520,000

Required

1. Compute the East Division's ROI for last year; also compute the ROI as it will appear if the new product line is added.
2. If you were in Fred Halloway's position, would you be inclined to accept or reject the new product line? Explain.
3. Why do you suppose "headquarters" is anxious for the East Division to add the new product line?
4. Suppose that the company views a return of 15 percent on invested assets as being the minimum that any division should earn and that performance is evaluated by the residual income approach.
   a. Compute the East Division's residual income for last year; also compute the residual income as it will appear if the new product line is added.
   b. Under these circumstances, if you were in Fred Halloway's position would you accept or reject the new product line? Explain.

P11–14 Basic Transfer Pricing Computations Unless indicated otherwise, assume that each of the following situations is independent:

1. The following data are provided for a product manufactured by North Division:

Selling price on the intermediate market	$60
Variable costs per unit	45
Fixed costs per unit (based on capacity)	9
Capacity in units	100,000

North Division is selling all it can produce to outside customers on the intermediate market. Another division in the company, South Division, is currently purchasing 30,000 units of an identical product from an outside supplier at a price of $60 per unit, less a 5 percent quantity discount. If North Division begins selling to South Division, $12 per unit in sales commissions and shipping costs can be avoided. From the standpoint of the company as a whole, any sales made by North Division to South Division should be priced at what amount per unit?

2. Refer to the data in (1) above. Assume that North Division offers to sell 30,000 units to South Division each year at a price of $54 per unit. If South Division accepts this offer, what will be the effect on the profits of the company as a whole?
3. The following data are provided for product X, which is produced and sold by Division A:

Selling price on the intermediate market	$95
Variable costs per unit of product X	70
Fixed costs per unit (based on capacity)	16
Capacity in units of product X	25,000

Division A is currently operating at full capacity, producing 25,000 units of product X each period and selling them to outside customers. Division B would like Division A to start producing 5,000 units of a new product—product Y—for it each period. This would require that Division A cut back production of product X by 40 percent, to only 15,000 units each period. Division A has estimated the following cost per unit for the new product Y:

Selling price to Division B.	$?
Variable costs per unit of product Y . . .	80
Fixed costs per unit	32

Division A would use existing personnel and equipment to produce product Y. What transfer price should Division A charge Division B for each unit of product Y?

P11–15 ROI Analysis The income statement for Westex, Inc., for its most recent period is given below:

	Total	Unit
Sales	$1,000,000	$50.00
Less variable expenses	600,000	30.00
Contribution margin	400,000	20.00
Less fixed expenses	320,000	16.00
Net operating income.	80,000	4.00
Less income taxes (40%)	32,000	1.60
Net income	$ 48,000	$ 2.40

The company had average operating assets of $500,000 during the period.

Required 1. Compute the company's ROI for the period, using the ROI formula.

For each of the following questions, indicate whether the margin and turnover will increase, decrease, or remain unchanged as a result of the events described, and then compute the new ROI figure. Consider each question separately, starting in each case from the original ROI computed in (1) above.

2. The company is able to achieve a cost savings of $10,000 per period by using less costly labor inputs.
3. By use of JIT to control the purchase of some items of raw materials, the

company is able to reduce the average level of inventory by $100,000. (The released funds are used to pay off bank loans.)

4. Sales are increased by $100,000; operating assets remain unchanged.
5. The company issues bonds and uses the proceeds to purchase $125,000 in machinery and equipment. Interest on the bonds is $15,000 per period. Sales remain unchanged. The new, more efficient equipment reduces production costs by $5,000 per period.
6. The company invests $180,000 of cash (received on accounts receivable) in a plot of land that is to be held for possible future use as a plant site.
7. Obsolete items of inventory carried on the records at a cost of $20,000 are scrapped and written off as a loss, since they are unsalable.

P11–16 Choosing an Appropriate Transfer Price Top-Value Products, Inc., has just acquired a small company that manufactures electrical pumps. The company will operate as a division of Top-Value Products, Inc., under the name of the Pump Division. The pumps that are manufactured by the Pump Division are used primarily in dishwashers and are sold to various dishwasher manufacturers across the nation. The pumps sell for $60 each. Top-Value Products, Inc., has an Appliances Division that manufactures dishwashers, and the president of Top-Value products, Inc., feels that the Appliances Division should begin to purchase its pumps from the newly acquired Pump Division.

The Appliances Division is currently purchasing 30,000 pumps each year from an outside supplier. The price is $57 per pump, which represents the normal $60 price less a 5 percent quantity discount.

The Pump Division's cost per pump is given below:

Direct materials	$20
Direct labor	14
Variable overhead	6
Fixed overhead	5*
Total cost per pump	$45

* Based on 100,000 units capacity.

The president of Top-Value Products, Inc., is unsure what transfer price should control sales between the two divisions.

Required

1. Assume that the Pump Division has sufficient idle capacity to supply 30,000 pumps each year to the Appliances Division. Explain why each of the following transfer prices would or would not be an appropriate price to charge the Appliances Division on the intracompany sales:
   a. $60.00.
   b. $57.00.
   c. $48.50.
   d. $45.00.
   e. $40.00.
2. Assume that the Pump Division is currently selling all the pumps it can produce to outside customers. Under these circumstances, explain why each of the transfer prices given in (1*a*) through (1*e*) above would or would not be an appropriate price to charge the Appliances Division on the intracompany sales.

P11–17 ROI and Residual Income Lawton Industries has manufactured prefabricated houses for over 20 years. The houses are constructed in sections to be assembled on customers' lots.

Lawton expanded into the precut housing market several years ago when it acquired Presser Company, one of its suppliers. In this market, various types of lumber are precut into the appropriate lengths, banded into packages, and shipped to customers' lots for assembly. Lawton decided to maintain Presser's separate identity and therefore established the Presser Division as an investment center of Lawton.

Lawton uses ROI as a performance measure. Management bonuses are based in part on ROI. All investments in operating assets are expected to earn a minimum return of 15 percent before income taxes.

Presser's ROI has ranged from 19 to 22 percent since it was acquired by Lawton. During the past year, Presser had an investment opportunity that had an estimated ROI of 18 percent. Presser's management decided against the investment because it believed the investment would decrease the division's overall ROI.

Last year's (19x5) income statement for Presser Division is given below. The division's operating assets employed were $15,500,000 at the end of the year, which represents a 24 percent increase over the 19x4 year-end balance. (Several purchases of new equipment were made during the year.)

PRESSER DIVISION
Divisional Income Statement
For the Year Ended December 31, 19x5

Sales		$35,000,000
Cost of goods sold		24,600,000
Gross margin		10,400,000
Less operating expenses:		
Selling expenses	$5,700,000	
Administrative expenses	1,900,000	7,600,000
Net operating income		$ 2,800,000

Required

1. Calculate the following performance measures for 19x5 for Presser Division:
   a. ROI. (Remember, ROI is based on the *average* operating assets, computed from the beginning-of-year and end-of-year balances.)
   b. Residual income.
2. Would the management of Presser Division have been more likely to accept the investment opportunity it had in 19x5 if residual income were used as a performance measure instead of ROI? Explain.
3. The Presser Division is a separate investment center within Lawton Industries. Identify the items Presser Division must be free to control if it is to be evaluated fairly by either the ROI or residual income performance measures.

(CMA, Heavily Adapted)

P11–18 Negotiated Transfer Price Pella Company has several independent divisions. The company's Compressor Division produces a high-quality compressor that is sold to various users. The division's income statement for the most recent month, in which 500 compressors were sold, is given below:

	Total	Unit
Sales	$125,000	$250
Less cost of goods sold	75,000	150
Gross margin	50,000	100
Less selling and administrative expenses	30,000	60
Divisional net income	$ 20,000	$ 40

As shown above, it costs the division $150 to produce a compressor. This figure consists of the following costs:

Direct materials	$ 50
Direct labor	60
Overhead (50% fixed)	40
Total cost	$150

The division has fixed selling and administrative expenses of $25,000 per month and variable selling and administrative expenses of $10 per compressor.

Another division of Pella Company, the Home Products Division, uses compressors as a component part of air-conditioning systems that it installs. The Home Products Division has asked the Compressor Division to sell it 40 compressors each month of a somewhat different design. The Compressor Division has estimated the following cost for each of the new compressors:

Direct materials	$ 60
Direct labor	90
Overhead (two thirds fixed)	75
Total cost	$225

In order to produce the new compressors, the Compressor Division would have to reduce production of its present compressors by 100 units per month. However, all variable selling and administrative expenses could be avoided on the intracompany business. Total fixed overhead costs would not change.

Required

1. What price should be charged by the Compressor Division for the new compressor? Show all computations.
2. Suppose the Home Products Division has found a supplier that will provide the new compressors for only $350 each. If the Compressor Division meets this price, what will be the effect on the profits of the company as a whole?

P11–19 Cost Volume Profit Analysis; ROI; Transfer Pricing The Bearing Division of Timkin Company produces a small bearing that is used by a number of companies as a component part in the manufacture of their products. Timkin Company operates its divisions as autonomous units, giving its divisional managers great discretion in pricing and other decisions. Each division is expected to generate a return on its assets of at least 12 percent. The Bearing Division has operating assets as follows:

Cash	$ 7,000
Accounts receivable	60,000
Inventories	108,000
Plant and equipment (net)	125,000
Total assets	$300,000

The bearings are sold for $4 each. Variable costs are $2.50 per bearing, and fixed costs total $234,000 each period. The division's capacity is 200,000 bearings each period.

Required

1. How many bearings must be sold each period for the division to obtain the desired rate of return on its assets?
   a. What is the margin earned at this sales level?
   b. What is the turnover of assets at this sales level?
2. The divisional manager is considering two ways of increasing the ROI figure:
   a. Market studies suggest that an increase in price to $4.25 per bearing would result in sales of 160,000 units each period. The decrease in units sold would allow the division to reduce its investment in assets by $10,000, due to the lower level of inventories and receivables that would be needed to support sales. Compute the margin, turnover, and ROI if these changes are made.
   b. Other market studies suggest that a reduction in price to $3.75 per bearing would result in sales of 200,000 units each period. However, this would require an increase in total assets of $10,000, due to the somewhat larger inventories and receivables that would be carried. Compute the margin, turnover, and ROI if these changes are made.

3. Refer to the original data. Assume that the normal volume of sales is 180,000 bearings each period at a price of $4 per bearing. Another division of Timkin Company is currently purchasing 20,000 bearings each period from an overseas supplier at $3.25 per bearing. The manager of the Bearing Division says that this price is "ridiculous" and refuses to meet it, since doing so would result in a loss of $0.42 per bearing for her division:

Selling price		$ 3.25
Cost per bearing:		
Variable cost	$2.50	
Fixed cost ($234,000 ÷ 200,000 bearings)	1.17	3.67
Loss per bearing		$(.42)

You may assume that sales to the other division would require an increase of $25,000 in the total assets carried by the Bearing Division. Would you recommend that the Bearing Division meet the $3.25 price and start selling 20,000 bearings per period to the other division? Support your answer with ROI computations.

P11–20 Impact of Transfer Price on Marketing Decisions Damico Company's Board Division manufactures an electronic control board that is widely used in compact disc (CD) players. The cost per control board is as follows:

Variable cost per board	$120
Fixed cost per board	30*
Total cost per board	$150

* Based on a capacity of 80,000 boards per year.

Part of the Board Division's output is sold to outside manufacturers of CD players, and part is sold to Damico Company's Consumer Products Division, which produces a CD player under the Damico name. The Board Division charges a selling price of $190 per control board for all sales, both internally and externally.

The costs, revenues, and net income associated with the Consumer Products Division's CD player is given below:

Selling price per player		$580
Less variable costs per player:		
Cost of the control board	$190	
Variable cost of other parts	230	
Total variable costs		420
Contribution margin		160
Less fixed costs per player		85*
Net income per player		$ 75

* Based on a capacity of 20,000 CD players per year.

The Consumer Products Division has an order from an overseas distributor for 5,000 CD players. The distributor wants to pay only $400 per CD player.

Required

1. Assume that the Consumer Products Division has enough idle capacity to fill the 5,000-unit order. Is the division likely to accept the $400 price, or to reject it? Explain.
2. Assume that both the Board Division and the Consumer Products Division have idle capacity. Under these conditions, would rejecting the $400 price be an

advantage to the company as a whole, or would it result in the loss of potential profits? Show computations to support your answer.

3. Assume that the Board Division is operating at capacity and could sell all of its control boards to outside manufacturers of CD players. Assume, however, that the Consumer Products Division has enough idle capacity to fill the 5,000-unit order. Under these conditions, compute the dollar advantage or disadvantage of accepting the order at the $400 price.
4. What kind of transfer pricing information is needed by the Consumer Products Division in making decisions such as these?

P11–21 Critique of a Performance Evaluation Program ATCO Company purchased the Dexter Company three years ago. Prior to the acquisition, Dexter manufactured and sold plastic products to a wide variety of customers. Dexter has since become a division of ATCO, and now it manufactures plastic components only for products made by ATCO's Macon Division. Macon sells its products to hardware wholesalers.

ATCO's corporate management gives the Dexter Division management a considerable amount of authority in running the division's operations. However, corporate management retains authority for decisions regarding capital investments, price setting of all products, and the quantity of each product to be produced by the Dexter Division.

ATCO has a formal performance evaluation program for the management of all its divisions. The performance evaluation program relies heavily on each division's ROI. The income statement of Dexter Division presented below provides the basis for the evaluation of Dexter's divisional management.

DEXTER DIVISION OF ATCO COMPANY
Income Statement
For the Year Ended October 31, 19x5
(in thousands)

Sales		$4,000
Costs and expenses:		
Product costs:		
Direct materials	$ 500	
Direct labor	1,100	
Factory overhead	1,300	
Total product costs	2,900	
Less increase in inventory	350	2,550
Engineering and research		120
Shipping and receiving		240
Division administration:		
Manager's office	210	
Cost accounting	40	
Personnel	82	332
Corporate costs:		
Computer	48	
General services	230	278
Total costs and expenses		3,520
Divisional operating income		$ 480
Net plant investment		$4,000
Return on investment		12%

The financial statements for the divisions are prepared by the corporate accounting staff. The corporate general services costs are allocated on the basis of sales dollars, and the computer department's actual costs are apportioned among the divisions on the basis of use. The net division investment includes division fixed assets at net book value (cost less depreciation), division inventory, and corporate working capital apportioned to the divisions on the basis of sales dollars.

Required

1. Discuss fully whether the financial reporting and performance evaluation program discussed above is an appropriate basis for measuring performance in the Dexter Division.
2. Based on your response to (1) above, recommend appropriate revisions of the financial information and reports used to evaluate the performance of Dexter's divisional management. If revisions are not necessary, explain why this is so.

(CMA, Adapted)

P11–22 Transfer Pricing with and without Idle Capacity Division X manufactures an electronic relay device that can be sold either to outside customers or to Division Y. Selected operating data on the two divisions are given below:

Division X:	
Unit selling price to outside customers	$ 30
Variable production cost per unit	16
Variable selling and administrative expense per unit	4
Fixed production cost in total	500,000*
Division Y:	
Outside purchase price per unit (before any quantity discount)	30

* Capacity 100,000 units per year.

Division Y now purchases the relay from an outside supplier at the regular $30 intermediate price less a 10 percent quantity discount. Since the relay manufactured by Division X is of the same quality and type used by Division Y, consideration is being given to buying internally rather than from the outside supplier.

The controller of Division X has determined that half of the variable selling and administrative costs can be avoided on any intracompany sales. Top management wants to treat each division as an autonomous unit with independent profit responsibility.

Required

1. Assume that Division X is currently selling only 60,000 units per year to outside customers and that Division Y needs 40,000 units per year.
   a. What is the lowest transfer price that can be justified between the two divisions? Explain.
   b. What is the highest transfer price that can be justified between the two divisions? Explain.
   c. Assume that Division Y finds an outside supplier that will sell the needed relays for only $26 per unit. Should Division X be required to meet this price? Explain.
   d. Refer to the original data. Assume that Division X decides to raise its price to $35 per unit. If Division Y is forced to pay this price and to start purchasing from Division X, will this result in greater or less total corporate profits? How much per unit?
   e. Under the circumstances posed in *(d)* above, should Division Y be forced to purchase from Division X? Explain.
2. Assume that Division X can sell all that it produces to outside customers. Repeat *(a)* through *(e)* above.

CASES

C11–23 Transfer Pricing; Divisional Performance; Behavioral Problems Stanco, Inc., is a decentralized organization containing five divisions. The company's Electronics Division produces a variety of electronics items, including an XL5 circuit board. The division (which is operating at capacity) sells the XL5 circuit board to regular customers for $12.50 each. The circuit boards have a variable production cost of $8.25 each.

The company's Clock Division has asked the Electronics Division to supply it with a large quantity of XL5 circuit boards for only $9 each. The Clock Division, which is operating at only 60 percent of capacity, will put the circuit boards into a timing device that it will produce and sell to a large oven manufacturer. The cost of the timing device being manufactured by the Clock Division follows:

XL5 circuit board (desired cost)	$ 9.00
Other purchased parts (from outside vendors)	30.00
Direct labor	16.50
Variable overhead	4.25
Fixed overhead and administrative costs	10.00
Total cost per timing device	$69.75

The manager of the Clock Division feels that she can't quote a price greater than $70 per timing device to the oven manufacturer if her division is to get the job. As shown above, in order to keep the price at $70 or less, she can't pay more than $9 per unit to the Electronics Division for the XL-5 circuit boards. Although the $9 price for the XL-5 circuit boards represents a substantial discount from the normal $12.50 price, she feels that the price concession is necessary for her division to get the oven manufacturer contract and thereby keep its core of highly trained people.

The company uses ROI and dollar profits in measuring divisional performance.

Required

1. Assume that you are the manager of the Electronics Division. Would you recommend that your division supply the XL5 circuit boards to the Clock Division for $9 each as requested? Why or why not? Show all computations. (Ignore income taxes.)
2. Would it be to the short-run economic advantage of the company as a whole for the Electronics Division to supply the Clock Division with the circuit boards for $9 each? Explain your answer. (Ignore income taxes.)
3. Discuss the organizational and manager behavior problems, if any, inherent in this situation. As the Stanco, Inc., company controller, what would you advise the company's president to do in this situation?

C11–24 Negotiated Transfer Price National Industries is a diversified corporation with separate and distinct operating divisions. Each division's performance is evaluated on the basis of total dollar profits and return on division investment.

The WindAir Division manufactures and sells air conditioner units. The coming year's budgeted income statement, based on a sales volume of 15,000 units, appears below:

WINDAIR DIVISION
Budgeted Income Statement
For the Year 1993

	Total	Per Unit
Sales revenue	$6,000,000	$400
Less cost of goods sold	3,210,000	214
Gross margin	2,790,000	186
Less operating expenses:		
Variable selling	270,000	18
Fixed selling	1,035,000	69
Fixed administrative	570,000	38
Total operating expenses	1,875,000	125
Net income	$ 915,000	$ 61

The division's $214 per unit cost of goods sold consists of the following items:

Compressor	$ 70
Other material and parts	37
Direct labor	30
Variable overhead	45
Fixed overhead	32
Total cost per unit	$214

WindAir Division's manager believes that sales can be increased if the unit selling price of the air conditioners is reduced. A market research study conducted by an independent firm at the request of the manager indicates that a 5 percent reduction in the selling price ($20) would increase sales volume 16 percent, or 2,400 units. WindAir has sufficient production capacity to manage this increased volume with no increase in fixed costs.

At present, WindAir uses a compressor in its units that it purchases from an outside supplier at a cost of $70 per compressor. The division manager of WindAir has approached the manager of the Compressor Division regarding the sale of a compressor unit to WindAir. The Compressor Division currently manufactures and sells a unit exclusively to outside firms that is similar to the unit used by WindAir. The specifications of the WindAir compressor are slightly different, which would reduce the Compressor Division's raw material cost by $1.50 per unit. In addition, the Compressor Division would not incur any variable selling costs in the units sold to WindAir. The manager of WindAir wants all of the compressors it uses to come from one supplier and has offered to pay $50 for each compressor unit.

The Compressor Division has the capacity to produce 75,000 units. The coming year's budgeted income statement for the Compressor Division, shown below, is based on a sales volume of 64,000 units without considering WindAir's proposal.

COMPRESSOR DIVISION
Budgeted Income Statement
For the Year 1993

	Total	Per Unit
Sales revenue	$6,400,000	$100
Less cost of goods sold	2,624,000	41
Gross margin	3,776,000	59
Less operating expenses:		
Variable selling	832,000	13
Fixed selling	1,024,000	16
Fixed administrative	512,000	8
Total operating expenses	2,368,000	37
Net income	$1,408,000	$ 22

The division's $41 cost of goods sold consists of the following items:

Raw materials	$12
Direct labor	8
Variable overhead	10
Fixed overhead	11
Total cost per compressor	$41

Required

1. Should WindAir Division institute the 5 percent price reduction on its air conditioner units even if it cannot acquire the compressors internally for $50 each? Support your conclusion with appropriate calculations.
2. Without prejudice to your answer to (1) above, assume that WindAir needs

17,400 units. Should the Compressor Division be willing to supply the compressor units for $50 each? Support your conclusions with appropriate calculations.

3. As the manager of the Compressor Division, what is the minimum transfer price that you could charge for the new compressor? Show computations.
4. Without prejudice to your answer to (1) above, assume that WindAir needs 17,400 units. Would it be in the best interest of National Industries for the Compressor Division to supply the compressor units at $50 each to the WindAir Division? Support your conclusions with appropriate calculations.

(CMA, Adapted)

C11–25 Transfer Pricing Dispute; Suboptimization; Behavioral Problems Gheen Electric Company manufactures a large variety of systems and components for the electronics industry. The firm is organized into several divisions with divisional managers given the authority to make virtually all operating decisions. Management control over divisional operations is maintained by a system of divisional profit and ROI measures which are reviewed regularly by top management. The top management of Gheen Electric has been quite pleased with the effectiveness of the system they have been using and believe that it is responsible for the company's improved profitability over the last few years.

The company's Circuit Division manufactures solid-state devices and is operating at capacity. The company's Systems Division has asked the Circuit Division to supply it with 150,000 units of integrated circuit IC378. The Circuit Division currently is selling this circuit to its regular customers at a price of $4 per unit.

The Systems Division, which is currently operating at only 60 percent of capacity, wants this particular circuit for a digital clock system. It has an opportunity to supply 150,000 of these clock systems to Centonic Products, a major producer of clock radios and other popular electronic equipment. This is the first opportunity any of the Gheen divisions have had to do business with Centonic Products. Centonic has offered to pay the Systems Division $11.50 per clock system.

The Systems Division has prepared an analysis of the probable costs to produce the clock system for Centonic. The division's cost analysis is shown below:

Proposed price per system		$11.50
Costs, excluding the required integrated circuit (IC378) from the Circuit Division:		
Components purchased from other suppliers	$4.20	
Circuit board etching—labor and variable overhead	0.50	
Assembly, testing, and packaging—labor and variable overhead	0.70	
Fixed overhead allocation	3.00	
Profit margin	0.60	9.00
Amount which can be paid for the integrated circuit (IC378) from the Circuit Division		$ 2.50

The $2.50 amount above that can be paid to the Circuit Division for IC378 was determined by working backwards from the proposed selling price to Centonic. The cost estimates used by the Systems Division in the above analysis represent the highest amounts that the Systems Division can incur for the various cost components and still realize a small profit margin.

As a result of this analysis, the Systems Division has offered the Circuit Division a price of $2.50 for each unit of IC378. This bid was refused by Tom Belcher, manager of the Circuit Division, because he felt that the Systems Division should at least meet the $4 per circuit price that regular customers pay. When the Systems Division found that it could not obtain a comparable integrated circuit from outside vendors, the situation was brought to an arbitration committee which has been set up to review such problems.

The arbitration committee prepared an analysis which showed that a price of $1.80 per unit for IC378 would cover the Circuit Division's variable costs of producing the circuit. A price of $2.75 per unit would cover the division's full costs, including fixed overhead, and a price of $3.50 per unit would cover all costs plus provide a profit margin on each circuit that was equal to the average profit margin on all circuits produced and sold by the Circuit Division.

Sue Adams, manager of the Systems Division, reacted to the committee's finding by saying, "Tom Belcher could sell us that integrated circuit for $2.50 per unit and still earn a positive contribution toward profits. In fact, he should be required to sell at his variable cost—$1.80 per unit—and not be allowed to take advantage of us."

Tom Belcher countered by arguing, "It doesn't make sense to sell IC378 to the Systems Division for $2.50 per unit when we can get $4 per unit from our regular customers on all we can produce. In fact, the Systems Division could pay us as much as $5 per unit for IC378, and they would still have a positive contribution to profit. Why should we be forced to subsidize their inability to compete?"

The arbitration committee recommended a price of $3.50 per unit for IC378 so that the Circuit Division could earn a "fair" profit on the business. However, this price was rejected by both divisional managers. Consequently, the problem has been brought to the attention of the vice president of operations.

Required

1. What transfer price should control the sale of IC378 to the Systems Division? Show computations to support your position.
2. What would be the effect on the profits of Gheen Electric as a whole if transfers are made at the $3.50 per unit price recommended by the arbitration committee? What would be the effect if transfers are made at $5 per unit?
3. Identify the organizational and behavioral difficulties, if any, that are inherent in this situation. As the vice president of operations, what would you advise Gheen Electric's president to do to resolve the problem?

(CMA, Heavily Adapted)

PART III

THE CAPSTONE
USING COST DATA IN DECISION MAKING

12

Pricing of Products and Services

LEARNING OBJECTIVES

After studying Chapter 12, you should be able to:

1. Explain how the price of a product or service is obtained by using the economist's total revenue and total cost concepts and marginal revenue and marginal cost concepts.
2. Define price elasticity and explain how it impacts on the pricing decision.
3. Compute the target selling price for a product by use of cost-plus pricing under either the absorption or the contribution approach.
4. Derive the markup percentage needed to achieve a target ROI for a product.
5. Compute the target selling price for a service by use of time and material pricing.
6. Make special pricing decisions under the contribution approach, using the range of flexibility concept.
7. Define or explain the key terms listed at the end of the chapter.

Many firms have no pricing problems at all. They make a product that is in competition with other, similar products for which a market price already exists. Customers will not pay more than this price, and there is no reason for any firm to charge less. Under these circumstances, no price calculations are necessary. Any firm entering the market simply charges the price that the market directs it to accept. To a large extent, farm products follow this type of pattern. In these situations, the question isn't what price to charge; the question is simply how much to produce.

In this chapter, we are concerned with the more common situation in which a firm is faced with the problem of setting its own prices, as well as deciding how much to produce. The pricing decision is considered by many to be the single most important decision that a manager has to make. The reason is that the pricing of products isn't just a marketing decision or a financial decision; rather, it is a decision touching on *all* aspects of a firm's activities, and as such it affects the entire enterprise. Since the prices charged for a firm's products largely determine the quantities customers are willing to purchase, the setting of prices dictates the inflows of revenues into a firm. If these revenues consistently fail to cover all the costs of the firm, then in the long run the firm cannot survive. This is true regardless of how carefully costs may be controlled or how innovative the managers of the firm may be in the discharge of their other responsibilities.

Cost is a key factor in the pricing decision. As we have already seen, however, *cost* is a somewhat fluid concept that is sometimes hard to pin down. Our purpose in this chapter is to look at some of the cost concepts developed in earlier chapters and to see how these concepts can be applied in the pricing decision. This chapter is not intended to be a comprehensive guide to pricing; rather, its purpose is to integrate those cost concepts with which we are already familiar into a general pricing framework.

THE ECONOMIC FRAMEWORK FOR PRICING

A large part of microeconomic theory (theory of the firm) is devoted to the matter of pricing. In order to establish a framework for the pricing decision, it will be helpful to review certain concepts of microeconomic theory. This review will also assist us in showing the relationship between the models involved in microeconomic theory and the concept of incremental analysis discussed in preceding chapters.

Total Revenue and Total Cost Curves

Microeconomic theory states that the best price for a product is the price that maximizes the difference between total revenue and total costs. The economist illustrates this concept by constructing a model such as that shown in Exhibit 12–1.

This model is based on a number of assumptions. The economist assumes, first, that it is not possible to sell an unlimited number of units at the same price. If an unlimited number of units could be sold at the same price, then the total revenue *(TR)* curve would appear as a straight line, beginning at the origin of the graph. Since the economist assumes that at some point price reductions will be necessary to sell more units, the *TR* curve is shown increasing at a decreasing rate as quantity sold increases. That is, as price is reduced to stimulate more sales, total revenue will continue to increase for each unit sold, but the *rate* of this increase will begin to decline. As price is reduced more and more, the increase in total revenue will continue to decline, as depicted by the flattening tendency in the *TR* curve in Exhibit 12–1.

The total cost *(TC)* curve in Exhibit 12–1 assumes that the cost of producing additional units of product is not constant, but rather increases as attempts are made to squeeze more and more production out of a given set of productive facilities. So long as the rate of this increase is less than the rate of increase in total revenue, the company can profit by producing and selling more units of product. At some point, however, the rate of increase in total cost will become equal to the rate of increase in total revenue—that is, at some point the two lines will become parallel to each other. At this point, the increase to total cost from producing and selling one more unit of product is exactly equal to the increase to total revenue from that unit of product, and its production and sale yield zero increase in total profits in the firm. This point is shown in the graph in Exhibit 12–1 as quantity Q_0, representing the optimum volume of production and sales for the firm.

At Q_0 volume of units, the difference between total revenue and total cost is maximized. If we move to the right of Q_0 volume, then total cost is increasing more rapidly than total revenue, and therefore total profits would

EXHIBIT 12–1
Total Revenue and Total Cost Curves

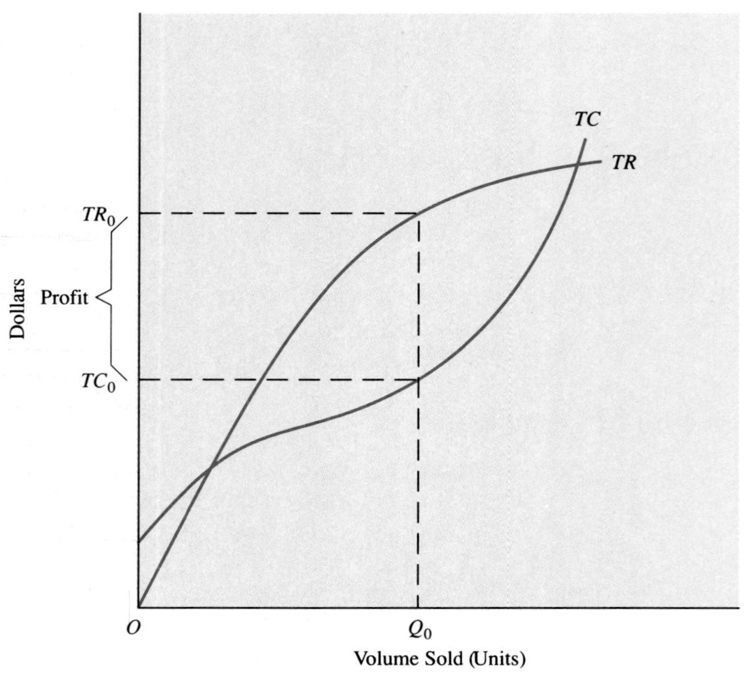

be decreased. If we move to the left of Q_0 volume, then total revenue is increasing more rapidly than total cost, and the company can profit by further expanding output up to Q_0 level of activity. In sum, Q_0 represents the optimum volume of sales for the firm, and the correct price to charge is the price that will allow the firm to sell this volume of units.

Marginal Revenue and Marginal Cost Curves

These same concepts can be shown in terms of marginal revenue and marginal cost. **Marginal revenue** can be defined as the addition to total revenue resulting from the sale of one additional unit of product. **Marginal cost** can be defined as the addition to total cost resulting from the production and sale of one additional unit of product. The economist expresses these concepts in model form as shown in Exhibit 12–2.

The marginal revenue *(MR)* and marginal cost *(MC)* curves in Exhibit 12–2 have their basis in the economist's assumption that the total revenue and total cost curves behave in the way depicted earlier in Exhibit 12–1. That is, the marginal revenue and marginal cost curves are derived by measuring the rate of *change* in total revenue and total cost at various levels of activity, and by plotting this change in graph form. Since the total revenue curve in Exhibit 12–1 depicts a declining rate of increase in total revenue, the marginal revenue curve in Exhibit 12–2 slopes downward to the right. And since the total cost curve in Exhibit 12–1 depicts total cost as first increasing at a decreasing rate, then flattening out somewhat, and then increasing at an increasing rate, the marginal cost curve in Exhibit 12–2 slopes downward initially, bottoms out, and then slopes upward to the right. As

EXHIBIT 12–2
Marginal Revenue and Marginal Cost Curves

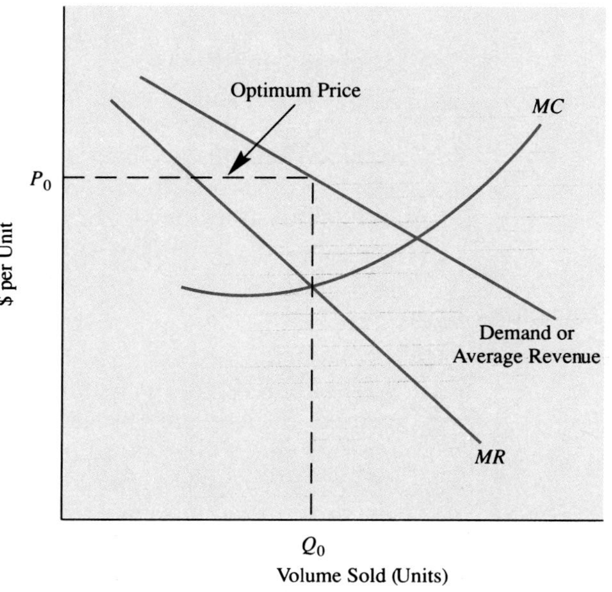

discussed in Chapter 2, the economist's marginal concept is basically the same as the accountant's incremental concept.

The optimum price to charge is determined by the intersection of the marginal revenue and the marginal cost curves. The intersection of these two curves occurs at volume Q_0. This is the same volume as shown earlier in Exhibit 12–1, depicting the point of maximum difference between total revenues and total costs. At volume Q_0, price P_0 should be charged for each unit sold.

Elasticity of Demand

A product's price elasticity is a key concept in any pricing decision. **Price elasticity** measures the degree to which volume of sales is affected by a change in price per unit. Demand for a product is price inelastic if a change in price has little or no effect on the volume of units sold. Demand is price elastic if a change in price has a substantial effect on the volume of units sold. Salt is a good example of a product that tends to be price inelastic. Raising or lowering the price of salt would probably have little or no effect on the amount of salt sold in a given year.

Whether demand for a product tends to be price elastic or price inelastic can be a crucial factor in a decision relating to a change in price. The problem is that measuring the degree of price elasticity is an extremely difficult thing to do. It's one thing to observe generally that a given product tends to be price elastic, and it's another thing to determine the exact *degree* of that elasticity—that is, to determine what change in volume of sales will take place as a result of specific changes in price. Yet this is exactly the kind of information that managers need in their pricing decisions, and the kind of information that they attempt to obtain by carefully planned marketing research programs.

Pricing decisions are further complicated by the fact that cross-elasticity often exists in the demand for certain products. *Cross-elasticity* measures the degree to which demand for one product is affected by a change in the price of a substitute product. For example, as the price of galvanized pipe goes up, consumers may switch to plastic pipe. One of the problems in measuring cross-elasticity is trying to identify the substitutes for a particular product, and the willingness of consumers to accept those substitutes in place of the product itself. Although problems of this type are often difficult to quantify, the concept of cross-elasticity of demand is an important concept and cannot be disregarded in the pricing decision.

Limitations of the General Models

Although the models in Exhibits 12–1 and 12–2 do a good job of showing the general outlines of the incremental profit approach to pricing, they must be viewed as being only broad, conceptual guides in pricing decisions. There are several reasons why. First, the cost and revenue data available to managers are generally sufficient to provide only rough approximations of the shape of the various cost and revenue curves depicted in the models. As our methods of measurement are improved and refined in years to come, this situation may change, but at present managers usually have only a general idea of the shape of the demand curve that they are facing.

Second, the models are directly applicable only in conditions of **monopoly** (no directly competing product in the market) and **monopolistic competition** (many sellers of similar products, with no one seller having a large enough share of the market for other sellers to be able to discern the effect of its pricing decision on their sales). The models are not applicable between these two extremes, where the market is characterized by situations of **oligopoly** (a few large sellers competing directly with one another). The reason is that the models make no allowance for retaliatory pricing decisions by competing firms, and retaliatory pricing is a prime characteristic of oligopolistic industries.

A third limitation of the general models arises from the fact that price is just one element in the marketing of a product. Many other factors must also be considered that can have a significant impact on the number of units of a product that can be sold at a given price. Among these factors are promotional strategy, product design, intensity of selling effort, and the selection of distribution channels.

A final limitation of the general models is that even if business firms had a precise knowledge of the shape of their demand curves, we cannot automatically assume that they would price in such a way as to maximize profits. The reason is that this might bring accusations from the public of ''profiteering'' and ''charging all that the traffic will bear.'' Rather than attempting to maximize profits, many firms seek only to earn a ''satisfactory'' profit for the company. They think in terms of a reasonable return on the investment that has been made in the company, and they strive to set prices in such a way as to earn that return. The concept of a satisfactory profit underlies the actions of a great many business firms today.

Although the limitations discussed above preclude the *direct* use of the economic pricing models in pricing decisions, these models are nonetheless highly useful in providing the general framework within which the price setter must work. They state the pricing problem in *conceptual* terms, and as such they constitute the starting point in any pricing decision.

PRICING STANDARD PRODUCTS

Not all pricing decisions are approached in the same way. Some pricing decisions relate to the pricing of standard products that are sold to customers in the routine day-to-day conduct of business activities. Other pricing decisions relate to special orders of standard or near-standard products, and still others relate to the pricing of special products that have been taken on in an effort to fill out unused productive capacity. In this section, we consider the pricing of standard products. The pricing of special orders of various types is reserved for a later section.

Cost-Plus Pricing Formulas

In pricing standard products, the key concept is to recognize that selling prices must be sufficient in the long run to cover *all* costs of production, administration, and sales, both fixed and variable, as well as to provide for a reasonable return on the stockholders' investment, if a firm is to survive and grow. This point is often missed by some pricing enthusiasts who seem to imply in their writings that any price above variable or incremental costs is an acceptable price for any product under any circumstances.[1]

In setting normal long-run prices on standard products, *all costs* are relevant to the pricing decision and must be explicitly considered by the price setter if long-run profit goals are to be met. This means that a portion of the fixed costs must be considered along with the variable costs, and that the costs of administration and sales must be weighted in along with the costs of production as prices are set.

The most common approach to the pricing of standard products is to employ some type of **cost-plus pricing** formula.[2] The approach is to compute a "cost" base and then to add to this base some predetermined **markup** to arrive at a target selling price. The "cost" in cost-plus pricing is defined according to the method being used to cost units of product. In Chapters 3 and 7, we found that units of product can be costed in two different ways—by the absorption approach or by the contribution approach (with direct costing). We consider both costing methods below, and the approach that each takes to cost-plus pricing of standard products.

The Absorption Approach

Under the absorption approach to cost-plus pricing, the cost base is defined as the cost to manufacture one unit of product. Selling and administrative costs are not included in this cost base, but rather are provided for through the markup that is added on to arrive at the target selling price. Thus, the markup must be high enough to cover these costs as well as to provide the company with a "satisfactory" profit margin.

To illustrate, let us assume that Ritter Company is in the process of setting a selling price on one of its standard products, which has just undergone some slight modifications in design. The accounting department has accumulated the following cost data on the redesigned product:

	Per Unit	Total
Direct materials	$6	
Direct labor	4	
Variable overhead	3	
Fixed overhead (based on 10,000 units)	7	$70,000
Variable selling and administrative expenses . . .	2	
Fixed selling and administrative expenses (based on 10,000 units)	1	10,000

The first step is to compute the cost to manufacture one unit of product. For Ritter Company, this amounts to $20 per unit, computed as follows:

Direct materials	$ 6
Direct labor	4
Overhead ($3 variable plus $7 fixed, or 250% of direct labor cost)	10
Total absorption cost to manufacture one unit . . .	$20

[1] For a discussion of the circumstances under which variable or incremental costs are useful as a pricing guide, see the section "Special Pricing Decisions."

[2] For a study documenting the use of cost-plus pricing, see Lawrence A. Gordon, Robert Cooper, Haim Falk, and Danny Miller, *The Pricing Decision* (New York: National Association of Accountants, 1981), p. 23.

EXHIBIT 12–3
Price Quotation Sheet—Absorption Basis

Direct materials	$ 6
Direct labor	4
Overhead at 250% of direct labor cost	10
Total cost to manufacture	20
Markup to cover selling and administrative expenses and desired profit—50% of cost to manufacture	10
Target selling price	$30

Let us assume that in order to obtain its target selling price, Ritter Company has a general policy of adding a markup equal to 50 percent of the cost to manufacture. A price quotation sheet for the company prepared under this assumption is presented in Exhibit 12–3.

As shown in Exhibit 12–3, even though this pricing approach is termed cost-plus, part of the costs involved are buried in the *plus,* or markup, part of the formula. The buried costs are those associated with the selling and administrative activities. Some firms break these costs out separately and add them to the cost base along with the cost to manufacture, and then apply a markup to this base that represents the expected profit on the goods being sold.[3] Other firms, however, such as Ritter Company in our example, prefer not to include the selling and administrative expenses in the cost base. This is because of the problems involved in trying to allocate the common selling and administrative expenses among the various products of the firm. For example, the salary of the company's president is a cost that is common to all products. It would be difficult to allocate the president's salary to these products in any meaningful way. Therefore, firms often provide for such costs in final, target selling prices by simply expanding the markup over cost to manufacture to include them as well as the desired profit, as we have done in Exhibit 12–3. This means, of course, that the markup must be structured with great care in order to ensure that it is sufficient to cover all that it is supposed to cover. More is said on this point a little later.

If Ritter Company produces and sells 10,000 units of its product at a selling price of $30 per unit, the income statement will appear as shown in Exhibit 12–4.

The Contribution Approach

The contribution approach to cost-plus pricing differs from the absorption approach in that it emphasizes costs by behavior rather than by function. Thus, under the contribution approach, the cost base consists of the variable expenses associated with a product. Included are the variable selling and administrative expenses, as well as the variable manufacturing expenses. Since no element of fixed cost is included in the base, the markup that is

[3] For a study showing the various bases used in cost-plus pricing, see V. Govindarajan and Robert N. Anthony, "How Firms Use Cost Data in Pricing Decisions," *Management Accounting* 65, no. 1 (July 1983), pp. 30–36.

EXHIBIT 12–4

RITTER COMPANY
Income Statement
Absorption Basis

Sales (10,000 units at $30)	$300,000
Cost of goods sold (10,000 units at $20)	200,000
Gross margin	100,000
Selling and administrative expenses (10,000 units at $2 variable and $1 fixed)	30,000
Net income	$ 70,000

EXHIBIT 12–5
Price Quotation Sheet—Contribution Basis

Direct materials	$ 6
Direct labor	4
Variable overhead	3
Variable selling and administrative expenses	2
Total variable expenses	15
Markup to cover fixed expenses and desired profit—100% of variable expenses	15
Target selling price	$30

added must be adequate to cover the fixed costs, as well as to provide the desired profit per unit.

To illustrate, refer again to the cost data for Ritter Company. The base to use in cost-plus pricing under the contribution approach would be $15, computed as follows:

Direct materials	$ 6
Direct labor	4
Variable overhead	3
Variable selling and administrative expenses	2
Total variable expenses	$15

Let us assume Ritter Company has found that a markup of 100 percent of variable expenses is adequate to cover its fixed expenses and to provide the desired profit per unit. A price quotation sheet prepared under this assumption is shown in Exhibit 12–5.

Notice again that even though this pricing method is termed *cost*-plus pricing, a portion of the costs are buried in the *plus,* or markup, part of the formula. In this case, however, the buried costs are the fixed costs rather than the selling and administrative costs. Again, the reason for not including the fixed costs in the base can be traced to the time and difficulty that would be involved in any attempt to allocate. As a practical matter, there is no way to equitably allocate many common fixed costs, as discussed in Chapter 7. Any attempt to do so may result in less usable cost data for pricing, rather than more usable data. In addition, users of the contribution approach to

EXHIBIT 12-6

RITTER COMPANY
Income Statement
Contribution Basis

Sales (10,000 units at $30)		$300,000
Less variable expenses (10,000 units at $15)		150,000
Contribution margin		150,000
Less fixed expenses:		
Production	$70,000	
Selling and administrative	10,000	80,000
Net income		$ 70,000

pricing argue that keeping the cost base free of any element of fixed costs facilitates pricing in special and unusual situations. This point is discussed further in a following section dealing with special pricing problems.

Compare the contribution approach to cost-plus pricing in Exhibit 12–5 with the absorption approach in Exhibit 12–3. Although both approaches are employing the cost-plus concept, notice the difference in the way in which they handle the cost data and structure the price quotation sheet. Also notice that the Ritter Company can attain the *same* $30 target selling price by using either costing method.

In order to conclude the Ritter Company example, let us again assume that the company produces and sells 10,000 units of product at a selling price of $30 per unit. The company's income statement as it would appear under the contribution approach is shown in Exhibit 12–6.

Determining the Markup Percentage

By far the most crucial element in the cost-plus pricing formulas is the percentage markup added to the cost base. We have found that under both the absorption and the contribution approaches some elements of cost are buried in the markup figure. This means that the markup must be sufficient to cover these buried costs, as well as to provide a satisfactory return on assets employed, if long-run profit goals are to be met. How does the manager determine the "right" markup percentage to use in setting target selling prices? The markup chosen is a function of a number of variables, one of which is the company's desired return on investment (ROI).

Markup Formulas ROI is widely used by firms as a basis for determining the appropriate markup to add to products. The approach is to set a target ROI figure and then to structure the markup so that this target figure is achieved. A formula exists that can be used to determine the appropriate markup percentage, given the ROI figure that management wishes to obtain for the organization. Assuming use of the absorption approach to costing, the formula is:

$$\text{Markup percentage} = \frac{\text{Desired return on assets employed} + \text{Selling and administrative expenses}}{\text{Volume in units} \times \text{Unit cost to manufacture}} \quad (1)$$

If the contribution approach to costing is used, the formula becomes:

$$\text{Markup percentage} = \frac{\begin{array}{c}\text{Desired return on}\\ \text{assets employed}\end{array} + \text{Fixed costs}}{\text{Volume in units} \times \text{Unit variable expenses}} \qquad (2)$$

Using the Formulas To show how the basic formula in (1) above is applied, assume Hart Company has determined that an investment of $2,000,000 is necessary to produce and market 50,000 units of product X each year. The $2,000,000 investment would cover purchase of equipment and provide funds needed to carry inventories and accounts receivable. In all, the company's accounting department estimates that the following costs and activity will be associated with the manufacture and sale of product X:

Number of units sold annually.	50,000
Required investment in assets	$2,000,000
Cost to manufacture one unit	30
Selling and administrative expenses . . .	700,000

If Hart Company desires a 25 percent ROI, then the required markup for the product will be [using formula (1) above]:

$$\text{Markup percentage} = \frac{\begin{array}{c}\text{Desired return on}\\ \text{assets employed}\end{array} + \begin{array}{c}\text{Selling and adminis-}\\ \text{trative expenses}\end{array}}{\text{Volume in units} \times \text{Unit cost to manufacture}}$$

$$\text{Markup percentage} = \frac{(25\% \times \$2{,}000{,}000) + \$700{,}000}{50{,}000 \text{ units} \times \$30}$$

$$= \frac{\$1{,}200{,}000}{\$1{,}500{,}000} = 80\%$$

Using this markup percentage, the selling price of a unit of product X would be set at $54:

Cost to manufacture.	$30
Add markup—80% × $30 . . .	24
Target selling price	$54

As proof that the $54 selling price for product X will permit Hart Company to achieve a 25 percent ROI, the company's income statement and a computation of its projected ROI are presented in Exhibit 12–7.

As a concluding note, in our example we have focused on formula (1) given earlier. Formula (2) is applied in the same way, except that it is used when the manager prefers to base markups on variable costs and to use the contribution approach in preparing statements.

Adjusting Prices to Market Conditions

Although the cost-plus approach that we have been discussing can be of great assistance to the manager in determining target selling prices, care must be taken not to apply the cost-plus formulas too rigidly. The reason is that they tend to ignore the relationship between price and volume, and if

EXHIBIT 12–7
Income Statement and ROI Analysis—Hart Company

HART COMPANY
Budgeted Income Statement

Sales (50,000 units × $54)	$2,700,000
Less cost of goods sold (50,000 units × $30)	1,500,000
Gross margin	1,200,000
Less selling and administrative expenses	700,000
Net operating income	$ 500,000

Projected ROI (based on $2,000,000 in assets employed):

$$\frac{\text{Net operating income}}{\text{Sales}} \times \frac{\text{Sales}}{\text{Average operating assets}} = \text{ROI}$$

$$\frac{\$500{,}000}{\$2{,}700{,}000} \times \frac{\$2{,}700{,}000}{\$2{,}000{,}000} = \text{ROI}$$

$$18.52\%^{*} \times 1.35 = 25\%$$

* Rounded.

applied too rigidly might result in less profits, rather than more profits, for the firm. For example, in the preceding illustration the competitive situation might be such for product X that a selling price of $54 would result in far less than 50,000 units being sold each year. On the other hand, at a $54 selling price, demand might be so great that the company would be swamped with orders.

In order to make cost-plus pricing formulas workable, companies usually do three things. First, they rarely price a product exactly at the target price suggested by the cost-plus formula. The costs used in the formula serve as a basis for establishing prices at their *lower limit*—the actual final selling price may be much higher than this minimum target figure. Many people have the mistaken notion that price is purely a function of cost, when in reality cost serves in large part simply to define the lower limit that can be set. Noncost factors, such as competitive position, promotional strategy, packaging, and ability to achieve long-term product differentiation, may permit a manager to set a price significantly higher than the minimum target figure provided by use of the cost formulas. The mark of real executives in pricing can be found in their ability to sense the market situation and to know when price adjustments can and should be made. If such executives sense that their competitive position is strong, they will adjust the prices upward; if they sense a strengthening of opposing competitive forces, then they will either shade the prices downward or attempt to further differentiate the product.

Second, the price setter must recognize that even if a particular margin has been obtainable for the last 20 or 30 years, this is no assurance that it will continue to be obtainable. For example, the neighborhood grocery stores suddenly discovered in the 1940s that the margins they had been obtaining for many decades were no longer obtainable because of the development of large chain supermarkets. In turn, the chain supermarkets discovered in the 1970s that the margins they had enjoyed for nearly three decades were being undercut by the self-service discount food outlets. In order to achieve target ROI figures, managers are often required to trade off some margin in favor of a higher turnover of assets. This means that markups must sometimes be reduced in the hope of stimulating the overall volume of sales.

Third, companies will not use the same markup for all product lines, but rather will vary the markup according to custom, need, or general industry practice. For example, one product line may carry a markup of 20 percent, whereas another may carry a markup of 60 percent. This is typical of clothing and department stores, where the percentage markup varies by department and occasionally even by item. Jewelry generally has a high markup, whereas stockings carry a relatively low markup.

Why Use Cost Data in Pricing?

If pricing executives end up setting prices according to how they sense the market, then an obvious question at this point is, "Why bother using cost data in the pricing decision?" Several reasons can be advanced in favor of computing target selling prices by means of the cost-plus formulas even if the resulting prices are later modified. First, in making pricing decisions, the manager is faced with a myriad of uncertainties. Cost-plus target prices represent a *starting point,* a way of perhaps removing some of the uncertainties and shedding some light on others. By this means, the manager may be able to feel his or her way more easily through the thicket and come up with a price that will be acceptable given the constraints at hand.

Second, cost might be viewed as a floor of protection, guarding the price setter from pricing too low and incurring losses. Although this line of reasoning is appealing and reassuring, the protection offered by the cost floor is more illusory than real. For one thing, we have already noted that neither the absorption approach nor the contribution approach includes all costs in the cost base. For another thing, unit cost depends on volume. This is because many costs are fixed, and unit cost will therefore depend on the number of units produced and sold. Even though selling prices may be set above total costs, losses may still be incurred if the volume of sales is less than estimated, thereby forcing per unit costs upward to the point that they exceed the selling price.

Third, formula-based target selling prices may give the price setter some insights into competitors' costs, or help him to predict what a competitive price will be. For example, if a company is operating in an industry where 30 percent markups over cost to manufacture are common, then the company may be able to assume that this same pattern will hold for new products, and thereby either predict competitors' prices or price in such a way as to gain quick acceptance of a new product line. On the other hand, by following standard markups over cost, a company may be able to largely *neutralize* the pricing issue and concentrate on competing in other ways, such as in delivery or in credit terms.

Finally, many firms have such a wide range of products that they simply don't have the time to do a detailed cost-volume-profit analysis on every item in every product line. Cost-plus pricing formulas provide a quick and direct way to reach at least a tentative price that can be further refined as time and circumstances permit.

TIME AND MATERIAL PRICING

Instead of computing prices by means of a cost-plus formula, some companies use an alternative approach called **time and material pricing.** Under this method, two pricing rates are established—one based on direct labor time and the other based on direct material used. In each case, the rate is constructed so that it includes an allowance for selling and administrative expenses, for other direct costs, and for a desired profit. This pricing method is widely used in television and appliance repair shops, in automobile repair shops, in printing shops, and in similar types of service organizations. In addition, it is used by various kinds of professionals, including accountants, attorneys, physicians, and consultants.

Time Component

The time component is typically expressed as a rate per direct labor-hour. The rate is computed by adding together three elements: (1) the direct costs of the employee, including salary and fringe benefits; (2) a pro rata allowance for selling and administrative expenses of the organization; and (3) an allowance for a desired profit per hour of employee time. In some organizations (such as a repair shop), the same hourly rate will be charged regardless of which employee is assigned to complete a job; in other organizations, the rate may vary by employee. For example, in an accounting firm, the rate charged for a new assistant accountant's time will generally be less than the rate charged for an experienced senior accountant or for a partner.

Material Component

The material component is determined by adding a *material loading charge* to the invoice price of any materials used on the job. The **material loading charge** is designed to cover the costs of ordering, handling, and carrying materials in stock, plus a profit margin on the materials themselves. Typically, a material loading charge will fall somewhere between 30 percent and 50 percent of the invoice cost of the materials.

An Example of Time and Material Pricing

To provide a numerical example of time and material pricing, assume the following data:

The Quality Auto Shop uses time and material pricing for all of its repair work. The following costs have been budgeted for the coming year:

	Repairs	Parts
Mechanics—wages	$300,000	$ —
Service manager—salary	40,000	—
Parts manager—salary	—	36,000
Clerical assistant—salary	18,000	15,000
Retirement and insurance— 16% of salaries and wages	57,280	8,160
Supplies	720	540
Utilities	36,000	20,800
Property taxes	8,400	1,900
Depreciation	91,600	37,600
Invoice cost of parts used	—	400,000
Total budgeted cost	$552,000	$520,000

The company employs 12 mechanics who work a 40-hour week, 50 weeks per year. A profit of $7 per hour of repair time is considered to be a reasonable return to the company. For parts, the company wants to earn a profit equal to 15 percent of the invoice cost of parts used.

Computations showing the billing rate and the material loading charge that should be used over the next year are presented in Exhibit 12–8. Note from the exhibit that the billing rate, or time component, should be $30 per hour of repair time and that the material loading charge should be 45 percent of the invoice cost of parts used. Using these rates, a repair job that required 4.5 hours of mechanic's time and $200 in parts would be billed as follows:

Labor time: 4.5 hours × $30		$135
Parts used:		
Invoice cost	$200	
Material loading charge: 45% × $200 . . .	90	290
Total price of the job		$425

Rather than using labor-hours as a basis for computing the time rate, a machine shop, a printing shop, or a similar organization might use machine-hours. Some organizations might charge a different rate per machine-hour, depending on the type of machine used.

EXHIBIT 12–8
Time and Material Pricing

	Time Component: Repairs		Parts: Material Loading Charge	
	Total	**Per Hour***	**Total**	**Percent†**
Cost of mechanics' time:				
Mechanics' wages	$300,000			
Retirement and insurance (16% of wages)	48,000			
Total costs.	348,000	$14.50		
For repairs—other cost of repair service. For parts—costs of ordering, handling, and storing parts:				
Repairs service manager—salary	40,000		$ —	
Parts manager—salary	—		36,000	
Clerical assistant—salary	18,000		15,000	
Retirement and insurance (16% of salaries) . . .	9,280		8,160	
Supplies	720		540	
Utilities	36,000		20,800	
Property taxes	8,400		1,900	
Depreciation	91,600		37,600	
Total costs.	204,000	8.50	120,000	30
Desired profit:				
24,000 hours × $7	168,000	7.00	—	
15% × $400,000	—		60,000	15
Total amount to be billed	$720,000	$30.00	$180,000	45

* Based on 24,000 hours (12 mechanics × 40 hours × 50 weeks = 24,000 hours).

† Based on $400,000 invoice cost of parts. The charge for ordering, handling, and storing parts, for example, is computed as follows: $120,000 cost ÷ $400,000 invoice cost = 30%.

PRICING NEW PRODUCTS

New products easily present the most challenging pricing problems, for the reason that the uncertainties involved are so great. If a new product is unlike anything currently on the market, then demand will be uncertain. If the new product is similar to products already being sold, then uncertainty will exist as to the degree of substitution that will develop between the new product and the already available products. Uncertainty will also exist over ultimate marketing costs, and so forth. In order to reduce the level of these uncertainties, a firm will often resort to some type of experimental or test marketing.

Test Marketing of Products

Many firms have used **test marketing** with great success in order to gain data relative to the pricing decision. The approach is to introduce the new product in selected areas only, generally at different prices in different areas. By this means, a company can gather data on the competition that the product will encounter, on the relationship between volume and price, and on the contribution to profits that can be expected at various selling prices and volumes of sales. A price can then be selected that will result in the greatest overall contribution to profits, or that seems best in relation to the company's long-run objectives.

Of course, test marketing is not the same thing as the full-scale production and marketing of a product, but it can provide highly useful information that can help to ensure that the full-scale effort will be successful. An added benefit can be found in the fact that through test marketing it may be possible to keep any errors in pricing on a small scale, rather than nationwide.

Pricing Strategies

Two basic pricing strategies are available to the price setter in pricing new products. These pricing strategies are known as **skimming pricing** and **penetration pricing.**

Skimming pricing involves setting a high initial price for a new product, with a progressive lowering of the price as time passes and as the market broadens and matures. The purpose of skimming pricing is to maximize short-run profits. In effect, it represents a direct application of the economist's pricing models discussed earlier in the chapter.

Penetration pricing involves setting low initial prices in order to gain quick acceptance in a broad portion of the market. It calls for the sacrifice of some short-run profits in order to achieve a better long-run market position. Whether a firm adopts the skimming strategy or the penetration strategy will depend on what it is trying to accomplish and on which approach appears to offer the greatest chance for success.

For example, many new products have a certain novelty appeal that causes demand to be quite price inelastic. In these cases, high initial prices are often set and maintained until competitors develop competing products and begin price cutting. As sales volume becomes more sensitive to sales price, prices are slowly reduced until the point is reached where a penetration price is possible that permits access to a mass market. A good example of this type of skimming strategy can be found in the marketing of electronic calculators. Prices of hand-sized calculators started at about $300 in the early 1970s and dropped to less than $25 in about three years' time, finally permitting access to a market so wide that it included the purchasing of calculators for use in weekly grocery shopping. Television sets, stereo sets, automobiles, electronic ovens, and some drug products all went through a similar skimming pricing period before prices were eventually lowered to a mass market penetration level.

One strong argument in favor of skimming pricing is that it offers some protection against unexpected costs in the production and marketing of a product. If a new product is priced on a penetration basis and costs are unexpectedly high, then the company may be forced to raise prices later—not an easy thing to do when you are trying to gain wide market acceptance of a new product. On the other hand, if a new product is priced initially on a skimming level, the company has a layer of protection that can be used to absorb any unexpected costs or cost increases. Even if this later causes price reductions to be less than expected, the company will still be in the more favorable position of reducing prices rather than raising them.

Skimming pricing is most effective in those markets where entry is relatively difficult because of the technology or investment required. The easier that market entry becomes, the smaller is the likelihood that skimming can be carried off very effectively, or at least for a very long period of time. For example, skimming pricing was possible for many years in the computer industry because of technological barriers to entry. By contrast, it is doubtful whether skimming pricing was ever much of a factor in the marketing of household cleaning products.

Target Costs and Product Pricing

Our discussion thus far has presumed that a product has already been developed, has been costed, and that it is ready to be marketed as soon as a price is set. In many cases, the sequence of events is just the reverse. That is, the company will already *know* what price should be charged, and the problem will be to *develop* a product that can be marketed profitably at the desired price. Even in this situation, where the normal sequence of events is reversed, cost is still a crucial factor. The company's approach will be to set **target costs** that can be used as guides in developing a product that can be sold within the desired price range.

This approach is used widely in the household appliance industry, where a company will determine in advance the price range in which it wants a particular product model to sell and then will set about to develop the model. Component parts will be designed and then costed item by item to see whether the total cost is compatible with the target cost already set. If not, the parts will be redesigned and recosted, and features will be changed or eliminated until the expected costs fall within the desired targets. Prototypes will then be developed, and again costs will be carefully analyzed to be sure that the desired targets are being met. In these types of situations, the accountant can be of great help to management by continually pointing out the relationships between cost and volume, by segregating relevant costs where needed, and by assisting in the organization and interpretation of cost data.

To provide a numerical example of how to compute a target cost figure, assume the following situation:

Handy Appliance Company wants to produce a hand mixer that will sell for $29. In order to produce 25,000 mixers a year, an investment of $625,000 would be required. The company desires a 15 percent ROI. Selling and administrative costs associated with the mixer would total $200,000 per year. Given these data, the target cost to manufacture one mixer would be:

Projected sales (25,000 mixers × $29)		$725,000
Less required markup:		
Selling and administrative expenses	$200,000	
Desired ROI (15% × $625,000)	93,750	
Total markup		293,750
Target cost to manufacture 25,000 mixers		$431,250
Target cost to manufacture one mixer: $431,250 ÷ 25,000		$17.25

Thus, the company should produce the new mixer only if it can be manufactured at a target cost of $17.25 or less per unit.

SPECIAL PRICING DECISIONS

When faced with a pricing decision, which pricing method should the manager use—the absorption approach illustrated in Exhibit 12–3 or the contribution approach illustrated in Exhibit 12–5? If all pricing decisions were related to the pricing of *standard* products, the answer would be that it really wouldn't matter which method was used.[4] We have already seen that the same target selling price for a standard product can be obtained using either method. The choice would probably depend on which method was otherwise being used to cost units of product. If the absorption method was otherwise in use, then it would be simpler to go ahead and use it as a basis for pricing decisions as well; the opposite would be the case if contribution costing was otherwise in use.

But not all pricing decisions relate to standard products; many pricing decisions relate to special or unusual situations. For example, a company may get a large order for a product but be asked to quote a special, one-time-only price. Or a special order may come in from a foreign customer who wants a special price on a standard item on a continuing basis because his or her order represents business that the company otherwise wouldn't have. A company may have substantial idle capacity and be faced with the problem of pricing special products that are not a part of the regular line and that are being produced on a limited basis. Finally, a company may be in a competitive bidding situation and forced to bid on many unlike jobs, some of which will be on a more or less continuing basis and others will be one-time-only affairs.

[4] The Govindarajan and Anthony study cited earlier found that 83 percent of the 504 companies in the study used some form of full cost (either absorption cost or absorption cost plus selling and administrative expenses) as a basis for normal, long-run pricing. The remaining 17 percent used only variable costs as a basis for pricing decisions. Ibid., p. 31.

All of these situations present *special* pricing problems of one kind or another. Some managers believe that special problems such as these can be handled more easily by the contribution approach than by the absorption approach to pricing.[5] The reasons are twofold. First, advocates of the contribution approach argue that it provides the price setter with more detailed information than does the absorption approach, and that the information it provides is structured in a way that parallels the way in which the price setter is used to thinking—in terms of cost-volume-profit relationships. And second, it is argued that the contribution approach provides the price setter with a flexible framework that is immediately adaptable to *any* pricing problem, without the necessity of doing a lot of supplementary analytical work.

Pricing a Special Order

To illustrate the adaptability of the contribution approach to special pricing situations and to show how the data it presents guides the price setter in decisions, let us assume the following price quotation sheets for Helms Company:

Absorption Method

Direct materials	$ 6
Direct labor	7
Overhead at 100% of direct labor	7
Total cost to manufacture	20
Markup—20%	4
Target selling price	$24

Contribution Method

Direct materials	$ 6
Direct labor	7
Variable overhead	2
Variable selling and administrative	1
Total variable expenses	16
Markup—50%	8
Target selling price	$24

These price quotation sheets relate to a vacuum pump that Helms Company manufactures and markets through jobbers. The company has never been able to sell all of the pumps that it can produce, and for this reason it is constantly on the lookout for new business. Let us assume that Helms Company has just been approached by a foreign distributor who wants to purchase 10,000 pumps at a price of $19 per pump. Should the company accept the offer?

The Absorption Method The price quotation sheet prepared above by the absorption method is of little help in making the decision. If Helms Company tries to relate the $20 "cost to manufacture" to the proposed $19 price, then the offer is clearly not attractive:

Sales (10,000 units at $19)	$190,000
Less absorption cost to manufacture (10,000 units at $20)	200,000
Net loss from the order	$ (10,000)

On the other hand, since there is idle capacity in the plant, management may be tempted to accept the offer. The dilemma is that no one really *knows* from looking at the price quotation sheet which course of action is best. The

[5] See Thomas M. Bruegelmann, Gaile Haessly, Claire P. Wolfangel, and Michael Schiff, "How Variable Costing Is Used in Pricing Decisions," *Management Accounting* 66, no. 10 (April 1985), pp. 58–65.

pricing system doesn't provide the essential keys that are needed to move in an intelligent way. As a result, whatever decision is made will be made either on a "seat of the pants" basis or only after much effort has been expended in trying to dig into the cost records for additional information.

The Contribution Method By contrast, the price quotation sheet prepared by the contribution method provides the company with exactly the framework that it needs in making the decision. Since this price quotation sheet is organized by cost behavior, it dovetails precisely with cost-volume-profit concepts, and it enables the decision maker to reach his or her decisions without having to do all kinds of added digging and analytical work in the cost records.

Consider the Helms Company data. Since the company has idle capacity (for which there is apparently no other use), fixed overhead costs are irrelevant to the decision over whether to accept the foreign distributor's offer. Any amount received over unit variable costs (and any *incremental* fixed costs[6]) will increase overall profitability; therefore, rather than relating the proposed purchase price to the $20 "cost to manufacture," the company should relate it to the unit variable costs involved. This is easy to do if the regular price quotation sheet on a product is organized by cost behavior, such as shown above under the contribution method. In the case of Helms Company, the unit variable costs are $16. Assuming that the unit variable costs associated with the special order will be the same as those associated with regular business, the analysis would be:

Sales (10,000 units at $19)	$190,000
Less variable expenses (10,000 units at $16)	160,000
Contribution margin promised by the order (and also increased net income, if the fixed costs don't change)	$ 30,000

In sum, by using the price quotation sheet prepared by the contribution method, the Helms Company will be able to see a clear-cut, short-run advantage to accepting the foreign distributor's offer. Before any final decision can be made, however, Helms Company will have to weigh long-run considerations very carefully, particularly the impact that accepting this offer might have on future efforts to secure a position in foreign markets. Accepting the $19 price might seriously undermine future negotiations with foreign dealers and cause disruptions in the long-run profitability of the firm. Helms Company may feel that it would be better to forgo the short-run $30,000 increase in contribution margin in order to protect its future long-run market position.

The essential point of our discussion is that the contribution approach to pricing contains a ready-made framework within which the price setter can operate in special pricing situations. By organizing costs in a way that is compatible with cost-volume-profit concepts, this approach to structuring price quotation sheets assists the manager in isolating those costs that are relevant in special pricing decisions and guides the manager in those decisions from a cost point of view.

[6] That is, any added fixed costs that are incurred solely as a result of the added sales.

The Variable Pricing Model

The contribution approach to pricing can be presented in general model form, as shown in Exhibit 12–9.

The contribution approach provides a **ceiling** and a **floor** between which the price setter operates. The ceiling represents the price that the manager would *like* to obtain, and indeed *must* obtain on the bulk of the sales over the long run. But under certain conditions, the model shows that the manager can move within the **range of flexibility** as far down as the floor of variable costs in quoting a price to a prospective customer. What are the conditions under which a price based on variable costs alone might be appropriate? We can note three:

1. When idle capacity exists, as in the case of Helms Company.
2. When operating under distress conditions.
3. When faced with sharp competition on particular orders under a competitive bidding situation.

When any of these conditions exist, it may be possible to increase overall profitability by pricing *some* jobs, products, or orders at *any amount* above variable costs, even if this amount is substantially less than the normal markup.

We will now examine each of the three special conditions listed above more closely to see how each relates to the range of flexibility depicted in Exhibit 12–9.

Idle Capacity There is no need to be concerned about the range of flexibility depicted in Exhibit 12–9 so long as a company can sell all that it can produce at regular prices. That is, no company is going to sell at less than regular prices if regular prices are obtainable.

However, a different situation exists if a company has idle capacity that can't be used to expand regular sales at regular prices. Under these conditions, any use to which the idle capacity can be put that increases revenues more than variable costs (and any *incremental* fixed costs) will increase overall net income.

The use might come in the form of a special order for a regular product from a customer that the company does not usually supply (such as a foreign market). Or the use might come in the form of a slight modification of a regular product to be sold under a new customer's own brand name. Alterna-

EXHIBIT 12–9
The Contribution Approach to Pricing: A General Model

Variable costs:			
Direct materials	$ XX		
Direct labor	XX		
Variable overhead	XX		
Variable selling and administrative	XX		
Total variable costs	XXX	Floor	Range of flexibility
Markup (to cover the fixed costs and desired profit)	XX		
Target selling price	$XXX	Ceiling	

tively, the use might come in the form of a special order for a product that the company does not usually produce. In any of these situations, so long as the price received on the extra business exceeds the variable costs (and any *incremental* fixed costs) involved, overall net income will be increased by utilizing the idle capacity.

Helms Company is a good example of the sort of situation we are talking about. The company has idle capacity, and there is no prospect of using the idle capacity for regular business. Under these conditions, nothing will be lost by quoting a price to the foreign distributor that is below full cost, or even relaxing the price down very close to the floor of variable costs, if necessary.

Distress Conditions Occasionally a company is forced to operate under distress conditions when the market for its product has been adversely affected in some way. For example, demand may virtually dry up overnight, forcing the company to drop its prices sharply downward. Under these conditions, any contribution that can be obtained to help cover fixed costs may be preferable to ceasing operations altogether. If operations cease, then *no* contribution will be available to apply toward fixed costs.

Competitive Bidding The pricing model illustrated in Exhibit 12–9 is particularly useful in competitive bidding situations. Competition is often hot and fierce in situations where bidding is involved, so companies can't afford to be inflexible in their pricing. Unfortunately, many companies refuse to cut prices in the face of stiff competition, adamantly stating that they price only on a "full-cost" basis and don't want the business unless they can get a "decent price" for the work. There are several problems associated with taking this kind of position on pricing. First, it involves faulty logic. The so-called decent price is obtained by adding some markup onto "full cost." But cost is dependent on *volume* of sales, which in turn is dependent on selling price.

Second, as discussed in Chapter 11, there are *two* determinants of profitability—margin and turnover. The "decent price" attitude ignores the turnover factor and focuses entirely on the margin factor. Yet many companies have demonstrated that a more modest margin combined with a faster turnover of assets can be highly effective from a profitability point of view. One way to increase turnover, of course, is to be flexible in bidding by shading prices in situations where competition is keen.

Finally, in situations where fixed costs are high, a company can't *afford* to be inflexible in its pricing policies. Once an investment in plant and other fixed productive facilities has been made, a company's strategy must be to generate every dollar of contribution that it can to assist in the covering of these costs. Even if a company is forced to operate at an accounting loss, this might be preferable to having no contribution at all toward recovery of investment.

CRITICISMS OF THE CONTRIBUTION APPROACH TO PRICING

Not all managers are enthusiastic about the contribution approach to pricing. Some argue that the contribution approach, with its reliance on variable costs, can lead to setting prices too low and to eventual bankruptcy. These managers argue that the absorption approach to pricing is superior to the contribution approach since it includes an element of fixed overhead cost in the pricing base, whereas the contribution approach includes only the variable costs. Including an element of fixed overhead cost in the pricing base is said to make the absorption approach safer in terms of long-run pricing. Managers who argue in this way feel that if variable costs alone are used in pricing, the price setter may be misled into accepting *any* price over variable costs on a long-run basis for any product.

This argument can be criticized on several points. We should note first that the absorption approach to pricing excludes as many costs from the pricing base as does the contribution approach. It just excludes *different* costs. For example, the absorption approach doesn't consider selling and administrative costs in its base, since the base typically consists of "costs to manufacture." By contrast, the contribution approach does include variable selling and administrative expenses along with variable production expenses in developing a base for pricing.

Whether or not *any* pricing mechanism results in intelligent pricing decisions will depend in large part on the ability of the price setter to use the available data. As a practical matter, this means that pricing decisions must be restricted to managers who are qualified to make them. This point has been made very well in an NAA study of actual pricing practices:

> No instance of unprofitable pricing attributable to direct costing was reported, but on the contrary, opinion was frequently expressed to the effect that direct costing had contributed to better pricing decisions. However, companies restrict product cost and margin data to individuals qualified to interpret such data and responsible for pricing policy decisions.[7]

On the other hand, no matter how expert a decision maker may be, the decisions will be faulty if the cost information with which he or she is working is irrelevant, unclear, or inadequate. Firms that have adopted the contribution approach to pricing have found that the old pricing system often led to incorrect pricing decisions because of faulty data:

> Instances were cited in which management had unknowingly continued selling products below out-of-pocket cost or had decided to withdraw from the market when a substantial portion of the period costs would have been recovered. . . .
>
> In one interview . . . when direct costing was introduced, analysis demonstrated that contracts which would have contributed to period costs had often been refused at times when the company had a large amount of idle capacity.[8]

PRICE DISCRIMINATION

In structuring a pricing policy, firms must take care to keep their actions within the requirements of the various laws that deal with price setting and with price discrimination. The most widely known of these is the **Robinson-**

[7] National Association of Accountants, *Research Report No. 37,* "Current Applications of Direct Costing" (New York, January 1961), p. 55.

[8] Ibid.

Patman Act of 1936. The act forbids quoting different prices to competing customers unless the difference in price can be traced directly to "differences in the cost of manufacture, sale, or delivery resulting from the differing methods or quantities in which commodities are to such purchasers sold or delivered." Both the Federal Trade Commission and the courts have consistently held that "cost" is to be interpreted as full cost and not just incremental or variable costs. This means that in the case of *competing* customers for the *same* goods, price differences cannot be defended on the basis of covering incremental costs alone. Note, though, that we are talking about *competing* customers for the *same* goods. We are not talking about a competitive bidding situation, nor are we talking about a situation in which idle capacity might be used to produce for a noncompeting market or for some purpose other than production of regular products.

In addition to the Robinson-Patman Act, all states have laws prohibiting the sale of goods or services below "cost." Cost is normally either specified as full cost or is so interpreted by the regulating agencies. Although these state laws might appear to greatly restrict the flexibility of management in pricing decisions, they are often interpreted to apply to a company's products *as a whole,* rather than to individual products. For example, a store may be able to sell bread below cost (often called a loss leader) so long as it sells its products *as a whole* over cost. These laws do suggest, however, that firms should keep careful records of their costs and of the way their prices are structured in order to be able to answer questions of regulatory bodies.

An international law relating to pricing exists in the form of the Anti-Dumping Law of 1932. This law prohibits the sale of products below cost in international markets. Again, cost is interpreted as full cost, including fully allocated fixed costs. The law is designed to protect a domestic manufacturer in its home market in those instances where it is in direct competition with a foreign supplier.

SUMMARY

The general pricing models of the economist contain the basic framework for pricing decisions. Since these models are conceptual in nature, and since the specific information required for their direct application is rarely available, firms normally rely on pricing formulas to implement the ideas that the models contain. Pricing decisions can be divided into three broad groups:

1. Pricing standard products.
2. Pricing new products.
3. Pricing special orders.

The pricing of standard and new products is generally carried out through cost-plus pricing formulas. Such formulas require a cost base, to which a markup is added to derive a target selling price. Cost-plus pricing can be carried out equally well using either the absorption approach or the contribution approach.

Service-type organizations, such as repair shops and professional firms, use a pricing method known as time and material pricing. Under this approach, two pricing rates are established—one rate for time spent on a job, such as labor time or machine time, and another rate for materials used. In each case, the rate is structured so as to include a profit element as well as the direct costs of the time and material involved.

The pricing of special orders is somewhat different from the pricing of regular products or services in that in some situations full costs may not be applicable in setting prices. Circumstances may exist in which the price setter may be justified in pricing simply on a basis of variable or incremental costs. In these special pricing situations, price setters often find the contribution approach, with its emphasis on cost behavior, more useful than the absorption approach, which may require considerable reworking of data in order to generate the information needed for a pricing decision.

KEY TERMS FOR REVIEW

Ceiling A term used in relation to the range of flexibility that denotes the price that is obtained by adding a normal markup to the cost base in cost-plus pricing. (p. 524)

Cost-plus pricing A pricing method in which some predetermined markup is added to a cost base in determining a target selling price. (p. 510)

Floor A term used in relation to the range of flexibility that denotes the variable costs associated with a product. (p. 524)

Marginal cost A term used in economics that means the addition to total cost resulting from the production and sale of one additional unit of product. (p. 507)

Marginal revenue A term used in economics that means the addition to total revenue resulting from the sale of one additional unit of product. (p. 507)

Markup The amount added to a cost base in determining the target selling price in cost-plus pricing. (p. 510)

Material loading charge An amount added to the invoice cost of materials that is designed to cover (1) the costs of ordering, handling, and carrying the materials in stock; and (2) a profit margin on the materials themselves. (p. 517)

Monopolistic competition A term used in economics that denotes a situation in which there are many sellers of similar products, with no one seller having a large enough share of the market for other sellers to be able to discern the effect of its pricing decisions on their sales. (p. 509)

Monopoly A term used in economics that denotes the absence of a directly competing product in the market. (p. 509)

Oligopoly A term used in economics that denotes a situation in which a few large sellers of a product are competing directly with one another. (p. 509)

Penetration pricing The setting of a low initial price for a product in order to gain quick acceptance in a broad portion of the market. (p. 519)

Price elasticity A term used in economics that means the degree to which volume of sales is affected by a change in price per unit. (p. 508)

Range of flexibility The range between the "floor" of variable costs and the "ceiling" of a normal target selling price in which a manager has to operate in special pricing decisions. (p. 524)

Robinson-Patman Act A federal law that prohibits discrimination in pricing between competing customers for a good or service. (p. 526)

Skimming pricing The setting of a high initial price for a product, with a progressive lowering of the price as time passes and as the market broadens and matures. (p. 519)

Target cost A maximum amount of production cost, which is used as a guide in developing a product that can be sold within a desired price range. (p. 520)

Test marketing The introduction of a product in selected areas in order to gain data on customer acceptance, volume of activity at various prices, and so forth. (p. 519)

Time and material pricing A pricing method, often used in service-type organizations, in which two pricing rates are established—one based on labor time and the other based on materials used. (p. 517)

QUESTIONS

12–1 Why does the economist depict a slowing down of the rate of increase in total revenue as more and more units are sold?

12–2 As depicted by the total revenue and total cost curves, what is the optimum point of production and what is the optimum price to be charged for a product?

12–3 According to the marginal revenue and marginal cost curves, what is the optimum point of production and what is the optimum price to charge for a product?

12–4 What is meant by price elasticity? Contrast a product that is price inelastic with a product that is price elastic.

12–5 Identify four limitations of the economic pricing models.

12–6 What costs are relevant in long-run pricing decisions?

12–7 What is meant by the term *cost-plus pricing?* Distinguish between the absorption and contribution approaches to cost-plus pricing.

12–8 In what sense is the term *cost-plus pricing* a misnomer?

12–9 "Full cost can be viewed as a floor of protection. If a firm always sets its prices above full cost, it will never have to worry about operating at a loss." Discuss.

12–10 In cost-plus pricing, what elements must be covered by the markup when the cost base consists of the cost to manufacture a product? What elements must be covered when the cost base consists of a product's variable expenses?

12–11 What is time and material pricing? What type of organization would use time and material pricing?

12–12 What is a material loading charge?

12–13 Distinguish between skimming pricing and penetration pricing. Which strategy would you probably use if you were introducing a new product that was highly price inelastic? Why?

12–14 What are *target costs,* and how do they enter into the pricing decision?

12–15 What problem is sometimes encountered in trying to price special orders under absorption costing?

12–16 Identify those circumstances under which the manager might be justified in pricing at any amount above variable costs.

12–17 In what ways does the Robinson-Patman Act influence pricing decisions?

EXERCISES

E12–1 Meridian Company must determine a target selling price for one of its products. Cost data relating to the product are as follows:

	Per Unit	Total
Direct materials	$ 6	
Direct labor	10	
Variable overhead	3	
Fixed overhead	5	$450,000
Variable selling and administrative expenses	1	
Fixed selling and administrative expenses	4	360,000

The costs above are based on an anticipated volume of 90,000 units produced and sold each period. The company uses cost-plus pricing, and it has a policy of obtaining target selling prices by adding a markup of 50 percent of cost to manufacture or by adding a markup of 80 percent of variable costs.

Required

1. Assuming that the company uses absorption costing, compute the target selling price for one unit of product.
2. Assuming that the company uses the contribution approach to costing, compute the target selling price for one unit of product.

E12–2 Naylor Company is considering the introduction of a new product. As one step in its study of the new product, the company has gathered the following information:

Number of units to be produced and sold each year	12,500
Cost to manufacture one unit of product	$ 30
Projected annual selling and administrative expenses	60,000
Estimated investment required by the company	500,000
Desired ROI	18%

The company uses cost-plus pricing and the absorption costing method.

Required

1. Compute the markup the company will have to use to achieve the desired ROI.
2. Compute the target selling price per unit.

E12–3 Rolex, Inc., is anxious to introduce a new product on the market and is trying to determine what price to charge. The new product has required a $500,000 investment in equipment and working capital. The company wants a 10 percent ROI on all products. The following costs are traceable to the new product:

	Per Unit	Annual Total
Variable production costs (direct materials, direct labor, and variable overhead)	$19	—
Fixed overhead costs	—	$250,000
Variable selling and administrative expenses	1	—
Fixed selling and administrative expenses	—	150,000

The company uses cost-plus pricing and the contribution approach to costing.

Required

1. Assume that the company expects to sell 50,000 units each year. What percentage markup would be required to achieve the target ROI? Using this markup, what would be the selling price per unit?
2. Repeat the computations in (1) above, assuming that the company expects to sell 30,000 units each year.

E12–4 Riteway Plumbing Company does extensive plumbing repair work. The company incurs the following costs in its repair operations:

Plumbers:	
Wage rate per hour	$ 14
Fringe benefits per hour	3
Desired profit per hour of plumber time	5
Selling, administrative, and other costs of the repairs operation per year.	160,000
Materials:	
Costs of ordering, handling, and storing parts	15% of invoice cost
Desired profit on parts	30% of invoice cost

In total, the company logs 20,000 hours of repair time each year.

Required

1. Assume that the company uses time and material pricing. Compute the time rate and the material loading charge that should be used to bill jobs.
2. One of the company's plumbers has just completed a repair job that required three hours of time and $40 in parts (invoice cost). Compute the amount that should be billed for the job.

E12–5 Mead Company has always used the absorption approach for product costing and for pricing. The company's price quote sheet on its microwave oven is given below (per oven):

Direct materials	$ 75
Direct labor.	60
Overhead ($5 variable + $40 fixed) . . .	45
Total cost to manufacture	$180
Markup: 33⅓%	60
Target selling price	$240

The company incurs $10 in variable selling costs per unit and $150,000 annually in fixed selling and administrative costs. It produces and sells 5,000 ovens each year. The sales manager is curious as to what the price quote sheet would look like if the company used the contribution approach to pricing instead of the absorption approach.

Required

1. The accounting department has determined that the company would have to use a markup of 60 percent if the contribution approach were used in determining target selling prices. Prepare a price quote sheet for a microwave oven using the contribution approach.
2. Identify the ceiling and the floor on the price quote sheet that you have prepared and explain their significance to the manager.
3. Assume that the company has idle capacity and would like to run a special on microwave ovens for $179 each. Does it appear that this price would add to the company's overall profits? Explain.

E12–6 The selling price that must be obtained on a product will be dependent in part on the number of units that can be sold. Consider the following data on a new product:

Variable production cost per unit	$ 24
Variable selling and administrative expenses per unit . . .	6
Fixed production cost (total)	800,000
Fixed selling and administrative expenses (total)	1,000,000
Desired markup	75%

The company uses the absorption costing method for product costing and for pricing.

Required 1. What would be the target selling price per unit if the company can produce and sell *(a)* 25,000 units each period and *(b)* 50,000 units each period?
2. If the company charges the prices that you computed in (1) above, will it be assured that no losses will be sustained? Explain.

E12–7 Auto Supply, Inc., is a producer and distributor of auto accessories. The company is anxious to enter the rapidly growing market for long-life batteries. Management believes that to be fully competitive, the battery that the company produces and markets can't be priced at more than $75. At this price, management is sure that the company can sell 40,000 batteries a year.

A study has indicated that the following costs and other data would be associated with the new battery line:

Permanent investment required	$ 800,000
Annual selling and administrative expenses	1,500,000
Required ROI	25%

Required Compute the target cost to manufacture one battery.

E12–8 Reeder Company is contemplating entry into a new market. Costs and other information associated with the new product are given below:

Projected annual sales in units	60,000
Projected variable costs per unit:	
Production	$ 12
Selling and administrative	3
Projected fixed costs in total:	
Production	350,000
Selling and administrative	170,000

As a first approximation to a selling price, the company normally uses a markup of 60 percent on variable costs, which represents the markup typically used in the industry.

Required 1. Compute the target selling price for the new product, using the contribution approach.
2. Assume that the company will not add a new product line unless it promises a return on investment of at least 20 percent. The new product would require an investment in equipment and other assets totaling $1,000,000. What markup percentage would be required on the new product to provide the desired ROI? (Assume that the company uses the contribution approach to pricing.)

PROBLEMS

P12–9 **Percentage Markups and Price Quotation Sheets** Aspen Company produces and markets a number of consumer products, including a toaster. Cost and revenue data on the toaster for 19x5, the most recent year, are given below:

	10,000 Units Sold	
	Total	**Per Unit**
Sales	$300,000	$30
Cost of goods sold	180,000	18*
Gross margin	120,000	12
Selling and administrative expenses	70,000	7
Net income	$ 50,000	$ 5

* Contains $3 per unit in direct materials, $4 per unit in direct labor, and $1 per unit in variable overhead.

Fixed overhead costs comprise $100,000 of cost of goods sold, and $50,000 of the selling and administrative expenses are fixed.

Required

1. Using the data from the income statement above, do the following:
   a. Compute the percentage markup on cost being used by the company (that is, the gross margin as a percentage of cost of goods sold).
   b. Prepare a model price quotation sheet for a single unit of product using the absorption approach.
2. Recast the income statement for 19x5 in the contribution format, and then do the following:
   a. Compute the percentage markup based on variable cost (that is, the contribution margin as a percentage of variable costs).
   b. Prepare a model price quotation sheet for a single unit of product using the contribution approach.
3. Assume that the company has sufficient capacity to produce 12,500 toasters each year. J-Mart, a regional discount chain located in the East, is willing to make a bulk purchase of 2,500 toasters at a price of $15 per toaster, if the toasters are imprinted with the J-Mart name. The sale of these toasters would not disturb regular sales.
   a. Using the model price quotation sheet prepared in (1) above, should the offer be accepted? Explain.
   b. Explain how the model price quotation sheet prepared in (2) above can be helpful to the manager in making special pricing decisions. Using this sheet as a guide, should the offer be accepted? Show computations.

P12–10 Computation of Markup Percentages Arborland Vineyards is in the process of developing a new wine. After considerable study, the following target costs have been set for a case of the new wine (based on 20,000 cases):

	Target Costs per Case	Target Annual Costs
Direct materials	$18.00	
Direct labor	3.60	
Variable overhead	2.40	
Fixed overhead—direct	6.00	$120,000
Variable selling	1.00	
Fixed selling and administrative	7.25	145,000

The company estimates that adding the new wine will require the following permanent investment of funds:

For working capital	$250,000
For equipment	150,000
Total investment	$400,000

The company has a 15 percent target return on funds invested in a product. Cost-plus pricing is in use.

Required

1. Assuming that the company uses absorption costing:
   a. Compute the markup percentage needed for the company to achieve its target ROI of 15 percent on funds invested in the new product.
   b. Using the markup percentage computed in (1*a*) above, compute the target selling price for a case of the new wine.
2. Assuming that the company uses the contribution approach:
   a. Compute the markup percentage needed for the company to achieve its target ROI of 15 percent on funds invested in the new product.
   b. Using the markup percentage computed in (2*a*) above, compute the target selling price for a case of the new wine.

3. Look at the formula used to compute the markup percentage in (1) above. Assume that management wants to reduce the markup percentage somewhat in order to meet competition, but it still wants to earn a 15 percent ROI. What lines of attack does the formula suggest that management can follow?

P12–11 Time and Material Pricing Superior TV Repair, Inc., employs 10 repair technicians who work a 40-hour week, 50 weeks per year. The company uses time and material pricing, and each year it reviews its rates in light of the actual costs incurred in the prior year. Actual costs incurred last year in connection with repair work and in connection with the company's parts inventory are given below:

	Repairs	Parts
Repair technicians—wages	$280,000	$ —
Repair service manager—salary	30,000	—
Parts manager—salary	—	26,000
Repairs and parts assistant—salary	16,000	4,000
Retirement benefits (20% of salaries and wages)	65,200	6,000
Health insurance (5% of salaries and wages)	16,300	1,500
Utilities	71,000	15,700
Truck operating costs	11,600	—
Property taxes	5,200	3,200
Liability and fire insurance	3,800	1,800
Supplies	900	300
Rent—building	24,000	16,500
Depreciation—trucks and equipment	36,000	—
Invoice cost of parts used	—	300,000
Total costs for the year	$560,000	$375,000

The company has a target profit of $4 per hour of repair service time and a target profit of 15 percent of the invoice cost of parts used. During the past year, the company billed repair service time at $27.50 per hour and added a material loading charge of 35 percent to parts. There is some feeling in the company that these rates may now be inadequate since costs have risen somewhat over the last year.

Required

1. Using the data above, compute the following:
   a. The rate that should be charged per hour of repair service time. Your rate should contain three cost elements, as discussed in the body of the chapter.
   b. The material loading charge that should be used in billing jobs. The material loading charge should be expressed as a percentage of the invoice cost of parts and should contain two elements, as discussed in the body of the chapter.
2. Are the time and material rates that the company has been using adequate to cover its costs and yield the desired profit margins? Explain. (No computations are necessary.)
3. Assume that the company adopts the rates that you have computed in (1) above. What should be the total price charged on a repair job that requires 1½ hours of service time and parts with an invoice cost of $69.50?

P12–12 Integrative Problem: Markup Percentages; Price Quote Sheets; Special Order Lemhi Products, Inc., manufactures a variety of electrical products. The company wants to introduce a new electric motor that would have the following cost characteristics (based on an activity level of 50,000 motors produced and sold each year):

	Per Motor	Total
Direct materials	$18	
Direct labor	40	
Variable overhead	7	
Fixed overhead	20	$1,000,000
Variable selling expense	5	
Fixed selling expense	16	800,000

After careful study, the company has determined that production of the new motor would require an investment of $3,250,000 in order to purchase equipment, carry inventories, and provide for other working capital needs. The company desires a 20 percent return on investment for all new products.

Required

1. Assume that the company uses the absorption costing method.
   a. Compute the markup percentage needed to achieve the company's desired 20 percent ROI.
   b. Using the markup percentage you have computed, prepare a price quote sheet for a single motor.
2. Assume that the company uses the contribution approach to costing.
   a. Compute the markup percentage needed to achieve the company's desired 20 percent ROI.
   b. Using the markup percentage you have computed, prepare a price quote sheet for a single motor.
3. Assume that production and sales drop off to only 45,000 motors per year due to a severe economic recession. A government contractor has offered to make a bulk purchase of 5,000 motors at a price of $82 per motor.
   a. Using the model price quote sheet prepared in (1*b*) above, should the offer be accepted? Explain.
   b. Explain how the model price quote sheet prepared in (2*b*) above can be helpful to the manager in making special pricing decisions. Using this sheet as a guide, should the offer be accepted? Explain.

P12–13 **Distress Pricing** Advance Toys, Inc., manufactures a broad line of toys, games, and puzzles. In 19x1, the company obtained the manufacturing and distribution rights to a new puzzle called a Hubic Cube. New equipment costing $800,000 was purchased to produce the cubes. The equipment was estimated to be capable of producing 1,000,000 cubes before it would have to be replaced in 19x5. The company felt that the market for the Hubic Cube would be stable for several years and that there would be little competition, due to the complex nature of the production process. The cubes were priced as follows (per unit):

Direct materials	$0.80
Direct labor	0.50
Overhead (1/6 variable)	1.20
Total cost to manufacture	2.50
Markup—60%	1.50
Target selling price	$4.00

Selling and administrative expenses relating to the cubes were:

Advertising and other fixed costs (per year)	$25,000
Commissions and shipping costs (per cube)	$0.10

In 19x1 and 19x2, the company produced and sold 300,000 Hubic Cubes each year. Early in 19x3, the market suddenly became flooded with similar cubes from several overseas sources, and the selling price quickly dropped to only $2.25 per cube.

The marketing vice president has recommended that the company stop producing the cubes and scrap the special equipment. "It would be insane to continue producing," she reasoned. "At a selling price of only $2.25 per cube, we would be losing $0.25 on every cube that comes off the production line, and that doesn't even consider our selling costs."

Required

1. Redo the price quote sheet above by placing it in the contribution format. (The appropriate markup would be 150 percent.)
2. Assume that due to increased competition the company can expect to sell only 100,000 units per year even at the lower price. Do you agree with the vice president's recommendation to stop production and scrap the special equipment? Explain.

P12–14 Time and Material Pricing Highland Appliance Company offers an extensive repair service through use of highly trained technicians and radio dispatched trucks. The company has been charging $30 per hour for repair time, but this rate has not been high enough to yield a satisfactory profit. The company wants to earn a profit of $7 per hour for repair time, and it wants to earn a profit on parts equal to 25 percent of their invoice cost.

An analysis of the costs incurred by the repair service over the past year has revealed the following:

a. The company employs one service manager over repair work who is paid $42,000 per year and one parts manager who is paid $36,000 per year. In addition, the service manager over repair work has a clerical assistant who is paid $19,000 per year, and the parts manager has an assistant who is paid $14,000 per year.

b. Fifteen repair technicians are employed for repair work; each technician works a 40-hour week, 50 weeks per year. Their combined wages totaled $420,000 last year.

c. Retirement benefits are equal to 12 percent of all wages and salaries paid. Medical insurance is equal to 3 percent of wages and salaries.

d. Property taxes for the year on equipment and inventories were allocable between repairs and parts as follows: repairs, $16,200; and parts, $4,800.

e. Costs for utilities incurred during the year: repairs, $81,000; and parts, $19,000.

f. The operating costs for the trucks used in repair service for the year totaled $35,700.

g. Liability insurance costs allocable to repair work totaled $9,100 for the year, and liability insurance costs allocable to parts totaled $3,700.

h. The repairs area incurred costs for cleaning supplies totaling $850 for the year.

i. Rent on the building totaled $32,000 for the year, of which $26,000 was chargeable to repairs and $6,000 was chargeable to parts.

j. Depreciation on equipment used in repair work totaled $148,000 for the year, and depreciation on equipment and storage bins used for parts totaled $17,000.

k. Parts with an invoice cost of $540,000 were used in repair work last year.

Required

1. Compute the rate that should be charged per hour of repair technician time, and the material loading charge that should be used (as a percentage of the invoice cost of parts). Your time rate should contain three cost elements, as discussed in the body of the chapter. Your material loading charge should contain two cost elements.
2. What should be the total price on a job that requires 1½ hours of repair time and $60 in parts?

P12–15 Pricing Potpourri Unless otherwise indicated, each of the following parts is independent. In all cases, show computations to support your answer.

1. Rockwell Company incurs the following unit costs in producing and selling 10,000 units of product X each year:

Production costs:	
Direct materials	$20
Direct labor	7
Variable overhead	5
Fixed overhead	13
Selling and administrative costs:	
Variable	4
Fixed	9

   Assume that the company uses the absorption approach to cost-plus pricing and desires a markup of 40 percent. Compute the target selling price per unit.

2. Refer to the data in (1) above. Assume that the company uses the contribution approach to cost-plus pricing and desires a markup of 75 percent. Compute the target selling price per unit.
3. Wildroot Products manufactures and sells 20,000 units of product Y each year. The company incurs the following unit costs at the 20,000-unit level of activity:

Direct materials	$30
Direct labor	9
Variable overhead	2
Fixed overhead	10
Variable selling and administrative expenses	6
Fixed selling and administrative expenses	8

   What is the "floor" below which the company should not go, even in special pricing decisions?

4. Caldwell, Inc., estimates that the following costs and activity would be associated with the manufacture and sale of product A:

Number of units sold annually	40,000
Required investment in assets	$850,000
Cost to manufacture one unit	15
Selling and administrative expenses (annual)	250,000

   The company uses the absorption approach to cost-plus pricing and desires a 20 percent ROI. What is the required markup in percentage terms?

5. Rohr Company requires a 16 percent return on investment. The company estimates that an investment of $2,500,000 would be needed to produce and sell 30,000 units of product B each year. Other costs associated with the product would be:

	Variable (per unit)	Fixed (total)
Production (materials, labor, and overhead)	$50	$200,000
Selling and administrative	10	600,000

   The company uses the contribution approach to cost-plus pricing. Given these data, what markup would be required to allow the company to achieve its target ROI?

6. You have just received a bill for $360 for materials used in doing some plumbing repair work on your home. You feel that this charge is unreasonable, and at your insistence the company has given you the following breakdown:

Invoice cost of materials	$225
Charge for ordering, handling, and storing materials	45
Profit margin on the materials	90
Total charge for materials	$360

Compute the material loading charge (in percentage terms) being used by the company.

7. Barker Company uses time and material pricing. The time rate is computed at $36 per hour. The material loading charge is computed at 20 percent for ordering, handling, and storing material and at 30 percent for a desired profit on these materials. Given these data, what is the total charge on a job that requires 2.5 hours of labor time and $140 in materials?
8. Dumas Company, a manufacturer of consumer products, wants to introduce a new hair dryer. To compete effectively, the dryer could not be priced at more than $40. The company requires a 16 percent ROI on all new products. In order to produce and sell 50,000 dryers each year, the company would need to make an investment of $750,000. Selling and administrative expenses would total $800,000 per year. Compute the target cost to manufacture one dryer.

P12–16 Competitive Bidding Hyer Machine Company designs and produces machine tools to customer specifications. The bulk of the company's business is obtained by competitive bidding. In the latter part of 19x5, the company was invited (along with several other companies) to bid on an order of 50 specially designed jigs needed by a manufacturing firm.

Hyer Machine Company was very happy to receive the invitation to bid, since business had been very slow for over a year, with no prospects for improvement. The company estimated the following costs relating to the 50 jigs:

	Total	Per Jig
Direct material	$ 50,000	$1,000
Direct labor	40,000	800
Variable overhead	10,000	200
Fixed overhead*	50,000	1,000
Design and cost study	5,000	100
Shipping	7,500	150
Total cost	$162,500	$3,250

* Allocated on a basis of machine-hours.

Based on these data, the company submitted a bid of $3,900 per jig. The price quotation sheet used to compute the bid is shown below:

Direct materials	$1,000
Direct labor	800
Manufacturing overhead	1,200
Total cost to manufacture	3,000
Markup desired—30%	900
Bid price per jig	$3,900

The manufacturer receiving the bid replied that the bid was too high and that no bid over $3,300 per jig would be considered. Upon hearing this, the president of Hyer Machine Company stated, "That lets us out. Our cost is $3,250 per jig. At a bid price of $3,300, the profit we'd make wouldn't be worth the effort."

Required What would you advise Hyer Machine Company to do? Show computations in good form.

P12–17 **Distress Pricing** Khater Industries operates a number of plants including one that manufactures a "super" chip that is used in many electronic products. The following data relate to the company's chip plant:

Number of chips produced per year . . .	90,000
Cost of materials per chip.	$20
Direct labor cost per chip	4
Shipping cost per chip	1

Manufacturing overhead is applied to the chips on a basis of 90 percent of the cost of materials. One sixth of the overhead cost is variable. The chips sell for $70 each.

In the past several months, the market has been flooded with chips from another country. As a result, the selling price per chip has dropped by one half. Khater Industries will have to meet the current price if it wants to retain its customers. After making a few computations, Khater's president stated, "We have no choice but to close down the chip plant. At the current price, we would lose $8 on every chip that we produced and sold. I'm afraid we're out of the chip business for awhile."

Required

1. How did the president compute the $8 per chip loss?
2. Prepare a price quotation sheet in the contribution format for one chip. (The appropriate markup would be 150 percent.) Do you agree with the president's decision to close the chip plant? Explain, and show computations to support your answer.

P12–18 **Integrative Problem: Standard Costs; Markup Computations; Pricing Decisions** Euclid Fashions, Inc., has designed a sports jacket that is about to be introduced on the market. A standard cost card has been prepared for the new jacket, as shown below:

	Standard Quantity or Hours	Standard Price or Rate	Standard Cost
Direct materials	2.0 yards	$ 4.60 per yard	$ 9.20
Direct labor	1.4 hours	10.00 per hour	14.00
Overhead (1/6 variable).	1.4 hours	12.00 per hour	16.80
Total standard cost per jacket . . .			$40.00

The following additional information relating to the new jacket is available:

a. The only variable selling or administrative costs on the jackets will be $4 per jacket for shipping. Fixed selling and administrative costs will be (per year):

Salaries	$ 90,000
Advertising and other . . .	384,000
Total.	$474,000

b. Since the company manufactures many products, it is felt that no more than 21,000 hours of labor time per year can be devoted to production of the new jackets.

c. An investment of $900,000 will be necessary to carry inventories and accounts receivable and to purchase some new equipment. The company desires a 24 percent ROI in new product lines.

d. Overhead costs are allocated to products on a basis of direct labor-hours.

Required

1. Assume that the company uses absorption costing.
   a. Compute the markup that the company needs on the jackets in order to achieve a 24 percent ROI.
   b. Using the markup you have computed, prepare a price quote sheet for a single jacket.

   c. Assume that the company is able to sell all of the jackets that it can produce. Prepare an income statement for the first year of activity, and compute the company's ROI for the year on the jackets, using the ROI formula from Chapter 11.

2. Assume that the company uses the contribution approach.
   a. Compute the markup that the company needs on the jackets in order to achieve a 24 percent ROI.
   b. Using the markup you have computed, prepare a price quote sheet for a single jacket.
   c. Prepare an income statement for the first year of activity.
3. After marketing the jackets for several years, the company is experiencing a falloff in demand due to an economic recession. A large retail outlet will make a bulk purchase of jackets if its label is sewn in and if an acceptable price can be worked out. Identify the range within which this price should fall.

P12–19 High-Low Analysis; Special Order Integrated Circuits, Inc. (ICI), is currently operating at 50 percent of capacity, producing 50,000 units annually of a patented electronic component. ICI has received an offer from a company in Yokohama, Japan, to purchase 30,000 components at $7 per unit, FOB ICI's plant. ICI has not previously sold components in Japan. Budgeted production costs for 50,000 and 80,000 units of output follow:

Units	50,000	80,000
Costs:		
Direct materials	$ 75,000	$120,000
Direct labor	200,000	320,000
Factory overhead	125,000	140,000
Total costs	$400,000	$580,000
Cost per unit	$8.00	$7.25

The sales manager thinks that the order should be accepted, even if this results in a loss of $1 per unit, because the sale may build up future markets. The production manager does not wish to have the order accepted, primarily because the order would show a loss of 25 cents per unit when computed on the new average unit cost.

Required

1. In terms of direct materials, direct labor, variable overhead, and fixed overhead, show the breakdown of the unit costs at the 50,000 and 80,000 unit levels of activity.
2. Assume that the normal target selling price is $10 per unit. Using the contribution approach, prepare a price quotation sheet for one unit of product. (The appropriate markup would be 66⅔ percent.) Indicate the ceiling, the floor, and the range of flexibility on your sheet.
3. On the basis of the information given in the problem and the information that you have computed above, should the order be accepted or rejected? Show computations to support your answer.
4. In addition to revenue and costs, what additional factors should be considered before making a final decision?

(CPA, Adapted)

P12–20 Integrative Problem: Missing Data; Markup Computations; Return on Investment; Pricing Rest Easy, Inc., has designed a new puncture proof, self-inflating sleeping pad that is unlike anything on the market. Because of the unique properties of the new sleeping pad, the company anticipates that it will be able to sell all the pads that it can produce. On this basis, the following budgeted income statement for the first year of activity is available:

Sales (__?__ pads at __?__ per pad)	$?
Less cost of goods sold (__?__ pads at __?__ per pad) . . .	4,000,000
Gross margin	?
Less selling and administrative expenses.	2,160,000
Net income	$?

Additional information on the new sleeping pad is given below:

a. The company will hire enough workers to commit 100,000 direct labor-hours to the manufacture of the pads.

b. A partially completed standard cost card for the new sleeping pad follows:

	Standard Quantity or Hours	Standard Price or Rate	Standard Cost
Direct materials	5 yards	$6 per yard	$30
Direct labor	2 hours	? per hour	?
Overhead (1/6 variable)	?	? per hour	?
Total standard cost per sleeping pad			$?

c. An investment of $3,500,000 will be necessary to carry inventories and accounts receivable and to purchase some new equipment needed in the manufacturing process. Management has decided that the design of the new pad is unique enough that the company should set a selling price that will yield a 24 percent return on investment.

d. Other information relating to production and costs follows:

Variable overhead cost (per pad)	$7
Variable selling cost (per pad)	5
Fixed overhead cost (total).	?
Fixed selling and administrative cost (total)	?
Number of pads produced and sold (per year) . . .	?

e. Overhead costs are allocated to production on a basis of direct labor-hours.

Required

1. Complete the standard cost card for a single pad.
2. Assume that the company uses absorption costing.
   a. Compute the markup that the company needs on the pads in order to achieve a 24 percent ROI.
   b. Using the markup you have computed, prepare a price quotation sheet for a single pad.
   c. Assume, as stated, that the company can sell all the pads that it can produce. Complete the income statement for the first year of activity, and then compute the company's ROI for the year, using the ROI formula from Chapter 11.
3. Assume that the company uses the contribution approach.
   a. Compute the markup that the company needs on the pads in order to achieve a 24 percent ROI.
   b. Using the markup you have computed, prepare a price quotation sheet for a single pad.
   c. Prepare an income statement for the first year of activity.

CASE

C12–21 Pricing a Bid; Opportunity Cost Azad Equipment, Inc., is a manufacturer of standard and custom-designed printing equipment. In March 19x1 the company was asked to bid on a custom-designed printing press which must be built and delivered to Riker Publishing Company by June 30, 19x1. Riker Publishing will choose a bidder by April 1, so Azad Equipment will have the entire second quarter to build the new press if its bid is accepted.

Azad Equipment has a policy of pricing custom-designed equipment at a price of 50 percent above cost to manufacture. Riker Publishing's specifications for the new press have been reviewed by Azad Equipment's engineering and cost accounting departments, and these departments have made the following estimates for raw materials and direct labor to build the new press:

Raw materials	$986,000
Direct labor (27,000 hours × $9) . . .	243,000

Manufacturing overhead is applied to products on a basis of direct labor-hours. Azad Equipment has budgeted to operate its plant at capacity during 19x1, which is 35,000 direct labor-hours per month or 420,000 hours for the year. The company's overhead application rate of $13 per hour for 19x1 is based on the following budgeted manufacturing overhead costs:

Variable overhead	$1,092,000
Fixed overhead	4,368,000
Total budgeted overhead . . .	$5,460,000

Although Azad Equipment had originally planned to operate its plant at 35,000 direct labor-hours per month during 19x1, business has been slower than anticipated and the company's production schedule calls for only 30,000 hours per month during the second quarter. Azad's production department is aware, however, that if Azad is awarded the bid for the new press, production of one of Azad's standard products will have to be cut back to some extent.

The product that will be cut back is a standard offset press that Azad manufactures in fairly large volume. This press has a unit sale price of $40,000 and the following cost structure:

Raw materials	$12,300
Direct labor (750 hours × $9) . . .	6,750
Overhead (750 hours × $13)	9,750
Total cost per press	$28,800

Although sales equal to the cutback in production would be lost during the second quarter, management is confident that the company could reenter the market during the third quarter with no damage to future sales.

In commenting on Azad's bid for the new press, Azad's president observed, "We don't want this job unless it improves our profits; otherwise, we're better off to just stick with our standard line of products."

Required

1. Determine the bid that Azad Equipment will submit on the new press if it follows its usual pricing policy for custom-designed equipment. Show all computations in good form.
2. Determine the minimum bid that Azad Equipment could submit on the new press if it wanted profits for the second quarter to be the same as if it just continued to produce and sell its standard products. Show all computations in good form.

13

Relevant Costs for Decision Making

LEARNING OBJECTIVES

After studying Chapter 13, you should be able to:

1 State a general rule for distinguishing between relevant and irrelevant costs in a decision-making situation.

2 Identify sunk costs and explain why they are not relevant in decision making.

3 Prepare an analysis showing whether a product line or other organizational segment should be dropped or retained.

4 Explain what is meant by a make or buy decision and prepare a well-organized make or buy analysis.

5 Make appropriate computations to determine the most profitable utilization of scarce resources in an organization.

6 Prepare an analysis showing whether joint products should be sold at the split-off point or processed further.

7 Construct a graph that shows the optimal solution to a linear programming problem.

8 Define or explain the key terms listed at the end of the chapter.

Decision making is one of the basic functions of a manager. Managers are constantly faced with problems of deciding what products to sell, what production methods to use, whether to make or buy component parts, what prices to charge, what channels of distribution to use, whether to accept special orders at special prices, and so forth. At best, decision making is a difficult and complex task. The difficulty of this task is usually increased by the existence of not just one or two but numerous courses of action that might be taken in any given situation facing a firm.

In decision making, *cost* is always a key factor. The costs of one alternative must be compared against the costs of other alternatives as one step in the decision-making process. The problem is that some costs associated with an alternative may not be *relevant* to the decision to be made. A **relevant cost** can be defined as a cost that is *applicable to a particular decision* in the sense that it will have a bearing on which alternative the manager selects.

To be successful in decision making, managers must have tools at their disposal to assist them in distinguishing between relevant and irrelevant costs so that the latter can be eliminated from the decision framework. The purpose of this chapter is to acquire these tools and to show their application in a wide range of decision-making situations.

COST CONCEPTS FOR DECISION MAKING

Three cost terms discussed in Chapter 2 are particularly applicable to this chapter. These terms are differential costs, opportunity costs, and sunk costs. The reader may find it helpful to turn back to Chapter 2 and refresh his or her memory of these terms before reading on.

Identifying Relevant Costs

What costs are relevant in decision making? The answer is easy. Any cost that is *avoidable* is relevant for decision purposes. An **avoidable cost** can be defined as a cost that can be eliminated (in whole or in part) as a result of choosing one alternative over another in a decision-making situation. *All* costs are considered to be avoidable, *except:*

1. Sunk costs.
2. Future costs that *do not differ* between the alternatives at hand.

As we learned in Chapter 2, a **sunk cost** is a cost that has already been incurred and that cannot be avoided regardless of which course of action a manager may decide to take. As such, sunk costs have no relevance to future events and must be ignored in decision making. Similarly, if a cost will be incurred regardless of which course of action a manager may take, then the cost cannot possibly be of any help in deciding which course of action is best. Such a cost is not avoidable, and hence it is not relevant to the manager's decision.

The term *avoidable cost* is synonymous with the term *differential cost* that we introduced in Chapter 2, and the terms are frequently used interchangeably. To identify the costs that are avoidable (differential) in a particular decision situation, the manager's approach to cost analysis should include the following steps:

1. Assemble *all* of the costs associated with *each* alternative being considered.
2. Eliminate those costs that are sunk.
3. Eliminate those costs that do not differ between alternatives.
4. Make a decision based on the remaining costs. These costs will be the **differential** or **avoidable costs,** and hence the costs relevant to the decision to be made.

Different Costs for Different Purposes

We need to recognize from the outset of our discussion that costs that are relevant in one decision situation are not necessarily relevant in another. Simply put, this means (as we've stated before) that *the manager needs different costs for different purposes*. For one purpose, a particular group of costs may be relevant; for another purpose, an entirely different group of costs may be relevant. Thus, in *each* decision situation the manager must examine the data at hand and then take the steps necessary to isolate the relevant costs. Otherwise, he or she runs the risk of being misled by irrelevant data.

The concept of ''different costs for different purposes'' is basic to managerial accounting; we shall see its application frequently in the pages that follow.

SUNK COSTS ARE NOT RELEVANT COSTS

One of the most difficult conceptual lessons that managers have to learn is that sunk costs are never relevant in decisions. The tendency to want to include sunk costs within the decision framework is especially strong in the case of book value of old equipment. We focus on book value of old equipment below, and then we consider other kinds of sunk costs in other parts of the chapter. We shall see that regardless of the kind of sunk cost involved, the conclusion is always the same—sunk costs are not avoidable, and therefore they must be eliminated from the manager's decision framework.

Book Value of Old Equipment

Assume the following data:

Old Machine		**Proposed New Machine**	
Original cost	$175,000	List price new	$200,000
Remaining book value	140,000	Expected life	4 years
Remaining life	4 years	Disposal value in four years	–0–
Disposal value now	90,000	Annual variable expenses to operate	300,000
Disposal value in four years	–0–	Annual revenue from sales	500,000
Annual variable expenses to operate	345,000		
Annual revenue from sales	500,000		

Should the old machine be disposed of and the new machine purchased?

Some managers would say no, since disposal of the old machine would result in a "loss" of $50,000:

Old Machine	
Remaining book value	$140,000
Disposal value now	90,000
Loss if disposed of now	$ 50,000

Given this potential loss if the old machine is sold, there is a general inclination for the manager to reason, "We've already made an investment in the old machine, so now we have no choice but to use it until our investment has been fully recovered." The manager will tend to think this way even though the new machine is clearly more efficient than the old machine. Although it may be appealing to think that an error of the past can be corrected by simply *using* the item involved, this, unfortunately, is not correct. The investment that has been made in the old machine is a sunk cost. The portion of this investment that remains on the company's books (the book value of $140,000) should not be considered in a decision about whether to buy the new machine. We can prove this assertion by the following analysis:[1]

	Total Costs and Revenues—Four Years		
	Keep Old Machine	**Differential Costs**	**Purchase New Machine**
Sales	$ 2,000,000	–0–	$ 2,000,000
Variable expenses.	(1,380,000)	$ 180,000	(1,200,000)
Cost (depreciation) of the new machine	—	(200,000)	(200,000)
Depreciation of the old machine or book value write-off.	(140,000)	–0–	(140,000)*
Disposal value of the old machine	—	90,000	90,000*
Total net income over the four years . . .	$ 480,000	$ 70,000	$ 550,000

* For external reporting purposes, the $140,000 remaining book value of the old machine and the $90,000 disposal value would be netted together and deducted as a single $50,000 "loss" figure.

Looking at all four years together, notice that the firm will be $70,000 better off by purchasing the new machine. Also notice that the $140,000 book value of the old machine had *no effect* on the outcome of the analysis. Since this book value is a sunk cost, it must be absorbed by the firm regardless of whether the old machine is kept and used or whether it is sold. If the old machine is kept and used, then the $140,000 book value is deducted in the form of depreciation. If the old machine is sold, then the $140,000 book value is deducted in the form of a lump-sum write-off. Either way, the company bears the same $140,000 deduction.

Focusing on Relevant Costs What costs in the example above are relevant in the decision concerning the new machine? Following the steps outlined

[1] The computations involved in this example are taken one step further in Chapters 14 and 15 where we discuss the time value of money and the use of present value in decision making.

earlier, we should eliminate (1) the sunk costs and (2) the future costs that do not differ between the alternatives at hand.

1. The sunk costs:
   a. The remaining book value of the old machine ($140,000).
2. The future costs that do not differ:
   a. The sales revenue ($500,000 per year).
   b. The variable expenses (to the extent of $300,000 per year).

The costs that remain will form the basis for a decision. The analysis is:

	Differential Costs— Four Years
Reduction in variable expense promised by the new machine ($45,000* per year × 4 years)	$ 180,000
Cost of the new machine	(200,000)
Disposal value of the old machine	90,000
Net advantage of the new machine	$ 70,000

* $345,000 − $300,000 = $45,000.

Note that the items above are the same as those in the middle column of the earlier analysis and represent those costs and revenues that are differential as between the two alternatives.

Depreciation and Relevant Costs Since the book value of old equipment is not a relevant cost in decision making, there is a tendency to assume that depreciation of *any* kind is irrelevant in the decision-making process. This is not a correct assumption. Depreciation is irrelevant in decisions only if it relates to a sunk cost. Notice from the comparative income statements in the preceding section that the $200,000 depreciation on the new machine appears in the middle column as a relevant item in trying to assess the desirability of the new machine's purchase. By contrast, depreciation on the old machine does not appear as a relevant cost. The difference is that the investment in the new machine has *not yet been made,* and therefore it does not represent depreciation of a sunk cost.

FUTURE COSTS THAT DO NOT DIFFER ARE NOT RELEVANT COSTS

Any future cost that does not differ between the alternatives in a decision situation is not a relevant cost so far as that decision is concerned. As stated earlier, if a company is going to sustain the same cost regardless of what decision it makes, then that cost can in no way tell the company which decision is best. The only way a future cost can help in the decision-making process is by being different as between the alternatives under consideration.

An Example of Irrelevant Future Costs

To illustrate the irrelevance of future costs that do not differ, let us assume that a firm is contemplating the purchase of a new laborsaving machine. The machine will cost $30,000 and have a 10-year useful life. The company's sales and cost structure on an annual basis with and without the new machine are shown below:

	Present Costs	Expected Costs with the New Machine
Units produced and sold	5,000	5,000
Sales price per unit	$ 40	$ 40
Direct materials cost per unit	14	14
Direct labor cost per unit	8	5
Variable overhead cost per unit	2	2
Fixed costs, other	62,000	62,000
Fixed costs, new machine	—	3,000

The new machine promises a saving of $3 per unit in direct labor costs ($8 − $5 = $3), but it will increase fixed costs by $3,000 per period. All other costs, as well as the total number of units produced and sold, will remain the same. Following the steps outlined earlier, the analysis is:

1. Eliminate the sunk costs. (No sunk costs are identified in this example.)
2. Eliminate the future costs (and revenues) that do not differ:
   a. The sales price per unit does not differ.
   b. The direct materials cost per unit does not differ.
   c. The variable overhead cost per unit does not differ.
   d. The total "fixed costs, other" do not differ.

This leaves just the per unit labor costs and the fixed costs associated with the new machine as being differential costs:

Savings in direct labor costs (5,000 units at a cost saving of $3 per unit)	$15,000
Less increase in fixed costs	3,000
Net annual cost savings promised by the new machine	$12,000

The accuracy of this solution can be proved by looking at *all* items of cost data (both those that are relevant and those that are not) under the two alternatives for a period and then comparing the net income results. This is done in Exhibit 13–1. Notice from the exhibit that we obtain the same $12,000 net advantage in favor of buying the new machine as we obtained above when we focused only on relevant costs. Thus, we can see that future costs that do not differ between alternatives are indeed irrelevant in the decision-making process and can be safely eliminated from the manager's decision framework.

Why Isolate Relevant Costs?

In the preceding example, we used two different approaches to show that the purchase of the new machine was desirable. First, we considered only the relevant costs; and second, we considered all costs, both those that were relevant and those that were not. We obtained the same answer under both approaches. When students see that the same answer can be obtained under either approach, they often ask, "Why bother to isolate relevant costs when total costs will do the job just as well?" The isolation of relevant costs is desirable for at least two reasons.

EXHIBIT 13–1
Differential Cost Analysis

	5,000 Units Produced and Sold		
	Present Method	**Differential Costs**	**New Machine**
Sales	$200,000	$ –0–	$200,000
Variable expenses:			
Direct materials	70,000	–0–	70,000
Direct labor	40,000	15,000	25,000
Variable overhead	10,000	–0–	10,000
Total variable expenses	120,000		105,000
Contribution margin	80,000		95,000
Less fixed expenses:			
Other	62,000	–0–	62,000
New machine	–0–	(3,000)	3,000
Total fixed expenses	62,000		65,000
Net income	$ 18,000	$12,000	$ 30,000

First, only rarely will enough information be available to prepare a detailed income statement such as we have done in the preceding examples. Since normally only limited data are available, the decision maker *must* know how to recognize which costs are relevant and which are not. Assume, for example, that you are called on to make a decision relating to a matter in a *single operation* of a multidepartmental, multiproduct firm. Under these circumstances, it would be virtually impossible to prepare an income statement of any type. You would have to rely on your ability to recognize which costs were relevant and which were not in order to assemble the data necessary to make a decision.

Second, the use of irrelevant costs mingled with relevant costs may confuse the picture and draw the decision maker's attention away from the matters that are really critical to the problem at hand. Furthermore, the danger always exists that an irrelevant piece of data may be used improperly, resulting in an incorrect decision. The best approach is to isolate the relevant items and to focus all attention directly on them and on their impact on the decision to be made.

Relevant cost analysis, combined with the contribution approach to the income statement, provides a powerful tool for making decisions in special, nonroutine situations. We will investigate various uses of this tool in the remaining sections of this chapter.

ADDING AND DROPPING PRODUCT LINES

Decisions relating to whether old product lines should be dropped and new product lines should be added are among the most difficult that a manager has to make. In such decisions, many factors must be considered that are both qualitative and quantitative in nature. Ultimately, however, any final decision to drop an old product line or to add a new product line is going to hinge primarily on the impact the decision will have on net income. In order to assess this impact, it is necessary to make a careful analysis of the costs involved.

An Illustration of Cost Analysis

As a basis for discussion, let us consider the product lines of the Discount Drug Company. The company has three major product lines—drugs, cosmetics, and housewares. Sales and cost information for the preceding month for each separate product line and for the store in total is given in Exhibit 13–2.

What can be done to improve the company's overall performance? One product line—housewares—shows a net loss for the month. Perhaps dropping this line would cause profits in the company as a whole to improve. In deciding whether the line should be dropped, management will need to reason as follows:

If the housewares line is dropped, then the company will lose $20,000 per month in contribution margin that is now available to help cover the fixed costs. By dropping the line, however, it may be possible to avoid certain of these fixed costs. It may be possible, for example, to discharge certain employees, or it may be possible to reduce advertising costs. If by dropping the housewares line the company is able to avoid more in fixed costs than it loses in contribution margin, then it will be better off if the line is eliminated, since overall net income should improve. On the other hand, if the company is not able to avoid as much in fixed costs as it loses in contribution margin, then the housewares line should be retained. In short, in order to identify the differential costs in decisions of this type, the manager must ask, "What costs can I avoid to offset my loss of revenue (or loss of contribution margin) if I drop this product line?"

As we have seen from our earlier discussion, not all costs are avoidable. For example, some of the costs associated with a product line may be sunk

EXHIBIT 13–2
Discount Drug Company Product Lines

		Product Line		
	Total	Drugs	Cosmetics	Housewares
Sales	$250,000	$125,000	$75,000	$50,000
Less variable expenses	105,000	50,000	25,000	30,000
Contribution margin	145,000	75,000	50,000	20,000
Less fixed expenses:				
Salaries	50,000	29,500	12,500	8,000
Advertising	15,000	1,000	7,500	6,500
Utilities	2,000	500	500	1,000
Depreciation—fixtures	5,000	1,000	2,000	2,000
Rent	20,000	10,000	6,000	4,000
Insurance	3,000	2,000	500	500
General administrative	30,000	15,000	9,000	6,000
Total fixed expenses	125,000	59,000	38,000	28,000
Net income (loss)	$ 20,000	$ 16,000	$12,000	$ (8,000)

costs. Other costs may be allocated common costs that will not differ in total regardless of whether the product line is dropped or retained. To show how the manager should proceed in a product line analysis, suppose that the management of the Discount Drug Company has analyzed the costs being charged to the three product lines and has determined the following:

1. The salaries represent salaries paid to employees working directly in each product line area. All of the employees working in housewares can be discharged if the line is dropped.
2. The advertising represents direct advertising of each product line and is avoidable if the line is dropped.
3. The utilities represent utilities costs for the entire company. The amount charged to each product line represents an allocation based on space occupied.
4. The depreciation represents depreciation on fixtures used for display of the various product lines. Although the fixtures are nearly new, they are custom-built and will have little resale value if the housewares line is dropped.
5. The rent represents rent on the entire building housing the company; it is allocated to the product lines on a basis of sales dollars. The monthly rent of $20,000 is fixed under a long-term lease agreement.
6. The insurance represents insurance carried on inventories maintained within each of the three product line areas.
7. The general administrative expense represents the costs of accounting, purchasing, and general management, which are allocated to the product lines on a basis of sales dollars. Total administrative costs will not change if the housewares line is dropped.

With this information, management can identify those costs that are avoidable and those costs that are not avoidable if the product line is dropped:

	Total Cost	Not Avoidable*	Avoidable
Salaries	$ 8,000		$ 8,000
Advertising	6,500		6,500
Utilities	1,000	$ 1,000	
Depreciation—fixtures	2,000	2,000	
Rent	4,000	4,000	
Insurance	500		500
General administrative	6,000	6,000	
Total fixed expenses	$28,000	$13,000	$15,000

* These costs represent either (1) sunk costs or (2) costs that will not change regardless of whether the housewares line is retained or discontinued.

To determine how dropping the line will affect the overall profits of the company, we can compare the contribution margin that will be lost against the costs that can be avoided if the line is dropped.

Contribution margin lost if the housewares line is discontinued (see Exhibit 13–2)	$(20,000)
Less fixed costs that can be avoided if the housewares line is discontinued (see above)	15,000
Decrease in overall company net income	$ (5,000)

In this case, the fixed costs that can be avoided by dropping the product line are less than the contribution margin that will be lost. Therefore, the housewares line should not be discontinued unless a more profitable use can be found for the floor and counter space that it is occupying.

A Comparative Format

Some managers prefer to approach decisions of this type by preparing comparative income statements showing the effects on the company as a whole of either keeping or dropping the product line in question. A comparative analysis of this type for the Discount Drug Company is shown in Exhibit 13–3.

As shown by column 3 in the exhibit, overall company net income will decrease by $5,000 each period if the housewares line is dropped. This is the same answer, of course, as we obtained in our earlier analysis.

Beware of Allocated Fixed Costs

Our conclusion that the housewares line should not be dropped seems to conflict with the data shown in Exhibit 13–2. Recall from the exhibit that the housewares line is showing a loss rather than a profit. Why keep a line that is showing a loss? The explanation for this apparent inconsistency lies at least in part with the common fixed costs that are being allocated to the product lines. As we observed in Chapter 7, one of the great dangers in allocating common fixed costs is that such allocations can make a product line (or other segment of a business) *look* less profitable than it really is. Consider the following example:

> A bakery distributed its products through route salesmen, each of whom loaded a truck with an assortment of products in the morning and spent the day calling on customers in an assigned territory. Believing that some items were more profitable than others, management asked for an analysis of product

EXHIBIT 13–3

A Comparative Format for Product Line Analysis

	Keep Housewares	Drop Housewares	Difference: Net Income Increase or (Decrease)
Sales	$50,000	$ -0-	$(50,000)
Less variable expenses	30,000	-0-	30,000
Contribution margin	20,000	-0-	(20,000)
Less fixed expenses:			
Salaries	8,000	-0-	8,000
Advertising	6,500	-0-	6,500
Utilities	1,000	1,000	-0-
Depreciation—fixtures	2,000	2,000	-0-
Rent	4,000	4,000	-0-
Insurance	500	-0-	500
General administrative	6,000	6,000	-0-
Total fixed expenses	28,000	13,000	15,000
Net income (loss)	$ (8,000)	$(13,000)	$ (5,000)

> costs and sales. The accountants to whom the task was assigned allocated all manufacturing and marketing costs to products to obtain a net profit for each product. The resulting figures indicated that some of the products were being sold at a loss, and management discontinued these products. However, when this change was put into effect, the company's overall profit declined. It was then seen that, by dropping some products, sales revenues had been reduced without commensurate reduction in costs because the joint manufacturing costs and route sales costs had to be continued in order to make and sell remaining products.[2]

The same thing has happened in the Discount Drug Company as happened in the bakery company. That is, by allocating the common fixed costs among all product lines, the Discount Drug Company has made the housewares line *look* as if it were unprofitable, whereas, in fact, dropping the line would result in a decrease in overall company net income. This point can be seen clearly if we recast the data in Exhibit 13–2 and eliminate the allocation of the common fixed costs. This recasting of data is shown in Exhibit 13–4 above.

Exhibit 13–4 gives us a much different perspective of the housewares line than does Exhibit 13–2. As shown in Exhibit 13–4, the housewares line is covering all of its own direct fixed costs and is generating a $3,000 segment margin toward covering the common fixed costs of the company. Unless

EXHIBIT 13–4

Discount Drug Company Product Lines—Recast in Contribution Format (from Exhibit 13–2)

		Product Line		
	Total	Drugs	Cosmetics	Housewares
Sales	$250,000	$125,000	$75,000	$50,000
Less variable expenses	105,000	50,000	25,000	30,000
Contribution margin	145,000	75,000	50,000	20,000
Less traceable fixed expenses:				
Salaries	50,000	29,500	12,500	8,000
Advertising	15,000	1,000	7,500	6,500
Depreciation—fixtures	5,000	1,000	2,000	2,000
Insurance	3,000	2,000	500	500
Total	73,000	33,500	22,500	17,000
Product line segment margin	72,000	$ 41,500	$27,500	$ 3,000*
Less common fixed expenses:				
Utilities	2,000			
Rent	20,000			
General administrative	30,000			
Total	52,000			
Net income	$ 20,000			

* If the housewares line is dropped, this $3,000 in segment margin will be lost to the company. In addition, we have seen that the $2,000 depreciation on the fixtures is a sunk cost that cannot be avoided. The sum of these two figures ($3,000 + $2,000 = $5,000) represents another way of obtaining the $5,000 figure that we found earlier would be the decrease in the company's overall profits if the housewares line were discontinued.

[2] Walter B. McFarland, *Concepts for Management Accounting* (New York: National Association of Accountants, 1966), p. 46.

another product line can be found that will generate a greater segment margin than this, then, as we have noted, the company will be better off to keep the housewares line. By keeping the line, the company will get at least some contribution toward the common fixed costs of the organization from the space it is occupying.

When we talk about another product to replace housewares, we are talking about the *opportunity cost* of space. As a next step, management should explore alternative uses for the space in the store, such as adding a new product, expanding the existing products, or even renting the space out that is now being occupied by housewares.

To conclude, we should note that even in those situations where the contribution of a particular product line is small in comparison with other products, managers will often retain the line instead of replacing it, if the line is necessary to the sale of other products or if it serves as a "magnet" to attract customers. Bread, for example, is not an especially profitable line in food stores, but customers expect it to be available, and many would undoubtedly shift their buying elsewhere if a particular store decided to stop carrying it.

THE MAKE OR BUY DECISION

Many steps are involved in getting a finished product into the hands of a consumer. First, raw materials must be obtained through mining, drilling, growing crops, raising animals, and so forth. Second, these raw materials must be processed to remove impurities or to extract the desirable and usable materials from the bulk of materials available. Third, the usable materials must be fabricated into desired form to serve as basic inputs for manufactured products. Fourth, the actual manufacturing of the finished product must take place, with several products perhaps coming from the same basic raw materials input (as, for example, several different items of clothing coming from the same basic cloth input). And finally, the finished product must be distributed to the ultimate consumer.

When a company is involved in more than one of these steps, it is following a policy of **vertical integration.** Vertical integration is very common. Some firms go so far as to control *all* of the activities relating to their products, from the mining of raw materials or the raising of crops right up to the final distribution of finished goods. Other firms are content to integrate on a less grand scale, and perhaps they will produce only certain fabricated parts that go into their finished products.

A decision to produce a fabricated part internally, rather than to buy the part externally from a supplier, is often called a **make or buy decision.** Actually, any decision relating to vertical integration is a make or buy decision, since the company is deciding whether to meet its own needs internally rather than to buy externally.

The Advantages of Integration

Certain advantages arise from integration. The integrated firm is less dependent on its suppliers and may be able to ensure a smoother flow of parts and materials for production than the nonintegrated firm. For example, a strike against a major parts supplier might cause the operations of a nonintegrated firm to be interrupted for many months, whereas the integrated firm that is producing its own parts might be able to continue operations. Also, many firms feel that they can control quality better by producing their own parts and materials, rather than by relying on the quality control standards of outside suppliers. In addition, the integrated firm realizes profits from the parts and materials that it is "making" rather than "buying," as well as profits from its regular operations.

The advantages of integration are counterbalanced by a number of hazards. A firm that produces all of its own parts runs the risk of destroying long-run relationships with suppliers, which may prove harmful and disruptive to the firm. Once relationships with suppliers have been severed, they are often difficult to reestablish. If product demand becomes heavy, a firm may not have sufficient capacity to continue producing all of its own parts internally, but then it may experience great difficulty in its efforts to secure assistance from a severed supplier. In addition, changing technology often makes continued production of one's own parts more costly than purchasing them from the outside, but this change in cost may not be obvious to the firm. In sum, these factors suggest that although certain advantages may accrue to the integrated firm, the make or buy decision should be weighed very carefully before any move is undertaken that may prove to be costly in the long run.

An Example of Make or Buy

How does a firm approach the make or buy decision? Basically, the matters that must be considered fall into two broad categories—qualitative and quantitative. Qualitative matters deal with issues such as those raised in the preceding section. Quantitative matters deal with cost—what is the cost of producing as compared to the cost of buying? Several kinds of costs may be involved here, including opportunity costs.

To provide an illustration, assume that Bonner Company is now producing a small subassembly that is used in the production of one of the company's main product lines. Bonner Company's accounting department reports the following "costs" of producing the subassembly internally:

	Per Unit	8,000 Units
Direct materials	$ 6	$ 48,000
Direct labor	4	32,000
Variable overhead	1	8,000
Supervisor's salary	3	24,000
Depreciation of special equipment	2	16,000
Allocated general overhead	5	40,000
Total cost	$21	$168,000

Bonner Company has just received an offer from an outside supplier who will provide 8,000 subassemblies a year at a price of only $19 each. Should Bonner Company stop producing the subassemblies internally and start purchasing them from the outside supplier? To make this decision, the manager must again focus on the differential costs. As we have seen, the differential costs can be obtained by eliminating from the cost data those costs that are not avoidable—that is, by eliminating (1) the sunk costs and (2) the future costs that will continue regardless of whether the subassemblies are produced internally or purchased outside. The costs that remain after making these eliminations will be the costs that are avoidable to the company by purchasing outside. If these costs are less than the outside purchase price, then the company should continue to manufacture its own subassemblies and reject the outside supplier's offer. That is, the company should purchase outside only if the outside purchase price is less than the costs that can be avoided internally as a result of stopping production of the subassemblies.

Looking at the data above, notice first that depreciation of special equipment is one of the "costs" of producing the subassemblies internally. Since the equipment has already been purchased, this depreciation represents a sunk cost. Also notice that the company is allocating a portion of its general overhead costs to the subassemblies. Since these costs are common to all items produced in the factory, they will continue unchanged even if the subassemblies are purchased from the outside. These allocated costs, therefore, are not differential costs (since they will not differ between the make or buy alternatives), and they must be eliminated from the manager's decision framework along with the sunk costs.

The variable costs of producing the subassemblies (materials, labor, and variable overhead) are differential costs, since they can be avoided by buying the subassemblies from the outside supplier. If the supervisor can be discharged and his or her salary avoided by buying the subassemblies, then it too will be a differential cost and relevant to the decision. Assuming that both the variable costs and the supervisor's salary can be avoided by buying from the outside supplier, then the analysis takes the form shown in Exhibit 13–5.

Since it costs $5 less per unit to continue to make the subassemblies, Bonner Company should reject the outside supplier's offer. There is one

EXHIBIT 13–5
Make or Buy Analysis

	Production "Cost" per Unit	Per Unit Differential Costs		Total Differential Costs—8,000 Units	
		Make	Buy	Make	Buy
Direct materials	$ 6	$ 6		$ 48,000	
Direct labor	4	4		32,000	
Variable overhead	1	1		8,000	
Supervisor's salary	3	3		24,000	
Depreciation of special equipment	2	—		—	
Allocation of general overhead	5	—		—	
Outside purchase price			$19		$152,000
Total cost	$21	$14	$19	$112,000	$152,000
Difference in favor of continuing to make		$5		$40,000	

additional factor that the company may wish to consider before coming to a final decision, however. This factor is the opportunity cost of the space now being used to produce the subassemblies.

The Matter of Opportunity Cost

If the space now being used to produce the subassemblies *would otherwise be idle,* then Bonner Company should continue to produce its own subassemblies and the supplier's offer should be rejected, as we stated above. Idle space that has no alternative use has an opportunity cost of zero.

But what if the space now being used to produce subassemblies would not sit idle, but rather could be used for some other purpose? In this case, the space would have an opportunity cost that would have to be considered in assessing the desirability of the supplier's offer. What would this opportunity cost be? It would be the segment margin that could be derived from the best alternative use of the space.

To illustrate, assume that the space now being used to produce subassemblies could be used to produce a new product line that would generate a segment margin of $60,000 per year. Under these conditions, Bonner Company would be better off to accept the supplier's offer and to use the available space to produce the new product line:

	Make	Buy
Differential cost per unit (see prior example)	$ 14	$ 19
Number of units needed annually	× 8,000	× 8,000
Total annual cost	112,000	152,000
Opportunity cost—segment margin forgone on a potential new product line.	60,000	
Total cost	$172,000	$152,000
Difference in favor of purchasing from the outside supplier	$20,000	

Perhaps we should again emphasize that opportunity costs are not recorded in the accounts of an organization. They do not represent actual dollar outlays. Rather, they represent those economic benefits that are *forgone* as a result of pursuing some course of action. The opportunity costs of Bonner Company are sufficiently large in this case to make continued production of the subassemblies very costly from an economic point of view.

UTILIZATION OF SCARCE RESOURCES

Firms are often faced with the problem of deciding how scarce resources are going to be utilized. A department store, for example, has a limited amount of floor space and therefore cannot stock every product line that may be available. A manufacturing firm has a limited number of machine-hours and a limited number of direct labor-hours at its disposal. When capacity becomes pressed, the firm must decide which orders it will accept and which orders it will reject. In making these decisions, the contribution approach is necessary, since the firm will want to select the course of action that will maximize its *total* contribution margin.

Contribution in Relation to Scarce Resources

To maximize total contribution margin, a firm may not necessarily want to promote those products that have the highest *individual* contribution margins. Rather, total contribution margin will be maximized by promoting those products or accepting those orders that promise the highest contribution margin *in relation to the scarce resources of the firm*. This concept can be demonstrated by assuming that a firm has two product lines, A and B. Cost and revenue characteristics of the two product lines are given below:

	Product Line	
	A	B
Sales price per unit	$25	$30
Variable cost per unit	10	18
Contribution margin per unit	$15	$12
CM ratio	60%	40%

Product line A appears to be much more profitable than product line B. It has a $15 per unit contribution margin as compared to only $12 per unit for product line B, and it has a 60 percent CM ratio as compared to only 40 percent for product line B.

But now let us add one more piece of information—it takes two machine-hours to produce one unit of A and only one machine-hour to produce one unit of B. The firm has only 18,000 machine-hours of capacity available in the plant per period. If demand becomes strong, which orders should the firm accept, those for product line A or those for product line B? The firm should accept orders for product line B. Even though product line A has the highest *per unit* contribution margin, product line B provides the highest contribution margin in relation to the scarce resource of the firm, which in this case is machine-hours available.

	Product Line	
	A	B
Contribution margin per unit (above) *(a)*	$15.00	$12
Machine-hours required to produce one unit *(b)*	2 hours	1 hour
Contribution margin per machine-hour, *(a)* ÷ *(b)*	$ 7.50	$12
Total contribution margin promised:		
Total machine-hours available	18,000	18,000
Contribution margin per machine-hour	× $7.50	× $12
Total contribution margin	$135,000	$216,000

This example shows clearly that looking at unit contribution margins alone is not enough; the contribution margin promised by a product line must be viewed in relation to whatever resource constraints a firm may be working under.

One of the most common resource constraints is advertising dollars available. Firms typically concentrate their efforts on those product lines that promise the greatest contribution margin per dollar of advertising expended. Another common resource constraint is floor space. Various discount retail outlets and discount food chains have utilized the concept of maximum contribution margin per square foot by concentrating on those product lines that have a rapid turnover, thereby generating large amounts of contribution in small amounts of space available.

The Problem of Multiple Constraints

What does a firm do if it is operating under *several* scarce resource constraints? For example, a firm may have limited raw materials available, limited direct labor-hours available, limited floor space, and limited advertising dollars to spend on product promotion. How would it proceed to find the right combination of products to produce under such a variety of constraints? The proper combination or "mix" of products can be found by use of a quantitative method known as *linear programming*. Linear programming, a very powerful analytical tool, is illustrated in the appendix to this chapter.

JOINT PRODUCT COSTS AND THE CONTRIBUTION APPROACH

The manufacturing processes of some firms are such that several end products are produced from a single raw material input. The meat-packing industry, for example, inputs a pig into the manufacturing process and comes out with a great variety of end products—bacon, ham, spare ribs, pork roasts, and so on. Firms that produce several end products from a common input (e.g., a pig) are faced with the problem of deciding how the cost of that input is going to be divided among the end products (bacon, ham, pork roasts, and so on) that result. Before we address ourselves to this problem, it will be helpful to define three terms—joint products, joint product costs, and split-off point.

Two or more products that are produced from a common input are known as **joint products.** The term **joint product costs** is used to describe those manufacturing costs that are incurred in producing joint products up to the split-off point. The **split-off point** is that point in the manufacturing process at which the joint products (bacon, ham, spare ribs, and so on) can be recognized as individual units of output. At that point, some of the joint products will be in final form, ready to be marketed to the consumer. Others will still need further processing on their own before they are in marketable form. These concepts are presented graphically in Exhibit 13–6.

The Pitfalls of Allocation

Joint product costs are really common costs incurred to simultaneously produce a variety of end products. Traditional cost accounting books contain various approaches to allocating these common costs among the different products at the split-off point. The most usual approach is to allocate the joint product costs according to the relative sales value of the end products.

Although allocation of joint product costs is needed for some purposes, such as balance sheet inventory valuation, allocations of this kind should be used with great caution *internally* in the decision-making process. Unless a manager proceeds with care, he or she may be led into incorrect decisions as

EXHIBIT 13–6
Joint Products

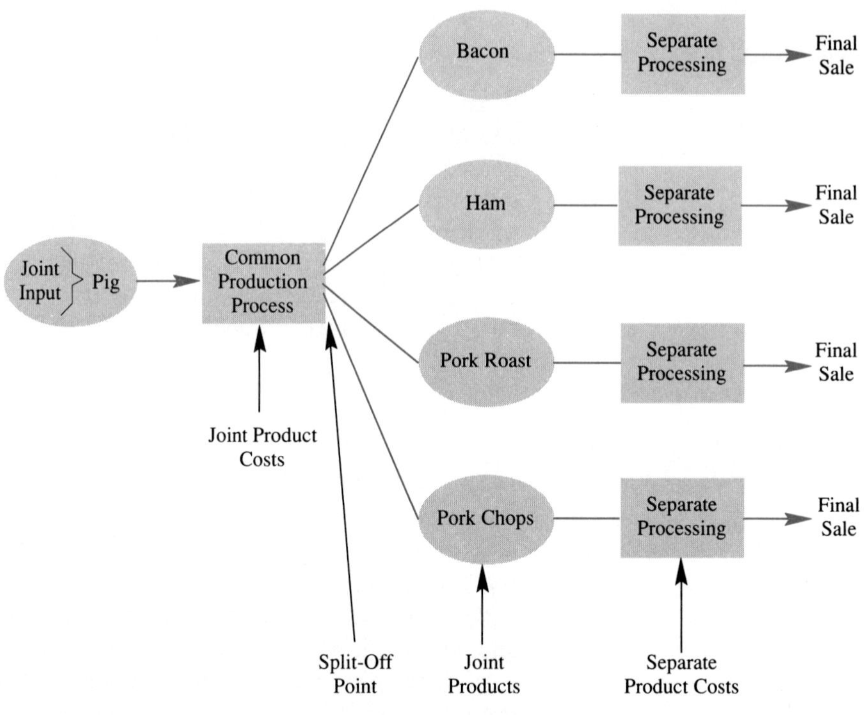

a result of relying on allocated common costs. Consider the following situation, which occurred in a firm several years ago:

> A company located on the Gulf of Mexico is a producer of soap products. Its six main soap product lines are produced from common inputs. Joint product costs up to the split-off point constitute the bulk of the production costs for all six product lines. These joint product costs are allocated to the six product lines on the basis of the relative sales value of each line at the split-off point.
>
> The company has a waste product that results from the production of the six main product lines. Until a few years ago, the company loaded the waste onto barges and dumped it into the Gulf of Mexico, since the waste was thought to have no commercial value. The dumping was stopped, however, when the company's research division discovered that with some further processing the waste could be made commercially salable as a fertilizer ingredient. The further processing was initiated at a cost of $175,000 per year. The waste was then sold to fertilizer manufacturers at a total price of $300,000 per year.
>
> The accountants responsible for allocating manufacturing costs included the sales value of the waste product along with the sales value of the six main product lines in their allocation of the joint product costs at the split-off point. This allocation resulted in the waste product being allocated $150,000 in joint product cost. This $150,000 allocation, when added to the further processing costs of $175,000 for the waste, caused the waste product to show a net loss:

Sales value of the waste product after further processing	$300,000
Less costs assignable to the waste product . . .	325,000
Net loss.	$ (25,000)

When presented with this analysis, the company's management decided that further processing of the waste was not desirable after all. The company went back to dumping the waste in the Gulf.

Sell or Process Further Decisions

Joint product costs are irrelevant in decisions regarding what to do with a product from the split-off point forward. The reason is that by the time one arrives at the split-off point, the joint product costs have already been incurred and therefore are sunk costs. In the case of the soap company example above, the $150,000 in allocated joint product costs should not have been permitted to influence what was done with the waste product from the split-off point forward. The analysis should have been:

	Dump in Gulf	Process Further
Sales value	–0–	$300,000
Additional processing costs	–0–	175,000
Contribution margin	–0–	$125,000
Advantage of processing further	$125,000	

Decisions of this type are known as **sell or process further decisions.** As a general guide, it will always be profitable to continue processing a joint product after the split-off point *so long as the incremental revenue from such processing exceeds the incremental processing costs.* Joint product costs that have already been incurred up to the split-off point are sunk costs, and are always irrelevant in decisions concerning what to do from the split-off point forward.

To provide a detailed example of a sell or process further decision, assume that three products are derived from a single raw material input. Cost and revenue data relating to the products are presented in Exhibit 13–7, along with an analysis of which products should be sold at the split-off point and which should be processed further. As shown in the exhibit, products B and C should both be processed further; product A should be sold at the split-off point.

EXHIBIT 13–7

Sell or Process Further Decision

	Product		
	A	B	C
Sales value at the split-off point	$120,000	$150,000	$60,000
Sales value after further processing	160,000	240,000	90,000
Allocated joint product costs	80,000	100,000	40,000
Cost of further processing	50,000	60,000	10,000
Analysis of sell or process further:			
Sales value after further processing	$160,000	$240,000	$90,000
Sales value at the split-off point	120,000	150,000	60,000
Incremental revenue from further processing	40,000	90,000	30,000
Cost of further processing	50,000	60,000	10,000
Profit (loss) from further processing	$(10,000)	$ 30,000	$20,000

SUMMARY

The accountant is responsible for seeing that relevant, timely data are available to guide management in its decisions, particularly those decisions relating to special, nonroutine situations. Reliance by management on irrelevant data can lead to incorrect decisions, reduced profitability, and inability to meet stated objectives. *All* costs are relevant in decision making, *except:*

1. Sunk costs.
2. Future costs that will not differ between the alternatives under consideration.

The concept of cost relevance has wide application. In this chapter, we have observed its use in equipment replacement decisions, in make or buy decisions, in discontinuance of product line decisions, in joint product decisions, and in decisions relating to the effective use of scarce resources. This list does not include all of the possible applications of the relevant cost concept. Indeed, *any* decision involving costs hinges on the proper identification and use of those costs that are relevant, if the decision is to be made properly. For this reason, we shall continue to focus on the concept of cost relevance in the following two chapters, where we consider long-run investment decisions.

KEY TERMS FOR REVIEW

Avoidable cost Any cost that can be eliminated (in whole or in part) as a result of choosing one alternative over another in a decision-making situation. This term is synonymous with *relevant cost* and *differential cost*. (p. 544)

Differential cost Any cost that is present under one alternative in a decision-making situation but is absent in whole or in part under another alternative. This term is synonymous with *avoidable cost* and *relevant cost*. (p. 545)

Joint product costs Those manufacturing costs that are incurred up to the split-off point in producing joint products. (p. 559)

Joint products Two or more items that are produced from a common input. (p. 559)

Make or buy decision A decision as to whether an item should be produced internally or purchased from an outside supplier. (p. 554)

Relevant cost A cost that is applicable to a particular decision in the sense that it will have a bearing on which alternative the manager selects. This term is synonymous with *avoidable cost* and *differential cost*. (p. 544)

Sell or process further decision A decision as to whether a joint product should be sold at the split-off point or processed further and sold at a later time in a different form. (p. 561)

Split-off point That point in the manufacturing process where some or all of the joint products can be recognized as individual units of output. (p. 559)

Sunk cost Any cost that has already been incurred and that cannot be changed by any decision made now or in the future. (p. 544)

Vertical integration The involvement by a company in more than one of the steps from extracting or otherwise securing basic raw materials to the manufacture and distribution of a finished product. (p. 554)

APPENDIX: LINEAR PROGRAMMING

Linear programming is a mathematical tool designed to assist management in making decisions in situations where constraining or limiting factors are present. The limiting factors might include, for example, a scarcity of raw materials needed in the production of a firm's products, or a plant with inadequate machine time to produce all of the products being demanded by a firm's customers. Linear programming is designed to assist the manager in putting together the "right mix" of products in situations such as these, so that the scarce resources of the firm (e.g., raw materials, machine time) can be utilized in a way that will maximize profits.

A Graphic Approach to Linear Programming

To demonstrate a linear programming analysis, let us assume the following data:

> A firm produces two products, X and Y. The contribution margin per unit of X is $8, and the contribution margin per unit of Y is $10. The firm has 36 hours of production time available each period. It takes 6 hours of production time to produce one unit of X and 9 hours of production time to produce one unit of Y.
>
> The firm has only 24 pounds of raw materials available for use in production each period. It takes 6 pounds of raw materials to produce one unit of X and 3 pounds to produce one unit of Y.
>
> Management estimates that no more than three units of Y can be sold each period. The firm is interested in maximizing contribution margin. What combination of X and Y should be produced and sold?

There are four basic steps in a linear programming analysis:

1. Determine the *objective function,* and express it in algebraic terms.
2. Determine the *constraints* under which the firm must operate, and express each constraint in algebraic terms.
3. Determine the *feasible production area* on a graph. This area will be bounded by the constraint equations derived in (2) above, after the constraint equations have been expressed on the graph in linear form.
4. Determine from the feasible production area the *product mix* that will maximize (or minimize) the objective function.

We will now examine each of these steps in order by relating them to the data in the example above.

1. Determine the objective function, and express it in algebraic terms.

The **objective function** represents the goal that management is trying to achieve. This goal might be to maximize total contribution margin, as in our example; alternatively, it might be to minimize total cost.

Looking at the data in our example, for each unit of X that is sold, $8 in contribution margin will be realized. For each unit of Y that is sold, $10 in contribution margin will be realized. Therefore, the total contribution margin for the firm can be expressed by the following **objective function equation:**

$$Z = \$8X + \$10Y \qquad (1)$$

where Z = the total contribution margin that will be realized with an optimal mix of X and Y, X = the number of units of product X that should be produced and sold to yield the optimal mix, and Y = the number of units of product Y that should be produced and sold to yield the optimal mix.

2. Determine the constraints under which the firm must operate, and express each constraint in algebraic terms.

A **constraint** is simply some limitation under which the company must operate, such as limited production time available or a limited amount of raw materials on hand. From the data in our example, we can identify three constraints. First, only 36 hours of production time are available. Since it requires six hours to produce one unit of X and nine hours to produce one unit of Y, this constraint can be expressed in algebraic terms in the form of a **constraint equation,** as follows:

$$6X + 9Y \leq 36 \tag{2}$$

Notice the inequality sign (≤) in the equation. This signifies that the total production of both products X and Y taken together cannot *exceed* the 36 hours available, but that this production *could* require *less* than the 36 hours available.

The second constraint deals with raw materials usage. Only 24 pounds are available each period. It takes 6 pounds of raw materials to produce one unit of X and 3 pounds to produce one unit of Y. This constraint can be expressed in the following algebraic terms:

$$6X + 3Y \leq 24 \tag{3}$$

The third constraint deals with market acceptance of product Y. The market can absorb only three units of Y each period. This constraint can be expressed as follows:

$$Y \leq 3 \tag{4}$$

3. Determine the feasible production area on a graph.

A graph containing the constraint equations [equations (2) through (4) above] is presented in Exhibit 13A–1. In placing these three equations on the graph, we have asked the questions "How much product X could be produced if all resources were allocated to it and none were allocated to product Y?" and "How much product Y could be produced if all resources were allocated to it and none were allocated to product X?" For example, consider equation (2), dealing with production capacity. A total of 36 hours of production time is available. If all 36 hours are allocated to product X, six units can be produced each period (since it takes 6 hours to produce one unit of X, and 36 hours are available). On the other hand, if all 36 hours are allocated to product Y, then four units of Y can be produced each period (since it takes 9 hours to produce one unit of Y, and 36 hours are available).

If All Production Capacity Is Allocated to Product X	If All Production Capacity Is Allocated to Product Y
$6X + 0 \leq 36$	$0 + 9Y \leq 36$
$X = 6$	$Y = 4$

Therefore, the line on the graph in Exhibit 13A–1 expressing the production constraint equation [equation (2)] extends from the six-unit point on the *X* axis to the four-unit point on the *Y* axis. Of course, production could fall *anywhere* on this constraint line; the points on the axes (6, 4) simply represent the *extremes* that would be possible.

The equation associated with the raw materials constraint [equation (3)] has been placed on the graph through a similar line of reasoning. Since 24 pounds of raw materials are available, the firm could produce either four units of X or eight units of Y if all of the raw materials were allocated to one or the other (since it takes 6 pounds to produce a unit of X and 3 pounds to produce a unit of Y). Therefore, the line expressing the equation extends from the four-unit point on the *X* axis to the eight-

EXHIBIT 13A–1
A Linear Programming Graphic Solution

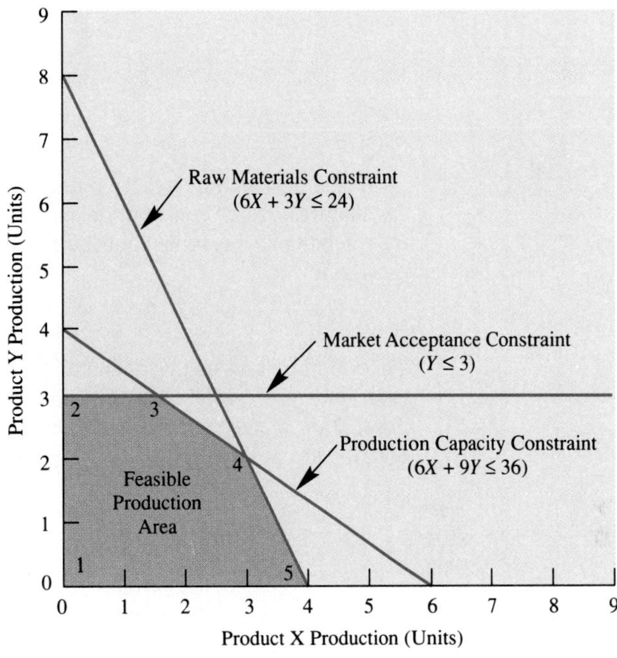

unit point on the Y axis. Again, production could fall *anywhere* on this constraint line; the points on the axes (4, 8) simply represent the *extremes* that would be possible.

Since the third constraint equation [equation (4)] concerns only product Y, the line expressing the equation on the graph does not touch the X axis at all. It extends from the three-unit point on the Y axis and runs horizontal to the X axis, thereby signifying that regardless of the number of units of X that are produced, there can never be more than three units of Y produced.

Having now plotted on the graph the lines representing the three constraint equations, we have isolated the **feasible production area.** This area has been shaded on the graph. Notice that the feasible production area is formed by the lines of the constraint equations. Each line has served to limit the size of the area to some extent. The reason, of course, is that these lines represent *constraints* under which the firm must operate, and thereby serve to *limit* the range of choices available. The firm could operate *anywhere* within the feasible production area. One point within this area, however, represents an optimal mix of products X and Y that will result in a maximization of the objective function (contribution margin). Our task now is to find precisely where that point lies.

4. Determine from the feasible production area the product mix that will maximize the objective function.

The **optimal product mix** will always fall on a *corner* of the feasible production area. If we scan the graph in Exhibit 13A–1, we can see that the feasible production area has five corners. The five corners will yield the following product mixes between X and Y (starting at the origin and going clockwise around the feasible production area):

Corner	Units Produced X	Y
1	0	0
2	0	3
3	1½	3
4	3	2
5	4	0

Which production mix is optimal? To answer this question, we will need to calculate the total contribution margin promised at each corner. We can do this by referring to the unit contribution margin data given in the objective function equation:

$$Z = \$8X + \$10Y \tag{1}$$

This equation tells us that each unit of X promises $8 of contribution margin and that each unit of Y promises $10 of contribution margin. Relating these figures to the production mixes at the five corners, we find that the following total contribution margins are possible:

X		Y		Total Contribution Margin
$8(0)	+	$10(0)	=	$ 0
8(0)	+	10(3)	=	30
8(1½)	+	10(3)	=	42
8(3)	+	10(2)	=	44
8(4)	+	10(0)	=	32

The firm should produce three units of X and two units of Y. This production mix will yield a maximum contribution margin of $44. Given the constraints under which the firm must operate, it is not possible to obtain a greater total contribution margin than this amount. Any production mix different from three units of X and two units of Y will result in *less* total contribution margin.

Why Always on a Corner?

It was stated earlier that we will always find the optimal product mix on a *corner* of the feasible production area. Why does the optimal mix always fall on a corner? Look again at the objective function equation [equation (1)]. This equation expresses a straight line with a −4/5 slope. Place a ruler on the graph in Exhibit 13A–1 extending from the 8-unit point on the *Y* axis to the 10-unit point on the *X* axis (a −4/5 slope). Now bring your ruler down toward the origin of the graph, taking care to keep it parallel to the line from which you started. Note that the first point that your ruler touches is the corner of the feasible production area showing a production mix of three units of X and two units of Y. Your ruler touches this point first because it is the farthest point from the origin in relation to the objective function line. Therefore, that point must yield the greatest total contribution margin for the firm. Any point closer to the origin would result in less total contribution margin.[3]

[3] The objective function line could coincide with one of the lines bounding the feasible production area. In this case, a number of different product combinations would be possible, each resulting in the same total contribution margin. However, our statement that the solution will always be found on a corner is still true even under these conditions, since the product mix at the corners of the line would yield the same total contribution margin as any point on the line.

Direction of the Constraint

Exhibit 13A–1 shows the direction of all the constraints to be *inward* toward the origin of the graph. The direction of the constraint will always be inward, so long as the constraint equation is stated in terms of less than or equal to (≤).

The direction of the constraint will be *outward,* away from the origin of the graph, whenever the constraint equation is stated in terms of greater than or equal to (≥). To illustrate, assume the following constraint:

X weighs 4 ounces, and Y weighs 9 ounces. X and Y must be mixed in such a way that their total weight is at least 72 ounces.

Constraint equation: $4X + 9Y \geq 72$ ounces

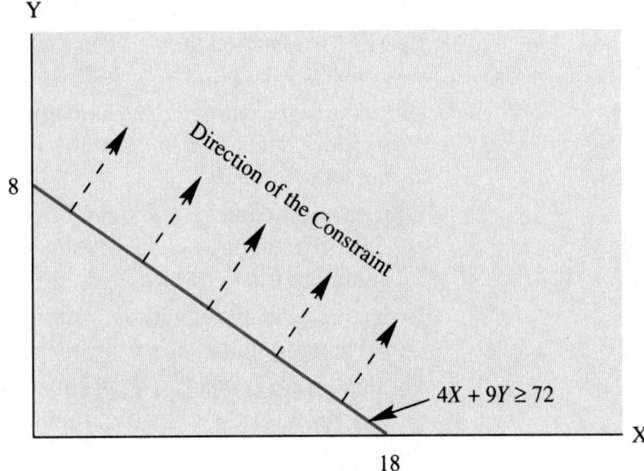

Since the direction of this constraint line is upward rather than downward, the feasible production area will be found *above* it rather than below it. Constraints expressed in terms of *greater than or equal to,* as illustrated above, can be found in any linear programming problem but are most common in *minimization* problems.

The Simplex Method

In our examples, we have dealt with only two products, X and Y. When more than two products are involved in a linear programming problem, the graphic method is no longer adequate to provide a solution. In these cases, a more powerful version of linear programming is needed. This more powerful version is commonly called the **simplex method.**

The simplex method is more complex in its operation than is the graphic method; however, the principles underlying the two methods are the same. Generally, linear programming simplex solutions are carried out on the digital computer. The mechanics of the simplex method are covered in most advanced managerial accounting texts.

Applications of Linear Programming

Linear programming has been applied to an extremely wide range of problems in many different fields. Decision makers have found that it is by far the best tool available for combining labor, materials, and equipment to the best advantage of a firm. Although the use of linear programming has been most extensive in the industrial, agricultural, and military sectors, it has also been applied to problems in economics, engineering, and the sciences. Problems to which linear programming has been successfully applied include gasoline blending, production scheduling to optimize the use of total facilities, livestock feed blending to obtain a desired nutritional mix at the least cost, the routing of boxcars to desired points at the least cost, the selection of sites for electrical transformers, forestry maintenance, and the choice of flight paths for space satellites.

KEY TERMS FOR REVIEW (APPENDIX)

Constraint A limitation under which a company must operate, such as limited machine time available or limited materials available. (p. 564)

Constraint equation An algebraic expression of one of the limitations (constraints) under which a company must operate. (p. 564)

Feasible production area The area on a linear programming graph, bounded by the constraint equations, within which production can take place. (p. 565)

Linear programming A mathematical tool designed to assist the manager in making decisions in situations where constraining or limiting factors are present. (p. 563)

Objective function A statement of the goal that management is trying to achieve. This goal might be, for example, to maximize total contribution margin or to minimize total cost. (p. 563)

Objective function equation An algebraic expression of the goal that management is trying to achieve in a linear programming analysis. (p. 563)

Optimal product mix The product mix that allows the firm to achieve the objective expressed in the objective function equation. (p. 565)

Simplex method A linear programming method that is designed to handle three or more variables in the objective function equation (for example, the optimal production mix of three or more products). (p. 567)

QUESTIONS

13–1 What is a *relevant cost?*

13–2 Define the following terms: incremental cost, opportunity cost, and sunk cost.

13–3 Are variable costs always relevant costs? Explain.

13–4 The book value of a machine (as shown on the balance sheet) is an asset to a company, but this same book value is irrelevant in decision making. Explain why this is so.

13–5 "Sunk costs are easy to spot—they're simply the fixed costs associated with a decision." Do you agree? Explain.

13–6 "Sometimes depreciation on equipment is a relevant cost in a decision, and sometimes it isn't." Do you agree? Explain.

13–7 "My neighbor offered me $25 for the use of my boat over the weekend, but I decided that renting it out is just too risky." What cost term would you use to describe the $25? Explain.

13–8 "Variable costs and differential costs mean the same thing." Do you agree? Explain.

13–9 "All future costs are relevant in decision making." Do you agree? Why?

13–10 Prentice Company is considering dropping one of its product lines. What costs of the product line would be relevant to this decision? Irrelevant?

13–11 Why is the term *avoidable cost* used in connection with product line and make or buy decisions?

13–12 "If a product line is generating a loss, then that's pretty good evidence that the product line should be discontinued." Do you agree? Explain.

13–13 What is the danger in allocating common fixed costs among product lines or other segments of an organization?

13–14 What is meant by the term *make or buy?*

13–15 How does opportunity cost enter into the make or buy decision?

13–16 Give four examples of limiting or scarce factors that might be present in an organization.

13–17 How will the relating of product line contribution margins to scarce resources help a company ensure that profits will be maximized?

13–18 Define the following terms: joint products, joint product costs, and split-off point.

13–19 From a decision-making point of view, what pitfalls are there in allocating common costs among joint products?

13–20 What guideline can be used in determining whether a joint product should be sold at the split-off point or processed further?

13–21 Airlines often offer reduced rates during certain times of the week to members of a businessperson's family if they accompany him or her on trips. How does the concept of relevant costs enter into the decision to offer reduced rates of this type?

13–22 (Appendix) Schloss Company has decided to use linear programming as a planning tool. The company can't decide whether to use contribution margin per unit or gross profit per unit in its linear programming computations. Which would you suggest? Why?

13–23 (Appendix) Define *objective function* and *constraint* as these concepts relate to linear programming.

13–24 (Appendix) Sever Company produces two products. Product A has a contribution margin per unit of $10. Product B has a contribution margin per unit of $8. Explain why a linear programming analysis might suggest that the company produce more of product B than product A. (Ample market exists for either product.)

13–25 (Appendix) What is meant by the term *feasible production area?*

EXERCISES

E13–1 Listed below are a number of "costs" incurred by Rialdo Company:

	Case 1		Case 2	
Item	Relevant	Not Relevant	Relevant	Not Relevant
a. Sales revenue				
b. Direct materials				
c. Direct labor				
d. Variable production overhead				
e. Depreciation—machine A				
f. Depreciation—machine B				
g. Fixed production overhead (general)				
h. Variable selling expense				
i. Fixed selling expense				
j. General administrative salaries				
k. Book value—machine A				
l. Market value—machine A (current resale)				
m. Market value—machine B (cost)				
n. Rate of return available from outside investments				

Required Copy the information above onto your answer sheet, and place an *X* in the appropriate column to indicate whether each item is relevant or not relevant in the following situations (requirement 1 relates to Case 1 above, and requirement 2 relates to Case 2):

1. Rialdo Company wants to purchase machine B to replace machine A (machine A will be sold). Both machines have the same capacity and a remaining life of five years. Machine B will reduce direct materials costs by 20 percent, due to less waste. Other production costs will not change.
2. Rialdo Company wants to purchase machine B to increase production and sales. Machine A will continue to be used.

E13–2 The costs associated with the acquisition and annual operation of a truck are given below:

Insurance	$1,600
Licenses	250
Taxes (vehicle)	150
Garage rent for parking (per truck) . . .	1,200
Depreciation ($9,000 ÷ 5 years).	1,800*
Gasoline, oil, tires, and repairs	0.07 per mile

* Based on obsolescence rather than on wear and tear.

Required 1. Assume that Hollings Company has purchased one truck, and that the truck has been driven 50,000 miles during the first year. Compute the average cost per mile of owning and operating the truck.
2. At the beginning of the second year, Hollings Company is unsure whether to use the truck or leave it parked in the garage and have all hauling done commercially. (The state requires the payment of vehicle taxes even if the vehicle isn't used.) What costs above are relevant to this decision?
3. Assume that the company decides to use the truck during the second year. Near year-end an order is received from a customer over 1,000 miles away. What costs above are relevant in a decision between using the truck to make the delivery and having the delivery done commercially?
4. Occasionally, the company could use two trucks at the same time. For this reason, some thought is being given to purchasing a second truck. The total miles driven would be the same as if only one truck were owned. What costs above are relevant to a decision over whether to purchase the second truck?

E13–3 Markham Company is considering the purchase of a high-speed lathe to replace a standard lathe that is now in use. Selected information on the two machines is given below:

	Standard Lathe	High-Speed Lathe
Original cost new	$40,000	$60,000
Accumulated depreciation to date. . . .	10,000	—
Current salvage value	8,000	—
Estimated cost per year to operate . . .	36,000	21,000
Remaining years of useful life	5 years	5 years

Required Prepare a computation covering the five-year period that will show the net advantage or disadvantage of purchasing the high-speed lathe. Ignore income taxes, and use only relevant costs in your analysis.

E13–4 Dexter Products, Inc., manufactures and sells a number of items, including an overnight case. The company has been experiencing losses on the overnight case for some time, as shown on the following income statement:

DEXTER PRODUCTS, INC.
Income Statement—Overnight Cases
For the Quarter Ended June 30, 19x5

Sales		$450,000
Less variable expenses:		
Variable manufacturing expenses	$130,000	
Sales commissions	48,000	
Freight-out	12,000	
Total variable expenses		190,000
Contribution margin		260,000
Less fixed expenses:		
Salary of line manager	21,000	
General factory overhead	104,000*	
Depreciation of equipment (no resale value)	36,000	
Advertising—traceable	110,000	
Insurance on inventories	9,000	
Purchasing department expenses	50,000†	
Total fixed expenses		330,000
Net loss		$ (70,000)

* Allocated on a basis of machine-hours.
† Allocated on a basis of sales dollars.

The discontinuance of the overnight cases would not affect sales of other product lines.

Required Would you recommend that the company discontinue the manufacture and sale of overnight cases? Support your answer with appropriate computations.

E13–5 Climate-Control, Inc., manufactures a variety of heating and air-conditioning units. The company is currently manufacturing all of its own component parts. An outside supplier has offered to produce and sell one component part to the company at a cost of $20 per part. In order to evaluate this offer, Climate-Control, Inc., has gathered the following information relating to its own "cost" of producing the part internally:

	Per Part	15,000 Parts per Year
Direct materials	$ 6	$ 90,000
Direct labor	8	120,000
Variable manufacturing overhead	1	15,000
Fixed manufacturing overhead, traceable	5*	75,000
Fixed manufacturing overhead, common, but allocated	10	150,000
Total cost	$30	$450,000

* 40 percent supervisory salaries; 60 percent depreciation of special equipment (no resale value).

Required

1. Assuming that the company has no alternative use for the facilities now being used to produce the part, should the outside supplier's offer be accepted? Show all computations.
2. Assuming that a new product that will generate a segment margin of $65,000 per year could be produced if the part were purchased, should the offer be accepted? Show computations.

E13–6 Rolex Company manufactures three products from a common input in a joint processing operation. Joint processing costs up to the split-off point total $100,000 per year. The company allocates these costs to the joint products on the basis of their total sales value at the split-off point. These sales values are: product X, $50,000; product Y, $90,000; and product Z, $60,000.

Each product may be sold at the split-off point or processed further. Additional processing requires no special facilities. The additional processing costs and the sales value after further processing for each product (on an annual basis) are:

Product	Additional Processing Costs	Sales Value
X	$35,000	$ 80,000
Y	40,000	150,000
Z	12,000	75,000

Required

1. Which product or products should be sold at the split-off point, and which product or products should be processed further? Show computations.
2. What general statement can be made with respect to joint costs and the decision to process further?

E13–7 Banner Company produces three products, A, B, and C. The selling price, variable costs, and contribution margin for one unit of each product follow:

	Product		
	A	B	C
Selling price	$60	$90	$80
Less variable expenses:			
Direct materials	27	14	40
Direct labor	12	32	16
Variable overhead	3	8	4
Total	42	54	60
Contribution margin	$18	$36	$20
Contribution margin ratio	30%	40%	25%

Due to a strike in the plant of one of its competitors, demand for the company's products far exceeds its capacity to produce. Management is trying to determine which product(s) to concentrate on next week in filling its backlog of orders. The direct labor rate is $8 per hour, and only 3,000 hours of labor time are available each week.

Required

1. Compute the amount of contribution margin that will be obtained per hour of labor time spent on each product.
2. Which orders would you recommend that the company work on next week—the orders for product A, product B, or product C? Show computations.

E13–8 Bill has just returned from a duck hunting trip. He has brought home eight ducks. Bill's wife detests cleaning ducks, and to discourage him from further duck hunting, she has presented him with the following cost estimate per duck:

Camper and equipment:	
Cost, $12,000; usable for eight seasons; 10 hunting trips per season	$150
Travel expense (pickup truck):	
100 miles at $0.12 per mile (gas, oil, and tires—$0.07 per mile; depreciation and insurance—$0.05 per mile)	12
Shotgun shells (two boxes)	20

Boat:	
Cost, \$320; usable for eight seasons; 10 hunting trips per season . . .	4
Fine paid for speeding on the way to the river	25
Hunting license:	
Cost, \$30 for the season; 10 hunting trips per season	3
Money lost playing poker:	
Loss, \$18 (Bill plays poker every weekend)	18
A fifth of Old Grandad:	
Cost, \$8 (used to ward off the cold)	8
Total cost.	\$240
Cost per duck (\$240 ÷ 8 ducks)	\$ 30

Required

1. Assuming that the duck hunting trip Bill has just completed is typical, what costs are relevant to a decision as to whether Bill should go duck hunting again this season?
2. Discuss the wife's computation of the cost per duck.

E13–9 Royal Company manufactures 20,000 units of part R-3 each year for use on its production line. The cost per unit for part R-3 is:

Direct materials	\$ 4.80
Direct labor	7.00
Variable overhead	3.20
Fixed overhead	10.00
Total cost per part	\$25.00

An outside supplier has offered to sell 20,000 units of part R-3 each year to Royal Company for \$23.50 per part. If Royal Company accepts this offer, the facilities now being used to manufacture part R-3 could be rented to another company at an annual rental of \$150,000. However, Royal Company has determined that \$6 of the fixed overhead being applied to part R-3 would continue even if part R-3 were purchased from the outside supplier.

Required Prepare computations to show the net dollar advantage or disadvantage of accepting the outside supplier's offer.

E13–10 Delphi Sports Equipment manufactures round, rectangular, and octagonal trampolines. Data on sales and expenses for the past month follow:

		Trampoline		
	Total	**Round**	**Rectangular**	**Octagonal**
Sales.	\$1,000,000	\$140,000	\$500,000	\$360,000
Less variable expenses	410,000	60,000	200,000	150,000
Contribution margin	590,000	80,000	300,000	210,000
Less fixed expenses:				
Advertising—traceable.	216,000	41,000	110,000	65,000
Depreciation of special equipment	95,000	20,000	40,000	35,000
Salary of line supervisor	19,000	6,000	7,000	6,000
General factory overhead*	200,000	28,000	100,000	72,000
Total fixed expenses.	530,000	95,000	257,000	178,000
Net income (loss)	\$ 60,000	\$(15,000)	\$ 43,000	\$ 32,000

* Allocated on a basis of sales dollars.

The data above are representative of the long-run trend of sales and costs. Management is concerned about the continued losses shown by the round trampolines and wants a recommendation as to whether or not the line should be discontinued. The special equipment used to produce the trampolines has no resale value.

Required

1. Should production and sale of the round trampolines be discontinued? Show computations to support your answer.
2. Recast the above data in a format that would be more usable to management in assessing the long-run profitability of the various product lines.

E13–11 (Appendix) Sweetwater Company manufactures two soft drinks, Zip and Pep. Each soft drink is manufactured in batches. The material requirements for a batch of each drink are as follows:

	Material A (gallons)	Material B (pounds)	Material C (ounces)
Zip usage per batch	10	24	40
Pep usage per batch	20	16	—
Total raw materials available each week	8,000	9,600	12,000

Each batch of Zip yields a total contribution margin of $75; each batch of Pep yields a total contribution margin of $90. The company wants to maximize contribution margin.

Required

1. Prepare equations to express the objective function and the constraints under which the company must operate.
2. Determine how many batches of Zip and how many batches of Pep should be produced each week. Use the linear programming graphic method, with Zip on the horizontal (X) axis and Pep on the vertical (Y) axis.

PROBLEMS

P13–12 **Dropping a Tour; Analysis of Operating Policy** Blueline Tours, Inc., operates a large number of tours throughout the United States. A careful study has indicated that some of the tours are not profitable, and consideration is being given to dropping these tours in order to improve the company's overall operating performance.

One such tour is a two-day Historic Mansions bus tour conducted in the southern states. An income statement from a typical Historic Mansions tour is given below:

Ticket revenue (100 seats × 40% occupancy × $75 ticket price)	$3,000	100%
Less variable expenses ($22.50 per person)	900	30
Contribution margin	2,100	70%
Less tour expenses:		
Tour promotion	600	
Salary of bus driver	350	
Fee, tour guide	800	
Fuel for bus	125	
Depreciation of bus	450*	
Liability insurance, bus	200	
Overnight parking fee, bus	50	
Room and meals, bus driver and tour guide	75	
Bus maintenance and preparation	300	
Total tour expenses	2,950	
Net loss	$ (850)	

* Based on obsolescence.

The following additional information is available about the tour:

a. Bus drivers are paid fixed annual salaries; tour guides are paid for each tour conducted.

b. The "Bus maintenance and preparation" cost above is an allocation of the salaries of mechanics and other service personnel who are responsible for keeping the company's fleet of buses in good operating condition.

Required

1. Prepare an analysis showing what the impact will be on the company's profits if this tour is discontinued.
2. The company's tour director has been criticized because only about 50 percent of the seats on Blueline's tours are being filled as compared to an average of 60 percent for the industry. The tour director has explained that Blueline's average seat occupancy could be improved considerably by eliminating about 10 percent of the tours, but that doing so would reduce profits. Explain how this could happen.

P13–13 Relevant Cost Analysis; Book Value Natural Products, Inc., is a manufacturer of various herb and vitamin capsules. One year ago the company purchased a new capsule press at a cost of $84,000. The press has been very satisfactory, but the company's production manager has just received information on a computer-operated press that is vastly superior to the press that has been purchased. The computer-operated press would slash annual operating costs by 70 percent, as shown below:

	Present Press	Proposed New Press
Purchase cost new	$84,000	$110,000
Estimated useful life new	6 years	5 years
Annual straight-line depreciation . . .	$14,000	$ 22,000
Remaining book value	70,000	—
Salvage value now	30,000	—
Annual costs to operate	40,000	12,000

The production manager would like to purchase the new press, but her enthusiasm has been dampened considerably by the following computation:

Remaining book value of the old press . . .	$70,000
Less salvage value of the old press	30,000
Net loss from disposal	$40,000

After considering the matter, the production manager commented, "There's no way we can buy that new capsule press. If the front office found out that we took a loss on the old press, somebody's head would roll."

Sales of capsule products are expected to remain unchanged at $200,000 per year, and selling and administrative expenses are expected to be $116,000 per year, regardless of which press is used.

Required

1. Prepare a summary income statement covering the next five years, assuming:
   a. That the new press is not purchased.
   b. That the new press is purchased.
2. Determine the desirability of purchasing the new press, using only relevant costs in your analysis.

P13–14 Sell or Process Further Decision (Prepared from a situation suggested by Professor John W. Hardy.) Lone Star Meat Packers is a major processor of beef and other meat products. The company has a large amount of T-bone steak on hand, and it is trying to decide whether to sell the T-bone steaks as they are initially cut or to process them further into filet mignon and the New York cut.

If the T-bone steaks are sold as initially cut, the company figures that a 1 pound T-bone steak would yield the following profit:

Selling price ($2.25 per pound) . . .	$2.25
Less joint product cost.	1.80
Profit per pound.	$0.45

Instead of being sold as initially cut, the T-bone steaks could be further processed into filet mignon and New York cut steaks. Cutting one side of a T-bone steak provides the filet mignon, and cutting the other side provides the New York cut. One 16-ounce T-bone steak thus cut will yield one 6-ounce filet mignon and one 8-ounce New York cut; the remaining ounces are waste. The cost of processing the T-bone steaks into these cuts is $0.25 per pound. The filet mignon can be sold for $4 per pound, and the New York cut can be sold for $2.80 per pound.

Required

1. Determine the profit per pound from further processing the T-bone steaks.
2. Would you recommend that the T-bone steaks be sold as initially cut or processed further? Why?

P13–15 Make or Buy Analysis "That old equipment for producing subassemblies is worn out," said Paul Taylor, president of Timkin Company. "We need to make a decision quickly." The company is trying to decide whether it should purchase new equipment and continue to make its subassemblies internally or whether it should discontinue production of its subassemblies and purchase them from an outside supplier. The alternatives are:

Alternative 1: New equipment for producing the subassemblies can be purchased at a cost of $350,000. The equipment would have a five-year useful life (the company uses straight-line depreciation) and a $50,000 salvage value.

Alternative 2: The subassemblies can be purchased from an outside supplier who has offered to provide them for $8 each under a five-year contract.

Timkin Company's present costs per unit of producing the subassemblies internally (with the old equipment) are given below. These costs are based on a current activity level of 40,000 subassemblies per year:

Direct materials.	$ 2.75
Direct labor	4.00
Variable overhead.	0.60
Fixed overhead ($0.75 supervision, $0.90 depreciation, and $2 general company overhead)	3.65
Total cost per unit	$11.00

The new equipment would be more efficient and, according to the manufacturer, would reduce direct labor costs and variable overhead costs by 25 percent. Supervision cost ($30,000 per year) and direct materials cost per unit would not be affected by the new equipment. The new equipment's capacity would be 60,000 subassemblies per year. The company has no other use for the space now being used to produce subassemblies.

Required

1. The president is unsure what the company should do and would like an analysis showing what unit costs and what total costs would be under each of the two alternatives given above. Assume that 40,000 subassemblies are needed each year. Which course of action would you recommend to the president?

2. Would your recommendation in (1) above be the same if the company's needs were: *(a)* 50,000 subassemblies per year, or *(b)* 60,000 subassemblies per year? Show computations in good form.
3. What other factors would you recommend that the company consider before making a decision?

P13–16 Relevant Cost Potpourri Unless otherwise indicated, each of the following parts is independent. In all cases, show computations to support your answer.

1. Boyle's Home Center has two departments, A and B. The most recent income statement for the company follows:

	Total	Department A	Department B
Sales	$5,000,000	$1,000,000	$4,000,000
Less variable expenses	1,900,000	300,000	1,600,000
Contribution margin	3,100,000	700,000	2,400,000
Less fixed expenses	2,700,000	900,000	1,800,000
Net income (loss)	$ 400,000	$ (200,000)	$ 600,000

A study indicates that $370,000 of the fixed expenses being charged to Department A are sunk costs and allocated costs that will continue even if Department A is dropped. In addition, the elimination of Department A would result in a 10 percent decrease in the sales of Department B. If Department A is dropped, what will be the effect on the income of the company as a whole?

2. Morrell Company produces several products from the processing of krypton, a rare mineral. Material and processing costs total $30,000 per ton, one third of which is allocable to product A. The amount of product A received from a ton of krypton can either be sold at the split-off point or processed further at a cost of $13,000 and then sold for $60,000. The sales value of product A at the split-off point is $40,000. Should product A be processed further or sold at the split-off point?
3. Shelby Company produces three products, X, Y, and Z. Cost and revenue characteristics of the three products follow (per unit):

	Product X	Product Y	Product Z
Selling price	$80	$56	$70
Less variable expenses:			
Direct materials	24	15	9
Labor and overhead	24	27	40
Total variable expenses	48	42	49
Contribution margin	$32	$14	$21
Contribution margin ratio	40%	25%	30%

Demand for the company's products is very strong, with far more orders on hand each month than the company has raw materials available to produce. The same material is used in each product. The material costs $3 per pound, with a maximum of 5,000 pounds available each month. Which orders would you advise the company to accept first, those for X, for Y, or for Z? Which orders second? Third?

4. For many years, Diehl Company has produced a small electrical part that it uses in the production of its standard line of diesel tractors. The company's cost of producing one part, based on a production level of 60,000 parts per year, is:

	Per Part	Total
Direct materials	$ 4.00	
Direct labor	2.75	
Variable overhead	0.50	
Fixed overhead, direct	3.00	$180,000
Fixed overhead, common (allocated on a basis of labor-hours)	2.25	135,000
Total cost per part	$12.50	

An outside supplier has offered to supply the electrical parts to the Diehl Company for only $10 per part. The company has determined that one third of the direct fixed costs represent supervisory salaries and other costs that can be eliminated if the parts are purchased. The other two thirds of the direct fixed costs represent depreciation of special equipment that has no resale value. The decision would have no effect on the common fixed costs of the company, and the space being used to produce the parts would otherwise be idle. Show the dollar advantage or disadvantage of accepting the supplier's offer.

5. Glade Company produces a single product. The cost of producing and selling a single unit of this product at the company's normal activity level of 8,000 units per month is:

Direct materials	$2.50
Direct labor	3.00
Variable overhead	0.50
Fixed overhead	4.25
Variable selling and administrative expenses . . .	1.50
Fixed selling and administrative expenses	2.00

The normal selling price is $15 per unit. The company's capacity is 10,000 units per month. An order has been received from an overseas source for 2,000 units at a price of $12 per unit. This order would not disturb regular sales. If the order is accepted, by how much will monthly profits be increased or decreased? (The order would not change the company's total fixed costs.)

6. Refer to the data in (5) above. Assume that the company has 500 units of this product left over from last year, which are inferior to the current model. The units must be sold through regular channels at reduced prices. What unit cost figure is relevant for establishing a minimum selling price for these units? Explain.

P13–17 Utilization of Scarce Resources; Product Mix Winkle Creations, Inc., manufactures a line of stuffed animals and a stuffed animal do-it-yourself kit. Sales are increasing, and management is concerned that the company may not have sufficient capacity to meet the expected demand for the coming year. The following sales and production data are available for planning purposes:

		Per Unit		
Product	Estimated Demand Next Year (units)	Selling Price	Direct Materials	Direct Labor
Monkey	80,000	$20.00	$6.91	$5.60
Teddy bear.	105,000	12.50	4.30	3.20
Panda	60,000	9.00	3.90	2.40
Beagle	48,000	14.75	6.50	4.00
Do-it-yourself kit	200,000	8.50	4.70	1.60

The following additional information is available:

a. Because of strong competition, the company feels that it can't increase its selling prices above those indicated.
b. The direct labor rate is $8 per hour; this rate is expected to remain unchanged during the coming year.
c. Fixed overhead costs total $640,000 per year. Variable overhead costs are equal to 25 percent of direct labor costs.
d. The company's plant has a capacity of 160,000 direct labor-hours per year on a single-shift basis. The company's present employees and equipment can produce all five products.
e. The company's present inventory of finished products is nominal and can be ignored.
f. All of the company's nonmanufacturing costs are fixed.

Required

1. Determine the contribution margin for a unit of each product.
2. Determine the contribution margin that will be realized per direct labor-hour expended on each product.
3. Prepare a schedule showing the total direct labor-hours that will be required to produce the units estimated to be sold during the coming year.
4. Examine the data that you have computed in (1) through (3). Indicate the product and the number of units to be increased or decreased so that total production time is equal to the 160,000 production hours available.
5. Assume that the company does not want to reduce sales of any product. Identify ways in which the company could obtain the additional output and any problems that might be encountered.

P13–18 **Discontinuance of a Department** "We've got to eliminate Department A," said Rob Hunter, vice president of Pringle's Department Store. "It's a drag on the entire organization. If anyone needs proof, just look at last quarter's income statement." The statement to which Mr. Hunter was referring is shown below:

PRINGLE'S DEPARTMENT STORE
Income Statement
For the Quarter Ending March 31, 19x5

		Department		
	Total	**A**	**B**	**C**
Sales	$1,500,000	$280,000	$700,000	$520,000
Less variable expenses	903,600	156,000	435,600	312,000
Contribution margin	596,400	124,000	264,400	208,000
Less fixed expenses:				
Direct advertising	97,500	26,000	40,000	31,500
General advertising*	30,000	5,600	14,000	10,400
Salaries	136,000	36,000	58,000	42,000
Rent on building†	76,500	19,000	31,500	26,000
Utilities	30,900	8,000	13,600	9,300
Employment taxes‡	20,400	5,400	8,700	6,300
Depreciation of fixtures	40,000	10,800	16,300	12,900
Insurance on inventory and fixtures	3,700	1,200	1,400	1,100
General office expenses	60,000	20,000	20,000	20,000
Service department expenses	45,000	15,000	15,000	15,000
Total fixed expenses	540,000	147,000	218,500	174,500
Net income (loss)	$ 56,400	$(23,000)	$ 45,900	$ 33,500

* Allocated on a basis of sales dollars.
† Allocated on a basis of space occupied.
‡ Based on salaries paid directly in each department.

You have been assigned the task of making a recommendation to the president as to whether or not Department A should be eliminated. You have gathered the following information:

a. All departments are housed in the same building. The store leases the entire building at a fixed annual rental rate.
b. One of the employees in Department A is Mary Collins, who has been with the company for many years. If Department A is eliminated, Ms. Collins will be transferred to another department. Her salary is $4,000 per quarter.
c. If Department A is eliminated, the fixtures in the department will be transferred to the other departments.
d. If Department A is eliminated, the utilities bill will be reduced by about $7,000 per quarter.
e. One fourth of the insurance in Department A relates to the fixtures in the department; the remainder relates to the department's merchandise inventory.
f. The company has two service departments—purchasing and warehouse. If Department A is eliminated, the company can discharge one full-time and one part-time person from these departments. The combined salaries and other employment costs of these employees is $5,300 per quarter. General office expenses will not change.

Required

1. Assume that the company has no alternative use for the space now being occupied by Department A. Prepare computations to show whether or not the department should be eliminated. (You may assume that eliminating Department A would have no effect on the sales of the other departments.)
2. Assume that the space being occupied by Department A is quite valuable and could be subleased at a rental rate of $60,000 per quarter. Would you advise the company to eliminate Department A and sublease the space? Show computations.

P13–19 Selected Relevant Cost Questions Barker Company has a single product called a Zet. The company normally produces and sells 80,000 Zets each year at a selling price of $40 per unit. The company's unit costs at this level of activity are given below:

Direct materials	$ 9.50	
Direct labor	10.00	
Variable overhead	2.80	
Fixed overhead	5.00	($400,000 total)
Variable selling expenses	1.70	
Fixed selling expenses	4.50	($360,000 total)
Total cost per unit	$33.50	

A number of questions relating to the production and sale of Zets are given below. Each question is independent.

Required

1. Assume that Barker Company has sufficient capacity to produce 100,000 Zets each year. The company could increase sales by 25 percent above the present 80,000 units each year if it were willing to increase the fixed selling expenses by $150,000. Would the increased fixed expenses be justified?
2. Assume again that Barker Company has sufficient capacity to produce 100,000 Zets each year. The company has an opportunity to sell 20,000 units in an overseas market. Import duties, foreign permits, and other special costs associated with the order would total $14,000. The only selling costs that would be associated with the order would be $1.50 per unit shipping cost. You have been asked by the president to compute the per unit break-even price on this order.
3. One of the materials used in the production of Zets is obtained from a foreign

supplier. Civil unrest in the supplier's country has caused a cutoff in material shipments that is expected to last for three months. Barker Company has enough of the material on hand to continue to operate at 25 percent of normal levels for the three-month period. As an alternative, the company could close the plant down entirely for the three months. Closing the plant would reduce fixed overhead costs by 40 percent during the three-month period; the fixed selling costs would continue at two thirds of their normal level while the plant was closed. What would be the dollar advantage or disadvantage of closing the plant for the three-month period?

4. The company has 500 Zets on hand that were produced last month and have small blemishes. Due to the blemishes, it will be impossible to sell these units at the regular price. If the company wishes to sell them through regular distribution channels, what unit cost figure is relevant for setting a minimum selling price?
5. An outside manufacturer has offered to produce Zets for Barker Company and to ship them directly to Barker's customers. If Barker Company accepts this offer, the facilities that it uses to produce Zets would be idle; however, fixed overhead costs would continue at 30 percent of their present level. Since the outside manufacturer would pay for all the costs of shipping, the variable selling costs would be reduced by 60 percent. Compute the unit cost figure that is relevant for comparison against whatever quoted price is received from the outside manufacturer.

P13–20 Shutdown versus Continue-to-Operate Decision (Note to the student: This type of decision is similar to that of dropping a product line, and the portion of the text dealing with the latter topic should be referred to, if needed.)

Hallas Company manufactures a fast-bonding glue in its Northwest plant. The company normally produces and sells 40,000 gallons of the glue each month. This glue, which is known as MJ-7, is used in the wood industry in the manufacture of plywood. The selling price of MJ-7 is $35 per gallon, variable expenses are $21 per gallon, fixed overhead costs in the plant total $230,000 per month, and the fixed selling costs total $310,000 per month.

Strikes in the mills that purchase the bulk of the MJ-7 glue have caused Hallas Company's sales to temporarily drop to only 11,000 gallons per month. Hallas Company's management estimates that the strikes will last for about two months, after which sales of MJ-7 should return to normal. Due to the current low level of sales, however, Hallas Company's management is thinking about closing down the Northwest plant during the two months that the strikes are on.

If Hallas Company does close down the Northwest plant, it is estimated that fixed overhead costs can be reduced to only $170,000 per month and that fixed selling costs can be reduced by 10 percent. Start-up costs at the end of the shutdown period would total $14,000. Since Hallas Company uses JIT production methods, no inventories are on hand.

Required

1. Assuming that the strikes continue for two months, as estimated, would you recommend that Hallas Company close the Northwest plant? Show computations in good form to support your answer.
2. At what level of sales (in gallons) for the two-month period would Hallas Company be indifferent between closing the plant or keeping it open? Show computations. (Hint: This is a type of break-even analysis, except that the fixed cost portion of your break-even computation should include only those fixed costs that are relevant [i.e., avoidable] over the two-month period.)

P13–21 Discontinuance of a Store Thrifty Markets, Inc., operates three stores in a large metropolitan area. The company's segmented income statement for the last quarter is given on the next page:

THRIFTY MARKETS, INC.
Income Statement
For the Quarter Ended March 31, 19x6

	Total	Uptown Store	Downtown Store	Westpark Store
Sales	$2,500,000	$900,000	$600,000	$1,000,000
Cost of goods sold	1,450,000	513,000	372,000	565,000
Gross margin	1,050,000	387,000	228,000	435,000
Operating expenses:				
Selling expenses:				
Direct advertising	118,500	40,000	36,000	42,500
General advertising*	20,000	7,200	4,800	8,000
Sales salaries	157,000	52,000	45,000	60,000
Delivery salaries	30,000	10,000	10,000	10,000
Store rent	215,000	70,000	65,000	80,000
Depreciation of store fixtures	46,950	18,300	8,800	19,850
Depreciation of delivery equipment	27,000	9,000	9,000	9,000
Total selling expenses	614,450	206,500	178,600	229,350
Administrative expenses:				
Store management salaries	63,000	20,000	18,000	25,000
General office salaries*	50,000	18,000	12,000	20,000
Utilities	89,800	31,000	27,200	31,600
Insurance on fixtures and inventory	25,500	8,000	9,000	8,500
Employment taxes	36,000	12,000	10,200	13,800
General office expenses—other*	25,000	9,000	6,000	10,000
Total administrative expenses	289,300	98,000	82,400	108,900
Total operating expenses	903,750	304,500	261,000	338,250
Net income (loss)	$ 146,250	$ 82,500	$ (33,000)	$ 96,750

* Allocated on a basis of sales dollars.

Management is very concerned about the Downtown Store's inability to show a profit, and consideration is being given to closing the store. The company has asked you to make a recommendation as to what course of action should be taken. The following additional information is available on the store:

a. The manager of the store has been with the company for many years; he would be retained and transferred to another position in the company if the store were closed. His salary is $6,000 per quarter.

b. The lease on the building housing the Downtown Store can be broken with no penalty.

c. The fixtures being used in the Downtown Store would be transferred to the other two stores if the Downtown Store were closed.

d. The company's employment taxes are 12 percent of salaries.

e. A single delivery crew serves all three stores. One delivery person could be discharged if the Downtown Store were closed; this person's salary is $3,000 per quarter.

f. One third of the Downtown Store's insurance relates to its fixtures.

g. The general office salaries and other expenses relate to the general management of Thrifty Markets, Inc. The employee in the general office who is responsible for the Downtown Store's accounting records would be discharged if the store were closed. This employee's salary is $5,000 per quarter.

Required

1. Prepare a schedule showing the change in revenues and expenses and the impact on overall company net income that would result if the Downtown Store were closed.

2. Based on your computations in (1) above, what recommendation would you make to the management of Thrifty Markets, Inc.?
3. Assume that if the Downtown Store were closed, sales in the Uptown Store would increase by $200,000 per quarter due to loyal customers shifting their buying to the Uptown Store. The Uptown Store has ample capacity to handle the increased sales, and its gross profit rate is 43 percent. What effect would these factors have on your recommendation concerning the Downtown Store? Show computations.

P13–22 **Make or Buy Decision** Rolex Company manufactures a variety of ballpoint pens. The company has just received an offer from an outside supplier to provide the ink cartridge for the company's Zippo pen line, at a price of $0.48 per dozen cartridges. The company is interested in this offer, since its own production of cartridges is at capacity.

Rolex Company estimates that if the supplier's offer were accepted, the direct labor and variable overhead costs of the Zippo pen line would be reduced by 10 percent and the direct materials cost would be reduced by 20 percent.

Under present operations, Rolex Company manufactures all of its own pens from start to finish. The Zippo pens are sold through wholesalers at $4 per box. Each box contains one dozen pens. Fixed overhead costs charged to the Zippo pen line total $50,000 each year. (The same equipment and facilities are used to produce several pen lines.) The present cost of producing one dozen Zippo pens (one box) is given below:

Direct materials	$1.50
Direct labor	1.00
Manufacturing overhead	0.80*
Total cost	$3.30

* Includes both variable and fixed overhead, based on capacity production of 100,000 boxes of pens each year.

Required

1. Should Rolex Company accept the outside supplier's offer? Show computations.
2. What is the maximum price that Rolex Company would be willing to pay the outside supplier per dozen cartridges?
3. Due to the bankruptcy of a competitor, assume that Rolex Company expects to sell 150,000 boxes of pens next year. Since the company only has enough capacity to produce 100,000 boxes per year, $30,000 in added fixed expenses would be needed each year if the company wanted to expand its capacity to 150,000 boxes. Under these circumstances, should the outside supplier's offer be accepted? For how many boxes of Zippo cartridges? Show computations to support your answer.
4. What nonquantifiable factors should the company consider before accepting the outside supplier's offer?

P13–23 **Sell or Process Further Decision** Cum-Clean Corporation produces a variety of cleaning compounds and solutions for both industrial and household use. While most of its products are processed independently, a few are related, such as the company's Grit 337 and its Sparkle silver polish.

Grit 337 is a coarse cleaning powder with many industrial uses. It costs $1.60 a pound to make, and it has a selling price of $2 a pound. A small portion of the annual production of Grit 337 is retained in the factory for further processing in the mixing department, where it is combined with several other ingredients to form a paste that is marketed as Sparkle silver polish. The silver polish sells for $4 per jar.

This further processing requires one-fourth pound of Grit 337 per jar of silver polish. Other ingredients added and labor costs involved in the processing of a jar of silver polish are:

Other ingredients . . .	$0.65
Direct labor.	1.48
Total cost	$2.13

Overhead costs associated with the processing of the silver polish are:

Variable overhead cost	25 percent of direct labor cost
Fixed overhead cost (per month):	
Production supervisor.	$1,600
Depreciation of mixing equipment . . .	1,400

The production supervisor has no duties other than to oversee production of the silver polish. The mixing equipment is special-purpose equipment acquired specifically to produce the silver polish. It has only a nominal resale value.

Advertising costs for the silver polish total $4,000 per month. Variable selling costs associated with the silver polish are 7.5 percent of sales.

Due to a recent decline in the demand for silver polish, the company is wondering whether its continued production is advisable. The sales manager feels that it would be more profitable to just sell all of the Grit 337 as a cleaning powder.

Required

1. What is the incremental contribution margin per jar from further processing of Grit 337 into silver polish?
2. What is the minimum number of jars of silver polish that must be sold each month to justify the continued processing of Grit 337 into silver polish? Show all computations in good form.

(CMA, Heavily Adapted)

P13–24 Break Even; Eliminating an Unprofitable Line Kathy Woods, president of the Eastern Company, wants guidance on the advisability of eliminating product C, one of the company's three similar products, in hope of improving the company's overall operating performance. The company's three products are manufactured in a single plant and occupy roughly equal amounts of floor space. Below is a condensed statement of operating income for the company and for product C for the quarter ended October 31, 19x6:

	All Three Products	Product C
Sales	$2,900,000	$315,000
Cost of sales:		
Raw materials	515,000	133,850
Direct labor	1,305,000	72,000
Fringe benefits (15% of labor)	195,750	10,800
Royalties (1% of product C sales).	3,500	3,150
Building rent and maintenance	6,000	4,000
Factory supplies	15,000	2,000
Depreciation (straight line)	75,200	19,100
Electrical power—machines	29,300	3,600
Total cost of sales	2,144,750	248,500
Gross margin	755,250	66,500
Selling and administrative expenses:		
Sales commissions	120,000	15,000
Officers' salaries	31,500	10,500
Product line managers' salaries	14,000	5,300
Fringe benefits (15% of salaries and commissions)	24,825	4,620
Shipping	81,225	9,350
Advertising.	227,000	37,300
Total selling and administrative expenses . . .	498,550	82,070
Net operating income (loss)	$ 256,700	$(15,570)

Inventories carried by the company are small and can be ignored. Each element of cost is entirely fixed or variable within the relevant range. The dropping of product C would have little (if any) effect on sales of the other two product lines.

Required

1. Before a decision is made on whether product C should be dropped, Ms. Woods would first like to know the overall break-even point for product C (in sales dollars), given the cost and revenue data shown above.
2. Would you recommend to Ms. Woods that product C be dropped? Prepare appropriate computations to support your answer. You may assume that the plant space now being used to produce product C would otherwise be idle. The equipment being used to produce product C has no resale value.

(CPA, Adapted)

P13–25 Accept or Reject Special Orders; Make or Buy; Utilization of Scarce Resources Each of the following parts is independent, unless stated otherwise.

1. Saxon Company produces a single product, Awls. Operating at capacity, the company can produce 50,000 Awls per year. Costs associated with this level of production and sales are given below:

	Unit	Total
Direct materials	$12	$ 600,000
Direct labor	3	150,000
Variable overhead	1	50,000
Fixed overhead	5	250,000
Variable selling expenses . . .	2	100,000
Fixed selling expenses	4	200,000
Total cost	$27	$1,350,000

The Awls sell for $32 each. A government agency would like to make a one-time-only purchase of 10,000 Awls. The agency would pay a fixed fee of $4 per unit, and in addition it would reimburse Saxon Company for all costs of production (variable and fixed) associated with the units. There would be no variable selling expenses associated with this order. You may assume that due to a recession, sales of Awls have slumped to only 40,000 units per year. If Saxon Company accepts the agency's business, by how much will profits be increased or decreased from what they would be if only 40,000 units were produced and sold?

2. Assume the same situation as that described in (1) above, except that the company is currently selling 50,000 Awls each year through regular channels. Thus, accepting the agency's business would require giving up regular sales of 10,000 units. If the agency's business is accepted, by how much will profits be increased or decreased from what they would be if the 10,000 units were sold through regular channels?
3. Dexter Company has been producing two bearings, D10 and D15, for use on its assembly line. Data relating to these bearings are presented below:

	D10	D15
Machine-hours required per unit . . .	2.5	4.0
Standard cost per unit:		
Direct materials	$ 7.00	$10.00
Direct labor	4.00	6.00
Manufacturing overhead:		
Variable*	2.00	3.00
Fixed†	5.00	8.00
Total cost per unit	$18.00	$27.00

* Variable overhead is applied on a basis of direct labor-hours.
† Fixed overhead is applied on a basis of machine-hours. One fourth of the fixed overhead consists of supervisory salaries for direct supervision of production of the bearings. The remainder consists of general factory overhead.

Dexter Company needs 8,000 units of the D10 bearing and 15,000 units of the D15 bearing each year. Dexter's management is thinking about devoting additional machine time to other product lines. If it does devote the extra time, only 60,000 machine-hours will be available each year for the production of bearings. An outside company has offered to sell Dexter Company all the bearings it needs at a price of $17 for the D10 and a price of $24 for the D15. The outside supplier will not accept an order for only part of Dexter's needs, so the 60,000 available machine-hours will be idle if Dexter purchases its bearings outside. What will be the net benefit or loss per unit for the D10 and the D15 if Dexter accepts the outside supplier's offer for all of its bearing needs?

4. Refer to the data in (3) above. Assume that a decision has been made to devote additional machine time to other product lines, and assume that the outside supplier has agreed to accept an order for only part of Dexter's bearing needs. Dexter Company wants to schedule the 60,000 available machine-hours in such a way as to minimize its total costs. One supervisor with an annual salary of $24,000 would be needed to oversee production of the bearings. How many units of the D10 and the D15 bearings should be manufactured in the available facilities and how many units should be purchased from the outside supplier? Be prepared to show computations and present reasoning in class to support your answer.

P13–26 Special Order; Relevant Costs Fred White operates a small machine shop. He manufactures one standard product that is available from many similar businesses, and he also manufactures products to customer order. His accountant prepared the annual income statement shown below:

	Custom Sales	Standard Sales	Total
Sales	$50,000	$25,000	$75,000
Materials used	9,100	8,400	17,500
Labor	20,000	9,000	29,000
Depreciation	6,300	3,600	9,900
Power used	2,000	900	2,900
Rent	6,000	1,000	7,000
Heat and light	600	100	700
Total costs	44,000	23,000	67,000
Net profit	$ 6,000	$ 2,000	$ 8,000

The depreciation charges are for machines used in the respective product lines. Mr. White has found that power used consistently equals 10 percent of labor cost. The rent is for the building space, which has been leased for 10 years at $7,000 per year. The rent and heat and light are apportioned to the product lines based on amount of floor space occupied. All other costs are current expenses identified with the product line causing them.

A valued custom-parts customer has asked Mr. White if he would manufacture 5,000 special units for her. Mr. White is working at capacity and would have to give up some other business in order to take this business. He can't renege on custom orders already agreed to, but he could reduce the output of his standard product about one half for one year while producing the specially requested custom part. The customer is willing to pay $7.25 for each part. The material cost will be about $2 per unit, and the labor cost will be $3.60 per unit. Mr. White will have to spend $2,000 for a special device that will be discarded when the job is done.

Required

1. Calculate the opportunity cost of taking the special order.
2. Would you advise Mr. White to take the order? Show appropriate computations to support your answer.

3. What nonquantitative factors should Mr. White consider before taking the special order?

(CMA, Adapted)

P13–27 **Optimum Production Mix to Maximize Profits** (Appendix) Ron Green has just retired and is anxious to open a small pottery business to occupy his time. Mr. Green has decided to produce just two items initially—pots and bowls. The local pottery supply house has indicated that because of shortages in supplies, Mr. Green can be allowed only 80 pounds of high-quality clay and only 11¼ gallons of glazing material each week.

Mr. Green has purchased a used kiln that he feels can be operated about 60 hours per week. His wife will package all finished products; she will have a maximum of 11 hours per week to work for the pottery business. Mr. Green has determined the following additional information:

Operation	Item Needed	Per Batch Pots	Per Batch Bowls
Molding	Clay	8 lbs.	5 lbs.
Glazing	Glaze	5 qts.	3 qts.
Firing.	—	4 hrs.	6 hrs.
Packaging	—	1 hr.	1 hr.

Mr. Green feels that no more than nine batches of bowls can be sold each week. The pots yield $50 in profits per batch, and the bowls yield $40 per batch. Mr. Green wishes to maximize his profits.

Required

1. Prepare linear programming equations to express the objective function and each of the constraints. Identify pots as X and bowls as Y.
2. Prepare a linear programming graph to determine how many batches of pots and how many batches of bowls should be produced each week. Place pots on the horizontal (X) axis and bowls on the vertical (Y) axis.

P13–28 **Linear Programming—Multiple Departments** (Appendix) Markov Company manufactures two industrial products—X–10, which sells for $90 a unit, and Y–12, which sells for $85 a unit. Each product is processed through both of the company's manufacturing departments. The limited availability of labor, material, and equipment capacity has restricted the ability of the firm to meet the demand for its products. The production department believes that linear programming can be used to routinize the production schedule for the two products.

The following data are available to the production department:

	Amount Required per Unit X-10	Amount Required per Unit Y-12
Direct material: Weekly supply limited to 1,800 pounds at $12 per pound	4 pounds	2 pounds
Direct labor:		
Department 1—weekly supply limited to 10 people at 40 hours each at an hourly rate of $6.	⅔ hour	1 hour
Department 2—weekly supply limited to 15 people at 40 hours each at an hourly rate of $8.	1¼ hours	1 hour
Machine time:		
Department 1—weekly capacity limited to 250 hours	½ hour	½ hour
Department 2—weekly capacity limited to 300 hours	0 hours	1 hour

The overhead costs for Markov Company are accumulated on a plant-wide basis. Overhead is assigned to products on the basis of the number of direct labor-hours required to manufacture them. This base is appropriate for overhead assignment because most of the variable overhead costs vary as a function of labor time. The estimated overhead cost per direct labor-hour is:

Variable overhead cost	$ 6
Fixed overhead cost.	6
Total overhead cost per direct labor-hour . . .	$12

The company wants to produce the mix of the two products that will allow it to maximize total contribution margin.

The production department formulated the following equations for the linear programming statement of the problem:

X = number of units of X–10 to be produced
Y = number of units of Y–12 to be produced

Objective function equation to minimize costs:

$$\text{Minimize:} \quad Z = \$85X + \$62Y$$

Constraint equations:

$$\text{Material:} \quad 4X + 2Y \leqslant 1{,}800 \text{ pounds}$$
$$\text{Department 1 labor:} \quad \tfrac{2}{3}X + Y \leqslant 400 \text{ hours}$$
$$\text{Department 2 labor:} \quad 1\tfrac{1}{4}X + Y \leqslant 600 \text{ hours}$$

Required

1. The linear programming equations as prepared by the company's production department contain a number of errors and omissions. Examine these equations, and explain what errors and omissions have been made.
2. Prepare the proper equations for the linear programming statement of the company's problem.
3. Using the equations that you prepared in (2) above, prepare a linear programming graphic solution to determine how many units of X–10 and Y–12 should be produced each week. (Place product X–10 on the horizontal axis and product Y–12 on the vertical axis.)

(CMA, Adapted)

P13–29 Optimal Candy Mixture; Cost Minimization (Appendix) (Based on a situation described by Miller and Starr, *Executive Decisions and Operations Research,* pp. 217–22.) Sterling Candy Company produces and sells a box of candy made up of caramels and creams. The company would like to find the optimal mixture of the two kinds of candy, in order to meet the specifications per box as outlined in the following table:

	Caramels	Creams	Per Box
Weight per piece	1.2 ozs.	0.6 ozs.	18.0 ozs. or more
Number of pieces	?	?	25 or more
Cost per piece	$0.03	$0.02	$0.66 maximum cost

The company wants at least six caramels in each box of candy. The company can produce either caramels or creams in unlimited numbers, so the objective is to minimize the cost of the candy going into each box. The mixture will not affect the selling price per box.

Required

1. Prepare equations expressing the objective function and the constraints under which the company must operate.

2. Determine the mix of caramels and creams that will minimize the total cost per box of candy. Use a linear programming graph, with caramels on the horizontal axis *(X)* and creams on the vertical axis *(Y)*.

CASES

C13–30 Sell or Process Further Decision Midwest Mills has a plant that can either mill wheat grain into a cracked wheat cereal or further mill the cracked wheat into flour. The company can sell all the cracked wheat cereal that it can produce at a selling price of $490 per ton. In the past, the company has sold only part of its cracked wheat as cereal and has retained the rest for further milling into the flour product. The flour has been selling for $700 per ton, but recently the price has become unstable and has dropped to $625 per ton. The costs and revenues associated with a ton of flour follow:

		Per Ton of Flour
Selling price		$625
Cost to manufacture:		
Raw materials:		
Enrichment materials	$ 80	
Cracked wheat	470	
Total raw materials	550	
Direct labor	20	
Manufacturing overhead	60	630
Manufacturing profit (loss)		$ (5)

Because of the weak price for flour, the sales manager believes that the company should discontinue the milling of flour and concentrate its entire milling capacity on the milling of cracked wheat to sell as cereal. (The same milling equipment is used for both products.) Current cost and revenue data on the cracked wheat cereal follow:

		Per Ton of Cracked Wheat
Selling price		$490
Cost to manufacture:		
Wheat grain	$390	
Direct labor	20	
Manufacturing overhead	60	470
Manufacturing profit		$ 20

The sales manager argues that since the present $625 per ton price for the flour results in a $5 per ton loss, the milling of flour should be discontinued and should not be resumed until the price per ton rises above $630.

The company assigns overhead cost to the two products on the basis of direct labor-hours. The same amount of time is required to either mill a ton of cracked wheat or to further mill a ton of cracked wheat into flour. Because of the nature of the plant, virtually all overhead costs are fixed. Materials and labor costs are variable.

Required

1. Do you agree with the sales manager that the company should discontinue milling flour and use the entire milling capacity to mill cracked wheat if the price of flour remains at $625 per ton? Support your answer with appropriate comments and computations.

2. What is the lowest price that the company should accept for a ton of flour? Again support your answer with appropriate comments and computations.

C13–31 Integrative Case: Relevant Costs; Pricing Jenco, Inc. manufactures a combination fertilizer-weed killer under the name Fertikil. This is the only product that Jenco produces at present. Fertikil is sold nationwide through normal marketing channels to retail nurseries and garden stores.

Taylor Nursery plans to sell a similar fertilizer-week killer compound through its regional nursery chain under its own private label. Taylor does not have manufacturing facilities of its own, so it has asked Jenco (and several other companies) to submit a bid for the price that would be charged for manufacturing and delivering a 25,000-pound order of the private brand compound to Taylor. While the chemical composition of the Taylor compound differs from that of Fertikil, the manufacturing processes are very similar.

The Taylor compound would be produced in 1,000-pound lots. Each lot would require 60 direct labor-hours and the following chemicals:

Chemicals	Quantity in Pounds
CW–3	400
JX–6.	300
MZ–8	200
BE–7	100

The first three chemicals (CW–3, JX–6, and MZ–8) are all used in the production of Fertikil. BE–7 was used in another compound that Jenco discontinued several months ago. The supply of BE–7 that Jenco had on hand when the other compound was discontinued was not discarded because BE–7 does not deteriorate and there have been adequate storage facilities available. Jenco could sell its supply of BE–7 at the prevailing market price less $0.10 per pound selling and handling expenses.

Jenco also has on hand a chemical called CN–5, which was manufactured for use in another product that is no longer produced. CN–5, which cannot be used in Fertikil, can be substituted for CW–3 on a one-for-one basis without affecting the quality of the Taylor compound. The CN–5 in inventory has a salvage value of $500.

Inventory and cost data for the chemicals that can be used to produce the Taylor compound are as shown below:

Raw Material	Pounds in Inventory	Actual Price per Pound When Purchased	Current Market Price per Pound
CW–3	22,000	$0.80	$0.90
JX–6	5,000	0.55	0.60
MZ–8	8,000	1.40	1.60
BE–7	4,000	0.60	0.65
CN–5	5,500	0.75	(Salvage)

The current direct labor rate is $7 per hour. The manufacturing overhead rate is established at the beginning of the year and is applied consistently throughout the year using direct labor-hours (DLH) as the base. The predetermined overhead rate for the current year, based on a two-shift capacity of 400,000 total DLH with no overtime, is as follows:

Variable manufacturing overhead	$2.25 per DLH
Fixed manufacturing overhead	3.75 per DLH
Combined rate	$6.00 per DLH

Jenco's production manager reports that the present equipment and facilities are adequate to manufacture the Taylor compound. However, Jenco is within 800 hours of its two-shift capacity this month before it must schedule overtime. If need be, the Taylor compound could be produced on regular time by shifting a portion of Fertikil production to overtime. Jenco's rate for overtime hours is 1½ times the regular pay rate, or $10.50 per hour. There is no allowance for any overtime premium in the manufacturing overhead rate.

Jenco's standard markup policy for new products is 40 percent of the full manufacturing cost.

Required

1. Assume that Jenco, Inc., has decided to submit a bid for a 25,000-pound order of Taylor's new compound. The order must be delivered by the end of the current month. Taylor has indicated that this is a one-time order that will not be repeated. Calculate the lowest price that Jenco could bid for the order without reducing its net income.
2. Refer to the original data. Assume that Taylor Nursery plans to place regular orders for 25,000-pound lots of the new compound during the coming year. Jenco expects the demand for Fertikil to remain strong again in the coming year. Therefore, the recurring orders from Taylor would put Jenco over its two-shift capacity. However, production could be scheduled so that 60 percent of each Taylor order could be completed during regular hours. As another option, some Fertikil production could be shifted temporarily to overtime so that the Taylor orders could be produced on regular time. Jenco's production manager has estimated that the prices of all chemicals will stabilize at the current market rates for the coming year; also, the variable and fixed overhead costs are expected to continue at the same rates per direct labor-hour.

   Calculate the price that Jenco, Inc., should quote Taylor Nursery for each 25,000-pound lot of the new compound, assuming that it is to be treated as a new product and that there will be recurring orders during the coming year.

(CMA, Adapted)

C13–32 Decentralization and Relevant Costs Whitmore Products consists of three decentralized divisions—Bayside Division, Cole Division, and Diamond Division. The president of Whitmore Products has given the managers of the three divisions the authority to decide whether they will sell to outside customers on the intermediate market or sell to other divisions within the company. The divisions are autonomous in that each divisional manager has power to set selling prices to outside customers and to set transfer prices to other divisions. Each divisional manager is anxious to maximize his or her division's contribution margin.

To fill out capacity for the remainder of the current year, the manager of the Cole Division is considering two alternative orders. Data on the orders are provided below:

a. The Diamond Division is in need of 3,000 motors that can be supplied by the Cole Division. To manufacture these motors, Cole would purchase component parts from the Bayside Division at a transfer price of $800 per part. (Each motor would require one part.) Bayside would incur variable costs for these parts of $400 each. In addition, each part would require 3.5 hours of machine time at a general fixed overhead rate of $40 per hour. Cole Division would then further process these parts and add other variable costs to the motors at a cost of $900 per motor. The motors would require seven hours of machine time each in Cole's plant at a general fixed overhead rate of $25 per hour.

   If the Diamond Division can't obtain the motors from the Cole Division, it will purchase the motors from London Company which has offered to supply the same motors to Diamond Division at a price of $2,000 per motor. In order to manufacture these motors, London Company would also have to purchase a component part from Bayside Division. This would be a different component part than that needed by the Cole Division. It would cost Bayside $250 in variable cost to produce and Bayside would sell it to London Company for $500 per part on an order of 3,000 parts. Because of its intricate design, this part would also require 3.5 hours of machine time to manufacture.

b. The Wales Company wants to place an order with the Cole Division for 3,500 units of a motor that is similar to the motor needed by the Diamond Division. The Wales Company has offered to pay $1,800 per motor. To manufacture these motors, Cole Division would again have to purchase a component part from the Bayside Division. This part would cost Bayside Division $200 per part in variable cost to produce, and Bayside would sell it to Cole Division at a transfer price of $400 per part. This part would require three hours of machine time to manufacture in Bayside's plant. Cole Division would further process these parts and add other variable costs to the motors at a cost of $1,000 per motor. This work would require six hours of machine time per motor to complete.

The Cole Division's plant capacity is limited, and the division can accept only the order from the Diamond Division or the order from the Wales Company, but not both. The president of Whitmore Products and the manager of the Cole Division both agree that it would not be beneficial to increase capacity at this time.

Required

1. If the manager of the Cole Division is anxious to maximize short-run profits, which order should be accepted—the order from the Diamond Division or the order from the Wales Company? Support your answer with appropriate computations.
2. For the sake of discussion, assume that the Cole Division decides to accept the order from the Wales Company. Determine if this decision is in the best interests of Whitmore Products *as a whole*. Again support your answer with appropriate computations.

(CMA, Heavily Adapted)

14

Capital Budgeting Decisions

LEARNING OBJECTIVES

After studying Chapter 14, you should be able to:

1 Explain the concept of present value and make present value computations with and without the present value tables.

2 Determine the acceptability of an investment project, using the net present value method.

3 Enumerate the typical cash inflows and cash outflows that might be associated with an investment project and explain how they would be used in a present value analysis.

4 Determine the acceptability of an investment project, using the time-adjusted rate of return method (with interpolation, if needed).

5 Explain how the cost of capital is used as a screening tool.

6 Make a capital budgeting analysis involving automated equipment.

7 Prepare a net present value analysis of two competing investment projects, using either the incremental-cost approach or the total-cost approach.

8 Prepare a net present value analysis where a least-cost decision is involved.

9 Determine the payback period for an investment, using the payback formula.

10 Compute the simple rate of return for an investment, using the simple rate of return formula.

11 Define or explain the key terms listed at the end of the chapter.

The term **capital budgeting** is used to describe actions relating to the planning and financing of capital outlays for such purposes as the purchase of new equipment, the introduction of new product lines, and the modernization of plant facilities. As such, capital budgeting decisions are a key factor in the long-run profitability of a firm. This is particularly true in situations where a firm has only limited investment funds available but has almost unlimited investment opportunities to choose from. The long-run profitability of the firm will depend on the skill of the manager in choosing those uses for limited funds that will provide the greatest return. This selection process is complicated by the fact that most investment opportunities are long term in nature, and the future is often distant and hard to predict.

To make wise investment decisions, managers need tools that will guide them in comparing the relative advantages and disadvantages of various investment alternatives. We are concerned in this chapter with gaining understanding and skill in the use of such tools.

CAPITAL BUDGETING—AN INVESTMENT CONCEPT

Capital budgeting is an *investment* concept, since it involves a commitment of funds now in order to receive some desired return in the future. When speaking of investments, one is inclined to think of a commitment of funds to corporate stocks and bonds. This is just one type of investment, however. The commitment of funds by a business to inventory, equipment, and related uses is *also* an investment in that the commitment is made with the expectation of receiving some return in the future from the funds committed.

Typical Capital Budgeting Decisions

What types of business decisions require capital budgeting analysis? Virtually any decision that involves an outlay now in order to obtain some return (increase in revenue or reduction in costs) in the future. Typical capital budgeting decisions encountered by the manager are:

1. Cost reduction decisions. Should new equipment be purchased in order to reduce costs?
2. Plant expansion decisions. Should a new plant, warehouse, or other facility be acquired in order to increase capacity and sales?
3. Equipment selection decisions. Would machine A, machine B, or machine C be the most cost-effective?
4. Lease or buy decisions. Should new plant facilities be leased or purchased?
5. Equipment replacement decisions. Should old equipment be replaced now or later?

Capital budgeting decisions tend to fall into two broad categories—*screening decisions* and *preference decisions*. **Screening decisions** are those relating to whether a proposed project meets some preset standard of acceptance. For example, a firm may have a policy of accepting cost reduction projects only if they promise a return of, say, 20 percent before taxes.

Preference decisions, by contrast, relate to selecting from among several *competing* courses of action. To illustrate, a firm may be considering five different machines to replace an existing machine on the assembly line. The choice as to which of the five machines to purchase is a *preference* decision.

In this chapter, we discuss ways of making screening decisions. The matter of preference decisions is reserved until the following chapter.

Characteristics of Business Investments

Business investments have two key characteristics that must be recognized as we begin our study of capital budgeting methods. These characteristics are (1) that most business investments involve *depreciable assets* and (2) that the returns on most business investments extend over long periods of time.

Depreciable Assets An important feature of depreciable assets is that they generally have little or no resale value at the end of their useful lives. By contrast, the original sum invested in a *non*depreciable asset will still exist when the project terminates. For example, if a firm purchases land (a nondepreciable asset) for $5,000 and rents it out at $750 a year for 10 years, at the end of the 10-year term the land will still be intact and should be salable for at least its purchase price. The computation of the rate of return on such an investment is fairly simple. Since the asset (the land) will still be intact at the end of the 10-year period, each year's $750 inflow is a return *on* the original $5,000 investment. The rate of return is therefore a straight 15 percent ($750 ÷ $5,000).

Computation of the rate of return on *depreciable* assets is more difficult, since the assets are "used up," so to speak, over their useful lives. Thus, any returns provided by such assets must be sufficient to do two things:

1. Provide a return *on* the original investment.
2. Return the total amount *of* the original investment itself.

To illustrate, assume that the $5,000 investment above was made in equipment rather than in land. Also assume that the equipment will reduce the firm's operating costs by $750 each year for 10 years. Is the return on the equipment a straight 15 percent, the same as it was on the land? The answer is no. The return being promised by the equipment is much less than the return being promised by the land. The reason is that part of the yearly $750 inflow from the equipment *must go to recoup the original $5,000 investment itself, since the equipment will be worthless at the end of its 10-year life.* Only what remains *after* recovery of this investment can be viewed as a return *on* the investment over the 10-year period.

The Time Value of Money As stated earlier, another characteristic of business investments is that they promise returns that are likely to extend over fairly long periods of time. Therefore, in approaching capital budgeting decisions, it is necessary to employ techniques that recognize *the time value of money.* Any business leader would rather receive a dollar today than a year from now. The same concept applies in choosing between investment projects. Those that promise returns earlier in time are preferable to those that promise returns later in time.

The capital budgeting techniques that recognize the above two characteristics of business investments most fully are those that involve *discounted cash flows*. We shall spend the remainder of this chapter illustrating the use of discounted cash flow methods in making capital budgeting decisions. Before starting this material, the reader should study Appendix A to this chapter, "The Concept of Present Value," if he or she is not familiar with discounting and with the use of present value tables.

DISCOUNTED CASH FLOWS—THE NET PRESENT VALUE METHOD

There are two approaches to making capital budgeting decisions by means of discounted cash flow. One is the *net present value method,* and the other is the *time-adjusted rate of return method* (sometimes called the *internal rate of return method*). The net present value method is discussed below; the time-adjusted rate of return method is discussed in a following section.

The Net Present Value Method Illustrated

Under the net present value method, the present value of all cash inflows is compared against the present value of all cash outflows that are associated with an investment project. The difference between the present value of these cash flows, called the **net present value,** determines whether or not the project is an acceptable investment. To illustrate, let us assume the following data:

Example A

Harper Company is contemplating the purchase of a machine capable of performing certain operations that are now performed manually. The machine will cost $5,000 new, and it will last for five years. At the end of the five-year period, the machine will have a zero scrap value. Use of the machine will reduce labor costs by $1,800 per year. Harper Company requires a minimum return of 20 percent before taxes on all investment projects.

Should the machine be purchased? To answer this question, it will be necessary first to isolate the cash inflows and cash outflows associated with the proposed project. In order to keep the example free of unnecessary complications, we have assumed only one cash inflow and one cash outflow. The cash inflow is the $1,800 annual reduction in labor costs. The cash outflow is the $5,000 initial investment in the machine.

The investment decision: Harper Company must determine whether a cash investment now of $5,000 can be justified if it will result in an $1,800 reduction in cost each year over the next five years, assuming that the company can get a 20 percent return on its money invested elsewhere.

To determine whether the investment is desirable, it will be necessary to discount the stream of annual $1,800 cost reductions to present value and to compare this discounted present value with the cost of the new machine. Since Harper Company requires a minimum return of 20 percent on all

EXHIBIT 14–1
Net Present Value Analysis of a Proposed Project

Initial cost	$5,000
Life of the project (years)	5
Annual cost savings	$1,800
Salvage value	-0-
Required rate of return	20%

Item	Year(s)	Amount of Cash Flow	20 Percent Factor	Present Value of Cash Flows
Annual cost savings	1–5	$ 1,800	2.991*	$ 5,384
Initial investment	Now	(5,000)	1.000	(5,000)
Net present value				$ 384

* From Table 14C–4 in Appendix C.

investment projects, we will use this rate in the discounting process. Exhibit 14–1 gives a net present value analysis of the desirability of purchasing the machine.

According to the analysis, Harper Company should purchase the new machine. The present value of the cost savings is $5,384, as compared to a present value of only $5,000 for the investment required (cost of the machine). Deducting the present value of the investment required from the present value of the cost savings gives a *net present value* of $384. Whenever the *net present value* is zero or greater, as in our example, an investment project is acceptable. Whenever the *net present value* is negative (the present value of the cash outflows exceeds the present value of the cash inflows), an investment project is not acceptable.

A full interpretation of the solution would be as follows: The new machine promises slightly more than the required 20 percent rate of return. This is evident from the positive net present value of $384. Harper Company could spend up to $5,384 for the new machine and still obtain the 20 percent rate of return it desires. The net present value of $384, therefore, shows the amount of "cushion" or "margin of error" that the company has in estimating the cost of the new machine. Alternatively, it also shows the amount of error that can exist in the present value of the cost savings, with the project remaining acceptable. That is, if the present value of the cost savings were only $5,000 rather than $5,384, the project would still promise the required 20 percent rate of return.

Emphasis on Cash Flows

In organizing data for making capital budgeting decisions, the reader may have noticed that our emphasis has been on cash flows and not on accounting net income. The reason is that accounting net income is based on accrual concepts that ignore the timing of cash flows into and out of an organization. As we stated earlier in the chapter, from a capital budgeting standpoint the timing of cash flows is important, since a dollar received today is more valuable than a dollar received in the future. Therefore, even though the accounting net income figure is useful for many things, it must be ignored in those capital budgeting computations that involve discounted cash flow analysis. Instead of determining accounting net income, the manager must concentrate on identifying the specific cash flows associated with various investment projects and on determining when these cash flows will take place.

In considering an investment project, what kinds of cash flows should the manager look for? Although the specific cash flows will vary from project to project, certain types of cash flows tend to recur and should be looked for, as explained in the following paragraphs.

Typical Cash Outflows Usually a cash outflow in the form of an initial investment in equipment or other assets will be present. This investment is often computed on an incremental basis, in that any salvage realized from the sale of old equipment is deducted from the cost of the new equipment, leaving only the net difference as a cash outflow for capital budgeting purposes. In addition to this type of investment, some projects require that a company expand its working capital to service the greater volume of business that will be generated. **Working capital** means the amount carried in cash, accounts receivable, and inventory (in excess of current liabilities) that is available to meet day-to-day operating needs. When a company takes on a new project, the balances in these accounts will often increase. For example, the opening of a new store outlet would require added cash to operate sales registers, increased accounts receivable to carry new customers, and more inventory to stock the shelves. Any such incremental working capital needs should be treated as part of the initial investment in a project. Also, many projects require periodic outlays for repairs and maintenance and for additional operating costs. These should all be treated as cash outflows for capital budgeting purposes.

Typical Cash Inflows On the cash inflow side, a project will normally either increase revenues or reduce costs. Either way, the amount involved should be treated as a cash inflow for capital budgeting purposes. (In regard to this point, notice that so far as cash flows are concerned, a *reduction in costs is equivalent to an increase in revenues.*) Cash inflows are also frequently realized from salvage of equipment when a project is terminated. In addition, upon termination of a project, any working capital that is released for use elsewhere should be treated as a cash inflow. Working capital is released, for example, when a company sells off its inventory, collects its receivables, and uses the resulting funds elsewhere in another investment project. (If the released working capital is not shown as a cash inflow at the termination of a project, then the project will go on being charged for the use of the funds forever!)

In summary, the following types of cash flows are common in business investment projects:

Cash outflows:

Initial investment (including installation costs).

Increased working capital needs.

Repairs and maintenance.

Incremental operating costs.

Cash inflows:
- Incremental revenues.
- Reduction in costs.
- Salvage value.
- Release of working capital.

Recovery of the Original Investment

When first introduced to present value analysis, students are often surprised by the fact that depreciation is not deducted in computing the profitability of a project. There are two reasons for not deducting depreciation.

First, depreciation is an accounting concept not involving a current cash outflow.[1] As discussed in the preceding section, discounted cash flow methods of making capital budgeting decisions focus on *flows of cash*. Although depreciation is a vital concept in computing accounting net income for financial statement purposes, it is not relevant in an analytical framework that focuses on flows of cash.

A second reason for not deducting depreciation is that discounted cash flow methods *automatically* provide for return of the original investment, thereby making a deduction for depreciation unnecessary. To demonstrate this point, let us assume the following data:

Example B

Carver Hospital is considering the purchase of an attachment for its X-ray machine that will cost $3,170. The attachment will be usable for four years, after which time it will have no salvage value. It is estimated that the attachment will increase net cash inflows by $1,000 per year in the X-ray department. The hospital's board of directors has instructed that no investments are to be made unless they promise an annual return of at least 10 percent.

A present value analysis of the desirability of purchasing the attachment is presented in Exhibit 14–2. Notice that the attachment promises exactly a

EXHIBIT 14–2

Net Present Value Analysis of X-Ray Attachment

Initial cost	$3,170
Life of the project (years)	4
Annual net cash inflow	$1,000
Salvage value.	-0-
Required rate of return	10%

Item	Year(s)	Amount of Cash Flow	10 Percent Factor	Present Value of Cash Flows
Annual net cash inflow. . . .	1–4	$ 1,000	3.170*	$ 3,170
Initial investment	Now	(3,170)	1.000	(3,170)
Net present value				$ -0-

* From Table 14C–4 in Appendix C.

[1] Although depreciation itself does not involve a cash outflow, it does have an effect on cash outflows for income taxes. We shall take a look at this effect in the following chapter, when we discuss the impact of income taxes on management planning.

EXHIBIT 14–3
The Carver Hospital—Breakdown of Annual Cash Inflows

Year	(1) Investment Outstanding during the Year	(2) Cash Inflow	(3) Return on Investment (1) × 10%	(4) Recovery of Investment during the Year (2) − (3)	(5) Unrecovered Investment at the End of the Year (1) − (4)
1.	$3,170	$1,000	$317	$ 683	$2,487
2.	2,487	1,000	249	751	1,736
3.	1,736	1,000	173	827	909
4.	909	1,000	91	909	-0-
Total investment recovered. . . .				$3,170	

10 percent return on the original investment, since the net present value is zero at a 10 percent discount rate.

Each annual $1,000 cash inflow arising from use of the attachment is made up of two parts. One part represents a recovery of a portion of the original $3,170 paid for the attachment, and the other part represents a return *on* this investment. The breakdown of each year's $1,000 cash inflow between recovery *of* investment and return *on* investment is shown in Exhibit 14–3.

The first year's $1,000 cash inflow consists of a $317 interest return (10 percent) *on* the $3,170 original investment, plus a $683 return *of* that investment. Since the amount of the unrecovered investment decreases over the four years, the dollar amount of the interest return also decreases. By the end of the fourth year, all $3,170 of the original investment has been recovered.

Limiting Assumptions

In working with discounted cash flows, at least two limiting assumptions are usually made. The first is that all cash flows occur at the end of a period. This is somewhat unrealistic in that cash flows typically occur somewhat uniformly *throughout* a period. The purpose of this assumption is just to simplify computations.

The second assumption is that all cash flows generated by an investment project are immediately reinvested in another project. It is further assumed that the second project will yield a rate of return at least as large as the discount rate used in the first project. Unless these conditions are met, the return computed for the first project will not be accurate. To illustrate, we used a discount rate of 10 percent for the Carver Hospital in Exhibit 14–2. Unless the funds released each period are immediately reinvested in another project yielding at least a 10 percent return, the return computed for the X-ray attachment will be overstated.

Choosing a Discount Rate

In using the net present value method, it is necessary to choose some rate of return for discounting cash flows to present value. In example A we used a rate of return of 20 percent before taxes, and in example B we used a rate of return of 10 percent. These rates were chosen somewhat arbitrarily simply for the sake of illustration.

As a practical matter, firms put much time and study into the choice of a discount rate. The rate generally viewed as being most appropriate is a firm's **cost of capital.** A firm's cost of capital is not simply the interest rate that it must pay for long-term debt. Rather, cost of capital is a broad concept, involving a blending of the costs of *all* sources of investment funds, both debt and equity. The mechanics involved in cost of capital computations are covered in finance texts and will not be considered here. The cost of capital is known by various names. It is sometimes called the **hurdle rate,** the **cutoff rate,** or the **required rate of return.**

Most finance people would agree that a before-tax cost of capital of 16 percent to 20 percent would be typical for an average industrial corporation. The appropriate after-tax figure would depend on the corporation's tax circumstances, but it would probably average around 10 to 12 percent.

An Extended Example of the Net Present Value Method

To conclude our discussion of the net present value method, we present below an extended example of how it is used in analyzing an investment proposal. This example will also help to tie together (and to reinforce) many of the ideas we have developed thus far.

Example C

Under a special licensing arrangement, Swinyard Company has an opportunity to market a new product in the western United States for a five-year period. The product would be purchased from the manufacturer, with Swinyard Company responsible for all costs of promotion and distribution. The licensing arrangement could be renewed at the end of the five-year period at the option of the manufacturer. After careful study, Swinyard Company has estimated that the following costs and revenues would be associated with the new product:

Cost of equipment needed	$ 60,000
Working capital needed	100,000
Salvage value of the equipment in five years	10,000
Overhaul of the equipment in four years	5,000
Annual revenues and costs:	
Sales revenues	200,000
Cost of goods sold	125,000
Out-of-pocket operating costs (for salaries, advertising, and other direct costs)	35,000

At the end of the five-year period, the working capital would be released for investment elsewhere if the manufacturer decided not to renew the licensing arrangement. Swinyard Company's cost of capital is 20 percent. Would you recommend that the new product be introduced? Ignore income taxes.

As shown by the data above, Example C involves a variety of cash inflows and cash outflows. The solution is given in Exhibit 14–4.

Notice particularly how the working capital is handled in the exhibit. Also notice how the sales revenues, cost of goods sold, and out-of-pocket costs are handled. **Out-of-pocket costs** are actual cash outlays made during the period for salaries, advertising, and other operating expenses. Depreciation would not be an out-of-pocket cost, since it involves no current cash outlay.

EXHIBIT 14–4
The Net Present Value Method—An Extended Example

Sales revenues	$200,000
Less cost of goods sold	125,000
Gross margin	75,000
Less out-of-pocket costs for salaries, advertising, etc.	35,000
Annual net cash inflows	$ 40,000

Item	Year(s)	Amount of Cash Flows	20 Percent Factor	Present Value of Cash Flows
Purchase of equipment	Now	$ (60,000)	1.000	$ (60,000)
Working capital needed	Now	(100,000)	1.000	(100,000)
Overhaul of equipment	4	(5,000)	0.482*	(2,410)
Annual net cash inflows from sales of the product line	1–5	40,000	2.991†	119,640
Salvage value of the equipment	5	10,000	0.402*	4,020
Working capital released	5	100,000	0.402*	40,200
Net present value				$ 1,450

* From Table 14C–3 in Appendix C.
† From Table 14C–4 in Appendix C.

Since the overall net present value is positive, the new product should be added, assuming that there is no better use for the investment funds involved.

DISCOUNTED CASH FLOWS—THE TIME-ADJUSTED RATE OF RETURN METHOD

The **time-adjusted rate of return** (or **internal rate of return**) can be defined as the true interest yield promised by an investment project over its useful life. It is sometimes referred to simply as the **yield** on a project. The time-adjusted rate of return is computed by finding the discount rate that will equate the present value of the investment (cash outflows) required by a project with the present value of the returns (cash inflows) that the project promises. In other words, the time-adjusted rate of return is that discount rate that will cause the net present value of a project to be equal to zero.

The Time-Adjusted Rate of Return Method Illustrated

Finding a project's time-adjusted rate of return can be very helpful to a manager in making capital budgeting decisions. To illustrate, let us assume the following data:

Example D

Glendale School District is considering the purchase of a large tractor-pulled lawn mower. If the large mower is purchased, it will replace the hiring of persons to mow with small, individual gas mowers. The large mower will cost $16,950 and will have a life of 10 years. It will have only a negligible scrap value, which can be ignored, and it will provide a savings of $3,000 per year in mowing costs because of the labor it will replace.

EXHIBIT 14–5
Evaluation of the Mower Purchase Using a 12 Percent Discount Rate

Initial cost	$16,950
Life of the project (years)	10
Annual cost savings	$ 3,000
Salvage value	–0–

Item	Year(s)	Amount of Cash Flow	12 Percent Factor	Present Value of Cash Flows
Annual cost savings	1–10	$ 3,000	5.650*	$ 16,950
Initial investment	Now	(16,950)	1.000	(16,950)
Net present value				$ –0–

* From Table 14C–4 in Appendix C.

To compute the time-adjusted rate of return promised by the new mower, it will be necessary to find the discount rate that will cause the net present value of the project to be zero. How do we proceed to do this? The simplest and most direct approach is to divide the investment in the project by the expected annual cash inflow. This computation will yield a factor from which the time-adjusted rate of return can be determined. The formula is:

$$\frac{\text{Investment in the project}}{\text{Annual cash inflow}} = \text{Factor of the time-adjusted rate of return} \quad (1)$$

The factor derived from formula (1) is then located in the present value tables to see what rate of return it represents. We will now perform these computations for Glendale School District's proposed project. Using formula (1), we get:

$$\frac{\$16{,}950}{\$3{,}000} = 5.650$$

Thus, the discount factor that will equate a series of $3,000 cash inflows with a present investment of $16,950 is 5.650. Now we need to find this factor in Table 14C–4 in Appendix C to see what rate of return it represents. If we refer to Table 14C–4 and scan along the 10-period line, we find that a factor of 5.650 represents a 12 percent rate of return. Therefore, the time-adjusted rate of return promised by the mower project is 12 percent. We can prove this by computing the project's net present value, using a 12 percent discount rate. This computation is made in Exhibit 14–5.

Notice from Exhibit 14–5 that using a 12 percent discount rate equates the present value of the annual cash inflows with the present value of the investment required in the project, leaving a zero net present value. The 12 percent rate therefore represents the time-adjusted rate of return promised by the project.

The Problem of Uneven Cash Flows

The technique just demonstrated works very well if a project's cash flows are even. But what if they are not? For example, what if a project will have some salvage value at the end of its life in addition to the annual cash inflows? Under these circumstances, a trial-and-error process is necessary to find the rate of return that will equate the cash inflows with the cash outflows. The trial-and-error process can be carried out by hand, or it can be carried out by means of computer software programs that perform the necessary computations in seconds. In short, simply because cash flows are erratic or uneven will not in any way prevent a manager from determining a project's time-adjusted rate of return.

The Process of Interpolation

Interpolation is the process of finding odd rates of return that do not appear in published interest tables. It is an important concept, since published interest tables are usually printed in terms of whole percentages (10 percent, 12 percent, and so forth), whereas projects often have rates of return that involve fractional amounts. To illustrate the process of interpolation, assume the following data:

Investment required	$6,000
Annual cost savings	1,500
Life of the project	10 years

What is the time-adjusted rate of return promised by this project? We can proceed as before and find that the relevant factor is 4.000:

$$\frac{\text{Investment required}}{\text{Annual cost savings}} = \frac{\$6,000}{\$1,500} = 4.000$$

Looking at Table 14C–4 in Appendix C and scanning along the 10-period line, we find that a factor of 4.000 represents a rate of return somewhere between 20 and 22 percent. To find the rate we are after, we will need to interpolate, as follows:

	Present Value Factors	
20% factor	4.192	4.192
True factor	4.000	
22% factor		3.923
Difference.	0.192	0.269

$$\text{Time-adjusted rate of return} = 20\% + \left(\frac{0.192}{0.269} \times 2\%\right)$$

$$\text{Time-adjusted rate of return} = 21.4\%$$

Using the Time-Adjusted Rate of Return

Once the time-adjusted rate of return has been computed, what does the manager do with the information? The time-adjusted rate of return is compared against whatever rate of return (usually the cost of capital) the organization requires on its investment projects. If the time-adjusted rate of return is *equal* to or *greater* than the cost of capital, then the project is acceptable.

If it is *less* than the cost of capital, then the project is rejected. A project is not a profitable undertaking if it can't provide a rate of return at least as great as the cost of the funds invested in it.

In the case of the Glendale School District example used earlier, let us assume that the district has set a minimum required rate of return of 10 percent on all projects. Since the large mower promises a rate of return of 12 percent, it clears this hurdle and would therefore be an acceptable investment.

THE COST OF CAPITAL AS A SCREENING TOOL

As we have seen in preceding examples, the cost of capital operates as a *screening* tool, helping the manager to screen out undesirable investment projects. This screening is accomplished in different ways, depending on whether the company is using the time-adjusted rate of return method or the net present value method in its capital budgeting analysis.

When the time-adjusted rate of return method is being used, the cost of capital takes the form of a **hurdle rate** that a project must clear for acceptance. If the time-adjusted rate of return on a project is not great enough to clear the cost of capital hurdle, then the project is rejected. We saw the application of this idea in the Glendale School District example, where the hurdle rate was set at 10 percent.

When the net present value method is being used, the cost of capital becomes the *actual discount rate* used to compute the net present value of a proposed project. Any project yielding a negative net present value is screened out and rejected unless nonquantitative factors such as social responsibility, employee morale, or improvements in a company's ability to compete are significant enough to require its acceptance. (This point is discussed further in a following section, "Investments in Automated Equipment.")

The operation of the cost of capital as a screening tool is summarized in Exhibit 14–6.

EXHIBIT 14–6
Capital Budgeting Screening Decisions

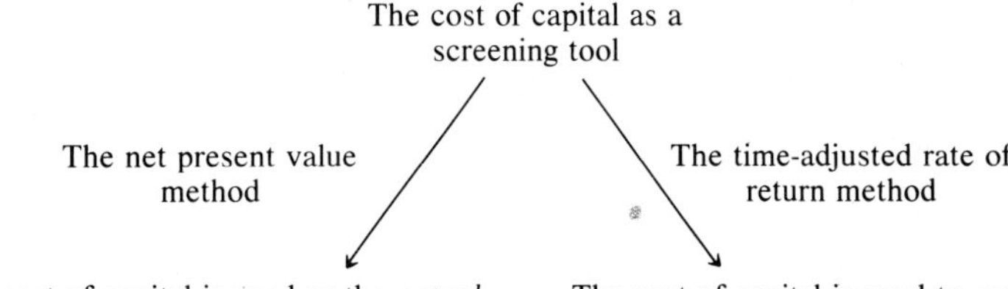

The cost of capital is used as the *actual* discount rate in computing the net present value of a project. Any project with a negative net present value is rejected unless social, environmental, or other nonquantitative factors dictate its acceptance.

The cost of capital is used to *compare against* the time-adjusted rate of return promised by a project. To be acceptable, the project's rate of return cannot be less than the cost of capital unless social, environmental, or other nonquantitative factors dictate its acceptance.

COMPARISON OF THE NET PRESENT VALUE AND THE TIME-ADJUSTED RATE OF RETURN METHODS

The net present value method has a number of advantages over the time-adjusted rate of return method of making capital budgeting decisions.

First, the net present value method is simpler to use. As explained earlier, the time-adjusted rate of return method often requires a trial-and-error process to find the exact rate of return that will equate a project's cash inflows and outflows. No such trial-and-error process is necessary when working with the net present value method.

Second, using the net present value method makes it easier to adjust for risk. The point was made earlier in the chapter that the longer one has to wait for a cash inflow, the greater is the risk that the cash inflow will never materialize. To show the greater risk connected with cash flows that are projected to occur many years in the future, firms often discount such amounts at higher discount rates than the discount rates used for flows that are projected to occur earlier in time. For example, a firm might anticipate that a project will provide cash inflows of $10,000 per year for 15 years. If the firm's cost of capital is 18 percent before taxes, then it might discount the first five years' inflows at this rate. The discount rate might then be raised to, say, 20 percent for the next five years and then to, say, 25 percent for the last five years. This successive raising of the discount rate would show the greater risk connected with the cash flows that are projected to be received far into the future.

No such selective adjustment of discount rates is possible under the time-adjusted rate of return method. About the only way to adjust for risk is to raise the hurdle rate that the rate of return for a project must clear for acceptance. This is a somewhat crude approach to the risk problem in that it attaches the same degree of increased risk to *all* of the cash flows associated with a project—those that occur earlier in time as well as those that occur later in time.

Third, the net present value method provides more usable information than does the time-adjusted rate of return method. The dollar net present value figure generated by the net present value method is viewed as being particularly useful for decision-making purposes. This point is considered further in the following chapter.

CAPITAL BUDGETING AND NONPROFIT ORGANIZATIONS

The capital budgeting concepts that we have been studying have equal application to all types of organizations, regardless of whether they are profit or nonprofit in nature. Note, for example, the different types of organizations used in the examples in this chapter. These organizations include a hospital, a company working under a licensing agreement, a school district, a company operating a ferryboat service, and a manufacturing company. The diversity of these examples shows the range and power of the capital budgeting model.

The only real problem in the use of capital budgeting by nonprofit organizations is determining the proper discount rate to use in the analysis of data.

Some nonprofit organizations use the rate of interest paid on special bond issues (such as an issue for street improvements or an issue to build a school) as their discount rate; others use the rate of interest that could be earned by placing money in an endowment fund rather than spending it on capital improvements; and still others use discount rates that are set somewhat arbitrarily by governing boards.

The greatest danger lies in using a discount rate that is too low. Most government agencies, for example, at one time used the interest rate on government bonds as their discount rate. It is now recognized that this rate is too low and has resulted in the acceptance of many projects that should not have been undertaken.[2] To resolve this problem, the Office of Management and Budget has specified that federal government units must use a discount rate of at least 10 percent on all projects.[3] For nonprofit units such as schools and hospitals, it is generally recommended that the discount rate should "approximate the average rate of return on private sector investments."[4] Since this rate would include the experience of thousands of companies, it undoubtedly would provide more satisfactory results as a discount rate than simply using the interest rate on a special bond issue or the interest return on an endowment fund.

INVESTMENTS IN AUTOMATED EQUIPMENT

Investments in automated equipment differ in several ways from investments in other types of equipment. First, such investments tend to be very large in dollar amount, even when only a few items are purchased. Second, automation is sometimes improperly viewed as being a cure-all for competitive deficiencies, so any purchases of automated equipment must be carefully evaluated in terms of a company's long-term goals and objectives. And third, the benefits from automated equipment are often indirect and intangible, and therefore hard to quantify. Each of these factors is discussed in the following sections.

Cost of Automation

The cost involved in automating a process is much greater than the cost of purchasing conventional equipment. Single pieces of automated equipment, such as a robot or a computerized numerical control machine, can cost $1 million or more. A flexible manufacturing system, involving one or more cells, can cost up to $50 million, and the cost of even a small, fully automated factory can exceed $100 million.

Even more important, the front-end investment in robots and other hardware usually constitutes no more than half of the total cost to automate. Some companies have discovered to their surprise that the costs of engineering, software development, and implementation of the system can equal or

[2] See *Federal Capital Budgeting: A Collection of Haphazard Practices,* GAO, P.O. Box 6015, Gaithersburg, MD, PAD-81-19, February 26, 1981.

[3] Office of Management and Budget Circular No. A-94, March 1972. The U.S. Postal Service is exempted from the 10 percent rate as are all water resource projects and all lease or buy decisions.

[4] Robert N. Anthony and David W. Young, *Management Control in Nonprofit Organizations,* 3rd ed. (Homewood, Ill: Richard D. Irwin, 1984), p. 325.

exceed the cost of the equipment itself. This suggests that before any equipment is ordered, management must take more than just an ordinary amount of care in assessing the potential costs that may be involved with getting (and keeping) the equipment in an operational mode.

Long-Term Objectives and Automation

The first step in any move toward automation is for management to carefully evaluate the company's products, the needs of its customers, the nature of its markets, and its position in relation to domestic and foreign competition. Goals and objectives should then be set, and a comprehensive long-term manufacturing strategy should be developed that will allow the company to meet these goals and objectives. Too often, automation is approached in a hodge-podge manner with no long-term manufacturing strategy in mind. The result in some cases has been a belated realization that automation was both unwise and unnecessary. One pair of management consultants has aptly observed:

> Although automation often is viewed as a "cure-all" for competitive deficiencies, this view is incorrect. The key to effective and successful automation is to first analyze, understand, and if necessary, redesign and simplify the manufacturing process. Many companies are achieving significant benefits, without significantly automating, by simply rearranging the plant floor, eliminating nonvalue activities such as inventory storage and material handling, and establishing more streamlined and flexible process flows.[5]

In short, automation isn't for everyone, or at the least it is often better if taken in small doses. Once a company has carefully studied, redesigned, and simplified its manufacturing process, then automated equipment can be added (if needed) to boost output, improve quality, or strengthen the company's competitive position. Because of its high cost and complexity of operation, automated equipment represents a much more risky investment than conventional equipment. Thus, it should be purchased only if it is compatible with a well-defined, long-term manufacturing strategy.

Benefits from Automation

Perhaps the most difficult task associated with a purchase of automated equipment lies in identifying the benefits that the equipment will provide. At least one of these benefits is obvious in that direct labor cost is generally reduced. But a reduction in direct labor cost is rarely sufficient in itself to justify the purchase of an expensive, automated machine. Consider the following situation:

> In 1982, Rockwell International Corp.'s Herman M. Reininga wanted to buy an $80,000 laser to etch contract numbers on communications systems sold to the Pentagon. But the division's financial staff laughed him out of the meeting. The laser would save only $4,000 in direct labor each year. At that rate, it would take 20 years to recover the cost.

....

[5] Robert A. Howell and Stephen R. Soucy, "Capital Investment in the New Manufacturing Environment," *Management Accounting* 69 (November 1987), p. 27.

> Three years later, Reininga got his laser. He presented data showing that finished radios sat around for two weeks waiting for an antique etching operation to finish identity plates. The laser would do the job in 10 minutes, moving shipments out faster—and saving the company $200,000 a year in inventory-holding costs.[6]

The literature is replete with examples of companies refusing to purchase automated equipment because of inadequate savings in labor costs. Managers often fail to recognize that the most significant benefits from automation are indirect—as in the example above—or intangible in nature. Indeed, the intangible benefits can be the most significant benefits of all. These include improved product quality, reduced throughput time, and increased manufacturing flexibility. Unfortunately, these benefits are difficult to quantify and therefore tend to be ignored in capital budgeting analyses.

An annotated listing of benefits to look for in evaluating a purchase of automated equipment is given below.

Tangible benefits:

1. *Reduced direct labor costs.* Direct labor cost is generally reduced when automated equipment is purchased. However, a reduction in labor cost is rarely sufficient to justify automation.

2. *Reduced inventory costs.* Automated equipment is more reliable, more consistent, and faster than conventional equipment. Therefore, it can reduce inventory costs in two ways—first, by reducing the quantity of inventory on hand; and second, by freeing the space in which inventory is stored. The reduced quantity of inventory means less money tied up in inventory and also reduced inventory carrying costs. The freed space means less rental cost to store inventory or, if the company owns its facilities, greater revenue from expanded output.

3. *Reduced cost-of-quality problems.* Due to greater reliability and consistency of output, automation results in less defects and in less waste, scrap, and rework costs. In turn, reductions in defects and related problems lead to reductions in warranty expenses. General Electric reports, for example, that automating its dishwasher operation resulted in a 50 percent reduction in its service call rate. Moreover, greater product uniformity and reliability through automation means that fewer inspections are needed. We have already noted that some automated companies have virtually eliminated manual inspections of their materials and products.

Intangible benefits:

1. *Faster throughput time.* The greater efficiency of an automated process will decrease the production throughput time and thereby increase the total output for a given period.

2. *Increased manufacturing flexibility.* Setup time can be reduced through automation, thereby increasing manufacturing flexibility. Also, the flexibility

---

[6] Reprinted from "The Productivity Paradox," *Business Week,* No. 3055 (June 6, 1988), p. 104, by special permission.

of automated equipment generally translates into a longer service life than conventional equipment.

3. *Faster response to market shifts*. Automated equipment allows a company to respond more quickly to shifts in customer tastes and needs, due to the flexibility of the equipment.

4. *Increased learning effects*. Automating a facility or a process is difficult, both in a technical and an operational sense. Much learning is required, and these learning effects can be of great value as new technology unfolds and becomes available. Companies that hold back, fearing the complexities of automation, soon fall behind their competitors in recognizing and in being able to utilize the newer technology as it comes onto the market.

5. *Avoiding capital decay*. **Capital decay** can be defined as a loss in market share resulting from technologically obsolete products and operations. Retention of market share—or even an increase in market share—is perhaps the most significant intangible benefit that can be gained from automation. Companies sometimes reject automation by assuming that sales will remain unchanged even if they don't automate. However, if a more efficient process is available, a competitor undoubtedly will invest in it, thereby gaining a competitive advantage. The correct assumption, therefore, is that if a company fails to take advantage of new technology, it will *not* face the status quo in terms of sales; rather, it will face declining sales due to capital decay.

6. *Higher quality of output*. Automation allows a higher quality of output that can greatly strengthen the image and competitive position of a company. High quality promotes confidence on the part of customers and creates an aura of reliability that can provide access to expanding, worldwide markets.

The reader should note that the tangible benefits above represent potential *cost savings,* whereas the intangible benefits represent potential *revenue enhancements*. Generally, it's easy to measure the amount of cost savings associated with an investment project, and that's why items such as reduced direct labor cost always show up in a capital budgeting analysis. But it's hard to measure the impact of a potential revenue enhancement such as greater flexibility or faster market response. As a result, managers tend to overlook such items when evaluating the benefits from automated equipment. The intangible benefits must be explicitly considered, however, or faulty decisions will follow.

Decision Framework for Automated Equipment

We now tie together the ideas developed on preceding pages by presenting a decision framework that can be used for purchases of automated equipment. This framework consists of five steps,[7] as follows:

[7] These steps are adapted from Robert E. Bennett and James A. Hendricks, "Justifying the Acquisition of Automated Equipment," *Management Accounting* 69 (July 1987), p. 46. This thoughtful and well-written article deserves careful study.

1. Determine the long-term strategic goals and objectives of the company, and determine a manufacturing strategy that will allow these goals and objectives to be achieved.
2. List all the expected benefits and costs associated with the automated equipment under consideration.
3. Quantify those items from step 2 that can be readily estimated.
4. Determine the net present value or time-adjusted rate of return for those items quantified in step 3. These computations may justify acquisition of the equipment under study. If not, then proceed to step 5.
5. Try to quantify the intangible benefits from step 2, and recompute the net present value or the time-adjusted rate of return. As an alternate step, determine the amount of additional cash flow per year that would be needed to make the project acceptable, and then ask the question, "Are the intangible benefits worth at least this much to the company?" If so, the project should be accepted; if not, it should be rejected.

To illustrate step 5, assume that a company with a 16 percent cost of capital is considering a piece of automated equipment that would have a 15-year useful life. By applying steps 1–4, the equipment shows a negative net present value of $223,000. Given these data, the amount of additional cash flow per year that would be needed to make the project acceptable can be computed as follows:

Net present value (negative)	$(223,000)
Factor for an annuity of 16% for 15 periods (from Table 14C–4 in Appendix C)	5.575

$$\frac{\text{Net present value, \$(223,000)}}{\text{Factor, 5.575}} = \$40,000$$

Thus, if intangible benefits such as greater flexibility, higher quality of output, and avoidance of capital decay are worth at least $40,000 a year to the company, then the automated equipment should be purchased. If, in the judgment of management, these intangible benefits are *not* worth $40,000 a year, then no purchase should be made.

EXPANDING THE NET PRESENT VALUE APPROACH

So far we have confined all of our examples to the consideration of a single investment alternative. We will now expand the net present value approach to include two alternatives. In addition, we will integrate the concept of relevant costs into discounted cash flow analysis.

There are two ways that the net present value method can be used to compare competing investment projects. One is the *total-cost approach,* and the other is the *incremental-cost approach.* Each approach is illustrated below.

The Total-Cost Approach

The total-cost approach is the most flexible and the most widely used method of making a net present value analysis of competing projects. To illustrate the mechanics of the approach, let us assume the following data:

Example E

Harper Ferry Company provides a ferry service across the Mississippi River. One of its ferryboats is in poor condition. This ferry can be renovated at an immediate cost of $20,000. Further repairs and an overhaul of the motor will be needed five years from now at a cost of $8,000. In all, the ferry will be usable for 10 years if this work is done. At the end of 10 years, the ferry will have to be scrapped at a salvage value of approximately $5,000. The scrap value of the ferry right now is $7,000. It will cost $16,000 each year to operate the ferry, and revenues will total $25,000 annually.

As an alternative, Harper Ferry Company can purchase a new ferryboat at a cost of $36,000. The new ferry will have a life of 10 years, but it will require some repairs at the end of 5 years. It is estimated that these repairs will amount to $2,500. At the end of 10 years, it is estimated that the ferry will have a scrap value of $5,000. It will cost $12,000 each year to operate the ferry, and revenues will total $25,000 annually.

Harper Ferry Company requires a return of at least 18 percent before taxes on all investment projects.

Should the company purchase the new ferry or renovate the old ferry? The solution is given in Exhibit 14–7.

Two points should be noted from the exhibit. First, observe that *all* cash inflows and *all* cash outflows are included in the solution under each alternative. No effort has been made to isolate those cash flows that are relevant to the decision and those that are not relevant. The inclusion of all cash flows

EXHIBIT 14–7
The Total-Cost Approach to Project Selection

	New Ferry	Old Ferry
Annual revenues	$25,000	$25,000
Annual cash operating costs . . .	12,000	16,000
Net annual cash inflows	$13,000	$ 9,000

Item	Year(s)	Amount of Cash Flows	18 Percent Factor*	Present Value of Cash Flows
Buy the new ferry:				
Initial investment	Now	$(36,000)	1.000	$(36,000)
Repairs in five years	5	(2,500)	0.437	(1,093)
Net annual cash inflows	1–10	13,000	4.494	58,422
Salvage of the old ferry	Now	7,000	1.000	7,000
Salvage of the new ferry	10	5,000	0.191	955
Net present value				29,284
Keep the old ferry:				
Initial repairs	Now	$(20,000)	1.000	(20,000)
Repairs in five years	5	(8,000)	0.437	(3,496)
Net annual cash inflows	1–10	9,000	4.494	40,446
Salvage of the old ferry	10	5,000	0.191	955
Net present value				17,905
Net present value in favor of buying the new ferry.				$ 11,379

* All factors are from Tables 14C–3 and 14C–4 in Appendix C.

associated with each alternative gives the approach its name—the *total-cost* approach.

Second, notice that a net present value figure is computed for each of the two alternatives. This is a distinct advantage of the total-cost approach in that an unlimited number of alternatives can be compared side by side to determine the most profitable course of action. For example, another alternative for Harper Ferry Company would be to get out of the ferry business entirely. If management desired, the net present value of this alternative could be computed to compare with the alternatives shown in Exhibit 14–7. Still other alternatives might be open to the company. Once management has determined the net present value of each alternative that it wishes to consider, it can select the course of action that will be most profitable. In the case at hand, given only the two alternatives, the data indicate that the most profitable course is to purchase the new ferry.[8]

The Incremental-Cost Approach

When only two alternatives are being considered, the incremental-cost approach offers a simpler and more direct route to a decision. Unlike the total-cost approach, it focuses only on differential costs.[9] The procedure is to include in the discounted cash flow analysis only those costs and revenues that *differ* between the two alternatives being considered. To illustrate, refer again to the data in Example E relating to Harper Ferry Company. The solution using only differential costs is presented in Exhibit 14–8.

Two things should be noted from the data in this exhibit. First, notice that the net present value of $11,379 shown in Exhibit 14–8 agrees with the net present value shown under the total-cost approach in Exhibit 14–7. This agreement should be expected, since the two approaches are just different roads to the same destination.

EXHIBIT 14–8

The Incremental-Cost Approach to Project Selection

Items	Year(s)	Amount of Cash Flows	18 Percent Factor*	Present Value of Cash Flows
Incremental investment required to purchase the new ferry	Now	$(16,000)	1.000	$(16,000)
Repairs in five years avoided	5	5,500	0.437	2,403
Increased net annual cash inflows	1–10	4,000	4.494	17,976
Salvage of the old ferry	Now	7,000	1.000	7,000
Difference in salvage value in 10 years	10	–0–	—	–0–
Net present value in favor of buying the new ferry				$ 11,379

* All factors are from Tables 14C–3 and 14C–4 in Appendix C.

[8] The alternative with the highest net present value is not always the best choice, although it is the best choice in this case. For further discussion, see the section "Preference Decisions—The Ranking of Investment Projects" in Chapter 15.

[9] Technically, the incremental-cost approach is misnamed, since it focuses on differential costs (that is, on both cost increases and decreases) rather than just on incremental costs. As used here, the term *incremental costs* should be interpreted broadly to include both cost increases and cost decreases.

Second, notice that the costs used in Exhibit 14–8 are just mathematical differences between the costs shown for the two alternatives in the prior exhibit. For example, the $16,000 incremental investment required to purchase the new ferry in Exhibit 14–8 is the difference between the $36,000 cost of the new ferry and the $20,000 cost required to renovate the old ferry from Exhibit 14–7. The other figures in Exhibit 14–8 have been computed in the same way.

Least-Cost Decisions

Revenues are not directly involved in some decisions. For example, a company that makes no charge for delivery service may need to replace an old delivery truck, or a company may be trying to decide whether to lease or to buy its fleet of executive cars. In situations such as these, where no revenues are involved, the most desirable alternative will be the one that promises the *least total cost*. Hence, these are known as least-cost decisions. To illustrate a least-cost decision, assume the following data:

Example F

Val-Tek Company is considering the replacement of an old threading machine that is used in the manufacture of a number of products. A new threading machine is available on the market that could substantially reduce annual operating costs. Selected data relating to the old and the new machines are presented below:

	Old Machine	New Machine
Purchase cost new	$20,000	$25,000
Salvage value now	3,000	—
Annual cash operating costs	15,000	9,000
Overhaul needed immediately	4,000	—
Salvage value in six years	-0-	5,000
Remaining life	6 years	6 years

Val-Tek Company's cost of capital is 10 percent.

EXHIBIT 14–9
The Total-Cost Approach (Least-Cost Decision)

Items	Year(s)	Amount of Cash Flows	10 Percent Factor*	Present Value of Cash Flows
Buy the new machine:				
Initial investment	Now	$(25,000)	1.000	$(25,000)†
Salvage of the old machine	Now	3,000	1.000	3,000†
Annual cash operating costs	1–6	(9,000)	4.355	(39,195)
Salvage of the new machine	6	5,000	0.564	2,820
Present value of net cash outflows . . .				(58,375)
Keep the old machine:				
Overhaul needed now	Now	$ (4,000)	1.000	(4,000)
Annual cash operating costs	1–6	(15,000)	4.355	(65,325)
Present value of net cash outflows . . .				(69,325)
Net present value in favor of buying the new machine				$ 10,950

* All factors are from Tables 14C–3 and 14C–4 in Appendix C.

† These two items could be netted into a single $22,000 incremental-cost figure ($25,000 − $3,000 = $22,000).

EXHIBIT 14–10
The Incremental-Cost Approach (Least-Cost Decision)

Items	Year(s)	Amount of Cash Flows	10 Percent Factor*	Present Value of Cash Flows
Incremental investment required to purchase the new machine.	Now	$(21,000)	1.000	$(21,000)†
Salvage of the old machine	Now	3,000	1.000	3,000†
Savings in annual cash operating costs	1–6	6,000	4.355	26,130
Difference in salvage value in six years	6	5,000	0.564	2,820
Net present value in favor of buying the new machine				$ 10,950

* All factors are from Tables 14C–3 and 14C–4 in Appendix C.
† These two items could be netted into a single $18,000 incremental-cost figure ($21,000 − $3,000 = $18,000).

An analysis of the alternatives, using the total-cost approach, is provided in Exhibit 14–9.

As shown in the exhibit, the new machine promises the lowest present value of total costs. An analysis of the two alternatives using the incremental-cost approach is presented in Exhibit 14–10. As before, the data going into this exhibit represent the differences between the alternatives as shown under the total-cost approach.

OTHER APPROACHES TO CAPITAL BUDGETING DECISIONS

The discounted cash flow methods of making capital budgeting decisions are relatively new. They were first introduced on a widespread basis in the 1950s, although their appearance in business literature predates this period by many years. Discounted cash flow methods have gained widespread acceptance as accurate and dependable decision-making tools. Other methods of making capital budgeting decisions are also available, however, and are preferred by some managers.

The Payback Method

The payback method centers on a span of time known as the *payback period.* The **payback period** can be defined as the length of time that it takes for an investment project to recoup its own initial cost out of the cash receipts that it generates. In business jargon, this period is sometimes spoken of as "the time that it takes for an investment to pay for itself." The basic premise of the payback method is that the more quickly the cost of an investment can be recovered, the more desirable is the investment.

The payback period is expressed in years. The formula used in computing the payback period is:

$$\text{Payback period} = \frac{\text{Investment required}}{\text{Net annual cash inflow*}} \tag{2}$$

* If new equipment is replacing old equipment, this becomes incremental net annual cash inflow.

To illustrate the mechanics involved in payback computations, assume the following data:

Example G

York Company needs a new milling machine. The company is considering two machines, machine A and machine B. Machine A costs $15,000 and will reduce operating costs by $5,000 per year. Machine B costs only $12,000 but will also reduce operating costs by $5,000 per year.

Required Which machine should be purchased? Make your calculations by the payback method.

$$\text{Machine A payback period} = \frac{\$15{,}000}{\$5{,}000} = 3.0 \text{ years}$$

$$\text{Machine B payback period} = \frac{\$12{,}000}{\$5{,}000} = 2.4 \text{ years}$$

According to the payback calculations, York Company should purchase machine B, since it has a shorter payback period than machine A.

Evaluation of the Payback Method

The payback method is not a measure of how profitable one investment project is as compared to another. Rather, it is a measure of *time* in the sense that it tells the manager how many years will be required to recover the investment in one project as compared to another. This is a major defect in the approach, since a shorter payback period is not always an accurate guide as to whether one investment is more desirable than another. To illustrate this point, consider again the two machines used in the example above. Since machine B has a shorter payback period than machine A, it *appears* that machine B is more desirable than machine A. But if we add one more piece of data, this illusion quickly disappears. Machine A has a projected 10-year life, and machine B has a projected 5-year life. It would take two purchases of machine B to provide the same length of service as would be provided by a single purchase of machine A. Under these circumstances, machine A would be a much better investment than machine B, even though machine B has a shorter payback period. Unfortunately, the payback method has no inherent mechanism for highlighting differences in useful life between investments for the decision maker. Such differences can be very subtle, and relying on payback alone can cause the manager to make incorrect decisions.

A further criticism of the payback method is that it does not consider the time value of money. A cash inflow to be received several years in the future is weighed equally with a cash inflow to be received right now. To illustrate, assume that for an investment of $8,000 you can purchase either of the two following streams of cash inflows:

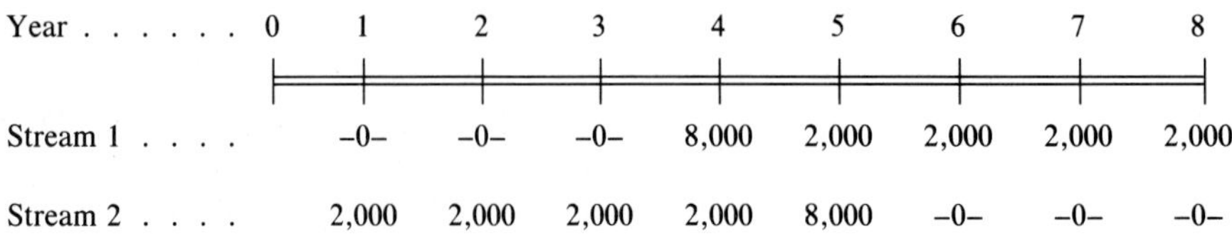

Year	0	1	2	3	4	5	6	7	8
Stream 1		-0-	-0-	-0-	8,000	2,000	2,000	2,000	2,000
Stream 2		2,000	2,000	2,000	2,000	8,000	-0-	-0-	-0-

Which stream of cash inflows would you prefer to receive in return for your $8,000 investment? Each stream has a payback period of 4.0 years. Therefore, if payback alone were relied on in making the decision, you would be forced to say that the streams are equally desirable. However, from the point of view of the time value of money, stream 2 is much more desirable than stream 1.

On the other hand, under certain conditions the payback method can be very useful to the manager. For one thing, it can help the manager to identify the "ballpark" in weeding out investment proposals. That is, it can be used as a screening tool to help answer the question "Should I consider this proposal further?" If a proposal doesn't provide a payback within some specified period, then there may be no need to consider it further. In addition, the payback period is often of great importance to new firms that are "cash poor." When a firm is cash poor, a project with a short payback period but a low rate of return might be preferred over another project with a high rate of return but a long payback period. The reason is that the company may simply need a faster return of its cash investment.

An Extended Example of Payback

As shown by formula (2) given earlier, the payback period is computed by dividing the investment in a project by the net annual cash inflows that the project will generate. If new equipment is replacing old equipment, then any salvage to be received on disposal of the old equipment should be deducted from the cost of the new equipment, and only the *incremental* investment should be used in the payback computation. In addition, any depreciation deducted in arriving at the net income promised by an investment project must be added back to obtain the project's expected net annual cash inflow. To illustrate, assume the following data:

Example H

Goodtime Fun Centers, Inc., operates many outlets in the eastern states. Some of the vending machines in one of its outlets provide very little revenue, so the company is considering the removal of the machines and the installation of equipment to dispense soft ice cream. The equipment would cost $80,000 and have an eight-year useful life. Incremental annual revenues and costs associated with the sale of ice cream would be:

Sales	$150,000
Less cost of ingredients	90,000
Contribution margin	60,000
Less fixed expenses:	
Salaries	27,000
Maintenance	3,000
Depreciation	10,000
Total fixed expenses	40,000
Net income	$ 20,000

The vending machines can be sold for a $5,000 scrap value. The company will not purchase equipment unless it has a payback of three years or less. Should the equipment to dispense ice cream be purchased?

EXHIBIT 14–11
Computation of the Payback Period

Step 1: *Compute the net annual cash inflow.* Since the net annual cash inflow is not given, it must be computed before the payback period can be determined:

Net income (given above)	$20,000
Add: Noncash deduction for depreciation . . .	10,000
Net annual cash inflow.	$30,000

Step 2: *Compute the payback period.* Using the net annual cash inflow figure from above, the payback period can be determined as follows:

$$\frac{\text{Cost of the new equipment} - \text{Salvage from the old machines}}{\text{Net annual cash inflow}} = \text{Payback period}$$

$$\frac{\$80,000 - \$5,000}{\$30,000} = 2.5 \text{ years}$$

An analysis as to whether the proposed equipment meets the company's payback requirements is given in Exhibit 14–11. Several things should be noted from the data in this exhibit. First, notice that depreciation is added back to net income to obtain the net annual cash inflow promised by the new equipment. As stated earlier in the chapter, depreciation does not represent a present cash outlay; thus, it must be added back to net income in order to adjust net income to a cash basis. Second, notice in the payback computation that the salvage value from the old machines has been deducted from the cost of the new equipment, and that only the incremental investment has been used in computing the payback period.

Since the proposed equipment has a payback period of less than three years, the company's payback requirement has been met and the new equipment should be purchased.

Payback and Uneven Cash Flows

When the cash flows associated with an investment project are erratic or uneven, the simple payback formula that we outlined earlier is no longer usable, and the computations involved in deriving the payback period can be fairly complex. Consider the following data:

Year	Investment	Cash Inflow
1	$4,000	$1,000
2		–0–
3		2,000
4	2,000	1,000
5		500
6		3,000
7		2,000
8		2,000

What is the payback period on this investment? The answer is 5.5 years, but to obtain this figure it is necessary to balance off the cash inflows against the investment outflows on a year-by-year basis. The steps involved in this

EXHIBIT 14–12
Payback and Uneven Cash Flows

Year	(1) Beginning Unrecovered Investment	(2) Additional Investment	(3) Total Unrecovered Investment (1) + (2)	(4) Cash Inflow	(5) Ending Unrecovered Investment (3) − (4)
1	$4,000		$4,000	$1,000	$3,000
2	3,000		3,000	–0–	3,000
3	3,000		3,000	2,000	1,000
4	1,000	$2,000	3,000	1,000	2,000
5	2,000		2,000	500	1,500
6	1,500		1,500	3,000	–0–
7	–0–		–0–	2,000	–0–
8	–0–		–0–	2,000	–0–

process are shown in Exhibit 14–12. By the middle of the sixth year, sufficient cash inflows will have been realized to recover the entire investment of $6,000 ($4,000 + $2,000).

The Simple Rate of Return Method

The **simple rate of return** method is another capital budgeting technique that does not involve discounted cash flows. The method is also known as the accounting rate of return, the unadjusted rate of return, and the financial statement method. It derives its popularity from the belief that it parallels conventional financial statements in its handling of investment data.

Unlike the other capital budgeting methods that we have discussed, the simple rate of return method does not focus on cash flows. Rather, it focuses on accounting net income. The approach is to estimate the revenues that will be generated by a proposed investment and then to deduct from these revenues all of the projected operating expenses associated with the project. This net income figure is then related to the initial investment in the project, as shown in the following formula:

$$\text{Simple rate of return} = \frac{\left(\text{Incremental revenues} - \text{Incremental expenses, including depreciation}\right) = \text{Net income}}{\text{Initial investment*}} \qquad (3)$$

* The investment should be reduced by any salvage from the sale of old equipment.

Or, if a cost reduction project is involved, formula (3) becomes:

$$\text{Simple rate of return} = \frac{\text{Cost savings} - \text{Depreciation on new equipment}}{\text{Initial investment*}} \qquad (4)$$

* The investment should be reduced by any salvage from the sale of old equipment.

Example I

Brigham Tea, Inc., is a processor of a nontannic acid tea product. The company is contemplating the purchase of equipment for an additional processing line. The additional processing line would increase revenues by $90,000 per year. Incremental cash operating expenses would be $40,000 per year. The equipment would cost $180,000 and have a nine-year life. No salvage value is projected.

Required

1. Compute the simple rate of return.
2. Compute the time-adjusted rate of return, and compare it to the simple rate of return.

Solution

1. By applying the formula for the simple rate of return found in equation (3), we can compute the simple rate of return to be 16.7 percent:

$$\text{Simple rate of return} = \frac{\begin{bmatrix}\$90{,}000 \\ \text{incremental} \\ \text{revenues}\end{bmatrix} - \begin{bmatrix}\$40{,}000 \text{ cash operating expenses} \\ + \$20{,}000 \text{ depreciation}\end{bmatrix} = \begin{matrix}\$30{,}000 \\ \text{net income}\end{matrix}}{\$180{,}000 \text{ initial investment}}$$

$$\text{Simple rate of return} = 16.7\%$$

2. The rate computed in (1) above, however, is far below the time-adjusted rate of return of approximately 24 percent:

$$\text{Time-adjusted rate of return} = \frac{\$180{,}000}{\$50{,}000^*} = \text{Factor of } 3.600$$

Time-adjusted rate of return = Approximately 24% from Table 14C–4 in Appendix C, scanning across the nine-year line

* $30,000 net income + $20,000 depreciation = $50,000; or, the annual cash inflow can be computed as: $90,000 increased revenues − $40,000 cash expenses = $50,000.

Example J

Midwest Farms, Inc., hires people on a part-time basis to sort eggs. The cost of this hand sorting process is $30,000 per year. The company is investigating the purchase of an egg sorting machine that would cost $90,000 and have a 15-year useful life. The machine would have only a nominal salvage value, and it would cost $10,000 per year to operate and maintain. The egg sorting equipment currently being used could be sold now for a scrap value of $2,500.

Required Compute the simple rate of return on the new egg sorting machine.

Solution A cost reduction project is involved in this situation. By applying the formula for the simple rate of return found in equation (4), we can compute the simple rate of return as follows:

$$\text{Simple rate of return} = \frac{\begin{matrix}\$20{,}000^* \text{ cost} \\ \text{savings}\end{matrix} - \begin{matrix}\$6{,}000^\dagger \text{ depreciation} \\ \text{on the new equipment}\end{matrix}}{\$90{,}000 - \$2{,}500}$$

$$= 16.0\%$$

* $30,000 − $10,000 = $20,000 cost savings.
† $90,000 ÷ 15 years = $6,000 depreciation.

Criticisms of the Simple Rate of Return

The most damaging criticism of the simple rate of return method is that it does not consider the time value of money. A dollar received 10 years from now is viewed as being just as valuable as a dollar received today. Thus, the manager can be misled in attempting to choose between competing courses of action if the alternatives being considered have different cash flow patterns. For example, assume that project A has a high simple rate of return but yields the bulk of its cash flows many years from now. Another project, B, has a somewhat lower simple rate of return but yields the bulk of its cash flows over the next few years. The manager would probably choose project A over project B because of its higher simple rate of return; however, project B might in fact be a much better investment if the time value of money were considered.

A further criticism of the simple rate of return method is that it often proves to be misleading in its basic approach. The method is supposed to parallel conventional financial statements in its handling of data. Yet studies show that this parallelism is rarely present.[10] The problem is that conventional accounting practice tends to write costs off to expense very quickly. As a result, the net income and asset structure actually reflected on financial statements may differ substantially from comparable items in rate of return computations, where costs tend to be expensed less quickly. This disparity in the handling of data is especially pronounced in those situations where rate of return computations are carried out by nonaccounting personnel.

The Choice of an Investment Base

In our examples, we have defined the investment base for simple rate of return computations to be the entire initial investment in the project under consideration [see formula (3)]. Actual practice varies between using the entire initial investment, as we have done, and using only the *average* investment over the life of a project. As a practical matter, which approach one chooses to follow is unimportant so long as consistency is maintained between projects and between years. If the average investment is used rather than the entire initial investment, then the resulting rate of return will be approximately doubled.

POSTAUDIT OF INVESTMENT PROJECTS

Postaudit of an investment project means a follow-up after the project has been approved to see whether or not expected results are actually realized. This is a key part of the capital budgeting process in that it provides management with an opportunity, over time, to see how realistic the proposals are that are being submitted and approved. It also provides an opportunity to reinforce successful projects as needed, to strengthen or perhaps salvage projects that are encountering difficulty, to terminate unsuccessful projects before losses become too great, and to improve the overall quality of future investment proposals.

In performing a postaudit, the same technique should be used as was used in the original approval process. That is, if a project was approved on a basis

[10] See National Association of Accountants, Research Report No. 35, "Return on Capital as a Guide to Managerial Decisions" (New York, December 1959), p. 64.

of a net present value analysis, then the same procedure should be used in performing the postaudit. However, the data going into the analysis should be *actual data* as observed in the actual operation of the project, rather than estimated data. This affords management with an opportunity to make a side-by-side comparison to see how well the project has worked out. It also helps assure that estimated data received on future proposals will be carefully prepared, since the persons submitting the data will know that their estimates will be given careful scrutiny in the postaudit process. Actual results that are far out of line with original estimates should be carefully reviewed by management, and corrective action taken as necessary. In accordance with the management by exception principle, those managers responsible for the original estimates should be required to provide a full explanation of any major differences between estimated and actual results.

SUMMARY

Decisions relating to the planning and financing of capital outlays are known as capital budgeting decisions. Such decisions are of key importance to the long-run profitability of a firm, since large amounts of money are usually involved and since whatever decisions are made may "lock in" a firm for many years.

A decision to make a particular investment hinges basically on whether the future returns promised by the investment can be justified in terms of the present cost outlay that must be made. A valid comparison between the future returns and the present cost outlay is difficult because of the difference in timing involved. This timing problem is overcome through use of the concept of present value and through employment of the technique of discounting. The future sums are discounted to their present value so that they can be compared on a valid basis with current cost outlays. The discount rate used may be the firm's cost of capital, or it may be some arbitrary rate of return that the firm requires on all investment projects.

There are two ways of using discounted cash flow in making capital budgeting decisions. One is the net present value method, and the other is the time-adjusted rate of return method. The net present value method simply involves the choosing of a discount rate, then the discounting of all cash flows to present value, as described in the preceding paragraph. If the present value of the cash inflows exceeds the present value of the cash outflows, then the net present value is positive and the project is acceptable. The opposite is true if the net present value is negative. The time-adjusted rate of return method finds the discount rate that equates the cash inflows and the cash outflows, leaving a zero net present value.

Instead of using discounted cash flow, some companies prefer to use either payback or the simple rate of return in evaluating investment proposals. Payback is determined by dividing a project's cost by the annual cash inflows that it will generate in order to find out how quickly the original investment can be recovered. The simple rate of return is determined by dividing a project's accounting net income either by the initial investment in the project or by the average investment over the life of the project. Both payback and the simple rate of return can be useful to the manager, so long as they are used with a full understanding of their limitations.

After an investment proposal has been approved, a postaudit should be performed to see whether expected results are actually being realized. This is a key part of the capital budgeting process, since it tends to strengthen the quality of the estimates going into investment proposals and affords management with an early opportunity to recognize any developing problems.

KEY TERMS FOR REVIEW

Capital budgeting Actions relating to the planning and financing of capital outlays for such purposes as the purchase of new equipment, the introduction of new product lines, and the modernization of plant facilities. (p. 594)

Capital decay A loss in market share resulting from technologically obsolete products and operations. (p. 610)

Cost of capital The overall cost to an organization of obtaining investment funds, including the cost of both debt sources and equity sources. (p. 601)

Cutoff rate This term is synonymous with *required rate of return*. (p. 601)

Hurdle rate This term is synonymous with *required rate of return*. (p. 601)

Internal rate of return The discount rate that will cause the net present value of an investment project to be equal to zero; thus, the internal rate of return represents the true interest return promised by a project over its useful life. This term is synonymous with *time-adjusted rate of return*. (p. 602)

Interpolation The process of finding odd rates of return (such as 12.6 percent or 9.4 percent) that do not appear in published interest tables. (p. 604)

Net present value The difference between the present value of the cash inflows and the cash outflows associated with an investment project. (p. 596)

Out-of-pocket costs The actual cash outlays made during a period for salaries, advertising, repairs, and similar costs. (p. 601)

Payback period The length of time that it takes for an investment project to recoup its own initial cost out of the cash receipts that it generates. (p. 615)

Postaudit The follow-up after a project has been approved and implemented to determine whether expected results are actually realized. (p. 621)

Preference decision A decision as to which of several competing acceptable investment proposals is best. (p. 595)

Required rate of return The minimum rate of return that an investment project must yield in order to be acceptable. (p. 601)

Screening decision A decision as to whether a proposed investment meets some preset standard of acceptance. (p. 594)

Simple rate of return The rate of return promised by an investment project when the time value of money is not considered; it is computed by dividing a project's annual net income by the initial investment required. (p. 619)

Time-adjusted rate of return The discount rate that will cause the net present value of an investment project to be equal to zero; thus, the time-adjusted rate of return represents the true interest return promised by a project over its useful life. This term is synonymous with *internal rate of return*. (p. 602)

Working capital The excess of current assets over current liabilities. (p. 598)

Yield A term synonymous with *internal rate of return* and *time-adjusted rate of return*. (p. 602)

APPENDIX A: THE CONCEPT OF PRESENT VALUE

The point was made in the main body of the chapter that a business leader would rather receive a dollar today than a year from now. There are two reasons why this is true. First, a dollar received today is more valuable than a dollar received a year from now. The dollar received today can be invested immediately, and by the end of a year it will have earned some return, making the total amount in hand at the end of the year *greater* than the investment started with. The person receiving the dollar a year from now will simply have a dollar in hand at that time.

Second, the future involves uncertainty. The longer people have to wait to receive a dollar, the more uncertain it becomes that they will ever get the dollar that they seek. As time passes, conditions change. The changes may be such as to make future payments of the dollar impossible.

Since money has a time value, the manager needs a method of determining whether a cash outlay made now in an investment project can be justified in terms of expected receipts from the project in future years. That is, the manager must have a means of expressing future receipts in present dollar terms so that the future receipts can be compared *on an equivalent basis* with whatever investment is required in the project under consideration. The theory of interest provides managers with the means of making such a comparison.

The Theory of Interest

If a bank pays $105 one year from now in return for a deposit of $100 now, we would say that the bank is paying interest at an annual rate of 5 percent. The relationships involved in this notion can be expressed in mathematical terms by means of the following equation:

$$F_1 = P(1 + r) \tag{5}$$

where F_1 = the amount to be received in one year, P = the present outlay to be made, and r = the rate of interest involved.

If the present outlay is $100 deposited in a bank savings account that is to earn interest at 5 percent, then P = $100 and $r = 0.05$. Under these conditions, F_1 = $105, the amount to be received in one year.

The $100 present outlay can be called the **present value** of the $105 amount to be received in one year. It is also known as the *discounted value* of the future $105 receipt. The $100 figure represents the value in present terms of a receipt of $105 to be received a year from now by an investor who requires a return of 5 percent on his money.

Compound Interest

What if the investor wants to leave his or her money in the bank for a second year? In that case, by the end of the second year the original $100 deposit will have grown to $110.25:

Original deposit	$100.00
Interest for the first year:	
$100 × 0.05	5.00
Amount at the end of the first year.	105.00
Interest for the second year:	
$105 × 0.05	5.25
Amount at the end of the second year . . .	$110.25

Notice that the interest for the second year is $5.25, as compared to only $5 for the first year. The reason for the greater interest earned during the second year is that during the second year, interest is being paid *on interest*. That is, the \$5 interest earned during the first year has been left in the account and has been added to the original \$100 deposit in computing interest for the second year. This concept is known as **compound interest.** The compounding we have done is annual compounding. Interest can be compounded on a semiannual, quarterly, or even more frequent basis. Many savings institutions are now compounding interest on a daily basis. Of course, the more frequently compounding is done, the more rapidly the invested balance will grow.

How is the concept of compound interest expressed in equation form? It is expressed by taking equation (5) and adjusting it to state the number of years, n, that a sum is going to be left deposited in the bank:

$$F_n = P(1 + r)^n \tag{6}$$

where n = years.

If $n = 2$ years, then our computation of the value of F in two years will be:

$$F_2 = \$100(1 + 0.05)^2$$
$$F_2 = \$110.25$$

Present Value and Future Value Exhibit 14A–1 shows the relationship between present value and future value as expressed in the theory of interest equations. As shown in the exhibit, if \$100 is deposited in a bank at 5 percent interest, it will grow to \$127.63 by the end of five years if interest is compounded annually.

Computation of Present Value

An investment can be viewed in two ways. It can be viewed either in terms of its future value or in terms of its present value. We have seen from our computations above that if we know the present value of a sum (such as our \$100 deposit), it is a relatively simple task to compute the sum's future value in n years by using equation

EXHIBIT 14A–1

The Relationship between Present Value and Future Value

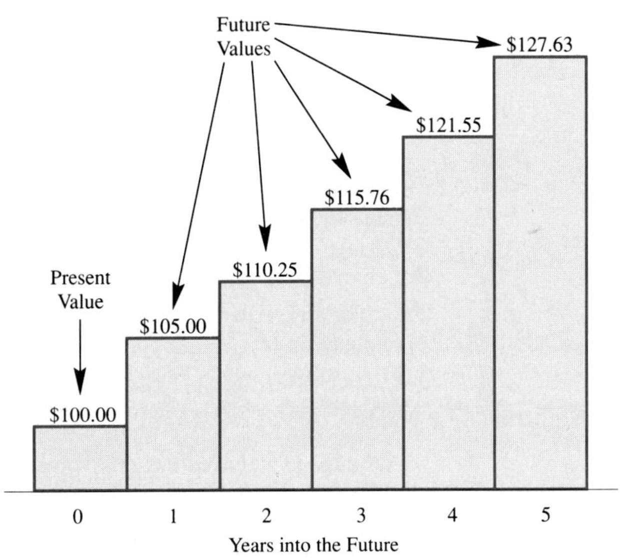

(6). But what if the tables are reversed, and we know the *future* value of some amount but we do not know its present value?

For example, assume that you are to receive $200 two years from now. You know that the future value of this sum is $200, since this is the amount that you will be receiving in two years. But what is the sum's present value—what is it worth *right now?* The present value of any sum to be received in the future can be computed by turning equation (2) around and solving for P:

$$P = \frac{F_n}{(1 + r)^n} \tag{7}$$

In our example, F = $200 (the amount to be received in the future), $r = 0.05$ (the rate of interest), and $n = 2$ (the number of years in the future that the amount is to be received).

$$P = \frac{\$200}{(1 + 0.05)^2}$$

$$P = \frac{\$200}{1.1025}$$

$$P = \$181.40$$

As shown by the computation above, the present value of a $200 amount to be received two years from now is $181.40 if an interest return of 5 percent is required. In effect, we are saying that $181.40 received *right now* is equivalent to $200 received two years from now if the investor requires a 5 percent return on his or her money. The $181.40 and the $200 are just two ways of looking at the same item.

The process of finding the present value of a future cash flow, which we have just completed, is called **discounting.** We have *discounted* the $200 to its present value of $181.40. The 5 percent interest figure that we have used to find this present value is called the **discount rate.** Discounting of future sums to their present value is a common practice in business. A knowledge of the present value of a sum to be received in the future can be very useful to the manager, particularly in making capital budgeting decisions. However, we need to find a simpler way of computing present value than using equation (7) every time we need to discount a future sum. The computations involved in using this equation are complex and time-consuming.

Fortunately, tables are available in which most of the mathematical work involved in the discounting process has been done. Table 14C–3 in Appendix C shows the discounted present value of $1 to be received at various periods in the future at various interest rates. The table indicates that the present value of $1 to be received two periods from now at 5 percent is 0.907. Since in our example we want to know the present value of $200 rather than just $1, we need to multiply the factor in the table by $200:

$$\$200 \times 0.907 = \$181.40$$

The answer we obtain is the same answer as we obtained earlier using the formula in equation (7).

Present Value of a Series of Cash Flows

Although some investments involve a single sum to be received (or paid) at a single point in the future, other investments involve a *series* of cash flows. A series (or stream) of cash flows is known as an **annuity.** To provide an example, assume that a firm has just purchased some government bonds in order to temporarily invest funds that are being held for future plant expansion. The bonds will yield interest of $15,000

EXHIBIT 14A–2
Present Value of a Series of Cash Receipts

Year	Factor at 12 Percent (Table 14C–3)	Interest Received	Present Value
1	0.893	$15,000	$13,395
2	0.797	15,000	11,955
3	0.712	15,000	10,680
4	0.636	15,000	9,540
5	0.567	15,000	8,505
			$54,075

each year and will be held for five years. What is the present value of the stream of interest receipts from the bonds? As shown in Exhibit 14A–2, the present value of this stream is $54,075 if we assume a discount rate of 12 percent compounded annually. The discount factors used in this exhibit were taken from Table 14C–3 in Appendix C.

Two points are important in connection with Exhibit 14A–2. First, notice that the farther we go forward in time, the smaller is the present value of the $15,000 interest receipt. The present value of $15,000 received a year from now is $13,395, as compared to only $8,505 for the $15,000 interest payment to be received five years from now. This point simply underscores the fact that money has a time value.

The second point is that even though the computations involved in Exhibit 14A–2 are accurate, they have involved unnecessary work. The same present value of $54,075 could have been obtained more easily by referring to Table 14C–4 in Appendix C. Table 14C–4 contains the present value of $1 to be received each year over a *series* of years at various interest rates. Table 14C–4 has been derived by simply adding together the factors from Table 14C–3. To illustrate, we used the following factors from Table 14C–3 in the computations in Exhibit 14A–2.

Year	Table 14C–3 Factors at 12 Percent
1	0.893
2	0.797
3	0.712
4	0.636
5	0.567
	3.605

The sum of the five factors above is 3.605. Notice from Table 14C–4 that the factor for $1 to be received each year for five years at 12 percent is also 3.605. If we use this factor and multiply it by the $15,000 annual cash inflow, then we get the same $54,075 present value that we obtained earlier in Exhibit 14A–2.

$$\$15,000 \times 3.605 = \$54,075$$

Therefore, when computing the present value of a series (or stream) of cash flows, Table 14C–4 should be used.

To summarize, the present value tables in Appendix C should be used as follows:

Table 14C–3: This table should be used to find the present value of a single cash flow (such as a single payment or receipt) occurring in the future.

Table 14C–4: This table should be used to find the present value of a series (or stream) of cash flows occurring in the future.

The use of both of these tables is illustrated in various exhibits in the main body of the chapter. *When a present value factor appears in an exhibit, the reader should take the time to trace it back into either Table 14C–3 or Table 14C–4 in order to get acquainted with the tables and how they work.* (Exercise 14–1 at the end of the chapter is designed for those readers who would like some practice in present value analysis before attempting other homework exercises and problems. A solution to Exercise 14–1 is provided immediately following the exercise itself.)

KEY TERMS FOR REVIEW (APPENDIX A)

Annuity A series, or stream, of cash flows of equal amounts. (p. 626)

Compound interest The process of paying interest on interest in an investment. (p. 625)

Discount rate The rate of return that is used to find the present value of a future cash flow. (p. 626)

Discounting The process of finding the present value of a future cash flow. (p. 626)

Present value The estimated value now of an amount that will be received in some future period. (p. 624)

APPENDIX B: INFLATION AND CAPITAL BUDGETING

Students frequently raise the question "What about inflation—doesn't it have an impact in a capital budgeting analysis?" The answer is a qualified yes in that inflation does have an impact on the *numbers* that are used in a capital budgeting analysis, but it does not have an impact on the *results* that are obtained. To show what we mean by this statement, assume the following data:

Example K

Martin Company wants to purchase a new machine that costs $36,000. The machine would provide annual cost savings of $20,000, and it would have a three-year life with no salvage value. For each of the next three years, the company expects a 10 percent inflation rate in cost items associated with its activities. If the company's cost of capital is 16 percent, should the new machine be purchased?

Two solutions to this example are provided in Exhibit 14B–1. In the first solution (solution A), inflation is ignored and the net present value of the proposed investment is computed in the same way as we have been computing it throughout the chapter. In the second solution (solution B), inflation is given full consideration.

Adjustments for Inflation

Several points should be noted about solution B. First, note that the annual cost savings are adjusted for the effects of inflation by multiplying each year's savings by a price-index number that reflects a 10 percent inflation rate. (Observe from the footnotes to the exhibit how the index number is computed for each year.)

Second, note that the cost of capital must also be adjusted for the effects of inflation. This is done by adding together three cost elements: the cost of capital itself, the inflation rate, and a combined factor that allows for the reinvestment of inflation-generated earnings. A frequent error in adjusting data for inflation is to omit

EXHIBIT 14B–1
Capital Budgeting and Inflation

Solution A: Inflation Not Considered

Items	Year(s)	Amount of Cash Flows	16 Percent Factor	Present Value of Cash Flows
Initial investment	Now	$(36,000)	1.000	$(36,000)
Annual cost savings	1–3	20,000	2.246	44,920
Net present value				$ 8,920

Solution B: Inflation Considered

Items	Year(s)	Amount of Cash Flows	Price Index Number	Price-Adjusted Cash Flows	27.6† Percent Factor	Present Value of Cash Flows
Initial investment	Now	$(36,000)	—	$(36,000)	1.0000	$(36,000)
Annual cost savings	1	20,000	1.10	22,000	0.7837‡	17,241
	2	20,000	1.21*	24,200	0.6142‡	14,864
	3	20,000	1.331*	26,620	0.4814‡	12,815
Net present value						$ 8,920

* Computation of the price-index numbers, assuming a 10 percent inflation rate each year: year 2, $(1.10)^2 = 1.21$; year 3, $(1.10)^3 = 1.331$.
† The inflation-adjusted cost of capital consists of three elements:

The basic cost of capital	16.0%
The inflation factor	10.0
The combined effect (16% × 10% = 1.6%)	1.6
Inflation-adjusted cost of capital	27.6%

‡ Discount factors are computed using the formula $1/(1 + r)^n$ where r = discount factor and n = number of years. For year 1, the computations are: $1/1.276 = 0.7837$; for year 2: $1/(1.276)^2 = 0.6142$; for year 3: $1/(1.276)^3 = 0.4814$. Computations have been carried to four decimal places to avoid a rounding error.

any adjustment at all to the cost of capital; or, if an adjustment is made, to simply add together the cost of capital and the inflation rate. Both of these procedures are incorrect and will yield erroneous results.[11]

Finally, note that the net present value obtained in solution B is *identical* to that obtained in solution A. It sometimes surprises students to learn that the same net present value will be obtained regardless of whether or not the data are adjusted for the effects of inflation. But if the reader will stop and reflect for a moment, this is a logical result. The reason is that in adjusting the data for the effects of inflation, we adjust *both* the cash flows and the discount rate, and thus the inflationary effects cancel themselves out. As a result, the net present value is the same as if no adjustments had been made.

How Practical Are Adjustments for Inflation?

In actual practice, not all companies make adjustments for inflation when doing a capital budgeting analysis. The reasons are obvious—the computations are very complex, and the same net present value can be obtained by using unadjusted data. The one advantage that is sometimes cited in favor of using inflation-adjusted data is

[11] The proper way to adjust the discount rate for inflationary effects is widely misunderstood. If the manager omits any adjustment to the cost of capital, or just adds together the cost of capital and the inflation rate, then the result will be to overstate the net present value of an investment project.

that it may be of more value in the postaudit process. It is argued that using inflation-adjusted data in the original capital budgeting analysis allows the manager to later compare like items in the postaudit, because *both* the estimated data and the actual data will contain the effects of inflation. If unadjusted data are used in the original capital budgeting analysis, then it is argued that the manager is forced to compare *unlike* items in the postaudit. Thus, the manager may be mislead in his or her evaluation of how the investment turned out.

Unfortunately, this "advantage" is more illusory than real. For one thing, if inflation-adjusted data are used in the original capital budgeting analysis, then these data and the actual data will be comparable only if the *same rate* of inflation is present in both. The likelihood of having the same rate present in both is small, since Inflation is very difficult to predict. Economists rarely agree on the expected rate for the next year, let alone several years into the future. In addition, the use of inflation-adjusted data may conceal sloppy estimates of cash flows by enabling the manager to hide behind the excuse that inflation rates turned out to be different than expected, thus throwing his or her estimates off.

To overcome these problems, a better approach is to use unadjusted data (because of its simplicity) in the original capital budgeting analysis, and then *in the postaudit* to adjust the actual data in order to remove the effects of any inflation that may have taken place. This approach will then allow for a comparison of like items, since neither the original data nor the actual data will contain any inflationary elements. It will also preclude the manager from hiding behind the excuse that his or her estimates were thrown off because the rate of inflation was different than expected.

Summary

Although it is possible to make adjustments for inflation in a capital budgeting analysis, it is a very difficult and complex process. Moreover, if the adjustments are properly done, the same net present value will be obtained as if no adjustments had been made. A simpler and more effective approach is to use unadjusted data in capital budgeting computations, as we have done in the chapter, and then to make adjustments to the actual data in the postaudit (when the actual rate of inflation is known), if it is thought that such adjustments are warranted.

APPENDIX C: FUTURE VALUE AND PRESENT VALUE TABLES

TABLE 14C-1

Future Value of \$1; $F_n = P(1 + r)^n$

Periods	4%	6%	8%	10%	12%	14%	20%
1	1.040	1.060	1.080	1.100	1.120	1.140	1.200
2	1.082	1.124	1.166	1.210	1.254	1.300	1.440
3	1.125	1.191	1.260	1.331	1.405	1.482	1.728
4	1.170	1.263	1.361	1.464	1.574	1.689	2.074
5	1.217	1.338	1.469	1.611	1.762	1.925	2.488
6	1.265	1.419	1.587	1.772	1.974	2.195	2.986
7	1.316	1.504	1.714	1.949	2.211	2.502	3.583
8	1.369	1.594	1.851	2.144	2.476	2.853	4.300
9	1.423	1.690	1.999	2.359	2.773	3.252	5.160
10	1.480	1.791	2.159	2.594	3.106	3.707	6.192
11	1.540	1.898	2.332	2.853	3.479	4.226	7.430
12	1.601	2.012	2.518	3.139	3.896	4.818	8.916
13	1.665	2.133	2.720	3.452	4.364	5.492	10.699
14	1.732	2.261	2.937	3.798	4.887	6.261	12.839
15	1.801	2.397	3.172	4.177	5.474	7.138	15.407
20	2.191	3.207	4.661	6.728	9.646	13.743	38.338
30	3.243	5.744	10.063	17.450	29.960	50.950	237.380
40	4.801	10.286	21.725	45.260	93.051	188.880	1469.800

TABLE 14C-2

Future Value of an Annuity of \$1 in Arrears; $F_n = \frac{(1 + r)^n - 1}{r}$

Periods	4%	6%	8%	10%	12%	14%	20%
1	1.000	1.000	1.000	1.000	1.000	1.000	1.000
2	2.040	2.060	2.080	2.100	2.120	2.140	2.220
3	3.122	3.184	3.246	3.310	3.374	3.440	3.640
4	4.247	4.375	4.506	4.641	4.779	4.921	5.368
5	5.416	5.637	5.867	6.105	6.353	6.610	7.442
6	6.633	6.975	7.336	7.716	8.115	8.536	9.930
7	7.898	8.394	8.923	9.487	10.089	10.730	12.916
8	9.214	9.898	10.637	11.436	12.300	13.233	16.499
9	10.583	11.491	12.488	13.580	14.776	16.085	20.799
10	12.006	13.181	14.487	15.938	17.549	19.337	25.959
11	13.486	14.972	16.646	18.531	20.655	23.045	32.150
12	15.026	16.870	18.977	21.385	24.133	27.271	39.580
13	16.627	18.882	21.495	24.523	28.029	32.089	48.497
14	18.292	21.015	24.215	27.976	32.393	37.581	59.196
15	20.024	23.276	27.152	31.773	37.280	43.842	72.035
20	29.778	36.778	45.762	57.276	75.052	91.025	186.690
30	56.085	79.058	113.283	164.496	241.330	356.790	1181.900
40	95.026	154.762	259.057	442.597	767.090	1342.000	7343.900

TABLE 14C–3
Present Value of \$1; $P = \dfrac{F_n}{(1 + r)^n}$

Periods	4%	5%	6%	8%	10%	12%	14%	16%	18%	20%	22%	24%	26%	28%	30%	40%
1	0.962	0.952	0.943	0.926	0.909	0.893	0.877	0.862	0.847	0.833	0.820	0.806	0.794	0.781	0.769	0.714
2	0.925	0.907	0.890	0.857	0.826	0.797	0.769	0.743	0.718	0.694	0.672	0.650	0.630	0.610	0.592	0.510
3	0.889	0.864	0.840	0.794	0.751	0.712	0.675	0.641	0.609	0.579	0.551	0.524	0.500	0.477	0.455	0.364
4	0.855	0.823	0.792	0.735	0.683	0.636	0.592	0.552	0.516	0.482	0.451	0.423	0.397	0.373	0.350	0.260
5	0.822	0.784	0.747	0.681	0.621	0.567	0.519	0.476	0.437	0.402	0.370	0.341	0.315	0.291	0.269	0.186
6	0.790	0.746	0.705	0.630	0.564	0.507	0.456	0.410	0.370	0.335	0.303	0.275	0.250	0.227	0.207	0.133
7	0.760	0.711	0.665	0.583	0.513	0.452	0.400	0.354	0.314	0.279	0.249	0.222	0.198	0.178	0.159	0.095
8	0.731	0.677	0.627	0.540	0.467	0.404	0.351	0.305	0.266	0.233	0.204	0.179	0.157	0.139	0.123	0.068
9	0.703	0.645	0.592	0.500	0.424	0.361	0.308	0.263	0.225	0.194	0.167	0.144	0.125	0.108	0.094	0.048
10	0.676	0.614	0.558	0.463	0.386	0.322	0.270	0.227	0.191	0.162	0.137	0.116	0.099	0.085	0.073	0.035
11	0.650	0.585	0.527	0.429	0.350	0.287	0.237	0.195	0.162	0.135	0.112	0.094	0.079	0.066	0.056	0.025
12	0.625	0.557	0.497	0.397	0.319	0.257	0.208	0.168	0.137	0.112	0.092	0.076	0.062	0.052	0.043	0.018
13	0.601	0.530	0.469	0.368	0.290	0.229	0.182	0.145	0.116	0.093	0.075	0.061	0.050	0.040	0.033	0.013
14	0.577	0.505	0.442	0.340	0.263	0.205	0.160	0.125	0.099	0.078	0.062	0.049	0.039	0.032	0.025	0.009
15	0.555	0.481	0.417	0.315	0.239	0.183	0.140	0.108	0.084	0.065	0.051	0.040	0.031	0.025	0.020	0.006
16	0.534	0.458	0.394	0.292	0.218	0.163	0.123	0.093	0.071	0.054	0.042	0.032	0.025	0.019	0.015	0.005
17	0.513	0.436	0.371	0.270	0.198	0.146	0.108	0.080	0.060	0.045	0.034	0.026	0.020	0.015	0.012	0.003
18	0.494	0.416	0.350	0.250	0.180	0.130	0.095	0.069	0.051	0.038	0.028	0.021	0.016	0.012	0.009	0.002
19	0.475	0.396	0.331	0.232	0.164	0.116	0.083	0.060	0.043	0.031	0.023	0.017	0.012	0.009	0.007	0.002
20	0.456	0.377	0.312	0.215	0.149	0.104	0.073	0.051	0.037	0.026	0.019	0.014	0.010	0.007	0.005	0.001
21	0.439	0.359	0.294	0.199	0.135	0.093	0.064	0.044	0.031	0.022	0.015	0.011	0.008	0.006	0.004	0.001
22	0.422	0.342	0.278	0.184	0.123	0.083	0.056	0.038	0.026	0.018	0.013	0.009	0.006	0.004	0.003	0.001
23	0.406	0.326	0.262	0.170	0.112	0.074	0.049	0.033	0.022	0.015	0.010	0.007	0.005	0.003	0.002	
24	0.390	0.310	0.247	0.158	0.102	0.066	0.043	0.028	0.019	0.013	0.008	0.006	0.004	0.003	0.002	
25	0.375	0.295	0.233	0.146	0.092	0.059	0.038	0.024	0.016	0.010	0.007	0.005	0.003	0.002	0.001	
26	0.361	0.281	0.220	0.135	0.084	0.053	0.033	0.021	0.014	0.009	0.006	0.004	0.002	0.002	0.001	
27	0.347	0.268	0.207	0.125	0.076	0.047	0.029	0.018	0.011	0.007	0.005	0.003	0.002	0.001	0.001	
28	0.333	0.255	0.196	0.116	0.069	0.042	0.026	0.016	0.010	0.006	0.004	0.002	0.002	0.001	0.001	
29	0.321	0.243	0.185	0.107	0.063	0.037	0.022	0.014	0.008	0.005	0.003	0.002	0.001	0.001	0.001	
30	0.308	0.231	0.174	0.099	0.057	0.033	0.020	0.012	0.007	0.004	0.003	0.002	0.001	0.001		
40	0.208	0.142	0.097	0.046	0.022	0.011	0.005	0.003	0.001	0.001						

TABLE 14C–4
Present Value of an Annuity of $1 in Arrears; $P_n = \frac{1}{r}\left[1 - \frac{1}{(1 + r)^n}\right]$

Periods	4%	5%	6%	8%	10%	12%	14%	16%	18%	20%	22%	24%	26%	28%	30%	40%
1	0.962	0.952	0.943	0.926	0.909	0.893	0.877	0.862	0.847	0.833	0.820	0.806	0.794	0.781	0.769	0.714
2	1.886	1.859	1.833	1.783	1.736	1.690	1.647	1.605	1.566	1.528	1.492	1.457	1.424	1.392	1.361	1.224
3	2.775	2.723	2.673	2.577	2.487	2.402	2.322	2.246	2.174	2.106	2.042	1.981	1.923	1.868	1.816	1.589
4	3.630	3.546	3.465	3.312	3.170	3.037	2.914	2.798	2.690	2.589	2.494	2.404	2.320	2.241	2.166	1.879
5	4.452	4.330	4.212	3.993	3.791	3.605	3.433	3.274	3.127	2.991	2.864	2.745	2.635	2.532	2.436	2.035
6	5.242	5.076	4.917	4.623	4.355	4.111	3.889	3.685	3.498	3.326	3.167	3.020	2.885	2.759	2.643	2.168
7	6.002	5.786	5.582	5.206	4.868	4.564	4.288	4.039	3.812	3.605	3.416	3.242	3.083	2.937	2.802	2.263
8	6.733	6.463	6.210	5.747	5.335	4.968	4.639	4.344	4.078	3.837	3.619	3.421	3.241	3.076	2.925	2.331
9	7.435	7.108	6.802	6.247	5.759	5.328	4.946	4.607	4.303	4.031	3.786	3.566	3.366	3.184	3.019	2.379
10	8.111	7.722	7.360	6.710	6.145	5.650	5.216	4.833	4.494	4.192	3.923	3.682	3.465	3.269	3.092	2.414
11	8.760	8.306	7.887	7.139	6.495	5.988	5.453	5.029	4.656	4.327	4.035	3.776	3.544	3.335	3.147	2.438
12	9.385	8.863	8.384	7.536	6.814	6.194	5.660	5.197	4.793	4.439	4.127	3.851	3.606	3.387	3.190	2.456
13	9.986	9.394	8.853	7.904	7.103	6.424	5.842	5.342	4.910	4.533	4.203	3.912	3.656	3.427	3.223	2.468
14	10.563	9.899	9.295	8.244	7.367	6.628	6.002	5.468	5.008	4.611	4.265	3.962	3.695	3.459	3.249	2.477
15	11.118	10.380	9.712	8.559	7.606	6.811	6.142	5.575	5.092	4.675	4.315	4.001	3.726	3.483	3.268	2.484
16	11.652	10.838	10.106	8.851	7.824	6.974	6.265	5.669	5.162	4.730	4.357	4.033	3.751	3.503	3.283	2.489
17	12.166	11.274	10.477	9.122	8.022	7.120	6.373	5.749	5.222	4.775	4.391	4.059	3.771	3.518	3.295	2.492
18	12.659	11.690	10.828	9.372	8.201	7.250	6.467	5.818	5.273	4.812	4.419	4.080	3.786	3.529	3.304	2.494
19	13.134	12.085	11.158	9.604	8.365	7.366	6.550	5.877	5.316	4.844	4.442	4.097	3.799	3.539	3.311	2.496
20	13.590	12.462	11.470	9.818	8.514	7.469	6.623	5.929	5.353	4.870	4.460	4.110	3.808	3.546	3.316	2.497
21	14.029	12.821	11.764	10.017	8.649	7.562	6.687	5.973	5.384	4.891	4.476	4.121	3.816	3.551	3.320	2.498
22	14.451	13.163	12.042	10.201	8.772	7.645	6.743	6.011	5.410	4.909	4.488	4.130	3.822	3.556	3.323	2.498
23	14.857	13.489	12.303	10.371	8.883	7.718	6.792	6.044	5.432	4.925	4.499	4.137	3.827	3.559	3.325	2.499
24	15.247	13.799	12.550	10.529	8.985	7.784	6.835	6.073	5.451	4.937	4.507	4.143	3.831	3.562	3.327	2.499
25	15.622	14.094	12.783	10.675	9.077	7.843	6.873	6.097	5.467	4.948	4.514	4.147	3.834	3.564	3.329	2.499
26	15.983	14.375	13.003	10.810	9.161	7.896	6.906	6.118	5.480	4.956	4.520	4.151	3.837	3.566	3.330	2.500
27	16.330	14.643	13.211	10.935	9.237	7.943	6.935	6.936	5.492	4.964	4.525	4.154	3.839	3.567	3.331	2.500
28	16.663	14.898	13.406	11.051	9.307	7.984	6.961	6.152	5.502	4.970	4.528	4.157	3.840	3.568	3.331	2.500
29	16.984	15.141	13.591	11.158	9.370	8.022	6.983	6.166	5.510	4.975	4.531	4.159	3.841	3.569	3.332	2.500
30	17.292	15.373	13.765	11.258	9.427	8.055	7.003	6.177	5.517	4.979	4.534	4.160	3.842	3.569	3.332	2.500
40	19.793	17.159	15.046	11.925	9.779	8.244	7.105	6.234	5.548	4.997	4.544	4.166	3.846	3.571	3.333	2.500

QUESTIONS

14–1 What is meant by the term *capital budgeting?*

14–2 Distinguish between capital budgeting screening decisions and capital budgeting preference decisions.

14–3 What is meant by the term *time value of money?*

14–4 What is meant by the term *discounting,* and why is it important to the business manager?

14–5 Why can't accounting net income figures be used in the net present value and time-adjusted rate of return methods of making capital budgeting decisions?

14–6 Why are discounted cash flow methods of making capital budgeting decisions superior to other methods?

14–7 What is net present value? Can it ever be negative? Explain.

14–8 One real shortcoming of discounted cash flow methods is that they ignore depreciation. Do you agree? Why or why not?

14–9 Identify two limiting assumptions associated with discounted cash flow methods of making capital budgeting decisions.

14–10 If a firm has to pay interest of 14 percent on long-term debt, then its cost of capital is 14 percent. Do you agree? Explain.

14–11 What is meant by an investment project's time-adjusted rate of return? How is the time-adjusted rate of return computed?

14–12 Explain how the cost of capital serves as a screening tool when dealing with *(a)* the net present value method and *(b)* the time-adjusted rate of return method.

14–13 Companies that invest in underdeveloped countries usually require a higher rate of return on their investment than they do when their investment is made in countries that are better developed and that have more stable political and economic conditions. Some people say that the higher rate of return required in the underdeveloped countries is evidence of exploitation. What other explanation can you offer?

14–14 Riskier investment proposals should be discounted at lower rates of return. Do you agree? Why or why not?

14–15 As the discount rate increases, the present value of a given future sum also increases. Do you agree? Explain.

14–16 Refer to Exhibit 14–4 in the book. Is the return promised by this investment proposal exactly 20 percent, slightly more than 20 percent, or slightly less than 20 percent? Explain.

14–17 If an investment project has a zero net present value, then it should be rejected since it will provide no return on funds invested. Do you agree? Why?

14–18 A machine costs $12,000. It will provide a cost savings of $3,000 per year. If the company requires a 16 percent rate of return, how many years will the machine have to be used to provide the desired 16 percent return?

14–19 Frontier Company is investigating the purchase of a piece of automated equipment, but after considering the savings in labor costs the machine has a negative net present value. If no other cost savings can be identified, should the company reject the equipment? Explain.

14–20 What is meant by the term *payback period?* How is the payback period determined?

14–21 Sharp Company is considering the purchase of certain new equipment in order to sell a new product line. Expected yearly net income from the new product line is given below. From these data, compute the net annual cash inflow that would be used to determine the payback period on the new equipment.

Sales		$150,000
Less cost of goods sold		45,000
Gross margin.		105,000
Less operating expenses:		
Advertising	$35,000	
Salaries and wages	50,000	
Depreciation	12,000	97,000
Net income		$ 8,000

14–22 In what ways can the payback method be useful to the manager?

14–23 What is the formula for computing the simple rate of return?

14–24 What is the major criticism of the payback and simple rate of return methods of making capital budgeting decisions?

EXERCISES

(Ignore income taxes in all exercises.)

E14–1 (The solution to this exercise is given below.) Each of the following situations is independent. Work out your own solution to each situation, and then check it against the solution provided.

1. John has just reached age 58. In 12 years, he plans to retire. Upon retiring, he would like to take an extended vacation, which he expects will cost at least $4,000. What lump-sum amount must he invest now in order to have the needed $4,000 at the end of 12 years if the desired rate of return is:
   a. Eight percent?
   b. Twelve percent?
2. The Morgans would like to send their daughter to an expensive music camp at the end of each of the next five years. The camp costs $1,000 each year. What lump-sum amount would have to be invested now in order to have the $1,000 at the end of each year if the desired rate of return is:
   a. Eight percent?
   b. Twelve percent?
3. You have just received an inheritance from your father's estate. You can invest the money and either receive a $20,000 lump-sum amount at the end of 10 years or receive $1,400 at the end of each year for the next 10 years. If the minimum desired rate of return is 12 percent, which alternative would you prefer?

Solution to Exercise 14–1

1. *a.* The amount that must be invested now would be the present value of the $4,000, using a discount rate of 8 percent. From Table 14C–3 in Appendix C, the factor for a discount rate of 8 percent for 12 periods is 0.397. Multiplying this discount factor times the $4,000 needed in 12 years will give the amount of the present investment required: $4,000 × 0.397 = $1,588.
   b. We will proceed as we did in *(a)* above, but this time we will use a discount rate of 12 percent. From Table 14C–3 in Appendix C, the factor for a discount rate of 12 percent for 12 periods is 0.257. Multiplying this discount factor times the $4,000 needed in 12 years will give the amount of the present investment required: $4,000 × 0.257 = $1,028.

   Notice that as the discount rate (desired rate of return) increases, the present value decreases.
2. This part differs from (1) above in that we are now dealing with an annuity rather than with a single future sum. The amount that must be invested now will be the

present value of the $1,000 needed at the end of each year for five years. Since we are dealing with an annuity, or a series of cash flows, we must refer to Table 14C–4 in Appendix C for the appropriate discount factor.

a. From Table 14C–4 in Appendix C, the discount factor for 8 percent for five periods is 3.993. Therefore, the amount that must be invested now in order to have $1,000 available at the end of each year for five years is: $1,000 × 3.993 = $3,993.

b. From Table 14C–4 in Appendix C, the discount factor for 12 percent for five periods is 3.605. Therefore, the amount that must be invested now in order to have $1,000 available at the end of each year for five years is: $1,000 × 3.605 = $3,605.

Again notice that as the discount rate (desired rate of return) increases, the present value decreases. This is logical, since at a higher rate of return we would expect to have to invest less than would have to be invested if a lower rate of return were being earned.

3. For this part we will need to refer to both Tables 14C–3 and 14C–4 in Appendix C. From Table 14C–3, we will need to find the discount factor for 12 percent for 10 periods, then apply it to the $20,000 lump sum to be received in 10 years. From Table 14C–4, we will need to find the discount factor for 12 percent for 10 periods, then apply it to the series of $1,400 payments to be received over the 10-year period. Whichever alternative has the highest present value is the one that should be selected.

$20,000 × 0.322 = $6,440
$1,400 × 5.650 = $7,910

Thus, you would prefer to receive the $1,400 per year for 10 years, rather than the $20,000 lump sum.

E14–2 Consider each of the following situations independently.

1. Annual cash inflows that will arise from two competing investment opportunities are given below. Each investment opportunity will require the same initial investment. You can invest money at a 20 percent rate of return. Compute the present value of the cash inflows for each investment.

	Investment	
Year	**X**	**Y**
1	$ 1,000	$ 4,000
2	2,000	3,000
3	3,000	2,000
4	4,000	1,000
	$10,000	$10,000

2. At the end of three years, when you graduate from college, your father has promised to give you a new car that will cost $9,000. What lump sum must he invest now in order to have the $9,000 at the end of three years, if he can invest money at:

a. Six percent?
b. Ten percent?

3. Mark has just won the grand prize on the "Hoot'n' Holler" quiz show. He has a choice between *(a)* receiving $50,000 immediately and *(b)* receiving $6,000 per year for eight years plus a lump sum of $20,000 at the end of the eight-year period. If Mark can get a return of 10 percent on his investments, which option would you recommend that he accept? (Use present value analysis, and show all computations.)

4. You have just learned that you are a beneficiary in the will of your late Aunt Susan. The executrix of her estate has given you three options as to how you may receive your inheritance:
   a. You may receive $50,000 immediately.
   b. You may receive $75,000 at the end of six years.
   c. You may receive $12,000 at the end of each year for six years (a total of $72,000).

   If you can invest money at a 12 percent return, which option would you prefer?

E14–3 Each of the following parts is independent.

1. Largo Freightlines plans to build a new garage in three years in order to have more space for repairing its trucks. The garage will cost $400,000. What lump-sum amount should the company invest now in order to have the $400,000 available at the end of the three-year period? Assume that the company can invest money at:
   a. Eight percent.
   b. Twelve percent.
2. Martell Products, Inc., can purchase a new copier that will save $5,000 per year in copying costs. The copier will last for six years and have no salvage value. What is the maximum purchase price that Martell Products would be willing to pay for the copier if the company's required rate of return is:
   a. Ten percent.
   b. Sixteen percent.
3. Sally has just won the million-dollar Big Slam jackpot at a gambling casino. The casino will pay her $50,000 per year for 20 years as the payoff. If Sally can invest money at a 10 percent rate of return, what is the present value of her winnings? Did she really win a million dollars? Explain.

E14–4 Consider each case below independently.

1. Minden Company requires a minimum return of 18 percent on all investments. The company can purchase a new machine at a cost of $40,350. The new machine would generate cash inflows of $15,000 per year and have a four-year life with no salvage value. Compute the machine's net present value. (Use the format shown in Exhibit 14–1.) Is the machine an acceptable investment? Explain.
2. Leven Products, Inc., is investigating the purchase of a new grinding machine that has a projected life of 15 years. It is estimated that the machine will save $20,000 per year in cash operating costs. What is the machine's time-adjusted rate of return if it costs $93,500 new?
3. Sunset Press has just purchased a new trimming machine that cost $14,125. The machine is expected to save $2,500 per year in cash operating costs and to have a 10-year life. Compute the machine's time-adjusted rate of return. If the company's cost of capital is 16 percent, did it make a wise investment? Explain.

E14–5 On January 2, 19x2, Fred Critchfield paid $18,000 for 900 shares of the common stock of Acme Company. Mr. Critchfield received an $0.80 per share dividend on the stock each year for four years. At the end of four years, he sold the stock for $22,500. Mr. Critchfield has a goal of earning a minimum return of 12 percent on all of his investments.

Required Did Mr. Critchfield earn a 12 percent return on the stock? Use the net present value method and the general format shown in Exhibit 14–1 in determining your answer. (Round all computations to the nearest whole dollar.)

E14–6 Scalia's Cleaning Service is investigating the purchase of an ultra-sound machine for cleaning window blinds. The machine would cost $136,700, including invoice cost, freight, and training of employees to operate it. Scalia's has estimated that the new machine would increase the company's cash flows, net of expenses, by $25,000 per year. The machine would have a 14-year useful life with no expected salvage value.

Required

1. Compute the machine's time-adjusted rate of return. (Do not round your computations.)
2. Compute the machine's net present value. Use a discount rate of 16 percent, and use the format shown in Exhibit 14–5. Why do you have a zero net present value? If the company's cost of capital is 15 percent, is this an acceptable investment? Explain.
3. Suppose that the new machine would increase the company's annual cash flows, net of expenses, by only $20,000 per year. Under these conditions, compute the time-adjusted rate of return. Interpolate as needed, and round your final answer to the nearest tenth of a percent.

E14–7 Pisa Pizza Parlor is investigating the purchase of a new delivery truck that would contain specially designed warming racks. The new truck would cost $22,300 and have a six-year useful life. It would save $1,400 per year over the present method of delivering pizzas. In addition, it would result in delivery of about 1,800 more pizzas each year. The company realizes a contribution margin of $2 per pizza.

Required

1. What would be the total annual cash inflows associated with the new truck for capital budgeting purposes?
2. Compute the time-adjusted rate of return promised by the new truck. Interpolate to the nearest tenth of a percent.
3. In addition to the data above, assume that due to the unique warming racks, the truck will have a $13,000 salvage value at the end of six years. Under these conditions, compute the time-adjusted rate of return to the nearest *whole* percent. (Hint: You may find it helpful to use the net present value approach; find the discount rate that will cause the net present value to be closest to zero. Use the format shown in Exhibit 14–4.)

E14–8 Sharp Company has $15,000 to invest. The company is trying to decide between two alternative uses of the funds. The alternatives are:

	Invest in Project A	Invest in Project B
Investment required	$15,000	$15,000
Annual cash inflows	4,000	—
Single cash inflow at the end of 10 years	—	60,000
Life of the project	10 years	10 years

Sharp Company's cost of capital is 16 percent.

Required Which investment would you recommend that the company accept? Show all computations using net present value. (Use the format shown in Exhibit 14–4. Prepare a separate computation for each investment.)

E14–9 Wriston Company has $300,000 to invest. The company is trying to decide between two alternative uses of the funds. The alternatives are:

	A	B
Cost of equipment required	$300,000	$ —
Working capital investment required	—	300,000
Annual cash inflows	80,000	60,000
Salvage value of equipment in seven years	20,000	—
Life of the project	7 years	7 years

The working capital needed for project B will be released for investment elsewhere at the end of seven years. Wriston Company's cost of capital is 20 percent.

Required Which investment alternative (if either) would you recommend that the company accept? Show all computations using the net present value format. (Prepare a separate computation for each project.)

E14–10 Solve thė three following present value exercises:

1. Mountain View Hospital has purchased new lab equipment that cost $134,650. The equipment is expected to last for three years and to provide cash inflows as follows:

Year 1	$45,000
Year 2	60,000
Year 3	?

   Assuming that the equipment will yield exactly a 16 percent rate of return, what is the expected cash inflow for year 3?
2. Lukow Products is investigating the purchase of a piece of automated equipment that will save $400,000 each year in direct labor and inventory carrying costs. This equipment costs $2,500,000 and is expected to have a 15-year useful life with no salvage value. The company requires a minimum 20 percent return on all equipment purchases. Management anticipates that this equipment will provide certain intangible benefits such as greater flexibility, higher quality of output, and a positive learning experience in automation. What dollar value per year would management have to attach to these intangible benefits in order to make the equipment an acceptable investment?
3. Worldwide Travel Service has made an investment in certain equipment that cost the company $307,100. The equipment is expected to generate cash inflows of $50,000 each year. How many years will the equipment have to be used in order to provide the company with a 14 percent return on its investment?

E14–11 The Heritage Amusement Park would like to construct a new ride called the Sonic Boom which the park management feels would be very popular. The ride would cost $450,000 to construct, and it would have a 10 percent salvage value at the end of its 15-year useful life. It is estimated that the following annual costs and revenues would be associated with the ride:

Ticket revenues		$250,000
Less operating expenses:		
Maintenance	$40,000	
Salaries	90,000	
Depreciation	27,000	
Insurance	30,000	
Total operating expenses . . .		187,000
Net income		$ 63,000

Required

1. Assume that the Heritage Amusement Park will not construct a new ride unless the ride promises a payback period of six years or less. Would you recommend that the Sonic Boom ride be constructed?
2. Compute the simple rate of return promised by the new ride. (Compute investment at initial cost.) If the amusement park's cost of capital is 12 percent, would you recommend that the new ride be constructed?

E14–12 Martin Company is considering the purchase of a new piece of equipment. Relevant information concerning the equipment follows:

Purchase cost	$180,000
Annual cost savings that will be provided by the equipment	37,500
Life of the equipment	12 years
Cost of capital	14%

Required

1. Compute the payback period for the equipment. If the company requires a maximum payback period of four years, would you recommend purchase of the equipment? Explain.
2. Compute the simple rate of return on the equipment. Use straight-line depreciation based on the equipment's useful life. Would you recommend purchase of the equipment? Explain.

PROBLEMS

P14–13 Basic Net Present Value Analysis Doughboy Bakery would like to buy a new machine for putting icing and other toppings on pastries. These are now put on by hand. The machine that the bakery is considering costs $90,000 new. It would last the bakery for eight years but would require a $7,500 overhaul at the end of the fifth year. After eight years, the machine could be sold for $6,000.

The bakery estimates that it will cost $14,000 per year to operate the new machine. The present hand method of putting toppings on the pastries costs $35,000 per year. In addition to reducing operating costs, the new machine will allow the bakery to increase its production of pastries by 5,000 packages per year. The bakery realizes a contribution margin of $0.60 per package. The bakery requires a 16 percent return on all investments in equipment.

Required (ignore income taxes)

1. What are the net annual cash inflows that will be provided by the new machine?
2. Compute the new machine's net present value. Use the incremental cost approach, and round all dollar amounts to the nearest whole dollar.

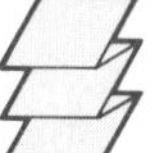

P14–14 Basic Net Present Value Analysis Renfree Mines, Inc., owns the mining rights to a large tract of land in a mountainous area. The tract contains a mineral deposit that the company believes might be commercially attractive to mine and sell. An engineering and cost analysis has been made, and it is expected that the following cash flows would be associated with opening and operating a mine in the area:

Cost of equipment required	$850,000
Net annual cash receipts	230,000*
Working capital required	100,000
Cost of road repairs in three years	60,000
Salvage value of equipment in five years . . .	200,000

* Receipts from sales of ore, less out-of-pocket costs for salaries, utilities, insurance, and so forth.

It is estimated that the mineral deposit would be exhausted after five years of mining. At that point, the working capital would be released for reinvestment elsewhere. The company's cost of capital is 14 percent.

Required (ignore income taxes) Determine the net present value of the proposed mining project. Should the project be undertaken? Explain.

P14–15 Time-Adjusted Rate of Return; Sensitivity Analysis Crescent Fabrics, Inc., is investigating purchase of an electronic loom to replace a mechanical loom in one of its plants. The electronic loom would cost $500,000, but studies have shown that it would save $80,000 per year in costs (mostly through reduced labor costs). If the new electronic loom is purchased, the old mechanical loom can be sold for its salvage value of $90,000. The manufacturer estimates that the new loom would have a service life of 10 years.

Required (ignore income taxes)

1. What would be the net initial (incremental) cost of the new electronic loom for capital budgeting purposes?
2. Using the investment cost figure computed in (1) above, compute the time-adjusted rate of return on the new loom. Interpolate to the nearest tenth of a percent.
3. Few electronic looms are in use, so the management of Crescent Fabrics, Inc., is unsure about the estimated 10-year life. Compute what the time-adjusted rate of return would be if the useful life of the new loom were *(a)* 7 years and *(b)* 13 years, instead of 10 years. Again interpolate to the nearest tenth of a percent.
4. Refer to the original data. Technology is moving rapidly in the electronics industry, and management may not want to keep the new loom for more than six years. If the new loom is disposed of at the end of six years, it would have a salvage value of $160,000.
   a. Again using the investment figure computed in (1) above, compute the time-adjusted rate of return to the nearest *whole* percent. (Hint: A useful way to proceed is to find the discount rate that will cause the net present value to be equal to, or near, zero.)
   b. If the company's cost of capital is 12 percent, would you recommend purchase? Explain.

P14–16 **Net Present Value Analysis; FMS/Automation Decision** Big Byte Computers, Inc., is considering the purchase of an automated etching machine for use in the production of its circuit boards. The machine would cost $900,000. An additional $650,000 would be required for installation costs and for software. Management believes that the automated machine would provide substantial annual reductions in costs, as shown below:

	Annual Reduction in Costs
Labor costs	$240,000
Material costs	96,000

The new machine would require considerable maintenance work to keep it in proper adjustment. The company's engineers estimate that maintenance costs would increase by $4,250 per month if the machine is purchased. In addition, the machine would require an overhaul at the end of the sixth year that the manufacturer estimates would cost $90,000.

The new etching machine would be usable for 10 years, after which it would be sold for its scrap value of $210,000. It would replace an old etching machine that can be sold now for its scrap value of $70,000. Big Byte Computers, Inc., requires a return of at least 18 percent on investments of this type.

Required (ignore income taxes)

1. Compute the net annual cost savings promised by the new etching machine.
2. Using the data from (1) above and other data from the problem, compute the new machine's net present value. (Use the incremental-cost approach.) Would you recommend purchase? Explain.
3. Assume that management can identify several intangible benefits associated with the new machine, including greater flexibility in shifting from one type of circuit board to another, improved quality of output, and faster delivery as a result of reduced throughput time. What dollar value per year would management have to attach to these intangible benefits in order to make the new etching machine an acceptable investment?

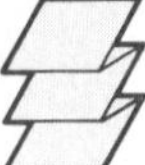

P14–17 Simple Rate of Return; Payback Lugano's Pizza Parlor is considering the purchase of a large oven and related equipment for mixing and baking "crazy bread." The oven and equipment would cost $120,000 delivered and installed. It would be usable for about 15 years, after which it would have a 10 percent scrap value. The following additional information is available:

a. Mr. Lugano estimates that purchase of the oven and equipment would allow the pizza parlor to bake and sell 72,000 loaves of crazy bread each year. The bread sells for $1.25 per loaf.
b. The cost of the ingredients in a loaf of bread is 40 percent of the selling price. Mr. Lugano estimates that other costs each year associated with the bread would be: salaries, $18,000; utilities, $9,000; and insurance, $3,000.
c. The pizza parlor uses straight-line depreciation on all assets and considers salvage value in computing depreciation deductions.
d. In order to purchase the oven and equipment, Mr. Lugano would have to liquidate some personal investments that yield a return of 12 percent.

Required (ignore income taxes)

1. Prepare an income statement showing the net income each year from production and sale of the crazy bread. Use the contribution format.
2. Compute the simple rate of return promised by the new oven and equipment. Should the oven and equipment be purchased?
3. Compute the payback period on the oven and equipment. If Mr. Lugano wants a maximum six-year payback on any equipment, should the purchase be made?

P14–18 Opening a Small Business; Net Present Value Frank White will retire in six years. He has $50,000 to invest, and he wants to open some type of small business operation that can be managed in the free time he has available from his regular occupation, but which can be closed easily when he retires. He is considering several investment alternatives, one of which is to open a laundromat.

After careful study, Mr. White has determined the following:

a. Washers, dryers, and other equipment needed to open the laundromat would cost $48,000. In addition, $2,000 in working capital investment would be required to purchase an inventory of soap, bleaches, and related items and to provide change for change machines. (The soap, bleaches, and related items would be sold to customers basically at cost.) After six years, the working capital would be released for investment elsewhere.
b. The laundromat would charge 50 cents per use for the washers and 25 cents per use for the dryers. (A regular wash cycle is 20 minutes, and a regular dryer cycle is 15 minutes.) Mr. White expects the laundromat to gross $600 each week from the washers and $375 each week from the dryers.
c. The only variable costs in the laundromat would be 7½ cents per use for water and electricity for the washers and 9 cents per use for gas and electricity for the dryers.
d. Fixed costs would be $1,000 per month for rent, $500 per month for cleaning, and $625 per month for maintenance, insurance, and other items.
e. The equipment would have a 10 percent disposal value in six years.

Mr. White will not open the laundromat unless it provides at least a 12 percent return, since this is the amount that he could earn from an alternative investment opportunity.

Required (ignore income taxes)

1. Assuming that the laundromat would be open 52 weeks a year, compute the expected net annual cash receipts from its operation (gross cash receipts less cash disbursements). (Do not include the cost of the equipment, the working capital, or the salvage values in these computations.)

2. Would you advise Mr. White to open the laundromat? Show computations using the net present value method of investment analysis. Round all dollar amounts to the nearest whole dollar.

P14–19 Time-Adjusted Rate of Return; Sensitivity Analysis Dr. Karen Black is the managing partner of the Crestwood Dental Clinic. Dr. Black is trying to determine whether or not the clinic should move patient files and other items out of a spare room in the clinic and use the room for dental work. She has determined that it would require an investment of $142,950 for equipment and related costs of getting the room ready for use. Based on receipts being generated from other rooms in the clinic, Dr. Black estimates that the new room would generate a net cash inflow of $37,500 per year. The equipment purchased for the room would have a seven-year estimated useful life.

Required (ignore income taxes)

1. Compute the time-adjusted rate of return on the equipment for the new room. Prove your answer by computing the net present value of the equipment, using the rate of return figure you have computed as the discount rate.
2. Assume that Dr. Black will not purchase the new equipment unless it promises a return of at least 14 percent. Compute the amount of annual cash inflow that would provide this return on the $142,950 investment.
3. Although seven years is the average life for dental equipment, Dr. Black knows that due to changing technology this life can vary substantially. Compute the time-adjusted rate of return if the life of the equipment were *(a)* five years, and *(b)* nine years, rather than seven years. Interpolate to the nearest tenth of a percent. Is there any information provided by these computations that you would be particularly anxious to show Dr. Black?
4. Dr. Black is unsure about the estimated $37,500 annual cash inflow from the room. She thinks that the actual cash inflow could be as much as 20 percent greater or less than this figure.
   a. Assume that the actual cash inflow each year is 20 percent greater than estimated. Recompute the time-adjusted rate of return. Interpolate to the nearest tenth of a percent.
   b. Assume that the actual cash inflow each year is 20 percent less than estimated. Recompute the time-adjusted rate of return. Again interpolate to the nearest tenth of a percent.
5. Refer to the original data. Assume that the equipment is purchased and that the room is opened for dental use. However, due to an increasing number of dentists in the area, the clinic is able to generate only $30,000 per year in net cash receipts from the new room. At the end of five years, the clinic closes the room and sells the equipment to a newly licensed dentist for a cash price of $61,375. Compute the time-adjusted rate of return (to the nearest *whole* percent) that the clinic earned on its investment over the five-year period. Round all dollar amounts to the nearest whole dollar. (Hint: A useful way to proceed is to find that discount rate which will cause the net present value of the investment to be equal to, or near, zero.)

P14–20 Simple Rate of Return; Payback Regal Machines, Inc., places electronic games and other amusement devices in supermarkets and similar outlets. Regal is investigating the purchase and placement of a new electronic game called Mystic Invaders. The manufacturer will sell Regal 150 games for a total price of $180,000. Regal has determined the following additional information about the game:

a. The game would have a five-year useful life and only a negligible salvage value. The company uses straight-line depreciation.

b. The game would replace other games that are unpopular and generating little revenue. These other games would be sold in bulk for a $30,000 sale price.

c. Regal estimates that Mystic Invaders would generate incremental revenues of $200,000 per year (total for all 150 games). Incremental out-of-pocket costs each year would be (in total): maintenance, $50,000; and insurance, $10,000. In addition, Regal would have to pay a commission of 40 percent of total revenues to the supermarkets and other outlets in which the games were placed.

d. Regal's cost of capital is 14 percent.

Required (ignore income taxes)

1. Prepare an income statement showing the net income each year from Mystic Invaders. Use the contribution approach.
2. Compute the simple rate of return on Mystic Invaders. Should the game be purchased?
3. Compute the payback period on Mystic Invaders. If the company requires a payback period of three years or less, should the game be purchased?

P14–21 Replacement Decision Eastbay Hospital has an auxiliary generator that is used when power failures occur. The generator is in bad repair and must be either overhauled or replaced with a new generator. The hospital has assembled the following information:

	Present Generator	New Generator
Purchase cost new	$16,000	$20,000
Remaining book value	9,000	—
Overhaul needed now	8,000	—
Annual cash operating costs	12,500	7,500
Salvage value—now	4,000	—
Salvage value—eight years from now . . .	3,000	6,000

If the company keeps and overhauls its present generator, then the generator will be usable for eight more years. If a new generator is purchased, it will be used for eight years, after which it will be replaced. The new generator would be diesel-powered, resulting in a substantial reduction in annual operating costs, as shown above.

The hospital computes depreciation on a straight-line basis. All equipment purchases are evaluated on a basis of a 16 percent rate of return.

Required (ignore income taxes)

1. Should Eastbay Hospital keep the old generator or purchase the new one? Use the total-cost approach to net present value in making your decision.
2. Redo (1) above, this time using the incremental-cost approach.

P14–22 Net Present Value Analysis of Securities On January 2, 19x5, Frank Vecci had $245,000 to invest. He used the funds to purchase the following three securities:

a. Preferred stock was purchased at its par value of $50,000. The stock paid a 7 percent dividend (based on par) each year for three years. At the end of three years, the stock was sold for $49,000.

b. Common stock was purchased at a cost of $95,000. The stock paid no dividends, but it was sold for $160,000 at the end of three years.

c. Bonds were purchased at a cost of $100,000. The bonds paid $6,000 in interest every six months. After three years, the bonds were sold for $113,400. (Note: In discounting a cash flow that occurs semiannually, the procedure is to halve the discount rate and double the number of periods. Use the same procedure in discounting the proceeds from the sale of the bonds.)

Mr. Vecci's goal is to earn a before-tax rate of return of at least 16 percent on his investments. Round all dollar amounts to the nearest whole dollar.

Required (ignore income taxes)

1. Compute the net present value of *each* of the three investments. On which investments did Mr. Vecci earn at least the desired 16 percent return?

2. Considering all three investments together, did Mr. Vecci earn the desired 16 percent return?
3. An insurance salesperson has approached Mr. Vecci with a proposal that Mr. Vecci invest the $322,400 proceeds from the sale of the securities ($49,000 + $160,000 + $113,400 = $322,400) in a 10-year annuity. The salesperson says that the annuity is guaranteed to yield an 18 percent return each year over the next 10 years. What net annual cash inflow would Mr. Vecci have to receive from the annuity in order to earn an 18 percent return on his investment?

P14–23 Simple Rate of Return; Payback; Time-Adjusted Rate of Return Honest John's Used Cars, Inc., has always hired students from the local university to wash the cars on the lot. Honest John is considering the purchase of an automatic car wash that would be used in place of the students. The following information has been gathered by Honest John's accountant in order to help Honest John make a decision on the purchase:

a. Payments to students for washing cars totals $15,000 per year at present.
b. The car wash would cost $21,000 installed, and it would have a ten-year useful life. Honest John uses straight-line depreciation on all assets. The car wash would have a negligible salvage value in 10 years.
c. Annual out-of-pocket costs associated with the car wash would be: wages of students to operate the wash, keep the soap bin full, and so forth, $6,300; utilities, $1,800; and insurance and maintenance, $900.
d. Honest John now earns a return of 20 percent before taxes on the funds invested in his inventory of used cars. He feels that he would have to earn an equivalent rate on the car wash in order for the purchase to be attractive.

Required (ignore income taxes)

1. Determine the annual savings that would be realized in cash operating costs if the car wash were purchased.
2. Compute the simple rate of return promised by the car wash. (Hint: Note that this is a cost reduction project.) Based on the simple rate of return, should the car wash be purchased?
3. Compute the payback period on the car wash. Honest John (who has a reputation for being somewhat of a nickel-nurser) will not purchase any equipment unless it has a payback of four years or less. Should the car wash be purchased?
4. Compute (to the nearest whole percent) the time-adjusted rate of return promised by the car wash. Based on this computation, does it appear that the simple rate of return would normally be an accurate guide in investment decisions?

P14–24 Net Present Value; FMS/Automated Equipment; Postaudit "If we can get that new robot to combine with our other automated equipment, we'll have a complete flexible manufacturing system in place in our Northridge plant," said Hal Swain, production manager for Diller Products.

"Let's just hope that reduced labor and inventory costs can justify its acquisition," replied Linda Wycoff, the controller. "Otherwise, we'll never get it. You know how the president feels about equipment paying for itself out of reduced costs."

Selected data relating to the robot are provided below:

Cost of the robot	$1,600,000
Software and installation	700,000
Annual savings in labor costs	?
Annual savings in inventory carrying costs	190,000
Monthly increase in power and maintenance costs	2,500
Salvage value in 12 years	90,000
Useful life	12 years

Engineering studies suggest that use of the robot will result in a savings of 40,000 direct labor-hours each year. The labor rate is $8 per hour. Also, the smoother work flow made possible by the FMS will allow the company to reduce the amount of inventory on hand by $300,000. This inventory reduction will take place in the first year of operation. The company requires a 20 percent return on all investments in automated equipment.

Required (ignore income taxes)

1. Determine the net *annual* cost savings if the robot is purchased. (Do not include the $300,000 inventory reduction or the salvage value in this computation.)
2. Compute the net present value of the proposed investment in the robot. Based on these data, would you recommend that the robot be purchased? Explain.
3. Assume that the robot is purchased. At the end of the first year, Linda Wycoff has found that some items didn't work out as planned. Software and installation costs were $125,000 more than estimated, due to unforseen problems; and direct labor has been reduced by only 35,000 hours per year, rather than by 40,000 hours. Assuming that all other items of cost data were accurate, does it appear that the company made a wise investment? Show computations, using the net present value format as in (2) above. (Hint: It might be helpful to place yourself back at the beginning of the first year, with the new data.)
4. Upon seeing your analysis in (3) above, the president stated, "That robot is the worst investment we've ever made. And here we'll be stuck with it for years."
   a. Explain to the president what benefits other than cost savings might accrue from use of the new robot and FMS.
   b. Compute for the president the dollar amount of cash inflow that would be needed each year from the benefits in *(a)* above in order for the equipment to yield a 20 percent rate of return.

P14–25 Lease or Buy Decision Blinko Products wants an airplane available for use by its corporate staff. The airplane that the company wishes to acquire, a Zephyr II, can be either purchased or leased from the manufacturer. The company has made the following evaluation of the two alternatives:

Purchase alternative. If the Zephyr II is purchased, then the costs incurred by the company would be:

Purchase cost of the plane	$850,000
Annual cost of servicing, licenses, and taxes.	9,000
Repairs:	
First three years, per year	3,000
Fourth year.	5,000
Fifth year.	10,000

The plane would be sold after five years. Based on current resale values, the company would be able to sell it for about one half of its original cost at the end of the five-year period.

Lease alternative. If the Zephyr II is leased, then the company would have to make an immediate deposit of $50,000 to cover any damage during use. The lease would run for five years, at the end of which time the deposit would be refunded. The lease would require an annual rental payment of $200,000 (payable in installments throughout the year). As part of this lease cost, the manufacturer would provide all servicing and repairs, license the plane, and pay all taxes. At the end of the five-year period, the plane would revert to the manufacturer, as owner.

Blinko Products' cost of capital is 18 percent.

Required (ignore income taxes)

1. Use the total-cost approach to determine the present value of the cash flows associated with each alternative.
2. Which alternative would you recommend that the company accept? Why?

P14–26 Payback; Simple Rate of Return; Discounted Cash Flow Tune-ups, Inc., operates a chain of service centers that provide tune-up work and minor repairs for automobiles. The company wants to open a new center and has found what appears to be an acceptable site. After careful study, the following estimates have been made of annual revenues and expenses for the new center:

Service revenue		$1,000,000
Less cost of parts		350,000
Contribution margin		650,000
Less fixed expenses:		
Advertising	$250,000	
Rent	70,000	
Salaries	110,000	
Insurance	6,000	
Depreciation	80,000*	
Other	14,000	
Total fixed expenses		530,000
Net income		$ 120,000

* $750,000 − $30,000 = $720,000; $720,000 ÷ 9 years = $80,000.

New equipment costing $750,000 would be purchased for the center. Since the equipment would be electronic in nature and therefore subject to rapid obsolescence, it would have no more than a nine-year useful life and only a $30,000 scrap value.

The company requires a return of 20 percent on all new centers. Also, the company will not open a new center unless it has a payback of four years or less.

Required (ignore income taxes)

1. What is the simple rate of return on the new center? Should the center be opened?
2. What is the payback period on the new center? Is the center an acceptable investment? Explain.
3. The president is uneasy about the results obtained by the simple rate of return and would like some further analysis done. Compute the net present value of the new center. Will the center provide the 20 percent return required by the company?

P14–27 Net Present Value; FMS/Automated Equipment; Postaudit "I know that $1.9 million sounds like a lot of money," said Jana Bywater, operations manager for Darrow Products. But that new automated equipment would let us create three cells in the Ogden plant and turn its assembly line into a state-of-the-art flexible manufacturing system."

"It doesn't just *sound* like a lot of money," replied Dan Carmack, the company's president. "It *is* a lot of money. And you seem to be forgetting that software and installation will cost another $750,000. But the key question is whether or not this equipment will pay for itself in labor savings. If it doesn't, then I'm not interested."

"The people in engineering figure that we'll need 40 less people a year on the assembly line," replied Jana. "And insurance, storage, and other inventory carrying costs will be reduced by $80,000 per year, since we will have less inventory on hand. In fact, the controller's office estimates that with the smoother flow and greater dependability of the FMS our inventory will be reduced by a half of a million dollars by the end of the first year."

"You operations people are eternal optimists," said Dan. "The savings in inventory carrying costs will be more than eaten up by increased maintenance and by the extra power that those robots will gobble up. In fact, the manufacturer admits that these increased costs will come to at least $240,000 a year. By the way, how much would we get out of our old equipment?"

"Only about $20,000," replied Jana, "because it's so obsolete. But the new automated equipment won't do much better. Right now technology is moving so fast that in 15 years it will be worth only about $70,000."

"I figure that sales will grow by 20 percent a year from our present $10 million level regardless of whether or not we buy the equipment," asserted Dan. "So that means the key is cost savings. Let's see, our assembly-line people work 40 hours a week, 50 weeks a year, and they're paid $7 per hour. If the new equipment has a 15-year useful life, like the manufacturer says, see how it stacks up against our 16 percent cost of capital."

Required (ignore income taxes)

1. Compute the net annual cost savings that will be provided by the new equipment.
2. Use the incremental-cost approach to determine the net present value of the new equipment. Based on these data, should the equipment be purchased?
3. Assume that the new equipment is purchased. Due to unforseen problems, installation costs are $130,000 greater than estimated. Also, at the end of the first year Dan Carmack is surprised to learn that only 35 people have been replaced on the assembly line, and he has requested that a postaudit be performed on the new equipment. Assuming that all other items of data were accurate, does it appear that the company made a wise investment? Show computations, using the net present value format, as in (2) above. (Hint: It might be helpful to place yourself back at the beginning of the first year, with the new data.)
4. Upon seeing your analysis in (3) above, Dan Carmack exclaims, "I said that labor savings was the key to this equipment, and I was right! We've never made a worse investment! I don't foresee a single benefit, and I'm amazed that our competitors are making the same mistake."
   a. Explain to the president what benefits other than cost savings might accrue from use of automated equipment.
   b. Compute for the president the dollar amount of cash inflow that would be needed each year from the benefits in *(a)* above in order for the equipment to yield a 16 percent rate of return.

P14–28 Lease or Buy Decision Flamingo Auto Parts, Inc., operates a chain of auto supply stores in the Midwest. The company plans to open a new store soon in a rapidly growing area, and an excellent site has been located for construction of a building. Flamingo Auto Parts has two alternatives as to how the desired site can be acquired, the building constructed, and needed fixtures obtained for use in the store.

Purchase alternative. The company could purchase the building site, construct the building, and purchase store fixtures at a total cost of $750,000. This alternative would require the immediate payment of $300,000 and then a payment of $150,000 each year for the next four years (including interest). Flamingo Auto Parts estimates that the annual costs associated with the property would be:

Property taxes	$ 9,000
Insurance	3,000
Repairs and maintenance	6,000
Total annual costs	$18,000

The company would occupy the property for 15 years. Based on prior experience, it is estimated that the property would have a resale value of about $400,000 at the end of the 15-year period.

Lease alternative. The Worldwide Insurance Company has offered to purchase the site, construct the building, and install fixtures to Flamingo Auto Parts' specifications. The insurance company would then lease the property back to Flamingo Auto Parts under a 15-year lease at an annual lease cost of $100,000. (The first payment would be due now, and the remaining payments would be due in years 1–14.) The insurance company would require a $15,000 security deposit immediately; this would be returned at the termination of the lease. Under the lease agreement, the insurance company would pay for the property taxes and insurance; thus, Flamingo Auto Parts would be required to pay only the repair and maintenance costs associated with the property.

Flamingo Auto Parts' cost of capital is 16 percent.

Required (ignore income taxes) Using discounted cash flow, determine whether Flamingo Auto Parts, Inc., should lease or buy the desired store facilities. Use the total-cost approach.

P14–29 Comprehensive Problem: Simple Rate of Return; Payback Bullrun Meatpackers is considering the purchase of two different items of equipment, as described below.

Machine A. A machine has come onto the market that would allow Bullrun Meatpackers to process and sell an item that was previously a waste product. The following information is available on the machine:

a. The machine would cost $350,000 and would have a 10 percent salvage value at the end of its 12-year useful life. The company uses straight-line depreciation and considers salvage value in computing depreciation deductions.

b. The new product from the machine would generate revenues of $500,000 per year. Variable manufacturing expenses would be 60 percent of sales.

c. Fixed expenses associated with the new product would be (per year): advertising, $36,000; salaries, $90,000; and insurance, $4,000.

Machine B. Another machine has come onto the market that would allow Bullrun Meatpackers to dispose of some antiquated, hand-operated wrapping equipment and replace it with a largely automatic wrapping process. The following information is available:

a. The new wrapping machine would cost $260,000 and would have negligible salvage value at the end of its 13-year useful life. The company would use straight-line depreciation on the new machine.

b. The old hand-operated wrapping equipment could be sold now for $10,000.

c. The new machine would provide substantial annual savings in cash operating costs. It would require an operator at an annual salary of $18,000, and it would require $4,500 in annual maintenance costs. The old hand-operated equipment costs $85,000 per year to operate.

Bullrun Meatpackers requires a return of 15 percent on all equipment purchases. Also, it will not purchase equipment unless the equipment has a payback period of 4.0 years or less.

Required (ignore income taxes)

1. For machine A:
   a. Prepare an income statement showing the expected net income each year from the new product. Use the contribution format.
   b. Compute the simple rate of return.
   c. Compute the payback period.
2. For machine B:
   a. Compute the simple rate of return.
   b. Compute the payback period.
3. Which machine, if either, should the company buy?

P14–30 Keep or Sell Rental Property Wesco Products owns a tract of land on which there is a small factory building. The property was purchased several years ago at a cost of $350,000 with the intention of tearing down the old building and constructing a new building on the land. However, the company decided to construct the new building elsewhere. As a result, the old building is being rented to another company. Consideration is now being given to selling the old building and land, rather than continuing to rent it. Wesco Products' alternatives are:

Keep the property. If Wesco Products keeps the property, it will continue to be rented. Annual revenues and expenses associated with the property follow:

Annual rental revenues		$90,000
Annual expenses:		
Property taxes	$16,500	
Insurance	8,900	
Repairs and maintenance	4,600	
Depreciation	20,000	50,000
Net income		$40,000

Wesco Products makes a $30,000 payment to its bank each year on a loan that was obtained to purchase the property. The loan will be paid off in seven more years. The building can be rented for only about 15 more years, after which the property could be sold for about $500,000.

Sell the property. A realty company has offered to purchase the property now. The realty company would pay $250,000 down on the property and then pay Wesco Products $32,500 per year for the next 15 years. If this option is accepted, Wesco Products would have to pay off its bank loan immediately. The remaining principal balance on the loan is $180,000.

Required (ignore income taxes)

1. Assume that Wesco Products' cost of capital is 14 percent. Compute the present value of the cash flows associated with each alternative. Use the total-cost approach.
2. Would you advise Wesco Products to accept the realty company's offer, or would you advise it to wait for a better offer? Explain.

P14–31 Net Present Value; New Product Line Atwood Company has an opportunity to produce and sell a revolutionary new smoke detector for homes. In order to determine whether this would be a profitable venture, the company has gathered the following data on probable costs and market potential:

a. New equipment would have to be acquired in order to produce the smoke detector. The equipment would cost $100,000 and be usable for 12 years. After 12 years, it would have a salvage value equal to 10 percent of the original cost.

b. Production and sales of the smoke detector would require a working capital investment of $40,000 in order to finance accounts receivable, inventories, and day-to-day cash needs.

c. An extensive marketing study projects sales in units over the next 12 years to be:

Year	Sales in Units
1	4,000
2	7,000
3	10,000
4–12	12,000

d. The smoke detectors would sell for $45 each; variable costs for production, administration, and sales would be $25 per unit.

e. In order to gain entry into the market, the company would have to advertise heavily in the early years of sales. The advertising program would be:

Year	Amount of Advertising
1–2	$70,000
3	50,000
4–12	40,000

f. Other fixed costs for salaries, insurance, maintenance, and straight-line depreciation on equipment would total $127,500 per year. (Depreciation is based on cost less salvage value.)

g. Atwood Company views the smoke detector as a somewhat risky venture; therefore, the company would require a minimum 20 percent rate of return in order to accept it as a new product line.

Required (ignore income taxes)

1. Compute the net cash inflow (cash receipts less yearly cash operating expenses) anticipated from sale of the smoke detectors for each year over the next 12 years.
2. Using the data computed in (1) above and other data provided in the problem, determine the net present value of the proposed investment. Would you recommend that Atwood Company accept the smoke detector as a new product line?

CASES

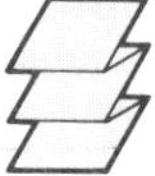

C14–32 **Discontinuing a Department; Relevant Costs; Present Value** You have just been hired as a management trainee by Marley's Department Store. Your first assignment is to determine whether the store should discontinue its housewares department and expand its appliances department. The store's vice-president believes that the housewares space could be better utilized selling appliances, since the appliances have a better markup and move more rapidly. The store's most recent income statement is presented below:

MARLEY'S DEPARTMENT STORE
Income Statement
For the Year Ended June 30, 19x1

		Department		
	Total	Appliances	Housewares	Clothing
Sales	$8,000,000	$3,600,000	$2,000,000	$2,400,000
Less variable expenses	2,930,000	1,080,000	1,250,000	600,000
Contribution margin	5,470,000	2,520,000	750,000	1,800,000
Less fixed expenses:				
Advertising	1,450,000	650,000	370,000	430,000
Salaries	770,000	410,000	90,000	270,000
General administration	460,000	207,000	115,000	138,000
Insurance	33,000	13,000	8,000	12,000
Depreciation	242,000	80,000	72,000	90,000
Utilities	690,000	320,000	130,000	240,000
Total fixed expenses	3,645,000	1,680,000	785,000	1,180,000
Net income (loss)	$1,425,000	$ 840,000	$ (35,000)	$ 620,000

In the course of your analytical work, you have determined the following:

a. If the housewares department is discontinued, sales of appliances could be expanded by 25 percent. Sales of clothing would be unaffected.

b. The store fixtures being used in the housewares department could not be used in the expanded appliances department. These fixtures have a book value of $180,000, but they can be sold now for only $70,000. In 10 years they will have no salvage value.

c. Since appliances are much more expensive than housewares items, the store would have to expand its working capital investment in inventories and accounts receivable by $250,000.

d. The added level of appliance sales would carry the same percentage of variable expenses (for cost of goods sold and for commissions) as are carried by current appliance sales.

e. Expanding the appliances department would require extensive remodeling and the purchase of new fixtures at a cost of $1,560,000. The store's lease has 10 years to run, after which the fixtures would have a salvage value of $90,000. The company uses straight-line depreciation.

f. Only one employee of the housewares department will be retained if the housewares department is discontinued. This employee's salary is $25,000 per year. No additional employees would be needed in the expanded appliances department.

g. Since the appliances department already has an extensive advertising program, it would not need to increase its advertising if it moves into the new space. Also, utilities for the space would be the same regardless of whether it was occupied by the housewares or the appliances department. Insurance costs for the space, however, would be $15,000 per year if the space is used to sell appliances rather than housewares.

h. The general administration costs represent costs of top management that are allocated to the departments on a basis of sales dollars. Total general administration costs will not change if the housewares department is dropped.

i. The store requires a return of 16 percent on all investments.

Required (ignore income taxes)

1. Compute the net *annual* change in cash flows if the housewares department is discontinued and the appliances department is expanded. (Do not include added investments or salvage values in this computation.)
2. Make a recommendation to the vice president as to whether the housewares department should be discontinued and the appliances department expanded. Use discounted cash flow and the incremental-cost approach. Show all computations in a neat, orderly form.

C14–33 Equipment Acquisition; Uneven Cash Flows Woolrich Company's market research division has projected a substantial increase in demand over the next several years for one of the company's products. To meet this demand, the company will need to produce units as follows:

Year	Production in Units
1	20,000
2	30,000
3	40,000
4–10	45,000

At present, the company is using a single model 2600 machine to manufacture this product. In order to increase its productive capacity, the company is considering two alternatives:

Alternative 1. The company could purchase another model 2600 machine that would operate along with the one it now owns. The following information is available on this alternative:

a. The model 2600 machine now in use cost $165,000 four years ago. Its present book value is $99,000, and its present market value is $90,000.
b. A new model 2600 machine costs $180,000 now. The currently owned model 2600 machine will have to be replaced in six years at a cost of $200,000. The replacement machine will have a market value of about $100,000 when it is four years old.
c. The variable cost required to produce one unit of product using the model 2600 machine is given under the "general information" below.
d. Repairs and maintenance costs each year on a single model 2600 machine total $3,000.

Alternative 2. The company could purchase a model 5200 machine and use the currently owned model 2600 machine as standby equipment. The model 5200 machine is a high-speed unit with double the capacity of the model 2600 machine. The following information is available on this alternative:
a. The cost of a new model 5200 machine is $250,000.
b. The variable cost required to produce one unit of product using the model 5200 machine is given under the "general information" below.
c. Due to its more complex operation, the model 5200 machine is more costly to maintain than the model 2600 machine. Repairs and maintenance on a model 5200 machine, with a model 2600 machine used as standby, would total $4,600 per year.

The following general information is available on the two alternatives:
a. Both the model 2600 machine and the model 5200 machine have a 10-year life from the time they are first used in production. The scrap value of both machines is nominal and can be ignored. Straight-line depreciation is used by the company.
b. The two machine models are not equally efficient in output. Comparative variable costs per unit of product are:

	Model 2600	Model 5200
Direct materials per unit	$0.36	$0.40
Direct labor per unit	0.50	0.22
Supplies and lubricants per unit	0.04	0.08
Total variable cost per unit	$0.90	$0.70

c. No other factory costs would change as a result of the decision between the two machines.
d. Woolrich Company's cost of capital is 18 percent.

Required (ignore income taxes)
1. Which alternative should the company choose? Show computations using discounted cash flow. (Round to the nearest whole dollar.)
2. Suppose that the cost of materials increases by 50 percent. Would this make the model 5200 machine more or less desirable? Explain. No computations are needed.
3. Suppose that the cost of labor increases by 25 percent. Would this make the model 5200 machine more or less desirable? Explain. No computations are needed.

C14–34 **CVP Analysis; Discounted Cash Flow** Mercury Transit, Inc., has decided to inaugurate express bus service between its headquarters city and a nearby suburb (one-way fare, 50 cents) and is considering the purchase of either 32- or 52-passenger buses, on which pertinent estimates are as follows:

	32-Passenger Bus	52-Passenger Bus
Number of each to be purchased	6	4
Useful life	8 years	8 years
Purchase price of each bus (paid on delivery)	$80,000	$110,000
Mileage per gallon	10	7½
Salvage value per bus	$ 6,000	$ 7,000
Drivers' hourly wage	3.50	4.20
Price per gallon of gasoline	1.50	1.50
Other annual cash expenses	52,000	47,000

During the four daily rush hours, all buses will be in service and all are expected to operate at full capacity (state law prohibits standees) in both directions of the route, each bus covering the route 12 times (six round trips) during the four-hour period. During the remaining 12 hours of the 16-hour day, 500 passengers would be carried and Mercury Transit would operate only four buses on the route. Part-time drivers would be employed to drive the extra hours during the rush hours. A bus traveling the route all day would go 480 miles each day, and one traveling only during rush hours would go 120 miles each day, during the 260-day year.

Required (ignore income taxes)

1. Prepare a schedule showing the computation of the estimated annual gross revenues from the new route for each alternative.
2. Prepare a schedule showing the computation of the estimated annual drivers' wages for each alternative.
3. Prepare a schedule showing the computation of the estimated annual cost of gasoline for each alternative.
4. Assume that your computations in (1), (2), and (3) above are as follows:

	32-Passenger Bus	52-Passenger Bus
Estimated annual revenues	$365,000	$390,000
Estimated annual drivers' wages	67,000	68,000
Estimated annual cost of gasoline	85,000	100,000

Assuming that a minimum rate of return of 14 percent before income taxes is desired and that all annual cash flows occur at the end of the year, determine whether the 32-passenger buses or the 52-passenger buses should be purchased. Use discounted cash flow and the total-cost approach.

(CPA, Adapted)

15

Further Aspects of Investment Decisions

LEARNING OBJECTIVES

After studying Chapter 15, you should be able to:

1 Compute the after-tax cost of a tax-deductible cash expense and the after-tax benefit from a taxable cash receipt.

2 Explain how depreciation deductions are computed under the Accelerated Cost Recovery System (ACRS).

3 Compute the tax savings arising from the depreciation tax shield, using both the ACRS tables and the optional straight-line method.

4 Compute the after-tax net present value of an investment proposal.

5 Determine the profitability index for an investment proposal.

6 Rank investment projects in order of preference under both the time-adjusted rate of return and net present value methods.

7 Define or explain the key terms listed at the end of the chapter.

We continue our discussion of capital budgeting in this chapter by focusing on two new topics. First, we focus on income taxes and their impact on the capital budgeting decision. And second, we focus on methods of ranking competing capital investment projects according to their relative desirability.

INCOME TAXES AND CAPITAL BUDGETING

In our discussion of capital budgeting in the preceding chapter, the matter of income taxes was omitted for two reasons. First, many organizations have no taxes to pay. Such organizations include schools, hospitals, and governmental units on local, state, and national levels. These organizations will always use capital budgeting techniques on a before-tax basis, as illustrated in the preceding chapter. Second, the topic of capital budgeting is somewhat complex, and it is best absorbed in small doses. Now that we have laid a solid groundwork in the concepts of present value and discounting, we can explore the effects of income taxes on capital budgeting decisions with little difficulty.

The Concept of After-Tax Cost

If someone were to ask you how much the rent is on your apartment, you would probably answer with the dollar amount that you pay out each month. If someone were to ask a business executive how much the rent is on a factory building, he or she might answer by stating a lesser figure than the dollar amount being paid out each month. The reason is that rent is a tax-deductible expense to a business firm, and expenses such as rent are often looked at on an *after-tax* basis rather than on a before-tax basis. The true cost of a tax-deductible item is not the dollars paid out; rather, it is the amount of net cash outflow that results *after* taking into consideration any reduction in income taxes that the payment will bring about. An expenditure net of its tax effect is known as **after-tax cost.**

After-tax cost is not a difficult concept. To illustrate the ideas behind it, assume that two companies, A and B, normally have sales of $850,000 each month and cash expenses of $700,000 each month. Company A is considering an advertising program that will cost $60,000 each month. The tax rate is 30 percent.[1] What will be the after-tax cost to Company A of the contemplated $60,000 monthly advertising expenditure? The computations needed to compute the after-tax cost figure are shown in Exhibit 15–1.

As shown in the exhibit, the after-tax cost of the advertising program would be only $42,000 per month. This figure must be correct, since it

[1] Under current tax law, the first $50,000 of corporate income is taxed at a 15 percent rate, the next $25,000 is taxed at a 25 percent rate, and any amount over $75,000 is taxed at a 34 percent rate. An additional 5 percent tax is levied on taxable income between $100,000 and $335,000. As a result of this additional tax, corporations with taxable income in excess of $335,000 effectively pay tax at a flat rate of 34 percent. When state income taxes are included, this figure can rise to well over 40 percent for some companies. For ease of computations, in this book we use an average, overall corporate tax rate of either 30 percent or 40 percent.

EXHIBIT 15–1
The Computation of After-Tax Cost

	Company	
	A	B
Sales	$850,000	$850,000
Less expenses:		
Salaries, insurance, and other	700,000	700,000
New advertising program	60,000	—
Total expenses	760,000	700,000
Income before taxes	90,000	150,000
Income taxes (30%)	27,000	45,000
Net income	$ 63,000	$105,000
After-tax cost of the new advertising program ($105,000 − $63,000)	$42,000	

measures the difference in net income between the two companies and since their income statements are identical except for the $60,000 in advertising paid by Company A. In effect, a $60,000 monthly advertising expenditure would *really* cost Company A only $42,000 *after taxes*.

A formula can be developed from these data that will give the after-tax cost of *any* tax-deductible cash expense.[2] The formula is:

(1 − Tax rate) × Cash expense = After-tax cost (net cash outflow) (1)

We can prove the accuracy of this formula by applying it to Company A's $60,000 advertising expenditure:

(1 − 0.30) × $60,000 = $42,000 after-tax cost of the advertising program

The concept of after-tax cost is very useful to the manager, since it measures the *actual* amount of cash that will be leaving a company as a result of an expenditure decision. As we now integrate income taxes into capital budgeting decisions, it will be necessary to place all cash expense items on an after-tax basis by applying the formula above.

The same reasoning applies to revenues and other *taxable* cash receipts. When a cash receipt occurs, the amount of cash inflow realized by an organization will be the amount that remains after taxes have been paid. The **after-tax benefit,** or net cash inflow, realized from a particular cash receipt can be obtained by applying a simple variation of the cash expenditure formula used above:

(1 − Tax rate) × Cash receipt = After-tax benefit (net cash inflow) (2)

We emphasize the term *taxable cash receipts* in our discussion because not all cash inflows are taxable. For example, the release of working capital at the termination of an investment project would not be a taxable cash inflow since it simply represents a return of original investment.

[2] This formula assumes that a company is operating at a profit; if it is operating at a loss, then the after-tax cost of an item is simply the amount paid, since no tax benefits will be realized.

The Concept of Depreciation Tax Shield

The point was made in the preceding chapter that depreciation deductions in and of themselves do not involve cash flows. For this reason, depreciation deductions were ignored in Chapter 14 in all discounted cash flow computations.

Even though depreciation deductions do not involve cash flows, they do have an impact on the amount of income taxes that a firm will pay, and income taxes *do* involve cash flows. Therefore, as we now integrate income taxes into capital budgeting decisions, it will be necessary to consider depreciation deductions to the extent that they affect tax payments.

A Cash Flow Comparison To illustrate the effect of depreciation deductions on tax payments, let us compare two companies, X and Y. Both companies have annual sales of $500,000 and cash operating expenses of $310,000. In addition, Company X has a depreciable asset on which the depreciation deduction is $90,000 per year. The tax rate is 30 percent. A cash flow comparison of the two companies is given at the bottom of Exhibit 15–2.

Notice from the exhibit that Company X's net cash inflow exceeds Company Y's by $27,000. Also notice that in order to obtain Company X's net cash inflow, it is necessary to add the $90,000 depreciation deduction back to the company's net income. This step is necessary since depreciation is a noncash deduction on the income statement.

Exhibit 15–2 presents an interesting paradox. Notice that even though Company X's net cash inflow is $27,000 *greater* than Company Y's, its net income is much *lower* than Company Y's (only $70,000, as compared to Company Y's $133,000). The explanation for this paradox lies in the concept of the *depreciation tax shield*.

EXHIBIT 15–2

The Impact of Depreciation Deductions on Tax Payments—A Comparison of Cash Flows

Income Statements

	Company X	Company Y
Sales	$500,000	$500,000
Expenses:		
Cash operating expenses	310,000	310,000
Depreciation expense	90,000	—
Total	400,000	310,000
Net income before taxes	100,000	190,000
Income taxes (30%)	30,000	57,000
Net income	$ 70,000	$133,000

Cash Flow Comparison

	Company X	Company Y
Cash inflow from operations:		
Net income, as above	$ 70,000	$133,000
Add: Noncash deduction for depreciation	90,000	—
Net cash inflow	$160,000	$133,000
Greater amount of cash available to Company X	$27,000	

The Depreciation Tax Shield Company X's greater net cash inflow comes about as a result of the *shield* against tax payments that is provided by depreciation deductions. Although depreciation deductions involve no outflows of cash, they are fully deductible in arriving at taxable income. In effect, depreciation deductions *shield* revenues from taxation and thereby *lower* the amount of taxes that a company must pay.

In the case of Company X, the $90,000 depreciation deduction taken involved no outflow of cash to the company. Yet this depreciation was fully deductible on the company's income statement and thereby *shielded* $90,000 in revenues from taxation. Were it not for the depreciation deduction, the company's income taxes would have been $27,000 higher, since the entire $90,000 in shielded revenues would have been taxable at the regular tax rate of 30 percent (30 percent × $90,000 = $27,000). In effect, the depreciation tax shield *has reduced Company X's taxes by $27,000,* permitting these funds to be retained within the company rather than going to the tax collector. Viewed another way, we can say that Company X has realized a $27,000 *cash inflow* (through reduced tax payments) as a result of its $90,000 depreciation deduction.

Because depreciation deductions shield revenues from taxation, they are generally referred to as a **depreciation tax shield.** The reduction in tax payments made possible by the depreciation tax shield will always be equal to the amount of the depreciation deduction taken, multiplied by the tax rate. The formula is:

$$\text{Tax rate} \times \text{Depreciation deduction} = \text{Tax savings from the depreciation tax shield} \quad (3)$$

We can prove this formula by applying it to the $90,000 depreciation deduction taken by Company X in our example:

0.30 × $90,000 = $27,000 reduction in tax payments (shown as "Greater amount of cash available to Company X" in Exhibit 15–2)

As we now integrate income taxes into capital budgeting computations, it will be necessary to consider the impact of depreciation deductions on tax payments by showing the tax savings provided by the depreciation tax shield.

The concepts that we have introduced in this section and in the preceding section are not complex and can be mastered fairly quickly. To assist you in your study, a summary of these concepts is given in Exhibit 15–3.

Accelerated Cost Recovery System (ACRS)

Historically, depreciation has been closely tied to the useful life of an asset, with year-by-year depreciation deductions typically computed by the straight-line method, the sum-of-the-years'-digits method, or the double-declining-balance method. Also, in computing depreciation deductions, companies have generally given recognition to an asset's expected salvage value by deducting the salvage value from the asset's cost and depreciating only the remainder. Although these concepts can still be used for computing depreciation deductions on financial statements, sweeping changes were

EXHIBIT 15–3
Tax Adjustments Required in a Capital Budgeting Analysis

Item	Treatment
Cash expense*	Multiply by (1 − Tax rate) to get after-tax cost.
Cash receipt*.	Multiply by (1 − Tax rate) to get after-tax cash inflow.
Depreciation deduction	Multiply by the tax rate to get the tax savings from the depreciation tax shield.

* Where cash receipts and cash expenses recur *each year*, the expenses should be deducted from the receipts and only the difference should be multiplied by (1 − Tax rate). See the example at the top of Exhibit 15–7.

made in 1981, and then modified somewhat in 1986, in the way that depreciation deductions are computed for tax purposes.

As enacted by Congress, the new approach, called the **Accelerated Cost Recovery System (ACRS),** largely abandons the concept of useful life and accelerates depreciation by placing all depreciable assets into one of eight property classes. Under ACRS, the only function of an asset's useful life is to determine the property class into which the asset should be placed. The various property classes under the ACRS rules are presented in Exhibit 15–4.

Two key points should be noted about the data in Exhibit 15–4. First, each ACRS property class has a prescribed life. This is the life that must be used to depreciate any asset within that property class, regardless of the asset's actual useful life. Thus, an asset with a useful life of, say, 12 years, would be in the 7-year property class and would therefore be depreciated over 7 years rather than over 12 years. (Remember, the only function of an asset's useful life is to place it in the correct ACRS property class.) These property classes make it possible to depreciate assets over quite short periods of time. Office equipment, for example, typically has a useful life of 10 years or more, but it is in the ACRS 7-year property class. Therefore, the ACRS rules permit office equipment to be depreciated over a period equal to about 70 percent of its actual useful life. Similarly, an office building generally has a useful life of about 40 years, but it is depreciated over a 31.5-year period under ACRS.

Second, note from Exhibit 15–4 that the ACRS property classes utilize various depreciation methods and rates. To simplify depreciation computations, preset tables are available that show allowable depreciation deductions by year for each of the ACRS property classes. These tables are presented in Exhibit 15–5.[3] The percentage figures used in the tables are based on the declining-balance method of depreciation. A 200 percent rate was

[3] For ease of computations, percentage figures in the tables have been rounded to three decimal places (e.g., 33.3 percent for three-year property would be 0.333 in decimal form). Tables prepared by the Internal Revenue Service carry these computations to either four or five decimal places, depending on the property class (no official tables were provided by Congress in the Tax Reform Act). In preparing tax returns and other data for the Internal Revenue Service, the IRS tables should be used.

EXHIBIT 15–4
ACRS Property Classes

ACRS Property Class and Depreciation Method	Useful Life of Assets Included in This Class	Examples of Assets Included in This Class
3-year property 200% declining balance	4 years or less	Most small tools are included; the law specifically *excludes* autos and light trucks from this property class.
5-year property 200% declining balance	More than 4 years to less than 10 years	Autos and light trucks, computers, typewriters, copiers, duplicating equipment, heavy general-purpose trucks, and research and experimentation equipment are included.
7-year property 200% declining balance	10 years or more to less than 16 years	Office furniture and fixtures, and most items of machinery and equipment used in production are included.
10-year property 200% declining balance	16 years or more to less than 20 years	Various machinery and equipment, such as that used in petroleum distilling and refining and in the milling of grain, are included.
15-year property 150% declining balance	20 years or more to less than 25 years	Sewage treatment plants, telephone and electrical distribution facilities, and land improvements are included.
20-year property 150% declining balance	25 years or more	Service stations and other real property with a useful life of less than 27.5 years are included.
27.5-year property Straight line	Not applicable	All residential rental property is included.
31.5-year property Straight line	Not applicable	All nonresidential real property is included.

used to develop the figures dealing with the 3-, 5-, 7-, and 10-year property classes; and a 150 percent rate was used to develop the figures dealing with the 15- and 20-year property classes. In all cases, the tables automatically switch to straight-line depreciation at the point where depreciation deductions would be greater under that method. The tables in Exhibit 15–5 apply to both new and used property.

Factors in the Implementation of ACRS When computing depreciation deductions under the ACRS approach, taxpayers are permitted to take only a half year's depreciation in the first year and the last year of an asset's life. This is known as the **half-year convention;** in effect, it adds a full year onto the recovery period for an asset, as shown in the tables in Exhibit 15–5. Note from the exhibit, for example, that assets in the three-year property class are depreciated over *four* years with only a half year's depreciation being allowed in the first and fourth years. In like manner, assets in the five-year property class are depreciated over *six* years, with the same pattern holding true for all other property classes.

EXHIBIT 15–5
ACRS Depreciation Tables by Property Class

Year	Property Class					
	3-Year	5-Year	7-Year	10-Year	15-Year	20-Year
1.	33.3%	20.0%	14.3%	10.0%	5.0%	3.8%
2.	44.5	32.0	24.5	18.0	9.5	7.2
3.	14.8*	19.2	17.5	14.4	8.6	6.7
4.	7.4	11.5*	12.5	11.5	7.7	6.2
5.		11.5	8.9*	9.2	6.9	5.7
6.		5.8	8.9	7.4	6.2	5.3
7.			8.9	6.6*	5.9*	4.9
8.			4.5	6.6	5.9	4.5*
9.				6.5	5.9	4.5
10.				6.5	5.9	4.5
11.				3.3	5.9	4.5
12.					5.9	4.5
13.					5.9	4.5
14.					5.9	4.5
15.					5.9	4.5
16.					3.0	4.4
17.						4.4
18.						4.4
19.						4.4
20.						4.4
21.						2.2
Total	100.0%	100.0%	100.0%	100.0%	100.0%	100.0%

* Denotes the year of changeover to straight-line depreciation.

Another factor in the implementation of ACRS is that salvage value is not considered in computing depreciation deductions. Thus, depreciation deductions are computed on a basis of the full, original cost of an asset without any offset for the asset's expected salvage value. This is actually a benefit to an organization, since it allows the entire cost of an asset to be written off as depreciation expense. However, since the entire cost of an asset is written off, any salvage value realized from sale of the asset at the end of its useful life is fully taxable as income.

Using the ACRS Tables To illustrate how the tables in Exhibit 15–5 are used to compute depreciation deductions, assume that Wendover Company purchased a piece of new equipment on January 2, 1990. Cost and other data relating to the equipment follow:

Cost of the equipment	$200,000
Salvage value	3,000
Useful life	14 years

Since the equipment has a useful life of 14 years, it will be in the ACRS 7-year property class (see Exhibit 15–4). Under ACRS, salvage value is ignored in computing depreciation deductions; therefore, Wendover Company's depreciation deductions for tax purposes will be computed on the equipment's full $200,000 original cost, as follows:

Year	Equipment Cost	ACRS Percentage*	Depreciation Deduction
1	$200,000	14.3%	$ 28,600
2	200,000	24.5	49,000
3	200,000	17.5	35,000
4	200,000	12.5	25,000
5	200,000	8.9	17,800
6	200,000	8.9	17,800
7	200,000	8.9	17,800
8	200,000	4.5	9,000
		100.0%	$200,000

* From the table for seven-year property in Exhibit 15–5.

Note that eight years are involved in the depreciation process, as discussed earlier, since the tables provide for only a half year's depreciation in the first and last years.

Optional Straight-Line Method ACRS allows flexibility to the extent that a company can elect to compute depreciation deductions by the **optional straight-line method** if it desires. Under the optional straight-line method, a company is permitted to ignore the ACRS tables and to spread its depreciation deductions somewhat evenly over an asset's property class life.

To provide an example, assume that Emerson Company purchases duplicating equipment at a cost of $10,000 on April 1, 1991. The equipment has a $600 salvage value, and it has a useful life of eight years. Thus, according to the data in Exhibit 15–4, it is in the ACRS five-year property class. If the company elects to use the optional straight-line method, it can deduct $1,000 depreciation in 1991:

$$\$10{,}000 \div 5 \text{ years} = \$2{,}000 \text{ per year; } \$2{,}000 \times 1/2 = \$1{,}000$$

For 1992–95 (the next four years) the company can deduct $2,000 depreciation each year, and in 1996 it can deduct the final $1,000 amount, as shown below:

Year	Depreciation Deduction
1991 (half year's depreciation)	$1,000
1992	2,000
1993	2,000
1994	2,000
1995	2,000
1996 (half year's depreciation)	1,000

Note that the half-year convention must be observed when using the optional straight-line method, the same as with the ACRS tables. Also note that in accordance with the ACRS rules, the asset's salvage value was not considered in computing the depreciation deductions.

The option of being able to use the straight-line method in lieu of the percentages in the ACRS tables is of particular value to new firms and to firms experiencing economic difficulties. The reason, of course, is that such firms often have little or no income and thus may prefer to stretch out depreciation deductions rather than to accelerate them.

The Choice of a Depreciation Method

As stated earlier, companies can still use any depreciation method they want (including sum-of-the-years' digits) on financial statements, even though they must use the ACRS rules for tax purposes. If a company uses a different depreciation method on its financial statements than it does for tax purposes, which method should be used in a capital budgeting analysis? Since capital budgeting is concerned with *actual cash flows,* the answer is that the same depreciation method should be used for capital budgeting purposes as is being used for tax purposes. Under the new law, this will be either the ACRS tables or the ACRS optional straight-line method.

For tax purposes, most companies will choose the ACRS tables, since this highly accelerated approach to depreciation will be more advantageous than the optional straight-line method from a present value of tax savings point of view. To illustrate, refer to the data in Exhibit 15–6. This exhibit compares the two depreciation methods in terms of the present value of the tax savings that they provide on a hypothetical asset costing $300,000.

As shown by Exhibit 15–6, the ACRS table approach (which is based on declining-balance depreciation) provides a larger present value of tax sav-

EXHIBIT 15–6
Tax Shield Effects of Depreciation

Cost of the asset	$300,000
Useful life	9 years
Property class life	5 years
Salvage value	-0-
Cost of capital	14% after taxes
Income tax rate	30%

Straight-Line Depreciation, with Half-Year Convention:

Year	Depreciation Deduction	Tax Shield: Income Tax Savings at 30 Percent	14 Percent Factor	Present Value of Tax Savings
1	$30,000	$ 9,000	0.877	$ 7,893
2	60,000	18,000	0.769	13,842
3	60,000	18,000	0.675	12,150
4	60,000	18,000	0.592	10,656
5	60,000	18,000	0.519	9,342
6	30,000	9,000	0.456	4,104
				$57,987

ACRS Tables, Five-Year Property Class:

Year	Cost	ACRS Percentage	Depreciation Deduction	Tax Shield: Income Tax Savings at 30 Percent	14 Percent Factor	Present Value of Tax Savings
1	$300,000	20.0%	$60,000	$18,000	0.877	$15,786
2	300,000	32.0	96,000	28,800	0.769	22,147
3	300,000	19.2	57,600	17,280	0.675	11,664
4	300,000	11.5	34,500	10,350	0.592	6,127
5	300,000	11.5	34,500	10,350	0.519	5,372
6	300,000	5.8	17,400	5,220	0.456	2,380
						$63,476

ings than does the optional straight-line method. This example goes far to explain why companies often prefer the accelerated method of depreciation over the straight-line method for tax purposes. Since the accelerated method provides more of its tax shield early in the life of an asset, the present value of the resulting tax savings will always be greater than the present value of the tax savings under the straight-line method.

Example of Income Taxes and Capital Budgeting

Armed with an understanding of the new ACRS depreciation rules, and with an understanding of the concepts of after-tax cost, after-tax revenue, and depreciation tax shield, we are now prepared to examine a comprehensive example of income taxes and capital budgeting. Assume the following data:

Holland Company owns the mineral rights to land on which there is a deposit of ore. The company is uncertain as to whether it should purchase equipment and open a mine on the property. After careful study, the following data have been assembled by the company:

Cost of equipment needed	$300,000
Working capital needed	75,000
Estimated annual cash receipts from sales of ore	250,000
Estimated annual cash expenses for salaries, insurance, utilities, and other cash expenses of mining the ore	170,000
Cost of road repairs needed in 6 years	40,000
Salvage value of the equipment in 10 years	100,000
Useful life of the equipment	15 years

The ore in the mine would be exhausted after 10 years of mining activity, at which time the mine would be closed. The equipment would then be sold for its salvage value. Holland Company uses the ACRS tables in computing depreciation deductions. The company's after-tax cost of capital is 12 percent, and its tax rate is 30 percent.

Should Holland Company purchase the equipment and open a mine on the property? The solution to the problem is given in Exhibit 15–7. The reader should go through this solution item by item and note the following points:

Cost of new equipment. The initial investment of $300,000 in the new equipment is included in full, with no reductions for taxes. The tax effects of this investment are considered in the depreciation deductions.

Working capital. Observe that the working capital needed for the project is included in full, with no reductions for taxes. This represents an *investment,* not an expense, so no tax adjustment is needed. (Only revenues and expenses are adjusted for the effects of taxes.) Also observe that no tax adjustment is needed when the working capital is released at the end of the project's life. The release of working capital would not be a taxable cash inflow, since it merely represents a return of investment funds back to the company.

Net annual cash receipts. The net annual cash receipts from sales of ore are adjusted for the effects of income taxes, as discussed earlier in the chapter. Note at the top of Exhibit 15–7 that the annual cash expenses are deducted from the annual cash receipts to obtain a net cash receipts figure. This just simplifies computations. (Many of the exercises and problems that follow already provide a net annual cash receipts figure, thereby eliminating the need to make this computation.)

Road repairs. Since the road repairs occur just once (in the sixth year), they are treated separately from other expenses. Road repairs would be a tax-deductible cash expense, and therefore they are adjusted for the effects of income taxes, as discussed earlier in the chapter.

Depreciation deductions. Since the equipment has a 15-year useful life, it is in the ACRS 7-year property class. The tax savings provided by depreciation deductions under the ACRS rules are included in the present value computations in the same way as was illustrated earlier in the chapter (see Exhibit 15–6). Note that depreciation deductions are kept separate from cash expenses. These are unlike items, and they should be treated separately in a capital budgeting analysis.

Salvage value of equipment. Since under the ACRS rules a company does not consider salvage value in computing depreciation deductions, book value will be zero at the end of the life of an asset. Thus, any salvage value received is fully taxable as income to the company. The after-tax benefit is determined by multiplying the salvage value by (1 − Tax rate), as discussed earlier.

Since the net present value of the proposed mining project is positive, the equipment should be purchased and the mine opened. The reader should study Exhibit 15–7 until all of its points are thoroughly understood. *Exhibit 15–7 is a key exhibit in the chapter!*

The Total-Cost Approach and Income Taxes

As stated in the preceding chapter, the total-cost approach is used to compare two or more competing investment proposals. To provide an example of this approach when income taxes are involved, assume the following data:

The *Daily Globe* has an auxiliary press that was purchased two years ago. The newspaper is thinking about replacing this old press with a newer, faster model. The alternatives are:

Buy a new press. A new press could be purchased for $150,000. It would have a useful life of eight years, after which time it would be salable for $10,000. The old press could be sold now for $40,000. (The book value of the old press is $63,000.) If the new press is purchased, it would be depreciated using the ACRS tables and would be in the five-year property class. The new press would cost $60,000 each year to operate.

Keep the old press. The old press was purchased two years ago at a cost of $90,000. The press is in the ACRS five-year property class and is being depreciated by the optional straight-line method. The old press will last for eight more years, but it will need an overhaul in five years that will cost $20,000. Cash operating costs of the old press are $85,000 each year. The old press will have a salvage value of $5,000 at the end of eight more years.

The tax rate is 30 percent. The *Daily Globe* requires an after-tax return of 10 percent on all investments in equipment.

EXHIBIT 15–7

Example of Income Taxes and Capital Budgeting

	Per Year
Cash receipts from sales of ore	$250,000
Less payments for salaries, insurance, utilities, and other cash expenses	170,000
Net cash receipts	$ 80,000

Items and Computations				Year(s)	(1) Amount	(2) Tax Effect*	After-Tax Cash Flows (1) × (2)	12 Percent Factor	Present Value of Cash Flows
Cost of new equipment				Now	$(300,000)	—	$(300,000)	1.000	$(300,000)
Working capital needed				Now	(75,000)	—	(75,000)	1.000	(75,000)
Net annual cash receipts (above)				1–10	80,000	1 − 0.30	56,000	5.650	316,400
Road repairs				6	(40,000)	1 − 0.30	(28,000)	0.507	(14,196)
Depreciation deductions:									
Year	Cost	ACRS Percentage	Depreciation Deduction						
1	$300,000	14.3%	$42,900	1	42,900	0.30	12,870	0.893	11,493
2	300,000	24.5	73,500	2	73,500	0.30	22,050	0.797	17,574
3	300,000	17.5	52,500	3	52,500	0.30	15,750	0.712	11,214
4	300,000	12.5	37,500	4	37,500	0.30	11,250	0.636	7,155
5	300,000	8.9	26,700	5	26,700	0.30	8,010	0.567	4,542
6	300,000	8.9	26,700	6	26,700	0.30	8,010	0.507	4,061
7	300,000	8.9	26,700	7	26,700	0.30	8,010	0.452	3,621
8	300,000	4.5	13,500	8	13,500	0.30	4,050	0.404	1,636
Salvage value of equipment				10	100,000	1 − 0.30	70,000	0.322	22,540
Release of working capital				10	75,000	—	75,000	0.322	24,150
Net present value									$ 35,190

* Taxable cash receipts and tax-deductible cash expenses are multiplied by (1 − Tax rate) to get the after-tax cash flow. Depreciation deductions are multiplied by the tax rate itself to get the cash flow figure (i.e., tax savings from the depreciation tax shield).

EXHIBIT 15–8

Income Taxes and Capital Budgeting: Total-Cost Approach

Items and Computations	Cost	ACRS Percentage	Depreciation Deduction	Year(s)	(1) Amount	(2) Tax Effect	After-Tax Cash Flows (1) × (2)	10 Percent Factor	Present Value of Cash Flows
Buy the new press:									
Cost of the new press				Now	$(150,000)	—	$(150,000)	1.000	$(150,000)
Annual cash operating costs				1–8	(60,000)	1 − 0.30	(42,000)	5.335	(224,070)
Depreciation deductions:									
Year	Cost	ACRS Percentage	Depreciation Deduction						
1	$150,000	20.0%	$30,000	1	30,000	0.30	9,000	0.909	8,181
2	150,000	32.0	48,000	2	48,000	0.30	14,400	0.826	11,894
3	150,000	19.2	28,800	3	28,800	0.30	8,640	0.751	6,489
4	150,000	11.5	17,250	4	17,250	0.30	5,175	0.683	3,535
5	150,000	11.5	17,250	5	17,250	0.30	5,175	0.621	3,214
6	150,000	5.8	8,700	6	8,700	0.30	2,610	0.564	1,472
Cash flow from sale of the old press:									
Cash received from the sale				Now	40,000	—	40,000	1.000	40,000
Tax savings from the loss on sale:									
Present book value			$63,000						
Sale price (above)			40,000						
Loss on the sale			$23,000	1	23,000	0.30	6,900	0.909	6,272
Salvage value of the new press				8	10,000	1 − 0.30	7,000	0.467	3,269
Present value of cash flows									$(289,744)
Keep the old press:									
Annual cash operating costs				1–8	$(85,000)	1 − 0.30	$(59,500)	5.335	$(317,433)
Overhaul needed				5	(20,000)	1 − 0.30	(14,000)	0.621	(8,694)
Depreciation deductions:									
Year	Cost	Depreciation Deduction							
1	$90,000	$18,000*		1	18,000	0.30	5,400	0.909	4,909
2	90,000	18,000		2	18,000	0.30	5,400	0.826	4,460
3	90,000	18,000		3	18,000	0.30	5,400	0.751	4,055
4	90,000	9,000		4	9,000	0.30	2,700	0.683	1,844
Salvage value of the old press				8	5,000	1 − 0.30	3,500	0.467	1,635
Present value of cash flows									$(309,224)
Net present value in favor of purchasing the new press									$ 19,480

* $90,000 ÷ 5 years = $18,000 per year. Two years' depreciation has already been taken on the old press.

Should the *Daily Globe* keep its old press or buy the new press? The solution using the total-cost approach is presented in Exhibit 15–8. Most of the items in this exhibit have already been discussed in connection with Exhibit 15–7. Only a couple of points need elaboration:

Annual cash operating costs. Since there are no revenues identified with the project, we simply place the cash operating costs on an after-tax basis and discount them as we did in Chapter 14.

Sale of the old press. The computation of the cash inflow from sale of the old press is somewhat more involved than the other items in Exhibit 15–8. Note that *two* cash inflows are connected with this sale. The first is a \$40,000 cash inflow in the form of the sale price. The second is a \$6,900 cash inflow in the form of a reduction in income taxes, resulting from the tax shield provided by the loss sustained on the sale. This tax shield functions in the same way as the tax shield provided by depreciation deductions. That is, the \$23,000 loss shown in the exhibit on sale of the old press (the difference between the sale price of \$40,000 and the book value of \$63,000) is fully deductible from income in the year the loss is sustained. This loss shields income from taxation, thereby causing a reduction in the income taxes that would otherwise be payable. The tax savings resulting from the loss tax shield are computed by multiplying the loss by the tax rate (the same procedure as for depreciation deductions): \$23,000 × 0.30 = \$6,900.

A second solution to this problem is presented in Exhibit 15–9, where the incremental-cost approach is used. Notice both from this exhibit and from Exhibit 15–8 that the net present value is \$19,480 in favor of buying the new press.

PREFERENCE DECISIONS—THE RANKING OF INVESTMENT PROJECTS

In the preceding chapter, we indicated that there are two types of decisions that must be made relative to investment opportunities. These are screening decisions and preference decisions. Screening decisions have to do with whether or not some proposed investment is acceptable to a firm. We discussed ways of making screening decisions in the preceding chapter, where we studied the use of the cost of capital as a screening tool. Screening decisions are very important in that many investment proposals come to the attention of management, and those that are not worthwhile must be screened out.

Preference decisions come *after* screening decisions and attempt to answer the following question: "How do the remaining investment proposals, all of which have been screened and provide an acceptable rate of return, rank in terms of preference? That is, which one(s) would be *best* for the firm to accept?" Preference decisions are more difficult to make than screening decisions. The reason is that investment funds are usually limited, and this often requires that some (perhaps many) otherwise very profitable investment opportunities be forgone.

Preference decisions are sometimes called *ranking* decisions, or *rationing* decisions, because they attempt to ration limited investment funds among

EXHIBIT 15–9

Income Taxes and Capital Budgeting: Incremental-Cost Approach

Items and Computations				Year(s)	(1) Amount	(2) Tax Effect	After-Tax Cash Flows (1) × (2)	10 Percent Factor	Present Value of Cash Flows
Cost of the new press				Now	$(150,000)	—	$(150,000)	1.000	$(150,000)
Savings in annual cash operating costs				1–8	25,000	1 − 0.30	17,500	5.335	93,363
Overhaul avoided				5	20,000	1 − 0.30	14,000	0.621	8,694
Difference in depreciation:									
	Depreciation Deduction								
Year	New Press	Old Press	Difference						
1	$30,000	$18,000	$12,000	1	12,000	0.30	3,600	0.909	3,272
2	48,000	18,000	30,000	2	30,000	0.30	9,000	0.826	7,434
3	28,800	18,000	10,800	3	10,800	0.30	3,240	0.751	2,433
4	17,250	9,000	8,250	4	8,250	0.30	2,475	0.683	1,690
5	17,250	—	17,250	5	17,250	0.30	5,175	0.621	3,214
6	8,700	—	8,700	6	8,700	0.30	2,610	0.564	1,472
Cash flow from sale of the old press:									
Cash received from the sale				Now	40,000	—	40,000	1.000	40,000
Tax savings from the loss on sale (see Exhibit 15–8)				1	23,000	0.30	6,900	0.909	6,272
Difference in salvage value in eight years:									
Salvage from the new press			$10,000						
Salvage from the old press			5,000						
Difference			$ 5,000	8	5,000	1 − 0.30	3,500	0.467	1,635
Net present value in favor of purchasing the new press									$ 19,480

Note: The figures in this exhibit are derived from the *differences* between the two alternatives given in Exhibit 15–8.

many competing investment opportunities. The choice may be simply between two competing alternatives, or many alternatives may be involved that must be ranked according to their overall desirability. Either the time-adjusted rate of return method or the net present value method can be used in making preference decisions.

Time-Adjusted Rate of Return Method

When using the time-adjusted rate of return method to rank competing investment projects, the preference rule is: *The higher the time-adjusted rate of return, the more desirable the project.* If one investment project promises a time-adjusted rate of return of 18 percent, then it is preferable over another project that promises a return of only 15 percent.

Ranking projects according to time-adjusted rate of return is a widely used means of making preference decisions. The reasons are probably twofold. First, no additional computations are needed beyond those already performed in making the initial screening decisions. The rates of return themselves are used to rank acceptable projects. Second, the ranking data are easily understood by management. Rates of return are very similar to interest rates, which the manager works with every day.

Net Present Value Method

If the net present value method is being used to rank competing investment projects, the net present value of one project cannot be compared directly to the net present value of another project unless the investments in the projects are of equal size. For example, assume that a company is considering two competing investments, as shown below:

	Investment	
	A	B
Investment required	$(80,000)	$(5,000)
Present value of cash inflows . . .	81,000	6,000
Net present value	$ 1,000	$ 1,000

Each project has a net present value of $1,000, but the projects are not equally desirable. A project requiring an investment of only $5,000 that produces cash inflows with a present value of $6,000 is much more desirable than a project requiring an investment of $80,000 that produces cash flows with a present value of only $81,000. In order to compare the two projects on a valid basis, it is necessary in each case to divide the present value of the cash inflows by the investment required. The ratio that this computation yields is called the **profitability index.** The formula for the profitability index is:

$$\frac{\text{Present value of cash inflows}}{\text{Investment required}} = \text{Profitability index (PI)}$$

The profitability indexes for the two investments above would be:

	Investment	
	A	B
Present value of cash inflows . . .	$81,000 *(a)*	$6,000 *(a)*
Investment required	$80,000 *(b)*	$5,000 *(b)*
Profitability index, *(a)* ÷ *(b)*	1.01	1.20

The preference rule to follow when using the profitability index to rank competing investment projects is: *The higher the profitability index, the more desirable the project*. Applying this rule to the two investments above, investment B should be chosen over investment A.

In computing the "Investment required" in a project, the amount of cash outlay should be reduced by any salvage recovered from the sale of old equipment. Also, the "Investment required" includes any working capital that the project may need, as explained in the preceding chapter. Finally, we should note that the "Present value of cash inflows" figure used in the PI formula is often a "net" amount. For example, if a project has small *out*flows (such as for repairs or for an overhaul) that occur after the project starts, then the present value of these small outflows should be deducted from the present value of the project's inflows and the resulting net figure used in the PI computation.

Comparing the Preference Rules

The profitability index is conceptually superior to the time-adjusted rate of return as a method of making preference decisions. This is because the profitability index will always give the correct signal as to the relative desirability of alternatives, even if the alternatives have different lives and different patterns of earnings. By contrast, if lives are unequal, the time-adjusted rate of return method can lead the manager to make incorrect decisions.

Assume the following situation:

Parker Company is considering two investment proposals, only one of which can be accepted. Project A requires an investment of $5,000 and will provide a single cash inflow of $6,000 in one year. Therefore, it promises a time-adjusted rate of return of 20 percent. Project B also requires an investment of $5,000. It will provide cash inflows of $1,360 each year for six years. Its time-adjusted rate of return is 16 percent. Which project should be accepted?

Although project A promises a time-adjusted rate of return of 20 percent, as compared to only 16 percent for project B, project A is not necessarily preferable over project B. It is preferable *only* if the funds released at the end of the year under project A can be reinvested at a high rate of return in some *other* project for the five remaining years. Otherwise, project B, which promises a return of 16 percent over the *entire* six years, is more desirable.

Let us assume that the company in the example above has a cost of capital of 12 percent. The net present value method, with the profitability index, would rank the two proposals as follows:

	Project A	Project B
Present value of cash inflows:		
$6,000 received at the end of one year at 12% (factor of 0.893)	$5,358 *(a)*	
$1,360 received at the end of each year for six years at 12% (factor of 4.111).		$5,591 *(a)*
Investment required	$5,000 *(b)*	$5,000 *(b)*
Profitability index, *(a)* ÷ *(b)*	1.07	1.12

The profitability index indicates that project B is more desirable than project A. This is in fact the case if the funds released from project A at the end of one year can be reinvested at only 12 percent (the cost of capital). Although the computations will not be shown here, in order for project A to be more desirable than project B, the funds released from project A would have to be reinvested at a rate of return *greater* than 14 percent for the remaining five years.

In short, the time-adjusted rate of return method of ranking tends to favor short-term, high-yield projects, whereas the net present value method of ranking (using the profitability index) tends to favor longer-term projects.

SUMMARY

Unless a company is a tax-exempt organization, such as a school or a governmental unit, income taxes should be considered in making capital budgeting computations. When income taxes are a factor in a company, tax-deductible cash expenditures must be placed on an after-tax basis by multiplying the expenditure by (1 − Tax rate). Only the after-tax amount is used in determining the desirability of an investment proposal. Similarly, taxable cash inflows must be placed on an after-tax basis by multiplying the cash inflow by the same formula.

Although depreciation deductions do not involve a present outflow of cash, they are valid expenses for tax purposes and as such affect income tax payments. Depreciation deductions shield income from taxation, resulting in decreased taxes being paid. This shielding of income from taxation is commonly called a depreciation tax shield. The savings in income taxes arising from the depreciation tax shield are computed by multiplying the depreciation deduction by the tax rate itself. Since accelerated methods of depreciation provide the bulk of their tax shield early in the life of an asset, they are superior to the straight-line method of depreciation, from a present value of tax savings point of view.

Preference decisions relate to ranking two or more investment proposals according to their relative desirability. This ranking can be performed using either the time-adjusted rate of return or the profitability index. The profitability index, which is the ratio of the present value of a proposal's cash inflows to the investment required, is generally regarded as the best way of making preference decisions when discounted cash flow is being used.

KEY TERMS FOR REVIEW

Accelerated Cost Recovery System (ACRS) A method of depreciation required for income tax purposes that places a depreciable asset into one of eight property classes according to the asset's useful life. (p. 660)

After-tax benefit The amount of net cash inflow realized by an organization from a taxable cash receipt after income tax effects have been considered. The amount is determined by multiplying the cash receipt by (1 − Tax rate). (p. 657)

After-tax cost The amount of net cash outflow resulting from a tax-deductible cash expense after income tax effects have been considered. The amount is determined by multiplying the cash expense by (1 − Tax rate). (p. 656)

Depreciation tax shield A reduction in the amount of income subject to tax that results from the presence of depreciation deductions on the income statement. The reduction in tax is computed by multiplying the depreciation deduction by the tax rate. (p. 659)

Half-year convention A requirement under the Accelerated Cost Recovery System that permits a company to take only a half year's depreciation in the first and last years of an asset's depreciation period. (p. 661)

Optional straight-line method A method of computing depreciation deductions under ACRS that can be used by an organization in lieu of the ACRS tables. (p. 663)

Profitability index The ratio of the present value of a project's cash inflows to the investment required. (p. 671)

QUESTIONS

15–1 Some organizations will always use capital budgeting techniques on a before-tax basis rather than on an after-tax basis. Name several such organizations.

15–2 What is meant by after-tax cost, and how is the concept used in capital budgeting decisions?

15–3 What is a depreciation tax shield, and how does it affect capital budgeting decisions?

15–4 The three most widely used depreciation methods are straight line, sum-of-the-years' digits, and double-declining balance, with the depreciation period based on the asset's actual useful life. Explain why a company might use one or more of these methods, instead of the Accelerated Cost Recovery System, for computing depreciation expense in its published financial statements.

15–5 Why are accelerated methods of depreciation superior to the straight-line method of depreciation from an income tax point of view?

15–6 Ludlow Company is considering the introduction of a new product line. Would an increase in the income tax rate tend to make the new investment more or less attractive? Explain.

15–7 Assume that an old piece of equipment is sold at a loss. From a capital budgeting point of view, what two cash inflows will be associated with the sale?

15–8 Assume that a new piece of equipment costs $40,000 and that the tax rate is 30 percent. Should the new piece of equipment be shown in the capital budgeting analysis as a cash outflow of $40,000, or should it be shown as a cash outflow of $28,000 [$40,000 × (1 − 0.30)]? Explain.

15–9 Assume that a company has cash operating expenses of $15,000 and a depreciation expense of $10,000. Can these two items be added together and treated as one in a capital budgeting analysis, or should they be kept separate? Explain.

15–10 Distinguish between capital budgeting screening decisions and capital budgeting preference decisions. Why are preference decisions more difficult to make than screening decisions?

15–11 Why are preference decisions sometimes called *rationing* decisions?

15–12 How is the profitability index computed, and what does it measure?

15–13 What is the preference rule for ranking investment projects under the net present value method?

15–14 Can an investment with a profitability index of less than 1.00 be an acceptable investment? Explain.

15–15 What is the preference rule for ranking investment projects under time-adjusted rate of return?

EXERCISES

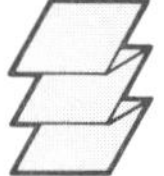

E15–1 *a.* Stoffer Company has hired a management consulting firm to review and make recommendations concerning Stoffer's organizational structure. The consulting firm's fee will be $100,000. What will be the after-tax cost of the consulting firm's fee if Stoffer's tax rate is 30 percent?

b. The Green Hills Riding Club has redirected its advertising toward a different sector of the market. As a result of this change in advertising, the club's annual revenues have increased by $40,000. If the club's tax rate is 25 percent, what is the after-tax benefit from the increased revenues?

c. The Golden Eagles Basketball Team has just installed an electronic scoreboard in its playing arena at a cost of $210,000. The scoreboard has an estimated 15-year useful life and a salvage value of $14,000. Using the optional straight-line method, determine the yearly tax savings from the depreciation tax shield. Assume that the income tax rate is 30 percent.

d. Repeat (*c*) above, this time using the ACRS tables in Exhibit 15–5.

E15–2 Various assets used by organizations are listed below.

	Assets	Useful Life
a.	A pickup truck used by a construction company	5 years
b.	An office building used by an advertising agency	50 years
c.	Power lines used in distribution of electricity	22 years
d.	Small tools used on the assembly line of an auto plant	? years
e.	Petroleum distilling equipment	16 years
f.	An apartment house rented to college students	180 years*
g.	A computer used by an airline to schedule flights	? years
h.	A desk in the office of an attorney	10 years
i.	Shrubbery and trees planted around a new medical clinic	? years
j.	A printing press used by a newspaper	18 years
k.	A frozen food display case used by a retail market	15 years
l.	Lab equipment used by a pharmaceutical company in cancer research	7 years

* We're just kidding; it's really 45 years.

Required Indicate the ACRS property class into which each of the assets above should be placed for depreciation purposes.

E15–3 Swick Company would like to purchase equipment that would allow the company to penetrate a new market. The equipment would cost $60,000 and have a four-year useful life. It would be depreciated using the ACRS tables and have a salvage value of $9,000.

Use of the equipment would generate before-tax net cash receipts of $25,000 per year. The equipment would require repairs in the third year that would cost $12,000. The company's tax rate is 30 percent, and its after-tax cost of capital is 10 percent.

Required 1. Compute the net present value of the proposed investment in new equipment. (Round all dollar amounts to the nearest whole dollar.)
2. Would you recommend that the equipment be purchased? Explain.

E15–4 Dwyer Company is considering two investment projects. Relevant cost and cash flow information on the two projects is given below:

	Project	
	A	B
Investment in heavy trucks	$130,000	
Investment in working capital . . .		$130,000
Net annual cash inflows	25,000	25,000
Life of the project	9 years*	9 years

* Useful life of the trucks.

The trucks will have a $15,000 salvage value in nine years, and they will be depreciated using the optional straight-line method. At the end of nine years, the working capital will be released for use elsewhere. The company requires an after-tax return of 12 percent on all investments. The tax rate is 30 percent. (Be sure you place the trucks in the correct property class for depreciation purposes.)

Required Compute the net present value of each investment project. (Round all dollar amounts to the nearest whole dollar.)

E15–5 (This exercise should be assigned only if Exercise 15–4 is also assigned.) Refer to the data in Exercise 15–4.

Required 1. Compute the profitability index for each investment project.
2. Is an investment project with a profitability index of less than 1.0 an acceptable project? Explain.

E15–6 Press Publishing Company hires students from the local university to collate pages on various printing jobs. This collating is all done by hand, at a cost of $60,000 per year. A collating machine has just come onto the market that could be used in place of the student help. The machine would cost $170,000 and have a 15-year useful life. It would require an operator at an annual cost of $18,000 and have annual maintenance costs of $7,000. New roller pads would be needed on the machine in six years at a total cost of $20,000. The salvage value of the machine in 15 years would be $40,000.

The company uses the ACRS tables for depreciation purposes. Management requires a 14 percent after-tax return on all equipment purchases. The company's tax rate is 30 percent.

Required 1. Determine the before-tax net annual cost savings that the new collating machine will provide.
2. Using the data from (1) above and other data from the exercise, compute the collating machine's net present value. (Round all dollar amounts to the nearest whole dollar.) Would you recommend that the machine be purchased?

E15–7 Information on four investment proposals is given below:

	Investment Proposal			
	A	B	C	D
Investment required	$ (85,000)	$(200,000)	$ (90,000)	$(170,000)
Present value of cash inflows	119,000	184,000	135,000	221,000
Net present value	$ 34,000	$ (16,000)	$ 45,000	$ 51,000
Life of the project	5 years	7 years	6 years	6 years

Required

1. Compute the profitability index for each investment proposal.
2. Rank the proposals in terms of preference.

PROBLEMS

P15–8 Basic Net Present Value Analysis Rapid Parcel Service has been offered an eight-year contract to deliver mail and small parcels between army installations. In order to accept the contract, the company would have to purchase several new delivery trucks at a total cost of $450,000. Other data relating to the contract follow:

Net annual cash receipts (before taxes) from the contract	$108,000
Cost of overhauling the motors in the trucks in five years	45,000
Salvage value of the trucks at termination of the contract	20,000

The trucks would be in the "light truck" category for tax purposes. If the contract were accepted, several old, fully depreciated trucks would be sold at a total price of $30,000. These funds would be used in purchasing the new trucks. The company uses the ACRS tables to compute depreciation and requires a 12 percent after-tax return on all equipment purchases. The tax rate is 30 percent.

Required Compute the net present value of this investment opportunity. Round all dollar amounts to the nearest whole dollar. Would you recommend that the contract be accepted?

P15–9 Straightforward Net Present Value Analysis The Crescent Drilling Company owns the drilling rights to several tracts of land on which natural gas has been found. The amount of gas on some of the tracts is somewhat marginal, and the company is unsure whether it would be profitable to extract and sell the gas which these tracts contain. One such tract is tract 410, on which the following information has been gathered:

Investment in equipment needed for extraction work	$600,000
Working capital investment needed	85,000
Annual cash receipts from sale of gas, net of related cash operating expenses (before taxes)	110,000
Cost of restoring land at completion of extraction work	70,000

The natural gas in tract 410 would be exhausted after 10 years of extraction work. The equipment would have a useful life of 15 years, but it could be sold for only 15 percent of its original cost when extraction was completed. The company uses the

ACRS tables in computing depreciation deductions. The tax rate is 30 percent, and the company's after-tax cost of capital is 10 percent. The working capital would be released for use elsewhere at the completion of the project.

Required
1. Compute the net present value of tract 410. Round all dollar amounts to the nearest whole dollar.
2. Would you recommend that the investment project be undertaken?

P15–10 Various Depreciation Methods; Net Present Value Vitro Company has been offered an eight-year contract to produce a key part for a government agency. Management has determined that the following costs and revenues would be associated with the contract:

Cost of special equipment	$700,000
Working capital needed to carry inventories	90,000
Annual revenues from the contract	450,000
Annual out-of-pocket costs for materials, salaries, and so forth	261,500
Salvage value of the equipment in eight years	25,000

Although the equipment would have a useful life of nine years, the company would sell it at the end of the contract period. Vitro Company's after-tax cost of capital is 14 percent, and its tax rate is 30 percent. At the end of the contract period, the working capital would be released for use elsewhere.

Required
1. Assume that Vitro Company uses the ACRS optional straight-line depreciation method. Determine the net present value of the proposed contract. (Round all dollar amounts to the nearest whole dollar.)
2. Assume that Vitro Company uses the ACRS tables to compute depreciation deductions. Determine the net present value of the proposed contract. (Round all dollar amounts to the nearest whole dollar.).

P15–11 Preference Ranking of Investment Projects Austin Company is investigating five different investment opportunities. Information on the five projects under study is given below:

	Project Number				
	1	**2**	**3**	**4**	**5**
Investment required	$(480,000)	$(360,000)	$(270,000)	$(450,000)	$(400,000)
Present value of cash inflows at a 10% discount rate	567,270	433,400	336,140	522,970	379,760
Net present value	$ 87,270	$ 73,400	$ 66,140	$ 72,970	$ (20,240)
Life of the project	6 years	12 years	6 years	3 years	5 years
Time-adjusted rate of return	16%	14%	18%	19%	8%

Since the company's cost of capital is 10 percent, a 10 percent discount rate has been used in the present value computations above. Limited funds are available for investment, so the company can't accept all of the projects available.

Required
1. Compute the profitability index for each investment project.
2. Rank the five projects according to preference, in terms of:
   a. Net present value.
   b. Profitability index.
   c. Time-adjusted rate of return.
3. Which ranking do you prefer? Why?

P15–12 Various Depreciation Methods; Profitability Index Stokes Broadcasting, Inc., operates several communications businesses, including a TV station. The company is considering the replacement of one of the cameras in the station with a more sophisticated model. Although the old camera is fully depreciated and has a negligible salvage value, it is in good operating condition and will be donated to a local university if the new camera is purchased. Management is considering two cameras as a replacement, only one of which can be purchased. Cost and other data on the two cameras are given below:

	Camera	
	1	2
Cost of the camera	$150,000	$225,000
Annual savings in cash operating costs . . .	40,000	56,000
Parts replacement in four years.	9,000	15,000
Salvage value	10,000	30,000
Useful life	8 years	8 years
Depreciation method to be used	SL*	ACRS tables

* Optional straight-line method, as allowed under ACRS.

Stokes Company's after-tax cost of capital is 12 percent. The company's tax rate is 30 percent. Round all dollar amounts to the nearest whole dollar.

Required

1. Compute the net present value of each investment alternative. Based on these data, which camera should be purchased?
2. Compute the profitability index for each investment alternative. Based on these data, which camera should be purchased?

P15–13 Preference Ranking of Investment Projects Yancey Company has limited funds available for investment and must ration the funds among five competing projects. Selected information on the five projects follows:

Project	Investment Required	Net Present Value	Life of the Project (years)	Time-Adjusted Rate of Return (percent)
A	$800,000	$221,615	7	18
B	675,000	210,000	12	16
C	500,000	175,175	7	20
D	700,000	152,544	3	22
E	900,000	(52,176)	6	8

Yancey Company's cost of capital is 10 percent. (The net present values above have been computed using a 10 percent discount rate.) The company wants your assistance in determining which project to accept first, which to accept second, and so forth.

Required

1. Compute the profitability index for each project.
2. Rank the five projects in order of preference, in terms of:
   a. Net present value.
   b. Profitability index.
   c. Time-adjusted rate of return.
3. Which ranking do you prefer? Why

P15–14 Net Present Value Analysis Fran's Travel Service is located in Orlando, Florida. The company, which specializes in local, scenic tours, has an opportunity to purchase several buses that were recently repossessed by a bank. Although the buses cost

$800,000 new and are only three years old, they can be purchased by Fran's for the remaining amount unpaid, which is only $610,000. Moreover, the bank will allow Fran's to pay $400,000 immediately and $70,000 each year for three years, without interest.

Fran's president, Vera Costeau, estimates that the buses could be operated 300 days per year, carrying 180 tourists per day. The company charges $7.50 per person for its tours. Ms. Costeau estimates that the following expenses would be associated with the buses each year:

Salaries for bus operators and tour guides	$130,000
Insurance	9,000
Fuel	85,000
Bank payments	70,000*
Promotion for the tours	21,000
Rent for parking the buses	7,200
Maintenance	53,000
Fees and highway taxes	4,800
Depreciation	37,333†
Total expenses	$417,333

* For the first three years only.
† $610,000 cost − $50,000 estimated salvage value = $560,000 depreciable cost; $560,000 ÷ 15 years = $37,333 per year.

The owner of the property on which the buses would be parked at night would require a deposit of $1,800, which is equal to three months' rent. This deposit would be refunded at the end of the buses' 15-year remaining useful life. In nine years, the buses would need to have all seat coverings replaced at a cost of $35,000.

If the buses are purchased, Fran's will use the ACRS tables to compute depreciation for tax purposes. The company's after-tax cost of capital is 10 percent, and the tax rate is 30 percent.

Required

1. Compute the net cash receipts (before income taxes) each year from operating the buses.
2. By use of the net present value method, determine whether the buses should be purchased. (Round all dollar amounts to the nearest whole dollar.)

P15–15 Comprehensive Problem: Various Depreciation Methods; Net Present Value Eric Giacardi, vice president of Dicer Products, would like to purchase an automated kiln for use in the manufacture of one of the company's product lines. Selected information about the kiln follows:

Cost of the kiln	$900,000
Annual savings provided by the kiln in cash operating costs (before taxes)	230,000
Salvage value of the kiln (5% of cost)	45,000
Cost of relining the kiln in 5 years	130,000

The company would have to increase its working capital by $60,000 in order to support the operation of the new kiln.

An analysis that Mr. Giacardi has just received from his staff indicates that the new kiln will not provide the 14 percent after-tax return required by the company. In doing the analysis, Mr. Giacardi had instructed his staff to depreciate the kiln by the optional straight-line method, since the company always uses straight-line depreciation for accounting purposes. Dicer Products' tax rate is 30 percent. The useful life of the kiln is estimated to be nine years.

Upon seeing the analysis done by Mr. Giacardi's staff, Robyn Hafen, president of Dicer Products, suggested that the analysis be redone using the ACRS tables rather than the optional straight-line method. Somewhat surprised by this suggestion, Mr. Giacardi stated, "What difference does it make how we compute the depreciation? We have the same total depreciation either way. This new kiln simply doesn't meet our rate of return requirements."

Required

1. Compute the net present value of the kiln using the optional straight-line method for depreciation deductions. (Round all dollar amounts to the nearest whole dollar.)
2. Compute the net present value of the kiln using the ACRS tables in Exhibit 15–5 for depreciation deductions, as suggested by Ms. Hafen. (Again round all dollar amounts to the nearest whole dollar.)
3. Explain to Mr. Giacardi how the depreciation method used can affect the rate of return generated by an investment project.

P15–16 Uneven Cash Flows; Net Present Value "I know the salt in the Heber tract contains some contaminants, but I still think it's worth going after," said Bryce Wasser, chief engineer for Emory Mines.

"I'm not so sure," replied Erika Kretchow, the company's vice president. "The best we can hope to get for salt is $21 a ton, and the accounting people say that it will cost at least $15 a ton to remove the contaminants and process the salt into usable form. That doesn't leave much in the way of contribution margin."

"I know the contribution per ton will be low," replied Bryce, "but our studies show that we have 1,275,000 tons of salt in the Heber tract. I figure we can extract 70,000, 100,000, and 160,000 tons the first three years, respectively, and then the remainder evenly over the next seven years. Even at only $21 a ton, that will really enhance our cash flow."

"Yes, but what about all the other costs?" asked Erika. "Fixed costs for salaries, insurance, and so forth directly associated with the extraction of the salt would be $530,000 a year. In addition, we would have to pay out an additional $275,000 at the end of the project to level and fill the land. You know how tough those environmental people can be if a project isn't handled right. And all of this doesn't even consider the $800,000 cost of special equipment that we would need or the $90,000 in working capital that would be required to carry inventories and accounts receivable. I think we should just forget the whole idea and concentrate our resources on existing projects."

"You're suffering from tunnel vision," quipped Bryce. "The new tax laws allow us to depreciate equipment really fast, so we'll save tens of thousands of dollars in taxes at our 30 percent tax rate. Besides that, since the equipment would have a 15-year useful life, it would still have some use left when the salt was all extracted and we closed the area. Based on experience, I'm sure we could sell it to someone for at least 5 percent of its original cost."

"I'll admit the project has some tempting features, Bryce, but I'll still bet that it won't provide the 16 percent after-tax return we require on high-risk investments. Let's give our figures to the people in the New Projects Division and have them do a present value analysis for us."

Required

1. Compute the before-tax net cash receipts each year from the extraction, processing, and sale of the salt. (Do not include the cost of leveling and filling the land in this computation.)
2. Using the data from (1) above and other data from the problem as needed, prepare a net present value analysis to determine whether the company should purchase the equipment and extract the salt. (Round all dollar amounts to the nearest whole dollar.) You may assume that for the company *as a whole,* there

will be a positive taxable income in every year, so that a tax benefit would be realized from any operating losses associated with the salt-extraction project.

P15–17 Equipment Replacement; Incremental-Cost Approach "Those new golf carts are simply beautiful," exclaimed Bonnie Weskow, operations manager for Coral Lake Resort. "No wonder the Board of Directors is so anxious to buy them."

"All of the Board except me," replied Harvey Delgado, chairman of the Board. "Everyone seems to forget that we purchased our present carts just two years ago at a cost of $260,000. Those new carts will cost a cool $350,000. The worst part is that we can only get $110,000 out of our old carts if we sell them now. That's quite a loss for the resort to absorb."

"We can make up the loss very quickly," countered Bonnie. "Mountain Hills Resort in the northern part of the state says that usage of their carts increased by 20 percent when they purchased these new carts. I've gathered a lot of information about the new carts and I'll have a recommendation ready for the Board tomorrow."

The information to which Bonnie was referring is provided below:

a. Both the old and the new carts are in the ACRS five-year property class. The new carts have an estimated useful life of eight years. Although the old carts have already been used for two years, Coral Lake's maintenance engineer is confident that with proper maintenance and with some extra care the old carts can be kept usable for an additional eight years.

b. The old carts are being depreciated by the optional straight-line method. Two years' depreciation has been taken on the old carts; thus, their book value is now $182,000. Depreciation over the next four years will be: years 1–3, $52,000 per year; and year 4, $26,000.

c. The new carts would be depreciated using the ACRS tables. Bonnie estimates that the new carts could be sold for 10 percent of their original cost in eight years. The old carts will be worth nothing at the end of eight more years.

d. The old carts are being rented an average of 45,000 hours per year. Coral Lake Resort charges $7 per hour for use of a cart.

e. To keep the new carts operating at peak efficiency, Coral Lake Resort would purchase a maintenance contract that would cost $8,000 more per year than the present maintenance contract. In addition, the resort would have to make a $4,000 maintenance deposit immediately. This deposit would be refunded at the end of the carts' useful life.

f. The new carts have a unique, high-powered motor that would have to be rewound in five years at a total cost of $90,000.

g. Coral Lake Resort has a tax rate of 30 percent and requires an after-tax return of 10 percent on all investments.

Required

1. Compute the incremental net annual cash receipts (before taxes) expected from use of the new carts. (Do not include the cost of rewinding the motors or any salvage value in this computation.)
2. Use discounted cash flow to determine whether the new carts should be purchased. Use the incremental-cost approach. (Round all dollar amounts to the nearest whole dollar.) Are there any nonquantitative factors that should be considered in this decision?

P15–18 A Comparison of Investment Alternatives; Total-Cost Approach Julia Vanfleet is professor of mathematics at a western university. She has received a $225,000 inheritance from her father's estate, and she is anxious to invest it between now and the time she retires in 12 years. Professor Vanfleet's position with the university pays a salary of $60,000 per year. Since the state in which the university is located is experiencing extreme budgetary problems, this salary is expected to remain unchanged in the foreseeable future. Professor Vanfleet is considering two alternatives for investing her inheritance.

Alternative 1. Municipal bonds can be purchased that mature in 12 years and that bear interest at 8 percent. This interest would be tax-free and paid semiannually. (In discounting a cash flow that occurs semiannually, the procedure is to halve the interest rate and double the number of periods. Use the same procedure for discounting the principal returned when the bonds reach maturity.) This alternative would permit Professor Vanfleet to stay with the university.

Alternative 2. A small retail business is available for sale that can be purchased for $225,000. The following information relates to this alternative:

a. Of the purchase price, $80,000 would be for fixtures and other depreciable items. The remainder would be for the company's working capital (inventory, accounts receivable, and cash). The fixtures and other depreciable items would have a remaining useful life of at least 12 years and would be in the ACRS 7-year property class. At the end of 12 years these depreciable items would have a negligible salvage value; however, the working capital would be recovered (either through sale or liquidation of the business) for reinvestment elsewhere.

b. The store building would be leased. At the end of 12 years, if Professor Vanfleet could not find someone to buy out the business it would be necessary to pay $2,000 to the owner of the building in order to break the lease.

c. The ACRS tables would be used for depreciation purposes.

d. Store records indicate that sales have averaged $850,000 per year and out-of-pocket costs (including rent on the building) have averaged $760,000 per year (*not* including income taxes).

e. Since Professor Vanfleet would operate the store herself, it would be necessary for her to leave the university if this alternative were selected. Professor Vanfleet's tax rate is 20 percent, and she wants an after-tax return of at least 8 percent on her investment.

Required Advise Professor Vanfleet as to which alternative should be selected. Use the total-cost approach to discounted cash flow in your analysis. (Round all dollar amounts to the nearest whole dollar.)

P15–19 Comparison of Total-Cost and Incremental-Cost Approaches Viking Foods, Inc., provides hot, ready-to-eat dinners for airlines. The company is considering the purchase of several new trucks to replace an equal number of old trucks now in use in delivering dinners to flights at airports. The new trucks would cost $430,000, but they would require only one operator per truck (as compared to two operators for the trucks now being used), as well as provide other cost savings. A comparison of total annual cash operating costs between the old trucks that would be replaced and the new trucks is provided below:

	Old Trucks	New Trucks
Salaries—operators	$120,000	$ 60,000
Fuel	80,000	75,000
Insurance	9,000	27,000
Maintenance	11,000	8,000
Total operating costs	$220,000	$170,000

If the new trucks are purchased, the old trucks will be sold to another company for $80,000. These trucks cost $350,000 when they were new, have a current book value of $105,000, and have been used for four years. They are in the ACRS five-year property class, and the optional straight-line method is being used to depreciate these trucks for tax purposes.

If the new trucks are not purchased, the old trucks will be used for eight more years and then sold for an estimated salvage value of $10,000. However, in order to keep the old trucks operating, extensive repairs would be needed in one year that will cost an estimated $100,000. These repairs will be expensed for tax purposes in the year incurred.

The new trucks would have a useful life of eight years and would be depreciated using the ACRS tables. They would have an estimated $40,000 salvage value at the end of their useful life. The company's tax rate is 30 percent, and its after-tax cost of capital is 12 percent.

Required

1. By use of the total-cost approach to discounted cash flow, determine whether the new trucks should be purchased. (Round all dollar amounts to the nearest whole dollar.)
2. Repeat the computations in (1) above, this time using the incremental-cost approach to discounted cash flow.

P15–20 Net Present Value; Incremental-Cost Approach Zeppo Company makes cookies for its chain of snack food stores. On January 2, 19x0, the company purchased a special cookie-cutting machine. This machine has been utilized for two years. Zeppo Company is now considering the purchase of a newer, more efficient machine. If purchased, this new machine would be acquired on January 2, 19x2. Since the machine now in use is only two years old, management is reluctant to replace it—particularly in view of the fact that it can be sold for only half of its original cost. The following information has been assembled to help management decide whether to keep the old machine or buy the new one:

	Old Machine	New Machine
Original cost at acquisition	$140,000	$200,000
Useful life from date of acquisition	12 years	10 years
Expected annual cash operating expenses:		
Variable cost per dozen cookies	$0.21	$0.14
Total fixed costs	$ 37,000	$ 30,000
Depreciation method used for tax purposes	Straight line*	ACRS tables
Estimated salvage value of the machines:		
Now (January 2, 19x2)	$ 70,000	$ —
In 10 years	5,000	20,000

* By "straight line" we mean the optional straight-line method as allowed under the ACRS rules.

The company expects to sell 300,000 dozen cookies in each of the next 10 years. The selling price of the cookies is expected to average 50 cents per dozen.

The company is subject to an overall income tax rate of 30 percent. Assume that any gain or loss on the sale of equipment is treated as an ordinary tax item. Zeppo Company requires an after-tax return of 10 percent on all equipment purchases.

Required

1. Compute the expected savings in cash operating costs (before taxes) each year from use of the new machine.
2. Using the data from (1) above and other data provided in the problem, compute the net present value of purchasing the new machine. Use the incremental-cost approach.
3. Assume that the quantitative differences are so slight between the two alternatives that Zeppo Company is indifferent to the two proposals. Identify and discuss the nonquantitative factors that are important to this decision and that the company should consider.

(CMA, Heavily Adapted)

CASES

C15–21 Replacement of Dairy Herd; Net Present Value "Unless we move quickly, someone else will snap up that herd of Guernsey cows," said Krissy Sequist, operations vice president for Consolidated Foods. "They're available for a good price, and the Guernsey breed is so productive that these cows could increase the income at our Paradise Dairy by 25 percent a year."

The income figures to which Krissy was referring are given below:

	Present Cows	Guernsey Cows
Revenue from sale of milk	$360,000	$410,000
Less operating expenses:		
Salaries—dairy manager and workers	75,000	75,000
Feed	16,000	24,000
Insurance on the cows	8,000	12,500
Depreciation, barns and equipment	140,000	140,000
Depreciation, cows	30,000*	50,000†
Utilities	21,000	21,000
Total operating expenses	290,000	322,500
Income before income taxes	70,000	87,500
Less income taxes (30%)	21,000	26,250
Net income	$ 49,000	$ 61,250

* $300,000 cost ÷ 10-year useful life = $30,000 per year.
† $420,000 cost − $20,000 resale value = $400,000; $400,000 ÷ 8-year useful life = $50,000 per year.

"Your income figures are impressive," replied Sam McDonald, the financial vice president. "But do you call $420,000 a good price? That's 40 percent more than we paid for the present herd at Paradise Dairy, and we purchased those cows just two years ago. I doubt that the Guernsey cows would meet the 8 percent after-tax return that we require on investments."

"They would more than triple the 8 percent return," replied Krissy, as she showed Sam the following computation:

$$\frac{\text{Net income}}{\text{Initial investment} - \text{Sale of the present cows}} = \text{Simple rate of return}$$

$$\frac{\$61,250}{\$420,000 - \$170,000} = 24.5\%$$

"That return is incredible," said Sam. "But something seems odd about the computation. Let me dig up some additional data and I'll be back with you in a day or two."

After some effort, Sam has accumulated the following additional data relating to the cows:

a. Both the cows now owned by Paradise Dairy and the Guernsey cows are in the ACRS five-year property class. For tax purposes, the company is using the optional straight-line method to compute depreciation on the cows now owned by the dairy.

b. If the Guernsey cows are purchased, they will be depreciated by use of the ACRS tables. These cows have a remaining useful life of eight years.

c. The cows now owned by Paradise Dairy will have no resale value at the end of their 10-year useful life.

d. The Guernsey cows would be registered. To maintain this registration, the dairy would have to pay a renewal fee of $5,000 four years from now.

e. To maximize production, the Guernsey cows would require a special feed that would increase working capital requirements by $3,000 to carry an inventory of the feed on hand.

Required

1. By use of net present value analysis, determine whether the Guernsey cows should be purchased. Use the incremental-cost approach, and round all dollar amounts to the nearest whole dollar.
2. Do you agree with Sam that something is "odd" about Krissy's simple rate of return computation? Explain.

C15–22 **Integrative Case: Make or Buy; Discounted Cash Flow** "According to my figures, it would be a mistake to buy those new tools and to continue manufacturing the K96 relay," said Allen Dusak, production manager for Midway Electronics. "If we do buy the new tools, then our cost for the K96 relay will jump from $38 to well over $40 per unit, and that's more than we would have to pay an outside supplier to manufacture the relay for us."

Midway Electronics manufactures several products, including many of the component parts (such as the K96 relay) that go into these products. The K96 relay requires specialized tools in its manufacture and the tools presently in use are worn out. Rather than replace the tools, management is considering whether the K96 relay should be purchased from an outside source. A supplier is willing to provide the relays at a unit sales price of $40 if at least 150,000 units are ordered each year. However, Midway Electronics is reluctant to accept this offer, since it has no alternative use for the space now being used to manufacture the K96 relay.

Midway Electronics has produced 160,000 K96 relays each year for the past four years. Sales forecasts suggest that this volume will remain constant for at least four more years. In the past, the relays have cost $38 each to manufacture, as shown by the following data:

Direct materials	$20.00
Direct labor	4.60
Variable overhead	1.40
Fixed overhead	12.00*
Total unit cost	$38.00

* Depreciation of tools accounts for one fourth of the fixed overhead. These tools must now be replaced. The balance of this $12 is for general fixed overhead costs of the factory that require cash expenditures.

If the specialized tools are purchased, they will cost $5,000,000 and will have a disposal value of $200,000 at the end of their four-year useful life. Straight-line depreciation would be used for book purposes, but the ACRS tables would be used for tax purposes. Midway Electronics has a 30 percent tax rate, and management requires a 14 percent after-tax return on investment for any purchases of tools and equipment.

"I know the new tools are costly," said Marci Cantrell, sales representative for the manufacturer of the tools. "But they will allow direct labor and variable overhead to be reduced by $1.30 per unit for the K96 relay. I know this $1.30 figure is accurate because another company we sell to is using these same tools to produce a K96 relay of its own under operating conditions that are identical to Midway's."

"I agree that direct labor and variable overhead would be reduced by $1.30 per unit with the new tools," replied Allen Dusak. "The other company you mention was kind enough to provide me with a cost breakdown for its relay, as follows:

Direct materials	$21.80
Direct labor	4.00
Variable overhead	0.70
Fixed overhead	13.20
Total unit cost	$39.70

The thing you haven't mentioned, Marci, is that the other company's direct material cost went up by $1.80 per unit, due to the higher quality of material that must be used with the new tools. Our materials cost would go up by the same amount, which would more than offset the $1.30 reduction in labor and variable overhead. Also, you haven't considered the difference in volume between the other company and us. They produce 200,000 relays a year. When you consider our lower volume, I'm sure that with the new tools our unit cost would jump to well over $40."

Although the old tools being used by Midway Electronics are now fully depreciated, they have a salvage value of $30,000. These tools will be sold if the new tools are purchased. However, if the new tools are not purchased, then the old tools will be retained as standby equipment in case of a supply breakdown. Midway's accounting department has confirmed that total fixed overhead costs, other than depreciation, will not change regardless of the decision made concerning the relays. However, accounting has estimated that working capital needs will increase by $85,000 if the new tools are purchased due to the higher quality of material required in the manufacture of the relays.

Required

1. Prepare a discounted cash flow analysis that will help Midway Electronics' management decide whether the new tools should be purchased. Use the incremental-cost approach, and round all dollar amounts to the nearest whole dollar.
2. Identify additional factors that Midway's management should consider before a decision is made about whether to manufacture or buy the K96 relays.

PART IV

SELECTED TOPICS FOR FURTHER STUDY

16

Service Department Cost Allocations

LEARNING OBJECTIVES

After studying Chapter 16, you should be able to:

1 Explain what is meant by a service department, and explain why it is necessary to allocate service department costs to operating departments.

2 Allocate service department costs to other departments, using *(a)* the step method and *(b)* the direct method.

3 Explain why variable service department costs should be allocated separately from fixed service department costs, and give the allocation guidelines for each type of cost.

4 Explain why fixed service department costs should always be allocated in lump-sum amounts.

5 Prepare an allocation schedule involving several service departments and several operating departments.

6 Define or explain the key terms listed at the end of the chapter.

As stated in Chapter 1, most organizations have one or more service departments that carry on critical auxiliary services for the entire organization. In this chapter, we look more closely at service departments and consider how their costs are allocated to the units they serve for planning, costing, and other purposes.

THE NEED FOR COST ALLOCATION

Departments within an organization can be divided into two broad classes: (1) operating departments and (2) service departments. **Operating departments** include those departments or units where the central purposes of the organization are carried out. Examples of such departments or units would include the surgery department in a hospital; the undergraduate and graduate programs in a university; various flight groups in an airline; and producing departments such as milling, assembly, and painting in a manufacturing company.

Service departments, by contrast, do not engage directly in operating activities. Rather, they provide services or assistance that facilitate the activities of the operating departments. Examples of such services include cafeteria, internal auditing, personnel, X ray, cost accounting, and purchasing. Although service departments do not engage directly in the operating activities of an organization, the costs that they incur are generally viewed as being part of the cost of the final product or service, the same as are materials, labor, and overhead in a manufacturing company or medications in a hospital.

Equity in Allocation

The major question that we must consider in this chapter is: How does the manager determine how much of a service department's cost is to be allocated to each of the units that it serves? This is an important question, since the amount of service department cost allocated to a particular unit can have a major impact on the cost of the goods or services that the unit is providing. As we shall see, many factors must be considered if allocations are to be equitable between departments or other units that receive services during a period.

GUIDELINES FOR COST ALLOCATION

There are several basic guidelines to follow in service department cost allocation. These guidelines relate to (1) selecting the proper allocation base, (2) allocating the costs of interdepartmental services, (3) allocating costs by behavior, (4) avoiding certain allocation pitfalls, and (5) deciding whether to allocate budgeted or actual costs. These topics are covered in order in the following five sections.

Selecting Allocation Bases

Costs of service departments are allocated to other departments by means of some type of *allocation base*. An **allocation base** is a measure of activity that acts as a *cost driver* for the department involved. Allocation bases (cost drivers) may include labor-hours, number of employees, square footage of floor space, or any other measure of activity. Managers try to select allocation bases that reflect as accurately as possible the benefits that are being received by the various departments within the company from the services involved. A number of such bases may be selected according to the nature of the services. Examples of allocation bases that are frequently used are presented in Exhibit 16–1.

Once allocation bases have been chosen, they tend to remain unchanged for long periods of time. The selection of an allocation base represents a *major policy decision* that is normally reviewed only at very infrequent intervals or when it appears that some major inequity exists.

As we stated earlier, the way in which service department costs are allocated to other departments can have a major impact on their performance or on the cost of the goods or services they are providing, so the selection of an allocation base is no minor decision. The criteria for making selections may include: (1) direct, traceable benefits from the service involved, as measured, for example, by the number of service orders handled;

EXHIBIT 16–1
Bases Used in Allocating Service Department Costs

Service Department	Bases (Cost Drivers) Involved
Laundry	Pounds of laundry; number of items processed
Airport ground services	Number of flights
Cafeteria	Number of employees
Medical facilities	Periodic analysis of cases handled; number of employees; hours worked
Materials handling	Hours of service; volume handled
Custodial services (building and grounds)	Measure of square footage occupied
Engineering	Periodic analysis of services rendered; direct labor-hours
Production planning and control	Periodic analysis of services rendered; direct labor-hours
Cost accounting	Labor-hours; clients or patients serviced
Power	Measured usage (in kwh); capacity of machines
Personnel and employment	Number of employees; turnover of labor; periodic analysis of time spent
Receiving, shipping, and stores	Units handled; number of requisition and issue slips; square or cubic footage occupied
Factory administration	Total labor-hours
Maintenance	Machine-hours; total labor-hours (in order of preference)

and (2) the extent to which space or equipment is made available to a department, as measured, for example, by the number of square feet occupied in a building. In addition to these criteria, the manager must take care to assure that allocations are clear and straightforward, since complex allocation computations run the risk of yielding negative returns. That is, if allocation computations become too complex, the cost of the computations may exceed any benefits that they are trying to bring about. Allocation formulas should be simple and easily understood by all involved, particularly by the managers to whom the costs are being allocated.

Interdepartmental Services

Many service departments provide services for each other, as well as for operating departments. The cafeteria, for example, provides food for all employees, including those assigned to other service departments. In turn, the cafeteria may receive services from other service departments, such as from custodial services or from personnel. Services provided between service departments are known as **interdepartmental** or **reciprocal services.**

Two basic approaches are used to allocate the costs of service departments to other departments. These are known as the *direct method* and the *step method*. Both methods are discussed in the following sections.

Direct Method The **direct method** is a very simple allocation approach in that it ignores the costs of services between service departments and allocates all costs directly to operating departments. Even if a service department (such as personnel) renders a large amount of service to another service department (such as the cafeteria), no allocations are made between the two departments. Rather, all costs would go directly to the operating departments of the company. Hence the term *direct method*.

To provide a numerical example of the direct method, assume that Mountain View Hospital has two service departments and two operating departments as shown below:

	Service Department		Operating Department		
	Hospital Administration	Custodial Services	Laboratory	Daily Patient Care	Total
Departmental costs before allocation	$360,000	$90,000	$261,000	$689,000	$1,400,000
Labor-hours	—	6,000	18,000	30,000	54,000
Proportion of labor-hours	—	1/9	3/9	5/9	9/9
Space occupied—square feet . . .	10,000	—	5,000	45,000	60,000
Proportion of space occupied . . .	2/12	—	1/12	9/12	12/12

Allocation of the hospital's service department costs by the direct method to the operating departments is shown in Exhibit 16–2. Note that after all allocations have been made, all of the departmental costs are contained in the two operating departments. These costs will form the basis for preparing overhead rates and for determining the overall profitability of the operating departments in the hospital.

Although the direct method is simple, it is highly inaccurate since it ignores interdepartmental services. This can be a major defect in that overhead rates can be affected if the resulting errors in allocation are significant.

EXHIBIT 16–2
Direct Method of Allocation

	Service Department		Operating Department		
	Hospital Administration	Custodial Services	Laboratory	Daily Patient Care	Total
Departmental costs before allocation	$ 360,000	$ 90,000	$261,000	$689,000	$1,400,000
Allocation:					
Hospital administration costs (3/8, 5/8)*	(360,000)		135,000	225,000	
Custodial services costs (1/10, 9/10)†		(90,000)	9,000	81,000	
Total costs after allocation	$ -0-	$ -0-	$405,000	$995,000	$1,400,000

* Based on the labor-hours in the two operating departments, which are: 18,000 hours + 30,000 hours = 48,000 hours.
† Based on the space occupied by the two operating departments, which is: 5,000 square feet + 45,000 square feet = 50,000 square feet.

In turn, incorrect overhead rates can lead to distorted product and service costs and to ineffective pricing. Even so, many organizations use the direct method because of its ease of application.

Step Method Unlike the direct method, the **step method** provides for allocation of a service department's costs to other service departments, as well as to operating departments, in a sequential manner. The sequence typically begins with the department that provides the greatest amount of service to other departments. After its costs have been allocated, the process continues, step by step, ending with the department that provides the least amount of services to other service departments. This step procedure is illustrated in graphic form in Exhibit 16–3.

A numeric example of the step method is provided in Exhibit 16–4. The data in this exhibit are the same as that used earlier in connection with the direct method in Exhibit 16–2.

Since hospital administration provides the greatest amount of service to other departments, its costs are allocated first. This allocation is on a basis of labor-hours in other departments. The costs of custodial services are then allocated on a basis of square footage of space occupied.

Two things should be noted about these allocations. First, note that the costs of hospital administration are borne by another service department (custodial services) as well as by the operating departments. Second, note that those hospital administration costs that have been allocated to custodial services *are included with custodial services costs,* and that the total ($90,000 + $40,000 = $130,000) is allocated only to subsequent departments. That is, no part of custodial services' costs are reallocated back to hospital administration, even though custodial services may have provided services to hospital administration during the period. This is a key idea associated with the step method: After the allocation of a service department's costs has been completed, costs of other service departments are not reallocated back to it.

EXHIBIT 16–3
Graphic Illustration—Step Method

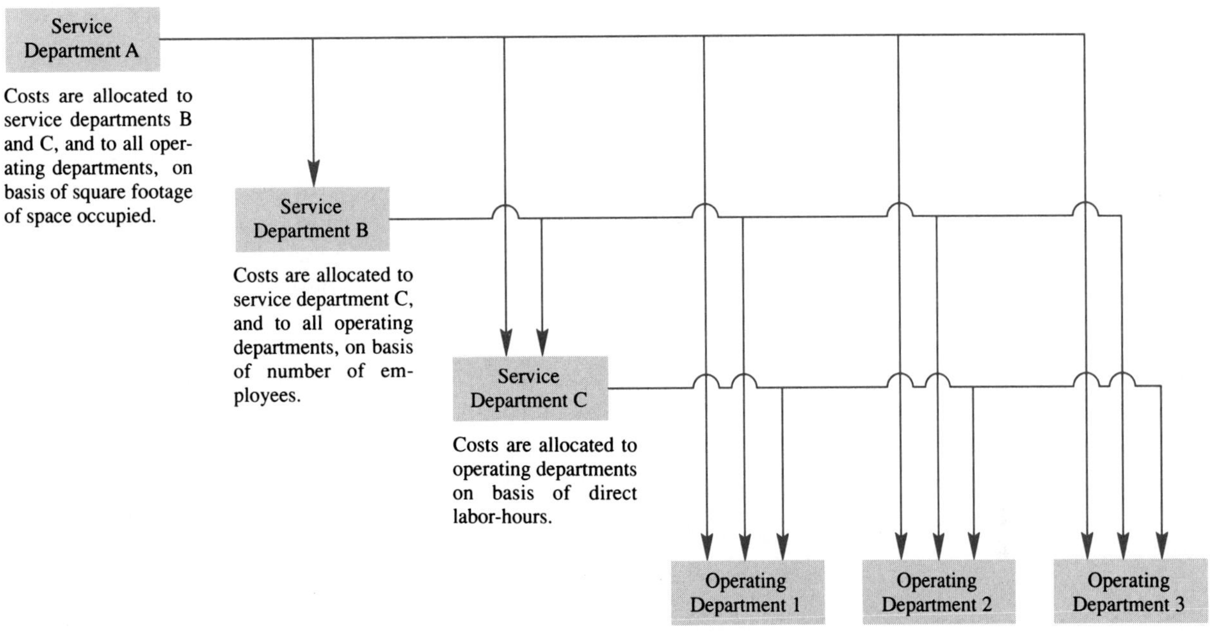

EXHIBIT 16–4
Step Method of Allocation

	Service Department		Operating Department		
	Hospital Administration	**Custodial Services**	**Laboratory**	**Daily Patient Care**	**Total**
Departmental costs before allocation	$ 360,000	$ 90,000	$261,000	$ 689,000	$1,400,000
Allocation:					
Hospital administration costs (1/9, 3/9, 5/9)	(360,000)	40,000	120,000	200,000	
Custodial services costs (1/10, 9/10)*		(130,000)	13,000	117,000	
Total costs after allocation	$ -0-	$ -0-	$394,000	$1,006,000	$1,400,000

* As in Exhibit 16–2, this allocation is based on the space occupied by the two operating departments.

In conclusion, for both the direct method and the step method, we should state that although most service departments are simply cost centers and thus generate no revenues, a few, such as the cafeteria, may charge employees or other outside parties for the services they perform. If a service department (such as the cafeteria) generates revenues, these revenues should be offset against the department's costs, and only the net amount of cost remaining after this offset should be allocated to other departments within the organization. In this manner, the other departments will not be required to bear costs for which the service department has already been reimbursed.

Allocating Costs by Behavior

Whenever possible, service department costs should be separated into variable and fixed classifications and allocated separately. This approach is necessary to avoid possible inequities in allocation, as well as to provide more useful data for planning and control of departmental operations.

Variable Costs Variable costs represent direct costs of providing services and will generally vary in total in proportion to fluctuations in the level of service consumed. Food cost in a cafeteria would be a variable cost, for example, and one would expect this cost to vary proportionately with the number of persons using the cafeteria over a given period of time.

As a general rule, variable costs should be charged to consuming departments according to whatever activity base controls the incurrence of the cost involved. If, for example, the variable costs of a service department such as maintenance are incurred according to the number of machine-hours worked in the producing departments, then variable maintenance costs should be allocated to the producing departments on a machine-hours basis. By this means, the departments directly responsible for the incurrence of servicing costs are required to bear them in proportion to their actual usage of the service involved.

Technically, the assigning of variable servicing costs to consuming departments can more accurately be termed *charges* than allocations, since the service department is actually charging the consuming departments at some fixed rate per unit of service provided. In effect, the service department is saying, "I'll charge you *X* dollars for every unit of my service that you consume. You can consume as much or as little as you desire; the total charge you bear will vary proportionately."

Fixed Costs The fixed costs of service departments represent the cost of having long-run service capacity available. As such, these costs are most equitably allocated to consuming departments on a basis of *predetermined lump-sum amounts*. By "predetermined lump-sum amounts" we mean that the amount charged to each consuming department is determined in advance and, once determined, does not change from period to period. Typically, the lump-sum amount charged to a department is based either on the department's peak-period or long-run average servicing needs. The logic behind lump-sum allocations of this type is as follows:

When a service department is first established, some basic capacity is built into it according to the observed needs of the other departments that it will service. This basic capacity may reflect the peak-period needs of the other departments, or it may reflect their long-run average or "normal" servicing needs. Depending on how much servicing capacity is provided for, it will be necessary to make a commitment of resources to the servicing unit, which will be reflected in its fixed costs. It is generally felt that these fixed costs should be borne by the consuming departments whose servicing needs have made the creation of the service department necessary, and that the costs should be borne in proportion to the individual servicing needs that have been provided for. That is, if available capacity in the service department has been provided to meet the peak-period needs of consuming departments, then the fixed costs of the service department should be allocated in predetermined lump-sum amounts to consuming departments on this basis.

If available capacity has been provided only to meet "normal" or long-run average needs, then the fixed costs should be allocated on this basis.

Once set, allocations should not vary from period to period, since they represent each consuming department's "fair share" of having a certain level of service capacity available and on line. The fact that a consuming department does not need a peak level or even a "normal" level of servicing every period is immaterial; if it requires such servicing at certain times, then the capacity to deliver it must be available. It is the responsibility of the consuming departments to bear the cost of that availability.

To illustrate this idea, assume that Novak Company has just organized a maintenance department to service all machines in the cutting, assembly, and finishing departments. In determining the capacity that should be built into the newly organized maintenance department, the company recognized that the various producing departments would have the following peak-period needs for maintenance:

Department	Peak-Period Maintenance Needs in Terms of Number of Hours of Maintenance Work Required	Percent of Total Hours
Cutting	900	30
Assembly	1,800	60
Finishing	300	10
	3,000	100

Therefore, in allocating the maintenance department fixed costs to the producing departments, 30 percent should be allocated to the cutting department, 60 percent to the assembly department, and 10 percent to the finishing department. These lump-sum allocations *will not change* from period to period unless there is some shift in servicing needs due to structural changes in the organization.

Pitfalls in Allocating Fixed Costs

Rather than allocate fixed costs in predetermined lump-sum amounts, some firms allocate them by use of a *variable* allocation base. What's wrong with this practice? The answer is that it can create serious inequities between departments. The inequities will arise from the fact that the fixed costs allocated to one department will be heavily influenced by what happens in *other* departments or segments of the organization.

To illustrate, assume that Kolby Products has an auto service center that provides maintenance work on the fleet of autos used in the company's two sales territories. The auto service center costs are all fixed. Contrary to good practice, the company allocates these fixed costs to the sales territories on the basis of miles driven (a variable base). Selected cost data for the last two years are given below:

	Year 1	Year 2
Auto service center costs (all fixed) . . .	$120,000 *(a)*	$120,000 *(a)*
Sales territory A—miles driven	1,500,000	1,500,000
Sales territory B—miles driven	1,500,000	900,000
Total miles driven	3,000,000 *(b)*	2,400,000 *(b)*
Allocation rate per mile, *(a)* ÷ *(b)*	$0.04	$0.05

Notice that sales territory A maintained an activity level of 1,500,000 miles driven in both years. On the other hand, sales territory B allowed its activity to drop off from 1,500,000 miles in year 1 to only 900,000 miles in year 2. The auto service center costs that would have been allocated to the two sales territories over the two-year span are as follows:

Year 1:	
Sales territory A: 1,500,000 miles at $0.04 . . .	$ 60,000
Sales territory B: 1,500,000 miles at $0.04 . . .	60,000
Total cost allocated	$120,000
Year 2:	
Sales territory A: 1,500,000 miles at $0.05 . . .	$ 75,000
Sales territory B: 900,000 miles at $0.05	45,000
Total cost allocated	$120,000

In year 1, the two sales territories share the service department costs equally. In year 2, however, the bulk of the service department costs are allocated to sales territory A. This is not because of any increase in activity in sales territory A; rather, it is because of the *decrease* in effort in sales territory B, which did not maintain its activity level during year 2. Even though sales territory A maintained the same level of activity in both years, the use of a variable allocation base has caused it to be penalized with a heavier cost allocation in year 2 because of what has happened in *another* territory of the company.

This kind of inequity is almost inevitable when a variable allocation base is used to allocate fixed costs. The manager of sales territory A undoubtedly will be upset about the inequity forced on his territory, but he will feel powerless to do anything about it. The result will be a loss of confidence in the system and the accumulation of a considerable backlog of ill feeling.

Should Actual or Budgeted Costs Be Allocated?

Should a service department allocate its *actual* costs to operating departments, or should it allocate its *budgeted* costs? The answer is that budgeted costs should be allocated. What's wrong with allocating actual costs? Allocating actual costs burdens the operating departments with the inefficiencies of the service department managers. If actual costs are allocated, then any lack of cost control on the part of the service department manager is simply buried in a routine allocation to other departments.

Any variance over budgeted costs should be retained in the service department and closed out at year-end against the company's revenues or against cost of goods sold, along with other variances. Operating department managers rarely complain about being allocated a portion of service department costs, but they complain bitterly if they are forced to absorb service department inefficiencies.

EFFECT OF ALLOCATIONS ON OPERATING DEPARTMENTS

Once allocations have been completed, what do the operating departments do with the allocated service department costs? Since the amounts allocated are presumed to represent each department's "fair share" of the cost of services provided for it, the allocations are included in performance evalua-

EXHIBIT 16–5
Effect of Allocations on Products and Services

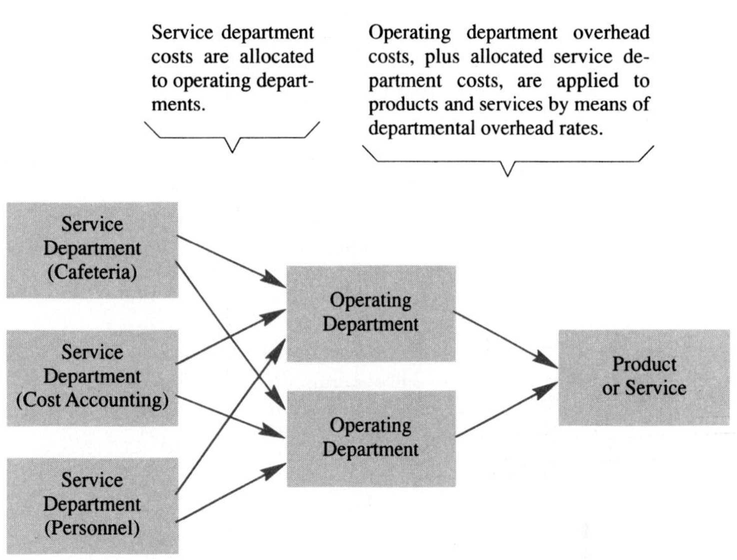

tions of the operating departments and also included in determining their individual profitability.

In addition, if the operating departments are responsible for developing overhead rates for costing of products or billing of services, then the allocated costs are combined with the other costs of the operating departments, and the total is used as a basis for rate computations. This rate development process is illustrated in Exhibit 16–5. Observe from the exhibit that the term *allocated* is used to describe the movement of service department costs to operating departments, whereas the term *applied* is used to describe the attaching of these costs (along with operating department costs) to products and services.

Typically, the flexible budget serves as the means for combining allocated service department costs with operating department costs and for computing overhead rates. An example of the combining of these costs on a flexible budget is presented in Exhibit 16–6. Note from the exhibit that both variable and fixed service department costs have been allocated to Superior Company's milling department and are included on the latter's flexible budget. Since allocated service department costs become an integral part of the flexible budget, they are automatically included in overhead rate computations, as shown at the bottom of the exhibit. If this had been the flexible budget of an operating department in a service company, rather than a manufacturing company, then the overhead rate computation would have been for purposes of developing an appropriate billing rate for services.

A SUMMARY OF COST ALLOCATION GUIDELINES

To summarize the material covered in preceding sections, we can note five key points to remember about allocating service department costs:

EXHIBIT 16–6
Flexible Budget Containing Allocated Service Department Costs

SUPERIOR COMPANY
Flexible Budget—Milling Department

Budgeted direct labor-hours 50,000

Overhead Costs	Cost Formula (per hour)	Direct Labor-Hours 40,000	50,000	60,000
Variable costs:				
Indirect labor	$1.45	$ 58,000	$ 72,500	$ 87,000
Indirect material	0.90	36,000	45,000	54,000
Utilities	0.10	4,000	5,000	6,000
Allocation—cafeteria	0.15	6,000	7,500	9,000
Total variable costs	$2.60	104,000	130,000	156,000
Fixed costs:				
Depreciation		85,000	85,000	85,000
Supervisory salaries		110,000	110,000	110,000
Property taxes		9,000	9,000	9,000
Allocation—cafeteria		21,000	21,000	21,000
Allocation—personnel department .		45,000	45,000	45,000
Total fixed costs		270,000	270,000	270,000
Total overhead costs		$374,000	$400,000	$426,000

$$\text{Predetermined overhead rate} = \frac{\$400{,}000}{50{,}000\ \text{DLH}} = \$8 \text{ per direct labor-hour}$$

1. If possible, the distinction between variable and fixed costs in service departments should be maintained.
2. Variable costs should be allocated at the budgeted rate, according to whatever activity measure (miles driven, direct labor-hours, number of employees) controls the incurrence of the cost involved.
   a. If the allocations are being made at the beginning of the year, they should be based on the budgeted activity level planned for the consuming departments. The allocation formula would be:

   $$\text{Budgeted rate} \times \text{Budgeted activity} = \text{Cost allocated}$$

   b. If the allocations are being made at the end of the year, they should be based on the actual activity level that has occurred during the year. The allocation formula would be:

   $$\text{Budgeted rate} \times \text{Actual activity} = \text{Cost allocated}$$

   Allocations made at the beginning of the year would be to provide data for computing overhead rates for costing of products and billing of services in the operating departments. Allocations made at the end of the year would be to provide data for comparing actual performance against planned performance.
3. Fixed costs represent the costs of having service capacity available. Where feasible, these costs should be allocated in predetermined lump-sum amounts. The lump-sum amount going to each department should be in proportion to the servicing needs that gave rise to the investment in

the service department in the first place. (This might be either peak-period needs for servicing or long-run average needs.) Budgeted fixed costs, rather than actual fixed costs, should always be allocated.

4. If it is not feasible to maintain a distinction between variable and fixed costs in a service department, then the costs of the department should be allocated to consuming departments according to the base that appears to provide the best measure of benefits received.
5. Where possible, reciprocal services between departments should be recognized.

IMPLEMENTING THE ALLOCATION GUIDELINES

We will now show the implementation of these guidelines by the use of specific examples. We will focus first on the allocation of costs for a single department, and then develop a more extended example where multiple departments are involved.

Basic Allocation Techniques

For purposes of illustration, assume that Seaboard Airlines is divided into a Freight Division and a Passenger Division. The company has a single aircraft maintenance department that provides servicing to both divisions. Variable servicing costs are budgeted at $10 per flight-hour. The fixed costs of the department are budgeted at $750,000 per year. Peak-period flight-hours per year and budgeted flight-hours for the coming year are shown below:

	Flight-Hours	
	Peak Period	Budgeted
Freight Division	12,000	9,000
Passenger Division	18,000	15,000
Total flight-hours	30,000	24,000

Given these data, the amount of cost that would be allocated to each division from the aircraft maintenance department at the beginning of the coming year would be:

	Division	
	Freight	Passenger
Variable cost allocation:		
$10 × 9,000 flight-hours	$ 90,000	
$10 × 15,000 flight-hours		$150,000
Fixed cost allocation:		
40%* × $750,000	300,000	
60%* × $750,000		450,000
Total cost allocated	$390,000	$600,000

* These allocations are based on peak-period flight-hours in each division:

Freight Division: 12,000 flight-hours ÷ 30,000 flight-hours = 40%.
Passenger Division: 18,000 flight-hours ÷ 30,000 flight-hours = 60%.

As explained earlier, these allocations would be placed on the flexible budgets of the respective divisions and included in the computation of divisional overhead rates.

At the end of the year, Seaboard Airlines' management may want to make a second allocation, this time based on actual activity, in order to compare actual performance for the year against planned performance. To illustrate, assume that year-end records show that actual costs in the aircraft maintenance department for the year were: variable costs, $290,000; and fixed costs, $780,000. We will assume that one division logged more flight-hours during the year than planned and the other one logged less flight-hours than planned.

	Flight-Hours	
	Budgeted (see above)	**Actual**
Freight Division	9,000	8,000
Passenger Division	15,000	17,000
Total flight-hours	24,000	25,000

The amount of actual service department cost chargeable to each division for the year would be as follows:

	Division	
	Freight	**Passenger**
Variable cost allocation:		
$10 × 8,000 flight-hours	$ 80,000	
$10 × 17,000 flight-hours		$170,000
Fixed cost allocation:		
40% × $750,000	300,000	
60% × $750,000		450,000
Total cost allocated	$380,000	$620,000

Notice that the variable cost is allocated according to the budgeted rate ($10 per hour) times the *actual activity* for the year, and that the fixed cost is allocated according to the original budgeted amount. As stated in the guidelines given earlier, allocations are always based on budgeted rates and amounts in order to avoid the passing on of inefficiency from one department to another. Thus, a portion of the actual costs of the aircraft maintenance department for the year will not be allocated, as shown below:

	Variable	**Fixed**
Total actual costs incurred	$290,000	$780,000
Costs allocated (above)	250,000*	750,000
Spending variance—not allocated	$ 40,000	$ 30,000

* $10 per flight-hour × 25,000 actual flight-hours = $250,000.

These variances will be closed out against the company's overall revenues for the year, along with any other variances that may occur.

An Extended Example

Proctor Company has three service departments—building maintenance, cafeteria, and inspection. The company also has two operating departments—shaping and assembly. The service departments provide services to each other, as well as to the operating departments. Types of costs in the service departments and bases for allocation are:

Department	Type of Cost	Base for Allocation
Building maintenance . . .	Fixed costs	Square footage occupied
Cafeteria	Variable costs	Number of employees
	Fixed costs	10% to inspection, 40% to shaping, and 50% to assembly
Inspection	Variable costs	Direct labor-hours
	Fixed costs	70% to shaping and 30% to assembly

Proctor Company allocates service department costs by the step method in the following order:

1. Building maintenance.
2. Cafeteria.
3. Inspection.

Assume the following budgeted cost and operating data for 19x1:

Department	Variable Cost	Fixed Cost
Building maintenance . . .	—	$130,000
Cafeteria	$200 per employee	250,000
Inspection	$0.06 per direct labor-hour	548,000

Department	Number of Employees	Direct Labor-Hours	Square Footage of Space Occupied (square feet)
Building maintenance . . .	6*	—	3,000
Cafeteria	9*	—	4,000
Inspection	30	—	1,000
Shaping	190	300,000	8,000
Assembly	250	500,000	13,000
Total.	485	800,000	29,000

* Although there are employees in both of these service departments, under the step method costs are only allocated *forward*—never backward. For this reason, the costs of the cafeteria will be allocated *forward* on the basis of the number of employees in the inspection, shaping, and assembly departments.

In addition to the service department costs listed above, the company's shaping department has budgeted $1,340,000 in overhead costs for 19x1, and its assembly department has budgeted $1,846,000 in overhead costs.

Cost allocations from the service departments to the operating departments would be as shown in Exhibit 16–7 on the following page. To save space, we have computed the operating department's predetermined overhead rates at the bottom of the exhibit.

EXHIBIT 16–7

THE PROCTOR COMPANY
Beginning-of-Year Cost Allocations for Purposes of Preparing Predetermined Overhead Rates

	Building Maintenance	Cafeteria	Inspection	Shaping	Assembly
Variable costs to be allocated	$ -0-	$ 94,000	$ 42,000	$ —	$ —
Cafeteria allocation at $200 per employee:					
30 employees × $200	—	(6,000)	6,000	—	—
190 employees × $200	—	(38,000)	—	38,000	—
250 employees × $200	—	(50,000)	—	—	50,000
Inspection allocation at $0.06 per direct labor-hour:					
300,000 DLH × $0.06	—	—	(18,000)	18,000	—
500,000 DLH × $0.06	—	—	(30,000)	—	30,000
Total	-0-	-0-	-0-	56,000	80,000
Fixed costs to be allocated	130,000	250,000	548,000		
Building maintenance allocation at $5 per square foot:*					
4,000 square feet × $5	(20,000)	20,000	—	—	—
1,000 square feet × $5	(5,000)	—	5,000	—	—
8,000 square feet × $5	(40,000)	—	—	40,000	—
13,000 square feet × $5	(65,000)	—	—	—	65,000
Cafeteria allocation:†					
10% × $270,000	—	(27,000)	27,000	—	—
40% × $270,000	—	(108,000)	—	108,000	—
50% × $270,000	—	(135,000)	—	—	135,000
Inspection allocation:‡					
70% × $580,000	—	—	(406,000)	406,000	—
30% × $580,000	—	—	(174,000)	—	174,000
Total	-0-	-0-	-0-	554,000	374,000
Total allocated costs	$ -0-	$ -0-	$ -0-	610,000	454,000
Other flexible budget costs at the planned activity level				1,340,000	1,846,000
Total overhead costs				$1,950,000	$2,300,000 *(a)*
Budgeted direct labor-hours				300,000	500,000 *(b)*
Predetermined overhead rate, *(a)* ÷ *(b)*				$6.50	$4.60

*Square footage of space	29,000 square feet
Less building maintenance space	3,000 square feet
Net space for allocation	26,000 square feet

$$\frac{\text{Building maintenance fixed costs, \$130,000}}{\text{Net space for allocation, 26,000 square feet}} = \text{\$5 per square foot}$$

†Cafeteria fixed costs	$250,000
Allocated from building maintenance	20,000
Total cost to be allocated	$270,000

Allocation percentages are given in the problem.

‡Inspection fixed costs	$548,000
Allocated from building maintenance	5,000
Allocated from cafeteria	27,000
Total cost to be allocated	$580,000

Allocation percentages are given in the problem.

No Distinction Made between Fixed and Variable Costs

As stated in the guidelines given earlier, in some cases it may not be feasible to maintain a distinction between fixed and variable service department costs. We noted that in such cases the costs should be allocated to operating departments according to the base that appears to provide the best measure of benefits received. An example of such an allocation was given earlier in Exhibit 16–4, where we first illustrated the step method. The reader may wish to turn back and review this example before reading on.

Should All Costs Be Allocated?

As a general rule, any service department costs that are incurred as a result of specific services provided to operating departments should be allocated back to these departments and used to compute overhead rates and to measure profitability. The only time when this general rule is not followed is in those situations where in the view of management, allocation would result in an undesirable behavioral response from operating departments. There are some servicing costs, for example, that are clearly beneficial to operating departments but which these departments may not utilize as fully as they should, particularly in times of cost economizing. Systems design is a good example of such a cost. Utilization of systems design services may be very beneficial to operating departments in terms of improving overall efficiency, reducing waste, and assuring adherence to departmental policies. But if a department knows that it will be charged for the systems design services it uses, it may be less inclined to take advantage of the benefits involved, especially if the department is feeling some pressure to trim costs. In short, the departmental manager may opt for the near-term benefit of avoiding a direct charge, in lieu of the long-term benefit of reduced waste and greater efficiency.

To avoid discouraging use of a service that is helpful to the entire organization, some firms do not charge for the service at all. These managers feel that by making such services a "free" commodity, departments will be more inclined to take full advantage of their benefits.

Other firms take a somewhat different approach. They agree that charging according to usage may discourage utilization of such services as systems design, but they argue that such services should not be free. Instead of providing free services, these firms take what is sometimes called a **retainer fee approach.** Each department is charged a flat amount each year, regardless of how much or how little of the service it utilizes. The thought is that if a department knows that it is going to be charged a certain amount for systems design services, *regardless of usage,* then it will probably utilize the services at least to that extent.

Beware of Sales Dollars as an Allocation Base

Over the years, sales dollars (or total revenues) have been a favorite allocation base for service department costs. One reason is that sales dollars are simple, straightforward, and easy to work with. Another reason is that people tend to view sales dollars as being a measure of well-being, or "ability to pay," and, hence, as being a measure of how extensively costs can be absorbed from other parts of the organization.

Unfortunately, sales dollars often constitute a very poor allocation base, for the reason that sales dollars vary from period to period, whereas the costs being allocated are often largely *fixed* in nature. As discussed earlier, if a variable base is used to allocate fixed costs, inequities can result between departments since the costs being allocated to one department will depend in large part on what happens in *other* departments. For example, a letup in sales effort in one department will shift allocated costs off that department and onto other, more productive departments. In effect, the departments putting forth the best sales efforts are penalized in the form of higher allocations, simply because of inefficiencies elsewhere that are beyond their control. The result is often bitterness and resentment on the part of the managers of the better departments.

Consider the following situation encountered by the author:

A large men's clothing store has one service department and three sales departments–suits, shoes, and accessories. The service department's costs total $60,000 per period and are allocated to the three sales departments according to sales dollars. A recent period showed the following allocation:

	Department			
	Suits	**Shoes**	**Accessories**	**Total**
Sales by department	$260,000	$40,000	$100,000	$400,000
Percentage of total sales.	65%	10%	25%	100%
Allocation of service department costs, based on percentage of total sales	$ 39,000	$ 6,000	$ 15,000	$ 60,000

In a following period, the manager of the suit department launched a very successful program to expand sales by $100,000 in his department. Sales in the other two departments remained unchanged. Total service department costs also remained unchanged, but the allocation of these costs changed substantially, as shown below:

	Department			
	Suits	**Shoes**	**Accessories**	**Total**
Sales by department	$360,000	$40,000	$100,000	$500,000
Percentage of total sales.	72%	8%	20%	100%
Allocation of service department costs, based on percentage of total sales	$ 43,200	$ 4,800	$ 12,000	$ 60,000
Increase (or decrease) from prior allocation	4,200	(1,200)	(3,000)	—

The manager of the suit department complained that as a result of his successful effort to expand sales in his department, he was being forced to carry a larger share of the service department costs. On the other hand, the managers of the departments that showed no improvement in sales were being relieved of a portion of the costs that they had been carrying. Yet there had been no change in the amount of services provided for any department.

The manager of the suit department viewed the increased service department cost allocation to his department as a penalty for his outstanding performance, and he wondered whether his efforts had really been worthwhile after all in the eyes of top management.

Sales dollars should be used as an allocation base only in those cases where there is a direct causal relationship between sales dollars and the service department costs being allocated. In those situations where service department costs are fixed in nature, they should be allocated according to the guidelines discussed earlier in the chapter.

SUMMARY

Service departments are organized to provide some needed service in a single, centralized place, rather than to have all units within the organization provide the service for themselves. Although service departments do not engage directly in production or other operating activities, the costs that they incur are vital to the overall success of an organization and therefore are properly included as part of the cost of its products and services.

Service department costs are charged to operating departments by an allocation process. In turn, the operating departments include the allocated costs within their flexible budgets, from which overhead rates are computed for purposes of costing of products or billing of services.

In order to avoid inequity in allocations, variable and fixed service department costs should be allocated separately. The variable costs should be allocated according to whatever activity measure controls their incurrence. The fixed costs should be allocated in predetermined lump-sum amounts according to either the peak-period or the long-run average servicing needs of the consuming departments. Budgeted costs, rather than actual costs, should always be allocated, in order to avoid the passing on of inefficiency between departments. Any variances between budgeted and actual service department costs should be kept within the service departments for analysis purposes, then written off against revenues or against cost of goods sold, along with other variances.

KEY TERMS FOR REVIEW

Allocation base Any measure of activity (such as labor-hours, number of employees, or square footage of space) that is used to charge service department costs to other departments. (p. 692)

Direct method The allocation of all of a service department's costs directly to operating departments without recognizing services provided to other service departments. (p. 693)

Interdepartmental services Services provided between service departments. Also see *Reciprocal services*. (p. 693)

Operating department A department or similar unit in an organization within which the central purposes of the organization are carried out. (p. 691)

Reciprocal services Services provided between service departments. Also see *Interdepartmental services*. (p. 693)

Retainer fee approach A method of allocating service department costs in which other departments are charged a flat amount each period regardless of usage of the service involved. (p. 705)

Service department A department that provides support or assistance to operating departments and that does not engage directly in production or in other operating activities of an organization. (p. 691)

Step method The allocation of a service department's costs to other service departments as well as to operating departments in a sequential manner. The sequence starts with the service department that provides the greatest amount of service to other departments. (p. 694)

QUESTIONS

16–1 What is the difference between a service department and an operating department? Give several examples of service departments.

16–2 In what way are service department costs similar to such costs as lubricants, utilities, and factory supervision?

16–3 "Products and services can be costed equally well with or without allocations of service department costs." Do you agree? Why or why not?

16–4 How do service department costs enter into the final cost of products and services?

16–5 What criteria are relevant to the selection of allocation bases for service department costs?

16–6 What are interdepartmental service costs? How are such costs allocated to other departments under the step method?

16–7 How are service department costs allocated to other departments under the direct method?

16–8 If a service department generates revenues of some type, how do these revenues enter into the allocation of the department's costs to other departments?

16–9 What guidelines should govern the allocation of fixed service department costs to other departments? The allocation of variable service department costs?

16–10 "A variable base should never be used in allocating fixed service department costs to operating departments." Explain.

16–11 Why might it be desirable not to allocate some service department costs to operating departments?

16–12 What is the purpose of the retainer fee approach to cost allocation?

EXERCISES

E16–1 Arbon Company has three service departments and two operating departments. Selected data on the five departments are presented below:

	Service Department			Operating Department		
	X	**Y**	**Z**	**1**	**2**	**Total**
Overhead costs	$84,000	$67,800	$36,000	$256,100	$498,600	$942,500
Number of employees	80	60	240	600	300	1,280
Square feet of space occupied	3,000	12,000	10,000	20,000	70,000	115,000
Machine-hours	—	—	—	10,000	30,000	40,000

The company allocates service department costs by the step method in the following order: X (number of employees), Y (space occupied), and Z (machine-hours). The company makes no distinction between fixed and variable service department costs.

Required Using the step method, make the necessary allocations of service department costs.

E16–2 Refer to the data for Arbon Company in Exercise 16–1. Assume that the company allocates service department costs by the direct method, rather than by the step method.

Required Assuming that the company uses the direct method, how much overhead cost would be chargeable to each operating department? Show computations in good form.

E16–3 Gutherie Oil Company has a transport services department that provides trucks to transport crude oil from eastern docks to the company's Arbon Refinery and Beck Refinery. The transport services department has sufficient capacity to handle peak-period needs of 270,000 gallons per year for the Arbon Refinery and 180,000 gallons per year for the Beck Refinery. At this level of activity, budgeted costs for the transport services department total $335,000 per year, consisting of $0.30 per gallon variable cost and $200,000 fixed cost.

During 19x5, the coming year, 270,000 gallons of crude oil are budgeted to be hauled to the Arbon Refinery and 130,000 gallons of crude oil to the Beck Refinery.

Required Compute the amount of transport services cost that should be allocated to each refinery at the beginning of 19x5, for purposes of computing predetermined overhead rates. (The company allocates variable and fixed costs separately.)

E16–4 Refer to the data in Exercise 16–3. Assume that it is now the end of 19x5. During the year, the transport services department actually hauled the following amounts of crude oil for the two refineries: Arbon Refinery, 260,000 gallons; and Beck Refinery, 140,000 gallons. The transport services department incurred $365,000 in cost during the year, of which $148,000 was variable cost and $217,000 was fixed cost.

Management wants end-of-year service department cost allocations in order to compare actual performance against planned performance.

Required

1. Determine how much of the $148,000 in variable cost should be allocated to each refinery.
2. Determine how much of the $217,000 in fixed cost should be allocated to each refinery.
3. Will any of the $365,000 in transport services cost not be allocated to the refineries? Explain.

E16–5 Reed Company operates a medical services department for its employees. The variable costs of the department are allocated to using departments on a basis of the number of employees in each department. Budgeted and actual data for 19x8 are given below:

	Variable Costs—19x8	
	Budgeted	**Actual**
Medical services department . . .	$60 per employee	$72 per employee

The budgeted and actual number of employees in each operating department during 19x8 follows:

	Department		
	Cutting	**Milling**	**Assembly**
Budgeted number of employees . . .	600	300	900
Actual number of employees	500	400	800

Required Determine the amount of medical services department variable cost that should be allocated to each of the three operating departments at the end of 19x8, for purposes of comparing actual performance against planned performance.

E16–6 Refer to Reed Company in Exercise 16–5. In addition to the medical services department, the company also has a janitorial services department that provides services to all other departments in the company. The fixed costs of the two service departments are allocated on the following bases:

Department	Basis for Allocation	
Janitorial services . . .	Square footage of space occupied:	
	Medical services department	6,000 square feet
	Cutting department	30,000 square feet
	Milling department	24,000 square feet
	Assembly department	90,000 square feet
Medical services	Long-run average number of employees:	
	Janitorial services department . . .	20 employees
	Cutting department	600 employees
	Milling department	400 employees
	Assembly department	1,000 employees

Budgeted and actual fixed costs in the two service departments for 19x8 follow:

	Janitorial Services	Medical Services
Budgeted fixed costs	$350,000	$596,000
Actual fixed costs	361,000	605,000

Required

1. Show the allocation of the fixed costs of the two service departments at the beginning of 19x8 for purposes of computing overhead rates in the operating departments. The company uses the step method of allocation, starting with the janitorial services department.
2. Show the allocation of the fixed costs of the two service departments at the end of 19x8 for purposes of comparing actual performance against planned performance.

E16–7 Lacey's Department Store allocates its fixed administrative expenses to its four departments on a basis of sales dollars. During 19x1, the fixed administrative expenses totaled $900,000. These expenses were allocated as follows:

	Department				
	1	2	3	4	Total
Total sales—19x1 . . .	$600,000	$1,500,000	$2,100,000	$1,800,000	$6,000,000
Percentage of total sales	10%	25%	35%	30%	100%
Allocation (based on the above percentages)	$ 90,000	$ 225,000	$ 315,000	$ 270,000	$ 900,000

During 19x2, the following year, Department 2 doubled its sales. The sales levels in the other three departments remained unchanged. As a result of Department 2's sales increase, the company's 19x2 sales data appeared as follows:

	Department				
	1	2	3	4	Total
Total sales—19x2 . . .	$600,000	$3,000,000	$2,100,000	$1,800,000	$7,500,000
Percentage of total sales	8%	40%	28%	24%	100%

Fixed administrative expenses in the company remained unchanged at $900,000 during 19x2.

Required

1. Using sales dollars as an allocation base, show the allocation of the fixed administrative expenses between the four departments for 19x2.
2. Compare your allocation from (1) above to the allocation for 19x1. As the manager of Department 2, how would you feel about the allocation that has been charged to you for 19x2?
3. Comment on the usefulness of sales dollars as an allocation base.

PROBLEMS

P16–8 Various Allocation Methods Northstar Company consists of a Machine Tools Division and a Special Products Division. The company has a maintenance department that services the equipment in both divisions. The costs of operating the maintenance department are budgeted at $80,000 per month plus $0.50 per machine-hour. The maintenance department has a capacity to service 200,000 machine-hours per month—based on peak needs of 130,000 machine-hours per month in the Machine Tools Division and 70,000 machine-hours per month in the Special Products Division.

For October, the Machine Tools Division has estimated that it will operate at a 90,000 machine-hours level of activity and the Special Products Division has estimated that it will operate at a 60,000 machine-hours level of activity.

Required

1. At the beginning of October, how much maintenance department cost should be allocated to each division for flexible budget planning purposes?
2. Assume that it is now the end of October. Cost records in the maintenance department show that actual fixed costs for the month totaled $85,000 and that actual variable costs totaled $78,000. Due to labor unrest and an unexpected strike, the Machine Tools Division worked only 60,000 machine-hours during the month. The Special Products Division also worked 60,000 machine-hours, as planned. How much of the actual maintenance department costs for the month should be allocated to each division? (Management uses these end-of-month allocations to compare actual performance against planned performance.)
3. Refer to the data in (2) above. Assume that the company follows the practice of allocating *all* maintenance department costs each month to the divisions in proportion to the actual machine-hours recorded in each division for the month. On this basis, how much cost would be allocated to each division for October?
4. What criticisms can you make of the allocation method used in (3) above?
5. If managers of producing departments know that fixed service department costs are going to be allocated on a basis of long-run average usage of the service involved, what will be their probable strategy as they report their estimate of this usage to the company's budget committee? As a member of top management, what would you do to neutralize any such strategies?

P16–9 Cost Allocation: Step Method versus Direct Method Harker Products, Inc., has budgeted costs in its various departments as follows for the coming year:

Factory administration	$ 540,000
Custodial services	137,520
Personnel	57,680
Maintenance	90,400
Stamping—overhead	752,600
Assembly—overhead	351,800
Total cost	$1,930,000

The company allocates service department costs to other departments, *in the order listed below*. Bases for allocation are to be chosen from the following:

	Number of Employees	Total Labor-Hours	Square Feet of Space Occupied	Direct Labor-Hours	Machine-Hours
Factory administration	22	—	5,000	—	—
Custodial services	8	6,000	2,000	—	—
Personnel	10	10,000	3,000	—	—
Maintenance	50	44,000	10,000	—	—
Stamping—overhead	80	60,000	70,000	40,000	140,000
Assembly—overhead	120	180,000	20,000	160,000	20,000
	290	300,000	110,000	200,000	160,000

Stamping and assembly are operating departments; the other departments all act in a service capacity. The company does not make a distinction between fixed and variable service department costs. Allocations are made to using departments according to the base that appears to provide the best measure of benefits received (as discussed in the book).

Required

1. Allocate service department costs to using departments by the step method. Then compute predetermined overhead rates in the operating departments, using a machine-hours basis in stamping and a direct labor-hours basis in assembly.
2. Repeat (1) above, this time using the direct method. Again compute predetermined overhead rates in stamping and assembly.
3. Assume that the company doesn't want to bother with allocating service department costs but simply wants to compute a single plantwide overhead rate based on total overhead costs (both service department and operating department) divided by total direct labor-hours. Compute the appropriate overhead rate.
4. Suppose that the company wants to bid on a job during the year that will require machine and labor time as follows:

	Machine-Hours	Direct Labor-Hours
Stamping department	190	25
Assembly department	10	75
Total hours	200	100

Using the overhead rates computed in (1), (2), and (3) above, compute the amount of overhead cost that would be assigned to the job if the overhead rates were developed using the step method, the direct method, and the plantwide method. (Round allocations to the nearest whole dollar.)

P16–10 End-of-Year Cost Allocations Mangum Products, Inc., operates a power services department that provides electrical power to other departments within the company. Budgeted costs in the power services department for 19x3 total $162,000, of which $150,000 represents fixed costs.

Power consumption in the company is measured in kilowatt-hours (kwh) used. Data relating to budgeted and actual usage of power are given below for 19x3, along with data relating to the peak-period needs in the various departments (in kwh):

	Service Department		Operating Department		
	Engineering	Maintenance	Shaping	Assembly	Total
Budgeted for 19x3	10,000	30,000	252,000	108,000	400,000
Used during 19x3	10,800	21,600	234,000	93,600	360,000
Peak-period needs	20,000	50,000	300,000	130,000	500,000

During 19x3, the power services department incurred $12,600 in variable costs and $153,000 in fixed costs. The department allocates variable and fixed costs separately.

Required

1. Assume that management makes an allocation of power costs at the end of each year to the four departments listed above in order to compare actual performance against budgeted performance. How much of the power services department's actual costs for 19x3 would be allocated to each department?
2. Will any portion of the year's power costs not be allocated to the four departments? Explain.

P16–11 Beginning- and End-of-Year Allocations Decker Company has only one service department—a cafeteria, in which meals are provided for employees in the company's milling and finishing departments. The costs of the cafeteria are all paid by the company as a fringe benefit to its employees. These costs are allocated to the milling and finishing departments on a basis of meals served in each department. Cost and other data relating to the cafeteria and to the milling and finishing departments for 19x1 are provided below.

Cafeteria:

	19x1	
	Budget	**Actual**
Variable costs for food . . .	$300,000*	$384,000
Fixed costs	200,000	215,000

* Budgeted at $2 per meal served.

Milling and finishing departments:

	Number of Meals Served		
		19x1	
	Peak-Period Needs	**Budget**	**Actual**
Milling department	140,000	100,000	120,000
Finishing department	60,000	50,000	40,000
Total meals	200,000	150,000	160,000

The company allocates variable and fixed costs separately.

Required

1. Assume that it is the beginning of 19x1. An allocation of cafeteria costs must be made to the milling and finishing departments to assist in computing predetermined overhead rates. How much of the budgeted cafeteria cost above would be allocated to each department?
2. Assume that it is now the end of 19x1. Management would like data to assist in comparing actual performance against planned performance in the cafeteria and in the other departments.
   a. How much of the actual cafeteria costs above would be allocated to the milling department and to the finishing department?
   b. Would any portion of the actual cafeteria costs not be allocated to the other departments? If so, compute the amount that would not be allocated, and explain why it would not be allocated.

P16–12 Cost Allocation in a Hospital; Step Method Pleasant View Hospital has three service departments—food services, administrative services, and X-ray services. The costs of these departments are allocated by the step method, using the bases and in the order shown on the following page:

Service Department	Costs Incurred	Base for Allocation
Food services	Variable	Meals served
	Fixed	Peak-period needs—meals
Administrative services	Variable	Files processed
	Fixed	10% X-ray services, 20% Outpatient Clinic, 30% OB Care, and 40% General Hospital
X-ray services	Variable	X rays taken
	Fixed	Analysis of long-term usage

Estimated cost and operating data for all departments in the hospital for the forthcoming month are presented in the following table:

	Food Services	Admin. Services	X-Ray Services	Outpatient Clinic	OB Care	General Hospital	Total
Variable costs	$ 73,150	$ 6,800	$38,100	$11,700	$ 14,850	$ 53,400	$198,000
Fixed costs.	48,000	33,040	59,520	26,958	99,738	344,744	612,000
Total costs	$121,150	$39,840	$97,620	$38,658	$114,588	$398,144	$810,000
Files processed	—	—	1,500	3,000	900	12,000	17,400
X rays taken	—	—	—	1,200	350	8,400	9,950
Long-term average X-ray needs	—	—	—	1,560	360	10,080	12,000
Meals served	—	1,000	500	—	7,000	30,000	38,500
Peak-period needs—meals	—	1,000	500	—	8,500	40,000	50,000

All billing in the hospital is done through the Outpatient Clinic, OB Care, or General Hospital. The hospital's administrator wants the costs of the three service departments allocated to these three billing centers.

Required Prepare the cost allocation desired by the hospital administrator. Include under each billing center the direct costs of the center, as well as the costs allocated from the service departments.

P16–13 Allocating Costs Equitably between Divisions Precision Plastics maintains its own computer to service the needs of its three divisions. The company assigns the costs of the computer center to the three divisions on a basis of the number of lines of print prepared for each division during the month.

In July 19x6, Carol Benz, manager of Division A, came to the company's controller seeking an explanation as to why her division had been charged a larger amount for computer services in June than in May, although her division had used the computer less in June. During the course of the discussion, the following data were referred to by the controller:

		Division		
	Total	A	B	C
May actual results:				
Lines of print	200,000	80,000	20,000	100,000
Percentage of total	100%	40%	10%	50%
Computer cost assigned . . .	$182,000	$72,800	$18,200	$91,000
June actual results:				
Lines of print	150,000	75,000	30,000	45,000
Percentage of total	100%	50%	20%	30%
Computer cost assigned . . .	$179,000	$89,500	$35,800	$53,700

"You see," said Eric Weller, the controller, "the computer center has large amounts of fixed costs that continue regardless of how much the computer is used.

We have built into the computer enough capacity to handle the divisions' peak-period needs, and this cost must be absorbed by someone. I know it hurts, but the fact is that during June your division received a greater share of the computer's output than it did during May; therefore, it has been allocated a greater share of the cost."

Carol Benz was unhappy with this explanation. "I still don't understand why I would be charged more for the computer, when I used it less," she said. "There must be a better way to handle these cost allocations."

The computer center has enough capacity to handle 250,000 lines of print each month. This represents expected peak-period needs of 100,000 lines in Division A, 30,000 lines in Division B, and 120,000 lines in Division C.

Required

1. Is there any merit to Carol Benz's complaint? Explain.
2. By use of the high-low method, determine the monthly cost of the computer in terms of a variable rate per line of print and total fixed cost.
3. Reallocate the computer center costs for May and June in accordance with the cost allocation principles discussed in the chapter. Allocate the variable and fixed costs separately.

P16–14 Cost Allocation in a Hotel; Step Method The Coral Lake Hotel has three service departments—grounds and maintenance, general administration, and laundry. The costs of these departments are allocated by the step method, using the bases and in the order shown below:

Grounds and maintenance:
Fixed costs—allocated on a basis of square feet of space occupied.

General administration:
Variable costs—allocated on a basis of number of actual employees.
Fixed costs—allocated 20% to laundry, 14% to convention center, 36% to food services, and 30% to lodging.

Laundry:
Variable costs—allocated on a basis of number of items processed.
Fixed costs—allocated on a basis of peak-period needs for items processed.

Cost and operating data for all departments in the hotel for a recent month are presented in the table below:

	Grounds and Maintenance	General Administration	Laundry	Convention Center	Food Services	Lodging	Total
Variable costs	-0-	$ 915	$13,725	-0-	$ 48,000	$ 36,450	$ 99,090
Fixed costs	$17,500	12,150	18,975	$28,500	64,000	81,000	222,125
Total overhead costs	$17,500	$13,065	$32,700	$28,500	$112,000	$117,450	$321,215
Square feet of space	2,000	2,500	3,750	15,000	6,250	97,500	127,000
Number of employees	9	5	10	5	25	21	75
Laundry items processed	—	—	—	1,000	5,250	40,000	46,250
Peak-period needs—items processed	—	—	—	1,500	6,500	42,000	50,000

All billing in the hotel is done through the convention center, food services, and lodging. The hotel's general manager wants the costs of the three service departments allocated to these three billing centers.

Required Prepare the cost allocation desired by the hotel's general manager. Include under each billing center the direct costs of the center, as well as the costs allocated from the service departments.

P16–15 Service Department Allocations; Predetermined Overhead Rates; Unit Costs Apsco Products has two service departments and two producing departments. The service departments are medical services and maintenance. Estimated monthly cost and operating data for the coming year are given below. These data have been prepared for purposes of computing predetermined overhead rates in the producing departments.

	Medical Services	Maintenance	Producing A	Producing B
Direct labor cost	—	—	$ 30,000	$ 40,000
Maintenance labor cost	—	$ 5,000	—	—
Direct materials	—	—	50,000	80,000
Maintenance materials	—	7,536	—	—
Medical supplies	$ 3,630	—	—	—
Miscellaneous overhead costs	7,500	6,000	104,000	155,000
Total costs	$11,130	$18,536	$184,000	$275,000
Direct labor-hours	—	—	6,000	10,000
Number of employees:				
Currently employed	3	8	38	64
Long-run employee needs	3	10	60	80
Floor space occupied—square feet	800	1,500	8,000	12,000

The Apsco Company allocates service department costs to producing departments for product costing purposes. The step method is used, starting with medical services. Allocation bases for the service departments are:

Department	Costs Incurred	Base for Allocation
Medical services	Variable	Currently employed workers
	Fixed	Long-run employee needs
Maintenance	Variable	Direct labor-hours
	Fixed	Square footage of floor space occupied

The behavior of various costs is shown below:

	Medical Services	Maintenance
Maintenance labor cost	—	V
Maintenance materials	—	V
Medical supplies	V	—
Miscellaneous overhead costs	F	F

V = Variable.
F = Fixed.

Required

1. Show the allocation of the service department costs for the purpose of computing predetermined overhead rates. Round all allocations to the nearest whole dollar.
2. Compute the predetermined overhead rate to be used in each of the producing departments (overhead rates are based on direct labor-hours).
3. Assume that production in Department B is planned at 20,000 units for the month. Compute the planned cost of one unit of product in Department B.

CASES

C16–16 **Step Method versus Direct Method** "I can't understand what's happening here," said Mike Holt, president of Severson Products, Inc. "We always seem to bid too high on jobs that require a lot of labor time in the finishing department, and we always seem to get every job we bid on that requires a lot of machine time in the milling department. Yet we don't seem to be making much money on those milling department jobs. I wonder if the problem is in our overhead rates.''

Severson Products manufactures high-quality wood products to customers' specifications. Some jobs take a large amount of machine work in the milling department, and other jobs take a large amount of hand finishing work in the finishing department. In addition to the milling and finishing departments, the company has three service departments. The costs of these service departments are allocated to other departments *in the order listed below*. (For each service department, use the allocation base that provides the best measure of service provided, as discussed in the chapter.)

	Total Labor-Hours	Square Feet of Space Occupied	Number of Employees	Machine-Hours	Direct Labor-Hours
Cafeteria	16,000	12,000	25	—	—
Custodial services	9,000	3,000	40	—	—
Maintenance	15,000	10,000	60	—	—
Milling	30,000	40,000	100	160,000	20,000
Finishing	100,000	20,000	300	40,000	70,000
	170,000	85,000	525	200,000	90,000

Budgeted overhead costs in each department for the current year are as follows (no distinction is made between variable and fixed costs):

Cafeteria	$ 320,000*
Custodial services	65,400
Maintenance	93,600
Milling	416,000
Finishing	166,000
Total budgeted costs	$1,061,000

* This represents the amount of cost subsidized by the company.

The company has always allocated service department costs to the producing departments (milling and finishing) using the direct method of allocation, because of its simplicity.

Required

1. Allocate service department costs to using departments by the step method. Then compute predetermined overhead rates in the producing departments for the current year, using a machine-hours basis in the milling department and a direct labor-hours basis in the finishing department.
2. Repeat (1) above, this time using the direct method. Again compute predetermined overhead rates in the milling and finishing departments.
3. Assume that during the current year the company bids on a job that requires machine and labor time as follows:

	Machine-Hours	Direct Labor-Hours
Milling department	2,000	1,600
Finishing department	800	13,000
Total hours	2,800	14,600

a. Determine the amount of overhead that would be assigned to the job if the company used the overhead rates developed in (1) above. Then determine the amount of overhead that would be assigned to the job if the company used the overhead rates developed in (2) above.

b. Explain to the president why the step method would provide a better basis for computing predetermined overhead rates than the direct method.

C16–17 Direct Method; Plantwide Overhead Rates versus Departmental Overhead Rates Hobart Products manufactures a complete line of fiberglass attaché cases and suitcases. Hobart has three manufacturing departments—molding, component, and assembly—and two service departments—power and maintenance.

The sides of the cases are manufactured in the molding department. The frames, hinges, locks, and so forth, are manufactured in the component department. The cases are completed in the assembly department. Varying amounts of materials, time, and effort are required for each of the various cases. The power department and maintenance department provide services to the manufacturing departments.

Hobart has always used a plantwide overhead rate. Direct labor-hours are used to assign the overhead to products. The overhead rate is computed by dividing the company's total estimated overhead cost by the total estimated direct labor-hours to be worked in the three manufacturing departments.

Whit Portlock, manager of cost accounting, has recommended that the company use departmental overhead rates rather than a single, plantwide rate. Planned operating costs and expected levels of activity for the coming year have been developed by Mr. Portlock and are presented below:

	Service Department	
	Power	**Maintenance**
Departmental activity measures:		
Maximum capacity	100,000 kwh	Adjustable*
Estimated usage in the coming year	80,000 kwh	12,500 hours*
Departmental costs:		
Materials and supplies	$ 500,000	$ 25,000
Variable labor	140,000	–0–
Fixed overhead	1,200,000	375,000
Total service department costs	$1,840,000	$400,000

* Hours of maintenance time.

	Manufacturing Department		
	Molding	**Component**	**Assembly**
Departmental activity measures:			
Direct labor-hours	50,000	200,000	150,000
Machine-hours	87,500	12,500	–0–
Departmental costs:			
Raw materials	$1,630,000	$3,000,000	$ 125,000
Direct labor	350,000	2,000,000	1,300,000
Variable overhead	210,500	1,000,000	1,650,000
Fixed overhead	1,750,000	620,000	749,500
Total departmental costs	$3,940,500	$6,620,000	$3,824,500
Use of service departments:			
Maintenance:			
Estimated usage in hours of maintenance time for the coming year	9,000	2,500	1,000
Long-run average usage in hours of maintenance time	10,500	3,000	1,500
Power:			
Estimated usage in kilowatt-hours for the coming year	36,000	32,000	12,000
Peak-period needs in kilowatt-hours	50,000	35,000	15,000

Required

1. Assume that the company will use a single, plantwide overhead rate for the coming year, the same as in the past. Under these conditions, compute the plantwide rate that should be used.
2. Assume that Whit Portlock has been asked to develop departmental overhead rates for the three manufacturing departments for comparison with the plantwide rate. In order to develop these rates, do the following:
   a. By use of the direct method, allocate the service department costs to the manufacturing departments. In each case, allocate the variable and fixed costs separately.
   b. Compute overhead rates for the three manufacturing departments for the coming year. In computing the rates, use a machine-hours basis in the molding department and a direct labor-hours basis in the other two departments.
3. Assume that Hobart Products has one small attaché case that has the following annual requirements for machine time and direct labor time in the various departments:

	Machine-Hours	Direct Labor-Hours
Molding department	3,000	1,000
Component department	800	2,500
Assembly department	—	4,000
Total hours.	3,800	7,500

   a. Compute the amount of overhead cost that would be allocated to this attaché case if a plantwide overhead rate is used. Repeat the computation, this time assuming that departmental overhead rates are used.
   b. Management is concerned because this attaché case is priced well below competing products of competitors. On the other hand, certain other of Hobart's products are priced well above the prices of competitors with the result that profits in the company are deteriorating because of declining sales. Looking at the computations in *(a)* above, what effect is the use of a plantwide rate having on the costing of products and therefore on selling prices?
4. What additional steps could Hobart Products take to improve its overhead costing?

(CMA, Heavily Adapted)

17

"How Well Am I Doing?" Statement of Cash Flows

LEARNING OBJECTIVES

After studying Chapter 17, you should be able to:

1 Describe the purpose of a statement of cash flows.

2 State the general rules for determining whether transactions should be classified as operating activities, investing activities, or financing activities.

3 Explain what is meant by a direct exchange transaction and explain how such a transaction is reported to statement users.

4 Compute the cash provided by operating activities, using the indirect method.

5 Prepare working papers to gather data for a statement of cash flows.

6 Prepare a statement of cash flows in good form.

7 Adjust the income statement to a cash basis, using the direct method.

8 Define or explain the key terms listed at the end of the chapter.

Three major statements are prepared annually by most companies—an income statement, a balance sheet, and a statement of cash flows. The statement of cash flows is less well known than the income statement or the balance sheet, but many view it as being equal in importance. This importance is underscored by the fact that the Financial Accounting Standards Board (FASB) requires that a statement of cash flows be provided whenever a balance sheet and an income statement are made available to users of financial data. In this chapter, our focus is on the development of the statement of cash flows and on its use as a tool for assessing the well-being of a company.

PURPOSE AND USE OF THE STATEMENT

The purpose of the **statement of cash flows** is to highlight the major activities that have provided cash and that have used cash during a period, and to show the resulting effect on the overall cash balance. The statement is a powerful analytical tool that can be used by managers, investors, and creditors in the following ways:

1. To determine the amount of cash provided by operations during a period and to reconcile this amount with net income.
2. To assess an organization's ability to meet its obligations as they come due and to assess its ability to pay cash dividends.
3. To determine the amount of investment in new plant, equipment, and other noncurrent assets during a period.
4. To determine the type and extent of financing required to expand the investment in long-term assets or to bolster operations.
5. To assess an organization's ability to generate a positive cash flow in future periods.

For the statement of cash flows to be useful to managers and others in gathering information such as that above, it is important that companies employ a common definition of cash and organize the statement in a consistent manner. Questions relating to the definition of cash and to the organization of the statement are considered in the following two sections.

Definition of Cash

In preparing a statement of cash flows for inclusion in an annual report, the FASB has stated that the term *cash* must be broadly defined to include both cash and cash equivalents. **Cash equivalents** consist of short-term, highly liquid investments such as treasury bills, commercial paper, and money market funds. These items are termed *marketable securities* on the balance sheet. Investments of this type are considered to be "equivalent" to cash in that they are made solely for the purpose of generating a return on cash that is temporarily idle. Because short-term investments are just temporary uses of cash and therefore part of a company's overall cash management program, they are included with cash in preparing a statement of cash flows.

In the past, some companies have used the term *funds* in lieu of the term *cash* in describing the contents of a statement of cash flows. Since the term *funds* often means different things to different people, the FASB has stated that its use should be discontinued and that more descriptive terms, such as *cash,* or *cash and cash equivalents,* should be used in its place.

ORGANIZATION OF THE STATEMENT

For many years, companies have had wide latitude in organizing the content of a statement of cash flows. One popular format has been to divide the statement into two sections—one titled "Sources of cash" and the other titled "Uses of cash"—and to classify all cash flows under one of these two heads. Generally, this format has provided a separate figure for the amount of cash generated by operations, but it has provided little else in the way of organized data; as a result, investors and creditors have had difficulty in comparing one company with another.

To provide greater comparability of data, the FASB now requires that the statement of cash flows be divided into three sections. The first section must contain all cash flows relating to *operating activities* for a period; the next section must contain all cash flows relating to *investing activities;* and the final section must contain all cash flows relating to *financing activities.* Below we discuss the guidelines to be followed in classifying a company's cash flows under these three heads.

Operating Activities

As a general rule, any transactions that enter into the determination of net income are classified as **operating activities.** These transactions can result in either cash inflows or cash outflows.

Cash inflows come from the sale of goods or the providing of services; interest received from *all* sources; dividends received on stock held as an investment; and cash received from miscellaneous sources, such as rental income.

In reading this list of cash inflows, the reader may wonder why dividends received on stock held as an investment is treated as an *operating* item when the stock itself obviously represents an *investment* item. The reasons are twofold: first, the dividends enter into the determination of income; and second, investing activities are narrowly defined to include only the *principal amount* of stock purchased or sold. Thus, the income from an investment item such as stock is classified as part of operating activities even though the stock itself is classified under a different heading.

Cash outflows that are classified as operating activities consist of payments made for items *that appear as expenses on the income statement.* These would include payments to suppliers for inventory; payments to employees for services; payments to other entities for insurance, utilities, rent, and so forth; and payments to governmental agencies for taxes. In addition, payments to banks and other lenders for interest are included as part of operating activities even though the loans themselves are part of a company's financing activities. The reasons for this apparent inconsistency are the same as those given above for dividends: interest enters into the determination of income, and financing activities are narrowly defined to include only the principal amount borrowed or repaid.

The cash inflows and outflows discussed above are summarized in Exhibit 17–1.

Investing Activities

Generally speaking, any transactions that are involved in the acquisition or disposition of noncurrent assets are classified as **investing activities.** These transactions include acquiring or selling property, plant, and equipment; acquiring or selling securities held for long-term investment, such as bonds and stocks of other companies; and the lending of money to another entity

EXHIBIT 17–1
A Summary of Operating, Investing, and Financing Activities

Operating Activities

General rule: Any transactions that enter into the determination of net income are classified as operating activities. These transactions include:

Cash receipts from:
- Sale of goods or providing of services
- Interest (from all sources)
- Dividends (on stock of other companies)
- Miscellaneous income, such as from rentals

Cash payments to:
- Suppliers for purchases of inventory
- Employees for services
- Other entities for insurance, utilities, rent, and so forth
- Creditors for interest on debt
- Government agencies for taxes

Investing Activities

General rule: Any transactions that are involved in the acquisition or disposition of noncurrent assets are classified as investing activities. These transactions include:

Cash provided by:
- Sale of property, plant, and equipment
- Sale of securities, such as bonds and stocks of other companies, that are not cash equivalents
- Collection of a loan made to another company

Cash used to:
- Purchase property, plant, and equipment
- Purchase securities, such as bonds and stocks of other companies, that are not cash equivalents
- Lend money to another company, such as to a subsidiary

Financing Activities

General rule: Any transactions involving borrowing from creditors (other than the payment of interest), and any transactions involving the owners of a company (except stock dividends and stock splits), are classified as financing activities. These transactions include:

Cash provided by:
- Borrowing from short-term or long-term creditors through notes, bonds, mortgages, and similar forms of debt
- Sale of capital stock to owners

Cash used to:
- Retire notes, bonds, mortgages and similar forms of short-term and long-term debt
- Repurchase capital stock from owners
- Pay cash dividends to owners

(such as to a subsidiary) and the subsequent collection of the loan. Exhibit 17–1 provides a tabular summary of the cash inflows and cash outflows relating to investing activities.

Financing Activities

As a general rule, any transactions involving borrowing from creditors (other than the payment of interest), and any transactions involving the owners of a company (except stock dividends and stock splits), are classified as **financing activities.**

Cash inflows from financing activities include amounts obtained from creditors through the issuance of notes, bonds, mortgages, and similar forms of short-term and long-term debt. Amounts obtained from owners come from the sale of capital stock (preferred and common).

Cash outflows from financing activities include the repayment of amounts borrowed from short-term and long-term creditors, the repurchase of stock held by the owners of a company, and the payment of cash dividends to owners. The payment of cash dividends is classified as a financing item, rather than as an operating item, because dividends do not enter into the determination of income. In repaying creditors for amounts borrowed, if a gain or a loss is involved (such as retiring bonds for less than their carrying value), then the gain or loss should be classified as a financing item along with the debt to which it relates.

Refer to Exhibit 17–1 for a summary of the cash inflows and cash outflows relating to financing activities. Note from this exhibit that accounts payable is not included among the forms of debt representing financing activities. This is because accounts payable is used to obtain *goods and services* rather than to obtain cash. Also the goods and services obtained (such as inventory, utilities, and supplies) relate to a company's day-to-day operating activities rather than to its financing activities. The reader should also note that stock dividends and stock splits are not included as financing activities. This is because neither stock dividends nor stock splits involve the use of cash and therefore do not appear on a statement of cash flows.

DIRECT EXCHANGE TRANSACTIONS

Companies sometimes acquire assets or dispose of liabilities through **direct exchange transactions.** Examples of direct exchange transactions include the issue of capital stock in exchange for property and equipment, the conversion of long-term debt or preferred stock into common stock, and the acquisition of property and equipment under a long-term lease agreement.

Such exchanges have a common identifying characteristic in that they affect only noncurrent balance sheet accounts and have no effect on cash. Even though direct exchange transactions have no effect on cash, they must still be considered when the statement of cash flows is prepared. This is because these exchanges involve significant financing and investing activities, the existence of which must be made known to statement users. However, rather than being reported as part of a statement of cash flows, direct exchanges are reported in a separate, accompanying schedule. To illustrate how this is done, assume the following situation:

Delsey Company acquired a tract of land to be used as a building site and paid for it in full by issuing 5,000 shares of its own common stock, which had a par value of $100 per share. Since the stock was selling for $120 per share at the time the land was acquired, the exchange was recorded as follows:

Land (5,000 shares × $120)	600,000	
Common Stock, $100 par (5,000 shares × $100)		500,000
Paid-In Capital in Excess of Par (5,000 shares × $20)		100,000

This transaction had no effect on cash, but it did involve both an investing activity (the acquisition of land) and a financing activity (the issue of common stock) through a direct exchange. To report this exchange to statement users, Delsey Company should provide the following information in a separate schedule:

Schedule of noncash investing and financing activities:	
Common stock issued to acquire land for a building site	$600,000

OTHER FACTORS IN PREPARING THE STATEMENT OF CASH FLOWS

We must consider two other factors before we can illustrate the preparation of a statement of cash flows. These two factors are (1) whether amounts on the statement should be presented gross or net, and (2) whether operating activities should be presented by use of the direct method or the indirect method.

Cash Flows: Gross or Net?

For both *financing* and *investing* activities, items on the statement of cash flows should be presented in gross amounts rather than in net amounts. To illustrate, assume that a company purchases $500,000 in property during a year and sells other property for $300,000. Instead of showing a $200,000 net investment in property for the year, the company must show the gross amounts of both the purchases and the sales. In like manner, if a company receives $800,000 from the issue of bonds and then pays out $600,000 to retire other bonds, the receipts and the payments should be shown in their gross amounts, rather than being netted against each other.

The gross method of reporting does not extend to *operating* activities, where it is often necessary to net items against each other. For example, if $400,000 is added to accounts receivable as a result of sales during a year, and if $300,000 of receivables is collected, then only the $100,000 net difference would be used in determining the cash flow from operating activities for the year.

Operating Activities: Direct or Indirect Reporting?

The net result of the cash inflows and outflows arising from day-to-day operations is known formally as the **Net cash provided by operating activities.** It is possible to compute this figure by either the *direct method* or the *indirect method.*

Under the **direct method,** the income statement is reconstructed on a cash basis from top to bottom. In place of sales, we have cash collected from customers; in place of cost of goods sold, we have payments to suppliers for inventory; and in place of operating expenses, we have payments to employees for services, payments for insurance, and so forth. The net result between the cash receipts and the cash payments represents the "Net cash provided by operating activities" for the period.

Under the **indirect method,** the "Net cash provided by operating activities" is computed by starting with net income (as reported on the income statement) and adjusting the net income figure to a cash basis. That is, rather than making *direct* adjustments to sales, cost of goods sold, and other income statement items in order to compute the "Net cash provided by operating activities," these adjustments are made *indirectly* through the net income figure. Thus the term, *indirect method.* The indirect method has an advantage over the direct method in that it shows the reasons for any differences between net income and the "Net cash provided by operating activities." The indirect method is also known as the **reconciliation method.**

In preparing a statement of cash flows, should the manager use the direct method or the indirect method? For external reporting purposes, the FASB *recommends* and *encourages* the use of the direct method. But we must note that the indirect method is preferred by most companies, and therefore it is used most often in actual practice. If a company follows the FASB's recommendation and uses the direct method, then the FASB *requires* that a reconciliation between net income and the "Net cash provided by operating activities"—as determined by the indirect method—also be presented in a separate schedule accompanying the statement of cash flows. That is, when a company elects to use the direct method, it must also present computations by the indirect method as supplementary data.

We have already noted that the direct and indirect methods are very different in their approach. We will be most effective in our study, therefore, if we discuss the two methods separately. Since many people find the indirect method to be the easiest of the two methods to apply, we will discuss it first. The indirect method also lends itself readily to working papers, so we will use it as a base for illustrating the use of working papers in preparing a statement of cash flows. After laying this foundation, we will then turn our attention to the direct method and show how the income statement can be adjusted to a cash basis for external reporting purposes.

THE INDIRECT METHOD OF DETERMINING THE "NET CASH PROVIDED BY OPERATING ACTIVITIES"

The items for which adjustments must be made to determine the "Net cash provided by operating activities" can be grouped into five broad categories, as follows:

1. Depreciation, depletion, and amortization.
2. Changes in current asset accounts affecting revenue or expense.
3. Changes in current liability accounts affecting revenue or expense.
4. Gains or losses on sales of assets.
5. Changes in the Deferred Income Taxes account.

EXHIBIT 17–2
General Model: Indirect Method of Determining the "Net Cash Provided by Operating Activities"

	Add (+) or Deduct (−) to Adjust Net Income
Net income	$XXX
Adjustments needed to convert net income to a cash basis:	
Depreciation, depletion, and amortization expense	+
Add (deduct) changes in current asset accounts affecting revenue or expense:*	
Increase in the account	−
Decrease in the account	+
Add (deduct) changes in current liability accounts affecting revenue or expense:†	
Increase in the account	+
Decrease in the account	−
Add (deduct) gains or losses on sales of assets:	
Gain on sales of assets	−
Loss on sales of assets	+
Add (deduct) changes in the Deferred Income Taxes account:	
Increase in the account	+
Decrease in the account	−
Net cash provided by operating activities	$XXX

* Examples include accounts receivable, accrued receivables, inventory, and prepaid expenses.
† Examples include accounts payable, accrued liabilities, and deferred revenue.

A simple model is available that starts with net income and shows the adjustments that must be made for each of the items listed above in computing a cash flow figure under the indirect method. This model is presented in Exhibit 17–2. The various parts of the model are discussed in the following sections.

Depreciation, Depletion, and Amortization

As shown in Exhibit 17–2, depreciation and related items are added back to net income in computing the cash provided by operating activities. The mechanics of this process sometimes leads people to the hasty conclusion that depreciation is a source of cash to an organization. We must state emphatically that depreciation is not a source of cash. We add it back to net income for the reason that it requires no cash outlay during a period, yet it is deducted as an expense in arriving at net income. Thus, by adding it back, we are able to cancel out its effect and leave as part of net income only those items of revenue and expense that *do* affect the amount of cash provided during a period.

Besides depreciation, other deductions that reduce net income without involving an outflow of cash include depletion of natural resources and amortization of goodwill, patents, and similar items. Like depreciation, these items are added back to net income under the indirect method in computing the amount of cash provided by operating activities.

Changes in Current Asset and Current Liability Accounts

In adjusting the net income figure to a cash basis, the model in Exhibit 17–2 shows that certain additions and deductions must be made for changes in the current asset and current liability accounts. An explanation is provided in

EXHIBIT 17–3

Explanation of Adjustments for Changes in Current Asset and Current Liability Accounts (see Exhibit 17–2)

	Change in the Account	This Change Means that . . .	Therefore, to Adjust to a Cash Basis under the Indirect Method, We Must . . .
Accounts Receivable and Accrued Receivables	Increase	Sales (revenues) have been reported for which no cash has been collected.	Deduct the amount from net income to show that cash-basis sales are less than reported sales (revenues).
	Decrease	Cash has been collected for which no sales (revenues) have been reported for the current period.	Add the amount to net income to show that cash-basis sales are greater than reported sales (revenues).
Inventory	Increase	Goods have been purchased that are not included in cost of goods sold (COGS).	Deduct the amount from net income to show that cash-basis COGS is greater than reported COGS.
	Decrease	Goods have been included in COGS that were purchased in a prior period.	Add the amount to net income to show that cash-basis COGS is less than reported COGS.
Prepaid Expenses	Increase	More cash has been paid out for services than has been reported as expense.	Deduct the amount from net income to show that cash-basis expenses are greater than reported expenses.
	Decrease	More has been reported as expense for services than has been paid out in cash.	Add the amount to net income to show that cash-basis expenses are less than reported expenses.
Accounts Payable and Accrued Liabilities	Increase	More has been reported as expense for goods and services than has been paid out in cash.	Add the amount to net income to show that cash-basis expenses for goods and services are less than reported expenses.
	Decrease	More cash has been paid out for goods and services than has been reported as expense.	Deduct the amount from net income to show that cash-basis expenses for goods and services are greater than reported expenses.
Deferred Revenue	Increase	More cash has been received than has been reported as revenue.	Add the amount to net income to show that cash-basis revenue is greater than reported revenue.
	Decrease	More has been reported as revenue than has been received in cash.	Deduct the amount from net income to show that cash-basis revenue is less than reported revenue.

Exhibit 17–3 as to what the changes in these accounts mean and why the adjustments are needed. This exhibit should be studied with care, and the "Add" and "Deduct" signal in the last column should be traced back into Exhibit 17–2.

Gains and Losses on Sales of Assets

Observe from Exhibit 17–2 that gains on sales of assets are deducted from net income in computing the cash provided by operating activities. The reason is that such gains represent part of the total cash proceeds from sale of the asset involved, and these proceeds must be included in full under *investing* activities. If gains are not deducted from net income, then double counting will result since the gain will be counted once as part of net income and then counted a second time as part of the cash proceeds arising from the sale transaction.

Losses are added back to net income to adjust it to a cash basis. This is because losses are noncash deductions and, like depreciation, reduce net income but do not involve an outflow of cash.

Changes in the Deferred Income Taxes Account

Deferred income taxes represent amounts deducted currently on the income statement as income tax expense but not remitted to the Internal Revenue Service until a later time (perhaps several years later). Such taxes are generally carried as a long-term liability on the balance sheet. In adjusting the net income figure to a cash basis, changes in the Deferred Income Taxes account follow the same rules as for current liabilities. An increase in the account means that more expense has been shown on the income statement for taxes than has been paid out in cash. Therefore, in accordance with the rules already discussed (in Exhibit 17–3), we must add the increase back to net income to show that cash-basis expenses are less than reported expenses. The opposite will be true for a decrease in the Deferred Income Taxes account—the decrease must be deducted from net income to show that the amount of cash paid out was greater than reported expenses.

AN EXAMPLE OF THE STATEMENT OF CASH FLOWS

To pull together the ideas developed in preceding sections, we turn now to the financial statements of Imperial Company presented in Exhibits 17–4, 17–5, and 17–6 and prepare a statement of cash flows. The numbers in these exhibits have been simplified for ease of computation and discussion.

Four Basic Steps to the Statement of Cash Flows

There are four basic steps to follow in preparing a statement of cash flows. These steps are:

1. Find the change that took place in the Cash account during the year.
2. Determine the "Net cash provided by operating activities" by analyzing the changes in the appropriate balance sheet accounts and by following the model given in Exhibit 17–2 (or by following the model given for the direct method later in the chapter).

EXHIBIT 17–4

IMPERIAL COMPANY
Comparative Balance Sheet
December 31, 19x2, and 19x1

	19x2	19x1
Assets		
Current assets:		
Cash	$ 900	$ 3,000
Accounts receivable	7,000	5,500
Inventory	8,000	10,000
Prepaid expenses	600	500
Total current assets	16,500	19,000
Long-term investments	2,000	5,000
Plant and equipment	80,000	60,000
Less accumulated depreciation	8,000	4,000
Net plant and equipment	72,000	56,000
Total assets	$90,500	$80,000
Liabilities and Stockholders' Equity		
Current liabilities:		
Accounts payable	$ 5,000	$ 8,000
Accrued liabilities	1,000	—
Total current liabilities	6,000	8,000
Bonds payable	24,000	10,000
Stockholders' equity:		
Common stock	20,000	25,000
Retained earnings	40,500	37,000
Total stockholders' equity	60,500	62,000
Total liabilities and stockholders' equity	$90,500	$80,000

EXHIBIT 17–5

IMPERIAL COMPANY
Income Statement
For the Year Ended December 31, 19x2

Sales		$70,000
Less cost of goods sold		40,000
Gross margin		30,000
Less operating expenses:		
Selling expenses	$ 9,000	
Administrative expenses	10,500	
Depreciation expense	4,000	
Total operating expenses		23,500
Net income		$ 6,500

3. Analyze each additional balance sheet account and determine whether the change in the account was the result of an investing activity or a financing activity.
4. Summarize the cash flows obtained in steps 2 and 3 into operating, investing, and financing activities. The net result of the cash flows for these three activities will equal the change in cash obtained in step 1.

EXHIBIT 17–6

IMPERIAL COMPANY
Statement of Retained Earnings
For the Year Ended December 31, 19x2

Retained earnings, December 31, 19x1	$37,000
Add: Net income	6,500
	43,500
Deduct: Dividends paid	3,000
Retained earnings, December 31, 19x2	$40,500

For step 1, we can determine from Imperial Company's comparative balance sheet in Exhibit 17–4 that the Cash account has decreased by $2,100 during 19x2. By following the remaining steps above, we can prepare a statement of cash flows and find the reasons for this decrease.

Cash Provided by Operating Activities

Imperial Company's income statement shows that net income was $6,500 for 19x2. Starting with this figure and using the model presented in Exhibit 17–2 as a guide, an analysis of the cash provided by operating activities for 19x2 is given below:

Operating Activities	
Net income	$ 6,500
Adjustments needed to convert net income to a cash basis:	
Depreciation expense for the year	4,000
Add (deduct) changes in current assets:	
Increase in accounts receivable	(1,500)
Decrease in inventory	2,000
Increase in prepaid expenses	(100)
Add (deduct) changes in current liabilities:	
Decrease in accounts payable	(3,000)
Increase in accrued liabilities	1,000
Net cash provided by operating activities	$ 8,900

The $4,000 depreciation expense figure used above is taken from Imperial Company's income statement. Note that this amount also agrees with the change in the Accumulated Depreciation account on the company's balance sheet in Exhibit 17–4.

Looking further at the balance sheet, the company has three current asset accounts in addition to Cash—Accounts Receivable, Inventory, and Prepaid Expenses. Adjustments have been made above for changes in these accounts (and for changes in the current liabilities) according to the guidelines given in Exhibit 17–3. These adjustments are summarized as follows: Accounts Receivable has increased by $1,500; since an increase in Accounts Receivable represents sales for which no cash has been received, the $1,500 is deducted from net income above in determining the cash provided by operating activities. Inventory has decreased by $2,000; as discussed in Exhibit 17–3, this decrease means that items have been included in Cost of Goods Sold that were purchased in a prior year. Since no cash was disbursed this year for these items, the $2,000 is added back to net income. Finally, Prepaid Expenses have increased by $100; this $100 represents payments for services (such as rent) that are not included as expenses on the income statement. The $100 is therefore deducted from the net income figure above to show that cash-basis expenses are greater than reported expenses.

Imperial Company has two current liability accounts—Accounts Payable and Accrued Liabilities. Accounts Payable has decreased by $3,000; this decrease means that the company made payment for goods and services that were acquired in a preceding year. Since the cash payment was made this year, we must deduct the $3,000 from net income to show that cash basis expenses for goods and services are greater than reported expenses. Finally, the Accrued Liabilities account has increased by $1,000; this $1,000 represents items such as salaries that have been recorded as an expense but for which no cash payment has been made. Therefore, the $1,000 is added back to net income to show that cash expenses are less than reported expenses.

Changes in Other Balance Sheet Accounts

Having analyzed the current asset and current liability accounts and determined the cash provided by operating activities, we must now analyze each remaining balance sheet account and determine whether the change in the account was caused by an investing activity or a financing activity. So far as the end result is concerned, it makes no difference which of the remaining accounts we analyze first, nor does it matter in which order we proceed. This is simply a matter of choice. Since the Retained Earnings account usually contains a number of significant changes, managers often start with it.

Retained Earnings From the comparative balance sheet in Exhibit 17–4, we can see that Retained Earnings has increased by $3,500 during 19x2. To determine the cause of this change, we need to look at another exhibit—Exhibit 17–6—that contains an analysis of the Retained Earnings account. We can see from this exhibit that the $3,500 increase in Retained Earnings is a net result of $6,500 in net income for the year and $3,000 in dividends paid during the year. The net income figure has already been used in our computation of the cash provided by operating activities; the $3,000 dividends paid would be classified as a financing activity, as discussed earlier in Exhibit 17–1.

Financing Activities	
Cash was provided by:	
Cash was used to:	
Pay dividends to owners	$3,000

Long-Term Investments Imperial Company's comparative balance sheet in Exhibit 17–4 show that long-term investments decreased by $3,000 during 19x2. Long-term investments generally consist of securities (stocks and bonds) of other companies that are being held for some reason. If the amount of these investments decreases during a period, the most likely conclusion is that they were sold. From the guidelines given in Exhibit 17–1, any transaction involving the disposition of a noncurrent asset would be an investing activity. Since we have no evidence of any gain or loss on the sale, the entry on the cash flow statement would be as follows:

Investing Activities

Cash was provided by:	
Sale of long-term investments	$3,000
Cash was used to:	

Plant and Equipment The Plant and Equipment account has increased by $20,000 during 19x2, as shown by the comparative balance sheet in Exhibit 17–4. Since there is nothing on Imperial Company's statements to indicate that there were any sales of plant and equipment during 19x2, we can assume that this $20,000 represents the company's gross purchases for the year. (Remember, we can't "net" sales and purchases of assets off against each other; all amounts must be shown "gross" on the statement of cash flows.) The guidelines in Exhibit 17–1 indicate that a purchase of plant and equipment would be an investing activity.

Investing Activities

Cash was provided by:	
Sale of long-term investments . . .	$ 3,000
Cash was used to:	
Purchase plant and equipment . . .	20,000

Accumulated Depreciation Imperial Company's Accumulated Depreciation account has increased by $4,000 during 19x2, as shown in Exhibit 17–4. This change was accounted for earlier in our computation of the cash provided by operating activities.

Bonds Payable Moving down Imperial Company's 19x2 balance sheet in Exhibit 17–4, we find that Bonds Payable increased $14,000 during the year. Since we see no evidence of any bonds having been retired during the year, we can assume that the $14,000 represents the gross amount of bonds issued. The guidelines in Exhibit 17–1 show that an issue of long-term debt is a financing activity.

Financing Activities

Cash was provided by:	
Issue of bonds	$14,000
Cash was used to:	
Pay dividends to owners	3,000

Common Stock Imperial Company's Common Stock account decreased by $5,000 during 19x2. Since we see no evidence of any stock having been issued during the year, we can assume that the $5,000 represents the company's only stock transaction. The most likely explanation for a $5,000 decrease in the Common Stock account is a repurchase of stock from the owners. Such a repurchase would be a financing activity, as shown in Exhibit 17–1.

Financing Activities

Cash was provided by:	
Issue of bonds	$14,000
Cash was used to:	
Pay dividends to owners	3,000
Repurchase common stock	5,000

The Completed Statement of Cash Flows

We can now organize the results of our analytical work into statement form. Using the data we have developed, a complete statement of cash flows for Imperial Company is presented in Exhibit 17–7.

We noted at the beginning of this example that Imperial Company's Cash account had decreased by $2,100 during the year. We have now isolated the reasons for this decrease, as shown in the company's statement of cash flows.

The Statement of Cash Flows as a Planning Tool

The statement of cash flows is highly regarded as a management planning tool. Although it deals with historical costs, any lack of forward planning, coordination, or balance in working toward long-run objectives becomes quickly evident in the story it has to tell. For example, a company may have as its stated objective to double plant capacity in five years using only cash provided by operating activities. If the company at the same time is paying

EXHIBIT 17–7

IMPERIAL COMPANY
Statement of Cash Flows
For the Year Ended December 31, 19x2

Operating Activities		
Net income		$ 6,500
Adjustments needed to convert net income to a cash basis:		
Depreciation expense for the year		4,000
Add (deduct) changes in current assets:		
Increase in accounts receivable		(1,500)
Decrease in inventory		2,000
Increase in prepaid expenses		(100)
Add (deduct) changes in current liabilities:		
Decrease in accounts payable		(3,000)
Increase in accrued liabilities		1,000
Net cash provided by operating activities		8,900
Investing Activities		
Cash was provided by:		
Sale of long-term investments	$ 3,000	
Cash was used to:		
Purchase plant and equipment	(20,000)	
Net cash used for investing activities		(17,000)
Financing Activities		
Cash was provided by:		
Issue of bonds	14,000	
Cash was used to:		
Pay dividends to owners	(3,000)	
Repurchase common stock	(5,000)	
Net cash provided by financing activities		6,000
Net decrease in cash		(2,100)
Cash balance, January 1, 19x2		3,000
Cash balance, December 31, 19x2		$ 900

dividends equal to half of its earnings and is retiring large amounts of long-term debt, the discrepancy between long-run plans and current actions will be brought to light very quickly by the information contained in the statement of cash flows.

Some of the more significant ways in which managers use the statement for planning purposes include:

1. To coordinate dividend policy with other actions of the company.
2. To plan the financing of new product lines, additional plant and equipment, or acquisitions of other companies.
3. To find ways of strengthening a weak cash position and thereby strengthening credit lines.

A WORKING PAPER APPROACH TO THE STATEMENT OF CASH FLOWS

The procedure relied on to this point of simply developing a statement of cash flows through logic has allowed us to concentrate our efforts on learning basic concepts, with a minimum of time expended on mechanics. For some companies, this simple logic procedure is completely adequate as a means of developing a statement of cash flows.

For other companies, however, the balance sheet is so complex that working papers are needed to help organize the changes in the various accounts into statement form. A number of working paper approaches to the statement of cash flows are available. The one we have chosen to illustrate relies on the use of T-accounts to assist in the analysis and organization of data. In order to illustrate the T-account approach to working paper preparation, we will use the financial statements of Universal Company found in Exhibits 17–8 and 17–9.

The T-Account Approach

Note from Universal Company's comparative balance sheet (Exhibit 17–8) that cash and cash equivalents (marketable securities) have increased from $10,000 ($3,000 + $7,000) in 19x4 to $16,000 ($11,000 + $5,000) in 19x5—an increase of $6,000. To determine the reasons for this change we will again prepare a statement of cash flows. As before, our basic analytical approach will be to analyze the changes in the various balance sheet accounts. The only function the T-accounts will serve will be to assist us in the mechanical process of organizing our information as it develops.

In Exhibit 17–10 on page 738, we have prepared T-accounts and entered into these T-accounts the beginning and ending balances for every account on Universal Company's comparative balance sheet, except for Cash and Marketable Securities. The exhibit also contains a T-account titled "Cash," which we will use to accumulate the cash "Provided" and the cash "Used" as these amounts develop through our analysis of the other accounts.

The procedure is to make entries directly in the T-accounts to explain the actions that have caused the changes in the various account balances. To the extent that these changes have affected cash, appropriate entries are made in the T-account representing Cash.

EXHIBIT 17–8

UNIVERSAL COMPANY
Comparative Balance Sheet
December 31, 19x5, and 19x4

	19x5	19x4
Assets		
Current assets:		
Cash	$ 11,000	$ 3,000
Marketable securities	5,000	7,000
Accounts receivable	72,000	81,000
Inventory	103,000	93,000
Prepaid expenses	2,000	6,000
Total current assets	193,000	190,000
Investment in Company Y (note 1)	79,000	85,000
Plant and equipment (note 2)	340,000	295,000
Less accumulated depreciation	110,000	180,000
Net plant and equipment	230,000	115,000
Total assets	$502,000	$390,000
Liabilities and Stockholders' Equity		
Current liabilities:		
Accounts payable	$105,000	$ 90,000
Accrued liabilities	6,000	12,000
Total current liabilities	111,000	102,000
Deferred income taxes	15,000	10,000
Long-term notes payable	78,000	28,000
Total liabilities	204,000	140,000
Stockholders' equity:		
Common stock	175,000	140,000
Retained earnings	123,000	110,000
Total stockholders' equity	298,000	250,000
Total liabilities and stockholders' equity	$502,000	$390,000

Note 1: Part of the investment in Company Y was sold during the year at a selling price of $8,000.

Note 2: Equipment that had cost $160,000 new, and on which there was accumulated depreciation of $87,000, was sold during the year for $70,000.

Retained Earnings As we stated earlier in the chapter, the Retained Earnings account is generally the most useful starting point in developing a statement of cash flows. A detail of the change in Universal Company's Retained Earnings account is presented in Exhibit 17–9. We can note from the exhibit that net income of $63,000 was added to Retained Earnings during 19x5 and that dividends of $50,000 were charged against Retained Earnings. The dividends consisted of $40,000 in cash dividends and $10,000 in stock dividends.

Exhibit 17–11 on page 739 contains a second set of T-accounts for Universal Company in which entries have been made to show the effect of the year's activities on the company's Cash account. These entries for Retained Earnings are as follows: Entry (1) shows the increase in Retained Earnings that resulted from the net income reported for 19x5 and the corresponding increase that would have taken place in the Cash account:

EXHIBIT 17–9

UNIVERSAL COMPANY
Income Statement and
Reconciliation of Retained Earnings
For the Year Ended December 31, 19x5

Sales		$500,000
Less cost of goods sold		300,000
Gross margin		200,000
Less operating expenses (note 3)		109,000
Net operating income		91,000
Nonoperating items:		
Gain on sale of investments	$ 2,000	
Loss on sale of equipment	3,000	1,000
Income before taxes		90,000
Less income taxes (30%)		27,000
Net income		63,000
Retained earnings, January 1, 19x5		110,000
Total		173,000
Less dividends distributed:		
Cash dividends	40,000	
Stock dividends, common	10,000	50,000
Retained earnings, December 31, 19x5		$123,000

Note 3: Operating expenses contain $17,000 of depreciation expense.

(1)		
Cash—Provided	63,000	
Retained Earnings		63,000

Entry (2) records the payment of cash dividends on common stock and the corresponding drain on Cash:

(2)		
Retained Earnings	40,000	
Cash—Used		40,000

Entry (3) records the distribution of a stock dividend to common stockholders. A stock dividend has no effect on Cash. It simply capitalizes a portion of Retained Earnings and results in no outflow of assets:

(3)		
Retained Earnings	10,000	
Common Stock		10,000

The reader should trace all three of these entries into the T-accounts in Exhibit 17–11.

EXHIBIT 17–10

T-Accounts Showing Changes in Account Balances—Universal Company

Cash

Provided	Used

Accounts Receivable

Debit		Credit	
Bal.	81,000		
Bal.	72,000		

Inventory

Debit		Credit	
Bal.	93,000		
Bal.	103,000		

Prepaid Expenses

Debit		Credit	
Bal.	6,000		
Bal.	2,000		

Investment in Company Y

Debit		Credit	
Bal.	85,000		
Bal.	79,000		

Plant and Equipment

Debit		Credit	
Bal.	295,000		
Bal.	340,000		

Accumulated Depreciation

Debit		Credit	
		Bal.	180,000
		Bal.	110,000

Accounts Payable

Debit		Credit	
		Bal.	90,000
		Bal.	105,000

Accrued Liabilities

Debit		Credit	
		Bal.	12,000
		Bal.	6,000

Deferred Income Taxes

Debit		Credit	
		Bal.	10,000
		Bal.	15,000

Long-Term Notes Payable

Debit		Credit	
		Bal.	28,000
		Bal.	78,000

Common Stock

Debit		Credit	
		Bal.	140,000
		Bal.	175,000

Retained Earnings

Debit		Credit	
		Bal.	110,000
		Bal.	123,000

EXHIBIT 17–11

T-Accounts after Posting of Account Changes—Universal Company

Cash

	Provided		Used		
Net income	(1)	63,000	(5)	10,000	Increase in inventory
Decrease in accounts receivable	(4)	9,000	(7)	2,000	Gain on sale of investments
Decrease in prepaid expenses	(6)	4,000	(12)	6,000	Decrease in accrued liabilities
Loss on sale of equipment	(8)	3,000			
Depreciation expense	(10)	17,000			
Increase in accounts payable	(11)	15,000			
Increase in deferred income taxes	(13)	5,000			
Net cash provided by operating activities		98,000			
Sale of Company Y investment	(7)	8,000	(2)	40,000	Payment of cash dividends
Sale of equipment	(8)	70,000	(9)	205,000	Purchase of plant and equipment
Issue of long-term notes	(14)	50,000			
Sale of common stock	(15)	25,000			

Accounts Receivable

Bal.	81,000	(4)	9,000
Bal.	72,000		

Inventory

Bal.	93,000		
(5)	10,000		
Bal.	103,000		

Prepaid Expenses

Bal.	6,000	(6)	4,000
Bal.	2,000		

Investment in Company Y

Bal.	85,000	(7)	6,000
Bal.	79,000		

Plant and Equipment

Bal.	295,000		
(9)	205,000	(8)	160,000
Bal.	340,000		

Accumulated Depreciation

		Bal.	180,000
(8)	87,000	(10)	17,000
		Bal.	110,000

Accounts Payable

		Bal.	90,000
		(11)	15,000
		Bal.	105,000

Accrued Liabilities

		Bal.	12,000
(12)	6,000		
		Bal.	6,000

Deferred Income Taxes

		Bal.	10,000
		(13)	5,000
		Bal.	15,000

Long-Term Notes Payable

		Bal.	28,000
		(14)	50,000
		Bal.	78,000

Common Stock

		Bal.	140,000
		(3)	10,000
		(15)	25,000
		Bal.	175,000

Retained Earnings

		Bal.	110,000
(2)	40,000	(1)	63,000
(3)	10,000		
		Bal.	123,000

Observe from Exhibit 17–11 that these three entries fully explain the change that has taken place in the Retained Earnings account during 19x5. We can now proceed through the remainder of the accounts in the exhibit, analyzing the change between the beginning and ending balances in each account, and recording the appropriate entries in the T-accounts.

Current Asset Accounts The use of T-accounts greatly simplifies the computation of the "Net cash provided by operating activities." This is because the T-accounts automatically show the correct adjustment to make for the changes in the current asset and current liability accounts in order to adjust the net income figure to a cash basis. To demonstrate, Universal Company's Accounts Receivable has decreased by $9,000; the entry to record this change would be:

(4)		
Cash—Provided	9,000	
Accounts Receivable		9,000

The Inventory account has increased by $10,000; the entry to record this change would be:

(5)		
Inventory	10,000	
Cash—Used		10,000

Finally, the Prepaid Expenses account has decreased by $4,000; the entry to record this change would be:

(6)		
Cash—Provided	4,000	
Prepaid Expenses		4,000

As before, the reader should trace all three of these entries into the T-accounts in Exhibit 17–11. Note that by posting the change to the appropriate account (e.g., Accounts Receivable has been credited for $9,000 to show the decrease in the account), we *automatically* show the correct adjustment to cash as an offsetting entry. *Thus, the model given in Exhibit 17–2 for computing the cash provided by operating activities is not needed when working papers are prepared, since the adjustments shown in the model are made within the working papers themselves.*

Observe that in arranging the data on the working papers we have placed all operating items near the top of the Cash T-account, clustered around the net income figure. Then we have placed all investing and financing items in the lower portion of the Cash T-account. This helps us to assemble our data in an orderly manner.

Investment in Company Y The next account on Universal Company's comparative balance sheet is its investment in Company Y. This investment has decreased by $6,000 during 19x5. Since note 1 on the comparative balance sheet indicates that this decrease represents a sale from which the company received $8,000, the entry to record the transaction would be as follows:

(7)		
Cash—Provided	8,000	
Investment in Company Y		6,000
Gain on Sale of Investments		2,000

Note from the income statement in Exhibit 17–9 that the $2,000 gain on this sale is included as part of the company's $63,000 net income for the year. Thus, the gain is entered in the working papers in Exhibit 17–11 as a deduction from the net income figure. This deduction will avoid double counting of the gain and will allow all $8,000 of the sale price to be treated as an investing item.

Plant and Equipment The next account to be analyzed is Plant and Equipment. The T-accounts in Exhibit 17–11 show that this account has increased by $45,000 during 19x5. The increase could simply represent $45,000 in plant and equipment purchases. On the other hand, there may have been retirements or sales during the year that are concealed in this net change.

From the footnote 2 to the balance sheet, we find that certain items of equipment were, indeed, sold during 19x5 at a sale price of $70,000. The entry to record this sale and its effect on Cash would be:

(8)		
Cash—Provided	70,000	
Accumulated Depreciation	87,000	
Loss on Sale of Equipment	3,000	
Plant and Equipment		160,000

Note that the loss recorded above appears as a deduction on the company's income statement in Exhibit 17–9. Since this deduction is similar to depreciation and does not involve an outflow of cash, the loss is added back to net income in the working papers in Exhibit 17–11.

How much did the company expend on plant and equipment purchases during the year? Overall, we know that the Plant and Equipment account increased by $45,000. Since this $45,000 increase is what remains *after* the $160,000 retirement of equipment recorded above, then purchases during the year must have amounted to $205,000 ($45,000 + $160,000 = $205,000). Entry (9) records these purchases in the T-accounts:

(9)		
Plant and Equipment	205,000	
Cash—Used		205,000

Accumulated Depreciation The note on Universal Company's income statement indicates that depreciation expense totaled $17,000 for the year. The entry to record this depreciation in the T-accounts would be:

(10)		
Cash—Provided	17,000	
Accumulated Depreciation		17,000

This entry, along with entry (8) above, explains the change in the Accumulated Depreciation account for the year.

Current Liabilities The T-accounts in Exhibit 17–11 show that Universal Company has two current liability accounts—Accounts Payable and Accrued Liabilities. Accounts Payable has increased by $15,000 during 19x5. The entry in the T-accounts to show this increase would be:

(11)		
Cash—Provided	15,000	
Accounts Payable		15,000

The Accrued Liabilities account has decreased by $6,000; the entry to record this change would be:

(12)		
Accrued Liabilities	6,000	
Cash—Used		6,000

Since both of these changes are used to adjust net income to a cash basis, their cash effect is included in the upper portion of the Cash T-account along with the other operating items.

Deferred Income Taxes Universal Company's Deferred Income Taxes account has increased by $5,000 during 19x5. This means that the company has paid out *less* in taxes during the year than has been reported as expense on the income statement. The entry to record this $5,000 increase in deferred taxes and to adjust net income to a cash basis would be:

(13)		
Cash—Provided	5,000	
Deferred Income Taxes		5,000

Long-Term Notes Payable Universal Company's financial statements give no indication of any long-term notes having been retired during the year. Therefore, we must assume that the $50,000 increase in the Long-Term Notes

Payable account represents the gross amount of borrowing for the year. The entry to record this borrowing would be:

	(14)	
Cash—Provided	50,000	
Long-Term Notes Payable		50,000

Common Stock Universal's Common Stock account has increased by $35,000 during 19x5. We have already accounted for $10,000 of this increase in entry (3) above where we recorded a stock dividend paid in common stock. Since we have no information to the contrary, we must assume that the remaining $25,000 represents a sale of common stock to owners. The entry to record this sale would be:

	(15)	
Cash—Provided	25,000	
Common Stock		25,000

With entry (15), our analysis of changes in Universal Company's balance sheet accounts is complete.

Preparing the Statement of Cash Flows from the Completed T-Accounts

The Cash T-account in Exhibit 17–11 now contains the entries for those transactions that have affected Universal Company's cash position during the year. Our only remaining task is to organize these data into a formal statement of cash flows. This statement is easy to prepare, since the data relating to operating activities are grouped in the upper portion of the Cash T-account and the data relating to investing and financing activities are grouped in the lower portion of the account. Following the guidelines given earlier (Exhibit 17–1), these data have been organized into a formal statement of cash flows in Exhibit 17–12. As an exercise, the reader should review the contents of this statement and explain in his or her own words why cash increased by $6,000 during 19x5.

THE DIRECT METHOD OF DETERMINING THE "NET CASH PROVIDED BY OPERATING ACTIVITIES"

As stated earlier in the chapter, to compute the "Net cash provided by operating activities" under the direct method, we must reconstruct the income statement on a cash basis from top to bottom. A model is presented in Exhibit 17–13 that shows the adjustments that must be made to sales, expenses, and so forth to adjust each to a cash basis. To illustrate the computations involved, we have included in the exhibit the data just used for Universal Company.

Note that Universal Company's "Net cash provided by operating activities" figure ($98,000) agrees with the amount computed above by the indirect method. We would expect the two amounts to agree, since the direct and

EXHIBIT 17–12

UNIVERSAL COMPANY
Statement of Cash Flows
For the Year Ended December 31, 19x5

Operating Activities		
Net income		$ 63,000
Adjustments needed to convert net income to a cash basis:		
Depreciation expense for the year		17,000
Add (deduct) changes in current assets:		
Decrease in accounts receivable		9,000
Decrease in prepaid expenses		4,000
Increase in inventory		(10,000)
Add (deduct) changes in current liabilities:		
Increase in accounts payable		15,000
Decrease in accrued liabilities		(6,000)
Add (deduct) gains and losses on sales of assets:		
Gain on sale of investments		(2,000)
Loss on sale of equipment		3,000
Add the increase in deferred income taxes		5,000
Net cash provided by operating activities		98,000
Investing Activities		
Cash was provided by:		
Sale of Company Y stock	$ 8,000	
Sale of equipment	70,000	
Cash was used to:		
Purchase plant and equipment	(205,000)	
Net cash used for investing activities		(127,000)
Financing Activities		
Cash was provided by:		
Issue of long-term notes	50,000	
Sale of common stock	25,000	
Cash was used to:		
Pay dividends to owners	(40,000)	
Net cash provided by financing activities		35,000
Net increase in cash and cash equivalents		6,000
Cash and cash equivalents, January 1, 19x5		10,000
Cash and cash equivalents, December 31, 19x5		$ 16,000

indirect methods are just different roads to the same destination. The ''Operating activities'' section of Universal Company's statement of cash flows—prepared under the direct method—is presented below. (The investing and financing sections of the statement will be the same as shown for the indirect method in Exhibit 17–12.)

Operating Activities		
Cash received from customers		$509,000
Less cash disbursements for:		
Cost of merchandise purchased	$295,000	
Operating expenses	94,000	
Income taxes	22,000	
Total cash disbursements		411,000
Net cash provided by operating activities		$ 98,000

EXHIBIT 17–13

General Model: Direct Method of Determining the "Net Cash Provided by Operating Activities"

Revenue or Expense Item	Add (+) or Deduct (−) to Adjust to a Cash Basis	Illustration—Universal Company	
Sales revenue (as reported)		$500,000	
Adjustments to a cash basis:			
1. Increase in accounts receivable	−		
2. Decrease in accounts receivable	+	+9,000	$509,000
Cost of goods sold (as reported)		300,000	
Adjustments to a cash basis:			
3. Increase in inventory	+	+10,000	
4. Decrease in inventory	−		
5. Increase in accounts payable	−	−15,000	
6. Decrease in accounts payable	+		295,000
Operating expenses (as reported)		109,000	
Adjustments to a cash basis:			
7. Increase in prepaid expenses	+		
8. Decrease in prepaid expenses	−	−4,000	
9. Increase in accrued liabilities	−		
10. Decrease in accrued liabilities	+	+6,000	
11. Period's depreciation, depletion, and amortization	−	−17,000	94,000
Income tax expense (as reported)		27,000	
Adjustments to a cash basis:			
12. Increase in accrued taxes payable	−		
13. Decrease in accrued taxes payable	+		
14. Increase in deferred income taxes	−	−5,000	
15. Decrease in deferred income taxes	+		22,000
Net cash provided by operating activities			$ 98,000

Similarities and Differences in the Handling of Data

Although we arrive at the same destination under either the direct or the indirect methods, not all data are handled in the same way in the adjustment process. Stop for a moment, flip back to the general model for the indirect method on page 727, and compare the adjustments made in that model to the adjustments made for the direct method in Exhibit 17–13. The adjustments for accounts that affect revenue are the same in the two models. In either case, we adjust our figures to a cash basis by deducting increases in the accounts and adding decreases in the accounts. The adjustments for accounts that affect expenses, however, are handled in *opposite* ways in the two models. This is because under the indirect method we are making our adjustments to *net income,* whereas under the direct method we are making our adjustments to the *expense accounts* themselves.

To illustrate this difference, note the handling of prepaid expenses and depreciation in the two models. Under the indirect method (Exhibit 17–2), an increase in the Prepaid Expenses account is *deducted* from net income in computing the amount of cash provided by operations. Under the direct method (Exhibit 17–13), an increase in Prepaid Expenses is *added* to operating expenses. The reason for the difference can be explained as follows: An increase in Prepaid Expenses means that more cash has been paid out for items such as insurance than has been included as expense for the period. Therefore, to adjust net income to a cash basis we must either deduct this increase from net income (indirect method) or we must add this increase to operating expenses (direct method). Either way, we will end up with the same figure for cash provided by operations. In like manner, depreciation is added to net income under the indirect method to cancel out its effect (Exhibit 17–2), whereas it is deducted from operating expenses under the direct method to cancel out its effect (Exhibit 17–13). These same differences in the handling of data are true for all other expense items in the two models.

In the matter of gains and losses on sales of assets, no adjustments are needed at all under the direct method. These gains and losses are simply ignored, since they are not part of sales, cost of goods sold, operating expenses, or income taxes. For example, observe from Exhibit 17–13 that Universal Company's $2,000 gain on sale of investments and $3,000 loss on sale of equipment were not involved in the adjustment of the company's income statement to a cash basis. In this sense, the direct method is somewhat simpler than the indirect method.

Special Rules—Direct and Indirect Methods

When using the direct method to compute the cash provided by operating activities, companies are required, at a minimum, to present the following breakdowns of cash received and cash paid out:

Cash receipts:

1. Cash collected from customers.
2. Interest and dividends received.
3. Other operating cash receipts, if any.

Cash Payments:

1. Cash paid to employees and to suppliers for goods and services (for inventory, utilities, and so forth).
2. Interest paid.
3. Income taxes paid.
4. Other operating cash payments, if any.

If a company chooses to use the indirect method rather than the direct method, then it must also provide a special breakdown of data. In addition to the reconciliation between net income and the "Net cash provided by operating activities," the company must provide a separate disclosure of the amount of interest paid and the amount of income taxes paid during the year. The FASB requires this separate disclosure so that users can take the data provided by the indirect method and make estimates of what the amounts for sales, income taxes, and so forth, would have been if the direct method had been used instead.

Comparison of the Direct and Indirect Methods

Historically, *when a choice between the direct and indirect methods has been available,* few companies have chosen the direct method. We can cite three reasons why. First, it is argued that the direct method is more difficult to use than the indirect method because it involves a complete restructuring of the income statement. Moreover, this restructuring can't be integrated readily into working papers. Second, since the direct method adjusts all figures on the income statement to a cash basis, there is concern it may imply that the cash basis of reporting is a better measure of performance than the accrual basis. Third, although the direct method shows the amount of cash provided by operating activities, it does not tell statement users *why* the cash provided differs from net income. Statement users are left on their own to reconcile the two figures (which may pose an almost impossible task for some users). The indirect method, by contrast, *starts* with the net income figure and shows why the "Net cash provided by operating activities" figure is different.

On the other hand, managers who argue in favor of the direct method state that by restructuring the income statement to a cash basis, statement users can see clearly how cash is generated by operations without having the picture blurred by irrelevant, noncash items such as depreciation. These managers argue that including depreciation on the statement of cash flows confuses and may even mislead statements users. This confusion is avoided under the direct method, it is argued, since the direct method deals only with actual cash receipts and cash payments.

SUMMARY

The statement of cash flows is one of the three major statements prepared by business firms. Its purpose is analytical in that it attempts to explain how cash has been provided and used during a period. As such, the statement of cash flows is highly regarded as a tool for assessing the well-being of a firm and for assessing how well its management is performing.

The statement of cash flows is organized in terms of operating, investing, and financing activities. Operating activities encompass those transactions involved in the determination of net income, investing activities encompass those transactions involved in the acquisition or disposition of noncurrent assets, and financing activities encompass those transactions involved with owners and involved with borrowing from creditors. As this list of transactions suggests, to determine the reason for any change in the Cash account, we must analyze changes in all other balance sheet accounts.

The net result of cash flows arising from day-to-day operations is known as the "Net cash provided by operating activities." This figure can be computed by either the direct method or the indirect method. Under the direct method, the income statement is reconstructed on a cash basis. Under the indirect method, adjustments for sales, cost of goods sold, and other income statement items are made indirectly through the net income figure.

KEY TERMS FOR REVIEW

Cash equivalents Short-term, highly liquid investments such as treasury bills, commercial paper, and money market funds that are made solely for the purpose of generating a return on funds that are temporarily idle. (p. 721)

Net cash provided by operating activities The net result of the cash inflows and cash outflows that arise from day-to-day operations. (p. 725)

Direct exchange transactions Transactions involving only noncurrent accounts, such as the issue of capital stock in exchange for property or equipment, the conversion of long-term debt into common stock, and the acquisition of property under a long-term lease agreement. (p. 724)

Direct method A method of computing the cash provided by operating activities in which the income statement is reconstructed on a cash basis. (p. 726)

Financing activities A section on the statement of cash flows that includes all transactions (other than payment of interest) involving borrowing from creditors and all transactions (except stock dividends and stock splits) involving the owners of a company. (p. 724)

Indirect method A method of computing the cash provided by operating activities that starts with net income (as reported on the income statement) and adjusts the net income figure to a cash basis. It is also known as the *reconciliation method.* (p. 726)

Investing activities A section on the statement of cash flows that includes any transactions that are involved in the acquisition or disposition of noncurrent assets. (p. 723)

Operating activities A section on the statement of cash flows that includes any transactions that enter into the determination of income. (p. 722)

Reconciliation method See *Indirect method.* (p. 726)

Statement of cash flows A statement designed to highlight the major activities that have provided cash and that have used cash during a period, and that shows the resulting effect on the overall cash balance. (p. 721)

QUESTIONS

17–1 What is the purpose of a statement of cash flows?

17–2 What are *cash equivalents,* and why are they included with cash on a statement of cash flows?

17–3 What are the three major sections on a statement of cash flows, and what are the general rules that determine the transactions that should be included in each section?

17–4 Why is interest paid on amounts borrowed from banks and other lenders considered to be an operating activity when the amounts borrowed are financing activities?

17–5 If an asset is sold at a gain, why is the gain deducted from net income when computing the cash provided by operating activities figure under the indirect method?

17–6 Why aren't transactions involving accounts payable considered to be financing activities?

17–7 Give an example of a direct exchange, and explain how such exchanges are handled when preparing a statement of cash flows.

17–8 Assume that a company repays a $300,000 loan from its bank and then later in the same year borrows $500,000. What amount(s) would appear on the statement of cash flows?

17–9 How do the direct and the indirect methods differ in their approach to computing the cash provided by operating activities?

17–10 In determining the cash provided by operating activities under the indirect method, why is it necessary to add depreciation back to net income? What other income statement items are similar to depreciation and must be handled in the same way?

17–11 A business executive once stated, "Depreciation is one of our biggest sources of cash." Do you agree that depreciation is a source of cash? Explain.

17–12 If the balance in Accounts Receivable increases during a period, how will this increase be handled under the indirect method in computing the cash provided by operating activities?

17–13 If the balance in Accounts Payable decreases during a period, how will this decrease be handled under the direct method in computing the cash provided by operating activities?

17–14 During the current year, a company declared and paid a $60,000 cash dividend and a 10 percent stock dividend. How will these two items be treated on the current year's statement of cash flows?

17–15 Would a sale of equipment for cash be considered a financing activity or an investing activity? Why?

17–16 A merchandising company showed $250,000 in cost of goods sold on its income statement. The company's beginning inventory was $75,000, and its ending inventory was $60,000. Accounts payable for merchandise were $50,000 at the beginning of the year and $40,000 at the end of the year. Using the direct method, adjust the company's cost of goods sold to a cash basis.

EXERCISES

E17–1 For the year ended December 31, 19x3, Strident Company reported a net income of $84,000. Balances in the company's current asset and current liability accounts at the beginning and end of the year were:

	December 31	
	19x3	19x2
Current assets:		
Cash	$ 60,000	$ 80,000
Accounts receivable, net	250,000	190,000
Inventory	437,000	360,000
Prepaid expenses	12,000	14,000
Current liabilities:		
Accounts payable	420,000	390,000
Accrued liabilities	8,000	12,000

The Deferred Income Taxes account on the balance sheet increased by $6,000 during the year, and $50,000 in depreciation expense was deducted on the income statement.

Required By use of the indirect method, determine the cash provided by operating activities for the year.

E17–2 Refer to the data for Strident Company in Exercise 17–1. Assume that the company's income statement for 19x3 was as follows:

Sales	$1,000,000
Less cost of goods sold	580,000
Gross margin	420,000
Less operating expenses	300,000
Income before taxes	120,000
Less income taxes (30%)	36,000
Net income	$ 84,000

Required Using the direct method (and the data from Exercise 17–1), convert the company's income statement to a cash basis.

E17–3 Below are certain transactions that took place in Placid Company during the past year:

a. Equipment was purchased at a cost of $30,000.
b. An $8,000 cash dividend was declared and paid.
c. Sales for the year totaled $1,000,000.
d. Short-term investments were purchased at a cost of $10,000.
e. Equipment was sold during the year.
f. A gain was realized on the equipment sold in *(e)*.
g. Preferred stock was sold to investors.
h. A $6,000 stock dividend was declared and issued.
i. Interest was paid to long-term creditors.
j. Salaries and wages were paid to employees.
k. Stock of another company was purchased.
l. Bonds were issued that will be due in 10 years.
m. Rent was received from subleasing of space.
n. Common stock was repurchased and retired.

Required Prepare an answer sheet with the following headings:

	Activity			
Transaction	**Operating**	**Investing**	**Financing**	**Not Reported**
a.				
b.				
Etc.				

Enter the transactions above on your answer sheet and indicate how the effects of each transaction would be reported on a statement of cash flows by placing an *X* in the appropriate column.

E17–4 Comparative financial statement data for Holly Company are given below:

	December 31	
	19x8	**19x7**
Cash	$ 4	$ 7
Accounts receivable	36	29
Inventory	75	61
Plant and equipment	210	180
Accumulated depreciation	(40)	(30)
Total assets	$285	$247
Accounts payable	$ 45	$ 39
Common stock	90	70
Retained earnings	150	138
Total liabilities and stockholders' equity	$285	$247

For 19x8, the company reported net income as follows:

Sales	$500
Less cost of goods sold	300
Gross margin	200
Less operating expenses	180
Net income	$ 20

Dividends of $8 were declared and paid during 19x8. Depreciation expense for the year was $10.

Required By use of the indirect method, prepare a statement of cash flows for 19x8.

E17–5 Refer to the data for Holly Company in Exercise 17–4.

Required By use of the direct method, convert the company's income statement to a cash basis.

E17–6 Changes in various accounts and gains and losses on sales of assets during 19x5 for Weston Company are given below:

Item	Amount
Accounts Receivable	$ 70,000 decrease
Accrued Interest Receivable	6,000 increase
Inventory	110,000 increase
Prepaid Expenses	3,000 decrease
Accounts Payable	40,000 decrease
Accrued Liabilities	9,000 increase
Deferred Income Taxes	15,000 increase
Sale of equipment	8,000 gain
Sale of long-term investments	12,000 loss

Required For each item, place an *X* in the "Add" or "Deduct" column to indicate whether the dollar amount should be added to or deducted from net income under the indirect method in computing the cash provided by operating activities for the year. Use the following column headings in preparing your answers:

Item	Amount	Add	Deduct

E17–7 The income statement for Heller Company for the current year is given below:

HELLER COMPANY
Income Statement
For the Year Ended December 31, 19x2

Sales	$400,000
Less cost of goods sold	230,000
Gross margin	170,000
Less operating expenses	90,000*
Income before taxes	80,000
Less income taxes	24,000
Net income	$ 56,000

* Includes $15,000 depreciation expense.

Amounts from selected balance sheet accounts follow:

	19x2 December 31	19x2 January 1
Accounts Receivable	$100,000	$ 70,000
Inventory	150,000	110,000
Prepaid Expenses	8,000	14,000
Accounts Payable	130,000	125,000
Accrued Liabilities	42,000	50,000
Income Taxes Payable	6,000	7,000
Deferred Income Taxes	35,000	28,000

Required 1. Using the direct method, determine the cash provided by operating activities by converting the company's income statement to a cash basis. Show all computations.
2. Assume that the company had a $9,000 gain on sale of investments during the year and a $3,000 loss on sale of equipment. How would these two items have affected your computations in (1) above? Explain.

E17–8 The following changes took place during 19x8 in Pavolik Company's balance sheet accounts:

Cash	$ 5 D	Accounts Payable	$ 35 I
Accounts Receivable	110 I	Accrued Liabilities	4 D
Inventory	70 D	Bonds Payable	150 I
Prepaid Expenses	9 I	Deferred Income Taxes	8 I
Long-Term Investments	6 D	Common Stock	80 D
Plant and Equipment	200 I	Retained Earnings	54 I
Accumulated Depreciation	(60) I		
Land	15 D		

D = Decrease; I = Increase.

Long-term investments that had cost the company $6 were sold during the year for $16, and land that had cost $15 was sold for $9. In addition, the company declared and paid $30 in cash dividends during the year. No sales or retirements of plant and equipment took place during 19x8.

The company's income statement for the year follows:

Sales		$700
Less cost of goods sold		400
Gross margin		300
Less operating expenses		184
Net operating income		116
Nonoperating items:		
Gain on sale of investments	$10	
Loss on sale of land	6	4
Income before taxes		120
Less income taxes		36
Net income		$ 84

The company's cash balance on January 1, 19x8, was $90, and its balance on December 31, 19x8, was $85.

Required 1. Use the indirect method to determine the cash provided by operating activities for the year.
2. Prepare a statement of cash flows for the year.

E17–9 Refer to the data for Pavolik Company in Exercise 17–8.

Required Use the direct method to convert the company's income statement for 19x8 to a cash basis.

PROBLEMS

P17–10 **Indirect Method; Statement of Cash Flows without Working Papers** Comparative financial statements for Eaton Company follow:

EATON COMPANY
Comparative Balance Sheet
December 31, 19x5, and 19x4

	19x5	19x4
Assets		
Cash	$ 4	$ 11
Accounts receivable	310	230
Inventory	160	195
Prepaid expenses	8	6
Plant and equipment	500	420
Accumulated depreciation	(85)	(70)
Long-term investments	31	38
Total assets	$928	$830
Liabilities and Stockholders' Equity		
Accounts payable	$300	$225
Accrued liabilities	70	80
Bonds payable	195	170
Deferred income taxes	71	63
Common stock	160	200
Retained earnings	132	92
Total liabilities and stockholders' equity	$928	$830

EATON COMPANY
Income Statement
For the Year Ended December 31, 19x5

Sales		$750
Less cost of goods sold		450
Gross margin		300
Less operating expenses		223*
Net operating income		77
Nonoperating items:		
Gain on sale of investments	$5	
Loss on sale of equipment	2	3
Income before taxes		80
Less income taxes		24
Net income		$ 56

* Contains $25 depreciation expense.

During 19x5, the company sold some equipment for $18 that had cost $30 and on which there was accumulated depreciation of $10. In addition, the company sold long-term investments for $12 that had cost $7 when purchased several years ago. Cash dividends totaling $16 were paid during 19x5.

Required

1. By use of the indirect method, determine the cash provided by operating activities for 19x5.
2. Use the information in (1) above, along with an analysis of the remaining balance sheet accounts, and prepare a statement of cash flows for 19x5.

P17–11 Direct Method; Statement of Cash Flows without Working Papers Refer to the financial statement data for Eaton Company in Problem 17–10.

Required

1. By use of the direct method, adjust the company's income statement for 19x5 to a cash basis.
2. Use the information obtained in (1) above, along with an analysis of the remaining balance sheet accounts, and prepare a statement of cash flows for 19x5.

P17–12 **Indirect Method; Statement of Cash Flows without Working Papers** Balance sheet accounts for Foxboro Company contained the following amounts at the end of years 1 and 2:

	Year 2	Year 1
Debits		
Cash	$ 11,000	$ 19,000
Accounts Receivable, net	250,000	180,000
Inventory	318,000	270,000
Prepaid Expenses	7,000	16,000
Loan to Harker Company	40,000	—
Plant and Equipment	620,000	500,000
Total debits	$1,246,000	$985,000
Credits		
Accumulated Depreciation	$ 165,000	$130,000
Accounts Payable	310,000	260,000
Accrued Liabilities	42,000	50,000
Bonds Payable	190,000	100,000
Deferred Income Taxes	84,000	80,000
Common Stock	335,000	275,000
Retained Earnings	120,000	90,000
Total credits	$1,246,000	$985,000

The company's income statement for year 2 follows:

Sales	$700,000
Less cost of goods sold	400,000
Gross margin	300,000
Less operating expenses	216,000
Net operating income	84,000
Gain on sale of equipment	6,000
Income before taxes	90,000
Less income taxes	27,000
Net income	$ 63,000

Equipment that had cost $30,000 and on which there was accumulated depreciation of $10,000 was sold during year 2 for $26,000. Cash dividends totaling $33,000 were declared and paid during year 2, and depreciation expense totaled $45,000 for the year.

Required

1. By use of the indirect method, compute the cash provided by operating activities for year 2.
2. Prepare a statement of cash flows for year 2.
3. Prepare a brief explanation as to why cash declined so sharply during the year.

P17–13 **Direct Method; Statement of Cash Flows without Working Papers** Refer to the financial statement data for Foxboro Company in Problem 17–12. Mike Perry, president of the company, considers $15,000 to be a minimum cash balance for operating purposes. As can be seen from the balance sheet data, only $11,000 in cash was available at the end of the current year. The sharp decline is puzzling to Mr. Perry, particularly since sales and profits are at a record high.

Required

1. By use of the direct method, adjust the company's income statement to a cash basis for year 2.
2. Using the data from (1) above and other data from the problem as needed, prepare a statement of cash flows for year 2.
3. Explain to Mr. Perry why cash declined so sharply during the year.

P17–14 Classifying Transactions on a Statement of Cash Flows Below are a number of transactions that took place in Seneca Company during the past year.

a. Common stock was sold for cash.
b. Interest was paid on a note that will be due in two years.
c. Bonds were retired at a loss.
d. A long-term loan was made to a subsidiary.
e. Interest was received on the loan in *(d)*.
f. A 10 percent stock dividend was declared and issued on common stock.
g. A building was acquired by the issue of 30,000 shares of common stock.
h. Equipment was sold for cash.
i. A gain was realized on the sale of equipment in *(h)*.
j. Because of a need to pay obligations, short-term investments were sold.
k. Cash dividends were declared and paid.
l. Preferred stock was converted into common stock.
m. Deferred income taxes were paid; the taxes had been carried as a long-term liability.
n. Dividends were received on stock of another company held as an investment.
o. Equipment was purchased by giving a long-term note to the seller.

Required Prepare an answer sheet with the following column headings:

Transaction	Cash Provided, Used, or Neither	Activity			Reported in a Separate Schedule	Not on the Statement
		Operating	Investing	Financing		

Enter the letter of the transaction in the left column, and indicate whether the transaction would have provided cash, used cash, or neither. Then place an *X* in the appropriate column to show the proper classification of the transaction on the statement of cash flows, or to show if it would not appear on the statement at all.

P17–15 Indirect Method; Statement of Cash Flows without Working Papers Sharon Feldman, president of Allied Products, considers $20,000 to be a minimum cash balance for operating purposes. As can be seen from the statements below, only $15,000 in cash was available at the end of 19x2. Since the company reported a large net income for the year, and also issued bonds and sold some long-term investments, the sharp decline in cash is puzzling to Ms. Feldman.

ALLIED PRODUCTS
Comparative Balance Sheet
December 31, 19x2, and 19x1

	19x2	19x1
Assets		
Current assets:		
Cash	$ 15,000	$ 33,000
Accounts receivable, net	300,000	210,000
Inventory	250,000	196,000
Prepaid expenses	7,000	15,000
Total current assets	572,000	454,000
Long-term investments	90,000	120,000
Plant and equipment	860,000	750,000
Less accumulated depreciation	210,000	190,000
Net plant and equipment	650,000	560,000
Total assets	$1,312,000	$1,134,000

Liabilities and Stockholders' Equity		
Current liabilities:		
Accounts payable	$ 275,000	$ 230,000
Accrued liabilities	8,000	15,000
Total current liabilities	283,000	245,000
Bonds payable	200,000	100,000
Deferred income taxes	42,000	39,000
Total liabilities	525,000	384,000
Stockholders' equity:		
Common stock	595,000	600,000
Retained earnings	192,000	150,000
Total stockholders' equity	787,000	750,000
Total liabilities and stockholders' equity	$1,312,000	$1,134,000

ALLIED PRODUCTS
Income Statement
For the Year Ended December 31, 19x2

Sales		$800,000
Less cost of goods sold		500,000
Gross margin		300,000
Less operating expenses		214,000
Net operating income		86,000
Nonoperating items:		
Gain on sale of investments	$20,000	
Loss on sale of equipment	6,000	14,000
Income before taxes		100,000
Less income taxes		30,000
Net income		$ 70,000

The following additional information is available for the year 19x2:

a. The company sold long-term investments during the year at a selling price of $50,000.

b. Equipment that had cost $90,000 and on which there was $40,000 in accumulated depreciation was sold during the year for $44,000.

c. Cash dividends totaling $28,000 were declared and paid during the year.

d. The stock of a dissident stockholder was repurchased and retired during the year. No issues of stock were made.

Required

1. By use of the indirect method, compute the cash provided by operating activities for 19x2.
2. Using the data from (1) above and other data from the problem as needed, prepare a statement of cash flows for 19x2.
3. Explain to the president the major reasons for the decline in the company's cash position.

P17–16 Direct Method; Statement of Cash Flows without Working Papers Refer to the financial statements for Allied Products in Problem 17–15. Since the Cash account decreased substantially during 19x2, the company's executive committee is anxious to see how the income statement would appear on a cash basis.

Required

1. By use of the direct method, adjust the company's income statement for 19x2 to a cash basis.
2. Using the data from (1) above and other data from the problem as needed, prepare a statement of cash flows for 19x5.

3. Prepare a brief explanation for the executive committee, setting forth the major reasons for the decline in cash during the year.

P17–17 **Indirect Method; Working Papers; Statement of Cash Flows** Aquatech, Inc., is a supplier of water purification equipment for home and commercial use. The company is in an aggressive expansion program and will continue to expand if adequate financing can be obtained from its bank. A comparative balance sheet containing data for the last two years follows:

AQUATECH, INC.
Comparative Balance Sheet
December 31, 19x5, and 19x4

	19x5	19x4
Assets		
Current assets:		
Cash	$ (9,000)	$ 36,000
Accounts receivable, net	370,000	260,000
Inventory	275,000	190,000
Prepaid expenses	41,000	45,000
Total current assets	677,000	531,000
Loan to Facer Company	52,000	17,000
Plant and equipment	940,000	740,000
Less accumulated depreciation	(405,000)	(380,000)
Net plant and equipment	535,000	360,000
Goodwill, net of amortization	57,000	62,000
Total assets	$1,321,000	$970,000
Liabilities and Stockholders' Equity		
Current liabilities:		
Accounts payable	$ 340,000	$270,000
Accrued liabilities	26,000	35,000
Total current liabilities	366,000	305,000
Bonds payable	250,000	100,000
Deferred income taxes	70,000	60,000
Stockholders' equity:		
Common stock	510,000	400,000
Retained earnings	125,000	105,000
Total stockholders' equity	635,000	505,000
Total liabilities and stockholders' equity	$1,321,000	$970,000

The company's income statement for 19x5 is given below:

AQUATECH, INC.
Income Statement
For the Year Ended December 31, 19x5

Sales	$1,500,000
Less cost of goods sold	900,000
Gross margin	600,000
Less operating expenses	490,000*
Net operating income	110,000
Gain on sale of equipment	20,000
Income before taxes	130,000
Less income taxes	40,000
Net income	$ 90,000

* Contains $63,000 in depreciation expense and $5,000 amortization of goodwill.

Rafael Sanchez, president of Aquatech, was surprised to see that the company's Cash account was overdrawn at the end of 19x5. After studying the statements for awhile, he said, "There's something strange going on here. We reported a healthy profit for the year, plus we issued bonds and sold stock. Our cash inflow should have been more than enough to finance the two new warehouses that we purchased during the year. That Cash account can't be overdrawn unless someone has their hand in the till."

The following additional information is available for the year 19x5:

a. Equipment that had cost $60,000 and on which there was $38,000 in accumulated depreciation was sold for $42,000.
b. The company declared and paid $30,000 in cash dividends.
c. A $40,000 stock dividend was declared and issued during the year.
d. The only plant and equipment purchases during the year were the two warehouses mentioned by Mr. Sanchez.
e. There were no retirements of stock during the year.

Required

1. Prepare T-account working papers for a statement of cash flows.
2. Using the indirect method and the data from your working papers, prepare a statement of cash flows for 19x5.
3. Write a brief memo to Mr. Sanchez explaining the reasons for the decrease in cash during the year.

P17–18 Direct Method; Adjusting the Income Statement to a Cash Basis Refer to the data for Aquatech, Inc., in Problem 17–17. The company has approached its bank seeking a five-year loan to finance an expansion program. However, the loan officer at the bank is concerned about the company's overdraft and has asked to see the income statement for 19x5 converted to a cash basis.

Required By use of the direct method, adjust the company's income statement for 19x5 to a cash basis.

P17–19 Indirect Method; Working Papers; Statement of Cash Flows Linda Allen, president of Marcroft Company, is elated that the company's cash position improved during the last year, but she is puzzled as to why it happened. Comparative balance sheet data and the company's income statement for last year (19x2) follow:

MARCROFT COMPANY
Comparative Balance Sheet
December 31, 19x2, and 19x1

	19x2	19x1
Assets		
Current assets:		
Cash	$ 108,000	$ 60,000
Accounts receivable, net	320,000	235,000
Inventory	450,000	510,000
Prepaid expenses	27,000	30,000
Total current assets	905,000	835,000
Long-term investments	200,000	100,000
Plant and equipment	1,100,000	950,000
Less accumulated depreciation	(440,000)	(370,000)
Net plant and equipment	660,000	580,000
Goodwill	35,000	45,000
Total assets	$1,800,000	$1,560,000

Liabilities and Stockholders' Equity		
Current liabilities:		
Accounts payable	$ 570,000	$ 400,000
Accrued liabilities	20,000	38,000
Total current liabilities	590,000	438,000
Bonds payable	380,000	100,000
Stockholders' equity:		
Common stock	710,000	750,000
Retained earnings	120,000	272,000
Total stockholders' equity	830,000	1,022,000
Total liabilities and stockholders' equity	$1,800,000	$1,560,000

MARCROFT COMPANY
Income Statement
For the Year Ended December 31, 19x2

Sales	$2,500,000
Less cost of goods sold	1,630,000
Gross margin	870,000
Less operating expenses	950,000
Net operating loss	(80,000)
Loss on sale of equipment	(30,000)
Net loss	$ (110,000)

Upon reviewing these statements, Ms. Allen observed, "With our $110,000 loss, our continued payment of dividends, the doubling of our investment in Wicks Company, and our large equipment purchases, I was sure that we would end the year with almost nothing in the bank. But I find our cash position stronger than it has ever been. I would like a detailed analysis of exactly what happened in the Cash account during the year."

The following information is available for the year:

a. The company has the longest unbroken dividend record in its industry. To maintain this record, cash dividends of $12,000 were declared and paid during the year.
b. Equipment with an original cost of $200,000, and on which there was accumulated depreciation of $130,000, was sold during the year for $40,000.
c. During the year, the company repurchased the stock of a dissident stockholder. The shares were repurchased at their original issue price of $70,000.
d. Since cash dividends were very small, the company decided to issue a $30,000 stock dividend during the year as well.
e. The goodwill is being amortized against earnings.
f. There were no retirements of bonds during the year.

Required

1. Prepare T-account working papers for a statement of cash flows.
2. Using the indirect method, prepare a statement of cash flows for the year 19x2.
3. Prepare a brief explanation for Ms. Allen as to why cash increased during the year.

P17–20 Direct Method; Adjusting the Income Statement to a Cash Basis Refer to the data for Marcroft Company in Problem 17–19. Upon receiving a copy of the company's 19x2 financial statements, a loan officer at the company's bank stated, "There's something odd here. Marcroft Company lost $110,000 last year and paid out $12,000 in cash dividends. But yet the Cash account increased by $48,000. I want the company to adjust its income statement to a cash basis so that we can see what's really happening with operations."

Required

1. Using the direct method, adjust the company's income statement for 19x2 to a cash basis.
2. Which would be of greater value to the bank, to see the cash provided by operating activities figure computed by the direct method or by the indirect method? Explain your position.

P17–21 Missing Data; Indirect Method; Statement of Cash Flows Damocles Company is a manufacturer of fine swords. Below are listed the *net changes* in the company's balance sheet accounts for the past year (19x5):

	Debits	Credits
Cash	$ 51,000	
Accounts Receivable	170,000	
Inventory		$ 63,000
Prepaid Expenses	4,000	
Loans to Subsidiaries		80,000
Long-Term Investments	90,000	
Plant and Equipment	340,000	
Accumulated Depreciation		65,000
Accounts Payable		48,000
Accrued Liabilities	5,000	
Bonds Payable		200,000
Deferred Income Taxes Payable		9,000
Preferred Stock	180,000	
Common Stock		300,000
Retained Earnings		75,000
	$840,000	$840,000

The following additional information is available about last year's activities:

a. Net income for the year was $___?___.
b. The company sold equipment during the year for $35,000. The equipment had cost the company $160,000 when purchased and it had $145,000 in accumulated depreciation at the time of sale.
c. The company declared and paid $10,000 in cash dividends during the year.
d. Depreciation expense for the year was $___?___.
e. The opening and closing balances in the Plant and Equipment and Accumulated Depreciation accounts for 19x5 are given below:

	Opening	Closing
Plant and Equipment	$2,850,000	$3,190,000
Accumulated Depreciation	975,000	1,040,000

f. There were no stock dividends, stock splits, or stock conversions (i.e., one class of stock converted to another class) during the year.
g. The balance in the Cash account at the beginning of 19x5 was $109,000; the balance at the end of the year was $___?___.
h. If data are not given explaining the change in an account, make the most logical assumption as to the cause of the change.

Required Using the indirect method, prepare a statement of cash flows for the year 19x5. Show all computations for items that appear on your statement.

P17–22 **Comprehensive Problem; Indirect Method; Statement of Cash Flows** A comparative balance sheet for Alcorn Products containing data for the last two years is given below:

ALCORN PRODUCTS
Comparative Balance Sheet
December 31, 19x2, and 19x1

	19x2	19x1
Assets		
Current assets:		
Cash	$ 45,000	$ 33,000
Marketable securities	26,000	17,000
Accounts receivable, net	590,000	410,000
Inventory	608,000	620,000
Prepaid expenses	10,000	5,000
Total current assets	1,279,000	1,085,000
Long-term investments	80,000	130,000
Loans to subsidiaries	120,000	70,000
Plant and equipment	2,370,000	1,800,000
Less accumulated depreciation	615,000	560,000
Net plant and equipment	1,755,000	1,240,000
Goodwill	84,000	90,000
Total assets	$3,318,000	$2,615,000
Liabilities and Stockholders' Equity		
Current liabilities:		
Accounts payable	$ 870,000	$ 570,000
Accrued liabilities	25,000	42,000
Total current liabilities	895,000	612,000
Long-term notes	620,000	400,000
Deferred income taxes	133,000	118,000
Total liabilities	1,648,000	1,130,000
Stockholders' equity:		
Common stock	1,150,000	1,000,000
Retained earnings	520,000	485,000
Total stockholders' equity	1,670,000	1,485,000
Total liabilities and stockholders' equity	$3,318,000	$2,615,000

The following additional information is available about the company's activities during 19x2, the current year:

a. Equipment costing $100,000 was acquired by giving a note to the seller that will be due in two years.
b. A stock dividend totaling $60,000 was declared and issued to the common stockholders.
c. Cash dividends declared and paid to the common stockholders totaled $75,000.
d. Some $380,000 in long-term notes outstanding on January 1, 19x2, were repaid during the year.
e. Equipment was sold during the year for $70,000. The equipment had cost $130,000 and had $40,000 in accumulated depreciation on the date of sale.
f. Long-term investments were sold during the year for $110,000. These investments had cost $50,000 when purchased several years ago.

g. The company reported sales, expenses, and net income during 19x2 as follows:

Sales		$3,000,000
Less cost of goods sold		1,860,000
Gross margin		1,140,000
Less operating expenses		930,000*
Net operating income		210,000
Nonoperating items:		
Gain on sale of investments	$60,000	
Loss on sale of equipment	20,000	40,000
Income before taxes		250,000
Less income taxes		80,000
Net income		$ 170,000

* Contains $95,000 in depreciation expense and $6,000 in amortization of goodwill.

Required

1. Prepare T-account working papers for a statement of cash flows.
2. Using the indirect method, prepare a statement of cash flows for the year.
3. What problems relating to the company's activities are revealed by the statement of cash flows that you have prepared?

P17–23 Direct Method; Adjusting the Income Statement to a Cash Basis Refer to the data for Alcorn Products in Problem 17–22. All of the long-term notes issued during 19x2 (other than the note issued for the purchase of equipment) are being held by Alcorn's bank. The bank's management wants the income statement adjusted to a cash basis to see how the cash basis statement compares to the accrual basis statement.

Required Use the direct method to convert Alcorn Product's 19x2 income statement to a cash basis.

P17–24 Missing Data; Indirect Method; Statement of Cash Flows Oxident Products is the manufacturer of a vitamin supplement. Listed below are the *changes* that have taken place in the company's balance sheet accounts as a result of the past year's activities:

Debit Balance Accounts	Net Increase (Decrease)
Cash	$ (10,000)
Accounts Receivable, net	(81,000)
Inventory	230,000
Prepaid Expenses	(6,000)
Loans to Subsidiaries	100,000
Long-Term Investments	(120,000)
Plant and Equipment	500,000
Net increase	$ 613,000
Credit Balance Accounts	
Accumulated Depreciation	$ 90,000
Accounts Payable	(70,000)
Accrued Liabilities	35,000
Bonds Payable	400,000
Deferred Income Taxes	8,000
Preferred Stock	(180,000)
Common Stock	270,000
Retained Earnings	60,000
Net increase	$ 613,000

The following additional information is available about last year's activities:

a. There were no stock dividends, stock splits, or stock conversions (i.e., one class of stock converted into another class) during the year.
b. The company sold equipment during the year for $40,000. The equipment had cost the company $100,000 when purchased and it had $70,000 in accumulated depreciation at the time of sale.
c. Net income for the year was $___?___.
d. The balance in the Cash account at the beginning of the year was $52,000; the balance at the end of the year was $___?___.
e. The company declared and paid $30,000 in cash dividends during the year.
f. Long-term investments that had cost $120,000 were sold during the year for $80,000.
g. Depreciation expense for the year was $___?___.
h. The opening and closing balances in the Plant and Equipment and Accumulated Depreciation accounts for the past year are given below:

	Opening	Closing
Plant and Equipment	$2,700,000	$3,200,000
Accumulated Depreciation . . .	1,410,000	1,500,000

i. If data are not given explaining the change in an account, make the most logical assumption as to the cause of the change.

Required Using the indirect method, prepare a statement of cash flows for the past year. Show all computations for items that appear on your statement.

18

"How Well Am I Doing?" Financial Statement Analysis

LEARNING OBJECTIVES

After studying Chapter 18, you should be able to:

1 Explain the need for and limitations of financial statement analysis.

2 Prepare financial statements in comparative form and explain how such statements are used.

3 Place the balance sheet and the income statement in common-size form and properly interpret the results.

4 State what ratios are used to measure the well-being of the common stockholder and give the formula for each ratio.

5 Tell what is meant by the term *financial leverage* and explain how financial leverage is measured.

6 Enumerate the ratios used to analyze working capital and the well-being of creditors and give the formula for each ratio.

7 Define or explain the key terms listed at the end of the chapter.

No matter how carefully prepared, all financial statements are essentially historical documents. They tell what *has happened* during a particular year or series of years. The most valuable information to most users of financial statements, however, concerns what probably *will happen* in the future. The purpose of financial statement analysis is to assist statement users in *predicting the future* by means of comparison, evaluation, and trend analysis.

THE IMPORTANCE OF STATEMENT ANALYSIS

Virtually all users of financial data have concerns that can be resolved to some degree by the predictive ability of statement analysis. The stockholders are concerned, for example, about such matters as whether they should hold or sell their shares of stock, whether the present management group should remain or be replaced, and whether the company should have their approval to sell a new offering of senior debt. The creditors are concerned about such matters as whether income will be sufficient to cover the interest due on their bonds or notes, and whether prospects are good for their obligations to be paid at maturity. The managers are concerned about such matters as dividend policy, the availability of funds to finance future expansion, and the probable future success of operations under their leadership.

The thing about the future that statement users are most interested in predicting is profits. It is profits, of course, that provide the basis for an increase in the value of the stockholder's stock and that encourage the creditor to risk his or her money in an organization. And it is largely profits that make future expansion possible. The dilemma is that profits are uncertain. For this reason, one must have various analytical tools to assist in interpreting the key relationships and trends that serve as a basis for judgments of potential future success. Without financial statement analysis, the story that key relationships and trends have to tell may remain buried in a sea of statement detail.

In this chapter, we consider some of the more important ratios and other analytical tools that analysts use in attempting to predict the future course of events in business organizations.

Importance of Comparisons

Financial statements are not only historical documents but they are also essentially static documents. They speak only of the events of a single period of time. However, statement users are concerned about more than just the present; they are also concerned about the *trend of events* over time. For this reason, financial statement analysis directed toward a single period is of limited usefulness. The results of financial statement analysis for a particular period are of value only when viewed in *comparison* with the results of other periods and, in some cases, with the results of other firms. It is only through comparison that one can gain insight into trends and make intelligent judgments as to their significance.

Unfortunately, comparisons between firms within an industry are often made difficult by differences in accounting methods in use. For example, if one firm values its inventories by LIFO and another firm values its inventories by average cost, then direct dollar-for-dollar comparisons between the two firms may not be possible. In such cases, comparisons can still be made, but they must focus on data in a broader, more relative sense. Although the analytical work required here may be tougher, it is often necessary if the manager is to have any data available for comparison purposes.

The Need to Look beyond Ratios

There is a tendency for the inexperienced analyst to assume that ratios are sufficient in themselves as a basis for judgments about the future. Nothing could be further from the truth. The experienced analyst realizes that the best-prepared ratio analysis must be regarded as tentative in nature and never as conclusive in itself. Ratios should not be viewed as an end, but rather they should be viewed as a *starting point,* as indicators of what to pursue in greater depth. They raise many questions, but they rarely answer any questions by themselves.

In addition to looking at ratios, the analyst must look at other sources of data in order to make judgments about the future of an organization. The analyst must look, for example, at industry trends, at technological changes that are anticipated or that are in process, at changes in consumer tastes, at regional and national changes in economic factors, and at changes that are taking place within the firm itself. A recent change in a key management position, for example, might rightly serve as a basis for much optimism about the future, even though the past performance of the firm (as shown by its ratios) may have been very mediocre.

STATEMENTS IN COMPARATIVE AND COMMON-SIZE FORM

As stated above, few figures appearing on financial statements have much significance standing by themselves. It is the relationship of one figure to another and the amount and direction of change from one point in time to another that are important in financial statement analysis. How does the analyst key in on significant relationships? How does the analyst dig out the important trends and changes in a company? Three analytical techniques are in widespread use:

1. Dollar and percentage changes on statements.
2. Common-size statements.
3. Ratios.

All three techniques are discussed in following sections.

Dollar and Percentage Changes on Statements

A good beginning place in financial statement analysis is to put statements in comparative form. This consists of little more than putting two or more years' data side by side. Statements cast in comparative form will underscore movements and trends and may give the analyst valuable clues as to what to expect in the way of financial and operating performance in the future.

An example of financial statements placed in comparative form is given in Exhibits 18–1 and 18–2. These are the statements of Brickey Electronics, a hypothetical firm. The data on these statements are used as a basis for discussion throughout the remainder of the chapter.

Horizontal Analysis Comparison of two or more years' financial data is known as **horizontal analysis.** Horizontal analysis is greatly facilitated by showing changes between years in both dollar *and* percentage form, as has been done in Exhibits 18–1 and 18–2. Showing changes in dollar form helps the analyst to zero in on key factors that have affected profitability or

EXHIBIT 18–1

BRICKEY ELECTRONICS
Comparative Balance Sheet
December 31, 19x2, and 19x1
(dollars in thousands)

			Increase (Decrease)	
	19x2	**19x1**	**Amount**	**Percent**
Assets				
Current assets:				
Cash	$ 1,200	$ 2,350	$(1,150)	(48.9)
Accounts receivable, net	6,000	4,000	2,000	50.0
Inventory	8,000	10,000	(2,000)	(20.0)
Prepaid expenses	300	120	180	150.0
Total current assets	15,500	16,470	(970)	(5.9)
Property and equipment:				
Land	4,000	4,000	–0–	–0–
Buildings and equipment, net	12,000	8,500	3,500	41.2
Total property and equipment	16,000	12,500	3,500	28.0
Total assets	$31,500	$28,970	$ 2,530	8.7
Liabilities and Stockholders' Equity				
Current liabilities:				
Accounts payable	$ 5,800	$ 4,000	$ 1,800	45.0
Accrued payables	900	400	500	125.0
Notes payable, short term	300	600	(300)	(50.0)
Total current liabilities	7,000	5,000	2,000	40.0
Long-term liabilities:				
Bonds payable, 8%	7,500	8,000	(500)	(6.3)
Total liabilities	14,500	13,000	1,500	11.5
Stockholders' equity:				
Preferred stock, $100 par, 6%, $100 liquidation value	2,000	2,000	–0–	–0–
Common stock, $12 par	6,000	6,000	–0–	–0–
Additional paid-in capital	1,000	1,000	–0–	–0–
Total paid-in capital	9,000	9,000	–0–	–0–
Retained earnings	8,000	6,970	1,030	14.8
Total stockholders' equity	17,000	15,970	1,030	6.4
Total liabilities and stockholders' equity	$31,500	$28,970	$ 2,530	8.7

EXHIBIT 18–2

BRICKEY ELECTRONICS
Comparative Income Statement and Reconciliation of Retained Earnings
For the Years Ended December 31, 19x2, and 19x1
(dollars in thousands)

			Increase (Decrease)	
	19x2	**19x1**	**Amount**	**Percent**
Sales	$52,000	$48,000	$4,000	8.3
Cost of goods sold	36,000	31,500	4,500	14.3
Gross margin	16,000	16,500	(500)	(3.0)
Operating expenses:				
Selling expenses	7,000	6,500	500	7.7
Administrative expenses	5,860	6,100	(240)	(3.9)
Total operating expenses	12,860	12,600	260	2.1
Net operating income	3,140	3,900	(760)	(19.5)
Interest expense	640	700	(60)	(8.6)
Net income before taxes	2,500	3,200	(700)	(21.9)
Less income taxes (30%)	750	960	(210)	(21.9)
Net income	1,750	2,240	$ (490)	(21.9)
Dividends to preferred stockholders, $6 per share (see Exhibit 18–1)	120	120		
Net income remaining for common stockholders	1,630	2,120		
Dividends to common stockholders, $1.20 per share	600	600		
Net income added to retained earnings	1,030	1,520		
Retained earnings, beginning of year	6,970	5,450		
Retained earnings, end of year	$ 8,000	$ 6,970		

financial position. For example, observe in Exhibit 18–2 that sales for 19x2 were up $4 million over 19x1, but that this increase in sales was more than negated by a $4.5 million increase in cost of goods sold.

Showing changes between years in percentage form helps the analyst to gain *perspective* and to gain a feel for the *significance* of the changes that are taking place. One would have a different perspective of a $1 million increase in sales if the prior year's sales were $2 million than he would if the prior year's sales were $20 million. In the first situation, the increase would be 50 percent—undoubtedly a significant increase for any firm. In the second situation, the increase would be only 5 percent—perhaps a reflection of just normal growth.

Trend Percentages Horizontal analysis of financial statements can also be carried out by computing *trend percentages*. **Trend percentages** state several years' financial data in terms of a base year. The base year equals 100 percent, with all other years stated as some percentage of this base. To illustrate, assume that Martin Company has reported the following sales and income data for the past five years:

	19x5	19x4	19x3	19x2	19x1
Sales	$725,000	$700,000	$650,000	$575,000	$500,000
Net income . . .	99,000	97,500	93,750	86,250	75,000

By simply looking at these data, one can see that both sales and net income have increased over the five-year period reported. But how rapidly have sales been increasing, and have the increases in net income kept pace with the increases in sales? By looking at the raw data alone, it is difficult to answer these questions. The increases in sales and the increases in net income can be put into proper perspective by stating them in terms of trend percentages, with 19x1 as the base year. These percentages are given below:

	19x5	19x4	19x3	19x2	19x1
Sales	145%	140%	130%	115%*	100%
Net income . . .	132	130	125	115	100

* For 19x2: $575,000 ÷ $500,000 = 115%; for 19x3: $650,000 ÷ $500,000 = 130%; and so forth.

Notice that the growth in sales dropped off somewhat between 19x3 and 19x4, and then dropped off even more between 19x4 and 19x5. Also notice that the growth in net income has not kept pace with the growth in sales. In 19x5, sales are 1.45 times greater than in 19x1, the base year; however, in 19x5, net income is only 1.32 times greater than in 19x1.

Common-Size Statements

Key changes and trends can also be highlighted by the use of *common-size statements*. A **common-size statement** is one that shows the separate items appearing on it in percentage form as well as in dollar form. Each item is stated as a percentage of some total of which that item is a part. The preparation of common-size statements is known as **vertical analysis.**

The Balance Sheet One application of the vertical analysis idea is to state the separate assets of a company as percentages of total assets. A common-size statement of this type is shown in Exhibit 18–3 for Brickey Electronics.

Notice from Exhibit 18–3 that placing all assets in common-size form clearly shows the relative importance of the current assets as compared to the noncurrent assets. It also shows that significant changes have taken place in the *composition* of the current assets over the last year. Notice, for example, that the receivables have increased in relative importance and that both cash and inventory have declined in relative importance. Judging from the sharp increase in receivables, the deterioration in the cash position may be a result of inability to collect from customers.

The Income Statement Another application of the vertical analysis idea is to place all items on the income statement in percentage form in terms of sales. A common-size statement of this type is shown in Exhibit 18–4.

By placing all items on the income statement in common size in terms of sales, it is possible to see at a glance how each dollar of sales is distributed between the various costs, expenses, and profits. For example, notice from

EXHIBIT 18–3

BRICKEY ELECTRONICS
Common-Size Comparative Balance Sheet
December 31, 19x2, and 19x1
(dollars in thousands)

			Common-Size Percentages	
	19x2	**19x1**	**19x2**	**19x1**
Assets				
Current assets:				
Cash	$ 1,200	$ 2,350	3.8	8.1
Accounts receivable, net	6,000	4,000	19.0	13.8
Inventory	8,000	10,000	25.4	34.5
Prepaid expenses	300	120	1.0	0.4
Total current assets	15,500	16,470	49.2	56.9
Property and equipment:				
Land	4,000	4,000	12.7	13.8
Buildings and equipment, net	12,000	8,500	38.1	29.3
Total property and equipment	16,000	12,500	50.8	43.1
Total assets	$31,500	$28,970	100.0	100.0
Liabilities and Stockholders' Equity				
Current liabilities:				
Accounts payable	$ 5,800	$ 4,000	18.4	13.8
Accrued payables	900	400	2.8	1.4
Notes payable, short term	300	600	1.0	2.1
Total current liabilities	7,000	5,000	22.2	17.3
Long-term liabilities:				
Bonds payable, 8%	7,500	8,000	23.8	27.6
Total liabilities	14,500	13,000	46.0	44.9
Stockholders' equity:				
Preferred stock, $100 par, 6%, $100 liquidation value	2,000	2,000	6.4	6.9
Common stock, $12 par	6,000	6,000	19.0	20.7
Additional paid-in capial	1,000	1,000	3.2	3.5
Total paid-in capital	9,000	9,000	28.6	31.1
Retained earnings	8,000	6,970	25.4	24.0
Total stockholders' equity	17,000	15,970	54.0	55.1
Total liabilities and stockholders' equity	$31,500	$28,970	100.0	100.0

Exhibit 18–4 that 69.2 cents out of every dollar of sales was needed to cover cost of goods sold in 19x2, as compared to only 65.7 cents in the prior year; also notice that only 3.4 cents out of every dollar of sales remained for profits in 19x2—down from 4.6 cents in the prior year.

Common-size statements are also very helpful in pointing out efficiencies and inefficiencies that might otherwise go unnoticed. To illustrate, in 19x2, Brickey Electronics' selling expenses increased by $500,000 over 19x1. A glance at the common-size income statement shows, however, that on a relative basis selling expenses were no higher in 19x2 than in 19x1. In each year, they represented 13.5 percent of sales.

EXHIBIT 18–4

BRICKEY ELECTRONICS
Common-Size Comparative Income Statement
For the Years Ended December 31, 19x2, and 19x1
(dollars in thousands)

			Common-Size Percentages	
	19x2	19x1	19x2	19x1
Sales	$52,000	$48,000	100.0	100.0
Cost of goods sold	36,000	31,500	69.2	65.7
Gross margin	16,000	16,500	30.8	34.3
Operating expenses:				
Selling expenses	7,000	6,500	13.5	13.5
Administrative expenses	5,860	6,100	11.2	12.7
Total operating expenses	12,860	12,600	24.7	26.2
Net operating income	3,140	3,900	6.0	8.1
Interest expense	640	700	1.2	1.5
Net income before taxes	2,500	3,200	4.8	6.6
Income taxes (30%)	750	960	1.4	2.0
Net income	$ 1,750	$ 2,240	3.4	4.6

RATIO ANALYSIS—THE COMMON STOCKHOLDER

The common stockholder has only a residual claim on the profits and assets of a corporation. It is only after all creditor and preferred stockholder claims have been satisfied that the common stockholder can step forward and receive cash dividends or a distribution of assets in liquidation. Therefore, a measure of the common stockholder's well-being provides some perspective of the depth of protection available to others associated with a firm.

Earnings per Share

An investor buys and retains a share of stock with the thought in mind of a return coming in the future in the form of either dividends or capital gains. Since earnings form the basis for dividend payments, as well as the basis for any future increases in the value of shares, investors are always interested in a company's reported *earnings per share*. Probably no single statistic is more widely quoted or relied on in investor actions than earnings per share, although it has some inherent dangers, as discussed below.

The computation of **earnings per share** is made by dividing net income remaining for common stockholders by the number of common shares outstanding. "Net income remaining for common stockholders" is equal to the net income of a company, reduced by the dividends due to the preferred stockholders.

$$\frac{\text{Net income} - \text{Preferred dividends}}{\text{Number of common shares outstanding}} = \text{Earnings per share}$$

Using the data in Exhibits 18–1 and 18–2, we see that the earnings per share for Brickey Electronics for 19x2 would be:

$$\frac{\$1{,}750{,}000 - \$120{,}000}{500{,}000 \text{ shares*}} = \$3.26 \qquad (1)$$

* \$6,000,000 ÷ \$12 = 500,000 shares.

Two problems can arise in connection with the computation of earnings per share. The first arises whenever an extraordinary gain or loss appears as part of net income. The second arises whenever a company has convertible securities on its balance sheet. These problems are discussed in the following two sections.

Extraordinary Items and Earnings per Share

If a company has extraordinary gains or losses appearing as part of net income, *two* earnings per share figures must be computed—one showing the earnings per share resulting from *normal* operations and one showing the earnings per share impact of the *extraordinary* items. This approach to computing earnings per share accomplishes three things. First, it helps statement users to recognize extraordinary items for what they are—unusual events that probably will not recur. Second, it eliminates the distorting influence of the extraordinary items from the basic earnings per share figure. And third, it helps statement users to properly assess the *trend* of *normal* earnings per share over time. Since one would not expect the extraordinary or unusual items to be repeated year after year, they should be given less weight in judging earnings performance than is given to profits resulting from normal operations.

In addition to reporting extraordinary items separately, the accountant also reports them *net of their tax effect*. By "net of their tax effect," we mean that whatever impact the unusual item has on income taxes is *deducted from* the unusual item on the income statement. Only the net, after-tax gain or loss is used in earnings per share computations.

To illustrate these ideas, let us assume that Amata Company has suffered a fire loss of \$6,000 and that management is wondering how the loss should be reported on the company's income statement. The correct and incorrect approaches to reporting the loss are shown in Exhibit 18–5.

As shown under the "Correct Approach" in the exhibit, the \$6,000 loss is reduced to only \$4,200 after tax effects are taken into consideration. The reasoning behind this computation is as follows: The fire loss is fully deductible for tax purposes. Therefore, this deduction will reduce the firm's taxable income by \$6,000. If taxable income is \$6,000 lower, then income taxes will be \$1,800 *less* (30% × \$6,000) than they *otherwise* would have been. In other words, the fire loss of \$6,000 saves the company \$1,800 in taxes that otherwise would have been paid. The \$1,800 savings in taxes is deducted from the loss that caused it, leaving a net loss of only \$4,200. This same \$4,200 figure could have been obtained by multiplying the original loss by the formula (1 − Tax rate): [\$6,000 × (1 − 0.30) = \$4,200]. *Any* before-tax item can be put on an after-tax basis by use of this formula.

This same procedure is used in reporting extraordinary gains. The only difference is that extraordinary gains *increase* taxes; thus, any tax resulting

EXHIBIT 18–5

Reporting Extraordinary Items Net of Their Tax Effects

Incorrect Approach

Sales		$100,000	
Cost of goods sold		60,000	Extraordinary gains and losses should not be included with normal items of revenue and expense. This distorts a firm's normal income-producing ability.
Gross margin		40,000	
Operating expenses:			
Selling expenses	$18,000		
Administrative expenses	12,000		
Fire loss	6,000	36,000	
Net income before taxes		4,000	
Income taxes (30%)		1,200	
Net income		$ 2,800	

Correct Approach

Sales		$100,000	Reporting the extraordinary item separately and net of its tax effect leaves the normal items of revenue and expense unaffected.
Cost of goods sold		60,000	
Gross margin		40,000	
Operating expenses:			
Selling expenses	$18,000		
Administrative expenses	12,000	30,000	
Net operating income		10,000	
Income taxes (30%)		3,000	
Net income before extraordinary item		7,000	
Extraordinary item:			
Fire loss, net of tax		4,200	
Net income		$ 2,800	

Original loss	$6,000
Less reduction in taxes at a 30% rate	1,800
Loss, net of tax	$4,200

from a gain must be deducted from it, with only the net gain reported on the income statement.

To continue our illustration, assume that the company in Exhibit 18–5 has 2,000 shares of common stock outstanding. Earnings per share would be reported as follows:

Earnings per share on common stock:	
On net income before extraordinary item ($7,000 ÷ 2,000 shares)*	$ 3.50
On extraordinary item, net of tax ($4,200 ÷ 2,000 shares)	(2.10)
Net earnings per share	$ 1.40

* Sometimes called the *primary* earnings per share.

In sum, computation of earnings per share as we have done above is necessary to avoid misunderstanding of a company's normal income-producing ability. Reporting *only* the flat $1.40 per share figure would be misleading and perhaps cause investors to regard the company less favorably than they should.

Fully Diluted Earnings per Share

A problem sometimes arises in trying to determine the number of common shares to use in computing earnings per share. Until recent years, the distinction between common stock, preferred stock, and debt was quite clear.

The distinction between these securities has now become somewhat diffused, however, due to a growing tendency to issue convertible securities of various types. Rather than simply issuing common stock, firms today often issue preferred stock or bonds that carry a **conversion feature** allowing the purchaser to convert holdings into common stock at some future time.

When convertible securities are present in the financial structure of a firm, the question arises as to whether these securities should be retained in their unconverted form or treated as common stock in computing earnings per share. The American Institute of Certified Public Accountants has taken the position that convertible securities should be treated *both* in their present and prospective forms. This requires the presentation of *two* earnings per share figures for firms that have convertible securities outstanding, one showing earnings per share assuming no conversion into common stock and the other showing full conversion into common stock. The latter figure is known as the **fully diluted earnings per share.**

To illustrate the computation of a company's fully diluted earnings per share, let us assume that the preferred stock of Brickey Electronics in Exhibit 18–1 is convertible into common on the basis of five shares of common for each share of preferred. Since 20,000 shares of preferred are outstanding, conversion would require issuing an additional 100,000 shares of common stock. Earnings per share on a fully diluted basis would be:

$$\frac{\text{Net income}}{(\text{500,000 shares outstanding} + \text{100,000 converted shares})}$$

$$= \frac{\$1{,}750{,}000}{\text{600,000 shares}} = \$2.92 \quad (2)$$

In comparing equation (2) with equation (1), on page 772, we can note that the earnings per share figure has dropped by 34 cents. Although the impact of full dilution is relatively small in this case, it can be very significant in situations where large amounts of convertible securities are present.

Price-Earnings Ratio

The relationship between the market price of a share of stock and the stock's current earnings per share is often quoted in terms of a **price-earnings ratio.** If we assume that the current market price for Brickey Electronics' stock is $40 per share, the company's price-earnings ratio would be computed as follows:

$$\frac{\text{Market price per share}}{\text{Earnings per share}} = \text{Price-earnings ratio}$$

$$\frac{\$40}{\$3.26\ [\text{see equation (1)}]} = 12.3 \quad (3)$$

The price-earnings ratio is 12.3; that is, the stock is selling for about 12.3 times its current earnings per share.

The price-earnings ratio is widely used by investors as a general guideline in gauging stock values. Investors increase or decrease the price-earnings ratio that they are willing to accept for a share of stock according to how they view its *future prospects.* Companies with ample opportunities for growth generally have high price-earnings ratios, with the opposite being true for companies with limited growth opportunities. If investors decided that Brickey Electronics had greater than average growth prospects, then undoubtedly the price of the company's stock would begin to rise. If the price increased to, say, \$52 per share, then the price-earnings ratio would rise to 16 (\$52 price ÷ \$3.26 EPS = 16.0 P-E ratio).

Dividend Payout and Yield Ratios

Investors hold shares of one stock in preference to shares of another stock because they anticipate that the first stock will provide them with a more attractive return. The return sought isn't always dividends. Many investors prefer not to receive dividends. Instead, they prefer to have the company retain all earnings and reinvest them internally in order to support growth. The stocks of companies that adopt this approach, loosely termed *growth stocks,* often enjoy rapid upward movement in market price. Other investors prefer to have a dependable, current source of income through regular dividend payments and prefer not to gamble on the fortunes of stock prices to provide a return on their investment. Such investors seek out stocks with consistent dividend records and payout ratios.

The Dividend Payout Ratio

The **dividend payout ratio** gauges the portion of current earnings being paid out in dividends. Investors who seek growth in market price would like this ratio to be small, whereas investors who seek dividends prefer it to be large. This ratio is computed by relating dividends per share to earnings per share for common stock:

$$\frac{\text{Dividends per share}}{\text{Earnings per share}} = \text{Dividend payout ratio}$$

For Brickey Electronics, the dividend payout ratio for 19x2 was:

$$\frac{\$1.20 \text{ (see Exhibit 18–2)}}{\$3.26 \text{ [see equation (1)]}} = 36.8\% \qquad (4)$$

There is no such thing as a "right" payout ratio, even though it should be noted that the ratio tends to be somewhat the same for the bulk of firms within a particular industry. Industries with ample opportunities for growth at high rates of return on assets tend to have low payout ratios, and the reverse tends to be true for industries with limited reinvestment opportunities.

The Dividend Yield Ratio

The **dividend yield ratio** is obtained by dividing the current dividends per share by the current market price per share:

$$\frac{\text{Dividends per share}}{\text{Market price per share}} = \text{Dividend yield ratio}$$

If we continue the assumption of a market price of \$40 per share for Brickey Electronics' stock, the dividend yield is:

$$\frac{\$1.20}{\$40} = 3.0\% \qquad (5)$$

In making this computation, note that we used the current market price of the stock rather than the price the investor paid for the stock initially (which might be above or below the current market price). By using current market price, we recognize the opportunity cost[1] of the investment in terms of its yield. That is, this is the yield that would be lost or sacrificed if the investor sold the stock for $40 and bought a new security in its place.

Return on Total Assets

Managers have two basic responsibilities in managing a firm—*financing* responsibilities and *operating* responsibilities. Financing responsibilities relate to how one *obtains* the funds needed to provide for the assets in an organization. Operating responsibilities relate to how one *uses* the assets once they have been obtained. Proper discharge of both responsibilities is vital to a well-managed firm. However, care must be taken not to confuse or mix the two in assessing the performance of a manager. That is, whether funds have been obtained partly from creditors and partly from stockholders or entirely from stockholders should not be allowed to influence one's assessment of *how well* the assets have been employed since being received by the firm.

The **return of total assets** is a measure of how well assets have been employed; that is, it is a measure of operating performance. The formula is:

$$\frac{\text{Net income} + [\text{Interest expense} \times (1 - \text{Tax rate})]}{\text{Average total assets}} = \text{Return on total assets}$$

By adding interest expense back to net income, we derive a figure that shows earnings before any distributions have been made to either creditors or stockholders. Thus, we eliminate the matter of how the assets were financed from influencing the measurement of how well the assets have been employed. Notice that before being added back to net income, the interest expense must be placed on an after-tax basis by multiplying the interest figure by the formula (1 − Tax rate).

The return on total assets for Brickey Electronics for 19x2 would be (from Exhibits 18–1 and 18–2):

Net income	$ 1,750,000	
Add back interest expense: $640,000 × (1 − 0.30)	448,000	
Total	$ 2,198,000 *(a)*	
Assets, beginning of year	$28,970,000	
Assets, end of year	31,500,000	
Total	$60,470,000	
Average total assets: $60,470,000 ÷ 2	$30,235,000 *(b)*	
Return on total assets, *(a)* ÷ *(b)*	7.3%	(6)

Brickey Electronics has earned a return of 7.3 percent on average assets employed over the last year.

[1] Opportunity cost is the potential benefit that is lost or sacrificed when the selection of one course of action makes it necessary to give up a competing course of action.

Return on Common Stockholders' Equity

One of the primary reasons for operating a corporation is to generate income for the benefit of the common stockholders. One measure of a company's success in this regard is the rate of **return on common stockholders' equity** that it is able to generate. The formula is:

$$\frac{\text{Net income} - \text{Preferred dividends}}{\text{Average common stockholders' equity (Average total stockholders' equity} - \text{Preferred stock)}} = \text{Return on common stockholders' equity}$$

For Brickey Electronics, the return on common stockholders' equity is 11.3 percent for 19x2, as shown below:

Net income	$ 1,750,000	
Deduct preferred dividends	120,000	
Net income remaining for common stockholders	$ 1,630,000 *(a)*	
Average stockholders' equity	$16,485,000*	
Deduct preferred stock	2,000,000	
Average common stockholders' equity	$14,485,000 *(b)*	
Return on common stockholders' equity, *(a)* ÷ *(b)*	11.3%	(7)

* $15,970,000 + $17,000,000 = $32,970,000; $32,970,000 ÷ 2 = $16,485,000.

Compare the return on common stockholders' equity above (11.3 percent) with the return on total assets computed in the preceding section (7.3 percent). Why is the return on common stockholders' equity so much higher? The answer lies in the principle of *financial leverage* (sometimes called "trading on the equity").

The Concept of Financial Leverage **Financial leverage** (often called "leverage" for short) involves the financing of assets in a company with funds that have been acquired from creditors or from preferred stockholders at a fixed rate of return. If the assets in which the funds are invested are able to earn a rate of return *greater* than the fixed rate of return required by the suppliers of the funds, then financial leverage is **positive** and the common stockholders benefit.

For example, assume that a firm is able to earn an after-tax return of 12 percent on its assets. If that firm can borrow from creditors at a 10 percent interest rate in order to expand its assets, then the common stockholders can benefit from positive leverage. The borrowed funds invested in the business will earn an after-tax return of 12 percent, but the after-tax interest cost of the borrowed funds will be only 7 percent [10% interest rate × (1 − 0.30) = 7%]. The difference will go to the common stockholders.

We can see this concept in operation in the case of Brickey Electronics. Notice from Exhibit 17–1 that the company's bonds payable bear a fixed interest rate of 8 percent. The after-tax interest cost of these bonds is only 5.6 percent [8% interest rate × (1 − 0.30) = 5.6%]. The company's assets (which would contain the proceeds from the original sale of these bonds) are generating an after-tax return of 7.3 percent, as we computed earlier. Since this return on assets is greater than the after-tax interest cost of the bonds, leverage is positive, and the difference accrues to the benefit of the common stockholders. This explains in part why the return on common stockholders' equity (11.3 percent) is greater than the return on total assets (7.3 percent).

Sources of Financial Leverage Financial leverage can be obtained from several sources. One source is long-term debt, such as bonds payable or notes payable. Two additional sources are current liabilities and preferred stock. Current liabilities are always a source of positive leverage in that funds are provided for use in a company with no interest return required by the short-term creditors involved. For example, when a company acquires inventory from a supplier on account, the inventory is available for use in the business, yet the supplier requires no interest return on the amount owed to him.

Preferred stock can also be a source of positive leverage so long as the dividend payable to the preferred stockholders is less than the rate of return being earned on the total assets employed. In the case of Brickey Electronics, positive leverage is being realized on the preferred stock. Notice from Exhibit 18–1 that the preferred dividend rate is only 6 percent, whereas the assets in the company are earning at a rate of 7.3 percent, as computed earlier. Again, the difference goes to the common stockholders, thereby helping to bolster their return to the 11.3 percent computed above.

Unfortunately, leverage is a two-edged sword. If assets are unable to earn a high enough rate to cover the interest costs of debt, or to cover the preferred dividend due to the preferred stockholders, *then the common stockholder suffers*. The reason is that part of the earnings from the assets that the common stockholder has provided to the company will have to go to make up the deficiency to the long-term creditors or to the preferred stockholders, and the common stockholder will be left with a smaller return than would otherwise have been earned. Under these circumstances, financial leverage is said to be **negative.**

The Impact of Income Taxes Long-term debt and preferred stock are not equally efficient in generating positive leverage. The reason is that interest on long-term debt is tax deductible, whereas preferred dividends are not. This makes long-term debt a much more effective source of positive leverage than preferred stock.

To illustrate this point, assume that a company is considering three ways of financing a $100,000 expansion of its assets:

1. $100,000 from an issue of common stock.
2. $50,000 from an issue of common stock, and $50,000 from an issue of preferred stock bearing a dividend rate of 8 percent.
3. $50,000 from an issue of common stock, and $50,000 from an issue of bonds bearing an interest rate of 8 percent.

Assuming that the company can earn an additional $15,000 each year before interest and taxes as a result of the expansion, the operating results under each of the three alternatives are shown in Exhibit 18–6.

If the entire $100,000 is raised from an issue of common stock, then the return to the common stockholders will be only 10.5 percent, as shown under alternative 1 in the exhibit. If half of the funds are raised from an issue of preferred stock, then the return to the common stockholders increases to 13 percent, due to the positive effects of leverage. However, if half of the

EXHIBIT 18–6
Leverage from Preferred Stock and Long-Term Debt

	Alternatives: $100,000 Issue of Securities		
	Alternative 1: $100,000 Common Stock	**Alternative 2: $50,000 Common Stock; $50,000 Preferred Stock**	**Alternative 3: $50,000 Common Stock; $50,000 Bonds**
Earnings before interest and taxes	$ 15,000	$15,000	$15,000
Deduct interest expense (8% × $50,000)	—	—	4,000
Net income before taxes	15,000	15,000	11,000
Deduct income taxes (30%)	4,500	4,500	3,300
Net income	10,500	10,500	7,700
Deduct preferred dividends (8% × $50,000)	—	4,000	—
Net income remaining for common *(a)*	$ 10,500	$ 6,500	$ 7,700
Common stockholders' equity *(b)*	$100,000	$50,000	$50,000
Return on common stockholders' equity, *(a)* ÷ *(b)*	10.5%	13.0%	15.4%

funds are raised from an issue of bonds, then the return to the common stockholders jumps to 15.4 percent, as shown under alternative 3. Thus, long-term debt is much more efficient in generating positive leverage than is preferred stock. The reason is that the interest expense on long-term debt is tax deductible, whereas the dividends on preferred stock are not.

The Desirability of Leverage The leverage principle amply illustrates that having some debt in the capital structure can substantially benefit the common stockholder. For this reason, most companies today try to keep a certain level of debt within the organization—a level at least equal to that which is considered to be "normal" within the industry. Occasionally one comes across a company that boasts of having no debt outstanding. Although there may be good reasons for a company to have no debt, in view of the benefits that can be gained from positive leverage the possibility always exists that such a company is shortchanging its stockholders. As a practical matter, many companies, such as commercial banks and other financial institutions, rely heavily on leverage to provide an attractive return on their common shares.

Book Value per Share

Another statistic frequently used in attempting to assess the well-being of the common stockholder is book value per share. The **book value per share** measures the amount that would be distributed to holders of each share of common stock if all assets were sold at their balance sheet carrying amounts and if all creditors were paid off. Thus, book value per share is based entirely on historical costs. The formula for computing it is:

$$\frac{\text{Common stockholders' equity (Total stockholders' equity} - \text{Preferred stock)}}{\text{Number of common shares outstanding}} = \text{Book value per share}$$

The book value of Brickey Electronics' common stock is:

$$\frac{\$17{,}000{,}000 - \$2{,}000{,}000}{500{,}000 \text{ shares}} = \$30 \qquad (8)$$

If this book value is compared with the $40 market value that we have assumed in connection with the Brickey Electronics stock, then the stock appears to be somewhat overpriced. It is not necessarily true, however, that a market value in excess of book value is an indication of overpricing. As we discussed earlier, market prices are geared toward future earnings and dividends. Book value, by contrast, purports to reflect nothing about the future earnings potential of a firm. As a practical matter, it is actually geared to the *past* in that it reflects the balance sheet carrying value of already completed transactions.

Of what use, then, is book value? Unfortunately, the answer must be that it is of limited use so far as being a dynamic tool of analysis is concerned. It probably finds its greatest application in situations where large amounts of liquid assets are being held in anticipation of liquidation. Occasionally some use is also made of book value per share in attempting to set a price on the shares of closely held corporations.

RATIO ANALYSIS—THE SHORT-TERM CREDITOR

Although the short-term creditor is always well advised to keep an eye on the fortunes of the common stockholder, as expressed in the ratios of the preceding section, the short-term creditor's focus of attention is normally channeled in another direction. The short-term creditor is concerned with the near-term prospects of having obligations paid on time. As such, he or she is much more interested in cash flows and in working capital management than in how much accounting net income a company is reporting.

Working Capital

The excess of current assets over current liabilities is known as **working capital.** The working capital for Brickey Electronics is given below:

	19x2	19x1	
Current assets	$15,500,000	$16,470,000	
Current liabilities	7,000,000	5,000,000	
Working capital	$ 8,500,000	$11,470,000	(9)

The amount of working capital available to a firm is of considerable interest to short-term creditors, *since it represents assets financed from long-term capital sources that do not require near-term repayment.* Therefore, the greater the working capital, the greater is the cushion of protection available to short-term creditors and the greater is the assurance that short-term debts will be paid when due.

Although it is always comforting to short-term creditors to see a large working capital balance, their joy becomes full only after they have been satisfied that the working capital is turning over at an acceptable rate of speed, and that their obligations could be paid even under stringent operating conditions. The reason is that a large working capital balance standing by itself is no assurance that debts will be paid when due. Rather than being a sign of strength, a large working capital balance may simply mean that stagnant or obsolete inventory is building up. Therefore, to put the working capital figure into proper perspective, it must be supplemented with other analytical work. The following four ratios (the current ratio, the acid-test ratio, the accounts receivable turnover, and the inventory turnover) should all be used in connection with an analysis of working capital.

Current Ratio

The elements involved in the computation of working capital are frequently expressed in ratio form. A company's current assets divided by its current liabilities is known as the **current ratio:**

$$\frac{\text{Current assets}}{\text{Current liabilities}} = \text{Current ratio}$$

For Brickey Electronics, the current ratio for 19x1 and 19x2 would be:

19x2	**19x1**	
$\frac{\$15{,}500{,}000}{\$7{,}000{,}000} = 2.21 \text{ to } 1$	$\frac{\$16{,}470{,}000}{\$5{,}000{,}000} = 3.29 \text{ to } 1$	(10)

Although widely regarded as a measure of short-term debt-paying ability, the current ratio must be interpreted with a great deal of care. A *declining* ratio, as above, might be a sign of a deteriorating financial condition. On the other hand, it might be the result of a paring out of obsolete inventories or other stagnant assets. An *improving* ratio might be the result of an unwise stockpiling of inventory, or it might point up an improving financial situation. In short, the current ratio is useful, but tricky to interpret. To avoid a blunder, the analyst must take a hard look at the individual items of assets and liabilities involved.

The general rule of thumb calls for a current ratio of 2 to 1. This rule, of course, is subject to many exceptions, depending on the industry and the firm involved. Some industries can operate quite successfully on a current ratio of slightly over 1 to 1. The adequacy of a current ratio depends heavily on the *composition* of the assets involved. For example, although Company X and Company Y below both have current ratios of 2 to 1, one could hardly say that they are in comparable financial condition. Company Y most certainly will have difficulty in meeting its obligations as they come due.

	Company	
	X	**Y**
Current assets:		
Cash	$ 25,000	$ 2,000
Accounts receivable	60,000	8,000
Inventory	85,000	160,000
Prepaid expenses	5,000	5,000
Total current assets	$175,000	$175,000
Current liabilities	$ 87,500	$ 87,500
Current ratio	2 to 1	2 to 1

Acid-Test Ratio

A much more rigorous test of a company's ability to meet its short-term debts can be found in the **acid-test,** or **quick, ratio.** Merchandise inventory and prepaid expenses are excluded from the total of current assets, leaving only the more liquid (or "quick") assets to be divided by current liabilities.

$$\frac{\text{Cash + Marketable securities + Current receivables*}}{\text{Current liabilities}} = \text{Acid-test ratio}$$

* This would include both accounts receivable and any short-term notes receivable.

The acid-test ratio is designed to measure how well a company can meet its obligations without having to liquidate or depend too heavily on its inventory. Since inventory is not an immediate source of cash and may not even be salable in times of economic stress, it is generally felt that to be properly protected each dollar of liabilities should be backed by at least $1 of quick assets. Thus, an acid-test ratio of 1 to 1 is broadly viewed as being adequate in many firms.

The acid-test ratios for Brickey Electronics for 19x1 and 19x2 are given below:

	19x2	19x1	
Cash	$1,200,000	$2,350,000	
Accounts receivable . . .	6,000,000	4,000,000	
Total quick assets	$7,200,000	$6,350,000	
Current liabilities.	$7,000,000	$5,000,000	
Acid-test ratio	1.03 to 1	1.27 to 1	(11)

Although Brickey Electronics has an acid-test ratio for 19x2 that is within the acceptable range, an analyst might be concerned about several disquieting trends revealed in the company's balance sheet. Notice that short-term debts are rising, while the cash position seems to be deteriorating. Perhaps the weakened cash position is a result of the greatly expanded volume of accounts receivable. One wonders why the accounts receivable have been allowed to increase so rapidly in so brief a time.

In short, as with the current ratio, to be used intelligently the acid-test ratio must be interpreted with one eye on its basic components.

Accounts Receivable Turnover

The **accounts receivable turnover** is a measure of how many times a company's accounts receivable have been turned into cash during the year. It is frequently used in conjunction with an analysis of working capital, since a smooth flow from accounts receivable into cash is an important indicator of the "quality" of a company's working capital and is critical to its ability to operate. The accounts receivable turnover is computed by dividing sales on account by the average accounts receivable balance for the year.

$$\frac{\text{Sales on account}}{\text{Average accounts receivable balance}} = \text{Accounts receivable turnover}$$

The accounts receivable turnover for Brickey Electronics for 19x2 is:

$$\frac{\text{Sales on account}}{\text{Average accounts receivable balance}} = \frac{\$52{,}000{,}000}{\$5{,}000{,}000^*} = 10.4 \text{ times} \quad (12)$$

* $4,000,000 + $6,000,000 = $10,000,000; $10,000,000 ÷ 2 = $5,000,000 average.

The turnover figure can then be divided into 365 to determine the average number of days being taken to collect an account (known as the **average collection period**).

$$\frac{\text{365 days}}{\text{Accounts receivable turnover}} = \frac{365}{\text{10.4 times}} = \text{35 days} \quad (13)$$

Whether the average of 35 days taken to collect an account is good or bad depends on the credit terms Brickey Electronics is offering its customers. If the credit terms are 30 days, then a 35-day average collection period would be viewed as being very good. Most customers will tend to withhold payment for as long as the credit terms will allow and may even go over a few days. This factor, added to the ever-present few slow accounts, can cause the average collection period to exceed normal credit terms by a week to 10 days and should not be a matter for too much alarm.

On the other hand, if the company's credit terms are 10 days, then a 35-day average collection period may be a cause for some concern. The long collection period may be a result of the presence of many old accounts of doubtful collectibility, or it may be a result of poor day-to-day credit management. The firm may be making sales with inadequate credit checks on the companies to which the sales are being made, or perhaps no follow-ups are being made on slow accounts.

Inventory Turnover

The **inventory turnover ratio** measures how many times a company's inventory has been sold during the year. It is computed by dividing the cost of goods sold by the average level of inventory on hand:

$$\frac{\text{Cost of goods sold}}{\text{Average inventory balance}} = \text{Inventory turnover}$$

The average inventory figure is usually computed by taking the average of the beginning and ending inventory figures. Since Brickey Electronics has a beginning inventory figure of $10,000,000 and an ending inventory figure of $8,000,000, its average inventory for the year would be $9,000,000. The company's inventory turnover for 19x2 would be:

$$\frac{\text{Cost of goods sold}}{\text{Average inventory balance}} = \frac{\$36{,}000{,}000}{\$9{,}000{,}000} = \text{4 times} \quad (14)$$

The number of days being taken to sell the entire inventory one time (called the **average sale period**) can be computed by dividing 365 by the inventory turnover figure:

$$\frac{\text{365 days}}{\text{Inventory turnover}} = \frac{365}{\text{4 times}} = 91\tfrac{1}{4} \text{ days} \quad (15)$$

Grocery stores tend to turn their inventory over very quickly, perhaps as often as every 12 to 15 days. On the other hand, jewelry stores tend to turn their inventory over very slowly, perhaps only a couple of times each year.

If a firm has a turnover that is much slower than the average for its industry, then there may be obsolete goods on hand, or inventory stocks may be needlessly high. Excessive inventories simply tie up funds that could be used elsewhere in operations. Managers sometimes argue that they must buy in very large quantities in order to take advantage of the best discounts being offered. But these discounts must be carefully weighed against the added costs of insurance, taxes, financing, and risks of obsolescence and deterioration that result from carrying added inventories.

An inventory turnover that is substantially faster than the average is usually an indication that inventory levels are inadequate.

RATIO ANALYSIS—THE LONG-TERM CREDITOR

The position of long-term creditors differs from that of short-term creditors in that they are concerned with both the near-term *and* the long-term ability of a firm to meet its commitments. They are concerned with the near term since whatever interest they may be entitled to is normally paid on a current basis. They are concerned with the long term from the point of view of the eventual retirement of their holdings.

Since the long-term creditor is usually faced with somewhat greater risks than the short-term creditor, firms are often required to make various restrictive covenants for the long-term creditor's protection. Examples of such restrictive covenants would include the maintenance of minimum working capital levels and restrictions on payment of dividends to common stockholders. Although these restrictive covenants are in widespread use, they must be viewed as being a poor second to *prospective earnings* from the point of view of assessing protection and safety. Creditors do not want to go to court to collect their claims; they would much prefer staking the safety of their claims for interest and eventual repayment of principal on an orderly and consistent flow of funds from operations.

Times Interest Earned Ratio

The most common measure of the ability of a firm's operations to provide protection to the long-term creditor is the **times interest earned ratio.** It is computed by dividing earnings *before* interest expense and income taxes by the yearly interest charges that must be met:

$$\frac{\text{Earnings before interest expense and income taxes*}}{\text{Interest expense}} = \text{Times interest earned}$$

* This amount is the same as *net operating income* on many financial statements.

For Brickey Electronics, the times interest earned ratio for 19x2 would be:

$$\frac{\$3{,}140{,}000}{\$640{,}000} = 4.9 \text{ times} \qquad (16)$$

Earnings before income taxes must be used in the computation since interest expense deductions come *before* income taxes are computed. Income taxes are secondary to interest payments in that the latter have first claim on earnings. Only those earnings remaining after all interest charges have been provided for are subject to income taxes.

Various rules of thumb exist to gauge the adequacy of a firm's times interest earned ratio. Generally, earnings are viewed as adequate to protect long-term creditors if the times interest earned ratio is 2 or more. Before making a final judgment, however, it would be necessary to look at a firm's long-run *trend* of earnings, then decide how vulnerable the firm is to cyclical changes in the economy.

Debt-to-Equity Ratio

Although long-term creditors look primarily to prospective earnings and budgeted cash flows in attempting to gauge the risk of their position, they cannot ignore the importance of keeping a reasonable balance between the portion of assets being provided by creditors and the portion of assets being provided by the stockholders of a firm. This balance is measured by the **debt-to-equity ratio:**

$$\frac{\text{Total liabilities}}{\text{Stockholders' equity}} = \text{Debt-to-equity ratio}$$

	19x2	19x1	
Total liabilities	$14,500,000	$13,000,000 *(a)*	
Stockholders' equity	17,000,000	15,970,000 *(b)*	
Debt-to-equity ratio, *(a)* ÷ *(b)*	0.85 to 1	0.81 to 1	(17)

The debt-to-equity ratio indicates the amount of assets being provided by creditors for each dollar of assets being provided by the owners of a company. In 19x1, creditors of Brickey Electronics were providing 81 cents of assets for each $1 of assets being provided by stockholders; the figure increased only slightly to 85 cents by 19x2.

It should come as no surprise that creditors would like the debt-to-equity ratio to be relatively low. The lower the ratio, the larger is the amount of assets being provided by the owners of a company and the greater is the buffer of protection to creditors. By contrast, common stockholders would like the ratio to be relatively high, since through leverage common stockholders can benefit from the assets being provided by creditors.

In most industries, norms have developed over the years that serve as guides to firms in their decisions as to the "right" amount of debt to include in the capital structure. Different industries face different risks. For this reason, the level of debt that is appropriate for firms in one industry is not necessarily a guide to the level of debt that is appropriate for firms in a different industry.

SUMMARY OF RATIOS AND SOURCES OF COMPARATIVE RATIO DATA

As an aid to the reader, Exhibit 18–7 contains a summary of the ratios discussed in this chapter. Included in the exhibit are the formula for each ratio and a summary comment on each ratio's significance to the manager.

EXHIBIT 18–7
Summary of Ratios

Ratio	Formula	Significance
Earnings per share (of common stock)	(Net income − Preferred dividends) ÷ Number of common shares outstanding	Tends to have an effect on the market price per share, as reflected in the price-earnings ratio
Fully diluted earnings per share	Net income ÷ (Number of common shares outstanding + Common stock equivalent of convertible securities)	Shows the potential effect on earnings per share of converting convertible securities into common stock
Price-earnings ratio	Market price per share ÷ Earnings per share	An index of whether a stock is relatively cheap or relatively expensive in relation to current earnings
Dividend payout ratio	Dividends per share ÷ Earnings per share	An index showing whether a company pays out most of its earnings in dividends or reinvests the earnings internally
Dividend yield ratio	Dividends per share ÷ Market price per share	Shows the dividend return being provided by a stock, which can be compared to the return being provided by other stocks
Return on total assets	Net income + [Interest expense × (1 − Tax rate)] ÷ Average total assets	Measure of how well assets have been employed by management
Return on common stockholders' equity	(Net income − Preferred dividends) ÷ Average common stockholders' equity (Average total stockholders' equity − Preferred stock)	When compared to the return on total assets, measures the extent to which financial leverage is being employed for or against the common stockholders
Book value per share	Common stockholders' equity (Total stockholders' equity − Preferred stock) ÷ Number of common shares outstanding	Measures the amount that would be distributed to holders of each share of common stock if all assets were sold at their balance sheet carrying amounts and if all creditors were paid off
Working capital	Current assets − Current liabilities	Represents current assets financed from long-term capital sources that do not require near-term repayment
Current ratio	Current assets ÷ Current liabilities	Test of short-term debt-paying ability
Acid-test (quick) ratio	(Cash + Marketable securities + Current receivables) ÷ Current liabilities	Test of short-term debt-paying ability without having to rely on inventory
Accounts receivable turnover	Sales on account ÷ Average accounts receivable balance	Measure of how many times a company's accounts receivable have been turned into cash during the year
Average collection period (age of receivables)	365 days ÷ Accounts receivable turnover	Measure of the average number of days taken to collect an account receivable
Inventory turnover	Cost of goods sold ÷ Average inventory balance	Measure of how many times a company's inventory has been sold during the year
Average sale period (turnover in days)	365 days ÷ Inventory turnover	Measure of the average number of days taken to sell the inventory one time
Times interest earned	Earnings before interest expense and income taxes ÷ Interest expense	Measure of the likelihood that creditors will continue to receive their interest payments
Debt-to-equity ratio	Total liabilities ÷ Stockholders' equity	Measure of the amount of assets being provided by creditors for each dollar of assets being provided by the stockholders

EXHIBIT 18–8
Published Sources of Financial Ratios

Source	Content
Almanac of Business and Industrial Financial Ratios. Prentice-Hall. Published annually.	An exhaustive source that contains common-size income statements and financial ratios by industry and by size of companies within each industry.
Annual Statement Studies. Robert Morris Associates. Published annually.	A widely used publication that contains common-size statements and financial ratios on individual companies. The companies are arranged by industry.
Moody's Industrial Manual and *Moody's Bank and Finance Manual*. Dunn & Bradstreet. Published annually.	An exhaustive source that contains financial ratios on all companies listed on the New York Stock Exchange, the American Stock Exchange, and regional American exchanges.
Key Business Ratios. Dun & Bradstreet. Published annually.	Fourteen commonly used financial ratios are computed for major industry groupings. This source contains data on over 800 lines of business.
Standard & Poor's Industry Survey. Standard & Poor's. Published annually.	Various statistics, including some financial ratios, are provided by industry and on leading companies within each industry grouping.

Exhibit 18–8 contains a listing of published sources that provide comparative ratio data organized by industry. These sources are used extensively by managers, investors, and analysts in doing comparative analyses and in attempting to assess the well-being of companies.

SUMMARY

The data contained in financial statements represent a quantitative summary of a firm's operations and activities. If a manager is skillful at taking these statements apart, he or she can learn much about a company's strengths, its weaknesses, its developing problems, its operating efficiency, its profitability, and so forth.

Many analytical techniques are available to assist managers in taking financial statements apart and in assessing the direction and importance of trends and changes. In this chapter, we have discussed three such analytical techniques—dollar and percentage changes in statements, common-size statements, and ratio analysis. The reader should refer to Exhibit 18-7 for a detailed listing of the ratios that we have discussed. This listing also contains a brief statement as to the significance of each ratio involved.

KEY TERMS FOR REVIEW

(Note: Definitions and formulas for all financial ratios are given in Exhibit 18–7. These definitions and formulas are not repeated here.)

Common-size statements A statement that shows the items appearing on it in percentage form as well as in dollar form. On the income statement, the percentages are based on total sales; on the balance sheet, the percentages are based on total assets or total equities. (p. 769)

Conversion feature The ability to exchange either bonds or preferred stock for common stock at some future time. (p. 774)

Financial leverage The financing of assets in a company with funds that have been acquired from creditors or from preferred stockholders at a fixed rate of return. (p. 777)

Horizontal analysis A side-by-side comparison of two or more years' financial statements. (p. 767)

Negative financial leverage A situation in which the fixed return to a company's creditors and preferred stockholders is greater than the return on total assets. In this situation, the return on common stockholders' equity will be *less* than the return on total assets. (p. 778)

Positive financial leverage A situation in which the fixed return to a company's creditors and preferred stockholders is less than the return on total assets. In this situation, the return on common stockholders' equity will be *greater* than the return on total assets. (p. 777)

Trend percentages The expression of several years' financial data in percentage form in terms of a base year. (p. 768)

Vertical analysis The presentation of a company's financial statements in common-size form. (p. 769)

QUESTIONS

18–1 What three analytical techniques are used in financial statement analysis?

18–2 Distinguish between horizontal and vertical analysis of financial statement data.

18–3 What is the basic objective in looking at trends in financial ratios and other data? Rather than looking at trends, to what other standard of comparison might a statement user turn?

18–4 In financial analysis, why does the analyst compute financial ratios rather than simply studying raw financial data? What dangers are there in the use of ratios?

18–5 What pitfalls are involved in computing earnings per share? How can these pitfalls be avoided?

18–6 What is meant by reporting an extraordinary item on the income statement net of its tax effect? Give an example of both an extraordinary gain and an extraordinary loss net of its tax effect. Assume a tax rate of 30 percent.

18–7 Assume that two companies in the same industry have equal earnings. Why might these companies have different price-earnings ratios? If a company has a price earnings ratio of 20 and reports earnings per share for the current year of $4, at what price would you expect to find the stock selling on the market?

18–8 Armcor, Inc., is in a rapidly growing technological industry. Would you expect the company to have a high or a low dividend payout ratio?

18–9 Distinguish between a manager's *financing* and *operating* responsibilities. Which of these responsibilities is the return on total assets ratio designed to measure?

18–10 What is meant by the dividend yield on a common stock investment? In computing dividend yield, why do you use current market value rather than original purchase price?

18–11 What is meant by the term *financial leverage?*

18–12 The president of a medium-sized plastics company was recently quoted in a business journal as stating, "We haven't had a dollar of interest-paying debt in over 10 years. Not many companies can say that." As a stockholder in this firm, how would you feel about its policy of not taking on interest-paying debt?

18–13 Why is it more difficult to obtain positive financial leverage from preferred stock than from long-term debt?

18–14 If a stock's market value exceeds its book value, then the stock is overpriced. Do you agree? Explain.

18–15 Weaver Company experiences a great deal of seasonal variation in its business activities. The company's high point in business activity is in June; its low point is in January. During which month would you expect the current ratio to be highest? At what point would you advise the company to end its fiscal year? Why?

18–16 A company seeking a line of credit at a bank was turned down. Among other things, the bank stated that the company's 2 to 1 current ratio was not adequate. Give reasons why a 2 to 1 current ratio might not be adequate.

18–17 If you were a long-term creditor of a firm, would you be more interested in the firm's long-term or short-term debt-paying ability? Why?

18–18 A young college student once complained to the author, "The reason that corporations are such big spenders is that Uncle Sam always picks up part of the tab." What did he mean by this statement?

EXERCISES

E18–1 A comparative income statement is given below for Ryder Company:

RYDER COMPANY
Comparative Income Statement
For the Years Ended June 30, 19x2, and 19x1

	19x2	19x1
Sales	$5,000,000	$4,000,000
Less cost of goods sold	3,160,000	2,400,000
Gross margin	1,840,000	1,600,000
Selling expenses	900,000	700,000
Administrative expenses	680,000	584,000
Total expenses	1,580,000	1,284,000
Net operating income	260,000	316,000
Interest expense	70,000	40,000
Net income before taxes	$ 190,000	$ 276,000

The president is concerned that net income is down in 19x2 even though sales have increased during the year. The president is also concerned that administrative expenses have increased, since the company made a concerted effort during 19x2 to pare "fat" out of the organization.

Required

1. Express each year's income statement in common-size percentages. Carry computations to one decimal place.
2. Comment briefly on the changes between the two years.

E18–2 Noble Company's current assets, current liabilities, and sales have been reported as follows over the last five years:

	19x5	19x4	19x3	19x2	19x1
Sales	$2,250,000	$2,160,000	$2,070,000	$1,980,000	$1,800,000
Cash	$ 30,000	$ 40,000	$ 48,000	$ 65,000	$ 50,000
Accounts receivable	570,000	510,000	405,000	345,000	300,000
Inventory	750,000	720,000	690,000	660,000	600,000
Total	$1,350,000	$1,270,000	$1,143,000	$1,070,000	$ 950,000
Current liabilities	$ 640,000	$ 580,000	$ 520,000	$ 440,000	$ 400,000

Required

1. Express the asset, liability, and sales data in trend percentages. (Show percentages for each item.) Use 19x1 as the base year, and carry computations to one decimal place.
2. Comment on the results of your analysis.

E18–3 Recent financial statements for Madison Company are given below:

MADISON COMPANY
Balance Sheet
June 30, 19x4

Assets

Current assets:		
Cash		$ 21,000
Accounts receivable, net		160,000
Merchandise inventory		300,000
Prepaid expenses		9,000
Total current assets		490,000
Property and equipment, net		810,000
Total assets		$1,300,000

Liabilities and Stockholders' Equity

Liabilities:		
Current liabilities		$ 200,000
Bonds payable, 10%		300,000
Total liabilities		500,000
Stockholders' equity:		
Common stock, $5 par value	$100,000	
Retained earnings	700,000	
Total stockholders' equity		800,000
Total liabilities and stockholders' equity		$1,300,000

MADISON COMPANY
Income Statement
For the Year Ended June 30, 19x4

Sales	$2,100,000
Less cost of goods sold	1,260,000
Gross margin	840,000
Less operating expenses	660,000
Net operating income	180,000
Less interest expense	30,000
Net income before taxes	150,000
Less income taxes	45,000
Net income	$ 105,000

Account balances at the beginning of the company's fiscal year (July 1, 19x3) were: accounts receivable, $140,000; and inventory, $260,000. All sales were on account.

Required

Compute financial ratios as follows:

1. Current ratio. (Industry average: 2.3 to 1.)
2. Acid-test ratio. (Industry average: 1.2 to 1.)
3. Accounts receivable turnover in days. (Terms: 2/10, n/30.)
4. Inventory turnover in days. (Industry average: 72 days.)
5. Debt-to-equity ratio.
6. Times interest earned.
7. Book value per share. (Market price: $63.)

E18–4 Refer to the financial statements for Madison Company in Exercise 18–3. In addition to the data in these statements, assume that Madison Company paid dividends of $3.15 per share during the year ended June 30, 19x4. Also assume that the company's common stock had a market price of $63 per share on June 30.

Required Compute the following:

1. Earnings per share.
2. Dividend payout ratio.
3. Dividend yield ratio.
4. Price-earnings ratio. (Industry average: 10.)

E18–5 Refer to the financial statements for Madison Company in Exercise 18–3. Assets at the beginning of the year totaled $1,100,000, and the stockholders' equity totaled $725,000.

Required Compute the following:

1. Return on total assets.
2. Return on common stockholders' equity. (Industry average: 12.5 percent.)
3. Was financial leverage positive or negative for the year? Explain.

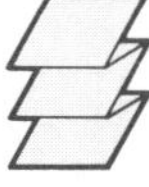

E18–6 Rightway Products had a current ratio of 2.5 to 1 on June 30 of the current year. On that date, the company's assets were:

Cash		$ 80,000
Accounts receivable	$530,000	
Less allowance for doubtful accounts	70,000	460,000
Inventory		750,000
Prepaid expenses		10,000
Plant and equipment, net		1,900,000
Total assets		$3,200,000

Required

1. What was the company's working capital on June 30?
2. What was the company's acid-test ratio on June 30?
3. The company paid an account payable of $100,000 immediately after June 30.
   a. What effect did this transaction have on working capital? Show computations.
   b. What effect did this transaction have on the current ratio? Show computations.

E18–7 Midwest Products, Inc., reported income as follows for the past year:

MIDWEST PRODUCTS, INC.
Income Statement
For the Year Ended May 31, 19x9

Sales	$800,000
Cost of goods sold	500,000
Gross margin	300,000
Operating expenses	210,000
Net income before taxes	90,000
Income taxes (30%)	27,000
Net income	$ 63,000

Included in the operating expenses above is a $30,000 loss resulting from a fire in the company's warehouse.

Required

1. Redo the company's income statement by showing the loss net of tax.
2. Assume that the company has 20,000 shares of common stock outstanding. Compute the earnings per share as it should appear in the company's annual report to its stockholders.

E18–8 Selected financial data from the September 30, 19x7, year-end statements of Kosanka Company are given below:

Total assets	$5,000,000
Long-term debt (12% interest rate)	750,000
Preferred stock, $100 par, 7%	800,000
Total stockholders' equity	3,100,000
Interest paid on long-term debt	90,000
Net income	470,000

Total assets at the beginning of the year were $4,800,000; total stockholders' equity was $2,900,000. There has been no change in the preferred stock during the year. The company's tax rate is 30 percent.

Required

1. Compute the return on total assets.
2. Compute the return on common stockholders' equity.
3. Is the company's financial leverage positive or negative? Explain.

PROBLEMS

P18–9 **Ratio Analysis and Common-Size Statements** Modern Building Supply sells various building materials to retail outlets. The company has just approached Linden State Bank requesting a $300,000 loan to strengthen the Cash account and to pay certain pressing short-term obligations. The company's financial statements for the most recent two years follow:

MODERN BUILDING SUPPLY
Comparative Balance Sheet

	This Year	Last Year
Assets		
Current assets:		
Cash	$ 90,000	$ 200,000
Marketable securities	—	50,000
Accounts receivable, net	650,000	400,000
Inventory	1,300,000	800,000
Prepaid expenses	20,000	20,000
Total current assets	2,060,000	1,470,000
Plant and equipment, net	1,940,000	1,830,000
Total assets	$4,000,000	$3,300,000
Liabilities and Stockholders' Equity		
Liabilities:		
Current liabilities	$1,100,000	$ 600,000
Bonds payable, 12%	750,000	750,000
Total liabilities	1,850,000	1,350,000
Stockholders' equity:		
Preferred stock, $50 par, 8%	200,000	200,000
Common stock, $10 par	500,000	500,000
Retained earnings	1,450,000	1,250,000
Total stockholders' equity	2,150,000	1,950,000
Total liabilities and stockholders' equity	$4,000,000	$3,300,000

MODERN BUILDING SUPPLY
Comparative Income Statement

	This Year	Last Year
Sales	$7,000,000	$6,000,000
Less cost of goods sold	5,400,000	4,800,000
Gross margin	1,600,000	1,200,000
Less operating expenses	970,000	710,000
Net operating income	630,000	490,000
Less interest expense	90,000	90,000
Net income before taxes	540,000	400,000
Less income taxes (40%)	216,000	160,000
Net income	324,000	240,000
Dividends paid:		
Preferred dividends	16,000	16,000
Common dividends	108,000	90,000
Total dividends paid	124,000	106,000
Net income retained	200,000	164,000
Retained earnings, beginning of year	1,250,000	1,086,000
Retained earnings, end of year	$1,450,000	$1,250,000

During the past year, the company has expanded the number of lines that it carries in order to stimulate sales and increase profits. It has also moved aggressively to acquire new customers. Sales terms are 2/10, n/30. All sales are on account.

Assume that the following ratios are typical of firms in the building supply industry:

Current ratio	2.5 to 1
Acid-test ratio	1.2 to 1
Average age of receivables	18 days
Inventory turnover in days	50 days
Debt-to-equity ratio	0.75 to 1
Times interest earned	6.0 times
Return on total assets	10%
Price-earnings ratio	9
Net income as a percentage of sales	4%

Required

1. Linden State Bank is uncertain whether the loan should be made. To assist it in making a decision, you have been asked to compute the following ratios for both this year and last year:
   a. The amount of working capital.
   b. The current ratio.
   c. The acid-test ratio.
   d. The average age of receivables. (The accounts receivable at the beginning of last year totaled $350,000.)
   e. The inventory turnover in days. (The inventory at the beginning of last year totaled $720,000.)
   f. The debt-to-equity ratio.
   g. The number of times interest was earned.
2. For both this year and last year (carry computations to one decimal place):
   a. Present the balance sheet in common-size form.
   b. Present the income statement in common-size form down through net income.
3. From your analysis in (1) and (2) above, what problems or strengths do you see existing in Modern Building Supply? Make a recommendation as to whether the loan should be approved.

P18–10 Investor Ratios; Analysis of Whether to Retain or Sell Stock Refer to the financial statements and other data in Problem 18–9. Assume that you have just inherited several hundred shares of Modern Building Supply stock. Not being acquainted with the company, you decide to do some analytical work before making a decision about whether to retain or sell the stock you have inherited.

Required

1. You decide first to assess the well-being of the common stockholders. For both this year and last year, compute:
   a. The earnings per share.
   b. The fully diluted earnings per share. The preferred stock is convertible into common stock at the rate of 2.5 shares of common for each share of preferred. The bonds are not convertible.
   c. The dividend yield ratio for common. The company's common stock is currently selling for $45 per share; last year it sold for $36 per share.
   d. The dividend payout ratio for common.
   e. The price-earnings ratio. How do investors regard Modern Building Supply as compared to other firms in the industry? Explain.
   f. The book value per share of common. Does the difference between market value and book value suggest that the stock at its current price is too high? Explain.
2. You decide next to assess the rate of return that the company is generating. Compute the following for both this year and last year:
   a. The return on total assets. (Total assets at the beginning of last year were $2,700,000.)
   b. The return on common equity. (Stockholders' equity at the beginning of last year was $1,786,000.)
   c. Is the company's financial leverage positive or negative? Explain.
3. Based on your analytical work (and assuming that you have no immediate need for cash), would you retain or sell the stock you have inherited? Explain.

P18–11 Effect of Leverage on the Return on Common Equity Vince Zolta and several other investors are in the process of organizing a new company to produce and distribute a household cleaning product. Mr. Zolta and his associates feel that $500,000 would be adequate to finance the new company's operations, and the group is studying three methods of raising this amount of money. The three methods are:

Method A: All $500,000 obtained through issue of common stock.

Method B: $250,000 obtained through issue of common stock and the other $250,000 obtained through issue of $100 par value, 10 percent preferred stock.

Method C: $250,000 obtained through issue of common stock and the other $250,000 obtained through issue of bonds carrying an interest rate of 10 percent.

Mr. Zolta and his associates are confident that the company can earn $100,000 each year before interest and taxes. The tax rate is 30 percent.

Required

1. Assuming that Mr. Zolta and his associates are correct in their earnings estimate, compute the net income that would go to the common stockholders under each of the three financing methods listed above.
2. Using the income data computed in (1) above, compute the return on common equity under each of the three methods.
3. Why do methods B and C provide a greater return on common equity than does method A? Why does method C provide a greater return on common equity than method B?

P18–12 Effect of Transactions on Various Ratios Selected amounts from Reingold Company's December 31, 19x1, balance sheet follow:

Cash	$ 70,000
Marketable securities	12,000
Accounts receivable, net	350,000
Inventory	460,000
Prepaid expenses	8,000
Plant and equipment, net	950,000
Accounts payable	200,000
Accrued liabilities	60,000
Notes due within one year	100,000
Bonds payable in five years	140,000

During the next year (19x2), the company completed the following transactions:

x. Purchased inventory on account, $50,000.
a. Declared a cash dividend, $30,000.
b. Paid accounts payable, $100,000.
c. Collected cash on accounts receivable, $80,000.
d. Purchased equipment for cash, $75,000.
e. Paid a cash dividend previously declared, $30,000.
f. Borrowed cash on a short-term note with the bank, $60,000.
g. Sold inventory costing $70,000 for $100,000, on account.
h. Wrote off uncollectible accounts in the amount of $10,000.
i. Sold marketable securities costing $12,000 for cash, $9,000.
j. Issued additional shares of capital stock for cash, $200,000.
k. Paid off all short-term notes due, $160,000.

Required

1. Compute the following amounts and ratios as of December 31, 19x1:
   a. Working capital.
   b. Current ratio.
   c. Acid-test ratio.
2. For 19x2, indicate the effect of each of the transactions given above on working capital, the current ratio, and the acid-test ratio. Give the effect in terms of increase, decrease, or none. Item (*x*) is given below as an example of the format to use:

	The Effect on		
Transaction	**Working Capital**	**Current Ratio**	**Acid-Test Ratio**
(*x*) Purchased inventory on account	None	Decrease	Decrease

P18–13 **Ratio Analysis; Comparison of Two Companies** Company A and Company B are in the same industry. The current year-end balance sheets for the two companies are given below:

Comparative Balance Sheets
December 31, 19x5

	Company	
	A	**B**
Cash	$ 15,000	$ 10,000
Accounts receivable	49,500	89,500
Inventory	55,000	117,000
Plant and equipment, net	150,000	240,000
Total assets	$269,500	$456,500
Current liabilities	$ 56,900	$101,000
Bonds payable	100,000	100,000
Preferred stock, 6%, $100 par	35,000	40,000
Common stock, $10 par	50,000	100,000
Retained earnings	27,600	115,500
Total liabilities and stockholders' equity	$269,500	$456,500

Selected data from the companies' current year-end income statements and other selected data follow:

Data from the Current Year-End Income Statements

	Company	
	A	B
Sales	$500,000	$700,000
Cost of goods sold	325,000	455,000
Interest expense	7,500	8,000
Net income before taxes	30,000	45,000
Net income	18,000	27,000
Tax rate	40%	40%

Beginning-of-the-Year-Data

	Company	
	A	B
Accounts receivable	$ 45,500	$ 85,500
Inventory	51,000	113,000
Total assets	250,000	425,000
Common stockholders' equity	71,300	206,900

Industry Averages

Current ratio	2.1 to 1
Acid-test ratio	1.1 to 1
Accounts receivable turnover	10.0 times
Inventory turnover	5.7 times
Times interest earned	6 times
Debt-to-equity ratio	0.9 to 1

Required

1. Compute the following amounts and ratios for each company:
   a. Working capital.
   b. Current ratio.
   c. Acid-test ratio.
   d. Accounts receivable turnover. (All sales are on account.)
   e. Average collection period for receivables. (Terms: n/30.)
   f. Inventory turnover.
   g. By use of these ratios, explain which company is the better short-term credit risk.
2. Compute the following ratios for each company:
   a. Times interest earned.
   b. Debt-to-equity ratio.
   c. By use of these ratios and any ratios from (1) above, explain which company could better take on *additional* long-term debt.

P18–14 Stockholder Ratio Analysis; Comparison with Industry Averages Refer to the financial statement data for Company A and Company B in Problem 18–13. Assume the following additional data for these two companies for the current year:

	Company A	Company B
Dividends paid:		
On preferred stock	$2,100	$ 2,400
On common stock	9,600	16,000
Market price per share (common)	48	45
Industry Ratios (Averages)		
Dividend yield	4%	
Price-earnings ratio	15	
Dividend payout ratio	60%	
Return on total assets	8%	
Return on common equity	12%	

Required

1. Compute the following ratios for each company for the current year:
   a. Earnings per share.
   b. Dividend yield ratio.
   c. Price-earnings ratio.
   d. Dividend payout ratio.
   e. Return on total assets.
   f. Return on common equity.
2. Is financial leverage positive or negative in the two companies? Explain.
3. By use of the ratios in (1) above, explain which company's stock is the better buy.

P18–15 Comprehensive Problem on Ratio Analysis You have just been hired as a loan officer at Fairfield State Bank. Your supervisor has given you a file containing a request from Hedrick Company for a $1,000,000, five-year loan. Financial statement data on the company for the last two years are given below:

HEDRICK COMPANY
Comparative Balance Sheet

	This Year	Last Year
Assets		
Current assets:		
Cash	$ 320,000	$ 420,000
Marketable securities	-0-	100,000
Accounts receivable, net	900,000	600,000
Inventory	1,300,000	800,000
Prepaid expenses	80,000	60,000
Total current assets	2,600,000	1,980,000
Plant and equipment, net	3,100,000	2,980,000
Total assets	$5,700,000	$4,960,000
Liabilities and Stockholders' Equity		
Liabilities:		
Current liabilities	$1,300,000	$ 920,000
Bonds payable, 10%	1,200,000	1,000,000
Total liabilities	2,500,000	1,920,000
Stockholders' equity:		
Preferred stock, 8%, $30 par value	600,000	600,000
Common stock, $40 par value	2,000,000	2,000,000
Retained earnings	600,000	440,000
Total stockholders' equity	3,200,000	3,040,000
Total liabilities and stockholders' equity	$5,700,000	$4,960,000

HEDRICK COMPANY
Comparative Income Statement

	This Year	Last Year
Sales (all on account)	$5,250,000	$4,160,000
Less cost of goods sold	4,200,000	3,300,000
Gross margin	1,050,000	860,000
Less operating expenses	530,000	520,000
Net operating income	520,000	340,000
Less interest expense	120,000	100,000
Net income before taxes	400,000	240,000
Less income taxes (30%)	120,000	72,000
Net income	280,000	168,000
Dividends paid:		
Preferred stock	48,000	48,000
Common stock	72,000	36,000
Total dividends paid	120,000	84,000
Net income retained	160,000	84,000
Retained earnings, beginning of year	440,000	356,000
Retained earnings, end of year	$ 600,000	$ 440,000

Marva Rossen, who just two years ago was appointed president of Hedrick Company, admits that the company has been "inconsistent" in its performance over the past several years. But Rossen argues that the company has its costs under control and is now experiencing strong sales growth, as evidenced by the more than 25 percent increase in sales over the last year. Rossen also argues that investors have recognized the improving situation at Hedrick Company, as shown by the jump in the price of its common stock from $20 per share last year to $36 per share this year. Rossen believes that with strong leadership and with the modernized equipment that the $1,000,000 loan will permit the company to buy, profits will be even stronger in the future.

Anxious to impress your supervisor, you decide to generate all the information that you can about the company. You determine that the following ratios are typical of companies in Hedrick's industry:

Current ratio	2.3 to 1
Acid-test ratio	1.2 to 1
Average age of receivables	31 days
Inventory turnover	60 days
Return on assets	9.5%
Debt-to-equity ratio	0.65 to 1
Times interest earned	5.7
Price-earnings ratio	10

Required

1. You decide first to assess the rate of return which the company is generating. Compute the following for both this year and last year:
   a. The return on total assets. (Total assets at the beginning of last year were $4,320,000.)
   b. The return on common equity. (Stockholders' equity at the beginning of last year totaled $3,016,000.)
   c. Is the company's leverage positive or negative? Explain.
2. You decide next to assess the well-being of the common stockholders. For both this year and last year, compute:
   a. The earnings per share.
   b. The fully diluted earnings per share. The preferred stock is convertible into common at the rate of two shares of common for each share of preferred.

   c. The dividend yield ratio for common.
   d. The dividend payout ratio for common.
   e. The price-earnings ratio. How do investors regard Hedrick Company as compared to other firms in the industry? Explain.
   f. The book value per share of common. Does the difference between market value per share and book value per share suggest that the stock at its current price is a bargain? Explain.
3. You decide, finally, to assess creditor ratios to determine both short-term and long-term debt paying ability. For both this year and last year, compute:
   a. Working capital.
   b. The current ratio.
   c. The acid-test ratio.
   d. The average age of receivables. (The accounts receivable at the beginning of last year totaled $520,000.)
   e. The inventory turnover. (The inventory at the beginning of last year totaled $640,000.)
   f. The debt-to-equity ratio.
   g. The number of times interest was earned.
4. Evaluate the data computed in (1) to (3) above, and using any additional data provided in the problem, make a recommendation to your supervisor as to whether the loan should be approved.

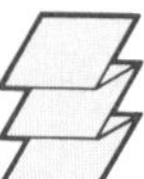

P18–16 **Common-Size Financial Statements** Refer to the financial statement data for Hedrick Company given in Problem 18–15.

Required For both this year and last year:

1. Present the balance sheet in common-size format.
2. Present the income statement in common-size format down through net income.
3. Comment on the results of your analysis.

P18–17 **Determining the Effect of Transactions on Various Financial Ratios** In the right-hand column below, certain financial ratios are listed. To the left of each ratio is a business transaction or event relating to the operating activities of Delta Company.

	Business Transaction or Event	Ratio
1.	The company declared a cash dividend.	Current ratio
2.	Sold inventory on account at cost.	Acid-test ratio
3.	The company issued bonds with an interest rate of 8%. The company's return on assets is 10%.	Return on common stockholders' equity
4.	The company's net income decreased by 10% between last year and this year. Long-term debt remained unchanged.	Times interest earned
5.	A previously declared cash dividend was paid.	Current ratio
6.	The market price of the company's common stock dropped from 24½ to 20. The dividend paid per share remained unchanged.	Dividend payout ratio
7.	Obsolete inventory totaling $100,000 was written off as a loss.	Inventory turnover ratio
8.	Sold inventory for cash at a profit.	Debt-to-equity ratio
9.	Changed customer credit terms from 2/10, n/30 to 2/15, n/30 to comply with a change in industry practice.	Accounts receivable turnover ratio
10.	Issued a common stock dividend on common stock.	Book value per share
11.	The market price of the company's common stock increased from 24½ to 30.	Book value per share
12.	The company paid $40,000 on accounts payable.	Working capital
13.	Issued a common stock dividend to common stockholders.	Earnings per share
14.	Paid accounts payable.	Debt-to-equity ratio

15.	Purchased inventory on open account.	Acid-test ratio
16.	Wrote off an uncollectible account against the Allowance for Bad Debts.	Current ratio
17.	The market price of the company's common stock increased from 24½ to 30. Earnings per share remained unchanged.	Price-earnings ratio
18.	The market price of the company's common stock increased from 24½ to 30. The dividend paid per share remained unchanged.	Dividend yield ratio

Required Indicate the effect that each business transaction or event would have on the ratio listed opposite to it. State the effect in terms of increase, decrease, or no effect on the ratio involved, and give the reason for your choice of answer. In all cases, assume that the current assets exceed the current liabilities both before and after the event or transaction. Use the following format for your answers:

	Effect on Ratio	Reason for Increase, Decrease, or No Effect
1.		
Etc.		

P18–18 Extraordinary Gains and Losses; Earnings per Share Rusco Products, Inc., has 20,000 shares of no-par common stock outstanding. The company's income statement for 19x7 as prepared by the company's accountant is given below:

Sales		$750,000
Less cost of goods sold		400,000
Gross margin		350,000
Less operating expenses:		
Selling expenses	$140,000	
Administrative expenses	90,000	
Loss from sale of unused plant	50,000	280,000
Income before taxes		70,000
Less income taxes (30%)		21,000
Net income		$ 49,000

The earnings per share for the company's common stock over the past three years is given below:

	19x4	19x5	19x6
Earnings per share—common	$2.40	$3.00	$3.60

Required

1. Consider the income statement as prepared by the company's accountant. Why might an investor have difficulty in interpreting this statement so far as determining Rusco Products, Inc.'s ability to generate normal after-tax earnings is concerned?
2. Recast the company's income statement in better form, showing the loss from unused plant net of tax.
3. Assume that rather than having a $50,000 loss, the company has a $50,000 gain from sale of unused plant. Redo the income statement, showing the gain net of tax.
4. Using the income statements that you prepared in (2) and (3) above, compute the earnings per share of common stock.
5. Explain how your computation of earnings per share would be helpful to an investor trying to evaluate the trend of Rusco Products, Inc.'s earnings over the past few years.

P18–19 **Interpretation of Already Completed Ratios** Being a prudent investor, Sally Perkins always investigates a company thoroughly before purchasing shares of its stock for investment. At present, Ms. Perkins is interested in the common stock of Plunge Enterprises. All she has available on the company is a copy of its annual report for the current year (19x3), which contains the 19x3 financial statements and the summary of ratios given below:

	19x1	19x2	19x3
Current ratio	2.0 to 1	2.5 to 1	2.8 to 1
Acid-test ratio	1.2 to 1	0.9 to 1	0.7 to 1
Accounts receivable turnover	10.4 times	9.5 times	8.6 times
Inventory turnover	6.8 times	5.7 times	5.0 times
Sales trend	100.0	118.0	130.0
Dividends paid per share*	$2.50	$2.50	$2.50
Dividend yield ratio	3%	4%	5%
Dividend payout ratio	60%	50%	40%
Return on total assets	10.4%	11.8%	13.0%
Return on common equity	9.0%	14.5%	16.2%

* There were no issues or retirements of common stock over the three-year period.

Ms. Perkins would like answers to a number of questions about the trend of events over the last three years in Plunge Enterprises. Her questions are:

a. Is the market price of the company's stock going up or down?
b. Is the amount of the earnings per share increasing or decreasing?
c. Is the price-earnings ratio going up or down?
d. Is the company employing financial leverage to the advantage of the common stockholders?
e. Is it becoming easier for the company to pay its bills as they come due?
f. Are customers paying their bills at least as fast now as they did in 19x1?
g. Is the total of the accounts receivable increasing, decreasing, or remaining constant?
h. Is the level of inventory increasing, decreasing, or remaining constant?

Required Answer each of Ms. Perkins' questions, using the data given above. In each case, explain how you arrived at your answer.

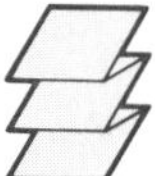

P18–20 **Comprehensive Problem—Part 1: Investor Ratios** (Problems 18–21 and 18–22 delve more deeply into the data presented below. Each problem is independent.) Microswift, Inc., was organized several years ago to develop and market computer software programs. The company is small but growing, and you are considering the purchase of some of its common stock as an investment. The following data on the company are available for the past two years:

MICROSWIFT, INC.
Comparative Income Statement
For the Years Ended December 31, 19x2, and 19x1

	19x2	19x1
Sales	$10,000,000	$7,500,000
Less cost of goods sold	6,500,000	4,500,000
Gross margin	3,500,000	3,000,000
Less operating expenses	2,630,000	2,280,000
Net operating income	870,000	720,000
Less interest expense	120,000	120,000
Net income before taxes	750,000	600,000
Less income taxes (30%)	225,000	180,000
Net income	$ 525,000	$ 420,000

MICROSWIFT, INC.
Comparative Retained Earnings Statement
For the Years Ended December 31, 19x2, and 19x1

	19x2	19x1
Retained earnings, January 1	$1,200,000	$ 980,000
Add net income (above)	525,000	420,000
Total	1,725,000	1,400,000
Deduct cash dividends paid:		
Preferred dividends	60,000	60,000
Common dividends	180,000	140,000
Total dividends paid	240,000	200,000
Retained earnings, December 31	$1,485,000	$1,200,000

MICROSWIFT, INC.
Comparative Balance Sheet
December 31, 19x2, and 19x1

	19x2	19x1
Assets		
Current assets:		
Cash	$ 100,000	$ 200,000
Accounts receivable, net	750,000	400,000
Inventory	1,500,000	600,000
Prepaid expenses	50,000	50,000
Total current assets	2,400,000	1,250,000
Plant and equipment, net	2,585,000	2,700,000
Total assets	$4,985,000	$3,950,000
Liabilities and Stockholders' Equity		
Liabilities:		
Current liabilities	$1,250,000	$ 500,000
Bonds payable, 12%	1,000,000	1,000,000
Total liabilities	2,250,000	1,500,000
Stockholders' equity:		
Preferred stock, 8%, $10 par	750,000	750,000
Common stock, $5 par	500,000	500,000
Retained earnings	1,485,000	1,200,000
Total stockholders' equity	2,735,000	2,450,000
Total liabilities and stockholders' equity	$4,985,000	$3,950,000

After some research, you have determined that the following ratios are typical of companies in the computer software industry:

Dividend yield ratio	3%
Dividend payout ratio	40%
Price-earnings ratio	16
Return on total assets	13.5%
Return on common equity	20%

The company's common stock is currently selling for $60 per share. During 19x1, the stock sold for $45 per share.

Required

1. In analyzing the company, you decide first to compute the earnings per share and related ratios. For both 19x1 and 19x2, compute:
   a. The earnings per share.
   b. The fully diluted earnings per share. Assume that each share of the preferred stock is convertible into two shares of common stock. The bonds are not convertible.

   c. The dividend yield ratio.
   d. The dividend payout ratio.
   e. The price-earnings ratio.
   f. The book value per share of common stock.
2. You decide next to determine the rate of return which the company is generating. For both 19x1 and 19x2, compute:
   a. The return on total assets. (Total assets were $3,250,000 on January 1, 19x1.)
   b. The return on common stockholders' equity. (Common stockholders' equity was $1,450,000 on January 1, 19x1.)
   c. Is financial leverage positive or negative? Explain.
3. Based on your work in (1) and (2) above, does the company's common stock seem to be an attractive investment? Explain.

P18–21 Comprehensive Problem—Part 2: Creditor Ratios Refer to the data in Problem 18–20. Although Microswift, Inc., has been very profitable since it was organized several years ago, the company is beginning to experience some difficulty in paying its bills as they come due. Management has approached Guaranty National Bank requesting a two-year $250,000 loan to bolster the cash account.

Guaranty National Bank has assigned you to evaluate the loan request. You have gathered the following data relating to companies in the computer software industry:

Current ratio.	2.4 to 1
Acid-test ratio	1.2 to 1
Average age of receivables . . .	16 days
Inventory turnover in days . . .	40 days
Times interest earned.	7 times
Debt-to-equity ratio	0.70 to 1

The following additional information is available on Microswift, Inc.:

a. All sales are on account.
b. On January 1, 19x1, the accounts receivable balance was $300,000 and the inventory balance was $500,000.

Required

1. Compute the following amounts and ratios for both 19x1 and 19x2:
   a. The working capital.
   b. The current ratio.
   c. The acid-test ratio.
   d. The accounts receivable turnover (average collection period) in days.
   e. The inventory turnover (average sale period) in days.
   f. The times interest earned.
   g. The debt-to-equity ratio.
2. Comment on the results of your analysis in (1) above.
3. Would you recommend that the loan be approved? Explain.

P18–22 Comprehensive Problem—Part 3: Common-Size Statements Refer to the data in Problem 18–20. The president of Microswift, Inc., is very concerned. Sales increased by $2.5 million during 19x2, yet the company's net income increased by only $105,000. Also, the company's operating expenses went up in 19x2, even though a major effort was launched during the year to cut costs.

Required

1. For both 19x1 and 19x2, prepare the income statement and the balance sheet in common-size form. (Round computations to one decimal place.)
2. From your work in (1) above, explain to the president why the increase in profits was so small in 19x2. Were any benefits realized from the company's cost-cutting efforts? Explain.

P18–23 Interpretation of Ratios Thorpe Company is a wholesale distributor of professional equipment and supplies. The company's sales have averaged about $900,000 annually for the three-year period 19x3–x5. The firm's total assets at the end of 19x5 amounted to $850,000.

The president of Thorpe Company has asked the controller to prepare a report summarizing the financial aspects of the company's operations for the past three years. This report will be presented to the board of directors at their next meeting.

In addition to comparative financial statements, the controller has decided to present a number of relevant financial ratios that can assist in the identification and interpretation of trends. At the request of the controller, the accounting staff has calculated the following ratios for the three-year period 19x3–x5:

	19x3	19x4	19x5
Current ratio	2.00	2.13	2.18
Acid-test ratio	1.20	1.10	0.97
Accounts receivable turnover	9.72	8.57	7.13
Percent of total debt to total assets	44%	41%	38%
Ratio of sales to fixed assets (sales divided by fixed assets)	1.75	1.88	1.99
Sales as a percent of 19x3 sales (trend analysis)	100%	103%	106%
Gross margin percentage	40.0%	38.6%	38.5%
Net income to sales	7.8%	7.8%	8.0%
Return on total assets	8.5%	8.6%	8.7%
Return on common stockholders' equity	15.1%	14.6%	14.1%
Inventory turnover	5.25	4.80	3.80
Percent of long-term debt to total assets	25%	22%	19%

In the preparation of his report, the controller has decided first to examine the financial ratios independently of any other data to determine if the ratios themselves reveal any significant trends over the three-year period.

Required Answer the following questions. Indicate in each case which ratio(s) you used in arriving at your conclusion.

1. The current ratio is increasing while the acid-test ratio is decreasing. Using the ratios provided, identify and explain the contributing factor(s) for this apparently divergent trend.
2. In terms of the ratios provided, what conclusion(s) can be drawn regarding the company's use of financial leverage during the 19x3–x5 period?
3. Using the ratios provided, what conclusion(s) can be drawn regarding the company's net investment in plant and equipment?

(CMA, Adapted)

P18–24 Incomplete Statements; Analysis of Ratios Incomplete financial statements for Tanner Company are given below:

TANNER COMPANY
Income Statement
For the Year Ended December 31, 19x4

Sales	$2,700,000
Less cost of goods sold	?
Gross margin	?
Less operating expenses	?
Net operating income	?
Less interest expense	45,000
Net income before taxes	?
Less income taxes (40%)	?
Net income	$?

TANNER COMPANY
Balance Sheet
December 31, 19x4

Current assets:	
Cash	$?
Accounts receivable, net	?
Inventory	?
Total current assets	?
Plant and equipment, net	?
Total assets	$?
Current liabilities	$250,000
Bonds payable, 10%	?
Total liabilities	?
Stockholders' equity:	
Common stock, $2.50 par value	?
Retained earnings	?
Total stockholders' equity	?
Total liabilities and stockholders' equity	$?

The following additional information is available about the company:

a. Selected financial ratios computed from the statements above are:

Current ratio	2.40 to 1
Acid-test ratio	1.12 to 1
Accounts receivable turnover	15.0 times
Inventory turnover	6.0 times
Debt-to-equity ratio	0.875 to 1
Times interest earned	7.0 times
Earnings per share	$4.05
Return on total assets	14%

b. All sales during the year were on account.

c. The interest expense on the income statement relates to the bonds payable; the amount of bonds outstanding did not change throughout the year.

d. There were no issues or retirements of common stock during the year.

e. Selected balances at the *beginning* of the current year (January 1, 19x4) were:

Accounts receivable	$ 160,000
Inventory	280,000
Total assets	1,200,000

Required Compute the missing amounts on the company's financial statements. (Hint: You may find it helpful to think about the difference between the current ratio and the acid-test ratio.)

Index

A

B

C

D

E

F

G-H

I

V

W-Z